Abnormal
Psychology

Michael J. Goldstein
University of California, Los Angeles

Bruce L. Baker
University of California, Los Angeles

Kay R. Jamison
University of California, Los Angeles

Abnormal Psychology

Experiences, Origins, and Interventions

Little, Brown and Company
Boston   Toronto

Library of Congress Catalog Card No. 79-87606

First Printing

Published simultaneously in Canada by Little, Brown & Company (Canada) Limited

Printed in the United States of America

Illustrators: Douglas Gilbert, George Hughes, Arthur Polonski

ACKNOWLEDGMENTS

Title page: Alfred Eisenstadt, © Time-Life.

UNIT 1 opening photo: © Lennart Nilsson, *Behold Man,* Little, Brown and Company, 1974.

CHAPTER 1. *Table 1.1:* Reprinted by permission. *Fig. 1.3 (top):* The Granger Collection. *Fig. 1.3 (bottom):* Photo Researchers, © Margot Granitsas. *Table 1.2:* Excerpted from a draft version of *Diagnostic and Statistical Manual of Mental Disorders,* Third Edition, by permission of the American Psychiatric Association. The final version of these definitions appears in *Diagnostic and Statistical Manual of Mental Disorders,* Third Edition (Washington, D.C.: American Psychiatric Association, 1980). *Fig. 1.4:* Courtesy of the Museum of the American Indian, Heye Foundation. *Fig. 1.5:* Dr. Jane Murphy. *Fig. 1.6:* National Association of Mental Health.

CHAPTER 2. *Fig. 2.2:* The Bettmann Archive. *Fig. 2.3:* The Bettmann Archive. *Fig. 2.4 and excerpt on pages 39–40:* Material is reprinted from *New Introductory Lectures on Psychoanalysis* by Sigmund Freud, translated by James Strachey; used by permission of W. W. Norton & Company, Inc. Copyright 1933 by Sigmund Freud. Copyright renewed 1961 by W. J. H. Sprott. Copyright © 1965, 1964 by James Strachey. *Fig. 2.5 (top):* Mary Evans Picture Library, Sigmund Freud Copyrights. *Fig. 2.5 (bottom):* Nina Leen, © Time-Life. *Fig. 2.6:* From Howard Gardner, *Developmental Psychology: An Introduction,* p. 82. Copyright © 1978 by Little, Brown and Company (Inc.). Adapted by permission. *Fig. 2.7:* From Howard Gardner, *Developmental Psychology: An Introduction,* p. 84. Copyright © 1978 by Little, Brown and Company (Inc.). Adapted by permission. *Fig. 2.8 (top):* Magnum, Burk Uzzle. *Fig. 2.8 (bottom):* The Bettmann Archive.

CHAPTER 3. *Fig. 3.1:* Judith Sedwick. *Table 3.1:* From R. L. Spitzer and J. Endicott, *Current and Past Psychopathology Scales (CAPPS)* (New York: New York State Psychiatric Institute, 1968). Reprinted by permission of the authors. *Fig. 3.2:* © The Psychological Corporation. *Fig. 3.4:* Eliot H. Rodnick, UCLA. *Fig. 3.6:* Richard Brightman. *Fig. 3.7:* Freelance Photographers Guild, C. Fisher.

CHAPTER 4. *Fig. 4.1 (top):* Frank Siteman. *Fig. 4.1 (bottom):* Magnum, Charles Harlbutt. *Fig. 4.2:* From John M. Neale, Robert M. Liebert, *Science and Behavior: An Introduction to Methods of Research,* © 1973, p. 78. Adapted by permission of Prentice-Hall, Inc., Englewood Cliffs, New Jersey. *Table 4.1:* Copyright © 1978 by John Wiley & Sons, Inc. Reprinted by permission of John Wiley & Sons, Inc. *Fig. 4.4:* Montreal Gazette. *Fig. 4.5:* From G. D. Ellison, "Animal Models of Psychopathology: The Low-Norepinephrine and Low-Serotonin Rat," *American Psychologist,* 32:2 (December 1977), p. 1041. Copyright 1977 by the American Psychological Association. Reprinted by permission. *Fig. 4.6:* From R. V. Hall, D. Lund, and D. Jackson, "Effects of Teacher Attention on Study Behavior," *Journal of Applied Behavior Analysis,* vol. 1 (1968), p. 3. Copyright 1968 by the Society for the Experimental Analysis of Behavior, Inc. Reprinted by permission. *Excerpt, pages 89–90:* From D. T. Campbell, "Reforms as Experiments," *American Psychologist* 24, no. 4 (1969), p. 413. Copyright 1969 by the American Psychological Association. Reprinted by permission.

UNIT 2 opening photo: Alfred Eisenstadt, © Time-Life.

CHAPTER 5. *Excerpt, pages 99, 103, 112:* From M. B. Bowers, Jr., *Retreat From Sanity.* Copyright © 1974 by Human Sciences Press. Reprinted by permission of Human Sciences Press, 72 Fifth Avenue, New York, N.Y. 10011. *Fig. 5.2:* Schizophrenia Bulletin, National Institute of Mental Health. *Fig. 5.3:* Schizophrenia Bulletin, National Institute of Mental Health. *Table 5.2:* Copyright 1973 by the American Psychological Association. Reprinted by permission. *Excerpt, page 105:* From Norma MacDonald, "Living with Schizophrenia," *The Canadian Medical Association Journal,* vol. 82, 1960. Reprinted by permission. *Excerpt, pages 106–107:* From *The Eden Express* by Mark Vonnegut. © 1975 by Praeger Publishers, Inc. Reprinted by permission of Holt, Rinehart and Winston. *Fig. 5.4:* From M. Bleuler, "A 23-year longitudinal study of 208 schizophrenics and impressions in regard to the nature of schizophrenia," in D. Rosenthal and S. S. Kety (eds.), *The Transmission of Schizophrenia* (Oxford: Pergamon Press Ltd., 1968), p. 5. Adapted by permission of Pergamon Press Ltd. *Fig. 5.5:* From B. J. Garland et al., "Cross-national Study of Diagnosis of the Mental Disorders: Some Comparisons of Diagnostic Criteria from the First Investigation," *American Journal of Psychiatry,* vol. 125 (1969), p. 32. Copyright 1969, the American Psychiatric Association. Reprinted by permission. *Excerpt, pages 111–112:* From a draft version of *Diagnostic and Statistical Manual of Mental Disorders,* Third Edition, by permission of the American Psychiatric Association. The material appears in its final form in *Diagnostic and Statistical Manual of Mental Disorders,* Third Edition (Washington, D.C.: American Psychiatric Association, 1980). *Fig. 5.6:* Schizophrenia Bulletin, National Institute of Mental Health. *Fig. 5.7:* New York Times News Service. *Excerpt, page 116:* From Michael J. Goldstein and James O. Palmer, *The Experience of Anxiety: A Casebook,* Second Edition. Copyright © 1963, 1975 by Michael J. Goldstein and James O. Palmer. Reprinted by permission of Oxford University Press, Inc. *Fig. 5.8:* Rockland Research Institute. *Table 5.3:* Copyright 1975 by the American Psychological Association. Reprinted by permission.

Acknowledgments continued on page liii.

Preface

The field of abnormal psychology is in a period of exciting but often very confusing change. The umbrella theories that formerly sought to explain all psychological deviance are giving way to more problem-specific and theoretically mixed explanations. And treatments once limited to the psychoanalytic couch or the institutional bed are being challenged by a host of new intervention and prevention alternatives. The search for causes and treatments increasingly has meant looking both inward to biological mechanisms and outward to the social context. So it is understandable that the student in search of "facts" might become disillusioned. It has been our goal in writing this book to capture the excitement and substance of a changing field as well as to be sensitive to the student's need for some order.

Quite naturally, the distinguishing characteristics of the book evolve from our own orientations and activities. Therefore our book has an eclectic perspective. Our own theoretical orientations vary considerably from behavioral to psychodynamic to biological perspectives on abnormal behavior. Hence we do not give undue emphasis to any single viewpoint. Freud and the psychoanalysts who followed, Watson and his disciples by way of Skinner, and many biological theorists during the period 1946–70 all claimed to be able to account for much abnormal behavior. Currently, we feel, there is a need for selective application of theories and for a synthesis of psychological and biological explanations. We have attempted not just to give "equal time" to each perspective but also to emphasize each where it is most appropriate and to seek integration where possible.

We emphasize the personal experience of psychological abnormality because as practicing clinical psychologists and active researchers in abnormal psychology, as well as teachers, the three of us feel strongly that a meaningful way to introduce students to this field is to weave personal reports, clinical observations, and research findings together. Understanding the phenomena of abnormal behavior — how it is viewed by clients, their families, and those who seek to help them — is a precondition for meaningful research. Many a foolish research hypothesis disintegrates as a result of a brief conversation with a disturbed person, and promising research ideas come from carefully listening to and observing the same persons. Therefore we have tried to communicate the inner experiences of individuals — their fears, struggles, and triumphs — in an attempt to develop compassion as well as understanding of the impact of these states on all of us.

We have also given the book a unique organization based on the instructional approach that our experience suggests is most effective. Following an introductory unit concerning current issues, historical roots, and approaches to assessment and research are five major units on types of abnormal behavior: schizophrenia, mood disorders, anxiety disorders, social deviance, and disorders of childhood. We have begun with the most obvious and severe disorder, schizophrenia, and then moved to more common types of psychopathology, because students readily grasp the extreme abnormality of schizophrenic behavior and because the varied research approaches applied to this problem provide a good point of departure for studying other, more common disorders. Of course, instructors need not follow this plan of organization. The units are relatively self-contained and lend themselves to different sequences, including the common practice of beginning with anxiety disorders.

Another organizational feature derives from our own extensive involvement in clinical practice. Each unit contains a whole chapter on intervention. Generally, abnormal psychology texts discuss treatment approaches apart from specific behavior patterns. We do not believe that this practice accurately reflects the current state of the field. In reality, intervention programs are increasingly targeted to specific abnormal behavior patterns; forms of psychological or drug therapy that seem to help with one disorder have proven useless with others. Therefore, for each problem area we describe interventions that are most promising. Consequently, key themes emerge repeatedly. For example, rather than writing a separate chapter on

community mental health, we chose to examine the shift from institutional to community-level intervention in the contexts of aftercare treatment of schizophrenia, prevention programs for retardation, and self-help programs for drug abusers.

Finally, we have added to the traditional areas of coverage in abnormal psychology content that we deem especially timely. We devoted a chapter to research approaches in abnormal behavior, because we believe that it is important that a student, as an informed consumer, appreciate how knowledge is acquired and how to evaluate research reports. Our extensive coverage of mood disorders is consistent with the recent increase in clinical and research interest in these problems. We stress the role of the family in producing abnormal behavior, in responding to a deviant member, and in treating the disturbance. We give considerable attention to the areas of mental retardation and childhood disorders because trends in behavioral treatment and community mental health have heightened interest in them. And we highlight a number of social problems, including child abuse, wife beating, and rape, three types of behavior that are just beginning to receive serious psychological attention.

We would like to acknowledge those people who made very significant and special contributions to this book. Numerous people at Little, Brown have contributed immeasurably: Marian Ferguson, who initially had faith in the project and shepherded it to completion with enthusiasm and kindly direction; Patrice Boyer, who organized the art program; Lee Ripley, who provided chapter summaries; Barbara Garrey and Barbara Sonnenschein, who ably directed the book's production; but most particularly Judith Kromm, who, in many ways, deserves coauthor status for her superb organizational, stylistic, and substantive advice and assistance.

Numerous colleagues have helped immeasurably. We would particularly like to acknowledge the assistance of Paul Abramson, Robert Asarnow, Richard Brightman, Andrew Christensen, Constance Hammen, Steven Hinshaw, Christine Padesky, N. Dickon Reppucci, and Kay Rowland in providing us with either helpful reviews or special materials. Dr. Jamison is especially grateful to Frederick K. Goodwin for his invaluable support and his critique of the affective disorders section of the text. We are also indebted to Irving H. Bieman, Alan J. Brightman, Anthony Davids, Dean Funabiki, Robert Holmstrom, Richard L. Kellogg, Sandra L. Kirmeyer, Herbert Krauss, Bruce Palmer, Edward H. Selden, Gary B. Seltzer, Marcia M. Seltzer, Robert D. Singer, C. R. Snyder, Ed Thrasher, Norris D. Vestre, Jay M. Weiss, and Herbert N. Weissman, whose helpful critiques aided us in revising early versions of the book. And without Jennifer Carter and Eleanor Walker we could not possibly have gotten accurate manuscripts to the publisher on time; they also provided sorely needed emotional support at all times.

The Authors

Michael J. Goldstein

Michael J. Goldstein received his Ph.D. in clinical psychology from the University of Washington in 1957. Since then his affiliation has been the University of California, Los Angeles. At UCLA he has taught the undergraduate abnormal psychology course for twenty two years in addition to various graduate courses in clinical psychology. He has also pursued a vigorous research career in several areas, but his most significant efforts have gone into developing multimodal treatments for schizophrenics and prospective-longitudinal studies of family factors in schizophrenia and other forms of adult psychopathology. In recognition of his contributions, the American College of Neuropharmacology admitted him as a fellow and the World Health Organization engaged him as a consultant on schizophrenia prevention.

During 1960–61 Dr. Goldstein was a Fulbright Research Professor at the University of Copenhagen. He also has served as a member of numerous national advisory committees, most notably as member (1969–75) and chairman of the Clinical Projects Review Committee of the National Institute of Mental Health.

In addition to being the author of four books and more than sixty articles, Dr. Goldstein has served on the editorial boards of the *Journal of Abnormal Psychology, Family Process, Law and Human Behavior,* and other journals. He maintains an active clinical practice, working mostly with families of disturbed adolescents from a systems point of view.

Bruce L. Baker

Kay R. Jamison

Bruce L. Baker received his Ph.D. in clinical psychology from Yale University. He taught for nine years at Harvard University before moving to the University of California, Los Angeles, where he is currently professor of psychology.

Dr. Baker teaches graduate seminars in behavior modification with children and community psychology. At the undergraduate level, he teaches abnormal psychology and a special off-campus program in special education. His primary research interests have been in behavior therapy and mental retardation. In the last eight years, with grants from the National Institute of Child Health and Human Development, he has studied training of parents as teachers of their retarded children. The coauthor of a series of instructional manuals for parents *(Steps to Independence Series),* Dr. Baker has also written a book on institutional alternatives *(As Close as Possible: Community Residences for Retarded Adults).* He is on the editorial board of the *Journal of Behavior Therapy and Experimental Psychiatry* and an editorial advisor for *Family Process.*

Dr. Baker is active in clinical work with children and families, as well as consultation to professional agencies. In 1969 he founded Camp Freedom, an educational and therapeutic residential program for retarded and disturbed children, which he directed through 1975.

Kay Redfield Jamison received her Ph.D. in clinical psychology from the University of California, Los Angeles. She also studied zoology and neurophysiology at the University of St. Andrews, Scotland, and clinical observation at the University of London's Maudsley Hospital. Currently Dr. Jamison is an assistant professor in the UCLA Department of Psychiatry, where she teaches undergraduate and graduate psychology students, interns, and residents about depression and manic-depression. She is also director of the UCLA Affective Disorders Clinic, and she maintains a clinical practice composed largely of patients with mood disorders.

Dr. Jamison's major clinical and research interest is manic-depressive illness — its psychology and phenomenology, its relationship to creativity, and interactions between psychological and biological forms of treatment. In addition, she has done research in substance abuse and currently is a member of the federal Controlled Substances/Drug Abuse Research Advisory Committee of the Food and Drug Administration.

Brief Contents

Unit 1 | **Introduction**

Chapter **1**   Abnormality: Definition and Issues of Classification   *3*

Chapter **2**   Evolving Models of Abnormal Behavior   *24*

Chapter **3**   Assessment   *53*

Chapter **4**   Research Approaches   *70*

Unit 2 | **The Schizophrenias**

Chapter **5**   The Nature of Schizophrenia   *99*

Chapter **6**   Origins of Schizophrenia   *123*

Chapter **7**   Intervention in Schizophrenia   *149*

Unit 3 | **The Mood Disorders**

Chapter **8**   The Depressive Disorders   *176*

Chapter **9**   Manic-Depressive Illness   *201*

Chapter **10**   Suicide   *218*

Chapter **11**   Treatment of Mood Disorders   *241*

Unit 4 | **Organic Disorders**

Chapter **12** Organic Brain Syndromes *266*

Unit 5 | **Anxiety and Psychophysiological Disorders**

Chapter **13** Anxiety Disorders and the Borderline Syndrome *295*

Chapter **14** Psychophysiological Dysfunction *324*

Chapter **15** Intervention in Anxiety and Psychophysiological Disorders *350*

Unit 6 | **Social Deviance**

Chapter **16** Substance Abuse *390*

Chapter **17** Sociopathy, Delinquency, and Family Violence *427*

Chapter **18** Sexual Deviance *460*

Chapter **19** Intervention with Social Deviance *486*

Unit 7 | **Disorders of Childhood**

Chapter **20** Mental Retardation *519*

Chapter **21** Childhood Behavior Disorders *551*

Chapter **22** Intervention with Children *578*

Unit 8 | **Mental Health Law and Clients' Rights**

Chapter **23** Mental Health Law and Clients' Rights *606*

Glossary *i*
References *xii*
Name Index *lvii*
Subject Index *lx*

Contents

Unit 1
Introduction

Chapter 1
Abnormality: Definition and Issues of Classification *3*

Definition of Abnormal Behavior *6*

Characteristics of Abnormal Behavior *8*
   Social Deviance / Subjective Distress /
   Psychological Handicap

Classifying Abnormal Behavior *10*
   DSM-III: A New Look at an Old Problem /
   Classification vs. Labeling Theory / Primary
   Labeling Theory / Secondary Labeling Theory

Facts About Abnormal Behavior *20*

The Goals of this Book *21*

Summary *22*

Chapter 2
Evolving Models of Abnormal Behavior *24*

Biological Themes *25*
   Decline and Renaissance / Contemporary
   Biological Models

Psychological Themes *32*
   Medieval Demonology / Challenge to
   Witchcraft / Roots of Modern Psychological
   Theories / Freudian Psychoanalysis (Structural
   theory / Developmental theory / Influence of
   Freudian theory) / Behaviorism and the Social
   Learning Approach / Behavioral-Psychoanalytic
   Rapprochement

Mental Institutions: The Era of "Moral
Treatment" *46*

Community Mental Health Centers *50*

A Contemporary Problem: Synthesizing
Divergent Models *50*

Summary *51*

Chapter 3
Assessment *53*

Assessment Criteria *54*

Assessment Techniques *56*
   The Interview / Psychological Tests (Intelligence
   tests / Personality tests) / Direct Observation /
   Psychophysiological Recording / Assessing
   Environments

Summary *68*

Chapter 4
Research Approaches   70

Design Considerations   71
  Internal Validity / External Validity (Sample /
  Situation)

Research Approaches   76
  Descriptive Studies (Case studies / Surveys) /
  Correlational Studies (Developmental studies) /
  Experimental Studies (Analogue experiments /
  Single-subject studies) / Mixed Designs

Ethical Issues in Research   92

Summary   94

Unit 2
The Schizophrenias

Chapter 5
The Nature of Schizophrenia   99

Concept of Schizophrenia   100

Process of Schizophrenic
Disorganization   102

The Subjective Experience of
Schizophrenia   104

Course of a Schizophrenic Psychosis   105

Diagnostic Reliability in Schizophrenia   108

DSM-III Criteria for Schizophrenia   111

Paranoid Schizophrenia   113

Catatonic Schizophrenia   114

Hebephrenic Schizophrenia   116

Schizo-Affective Reactions   117

Diagnosis by Computer: The Ultimate
Solution?   118

Predictors of Schizophrenia Outcome   119
  Specific Symptoms / Premorbid Adjustment /
  Detectable Life Crises / Family Attitudes

Summary   122

Chapter 6
Origins of Schizophrenia   123

Biological Perspective   124
  Biochemical Theories of Schizophrenia (Research
  limitations / An inborn error of metabolism? / The
  dopamine theory) / Genetic Predisposition (Twin
  studies / Schizotaxia / Adoption studies) /
  Overview of Biological Research on
  Schizophrenia

Interactive Models and High-Risk
Studies   133
  The Stress-Diathesis Model / The Mednick
  High-Risk Project

Psychosocial Stress   136
  Distortions in Family Relationships (Distortions in
  focusing attention and communication / Distortions
  in role relationships / Distortions in emotional
  climate / Implications and limitations of the family
  distortion model) / Sociological Status and
  Schizophrenia / A High-Risk Study of Family
  Relationships

A Concluding Word About Stress-Diathesis
Theory   147

Summary   147

Chapter 7
Intervention in Schizophrenia   149

Current Approach to Treatment   150

Biological Treatment of Schizophrenia   151
  Drugs and Aftercare

Psychological Approaches to Treatment   156
  Traditionally Oriented Psychotherapy /
  Existential Therapy (Laing's Treatment Model) /
  Behavior Therapy / Family Therapy

Multimodal Approaches   165

Preventive Efforts   170
  Genetic Counseling / Preventive Interventions of
  a Psychological Type

Summary   171

Unit 3
The Mood Disorders

Chapter 8
The Depressive Disorders *176*

Clinical Description and Diagnosis *176*
  Diagnostic Criteria / Interpersonal Aspects of Depression

Incidence of Depression *187*

Causes of Depression *187*
  Psychological Theories (Psychoanalytic theories / Personality theory / Behavioral Theories / Cognitive theory) / **Biological Theories**

Summary *198*

Chapter 9
Manic-Depressive Illness *201*

Clinical Description *204*

Diagnosis *206*

The Manic-Depressive Experience *208*

Genetic Theories of Manic-Depressive Illness *214*

Summary *216*

Chapter 10
Suicide *218*

Types of Suicidal Behavior *219*

Historical and Cultural Perspectives *220*

Statistics on Suicide *221*

Phenomenological Perspectives *222*

Theories of Suicide *226*
  Psychological Theories / **Biological Theories** / **Sociological Theory** (Egotistic suicides / Altruistic suicides)

Psychiatric Illness and Suicide *232*

Suicide and College Students *236*

Summary *239*

Chapter 11
Treatment of Mood Disorders *241*

Biological Approaches *243*
  Drugs I: Lithium / Drugs II: Antidepressants / Electroconvulsive Therapy (ECT) / Sleep Deprivation

Psychological Approaches *252*
  Cognitive Therapy / Behavior Therapy

Multimodal Interventions *256*
  Combined Treatment with Drugs and Psychotherapy / Mood Disorders Clinics

Suicide Prevention *259*

Summary *263*

Unit 4
Organic Disorders

Chapter 12
Organic Brain Syndromes *266*

Clinical Features *268*

Injuries to the Brain *270*
  Types of Trauma (Concussion / Contusion / Laceration) / Posttraumatic Complications

Brain Tumors *274*

Brain Infections *276*

Endocrine Disorders *278*
  Thyroid Disorders / Adrenal Disorders

Syndromes Associated with Aging *279*
  Presenile Degenerative Disorders (Alzheimer's disease / Parkinson's disease / Huntington's chorea) / Senile Dementia / Pseudodementia / Circulatory Disturbances / Problems in Treating the Elderly

Epilepsy *287*
  Grand Mal / Petit Mal / Psychomotor Epilepsy / Treatment of Epilepsy

Summary *289*

Unit 5
Anxiety and Psychophysiological Disorders

Chapter 13
Anxiety Disorders and the Borderline Syndrome   295

Measures of Anxiety   296
 Self-report of Anxiety / Biological Measures of Anxiety / Behavioral Signs of Anxiety / Relationship Among Indices of Anxiety

Anxiety Disorders: Patterns of Expression   300
 Symptomatic Disorders (Generalized anxiety disorders / Panic disorder / Phobic disorders / Obsessive-compulsive disorder / Conversion and dissociative disorders and multiple personality) / Personality Disorders (Compulsive personality disorders / Histrionic (hysterical) personality / Borderline syndrome) / Onset and Course of Anxiety Disorders

Theories on Development of Anxiety Disorders   317
 Psychoanalytic Model / Behavioral Model

Summary   322

Chapter 14
Psychophysiological Dysfunction   324

Stress and Coping   326
 Nonspecific Stress Theories / Specific Theories of Life Stress (Situational specificity / Attitudinal specificity / Personality specificity)

Biological Predisposition to Psychophysiological Disorders   340

Understanding Psychophysiological Disorders by Treating Them   341

Sexual Dysfunction   344
 Preparatory Phase / Coital Culmination / Origins of Sexual Dysfunction / Effect of Sexual Dysfunction on Relationships

Summary   348

Chapter 15
Intervention in Anxiety and Psychophysiological Disorders   350

Nonspecific Features of Psychological Therapies   352

Psychoanalytic Approach   353
 Client-Therapist Relationship / The Psychoanalytic Therapist / Transference / Dream Interpretation / Extensions of the Psychoanalytic Model—Groups and Families

Existential-Humanistic Approaches   360
 The Inner Experience / Client's Responsibility for Change / The Humanistic-Existential Therapist / Client-Centered Therapy / Gestalt Therapy

Behavior Therapy   365
 Behavioral Assessment of Anxiety Disorders / Anxiety Reduction Techniques (Systematic desensitization / Improving communication skills / Cognitive strategies)

Effectiveness of Psychological Therapies   383
 Effects of Different Therapies / Specific Therapies for Specific Problems

Preventing Anxiety Disorders   384

Summary   385

Unit 6
Social Deviance

Chapter 16
Substance Abuse   390

Criteria for Abuse   391
 Psychological Dependence / Negative Social Effects / DSM-III Criteria

Causes of Abuse   394

Opiate Addiction *395*

Theories of Addiction / Factors Leading to Opiate Addiction (Availability of the drug / Attributes of the person / The social environment) / Continuing Use of Narcotics (Attributes of the drug / Genetic predisposition / The social situation)

Central Nervous System Depressants: Alcohol *406*

Alcohol / Theories of Alcoholism / Factors Leading to Alcoholism (Availability of the drug / Attributes of the person)

Stimulants of the Central Nervous System *414*

Amphetamines / Cocaine / Caffeine

Hallucinogens *417*

Marijuana *422*

Patterns of Use / Therapeutic Uses / Social Policy

Summary *425*

Chapter 17
Sociopathy, Delinquency, and Family Violence *427*

Crime in America *428*

Crime Rates / Increases in Crime Rates / Types of Criminals (Organized crime / White collar crime) Causes of Criminal Behavior / (Genetic-biological factors / Family and environment / Cultural values)

Sociopathy *434*

Clinical Characteristics / Causes of Sociopathy (Failure to learn to avoid punishment / Lack of emotional response / Underarousal and stimulus-seeking / Learning to avoid punishment (revisited) / Brain-wave aberrations)

Juvenile Delinquency *442*

Types of Delinquents / Causes of Delinquency (Environmental influences: living conditions / Affluence, alienation, and self-esteem / Peer pressure and the gang / Family relationships)

Family Violence *448*

Child Abuse / Spouse Abuse / Murder / Legal Status and Powerlessness / Causes of Family Violence (Psychosocial functions / Cultural acceptance of violence)

Summary *458*

Chapter 18
Sexual Deviance *460*

Social Mores and Laws *461*

Actual Sexual Practices *461*

Psychological Abnormality *462*

Gender Identity Disorders *462*

Transvestism / Transsexualism / Causes of Gender Identity Disorders

Alternative Sexual Activities: I *470*

Fetishism / Voyeurism / Exhibitionism / Causes of Alternative Activities

Alternative Sexual Activities: II *474*

Pedophilia / Incest / Rape (The experience of rape / Who commits rape? / Rape and American society)

Summary *484*

Chapter 19
Intervention with Social Deviance *486*

Criminal Justice System *487*

Mental Health and Criminal Justice *488*

Rehabilitation Programs *489*

Psychotherapy / Behavior Therapy (Aversion therapy / Unresolved questions about aversion techniques / Increasing coping behaviors) / Family Therapy / Residential Programs / Community-based Programs (Self-help groups / Therapeutic communities / Methadone maintenance)

Help for Victims *510*
    Support and Counseling / Protection from
    Further Harm
Prevention *514*
Summary *515*

Unit 7
Disorders of Childhood

Chapter **20**
Mental Retardation *519*

History *520*

Diagnosis and Classification *521*
    IQ as a Measure of Retardation / **Adaptive**
    Behavior / **Classification** (Mild retardation /
    Moderate retardation / Severe and profound
    retardation)

Experience of the Family *526*

Causes of Retardation *528*
    Genetic Causes (Down's syndrome /
    Phenylketonuria) / **Physical and Environmental**
    Causes (Congenital rubella syndrome / Nutrition
    and drugs / Poisoning and head injury)
    Psychosocial Causes (Deficiencies in health
    care / Deficiencies in cognitive stimulation)

Characteristics of Retarded Persons *539*
    Learning / **Personality and Interpersonal**
    Experiences (Anxiety and frustration / Routine and
    rules / Dependence on others / Low self-esteem)

Growing Up *542*
    Education / **Social Acceptance** / **Adulthood** /
    (Vocation / Marriage / Residence)

Summary *549*

Chapter **21**
Childhood Behavior Disorders *551*

Experiencing Childhood Behavior
Disorders *552*

Diagnostic Issues *554*
    Eye of the Beholder / Variability in Children's
    Behavior

Classification of Childhood Behavior
Disorders *554*

Developmental Disorders: Enuresis *555*
    Adjustment of Enuretics / Treatment /
    Adjustment Following Conditioning Treatment /
    Life Course

Anxiety Disorders *558*
    Developmental Trends / School Phobia

Hyperactivity *565*
    Incidence / Description / Etiology / Life Course

Childhood Psychoses *568*
    A Description of Infantile Autism (Disturbances in
    relating / Insistence on preserving sameness /
    Disturbances in speech and language /
    Disturbances in motility / Disturbances in
    perception) / **Etiology of Autism** (Psychological
    explanations / Biological explanations) / **Life**
    Course of Autism

Summary *576*

Chapter **22**
Intervention with Children *578*

Psychotherapy *580*
    Psychoanalytic Play Therapy / Nondirective Play
    Therapy / Outcome of Child Psychotherapy /
    Family Therapy

Behavior Therapies *586*
    Anxiety Reduction (Systematic desensitization /
    Modeling / Reinforcement / Combined
    approaches) / **Behavior Management** (Classroom
    behavior management / Cognitive training) / **Skill**
    Training (Language training / Social skills
    training / Parent training)

Drug Therapy *598*

Early Intervention and Prevention *600*
    Moderate to Severe Retardation / Mild or
    Borderline Retardation / Behavior Disorders

Summary *603*

Unit 8
Mental Health Law and Clients' Rights

Chapter 23
Mental Health Law and Clients' Rights *606*

Access to Mental Health Services *607*

Paradoxes

Rights of Mental Patients *609*

Donaldson v. *O'Connor* / Civil Commitment and Right to Liberty (*Parens patriae* / Dangerousness / Paradoxes) / **Rights in Institutions** (Right to treatment / Least restrictive alternative / Paradoxes) / **Right to Refuse Treatment**

Acceptance in the Community *619*

Summary *621*

Glossary *i*

References *xii*

Name Index *lvii*

Subject Index *lx*

Abnormal Psychology

Unit 1 | **Introduction**

Chapter 1

Abnormality: Definition and Issues of Classification

Definition of Abnormal Behavior

Characteristics of Abnormal Behavior
Social Deviance
Subjective Distress
Psychological Handicap

Classifying Abnormal Behavior
DSM-III: A New Look at an Old Problem
Classification vs. Labeling Theory
Primary Labeling Theory
Secondary Labeling Theory

Facts About Abnormal Behavior

The Goals of This Book

Summary

Nancy G. sat between her parents in the hospital clinic office. Her mother and father had removed their coats, but Nancy remained wrapped in a heavy jacket, her hands thrust deep into her pockets. An extremely straight part divided Nancy's long black hair. Her skin was sallow, and she had dark circles under her eyes. Nancy was 14 years old, 62 inches tall, and weighed 68 pounds. She was starving to death. . . .

Last fall Nancy enrolled in a ninth-grade course in nutrition. She quickly became engrossed in the subject. She spent most of her allowance on calorie charts and health food books. She began helping her mother in the kitchen and enjoyed experimenting with novel recipes. . . . Initially, Mrs. G. was delighted with her daughter's interest. . . . Dr. G. also was pleased at first by Nancy's new activities. . . . It was not until the Christmas holidays that either of her parents took note of Nancy's excessive loss of weight. In three months she had lost 25 pounds. Both of them admonished her to quit dieting and, for a while, they reasoned patiently with her, trying to tempt her with her favorite foods. Mrs. G. resumed cooking dishes that had enticed Nancy in the past and began monitoring her daughter's food intake. In spite of parental efforts, however, Nancy continued to lose weight. By her fourteenth birthday in January, Nancy's weight decreased another 10 pounds. All efforts to make her eat were met first with arguments and then with tears.

As Nancy's weight decreased, there were increasing manifestations of emotional disturbance and personality change. She began to isolate herself from everyone in the family, particularly her brother and sister. In fact, she became quite agitated whenever she was in the same room with either of her siblings. Nancy had always been a fussy, perfectionistic child, but now her need for order and routine became an obsession. Her performance in school continued to be superior, but she worried endlessly about every assignment. In spite of her fragile physique, she continued to engage actively in sports, which she had always enjoyed. At school she played basketball vigorously. After school when she wasn't studying or working in the kitchen, she was riding her bicycle or running with her dog. A comprehensive physical exam revealed no signs of a physical illness that could account for her weight loss or hyperactivity.

What particularly disturbed her parents was that Nancy would frequently scrutinize her figure in the mirror and say things like, "How fat I am! Look at this disgusting stomach and these fat thighs." To her parents, this view Nancy had of herself was bizarre. Nancy reminded them of a concentration camp victim, emaciated and wasting away. They were also concerned because the girl's menstrual periods, which had started when she was 12, stopped completely soon after she began dieting (Goldstein and Palmer 1975, pp. 121–123).

Nancy's tragic attempt to achieve her bizarre conception of a "perfect body" clearly highlights a key aspect of abnormal behavior: it is perplexing and confusing to the observer. How could Nancy continue to refuse food when everyone else could see that she was wasting away? By what alterations of perception did she look at her body in the mirror and see something so drastically different from the girl other people saw? What rewards sustained these attitudes and behavior? Why did she resist incentives to eat?

Abnormal behavior has a compelling quality because it violates our assumptions and expectations about behavior. Lots of people diet — or try to — at one time or another in their lives, and we assume that they will have little trouble deciding when to stop. Yet for Nancy, an apparently "normal" image in the mirror or a scale reading that is "normal" for her build and height failed to elicit the typical response of a trip to the local pizza parlor or ice cream shop for a long-anticipated "reward." Quite the opposite happened. The more weight she lost, the more determined she was to lose more and the more anxious and dissatisfied she felt about her appearance.

Because Nancy's behavior violates an expectation about a "normal" response to weight loss, we struggle with many puzzling questions about her. Was her dieting behavior ever rationally motivated, despite appearances? Were her reasons for dieting quite complex and not always ascertainable? Was there a time in her dieting when her motivation shifted from normal to abnormal? Was Nancy's dieting a symptom of a deep-seated emotional conflict or did it arise from some as yet undiscovered biological anomaly?

Almost all patterns of abnormal behavior pose similar puzzles, particularly because most people who are emotionally disturbed are not abnormal in all facets of their behavior. Even the most bizarre psychotic will occasionally give relevant answers to questions. If you were to ask Nancy about something other than food, dieting, or her body, she would have answered you much as any other teenager would. She worried about her schoolwork, boys, and peer-group acceptance. Anyone whose behavior is somehow abnormal manifests numerous "islands" of normal behavior with which we can identify and feel empathy. It is this capacity to see parts of ourselves in disturbed individuals that makes the study of abnormal behavior so provocative. We recognize that by understand-

we all go through
short-lived periods
of depression
∴ can identify with
anorexia, long-term illness

∴ "medical students disease"

Fig. 1.1. A key aspect of anorexia is a distortion in the perception of one's own body.

ing the origins of abnormality, we can deepen our insight into ourselves and those around us.

We all go through episodes of greater-than-normal anxiety, periods of depression or withdrawal from others. Ordinarily, these periods of disturbance are short-lived responses to something in our environment. A new date, a good grade, a good job, or some positive change in the environment can quickly turn things around. From our own low points, however, we can recognize that the more chronic, persistent patterns of abnormal behavior observed in others are not far from our experience. This awareness is one possible reason why some students who read textbooks on abnormal psychology come down with "medical student's" disease and imagine themselves as alternately depressive, manic, schizophrenic, and so on, in the order of the chapters assigned. It is easy to see similarities and lose sight of differences.

Definition of Abnormal Behavior

As we have indicated, direct immediate experience with abnormal behavior is compelling and disturbing. We frequently know it when we see it. But scientific study of a subject requires more than immediate, emotional reactions. It requires a more precise definition. Is there a precise line or point of demarcation between normal and abnormal behavior? Most psychologists would answer with a resounding "no!" The division is arbitrary and depends somewhat on social conventions in a culture.

Because there is no clear division between normal and abnormal behavior, most psychologists accept the *continuum,* an imperceptibly changing scale of behavior with effective functioning at one end and severe personality disorganization at the other. Between these extremes are numerous gradations and variations within the range of abnormal behavior. Psychologists judge the severity of an abnormal behavior pattern by three criteria: (1) bizarreness of the behavior, (2) persistence of the behavior pattern, and (3) effect on social functioning (see Figure 1.2). Nancy's problem would

be considered a moderately severe form of abnormal behavior because of the disparity between her continual dieting and her current weight (bizarreness), because she failed to heed warnings that this self-starvation was life-threatening (persistence), and because her gradual social withdrawal disrupted her social and academic functioning.

The signs of abnormal behavior can be far less dramatic and obvious. Sometimes, only the disturbed individual or very intimate acquaintances may be aware that a problem exists, as in this illustration:

Gene approached the psychologist because of intense discomfort he had been experiencing with his girl friend, Debby. He loved her deeply and wanted to marry. During a recent episode of sexual experimentation with her, however, strange and disturbing thoughts of wanting to harm her intruded into his awareness. The thoughts were so powerful and disturbing that he lost all sexual desire and left hurriedly. The next two times Gene and Debby attempted to make love, the same thing happened, with the same conclusion. Gene had been feeling guilty about these thoughts and wondered if he was capable of giving in to them. He told no one about his turmoil, not even Debby, before consulting a psychologist.

Fig. 1.2. The line between normal and abnormal behavior is not a sharp one, but is better represented as a continuum. Abnormal behavior is judged to be more or less severe depending on its bizarreness, persistence, and impact on social functioning.

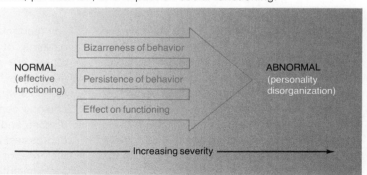

[Handwritten margin notes:]
MIDTOWN MANHATTAN STUDY put continuum to a test - to measure the prevalence of psychological disorders in a community (New York's East Side)

Treated & Untreated cases of abnormal behavior
- Scale for rating cases
1/ presence of psychological symptoms
2/ severity of the symptoms
3/ degree of impairment of relationships + social role

Conclusion: variation in psychological function was wide - if we consider the continuum we would have to consider that 1/4 are abnormal

Table 1.1. Incidence of mental health problems among 1660 respondents in Midtown Manhattan Study

Mental health category	Description of category	Percentage in category
Well	No evidence of symptom formation (symptom-free)	18.5
Mild symptoms	Mild symptom formation but functioning adequately	36.3
Moderate symptoms	Moderate symptom formation with no apparent interference in life adjustment	21.8
ADEQUATE FUNCTIONING		76.6 total
Marked symptoms	Moderate symptom formation with some interference in life adjustment	13.2
Severe symptoms	Serious symptom formation yet functioning with great difficulty	7.5
Incapacitated	Seriously incapacitated; unable to function	2.7
IMPAIRED FUNCTIONING		23.4 total

Source: Adapted from T. S. Langner and S. T. Michael, *Life Stress and Mental Health: The Midtown Manhattan Study,* p. 76. Copyright © 1963 by the Free Press of Glencoe, a division of the Macmillan Company. Reprinted by permission.

By our criteria, Gene's problem would be considered much less severely abnormal than Nancy's.

One advantage of the continuum approach to defining abnormal behavior is that it gives us greater flexibility to allow for individual variation when we evaluate behavior. In the *Midtown Manhattan Study* (Srole et al. 1962), a team of social and behavioral scientists put the continuum to the test. Their goal was to measure the prevalence of psychological disorders in a community, a residential section of New York City's East Side. For several years they gathered data on both treated and untreated cases of abnormal behavior of individuals living in the 400 blocks being studied. The study concluded, they devised a scale for rating cases that reflected a broad spectrum of mental health. The scale covered three factors: (1) presence of psychological symptoms, (2) severity of the symptoms, and (3) degree of impairment in everyday relationships and social role performance. Table 1.1 shows the results of their analysis. As the figures indicate, the variation in psychological functioning was indeed wide, ranging from 18.5 percent who were totally free of psychological symptoms to 2.7 percent totally disabled. You can see that if we consider the part of the continuum from *marked symptoms* to *incapacitated* as an index of major mental health problems in a community, we will have to conclude that about one person in four was abnormal.

Characteristics of Abnormal Behavior

Abnormal behavior violates all that we assume and expect about how people should act, whether that behavior is our own or someone else's. Psychologists have greater confidence defining behavior as abnormal when both the person in question *and* those around him concur that his behavior is an extreme departure from expectations. Sometimes we don't have this luxury, however, and most professionals would categorize as abnormal any behavior that includes at least one of these characteristics: (1) extreme social deviance, (2) subjective distress, or (3) psychological handicap.

Social Deviance

We call extreme and persistent behavior that disturbs people around us *social deviance*. Deviant behavior includes many patterns that we may not automatically think of as psychological disturbances, such as criminality and transvestism (dressing in clothes of the opposite sex), but insofar as they reflect inability to conform to socially approved rules, we often consider them psychological problems. Other examples of deviant behavior clearly suggest psychological problems. The case of Buddy A. is one:

Buddy's admission to the psychiatric ward of the county hospital was precipitated by the following events, which took place several hours earlier. He informed his mother that it would be necessary to sacrifice her in order for him to "attain Nirvana"; he threw her to the floor and, with his knee on her chest, began choking her. He later claimed in a rambling incoherent fashion that he was being "bombarded with knowledge" and had received

instructions from voices he heard to kill his mother. (Goldstein and Palmer 1975, p. 247)

The combination of Buddy's violent outburst, his belief that "voices" were telling him what to do, and his severely disorganized reasoning are such an extreme departure from appropriate social behavior that laymen and professionals alike viewed it as abnormal.

Some patterns of social deviance are highly dependent upon social values, which are subject to change as time passes. For a number of years our society looked upon homosexuality as a form of deviant behavior and designated it a "personality disorder." A sexual preference for members of one's own gender was considered a clear-cut symptom of emotional disorder and justified many social acts, including dismissal from a job and other forms of reproach. In 1973, the American Psychiatric Association voted to remove homosexuality from its list of disorders. Instead, it is now considered simply an alternative sexual choice. This act reflected not only changing social attitudes toward sexual freedom and variety but also scientific evidence that the range of emotional disorders is no greater among homosexuals than among heterosexuals (Weinberg and Williams 1974). It is just one example of the way our tolerance for deviant or unusual behavior varies from era to era, and the way designated patterns of abnormality usually reflect current values (see Figure 1.3).

Subjective Distress

For several months prior to her application for treatment, Veronica had been unable to leave her home without generalized feelings of panic, which she could not explain. "It is as if something dreadful would happen to me if I did not immediately go home," she said. Even after returning to the house, she would continue to feel shaken inside and would be unable to speak to anyone or do anything for an hour or so (Goldstein and Palmer 1975).

Fig. 1.3. Judgments of abnormality reflect social conventions of the times. Anne Hutchinson (left) was banished from the Massachusetts Bay Colony because she claimed to experience direct revelation from God. In contemporary society, members of religious groups (below) espousing more exotic beliefs and lifestyles are accepted.

Veronica defined her own excessive emotional reactions as abnormal, and most of us would agree with her. We assume that people can feel secure enough to walk out of the house without experiencing terror. When they cannot, we perceive that something is severely amiss. Self-reports of excessive fearfulness, depression, agitation, and other disturbing emotions ordinarily are considered valid criteria of abnormal psychological reactions.

Psychological Handicap

Phillip was very bright and academically talented as a teenager. He completed college with outstanding grades and began a career in merchandising. Within a few months after he started his first job, he became very unhappy with the job, and with his boss in particular, and quit suddenly. Numerous other jobs followed, but none lasted more than six months. At the age of 30, he seemed to be going nowhere in life. Wondering if his work pattern was indicative of a "neurotic problem," he sought psychological counseling.

A *psychological handicap,* which would seem to be Phillip's problem, is impaired ability to function adequately in everyday social and occupational roles because of emotional problems. The underlying problems may not be easy to identify, or they may be traceable directly to a specific life event, such as loss of a job or of a loved one. Subjective distress, if present at all, is not as intense as Veronica's.

Attributing unexplainable behavior to a psychological handicap involves value judgments: we must assume that we know what people — ourselves included — *should* be accomplishing. Many of the people who seek help from mental health professionals do it because they can't seem to meet their own standards for performance. They complain of not being able to find a love relationship, or to function as well as they think they should on the job, or to get close to other people, and so on.

Nancy, the self-starving teenager, showed many signs of *social deviance* in her eating, obsessive perfectionism, and hyperactivity. Also, her *subjective distress* was evident in her anxiety over excessive weight and failure to achieve the "perfect body." And she was *psychologically handicapped,* for her personal relationships deteriorated. The presence of all these characteristics is convincing justification for calling Nancy's behavior abnormal.

Classifying Abnormal Behavior

The definition of abnormal behavior as social deviance, subjective distress, or psychological handicap makes a general distinction between normal and abnormal behavior. Yet most psychologists and psychiatrists would like to make finer distinctions within the abnormal range. The difference between, say, Nancy's symptoms and Gene's disturbing sexual thoughts is so great that much is lost by considering them to represent one class of abnormal behavior. Over the years, professionals have devised many systems for classifying patterns of abnormal behavior. These systems have been mainly descriptive, because they group patients on the basis of similarities in their most prominent symptoms.

Most modern classification systems derive from the classic work of the German psychiatrist Emil Kraepelin, who years ago made the first scientific effort to classify patterns of abnormal behavior. Subsequently a great deal of time and energy has gone into developing psychiatric classification systems. Why expend so much effort forming more elegant pigeonholes for people? The answer is that a good classification system serves three purposes:

1. It allows us to predict the future course of a pattern of abnormal behavior, to make a *prognosis.*
2. It permits us to develop different *treatment* plans for distinct disorders.
3. It provides a way of studying the causes, or *etiologies,* of specific disorders.

Let's consider each of these in more detail by using Nancy once again.

Prognosis: Nancy's abnormal behavior pattern is classified as "anorexia nervosa" (literally, not eating for nervous causes). A large number of statistical studies (Halmi et al. 1973) have revealed that from 10 to 20 percent of people with this problem will die from self-starvation unless they receive intensive hospital treatment. Thus, if we know that Nancy manifests the key symptoms of this class, we also know that she runs a bad risk unless treated

comprehensively. We also know something else — that Nancy's risk from self-starvation is much greater than the risk for a depressed individual who also suffers from loss of appetite but who does not manifest the "relentless pursuit of thinness" (Bruch 1962) that Nancy does.

Differential treatment planning: Once we have recognized that Nancy is anorectic, we know that it is most essential to initiate treatment to get her eating again. Many anorectics require hospitalization and careful monitoring of food intake. Her emotional problems can wait until the danger of starvation has diminished. If, on the other hand, Nancy were judged to be neurotically depressed, hospitalizaton would not be critical for her survival, and she might begin an outpatient program of psychotherapy.

Etiology: Nancy's classification as anorectic does not now provide a definite system for understanding the cause of her disorder or distin-

The Mental Health Professions

The study and treatment of abnormal behavior is not the province of any one profession. A number of disciplines make significant contributions to this field. These are the disciplines, training, and typical activity:

1. **Psychology:** Psychologists receive a Ph.D. degree from a college of letters and science. All are trained in research methods, and many carry out basic and applied research relevant to abnormal behavior.

A special group called clinical psychologists also receive specialized training in applying psychological knowledge to diagnosis and treatment of abnormal behavior.

2. **Medicine:** A number of medical specialists, all with the M.D. degree from a college of medicine, are active in this field. Most prominent is the *psychiatrist,* who has completed a three-year specialized residency in the study and treatment of abnormal behavior. In addition to their training in applying psychological techniques, psychiatrists receive special training in biological treatments, such as drugs, for abnormal behavior.

Other medical specialties figure in this field. The *public health* physician studies the rate and course of abnormal behavior on a large scale to estimate how prevalent mental illness is in communities and even whole countries. Their research makes up the *epidemiology* of abnormal behavior.

3. **Social Work:** The social worker receives a professional degree, ordinarily the M.S.W. (Master of Social Work), from a school of social work. The psychiatric social worker takes specific training in social casework techniques for rehabilitating psychiatric patients.

4. **Nursing:** Nurses enter their profession after a two-year or four-year course of study in a school of nursing. Psychiatric nursing is a training specialty designed to qualify the nurse to work with emotionally disturbed patients. Psychiatric nurses are trained to use psychological techniques with patients, usually in hospitals, and are also qualified to administer medication, under a physician's direction.

guishing it from an adolescent depression. Nevertheless, isolating the pattern of symptoms classified as anorexia limits the number of etiological hypotheses for researchers to test. This method works not only for anorexia, but for many other classes of abnormal behavior as well.

In several notable cases, increasingly precise classification schemes have led to discovery of the cause behind a specific class of disorders. One dramatic example was the distinguishing of a form of psychosis called *paresis* from other disorders with similar symptoms when the specific bacterium that causes syphilis was discovered. The similarity between the symptoms of syphilis and the steady deterioration of both physical and mental abilities among some mental patients became a matter of record in 1798. The mental patients suffered multiple impairments, including delusions of grandeur and progressive paralysis, and they never recovered. Acceptance of Louis Pasteur's germ theory of disease in the 1870s sparked research efforts to find bacterial origins for just about every known disorder, including syphilis. In 1905 scientists finally identified the microorganism responsible for syphilis and, ultimately, for the symptoms of paresis, and the destruction of brain tissue it causes. The effect of this kind of success has been twofold: (1) it has spurred many researchers to look for a specific agent as the cause of a specific class of psychiatric disorder and to develop appropriate methods of prevention; and (2) it has encouraged efforts to devise better systems of classification and relate them to possible causes.

Although progress toward the discovery of specific etiologies for specific patterns of abnormal behavior has been slow, modern classification methods do provide a valuable aid in making recommendations for prognostic and differential treatment. In fact, progress has been so obvious that it influenced us in organizing this book. Relatively discrete clusters of abnormal behavior patterns are the subject in each of the next six units, and within each unit you will find a separate discussion of intervention or treatment that is specific for that cluster.

DSM-III: A New Look at an Old Problem

One of the most influential classification systems comes from the American Psychiatric Association (APA). Codified in *Diagnostic and Statistical Manuals (DSMs),* the system is periodically revised to take in the latest knowledge. The first and second editions, known as *DSM*-I (1952) and *DSM*-II (1968), have been used extensively in the United States to classify patients' behavior for clinical work and research. The APA is revising its classification system and *DSM*-III probably *will* have been adopted by the time you are reading this book.

The *DSM*-III edition is more closely linked to research on abnormal behavior than either of the previous editions, and has undergone extensive field testing. It goes beyond the other editions in specifying more precise behavioral criteria for clinical judgment; forms groups if possible, using firm knowledge about prognosis or differential response to specific treatments; and greatly increases the categories of abnormal behavior (*DSM*-I had 60, *DSM*-II had 145, and *DSM*-III has 230 separate categories).[1] Per-

---

[1] A number of writers (Zubin 1977; Garmezy 1978) have criticized this expansion of categories. Some have skeptically suggested that the APA is anticipating the arrival of national health insurance, and that ensuring that every behavior pattern has an official diagnosis of mental disorder means reimbursements for services will be more readily available. Spitzer et al. (1977) acknowledge that the added categories are not rooted in knowledge: "Because the *DSM*-III classification is designed for use for the entire profession and because knowledge about mental disorder is so limited, the Task Force has chosen to be *inclusive* rather than exclusive. In practice, this means that whenever a clinical condition can be described with clarity and relative distinctiveness, it is considered for inclusion."

diagnosis on 5 dimensions
Axis I — abnormal behavior in clear cut symptoms, anxiety etc
Axis II — 1/ personality disorders — recurring pattern of disturbed behavior in adults 2/ disorders in development in children & adolescents

haps the most significant change, however, is the multidimensional or *multiaxial* approach to diagnosis, which enables diagnosticians to assess a patient's behavior along five dimensions, or axes. A complex numerical code helps make the diagnosis more precise. Table 1.2 lists the general categories that comprise Axes I and II of *DSM*-III. Axis I describes abnormal behavioral patterns in terms of clear-cut symptoms (such as anxiety, depressions, psychosis). Axis II covers two areas: recurring patterns of disturbed life styles seen in adults and called *per-*

Table 1.2. Abbreviated draft of Axes I and II of *DSM*-III classification

AXIS I

ORGANIC MENTAL DISORDERS
(Symptoms include delusions, dementia, delirium, and/or depression.)

Senile and presenile dementias

Substance-induced
Alcohol
Barbiturate or similar-acting
   sedative or hypnotic
Opioid
Cocaine
Amphetamine or similar-acting
   stimulant
Hallucinogen
Cannabis
Tobacco
Caffeine
Other or unspecified substance
Cause unknown

SUBSTANCE-USE DISORDERS
Alcohol abuse
Alcohol dependence (alcoholism)
Barbiturate or similar-acting
   sedative or hypnotic abuse
Barbiturate or similar-acting
   sedative or hypnotic dependence
Opioid abuse
Opioid dependence
Cocaine abuse
Cocaine dependence
Amphetamine or similar-acting
   stimulant abuse
Amphetamine or similar-acting
   stimulant dependence
Hallucinogen abuse
Cannabis abuse

Cannabis dependence
Tobacco-use disorder
Other or unspecified
   substance-abuse
Other specified
   substance-dependence
Unspecified
   substance-dependence

SCHIZOPHRENIC DISORDERS
Disorganized (hebephrenic)
Catatonic
Paranoid
Undifferentiated
Residual

PARANOID DISORDERS
Paranoia
Shared paranoid disorder
Paranoid state

SCHIZOAFFECTIVE DISORDERS

AFFECTIVE DISORDERS
Episodic affective disorders
Manic disorder
Major depressive disorder
Bipolar affective disorder
   manic
   depressed
   mixed

Chronic affective disorders

Atypical affective disorders

PSYCHOSES NOT ELSEWHERE CLASSIFIED
Schizophreniform disorder
Brief reactive psychosis
Atypical psychosis

ANXIETY DISORDERS
Phobic disorders
Panic disorder
Obsessive compulsive disorder
Generalized anxiety disorder
Atypical anxiety disorder

FACTITIOUS (PSYCHOPHYSIOLOGICAL) DISORDERS
Factitious illness with
   psychological symptoms
Chronic factitious illness with
   physical symptoms

SOMATOFORM DISORDERS
Somatization disorder
Conversion disorder
Psychalgia
Atypical somatoform disorder

DISSOCIATIVE DISORDERS
Psychogenic amnesia
Psychogenic fugue
Multiple personality
Depersonalization disorder
Other

AXIS II

PERSONALITY DISORDERS
(Notice: These are coded on Axis II.)

Paranoid
Introverted
Schizotypal
Histrionic
Narcissistic
Antisocial
Borderline

sonality disorders, and specific *disorders of development* seen in children and adolescents. Axis III describes associated physical disorders. Axis IV assesses the severity of life stresses before the disorder appears, and Axis V the highest level of adaptive functioning before it appears. In most instances, the greater the life stress before onset and the better the social adaptation, the better the outcome. Therefore Axes IV and V are considered to be important predictors of the course of an abnormal behavior pattern, independent of its form.

Table 1.2. *(continued)*

Avoidant
Dependent
Compulsive
Passive-aggressive
Other or mixed

PSYCHOSEXUAL DISORDERS

Gender identity disorders

Paraphilias

Psychosexual dysfunctions

Other psychosexual disorders

DISORDERS USUALLY ARISING IN CHILDHOOD OR ADOLESCENCE
(This section lists conditions that usually first manifest themselves in childhood or adolescence. Any appropriate adult diagnosis can be used for diagnosing a child.)

Mental retardation

Pervasive developmental disorders
Infantile autism
Atypical childhood psychosis

Specific developmental disorders
(Notice: These are coded on Axis II.)
Specific reading disorder
Specific arithmetical disorder
Developmental language disorder
Developmental articulation
    disorder
Enuresis
Encopresis
Mixed
Other

Attention deficit disorders

Conduct disorders

Anxiety disorders of childhood or adolescence

Other disorders of childhood or adolescence

Disorders characteristic of late adolescence

Eating disorders

Speech disorders (stuttering)

Stereotyped movement disorders

REACTIVE DISORDERS NOT ELSEWHERE CLASSIFIED
Post-traumatic stress disorder

Adjustment disorders

DISORDERS OF IMPULSE CONTROL NOT ELSEWHERE CLASSIFIED
Pathological gambling
Kleptomania
Pyromania
Intermittent explosive disorder
Isolated explosive disorder
Other impulse-control disorder

SLEEP DISORDERS

Nonorganic

Organic

OTHER DISORDERS
Unspecified mental disorder (nonpsychotic)

Psychological factors affecting physical disorder

No mental disorder

CONDITIONS NOT ATTRIBUTABLE TO A MENTAL DISORDER
Malingering
Adult antisocial behavior
Childhood or adolescent antisocial
    behavior
Marital problem
Parent-child problem
Child abuse
Other interpersonal problem
Occupational problem
Uncomplicated bereavement
Noncompliance with medical
    treatment
Other life-circumstance problem

ADMINISTRATIVE CATEGORIES
Diagnosis deferred
Research subject
Boarder
Referral without need for
    evaluation

The new revision of the APA classification system is still in the pilot stage, and by the time you read this book many of the categories and category definitions probably will have been further modified in response to field test. Nevertheless, we will bring in *DSM*-III whenever possible in this book so that you will understand the latest attempts to sharpen criteria of classification.

Classification vs. Labeling Theory

Although use of the APA classification system is fairly standard in the United States, mental health professionals do not unanimously support *DSM*-III. Some object to the whole notion of defining anyone's behavior as abnormal, or pigeonholing them by assigning diagnostic labels. And *DSM*-III has evoked severe criticism (Garmezy 1978a) because it classifies so many problems in childhood behavior (reading disorders, for example) as mental disorders; the lifelong effect of acquiring this type of label as a child can be devastating. The whole system of classification implies acceptance of a particular model of abnormal behavior, the *medical* model, which views patterns of abnormal behavior in much the same way as physical diseases, having underlying causes and resultant observable "symptoms." Critics argue that abnormal behavior more often reflects "problems in living," which are hardly comparable to physical disease, and that the very use of diagnostic labels has a profoundly negative effect on a person's ability to resolve these problems (Szasz 1961).

Many criticize classification, but they all emphasize the negative consequences of assigning diagnostic labels such as anorexia, neurosis, or schizophrenia to people in turmoil. This view is the basis of *labeling theory* (Murphy 1976). Derived largely from sociology, labeling theory emphasizes that many of the behaviors we call deviant are quite normal in other cul-

tures (see Figure 1.4). Take someone who hears voices or sees things that aren't there. In our society, this type of behavior would earn a person the distinction of being abnormal and, possibly, a label to go with it. Many nonliterate cultures, on the other hand, would interpret the same behavior as a sign of a deep religious ex-

Fig. 1.4. Plains Indian men unable to function as warriors could find full acceptance dedicating themselves to female domestic and sexual specialties.

perience when carried out as part of the role of priest or *shaman*.

Primary Labeling Theory

In the context of cultural relativity, labeling theory has two variants, called *primary* and *secondary labeling*. Primary labeling theory purports that assigning labels actually *causes* a pattern of abnormal behavior to develop. Thus, it is argued, many patterns of unusual or deviant behavior that might run a benign course become entrenched patterns of abnormality once we have assigned diagnostic labels to them. Nancy may merely have been going through a disordered eating phase, but by labeling her "anorectic," we set in motion a chain of events within Nancy and those around her that set an inflexible pattern of abnormality. The label causes Nancy to think of herself differently — as abnormal and deviant — and consequently, she would assume the social role of the anorectic patient, which people around her would reinforce by their behavior toward her. Once the role of patienthood has been accepted, behavior is grooved in the abnormal direction and is less likely to change than it would be without the label. Some writers (Szasz 1961; Laing and Esterson 1964) have taken the theory a step further and have suggested that various forms of mental illness (including schizophrenia, manic-depressive illness, and sociopathy) are only *myths* created by society as it assigns labels that carry powerful emotional connotations.

Anthropologist Jane Murphy (1976) challenges a number of the assumptions underlying primary labeling theory. Her study of the phenomena of abnormal behavior in two cultures, the Eskimo of the Bering Sea area and the Egba Yorubas of Africa, questions the whole notion of cultural relativity. In both societies she found patterns of abnormal behavior that closely resemble a pattern our society has labeled

"schizophrenia," and milder patterns very much akin to our concept of anxiety disorders. Both of the cultures she investigated had a clear label for the former — *Nuthkavihak* in Eskimo and *Were* in Yoruba — but not for the latter (see Figure 1.5). As you will see later in this book, the Eskimo and the Yoruba classifications closely parallel our own, in that we have clearer and more coherent categories for severe forms of abnormal behavior than for the milder ones.

The symptoms of *Nuthkavihak* and *Were* are listed in Table 1.3. Eskimos describe *Nuthkavihak* as "being crazy," and the translation for *Were* is very similar. Curiously, both cultures differentiate these patterns from the altered states of consciousness manifested by priests or shamans. Murphy found that no *Nuthkavihak* or *Were* individuals had ever become priests or prophets.

Seeing, hearing, or believing things that are not seen, heard, or believed by all members of the group is sometimes considered abnormal behavior and sometimes a sign of great priestly power. In Eskimo culture a person's ability to control these states and use them for a specific social function, such as healing or prophecy, means that he is not *Nuthkavihak*. Asked to define the condition, one Eskimo said, "The mind does not control the person, he is *crazy*."

With these findings, Murphy has shattered one cornerstone of primary labeling theory, the idea that a pattern which our society labels abnormal, other cultures perceive differently. Still another blow to primary labeling theory came from Murphy's data on the incidence of *Nuthkavihak* in Eskimo culture. The number of Eskimos who manifested this schizophrenia-like syndrome was 8.8 per 1000; a careful 1940s study of a rural area in Sweden found the incidence to be 8.1 per 1000. Thus, if labels cause abnormal behavior, the Eskimos and the Swedish have an equal tendency to use them, which is highly unlikely.

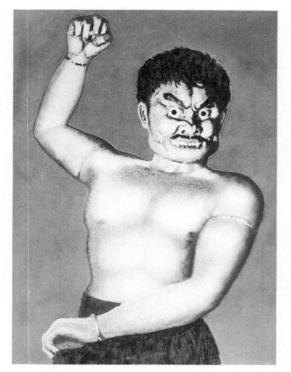 

Fig. 1.5. "This looks like the shaman in seance. He is out of his mind then, but *he* is not crazy." This statement was made by an Eskimo about a magazine picture (left) which has been retouched to show Eskimo clothing. Such an Eskimo shaman would not be considered abnormal because he controls and uses altered states for religious ritual. Right: An African said by members of his tribe and community to be insane because his altered states are in control of him.

Secondary Labeling Theory

Secondary labeling theory is more modest in scope than the primary variant. As the name implies, it accents the secondary consequences of diagnostic labeling. It assumes that a society has some patterns of abnormal behavior, but emphasizes that the names assigned to the behavior can catastrophically and unnecessarily stigmatize an individual. The stigma-

tizing consequences of the label, in turn, limit the possibililties for recovery or rehabilitation. A recent study by Rosenhan (1973) demonstrates how hard it is to shed a psychiatric label (see box, p. 19).

According to secondary labeling theory, a severe form of abnormal behavior such as manic-depressive illness arises according to a combination of biological and psychological factors (see Chapters 8 and 9 for a discussion of

Table 1.3. Symptoms of abnormal behavior in Eskimo and Yoruba cultures

Eskimo *Nuthkavihak*	Yoruba *Were*
1. Talking to one's self 2. Screaming at someone who does not exist 3. Belief that a child or husband was murdered by witchcraft, when no one else believes that 4. Belief that one is an animal 5. Refusal to eat because of fear that eating will kill one 6. Refusing to talk 7. Running away 8. Getting lost 9. Hiding in strange places 10. Making strange grimaces 11. Drinking urine 12. Becoming unusually strong and violent 13. Killing dogs 14. Threatening people for no reason	1. Hearing voices and trying to get others to see their source though no one can be seen 2. Laughing when there is nothing to laugh at 3. Talking all the time or not talking at all 4. Asking one's self questions and answering them 5. Picking up sticks and leaves for no purpose except to put them in a pile 6. Throwing away food because it is thought to contain *juju* 7. Tearing off one's clothes 8. Setting fires 9. Defecating in public and then mushing around in the feces 10. Taking up a weapon and then hitting someone for no reason 11. Breaking things in a state of being stronger than normal 12. Belief that an odor is continuously emitted from one's body

Source: J. M. Murphy, "Psychiatric Labeling in Cross-cultural Perspective," *Science*, 1976, 191, pp. 1019–1028.

these factors). The label "manic-depressive," however, has a negative effect not only on the patients but also on the people with whom they interact. Consider how you would feel if you sat down in class and the person next to you said, "Hi, I'm new here. Just got out of the hospital." You said, "What was wrong?" and she said, "I had a manic-depressive breakdown." Suddenly you would feel uncomfortable. Your discomfort would go beyond the excessive intimacy of the confidence shared. Perhaps you would be fearful: maybe she is dangerous or behaves oddly or, worse yet, will want to befriend you. Your emotional response to the label would affect your social behavior. You might change your seat or try to avoid sitting next to this person in the future. Rightly or wrongly, the label has stigmatized this ex-patient.

Secondary labeling theory applies not only to severe forms of mental illness but also to all other patterns of deviance. It is important because it describes how we formulate expectations about other people's behavior, expectations that may underestimate capability and become self-fulfilling prophecies. If you doubt the truth of this statement, think for a minute about the mentally retarded (Mercer 1973) and the blind (Scott 1969), for whom labels determine whether the individual accepts a normal or a deviant self-concept. Pressure has been exerted occasionally to change labels to avoid stigmatizing consequences. Relabeling mentally retarded children "exceptional" for educational purposes was an attempt to generate more optimistic expectations by using a less pessimistic label. Labels, it is clear, lead to rejection only because we are prone to reject those who are different; they also highlight differences. If we were raised to accept differences, labels would not matter. It's not the labels but our response to them that creates problems for others.

The label is still with us, but massive public education programs have been mounted to change the connotations. One of these is a long-term program of the National Association for Mental Health, started by a recovered psychiatric patient named Clifford Beers. It is meant to promote a more positive and more auspicious attitude about abnormal behavior with posters and radio and television advertising (see Figure 1.6).

Few would attempt to refute secondary labeling theory. It is obvious that anyone who uses diagnostic classification must be extremely cautious, so that the benefits of the information the diagnosis conveys are not outweighed by the negative effects of their application.

Psychiatric Labels Are Hard to Shake

An excellent illustration of the secondary consequences of branding people with psychiatric labels comes from a study by Rosenhan (1973).

Over a period of three years, Rosenhan arranged for a number of normal people to be admitted to several psychiatric hospitals in the United States. Care was taken to ensure that none of the participants had psychiatric problems. Each volunteer (called a "pseudo-patient") was instructed to appear at the admitting room of a psychiatric hospital complaining of hearing voices that said "empty," "hollow," and "thud." Other than this symptom, which indeed is one of the key symptoms of the severe psychiatric disorder known as schizophrenia, the pseudo-patients reported no false symptoms. They accurately described their own family histories and circumstances.

The strong effects of the psychiatric-hospital context on judgments of abnormality were very clear. All pseudo-patients were diagnosed as psychotic; for eleven of them the diagnosis was schizophrenia, and for one it was manic-depressive psychosis. On the basis of one reported symptom and without any objective confirmatory evidence, all the volunteers were judged abnormal and admitted to the hospital, where they stayed an average of nineteen days. It is hard to assume that a normal person would feign hallucinations to gain admission to a psychi-

atric hospital; the context makes that hypothesis highly unlikely.

The hospital also altered perceptions of the staff personnel with whom Rosenhan's "patients" came in contact after admission, when they stopped talking about the alleged hallucination and behaved in their usual (normal?) way. Once the label of schizophrenia or manic-depressive psychosis had been assigned, the consequences specified by the secondary labeling theory were observed. Behavior that was essentially normal was judged quite differently because of the label, because few would expect that someone who had acquired such a label could reverse their behavior so rapidly. Critics of psychiatric-classification systems argue that negative expectations generated by these labels can become self-fulfilling prophecies and drastically limit a patient's chances for full reintegration into society.

In no instance did any of the staff detect that the pseudo-patient was actually quite sane; in fact, the only people who recognized the deception were other psychiatric patients. Not only did normal behavior in the hospital context not lead to a changed attribution of normality, but at the time of discharge, most patients were diagnosed "schizophrenia — in remission," which implies that they were schizophrenic but did not show signs of the disorder at the time they were released.

Fig. 1.6. This typical ad from the National Association for Mental Health is designed to create greater awareness of emotional problems and the value of early intervention.

Facts About Abnormal Behavior

Despite the controversies that surround those who seek precise definitions for abnormality and classification, there are compelling reasons for identifying and studying abnormal behavior. The behavior is inherently fascinating and often personally relevant, but of greatest significance is the sheer magnitude of the social problem. We have come a long way in understanding abnormality, but the cures are few and the number of those requiring treatment is still very large.

As we have indicated, the Midtown Manhattan Study revealed that 25 percent of the population who were studied manifested strong signs of impairment resulting from abnormal behavior. Is Manhattan representative of other parts of the country? Evidently it is not very different in the prevalence of abnormal behavior. In a recent large study of a representative sample from the United States population (National Center for Health Statistics 1970), respondents answered questions about various symptoms of psychological distress. Almost 5 percent reported having had a "nervous breakdown," and 13 percent reported feeling close to the edge of such a breakdown at some time in their lives. Thus, a total of 18 percent suffered, by their own admission, from extreme abnormal behavioral reactions. The difference between 18 percent and the 25 percent figure that came from the Midtown Manhattan Study is not very great.

A survey on the incidence of emotional dysfunction among schoolchildren taken for the Joint Commission for Mental Illness and Health in Children (Glidewell and Swallow 1969) showed that 10 percent of the nation's elementary school children are sufficiently maladjusted to require professional assistance, and that 30 percent suffer identifiable difficulties in school adjustment. The latter figure is consistent with another study of primary school children carried out in Rochester, New York (Cowen et al. 1963). Although it is arbitrary to equate school maladjustment with abnormal behavior, the tragic consequences of urban ghetto life are revealed by the 70 percent figure of school maladjustment found among that population (Kellam and Schiff 1967).

Thus, from a very conservative point of view, at least one person in four suffers from some pattern of psychological disturbance. These studies translate into an approximate total of 40 million Americans whose psychological functioning is markedly to severely impaired.

The personal suffering and economic loss to society attributable to psychological impairment is truly staggering. The National Institute of Mental Health (1976) estimated the cost of abnormal behavior to the United States in 1974 to be approximately $38 billion. Direct costs for mental health care accounted for $14.5 billion. Indirect costs, such as earnings lost, related deaths and disabilities, and time lost to outpatient therapy accounted for $19.8 billion of the total. This society simply cannot allow so large a problem to persist; we must make every effort to eliminate it.

The Goals of This Book

If we believe that abnormal behavior is a major social problem that we must face in one way or another, what can this book do to help you comprehend and formulate opinions about relevant issues? First, we hope to provide you with an awareness of the diverse patterns of abnormal behavior. A major focus of the book is description, both from the observer's perspective and from the subjective point of view. The latter is particularly crucial, for only by entering the inner world of the disturbed individual can we develop the understanding necessary for compassionate empathy. Throughout this book, we provide you with personal reports of the inner experience of anxiety, depression, psychosis, and so on, to convey the value of understanding inner experience.

To enhance our understanding we must go beyond description to find the reasons that make people behave in abnormal ways. What makes a person who appears normal change into a terrified and frightened individual? Why do people sometimes experience deep and prolonged depression when things seem to be going so well for them? Why can't an autistic child respond to people as more normal children do?

A second major focus of this book is current knowledge on the answers to questions of this sort. What do we currently know about the causes, or etiologies, of abnormal behavior? In each section of the book, we review current theories about these causes, as well as the supporting and contradictory evidence. Where there are great gaps in our knowledge, we will recognize those.

The third focus of the book is treatment, or, as it is frequently called, *intervention* with abnormal behavior. What is available, how well does it work, and what are the side effects and key issues? No intervention, whether psychological or biological, is without its cost, and we need to know something about the relative costs and hazards of modern interventions to appraise their "risk-benefit ratio." We shall see in these chapters that we are entering a new era in the treatment of abnormal behavior. Single treatments such as drugs, individual psychotherapy, and residential care are less likely to stand alone in the future. *Multimodal* or combined approaches are increasingly popular, and we will deal with the issue of combining modalities of treatment wherever appropriate.

A final goal of this book is to provide an appreciation of how knowledge is acquired in this field. As you will see in Chapter 3, research on abnormal behavior has much in common with all research on human behavior. There are, however, special problems in studying abnormal behavior that relate to the disturbed and altered states of our human subjects. Many of the techniques for gathering information about human behavior require modification for use with abnormal, disturbed individuals.

In addition to discussions of research strategies, we shall present major findings derived from scientific research. This is not to say, however, that we shall present only well-docu-

mented "facts" about abnormality — to do so would give a very thin book. In studying abnormal psychology we confront a special dilemma. On the one hand, facts are especially difficult to come by, because the phenomena that interest us are quite elusive. Unconscious processes, early experiences, feelings, and sources of stress are difficult to define and to measure. Furthermore, their quality is apt to be distorted, as we shall see, by the ways in which they are measured. Also, the study of real clinical problems raises a host of procedural and ethical obstacles. On the other hand, in this field we cannot afford to wait until all the evidence is in to act. Clinical decisions that affect people's lives must be made daily, and they demand our best judgment, based on the best available evidence. Therefore, the clinical psychologist or psychiatrist is in the awkward position of being trained to be scientifically skeptical and clinically responsive. You may share some of their frustration, in reading this book, as you become aware of the very real problems that people suffer and the equally real limits of our present knowledge.

Summary

1. The division between normal and abnormal behavior is arbitrary and changes with social values. Therefore, psychologists view behavior as a continuum ranging from effective functioning to severe personality disorganization. Three criteria measure the severity of an abnormal behavior pattern: the bizarreness of the behavior, the persistence of the pattern, and the effect on social functioning.

2. Data collected from a large sample of residents of New York's East Side for the Midtown Manhattan Study revealed a broad spectrum of mental health among the population. One of every four persons in the study showed signs of major mental health problems.

3. Behavior is categorized as abnormal if it has at least one of three characteristics: extreme social deviance, reflecting an inability to conform to socially approved rules; subjective distress, or self-awareness of feelings of excessive fearfulness, agitation, or other disturbing emotions; and psychological handicap, defined as impaired ability to function adequately in everyday social and occupational roles because of emotional problems.

4. Classification of abnormal behavioral patterns facilitates: (1) prognosis — it allows us to predict the future course of these patterns; (2) treatment — it permits us to develop different treatment plans for distinct disorders; and (3) etiological research — it provides a basis for studying the causes of specific disorders.

5. The latest classification system developed by the American Psychiatric Association,

DSM-III, enables diagnosticians to assess patients' behavior along five axes, ranging from Axis I, which describes abnormal behavioral patterns, through Axis V, which describes the highest level of adaptive functioning before the disorder appeared.

6. The main objection to a classification system such as *DSM*-III is that it pigeonholes people by assigning them labels. There are two variants of labeling theory. (1) Primary labeling theory contends that the assignment of labels actually causes a pattern of abnormal behavior to develop. (2) Secondary labeling theory emphasizes that the names assigned to the behavior can stigmatize individuals in society's view and in the way they see themselves, and thereby can limit the possibilities for recovery or rehabilitation.

7. The primary reasons for studying abnormal behavior are its magnitude as a social problem (one in four people), and the great personal suffering and economic loss to society attributable to psychological impairment.

[Handwritten margin notes:]

Rosenhan

1/ a . b
2/ psychological disorder
+ develop ment disorders in children
3/ associated physical disorder
4/ life stress before the disorder
5/ highest level of adaptive functioning before the disorder

Beers
- helps to stop labeling

U.S study supports the Manhatan Study
,18%
25%

assumes that cultural ideas of abnormal behavior varies
vs Murphy
∴ # of a b cases must vary
Eskimo = Sweden.

Murphy
Beers

Chapter 2

Evolving Models of Abnormal Behavior

Biological Themes
Decline and Renaissance
Contemporary Biological Models

Psychological Themes
Medieval Demonology
Challenge to Witchcraft
Roots of Modern Psychological Theories
Freudian Psychoanalysis
Behaviorism and the Social Learning Approach
Behavioral-Psychoanalytic Rapprochement

Mental Institutions: The Era of "Moral Treatment"

Community Mental Health Centers

A Contemporary Problem: Synthesizing Divergent Models

Summary

He scratched on the doors of the gate and let his spittle fall down upon his beard. Then said Achish unto his servants, ''Lo, ye see this man is mad; wherefore have ye brought him to me?''

—I Sam. 21:13–14

This passage from the Bible clearly indicates that some patterns of behavior were considered abnormal as far back as Biblical times. Abnormal behavior disturbed onlookers then, as now; it was mysterious, unsavory, and frightening. Humankind has long sought explanations for behavior that arouses such distress in the onlooker. Despite the strong desire for understanding, however, the explanations have been very hard to find. As we saw in Chapter 1, even today we are forced to make guesses about underlying causes. In prescientific times these guesses invoked popular myths and legends to account for aberrant behavior and to prescribe treatment.

The transition between prescientific and scientific explanations of abnormality is not as sharp as we would like to believe. As late as the nineteenth century, a prominent American physician, Benjamin Rush (1745–1813), believed that one way to cure mental illness was to terrorize the patient, a "therapeutic" procedure originally advocated in ancient Rome (Deutsch 1965). A few themes have appeared again and again throughout history, each time in more sophisticated form, as our knowledge about the natural world has grown. Among these are: (1) that abnormal behavior reflects an underlying biological deviation, and (2) that it reflects an underlying deviation in psychological function. In this chapter we will trace the development of each of these themes, from prehistory to the present, the models to which they gave rise, and the types of treatment they spawned.

Biological Themes

Theories that abnormal behavior grows out of biological deviations go back to the writings of the ancient Greeks. Empedocles (490–430 B.C.) suggested that all illness arises from an imbalance in body chemicals known as *humors*. Empedocles based his theory on the four elements (fire, earth, water, and air), which manifest different qualities (heat, dryness, moisture, and cold, respectively). Each element was thought to correspond to a bodily chemical or humor: blood in the heart, phlegm in the brain, yellow bile in the liver, and black bile in the spleen. Any imbalance among these humors made the body vulnerable to disease.

Hippocrates (460–377 B.C.), father of Greek medicine, expanded Empedocles' humors theory to explain abnormal behavior. He conceived normal brain functioning, and therefore mental health, as dependent upon a delicate balance among the four humors. If a person was sluggish or dull, the body supposedly contained a predominance of phlegm. Too much black bile caused melancholia, or depression, too much yellow bile explained irritability, and too much

blood was the source of bad temperament. Hippocrates' biological view of abnormal behavior was based upon the very limited knowledge of physiology at that time. It has, of course, not stood the test of subsequent scientific scrutiny. It is significant, however, because of the hypothesis that abnormal behavior is a direct effect of alterations in brain structure or functioning.

During ancient times when the theory of humors was predominant, drugs were the major recommended treatment. The most popular of these was the black hellebore, or Christmas rose. The afflicted ingested the powdered roots of this plant, which is a drastic laxative and poisonous when taken in large doses. Its use persisted throughout the Middle Ages.

A more complete analysis of how an imbalance of humors caused mental illness came later from Benjamin Rush (1745–1813). Often referred to as "father of American psychiatry," Rush believed that mental illness resulted from "a great morbid excitement or inflammation of the brain; that an unrestrained appetite caused the blood vessels to be overcharged with blood; and that it is important to relieve the brain before obstruction and disorganization take place" (Deutsch 1965, p. 78). Consequently, the treatment for mental illness was to drain great amounts of blood from people judged to be mentally ill. Rush reported bleeding more than six quarts from one person over a few months and he took nearly four gallons from another in forty-seven bleedings. In all probability, bleeding was effective from the doctor's point of view, because it so weakened patients that they were less agitated and easier to manage.

After the decline of Greek civilization, the major contributions in the study of abnormal behavior came from the Roman Empire, most notably from Galen (A.D. 130–200), a Greek physician whose enormous influence over medical thought endured centuries after his death. According to Galen, the brain was the center of psychological functions, which included internal functions (imagination, judgment, memory, apperception [recognition], and movement) and external functions (consisting of the five senses). In addition, there were two emotional souls — which he called "irrational" — one in the heart and the other in the liver. Specifically, Galen believed that abnormal behavior arose either because the brain itself was diseased or as an indirect consequence of a disorder in another organ. For example, mania and melancholia resulted from an actual disease of the brain. Drunkenness occurred when wine filled the entire body with "warm vapors," which disrupted the function of the two irrational souls and indirectly impaired the brain's ability to make clear judgments. It is for this concept — that disorders of peripheral organs can profoundly impair functioning of the central nervous system — that modern psychology is indebted to the Greek doctor.

Decline and Renaissance

The fall of Rome abruptly put an end to the scientific quest for the biological origins of psychopathology. Throughout the medieval period, the science that was taught was that of ancient Greece and Rome, and antirationalism dominated. Recourse to faith, not empirical evidence, was the rule. Although the Renaissance began in the fifteenth century, no progress was made developing biological theories of abnormal behavior until the middle of the nineteenth century.

The reemergence of a biological viewpoint then began, with the German physician, Wilhelm Griesinger, insisting that any diagnosis of emotional disorder specify a physiological cause. Few valid clues to these physiological causes appeared however until Louis Pasteur

introduced the germ theory of disease in the 1860s and 1870s. Following Galen's dictum that abnormal behavior arises from disease in the brain or in peripheral organs that impact on brain processes, clinicians and scientists searched for signs that bacterial infection underlay various patterns of abnormal behavior. They hoped for specificity — a specific microbe that caused a specific pattern of abnormality — as in diphtheria, cholera, and other infectious diseases. We mentioned in Chapter 1 the one major triumph that these investigations produced, linking the psychiatric disorder general paresis to the spirochete that causes syphilis. No discovery in modern history gave more incentive to biological research into psychiatric disorders. Unfortunately, subsequent efforts to implicate infectious agents in the generation of mental illness proved futile.

During the period when infection figured prominently in theories of abnormal behavior, an interest in biological treatments also revived. One new approach was to induce fever to produce convulsions. Insulin-coma treatments to artificially lower blood sugar and electroconvulsive treatments (ECT), in which an electric current is passed through the brain from outside the skull, were common methods of inducing convulsions at the time. The use of ECT continues today because it has frequently been effective in treating severe depressive disorders, although no one knows how it works. Perhaps the most radical biological treatment developed in recent history — because it is irreversible — is the lobotomy, a surgical procedure during which the connecting fibers between the frontal and prefrontal lobes of the brain are severed (Figure 2.1).

The conviction that some patterns of abnormal behavior have biological causes persisted despite the abandonment of the infection model. But what avenues of research should be explored? Many stops and starts were made in

Overview: The Biology of Behavior

In recent years scientists have made many discoveries about the structure and function of the human nervous system, but particularly of the brain. One consequence of their quest to understand the biochemical mechanisms of the brain has been a renewal of interest among psychologists in the relationship between brain function and behavior, and, as the text points out, a number of contemporary theorists attribute the causes of certain types of abnormal behavior to malfunctions in newly described brain mechanisms.

The human nervous system has two parts: the central nervous system, made up of the brain and spinal cord, and the peripheral nervous system, which comprises all nerves outside the brain and spinal cord. The central nervous system interprets informational or sensory stimuli that it receives from the peripheral nervous system and dictates appropriate motor responses. Thus, the central nervous system governs behavior. The spinal cord functions primarily to relay messages between the brain and the peripheral nervous system. Its repertoire of responses is limited to "involuntary" motor responses, or reflexes, which require no conscious decision making (for example, jerking when the doctor strikes your knee with a mallet, blinking at a sudden burst of bright light, and jumping in response to an unexpected noise), and so the brain is actually the source of most behavior.

The structural basis of the nervous system is the individual nerve cell, which scientists believe is the key to understanding behavior. The brain is composed of tens of billions of nerve cells, or neurons, whose function is to transmit messages in the form of electrical impulses from one part of the brain to another. Figure 1 illustrates how an impulse travels through one nerve cell to the next nerve cell in its path. As the figure shows, most neurons have a cell body, a cell nucleus, impulse receptors called dendrites, and impulse transmitters called axons. The cell body produces electrical impulses, which it sends through the axon for transmission to the receptor site on an adjacent neuron. When a neuron "fires," it signals the axon and its terminal bulbs that an electrical impulse is on the way and sets off a series of chemical changes that determine whether or not the impulse will be able to jump across the synapse separating the transmitting — presynaptic — neuron and the potential receptor — postsynaptic — neuron (see Fig. 1 inset). In the terminal bulb a group of so-called synaptic vesicles release into the synapse either a neurotransmitter substance that completes the connection and allows the impulse to keep going or one that inhibits the transmission. Subsequently the terminal bulbs recover the neurotransmitter substance and the mitochondrion chemically breaks it down for elimination or reuse within the cell.

Neurotransmitter substances are the focus of a great deal of current research. Evidence of their existence is recent and the number of known neurotransmitter chemicals continues to grow, but scientists still know few of the details about how and why they work. Nevertheless, on the basis of what they know they speculate that malfunctions in the production, release, or reclamation of neurotransmitters are the cause, in part, of several types of abnormal behavior. Within the brain, each of these chemicals is confined to specific areas, to tracts of nerve cells that can accept only substances having the right chemical composition (see Figs. 4, 6.2, and 8.6). Therefore, each might be specific for a different type of behavior, and a malfunction involving one neurotransmitter might produce behavioral symptoms of manic-depressive illness whereas a malfunction affecting another neurotransmitter might be linked to symptoms of schizophrenia.

Further research on the brain is necessary to confirm or refute the theory. If it is true and if relationships between specific neurotransmitters and specific disorders can be firmly established, mental health professionals will be better able to treat these disorders in the future. Revealing the chemical mechanism responsible for behavioral symptoms, however, would not explain *why* some people fall victim to particular behavior disorders in the first place. There are many theories that attempt to explain the origins of abnormal behavior, as you will discover by reading this book, just as there are different viewpoints regarding neurotransmitter theories, and many of the clues that could confirm or refute them as yet remain locked inside the brain.

Fig. 1. The structure of a nerve cell and synapse (inset).

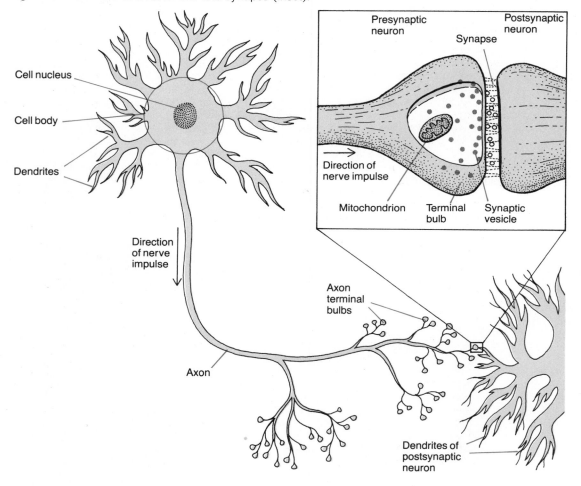

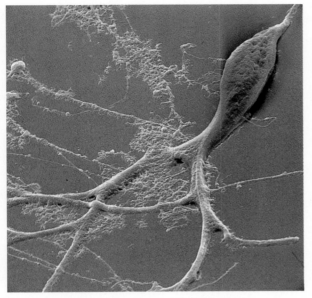

Fig. 2. A single nerve cell magnified 30,000 times.

Fig. 3. Plexiglas model of nerve endings shows nerve impulse traveling through axon (yellow) to terminal bulb, where synaptic vesicles (red) prepare to release neurotransmitter substance into synapse.

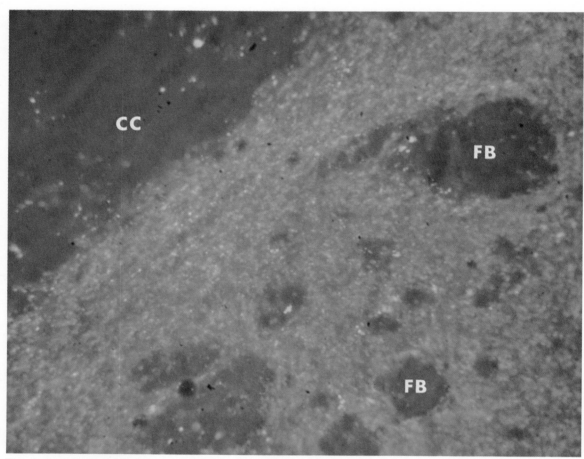

Fig. 4. Scientists can delineate specific neuron tracts by a technique known as histofluorescence. Here, dopaminergic tracts in a rat brain appear green when so treated. Each green dot represents an individual dopamine neuron terminal. (FB = a nonfluorescent (lacking dopamine) fiber bundle; CC = corpus callosum, a band of nonfluorescent fibers.)

[handwritten margin notes: biochemical model — focused on the mode by which impulses are transmitted within the brain — transmitted by neurons the presynaptic neurons produces neurotransmitter substance into the synaptic cleft which receptors in postsynaptic neuron + neuron cause the neuron to fire causing to transmit the impulse further]

[handwritten top margin notes: New discoveries; one of few neurotransmitters in the brain activate specific areas in the brain, particular the midbrain area, controls emotional behavior; 2/ The amount of neurotransmitter substance available at the synaptic cleft whether neural determines transmission occurs correctly, too much or too little may affect behavior.]

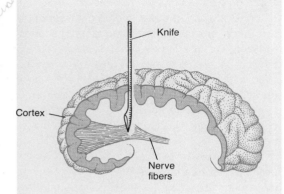

Fig. 2.1. In the 1930s the prefrontal lobotomy came into use as a means of controlling violent patients. Since then less drastic methods of treating behavior disorders have largely replaced this type of brain surgery.

the first half of the twentieth century, but no promising leads came until the 1950s. Many investigators felt that Hippocrates was on the right track but that he just didn't know enough about the biochemistry of behavior to create accurate theories. Great advances in biochemistry between 1920 and 1940 opened up the possibility of understanding how nerve impulses are transmitted. With the benefit of modern biochemical knowledge and recent clarification of the relationships among different parts of the brain and the way the brain interacts with other organs of the body, researchers have made significant strides toward disclosing the biological mechanisms involved in abnormal behavior.

Contemporary Biological Models

Models of abnormal behavior always reflect the current state of knowledge in an area. At this time, two approaches receiving considerable attention are a biochemical model and a

[handwritten margin note: biochemical model, genetic model]

genetic one. The favored biochemical model of abnormality focuses on the mode by which impulses are transmitted within the brain. Messages travel through the brain via individual nerve cells called *neurons.* For an impulse to pass from one neuron to another, the first cell, the *presynaptic neuron,* must release a chemical neurotransmitter substance into the *synaptic cleft* separating the two neurons. These neurotransmitters, in turn, activate receptor sites on the *postsynaptic neurons* and cause this neuron to fire and transmit the neural message in sequence to other neurons.

Two recent discoveries have made it possible to formulate relatively specific biochemical theories of abnormality. The first is that only one, or at most a few, of the large number of neurotransmitter substances in the brain activate specific areas of the brain, particularly the midbrain area, which controls emotional behavior. Consequently, any deviation in the amount of specific neurotransmitter substances can affect specific brain areas and, in turn, will lead to relatively specific alterations in mood or behavior. Second, the amount of neurotransmitter substance available at the synaptic cleft determines whether neural transmission occurs correctly. Either too much or too little of a neurotransmitter substance will alter perception, mood, thinking, and overt behavior. If too little neurotransmitter substance is available, receptor sites will call for more from the presynaptic neuron. The result may be overcompensation, leaving an excess of the substance in the synaptic cleft; behavior then becomes abnormal. Recent research on the effects of mind-altering (psychedelic) drugs on neurotransmitter substances has provided particularly valuable information about the role of these substances as behavior determinants, as we will see when we discuss biological theories of schizophrenia (Chapter 6) and mood disorders (Chapter 8).

Genetic theories also purport to explain abnormal behavior with biological reasoning. Based on the common observation that some families produce more emotionally disturbed offspring than others, these models postulate that children inherit the predisposition to abnormality from a parent. Research methods used to test genetic theories include family studies, twin studies, and adoption studies. *Family studies* simply chronicle how often particular forms of abnormal behavior occur in many generations of a family to uncover patterns that would support theories of genetic transmission. *Twin studies* contrast identical twins, who have identical genetic structure, with fraternal twins, who are carried at the same time but are no closer genetically than ordinary siblings. If a behavior pattern is genetically determined, it should show up in both identical twins or in neither of them. The incidence of similar abnormal behavior patterns in fraternal twins, on the other hand, should be about the same as it is among non-twin siblings. *Adoption studies* are an attempt to correct for the fact that family and twin studies cannot really separate genetic from environmental factors associated with being part of the same family. The assumption is that offspring of parents manifesting a form of abnormal behavior, even if they are adopted away at birth and reared by relatively normal parent figures, are more likely to develop abnormal behavior patterns than children of normal biological parents *if* genetic factors have some effect in producing abnormal behavior. In subsequent chapters, we shall examine evidence for genetic factors in various patterns of abnormal behavior that were found in family, twin, and adoption studies.

It should not surprise you to learn that emphasis on neurochemical research has thrust biological treatments into prominence once again. As you will see, therapists use drugs to quiet schizophrenic patients, raise the mood of the depressed, calm hyperkinetic children, and so on. Generally, modern biological treatments are much more effective than previous ones. Not only are pharmacological agents used extensively and effectively, but they are much applied in testing biological models as well. A drug that can reverse key symptoms of an abnormal behavior pattern can provide a clue to the biochemical cause that is producing these symptoms.

A fundamental problem with biological approaches to treatment is that as they become more precise and more effective, practitioners seem to lose sight of the whole person and his psychological needs. No matter how thoroughly they eliminate symptoms, drugs do little to help a person face life crises or problems that may very well have had something to do with the original breakdown. Frequently, clinicians who use biological treatments have difficulty shifting "mind sets" and considering behavior on a psychological level. Similarly, psychologically oriented practitioners have difficulty reconciling the use of drugs with psychological therapy. In this book, we shall present any evidence that is available on the interface between biological and psychological treatments and their relative contributions in reducing abnormal behavior patterns.

Psychological Themes

Psychological theories emphasize how significant emotions and inner conflicts are in the development of abnormal behavior. They also emphasize that much behavior, both normal and abnormal, is the result of one's learning history, and that, being learned, it can be unlearned.

The history of modern psychological theories of abnormality is stormy and ugly. Be-

[handwritten margin note: more women as witches, because their ability to tempt men sexually was taken as a sign of satanic possession / ability]

fore the late nineteenth century, social theorists attributed abnormal behavior to psychological factors, but these involved issues in ethics and religion in which judgments of good and evil were primary. We have seen that abnormal behavior is disturbing and frightening and that, therefore, it has given rise to all sorts of explanations. Primitive societies (Clements 1932) blame this frightening behavior on evil spirits. In these societies the disturbed individual is believed to behave strangely either because someone in the tribe is causing evil spirits to possess his mind or because he is sending out evil spirits to harm others. Naturally, the action taken to drive out the evil spirit depends on which explanation people accept.

Medieval Demonology

Following the decline of Rome, the church became the major social and political institution in the Western world. During the classic era of Greece and Rome, abnormal behavior had been largely the province of the physician. During the medieval period, however (Zilboorg and Henry 1941), the church left physical illness to the physician, but claimed that many forms of abnormality were disturbances of the spirit and therefore lay within the dominion of the church. Thus, treatment of the emotionally disturbed was generally in the hands of the priests, whose treatment consisted of praying, laying on of hands, and sprinkling the sufferer with holy water. The church taught that abnormal behavior was the product of *possession,* the taking over of a mind by demons. In early medieval times, the "possessed" were treated with kindness; however, the treatment changed markedly once deviant behavior came to be interpreted as a sign of satanic possession of the spirit.

At first, theology described two types of possession by the devil. In one form, the victim was believed to be unwillingly seized by the devil as God's punishment for sinning. These individuals the church considered to be mentally ill. Their possession was viewed as a personal misfortune. Priests would attempt to coax out the demon with elaborate rituals that most resemble the incantations of witch doctors in primitive societies. The priest would reason with the demon, cajole him, or curse him out if other methods failed. For these rituals, priests had access to books containing hundreds of pages of names and curses.

The second form of possession arose out of a voluntary and deliberate pact with the devil. These possessed individuals were called "witches," and were believed to be endowed with supernatural powers. As agents of the devil, they could injure their enemies, cause cattle to sicken, ruin crops, control the weather, make men impotent, and transform themselves into animals. By the end of the fifteenth century, the distinction between the two forms of demonic possession was blurred. Numerous individuals manifesting signs of conditions that we would recognize as mental illness were labeled "witches" or "heretics" and dealt with most harshly, usually being put through trial by fire to drive out Satan (see Figure 2.2).

It is curious that most of the so-called witches in medieval Europe were women. Generally, it was the women who were tortured and burned — in incredible numbers (Robbins 1959). Their ability to tempt men sexually was taken as a sure sign of satanic possession. At that time church doctrine labeled sexual yearnings sinful and targeted women, the descendants of Eve, as the source of man's temptation. *Malleus Maleficarum (The Witches' Hammer),* a popular guide to witch identification compiled by two Dominican monks late in the fifteenth century, has repeated references to women as the source of sin (Summers 1951). The devils, the manual says, "have six ways of injuring humanity. And one is to induce an evil love in a

[handwritten annotations in top margin: "Why attacked the Malleus — witches were really sick mentally or bodily; against them were wrong — inspired humanistic approach toward the mentally ill."]

Fig. 2.2. During the sixteenth century many women who were insane were accused of witchcraft and burned.

man for a woman." Perhaps the clearest statement of the antifeminist view in the *Malleus,* however, reads, "All witchcraft comes from carnal lust, which is in women insatiable." Using this rationale, the church caused hundreds of innocent, apparently mentally ill women to be burned at the stake during the next two centuries.

During the seventeenth century, witch hunting was also quite widespread in the colonies of the New World. The town of Danvers, near Salem, Massachusetts, became the center of these hunts in 1692. Within a few months, hundreds were arrested, nineteen were hanged, and one was burned to death. It seems that some of the people persecuted for satanic possession were mentally disturbed. Deutsch (1965) quotes the instance of a Boston family

servant who, during her trial for bewitching her employer's children, was asked whether anyone was standing by her. She replied that someone had been there, but looking very pertly in the air, she said, "No — he's gone" (p. 34). Evidently the woman was seeing things that weren't there, "hallucinating," we would call it today, and would probably be considered mentally ill by today's criteria. But in the seventeenth century her admission was considered a sign of witchcraft, and the woman was heartlessly punished.

Challenge to Witchcraft

It is hard to understand the enormous influence the *Malleus Maleficarum* had on Western European thinking. Revered by Catholics and Protestants alike, the manual was felt to be almost divinely inspired. For more than two hundred years it was heresy to challenge its doctrine or the dictum on witches. Johann Weyer (1515–1588), a physician, attacked this doctrine in an act of rare courage. He claimed that many, if not all, "witches" were really sick mentally or bodily and that the barbarous acts perpetrated against them were wrong. His influential book *De praestigiis daemonum* (1579) contained numerous clinical descriptions of abnormal behavior in short, sympathetic passages that stimulated compassion rather than scorn. He gave examples of a psychological approach in treating emotional disorders indicating that the radical techniques of the witch hunters were not necessary. Among them was this case that Weyer cited as *moral treatment:*

There was a melancholic girl in Burg who after having been conjured [interrogated] for a long time confessed that she was possessed by the spirit of Virgil. People believed this with so much more readiness since she was a simple and devout girl who had always lived at home; she was a Tuscanese who tried to speak Mantuan, that is to say the language of Lombardy, and she occasionally let drop a few words in Latin. After the conjurers had wasted time on her, a physician cured her by the Grace of God: First, in accordance with the precepts of his art, he gave her some purgative medicament used in cases of melancholia, then he administered some medicines which had the virtue of fortifying her and making her more comfortable. Thus, after the girl's body was purged, the minister of the Church was able to use his means more easily to expel the evil spirit. For with the natural obstacles removed, he could easily undertake the rest of the treatment (Zilboorg and Henry 1941, pp. 219–220).

Weyer, who is considered the father of psychiatry, inspired a humanistic approach toward the mentally ill that still strikes a sympathetic chord five centuries later.

Roots of Modern Psychological Theories

Theories of possession and witchcraft are psychological theories of abnormal behavior, but because they rely upon mystical conceptions of demons and spirits, they are not scientifically verifiable. For more than three hundred years after Weyer's outcry against the witchcraft interpretation of mental illness, the psychological perspective lay dormant. When it reappeared in the latter part of the nineteenth century, it was without the moral trappings of demonology. The new approach focused mainly on one pattern of abnormal behavior, *hysteria.*

For reasons that are not clear to us today, many people in eighteenth- and nineteenth-century Europe suffered from physical incapacities that make absolutely no anatomical sense, such as *glove anesthesia,* in which the person has no feeling in her hand, but does have sensation from the wrist up into the arm. (Chapter 13 has a detailed discussion of the class of conversion disorders to which glove anesthesia belongs.) From the time of the ancient Greeks, medical science believed glove anesthesia and other so-called hysterical reactions stemmed from a physical disorder. They further believed that only women had this disorder and alleged the cause to be a wandering uterus.

An Austrian physician, Friedrich Anton Mesmer (1734–1815), carried out highly controversial experiments to cure hysteria by the principles that he named *animal magnetism.* Mesmer, whose name gave us the word "mesmerize," believed that hysterical disorders were caused by a universal magnetic fluid in the body and that by changing the distribution of this fluid he could effect a change in behavior. He conducted mysterious meetings during which inflicted persons sat around a covered tub containing kettles of chemicals. Clothed in outlandish garments, Mesmer would enter the room, take from the tub the iron rods that protruded through the cover, and touch affected parts of the patients' bodies to transmit the curative animal magnetism (Figure 2.3). Review committees (Zilboorg and Henry 1941) could find no scientific basis for Mesmer's theory, but they could not dispute the fact that a number of hysterical people gained relief from their symptoms following Mesmer's treatment. Today it is generally recognized that Mesmer had stumbled on many of the techniques of hypnotism.

Jean Martin Charcot (1825–1893), a Parisian neurologist, also studied hysterical states. From research with blindness, deafness, paralysis, convulsive attacks, and gaps in memory brought on by hysteria, as well as anesthesia, he asserted that hysterical symptoms were caused by neurological dysfunctions. Charcot himself had never practiced hypnotism, but some of his associates became interested in the subject and did some research of their own. One day they demonstrated for Charcot that by means of hypnotism it was possible to produce all the typical bodily symptoms of hysteria, and afterward to remove them. By hypnotic suggestion they could render a patient's perfectly

Fig. 2.3. A group practicing Mesmer's techniques. Shown here is the baquet, a specially constructed table for magnetic connection between those taking part in the session.

healthy arm paralyzed or anesthetic. Charcot could not tell the difference between hypnotically induced and naturally occurring hysteria. The earlier success of Mesmer with these patients and these demonstrations by his students led Charcot to consider other psychological interpretations in which suggestion was significant. He came to believe that there was an intimate association between hysteria and hypnosis and that only hysterics were hypnotizable.

The latter part of Charcot's theory was shattered by two of his contemporaries practicing in the French provinces. A. A. Liebeault (1823–1904) and H. Bernheim (1837–1919) proved that most people can be hypnotized and that a wide variety of disorders improved as a result of suggestions implanted during the hypnotic trance.

The notion that hypnosis alters a person's state of consciousness received further support from Esdaile (cited in Bramwell 1921) in India, who showed that surgery can be carried out under hypnosis with no perceived pain. Evidence from three hundred major operations and many minor ones, all performed while the patients were in the hypnotic state, clearly showed that part of the mind can block awareness of physical pain while still in the waking state. The notion of levels of awareness or consciousness was a very significant outgrowth of experimentation with hypnosis and was critical to subsequent research.

Freudian Psychoanalysis

Sigmund Freud (1856–1939), a Viennese physician, gave up a career in neurological research to work with Josef Breuer (1842–1925), also a neurologist. From 1880–1882 Breuer treated a young, attractive hysteric named Bertha Pappenheim — known in the literature as Anna O. At one time or another, this woman displayed almost all the symptoms associated with hysteria: poor appetite, paralysis, a severe cough, multiple personality, and anesthesia. Because of the widely varied symptoms, her case intrigued Breuer, and he spent much time with her. Each evening she would talk over the events of the day with him. On one visit she related her memories about the first appearance of a symptom, and to Breuer's amazement, the symptom then seemed to disappear. Miss Pappenheim felt there was value in what she called "the talking cure," and Breuer shared her view. He referred to the process as *catharsis* because it seemed that the cure resulted from an emotional release similar to the one the ancient Greeks believed to be stimulated by a great tragic drama. Unfortunately,

Breuer's wife grew jealous of his relationship with Miss Pappenheim, and Breuer broke off the treatment rather abruptly. He discussed her case with Freud, who became deeply interested in hysteria and journeyed to Paris in 1885 to study at Charcot's clinic. Charcot's ability to bring on hysterical symptoms by hypnosis convinced Freud that whatever the neurological basis of the disease, the symptoms can be treated solely by verbal means.

After returning to Vienna, Freud researched his theory and in 1895 culminated his efforts with a landmark book, *Studies in Hysteria,* which he published jointly with Breuer. From these investigations and others that followed, Freud developed the *psychoanalytic* or, as it is sometimes called, the *psychodynamic* theory of abnormal behavior. Freud's data derive from individual and case studies, which he recorded with great style and detail. If Freud could be criticized, it would be because he drew far-reaching theoretical conclusions from one or two intensive case studies.

There is no simple integrated Freudian theory. Freud offered a series of theories, which he constantly modified with experience over a rich and productive career. We can break down his thinking into the psychoanalytic theory of the *structure* of the mind and the psychoanalytic theory of *development*.

STRUCTURAL THEORY

Freudian theory presumes that the mind has two levels of awareness, the conscious and the unconscious, and that they exist on a continuum ranging from total unconsciousness, through a region of dimly perceived awareness (preconsciousness), to full consciousness. Freud believed that the relationship between conscious and unconscious was a dynamic one in the sense that unconscious stimuli from the inner recesses of the mind press continuously for conscious awareness, but are suppressed by some filtering mechanism. If you consider the many kinds of stimuli impinging on you from within and without at this very moment and the impossibility of attending to them all, such a filtering mechanism makes good sense. In Freud's view, some stimuli are more actively blocked from awareness than others. These are painful, conflictual memories and primitive impulses related to past memories. Thus, when Anna O. recalled critical memories to Breuer, she permitted them access to consciousness and altered the dynamic balance between conscious and unconscious forces in the mind. Clearly, a key aspect of this part of Freudian theory is that conscious denial of critical memories and impulses from awareness produces abnormal symptoms.

Further clinical investigations revealed that a simple division of the mind into conscious and unconscious states was not sufficient. Therefore, Freud offered a second version of the structural model, a three-part organization consisting of *id, ego,* and *superego* (see Figure 2.4). Freud's concept of the id acknowledged the existence of a primitive part of the brain associated with the basic unconscious biological drives. Today, we would associate these drives with structures in the region of the midbrain, the area of the brain that is the focal point of the modern biochemical theory of abnormality. The id, Freud said, is the source of all energy and desire and persistently demands gratification. As infants, we are all id, crying for food immediately, demanding relief from wetness, and wanting warmth and body contact.

As the infant matures and becomes more alert to the external world, his ego develops. This is the part of the personality that is alert to reality and the consequences of different behaviors. According to Freud, the ego mediates between the demands of external reality and the continual pressure of the id for expression and gratification.

The superego, third part of the structural model, represents the internalization of values and standards designed to promote proper prosocial behavior and discourage antisocial behavior. It is the repository of society's mores and standards. Once the superego has developed, the ego must function as a double mediator. It must inhibit the demands of the id until the proper time and place for expression of impulse, and it must choose a mode of gratification acceptable to the superego. Thus, all individuals must continuously strive for compromise between the desires for immediate gratification and the constraints of reality. When an individual fails to effect this compromise or achieves it at too high a cost, his behavior will be abnormal.

An important component of the three-part model is the notion of a mechanism that prevents id impulses from reaching awareness. These mechanisms serve as gates or switches controlling access to past memories or current internal stimuli. Because they serve a protective or defensive function, these switches are called

Fig. 2.4. Freud's original schematic representation of his model of the mind. "pcpt.-cs." refers to the part of the ego that consciously perceives environmental stimuli. The other terms are defined in the text.

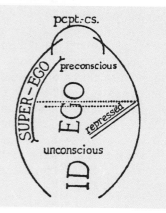

defense mechanisms. When early desires or memories become associated with anxiety (we will discuss how this occurs shortly), one way of coping with or reducing anxiety is to block these memories or desires from awareness. Try this extreme example: if mealtime has always been charged with anxiety for you, you may try to avert a painful experience by avoiding recognition of hunger as much as possible. Freud called this defensive blocking of impulses *repression.* It is one of a large number of defense mechanisms, which also include *projection,* the attribution of unwanted desires onto others; *reaction formation,* reversal of real desires, as when we are overly nice to someone we despise; and *isolation,* denial of feelings associated with feared desires, while remaining aware of their existence.

As long as the ego's defense mechanisms prevent the unconscious id impulses from reaching awareness, we see few signs of emotional disorder. The balance is delicate, however, because impulses are constantly searching for expression. The ego is self-monitoring, and any indication that the balance between id and superego is faltering sets off an anxiety response, a state of arousal preparatory for danger. Intense anxiety is a signal that the defense system is about to fail and that unacceptable desires are close to awareness. The anxiety response is terrifying as well as mysterious because there is no obvious external stimulus for it. A paradox of Freudian structural theory is that one part of the mind, the preconscious portion of the ego, senses the kind of impulses about to break through to awareness, but the fully conscious ego does not, and finds the experience mystifying and disorganizing.

Anxiety can become an enduring or persistent state or it may merely be a prelude to a breakdown of defenses and more extreme efforts to reestablish control that are recognizable symptoms of an emotional disorder. According to this model, then, symptoms are not arbitrary behaviors that just happen, but are motivated behaviors designed to stave off further disorganization.

DEVELOPMENTAL THEORY

Whereas structural Freudian theory covers *how* abnormal behavior occurs, the developmental model explains *why*. It is named a developmental theory because it is an attempt to trace personality development, both normal and abnormal, from infancy through adulthood.

From his case studies, Freud hypothesized that all abnormal behavior arises from inability to resolve conflicts about sexuality. Therefore, his theory of personality describes how sexual desires evolve and what sexual conflicts are.

Freud defined sexuality very broadly as a generalized sensation of pleasure, or *libido*. In mature individuals the libido is localized in the genital organs. Between birth and maturity, however, normal individuals pass through five stages of *psychosexual development*. At each of these stages, a different part of the body is most sensitive to stimulation. The first is the *oral stage*, during which the infant desires maximum gratification of id impulses by means of stimulation of nerve endings around the mouth. Sucking and feeding are the primary pleasures during this phase. In the second year of life, the child enters the *anal stage*, when enjoyment derives from the ability to control elimination and retention of feces. In the *phallic stage*,

Freud on Dreams

A crucial notion in Freudian theory is that conflictual unconscious wishes strive for conscious expression. Defenses limit their expression. Psychoanalytic therapy aims to bring feared infantile wishes into the conscious mind where they can be realistically appraised and exposed to the light of adult realities. Early in his clinical studies, Freud observed that dreams could be a useful tool in unlocking unconscious memories and desires. He looked upon dreams as a "royal road to the unconscious." In these passages, Freud discusses his approach to dream therapy:

The patient, then, has described a dream which we have to interpret. We have listened quietly without making use of our powers of reflection. We determine to bother our heads as little as possible over what we have heard — over the *manifest* dream . . . but for the present we must put it aside [the emotional quality and coherence of the dream] and travel along the main road which leads to the interpretation of the dream. This means that we ask the dreamer as well to free himself from the impression of the manifest dream, to switch his attention from the dream as a whole to individual parts of its content, and to tell us one after

another the things that occur to him in connection with these parts, what associations come into his mind when he turns his mental eye to each of them separately. . . .

And now let us consider these associations; they consist of the most varied material, memories of the day before, the "dream day," and memories of times long since past, deliberations, arguments for and against, admissions and questionings. A great many of them are poured out by the patient with ease, while he hesitates when he reaches others. Most of them show a clear connection with one of the elements of the dream . . . but it also happens that the patient introduces them with the words, "That doesn't seem to have anything to do with the dream at all; I say it because it comes into my head." When one listens to this flood of ideas, one soon notices that they have more in common with the content of the dream than the mere fact that it provided them with their origin. They throw an astonishingly clear light on all parts of the dream, they fill in the gaps between them, and they make their odd juxtapositions intelligible. . . . One cannot help observing the manifestations of . . . resistance during the interpretation. In many places the associations are given without hesitation. . . . In

which runs from ages three through six, sexual excitation occurs in self-manipulation of the genitalia. Between the ages of about six through twelve is a *latency period,* during which sexuality is believed dormant. Finally, upon reaching adolescence, the individual enters the *genital stage,* in which heterosexual interests predominate.

Conflicts can occur at each stage of development, depending upon the degree of sexual gratification permitted. Both overgratification and excessive deprivation during any stage may result in *fixation* at that stage. Fixation implies that the individual continues to seek sexual gratification in a more infantile manner than is appropriate for a chronological age. Fixations are important in Freudian theory because they limit the amount of energy available to resolve the key conflict, the *oedipal conflict,* which develops during the phallic stage.

The oedipal conflict, called *electra conflict* in females, is believed to be an inevitable part of human development. It arises from the fact that the child begins to have strong sexual fantasies about the parent of the opposite sex. Fearful of these fantasies and the desires they imply and fearful of punishment from the same-sex parent, the child may repress the entire conflict into the unconscious. Repression, rather than healthy resolution of the conflict by gender identification with the same-sex parent, sows the seed of subsequent abnormal development.

other places, the patient pauses and hesitates before he utters an association, and then one has to listen to a long chain of ideas before one gets anything which is of any use for the understanding of the dream. . . . But what is resistance doing here and what is it resisting? Now for us a resistance is the sure sign of a conflict. There must be a force present which is trying to express something and another which is striving to prevent its expression. What comes into being as the manifest dream may, therefore, be regarded as comprising all the solutions to which the battle between these two opposing forces can be reduced. . . .

It is as much the result of the archaic regression in the mental apparatus [during sleep] as of the demands of the censorship that so much use is made of the representation of certain objects and processes by means of symbols which have become strange to conscious thought. Such of them as have any point of contact are *condensed* into new unities. When the thoughts are translated into pictures, those forms are indubitably preferred which allow this type of telescoping or condensation; it is as though a force were at work which subjected the material to a process of pressure or squeezing together. As a result of condensation one element in a manifest dream may correspond to a number of elements of the dream thoughts; but conversely, one of the elements from among the dream thoughts may be represented by a number of pictures in the dream.

Even more remarkable is other processes of *displacement* or transference of accent, which in conscious thinking figures only as an error in thought or as a method employed in jokes. . . .

In the dream work, these ideas are separated from their affects [emotions]; the affects are treated separately. They may be transferred to something else, they may remain where they were, they may undergo transformation, or they may disappear from the dream entirely.

You can read an excerpt in which a Freudian psychotherapist interprets a patient's dream in Chapter 15. There you will see how Freud intended the principles just outlined to be used in searching for the emotional conflicts underlying the manifest dream.

Source: From S. Freud, *New Introductory Lectures on Psychoanalysis* 1933, pp. 20–35.

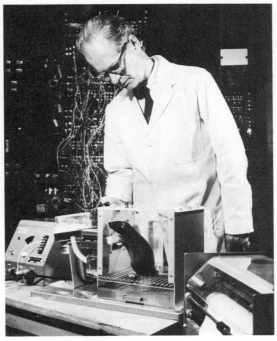

Fig. 2.5. Sigmund Freud (above) and B. F. Skinner (left), two major figures in the development of models of and interventions with abnormal behavior. Each is shown in the working environment that stimulated his theories: Freud in his study, Skinner in the laboratory.

In the Freudian model, drives repressed into the unconscious are not inert. Being id impulses, they strive relentlessly for expression and so require constant inhibition by the defense mechanisms. If these defenses fail because of increased life stress, anxiety and, in many instances, symptoms of abnormal behavior will develop.

INFLUENCE OF FREUDIAN THEORY

Freud's work has had enormous effects on the whole field of abnormal psychology for several reasons. First, it provided a relatively cohesive theory of psychological factors related to the appearance of abnormality. By providing a system of behavior constructs he made it possible to look at abnormal symptoms as rational and explainable, not as demons to be reacted to irrationally and fearfully. Clearly, the Freudian model created a more sympathetic climate for treating mental disorders simply because it is easier to feel compassion for something we can rationally comprehend. The second lasting creation was a developmental view of abnormal behavior that established the significance of events in early life and, in particular, of the ways in which family life affects the development of emotional conflict. Third, Freud offered a design for psychological treatment of abnormal behavior that followed from a consistent model of etiology. When we discuss the psychoanalytic model of treatment in Chapter 15, you will see the close relationship between Freud's model of abnormal development and therapeutic technique. Freud's influence on methods of treatment extends beyond his original model to a whole collection of therapeutic models based on psychodynamic principles. Also in Chapter 15, we shall consider this evolution of newer psychotherapies.

Although Freud's general contributions to abnormal psychology are quite important, the specific elements of his theory have not fared as well. It has proved difficult to validate the theory

of psychosexual development. Clinical experience indicates that not all patients have oedipal conflicts. Developmental conflicts involving dependency, aggression, and power, among others, do not necessarily derive from oedipal strivings. One eminent psychoanalyst (Marmor 1968) who evaluated the enduring aspects of Freud's theory in actual therapeutic practice concluded that some fundamental principles of his theory of psychosexual development have given way to more sophisticated ideas:

> Certain of his [Freud's] basic constructs such as those of conflict, repression, transference [the projection of feelings about early life figures upon the therapist] and the ''unconscious'' still constitute an extremely effective foundation for an understanding of human behavior and psychopathology. . . . What has become obsolete has been the cumbersome metapsychological superstructure that Freud erected upon these fundamental concepts — notably his theory of instincts, of libido, of the tripartite structure of the psyche and of psychic energy. This ''mythology'' of psychoanalysis, as Freud once called his theory of instincts, has been rendered untenable by newer developments and findings in the behavioral sciences (Marmor 1968, p. 6).

Behaviorism and the Social Learning Approach

For the first half of the twentieth century, the Freudian view was the only widely accepted psychological model of abnormal behavior. Concepts such as unconscious motivation, defense mechanisms, and anxiety were part of the mass consciousness of American culture. But perhaps the most generally espoused Freudian notion was the hypothesis that symptoms are symbolic expressions of unconscious conflicts and that only by unraveling the symbolism can one understand the conflict that lies beneath.

In the mid-1950s, another viewpoint challenged Freudian theory. The dissenters took issue specifically with two Freudian tenets —

the model of symptom evolution and the emphasis upon insight as the road to relief from overwhelming anxiety. Actually, the challenge did not appear suddenly but was the culmination of a movement that had been developing in fits and starts since the 1920s. It is known as *behaviorism* and began with John B. Watson (1919).

Watson rebelled against the psychology of his time, *structuralism,* which worked with the effects of specific stimuli upon our sensory experiences of sound, light, color, and so on. The main technique of structuralism was *introspection,* in which trained observers systematically recorded the details of their inner experience. Watson believed that a science of psychology must focus not on inner experience, but on *overt* behavior, which is observable and measurable. He rejected the notion that reports of inner experience — fantasies, dreams, sensations, or thoughts — are proper data for a science. In his view, psychology requires the same type of readily observable phenomena that form the foundations of other natural sciences. Thus, Watson rejected the phenomena — overt movements, secretions of glands or other physical acts — that were the core of the Freudian model as inadequate for a scientific psychology. Until recently, this viewpoint has divided behavioralism and psychoanalytic schools and made communication between their adherents difficult.

Although he disagreed about the value of inner experience, or *phenomenology,* Watson did concur with Freud in one way, and that was on the developmental theory of abnormal behavior. Watson believed that behavior is the result of learning and that normal and abnormal behavior are outcomes of specific learning experiences. His conviction came mostly from the experimental studies of Russian physiologist Ivan Pavlov (1927), who demonstrated that dogs can be taught new responses to neutral stimuli. This used a procedure which has come to be called *classical conditioning* (Figure 2.6). By systematically analyzing the conditioning process, Pavlov also proved that conditioned responses can be unlearned under the right circumstances. It is this deconditioning, or *extinction,* that has substantially influenced behavioral theories of abnormal psychology.

Picking up where Pavlov left off, Watson demonstrated in one classic experiment how human beings can learn fear by classical conditioning. For this study, Watson and his associate, Raynor (1920), chose an unusually healthy and unemotional 11-month-old boy named Albert. Before conditioning he had shown no signs of fear toward an array of mostly furry objects, including a white rat, a rabbit, a dog, and cotton. To condition fear, the researchers created an unexpected loud noise by striking a steel bar behind the infant.[1] In the first session, the bar was struck on two occasions when Albert reached out to touch a white rat. A week later, five more paired presentations of rat and noise occurred. On the eighth trial, only the rat was presented, but Albert immediately began to cry and to crawl away rapidly. When tested five days later, he showed *generalization* of the fear response not only toward the rat but toward other furry objects as well. Observing Albert's fear of furry objects might provoke psychoanalysts to suggest some theory of unconscious conflict. But in fact, the behaviorists said, Albert's behavior was a direct derivative of his learning history and did not require a more complex explanation.

Although the Watsonian view of abnormal behavior was provocative and simple, it gained few adherents among practitioners. It took the work of two later figures, B. F. Skinner (1953) and Joseph Wolpe (1958), to establish behaviorism as a possible alternative to the psychoanalytic view. Skinner is an exponent of *radical*

---

[1] Today, this type of study would raise strong ethical objections and would not be done.

behaviorism, which reduces all behavior to two processes of learning: classical conditioning and operant conditioning. The essence of *operant conditioning* is that the individual learns to make a response that *operates* on the environment so as to produce some favorable outcome or reward (Figure 2.7). Consequences that strengthen the likelihood of repeating a behavior pattern are *reinforcers.* Some forms of reinforcement are biological, including food, water, sleep, and sex. Others, such as praise, money, and social status, are social in origin.

Although some of the early psychologists, such as Thorndike (1911), knew of the operant conditioning process, Skinner elevated it to a high status. By careful experimentation with lower animals, Skinner demonstrated precisely how reinforcement patterns behavior. He for-

mulated a complex behavioral view of abnormality that went beyond the emotional conditioning to the mechanisms by which overt behaviors are learned or unlearned. By understanding the function of reinforcement, Skinner believes we can better appreciate what reinforces abnormal behavior and what might be necessary to unlearn it. Skinner did not work directly with people, but his ideas were carried forth by enthusiastic students who formed a therapeutic school now known as *behavior modification.* Interestingly, Skinner, like Watson, formed a developmental theory of abnormality that rejects the Freudian emphasis upon inner experience and the symbolic meaning of symptoms.

The second major figure in the modern development of the behavioristic perspective is

Fig. 2.6. In a familiar example of classical conditioning, a person who experiences a painful electric shock preceded by a bell soon shows anticipatory fear when only the bell sounds.

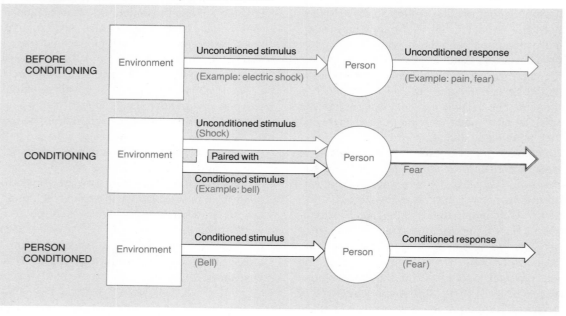

(Handwritten margin notes, top of page:)
SKINNER
Radical behaviorism: which reduced all behavior to 2 processes of learning. learns to make a response that operates on the environment so as to produce some favourable outcome or reward (CC) OC.
REINFORCERS: consequences that strengthen the likelihood of repeating a behavior pattern — biological / social

2nd figure in modern development of behaviorism is Wolpe — counterconditioning — unlearning that is learned conditions of maladaptive behavior fear and is subsequently avoidance of feared object requires reexposure to the original feared stimuli in a relaxed state — counter conditioning (desensitization)

(Handwritten margin notes, left side:)
careful experimentation of lower animals — the key he believed was reinforcement formulated Behavior Modification

Joseph Wolpe, a South African psychiatrist now living in the United States. In 1958, he published a most influential book, *Psychotherapy by Reciprocal Inhibition,* in which he described a program of behavior therapy that emphasized *counterconditioning,* Wolpe's name for deconditioning. He stressed that unlearning behavior that is learned under conditions of marked fear and is subsequently reinforced by avoidance of feared objects requires gradual reexposure to the original feared stimuli. Only when the original feared stimulus is reexperienced in a relaxed state can counterconditioning occur. In Chapter 15 we shall describe Wolpe's therapeutic approach in greater detail, for counterconditioning has proved very effective in extinguishing anxiety disorders like acrophobia (fear of heights) and other phobias.

Since 1958, the behavioral perspective has greatly changed abnormal psychology. Its major contributions are:

1. Additional support for a psychological model explaining the etiology of abnormal behavior.
2. Greater understanding of the learning processes in the development of abnormal emotions and behavior.
3. An alternative to the Freudian model of intervention or treatment. By removing the necessity for understanding unconscious conflicts in order to relieve symptoms, behavioral approaches have given us a new perspective and opened the way for intervention directed primarily at relieving symptoms.

Fig. 2.7. Once a classically conditioned fear response is established, we quickly learn to repeat behaviors (operants) that eliminate the painful stimulus.

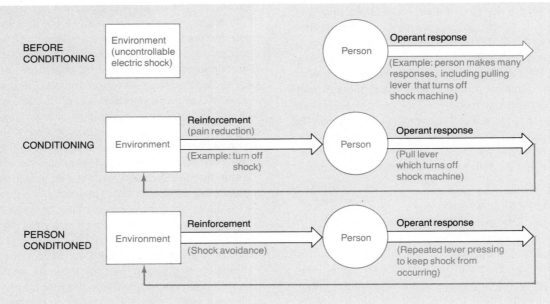

Behavioral-Psychoanalytic Rapprochement

For some time, the behavioral and psychoanalytic interpretations of abnormal behavior were worlds apart. If you adhered to one, you could not possibly view patient behavior from the perspective of the other. Only recently have there been signs of rapprochement (Wachtel 1977).

As long as the behaviorists held to the view that inner experiences are inadmissible data, and the heirs to Freudian theory denied the possibility of reducing the symptoms of abnormal behavior without first unburdening the unconscious mind, there was little basis for conciliation. But a new behavioral position known as *cognitive-behavioral theory* (Mahoney 1974) acknowledges that phenomenology may have a place in behavioral thinking. The cognitive behaviorists reconcile this apparent heresy by allowing that a person's perceptions and interpretations of events, called *cognitions,* are more important as determinants of behavior than the reality of the events. At the same time, some psychoanalytic writers have conceded that it may not be necessary to approach symptoms indirectly by uncovering unconscious conflicts (Marmor 1968). The search is now on for common positions to replace partisan rhetoric. Recent evidence that neither behavioral nor psychoanalytic therapy has a corner on the market of effectiveness has stimulated this desire to narrow the chasm between them in understanding and treating abnormal behavior.

Mental Institutions: The Era of "Moral Treatment"

Throughout history, a sizable proportion of emotionally disturbed individuals have been able to live in the community. Even though their behavior might appear odd and bizarre, if the community judged them to be *harmless,* they were free to do as they pleased. For a long time, these poor souls were responsible for their own survival, and abnormally disturbed individuals wandered about the countryside in desperate condition. If an individual was believed to be a danger to himself or others, then he was confined, usually in a jail-like institution where he would be chained and left to care for himself.

The mental hospital as an institution appeared in early medieval times and became prominent in Europe by the seventeenth century. Foucault (1965) suggests that this treatment model derived from the method for treating another public health problem — leprosy. Like lepers, the mentally ill were removed from society and placed in hospitals to protect the community from contamination.

In the seventeenth century, the precursors of our "hospitals" — places of confinement — sprang up in Europe. These institutions confined all manner of undesirables: criminals, "black sheep" of the family, idlers, and the mentally ill. They were not designed for treatment in any sense. In fact, many were amusement centers where the public could watch patients for a fee. In Paris and London, this form of entertainment assumed a ritual character. As late as 1815, it was reported to the English House of Commons that St. Mary of Bethlehem Hospital in London (a corruption of the name gave us our word "bedlam," meaning a place or scene of uproar or madness) made £400 in the preceding year by exhibiting the mentally ill. At the standard fee of one penny per visit, this sum represented 96,000 visits. Apparently, people visited the mental hospital in much the same spirit as they went to see animals in a zoo (Figure 2.8).

It was to just such a hospital, La Bicêtre, that Philippe Pinel, a young French physician, went as a staff member. Imbued with the French revolutionary spirit of liberty, equality, and frater-

Fig. 2.8. Modern mental hospitals (top) provide a marked and humane contrast to the horrors of Bedlam (bottom).

nity, Pinel was aghast at the abuses he found at La Bicêtre: "The unfortunate whose entire furniture consisted of the straw pallet, lying with head, feet and body pressed against the wall, could not enjoy sleep without being soaked by the water that trickled from that mass of stone" (Foucault 1965). The more dangerous the patient, the more restrictive the means of confinement. Chaining to a wall or bed was not uncommon.

Pinel pleaded for and received tacit approval to remove the chains. He also instituted a therapeutic program using kindness and sympathy, a program of *moral treatment.* Advocating humane and thoughtful treatment for the mentally ill, Pinel argued for the value of rehabilitation techniques designed to teach patients the value of work, recreation, social activities, and self-control. At the same time, he strove to improve their environment (Bockover 1963).

Curiously, in one of the strange parallels often found in history, during the same year (1792) that Pinel introduced his reforms, William Tuke, a Quaker tea merchant, took a similar step to alleviate horrifying conditions in English asylums. Tuke sought to establish a "retreat" in the tranquil English countryside where his fellow Quakers could receive wholesome and dignified care as an alternative to institutionalization. Out of his persistent efforts came York Retreat, where the troubled could escape the psychological stresses of everyday living while trying to return to a normal state without any of the biological treatments currently available. York was a radical treatment center for its time. Run by nonphysicians, its program relied on benign psychological techniques to promote recovery from mental disorders.

As a result of the work of Pinel and Tuke, moral treatment became the mode for many mental hospitals in the nineteenth century both in Europe and in America. In the United States, the Hartford (Connecticut) Retreat and Worcester (Massachusetts) State Hospital fol-

lowed Tuke's model. Both offered group living and combined work and play designed to encourage self-control and abandonment of undesirable activities. Between 1833 and 1852 Worcester State Hospital reported a "cure" rate of 60 to 75 percent of its patients, a figure that would be the envy of modern community mental health centers (Bockover 1963), although we must be very skeptical of recovery rates reported from the distant past because of ignorance about types of patients actually treated and imprecise criteria for improvement.

Despite optimistic figures, moral treatment programs came to be regarded as "unscientific," and during the second half of the nineteenth century, they slowly gave way to approaches supposedly more "scientific," particularly biological models. Impersonal, detached, objective, and "scientific" attitudes began to be held in high esteem among those working with the mentally ill. In the United States, construction of large state mental hospitals anticipated further "scientific" advances that would produce more cures for abnormal behavior. Unfortunately, putting these hospitals in remote rural areas kept the professional staffs from learning of new developments in their fields (Golann and Eisdorfer 1972). By the end of the nineteenth century, the humanitarianism of Pinel and Tuke appeared lost. Hope for early releases from these institutions floundered and sank, and mental hospitals became custodial institutions providing limited physical care for an indefinite period.

During the early part of the twentieth century, mental hospitals were custodial institutions wedded to the biological model but lacking effective biological treatments. Freud's followers soon extended his techniques, which Freud had originally applied mainly in treating mild disorders called neuroses, to the more disturbed psychotic patients. Two of the best-known hospitals to adopt the psychoanalytic model are the Menninger Foundation Hospital in Topeka, Kansas, and Chestnut Lodge in the Washington, D.C., area. Both turned away from the prevalent biological viewpoint to a purely psychological one based on the psychoanalytic theory that a psychosis is a primitive defense against overwhelming anxiety. These hospitals provided warm and supportive environments, staff encouraging return to reality, and individual therapy along psychoanalytic lines. One outgrowth of this approach was the establishment in the wards of therapeutic communities (Jones 1953), where patients developed maturity by participating in the governance of their hospital units.

Despite their many positive aspects, it was rarely possible for the general public hospitals to follow the leads of the psychoanalytic hospitals because they were very costly in manpower. With the swing of the pendulum back to biological treatment that accompanied introduction of the tranquilizing drugs (see Chapter 7) in 1955,

state hospitals again acquired a medical orientation and strong reliance upon biological treatment superseded psychosocial methods of rehabilitation.

Over the last twenty-five years, the philosophy underlying the design of treatment settings for the severely mentally ill has greatly changed. Strong pressure was applied in the early 1950s to return patients to their communities, where they might live more normally. This movement followed recognition that patients were languishing in mental hospitals. They had overaccommodated their behavior to the institutional environment and were apathetic, responding to the safety of an undemanding institution — a condition known as *institutionalism*. The new tranquilizing drugs, which provided a way of controlling agitation and hostility, reinforced demands for massive deinstitutionalization. As Figure 2.9 shows, between 1950 and 1974, large numbers of patients reentered their communi-

Fig. 2.9. During the last twenty-five years, the number of patients released from mental hospitals into the community has increased dramatically. This trend preceded but was greatly accelerated by the introduction of tranquilizing drugs. (From National Institute of Mental Health 1973, 1975.)

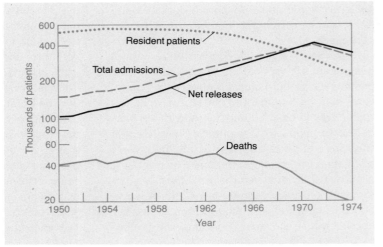

ties. Their release has solved one evil, but it has not provided a viable alternative — care for released patients and their families. In Chapters 7 and 22, we will look closely at the problems of deinstitutionalization, for they are still with us and they challenge our ability to design imaginative residential and community treatment programs. Without such programs, deinstitutionalization will replace one type of warehouse — the state hospital — with another — the downtown skid-row hotel.

Community Mental Health Centers

The federal government has been active in delivering mental health services since the end of World War II. In 1955, Congress enacted the National Mental Health Study Act, which created an interdisciplinary Joint Commission on Mental Illness and Health to study and recommend a national mental health program. The Commission's final report, issued in 1961, recommended establishment of local public treatment facilities. President John F. Kennedy's enthusiastic support was instrumental in the 1963 passage of the Community Mental Health Centers Act, providing federal funds for just that purpose.

The major goal of the community mental health center is to treat individuals within their community as outpatients whenever possible. Considered a treatment of last resort, hospitalization was to be used only for individuals dangerous to themselves or others. Their hospital stays were to be as brief as possible to prevent adaptation to the role of patient. The sooner a disturbed individual returns to a normal environment and can resume normal life at work, housekeeping, or as a student, the better the possibility of recovery. Therefore, the signifi-

cant part of any treatment program should take place at the outpatient level. This *aftercare* plan is the basic rationale of the community mental health center.

Another important idea in the 1963 legislation is emphasis upon preventing serious mental disorders. Perhaps, by identifying potential breakdowns earlier in life or intervening in life crises early, we can prevent debilitating reactions. Community mental health centers attempt to do just that in their crisis centers (where people seek immediate help during an acute crisis), suicide prevention centers, rape counseling centers, and so on. It is still too early to judge if these preventive programs are a success, but they have certainly spawned many imaginative and innovative concepts and programs for intervention. We have come a long way from *Bedlam and Bicêtre*.

A Contemporary Problem: Synthesizing Divergent Models

As we have remarked throughout this brief historical review, biological models of the causes and treatment of abnormal behavior and psychological models usually have alternated in importance. At present, the balance is unique. Both biological and psychological views are very prominent and have strong followings within the mental health establishment. Now the issue is how to synthesize these viewpoints to provide comprehensive models for the causes of abnormal behavior and appropriate multimodal programs for effective intervention. It seems that an either-or position is no longer tenable, because biological factors seem to underlie some disorders, but in others biological and psychological factors are both significant, and in still others, psychological factors seem to be overwhelmingly significant.

Summary

1. Two themes recur throughout the history of abnormal psychology: abnormal behavior reflects an underlying biological deviation; and abnormal behavior reflects serious psychological disturbance.

2. From the days of ancient Greece, early biological theories held that an imbalance of body chemicals caused abnormal behavior. Toward the end of the nineteenth century, Louis Pasteur's germ theory of disease gave a new direction to biological research into the causes of abnormality.

3. Currently, we have two types of biological theories of abnormal behavior. The first is a biochemical model based on knowledge about the way nerve impulses are transmitted in the brain. Recent research with neurotransmitter substances has led to specific biochemical theories of abnormality.

The second modern approach is a genetic model devised from the observation that, from generation to generation, some families produce more emotionally disturbed offspring than others. Data on this model derive from these sources: (1) family studies, (2) twin studies, and (3) adoption studies.

4. Early psychological theories of abnormal behavior had roots in moral and religious beliefs about good and evil. Late in the nineteenth century the discovery that hypnosis is an effective form of treatment for hysteria inspired research into the psychological causes of abnormal behavior.

5. Sigmund Freud began his study of abnormal behavior patterns after a colleague described to him the therapeutic effects of letting a young hysteria patient talk at length about her fears and emotions. Convinced that symptoms of abnormal behavior could be treated by verbal means alone, Freud developed the psychoanalytic theory of abnormal behavior.

6. Psychoanalytic theory has two primary components: structural and developmental. Freud's structural theory divides the mind into three parts: the id, the ego, and the superego. Defense mechanisms, such as repression and reaction formation, try to prevent id impulses from reaching awareness. When these defenses are about to fail, the individual experiences anxiety. Abnormal behavior patterns are motivated by the desire to prevent further disorganization.

Freud's developmental theory traces psychosexual development through five stages: oral, anal, phallic, latent, and genital. If overgratification or excessive deprivation occurs at any stage, the individual's psychosexual development ceases. According to Freud, the main conflict in each person's development occurs during the phallic stage and is called the *oedipal conflict.* It arises when the child begins to have sexual fantasies about the parent of the opposite sex and normally is resolved by identification with the parent of the same sex.

7. Freud's work has had great influence on the field because: (1) it provided a cohesive theory of psychological factors related to the appearance of abnormality; (2) it gave us a developmental view of abnormal behavior; and (3) it offered a design for psychological treatment based on a consistent etiology.

8. A twentieth-century challenge to Freud came from behaviorism, which regards all behavior — normal and abnormal — as the result of learning experiences. Behaviorist B. F. Skinner introduced the notion of radical behaviorism, according to which behavior is a consequence of classical (Pavlovian) conditioning and operant conditioning. Behavior-modification techniques grew out of Skinner's work. Joseph Wolpe developed a behavioral treatment model based on counterconditioning of feared stimuli by gradual reexposure to the stimuli.

9. Behaviorism's major contributions to

psychology have been: (1) greater understanding of the learning process; (2) additional support for a psychological model of the etiology of abnormal behavior; and (3) an alternative to the Freudian method of treatment that concentrates on relief of symptoms rather than on exploring unconscious causes of behavior.

10. Treatment of emotionally disturbed individuals has progressed from incarceration under inhuman conditions to more recent attempts at preventing mental disorders and helping to integrate the patient into the community as a functional member.

11. Today, neither the psychological nor the biological approach to research and treatment of abnormal behavior is predominant. Each side acknowledges that both psychological and biological factors are important in the development and treatment of behavior disorders.

Chapter 3

Assessment

Handwritten margin notes:

(16)

Purpose
1/ to make a diagnosis (classify)
2/ aid in planning an intervention program
  - not interested in overall diagnosis but specific problem
    + strengths
3/ gather data for research into the causes + correlates of abnormal behavior + the outcome of intervention

procedures used to systematically gather info about a person

Research ≠

1/ Interviews
2/ Psychological tests
3/ Observation
4/ Psychophysiological recordings

Assessment Criteria

Assessment Techniques

The Interview
Psychological Tests
Direct Observation
Psychophysiological Recording
Assessing Environment

Summary

Because we intend to convey what is known about abnormal behavior, we must consider how it all came to be "known." The next two chapters are about basic aspects of conducting research in abnormal psychology. In this chapter we consider the *assessment techniques* with which clinicians and researchers gather information about abnormal behavior. In Chapter 4, we discuss *research approaches* that determine how well we will be able to understand the data collected and whether we can derive from them general principles about abnormal behavior.

Assessment techniques are procedures used to systematically gather information about a person. In abnormal psychology, the primary techniques are interviews, psychological tests, direct observations, and psychophysiological recordings. Assessment in abnormal psychology serves several purposes, often all at the same time. The primary aim is to make a diagnosis. Consequently, many assessment techniques are designed to detect abnormality and to fit a person into a classification scheme. A second purpose is to aid in planning an intervention program. Here the clinician is less interested in an overall diagnosis than in finding specific indicators of the individual's problems and strengths. A third purpose of assessment, and the primary one here, is to gather data for research into the causes and correlates of abnormal behavior and the outcome of intervention.

Assessment Criteria

What makes assessment techniques good from a scientific point of view? Researchers apply three criteria in judging their value: how well they demonstrate (1) reliability, (2) validity, and (3) utility. *Reliability* is the degree to which a method of assessment yields consistent scores across varying conditions. There are several types of reliability, and the criteria that are relevant for a measure depend on its primary purpose. All measures should have good *inter-judge reliability* — two or more trained scorers or observers should show close agreement. Furthermore, if a measure is meant to assay a single trait, such as honesty, or intelligence, it should show *internal reliability:* a score on half of the test items should be similar to a score on the other half. Finally, if the test is measuring something that should remain stable for some time, such as intelligence, then the measure should also show good *test-retest reliability:* a testing of the same person today and next week should yield essentially the same score (Figure 3.1). The Wechsler Intelligence Scales, which we will describe, are well regarded, in part because they have very high reliability: two examiners utilizing the scoring system will derive very similar scores (inter-judge reliability); a score on half the items within a subscale is consistent with a score on the other half (internal reliability); and two testings several days or weeks

apart will yield similar scores (test-retest reliability).

A measure must be reliable to be usable, but reliability is not sufficient; it must also be valid. For *validity* we look beyond the test itself to ask whether it indeed measures what it is supposed to measure. If a scale appears to be representative of the variable it is supposed to measure, it has *content,* or *face validity.* An intelligence test that extensively measured only arithmetic skills would lack face validity, because it would not adequately represent the range of behaviors implied by the word "intelligence." It might, on the other hand, be considered valid as a measure of arithmetic skills. Hence, in asking whether a test is valid, we need to ask "For what?" "For whom?" and "Under what circumstances?" (Korchin 1976).

A measure might also be said to be valid if it relates to other independent indices of the same phenomena. A test with *concurrent validity* relates to other presently available measures of the phenomena, and a test with *predictive validity* successfully predicts related future behavior. A valid measure of intelligence would need to relate to other intelligence measures or predict an individual's performance in future situations requiring "intelligent" behavior, or both. In sum, reliability and validity both tell us whether an assessment technique gives a true picture of the variables we are studying.

If a test is both reliable and valid, and therefore acceptable for research, the investigator must then address a final question: *utility.* A much more practical consideration, a test's utility simply indicates whether the information acquired is worth the effort required to collect it in a particular situation. A test's utility depends on cost of administration, ease of scoring, difficulty of interpretation, ethical problems in using it, and many related characteristics. In practice, it is often a test's utility that determines how much it will be used.

judge reliability → 3 or more trained observers should show close agreement → for all measures
internal " → a score of ½ of test ≃ to a score on the other half.

↑ if measuring a single trait
test-retest-reliability → testing of the person today or a week later should have same results.

↑ if measuring a trait that is stable over a long time eg intelligence

eg Wechsler I.S.
reliability not sufficient
need validity
— they both tell us
whether an assessment
technique gives a true
picture of the variables
we are studying
∘ acceptable for research.

UTILITY:
whether the info acquired
is worth the effort required
to collect it in a
particular situation

UTILITY DEPENDS ON:
1/ cost
2/ ease of scoring
3/ difficulty of interpretation
4/ ethical problems using it
—it is often the test's utility that determines how much it will be used.

Fig. 3.1. This client is completing an item on the Block Design Subtest of the Wechsler Intelligence Scale For Children — Revised (WISC-R). The WISC-R is well regarded, in part because of its high interjudge reliability, internal reliability, and test-retest reliability.

Assessment Techniques

We will briefly discuss the primary techniques of assessment used to obtain data about abnormal behavior: the interview, psychological tests, direct observation, and psychophysiological recording. As we have said, all are likely to be used both by the clinician making a diagnosis or designing a treatment plan and by the researcher.

The Interview

The interview is the most commonly used method for gathering information in clinical practice. In the clinician-patient relationship, interviews are diagnostic or therapeutic in their intent, and they vary widely in orientation and amount of structure. Clinicians with a psychodynamic orientation might seek detail about the client's early experiences, dreams, fantasies, and thoughts in a rather loosely structured interview. A behavior therapist planning a treatment program might concentrate more on current life events and related past experiences and ask very specific questions. This directed conversation between expert clinician and client can yield rich and useful information; the clinician attends not only to the verbal content, but also to the client's nonverbal behavior, such as expressions of emotion and body posture during the session.

In utilizing the interview for research, however, some difficulties arise. A scoring problem lies in quantifying what people say in interviews in order to compare individuals. Validity is an inherent problem in the self-report format of the interview, which is open to considerable distortion. What people say is, at best, only a partial reflection of their experiences, influenced by their memories, by expectancies about what they ought to say, and by many other factors. Nonetheless, the interview is a common method for gathering epidemiological information (data on the distribution of behavior disorders in the population), family case histories, measures of mental status, and the like.

Two ways in which to make the interview format more acceptable for research are (1) to employ a standard set of questions with all subjects, and (2) to quantify responses to the interview with a scoring code. Rogler and Hollingshead (1965) conducted hours-long interviews with members of three generations from impoverished families in Puerto Rico. Their intent in asking wide-ranging questions was to detect differences in life history between families with a member who had recently experienced a schizophrenic breakdown and families that did not have a schizophrenic member. Scoring responses to the interview revealed that although the two groups of families had very similar early experiences, characterized by much stress, the families with breakdowns had experienced heightened stress in the year just prior to the breakdown. The lengthy interviews, which took place in these families' homes, unearthed much information about stresses that other information-gathering procedures might have missed. For studies of narrower scope, it is possible to use a highly standardized interview schedule, which is identical for all subjects. The *Current and Past Psychopathology Scales* (Spitzer and Endicott 1968) consists of a standardized interview schedule and precoded response types, which the interviewer rates as the interview proceeds (see Table 3.1).

Psychological Tests

Psychological tests present the subject with a standard set of demands, such as questions to answer or tasks to perform, and a narrower range of response options than the interview. These tests also have a standard system for scoring responses so that they will be useful for research purposes. Thus researchers can compare a subject with other individuals or with a

Table 3.1. Sample questions and scoring criteria from the current and Past Psychopathology Scales

The left column provides the interviewer questions to ask; the right column gives criteria for rating the responses.

INTERVIEW GUIDE   SCALES

ORIGINAL COMPLAINT
If a psychiatric patient: Now I would like to hear about
your problems or difficulties and how they led to
your coming to the (hospital, clinic).

GENERAL CONDITION
Tell me how you have been feeling recently.
    (Anything else been bothering you?)
PHYSICAL HEALTH

How is your physical condition?
Does any part of your body give you trouble?
Do you worry much about your health?

> The time period for this
> section is the past month.

PHYSICAL HEALTH
214 **SOMATIC CONCERNS**
Excessive concern with bodily functions; preoccupation with one or more real or imagined physical
complaints or disabilities; bizarre or unrealistic
feelings or beliefs about his body or parts of body.
Do not include mere dissatisfaction with appearance.

?   1   2   3   4   5   6

**If necessary, inquire for doctor's opinion about
symptoms or illnesses.**

When you are upset do you react physically...like
  [stomach trouble, diarrhea, headaches, sick
  feelings, dizziness]?

215 **CONVERSION REACTION**
Has a motor or sensory dysfunction which conforms
to the lay notion of neurological illness, for which
his doctors can find no organic basis (e.g., paralysis
or anesthesia).

?   1   2   3   4   5   6

216 **PSYCHOPHYSIOLOGICAL REACTIONS**
Is bothered by one or more psychophysiological
reactions to stress. Examples: backache,
headaches, hypertension, dizziness, asthma, spastic
bowel. **Note: the reaction may or may not involve
structural change.**

?   1   2   3   4   5   6

APPETITE-SLEEP-FATIGUE
**Disturbances in these areas are often associated
with Depression, Anxiety, or Somatic Concerns.**
What about your appetite for food?
Do you have any trouble sleeping or getting
  to sleep? (Why is that?)
How easily do you get tired?

MOOD
**This section covers several moods. The interviewer
must determine to what extent the symptoms are
associated with either one or the other or several
of the dimensions.**

What kinds of moods have you been in recently?

MOOD
217 **ELATED MOOD**
Exhibits or speaks of an elevated mood, exaggerated
sense of well being or optimism, or feelings of elation. Examples: Says "everything is great," jokes,
witticisms, silly remarks, singing, laughing, or trying
to get others to laugh or smile.

?   1   2   3   4   5   6

What kinds of things do you worry about?
  (How much do you worry?)

What kinds of fears do you have? (Any situation...
  activities...things?)

How often do you feel anxious or tense?
  (When you are this way, do you react physically...like sweating, dizziness, cramps?)

218 **ANXIETY**
Remarks indicate feelings of apprehension, worry,
anxiety, nervousness, tension, fearfulness, or panic.
When clearly associated with any of these feelings,
consider insomnia, restlessness, physical symptoms
(e.g., palpitations, sweating, dizziness, cramps), or
difficulty concentrating, etc.

?   1   2   3   4   5   6

Source: R. L. Spitzer and J. Endicott, *Current and Past Psychopathology Scales* (New York: New York State Psychiatric Institute and Biometrics Research, 1968).

representative group. The tests that primarily interest psychologists measure intelligence, personality traits, and psychopathology.

INTELLIGENCE TESTS

Although there are hundreds of psychological tests that measure specific abilities and achievements, intelligence tests are the most widely used. The clinical purpose is usually to help diagnose and place children or to assess intellectual deterioration in adults suffering from psychosis or organic brain damage. In research, intelligence measures often describe a study sample, because so much behavior relates to level of intelligence.

The tests in most common use are the Stanford-Binet and the Wechsler Scales, each administered individually by a trained examiner. The *Stanford-Binet* is primarily used with children; the examiner presents a series of developmentally graded tasks assessing memory, perception, information, verbal ability, and logical reasoning. The number of tasks that the child performs successfully establishes her mental age. Mental age compared to chronological age determines the child's intelligence quotient (IQ). Scales developed by psychologist David Wechsler (1958) measure the abilities of three age groups. They are the *Wechsler Adult Intelligence Scale* (WAIS), *Wechsler Intelligence Scale for Children-Revised* (WISC-R), and *Wechsler Preschool-Primary Scale of Intelligence* (WPPSI). These scales have a number of subtests, yielding a verbal and performance score, as well as an overall intelligence quotient. The verbal scales include measures of the person's vocabulary, information about the culture, social skills, abstract thinking, mental arithmetic, and short-term memory. The performance scales include measures of visual-motor coordination, perceptual acuity, concept formation, and planning ability, as well as ca-

pacity to work energetically on timed tasks. The separate verbal and performance IQs, as well as the particular pattern of subtest scores, are often more helpful than the Stanford-Binet score for pinpointing deficits. Illustrative items are shown in Figure 3.2.

Concerns expressed about intelligence tests particularly relate to their cultural bias and limited predictive validity. Some items and procedures best reflect the experiences and attributes of white, middle-class persons, putting minorities, in particular, at a potential disadvantage. With increased attention to this possibility, courts and legislatures have mandated that "culture-free" tests be used in a variety of settings, but constructing truly culture-free measures has proved extremely difficult. Predictive validity is another matter. Intelligence tests are rather good at predicting academic performance; they fall short mainly when they are misused to make predictions about an individual's adaptive functioning in other spheres. We shall discuss these problems at length in studying retarded functioning in children (Chapter 20).

PERSONALITY TESTS

An assumption underlying many psychological tests is that people have specific personality characteristics, or *traits,* that are relatively stable in different times and settings. We are accustomed to hearing people remark that "he's really tense," or "she's so outgoing," as if these are enduring attributes that would be manifest in every situation and at any time. Indeed, personality tests have been developed to measure such "traits." Another assumption in many tests is that people's responses to tests reflect something about how they would behave in other settings. Both of these assumptions — about enduring traits and the relationship of test responses to behavior — have been ques-

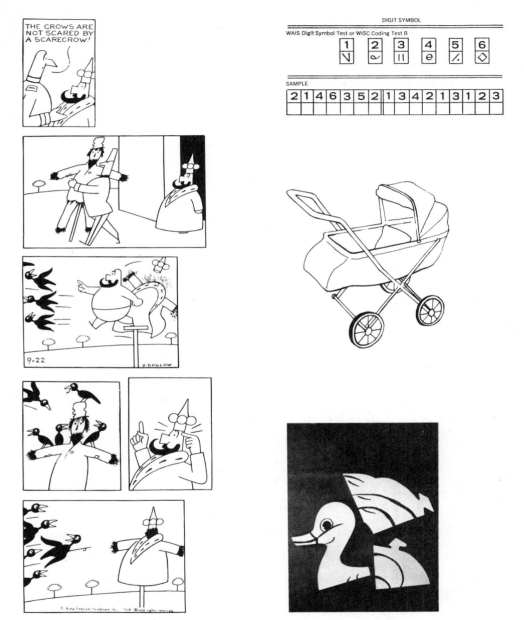

Fig. 3.2. These items are similar to those used in the Wechsler Performance scales. All items are timed. In Picture Arrangement (left), the examinee must put the panels in the correct order to tell a story. In Digit Symbol (top), he fills in the boxes with the correct symbol. In Picture Completion (middle), he points out what is missing. In Object Assembly (bottom), he puts puzzle pieces together to form a picture.

[handwritten margin notes, top: "① Rorscharch Inkblot test — 10 cards with symmetrical inkblots — 5 black + 5 coloured" ; "coding systems to interpret responses — but criticized for lacking reliability + validity." ; "Holtzman Inkblot Test. — 2 sets of 45 blots each — better system of administration + scoring + interpretation"]

[handwritten left margin: "with no correct answer" ; "ambiguous stimuli" ; "projection"]

tioned extensively (Mischel 1968). With these reservations in mind, we examine the two primary types of personality tests, projective tests and self-report inventories. These differ markedly in the types of responses they elicit.

[handwritten: "ambiguous" ; "reveals inner personality"]

PROJECTIVE TESTS. Psychologists often use techniques such as in–depth interviews, free association, dreams, and projective tests to probe the client's unconscious memories, drives, and conflicts. Of these attempts to reveal the inner personality, researchers have relied most heavily on projective tests. Here the examiner presents the client with ambiguous stimuli to which there are no correct answers, so that the client will not clearly perceive the purpose of the test and will "project" her private self into the responses.

The most popular projective test is the *Rorschach Psychodiagnostic Inkblot Test,* developed by Swiss psychiatrist Hermann Rorschach in 1921 and the subject of more than 3000 studies since then. The test contains ten cards with symmetrical ink blots, five black and five with various colors (see Figure 3.3 for sample blot). In the association phase of the test, the client is to examine each card and say aloud what she sees in it. In the inquiry phase, the client points out where on the blot she saw the images and what determined them (such as form, color, shading). Several formal scoring systems have been developed to code and interpret these responses. The clinician seeks in the pattern of responses indices of anxiety, hostility, sexual conflict, disordered thought, brain damage, and the like. Of special impor-

Fig. 3.3. An inkblot similar to those used in the Rorschach.

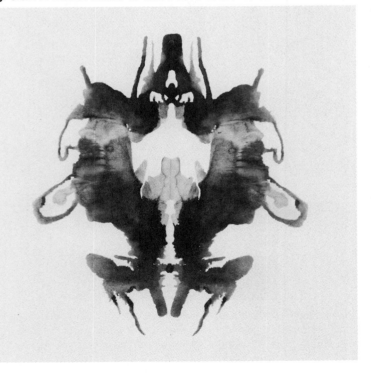

tance are recurrent themes and the individual's style of communciation.

Despite its popularity, the Rorschach test has been strongly criticized as lacking the reliability and validity required for a scientific instrument. A newer measure, the *Holtzman Inkblot Technique,* with two sets of forty-five blots each (Holtzman 1961) shows more promise, in that it has a better standardized system for administration, scoring, and interpretation.

The second most often used projective test is the *Thematic Apperception Test,* or *TAT* (Morgan and Murray 1935). A series of stimulus pictures, selected to elicit specific themes, depicts people engaged in varied activities. Though the TAT uses pictures, these are still ambiguous enough to allow considerable interpretation by the client (see Figure 3.4 for sample card). The

task for the client is to make up a story for each card and describe what is taking place, what the people are thinking and feeling, what led up to the event, and how it will turn out. A number of researchers have developed coding systems for TAT stories and similar assessment tools, especially for the motives they express. David McClelland, for one, has developed systems to score need for achievement, affiliation, and power. He has utilized these codes of expressed motives in studies as diverse as predicting the economic growth and decline of ancient cultures (by coding children's books, inscriptions on pottery, etc.) (McClelland 1961), to understanding men's and women's motives for drinking (by examining their TAT stories written under the influence of alcohol) (McClelland et al. 1972).

Fig. 3.4. A picture similar to those used in the TAT.

An adaptation of the TAT for children, the *Children's Apperception Test* (Bellak 1954) uses pictures of animals to elicit stories with themes related to Freudian psychosexual development theory. Another projective tool is the *Draw a Person Test,* for which the subject — usually a child — is asked to draw a person and, upon completion of the first figure, to draw one of the opposite sex; these productions can be scored for signs of intelligence or psychopathology (Machover 1949). The *Sentence Completion Test* (Rotter and Rafferty 1950) is an attempt to tap the inner personality by having the subject supply a word or phrase to complete sentence stems such as:

My greatest fear is . . .
A voice . . .
Mother . . .
I'm sad when . . .

Critics of projective tests have pointed out the general lack of validity in making huge leaps of inference from these perceptions and productions to speculations about the client's inner life. It has even been argued that the resultant psychological reports often tell more about the psychologist's worries than the client's. After reviewing literature on the Rorschach Zubin et al. (1965) concluded that "no other technique has captured the attention of so many on such little evidence" (p. 251). Nevertheless, many proponents of projective tests feel that the phenomena these tests are supposed to assess are so important to the study of abnormal psychology that this approach must be pursued, despite its scientific shortcomings.

SELF-REPORT INVENTORIES. Where the projective tests are intentionally ambiguous, self-report inventories present explicit statements about behaviors, thoughts, feelings, beliefs, experiences, and the like, and ask whether these describe the subject. You have undoubtedly filled out a self-report questionnaire of some type, because these are a major way of gathering information in our society.

The most frequently employed self-report inventory in abnormal psychology is the *Minnesota Multiphasic Personality Inventory* or MMPI (Hathaway and McKinley 1951), a printed list of 566 statements to which the subject responds "True," "False," or "?". The statements range from vocational and recreational preferences to bizarre experiences. Some sample items are:

I wake up fresh and rested most mornings
At times I feel like smashing things
My sex life is satisfactory
I am afraid of losing my mind
Someone has control over my mind
I love to go to dances

The MMPI's popularity is accounted for partly by its utility — it is self-administered and can be scored by computer. In developing the MMPI, a large pool of items was administered to samples of diagnosed psychiatric patients, and those items were retained which distinguished a diagnostic group (such as depressed persons) from other diagnostic subgroups and also from a nonpsychiatric sample. This type of empirical scale construction resulted in some items that have little face validity (they do not look as if they belong in a psychiatric test). Their incongruity has led to spoofs of the MMPI, such as the scale proposed by humorist Art Buchwald, which includes such items as: "Spinach makes me feel alone," "I salivate at the sight of mittens," and "I am never startled by a fish."

The MMPI is scored into ten clinical and personality scales, most of them related to the *DSM* categories used in constructing the test. There are also three control scales, which check the subject's falsification of responses, sloppiness in responding, or misunderstanding. The Lie Scale contains extreme items to detect the subject who is falsifying responses. A person who answers "true" to the item "I never put off until tomorrow what I ought to do today" is likely to be faking to look good.

A profile of scores is drawn up, indicating how much the subject deviates from the norm on each scale (see Figure 3.5). Although the MMPI was originally developed to assign subjects to diagnostic categories, it has come to be

used more as a general screening device (as in personnel selection) or as a personality measure, where the examiner interprets the pattern of scale scores. Hathaway and Meehl (1951) have published an atlas of coded profiles and case descriptions for almost a thousand patients, and computers have even been programmed to interpret the MMPI response pattern (Fowler 1969).

There are many other types of self-report inventories. The *Q-Sort* (Block 1961) has the

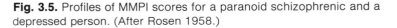

Fig. 3.5. Profiles of MMPI scores for a paranoid schizophrenic and a depressed person. (After Rosen 1958.)

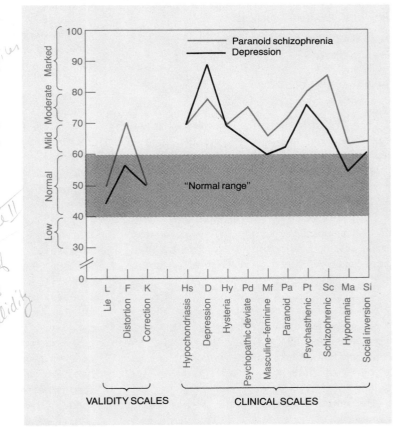

subject sort stimulus cards into piles, usually so that the number of cards in each pile will form a normal (bell-shaped) distribution on a graph. One use this method has been put to by researchers with a humanistic orientation has been to have the client sort self-statements from "most characteristic" to "least characteristic" of the actual self. The client then again sorts the cards according to his ideal self. A goal of therapy is to reduce this actual-ideal discrepancy (Butler and Haigh 1954).

Another type of inventory measures feelings or behaviors in a variety of situations. The *Fear Survey Schedule II,* or FSS II (Geer 1965), is used by behavior therapists, who have clients rate the extent of their unpleasant feelings in fifty-one situations, such as:

High places
Being teased
Thunder
Speaking in public
Prospect of a surgical operation

The FSS II has good concurrent validity — high, medium, and low scorers on selected items differed when exposed to actual behavioral tests in these situations.

Direct Observation

The assumption that people have personality traits which are fairly constant in different situations has been questioned by some psychologists, who argue that our behavior is, in fact, full of situational variability, and that to understand any behavior we must see it in context. Therefore, many researchers employ direct observation, both because it requires less inference than psychological tests and because it allows a study of relationships between behavior and setting.

Behavioral observations may be naturalistic or controlled. In *naturalistic observations,* individuals are observed, with a quantifiable scoring system and a minimum of intrusiveness by the observer, in their own settings: hospitals, schools, community facilities, at home. Such naturalistic observations often reveal behavior patterns we might not see from interviews or psychological tests. In *controlled observations,* the experimenter contrives a situation in the laboratory for behavioral observation under more standard conditions. In a study described in Chapter 13, Paul (1966) had students with public-speaking anxiety give a brief speech while trained raters looked for twenty indicators of anxiety. Behavior therapists working to reduce phobic, or irrationally fearful, behavior often use controlled observation to measure the progress of therapy; in behavior avoidance tests, patients are rated for the degree to which they cope with the fear (approach the snake, tolerate height, perform assertive responses).

Many types of procedures are used for observation. With *rating scales,* the examiner usually interviews a person or observes his behavior in a specific situation and then rates the person on a number of dimensions. In the Brief Psychiatric Rating Scale (Overall and Gorham 1962), patients are compared to the normal person on sixteen dimensions such as somatic complaint, anxiety, depressive mood, and motor ability. Each has specific rating criteria and a seven-point rating scale. For rating scales to have interjudge reliability, the criteria for scoring must be specifically delineated. Sources can be made more precise by *actual counts* of the frequency, duration, latency, or intensity of behaviors during brief intervals. Observation of behavior problems in classrooms may first involve training the observer to use a code for a number of off-task or inappropriate behaviors (blurts out, leaves seat, looks away). The trained observer might watch the "target child" for a specified brief period (20 seconds) and use the next 10 seconds to record the codes for any behaviors that occurred during that interval; this procedure is repeated for a period of time, several times a day. For studies in which the behaviors of interest are very well defined and easily counted, *self-recording* is employed. The patient who has a compulsion to wash her hands 150 times a day might wear a wrist counter and tally the number of hand-washings.

As a further aid to observation, behaviors can be recorded with audio- or videotape (Figure 3.6), with the advantage that later "micro" analysis can detect much that would be missed in the rapid flow of behavior. In one study, Goldstein and his associates (1978) asked families to discuss personally meaningful conflicts and recorded their discussions on videotape, for detailed analysis. One hypothesis was that parents with offspring who were considered high-risk prospects for schizophrenia would be less likely to acknowledge each others' remarks than families with low-risk offspring. To test this theory the observers coded each volley of conversation. These observations of family interaction supported the hypothesis; the high-risk individual's parents were more apt to disregard the intent or content of the prior speaker's remarks.

Psychophysiological Recording

Researchers have also been interested in the bodily changes that accompany psychological experiences, and technical advances have made it possible to measure many physiological responses. You are probably familiar with devices such as the blood-pressure cuff and the electrocardiograph, which are used to measure blood flow and heartbeat rate in routine physi-

Fig. 3.6. By videotaping this mother's interaction with her retarded child, researchers can later code behaviors they might have missed in direct observation.

cal examinations. Because such physiological responses are also known to vary with stress, these and other recording devices are utilized as assessment techniques in research on psychopathology.

Recordings are typically made of normal processes while the person is at rest or following some specific form of stimulation, such as a tone or light. A continuous record of a number of bodily responses or their associated electrical signals can be made on a moving paper chart. One example is the electrocardiogram (EKG), which is a record of discrete heartbeats. Change in the rate of these beats is frequently used as a sign of emotional response to stimulation. Similar records can be made with devices measuring respiration, muscle tension, skin temperature, or activity of sweat glands in the palms of the hand. Emotions such as anxiety increase palmar perspiration and increase the skin's electrical conductivity. The galvanic skin response (GSR) is an index of this increased sweat-gland activity, measured through electrodes attached to the hand and connected to a polygraph. Because emotional stimuli cause an increase in sweat-gland activity and increased secretion of acidic perspiration, they lower skin resistance. The GSR is popular with law enforcement agencies applying the lie-detector test to assess a strong emotional reaction to significant statements. But the validity of this test is still questioned: do recordings really indicate anxiety about lying? The pattern of bodily changes set off by a heightened emotional state actually seems quite diffuse. Research has been relatively unsuccessful in delineating specific patterns of response to emotional states; one response, such as an increase in heartbeat rate or palmar sweating, might accompany many emotions, such as anxiety, anger, or sexual arousal.

Advances in technology often make possible new areas of study. A recently developed recording device for male sexual arousal is the *penile plethysmograph,* a strain gauge that fits around the penis to measure blood flow. As the penis fills with blood during sexual arousal, the strain gauge stretches, and the changes are amplified and recorded on a polygraph. For women, sexual arousal can be assessed by a tamponlike device with a light at the tip, which is inserted into the vagina; the amount of light reflected from the vaginal walls indicates the amount of blood flow (Sintchak and Geer 1975). Certainly there is more to sexual arousal than the physiological responses these devices measure. However, because they are easy for the subject to attach in private, they have made it possible in recent years to study aspects of sexual response in the normal functioning adult as well as in those who are sexually dysfunctional or deviant.

Researchers have also been interested in cortical activity, electrical currents in the brain's cortex, the thin outer covering of gray matter on the cerebral hemisphere which can be measured by the electroencephalograph, or EEG (see Figure 3.7). Fluctuations in voltage on the cortical surface, just beneath the skull, can be detected by attaching electrodes to the scalp and amplifying and recording brain waves. Rhythms of several frequencies can be clearly distinguished. *Alpha rhythms,* of 8 to 12 cycles per second (cps) predominate when we are resting. When we are alert, *beta rhythms* (13 to 25 cps) predominate. Slow *delta rhythms* at fewer than 4 cps predominate during deep sleep. Frequencies much lower than those of alpha waves in the awake adult have been found to be associated with some behavioral abnormalities, such as sociopathy (see Chapter 17). Irregular or chaotic wave sequences, called *dysrhythmia,* may signify a cerebral lesion.

Assessing Environments

We have considered many techniques for gathering information about individuals, and

environmental influences
Moos — social climate scale
vastly different social settings can be described by somewhat similar attributes of social climate.

1/ Relationship dimensions
2/ Personal Development " — direction of personal growth — may vary along diff env.
3/ System Maintenance + System Change Dimension
— evaluation of orderliness, clarity of expectations, degree of control, + responsiveness to change.

another way of assessing environment is by direct observation — not relying on observation of people in it.

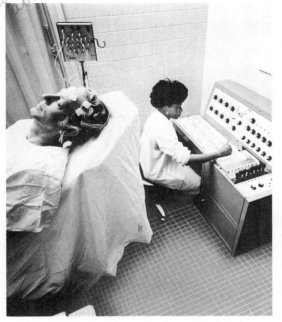

Fig. 3.7. Recording an electroencephalogram. Electrodes pasted to the subject's scalp detect minute amounts of electrical brain activity, which are amplified several million times and registered on moving graph paper by pen recorders.

Brigham
organizational components of Behavioral Modification

have seen that a person's behavior is often influenced by the setting in which it occurs, leading some investigators to measure how behavior varies in different settings. To understand a person's behavior more fully, we may want to go even further, and assess not just the individual but the setting. The *ecological approach* examines effects of the physical and social environment on people. "The social climate perspective assumes that environments, like people, have unique 'personalities'" (Moos 1976, p. 320).

We all have an intuitive sense about how the personality of environments affects our behavior. Your performance as a student is not always

the same — something about certain classes leads you to work harder, to ask more questions, and so forth. Similarly, many of the behavior disorders we shall discuss throughout this text vary in their occurrence from setting to setting. Some jobs, we shall see, have a higher risk for psychophysiological problems like high blood pressure, some families are more likely to raise delinquent children, and some mental hospitals are more conducive to improvement in the patients.

To assess environmental influences, Moos (1974, 1975, 1976) has developed *social climate scales,* for settings such as mental hospitals, correctional institutions, colleges, and families. Each individual in the setting indicates which of a list of descriptive statements are true and which are false for the setting as she views it (family members really help and support one another; we are generally very neat and orderly). Moos (1976) argues that vastly different social settings can be described by somewhat similar attributes of social climate:

1. *Relationship dimensions* identify the nature and intensity of personal relationships within the environment. They assess the extent to which people are involved in the environment, the extent to which they support and help one another, and the extent to which there is spontaneity and free and open expression among them.

2. *Personal Development dimensions* assess the basic directions along which personal growth and self-enhancement tend to occur in the particular setting. These dimensions vary somewhat among different environments depending on underlying purposes and goals.

3. *System Maintenance and System Change dimensions,* which are relatively similar in all the environments, evaluate orderliness, clarity of expectations, degree of control, and responsiveness to change.

One finding by Moos (1975) and his colleagues in correctional settings was that as emphasis on Relationship and Personal Development increased, residents liked one another and the staff more and felt they had greater opportunities for personal growth in the program.

Another approach to assessing environments is to observe characteristics of the setting directly, not relying on evaluations from the people in it. Brightman (1975) wanted to assess how well schools for retarded children were operating according to principles of behavior modification. He developed a scale called *Organizational Components of Behavior Modification,* for a trained observer to score after spending a day in the setting. The observer examined the use of physical space, materials, teacher-child interactions, case files, and the like and then scored the setting on twenty dimensions, such as how thoroughly the day was scheduled to meet individual needs, completeness of individual case records, or the teacher's use of rewards. This measure yielded a total score by which different settings could be compared.

These are a sampling of ways in which researchers gather information about individuals and settings. In Chapter 4 we will consider various research approaches and design considerations in evaluating this information and evolving more general principles about abnormal behavior.

Summary

1. The primary assessment techniques used to gather information in abnormal psychology are interviews, psychological tests, direct observations, and psychophysiological measures. Three reasons for using assessment techniques are: to make a diagnosis; to aid in planning an intervention program; and to gather data for research into causes and correlates of abnormal behavior and outcomes of intervention.

2. The value of an assessment technique is judged by these criteria: (1) reliability, (2) validity, and (3) utility.

3. The purpose of the *interview,* the most commonly used technique in a clinical setting, is to gather information about the individual with questions about early experiences, dreams, current life events, and so on. As the client responds, the interviewer examines nonverbal as well as verbal behavior. The interview format can be made more acceptable for research by: (1) employing standard questions with all subjects, and (2) quantifying interview responses with a scoring code.

4. *Psychological tests* have these characteristics: standard demands (answers to questions, tasks to be performed, etc.); narrower range of response options than the interview; and standard system for scoring responses. Tests that measure intelligence, personality traits, and psychopathology are included in this category.

5. The clinical purpose of intelligence tests is to diagnose and place children or to determine the extent of intellectual deterioration in adults suffering from psychosis or organic brain damage.

6. Personality tests work on the assumption that people have personality traits that are fairly constant. Two primary types of tests are: projective tests, such as the Rorschach Psychodiagnostic Inkblot Test and Thematic Apperception Test (TAT); and self-report inventories, which include the Minnesota Multiphasic Personality Inventory, Q-Sort, and Fear Survey Schedule II.

7. *Direct observation* requires less inference than psychological tests, and allows us to study the relationship between behavior and setting. It can be either naturalistic — in the pa-

tient's own setting with minimum intrusion by observers — or controlled — in a contrived laboratory situation where observing can be done under standardized conditions. Measures used during observation include: (1) rating scales, (2) actual counts, and (3) self-recording.

8. *Psychophysiological records* register physiological response to emotion-arousing stimuli. Examples are electrocardiograms, electroencephalograms, and measures of galvanic skin response.

9. Two major approaches are used in assessing the influence of physical and social environments on a patient's behavior. The first, developed by Moos, applies social climate scales to both family and institutional settings. Each individual scores his setting in three broad categories of climate: relationship; personal development; and system maintenance and system change. The second environmental assessment approach is to directly observe the characteristics of the setting, such as use of physical space, materials, and so on.

[handwritten annotations:]

no validity as a lie detector

cortical activity brain waves
1) Alpha — resting
2) Beta — alert
3) Delta — deep sleep

ecological approach
- examines effects of the physical + social environments on people

Breightman — observation

Critics
no validity
perceptions + productions to inner self

Rogers + Hollingsted
- interview format
Puerto Rico — scitzo

Moos — social climate scales
BREIGHAMN

Chapter 4

Research Approaches

Design Considerations
Internal Validity
External Validity

Research Approaches
Descriptive Studies
Correlational Studies
Experimental Studies
Mixed Designs

Ethical Issues in Research

Summary

The study of human behavior, especially behavior that differs from the norm, is scientifically unique in that everyone claims expertise. In our daily conversation, we all advance notions ranging from vague speculation to firm beliefs about why people do what they do. Indeed, as we saw in Chapter 2, opinions about abnormality throughout history have reflected observations filtered through the political, religious, economic, and social spirit of the time. Yet, as methods in the social sciences have gained sophistication, greater effort has been put into separating common beliefs from scientifically supported findings.

Scientific research differs from common-sense speculation; it relates new observations to an orderly body of knowledge and follows agreed-upon principles and procedures for acquiring knowledge. To be sure, creative insights are often derived from clinical observations by those who work with disturbed individuals and from those individuals' own reports of their experience, and we will give a great deal of attention to those observations. Ideas derived from subjective observations often lead to scientific research, ranging from purely exploratory investigation, wherein the investigator follows a hunch in an uncontrolled way to determine which factors might be worth further study, to the purely deductive investigation, wherein a clear causal hypothesis is stated and is tested in a carefully controlled experiment.

In this chapter we shall consider a variety of research approaches. We begin with *descriptive studies,* which seek primarily to describe a phenomenon as it is seen in nature. We next consider *correlational studies,* which assess the relationship between two or more variables. Finally we consider *experimental studies,* in which the researcher actually introduces a planned change or manipulation in a controlled setting and measures its effects. The choice of approach is determined by the questions the investigator wishes to ask, as well as practical and ethical limitations. Although experimental studies are the most scientifically desirable, usually manipulations that will experimentally produce psychopathology are not realistically possible.

Before we see specific research approaches, you need to consider several problems in designing a study, to be prepared to understand the various research approaches and to critically evaluate the research reported in the remainder of this book.

Design Considerations

Whatever research approach is followed, the investigator is guided by two primary considerations in designing the study. First, the study should afford a reasonably unambiguous interpretation of the findings; this criterion is called *internal validity.* Second, the findings should be generalizable beyond the specific study; this criterion is called *external validity.*

Internal Validity

A study has internal validity if it is designed so that only one cause for the effects observed is plausible. If several equally plausible explanations could be advanced to account for the findings, then the study is said to lack internal validity. Suppose that a group of severely disturbed patients in a mental hospital show improvement on a personality test after receiving a new drug. The staff would like to be able to conclude that the change was caused by the drug. It might also be argued, however, that the patients performed better because they had become familiar with the test, or that other changes in the ward accounted for the improvement. These rival hypotheses can be ruled out conclusively only in an experimental study, in which the investigator has control over the events — the experimenter could test another group of patients in the same ward who did not receive the drug, to see if they also changed. Later on, when we discuss experimental studies, we will see more ways of increasing internal validity. There is, however, one persistent threat to internal validity that can distort findings and make them difficult to interpret: the influence of the experimenter himself.

It is well documented that a wide array of the experimenter's attributes, such as age, sex, race, and numerous personality variables, can affect the way subjects respond. A general but more subtle threat to an experiment's internal validity is *experimenter bias* — the possibility that the experimenter's beliefs or expectations have influenced the results in some way (Rosenthal 1966). Apart from intentional misrepresentation, which we expect to be minimal, experimenters can unintentionally influence their results in several ways.

The experimenter's beliefs may lead him to misjudge or misrecord the phenomena he is studying. This is a problem when the object of the study is to determine the effects of new drugs or psychological therapies and the therapist is enthusiastic about the treatment and is attuned to seeing improvement, whether or not it occurs. Some advocates of megavitamin therapy (huge doses of B vitamins) for schizophrenia (e.g., Hoffer et al. 1957) have reported observing improvements that more skeptical observers have failed to detect. The treatment literature abounds with similar examples of strong beliefs influencing perceptions. To counteract this type of bias, researchers seek more objective measures and, consequently, will often use two or more observers or data coders and check their reliability often.

The experimenter may also unintentionally communicate an expectancy and actually influence the subject's behavior. Consider the historic feats of Clever Hans, a remarkable horse that solved arithmetic problems by tapping out the correct answer with his foot. After careful study of this behavior, Pfungst (1911) determined that as Hans approached the correct count, his master would look up at him. This response apparently was a signal for Hans to stop tapping his foot, an unintentional cue that went unnoticed by the master and countless observers. The phenomenon of unintentionally changing the events we are measuring to conform to our expectancies is called a *self-fulfilling prophecy*. Robert Rosenthal and his colleagues have demonstrated that the self-fulfilling prophecy is common in psychological research (Rosenthal 1966).

As a striking example of the self-fulfilling prophecy, consider academic underachievement in elementary school, a frequent reason for referrals to child-guidance clinics. Rosenthal and Jacobson (1968) gave urban elementary schoolchildren the "Harvard Test of Early Blooming." They selected five children in each grade who were likely to spurt ahead aca-

demically over the coming year, and so informed their teacher. In fact, it had been an intelligence test, and the names were chosen *at random.* Nonetheless, at posttesting a year later, the targeted children showed a dramatic gain in IQ, significantly greater than that of their classmates. This difference was most pronounced in the first and second grades, and with minority students — apparently these are students most influenced by the teacher's expectations and subsequent actions.

In school the teachers may have behaved very differently toward the target children. In research, where procedures are kept standard, these same effects are observed. How can these influences of the experimenter be explained? It seems possible that the experimenter conveys her expectations by what she says and how she says it, as well as by other social cues, such as smiles, nods, or posture. Probably no one cue pertains to all situations. Although some critics have argued that expectancy effects are not as strong as originally claimed (Barber and Silver 1968), the possibility is always there and we must be careful in designing experiments to minimize such effects. It is sometimes possible to automate the instructions and collection of data. Whenever possible, research staff unfamiliar with the hypotheses should be employed, so that the person taking measurements is *blind,* in other words does not know which condition the subject was in or even the hypotheses of the study.

We saw earlier that an experiment has internal validity if the effects observed have only one plausible cause. As you can see by now, this control is an ideal to strive for in conducting research, but it is not readily attained, especially when studying problems in abnormal psychology. Although one study will rarely afford unambiguous results, each can contribute something toward a more thorough understanding of a phenomenon.

[Handwritten marginal notes:] SAMPLE people — a pop'n which is randomly generalized · problems · bias · non-probability sample — first people he meets · better → probability sample — everyone has an equal chance of being chosen · most people who volunteer for a/b studies are patients passive & chronic · characteristics of experimental → not representative · SITUATION · research subjects usually know they are in an experiment — e.g. study of workers in chicago — productivity increased with each new condition caused by the knowledge that he is in an experiment · ∴ Hawthorne effect: change in a person's behavior caused by the knowledge that he is in an experiment. — investigation should be according to key variables — large # of subjects needed for not bias. · will try to understand the demands of the experiment + will react accordingly.

External Validity

[Handwritten:] generalizability of results to a larger pop'n + beyond experimental situation.

External validity means generalizability of the results. The investigator usually wishes to generalize from the results of an experiment to a larger population (such as all persons diagnosed schizophrenic) and beyond the experimental situation. Although a great many factors make generalization a problem, we shall consider two main classes: use of a sample population and the characteristics of the experimental situation.

SAMPLE

In selecting a sample to study, the researcher must first identify the population to which he wishes to generalize (all people in the United States, the residents of Elmwood). Even though he may have assigned subjects randomly to conditions and created an internally valid experiment, it is rare that the subjects are a random subsample of the entire population to which the researcher wants to generalize.

The investigator could study the first people he meets, but this *nonprobability sample* would be open to many sources of bias. A better method would be to sample the population in such a way that every member has an equal chance of being in the sample. This is a *probability sample*. To further ensure adequate representation of significant subgroups, investigators often stratify the sample on key variables, such as sex, race, or social class, and select a probability sample within each group. It is important in such cases to build in a high enough rate of participation that self-selection (who chooses to return the questionnaire) does not bias the results.

Many studies in abnormal psychology include volunteer subjects or chronic hospitalized patients. There is evidence that those who volunteer for psychological experiments are not a representative group and that they show more psychopathology than those who do not volunteer. A sample of hospitalized individuals is most likely to include patients who volunteer, who are cooperative and yet have little other therapeutic activity to conflict with the schedule of the experiment; in other words, those who are passive and chronic. The results may not be generalizable to others within the hospital and certainly, because the hospital experience is unique, not to psychotic individuals outside the hospital.

SITUATION

Findings might be limited not only to a particular group of subjects, but also to specific settings or conditions. One major factor that threatens external validity is the simple fact that research subjects usually know that they are in an experiment. They are not electrons, chemicals, or fossils, as in other sciences, but living people who know that they are being studied. Consequently they will attempt to understand the demands of the experiment and will react accordingly; some may comply, some will rebel, but all will react (see Figure 4.1).

Some years ago a study was made of factors affecting productivity of workers at the Western Electric Company (Roethlisberger and Dickson 1939). A small group of workers at the Hawthorne plant near Chicago was progressively exposed to varied working conditions (such as hours and temperature). The remarkable finding was that with each new condition, productivity increased; in fact, when the original conditions were reinstated, productivity increased still further! Apparently the workers tried to be good experimental subjects, and in so doing, limited the external validity of the studies. If the altered conditions had been implemented throughout the company's other plants without the workers' knowledge that an experiment was under way, the same increases in productivity would probably not have occurred. As a result

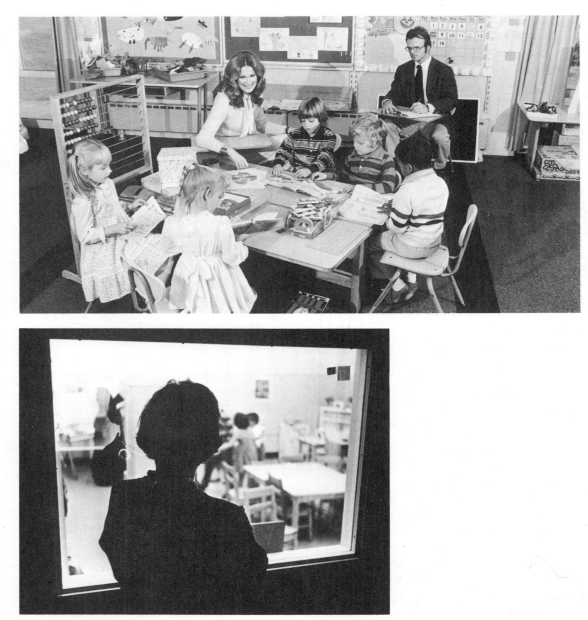

Fig. 4.1. Recording behavior by an observer in the room (top) and behind a one-way viewing window (bottom). When possible, researchers employ a one-way window to reduce subjects' reactivity to being observed.

of this study, the change in a person's behavior caused by knowing that he is in an experiment came to be known as the *Hawthorne effect.*

Martin Orne (1962) has said that experimental subjects will naturally attempt to assess the purposes of a study. He called the characteristics of the experimental situation that provide hints of expected behavior to subjects *demand characteristics.* As we have seen, the experi- menter may bias the results by somehow cuing the subject to the outcomes he desires. In other studies, the pretest will reveal the salient dimensions of the subsequent experiment. In still others, as the Hawthorne study showed, the expected outcome is obvious; surely the company would not try to decrease productivity. In deciding how well we can generalize results beyond the experimental situation, we must ask

Placebos

"I know *something* interesting is sure to happen," she said to herself, "whenever I eat or drink anything; so I'll just see what this bottle does."

— Lewis Carroll,
Alice's Adventures in Wonderland

A special type of demand characteristic is the *placebo effect* in drug and psychological treatments. It is commonly known that if an inert substance is given in a believable way, many people will experience reduction in a wide range of physical and behavioral symptoms (Frank 1961). A sugar pill said to be aspirin will relieve many tension headaches, and placebo agents can also activate healing of severely damaged tissues. One study of patients hospitalized with bleeding peptic ulcer found that 70 percent showed "excellent results lasting over a period of one year," when the doctor gave them an injection of distilled water and assured them it was a new medicine that would cure them. In a control group that received the placebo from a nurse, with the less encouraging explanation that it was an unproven experimental treatment, only 25 percent showed improvement (Volgyesi 1954). Also, it has been estimated that placebo response rate in outpatient trials of antidepressant and antianxiety drugs may be as high as 25 to 50 percent (Murphy et al. 1978). Because of the strong placebo effect, government approval of a new drug requires more than showing that the drug reduces symptoms; it must be shown to have greater effects than a placebo.

The placebo effect seems to depend in part upon the patient's expectation of positive results, enhanced by the physician's enthusiasm. Hence, in comparing effectiveness of a drug with that of a placebo, the patient must be kept blind as to which agent she is receiving, and the physician must also be kept blind as to which is being given. This is a *double-blind design.*

In studies of psychological treatment there has been interest in separating the specific effects of the treatment from nonspecific placebo effects. Many studies employ an *attention-placebo condition,* wherein clients receive a believable treatment containing many of the nonspecific aspects of the active therapy (such as contact with the therapist and belief in treatment), but where the supposedly active therapeutic ingredient is missing. Double-blind designs, however, are not easily implemented in psychological treatment studies.

Criticism has been continuous about the use of placebos in research, because they necessarily involve deception and are apt to deprive the patient of a more effective treatment (Lehmann 1978; O'Leary and Borkovec 1978). These ethical considerations have led some to advocate contrasting new drugs or psychological treatments with those already shown to be effective for the problem, rather than with placebo treatments.

[margin annotations:] Case study 1/ internal validity - lack of / 3/ bias — uncontrolled / unsystematic gathering of info/ but still used because of clinical techniques they illustrate + for the hypothesis they suggest. / lacks external validity / lack of generalization

[top right annotations: survey — 1/ may be primarily descriptive... 2/ may seek to compare the prevalence of a disorder in diff settings or types of respondents 3/ may seek to reveal trends in a disorder — seek info by 1/ questionnaires 2/ phone interviews 3/ direct — one threat of internal validity is experimental bias.]

whether demand characteristics peculiar to the experimental situation showed the subject how to respond.

As we consider the approaches followed in studying abnormal behavior, we will consider the problems of internal and external validity inherent in each.

Research Approaches

Descriptive Studies

[margin: describe a phenomena found in nature]

A basic objective of research is simply to describe a phenomenon as it is found in nature. The most popular descriptive approaches are the case study and the survey.

CASE STUDIES

[margin: describes in depth a person's current thoughts, feelings + behavior + how these relate to his life history.]

Traditionally, the major approach for studying psychopathology has been careful observation of individuals, reported in case studies. The case study usually describes in depth a person's current thoughts, feelings, and behavior and how these relate to life history. It may be used to illustrate an assessment or treatment technique, to describe a form of psychopathology, or to support a hypothesis about abnormality. The scientific limitations of the case study are obvious. It lacks internal validity because it is inherently uncontrolled and because evidence is usually gathered unsystematically and is biased by the perspectives of the clinician and client. It also lacks external validity; one can infer little about a larger population from a single case.

Nonetheless, case studies have been at the heart of research in psychopathology, not only for the clinical techniques they illustrate but also for the hypotheses they suggest. Kraepelin's early case studies provided descriptions of psychopathology that were critical to efforts at

classification, and Freud's detailed cases provided valuable descriptions of developmental antecedents to abnormal functioning and also suggested general principles about the human mind. More recently, researchers have tried to present more extensively quantified case studies, including some of the assessment techniques we have described. Throughout this book we shall draw heavily on descriptions by clinicians of individuals and also on autobiographical accounts.

[margin: researchers assess the relative prevalence or distribution of a variable in a large pop]

SURVEYS

Another type of descriptive study is the survey, with which researchers assess the relative prevalence or distribution of a variable in a large population. To illustrate some of the purposes of survey research, we shall consider studies of the very serious psychological problem of manic-depressive psychosis, a disorder characterized by extreme swings of mood between elation and depression (Chapter 8). A survey may be primarily descriptive. Eaton and Weil (1955) interviewed residents of the close-knit and strictly religious Hutterite farming communities in the North-Central United States and Canada for prevalence of psychiatric problems and found a strikingly high rate of manic-depressive psychosis relative to schizophrenia, which is fundamentally a disturbance of thought. A survey may also seek to compare the prevalence of a disorder in different settings or types of respondents. Surveys of hospital admission records reveal a much higher rate of diagnosed manic-depressive psychosis in England than in the United States and in women than in men. Finally, a survey may seek to reveal trends in a disorder. Surveys of hospital admission records have revealed a decreasing rate of manic-depressive psychosis in the United States from the early twentieth century to recent years.

one threat to external v. is representativeness of the sample

Surveys usually seek information with questionnaires, phone interviews, or direct interviews. As we have seen, however, one threat to the internal validity of such approaches is experimenter bias. In the interview and questionnaire study of mental disorders in persons living in Midtown Manhattan that we considered in Chapter 1, Srole and his associates (1962) found that more than 80 percent of respondents appeared to be at least mildly impaired psychologically. Undoubtedly the psychiatrically oriented interviewers communicated some feeling that they expected to find psychological problems, and this suggestion influenced the interviewees' responses. Some survey researchers utilize nonreactive measures, such as hospital records, to avoid the invalid responses obtained when subjects are surveyed directly as well as to study phenomena over some time. Even archival records, though, are

Nonreactive Measures

raise ethical problems

Nonreactive Measures, developed due to the problems of subjects reactivity being measured in an experiment / observation

> I can tell that you're a logger
> And not just a common bum,
> 'Cause nobody but a logger
> Stirs his coffee with his thumb.
>
> — ''My lover was a logger''
> Traditional American Folk Song

The problems of subjects' reactivity to being measured in an experiment have led to a search for nonreactive measures. One nonreactive technique is to observe people without their being aware of it. There is no telling what kind of a yarn the lady in our logger song would have received had she interviewed her man about his profession or presented him with a questionnaire to fill out. Her direct observation of his behavior told her what she wanted to know in a way he couldn't distort. Eugene Webb and his colleagues (1966) wrote a delightful argument for using more unobtrusive (and hence nonreactive) measures. They offer a plethora of measures taken from archives, from physical evidence, and from direct observation, which have allowed investigators to address questions without risking reactivity in their subjects. These are among their creative and often entertaining examples:

Webb / Archives: - library records etc

2/ Physical Evidence: Graffiti + sexual expression

3/ Observation / Racial attitudes / by behavior of blacks + whites in lecture hall

4/ Contrived observation / following a person (status) / on a traffic "wait" signal

1. Archives — Library borrowing records demonstrate the effect of introducing television into a community. Circulation of fiction titles dropped, but nonfiction titles were unaffected.
2. Physical evidence — Graffiti in public toilets were used to contrast sexual expression in the United States and the Philippines. Preoccupation with heterosexual and homosexual subjects was greater in the United States sample.
3. Observation — Racial attitudes in two colleges were contrasted by measuring how blacks and whites clustered in lecture halls.
4. Contrived observation — Conformity to a model dressed in high- or low-status clothing was measured by recording the number of people who followed a confederate when he walked against a ''wait'' traffic signal. More people followed the high-status dresser.

Unobtrusive measures can be added to other dependent measures for increased validity. A therapist treating insomniac college students might use a self-report from clients about their sleep habits (a very reactive measure), but might also record their attendance in early morning classes, a nonreactive index that should reflect sleep patterns. Despite the methodological advantage of nonreactive measures, most measures in human research, and particularly those which observe subjects unaware of the scrutiny, raise ethical problems, which we shall consider later in this chapter.

- unobtrusive measures can be added to other dependent measures for increased validity

Correlation — taking 2 or more observations of the same subjects.
direction strength of relationship = r = ±1.00
— often implemented with psychological tests as an index of their stability with diff raters or at diff time
- if correlation high → all = good.   reliability
- also used to study naturally occurring relationships in order to find indirect info.
about causes - if correlation reaches predetermined level of statistical significance

no better than the accuracy with which they were initially recorded, as illustrated by this whimsical observation:

> The Government is very keen on amassing statistics. They collect them, add them, raise them to the Nth power, take the cube root and prepare wonderful diagrams. But you must never forget that every one of these figures comes in the first instance from the village watchman, who just puts down what he pleases.
>
> — Sir Josiah Stamp

as they occur naturally

If one wishes to make inferences from a survey to a larger population, the main factor influencing external validity is the representativeness of the sample. Professional pollsters are able to gain a highly accurate picture of public opinion nationwide from a very small sample that they select to be representative. The Nielsen ratings of television programs, upon which the industry bases major decisions, sample only 700 of the 70 million households in the United States that have a television set, or 1 in 100,000.

studying vary variables that cannot be manipulated → experimentally → who to be studied

Correlational Studies

the way in which 2 or more variables co-vary.

Researchers attempting to understand abnormal behavior often want to go beyond simple description to study how several variables relate to one another. Many variables in which they are interested, such as age, sex, or child rearing, cannot be manipulated experimentally; they must be studied as they occur naturally. A researcher interested in the hypothesis that poverty influences juvenile delinquency might record delinquency rates and the extent of poverty in different areas of a city. Next she might correlate her descriptions of delinquency and poverty. If she finds a higher delinquency rate in poorer areas, a positive association or correlation is said to exist between delinquency rates and poverty.

type of correlational study is Developmental Study

A correlation describes the way in which two or more variables co-vary. Correlational methods address the question, "Do variable A and variable B relate to one another?" The study comparing delinquency and poverty in the city is correlational, as are these questions: "Is schizophrenia related to social class?" and "Does hyperactivity in childhood relate to delinquency in adolescence?"

Determining a correlation usually involves taking two (or more) observations on the same subjects. The strength of the relationship is often expressed statistically by an index, r. The value of r can vary from -1.00 to $+1.00$, and tells both the direction and strength of a relationship. When $r = 0.00$, there is no relationship at all between the two variables; knowing the value of one tells us nothing about the value of the other. As r approaches $+1.00$, there is an increasingly strong positive relationship; persons who have a high score on one variable are likely to score high on the other. Similarly, as r approaches -1.00, there is an increasingly strong negative relationship; a high score on one variable is likely to mean a low score on the other. See Figure 4.2 for a graphic representation of these relationships.

What is a "good" correlation? It depends on the question you are studying. Correlations are often employed with psychological tests, as an index of their stability with different raters or at different times (the characteristic we have described as reliability). For this purpose, a correlation needs to be rather high for the measure to be considered useful. Two raters simultaneously scoring the same nursery school children for aggressive behavior had almost perfect agreement: $r = +.97$ (Brown and Elliott 1965). Students taking a test of hypnotizability on two successive days had a consistency of $r = +.87$ (Hilgard 1961). These high correlations between raters and days increase our confidence in the measures.

Correlations are also used to study naturally

Problems

Correlational v.
1/directional problem
3/3rd variable - don't know which
came first (time-sequence)
in a correlation - it may be
due to a 3rd unmeasurable
variable

need to measure
or control for #3
variables that
may influence the
relationship

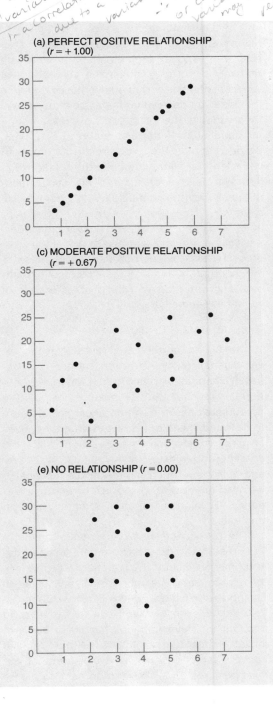

(a) PERFECT POSITIVE RELATIONSHIP
($r = +1.00$)

(c) MODERATE POSITIVE RELATIONSHIP
($r = +0.67$)

(e) NO RELATIONSHIP ($r = 0.00$)

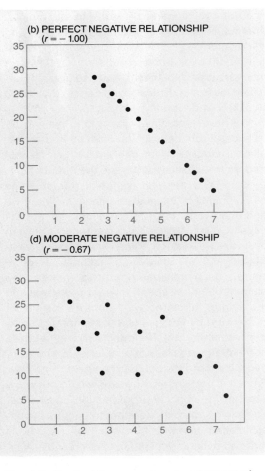

(b) PERFECT NEGATIVE RELATIONSHIP
($r = -1.00$)

(d) MODERATE NEGATIVE RELATIONSHIP
($r = -0.67$)

Fig. 4.2. Scatter diagrams showing degrees of relationship, which are described by the statistical index r. (After Neale and Liebert 1973.)

occurring relationships in order to find indirect information about causes. If we were studying the relationship between suicide and phases of the moon, even a low correlation would be of interest, provided that it reached a predetermined level of statistical significance (that it was not likely to be found by chance).

We have problems with logic in making inferences about causal relationships from correlational studies. Two inherent limitations that undermine internal validity are the *directionality problem* and the *third-variable problem*. The directionality problem arises because when we find that two factors are correlated, we cannot usually establish the time sequence between events — we do not know which came first. Klaber (1970), studying institutional care, scored each institution on two factors: the amount of money spent on ward programs and the amount of stereotyped behavior displayed in the ward by patients (such as constant rocking back and forth). He found a strong negative correlation — the less expenditure for programming, the more stereotyped behavior there was. From this correlation, however, we do not know whether the minimal programming caused patients to be idle and therefore to engage in self-stimulating behavior, or whether institutions that had patients with much stereotyped behavior deemed it a waste of money to introduce programs. We can guess about the direction of this relationship, but we cannot be certain. In some cases, the directionality problem is logically reduced or eliminated by the variables being studied. If children's sex is correlated with their choice of toys, we can be certain that the choice of toys did not make some children girls and some boys.

We are still left, however, with the third-variable problem. When any two variables are correlated, the association may actually be produced by a third, unmeasured variable. Stereotyped behavior and funding of programs

may be a misleading correlation. Perhaps institutions with a strong medical orientation consider recreational programming unnecessary and rely on drug treatment, a side effect of which might be stereotyped behavior. Hence the observed correlation might be caused by a third variable: the institution's degree of medical orientation. In correlational research, then, we need to measure or control for a number of variables that might influence the relationship, and we have sophisticated statistical techniques for assessing multiple relationships. We never know, however, if yet another "third variable" was not assessed, and some of the inherent limitations we have discussed are always present. Nevertheless, correlational studies can add to our confidence in an etiological hypothesis, and can indicate relationships worthy of further experimental study.

DEVELOPMENTAL STUDIES

One type of correlational research is the developmental study. Questions about how behavior changes in time are fundamental to abnormal psychology. Because some of the precursors of most psychopathologies are sure to be found in earlier years, a search for causes is partly a developmental question. Also, the age-appropriateness of behaviors, attitudes, and abilities is often important diagnostically; we need to know at what ages these are in evidence. Developmental studies employ several methods.

The *retrospective study* selects subjects in the present and goes back in time for their developmental history. Researchers used to ask people to recall events from earlier life, a method later widely criticized for yielding distorted data, even for a mother who was asked to recount the developmental history of her own child (Haggard et al. 1960). As the Chinese proverb says: "The palest ink is clearer than the best memory." It is better to go back to earlier records, say, from a clinic or school. Watt (1974) identified all the adult schizophrenics in Massachusetts who had attended one school system and then examined their elementary school records for indications of early disturbance. He found that contrary to the popular belief that schizophrenics are withdrawn as children, their teachers had seen these students as abrasive and aggressive in the classroom.

Two other developmental research strategies are more commonly used: the longitudinal and cross-sectional methods. The *longitudinal study* measures the same group of subjects over a long period, to study changes with age. This is the most direct way of assessing developmental changes and has been very useful despite several shortcomings. It is usually impractical for researchers to continue a study for years, and the attrition of subjects introduces bias into the sample. Also, subjects become fa-

miliar with the measurement procedures, which may give a distorted picture. In the Berkeley Growth Study, a longitudinal examination of intellectual functioning from infancy to age eighteen, most children were tested at least thirty-eight times (Bayley 1949).

Also, because most types of abnormal behavior occur with low frequency, it is not cost-effective to follow large groups of subjects for a long time just to detect the 1 percent who may, for example, become schizophrenic. For this reason, longitudinal studies often are designed to identify groups at high risk for a specific disorder. Among the longitudinal studies we will discuss in later chapters is Mednick and Schulsinger's (1968) tracking into their early adulthood of adolescents at risk for schizophrenia (Chapter 6). Interestingly, this prospective study supported the findings of Watt's retrospective study, in that adolescents rated aggressive in

Fig. 4.3. Developmental studies examine how behavior changes over time.

Drawing by David Pascal; © 1979 The New Yorker Magazine, Inc.

school were more likely to show signs of schizophrenia later.

The *cross-sectional study* examines people in different age groups at the same time. In Chapter 21 we will consider classic data on manifestation of fears across early childhood, evidence gathered by examining groups of children aged 1 to 2 years, 3 to 4 years, and 5 to 6 years (Jersild and Holmes 1935). The cross-sectional study is much more economical than the longitudinal study. A limitation of the cross-sectional study when the groups are far apart in age is separating effects of differences in age from differences in earlier experiences. A study measuring the effectiveness of behavioral therapy for women who had never experienced orgasm contrasted a group in their late twenties with one in their early forties (Schneidman and McGuire 1976). Therapy was more successful for the former, a finding that is clinically important but difficult to interpret, because these women (1) were younger, but also (2) had not experienced the problem as long, and (3) had grown up in a time of different sexual norms.

A recent attempt to enjoy the advantages of both the longitudinal and cross-sectional methods while circumventing their limitations combines these methods. Wynne and his co-workers (Garmezy 1978b) were interested in emotional and intellectual dysfunction between the ages of four and thirteen. They tested three groups of children, aged four, seven, and ten (cross-sectional) and then retested them three years later (longitudinal). The design appears in Table 4.1. Because two groups were tested at ages ten and thirteen, the experimenters can compare these for equivalence (dotted line) to see if their different backgrounds influenced results.

Experimental Studies

Experimental studies are conducted in controlled settings, where the researcher introduces a manipulation and measures its effect.

As we have seen, most research in abnormal psychology is descriptive or correlational, because it is impossible to manipulate some variables (age, for one) and impractical or unethical to manipulate others (severe stress to produce psychopathology). Experimental studies usually involve either efforts at treatment to reduce psychopathology or analogue studies to simulate psychopathology. We shall consider each. First, however, we discuss how to design a properly controlled experiment, and raise again the notion of internal validity.

In an experiment, the variables the researcher manipulates are called *independent variables,* and those he measures are *dependent variables.* In a study to test the hypothesis that higher drug dosages will result in more improvement of behavior in hyperactive schoolchildren, the drug dosage is the independent variable, and an index of hyperactive behavior is the dependent variable.

In doing experimental studies we try to control both the independent variable and extraneous factors that could account for observed changes. The research design should increase the plausibility of making causal interpretations — the internal validity. A good illustration of the need to control for alternative, or "rival," hypotheses is a classic study on the effects of early mothering experiences for institutionalized children. Skeels and Dye (1939) selected

Table 4.1. Age at testing

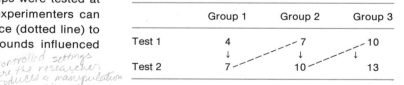

	Group 1	Group 2	Group 3
Test 1	4	7	10
Test 2	7	10	13

Source: N. Garmezy, "Current Status of a Sample of Other High-Risk Research Programs," in L. C. Wynne, R. L. Crowell, and S. Matthysse, eds., *The Nature of Schizophrenia: New Approaches to Research and Treatment.* (New York: John Wiley & Sons, 1978).

thirteen children under three years of age from an impoverished orphanage and placed them in the wards of a state institution for the mentally retarded. The adult women residents of the institution became quite attached to the children, giving them much care and attention. At the pretest, these children's average IQ was 64. By a post-test, after being in the wards for two years, their average IQ had risen to 93! The research design was:

Pretest — Treatment — Post-test

The dramatic rise in IQ, from mentally retarded to the normal range, has been attributed to the *individual care* given the children by the retarded adult-substitute mothers. Although this conclusion is appealing, it is not scientifically valid, because the design does not rule out plausible rival hypotheses that might explain the increase in IQ. Some of the most common threats to the internal validity of experiments are these (from Campbell and Stanley 1966):

1. *History.* Specific events other than the experimental treatment that occur between the pre and post-testing. In the Skeels and Dye study, the children experienced not only increased mothering from the retarded women but also a change in their environment, attention from institution staff, a different diet, and the like.
2. *Maturation.* Changes in the subjects' biological or psychological condition, including such factors as age, learning, fatigue, or boredom. The Skeels and Dye children were two years older at retesting.
3. *Testing.* How taking a test once affects performance at retesting. Intelligence scores have been shown to rise after initial exposure to a test (Anastasi 1968), so that these children might have been expected to perform better at the second testing.
4. *Instrumentation.* Changes in the way of measuring the dependent variable. A poly-

graph may lose its initial calibration, an observer may become bored or more skilled, or a tester may make subtle changes in the testing procedures. In the Skeels and Dye study the initial testing apparently was done in the orphanage, but the retesting was done in the state institution.

5. *Statistical regression.* The statistical tendency for extreme scores to become less extreme at retesting, because in part they reflect chance variation. Extremely high or low scoring groups are often selected for study, and part of their change at retesting is caused by statistical regression. The Skeels and Dye children had especially low initial IQs.

A good experimental design is meant to discount the most plausible rival hypotheses, by keeping conditions constant and using alternate (control) groups. A simple controlled experiment is the *pre-post control group design,* wherein an equivalent second group is tested at the same times as the experimental group but does not receive the experimental treatment. This research design is:

Experimental:
    Pretest — Treatment — Post-test
Control:
    Pretest ——————— Post-test

Ideally, once the research sample is selected, the experimenter randomly assigns people to groups, so that each person has an equal chance of being in the experimental or the control group. If groups are not equivalent to begin with, observed differences might be attributed to differences in a group's characteristics. Assume that the experimental and control groups are alike at the beginning of the study, and think about how this simple design controls each of these five threats to internal validity. Skeels and Dye (1939) did, in fact, report measures on a group of children who remained in the orphanage, and whose IQs decreased markedly. This control group seems to counter the rival hypothesis that the experimental group's improvement was caused by maturation or experience with the test. Yet this control does not allow conclusions about which aspects of the ward experience produced the changes, so that the conclusions about influences of mothering are still invalid (see Table 4.2). In designing a study we must decide which conclusions we would like to be able to draw, and then to rule out plausible rival hypotheses accordingly. An experimental study might have several conditions, to control for rival hypotheses.

> ANALOGUE EXPERIMENTS

Most experimental studies in psychopathology involve efforts to *reduce* abnormal behavior by treatment, because experimental studies of factors that might *cause* abnormal behavior have obvious practical and ethical limitations. Therefore, experimental studies of hypotheses about etiology are usually *analogues*. That is, they are designed to create under controlled conditions events and behaviors that are analogous to naturally occurring psychopathology. The researcher interested in studying hallucinations might produce these in normal volunteers with a drug like lysergic acid diethylamide (LSD) or by hypnosis. The difficulty, of course, is one of external validity — of generalizing from the analogue to the real phenomenon (as from drug-induced hallucinations to those in schizophrenia), and the greatest value of analogue studies may be in pointing up possible relationships for further study under more natural conditions.

SITUATION AND BEHAVIOR ANALOGUES. In studies using situation and behavior analogues, experimenters create conditions that will induce minor psychopathology-like symptoms in human subjects. A number of sensory deprivation studies have experimentally isolated subjects from sensory stimulation for long periods of time (see Figure 4.4). They might lie on a bed,

Table 4.2. How to evaluate an experiment: The Skeels and Dye study

What is the hypothesis?	IQ rises with increased individual care
What is the independent variable?	Placement of children, in an institution's wards or in an orphanage
What is the dependent variable?	IQ level of children
Does the experiment have internal validity?	No. The amount of individual care is not the only plausible cause of the rise in IQ. Other possible causes: 1. change in environment 2. maturation of children 3. improvement in test-taking ability 4. change in testing procedures 5. leveling of statistical extremes
Does the experiment have external validity?	No. The results may not generalize for several reasons, among them: 1. The children were a specially selected group of orphans 2. Everyone was aware that this was a research project

[handwritten margin notes: Haughton + Ayllon — compulsive-like behaviors from learning experiences ∴ possible causes; Orne + Scheibe could be caused by demand characteristics; but, a limit to what we can expose people to ∴ narrows inferences we can draw]

blindfolded, with arms and legs wrapped in cotton to reduce stimulation. The result of this isolation from stimulation was that subjects manifested a number of psychotic-like effects (Brownfield 1965).[1]

Haughton and Ayllon (1965) sought to demonstrate how compulsive-like behavior could result from learning experiences. For a demonstration that would raise ethical doubts today, they selected a schizophrenic woman who had been hospitalized for twenty-three years and who spent her days lying down and smoking. First they took away her cigarettes. They then taught her progressively that she could earn cigarettes by sweeping the floor with a broom, for longer and longer periods. Before long, her broom-carrying had become constant and resembled a compulsion; she would actively and aggressively resist if someone tried to take the broom away. Two examining psychiatrists, who did not know the behavior had been taught, saw broom-holding as a true compulsion and advanced very complex explanations about its

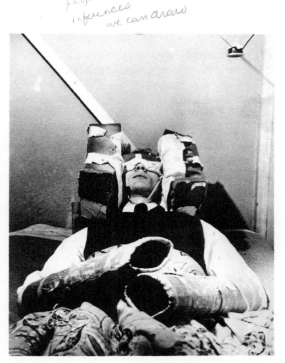

Fig. 4.4. This research subject, specially dressed for a sensory deprivation experiment, may begin to show behaviors analogous to psychotic symptoms.

[1] Orne and Scheibe (1964) hypothesized that some of these effects were caused by demand characteristics in the situation, which communicated to subjects that they should act in bizarre ways. In their study, subjects spent four hours sitting in a room with a window, with paper and pencil available on a table. The isolation was not nearly as extreme as in previous sensory deprivation experiments. Two groups of randomly assigned subjects, however, had been prepared for the experience differently. The control group was simply told that they were a control group for an experiment in sensory deprivation. For the demand characteristics group, an experimenter, in a white coat, took a medical history, while a tray of drugs labeled "emergency tray" was kept in full view. The experimenter stressed that the subjects should report any unusal experiences, had them sign release forms, and showed them a red "panic" button to push if they found the situation intolerable. This study showed that the demand characteristics group performed more poorly than the controls on a variety of perceptual, cognitive, and motor skills measures usually employed in sensory deprivation experiments. These subjects had complied with the obvious expectations of the experiment.

possible symbolic meaning for the patient. When the experimenters no longer gave cigarettes for broom-holding, the behavior vanished altogether. Analogue studies such as these give some indication about possible causes of abnormal behavior.

There are limits, however, to the degree of trauma to which we can expose human subjects. Because most of our theories of psychopathology postulate the existence of a relationship between fairly extreme personal stress and the development of abnormal behavior, the inability to re-create similar stress experimentally distinctly narrows the inferences we can draw.

[handwritten margin notes: Subject analogues — animals are used to broaden the researcher's range for inducing stress & give greater control over conditions ... to be valid ✓ the behaviors in the animals should be analogous to a type of abnormal behavior seen in human beings, ✓ in some way ... of experimental conditions should be analogous to conditions believed to be relevant to a form of human psychopathology. — operation at high levels of abstraction ... conflict between opposing response tendencies is an important general determinant of abnormal behavior ... eg "neurosis" — Pavlov not in common use but still ... especially lately]

SUBJECT ANALOGUES. In subject analogue studies, animals are used to broaden the researcher's range for inducing stress and give greater control over conditions. Research with animal analogues, to be valid, has to fulfill two requirements: the behaviors in the animal should be analogous in some way to a type of abnormal behavior seen in human beings, and experimental conditions should be analogous to conditions believed relevant to a form of human psychopathology. Psychophysiological disorders, such as peptic ulcers or cardiovascular conditions, are quite reproducible in animals (see Chapter 14). But what is the animal analogue of the delusions, disordered thinking, lack of emotional expression, and hallucinations of the schizophrenic patient?

The problem of simulating analogues to the conditions believed to produce psychopathology in research with lower animals is an even more formidable problem. It is difficult to imagine how one could create animal analogues for disturbed human family patterns, which are crucial in many theories of symptom formation. One way around this problem has been to operate at higher levels of abstraction. For example, if we posit that conflict between opposing response tendencies is an important general determinant of abnormal behavior, then we can define conflict so broadly that conditions comparable to the human level can be created for lower animals.

An important early example of an experimental conflict situation was Pavlov's (1927) accidental discovery that when dogs were given too difficult a problem to solve, they developed neurotic-like symptoms. While training a dog to discriminate between a circle and an ellipse, Pavlov made the shape of the ellipse progressively more like the circle. When the ellipse was almost circular, the dog performed pretty well for several weeks and then began to lose the discrimination altogether. At the same time, his

behavior changed markedly; he became agitated, squealed and struggled in the harness, and tried to avoid reentering the experiment room. Previously learned discriminations were also destroyed, and the dog's disturbance never did completely disappear, even after long periods of rest.

Many other researchers sought to create "experimental neurosis" in animals by exposing them to stressful conditions, especially conflict between an approach and an avoidance response (Masserman 1961; Liddell 1944; Wolpe 1958). Among other notable programs of animal analogue research are Harlow and Harlow's (1969) studies of early maternal deprivation and subsequent adjustment in monkeys and Ellison's (in press) studies of alcohol consumption or amphetamine intoxication in naturalistic colonies of rats (see Figure 4.5). Were these conditions analogous to the kinds of stress experienced by people who experience psychopathology? Were the animal responses similar to the human response of anxiety or depression or psychosis?

Again, the value of such studies may be primarily heuristic, leading to refined thinking about what might be true in naturalistic settings. In recent years, interest in animal analogue studies, except to investigate psychophysiological and biochemical hypotheses, has diminished.

[handwritten: a more internally valid understanding of a case study, taking objective & reliable measures of a person's behavior under varied conditions controlled by the researcher]

SINGLE-SUBJECT STUDIES

As we have seen, the case-study approach has contributed greatly to our understanding of abnormal behavior by elucidating individual dynamics and suggesting areas for more systematic study, but from a scientific point of view it lacks internal and external validity. In recent years, however, the study of the individual has been approached in ways that have made it a more internally valid undertaking. Single-subject research involves taking objective and reliable measures of a person's behavior under varied conditions controlled by the researcher. Sidman (1960) has argued that single-subject studies are preferable to group studies because group results often do not reflect the real behavior of any individual and at times can be very misleading. Single-subject research designs have been used in general to evaluate effectiveness of treatment, primarily in behavior therapy. The two designs most commonly used to control for problems of internal validity are the *reversal design* and the *multiple baseline design.*

REVERSAL DESIGN. In a reversal design, the effects of the program on a target behavior are demonstrated by alternately presenting and removing the program for a time. A target behavior is observed until a reasonably stable measure is obtained. This pretreatment record is called a *baseline.* Next, treatment conditions are introduced and usually continued until the

Fig. 4.5. An artist's conception of one of the UCLA rat colony environments, which are used to study animal analogues of psychopathology. On the left is the burrows area, where separate straw-lined burrows can be reached through individual tubes. In the middle is the behavioral arena, where various social behaviors can be observed occurring on the straw-covered floor. On the right is the feeding area, connected to the behavioral area by a large valve. One study examined the effects on rats' social behavior of continuous amphetamine intoxication; these effects provide a useful animal model of paranoid schizophrenia.

behavior has shown a clinically meaningful change and stabilized at a new level. Then treatment is withdrawn for a while, to determine whether the behavior will return toward its baseline level. Finally, treatment is reintroduced. This is also called an *ABAB* (or ABA'B') *design,* to denote the alternation of conditions. For a reversal design, consider a report of intervention with Robbie, a particularly disruptive third grader in an urban poverty-level school (Hall et al. 1968). As Figure 4.6 shows, Robbie was studying in only about 25 percent of observation intervals; in the remaining 75 percent he was snapping rubber bands, talking and laughing with classmates, and otherwise off-task. At B, the teacher introduced a systematic reinforcement procedure. She began paying a great deal of attention to Robbie when he was studying. The increase in his studying was dramatic; however, if the report had stopped here, we would not know why Robbie was studying more. Improvement did coincide with the pro-

gram, but remembering the types of rival hypotheses we have considered, Robbie's improved performance also might be attributable to some other event in his life, such as adaptation to a new classroom, or changes in the measurement procedures. At stage A', when the teacher withdraws the program (stops giving special attention to Robbie for studying) and his behavior deteriorates, we can begin to feel more nearly certain of a causal relationship between what the teacher is doing and what Robbie is doing. At B' the program is reintroduced and Robbie shows an immediate increase in studying.

Although the reversal design can be very effective, it does present problems. First, for some behaviors reversal is especially unethical or impractical. Most teachers, parents, and therapists are not comfortable about undoing their successes, even for a few days, and reversals are rare in true clinical practice. Second, even when the therapist agrees to a reversal, return-

Fig. 4.6. Reversal design, showing Robbie's study behavior when reinforcement is alternately given and withdrawn. (From Hall et al. 1968.)

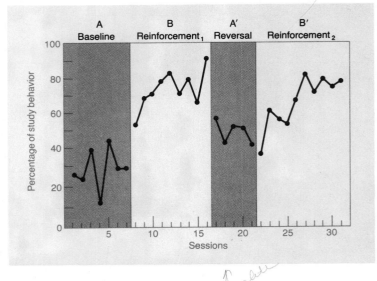

ing conditions to baseline is often quite difficult to do. One wonders how many examples of behavior deterioration during reversal are caused by a child's confusion at the adult's unnatural efforts to "make everything like before." A final dilemma is that although demonstrating that program gains disappear when the program is withdrawn may be a scientific success (a cause-effect relationship is established), it is a clinical failure (the program has had no lasting effect). A good clinical intervention should change the individual's behavior so that the effects persist after the treatment. In Robbie's case, the study behavior did not completely revert to baseline during reversal, indicating some lasting benefit. Ironically, though, had Robbie's gains in B been more lasting, the reversal design would not have accomplished its scientific purpose.

MULTIPLE-BASELINE DESIGN. The multiple-baseline design, though less frequently em-

Quasi-Experimental Designs

[handwritten margin note: Quasi-Experimental Design — Introduction of experimental control into the way that data are gathered.]

[handwritten margin note: Campbell + Stanley = quasi-E.D. for natural settings.]

An experimenter can observe many naturally occurring events in which full experimental control over assignment of subject or scheduling of the intervention is impossible. Nonetheless, we can introduce some experimental control into the way the data are gathered. Such approaches are referred to as *quasi-experimental designs.* Campbell and Stanley (1966) describe several of these designs for natural settings where better controlled experiments are not feasible.

When the researcher does not have complete control over subject assignment, she can use the *nonequivalent control group design.* This design resembles the pre-post control group design in that an experimental and control group are assessed before and after the intervention. The design here is quasi-experimental, however, because the groups are not randomly assigned, but represent some naturally occurring grouping, such as classrooms, hospital wards, towns, and the like. One classroom might be selected for a new program while a second classroom is assessed as a control. If the two classrooms are not equivalent, a number of rival hypotheses could be advanced to account for the differences. In this design, a control group is matched as closely as possible to the experimental group.

Where the researcher does not have control over the intervention, a *time-series design* may be employed. Here, rather than just

[handwritten margin notes: non-equivalent control group design — on naturally occurring group over there is no control of the subject assignment — control group closely matched to the exp. group as possible — pretest, posttest — Time-series Design — no control over the intervention — repeated measures before + after the intervention — measure should be over a long period of time — just on time of exposure to treatment — doesn't show the cause but helps to understand]

take a pretest and post-test measure, the experimenter takes repeated measures before and after the intervention. A special program to reduce traffic fatalities on Connecticut highways illustrates some evaluative problems also commonly found in community psychology projects. After a record high of 324 traffic deaths in 1955, Governor Ribicoff instituted a severe crackdown on speeding. In the first year of the new program only 284 died, leading the governor to conclude: "With the savings of 40 lives in 1956, a reduction of 12.3% from the 1955 motor vehicle death toll, we can say that the program is definitely worthwhile." This change is shown in graph (a) (p. 90).

Extending the measurement over several years, however, Campbell and Ross (1968; Campbell 1969) found less reason for enthusiasm. The time-series analysis is shown in graph (b). The dotted line presents the simple pre-post graph, which when examined alone in (a) indicated a successful program. The extended time series, though, shows instability prior to the program, and this variation makes the program's effect look relatively trivial. Indeed, the entire drop might be attributed to regression of extreme scores to less extreme ones upon the next testing, although in subsequent years the data in the highway program did begin to show some effect of the enforcement program. The time series is an important consid-

ployed than reversal design, has fewer problems. Two or more behaviors are measured until their baselines are stable. Daily measures might be taken of a child's pants-wetting, isolate behavior, and thumb-sucking. The experimental treatment is introduced for just one behavior; baseline continues for the other(s). If the target behavior changes and the other(s) do not, some experimental control is indicated. Subsequently, the experimental treatment is introduced for each other behavior.

Figure 4.7 illustrates the results of a progressive treatment program for Kevin. After seven days of baseline, a program was begun to reduce the number of times he wet his pants. Improvement was observed in his pants-wetting behavior (top graphs) but not in the other two problem behaviors until each was subsequently treated in turn. Hence it has been demonstrated that changes relate to the specific treatment and not to other factors, such as attention from the therapist.

eration in design because social experiments like this one are often begun just when a problem becomes extreme. A new reading program is introduced in a school system following a particularly poor showing on state-wide tests, or an innovative approach to

corrections is instituted following a rash of runaways from a boys' reformatory. Although the extended time-series design cannot rule out other explanations entirely, it does help us understand the program's effects.

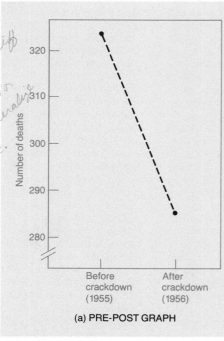

(a) PRE-POST GRAPH

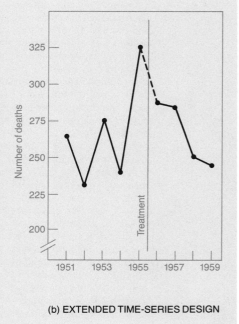

(b) EXTENDED TIME-SERIES DESIGN

(From Campbell 1969.)

Multiple-baseline designs can also take measures in different situations. We can measure a child's disruptive behavior in three classrooms, then introduce a program first in one, then the second, and finally the third.

The multiple-baseline design has the practical and ethical advantage of not requiring a reversal to demonstrate the relationship between an intervention and change in behavior. It does present a clinical and experimental dilemma similar to the one inherent in reversal design, in that change in one behavior or situation is likely to generalize somewhat to others. The child who becomes less disruptive in math class may begin to behave better in reading class as well. As generalization occurs, it weakens the experimental conclusions that can be drawn. The multiple-baseline design, though, is still an experimentally powerful and clinically feasible procedure.

Treatment for Kevin
— wetting of pants to the specific
changes relate to other factors.
treatment + not to other
(eg attention from therapist.

Fig. 4.7. Multiple baseline design, showing Kevin's successive reduction in problem behavior. The program was introduced first for wet pants, then for isolate behavior, and last for thumb-sucking. (From Madakacherry 1974.)

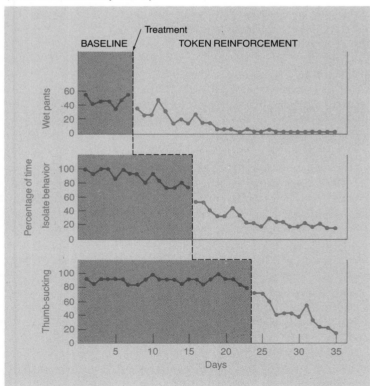

[handwritten margin notes, top:] to the Skeels + Dye exp. in diff → correlational (not manipulative) add boys + girls. treatments are diff for diff types of subjects. ... mixed

[handwritten:] experimental & correlational approaches

[handwritten, top right:] 3 diff subjects from 2 diff popln order 2 diff treatments.

[handwritten, top right:] Kelman — most psycho exp draw subjects from groups whose power is limited in our society — psych exp is a one-sided power arrangement

[handwritten, left margin:] important because an exp' treatment may be ✓ effective only for one type of persons + not for others.

Mixed Designs

Many studies in abnormal psychology combine experimental and correlational approaches in *mixed designs*. Neale and Libert define a mixed design as "one in which subjects from two or more discrete and typically non-overlapping populations are assigned to different treatments" (1973, p. 125). In the Skeels and Dye (1939) study, the experimental component was moving (or not moving) children from the orphanage to the ward; this was experimental because it could be manipulated by the investigator. If boys and girls had been assigned to each condition, the child's sex would have been a correlational component because it was a given characteristic, which could not be manipulated by the experimenter. The results could have been analyzed to see if the institutional mothering experience affected boys and girls differently.

Any study in which the researcher asks if the effects of an experimental treatment are different for different types of subjects (schizophrenics vs. normals; younger vs. older women) is a mixed design. Mixed designs are often important to employ, because an experimental treatment (such as a new form of therapy) might be effective for only one type of person and not for others. Even though we have discussed research approaches separately in this chapter, you will find that in practice various approaches are often combined.

Ethical Issues in Research

[handwritten:] ① threat to subjects' well-being. ② deception in exp. · invasion of privacy

The researcher in abnormal psychology confronts many ethical issues, some of which we have mentioned earlier in this chapter. The primary ones are the threats that studies might pose to a subject's well-being. Kelman (1972) points out that most psychological experiments

draw subjects from groups whose power is limited in our society, such as mental patients, children, prisoners, or students. Furthermore, the psychological experiment itself is a rather one-sided power arrangement, its subject implicitly pressured to comply with the experimenter's demands, for the sake of "science." It is, therefore, crucial to conduct research so that the subject's rights are protected, and the aims of research — acquiring useful knowledge — are also served. This is a delicate and often controversial balance.

One concern is that procedures might do physical or psychological harm. The medical literature is filled with old examples of extreme abuse, such as introducing live cancer cells into unknowing subjects (Langer 1966), giving people LSD without their knowledge, and sterilizing women without adequate consent. These types of subject abuse are better controlled today, but still the potential for psychological harm certainly remains in many studies that expose people to some form of stress. Treatment studies run the risk of doing psychological harm with control conditions that deprive people of needed treatment.

Other problems are recruiting of subjects and exerting pressure to volunteer, especially in settings like prisons, mental hospitals, or even universities, where subjects may be apprehensive about negative consequences if they do not comply, or may be encouraged with needed incentives to submit. Mitford (1974), in her exposé of conditions in the American prison system, describes how prisoners are used extensively to test new and often quite harmful drugs; because of the very low wages standard in prisons, volunteers are easily recruited for $1 a day.

Further ethical worries beset use of deception in experiments, giving subjects a false explanation of the study's purposes, and invasion of privacy, asking subjects very personal ques-

[handwritten marginalia at top of page:]
Human Subjects review committees to examine procedures for proposed research & the APA. established a Code of Ethics · 1/ Studied for /harmfulness/benefit to society 2/ to outweigh risks 3/ to be used in informed consent 4/ possibility of withdraw at any time - participation not to be used in accordance should be all info confidential. vs Gergen — the effects may not be as much as we expect . . . need systematic research on these guidelines

[right margin:] Resnick + Schwartz people want to be deceived.

tions, observing them without their knowing, and the like.

Consider the very common social-psychological studies that make a small manipulation in the community to observe people's reactions. Since the 1964 stabbing murder of Kitty Genovese on a New York City street while thirty-eight witnesses made no attempt to help her, psychologists have been interested in studying what makes some people help and others stand by when someone is in trouble. A typical study had two people simulate a fight on a public street, and observed passersby to see whether intervention related to the sex of the fighters (see Chapter 17). Kelman (1972) writes that this type of study is both deceptive and an invasion of privacy, because researchers observe people without their knowledge or consent and impose upon them, whether or not the subjects intervene to help. Such a study may also be psychologically harmful: some people will be upset by witnessing the fight, and those who pass by without helping may ruminate on the incident and experience lowered self-esteem for having been passive. In a study such as this one, "subjects" cannot be debriefed later about the experiment's purposes, nor can the investigator be available to provide help for any subsequent ill effects. It is clear that even this seemingly harmless study raises a cloud of ethical doubts.

Universities and others conducting research have established Human Subjects Review Committees, to examine procedures for proposed research. Also, the American Psychological Association has established a Code of Ethics for conducting research (APA 1973). The guidelines generally increase the investigator's responsibility to carefully consider and justify procedures. The primary consideration is that studies which may produce severe or lasting harm should be disallowed. Furthermore, studies are evaluated according to whether the potential benefits, to the subjects and society, outweigh the potential risks. Where deception is necessary, subjects are to be debriefed as soon and as thoroughly as possible. Usually, "informed consent" is to be sought, meaning that procedures and risks must be described to, and understood by, subjects, and their consent to participate must be obtained. The power of subjects is further increased by assurances that they are free to decline participation, to question procedures, or to withdraw at any time; in institutions, benefits such as early release are not to be made contingent upon participation in research. All information gathered about subjects must be kept confidential.

Most psychologists would agree that the increased regulation of research has been necessary. Yet in many instances simplistic enforcement or legitimate disagreement between committees and investigators about benefits and risks have hampered studies that some feel would be worthwhile. The need for informed consent is one of these. Some persons, such as children, persons who are retarded, or mental patients, are not fully able legally to give informed consent. The lengths to which the investigator must go to ensure informed consent sometimes create more difficulties than they prevent. In our own experience conducting brief interviews with retarded residents of halfway houses, we were required first to fully inform the residents of their right to refuse, the purposes of the study, the safeguards taken to ensure that the information they provided would not be used against them, and the like. Even the most thoroughly simplified explanation left many people far more confused or distraught than did the few questions in the interview itself.

Gergen (1973) has voiced reservations about the new ethical guidelines, saying that the effects of such factors as deception or fully informing subjects have not been studied and may at times be different from the effects we expect. He argues for more systematic research on these very factors, to better inform ethical decisions. In this spirit, Resnick and Schwartz (1973) decided to carry to its logical extreme the APA principle that the subject must be fully informed about all aspects of the experiment that might influence participation. An experimental group received painstakingly complete information on all the procedures and purposes of the experiment. Unexpectedly, their incentive to participate seemed to be destroyed by the effort — they became suspicious and missed a great many appointments. The authors conclude that this "suggests that people enjoy an element of risk and nondisclosure and become bored rapidly with the prospect of participating in something of which they already have full knowledge" (p. 137).

These ethical problems will never have easy answers, but the encouraging change in recent years is that issues are being raised, debated, and even studied more often.

Summary

1. We have three types of approaches to research in abnormal psychology: *descriptive studies,* which describe a phenomenon as it appears in nature; *correlational studies,* assessing the relationship between two or more variables; and *experimental studies,* in which the researcher intentionally introduces a change in a controlled setting and measures its effects. A study should be designed so that it has both internal and external validity.

2. A study has *internal validity* if only one cause for the effects observed is plausible. Experimenter bias can strongly affect internal validity if the researcher (1) misjudges or misrecords the phenomena because of preconceived beliefs, or (2) unintentionally communicates an expectancy to the subject.

3. A study has *external validity* if the results can be generalized to a larger population. Factors that affect this ability to generalize are choice of sample subjects, and the situation itself (the subjects know they are part of an experiment).

4. The most popular types of descriptive studies are: (1) case studies, which describe in depth an individual's current thoughts, feelings, and behavior, and how these relate to life history; and (2) surveys, which assess how common a variable is in a large population by questionnaires, phone interviews, or direct interviews.

5. Correlational studies look for relations between variables based on two or more observations of the same subjects. Correlational studies have two limitations: directionality (which variable came first), and third variable (a variable that has not been taken into account affects correlation). Developmental study is one form of correlational study that looks at how behavior changes in time.

6. Experimental studies are conducted in a controlled setting in which the researcher controls both the independent variable and extraneous factors that might affect results and internal validity. Several factors threaten the internal validity of experiments: (1) history (events other than experimental treatment); (2) maturation (changes in biological or psychological conditions); (3) testing (effects on performance that result from retesting the same subject); (4) instrumentation (changes in measuring); and (5) statistical regression (extreme scores become less extreme with retesting). One type of experimental study is the analogue experiment, in which researchers induce an abnormal behavior or event in mild form or with animal subjects, in order to study possible causes of this approximation to real abnormal behavior.

7. In single-subject studies, another type of

experimental study, two designs are commonly used to increase internal validity: reversal design, in which the effects of a treatment on a target behavior are demonstrated by alternately introducing and removing treatment; and multiple-baseline design, in which experimental control is demonstrated by showing that change in behavior relates to the independent variable introduced at different times.

8. The ethical issues in research studies involve: (1) direct risk to the subject's well-being; (2) recruiting of subjects and the pressure to volunteer; (3) use of deception in describing the study's purpose; and (4) invasion of privacy. The American Psychological Association has developed a code of ethics to deal with these issues, but ethical issues are still much debated.

[Handwritten annotations throughout margins, partially legible:]

Problem: reversal ethical / difficult / non-lasting / baseline / reinforcement / return

Gergen — these guidelines should be studied further. Resnick + Schwartz — people want to be deceived

Mixed designs — exp + correlational approaches → diff subjects from 2 diff poln + 2 diff treatments. eg. adding the division of boys & girls in the Skeels + Dye

Nonreactive measures
1/ Archives
2/ Physical features
3/ Observation
4/ Contrived observation

1/ Retrospective study — Watt, schizo's when children aggressive + abrasive
2/ Longitudinal study
3/ Cross-sectional study — examines people in diff age groups at same time. problems: diff experiences with diff ages.

Skeels + Dye
Control — no treatment. NO IV, EV.
Problem EV — generalizing from exp to real phenomena. Behavior Analogues — symptoms in human
1/ Situation — conditions that induce
Haughton + Ayllon — compulsive-like behavior from learning.
2/ Subject Analogues — animals used for broadening research. range for using stress + greater control over own conditions, should be analogous.
IV — behaviors & situation to human psychopathology
Taylor + experimental neurosis

Rosenhan + Jacobson
ORNE
Hawthorne
WATT — schizo's past
Skeels + Dye — orphanage
Gergen
Resnick + Schwartz
Analogue exp: compulsive — Haughton + Ayllon, Campbell + Stanley
Quasi exp. Design.

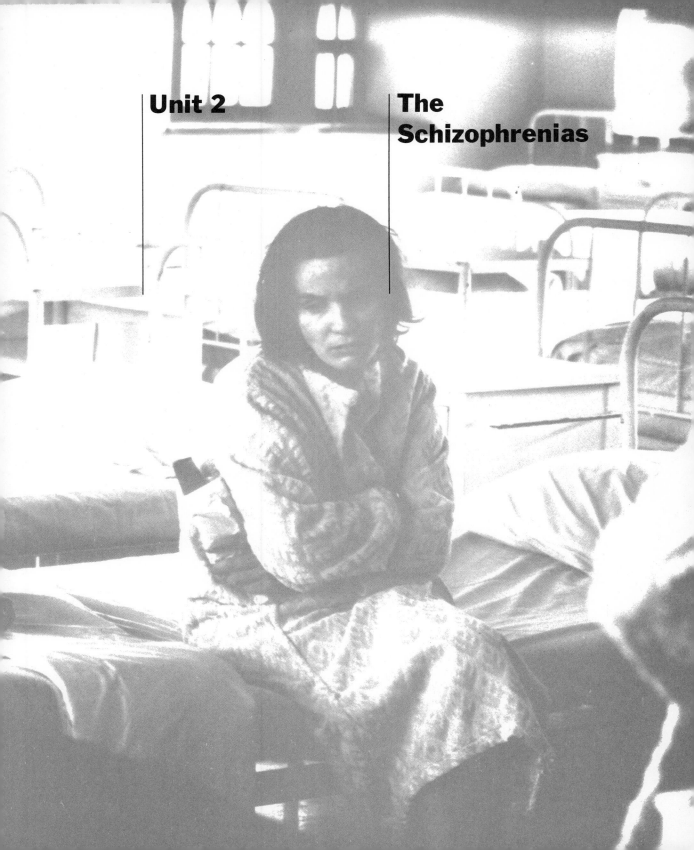

Unit 2

The Schizophrenias

The most disabling disorders of behavior are the psychoses. Asked to describe a psychotic, most lay people probably would use the word "mad" or "insane," for this is the way we perceive the bizarre behavior psychotics sometimes display. Psychologists characterize a psychotic breakdown as a radical change in consciousness, perception, thinking, and social behavior. The experience is often mystifying for the victim's family and friends, and also for the one to whom it is happening.

The schizophrenias, a group of psychoses that we will examine in this unit, are distinguished from other disorders primarily as disturbances in thinking that cause schizophrenics to say and do strange things.

Schizophrenic psychoses are a major mental health problem worldwide. They afflict about 1 percent of every nation's population. In any year, two million diagnosed schizophrenics live in the United States — 100,000 of whom are new cases in that year — and approximately 600,000 schizophrenics annually receive treatment. Schizophrenia occurs equally in males and females, most of them in their late teens or early twenties. It is the most common diagnosis among people eighteen to thirty-four years of age who enter public mental hospitals.

We begin our examination of specific patterns of abnormality with schizophrenia for two reasons. First, few question that the behavior pattern is abnormal. By studying an extreme deviation from normality, we can appreciate the more subtle variations of behavior. Second, the topic of schizophrenia places in high relief most of the issues discussed in Unit 1 — the vacillation between biological and psychological models of etiology, changing views on how the environment affects treatment of the mentally ill, current issues about interaction of biological and psychological treatment, the influence of family and community in fostering or inhibiting recovery, and so on. Once you recognize what these issues have to do with schizophrenia, you should

have little difficulty understanding their relation to other forms of abnormal behavior.

In Chapter 5 we will examine the schizophrenic psychoses from the point of view of both mental health experts and schizophrenics themselves, and their close friends and relatives. We will discuss the breaking down, the outlook for recovery, and the factors that affect the recovery rate. And we will see that there is more than one type of schizophrenia.

In Chapter 6 we examine theories of what causes a schizophrenic psychosis. We will review the evidence for and against several theories and consider whether we may find a different explanation for different behavior patterns that we currently categorize as types of schizophrenia.

In Chapter 7 we will discuss a number of treatment approaches to schizophrenia. Like theories of schizophrenia, these range from the purely biological to the purely psychological. As we will see, a combination of approaches may be the most effective method of intervention.

Chapter 5

23 pg.

The Nature of Schizophrenia

profound disorganization

Concept of Schizophrenia

Process of Schizophrenic Disorganization

The Subjective Experience of Schizophrenia

Course of a Schizophrenic Psychosis

Diagnostic Reliability in Schizophrenia

DSM-III Criteria for Schizophrenia

Paranoid Schizophrenia

Catatonic Schizophrenia

Hebephrenic Schizophrenia

Schizo-Affective Reactions

Diagnosis by Computer: The Ultimate Solution?

Predictors of Schizophrenia Outcome

Summary

A twenty-one-year-old college student, concerned about his parents and about a love affair, became quite guilt-ridden after a sexual experience with his girl friend. Soon thereafter, he felt that his life was completely changed. He experienced a sense of awareness of the world, which he soon saw ''as a completely wonderful place'' and stated, ''I began to experience goodness and love for the first time.'' He felt an intense benevolent quality which he had never felt before. He talked with friends frequently about the ''new life'' and about the way he now cares for and understands people. The feelings progressed to frank delusions that he was a religious messiah, and heralded an acute psychosis (Bowers 1974, p. 27).

Sandra, a twenty-three-year-old single woman, has had a long history of repeated failures in work, school, and in her personal relationships. Throughout her childhood she had been unable to make close friends or live up to her aspirations. Although she completed high school and had gone to college, she was expelled for failing work. She either quit or was discharged from numerous jobs within a few months of employment. . . . She continually fantasized wonderful things happening to her but developed illusions that she smelled bad, and that she had left a faucet open and consequently would be responsible for destroying a building, and that if she accidentally struck a match she would cause mass destruction and kill many people. Her associations between thoughts were very loose, confused, and she was suspicious of others (Grinker and Holzman 1973, pp. 173–174).

The two young people we've described could not be more different. The young man had been doing well in school, had a normal social life, and an intimate, if anxiety-producing, heterosexual relationship. Suddenly, it seems, something inside him snapped. The young woman's psychosis, on the other hand, developed gradually over a lifetime filled with personal failures. How do we account for the similar behavior of these two people following their breakdowns? What, if anything, can we say about their chances for recovery? Although you probably didn't recognize them, there are clues to the answers in the brief case histories you've just read. We will look at them a little later, when you know something about schizophrenic psychosis. Remember that schizophrenia is a profound form of behavioral disorganization that is difficult to diagnose and even more difficult to explain.

In this chapter we will define "schizophrenia" and consider some of the problems in diagnosing this disorder.

Concept of Schizophrenia

So far we have used "schizophrenia" and "schizophrenic psychosis" interchangeably. Before we get into a definition of schizophrenia, therefore, we had better explain that schizophrenia is a *functional psychosis,* a break from reality that we do not know to be caused by a physiological disease and believe to be a con-

sequence of something in one's life experience (see Figure 5.1). The so-called mood disorders (see Chapters 8–11) contain a second group of functional psychoses. The *organic psychoses* (Chapter 12) are breaks that we can attribute to a biological agent or physical cause; they include deterioration of the faculties, caused by old age (senile dementia) and progressive diseases such as Huntington's chorea.

The current description of schizophrenia holds that it is a disturbance in the way a person *thinks* as well as *feels.* Schizophrenics commonly report hallucinations and delusions, which they firmly believe. They also experience altered states of consciousness that most of us would associate with psychedelic drug use.

The definition of schizophrenia has been evolving since the beginning of this century, when Emil Kraepelin first called attention to the difference between the symptom patterns of schizophrenia and those typical of the mood disorders. He coined the term "dementia praecox" to describe cases with symptoms we now call "schizophrenic." The term reflects Kraepelin's belief that schizophrenia appeared early in life (praecox) and inevitably led to complete deterioration (dementia). He based the distinction between dementia praecox and mood disorders on the observation that between episodes, victims of mood disorders experience little residual impairment, whereas schizophrenics usually suffer residual symptoms and social and functional disabilities.

A few years after Kraepelin proposed the dementia classification, Swiss psychiatrist Eugen Bleuler (1950) noticed that dementia patients seemed to have in common a *primary,* or core pattern of symptoms accompanied by one or more of varied *secondary* symptoms, including delusions and hallucinations. The primary disturbance, Bleuler believed, was dissociation of thoughts from appropriate feelings caused by a splitting off (schizo) of parts of the self. Because of this schism, schizophrenics developed odd and irrational ways of communicating and relating to other people. Bleuler's conviction that this group of disorders was related by a common primary symptom pattern prompted him to refer to the disorder as "the group of schizophrenias."

Not only has Bleuler's term endured but his emphasis on the primacy of thought disturbance has also long served as the basis for diagnosis. The diagnostic criteria in use since 1968 (*DSM*-II) define the schizophrenias:

This large category includes a group of disorders manifested by characteristic disturbances of thinking, mood and behavior. Disturbances in thinking are marked by alterations of concept formation which may lead to misinterpretation of reality and sometimes to delusions (fixed but erroneous beliefs) and hallucinations (false sensory experiences), which frequently appear psychologically self-protective. Corollary mood changes include ambivalent, constricted and inappropriate emotional responsiveness and loss of empathy with others. Behavior may be withdrawn, regressive and bizarre. The schizophrenias, in which the mental status is attributable primarily to a *thought* disorder, are to be distinguished from the *major affective illnesses* which are dominated by a mood disorder (p. 33).

This general conception of schizophrenia is universal. When psychiatrists from both highly developed and underdeveloped countries recently diagnosed schizophrenic and other psychiatric patients for a World Health Organization study, their diagnoses showed that the term "schizophrenia" denotes the same class of symptoms worldwide. Table 5.1 lists these universal symptoms.

Fig. 5.1. Classifications of psychosis.

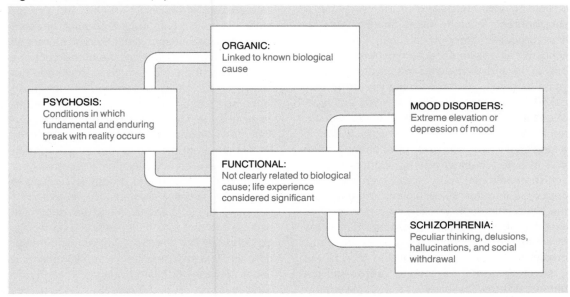

Table 5.1. Signs and symptoms recorded in schizophrenia patients worldwide

	Percentage of patients
Lack of insight that patient is mentally ill	97
Presence of auditory hallucinations	74
Ideas of reference (everything has personal meaning)	67
Suspiciousness	66
Flatness of affect (mood)	65
Voices speaking to patient	64
Delusions of persecution	64
Thoughts controlled by others	52

Source: Adapted from Sartorius et al., "The International Pilot Study of Schizophrenia," *Schizophrenia Bulletin,* 1974, Vol. 11, p. 31.

Process of Schizophrenic Disorganization

Psychologists have known for years that a schizophrenic episode takes time to develop and proceeds through stages. Often, the schizophrenic symptoms themselves appear only at the end. Sometimes the psychosis takes years to mature, as it did for the young woman described on page 99. Clinicians call this type of onset *insidious,* or gradual. Such individuals appear to have been sliding into a psychosis for a long time when some event, which they interpret in a very subjective way, triggers blatant schizophrenic reactions. *Acute,* or rapid onset described on page 99. Clinicians call this type the break occurs in weeks or even days. Research (Vaillant 1962) indicates that when onset is acute the likelihood of recovery is much greater than when it is insidious.

Regardless of how long it takes, schizophrenic disorganization seems to follow a fairly regular sequence. Bowers (1974) studied fifteen psychotic patients (most were schizophrenics) to determine the sequence of stages that precedes appearance of schizophrenic symptoms. Nearly all of the patients had been in a state of conflict and impasse immediately before breaking down. Many said things like, "I had nowhere to turn" or "there was no way out" when asked to describe how they felt. Actually, the crises that preceded their breakdowns were not unusual for the early adult period, which includes developmental crises involving career identity, heterosexual relationships, and autonomy from one's parents. The unique characteristic, however, was the feeling that they could not resolve the conflicts aroused by these developmental tasks.

The first sign that a developmental impasse is moving toward psychosis Bowers called *destructuring of perception and affect.* It has two components: experience of heightened awareness and ideas of reference and influence. Heightened awareness is a sensation that many people feel during severe crises. They describe it as a feeling of enormous urgency and a sense that something momentous is about to happen. They need less sleep and experience increased sensory acuity. Thoughts and perceptions occur faster than they can be assimilated. The mind seems to have just awakened during these times, so that people feel they are at their highest level. Nevertheless, their emotions may vacillate between intensely benign and highly fearful. Memories of childhood and long-forgotten events may surface. Occasionally, euphoria envelops the individual and produces a sense of triumphant mastery — sometimes in the most defeating circumstances. All of us who have had experiences like this have found them very exhilarating. For the potential schizophrenic, however, this state may persist, only to become one stage in the drift into psychosis (see Figure 5.2).

heightened
sense of self & identity
Same way to identity
- loss of immediate sense of self
dissolution
③ - Delusions → response to uncertainty
- provides coherence just when the
meaning just when the
individual's own sense
of identity seems to be
vanishing
- helps to reduce overwhelm
+ explain overwhelm
+ conflict
becomes quickly
resistant to change
and
fixed
— by the time delusions
become evident, other
symptoms of a schizo psychosis
are apparent as well.

Process of Schizophrenic Disorganization   **103**

Fig. 5.2. During the early stages of a schizophrenic breakdown, one experiences a euphoric feeling of happiness, energy, enthusiasm, and great talent. The woman who drew this picture said she was not ill but had an "acceleration of talent." She described the picture as "lively and festive" and went on to make many expansive and grandiose statements.

Bowers found that *ideas of reference,* or specialness, appear during the first stage of a schizophrenic break. Things and events take on hidden meanings that are apparent only to the patient. One of the participants in Bowers's study recalled:

One afternoon in the garden, I looked up to see a statue of Jesus in a "suffer little children to come unto me" pose with hand outstretched. He seemed to be speaking specifically to me saying

come here and kneel at my feet so I did (Bowers 1974, p. 163).

Another described the experience in the following way:

On the way to the store I had a flat tire. I thought this was planned also. At the gas station, the men smiled at me with twinkles in their eyes and I felt very good, and I saw men's faces in the sky and the stars twinkling in their eyes, I felt better than I ever had in my life (Bowers 1974, p. 149).

Almost inevitably, Bowers's subjects reported that the heightened sense of self gave way to *identity dissolution,* which Bowers describes as a progressive, continuing loss of the immediate sense of self. One man described it in this way:

I had the idea that I didn't know who I was and I had to find out. I kept looking at the patients in the room to find out which one I looked like. I saw the bad side of each one and became convinced this was the side I was similar to. I tried on other people's clothes. I said to myself, "If his clothes fit, then you must be like him" (Bowers 1974, p. 184).

Figure 5.3, drawn by a schizophrenic patient, expresses this sense of loss of self. Following the onset of this sensation, Bowers found the delusions began to appear — almost as a response to the intense feeling of chaotic uncertainty. A delusion, whether it is simply the belief that everyone is talking about you or the conviction that you are Jesus Christ, can be highly rewarding — it provides coherence and meaning just when the individual's own sense of identity seems to be vanishing. Because it helps to explain or to resolve overwhelming conflicts, a delusion quickly becomes fixed and resistant to change. By the time fixed delusions become evident, other characteristic symptoms of a schizophrenic psychosis (see Table 5.1) doubtless are apparent as well.

Fig. 5.3. An art therapist received this picture from a man who had seen a display of art by schizophrenic patients. The artist had been diagnosed as a paranoid schizophrenic. About the work he said, "To me it represents the butterfly or myself flying away from the depersonalization of the real world and soaring above it in its own realm of the universe."

The Subjective Experience of Schizophrenia

Once disorganization is complete and an individual has developed a relatively stable system of delusions and hallucinations, how does he experience the world? Some schizophrenic patients are able to communicate their feelings and perceptions very vividly through the medium of art, as Figures 5.2 and 5.3 show. More systematic efforts to elicit descriptions of the experience generally take the form of interviews with patients and former patients. In one particularly well-designed study, Freedman and Chapman (1973) talked to schizophrenic patients about their reactions to their illness. Table 5.2 summarizes some experiences common among these patients, including the observation that marked disruptions in thinking and perception caused them great anxiety.

Some writers (McGhie and Chapman 1961) have suggested that a primary aspect of acute schizophrenia is a breakdown in the filter system that keeps us from being overwhelmed by all the stimuli impinging upon us. Imagine being unable to focus your attention on one thing at a time, being constantly bombarded by stimuli, each as important as the one before it and the one after it. If you can do that, you have some idea of what McGhie and Chapman mean by a breakdown in the filter system.

Other researchers (Tucker et al. 1969; Bowers 1968; Freedman and Chapman 1973)

Table 5.2. Experiences reported by schizophrenic patients

1. *Disturbances in quality, clarity, or speed of thinking.*
   "I try to think and all of a sudden I can't say anything because it's like I turn off in my mind . . . emptiness."
2. *Changes in visual perception.*
   (a) *Blurring of perception* — "Maybe I'm not very sensitive to sight. . . . I keep thinking maybe I'm tired . . . the other night in front of the television, I felt a sort of blurring like that."
   (b) *Distortion of perception* — "My sister looked like the devil." "My eyes seem to disappear when I look in the mirror."
   (c) *Enhancement of perception* — "Things sound more intense . . . things feel or things sound louder. Interesting things sound louder and uninteresting things."
3. *Changes in the perception of speech.*
   "Say you're talking to another person. I don't understand a word what they're saying. Like they might be speaking some foreign language . . . because I can't understand it . . . if there's more than one person talking, I don't follow them because it goes too quickly."

Source: Adapted from B. Freedman and L. Chapman, *Journal of Abnormal Psychology*, 1973, 82(1), p. 49.

have not found these symptoms to be as universal among schizophrenic patients as McGhie and Chapman suggested. Apparently, changes in thought and perception do occur in some patients, but not universally enough to be labeled acute schizophrenia's *primary deficit* — the source of all other symptoms. That such changes can be vital in the subjective experience of a psychotic break is undeniable, as this account by a former schizophrenic patient indicates:

What I do want to explain, if I can, is the exaggerated state of awareness in which I lived before, during, and after my acute illness. At first it was as if parts of my brain "awoke" which had been dormant, and I became interested in a wide assortment of people, events, places, and ideas which normally would make no impression on me. Not knowing that I was ill, I made no attempt to understand what was happening, but felt that there was some overwhelming significance in all this, produced either by God or Satan, and I felt that I was duty-bound to ponder on each of these new interests, and the more I pondered, the worse it became. The walk of a stranger on the street could be a "sign" to me which I must interpret. Every face in the windows of a passing streetcar would be engraved on my mind, all of them concentrating on me and trying to pass me some sort of message. Now, many years later, I can appreciate what had happened. Each of us is capable of coping with a large number of stimuli invading our being through any one of the senses . . . it is obvious that we would be incapable of carrying on any of our daily activities if even one hundredth of all these available stimuli invaded us at once. So the mind must have a filter which functions without our conscious thought, sorting stimuli and allowing only those which are relevant to the situation in hand to disturb consciousness. And this filter must be working at a maximum efficiency at all times, particularly when we require a high degree of concentration. What had happened to me in Toronto was a breakdown in the filter. . . . New significance in people and places was not particularly unpleasant, though it got badly in the way of

my work, but the significance of the real or imagined feelings of people was very painful. . . . In this state, delusions can very easily take root and begin to grow. . . . By the time I was admitted to the hospital I had reached a stage of "wakefulness" when the brilliance of light on a window sill or the color of blue in the sky would be so important it could make me cry. I had very little ability to sort the relevant from the irrelevant. The filter had broken down. Completely unrelated events became intricately connected in my mind (MacDonald 1960, p. 218).

Course of a Schizophrenic Psychosis

Anyone who manifests all the signs of a schizophrenic psychosis faces a long siege. How long it will be before the symptoms *remit,* or become less intense, is hard to predict — as is the degree of social recovery he will achieve. Many factors are involved, as we shall see in Chapter 6, and the course of a psychosis varies widely. One person may recover completely and another not at all.

Manfred Bleuler (1968), an eminent Swiss psychiatrist (and son of Eugen Bleuler), has treated many schizophrenic patients and identified different patterns of onset and course. As Figure 5.4 shows, Bleuler grouped patients whom he had studied over twenty-five years in seven life classes, based on length of onset and how the psychosis proceeded. In the first four classes, an almost constant psychotic state follows the first psychotic episode. The groups differ in the length of time over which the first schizophrenic break developed. In classes 2 and 4, onset was gradual, whereas in 1 and 3 it was acute. The degree of psychosis evident years later varied, too, from complete psychosis to mild residual symptoms. Bleuler wrote that, compared to the early part of this century, fewer schizophrenic episodes now turn into lifelong psychoses. In Chapter 7 we will examine some new treatments of schizophrenia that have helped increase the rate of recovery.

Bleuler's experience suggests that most schizophrenic episodes begin with an *acute phase,* a distinct shift in the person's level of adjustment and function, followed by some improvement. In fact, 25 to 35 percent of the patients Bleuler studied recovered completely from their first schizophrenic episodes. Unfor-

Personal Account of a Schizophrenic Psychosis

Mark Vonnegut's excellent book, *The Eden Express,* recounts with great vividness the sequence of the author's schizophrenic episode. Much of his experience closely parallels Bowers's description of the stages in a breakdown. First came the euphoria and inexpressible energy:

Everything that had ever happened to me made perfect sense. I was sore at absolutely no one and nothing. Everything that had happened had happened just right. But where to go from here? As much as it was better to travel hopefully than to arrive, as much as I believed that and had lived by it, once you've arrived, you've arrived, and there's not much to be done about it. . . .

Things were still unbearably beautiful. I got this giddiness in my stomach and walked around completely overwhelmed by the incredible loveliness of the trees and the sky and the moss, infinitely delicate worlds within worlds, and people's faces and the way they moved and my own body and what a perfect machine it was and the stove and the floors and our funky house. And everything fit together so perfectly. It wasn't just in the way things looked. It was in the sounds of the wind and the stream and the way things felt, the ground gushing ever so slightly under my feet, the way everything smelled. It's everywhere, it's everywhere. And it keeps getting better and better. And I think to myself, Look Ma, no drugs.

People are all charming and silly. The idea of purpose cracks me up. The only thing that puzzles me is why it took me so long to catch on. How did I manage to keep a straight face for as long as I did? I vaguely remember pain and struggle but it seems so remote, so unnecessary, so absurd (p. 95).

Later he records destructuring of perception and affect:

Small tasks became incredibly intricate and complex. It started with pruning the fruit trees. One saw cut would take forever. I was completely absorbed in the sawdust floating gently to the ground, the feel of the saw in my hand, the incredible patterns in the bark, the muscles in my arm pulling back and then pushing forward. Everything stretched infinitely in all directions. Suddenly it seemed as if everything was slowing down and I would never finish sawing the limb. Then by some miracle that branch would be done and I'd have to rest, completely blown out. The same thing kept happening over and over. Then I found myself being unable to stick with any one tree. I'd take a branch here, a couple there. It seemed I had been working for hours and hours but the sun hadn't moved at all.

I began to wonder if I was hurting the trees and found myself apologizing. Each tree began to take on personality. I began to wonder if any of them liked me. I became completely absorbed in looking at each tree and began to notice that they were ever so slightly luminescent, shining with a soft inner light that played around the branches (p. 99).

Still later, ideas of reference appear while Vonnegut is in a cafe:

I started falling very deeply in love with the waitress and everyone else in the place. It seemed that they in turn were just as deeply in love with me. It was like something I couldn't get out of my eye.

I didn't understand it but I recognized it. There were all those little things that had happened occasionally between me and lovers be-

tunately, however, the first episode may not be the last one. Patients in Bleuler's classes 6 and 7 suffered a number of severe episodes during their lifetimes. Another study generally supports this view and offers hope for the future. All the patients in this study were first-time hospital admissions with a diagnosis of schizophrenia. Over a five-year follow-up period, 25 percent remained severely ill, 25 percent were moderately handicapped by residual symptoms, and

fore, but never this strong, never so lastingly, never with so many. I was completely in love, willing to die for or suffer incredibly for whatever they might want. A rush of warmth and emotion, spiritual and physical attraction, a wanting of oneness, a feeling of already oneness.

When I looked at someone they were everything. They were beautiful, breathtakingly so. They were all things to me. The waitress was Eve, Helen of Troy, all women of all times, the eternal female principle, heroic, beautiful, my mother, my sisters, every woman I had ever loved. Simon was Adam, Jesus, Bob Dylan, my father, every man I had ever loved. Their faces glowed with incredible light. It was impossible to focus, to hate, to fix. They were so mobile, all moving, all changing. They were whatever I needed and more. I loved them utterly.

I worried about how complicated this could make my life. Maybe it was enlightenment but it brought up not inconsequential problems of engineering. Who sleeps with whom was one, but there were lots of others. Like what if two people I loved wanted me to do different things? Who would I spend time with, who would I talk with, who would I dedicate my life to? If I loved everyone there was no way to focus any more, no reason to spend time with anyone in particular.

What would Virge think about all this? I had somehow fallen in love with Simon, Jack, Kathy, the waitress, and assorted passers-by more powerfully and completely than I ever had with her.

I worried about what my eyes might be doing to other people. Was I making them fall in love with me? (p. 117)

And finally came the hallucinations:

The Voices. Testing one, two, testing one. Checking out the circuits: "What hath God wrought. Yip di mina di zonda za da boom di yaidi yoohoo."

By this time the voices had gotten very clear.

At first I'd had to strain to hear or understand them. They were soft and working with some pretty tricky codes. Snap-crackle-pops, the sound of the wind with blinking lights and horns for punctuation. I broke the code and somehow was able to internalize it to the point where it was just like hearing words. In the beginning it seemed mostly nonsense, but as things went along they made more and more sense. Once you hear the voices, you realize they've always been there. It's just a matter of being tuned to them.

The voices weren't much fun in the beginning. Part of it was simply my being uncomfortable about hearing voices no matter what they had to say, but the early voices were mostly bearers of bad news. Besides, they didn't seem to like me much and there was no way I could talk back to them. Those were very one-sided conversations.

But later the voices could be very pleasant. They'd often be the voice of someone I loved, and even if they weren't, I could talk too, asking questions about this or that and getting reasonable answers. There were very important messages that had to get through somehow. More orthodox channels like phone and mail had broken down (pp. 136–137).

In Chapter 7 we will again look at Vonnegut's experience when we take up the treatment of schizophrenia.

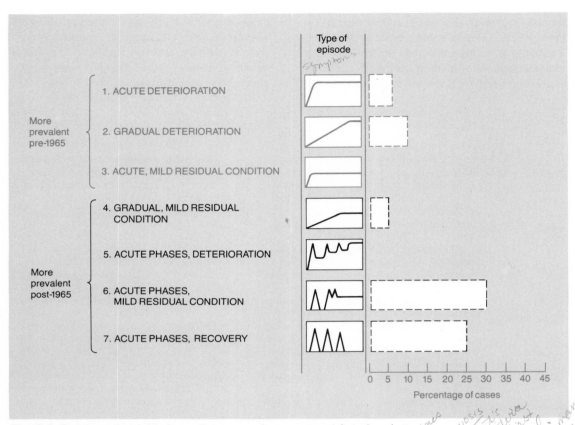

Fig. 5.4. Graph on the right shows the range of occurrence of each of the seven patterns Bleuler described. Code diagrams in the center indicate the nature of onset (acute or gradual) and the degree of residual symptoms. (After Bleuler 1968.)

50 percent had such a favorable five-year outlook that they would be no great burden to their family or community. In the published account of this research Wing concludes:

> Compared with the days when to enter hospital with a diagnosis of schizophrenia was almost tantamount to staying for a lifetime, it is possible now to be, if not optimistic, then at least not unreservedly gloomy about the prognosis of an early case (Wing 1966, pp. 17–18).

Diagnostic Reliability in Schizophrenia

When a clinician has complete data about the onset and course of a schizophrenic psychosis, she can easily diagnose the disorder accurately. Comprehensive histories are hard to find, however. Often, an acutely excited patient simply appears in a hospital's emergency room, accompanied by a policeman or distraught relative. The clinician's first step is pre-

[handwritten margin notes, top:] Reliability of Schizo: Diagnosis — agreement of diagnosis > 53%, 60, 74, 84 — rate of diagnostic agreement increases as the # of schizo in sample increased — diagnoses of long-term schizo are considerably more reliable. Noyes + Kolb — schizo nature more apparent when... confusion with mood disorders

dictable. She tries to match the patient's behavior with the criteria of a known psychiatric disorder (for example, identity dissolution accompanied by hallucinations). Today this initial diagnosis is especially important because of the many quite different programs of treatment; the diagnostician's findings determine which treatment the patient will undergo.

Considering the implications of the diagnosis, we might do well to ask how nearly certain we can be that the diagnostician will correctly label a patient. Is a diagnosis of schizophrenia proof that an individual *really* is schizophrenic? In recent years, investigators have sought to determine how reliable schizophrenia diagnoses are. The results have been rather disheartening. Four such reliability studies resulted in the same diagnosis being made by two psychiatrists only 53 percent of the time (Beck et al. 1962), 60 percent (Kaelbling and Volpe 1963), 74 percent (Sandifer et al. 1964), and 84 percent (Schmidt and Fonda 1956). These studies also showed that the rate of diagnostic agreement increased as the number

Schizophrenia Across Cultures: A Fascinating Finding

[handwritten margin notes, left:] WHO STUDY — less advanced countries had the greater percentage of favorable outcomes. Acute < UD > same rate of outcomes. Insidious — UD — much higher rate of favourable outcomes

Most empirical evidence about schizophrenia's course of development comes from the United States, the British Isles, and Western Europe. Recently, the World Health Organization (WHO) reported a two-year follow-up of 811 patients diagnosed as schizophrenic. The study contrasted the outcomes of cases from developing nations with those from more industrialized countries. Was the recovery rate better, as we might expect, in the developed countries, which have more professional and physical resources? No! As the graph shows, the so-called less advanced countries had the greater percentage of favorable outcomes.

A quick scan of the WHO data reveals another significant difference. Although acute-onset cases had the same rates of outcome in both groups of countries, gradual-onset cases had a much higher rate of favorable outcomes in the underdeveloped countries. Why? Researchers are now examining cultural differences and delivery systems for mental health care in an effort to account for this fascinating finding. (Sartorius et al. 1978.)

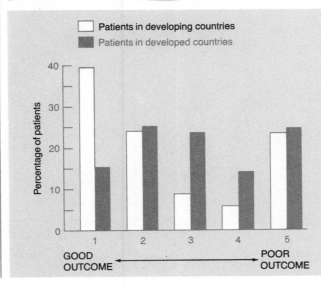

Categories of outcome described in two-year follow-up study of schizophrenics in developing and developed countries. Groups 1 and 2 showed total or near-total remission with no severe social impairment. Groups 3 and 4 experienced some degree of residual symptoms and/or severe social impairment. Patients in Group 5 suffered severe social impairment with or without residual symptoms. Outcomes were better for patients in developing countries. (After Sartorius et al. 1978.)

of schizophrenics in the sample increased. Nevertheless, the rate of agreement was hardly satisfactory. On the other hand, diagnoses of long-term schizophrenia are considerably more reliable. Noyes and Kolb (1963) suggest:

With recurring episodes, the schizophrenic nature of symptoms previously doubtful becomes more apparent with the result that confusion with manic-depressive (mood-disorder) symptomatology no longer exists (pp. 356–357).

Fig. 5.5. Observed patient behaviors recorded independently by U.K. and U.S. psychiatrists. They noted similar behaviors in patients diagnosed by a joint study team as having mood disorders and in patients judged schizophrenic. Thus differences in diagnosis at hospital admission must be due to differences in the way U.K. and U.S. psychiatrists interpret their observations. (After Gurland et al. 1969.)

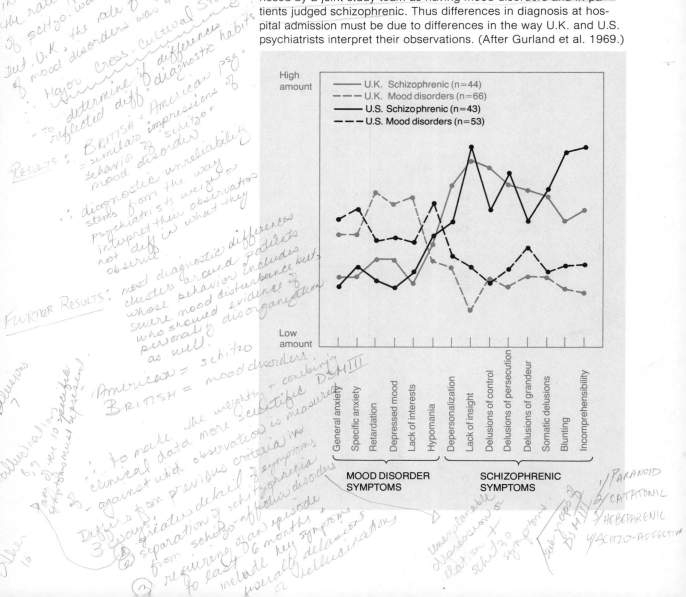

With long-term schizophrenia, the diagnostician has an additional aid: she knows the disorder's course for an extended time.

The reliability of diagnoses has raised many questions. Are the definitions of schizophrenia so general that different psychiatrists can interpret them differently? Are the descriptive terms clear, but the patients not so easily placed in categories? Or do diagnostic interviewers assign different weights to the same symptoms? Does one clinician consider delusions essential to a finding of schizophrenia but another require hallucinations? The noted biostatistician Morton Kramer (1969) found that in England and Wales the rate of first hospital admissions for schizophrenia was one-third lower than in the United States, but in the United Kingdom the rate for first admissions of patients having mood disorders was nine times higher than in the United States. A major cross-cultural study was launched (Joint U.S.–U.K. Study) to determine whether the differences reflected different diagnostic habits on opposite sides of the Atlantic (Gurland et al. 1969). Specifically, the study compared the diagnostic processes undergone by newly admitted psychiatric patients in similar public hospitals. Admitting psychiatrists used two devices to record clinical data: (1) a detailed behavior-rating scale that described specific patient behavior, and (2) an official psychiatric diagnosis, based on a commonly accepted international system. Using these two kinds of data, the investigators could establish whether British and American psychiatrists noticed the same patient behaviors and, if they did, whether they weighted them similarly in forming their overall diagnostic impressions.

In addition to the actual hospital diagnosis, the study included a joint United Kingdom–United States team, which diagnosed the same patients with a consistent diagnostic scheme. Figure 5.5 compares the clinical psychiatrists' behavior ratings and the study team's diagnoses of either schizophrenia or mood disorder.

The graphs show that British and American psychiatrists formed similar impressions of the schizophrenic behavior and the behavior of mood-disordered individuals. Thus, diagnostic unreliability seems to stem from the way psychiatrists weight, or interpret their observations, not from differences in what they observe.

Further analysis of the same data revealed that most diagnostic differences clustered around patients whose behavior included *severe* mood disturbance but who showed evidence of personality disorganization as well. American psychiatrists usually see such individuals as "schizophrenic," whereas their British counterparts diagnose "mood disorder." In these cases, the diagnosticians weighted mood disturbances very differently.

DSM-III Criteria for Schizophrenia

To make the weighting and combining of clinical data more scientific, the present draft of the APA's *Diagnostic and Statistics Manual* (*DSM*-III) sets out new diagnostic criteria against which to measure clinical observations. The *DSM*-III description of schizophrenia differs from previous criteria in three ways. First, it specifies the criteria for schizophrenia in much greater detail than does the list of symptoms we discussed earlier. The patient must display at least one of these ten symptoms during an active phase of the illness:

Delusions
1. Delusions of being controlled: Feels that an external force is directing his or her thoughts, actions, or emotions.
2. Thought broadcasting: Experiences thoughts as though they were being broadcast from his or her own head into the external world so that others can hear them.

3. Thought insertions: Feels that another's thoughts are being inserted into his or her mind (as did a young woman who claimed that radio waves from her neighbor's apartment were lodging obscene thoughts in her mind).
4. Thought withdrawal: Patient believes that thoughts have been removed from his or her head, leaving fewer thoughts.
5. Other bizarre delusions (clearly absurd, fantastic, or implausible).
6. Somatic, grandiose, religious, nihilistic, or other delusions, without persecutory or jealous content.
7. Delusions of any type if accompanied by hallucinations of any type.

Hallucinations
8. Auditory hallucinations: A voice makes a running commentary on the individual's continuing behavior or thought, or two or more voices converse. (One woman in her early thirties had become increasingly anxious about lasting marital problems. Each time she was about to make a decision, a voice said to her, "Go toward what makes you feel good." At other times it called her an "unfaithful bitch." The voices commented on her thoughts and behavior almost constantly.)
9. Auditory hallucinations: Hears one to several words on several occasions, content apparently unrelated to depression or elation.

Other Symptoms
10. Incoherence, derailment (loosening of associations), marked illogicality, or little speech content—if accompanied by blunted, flat, or inappropriate emotions; delusions or hallucinations; or grossly disorganized or catatonic behavior.

(*Diagnostic and Statistics Manual,* pp. 46–47.)

The Manual also recognizes as a symptom of schizophrenia the peculiar thought disorder that Eugen Bleuler believed was the primary disturbance in schizophrenia. Patients who have this problem miss or distort associations between objects and events of all kinds. In the

early stages of a psychotic episode, a schizophrenic's conversation may be "woolly" and vague and difficult to follow. In the more psychotic state, thinking seems to be directed by symbolic meanings or analogies. The following statement from a twenty-three-year-old man, hospitalized shortly before his marriage, is typical in its symbolism:

Before my marriage I was bothered by premature ejaculation. I tried to control this by developing my lower abdominal muscles. I became aware that my sexual ability was related to a burning sensation in my lower back. I worked for a man named Butch who was a very strong person. When Butch made certain movements with his feet, I would feel the burning sensation move into my loins. I really thought this should happen with my father. When these things are in the right place I feel alive and vibrant, there is something to push me (Bowers 1974, p. 183).

The second new feature of the *DSM*-III criteria is separation of schizophrenia from *schizo-affective disorders,* characterized by unexplainable depression or elation in addition to classic schizophrenic symptoms. This change reflects the findings of the United States–United Kingdom study and should increase the likelihood that different diagnosticians will arrive at the same conclusion.

Third, the *DSM*-III criteria for schizophrenia require that an episode have lasted at least six months and included key symptoms, usually delusions or hallucinations.[1]

The *DSM*-III criteria minimize the subjective bias that will enter into the initial diagnosis of

---

[1] A revised draft of *DSM*-III distributed in 1979 includes a new category, schizophreniform disorder, the criteria for which are identical to those for schizophrenia, except that the onset can be less than six months.

[handwritten marginal notes at top of page:]
PARANOID — prominent symptoms — delusions & persecutions type, but can become controlling to the point of eroding critical judgements + leading to unpredictable behavior.
delusions of persecution are the most common type — can be stable but often patients alter them to suit their own internal or external needs — in other cases delusions of self importance — other cases grandiosity — other cases extraordinary sexual potency — casanova complex — other type conjugal delusion. delusions & process unfaithfulness — other symptoms = Hallucinations

schizophrenia. A psychiatrist should have little difficulty deciding that a patient is schizophrenic, not suffering from a mood disorder, because any of ten specific symptoms must be present. Knowing how long the symptoms have persisted also makes it possible to rule out drugs as the cause of hallucinations or delusions (see Chapter 16 for a discussion of hallucinogenic drugs). Nevertheless, variations in behavior among patients whose symptoms fit the *DSM*-III scheme make it practical, for diagnosis, research, and treatment, to subdivide schizophrenia into more explicit categories, such as schizo-affective disorders. The subgroups in *DSM*-III, which are remarkably like the ones Kraepelin described in his pioneering clinical studies, are: paranoid schizophrenia; catatonic schizophrenia, hebephrenic schizophrenia; and schizo-affective disorder. We will examine the symptoms of each.

Paranoid Schizophrenia

The dominant symptom in paranoid schizophrenia is the delusion. Delusions of persecution are the most common type and may involve all sorts of ideas and plots. Paranoid schizophrenics with delusions of persecution believe that someone is trying to injure them (see Figure 5.6). Sometimes these delusions are stable, but more often patients alter them to suit their own internal or external needs. In other cases *delusions of self-importance* may dominate. The patient may believe he is the president or that she is a well-known female personage. *Grandiosity* is another common delusional trait. Hundreds of paranoid schizophrenics have declared themselves to be Jesus Christ, God the Father, and perhaps more modestly, Abraham Lincoln. Still another familiar delusion is ex-

traordinary sexual potency — sometimes lightly called the *Casanova complex*. One type of delusion that often reigns alone is the *conjugal delusion,* in which a married person fixedly believes that his or her mate is unfaithful, despite overwhelming evidence to the contrary.

In addition to these fixed beliefs, paranoid schizophrenics frequently hallucinate vivid sounds, sights, or smells. They may hear voices speaking to or about them, see or hear God, or witness their enemies plotting against them. They may feel x-rays, radio waves, or other invisible electric signals penetrating their bodies, destroying their will or their vital organs. One interesting and relatively common delusion is that these external agents cause a loss of control over one's thoughts.

The experience of a twenty-three-year-old married man named Chad resembles that of many paranoid schizophrenics. He entered the hospital complaining that he was a hypersensitive person who became very upset around people — and this included ''the whole country'' — who were not aware of his vulnerability. In the hospital he became violently angry when he witnessed aggressive behavior, particularly on television programs, which he believed were transmitted for him personally. The whole ''problem,'' he claimed, was the result of a plot by ''them'' to destroy his mind and ultimately to kill him.

Often these delusions become controlling in the patient's life, to the point of completely eroding critical judgment and leading to unpredictable behavior. Acting on their delusions or hallucinations, some patients will attack members of their family because ''God ordered me to.'' Paranoid schizophrenics who decide to destroy their ''persecutors'' can become particularly dangerous. We all have read about paranoids who have killed their children and spouse, and then committed suicide because of delusional beliefs.

<u>CATATONIC</u>
- like most schizo's experiences a period of gradual withdrawal and progressive emotional apathy before an acute and sudden break with reality.
- Jekyll + Hyde type
- withdrawn catatonics: adopt strange postures for long periods (his posture)
- agitated state
- when he is disrupted (his posture)
- dangerous state
- no warning
- not without contact with the world around them (secretive)
  - also attributed subjective meaning that justified their continued withdrawal.
- paranoid thinking is being controlled by massive passivity and negativism.
  - paranoid delusions
- evidence of magical thinking (imaginative)
- Diff between C + D schizo

<u>CATATONIC</u> - greater tendency to see the problem of control as an internal struggle - restless against internal dissolution
- personal responsibility ... +ve prognosis
- better chance to recover that other schizo's

<u>PARANOID</u> - conviction that external world is responsible to the inner terror ... highly rewarding and tension reducing ... more reluctant to leave such a state

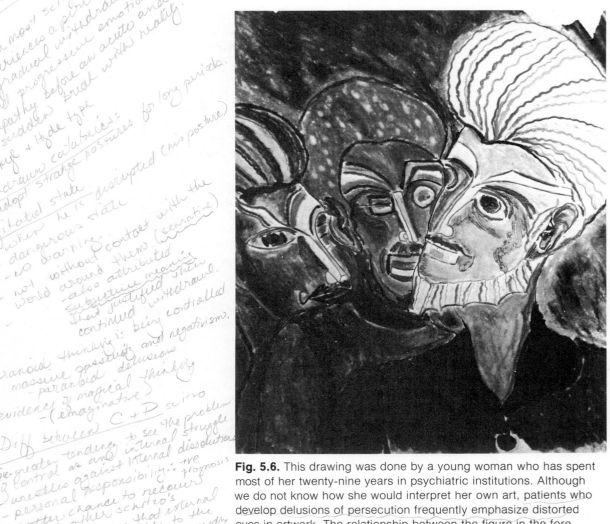

Fig. 5.6. This drawing was done by a young woman who has spent most of her twenty-nine years in psychiatric institutions. Although we do not know how she would interpret her own art, patients who develop delusions of persecution frequently emphasize distorted eyes in artwork. The relationship between the figure in the foreground and those in the background suggests a feeling of persecution by others.

Catatonic Schizophrenia

Like most schizophrenics, the catatonic often experiences a period of gradual withdrawal and progressive emotional apathy before an acute and sudden break with reality. The catatonic is a kind of Jekyll and Hyde type. One moment he may be completely withdrawn, negative and uncommunicative. Next you may see him greatly agitated and excited (see Figure 5.7). Withdrawn patients rarely show initiative or interest. Often they must be force-fed. They may adopt strange postures for long periods, resisting all attempts to move them or change their position. As a result of inactivity, they show signs of poor peripheral circulation, such as blue and swollen extremities. Without warning, the same patients may suddenly begin thrashing about with little purpose or orientation and destroy furniture or other objects. During an agitated stage, the patient can be quite dangerous to other patients or staff and requires considerable medication and personal care.

Withdrawn catatonics once were thought to be totally out of contact with the world around them. Interviews with former catatonic patients, however, have revealed that many were very sensitive to things and people. They also attrib-

uted strange, highly subjective meanings to things and events that they felt justified their continued withdrawal. Here is a former catatonic's description of his feelings that clearly shows an awareness — however distorted — of his environment:

Each time you would walk by, doctor, I'd notice the tie that you wore. If it was red or green, I'd think, "today is the day — the day that I'm to be killed" and I'd fight desperately to maintain any fixed posture and not let anyone touch or move me. If your tie was yellow or blue, I'd think "one more day, one more day to live" and I'd let the nurse feed me or change any posture — but not talk.

Besides illustrating the catatonic's sensitivity and subjective interpretation of ordinary things, this quotation illustrates considerable paranoid thinking, which the patient is trying to control by massive passivity and negativism. Withdrawn catatonics often have paranoid delusions such as this patient reported. Finally, this account shows evidence of magical thinking. Many catatonics have said that they believed they were about to explode into a destructive rage, and that small changes in posture or movement would unleash overwhelming forces. One patient felt he had to hold his hands out flat because, he said, the forces of "good and evil are waging a war of the world" there, and if he tilted his hands in any way, he would alter the precarious balance between good and evil.

A major difference between paranoid and catatonic patients is the catatonic's greater tendency to see the problem of control as an internal struggle. The catatonic wrestles against internal dissolution, but the paranoid sees the "enemy without." The catatonic's assumption of personal responsibility, implied in many reports, may be a key to this group's positive prognosis. They have a better chance of recovery than other schizophrenics. The paranoid's conviction that external forces are responsible

Fig. 5.7. During the withdrawn catatonic phase, the patient is unresponsive to others and adopts strange bodily positions. Despite their withdrawal, these patients may frequently be acutely aware of environmental events.

for her inner terror can be a highly rewarding and tension-reducing solution (Cameron 1959). Once the patient attains this viewpoint, she is very reluctant to give it up.

Buddy A. was a typical catatonic, as the details of his admission to the hospital vividly illustrate:

Buddy's admission to the psychiatric ward of the county hospital was precipitated by the following events, which took place several hours earlier. He informed his mother that it would be necessary to sacrifice her in order for him to "attain Nirvana"; he threw her to the floor and, with his knee on her chest, began choking her. After a violent struggle she was finally able to free herself and fled, screaming for the police. Buddy left the house and wandered about the streets. When the police located him he surrendered without protest.

His entrance into the hospital emergency room was most dramatic; a huge, muscular man, he strode across the lobby, dragging behind him two policemen to whom he was handcuffed. He was clad only in a filthy towel wrapped around his waist. His unkempt hair reached his shoulders and a massive beard covered most of his face. His body, hair, and beard were caked with dirt, and blood flowed from the scratches inflicted by his mother. Barely visible was the elaborate tatoo of a reverse swastika and of a heart-and-dagger. He voluntarily seated himself on a bench at the admission desk, forcing the officers also to sit. Aside from the glassy stare of his eyes, his face was expressionless. He paid no attention to questions addressed to him and said nothing to anyone. Staring at the ceiling he occasionally mumbled indistinctly to himself.

Released from the handcuffs, he allowed himself to be led to the general admitting ward where, for the next four hours, he squatted on his haunches at the foot of his bed, his head bowed as he muttered to himself. Several times the nursing attendants tried to get him to shower and dress in preparation for a physical examination. Finally, two of them attempted to lift him to his feet, hoping to lead him to the shower, at which time he savagely attacked them and began destroying the fur-

niture and bedding. Forcibly restrained and put in a separate room, he continued briefly to pound on the walls before he finally settled back into his buddha-like squat on the floor and resumed his trance-like appearance (Goldstein and Palmer 1975, pp. 247–248).

Hebephrenic Schizophrenia

This type of schizophrenia is most similar to the "dementia" described by Kraepelin. Hebephrenic reactions occur generally among young adults and involve more severe personality disintegration than other types of schizophrenia. Prior to a psychotic episode, the hebephrenic is reported to be odd, unscrupulous, and preoccupied with religious and philosophical matters. As teenagers these individuals frequently brood over sexual acts, such as masturbation, and things and events that they regard as sexual temptations. Hebephrenics have few close friends and often are preoccupied with their fantasies.

As the disorder progresses, behavior becomes increasingly antisocial. Emotional indifference and infantile reactions are evident, too. The person smiles often, but when asked what is funny, he shrugs, or gives irrelevant and silly explanations. Speech may become incoherent, and the individual may use a private language or *word salad,* which completely thwarts interpersonal communication. One such patient, when asked, "Why do you think people believe in God?" answered, "Well that's not a convinishment mount of diet, is it? Maybe his home is unfeedable or something."

Hallucinations, particularly imaginary sounds, are a common hebephrenic symptom. Patients may hear themselves accused of immoral practices or called vile names, often stemming from sexual practices. Typically obscene, immodest, and shameless, the hebephrenic's peculiar mannerisms become even more bizarre and apparent as the disorder continues.

Overall, hebephrenic case histories depict poorly adjusted young people who have little or no psychosocial competence and have retreated from life's stresses, particularly those of adolescence, into a personal fantasy world. Accompanying this marked withdrawal is disengagement from life as well as emotional distortion and emotional blunting.

Schizo-Affective Reactions

This relatively new category of schizophrenia, which we have mentioned, is significant for two reasons. First, it combines schizophrenic thought disturbance with mood disorders, intended to help resolve the problem of ambiguous diagnoses. Second, schizo-affective individuals are much more likely to recover than schizophrenics whose emotions are greatly muted or who seem completely apathetic. These people display a mixture of schizophrenic symptoms and severe depression or euphoria, as in this example:

A 25-year-old, single, graduate school drama teacher stated that she entered the hospital because she felt anxious, had poor control of her thoughts and felt electricity running through her body. She also believed that the Nazis and the Manson gang were after her. She screamed with anxiety and acted out her delusions. Her mind was flooded with thoughts that lacked organization. But, just as suddenly as she became immersed in her delusions, she returned to rational things and made plans for future teaching jobs. Before entering the hospital she had gone without sleep for long periods, was on an emotional high, made extravagant purchases and lost much weight (Grinker and Holzman 1973, p. 173).

The woman's delusions are symptomatic of schizophrenia, but because of the accompanying high and periods of relative normality, she was diagnosed "schizo-affective."

Schizophrenia — Why Use the Term?

Some writers, notably Thomas Szasz (1961) and Ronald Laing (1967), have criticized all attempts to develop a reliable diagnostic system. Schizophrenia, they say, may be a completely subjective determination, and all the checklists in the world will not make it into a scientific entity. In fact, diagnostic criteria may only sustain the belief that "schizophrenia" really does exist, whereas it is merely a socially convenient label for irritating, abrasive, and deviant behavior. Some observers (Scheff 1970) have actually suggested that schizophrenia is a label that the mental health community created and applies to deviant individuals who would function perfectly well if only society would leave them alone. Although it is true that the label can produce problems for former schizophrenic patients, it is equally apparent to anyone who has observed the terror, confusion, and distorted reasoning that they experience during a psychotic episode that they are not "perfectly well."

Meehl (1962) contends that the term "schizophrenia" is vague, but, he says, its definition does predict the length of illness and the degree of recovery. Most schizophrenics remain psychotic much longer than manic-depressives do. Though we must avoid self-fulfilling prophecies — in which a poor prognosis is likely to produce a poor outcome — we need descriptive information to plan treatment and social rehabilitation. Certainly the term "schizophrenic" is more helpful than many other possible descriptions, such as "upset individual."

Diagnosis by Computer: The Ultimate Solution?

The search for objective diagnoses can be carried one step further by eliminating the clinician's judgment entirely. Spitzer and Endicott (1968) reasoned that computers might classify patients more consistently and reliably than the human observer can. To test their theory, they developed a computer program to analyze the patient's behavioral data (recorded in quantitative form) by a series of binary (yes/no, true/false) decisions and to generate the most probable diagnosis (see Figure 5.8). In the most recent system, Diagno II, the computer asks: "Does this patient have delusions of persecution?" A "yes" answer from the programmer would lead the computer toward a schizophrenia diagnosis. If, however, the computer's search elicited a positive answer to the next question — "Did the patient recently suffer a severe head injury or physical illness affecting central nervous system tissue?" — the analysis would search with a new set of probes for organic psychoses.

Diagnosis by computer is an interesting attempt to standardize application of diagnostic systems. It should certainly be useful in research and statistical analyses, as in evaluating cross-national rates of psychopathology. Right

Fig. 5.8. Ratings on the Mental Status Examination Record (a portion of which is shown at left) are used to record patient behavior and symptoms in a systematic fashion. When fed into the computer, these ratings generate a diagnostic impression, a part of which is shown at right.

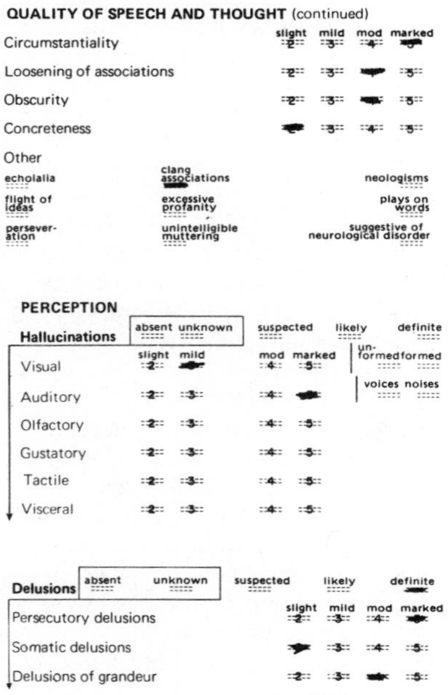


```
THE MOST LIKELY DIAGNOSIS IS-

  295.3  SCHIZOPHRENIA, PARANOID TYPE


FUNCTIONAL PSYCHOSIS IS STRONGLY SUGGESTED BY RATINGS OF
     -DELUSICNS
     -AT LEAST MODERATE LOOSENING OF ASSOCIATIONS
     -AT LEAST MODERATE IDEAS OF REFERENCE
     -AT LEAST MODERATE FLATNESS CF AFFECT
     -AT LEAST MILD INCOHERENCE
     -A SCCRE ON AN INDEX WHICH COMBINES UNCOOPERATIVE, WITHDRAWN,
      INAPPROPRIATE, SUSPICIOUS AND ANGRY BEHAVIOR, AND INABILITY TO
      FUNCTION IN GOAL DIRECTED ACTIVITIES, IN A PERSON OVER AGE 20
           CRITICAL VALUE = 19    PATIENT'S SCORE = 20
     -A SCORE ON AN INDEX OF THOUGHT DISORDER (WHICH COMBINES
      INCOHERENCE, IRRELEVANCE, BLOCKING, LOOSENING OF ASSOCIATIONS,
      AND CONCRETENESS)
           CRITICAL VALUE = 12    PATIENT'S SCORE = 16
     -AT LEAST MODERATE BLOCKING
     -CLANG ASSOCIATIONS
     -DELUSIONS OF INFLUENCE
     -A SCCRE ON AN INDEX WHICH COMBINES WITHDRAWN BEHAVIOR, FLATNESS
      OF AFFECT, INAPPROPRIATE BEHAVIOR, INAPPROPRIATE AFFECT,
      INCOHERENCE, IRRELEVANCE, LOOSENING OF ASSOCIATIONS,
      CONCRETENESS OF THOUGHT, IDEAS OF REFERENCE, BIZARRE THOUGHTS,
      DEPERSONALIZATION AND DEREALIZATION
           CRITICAL VALUE = 25    PATIENT'S SCORE = 39

CONTENT OF SPEECH AND THOUGHT
------- -- ------ --- -------

        THIS PATIENT HAS MARKED IDEAS OF REFERENCE, MODERATE BIZARRE
THOUGHTS, MILD GRANDIOSE THOUGHTS, AND SLIGHT PHOBIAS.  HE MANIFESTS
MARKED ALIENATION AND RESENTMENT TOWARDS OTHERS, MODERATE
DISTRUSTFULNESS AND FEELINGS OF ISOLATION, MILD INDECISIVENESS AND
CONCERN ABOUT DEATH, AND SLIGHT GUILT.  DELUSIONS ARE DEFINITELY
PRESENT, INCLUDING MARKED PERSECUTORY DELUSIONS, MARKED DELUSIONS OF
INFLUENCE, MODERATE DELUSIONS OF GRANDEUR, AND SLIGHT SOMATIC
DELUSICNS.  IN THE EXAMINER'S JUDGMENT THE PATIENT'S DELUSIONS HAVE
CCNSIDERABLE INFLUENCE ON HIS BEHAVIOR.
```

now, its applicability in day-to-day treatment of schizophrenics seems limited, however.

Predictors of Schizophrenia Outcome

We have mentioned several times that some schizophrenics are more likely to recover than others. Acute onset indicates a better chance for recovery than gradual onset, and more catatonics recover than paranoids. Course of onset and symptom patterns at the height of an episode are two of five factors believed to have prognostic significance. The other three are: the patient's pre-illness, or *premorbid* social adjustment; events that immediately preceded the break; and the attitudes of close friends and family members toward the patient.[2]

Specific Symptoms

Many suggestions appear in the literature that one or another cluster of symptoms (beyond catatonia or paranoia) forecast a bleak future for a patient. Schneider (1959) contends that there are *first-rank symptoms* — namely, thought withdrawal, thought insertion, thought broadcasting, and auditory hallucinations of a running commentary (see *DSM*-III definitions of these symptoms, pp. 111–112) — that portend an especially grim fate. Some observers have even argued that schizophrenics who manifest these symptoms are different from all other schizophrenics. But, *DSM*-III assigns no special significance to these symptoms. Nor does recent research (Strauss and Gift 1977) support this point of view. Five years after a schizophrenic episode, patients whose symptoms in-

cluded Schneider's first-rank symptoms had the same range of outcomes as patients with other symptoms.

Premorbid Adjustment

One way to assess a patient's premorbid adjustment is to compare his history with a scale developed by Leslie Phillips. This scale, shown in modified form in Table 5.3, yields a score, based on the capacity for two types of close relationships — heterosexual involvement, including quality and length, and relationships with peers of the same sex. The lower an individual's total score, the better his chance of recovery from a schizophrenic episode.

We can apply the Phillips scale to the two cases that opened this chapter, even though the amount of information given is not great. We would rate the male college student fairly low on the scale, from the evidence of a heterosexual relationship and friendships. The young woman, on the other hand, has a classically poor premorbid history with few, if any, friendships and no heterosexual relationships. Her score is high, so that we would expect her to be much less likely to recover fully.

Detectable Life Crises

Events that directly precede an episode's onset also can help predict outcome, particularly if they include a major, identifiable life stress, such as the loss of a loved one or a job. Episodes triggered by life events remit more rapidly than episodes for which causes are undetectable or highly subjective. Further, the patient who appears extremely disoriented and deeply depressed or elated following such a life crisis is more likely to recover than the patient who shows little or no emotion (Vaillant 1962).

Few of these predictive factors are entirely independent of one another. Patients with limited social life and the chronically withdrawn

[2] It is interesting that the same predictive factors also apply in many other cultures (Sartorius, Jablensky, and Shapiro 1978).

Table 5.3. Abbreviated form of Phillips Premorbid Adjustment Scale

I. Married, presently or formerly
   A. Married, only one marriage (or remarried only one time as a consequence of death of spouse), living as a unit
      1. Adequate heterosexual relations achieved   0
      2. Low sexual drive, difficult sexual relations, or extramarital affairs, either partner   1
   B. Married, more than one time, maintained a home in one marriage for at least 5 years
      1. Adequate sexual relations during at least one marriage   1
      2. Chronically inadequate sexual life   2
   C. Married and apparently permanently separated or divorced without remarriage, but maintained a home in one marriage for at least 5 years   2
   D. Same as (C), but maintained a home in one marriage for less than 5 years   3

II. Single (30 years or over)
   A. Has been engaged one or more times or has had a long-term relationship (at least 2 years) involving heterosexual relations or apparent evidence for a "love affair" with one person, but unable to achieve marriage   3
   B. Brief or short-term heterosexual or social dating experiences with one or more partners, but no long-lasting sexual experiences with a single partner   4
   C. Sexual and/or social relationships primarily with the same sex, but may have had occasional heterosexual contacts or dating experiences   5
   D. Minimal sexual or social interest in either men or women   6

III. Single (under 30 years, age 20–29)
   A. Has had at least one long-term "love affair" (minimum of 6 months to 1 year) or engagement, even though religious or other prohibitions or inhibitions may have prevented actual sexual union
      1. If ever actually engaged   1

      2. Otherwise   2
   B. Brief or short-term heterosexual or social dating experiences, "love affairs," with one or more partners, but no long-lasting sexual experiences with a single partner   3
   C. Casual sexual or social relationships with persons of either sex, with no deep emotional meaning   4
   D. Sexual and/or social relationships primarily with the same sex, but may have had occasional heterosexual contacts or dating experiences   5
   E. Minimal sexual or social interest in either men or women   6

Abbreviated Scale of Premorbid Social-Personal Adjustment

   A. A leader or officer in formally designated groups, clubs, organizations, or athletic teams in senior high school, vocational school, college, or in young adulthood   0
   B. An active and interested participant, but did not play a leading role in groups of friends, clubs, organizations, or athletic teams in senior high school, vocational school, college, or in young adulthood   1
   C. A nominal member, but had no involvement in, or commitment to, groups of friends, clubs, organizations, or athletic teams in senior high school, vocational school, college, or in young adulthood   2
   D. From adolescence through early adulthood, had only a few casual or close friends   3
   E. From adolescence through early adulthood, had no real friends, only a few superficial relationships or attachments to others   4
   F. From adolescence through early adulthood (i.e., after childhood) quiet, seclusive, preferred to be by self; minimal efforts to maintain any contact at all with others   5
   G. No desire to be with playmates, peers, or others, from early childhood. Either asocial or antisocial   6

Source: J. G. Harris, "An Abbreviated Form of the Phillips Rating Scale of Premorbid Adjustment in Schizophrenia," *Journal of Abnormal Psychology,* 1975, 84, p. 131.

(poor premorbids) are more likely to have drifted gradually into psychosis. Because of their limited interaction with others, it may be difficult to detect a significant pre-schizophrenic event, because such events usually involve important relationships. Although these factors do overlap somewhat, the distinctions are sufficient to compel us to keep them all in mind when attempting to predict how and when — and if — an individual will emerge from a schizophrenic episode.

Family Attitudes

Because schizophrenic symptoms are so acute and disorganizing, these powerfully affect a patient's relatives, particularly when they live with the patient. The schizophrenic's strange and frightening reactions, as well as the sporadic, fierce hostility — expressed directly and in delusions — make normal life with her all but impossible. In the past, when a schizophrenic was hospitalized for months or years, the family adapted by regrouping into a relatively stable unit accommodating to the absence of the afflicted child, parent, or spouse. The community mental health movement has made it possible to shorten the hospital stay to one or two weeks, because it allows a patient to return home partially recovered. Although rapid reentry into the community may facilitate the patient's recovery, it can present serious difficulties for the spouse, parents, and offspring.

Like the four predictive factors we discussed earlier, family attitudes toward a returning patient can help predict the course of the schizophrenic psychosis. In fact, recent research by Vaughn and Leff (1976a; 1976b) indicates that the way family members treat the patient affects the prognosis more than any of the other predictors. For their study, Vaughn and Leff intensively interviewed significant relatives living in the patients' homes — parents or spouse — before the patients' return from the hospital to assess what they called *expressed emotion*.

They found that some types of expressed emotion negatively affected the rate of relapse among the patients in the sample. In particular, relatives who criticized patients, who expressed hostility toward them, or who showed signs of being overprotective lowered the patients' chances for full recovery. The negative impact of criticism and hostility are easy to understand. Overprotectiveness, characterized by excessive care and attention, undermines the patient's autonomy. Alone or in combination, these expressed emotions portended that a patient was very likely (51 percent) to suffer a relapse and return to the hospital. When relatives did not display these negative emotions, the relapse rate was much lower (13 percent). We shall discuss this research in greater detail in Chapter 6, when we explore the relationship between family attitudes and the success of drug treatment for schizophrenics.

Meanwhile, it is encouraging to see how positive attitudes can foster recovery, as one family discovered:

The mother developed a paranoidal illness that began with strong erotic delusions that her doctor was in love with her. . . . She subsequently thought that the doctor's wife had hired some man to take her children away from her. . . . She refused to let her children out of her sight and they complained of her interference. . . . The father had a family council with his three children and discussed their strange situation. From then onward, he conducted what amounted to family therapy sessions as a result of which the . . . exasperation of the children turned into pity for the sick mother. Instead of fighting her paranoia, they discussed the persecution with her, neither contradicting nor acquiescing to its reality. One of the girls wrote a series of poems. . . . Another painted a large scale portrait of the family having a picnic together in happier days. All of these creations were presented to the mother on Mother's Day with the sensitive dedication "to the mother who wants to keep us safe." . . . This proved a turning point in her condition. . . . She (the mother) had always been slow to trust people but now she was much less suspicious and controlling. One of the children had become an A student and the family seemed better integrated than ever before (Anthony 1970, p. 149).

Summary

1. Schizophrenia can be defined as a functional psychosis characterized by disturbances in thinking and profound disorganization of behavior. It is difficult to diagnose and to explain.

2. Schizophrenia was first recognized by Emil Kraepelin, who distinguished the symptoms from those of the mood disorders. Kraepelin observed that schizophrenics have adjustment problems following an episode, whereas victims of mood disorders seem less troubled by residual symptoms.

3. A pattern of symptoms was enumerated several years later by Eugen Bleuler, a Swiss psychiatrist who coined the term "schizophrenia." He described the primary disturbance in schizophrenia as a dissociation of thoughts from appropriate feelings caused by a splitting off (schizo) of parts of the self. The secondary symptoms, which included odd and irrational ways of communicating and relating to others, developed as a result of this splitting off.

4. A schizophrenic episode develops through a sequence of stages. Onset can be insidious (gradual) or acute (rapid), but in either, the breakdown is immediately preceded by a state of *conflict and impasse.* This condition is followed by a *destructuring of perception and affect.* At this stage, the individual experiences acute awareness of everything in his environment without any ability to "filter" the inputs selectively. Long-forgotten memories may resurface, and a feeling of euphoria or specialness may envelop the individual. This stage gives way to *identity dissolution,* in which the individual's sense of self disintegrates. Now, he develops and clings to a *delusion* as the only

stable reality in the chaos he perceives around him. The presence of delusions is one criterion of a true schizophrenic psychosis.

5. Diagnostic criteria developed by the American Psychiatric Association for *DSM*-III differ in three ways from previously designated symptoms. (1) It specifies criteria for schizophrenia in great detail. A patient must display at least one of ten symptoms (e.g., auditory hallucinations) during the active phase of the illness. (2) The *DSM*-III distinguishes between schizophrenia and schizo-affective disorders. (3) A diagnosis of schizophrenia requires that an episode have lasted at least six months.

6. Four types of schizophrenia have been identified: *paranoid schizophrenia,* in which the patient feels threatened by external forces; *catatonic schizophrenia,* in which the basic problem is an internal struggle for control; *hebephrenic schizophrenia,* the most severe and damaging personality disturbance; and *schizoaffective reactions,* which include schizophrenic symptoms and severe depression or euphoria.

7. Five factors help to predict whether or not schizophrenia symptoms will remit: (1) The course of the episode's onset — psychoses that come on quickly are more likely to remit completely; (2) specific symptom characteristics at the height of the psychotic episode; (3) the individual's premorbid social adjustment — a patient who had close friendships and heterosexual involvements of some duration prior to onset has a better chance of recovering than one with few or no such relationships; (4) events in the individual's life directly preceding the onset — an episode brought on by a major identifiable life stress will remit more quickly than an episode with an obscure cause; and (5) the family's attitude toward the returning patient — hostile behavior by family members or, conversely, excessive care and attention, can undermine the patient's sense of autonomy and hinder recovery.

Chapter 6 (25) | The Origins of Schizophrenia

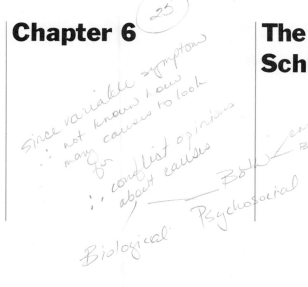

Biological Perspective
Biochemical Theories of Schizophrenia
Genetic Predisposition
Overview of Biological Research on Schizophrenia

Interactive Models and High-Risk Studies
The Stress-Diathesis Model
The Mednick High-Risk Project

Psychosocial Stress
Distortions in Family Relationships
A High-Risk Study of Family Relationships

A Concluding Word About Stress-Diathesis Theory

Summary

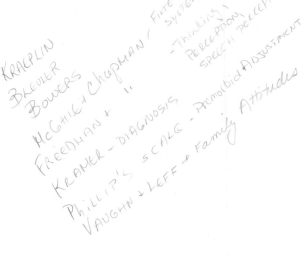

In Chapter 5 we looked at the inner experience of a schizophrenic episode, the observable symptoms, and the factors associated with the life course of adult schizophrenia, without paying much attention to what causes the break in the first place. How *can* we account for a schizophrenic breakdown, for the marked alterations in states of consciousness, the altered modes of thinking, and withdrawal from the external environment? Are they the result of some biological dysfunction, something akin to the effects produced by psychedelic drugs, which distort perception and thinking? Or do they grow out of an inherited tendency from which none can escape? Or do the symptoms of schizophrenia represent simply a final breakdown in a person's ability to cope with a stressful life? Perhaps the answer to each of these questions is "yes." Perhaps a person's physiological, genetic, *and* psychological makeup determine susceptibility to schizophrenia.

Research into causes of adult schizophrenia is a relatively new endeavor. Thus we do not yet have any clear-cut answers to the foregoing questions. Because the symptoms vary over a wide range, we do not even know how many causes to look for. It may be that some of the symptoms we observe in schizophrenia are secondary symptoms arising from a single factor. But it is possible, too, that the conditions we call "the schizophrenias" are distinct disorders that have distinct causes or etiologies, and that when we find the cause of, say, hebephrenic schizophrenia and catatonic schizophrenia, we will conclude that they are unrelated disorders. Similarly, cases of schizophrenia in which the patients have poor premorbid histories may arise from quite distinctive causes.

The uncertainty that pervades the field explains why we find conflicting opinions about what causes schizophrenia. Some researchers argue that it is a biological disorder. Others contend that the causes are psychosocial. The results of both types of research are inconclusive. The belief is growing, however, that both arguments have some validity and that a schizophrenic episode is the consequence of a combination of biological and environmental conditions. In this chapter we will examine all three viewpoints, along with some of the problems in the research and some of the implications for intervention and treatment.

Biological Perspective

A strong belief has persisted since ancient times that the profound alterations in consciousness, thinking, and mood observed during a schizophrenic episode must arise from some physiological malfunction in the central nervous system. Today there are two lines of biological research, one focusing on biochemical deviation and the other on the possibility that schizophrenia is the product of a genetic defect. The former is an attempt to explain how deviations in metabolism can radically alter

modes of perception and thought. The latter involves a search for evidence that some of us are more susceptible than others to a schizophrenic breakdown by virtue of our genetic makeup. These two biological positions can be linked, because biochemical deviations may represent the mediating mechanism through which a genetic predisposition ultimately produces abnormal behavior.

Biochemical Theories of Schizophrenia

Enormous modern advances in neurochemistry (the study of the chemical makeup and activity of the nervous system) have provided us with a clearer picture of normal brain chemistry and have stimulated research to determine how extensively neurochemical processes are involved in a schizophrenic breakdown. Particularly significant is our increased understanding of how nerve impulses travel from neuron to neuron within the brain through *neurotransmitters,* substances that the body then breaks down into harmless, excretable substances (see essay in Chapter 2). Now that we have this knowledge of normal brain processes, abnormal processes are more readily detectable.

Recent biochemical research on schizophrenia appears to follow one of two general hypotheses. One is that schizophrenics are victims of an inborn error of metabolism that alters the chemistry of the central nervous system. The second theory attributes the cause to a deviation in the amount of normal neurochemical substances in the brain. For fifteen years, the balance of support has shifted back and forth very rapidly between the two. No sooner have researchers produced evidence to substantiate one theory than others have published studies that refute the original finding (Wyatt et al. 1971). At this time, interest is stronger in the second explanation.

RESEARCH LIMITATIONS

Before we get to the major biochemical theories on schizophrenic psychosis, we need to consider the special limitations on this type of research. Medical researchers have the advantage of being able to study in lower animals physical disorders similiar to those we human beings suffer. Unfortunately, animals do not exhibit symptoms resembling human schizophrenia. Therefore, most schizophrenia researchers must use human subjects, a factor that limits our ability to study chemical processes in the living brain.

Many studies of brain biochemistry involve observing chemical processes that occur far from the brain. One way is to analyze metabolites (the products of metabolism) of brain chemicals that appear in the blood or urine. Although this kind of analysis is becoming more sophisticated, major problems retard the leap between the presence of a substance in the urine and the process in the brain that produced it.

A particular problem with human biochemical studies is that several factors other than brain chemicals affect the composition of metabolites in blood and urine. For example, diet and physical activity greatly influence these chemical assays. Many biochemical findings have been discovered later to be artifacts of some uncontrolled variable such as greater coffee intake by schizophrenic subjects.

Still another major problem has been that schizophrenic patients not only are psychotic but also tend to be extremely agitated or depressed. Furthermore, their emotional states may vary, so that a schizophrenic patient may be agitated for a few days and then may become very retarded. Both agitation and retardation have profound effects on biological processes, so that we must be careful to take frequent blood or urine samples for biochemical assays. Otherwise, what we judge to be significant biochemical differences between schizophrenic patients and nonschizophrenics may simply be a consequence of being acutely disturbed.

As these problems imply, most of the biochemical evidence on the causes of schizophrenia is likely to be indirect. As in a murder trial, the lines of circumstantial evidence are often impressive, but the critical evidence — a "smoking gun" — is lacking.

AN INBORN ERROR OF METABOLISM?

My arms sagged, pulling my shoulders down. My nose was running. I wiped it with the back of my hand and my upper lip was rubbed off. I wiped my face, and all the flesh was wiped off! I was melting. I jumped to my feet and tried to grab hold of something — anything. I felt as if my flesh was actually melting. In the midst of indescribable terror, I felt that the spongy wall was closing in on my face. I tried to shut my eyes, but they were fixed open. Something seemed to stop inside me. I saw Juan coming and I hated him. I wanted to tear him apart. I could have killed him then, but I could not move (Castenada 1968, pp. 97, 100).

A schizophrenic in the middle of an acute psychotic episode working toward a paranoid solution? It is very likely. This account is closely similar to the psychedelic experiences reported by Bowers's patients during the early stages of their psychotic breakdown (see Chapter 5). Actually, the case describes anthropologist Carlos Castenada's experience after taking the hallucinogenic mushroom *psilocybin*.

If a drug can produce experiences so much like those of a naturally occurring schizophrenic episode, isn't it possible that schizophrenia arises from some chemical change in the body? The idea that schizophrenia is a *toxic psychosis* (produced by a poisonous substance) is not new and, in fact, dates back to ancient Greece. In 1892, the chemist Thudichum expressed this hypothesis clearly:

> Many forms of insanity are unquestionably the external manifestations of the effects upon the brain substance of poisons fermented *within* the body, just as mental aberrations accompanying chronic alcoholic intoxication are the accumulated effects of a relatively simple poison fermented *out* of the body. These poisons we shall, I have no doubt, be able to isolate after we know the normal chemistry to its uttermost detail, and then will come in their turn the crowning discoveries to which our efforts must be ultimately directed, namely, the discoveries of antidotes to the poison and the fermenting causes and processes which produce them (Thudichum, J. W. L. 1884).

This view assumes that the body, by some error of metabolism, breaks down normal substances into toxic ones that, in turn, produce many of the symptoms of schizophrenia.

In recent years, this hypothesis has been the subject of thousands of investigations of steadily increasing sophistication. Systematic research on hallucinogenic, or psychedelic drugs such as LSD and mescaline has provided an array of data about external substances that can mimic some components of a schizophrenic episode. Understandably, this research has led investigators to look for internally produced hallucinogenic substances.

Experiments with mescaline, in particular, have sustained the idea that schizophrenia is caused by toxic chemicals in the brain. A direct chemical resemblance between mescaline and the neurotransmitter *norepinephrine* (Figure 6.1) has led researchers to suggest that, by some metabolic error, a schizophrenic's own system might manufacture enough mescaline, or a similar hallucinogen, to bring on psychotic symptoms (Osmond and Smythies 1953).

Normally, after an electrical impulse has

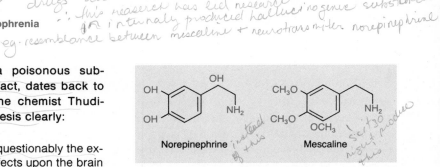

Fig. 6.1. Chemical structures of norepinephrine and mescaline.

passed from one neuron to another, the releasing neuron reabsorbs some part of the neurotransmitter and the body metabolizes, or breaks down, the rest for excretion in the urine (see pp. 27–30). Even a slight alteration in the breakdown of norepinephrine could produce a hallucinogenic substance, like mescaline, which would remain in the body and induce a kind of self-sustaining "trip," or schizophrenic psychosis. Despite this theory's attractiveness, researchers have not been able to find higher levels of hallucinogen-like substances in the blood or urine of schizophrenic patients. There is substantial evidence, however, of a relationship between norepinephrine and the mood disorders (see Chapter 8).

THE DOPAMINE THEORY

The second biochemical model also focuses on a neurotransmitter substance, *dopamine,* which is heavily concentrated in the limbic system of the brain. The evidence in favor of this theory likewise stems from drug research. The drugs that interest us here, *amphetamines* and *phenothiazines,* produce opposite effects. Amphetamines are stimulants that can induce a schizophrenia-like reaction in normal people if used excessively. Given to schizophrenic patients, amphetamines make the psychosis worse. Phenothiazines, on the other hand, are major tranquilizers that can cause partial and sometimes full remission of the symptoms of schizophrenia (Davis 1978).

Research with these drugs indicates that

both types affect a person's behavior primarily by altering the amount of dopamine in the synaptic cleft between neurons in the parts of the brain that control emotions (Figure 6.2). Studies with animals suggest that amphetamines *increase* the amount of dopamine in the junction by preventing reuptake by the firing neurons. As a result, the neurons fire at an excessive rate. In contrast, the phenothiazines block the dopamine receptor on the postsynaptic neuron (Figure 6.3), inhibiting the action of available dopamine in the synaptic cleft. Thus, the circumstantial evidence is strong that excess dopamine levels are involved in some way in schizophrenia, but the "smoking gun" is missing. No one has found direct evidence of higher levels of dopamine or its metabolites in the brains of schizophrenic patients. Post-mortem brain assays to estimate derivatives of dopamine at first seemed to reveal actual differences between schizophrenic subjects and controls (Stein and Wise 1977), but subsequent attempts to reproduce the results have failed (Wyatt et. al. 1975). Without such data, we must be cautious about accepting this model.

Genetic Predisposition

The idea that schizophrenia might be an inherited trait is not new. It is based on the clinical observation that the incidence of schizophrenia is higher among relatives of schizophrenics than among the general population. Research

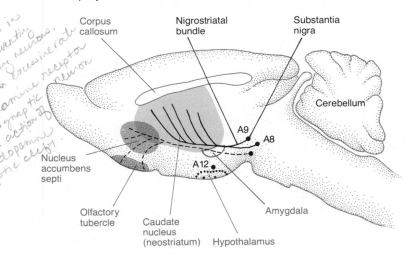

Fig. 6.2. Schematic drawing of dopaminergic pathways in the rat brain, which are believed to be very similar to those in the human brain. Nerve endings in these tracts release the neurotransmitter dopamine, which alters the activity of neurons containing receptors sensitive to it. The dots A8–A10 represent cell bodies in the midbrain where the tracts originate and from which they project to the forebrain. A12 represents cell bodies in the diencephalon area, which projects to an area of the brain called the infundibulum.

Corpus callosum
Nigrostriatal bundle
Substantia nigra
Cerebellum
A9
A8
A12
Nucleus accumbens septi
Olfactory tubercle
Caudate nucleus (neostriatum)
Hypothalamus
Amygdala

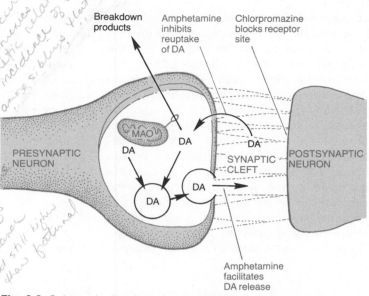

Breakdown products

Amphetamine inhibits reuptake of DA

Chlorpromazine blocks receptor site

MAO

DA

DA

DA

PRESYNAPTIC NEURON

SYNAPTIC CLEFT

DA

POSTSYNAPTIC NEURON

DA

DA

Amphetamine facilitates DA release

Fig. 6.3. Schematic drawing of a dopaminergic neuron illustrates the dopamine theory of schizophrenia. Amphetamines, which can produce schizophrenialike symptoms, *increase* the amount of dopamine (DA) in the synaptic cleft in two ways. They cause more dopamine to be released and increase concentration in the synaptic cleft by slowing reuptake into the presynaptic neuron. Chlorpromazine, a phenothiazine drug that suppresses schizophrenic symptoms, *reduces* the amount of effective dopamine by blocking the receptor site on the postsynaptic neuron.

data also show that odd and peculiar behaviors have occurred frequently among relatives who were not clinically schizophrenic. Systematic studies of the incidence of schizophrenia in family lines of schizophrenic and nonschizophrenic patients confirm earlier, informal observations. These studies show not only that schizophrenia is more likely to appear in the biological family line of a schizophrenic, but also that the closer the genetic relationship, the higher the incidence of schizophrenia. As Figure 6.4 shows, the incidence is fourteen times greater among siblings of schizophrenics than

among the general population, whereas for stepbrothers and stepsisters the rate is only twice as great.

To test the hypothesis that schizophrenia is an inherited trait, researchers have primarily studied the incidence of the disorder among twins and adopted children. So far, the results do implicate genetics.

TWIN STUDIES

Twin studies begin with the hypothesis that if inheritance is to blame for schizophrenia, identical twins have equal chances of becoming ill.

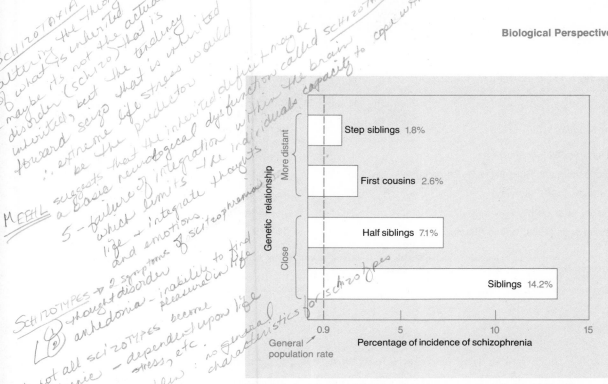

SCHIZOTAXIA

altering the theory of what is inherited

maybe it's not the actual disorder (schizo) that is inherited, but the tendency toward schizo that is inherited

∴ extreme life stress would be the predictor

MEEHL suggests that the inherited difficit may be a basic neurological dysfunction within the brain called SCHIZOTAXIA

5 - failure of integration within the individuals capacity to cope with life + integrate thoughts and emotions = schizophrenia

SCHIZOTYPES → 2 symptoms of schizophrenia
① thought disorder
② anhedonia - inability to find pleasure in life

but not all schizotypes become schizophrenic - dependent upon life stress, etc.

General characteristics for schizotypes

Problem : no general characteristics for schizotypes

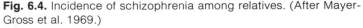

Fig. 6.4. Incidence of schizophrenia among relatives. (After Mayer-Gross et al. 1969.)

Identical twins begin life as a single egg, which divides shortly after fertilization. Thus, identical twins have identical genes guiding their growth and development. Fraternal twins, on the other hand, develop from two eggs that are fertilized at the same time. Therefore, they are no more closely related to each other, genetically speaking, than are nontwins from the same family. Because identical and fraternal twins share similar uterine environments and are reared at the same time in a family's history, however, they are appropriate subjects for genetic study.

Twin studies completed many years ago consistently show higher *concordance* — the number of instances in which both twins show the same pattern — for schizophrenia among identical twins than among fraternal twins. The results of several twin studies appear in Table 6.1. More recent findings indicate that the rate of concordance in identical twins is substan-

tially below the 100 percent concordance we would expect from a simple genetic model in which a single gene causes the disorder. One way in which researchers have attempted to deal with this discrepancy is by postulating more complex models to account for the data, including polygenetic models in which a number of interacting genes must be present to produce schizophrenia (Gottesman and Shields 1976). Although these theories are plausible, we have no reasonable way of testing their validity on the data available.

SCHIZOTAXIA

A second method of reconciling the limited fit between a genetic hypothesis and the findings of twin studies requires altering the theory of what is inherited. Most authors of studies assume that it is clinical schizophrenia — the actual disorder — that is inherited. But perhaps it is a *tendency* toward schizophrenia that is in-

Table 6.1. Concordance of schizophrenia among identical and fraternal twins in recent studies

Investigator	Number of pairs in sample	Concordance among identical twins	Number of pairs in sample	Concordance among fraternal twins
Tienari (1975, Finland)	17	0–36%	20	5–14%
Gottesman and Shields (1967, England)	22	40–50%	33	9–10%
Kringlen (1967, Norway)	55	25–38%[a]	90	4–10%
Fisher et al. (1969, Denmark)	21	24–48%[a]	41	10–19%
Pollin et al. (1969, United States)	95	14–27%	125	4–5%

Source: Adapted from I. I. Gottesman and J. Shields, "A Critical Review of Recent Adoption, Twin and Family Studies of Schizophrenia," *Schizophrenia Bulletin,* 1976, 2(3), pp. 360–398.
   [a] These figures vary depending on how narrowly schizophrenia is defined. The lower figure is for the narrower definition, which requires key symptoms to be present, such as thought withdrawal, thought insertion, thought broadcasting, or auditory hallucinations.

On the Trail of a Genetic Marker for Schizophrenia?

Family, twin, and adoption studies have suggested that a genetic factor operates in schizophrenia, but arguments over the mode of inheritance have continued unabated. Advocates of *monogenic* (single-gene inheritance) and *polygenic* (multiple-gene involvement) theories have mustered statistical evidence to support their positions. Yet, claims of genetic influence have been based on work with patients who were clinically schizophrenic at the time the studies began. If we had some way of determining whether or not an individual carried a gene or group of genes — a so-called *genetic marker* — then we could trace the patterns of inheritance more accurately. Because genetic markers do not necessarily bring on conditions like schizophrenia, they would enable researchers to better estimate the distribution of a trait and thereby figure out the mode of inheritance.

Soon we might be able to tell whether a person carries a gene (or genes) for schizophrenia by looking at his eyes. Psychologist Phillip Holzman et al. (1974) has discovered a potential behavioral genetic marker in the patterns of eye-tracking in schizophrenics, their relatives, other disordered groups, and normal controls. Holzman's task is very simple; it requires watching a pendulum as it swings back and forth. A machine that measures the subject's eye movements records the smoothness of the tracking and the number of arrests (stops in the tracking). The graphs illustrate the normal pattern of eye movement and one frequently found in schizophrenics. The schizophrenic record shows more irregular tracking (Channel 1) and more sudden changes in eye movements, called velocity arrests (Channels 2 and 3).

Not only are the disordered eye movements very common in schizophrenic patients, but Holzman has also found them in first-degree relatives of schizophrenics who themselves have never been schizophrenic. The implications of this research are very promising. Although we need more confirming studies, it is just possible that disordered eye movements will turn out to be a genetic marker for schizophrenia.

herited. It if were, extreme life stress might be the trigger that causes a predisposed individual to become schizophrenic. A relatively stress-free life would then protect some of the people whom the genetic theory predicts will become schizophrenic.

What form might this predisposition take and do we have a way of measuring it? The most provocative suggestion comes from Meehl (1962), who suggests that the inherited deficit may be a basic neurological dysfunction called *schizotaxia.* He says schizotaxia is a failure of integration within the brain that limits an individual's capacity to cope with life and to integrate thoughts and emotions. *Schizotypes,* Meehl's term for people who have schizotaxia, always manifest two fundamental symptoms of schizophrenia: thought disorder and *anhe-*

donia, the inability to find any pleasure in life. But, as we would expect, not all schizotypes would become schizophrenic. A multiplicity of factors, including recurrent life stress, would be necessary in order to trigger a schizophrenic episode.

A logical test of this theory would be to measure the number of schizotypes, rather than actual schizophrenics, in family lines of schizophrenics and nonschizophrenics. But we have one very basic problem: despite its simplicity and attractiveness, schizotaxia theory has failed to resolve the critical issue of how to recognize a schizotype. Although Meehl and his associates (1964) have tried to develop personality inventories that would identify schizotypes, genetic researchers have not tested them, nor have they gained wide acceptance.

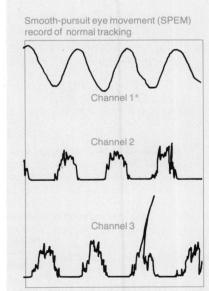

Smooth-pursuit eye movement (SPEM) record of normal tracking

Channel 1[a]

Channel 2

Channel 3

Smooth-pursuit eye movement of a schizophrenic patient

Channel 1

Channel 2

Channel 3

[a]Normal eye-tracking record: direct eye movement recording, channel 1; velocity of the eyes in the right and left directions, channels 2 and 3 respectively.

identical twins may receive treatment that is more uniform than fraternal, identical, more likely to react identically — to test environmental causes

ADOPTION STUDIES

One important factor that neither the twin studies nor Meehl's theory takes into account is the possibility that families with numerous generations of schizophrenics may be victims of a vicious circle of faulty family relationships, as well as inherited tendencies. Likewise, identical twins may receive treatment that is more uniform than the upbringing fraternal twins receive (identical dress, handling, parental attitudes, and so on), so that in a disturbed family environment they will be more likely to react identically. Consequently, environmntal factors might explain the greater likelihood that both identical twins will have a schizophrenic breakdown.

Because external influences cannot be discounted in earlier twin studies, genetically oriented investigators have increasingly studied children reared away from their biological parents for more conclusive data. In one classic study (Kety et al. 1975) of schizophrenic and psychiatrically normal adoptees, schizophrenia appeared most likely to occur in the biological relatives of schizophrenics even though these relatives had no part in child rearing. As Table 6.2 shows, this evidence strongly suggests that genetic factors are significant in increasing the vulnerability to schizophrenia. Further support for this hypothesis comes from the fact that, in this adoption study, *acute* schizophrenic adoptees (those who recovered quickly) had few, if any, biological relatives who were themselves schizophrenic, but *chronic* adoptee patients (those who took longer to recover or who were likely to remain ill indefinitely) tended to have schizophrenics among their biological relatives. This finding suggests that there may be a genetic predisposition to some forms of schizophrenia but not to others.

Adoption studies have provided significant evidence on the role of genetic factors in chronic schizophrenia, but what it is that disturbed individuals inherit is still not clear. Is it a tendency to develop schizophrenia, that is, a predisposition toward withdrawal under stress? Or is it brain dysfunction, as Meehl suggests? Before we can understand how genetic predisposition interacts with environmental forces as

Table 6.2. Incidence of schizophrenia and related conditions in the biological families of schizophrenic and control adoptees

This table indicates that even when individuals who developed schizophrenia were separated from their biological families shortly after birth and adopted away to nonrelatives, the incidence of schizophrenia and related disorders (the Spectrum of Schizophrenic Disorders) is substantially higher in the biological relatives of schizophrenics than in those of a control sample selected as free of mental illness.

		Extended schizophrenia spectrum		
	Definite schizophrenia	+ Uncertain schizophrenia	+ Schizoid or inadequate personality	= Total spectrum
Biological relatives of *schizophrenic* adoptees	6.4%	+ 7.5%	+ 7.5%	= 21.4%
Biological relatives of *control* adoptees	1.7%	+ 1.7%	+ 7.5%	= 10.9%

Source: Adapted from S. S. Kety, D. Rosenthal, P. H. Wender, and F. Schulsinger, "Studies based on a total sample of adopted individuals and their relatives: Why they were necessary, what they demonstrated and failed to demonstrate," *Schizophrenia Bulletin,* 1976, 2(3), p. 418.

[handwritten top-left: Interactive Models — accept the concept of biological predisposition, but add that environmental variables interact with genetic factors to produce biological or behavioral outcome]

[handwritten top-right: one interactive model — ROSENTHAL — Stress-Diathesis Model — assumes that biological vulnerability (diathesis) to schizo is much higher in some but life stress may be necessary to set off a schizo episode in a vulnerable individual — chronic life stress (family, etc) tends to produce vulnerable individuals who can't handle the acute stresses]

schizophrenia develops, we must resolve one all-important issue: *What is* the inherited trait or traits?

Overview of Biological Research on Schizophrenia

Current work on biological factors underlying schizophrenia has been very productive, although much of the evidence is indirect. Perhaps the greatest contribution of biochemical research has been to expand our understanding of how the brain operates and how drugs alter brain functioning and, ultimately, behavior. Theories that emphasize deviations in the availability of normal neurotransmitter substances, especially dopamine, have received more support than those emphasizing the self-manufacture of toxic, hallucinogenic substances.

Genetic theories of a predisposition to schizophrenia have been supported by adoption studies, particularly for chronic, nonremitting forms of the disorder. These studies indicate that not everybody *can* develop a schizophrenic psychosis; on the other hand, if you have a genetic predisposition, schizophrenia is not inevitable. Other factors are necessary for this predisposition to develop into a psychotic episode.

Interactive Models and High-Risk Studies

[handwritten: Both Bio + Psycho]

Scientific thinking is attracted by polarities, and in schizophrenia, we do not have to look far to find them. Schizophrenia is a biological disorder! No, schizophrenia is a psychological disorder! Of course, life is simple and neat when we can find unitary and exclusive determinants for some behavior pattern. Rarely does it happen, however. Most of the time we confront evidence suggesting that a multiplicity of factors combines to produce any psychopathological

pattern. Some argue that if there is a genetic factor in schizophrenia, the picture has no room for psychological or sociological factors. Yet, modern developmental theory supports proposed interactive theories, which accept the concept of biological predispositions, but add that environmental variables interact with genetic factors to produce a biological or behavioral outcome.

[handwritten right margin: PROBLEMS — 1) doesn't pinpoint the predisposition or diathesis — 2) not identify the life stresses]

The Stress-Diathesis Model

One interactive model, Rosenthal's *stress-diathesis* model, assumes that a biological vulnerability — or diathesis — to schizophrenia is much higher in some people than in others, but that life stress may be necessary to set off a schizophrenic episode in a vulnerable individual (Rosenthal 1970). In this model, the trigger may be chronic life stress in the form of persistent disturbed family relationships or acute temporary stress, as in rejection by a loved one. It is not uncommon to find elements of both in a patient's history. Chronic life stress tends to produce very vulnerable individuals who cannot handle the acute stresses of adult life.

The stress-diathesis model of schizophrenia suggests that biological and psychological explanations of schizophrenia, far from being incompatible with one another, can enrich our understanding of the interplay of many underlying factors in schizophrenia.

The stress-diathesis model had two problems, however. First, like strictly genetic theories, this one does not pinpoint the predisposition or diathesis, nor does it offer a way of identifying it. Second, it does not specify the life stresses that are likely to precipitate a schizophrenic breakdown. Solving the first problem is difficult because the solution demands that we find some behavioral or biochemical indicator telling us who carries the gene (or set of genes) that predispose them to schizophrenia. So far, efforts to find a reliable index have been unsuccessful, although there are some promising leads.

The schizotaxia model we discussed earlier clearly represents one attempt to define behavioral attributes that reflect the diathesis for schizophrenia. The best index of schizophrenia diathesis so far, though, is whether one or both of a person's biological parents have been schizophrenic. Approximately 10 percent of offspring who have one schizophrenic parent will ultimately develop schizophrenia and 40 percent of the offspring of two schizophrenic parents will do so. The problem with this index is that we have no way of evaluating which of the offspring of schizophrenics carry the diathesis and which are totally free of it. For this reason, a number of investigators have turned to a new research strategy for observing people judged to be at high risk for schizophrenia.

The Mednick High-Risk Project

High-risk studies locate children having at least one schizophrenic parent before the children themselves show signs or symptoms of schizophrenia. Researchers monitor these children through adulthood, when the appearance of schizophrenic symptoms is likely to occur. Most of these children have just one schizophrenic parent (Garmezy and Streitman 1974), but at least one study involves offspring of two schizophrenic parents (Erlenmeyer-Kimling and Cornblatt 1978). Some began when the subjects were infants. Others started with teenage offspring to reduce the time necessary for follow-up into adulthood (Garmezy and Streitman 1974). Because this type of investigation is relatively new (Mednick and McNeil first proposed it in 1968), results are available primarily

Vulnerability in Schizophrenia

This diagram from Zubin and Spring (1977) modifies the stress-diathesis theory, according to which individuals vary markedly in vulnerability to a schizophrenic episode. Here vulnerability is the result of genetic predisposition combined with early life experiences. Stress is represented as the number of "challenging events" encountered recently, as described in the Holmes-Rahe Scale discussed in Chapter 14. For highly vulnerable people, a small number of challenging events will precipitate a schizophrenic episode. Less vulnerable individuals will become schizophrenic only under incredibly stressful conditions. The graph implies that *everyone*, under some circumstances, will become schizophrenic, a suggestion that meets opposition from genetic theorists, who believe that the genetic predisposition must be present for the reaction to occur.

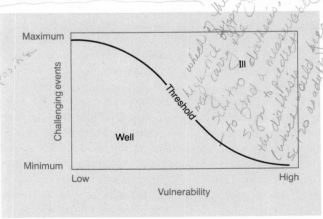

from studies that began with a teenage sample. We will look at one of the most extensive high-risk studies, the one Mednick undertook in Denmark, to see what we can learn about predicting which of the high-risk offspring may carry the schizophrenic diathesis.

The Mednick project (1968) involved 311 teenagers, 207 of them offspring of chronically schizophrenic mothers. The rest were carefully matched offspring of normal parents. Of particular interest were those with schizophrenic mothers, some of whom were assumed to carry the schizophrenic diathesis. The goal was to identify some measurable sign in the adolescent subjects that would predict which of them would become schizophrenic as adults.

Among the data Mednick collected on each teenager were birth history, school records, and behavioral as well as psychophysiological measures of sympathetic nervous system activity. The latter Mednick included because it is the sympathetic nervous system that activates in

response to threatening situations. Therefore, he believed that excessive responsivity would indicate a vulnerability to subsequent emotional breakdown. And, in fact, although potential schizophrenics differed from nonvulnerable offspring of schizophrenics on a number of measures, the best index was sympathetic nervous system activity.

For one psychophysiological test, the teenagers were exposed to a loud sound. Researchers measured changes in the subjects' skin resistance following a sound stimulus. The change in skin resistance is considered a measure of arousal. Normally, the response occurs within three to five seconds following stimulation, and then skin resistance gradually returns to the preexisting level.

Contrary to Mednick's hypothesis that the preschizophrenic would be excessively responsive to stimulation, he found that it was the rate of recovery to baseline level that discriminated. Preschizophrenics, as Figure 6.5 shows, recov-

Fig. 6.5. Schematic drawings of skin-resistance responses of adolescents who suffered schizophrenic breakdowns within five years after testing (left) and of adolescents who remained normal (right). (After Mednick and McNeil 1968.)

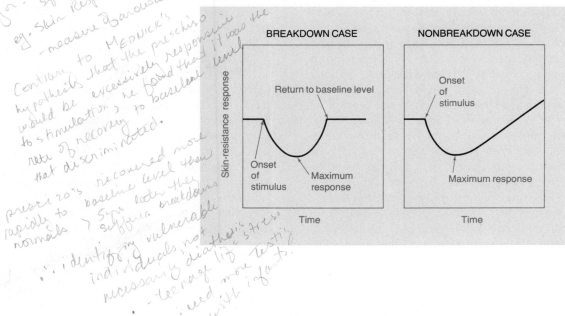

ered more rapidly than their normally developing controls. Five years after the tests had been done, subjects who showed recovery that Mednick called "abnormally fast" had suffered breakdowns.

If other researchers can replicate Mednick's findings, we will have a means for identifying vulnerable individuals. Similar results among other teenagers will not *prove* that the skin-resistance index is a measure of the diathesis, however, because by the teenage years it is impossible to rule out stress as a psychosocial variable affecting skin resistance response. But they will suggest a measure for use in future research with infants. By testing children periodically from infancy, psychologists could determine with assurance whether an abnormal skin-resistance response reflects the presence of the diathesis predisposing to schizophrenia.

Psychosocial Stress

As we have indicated, life stress interacts with the diathesis to raise the likelihood of a schizophrenic breakdown. The question we want to consider here is: Are certain life stresses more relevant than others for development of schizophrenia? You may recall from Chapter 5 that the kinds of developmental crisis that preceded schizophrenic breaks among patients studied by Bowers were quite typical of the crises that most young adults experience. Generally, at the time of their first breakdown, schizophrenics do not seem to be encountering an inordinate amount of stressful life events, and yet, when a clearly identifiable life crisis does precede the onset of schizophrenia, the prognosis for recovery is greater.

Because neither the level nor the kind of stress at the time of schizophrenic breakdown can account for the intensity of a person's reaction, psychosocial research has focused on

identifying prior life events that may increase vulnerability to normal stressors (stressful life events). Recently there has been a special interest in uncovering tensions within the family that influence the way a person learns to cope with stress. This research proceeds from the hypothesis that individuals from a disturbed family are extremely sensitive to such common human experiences as rejection, loneliness, and guilt. A young adult who grew up in a disturbed family environment does not have the strength that derives from well-integrated relationships with parents to cope with such stress (Faegerman 1963). Two examples from Bowers (1977) illustrate:

A young man with a close, symbiotic relationship with his mother and very limited heterosexual peer experience first moves away to attend college is greatly stressed by the level of development of heterosexual activity that he encounters.

Similarly, if a young person whose relationship with a parental figure has been particularly antagonistic and unsupportive leaves home to attend college or get a job, he may find that the level of confident assertion and self-protection that is required by this developmental level is more than he has acquired (p. 603).

Both cases seem to have had disturbed and damaging experiences in family relationships that lowered the threshold for subsequent schizophrenic breakdown.

Distortions in Family Relationships

Many people have disturbed family relationships. Is there something unique about the family environment of the person who becomes schizophrenic? Or does a biological predisposition to schizophrenia make an individual overly sensitive to nonspecific family tensions? Analysis of the familial factors in schizophrenia has become increasingly complex as data have accumulated. Initially, the focus of research in distorted family relationships was the mother-child relationship, which was thought to be the source of an individual's poor psychosocial adjustment. In current thinking, however, the entire pattern of family relationships is critical for normal adjustment.

The early concept of the *schizophrenogenic mother* (Fromm-Reichman 1950) reflected the belief that by combining overprotection and subtle rejection, mothers of potential schizophrenics so undermined their offsprings' self-esteem that they were unprepared to deal with normal life stress and ultimately broke down. As contact with families of schizophrenic patients has grown, both in numbers and intensity of contact, this hypothesis has proved to be simplistic. Even adding the concept of *schizophrenogenic father* failed to account for the complexity of disturbances in these families.

Most modern theorists look at the family for distortions in the total *system* of relationships and their effect upon the personality development of the offspring, particularly their progressive inability to cope with increasingly complex developmental tasks. These theorists suggest that three basic distortions in the family system contribute to offspring schizophrenic development: (1) distortions in focusing attention and communication, (2) distortions in role relationships, and (3) distortions in the emotional climate of the family. Although these factors are only partially independent, we will consider each separately.

DISTORTIONS IN FOCUSING ATTENTION AND COMMUNICATION

One of the fundamental symptoms of schizophrenia, the thought disorder, may develop from a family system in which communication is ambiguous and fragmented, and attention and meaning are blurred (Wynne and Singer 1965). Individual statements by family members may be reasonably "normal," but the flow of communication between family members can be discontinuous, as in this excerpt from a family therapy session:

Daughter (presenting patient, complainingly): Nobody will listen to me. Everybody is trying to still me.
Mother: Nobody wants to kill you.
Father: If you're going to associate with intellectual people, you're going to have to remember that still is a noun and not a verb (p. 195).

Conversations like that are typical of the condition Wynne and Singer name *transactional thought disorders,* which they contend are unique to families producing schizophrenic offspring (see Figure 6.6). When children are exposed consistently to this kind of disordered pattern of communications, they ultimately come to imitate bizarre "ways of thinking and deriving meaning, the points of anxiety, and the irrationality, confusion, and ambiguity" (Wynne and Singer 1963a, p. 192).

Although we can observe transactional thought disturbances in direct family interac-

Fig. 6.6. The Wynne-Singer theory of transactional thought disorder suggests that parental communication disorder can make offspring vulnerable to schizophrenic thought disorder.

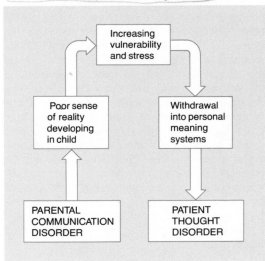

tion, Wynne and Singer suggest that the propensity for blurring meaning shows up even more clearly in psychological tests given to the parents of schizophrenics. For example, this can be seen in the following verbatim transcripts of two stories, one rated low in transactional thought disturbance and one rated high. Asked to tell a story based on an ambiguous picture from the Thematic Apperception Test (see Chapter 3) of a boy who is looking wistfully down at a violin on a table in front of him, the parent of one disturbed, but not psychotic child related these details:

LOW THOUGHT DISTURBANCE STORY

It's a child studying the violin, with many mixed emotions. The mother and father want them to — the child to uh — take violin lessons. The child would rather go out and play. He'll make an attempt for a short while and very soon it'll be put away and the child will go on about his own business and the violin will be forgotten.

A second parent, whose child was schizophrenic, offered this tale after looking at the same picture:

HIGH THOUGHT DISTURBANCE STORY

Well, actually — uh — these strings — I would picture *my* son in this . . . uh picture — and I would take his attitude in sitting there and thinking at the violin: "Oh boy, do I have to study again?" That's probably what's going through his mind — "Here we go again . . ." and you said, "What led up to it?" Will have to study what he's always resented. We gave him music lessons, piano lessons and — he loves music, he loves piano, but the thought of practicing is beyond his patience . . . and I could see him looking at the piano — as this boy is looking at the violin, and I'd assume to say that he practices just because he has to . . . (and how will it turn out?) well, it's uh with that attitude — same as any son being — if he wanted to he could — he'd get something out of it. If he just wasn't with it — he care less . . . . But that he wouldn't do it facetiously . . . .

Is the second parent talking about the boy in the picture, or her own son? Where does one theme start and the other leave off? Besides having difficulty developing a coherent story, the parent occasionally misused words ("I'd *assume* to say," "he wouldn't do it *facetiously*").

Evidence of transactional thought-disturbance styles appears in many contexts, including waiting-room conversations, test responses, and family therapy situations (Wynne and Singer 1963a, b). Therefore, we can assume that these distortions are not momentary reactions to the threat of being observed or tested but represent enduring conversational styles within the family. The child who learns to imitate these transactional thought-disturbance patterns is only a step away from the full-blown thought disturbance of schizophrenia.

A similar theory of schizophrenic development comes from British psychiatrist Ronald Laing (1965). He also emphasizes the manner in which the family communicate with one another, but his theory describes an additional dimension in the parent-child relationship, which he calls *mystification.* The process of mystification involves systematic denial of the reality of the child's feelings and perception about himself and the external world so that he comes to doubt and fear his hold upon reality. In Laing's theory, as in the Wynne-Singer theory, the schizophrenic reaction represents a final attempt to withdraw from a sense of hopeless confusion by an individual whose ability to test reality is poor. Interestingly, Laing has extended his conception of how familial forces shape a schizophrenic break to a treatment model, which relies heavily on a residential treatment program (see Chapter 7).

DISTORTIONS IN ROLE RELATIONSHIPS

In families with schizophrenic offspring, the roles of the children are often defined by the odd and distorted relationship between their parents. Although it is hard to say what normal family organization is, the patterns these families have developed are rarely within the gray area of normality. Lidz et al. (1957) have described two types of role distortions among families of schizophrenics, which they call *schism* and *skew*. In *schismatic* families, parents openly battle with each other. They try to coerce each other and they defy each other or, at best, submit temporarily with open hostility and resentment. Each parent undercuts the worth and self-esteem of the other. Their conflict creates an atmosphere of distrust and divides the family, as they try to force the children to take sides. Often the threat of family dissolution constantly hangs over the children, and it is left to them to maintain some sort of stability. Preoccupied with their marital problems, and lacking affection and support from the spouse, their parents often turn to them to fill their emotional needs. The effects on children of recurrent marital discord are many. It also provides negative models of spouse relationships and interferes with sex role identification and expectations about the opposite sex. As Lidz suggests, it increases personal conflict by frequently forcing one or more of the children into difficult alliances and roles.

Skewed families, on the other hand, have one strongly dominant parent who organizes family relationships in a deviant way. In many cases of marital skew, there is no sign of the overt parental discord characterizing the schismatic families. The Lidz study included families in which the focal parent dominated the family entirely and the other parent was typically passive and ineffectual. In the majority of skewed families in the sample, it was the mother who was dominant; the fathers participated only minimally in decision-making and in relating to the children. Less common was a marked skew in which the father completely dominated the family and based all decisions and actions en-

tirely on his needs. Mothers in these families tended to adopt an extremely childlike stance. Helpless and infantile, they were totally dependent upon their husbands for direction and nurture. The following description from the Lidz research illustrates this type of marital skew:

The father was an ingenious and successful foreign-born manufacturer, but at home he ruled his roost like an eastern potentate, a role for which he claimed divine sanction and inspiration via a special mystical cult that he shared only with a few select friends. . . . Father secluded himself in his room during most of the time he spent at home, with only his wife and the children's governess permitted to enter and attend to his needs. . . . He would sit there in his underclothes reading religious books by the hour. The entire household participated in the religious rites. The mother sharing his beliefs completely and continuing to do so even after his death, which according to the cult meant continuing life in a different plane. . . . Both the patient and his only sister were emotionally deprived children who were isolated from their parents *and* from the surrounding community because their family milieu was so aberrant (Lidz et al. 1957, pp. 337–338).

We could hardly expect people whose home life was so bizarre to develop normal personalities. And yet distorted role relationships usually have negative effects on some but not all the offspring in the family. How can we comfortably say that this kind of family system is schizogenic; that is, a causative factor in schizophrenia, if only one of the children becomes schizophrenic? Why isn't the system schizogenic for all the children in the family? We could fall back on the genetic hypothesis and say that some children in the family may be more biologically vulnerable to these distorted family systems, but because our knowledge of the biological mechanisms in schizophrenia is limited, we cannot readily accept this argument.

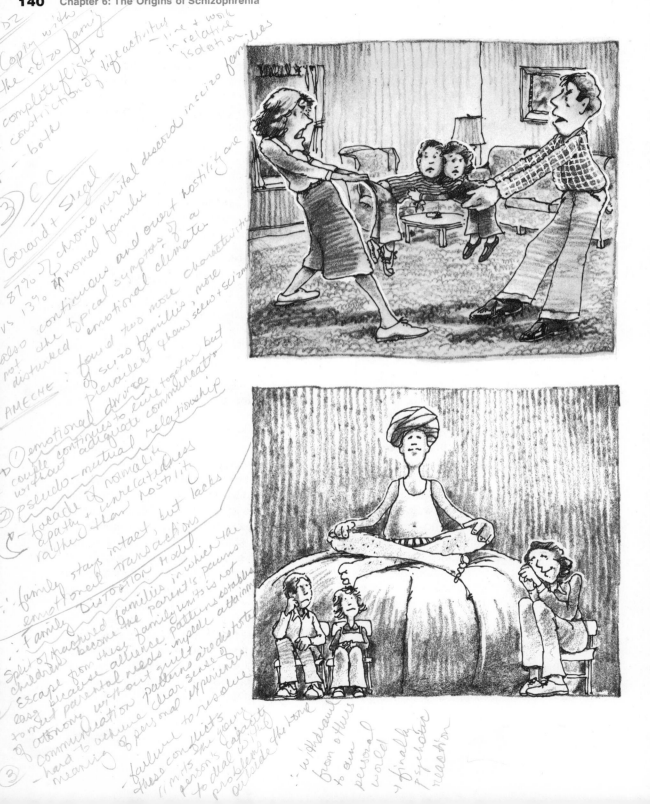

[Handwritten margin annotations:] Limitations to Family Theory — ① Small samples contracted — ② few studies contradict with other schizophrenic families who have children of other disturbances — ③ why do only one or a few members manifest it + why do some families produce schizophrenic + other psychopathological disorders — ④ Accounting for the problems to be in family + they cause by the disturbance in disturbance child — distortions — for both understanding of — = High Risk Study of family Relationship

There is some evidence that the child who does develop schizophrenia has a special and often critical role in maintaining the tenuous balance within the family system. Lidz et al. (1957) suggest that "the child who becomes schizophrenic is caught in the schism to a greater degree than are the others in a variety of ways." First, she may fulfill the role of "scapegoat," whose difficulties preoccupy her parents and mask their basic unhappiness with each other. Second, she may insert herself into the split to widen the gap between them and gain exclusive access to the love and attention of one parent. Third, she may continuously try to bridge the gap between her parents to bring about some peace. By adopting one of these roles, the schizophrenic child may make it possible for her siblings to escape the damaging consequences of the pathogenic environment. Which child falls into this role is often an accident of sequence in birth order, gender, or changes in the family situation.

In skewed families, the dominant parent commonly selects one of the children for a special relationship that is characterized by considerable parental interference in the child's life. Lidz and coauthors describe mothers who develop excessive, "symbiotic" attachments with their sons in order to satisfy their own needs. This symbiosis is so intense that it prevents the chlid from developing his own autonomy and also stimulates incestuous sexual ties. The other, more normal children in the family may resent this relationship, but they do avoid its invisible net.

Fig. 6.7. In marital schism (top), there is chronic discord between the parents in which the children are embroiled. Marital skew (bottom) refers to a family environment dominated by one highly eccentric parent.

Siblings of schizophrenic individuals may invent drastic methods of coping with life in a schizogenic family system. Some do make reasonably adequate adjustments, but a member will manifest severe problems later in life. In the small sample studies by the Lidz group (1963), siblings coped with their situation by *complete flight from the family* or *constriction of life activities* or both. The ones who fled literally moved great distances from their families and rarely, if ever, saw any family member. The others chose to live and work in relative isolation. Although these individuals noticeably limited their own emotional growth, perceptual development, and use of intellectual resources, constricting their lives enabled them to insulate themselves against emotionally demanding, overwhelming relationships.

DISTORTIONS IN EMOTIONAL CLIMATE

The patterns of family relationships we have been looking at obviously give rise to distorted emotional climates. A family in which the parents are forever arguing surely is not a healthy emotional environment for children, as the Lidz sample illustrates. But in another study, Gerard and Siegel (1950) found chronic marital discord characterized the families of 87 percent of 71 schizophrenic males, compared to 13 percent in a group of normal controls. Although chronic marital discord does beset schizophrenics' families, continuous and overt hostility are not the typical symptoms of a disturbed emotional climate. In schizophrenic families Nameche et al. (1964) found schism and skew less characteristic of the marital relationship in families with children who subsequently became schizophrenic adults than two more subtle patterns, *emotional divorce* and *pseudomutual relationships.*

In a climate of *emotional divorce* a couple continues to live together although the partners no longer relate to each other in any substantive manner, verbally or otherwise. In a *pseudo-mutual relationship,* husband and wife put up a façade of normality, to which they rigidly adhere despite deep dissatisfaction. The emotional climate in both types of families is apathy and unrelatedness rather than expressed hostility. The family unit remains intact but lacks the emotional transactions that can be such a satisfying side of family life. Under these circumstances, one parent may turn to one or more children for emotional gratification, but their closeness cannot alter the "gray" atmosphere.

IMPLICATIONS AND LIMITATIONS OF
THE FAMILY DISTORTION MODEL

Overall, the family studies we have discussed revealed consistent patterns among families having a schizophrenic offspring:

1. These families are typically split or fractured and children become their parents' pawns.
2. Escape from these family units is not easy because alliance patterns established to meet parental needs impede attainment of autonomy without guilt.
3. Communication patterns in these families are distorted. Diffuse or strangely literal modes of communication make it difficult to achieve a clear sense of the meaning of personal experiences.

These recurring findings suggest that the preschizophrenic offspring becomes trapped within a family system that gives rise to inner conflicts over dependency needs, autonomy, sexual identity, and self-confidence. Failure to resolve these conflicts limits the young person's capacity to deal with problems outside the home, particularly during adolescence and young adulthood. Faced with overwhelming

tasks, as he sees them, the preschizophrenic offspring reacts with relatively primitive coping mechanisms and withdraws from others into a private world where events have highly personal meaning. The end-stage is the psychotic reaction itself.

Despite many lines of evidence supporting the view that a distorted family system sets an individual on the path to schizophrenia, a number of issues require closer study. First, most sample populations studied have been relatively small. The Lidz group studied only fourteen families. Second, except for the Wynne-Singer studies, few researchers have tried to contrast families having a schizophrenic member with families containing other types of disturbed offspring. Consequently, we do not know whether these family patterns are unique for schizophrenic development or whether similar stressful environments produce different forms of psychopathology. Third, why is it that only one or very few of the children from a schizogenic family manifest schizophrenia, and why do some families produce not only schizophrenia but also quite different types of psychopathology, such as antisocial reactions? We dealt somewhat with this question in the section on skew and schism, but the Lidz data on siblings are largely speculative and do not provide rigorous data on the manner in which some offspring resist a pathogenic family environment. Finally, but not least significant, most family studies have involved families who already had the experience of living with a very disturbed offspring. Therefore it is difficult to discern which aspects of the fractured family patterns developed in reaction to this painful and guilt-producing experience, and which predate the offspring's breakdown. To gain better understanding of distortions in a schizogenic family, researchers have recently turned to high-risk studies.

A High-Risk Study of Family Relationships

The degree to which disturbed family relationships are merely reactive to psychotic behavior was the focus of one such study of nonschizophrenic teenagers (Goldstein et al. 1978). Sixty-five families that had at least one emotionally disturbed teenager were chosen for intensive evaluation. All the teenagers were undergoing outpatient treatment as the study began, but none was schizophrenic or close to it. Based on the hypothesis that failure to master the developmental stresses of adolescence increases the likelihood of severe adult psychopathology, the research group defined the teenagers as a high-risk group. They anticipated, however, that only a few of the sample were likely to be at risk for subsequent schizophrenia.

Five years after the initial analysis, a follow-up report did indeed record a broad range of outcomes with normal development at one end and schizophrenia at the other. Although the data are not yet complete for the entire sample, a comparison of earlier measures of deviance in parental transactional communication of the sort identified by Wynne and Singer with the psychiatric status of male teenagers after five years is revealing. Table 6.3 shows the relationship among three levels of deviance in parental transactional communication (estimated from TAT behavior) and subsequent level of functioning. The nonschizophrenia spectrum includes offspring whose adjustment was essentially normal and ranges include individuals diagnosed as having severe neurosis and personality disorders. The extended schizophrenia spectrum covers diagnoses of definite schizophrenia, probably schizophrenia, and borderline and severe personality disorders (after Kety et al. 1968). You can see in this table that in all but one case, the young men who fit into the extended schizophrenic spectrum came from families in which the parents, five years before breakdown, displayed a high degree of disorder in transactional communication of the sort Wynne and Singer observed in parents of schizophrenics. Furthermore, these difficulties in communication rarely showed up in parents of the men who were also disturbed but were

Table 6.3. Relationship between levels of parental transactional communication and level of offspring functioning[a]

Parental communication deviance level (estimated when offspring were teenagers)	Number of offspring subsequently diagnosed as:	
	Nonschizophrenia spectrum	Schizophrenia spectrum
High	2	6
Intermediate	6	1
Low	1	0

Source: M. J. Goldstein, E. H. Rodnick, et al., "Familial precursors of schizophrenia spectrum disorders," in L. C. Wynne, ed., *The Nature of Schizophrenia* (New York: John Wiley & Sons, 1978), p. 493.
[a] Relationship between levels of parental transactional communication index observed when offspring was a teenager and psychiatric status of offspring five years later.

Sociological Status and Schizophrenia

[handwritten margin notes: "incidence of schizo significantly higher among the lower socioeconomic groups" and "get more and available"]

The search for the stress component of the stress-diathesis equation has extended beyond the family unit to larger units of society. A major sociological variable is social class or social status, which reflect a person's position in the hierarchy of society. Common indices of social class include income level, residential area, educational level, and job position. As the accompanying table shows, a great deal of evidence points to a direct relationship between social class and schizophrenia. Figures on hospital admissions indicate that the incidence of schizophrenia is significantly higher among the lowest socioeconomic groups than for other groups.

Although the facts seem incontrovertible, we can account for the data in many ways. The most obvious explanation is the *social drift hypothesis,* which argues that as schizophrenia develops, individuals drift downward in occupation, income, and residence, and end in the lowest socioeconomic class at the time of admission to a hospital. Yet, recent evidence (Kohn 1973) indicates that even though some schizophrenic patients did suffer a downward socioeconomic slide, most came from families of lower-class origin, or failed to rise in social status as much as mentally healthy individuals born in similar circumstances. Thus, it seems clear that downward drift cannot account for the high representation of people from lower socioeconomic levels in schizophrenia wards.

A more sophisticated version of the social drift hypothesis uses genetic factors to account for the high rate of schizophrenia among the least fortunate classes. Over generations, its adherents argue, families having a high incidence of schizophrenia among close relatives decline in social position and, if family members marry, they not only transmit to offspring poor social circumstances but a higher genetic risk for schizophrenia as well. This theory assumes that the pool of genes carrying a predisposition to schizophrenia is gradually increasing among the lowest socioeconomic strata.

Kohn (1973) concludes that increasing genetic susceptibility may account for some part of the increased rate of schizophrenia at lower socioeconomic levels, but it cannot account for much. Because male schizophrenia patients have not actually fallen below their fathers' occupational levels but have lagged behind the general population in upward mobility, it is unlikely that genetically vulnerable individuals form a growing concentration in the lowest social classes.

What other explanation can we offer for the high rate of schizophrenia among the lower strata of society? By far the majority of lower-class families do not produce schizophrenic cases, so that there must be something special about those who do. One thing these families do seem to have in abundance is stress. Limited income, poor housing, deteriorating neighborhoods, and intense family pressures create stresses that are much greater for the impoverished than those experienced by the well-off. In a study of lower-class life in Puerto Rico, Rogler and Hollingshead (1965) found evidence that stress is indeed a factor in schizophrenia onset among the poor. During the year prior to appearance of schizophrenic symptoms in a family member, their research revealed greater stress in the patients' families than in matched lower-class families without psychiatric illness.

In essence, then, it is clear that the incidence of schizophrenia is greater in the lowest social strata of society. It is not so clear why. Stress obviously plays a role in schizophrenia, but we still need to identify the unique characteristics of families exposed to the stress of poverty who do and do not produce schizophrenic members.

Some principal U.S. studies of socioeconomic differentials in rates of serious mental disorder, particularly schizophrenia.

Investigator and locale	Criterion of mental disorder	Central findings
Faris & Dunham (1939, Map XI) Chicago, Ill.	First hospital admission, diagnosis of schizophrenia, 1922–1934, public and private hospitals combined.	The average annual rate per 100,000 population, aged 15–64, is 102.3 for the central city area of lowest socioeconomic status, with gradually diminishing rates to less than 25 in the highest-status areas at the periphery of the city.
Clark (1948, table 3) Chicago, Ill.	First hospital admission, diagnosis of schizophrenia, 1922–1934, public and private hospitals combined.	The rank-order correlation between occupational status and hospitalization rate for schizophrenia is 0.81, the rates increasing from less than 100/100,000 population for large owners, professionals, and "major salesmen" to more than 600/100,000 for semi-skilled and unskilled workers.
Hollingshead and Redlich (1958, table 17) New Haven, Conn.	(a) Incidence: First treatment by any psychiatric agency, diagnosis of schizophrenia, between May 31 and Dec. 1, 1950. (b) Prevalence: Persons in treatment by any psychiatric agency at any time from May 31–Dec. 1, 1950, diagnosis of schizophrenia.	(a) Using the Hollingshead Index of Social Position, which combines the education and occupational status of head of household and social status of neighborhood as the basis for classifying social-class position: Age- and sex-adjusted rates per 100,000 population are 6 for two highest social classes (combined), 8 for class 3, 10 for class 4, and 20 for class 5. (b) Age- and sex-adjusted rates per 100,000 population are: 111 for social classes 1 and 2 (combined), 168 for class 3, 300 for class 4, and 895 for class 5.
Srole et al. (1962, tables 12-1, 12-4, figure 5) Midtown, New York City	Psychiatric ratings of degree of impairment, based on structured interviews with a representative sample of the population, aged 20–59. (Fieldwork conducted in 1954.)	Using age-adjusted rates for white males, and occupational levels as the basis for classifying socioeconomic status, respondents judged to be "impaired, with severe symptom

Some principal U.S. studies of socioeconomic differentials in rates of serious mental disorder, particularly schizophrenia. *(continued)*

Investigator and locale	Criterion of mental disorder	Central findings
Srole et al. *(continued)*		formation'' or ''incapacitated,'' increase from 5.8% in the highest of 12 socioeconomic levels to 30.6% in the lowest; using respondents' fathers' educational and occupational levels, those severely impaired or incapacitated increase from 5.7% in the highest of 6 socioeconomic levels to 14.7% in the lowest.
Dunham (1965, tables 75, 76) Two small areas of Detroit, Mich. (one a high-rate area, the other a low-rate area).	First contact with any psychiatric facility, diagnosis of schizophrenia, during 1958.	Using the patients' own educational and occupational levels as the basis for classifying social-class position, the incidence of schizophrenia for the two areas combined is 0.0 for class 1, 0.32 for class 2, 0.35 for class 3, 0.21 for class 4, and 1.45 for class 5. Using patients' fathers' occupational levels (not education) as the basis for a comparable classification, the corresponding rates are 0.87, 0.79, 0.44, 0.43, and 0.69.
Turner and Wagenfeld (1967, table 1) Monroe County (Rochester), N.Y.	First contact with any psychiatric agency, diagnosis of schizophrenia, Jan. 1, 1960 to June 30, 1963. (Limited to white males, aged 20–50.)	Using patients' own occupational levels, the ratio of observed/expected number of schizophrenic patients is 0.4 for professionals, 0.8 for minor professionals and managerial personnel, 1.4 for clerical and sales personnel, 0.9 for skilled manual workers, 0.9 for semiskilled workers, and 3.1 for unskilled workers. The corresponding ratios, based on patients' fathers' occupational levels, are 0.6, 0.9, 0.8, 1.5, 0.6, and 2.5.
Rushing (1969, table 1) Washington State	First hospital admission (state hospitals only), diagnosis of schizophrenia, between Dec. 31, 1954 and April 31, 1965.	Using patients' occupational levels as the basis for classification, the average annual rates of first hospitalization for schizophrenia per 100,000 employed males, for males aged 21–65 are 21 in the highest of five socioeconomic levels, 39 in level 2, 49 in level 3, 64 in level 4, and 270 in level 5.

Source: Adapted from M. L. Kohn, ''Social Class and Schizophrenia: A Critical Review and a Reformulation,'' *Schizophrenia Bulletin,* 1973, 7, pp. 60–79.

not schizophrenic. These findings argue strongly against the theory that communication disturbances in parents of schizophrenics are simply reactions to schizophrenia in their offspring. They also provide some evidence for the theory that these problems are a relatively specific form of intrafamilial stress for individuals in the preschizophrenia spectrum.

Because all the data from this project are not in, we still do not know whether the other disturbed patterns of family relationship outlined above also precede the onset of schizophrenia. When this information is available we will be able to evaluate whether they are in fact life stresses that are unique to the experience of preschizophrenic individuals.

A Concluding Word About Stress-Diathesis Theory

Rosenthal's original theory was relatively simple: given a genetic predisposition — the diathesis — and some life stress, a schizophrenic breakdown will occur. With our current knowledge, however, perhaps this theory is simplistic. A more complex theory, which may fit the evidence better, is a cyclical model of human development in which diathesis and stress are constantly interacting. The cumulative effect would be heightened vulnerability to schizophrenia in early adulthood.

If a person with a genetic predisposition to schizophrenia is exposed to a pathogenic family environment, he fails to develop adequate means of coping with normal life stress. He passes successive developmental points without acquiring normal coping skills because of combined genetic vulnerability and impaired self-esteem. As the demands of life accelerate, the progressively impaired individual has to rely on more primitive coping mechanisms. When pressures for autonomy from the family unit,

self-assertion, and heterosexual relations culminate in early adulthood, the vulnerable person is incapable of dealing with them and finally withdraws into a schizophrenic psychosis.

Summary

1. The three theories about what causes schizophrenia are: it is a biological disorder; the causes are psychosocial; and it is caused by a combination of biological and environmental conditions. Research has been inconclusive, but the evidence so far favors the idea that both biological and environmental factors are involved.

2. The research on biological causes of schizophrenia falls into two areas: 1) *biochemical deviation,* which focuses on two general hypotheses, inborn errors of metabolism and neurochemical dysfunction; and 2) *genetic defects* — it is believed that some people may have a predisposition toward schizophrenia because of an inherited trait.

3. The research on inborn metabolic error has shown that the effects of hallucinogenic drugs such as mescaline can mimic aspects of schizophrenia. It has also been found that mescaline chemically resembles the neurotransmitter norepinephrine. Some researchers suggest that by metabolic error, a schizophrenic's body may be producing enough hallucinogen to cause psychotic symptoms.

4. Studies on neurochemical dysfunction show that a person's behavior may be affected by the rate at which nerve impulses fire. The neurotransmitter dopamine is affected by drugs (tranquilizers and stimulants) that either intensify or block the firing of neurons in the brain. Schizophrenic behavior, therefore, may be a reaction to the excessive sensory stimulation caused by this abnormal firing.

5. Theories of genetic predisposition are

based on the clinical observation that the incidence of schizophrenia in the relatives of schizophrenics is higher than it is among the general population. Using twin studies, though, researchers have not been able to verify that a single gene is responsible for schizophrenia. Therefore, it has been theorized that either several genes interact to produce schizophrenia, or simply that a tendency toward the illness is inherited.

6. Meehl has suggested the existence of an inherited neurological disorder called *schizotaxia* in which two symptoms of schizophrenia are present: thought disorder and anhedonia. Persons with schizotaxia would be much more likely to develop schizophrenia. Meehl did not suggest how one can identify a schizotype (a person with schizotaxia).

7. Rosenthal's *stress-diathesis* model is an interactive theory stating that with a genetic predisposition (diathesis) and some life stress, a schizophrenic breakdown is likely to occur. Rosenthal does not describe the diathesis or offer a way of identifying it.

8. The *Mednick Project* attempted to identify and monitor children having at least one schizophrenic parent before the child showed

any signs or symptoms of schizophrenia. In a psychophysiological test of skin resistance, Mednick found that preschizophrenics recovered more rapidly following stimulation than did the normal control subjects. If replicated, Mednick's findings may provide a means of identifying vulnerable individuals.

9. Three basic distortions in the family systems of schizophrenics have been identified as important factors in determining the likelihood of schizophrenic breakdown: 1) *distortions in focusing attention and communication* — children may learn to imitate bizarre patterns of communication that occur in the family system; 2) *distortions in the role relationships* — children may be forced into siding with one parent, becoming a "scapegoat," or being involved in an intense symbiotic relationship with one parent; and 3) *distortions in the emotional climate of the family* — constant hostility, emotional divorce, a pseudo-mutual relationship between the parents, have all been found detrimental to the child's mental health. Whether these factors are typical only of schizophrenics' families however, or if they also apply to families of other types of disturbed individuals, is something researchers have yet to determine.

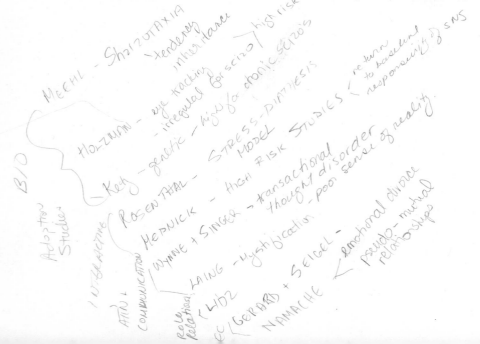

Chapter 7

Intervention in Schizophrenia

[handwritten annotations:]

for partially recovered patients

KRAEPLIN
- progressive + inevitable deterioration
- today, more optimism
1950's - decrease in schizo patients in hospital
- hospital as a therapeutic community because schizo symptoms were seen as a form of communication
active rehabilitation, not custodial care
- another outgrowth was preparation for reentry into society / halfway houses
mid 1950's - major tranquilizers - phenothiazines - control disorganized behavior + suppress schizo symptoms

Current Approach to Treatment

Biological Treatment of Schizophrenia
Drugs and Aftercare

Psychological Approaches to Treatment
Traditionally Oriented Psychotherapy
Existential Therapy (Laing's Treatment Model)
Behavior Therapy
Family Therapy

Multimodal Approaches

Preventive Efforts
Genetic Counseling
Preventive Interventions of a Psychological Type

Summary

"How long is the time until we know if we're going to make it or not?" Deborah asked.

"You kids are just in the honeymoon phase," said a girl sitting near them. "That takes about three months. I know, too. I've been in six hospitals. I've been analyzed, paralyzed, shocked, jolted, revolted, given Metrazol, Amatyl, and whatever else they make. All I need now is a brain operation and I'll have had the whole works. Nothing does any good, not this crap or anything else." She got up in the very doomed, dramatic way she had and left them, and Lactamaeon, second in command of Yr, whispered, *If one is to be doomed, one must be beautiful, or the drama is only a comedy. And therefore, Unbeautiful . . .*

Kill me, my lord, in the form of an eagle, Deborah said to him in the language of Yr. "How long has she been here?" she asked Carla in the language of Earth.

"More than a year, I think," Carla said.

"Is this . . . forever?"

"I don't know," Carla answered (Green 1964, pp. 47–48).

A schizophrenic episode appears to run a course that lasts anywhere from a few days to years. Until quite recently, we could do little to affect the course except to place a violent or disorganized individual in a mental hospital where she could be looked after and prevented from disturbing other members of society. Early in this century, when Kraepelin first delineated the syndrome we now call schizophrenia, pessimism was deep about the schizophrenic person's chances for recovery. Kraepelin's "dementia praecox" reflected the view that a schizophrenic episode leads to progressive and inevitable deterioration, or dementia. Now, workers in mental health are much more optimistic about the possibilities for altering the course of a schizophrenic breakdown and returning patients to their communities.

In the 1950s several breakthroughs altered the outlook for schizophrenia patients and led to a decrease in the number of people hospitalized with this disorder (Figure 7.1). First, psychoanalytic researchers recognized that much schizophrenic behavior is meaningful. However convoluted, it is a form of communication by which patients often express their reactions to the hospital environment. From this discovery came the concept of the hospital as a *therapeutic community* (Jones 1953), which would foster rather than inhibit recovery. Awareness of the hospital's therapeutic potential as a social setting caused professionals to rethink the role of hospitalization and raised hospital treatment to a new level for the first time since Philippe Pinel ushered in the Moral Era in the late eighteenth century (see Chapter 2). Henceforth, the emphasis would be on active rehabilitation, not custodial care.

Another outgrowth of this perspective was the establishment of *halfway houses,* sheltered-living environments in which partially recovered patients could prepare for reentry into society. Released from the hospital into these settings, patients who no longer required hospitalization but who were not yet ready to completely reintegrate into the community could acquire greater self-respect and personal responsibility.

The new approach to treatment received

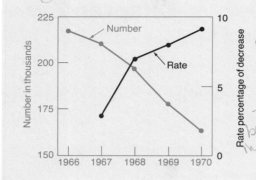

Fig. 7.1. Rate of decrease and decline in number of schizophrenic inpatients in state and county mental hospitals, 1966–70. (From Gunderson et al. 1974.)

enormous impetus from the discovery in the mid-1950s of the so-called *major tranquilizers,* especially the phenothiazines, which as we saw have provided insight into the causes of schizophrenia (see Chapter 6). Because these drugs control disorganized behavior and suppress schizophrenic symptoms and thus make patients less frightening to hospital staff and community residents, their availability strengthened the commitment to rehabilitative treatment.

Current Approach to Treatment

In Chapter 5, where we talked about the course of a schizophrenic episode, we pointed out that there are degrees of recovery and that the prognosis for each case depends on many variables. The degree to which an individual recovers from a schizophrenic episode is assessed by the *reduction in symptoms* and the *ability to function on a social level* that the patient gains once the symptoms are in remission. "Reduction in symptoms" means that the core symptoms have receded or that they have disappeared completely. By "ability to function on a social level" we mean the degree of life adjustment that a former patient is able to achieve. Unfortunately, treatment reduces symptoms far more often than it helps patients to find a socially and personally meaningful role in the community, particularly if premorbid adjustment was poor.

It is the goal of the first phase of treatment — the acute treatment stage — to reduce disorganizing psychotic symptoms and to reestablish contact with reality. Usually, this phase begins with the patient's admission to a hospital. Typically, at the time of admission, a patient is highly agitated, fearful, hostile, and tormented by hallucinations and delusional beliefs. Because of her confused state, she resists the notion that she needs help and arrives at the hospital with an escort of relatives, friends, or police who fear for her well-being or the safety of those around her. Here, many patients refuse hospitalization. For some, a legal action called *commitment* is necessary in order to hospitalize a patient against her expressed desire (see Chapter 23 for a discussion of current controversies about this process of commitment). The second phase of treatment, *aftercare,* is designed to permit a partially recovered patient to continue recovery while residing in the community. During this phase of treatment, the goal of integrating the former patient into society is combined with another important objective, preventing a relapse into psychosis — an ever-present hazard. In the United States, the duration of inpatient treatment has steadily diminished. Whereas ten years ago (as the quotation at the start of this chapter implies) a patient might have spent months or years in the hospital, now we can measure the stay in days or weeks. Consequently, many partially recovered schizophrenic patients reenter their communities. Frequently, although their delusions or hallucinations have disappeared or diminished,

many signs of anxiety, depression, and confusion are still present. Aftercare programs are meant to help patients deal with these problems.

Having sketched treatment procedures, we can turn to the types of treatment available for schizophrenia. In the pages that follow, you will recognize some of the same polarities we mentioned in Chapter 6 on the possible causes of schizophrenia. Just as we find biological and psychological theories of causation, so both biological and psychological approaches to the treatment of schizophrenia are used. We will study their methods separately and in combination, first as they apply to the acute phase of treatment and then in aftercare.

Biological Treatment of Schizophrenia

The history of biological treatments goes back about as far as the human race, to a time when primitive people believed that drilling a hole in the patient's skull would free the evil spirits responsible for his condition. At one time or another, almost every biological agent that has been used to treat disease has been tried on schizophrenia patients, without much success. Only in very recent times has any real progress been made.

The currently chosen biological treatment, drug therapy, is a radical departure from electroconvulsive (shock) therapy and lobotomy, the modes prevalent for thirty-five years. In electroconvulsive therapy, a constant electrical current is passed through the brain to induce convulsions. Its use in the treatment of schizophrenia has practically ceased because it is more hazardous and no more effective than other methods. Lobotomy, an operation that severs the tracts between frontal and prefrontal lobes of the brain, has proved ineffective.

Since the discovery of two types of powerful, antipsychotic tranquilizers — *phenothiazines* and *butyrophenones* — the biological treatment for schizophrenia has become almost entirely pharmacological. As indicated in Chapter 6, one significant biochemical effect of these drugs is to alter the dopamine levels in the brain. Clinically, they reduce fear and agitation, schizophrenic thinking, and delusions and hallucinations.

The ability of phenothiazine drugs to reduce symptoms varies from patient to patient. In some, they appear to completely eliminate vivid delusional beliefs and hallucinatory experiences so that the previous rational self reappears. One patient in drug treatment responded to a question about a strong belief that he was the object of a homicidal plot by a United Nations agency: "I can remember thinking that — but I was really crazy then — and of course

that's not true — I don't understand how I got into that weird state of mind!"

For some patients, the drugs seem merely to temper the effects of the schizophrenic process. A patient who formerly heard voices accusing him of "filthy sex desires" said that as a result of treatment, "I still hear the voices, but they simply don't bother me any more."

How well these drugs can reduce the overall schizophrenic symptomatology is evident from Figure 7.2, which derives from a nationwide, multihospital study of acute schizophrenics who received either an active drug (a phenothiazine) or a placebo. Generally, the patients who were on the active drug showed much less schizophrenic behavior at the end of the study period than those taking the placebo. Furthermore, drug-treated patients spent less time in the hospital and were more likely to return to their communities (May 1968). Without drugs,

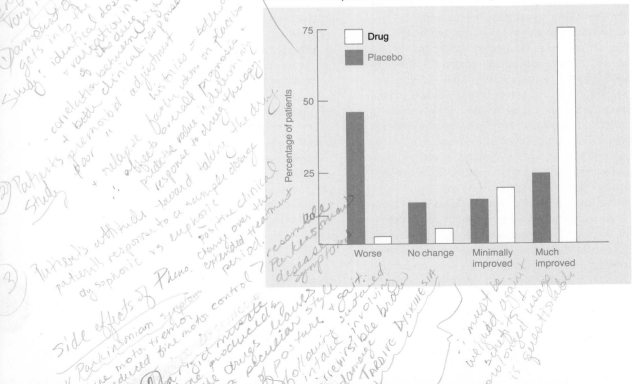

Fig. 7.2. Doctor's global rating of improvement in patients after treatment with phenothiazines or placebo. (From Davis 1978.)

many suicidal or overactive patients might injure themselves or others.

Interest is great in learning what accounts for this wide variety in clinical response to these drugs. One factor that has received close attention is the amount of the drug that actually gets into the patient's bloodstream. Because most phenothiazine drugs are swallowed, they must be absorbed into the blood from the intestinal tract. In one study (Curry 1971) schizophrenic patients who took identical doses of a phenothiazine drug showed a tenfold variation in subsequent blood levels of the drug. Researchers found a correlation between a higher level of absorption into the blood and better clinical response to the drug.

A patient's premorbid adjustment also affects response to antipsychotic drugs. In one study (Goldstein 1971) of the effects of phenothiazines on schizophrenic symptoms, patients with poor premorbid histories responded clearly and positively to the drugs and relapsed readily when shifted to placebo. On the other hand, patients with good premorbid histories did not show such a noticeable difference in behavior with either drug or placebo. Thus, a patient's premorbid psychosocial adjustment not only affects the overall prognosis (as we saw in Chapter 5), but also seems to have predictive value in determining the response to drug therapy.

Another possible explanation for the variation in drug response may lie in the patient's *attitude* toward taking the drug. Van Putten and May (1978) believe that a patient's response to a sample dosage of a phenothiazine drug indicates whether the long-term effects of treatment with the drug will be positive or negative. In their study, patients who reported that a sample dose of Chlorpromazine, a phenothiazine drug, administered on two consecutive days made them "goofy," "lazy," "mummified," "dull," or "fuzzy" responded poorly to a six-week treatment program with the drug. Van Putten and May labeled the reaction of these patients to the sample administration *dysphoric.* Characteristically, dysphoric patients manifested a drop in mood or slowed thought process. On the other hand, patients who reported a *euphoric* response to drug treatment claimed that the sample drug made them feel "calmer," "tranquil," "relaxed," "clearer," "mellow," or "less wound up." These patients showed positive clinical change over the extended treatment period. Additional research is necessary to determine how these subjective reactions relate to the blood level of the drug and to factors such as premorbid adjustment and patterns of symptoms.

As we often find with drug therapy, phenothiazines have disturbing side effects. The most common are a fine motor tremor and reduced fine motor control. Because these side effects mimic the symptoms of Parkinson's disease (a degenerative disease involving the dopamine tract in the brain) they are called *Parkinsonian symptoms.* Also, a rigid muscle tone produced by the drugs leaves a peculiar style of posture and gait. A condition called *tardive dyskinesia* appears in some patients following sustained intake of these drugs, involving symptoms of brain damage that apparently are irreversible.

Thus, advising schizophrenic patients to remain indefinitely on a maintenance dose of these drugs entails ethical and moral considerations that must be weighed against the benefits of controlling the symptoms of schizophrenia. Because of the side effects, patients often resist taking phenothiazine drugs, despite the possibility that their schizophrenic symptoms may worsen or return. Both the positive and negative effects of these drugs have generated legal and political controversies. We shall discuss these controversies in more detail in Chapter 23.

[handwritten marginalia: Hogarty & Goldberg — continuing the drug treatment greatly reduces relapses — 30% relapse — 68% placebo — sud/down the determine... — family environment to which the patient returns effects the outcome — HEE - great relapse]

Drugs and Aftercare

Phenothiazine drugs dramatically reduce symptoms during hospitalization, but that benefit has raised the question of whether patients should continue taking these drugs during the aftercare phase when discharged into the community. Numerous studies (Taube 1974) indicate that an average of 40 percent of patients discharged from hospitals return to the hospital within one year. But a series of other studies (Hogarty and Goldberg 1973; Hogarty et al. 1974a,b) strongly suggests that continuing the drug treatment greatly reduces the relapse rate. Hogarty and Goldberg found that over a two-year period following discharge from the hospital, only 30 percent of schizophrenic patients who continued on drug therapy relapsed, in contrast to 68 percent of those who received a placebo. Although drug maintenance significantly helps partially recovered schizophrenic

patients to return to the community, it does not solely determine whether they will adjust successfully. In fact, sometimes it does not make a noticeable difference. We have stated (see Chapter 5) that the emotional climate of the family environment to which a patient returns upon being discharged very much determines whether the patient sustains and builds upon gains made in the hospital, or regresses to a psychotic state. It also appreciably affects the success of an aftercare drug program, as Figure 7.3 shows. Here we see that the rate of relapse among patients who returned to benign, accepting home environments (Low Expressed Emotion) was extremely low and was not altered by drug therapy. On the other hand, patients who returned to homes where criticism, hostility, and emotional overinvolvement were present (High Expressed Emotion) had a generally high rate of relapse. Among the patients in the group believed to be at high risk for relapse,

[handwritten marginalia, right: For High Risk group drug therapy + limited face to face contact with family lowered relapse — family environment important too]

[handwritten marginalia, left: but only drug treatment is not enough because it eliminates symptoms but is not helpful in social adaptation]

Fig. 7.3. Relapse rates for patients returned to high and low Expressed Emotion (EE) home environments. Note that drug status and degree of family contact affect the relapse rates in high but not in low EE home environments. (After Leff 1976.)

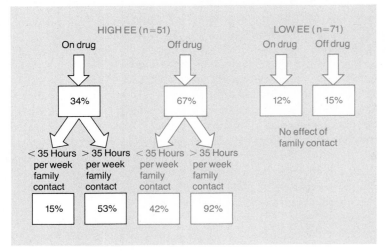

The Paradox of Maintenance Drug Therapy

There is pleasure sure,
in being mad,
which none but madmen know!

— John Dryden

Even though continued use of phenothiazine medication prevents patients who have been released into the community from suffering the recurrence of schizophrenia symptoms, many have difficulty continuing drug maintenance. The reasons for discontinuing medication are varied — a desire to deny the whole episode of psychosis, bitterness about being hospitalized, and residual paranoid suspicions, including the notion of being poisoned. Even patients who want to comply with the maintenance drug treatment often find some of the subjective effects of the drug difficult to tolerate. Mark Vonnegut's sensitive description of his own struggle with schizophrenia (see also Chapter 5) beautifully captures this common dilemma. Following hospitalization for a second breakdown, he says he wanted protection against recurrence of his horrifying symptoms, on the one hand, but on the other he found the method of protection disturbing:

Taking Thorazine was part of doing things right. I hated Thorazine but tried not to talk about hating it. . . . But Thorazine has a lot of unpleasant side effects. It makes you dizzy and faint when you stand up too quickly. If you go out in the sun your skin gets red and hurts like hell. It makes muscles rigid and twitchy.

The side effects were bad enough, but I liked what the drug was supposed to do even less. It's supposed to keep you calm, dull, uninterested and uninteresting. . . . What the drug is supposed to do is keep away hallucination. What I think it does is just fog up your mind so badly you don't notice the hallucinations or much else. . . . On Thorazine everything's a bore. Not a bore exactly. Boredom implies impatience. . . . When I did manage to get excited about some things, impatient with some things, interested in some things, it still didn't have the old zing to it (pp. 252–253).

Later Vonnegut describes another paradox of maintenance drug treatment: after stopping the drug, the patient feels much better, but only for a short while.

I managed to cheat on the Thorazine some. . . . I deliberately misinterpreted what some nurse had said and skipped a few days. I felt great. My mother and Virginia both remarked on how fast I was recovering and how chipper I was getting (p. 253).

Nevertheless, the patient who discontinues maintenance medication runs the risk of breaking down again. Vonnegut reports difficulty in convincing his psychiatrist of the benefits in stopping his medication:

He was so pleased. I was so pleased. . . . In this atmosphere of seemingly unanimous, unusual pleaseness, I told him I didn't need so much Thorazine. I told him, in fact, that at least part of the reason everyone was so pleased was that I had stopped taking it and I was sure that I could recover more quickly without it. . . . He called my mother and Virginia into the office. He explained that under no circumstances was he going to take any chances with my health. . . . So I was back on Thorazine again (p. 253).

True, the side effects of phenothiazine drugs, particularly the subjective ones, are adverse. Yet the drugs prevent additional breakdowns. Sometimes schizophrenic patients claim that they would rather be crazy again, if only to feel something, than to have their feelings blocked by drugs (Van Putten et al. 1976). The choice that both patients and their healers must make is definitely difficult (Vonnegut 1976).

however, drug therapy and limited face-to-face contact with the family kept the relapse rate down. Thus, it appears that a major effect of phenothiazine drugs in the aftercare phase is to protect the patient from a noxious home environment.

Helpful though they are in maintaining patients in the community, drugs hardly represent a "cure" for schizophrenia. Most patients whose aftercare treatment consists only of drugs are free of symptoms but show poor social adaptation. Many are unemployed — welfare cases who lead marginal lives. Add to this picture the known hazards associated with long use of the phenothiazines and it is clear that drug therapy does not merit unqualified endorsement.

Psychological Approaches to Treatment

The low level of social adjustment that undermines the positive effects of hospitalization for many discharged schizophrenic patients points to a need to help these people deal with psychological problems that may have brought them to the hospital in the first place. Psychological therapies appear to have value in treating schizophrenia, but where during treatment they are most beneficial and whether patients benefit more from a treatment program that includes both drugs and psychological therapy are questions that mental health professionals still debate. The attitudes of psychologically oriented therapists range, of course, from complete rejection of drugs at any stage of treatment to qualified acceptance. Because the evidence is not yet complete, we cannot say without hesitation that one group is more correct than the others. In describing the variety of psychological approaches in use, though, we

will cite some of the accumulated data and indicate the direction in which they seem to point.

Traditionally Oriented Psychotherapy

Psychological therapies require establishing a trusting relationship between therapist and patient (see Chapter 15 for a comprehensive discussion of psychological therapies). The schizophrenic patient is terrified, distorts her perceptions of others, and projects hostile intentions on to them, making it a big task for a psychotherapist to win the patient's trust during the hospital treatment. The difficulty of establishing personal contact with a withdrawn and fearful patient comes across in this excerpt from a therapy session between a schizophrenic patient and clinical psychologist Carl Rogers. Notice the prolonged silences and failures of acknowledgment that the therapist had to endure, and the devices used to transcend them.

T [therapist]: I see there are some cigarettes here in the drawer. Hm? Yeah, it is hot out. (Silence of 25 seconds.)

T: Do you look kind of angry this morning, or is that my imagination? (Client shakes his head slightly.) Not angry, huh? (Silence of 1 minute, 52 seconds.)

T: [softly] I kind of feel like saying that "If it would be of any help at all I'd like to come in." On the other hand if it's something you'd rather — if you just feel more like being within yourself, feeling whatever you're feeling within yourself, why that's O.K. too — I guess another thing I'm saying, really, in saying that is, "I do care. I'm not just sitting here like a stick." (Silence of 16 minutes, 41 seconds.)

T: I see I'm going to have to stop in a few minutes. (Silence of 20 seconds.)

T: It's hard for me to know how you've been feeling, but it looks as though part of the time maybe you'd rather I didn't know how you were feeling. Anyway it looks as though part of the time it just feels very good to let down and relax the tension. But as I say I don't

[handwritten margin notes: psychotherapy goals beyond reducing symptoms + try to assist the patient in assuming roles that are commensurate with their reasonably commensurate abilities and talents ... But Studies ... psychotherapy = affected by drugs ... significantly lower than drugs alone]

really know how you feel. It's just the way it looks to me. Have things been pretty bad lately? (Silence of 45 seconds.)

T: Maybe this morning you just wish I'd shut up — and maybe I should, but I just keep feeling I'd like to — I don't know, be in touch with you in some way. (Silence of 2 minutes, 21 seconds.) [*Jim yawns.*]

T: Sounds discouraged or tired. (Silence of 41 seconds.)

C: [client]: No. Just lousy.

T: Everything's lousy, huh? You feel lousy? (Silence of 39 seconds.)

T: Want to come in Friday at 12 at the usual time?

C: Yawns and mutters something unintelligible. (Silence of 48 seconds.)

T: Just kind of feel sunk way down deep in these lousy, lousy feelings, hm? — Is that something like it?

C: No. (Meador and Rogers 1973, pp. 140–141)

Only if the patient decides to trust the therapist can the two of them begin the arduous task of recontacting reality and exploring the terror that it holds for the schizophrenic patient.

Modern writers who have worked extensively with schizophrenic patients in a psychotherapeutic framework (Gunderson and Mosher 1976) conclude that the pursuit of insight and the interpretation of underlying conflicts that is so effective with some disorders is not as valuable with schizophrenia. More important is helping the patient to develop self-esteem and the capacity to deal more effectively with the inevitable life stresses, and here psychotherapy has been most successful (Gunderson and Mosher 1976).

We find poignant descriptions in the literature of the difficult and intricate process of psychotherapy with schizophrenia, but one of the most moving is the autobiographical account *I Never Promised You a Rose Garden.*

This session between the teenage patient, named Deborah, and her therapist, whom De-

borah had nicknamed Furii, occurred after Deborah had been hospitalized for some time.

"They said we were getting sicker; all of us. They said I was getting sicker."

"Well, do you think you are?" Furii said, lighting another cigarette.

"No games."

"I do not play games. I want you to think deeply and answer honestly."

"I don't want to think any more!" Deborah said, with her voice rising in the wind of her sudden anger. "I'm tired and scared and I just don't care any more what happens. Work in the dark and work in the cold and what for!"

"To get you out of this damn place, that's what for." Furii's voice was as loud as Deborah's.

"I won't tell you anything more. The more garbage I give away the more I have left. *You* can turn me off and go with your friends or write another paper and get another honor for it. I can't turn me off, so I'm turning the fight off, and don't you worry — I will be nice and docile and nothing more will go on the walls."

The cigarette gave a long puff before the doctor's face. "Okay," she said, almost amiably. "You quit, poor little girl, and you stay in a crazy house the rest of your life. You stay on a crowded disturbed ward all your days. . . . 'Poor darling,' the world will say, 'she could have been such a nice person . . . so talented . . . what a loss.'" The mobile features made a "tch-tch" purse of the mouth.

"And more talented than I really am because I'm here and will never test it!" Deborah shouted because the bonetruth gave such a fine sound, even from Hell.

"Yes, damn it, yes!" Furii said.

"Well, what!" Deborah said, good and loud.

"Well, did I ever say it would be easy? I cannot make you well and I do not want to make you well against your own wishes. If you fight with all the strength and patience you have, we will make it together."

"And what if I don't?"

"Well, there are lots of mental hospitals, and they build more every day."

"And if I fight, then for *what?*"

"For nothing easy or sweet, and I told you that last year and the year before that. For your own challenge, for your own mistakes and the punishment for them, for your own definition of love and of sanity — a good strong self with which to begin to live."

"You certainly don't go in for hyperbole."

"Look here, my dear girl," Furii said, and thumped the ash of her cigarette on the tray, "I am your doctor and I see these years how allergic you are to lying, so I try not to tell lies." She looked at Deborah with the familiar half-smile. "Besides, I like an anger that is not fearful and guilty and can come out in good and vigorous English."

They were quiet for a while and then Furii said, "I think it is time, and that you are ready, to answer for yourself the question that you raised before. Are you getting sicker? Don't be afraid — you will not have to hang for your answer, whatever it is."

Deborah saw herself as Noah, sending out a dove to scout the fearful country. After a time the dove came back, quaking with exhaustion. No green branch, but at least it was a return. "Not sicker," she said, "Not sicker at all" (Green 1964, pp. 185–186).

Case studies indicate that psychotherapy can go beyond reducing symptoms to assist the patients in assuming roles that are reasonably commensurate with their abilities and talents. Nevertheless, the evidence from controlled studies contrasting patients who received psychotherapy in the hospital (May 1968) and those treated with drugs alone have been very disappointing. Psychotherapy brought about no more improvement than a placebo drug, and the improvement was significantly less than drugs alone produced. It is possible that the reports of psychotherapeutic success come from experienced clinicians in private hospitals, whereas most of the controlled studies took place in public state hospitals. If we examine the factors that experienced therapists say favor success in psychotherapy, however (Table 7.1),

Table 7.1. Favorable prognostic factors identified by therapists highly experienced with schizophrenic patients

1. Sudden onset of the psychosis.
2. Known precipitating factor.
3. Psychosis is experienced as alien to self.
4. Displays pain or depression.
5. Has had employment or academic success outside family of origin.

Source: J. G. Gunderson and R. Hirschfield, "Factors influencing the selection of patients for individual psychotherapy," in J. G. Gunderson and L. R. Mosher, eds., *Psychotherapy of Schizophrenia* (New York: Jason Aronson, 1975), pp. 293–303 (table: p. 301).

we can see that they are very similar to the indices that predict a good outcome from schizophrenic psychosis with no treatment whatsoever.

Existential Therapy (Laing's Treatment Model)

Even if psychotherapy were very effective with schizophrenia, the amount of time and effort required makes it an impractical treatment for the many hospitalized schizophrenic patients. Recently there has been a movement toward developing therapeutic environments, staffed mainly by nonprofessionals or paraprofessionals who encourage patients to assist one another in recovery. Perhaps the most visible advocate of this type of treatment is Ronald Laing (1964). Likening a psychotic episode to a "bad trip" that a patient must pursue rather than abort in order to gain real personal recovery, Laing asserts that the schizophrenic episode is a purposeful attempt to reject and shed an outward, false self that gives the individual the appearance of being normal, yet bears little resemblance to the inner "secret" self. In this view, traditional therapeutic techniques, including phenothiazine therapy, can have only catastrophic consequences for the schizophrenia patient. These techniques, Laing believes, aim merely to restore the false self; they fail to help the true self. Consequently, Laing and his followers (Gilluly 1971) argue that therapists using traditional techniques are dehumanizing the individual by labeling his behavior ''crazy'' rather than trying to understand his way of experiencing reality and his disturbed behavior. They condemn traditional methods for denying schizophrenic individuals the opportunity to work through the split that has deformed their lives.

Laing maintains that acute schizophrenics need encouragement and guidance to explore the ''inner time and space'' of their psychotic world. He defines the appropriate therapeutic setting as one that fosters *creative regression;* that is, encourages the patient to regress into the psychotic state, instead of arresting the episode. In addition, the relationship between therapist and patient is two-sided and personal. In this environment, progress toward integration of the split-off aspects of the self will ultimately occur.

With a group of associates, Laing set up Kingsley Hall in London's East End in 1965 according to his therapeutic model. Until 1970, when the lease expired, Kingsley Hall was home for therapists and patients. Patients assumed responsibility for preparing meals and housekeeping duties and ministered to each other as therapists. Because they tolerated behavior that most clinics could not, the atmosphere was not as orderly as you might expect to find in a household.

Actually, Laing's model of the treatment of schizophrenia is not very new. During the late 1940s and 1950s, before phenothiazines were available, a number of psychoanalytically oriented psychiatric hospitals in the United States ran intensive interpersonally oriented treatment programs for acute schizophrenic individuals. Some of them (Rosen 1953) heartily endorsed the idea that the schizophrenic patient needs to go further into his psychosis, to regress if necessary in order to get well. Although these programs did produce clinical remission, they took enormous amounts of manpower and energy, and the long-term results were questionable. Two aspects of Laing's program that do differentiate it from earlier efforts are the environmental conditions and role relationships at Kingsley Hall. The communal life style is alien to the traditional hospital model, where patients have minimal responsibilities at all levels. Clearly, the Laing model can be very effective for redeveloping a sense of personal competence and self-worth, reducing alienation, and learning to give and take support from other people. These aspects are somewhat separate from the notion of creative regression, and the Laing emphasis on self-care has found application in the treatment and rehabilitation of other severely disordered individuals, such as drug addicts and alcoholics, and appears to have much merit (see Chapter 19 for a discussion of these programs).

Behavior Therapy

Behavioral psychologists have made important contributions to the treatment of hospitalized schizophrenic patients. The behavior therapist, from the perspective of the operant conditioning model discussed in Chapter 2, believes that much of the schizophrenic person's aberrant behavior is controlled by current contingencies in his environment. Although the symptoms of the withdrawal — poor self-care, inattention to matters of reality, and bizarre talk — may not have been directly caused by the environment, they are more apt to persist in an environment that reinforces such behavior and does not expect or reinforce more socially appropriate behaviors.

Behaviorists see the hospital environment,

with its emphasis on "sick" behavior and its custodial surroundings, as particularly conducive to schizophrenic symptoms; in fact, the depersonalization and apathy commonly associated with long institutionalization closely resemble some schizophrenic symptoms (Goffman 1961). Consequently, in behaviorally designed wards staff members reinforce patients for taking an interest in their surroundings and behaving in a socially appropriate manner by practicing good grooming, working at a job, participating in recreational activities, helping other patients, and so on (Ayllon and Azrin 1968). Unacceptable behavior, such as withdrawal, reports of delusions and hallucinations, and aggressive acts elicit punishment.

Attention from the staff is a simple means of reinforcing acceptable behavior. In more complex systems, called *token economies,* patients earn money or "tokens" for constructive be-

Soteria House: An American Variation of the Laing Model

Soteria (from the Greek, meaning "deliverance") is a house in the San Francisco Bay Area where ten people live together. Six are schizophrenia patients and four are nonprofessional staff. Designed to provide elements of a family atmosphere, Soteria's goal is to assist the patients through their psychotic crises with little or no use of drugs. Those people who are better integrated (patients on the road to recovery and staff) are available as caretakers and quasi-parental figures. At least two caretakers, one man and one woman, are continuously with any actively psychotic resident. This two-to-one ratio allows a disorganized, fragmented, psychotic person to live through, act out, talk out, and ultimately, work out many difficulties coming from her own family through these pseudo-parent caretakers. Unlike the patient's real family, however, these caretakers treat the schizophrenic reaction as an "altered state of consciousness" in an individual who is experiencing a major life crisis. They use the disruptive psychotic experience as an instrument for reintegration and growth, as this example illustrates:

Marjorie, a 21-year-old, single, ex-Catholic, second oldest of seven, part-time college student, was admitted to the house about a week before the events which will be described below. She had been brought to the local clinic by her roommates when they found her attempting to electrocute herself. A few days previously she had made three deep slashes in her wrists, requiring multiple sutures. On admission she exhibited many signs characteristic of schizophrenia: She was extremely quiet and withdrawn, showed little or no emotion, had a severe disorder of thought, and expressed the firm belief that she was "the devil" and that the TV had been giving her messages to "burn, baby, burn, feel the fire of hell." At 5:00 A.M. one morning the entire house was awakened to the smell of smoke. Marjorie was found sitting quietly in the dining-room with her hair burned, frizzled, and matted, with multiple burns in the smock she had worn to bed. She had intentionally set her mattress on fire with a cigarette and, as it had begun to burn her hair and smock, she changed her mind and went to find a staff member. The fire was quickly extinguished, another mattress was found, and another bed made for her. While others were taking care of these details, one staff member sat down with her at the dining-room table and began to explore exactly what it was that had happened which made her feel so bad that she wanted to kill herself. She reiterated again and again her feeling of being the "devil" and needing to feel the fires of hell. This staff member spent the next five hours (others also spent lesser amounts of time) with her exploring in detail recent events which might have resulted in her feeling like such a terrible person. At the time of the fire she looked like a zombie — affectless and motionless. Initially, the events she related were completely disorganized and incomprehensible. They were described with a kind of timelessness, randomness, and con-

havior and may be fined for inappropriate actions. *Token economies* attempt to simulate some conditions in the outside world by having patients exchange tokens for room and board and by allowing them to purchase cigarettes, cosmetics, and other incidental items and activities with their "earnings."

Some token economies operate on several levels, each of which has its specific reinforcement contingencies. An entering and very regressed patient may be placed on Level 1, where he will receive tangible items, such as meals and cigarettes, in exchange for basic self-care and appropriate ward behavior. The patient advances to Level 2 when staff personnel consider him ready to assume job responsibilities, for which the reinforcement is money and off-ward privileges. Finally the patient advances to Level 3, at which time he may get temporary leave from the hospital, counseling,

textlessness which made the staff member feel as though he were floating in space or in some vast expanse of ocean. He shared this feeling with her and, as he did so, she seemed to be better able to get a grasp on the events themselves, including very genuine affect. The precipitants of her crisis were the death of a maternal grandfather with whom she was extremely close some six months before, increased difficulties in her relationship with a sister of whom she'd always been jealous, and a spiraling cycle of sexual promiscuity. The discussion focused on these events, including her wish to have gone to her grandfather's funeral and feeling guilty for not having done so. She had decided not to go because she was afraid she would not be able to deal with her mother and sister and did not want to see her grandmother hurt and crying. Her grandfather had been cremated (she wondered where his ashes had been taken) and this attempt at self-destruction had been her way of joining him. In her relationship with her sister, Marjorie had always been the "bad one," "the irresponsible one," and the loser in the eyes of her mother as compared with her sister. Marjorie had been disturbed by the perverse pleasure she experienced when her favored sister had had to have a hysterectomy one year previously. These two events seemed to be related to her increasing sexual promiscuity, especially the bizarre turn it had taken after her grandfather's death. By mid-morning she was no longer disorganized in her thinking, was affectively very appropriate, and even able to smile and laugh occasionally.

She cried when speaking of her grandfather's death, was angry with her sister, and got very depressed discussing how she felt about her sex life. The change in her face and posture was striking: Her face was appropriately mobile and expressive, and she was able to move about in a very natural way. It seemed that getting in touch with these previously split-off and disavowed events and their associated affects had allowed her to recompensate, at least for a time. The staff member's role was one of support and reassurance (he quite often told her he felt her a worthwhile person), and a gentle guiding of her into herself, to help her identify and clarify the jumbled series of affects and ideas contained within. He tried to stay in her "space" with her, describing to her how he was experiencing it; by so doing, he validated her feelings and made it clear to her that they were real, comprehensible, and tolerable to him. This last point was made more by his staying with her (and lack of fear in the situation) than by any spoken word (Mosher et al. 1974, pp. 295–297).

Preliminary results of a study comparing Soteria House and a more traditional treatment center indicate that they are equally effective in reducing symptoms, but that former Soteria residents show signs of superior social adjustment in being capable of leaving home and returning to school or work.

and other privileges "free," provided the overall work and ward performance remain adequate. The progressive withdrawal of specific token contingencies may facilitate transfer to the outside community, which does not operate so predictably.

In environments like these, where patients receive encouragement and reinforcement for normal functioning and adaptive behaviors, many schizophrenic individuals show marked change in behavior. Figure 7.4 presents the results of an experiment to determine the effectiveness of this type of therapy (Ayllon and Azrin 1965). When tokens were contingent upon successful performance of ward and hospital jobs, schizophrenic patients performed well; when tokens were given randomly, patients' behavior deteriorated to former levels.

Token economies have proven most effective for rehabilitating chronic patients in the wards, but their use poses a dilemma for the behavior therapist. On the one hand, the most effective reinforcers are such "basics" as a bed in which to sleep, meals, visitors, and recreation. On the other hand, recent court decisions have decreed that an institution may not deny essentials to residents because it would infringe the patients' rights. The paradox, then, is that the very programs that might help chronic patients adjust so well that they can leave the institutions are becoming increasingly difficult to implement. We shall discuss this and related issues in Chapter 23.

If continued reinforcement of appropriate behavior is necessary for compliance, you might wonder whether the effects of this type of therapy are likely to endure once a patient has left the therapeutic environment. Experience with released patients who had been in a behavior therapy unit during the hospitalization suggests that behavioral improvement continues *only* while the environment supports it. In a comprehensive review of token economy pro-

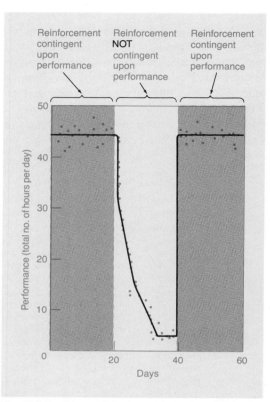

Fig. 7.4. In this study 44 patients were rewarded by ward personnel when they performed some assigned task properly. The tasks were such things as cleaning their room, making their bed, coming to the dining room on time, or doing some job in the hospital. As the graph shows, performance related directly to the reward structure. When rewards followed task performance, the patient continued to perform. In the absence of task-linked rewards, performance fell off rapidly. Behavioral theorists believe that many schizophrenic behaviors are continued because patients are not systematically rewarded for more normal behavior. The results of this study certainly support that position. (From Ayllon and Azrin 1965.)

[handwritten margin notes: Behavioral approaches have moved the beyond the simple token economy to planned rehabilitation programs that extend into the aftercare phase of treatment. 1, training. 2 social skills]

grams, Kazdin and Bootzin (1972) offer the pessimistic conclusion that "although token economies have been dramatically effective at changing behavior within the psychiatric hospital, there is little evidence that improvement is maintained outside of the hospital."

A clear challenge to behavioral treatment approaches is a plan to generalize gains achieved in the hospital to community life. Currently, numerous efforts are under way to devise such a program (Liberman 1976). Table 7.2 outlines a comprehensive behavioral program of treatment for chronic schizophrenic patients, the ones who ordinarily languish in institutions. It shows that behavioral approaches have moved beyond the simple token economy notion to planned rehabilitation programs that extend into the aftercare phase of treatment. This

work is particularly significant because (as we have said again and again) many schizophrenic patients lack the social skills necessary to maintain themselves in the community. Without active retraining programs they can only be dependent and inadequate members of society. The specificity of the behavioral approach combined with behavior monitoring and community support systems could, in the future, ease reentry into the community for many patients whose premorbid adjustment was poor.

Family Therapy

Family therapy differs from other psychological approaches in that it focuses attention on the family system and the distorted relationships among family members, not on the member who has suffered a schizophrenic break-

Table 7.2. Steps in the behavioral rehabilitation of chronic schizophrenics

Behavioral task	Required activity
Therapeutic goals	Define precisely the behavioral goals for each patient.
Therapeutic progress	Measure the frequency of the desired behaviors.
Reinforcement	Attach clear positive and negative consequences to adaptive and maladaptive behavior, respectively.
Shaping behavior	Use instructions and prompts to elicit the desired behaviors. Reinforce patients for making small, discrete steps in the desired direction.
Stimulus generalization	Structure the hospital setting to approximate the real world outside.
Training skills	Provide opportunities for patients to learn and practice vocational and housekeeping skills which have marketable value in the community or instrumental role value within the family.
Interpersonal goals	Prepare patients and significant others to live in mutually supportive ways in the community (prerelease training, aftercare). Teach significant others to use behavioral principles to maintain gains.
Community adjustment	Coordinate community resources to reinforce and back up the discharged patient's coping efforts.

Source: R. P. Liberman, "Behavior therapy for schizophrenia," in L. J. West and D. E. Flinn, eds., *Treatment of schizophrenia* (New York: Grune & Stratton, 1976), pp. 175–206.

- returning to an
emotionally neutral
environment
- Day Hospitals
- board & care homes

Behaviorism and Aftercare Treatment Center Reform

Since the phenothiazine drugs have become widely available and the negative effects of returning schizophrenic patients to an unsupportive family environment have become known, interest has grown in discharging them to a more emotionally neutral environment. Day hospitals, where patients spend the day in organized programs of occupational, art, and physical therapy designed to restore a sense of personal competence, and from which they return to their family homes at night, are one increasingly popular outgrowth of this awareness. Private residential treatment centers, or *board and care homes,* where schizophrenic patients live in hotel-like, supervised environments, also are becoming more and more common. It is an excellent plan in theory, but in fact, great vigilance is needed over such environments. All too frequently they become "warehouses" in the community where ex-patients vegetate and deteriorate, invisible to society at large. Such homes rarely appear to provide the active rehabilitation environment envisioned by those with whom the concept originated (Reich 1973).

Ordinarily, when we think of behavioral principles being applied to schizophrenic patients, we think of some behavior modifier attempting to stimulate more normal behavior in a patient by systematically using meaningful rewards and punishments. As more and more chronic schizophrenic patients are released to privately owned, extended-care facilities, however, similar incentives need to be built into these settings. Today owners of such facilities have few incentives to organize active rehabilitation programs. Thus, patients languish in these community facilities and rarely achieve any kind of independent existence.

Recently, Kohen and Paul (1976) have suggested applying principles of behavioral assessment and modification to ensure that proper rehabilitation procedures will be used in these environments, with bonuses contingent upon patients' progress toward independent living. As they envision the system, the state, which pays the bills for placement in extended care of chronic schizophrenic patients, would be the behavior modifier. Each facility would receive a bonus contingent upon evidence of patients' progress toward independence.

The Kohen-Paul plan starts with the notion that external observers monitor what residents do, changes in level of functioning by residents, and staff interactions with patients. Their plan has these components:

1. A behaviorally based assessment of patients' level of functioning at entry into the program. Funding per patient will be based on this assessment, and the agency will receive a higher rate for the poorer-functioning patients.
2. Repetition of this behavioral assessment carried out at regular intervals in order to chart patients' progress or the lack of it. Bonuses (rewards) will be paid to the extended-care home for each significant sign of behaviorally demonstrable progress.
3. Systematic monitoring of staff–patient interaction, based on clear behavioral categories by external observers. Operators who implement an approved program will continue to receive patient funding; those who do not will find their funds reduced.
4. Bonuses for successful release of patients from the facility to more independent living situations. These bonuses will be paid for three months after release to ensure that the patient has not simply been "dumped" to gain the bonus, and must be repaid if the patient returns within ninety days of release.

You can see that this program would rely heavily on behavioral principles to foster a structure that rewards patients' improvement and movement toward independence. It contrasts markedly with many contemporary systems in which the number of hospital beds filled determines the funding, and which thereby indirectly punish discharge and rehabilitation efforts.

down. By meeting with the family as a unit, the therapist attempts to modify patterns of role relationships, emotional tone, and communication among all family members. Many of the theories of the family's role in schizophrenia have arisen from observations of these therapy sessions.

Family centered treatment operates on the assumption (discussed in depth in Chapter 6) that the schizophrenic family member is trapped in a distorted system of relationships from which he perceives no escape. For him to recover, then, it is necessary to uncover and resolve deep-seated problems within the family that the parents denied or blurred by adopting peculiar styles of communication. Only after the family has acknowledged the problems between the parents and dealt with them can the schizophrenic offspring cease being the victim of family pathology. This refocusing of familial attention and subsequent disengagement of the schizophrenic son is described here:

A striking example from our own work in conjoint family therapy confirms and summarizes these views. The father and mother insisted for some time both that they were in agreement on all important matters and that everything was all right in their family — except, of course, the concern and worries caused by their son's schizophrenia. At this time he was almost mute, except for mumbling "I dunno" when asked questions. During several months of weekly family interviews, the therapist tried to get the parents to speak up more openly about some matters that were obviously family problems, such as the mother's heavy drinking. Both parents denied at some length that this was any problem. At last the father reversed himself and spoke out with only partially disguised anger, accusing his wife of drinking so much every afternoon with friends that she offered no companionship to him in the evenings. She retaliated rather harshly, accusing him both of dominating and of neglecting her, but in the course of this accusation she expressed some of her own feelings much

more openly and also spoke out on differences between them. This session was reviewed and discussed with the participants the next week (and a tape recording of the argument was played back). In the following session, the son began to talk fairly coherently and at some length about his desires to get out of the hospital and get a job, and thereafter he continued to improve markedly (Jackson 1960, p. 383).

Systematic evaluation of family therapy with schizophrenics resembles the literature on individual psychotherapy. Numerous clinical reports tell of successful cases in which family-level intervention has permitted a schizophrenic family member to improve and disengage from the pathological system, although there have been strikingly few controlled studies done on its effectiveness (Massie and Beels 1972). There are indications that family therapy has a negative effect when initiated during the acute phase of treatment (Guttman 1973), when the patient is very disturbed and his family is upset by his delusions, hallucinations, and hostility. In conclusion, then, family therapy can be considered a promising approach to the aftercare stage of treatment, but it requires systematic testing.

Multimodal Approaches

For the sake of clarity we have separated the approaches to treatment of schizophrenia by theoretical orientation. But, in practice, the modes of treatment that are likely to assist the schizophrenic patient's recovery are available in many combinations (see Figure 7.5). Perhaps the greatest controversy in schizophrenia treatment surrounds the combining of drugs and psychological treatment. A common argument against the use of drugs to facilitate psychotherapy, as we saw earlier, is that drug treat-

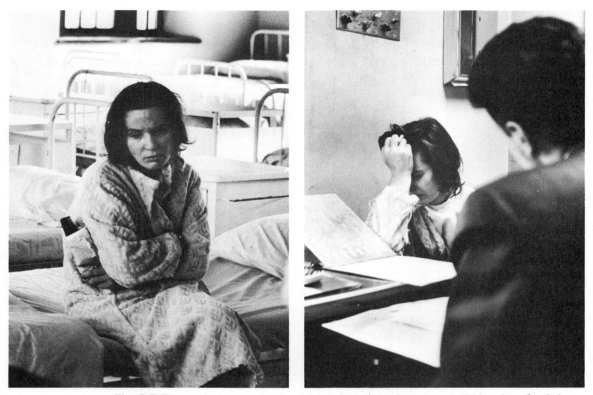

Fig. 7.5. These photos summarize selected phases of treatment of Mrs. Ann Clark (a fictitious name but a real person) who was brought to the hospital with symptoms indicative of schizophrenia: delusions of persecution and withdrawal. In the first photo (above, left) Ann has just arrived at Manhattan State Hospital and been helped into pajamas and a robe by nurses. Inwardly she is far more agitated than she appears. Shortly before, she had been weeping at being brought here; now she has withdrawn, convinced that everyone around her is hostile. Her behavior at home had been so strange that the police were called by a neighbor.

Dr. Dusan Mavrovic, Director of Female Admissions, tried to interview Ann and to reassure her that he wanted to help (above, right). Ann was very suspicious and fearful and gave only short, almost inaudible replies to his questions. After a while, she hid her face with her hand and only shrugged her shoulders when questioned.

Shortly thereafter Ann began a course of phenothiazine drug therapy designed to reduce her terror and her most acute psychotic symptoms. It was hoped that the drugs could make her more accessible to psychological intervention. In the third picture (p. 167, top left), Ann is shown taking a liquid dose of one such drug, chlorpromazine.

By the third day, Ann presents a different picture. She has become acclimated to the hospital environment and calmed by the drug treatment. In the next picture (p. 167, bottom left), she is able to tell her psychiatrist, Dr. Sparks, with animated gestures, of events that led to her hospitalization. At this stage she is still fearful of strangers, and the budding signs of trust in another person are an important step forward.

Discharged after almost seven weeks in the hospital (last picture), Ann was released with a specific aftercare program organized around regular visits to a community mental health clinic. In this program she will receive maintenance medication and will continue to work on improving her coping skills for dealing with the stresses that so overwhelmed her two months ago.

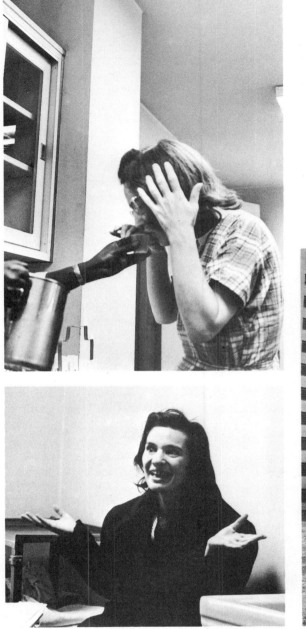

ment will inhibit a positive resolution of the psychotic crisis. Is there evidence to that effect?

A major study carried out during an extended inpatient phase (May 1968) indicated that adding psychoanalytically oriented therapy to phenothiazine drug treatment failed to produce any faster or better recovery than drugs alone. For the aftercare phase of treatment the reports are more positive. One impressive study by Hogarty et al. (1974a; 1974b) compared a maintenance drug-therapy program for released patients, and a psychological treatment program called Major Role Therapy (MRT), with the results of a program that provided both types of treatment.

The MRT technique was a reality-oriented counseling plan designed to help the patient conquer the very real problems of reentering the community, assuming a productive social role, and reestablishing satisfying personal relationships. The emphasis was on problem solving and not on resolving deep-seated conflicts, and the counselors assumed an active but progressively smaller role in helping patients make their own daily life decisions. Although this approach had some success, Hogarty and his colleagues found, after two years, that MRT combined with drug maintenance improved adjustment more than medication or MRT alone. Like the May study (1968), this one demonstrated that as an outpatient treatment, MRT alone was no better than the placebo condition, in which 80 percent of patients relapsed at the end of the two-year period.

The data on family therapy are very similar. In a recently completed study (Goldstein et al.

The Lodge: A Unique Rehabilitation Approach

A major problem for the mental health field is the rehabilitation of chronic schizophrenic patients who have recovered symptomatically but who lack basic job skills for meaningful reentry into the community. Without special rehabilitation programs, only 15 to 40 percent of these patients are able to support themselves while living in the community. Transitional living environments that bridge the gap between the dependency of the hospitalization period and an independent and productive existence are sadly lacking.

Fairweather (1969) designed an experiment to contrast a transitional environment with conventional procedures. It began in the ward with selection of a group of patients who, after some planning and preparation, moved together into an autonomous residence called "the lodge." In addition to providing living arrangements, the lodge established a business, a janitorial and gardening service. No professional people were regularly on the grounds. Instead, they acted as consultants, for a limited time. All profes-

sional help was gradually withdrawn until the patients were completely autonomous. Initially there were many mishaps, but a social structure did develop at the lodge and the janitorial and gardening business flourished.

Besides providing self-government and opportunities for work, the lodge's program emphasized drug maintenance. Peer supervision ensured that all residents took their prescribed medication. The cost of running the lodge was very low because the patient's income was used to defray expenses. After thirty months, the lodge was closed, and the remaining residents found new quarters and continued independently.

A forty-month follow-up showed that 40 to 70 percent of the former lodge members had full-time employment, a significant figure compared to a 2 percent average among a matched control group. Given proper structure and professional support, then, chronic schizophrenic patients might function socially as well as vocationally in the community.

1978), a short-term family therapy program was made available for a six-week period to patients leaving a community mental health center after a brief hospitalization. Like MRT, the family therapy was problem oriented and dealt with issues of the patient's reentry into the family unit and the larger community. Researchers divided patients into four groups for the study. One group received family therapy and an adequate dose of a phenothiazine drug. The second group participated in family therapy and took a minimal therapeutic dosage of the drug. The reason for giving a minimal dose instead of a placebo is that the use of placebo medication in such studies has raised grave questions about the ethics of denying patients an effective drug. The third group got only the adequate

drug dosage. And the fourth group received the minimal drug dose without family therapy.

You can see the result of this study in Figure 7.6. Fewest relapses occurred among patients who had both family therapy and the adequate maintenance drug dose, and the relapse rate was greatest for individuals who received neither family therapy nor an adequate dose of medication. These findings support the Hogarty results in the sense that they show how the combination of maintenance drug therapy and psychological therapy is the optimal treatment for preventing relapse in the aftercare phase of treatment.

Hogarty and Goldstein data both show also that when psychological therapies focus on the problem of reentry and are oriented toward

Fig. 7.6. Patient relapse during aftercare period, as a function of drug dose level and the presence of family therapy. (From Goldstein et al. 1978.)

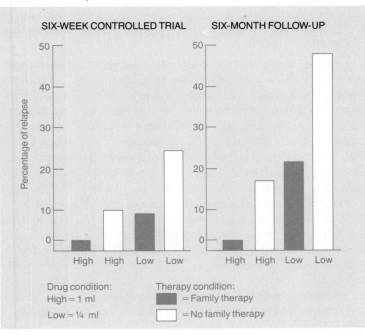

PREVENTIVE EFFORTS → Problems ① high rate for non-cres
" " of creativity among children of scizo.
① Genetic Counseling : encourage nonpregnancy ∴ 10-16% avoidance of scizo.
② fewer than 10% of scizos have one or more
scizo parents
③ can only affect those born after the scizo breakdown

170 Chapter 7: Intervention in Schizophrenia

solving real-life problems of the present, they are likely to be successful. Therapeutic programs that focus on the past, resolution of inner conflicts, or restructuring of long-standing family relationships are less likely to be helpful to discharged patients attempting to reestablish meaningful lives.

Preventive Efforts

So far, we have concentrated on methods of treating individuals who have suffered schizophrenic breakdowns. But a schizophrenic episode is such a disorganizing experience and recovery so arduous and unpredictable that it would clearly be preferable to prevent its occurrence in the first place. Therefore, the question we will consider here is: Are we far enough along that some effort at preventing schizophrenic episodes is likely to be effective?

Genetic Counseling

Looking at the results of genetic studies, some writers have suggested that a program of genetic counseling could be helpful in preventing schizophrenia. If parents who are or have been schizophrenic could be dissuaded from having children, then the 10 to 16 percent of their offspring likely to become schizophrenic would not be born at all. There are two problems with this approach. First, by far the majority of children of schizophrenics are not likely to become schizophrenic. Furthermore, the evidence is that many of those children who do not become psychotic show signs of unusual creativity (Schulsinger 1976; Karlson 1968).

The second problem with a genetic counseling approach is that fewer than 10 percent of schizophrenic patients have one or more

schizophrenic parents. Therefore, even if *all* schizophrenics rejected *all* child-bearing, the effect on the number of new cases of schizophrenics would be small. Furthermore, many of these children are born before their parents' first schizophrenic break, so that genetic counseling could affect only those offspring born after the parents had been identified as psychotic.

Preventive Interventions of a Psychological Type

Another approach to prevention is less radical. We can attempt to identify the individual who is at risk during childhood and set up a program to minimize the likelihood that subsequent life stress will bring on a schizophrenic break. However laudatory this goal, there are two intermediate requirements for instituting such preventive programming. First, we need a reasonably precise index for identifying the person at risk for subsequent schizophrenia long enough before the period of risk to begin treatment. Second, we need a model detailing what we can do to minimize the likelihood of subsequent schizophrenia.

You will recall that in Chapter 6 we described the high-risk methodology for identifying the individual at risk for schizophrenia. Most high-risk studies are still in progress and we do not yet know whether there is a way to identify, with precision, persons at risk for schizophrenia. Mednick's data on skin-resistance recovery (Mednick and Schulsinger 1968), however, provides preliminary evidence of one measure that experimenters might use to identify those at risk. In fact, such a program is under way on Mauritius, a small independent island nation in the Indian Ocean. Under the auspices of the World Health Organization, Mednick and Schulsinger (1973) administered skin-resistance tests to a broad sample of preschoolers to find children whose response patterns were comparable to those produced by Danish children who broke down in their original study (Mednick et al. 1979a,b). Notice that using these measures involves a major extrapolation of the original study, which included only children of schizophrenics. Whether the skin-resistance response has similar predictive value for a general population sample without schizophrenic parentage remains to be seen.

Once they had found a group of children who showed the abnormal response and a group of matched control children who showed normal skin-resistance patterns, Mednick and Schulsinger established a series of special nursery schools on Mauritius to train high-risk children in various competence skills that would foster personal adaptation to stress. These lessons involved cognitive training to prevent withdrawal into personal interpretations of events, social training to encourage good peer-group relationships, and training to reduce the intensity of emotional reactions to new or demanding situations. As a result of these nursery school experiences, Mednick and Schulsinger reasoned, the children would be less likely to experience subsequent social isolation and overly intense emotional reactions to normal life stress. This study has many years to run before its subjects reach early adulthood (the risk period for schizophrenia), but it is the first major attempt to apply knowledge from a high-risk study to a preventive effort. As more high-risk studies conclude, no doubt we will see other models for preventive intervention.

Summary

1. Several major breakthroughs in the treatment of schizophrenia occurred in the 1950s: (1) a change in emphasis from custodial care to rehabilitation in the hospital setting; (2) intro-duction of halfway houses to prepare patients for reentry into society; and (3) discovery of the major tranquilizers — the phenothiazines, in particular — which help to control schizophrenic behavior.

2. The treatment of schizophrenia is done in two phases. The goal for the first, or acute treatment stage, is planned to reduce disorganizing psychotic symptoms and to reestablish contact with reality. This phase begins with the patient's admission to the hospital. The goal of the second phase of treatment, aftercare, is to help the partially recovered patient continue recovery while residing in the community. Aftercare programs help the patient to deal with the anxiety, depression, and confusion that linger after the major symptoms have abated.

3. The two approaches to the treatment of schizophrenia are the biological and the psychological. Biological treatment consists almost exclusively of drug therapy. The antipsychotic tranquilizers — phenothiazines and butyrophenones — appear to alter dopamine levels in the brain to help reduce symptoms. The effectiveness of the drugs varies from patient to patient, possibly as a function of: (1) the amount that the blood absorbs, (2) the patient's premorbid adjustment, and (3) the patient's attitude toward taking the drug.

4. In aftercare, phenothiazine drug treatment helps to prevent a relapse into psychosis and to protect the patient from a home environment where criticism, hostility, and emotional overinvolvement reduce the patient's chances for complete recovery. Although the drugs control symptoms, they do not help the patient's social adjustment.

5. A variety of psychological approaches to the treatment of schizophrenia are in use. (1) Psychotherapy relies on establishing a trusting relationship between patient and therapist so that the therapist can help the patient develop self-esteem and the capacity to cope with inevitable life stresses. (2) Existential therapy (Laing's treatment model) is based on the theory that the schizophrenic needs to work through the psychotic episode, without drugs or traditional therapy, in order to recover. The communal environment of the Laing model is effective in helping the patient develop a sense of autonomy and learn to interact with others. (3) Behavior therapy is based on a reward-punishment system. Socially appropriate behavior, such as good grooming, is rewarded by tokens or privileges, and inappropriate behavior is punished by fines or loss of privileges. (4) Family therapy focuses on treating the family as a unit during aftercare. This type of therapy attempts to uncover and deal with deep-seated problems within the family so that the patient can cease being the victim of a family pathology. (5) Multimodal approaches comprising a combination of drug maintenance *and* psychological therapy are superior to either one alone. Psychological therapy programs that help the patient deal with reentry into the family unit and the community are generally more successful than the other types.

6. Schizophrenia prevention is just beginning to be explored. Two approaches have been suggested: (1) genetic counseling, and (2) early intervention for high-risk individuals. Genetic counseling is neither realistic nor likely to affect the majority of people who might develop schizophrenia. Training programs for high-risk youngsters are more promising, but are still in the testing stage.

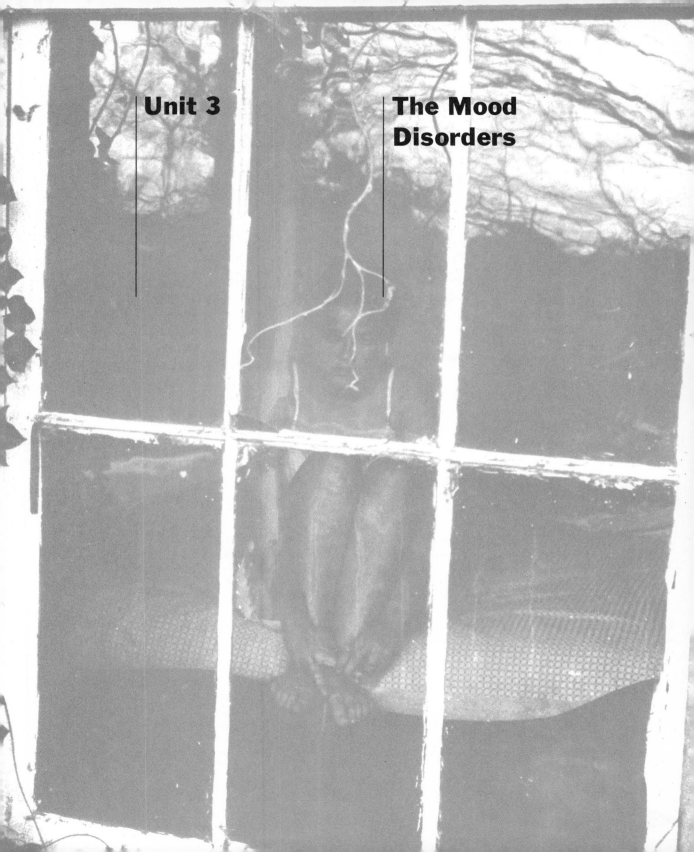

Unit 3

The Mood
Disorders

In this unit we will examine different mood, or *affective,* disorders — how they are identified and diagnosed, how people experience them, and how they can be treated. We will also include a chapter on the phenomenon of suicide, because of the close relationship between suicide and depression.

Of course, the word "mood" has many meanings. Generally, it refers to a pervasive and prolonged emotion that colors our perception of self and the world. Here we shall be interested specifically in the moods of depression and elation.

All of us get depressed and unhappy and can feel temporarily hopeless. We may be discouraged in love or school or work, sleep poorly or lose interest in food for a while, or cry more easily than usual. However painful and disturbing these emotions are, they usually disappear quickly, and most often they represent a direct response to some event. Similarly, we occasionally experience brief periods of intense excitement and happiness, when we feel we could conquer the world. These are normal reactions.

An additional range of feelings extends beyond the experiences of sadness and happiness into the realm of extreme disturbances. Severely depressed patients may require hospitalization and medical treatment and protection from the strong desire to kill themselves. At the opposite extreme are manic disturbances characterized by elation, great energy, irritability, and grandiosity. Some people swing back and forth, like the pendulum on a grandfather clock, between moods of severe depression and extreme mania (see Chapter 9). Research on these apparently dissimilar states has led to the development in recent years of methods of treatment that effectively limit the symptoms so that most individuals who suffer from these severe disorders of mood are able to live relatively normal lives (see Chapter 11).

Before long, modern methods of treating the severe mood disorders should, we hope, visibly affect the suicide rate, because statistics indicate that approximately one person in six with a manic-depressive disorder will commit suicide. More direct community programs of treatment and prevention of suicidal behavior may also help reduce suicides among the general population by helping people to cope with less extreme depressive reactions. We will discuss some of these programs in Chapter 11, too.

I hadn't washed my hair for three weeks.
I hadn't slept for seven nights.
My mother told me I must have slept, it was impossible not to sleep in all that time, but if I slept, it was with my eyes wide open, for I had followed the green, luminous course of the second hand and the minute hand and the hour hand of the bedside clock through their circles and semicircles, every night for seven nights, without missing a second, or a minute, or an hour.
The reason I hadn't washed my clothes or my hair was because it seemed so silly.
I saw the days of the year stretching ahead like a series of bright, white boxes, and separating one box from another was sleep, like a black shade. Only for me, the long perspective of shades that set off one box from the ˙next had suddenly snapped up, and I could see day after day after day glaring ahead of me like a white, broad, infinitely desolate avenue.

It seemed silly to wash one day when I would only have to wash again the next.
It made me tired just to think of it.
I wanted to do everything once and for all and be through with it (Sylvia Plath, *The Bell Jar,* pp. 104–105).

Depression is a word and a condition that everyone is familiar with, but how many of us could define it in a few precise words? Depression is . . . a mood. It is sadness and dejection. It is loss and lack of self-esteem. It is a natural part of life, something that occasionally seems to have some adaptive value, as in times of mourning. Depression may be any or all of these things, and unless the feelings persist more than a month or two, or are severe enough to remarkably impair normal functioning, or lead to a suicide attempt, generally the condition is not psychopathological.

Depression also may be a symptom of a psychopathological disorder. It may be present, for example, in schizophrenia (Chapter 5), alcoholism (Chapter 16), and personality disorders (Chapter 13). But in these disorders it is not a primary symptom, though it may be severe.

Depression also covers a distinct class of disorders belonging to the larger category known as mood disorders. In addition to severe and prolonged feelings of hopelessness, despair, low self-esteem, and a sense of self-blame, guilt, or worthlessness, clinical depression is characterized by psychomotor disturbance and a somatic component that includes a variety of bodily complaints and sleep disturbances. In this chapter, we will examine these components and look at the theories that psychologists and other scientists have put forth to try to explain what makes some people susceptible to severe and recurrent depression, sometimes alternating with periods of extreme euphoria.

Chapter 8  | # The Depressive Disorders

Clinical Description and Diagnosis
Diagnostic Criteria
Interpersonal Aspects of Depression

Incidence of Depression

Causes of Depression
Psychological Theories
Biological Theories

Summary

Clinical Description and Diagnosis

Depression can be a normal reaction to many events and life circumstances. The *normal reactive depression,* as described by Fieve (1975), is "simply a reaction to the vicissitudes and disappointments of day-to-day living . . . usually transitory, oftentimes related to loss or to disappointment or frustration in job, marriage, or social situations." This type of depression generally lifts rapidly in response to changes in the environment or, less dramatically, with the passage of time. It rarely requires psychological treatment. A second normal depressive reaction is the *normal grief reaction* that almost always accompanies a major loss (death of a spouse, child, or parent). The three primary depressive symptoms associated with this experience are depressed or sad mood, disturbed sleep, and frequent crying (Clayton et al. 1968). Also common are difficulty in concentration, loss of interest in people and events, and diminished appetite.

As you see in this statement by a man whose young wife had just died, the emptiness and

Fig. 8.1. This photo shows the sense of loss, loneliness, and despair often associated with an acute grief reaction.

despair of the normal depressive grief reaction can be profound:

How could things go on when the world had come to an end? How could things — how could I — go on in this void? How could one person, not very big, leave an emptiness that was galaxy-wide? Everything — every object — was pervaded by the void. . . . There were thousands of things and memories, each of which must be seen once in that piercingly bleak emptiness. . . . Under the surface of the visible world, there is an echoing hollowness, an aching void (Vanaukin 1977, p. 180).

The author's depression was clearly a response to a specific event. Almost everyone recovers from this normal reaction in a relatively short time (six to eight weeks) and without professional treatment.

Contrasting the normal experience of the widowed with the distorted perspective of extreme psychotic depression should leave no doubt in your mind that there are degrees of depression.

Fig. 8.2. Sorrowful sculpture commissioned by Henry Adams following his wife's suicide. He was incapacitated by grief for a year.

As long as I was able to attain unconsciousness at night and to maintain a fairly soporific state during the day I could just keep the horrors at bay. My whole conscious effort was now directed towards the aim of putting off the moment when I would disappear finally into Hell. I visualized this process as happening quite naturally. Some day, at some moment, the iron control I kept on my terrors would break. I should start shrieking in agony. Naturally the attendants would then shut me up in a side-room, probably in one of the worst wards. After that the process of torturing a human soul in the living flesh would just go on. I should shriek, but so do many lunatics; nobody would do anything for me; they would naturally think my pains were imaginary. But they would be real pains. . . . It did not matter much when I ''died'' in the body. I might spend days, months, or years shrieking in my side-room before they buried me. For me, it would all be the same process of eternal, progressively increasing torture. . . . There I was, shut in my own private universe, as it were, with no contact with real people at all, only with phantasmagoria who could at any moment turn into devils. I and all around me were utterly unreal. There in the reflection lay proof positive. My soul was finally turned into nothingness — except unending pain (Custance 1952, pp. 67–68).

If we apply to depression the continuum introduced in Chapter 1, we get a clearer picture of how severity of moods and symptoms can vary. Figure 8.3 illustrates one way of representing depressive symptoms on a continuum (Goodwin 1977). On the left are the mild symptoms of mood and cognition that are short-lived and do not interfere with normal functioning. The severe (and occasionally psychotic) symptoms appear at the extreme right. As the chart shows, the more severe disturbances often are prolonged, lasting months, infrequently years — and include *endogenous*, or physiological symptoms such as disturbances in sleep, energy, and appetite. Research has also implicated genetic and other biological factors in the etiology of severe, recurrent depression, whereas the mildest forms usually are reactions to discrete life changes. Of course, depression may also be brought on by combined environmental and biological factors, as the diagram shows. In severe depression, therapy generally includes some form of biological treatment such as drugs, although various forms of psychological treatment and multimodal approaches are used to treat forms of depression (see Chapter 11).

Sören Kierkegaard (1813–1855), Danish philosopher and theologian who was subject to severe recurrent depression, described his own symptoms quite simply:

> I do not care for anything. I do not care to ride, for the exercise is too violent. I do not care to walk, walking is too strenuous. I do not care to lie down, for I should either have to remain lying, and I do not care to do that, or I should have to get up again, and I do not care to do that either. . . . I do not care at all.

Fig. 8.3. Depression as a spectrum disorder, ranging from mild to severe reactions. (After Goodwin 1977.)

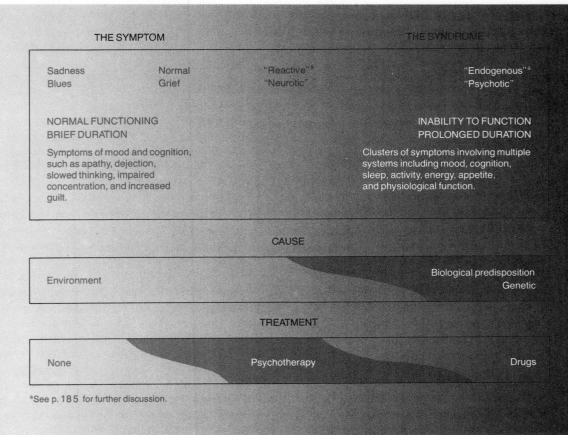

Although Kierkegaard's is a purely personal account, it encapsulates the general description of severe depression in *DSM*-III:

The essential feature of a depressive episode is either depressive mood or a pervasive loss of interest or pleasure. This disturbance is prominent and relatively persistent and associated with other symptoms of the depressive syndrome. These symptoms may include loss of interest or pleasure, sleep disturbance, appetite disturbance, change in weight, psychomotor agitation or retardation, cognitive disturbance, decreased energy, a feeling of worthlessness or guilt, and thoughts of death or suicide.

Specifically, *DSM*-III recognizes these changes in *mood, behavior,* and *cognitive functioning* as symptoms of depression:

Mood: A person with the depressive syndrome may describe his mood as *sad, hopeless, discouraged, down in the dumps,* or some other colloquial variant. Sometimes, however, the mood disturbance may not be expressed as a synonym for depressive mood but rather as a complaint of not caring any more, or a painful *inability to experience pleasure.* A loss of interest or pleasure is probably always present to some degree but sometimes the patient may not complain of this or even be aware of its existence except in retrospect.

Behavior: More typically there is *withdrawal from friends and family,* and *avocations* that used to be a source of pleasure *are neglected.* Early morning awakening is the most characteristic *sleep disturbance,* although initial insomnia, fitful sleep, or hypersomnia (increased sleep) also occur. Less commonly there is increased appetite with weight gain. *Psychomotor agitation* may take the form of pacing, handwringing, inability to sit still, pulling or rubbing of hair, skin, clothing, or other objects, outbursts of complaining or shouting, or talking incessantly. *Psychomotor retardation* may take the form of slowed speech, increased pauses before answering, low or monotonous speech, slowed body movements, or,

when severe, markedly decreased amount of speech or muteness.

Cognitive Functioning: Cognitive disturbance may manifest itself as *inability to concentrate, indecisiveness, slowed thinking,* or complaints of *poor memory.* The decrease in energy level is experienced as sustained tiredness or fatigue even in the absence of physical exertion. The sense of worthlessness varies from mild feelings of inadequacy to completely unrealistic evaluations of one's worth. The smallest task may seem difficult or impossible. Minor failings may be exaggerated and the environment searched for cues confirming a negative self-evaluation. *Guilt* may be expressed as an excessive reaction to either current or past failings or as a delusional conviction of sinfulness or responsibility for some untoward or tragic event. *Thoughts of death or suicide* may involve fears of dying, the belief that the patient or others would be better off if he were dead, or suicidal desires or plans. Often the symptoms are worse when the patient wakes up but improve slightly as the day progresses.

When the disturbance is mild, temporary improvement usually follows a positive change in the environment. But when it is severe, the syndrome generally is unrelentingly persistent despite environmental change.

Another general feature of major depressive disorders is that they are *recurrent.* Goodwin (1977) and Grof and colleagues (1973) write that nearly all patients who experience a severe depressive episode will undergo another sometime in their lives. At one time the estimate was that only one-half to two-thirds of such patients would suffer another serious depression, but more accurate histories and more extensive follow-up procedures make current figures more reliable. The *duration* of a severe depression varies considerably from individual to individual (although, for an individual with a recurrent disorder, the duration is relatively constant), but an episode generally lasts less than six months (Goodwin 1977).

Diagnostic Criteria

Current diagnostic systems emphasize a constellation of relatively clear signs and symptoms, together with a patient's history and current mental status, rather than listing assumed causes of clinical depression. Thus, *DSM*-III systematizes the general description of depression that appeared in earlier research, in order to make a diagnosis as clear-cut as possible. Table 8.1 summarizes the *DSM*-III diagnostic criteria for a major depressive disorder.

One of the more recent and the best-supported classification schemes for the mood disorders is the *unipolar-bipolar distinction. Unipolar* depression is a mood disorder characterized by periods of depression only. *Bipolar* depression has episodes of both depression and *mania,* which is characterized by extreme euphoria, or irritability and paranoia, and excessive mental and physical activity (see Chapter 9), or *hypomania,* a milder form of mania. Cases of unipolar mania, with no history of depression, are very rare. Much documentary evidence demonstrates that significant genetic, biochemical, psychosocial, and biological differences exist between patients having unipolar depression and those suffering from bipolar illness.

A patient's past and current functioning are primary in assessing any type of depression. To put together a thorough history, diagnosticians must assess: (1) prior evidence of depressive or manic episodes; (2) any stressful events that might have precipitated the episodes; (3) the patient's premorbid personality (was he "relatively normal," "maladjusted," or "depression prone?"), and (4) incidence of affective disorders, suicide, alcoholism, or psychiatric illness in the patient's family. An evaluation of

Poetry of Depression

The author of this poem was severely depressed when he wrote it. He palpably describes the invisible wall between his own colorless, frightened, flat, and depressed existence and the other, ineffably unattainable world of normal life.

A STUDY IN ORGANIC CONTRAST

They say the grass is tall
  on the other side of the river.
It is told that the sky is bluer
  that the mountains are made of
    whipping cream.
Rainbows are the face of a young maiden.
God created this half of the planet
for those who *cannot* see the golden grain
. . . or *will* not drink of the intoxicating waters.
Sheep run plentiful, the area is teeming —
That side of the river abounds in fish.
Here we live in a perpetual state of starvation,
There are no brightly colored butterflies here.
Our skies are black, theirs are blue-azure.

We can see them making love and music.
Our vocal chords are gone and so are our
  genitals. There is even an invisible
  barrier 'tween us.
We can hear them talking away endlessly
While we tearfully listen.
They smile, laugh and frolic with others
  over fields of dandelions and daisies.
We can only scowl at each other and throw
  stones.
The temperature over there is temperate,
  tropically so.
Our heat is scorching, with winds icy and
  snowy nights beyond toleration.
Once we, as a group, walked to the river's
  middle
They did the same
We reached out hands to touch . . .
Sparks arose from all hands.
Bolts of lightning were followed by booming
  thunder
All leapt back, terrified.
Nothing has ever changed.

[handwritten marginalia: Interpersonal Aspects of Depression — strongly influenced by features + consequences / difficulties with relationships are universally characteristic with depressed people — impaired social functioning is not usual — disruptive to interpersonal relationships / may persist even when depressive symptoms disappear with family + strangers]

current functioning completes the picture. Generally, this part of a patient's history records the importance of the depressive affect in the pattern of symptoms and describes any key somatic symptoms such as disturbed sleep, signs of psychosis, overall severity of the episode, and the other clinical features listed in Table 8.1 (Katz and Hirschfeld 1978).

As you saw in Chapter 3, diagnosticians commonly use a standard psychological inventory during the evaluation. Many psychological tests, including the Minnesota Multiphasic Personality Inventory (MMPI), the Rorschach, and the Thematic Apperception Test (TAT), measure depression. The Beck Depression Inventory and the Hamilton Depression Scale, however, are the tests that psychiatrists and psychologists use most frequently in clinical research on mood disorders. Originally both were intended for the clinician's use, but now pa-

Table 8.1. *DSM*-III criteria for a major depressive disorder

---

A. *Mood:* Dysphoria
B. *Behavioral changes* (at least 5):
   (1) anorexia or weight change (usually loss)
   (2) sleep disorder: initial insomnia, early morning awakening, or hypersomnia
   (3) loss of energy, fatigability
   (4) psychomotor agitation or retardation
   (5) loss of interest in usual activities (such as sex or work)
   (6) self-reproach or guilt
   (7) decreased concentration
   (8) recurrent thoughts of death or suicide
C. *Severity:* Sought help from someone during the dysphoric period or had impaired functioning socially (family, work, home).
D. *Duration:* At least 2–4 weeks.
E. *Exclusionary:* Presence of other preexisting psychiatric illness or life-threatening medical illness (within past year).

Source: Diagnostic and Statistics Manual, III, 1978.

tients frequently complete the Beck inventory themselves. Table 8.2 lists a few items from the Beck and Hamilton inventories; both scales cover psychopathological symptoms fairly extensively.

Interpersonal Aspects of Depression

It is so hard to explain how at different times you can do the same things, see the same people, go to the same places, and yet everything is so totally different. When I am my normal self I feel active, alive, able to enjoy things and to participate easily with other people; I eagerly seek them out. There is no question but that life and these experiences have great meaning to me. But when I get depressed it seems as though my friends require much more from me than I can ever possibly give, I seem a drain and a burden on them; the guilt and resentment is overwhelming. Everything I see, say, or do seems extraordinarily flat and pointless; there is no color, there is no point to anything. Things drag on and on, interminably. I am exhausted, dead inside. I want to sleep, to escape somehow, but there is always the thought that if I really could sleep, I must always and again awake to the dullness and apathy of it all. I doubt, completely, my ability to do anything well; it seems as though my mind has slowed down and burned out to the point of being virtually useless. The wretched convoluted thing works only well enough to torment me with a dreary litany of my inadequacies and shortcomings in character, and to haunt me with the total, the desperate hopelessness of it all. What is the point in going on like this; it is crazy. *I* am crazy, I say to myself. Others say "It's only temporary, it will pass, you will get over it," but of course they haven't any idea how I feel although they are certain they do. If I can't feel, move, think, or care then what on earth is the point?

That quotation comes from a depressed patient, and it clearly illustrates that interpersonal perceptions are strongly influenced by the features, severity, and consequences of depres-

Table 8.2. Sample items from the Beck and Hamilton Measures of Depression

THE BECK DEPRESSION INVENTORY

   21 categories of symptoms and attitudes related to depression ranging in severity from 0 (neutral) to 3 (maximum severity).

(0) I am not particularly discouraged about the future.
(1) I feel discouraged about the future.
(2) I feel I have nothing to look forward to.
(3) I feel that the future is hopeless and that things cannot improve.

(0) I don't have any thoughts of killing myself.
(1) I have thoughts of killing myself, but I would not carry them out.
(2) I would like to kill myself.
(3) I would kill myself if I had the chance.

THE HAMILTON DEPRESSION SCALE

   21 variables (including depression, guilt, suicidality, psychomotor activity, concentration, and sleep difficulties) are rated on a scale by either a psychiatrist or a psychologist.

Depressed mood (Sadness, hopeless, helpless, worthless)

0 Absent

1 These feeling states indicated only on questioning.

2 These feeling states spontaneously reported verbally.

3 Communicates feeling states nonverbally — i.e., through facial expression, posture, voice, and tendency to weep.

4 Patient reports VIRTUALLY ONLY these feeling states in his spontaneous verbal and non-verbal communication.

Work and activities

0 No difficulty

1 Thoughts and feelings of incapacity; fatigue or weakness related to activities, work or hobbies.

2 Loss of interest in activity, hobbies or work — either directly reported by patient, or indirect in listlessness, indecision, and vacillation *(feels he has to push self to work or activities).*

3 Decrease in actual time spent in activities or decrease in productivity. In hospital include in this category if patient does not spend at least three hours a day in activities *(hospital job or hobbies)* exclusive of ward chores.

4 Stopped working because of present illness. In hospital include in this category if patient engages in no activities except ward chores, or if patient fails to perform ward chores unassisted.

Top: From the Beck Depression Inventory. Copyright © 1978 by Aaron T. Beck, M.D. Reprinted by permission. *Bottom:* From Hamilton 1960. Reprinted by permission of the British Medical Association.

sion. Although impaired social functioning is usually not considered a definitive symptom of depression, reported or observed difficulties in relationships with other people are almost universally characteristic of depressed individuals. And much recent evidence tells us that depression is disruptive to interpersonal relationships. An extensive longitudinal study of mildly depressed women disclosed that impairment in social adjustment persisted even after depressive symptoms had diminished (Paykel and Weissman 1973; Bothwell and Weissman 1977). The most enduring interpersonal problems for those women were marital problems and general interpersonal friction. Similarly, study of unipolar and bipolar patients of both sexes disclosed that patients perceived that their depression was highly disruptive to their relation-

Eugène Mihaeso.

Fig. 8.4. Ad for antidepressant medication, entitled ''I'm just a shadow of what I used to be,'' stresses the long cold shadows and lack of pleasure in the depressive experience.

ships with spouses and children (Jamison et al. 1979). Apart from having a negative effect on relations with close family members, depression impairs interaction with relative strangers. Lewinsohn and coworkers have shown that depressed persons differ significantly from psychiatric and nonpsychiatric controls on a variety of interactional measures of nonverbal behavior and social skill, as well as self-reported discomfort in social situations (Youngren and Lewinsohn 1978).

The symptom patterns of depression shed some light on the possible causes of the interpersonal difficulties experienced by depressed persons. Depressed men and women are frequently very irritable and report diminished enjoyment of formerly gratifying activities, including relationships, and may withdraw from interpersonal contact. Many depressed persons display exaggerated dependency on others that is frequently frustrating for those from whom

they seek support, especially when their supportive efforts fail to relieve the despondency. Moreover, they may be especially sensitive to perceived rejection or criticism, no matter how slight it actually is; in fact they may invent such slights. The marked guilt and feelings of worthlessness and self-blame for social encounters they perceive in a negative way may intensify the depressive symptoms. All these behaviors are common in depression, and they can thwart the best intentions of friends and family members.

On top of the interpersonal difficulties that may arise directly from the sense of frustration that the depressed person may engender and experience in close relationships, some evidence in recent research suggests that, in general, depression elicits negative reactions in others. Coyne (1976) and Hammen and Peters (1978) found that interactions with depressed persons cause others to feel depressed. People

[Handwritten margin notes:]
Study HAMMEN PETER
- people tend to reject depressed people
- undesirable + potential friends or lovers.
+ perceived ↓ function poorly in various social roles
:. -ve judgement by others

MEN vs Women
- more men suffer rejection
- depressed people viewed as less masculine + more feminine than nondepressed
- may help to explain the more frequent diagnosis of depression in women than in men

Earlier Concepts of Depression

In modern clinical practice and research, the Research Diagnostic Criteria, which *DSM*-III incorporates, have virtually replaced older classification systems. But two of the earlier schemes, neurotic/psychotic depression and endogenous/reactive depression, made large contributions to research on mood disorders and are still used by some clinical researchers.

Neurotic/Psychotic Depression

Clinicians have long recognized that some depressions are more severe than others in reduced social competence, disorganized thought and behavior, and suicidal risk. Traditionally the distinction between *neurotic* and *psychotic* disorders focused on severity, impaired ability to distinguish between reality and nonreality, and disrupted day-to-day functioning. By these criteria, neurotic depressions comprise milder disorders characterized by anxiety, heightened reactivity to environmental stimuli, and a preexisting neurotic personality. Psychotic depressions are much more severe disorders with a different pattern of symptoms, which may include psychomotor retardation, an early morning-awakening pattern of sleep, delusions, and worsening of symptoms in the morning. The distinguishing feature of the psychotic depression is that the patient's thought patterns, behaviors, and delusional beliefs demonstrate a major distortion of reality. An individual may believe that he will be punished for past "crimes" for which no objective evidence exists. Or he may feel God has chosen him to suffer for all the sins of mankind. Retarded depressive patients may be so disabled that they withdraw entirely from the world and cease to move, to eat, or to eliminate waste. The concept of psychotic depression is still meaningful, but among the large samples of depressed patients surveyed in one study (Klerman 1971), fewer than 15 percent demonstrated manifestly psychotic features.

For the neurotic depressive patient, the depth of despair can be as great as in the psychotic reactions, but beliefs about the self do not diverge from reality. Nor is the functional inefficiency as marked in this disorder as in psychotic depression. Neurotic depressives may not perform their social roles well, but they do not show the total disruption in personal relationships and work responsibilities that the psychotic patient does.

Although the neurotic/psychotic distinction does provide a means for assessing the severity of depressive disorders and predicting response to treatment interventions (see Chapter 11), its usefulness is limited because the line between neurotic and psychotic depression is often unclear and somewhat arbitrary. It is not much help in determining the causes of a depressive episode or in judging recurrences.

Endogenous/Reactive Depressions

Late in the nineteenth century and early in the twentieth, many psychiatrists noticed that severe, psychotic depressions appeared in some patients without any noticeable precipitating life events. They named these depressions *endogenous,* meaning that they arose from factors within the patient. This concept of endogenous depression incorporated assumptions about its causes: they are genetic, constitutional, or metabolic. Furthermore, they said that the *form* (symptoms and causes) of an endogenous depression is different from and opposite to a *reactive,* or neurotic, depression, which is simply an exaggeration of the normal response of life events. For a psychologically vulnerable person, the loss of a loved one or of a job, a setback in financial status, or some other traumatic disruption might be the immediate cause of neurotic depression.

The endogenous/reactive distinction is popular (it is generally thought of as an either-or distinction), but clinicians have battled over its validity. Just what precipitating events have to do with depression remains uncertain, and the literature gives no clear-cut evidence that the separation is legitimate. Often it is difficult to tell whether depression caused an event to happen (for example, divorce or job loss), or resulted from it.

commonly report that depression is ''contagious,'' or that a friend's low mood ''brings me down,'' and indeed, these claims seem to hold some truth, although the reason for this phenomenon is not clear.

In a similar vein, some studies suggest that people tend to reject depressed individuals. Two experiments by Hammen and Peters (1977, 1978) revealed that depressed people are seen as undesirable potential friends or lovers, and are perceived to function poorly in various social roles. Depressed individuals elicited more rejection than did people with anxiety or unemotional, detached reactions to stress, and so it seems that in addition to emotional dysfunction something unique about depression results in negative judgments by others. Moreover, depressed men tended to suffer rejection more often than women, especially *by* women, and on the whole, depressed persons were viewed as less masculine and more feminine than nondepressed people — a result that may help to explain the relatively more frequent diagnosis of depression in women than men (see documentation of sex differences in Weissman and Klerman 1977).

The depressed person, then, not only experiences a paralyzing sense of futility, helplessness, and self-depreciation, but also probably faces one negative social encounter after another. It seems clear that, especially for individuals with recurrent experiences of depression, the cycle of upset and frustration in interpersonal situations may become self-perpetuating. From this perspective, it seems necessary to develop treatment programs that relieve the interpersonal manifestations and consequences of depression as well as mood and the cognitive and somatic symptoms of depression (see Chapter 11).

Depression in Leaders: Robert E. Lee

Robert E. Lee, commander-in-chief of the Confederate Army, was a complex, charismatic man and singular leader who suffered from periods of deep depression throughout his life. According to biographer Thomas Connelly (1977):

He seemed to believe that death would be a welcome release from the world. . . . Sometimes Lee's comments on the pleasant release of death revealed an almost suicidal tendency. After Gettysburg, when he brooded over the Confederate casualties, he remarked, ''My only consolation is that they are happier and we that are left are to be pitied.'' Or perhaps it was better said by Lee when he observed the encircling Federal lines shortly before the surrender at Appomattox. Realizing that he was defeated, he remarked, ''How easily I could be rid of this, and be at rest. I have only to ride along the line and all will be over!''

Lee's frequent mention of the release that death would provide revealed another element of his personality. Early biographers always lauded his serenity and self-possession. Actually Lee's mood of depression became a central part of his behavior. . . . He was convinced that his star had been ill-destined (p. 192).

Ironically, Lee's primary nonmilitary counterpart in the North, Abraham Lincoln, also suffered from severe, recurrent depressions. It is impossible to know how, or if, history would have been significantly different had Lee and Lincoln (and many other leaders, including Winston Churchill) not experienced such despair. Depression may have marred their judgment. On the other hand, perhaps it added a unique sensitivity and perspective to their use of power. Did they have remarkable leadership ability, in part, *because* of their mood swings, *in spite* of them, or totally *independently* of them? The possibilities are fascinating to contemplate.

Incidence of Depression

It is difficult to know accurately how many people suffer from depression because depressive disorders have so many types and degrees of severity. A recent study (Manheimer, cited in Daly 1978) estimates that during a given year, approximately 15 percent of the adult American population between ages eighteen and seventy-five manifest depressive symptoms. Research consistently indicates that one man in twenty and one woman in ten experience depression at some time. The reasons for the markedly higher rates of depression among women are not yet fully understood, and hypothetical explanations are generally complex. Weissman and Klerman (1977) reviewed the evidence gathered during the last forty years and drew several major conclusions:

1. International studies of diagnosed and treated depressed patients and community surveys that include both treated and untreated "cases" are consistent in their findings: women have a higher rate of depression in all countries and over all time periods.
2. There is no difference between the sexes in frequency of depressive symptoms following bereavement.
3. More women than men seek treatment for depression from all segments of the general health care system (use of outpatient facilities, visits to physicians, use of psychotropic medications, and so on).
4. Alcohol use and abuse (which mental health professionals believe are often equivalents to depression) are far more common in men.
5. No consistent relationship between hormone levels and depression has been found. "There is good evidence that premenstrual tension and use of oral contraceptives have an effect to increase rates, but these effects are probably of small magnitude. There is excellent evidence that the postpartum (post

childbirth) period does induce an increase in depression. Contrary to widely held views, there is good evidence that the menopause has no effect to increase rates of depression."
6. "As behaviors become more similar between the sexes, females may begin to employ modes of coping with stress that are similar to men. There are some indications that this may be occurring in that the female rates of alcoholism, suicide and crime (predominantly male behaviors) have begun to rise. Alternatively, the sex ratios for depression could become equal because of an increase of depression among men due to the stress produced by the change in the roles of women and by the uncertainty of the male role."

Causes of Depression

Currently, biological research on the causes of depression is moving somewhat more quickly than psychological research. As in schizophrenia, biological work has been helped along by rapid advances in brain neurochemistry. Research on the psychological causes of depression has proceeded more slowly, not only because of the ethical, moral, legal, and pragmatic restrictions on psychological experimentation, but also because we lack a universally accepted, specific system of classification.

Many theorists have attempted to relate psychological processes to the onset and maintenance of depression. Unfortunately, most have not specified the type of depression — unipolar or bipolar, among others — which their theories purport to explain. Consequently, the research literature is confused and somewhat contradictory, as one scientist bases claims for theory on research with a severely depressed patient population, and another attempts to apply the same theory to a group of mildly depressed undergraduate students. No wonder it is often difficult to collate the results of different studies. Future studies on the psychology of depression will have to attend to these diagnostic issues before anyone can propose and test meaningful hypotheses. In the meantime, keep in mind that the evidence for and against any of these theories is inconclusive.

First we will examine the psychological theories. Then we will look at the accumulating evidence implicating biological factors in clinical depression.

Psychological Theories

The major psychological theories of depression are: (1) psychoanalytic, or Freudian, (2) personality, (3) behavioral, and (4) cognitive.

PSYCHOANALYTIC THEORIES

Depression is a normal emotional response to a loss, and it is perhaps natural to theorize that all depressions, whether normal or pathological in intensity and duration, represent reactions to actual or theoretical losses of significant persons, objects, or status. Freud hypothesized that the difference between healthy mourning and pathological depression following loss lies in the prior emotional relationship to the lost person or object. If the relationship is basically positive and uncomplicated, then an individual will mourn the loss and ultimately adjust to it. If the relationship is ambivalent, with feelings of both hostility and emotional dependency, then a pathological depression is more likely. Faced with actual loss by death or threatened loss by separation or divorce, the depressed patient presumably experiences intense hostility toward the lost object, and this feeling gives rise to anger. By a complex intrapsychic mechanism, anger toward another is turned back against the self. The self-recriminations and guilt that characterize the depressed patient Freud construed as

hostility directed inward. He further speculated that traumatic experiences in early infancy create hypersensitivity to experiences of loss in the adult years. His theory originally purported that an ambivalent relationship with one's mother in the earliest feeding experiences preceded this combination of intense dependency and inhibited anger.

Generally, few data bear specifically on the relationship between early mother-infant relationships and adult depression. But many researchers have focused on a slightly different version of this hypothesis: that depressed patients may have experienced a greater-than-average number of losses of significant others in early life and developed hypersensitivity to object loss (Heinicke 1973). Levi et al. (1966) found that suicidal depressed patients reported a higher frequency of both recent and early separations than did a control group. Their data suggest that childhood separation may sensitize depression-prone individuals to adult experiences of loss, although other interpretations are certainly possible. Many theorists cite early death of a parent as a correlate of subsequent depression in children, but when parental deaths were due to suicide, an alternative explanation of the same finding is that genetic factors contributed to the offspring's disturbance.

Freud's original theory of depression has exerted a very significant and continuing influence upon clinicians and theorists. But it has been difficult to verify his hypotheses with scientific evidence. Part of the problem may be that the theory is correct for some milder forms of depression and totally inappropriate for others. Evidence on loss experiences must also necessarily be mostly retrospective. Nevertheless, some research findings appear to support Freud's interpretation of the significance of loss experiences as a risk factor in depression. Weissman and Paykel (1974) compared the life events reported by a sample of depressed

[handwritten annotations in top margin:]
PERSONALITY THEORY — depressives share maladaptive personality — excessive emotional dependency — are predisposed to have a greater than normal need for love + approval from others — whereby derive secondary qualities — envy, fear of competition — low self-esteem — lack of ability to deal with interpersonal nuances — related to FREUD's separation Hypothesis — bipolar manic-depressive — between periods of illness relatively normal + display somewhat extraverted personality pattern — vs Freud — only a coverup — depression is the subsequential loss + the reinforcers. Behavior SKINNER — response to interruption of established patterns of behavior that were previously reinforced by social environment

women, who were predominantly mildly to moderately depressed, with those of a normal control sample for the period immediately preceding onset of depression. The depressives reported more stressful life experiences than the control group did. Particularly common among the depressed women were loss experiences, broadly defined as separations, divorces, loss of status, and economic reversals. A significant methodological problem in this kind of research stems from the difficulty of ascertaining whether a stress such as divorce causes the depression or is, in fact, a result of it.

The second part of Freud's theory implies that potential depressives have great difficulty directing their anger outward at the source of their frustration — the lost person or object. Assessments of depressive women by Weissman and Paykel (1974) revealed that they were often overtly hostile to family members and other intimates, but less likely to express hostility toward therapists or professional interviewers. Perhaps, then, clinicians must consider the condition of hostility as well as its target in evaluating depressed patients.

Overall, the portion of Freud's theory that emphasizes loss experiences has received greater support than another aspect, which emphasizes inhibited aggression as an explanation for depression. It is possible that Freud was correct in attributing problems of aggression to the potential depressive, but less accurate in assuming that suppressing aggression leads to depressive reactions. Rather, the depressive may lack effective patterns of self-assertion that would permit him to channel aggressive impulses.

PERSONALITY THEORY

Personality theory suggests that individuals prone to develop clinical depression share maladaptive personality characteristics. The attribute cited most frequently in the psychological literature on depression is excessive emotional

dependency (Chodoff 1974). Predepressive personalities are thought to have a greater-than-normal need for love and approval from others. Secondary qualities believed to derive from excessive dependency are excessive envy, fear of competition, low self-esteem, and lack of interest in or ability to deal with interpersonal nuances. This hypothesis has arisen primarily from intensive psychoanalytic studies of clinical patients, but has not been validated by systematic studies using a large number of patients or control groups. Clearly, such a hypothesis relates well in a theoretical sense to Freud's separation hypothesis, because intense emotional dependency can be a major consequence of early separation experiences. Of course, dependency can be a symptom, as well as a cause, of depression.

The literature on bipolar manic-depressives consistently suggests that between periods of illness, these patients display relatively normal and somewhat extraverted personality patterns. Freudian theorists, however, question this judgment (Chodoff 1974) and suggest that although these patients may appear normal on the surface, they continue to have deep-seated problems of emotional dependency derived from earliest parent-child experiences, but manage to conceal them between episodes. This is an interesting hypothesis, but it is difficult to test because there have been no attempts to identify *potential* manic-depressives and study their early life experiences. To determine its validity, we need high-risk studies of depressive and manic-depressive individuals like current research with preschizophrenics (see Chapter 6).

BEHAVIORAL THEORIES

Behavioral theories of depression conceptualize depression as the result of a substantial loss of positive reinforcement. According to Skinner (1953), depression is a response to interruption of established patterns of behavior that were previously reinforced by the social environment. On the other hand, Ferster (1966) describes depressed persons as people who engage in fewer behaviors likely to evoke positive reinforcement. He also sees them as basically *passive* in their activities, that is, unable to act directly on their environments.

Lewinsohn (1974) believes that depressed behaviors themselves elicit positive reinforcement in the form of concern, interest, and kindness shown by others, although, as we mentioned earlier, several studies (Coyne 1976; Hammen and Peters 1978) indicate that, in fact, depressed people elicit many negative responses from those with whom they interact. Lewinsohn and his colleagues also postulate that a lack of social skills is crucial in development of depressive behavior (see Figure 8.5). Poor social skills may be important in some kinds of depression, but their role in the severe depressive disorders is unclear. Research indicates that the inability to socialize is a *state-dependent* phenomenon. In other words, appropriate social behaviors appear to reemerge as the depression clears. Likewise, studies of bipolar and unipolar patients conducted when the patients are not depressed do not show significant differences in social skills between normal persons and these groups, but when they are depressed they elicit less positive reinforcement from others, show less social ease, and engage in fewer behaviors likely to result in positive experiences (Lewinsohn 1975). Again, whether these changes in behavior and reinforcement schedules cause depression or merely reflect it is unclear.

One very important aspect of depression is a sense of helplessness, the belief that no one can or will do anything to alleviate the fundamental problem. A person who at one time ex-

Fig. 8.5. Schematic representation of Lewinsohn's theory of depressive behavior, which hypothesizes a feedback loop mechanism of depression. When depressed, individuals elicit less positive reinforcement from others, show less social ease, and engage in fewer behaviors likely to result in positive experiences. (After Lewinsohn and Shaffer 1971.)

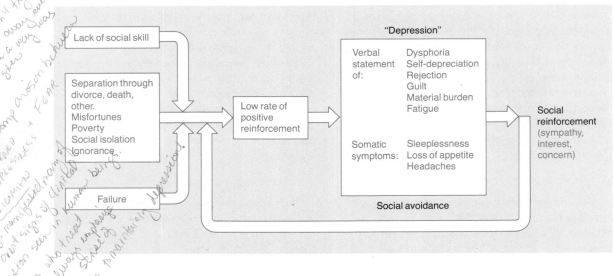

[handwritten annotations in top margin: "COGNITIVE THEORY — a way of perceiving oneself and others is the core feature of depression"; "BECK — disturbance in thinking (distortion) leads to mood (depression) or distorted cognitive self"]

perienced this feeling and found it extremely distressing may have expended considerable energy to avoid a recurrence of the feeling (Schmale 1973). In the face of a loss experience, however, the established defensive mechanisms may break down and the individual will reexperience the sense of helplessness. If he has never learned to cope effectively with this emotional state, he may suffer a depressive reaction. Seligman (1974) calls this reaction *learned helplessness* and suggests that it grows out of experiences in which the individual does not have control over traumatic occurrences.

Trying to substantiate the learned helplessness model, Seligman designed a research program to compare two groups of dogs that received traumatic shocks. Researchers trained one, the *escape group,* to press a panel with their noses whenever the unavoidable shock occurred so that the shock would end. Thus, they were not helpless in dealing with the unpleasant experience. The other experimental group, a *helplessness group,* experienced the same experimental situation, except that they could not do anything to terminate the shock. Twenty-four hours after this training experience, both groups were placed in a shuttle-box together with a control group of dogs that had not been exposed to any shocks prior to this part of the experiment. It was possible for all three groups to avoid electric shock by running into another section of the box. The escape group and the control group learned this skill very readily and ultimately were able to leave the shock box before the shock occurred. The helplessness group was very slow to learn in the new situation, and six of eight animals in the group never learned to escape the shock. Seligman concluded that the animals that had been exposed to unavoidable shock the day before had learned they were helpless to avoid painful shock and therefore did not try to escape it in the new situation.

Support for the comparison between learned helplessness and depression comes from two sources. First, Seligman's research team observed that the "helpless" dogs appeared to be depressed; that is, they manifested many of the overt signs of clinical depression seen in human beings (weight loss and undereating, lack of activity, decreased aggressiveness, lack of energy). Second, clinicians who treat depressed patients have repeatedly emphasized how important a sense of helplessness is in maintaining depressed thinking, affect, and behavior.

The learned helplessness model provides a useful approach to the study of what causes depression. Both the model's specificity for depression and its generalizability to other situations typically associated with depression are questioned, however. It is unclear whether learned helplessness is specific to depression or represents a general precondition for other forms of psychopathology as well. Also, Seligman's animal research emphasizes the ability to control *aversive,* or unpleasant, events, whereas for human beings a key factor in depression seems to be control (or lack of control) over *positive,* pleasurable events. Finally, it is unclear what type of depression — if any — the learned helplessness model best explains.

COGNITIVE THEORY

Scientific data that would conclusively identify one or two factors as psychological causes of depression are so scarce that, as we'd expect, what one theory calls a cause, another insists is a secondary effect, and vice versa. The theories we have examined generally purport to explain how a depressed mood leads to a negative way of thinking that, in turn, perpetuates the depressed state. Cognitive theorists, on the other hand, contend that a negative *cognitive set,* or way of perceiving oneself and others, is the core feature of depression. Beck (1967a, 1970) postulates that a disturbance in thinking leads to a disturbance in mood (specifically, depression). Individuals prone to depression, he says, tend to have a deprecatory and pessimistic attitude about themselves and, consequently, toward other people and events. During times of stress their cognitive sets become distorted and give way to the typical thinking patterns associated with depression — including an unrealistic sense of duty and responsibility, suicidal ideation, severe self-blame, and indecision. Beck and other cognitive theorists have defined several types of cognitive distor-

Primate Models of Depression

Most studies of human experiences of loss have been retrospective. Recently, programs of research with primates have been devised which attempt to develop animal models of depression. They are meant to study experimentally controlled loss experiences, and the majority (McKinney et al. 1977; Kaufman 1973) have concentrated on the immediate effects of separation from mother figures during infancy. Consistently, these researchers have found a pattern of reaction very similar to the one reported by psychiatrists John Bowlby (1969) and Renée Spitz (1965) in their studies of human infants' reaction to maternal separation. During the first stage of this reaction, the animals show great agitation and protest. Human beings as well as some other primates go through this so-called *protest stage,* which lasts for a relatively short time (one or two days). During the subsequent phase, *despair,* the animal's behavior is analogous in many ways to symptoms of clinical depression. Withdrawal, poor appetite, and a "sad" facial expression are common among "despairing" primates.

Research with these animal models of depression dovetails with other investigations into biological, pharmacological, and environmental processes in the treatment of depression. Despite the value of animal models, however, animal depressions lift relatively soon once the animal has been returned to either a mother figure or to a cage with peers. Also, the model does not hold for all species of primates, as Kaufman (1973) has demonstrated. He suggests that bonnet monkeys, one species that does not show such profound depressive reaction, may form less intense attachments to specific mother figures because of group parenting practices in that species.

Although these animal studies correspond closely to clinical observations of infants' reactions to separation, they do not demonstrate that loss during early life has a durable sensitizing effect influencing adult reactions to loss. On the same issue, one study carried out by Harlow's primate research group at the University of Wisconsin (Young et al. 1973) contrasted two groups of rhesus monkeys. One group had been separated from parents and peers at forty-five days of age. The other had not had significant separation experiences in early childhood. The separation, which lasted thirty days, was particularly traumatic because the monkeys were confined in a small vertical chamber with no opportunity for visual contact with other animals, or any other kind of involvement. (It is possible that this condition caused stress to be a major component in the monkeys' reactions to the experimental situation. And it is likely that their confinement inhibited normal developmental acquisition of social behavior.)

The researchers studied the two groups of animals again at approximately two years of age, during a four-week baseline period when they were separated from other monkeys for twenty-three hours a day and reunited with them for one hour. The resulting data are particularly dramatic, indicating that many behaviors rarely, if ever, occurred in the control sample during periods of separation or reunion, and were unique to the previously separated and distressed monkeys. Thus, the prior experience of separation did appear to leave these monkeys vulnerable to

tion. Chief among them are overgeneralization, selective abstraction, and inexact labeling.

OVERGENERALIZATION. An individual with a tendency to overgeneralize draws an unjustifiably general or illogical conclusion from a sin-

gle or very limited experience. Beck (1967a) gives this example:

A patient reported the following sequence of events occurring within a period of half an hour: His wife was upset because the children were slow

subsequent separation stress. Nevertheless, because of their early experience, which involved a very stressful period of social confinement and isolation in addition to separation, it is not clear whether this study reveals a relationship between early life stress and vulnerability to separation or a specific early separation and later problems in social adjustment. Further research ob-

viously is needed. A longitudinal study of the early separation monkeys, for example, would reveal what happens to them as they mature and reproduce. Perhaps it would also disclose whether the early effects are reversible after time and subsequent socializing and, if so, would give us some data to use in designing psychological treatment programs for depressed humans.

Box 8.4. Behaviors (huddling, self-clasping) associated with despair in rhesus monkeys. A monkey exhibiting despair in its severest form huddles and is inactive over long time periods even to the exclusion of eating or drinking.

[handwritten margin notes: "Biological Theories", "NEUROLOGICAL (CHEMICAL) EXPLANATIONS — once the transmission between the presynaptic + postsynaptic neuron has occurred much of the neurotransmitter is reabsorbed into the presynaptic neuron", "Breakthrough by accident — use of RESERPINE came with side effects of depression — depletes nerve endings of several important neurotransmitter substances.", "for lowering high blood pressure", "some returns to storage vesicles + the rest is metabolized by another enzyme (MAO.)", "enzyme reabsorption + breakdown of neurotransmitter substances are important to mood disorders."]

in getting dressed. He thought, "I'm a poor father because the children are not better disciplined." He then noticed a leaky faucet, and thought that this showed he was also a poor husband. While driving to work, he thought, "I must be a poor driver or other cars would not be passing me." As he arrived at work, he noticed some other personnel had already arrived. He thought, "I can't be very dedicated or I would have come earlier." When he noticed folders and papers piled up on his desk, he concluded, "I'm a poor organizer because I have so much work to do."

SELECTIVE ABSTRACTION. Sometimes depressed individuals will focus on a detail, out of context, and ignore other important features of a situation. A student reads a letter of recommendation written by her professor and notices the sentence, "Caroline needs to be more disciplined in her study habits." Caroline becomes preoccupied and depressed and obsesses over this one criticism. Meanwhile, she ignores the rest of the letter, which is highly flattering and extremely positive.

INEXACT LABELING. Some individuals overreact to a situation by mislabeling it, and then respond to the label, not to the event itself. Another example from Beck (1967a) illustrates this type of cognitive distortion:

> A man reported during his therapy hour that he was very upset because he had been "clobbered" by his superior. On further reflection, he realized that he had magnified the incident and that a more adequate description was that his supervisor "corrected an error" he had made. After reevaluating the event, he felt better. He also realized that whenever he was corrected or criticized by a person in authority he was prone to describe this as being "clobbered."

Many studies have demonstrated that, in fact, inexact labeling and other cognitive changes occur in depression. The theoretical issue of whether depressed moods precede or follow such alterations remains unresolved, however.

Biological Theories

During the past three decades progress has been remarkable in understanding what role biological factors play in depression and mania. We will look at the genetic theories in Chapter 9, concentrating here on neurochemical explanations.

If you read the essay in Chapter 2, you recall that nerve impulses travel through billions of neurons in the human nervous system, and that the substances making it possible for these impulses to move from one neuron to the next are neurotransmitters. Once the transmission between presynaptic neuron and postsynaptic neuron has occurred, much of the neurotransmitter is reabsorbed into the presynaptic neuron. Most of the reabsorbed neurotransmitter returns to the storage vesicles, but some is metabolized either by an enzyme in the mitochondria, monoamine oxidase (MAO), or by another enzyme. Reabsorption and breakdown of neurotransmitter substances are important in the biology of the mood disorders.

As often happens in clinical science, several of the first biological breakthroughs in the study of depression and mania came from chance observations, which generated more experimental and controlled systematic studies and findings. In the early 1950s, clinicians using the drug reserpine to treat high blood pressure noticed that a significant percentage of patients receiving the drug developed moderate to severe depression. Animal studies conducted during the same period showed that reserpine depletes nerve endings of several important neurotransmitter substances. Bit by bit, data have accumulated from clinical observations and biochemical investigations, and theories have evolved.

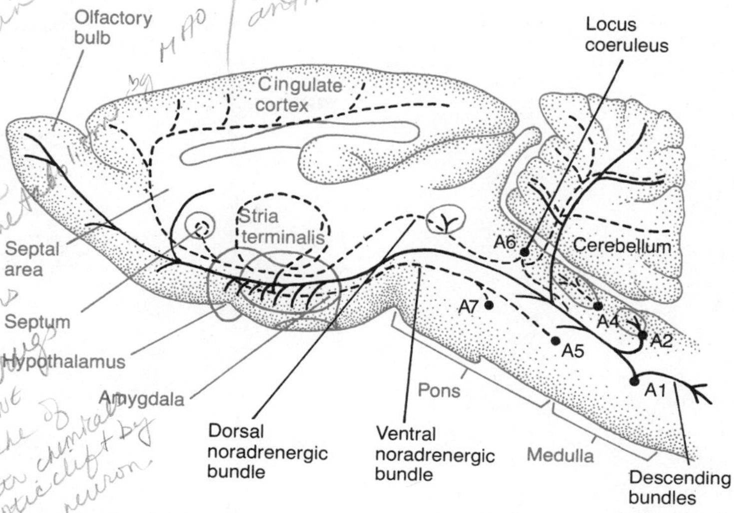

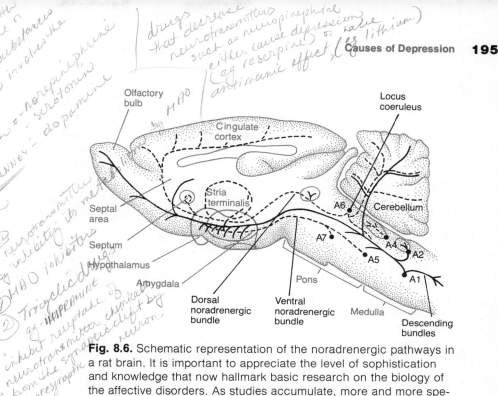

Fig. 8.6. Schematic representation of the noradrenergic pathways in a rat brain. It is important to appreciate the level of sophistication and knowledge that now hallmark basic research on the biology of the affective disorders. As studies accumulate, more and more specific information is acquired about neurochemical pathways within the brain and the central nervous system.

Schildkraut hypothesized in 1965 that clinical depression is associated with insufficient activity of one or more neurotransmitter substances in the central nervous system, whereas mania involves a functional excess. Schildkraut focused on the pivotal function of the neurotransmitter *norepinephrine* in this disorder, but subsequent studies have also implicated the neurotransmitter *serotonin* in depression and mania. Bunney et al. (1979) implicate the functional excess of another neurotransmitter, *dopamine* (see Chapter 6), in the manic process.

The clinical and scientific evidence that neurotransmitter imbalance is a key factor in mood disorders is substantial. Mood-elevating drugs increase neurotransmitter activity in the brain, for example. As Figure 8.7 shows, stimulants such as cocaine and amphetamines increase activity at the synapse. *Iproniazid,* a drug used in the 1950s to treat tuberculosis, elevates neurotransmitter levels by inhibiting its metabolism by monoamine oxidase (MAO) (Kline 1962; Davidson 1958). In the last two decades, MAO-inhibiting drugs have been used as antidepressant medications in the treatment of some kinds of depression (see Chapter 11). The other major class of antidepressants, the *tricyclic drugs* (e.g., imipramine) inhibit reuptake of neurotransmitter chemicals from the synaptic cleft by the presynaptic neuron. All these substances, then, increase the neurotransmitter available to interact with the receptor on the postsynaptic neuron (Glowinski and Axelrod 1964; Mendels et al. 1976). Drugs that decrease the functional availability of certain neurotransmitters, such as norepinephrine, either cause depression, as re-

PROBLEMS

1) — drugs that act as stimulants in normal people are not generally therapeutic with major depressive disorders + conversely

Explanation → difference of individuals to different substances

2) Lithium exerts both an antimanic + antidepressant effect if it operates mostly on norepinephrine

Explanation: mechanisms can effect similar changes in the CNS, the neurochemical hypothesis is valid + useful for conceptualizing research findings + generating new hypotheses.

2 ALTERNATIVE THEORIES of Mood Disorders

1) PERMISSIVE THEORY — abnormality in 2 neurotransmitter substances may be involved in depression

2) Two-disease Theory — two types of depressive illness one caused by deficit in one neuro + the other "another"

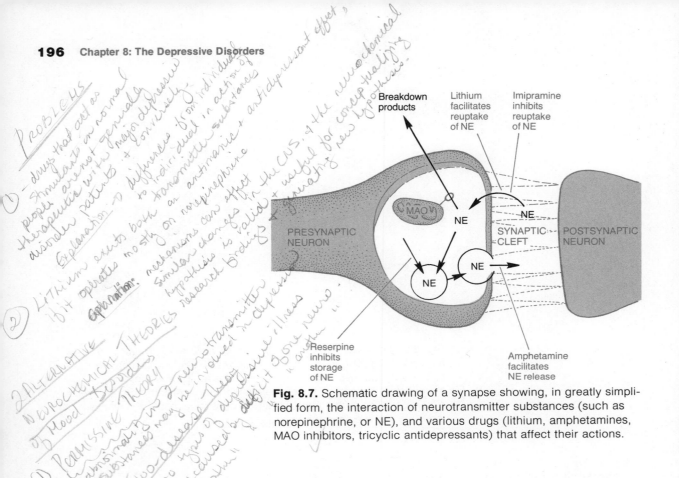

Fig. 8.7. Schematic drawing of a synapse showing, in greatly simplified form, the interaction of neurotransmitter substances (such as norepinephrine, or NE), and various drugs (lithium, amphetamines, MAO inhibitors, tricyclic antidepressants) that affect their actions.

serpine does, or have an antimanic effect, as lithium does.

Table 8.3 summarizes the therapeutic effects of treatments that alter norepinephrine activity in the brain. These effects support this neurochemical theory of depression. Nevertheless, this hypothesis is not flawless. Drugs that act as stimulants in normal individuals are not generally therapeutic in patients suffering from major depressive disorders; conversely, drugs that are therapeutic in depressed people do not produce stimulant effects in normal people. It is quite possible that the deviation in neurotransmitter function is qualitative rather than quantitative (Goodwin 1977); that is, there may be important differences (other than amounts) from individual to individual in the action of transmit-

ter substances. Quite a different problem is explaining how lithium exerts both an antimanic and antidepressant effect (see Chapter 11) if it operates mostly on norepinephrine. Of course, it may be that many mechanisms can effect similar changes in the central nervous sytem and that the neurochemical hypothesis is valid and useful for conceptualizing research findings and generating new hypotheses, yet ultimately it could be an incomplete explanation.

Two alternative neurochemical theories of mood disorders are the *permissive theory* and the *two-disease theory*. The permissive theory states that an abnormality in *two* neurotransmitter substances may be involved in depression (Prange 1970; Kety 1971). Like the norepinephrine theory, the permissive theory

[Handwritten margin notes:] ANOTHER / NEWER THEORY — neurotransmitter substances, psychosocial stress, + developmental factors, together affect an individual's risk for depression.

KRAMER + MCKINNEY — "the more AMPT required to produce 'depressive equivalents,' the less vulnerable to depression the monkeys are"

Results — Mother-reared = 4-8× as much to produce a peer-reared comparable effects with separation

— peer-reared = more susceptible to effects of AMPT without separation

Table 8.3. Effects of agents believed to alter norepinephrine levels in the brain

	Mechanism	Therapeutic effect
Tricyclic antidepressant	Increases amount of norepinephrine (NE) in synaptic cleft by preventing reuptake.	Benefits depression
MAO inhibitor	Raises the level of NE by inhibiting its metabolism by MAO.	Benefits depression
ECT	Increases NE synthesis.	Benefits depression
Reserpine	Lowers amount of NE in the brain by preventing storage.	Causes depression

Source: Adapted from J. M. Davis, "Central Biogenic Amines and Theories of Depression and Mania," in W. F. Fann, I. Karacan, A. D. Pokorny, and R. L. Williams, eds., *Phenomenology and Treatment of Depression* (New York: Spectrum Publications, 1977).

associates norepinephrine deficiency with depression and norepinephrine excess with mania. The permissive theory also holds, however, that serotonin levels must be low in both depression and mania. The two-disease theory postulates basically two types of depressive illness, one caused by functional deficits of serotonin, the other by functional deficits of norepinephrine. Some evidence supporting this differentiation comes from clinical studies showing that some patients respond better to drugs that primarily affect norepinephrine levels, and others to drugs that alter serotonin levels (Maas 1978; Asberg et al. 1976). See Table 8.4 for a summary of the functions of norepinephrine and serotonin in the three theories we have examined.

Yet another, newer theory suggests that neurotransmitter substances, psychosocial stress, and developmental factors together affect an individual's risk for depression. Kramer and McKinney (1979) recently reported on a study in which developmental and environmental differences affected the way monkeys reacted to AMPT (a drug that depletes norepin-

ephrine and dopamine in the brain). In their experiment, some monkeys were raised by their mothers until they were six months old, when they were housed with their peers. Others were raised with their peers and experienced either many separations from each other or few separations. Still others were raised by their mothers for six months and then isolated, and so on. Later, the researchers monitored the monkeys' behavior under different psychosocial situations (alone in a cage, in a group situation, or in a playroom with other monkeys). The dependent variable in the experiment was the dosage of AMPT that would bring about significant changes in the monkeys' huddling behaviors and decreased locomotion. Kramer and McKinney reasoned that the more AMPT required to produce "depressive equivalents," the less vulnerable to depression, or depression prone, the monkeys were. They found that mother-reared monkeys required four to eight times as much AMPT as peer-reared monkeys did to produce comparable effects on social and separation behaviors. Also, peer-related monkeys who had often been separated from the group were more

[handwritten margin notes:] Another way of conceptualizing mood disorders — Wehr & Goodwin — Biological rhythms ① disturbances ② long-term cyclicity

Table 8.4. Role of neurotransmitters in major biological theories of mood disorders

Norepinephrine (NE) theory
            Depression = low NE
            Mania   = high NE
Serotonin theory
            Depression = low serotonin
            Mania   = high serotonin
Permissive theory
            Depression = low NE, low serotonin
            Mania   = high NE, low serotonin
Two-Disease theory
            NE type
            Depression = low NE, normal serotonin
            No specific theory of mania
            Serotonin type
            Depression = low serotonin, normal NE
            No specific theory of mania

Source: Adapted from J. M. Davis, ''Central Biogenic Amines and Theories of Depression and Mania,'' in W. F. Fann, I. Karacan, A. D. Pokorny, and R. L. Williams, eds., *Phenomenology and Treatment of Depression* (New York: Spectrum Publications, 1977), p. 427.

susceptible to the effects of AMPT than peer-reared monkeys with few separations. Most strikingly, very large doses of AMPT (20–40 times as high as doses found to have behavioral effects in other groups and situations) were necessary to alter the social behavior of animals placed in a playroom environment if they normally lived alone. These findings, although preliminary, are exciting because they suggest that biological, psychosocial, and developmental factors together determine a person's susceptibility to depression and, interestingly, echo some current thinking about schizophrenia (see Chapter 6).

Finally, Wehr and Goodwin (1978) recently proposed yet another way of conceptualizing mood disorders. Based on a study of biological rhythms, they have suggested that:

Biological rhythms are involved in affective disorder in two ways. First disturbances in 24-hour (circadian) rhythms of activity, sleep, mood, and neuroendocrine function play an integral role in the pathophysiology of mania and depression. Second, the long-term cyclicity of the illness per se is a pathological example of a biological rhythm. More specifically, some cases of recurrent affective disorder appear to be pathological expressions of normal menstrual, seasonal, or annual rhythms (p. 2).

Summary

1. Depression is a mood disorder characterized by severe and/or prolonged feelings of hopelessness, despair, and low self-esteem, and a sense of self-blame, guilt, or worthlessness. Psychomotor disturbances, bodily complaints, and sleep disturbances are also features of clinical depression.

2. One type of depression is a normal human reaction and may take the form of: (1) a normal reactive depression to a disappointment or frustration in job or personal life; or (2) a

normal reactive depression to a disappointment or frustration in job or personal life; or (2) a normal grief reaction to the loss of a loved one. People usually recover from these forms of depression in a short time (six to eight weeks) and without professional treatment.

3. At the opposite end of a depression continuum are the severe, sometimes psychotic, depressive disorders. Symptoms of these forms may include functional disability and physiological problems. Major depressive disorders may last months and, more rarely, years.

4. Another general feature of major depressive disorders is that the patient is likely to experience a recurrence of serious depression.

5. A diagnosis of severe depression requires the presence of : (1) a dysphoric mood; (2) at least five behavior changes, including anorexia or weight change, sleep disorder, fatigability or loss of energy, psychomotor agitation or retardation, loss of interest in usual activities, self-reproach or guilt, decreased concentration, or recurrent thoughts of death or suicide; (3) sufficiently severe dysphoria for patient to seek help or noticeably impaired social functioning; (4) duration of at least two to four weeks; and (5) absence of other preexisting psychiatric illness or life-threatening medical illness in the year prior to onset.

6. Individuals having unipolar depression apparently differ genetically, biochemically, psychosocially, and biologically from bipolar patients diagnosed as having both depression and mania or hypomania.

7. Depression often has a negative effect on interpersonal relationships because of : (1) the frustration felt by both the depressed person and close friends and family in the interactions, and (2) the negative reactions that depression elicits from others.

8. Depression affects about 15 percent of American adults, more of whom are women than men.

9. There are both biological and psychological theories on the causes of depression, but because of modern advances in brain neurochemistry, biological theories are now rapidly expanding; both, however, can provide effective treatment modalities and theoretical perspectives.

10. The four major psychological theories of depression are: (1) *Psychoanalytic theories* which stem from Freud's hypothesis that pathological depression results from early loss experiences, and that the patient's hostility toward the lost person or object is redirected against the self. More recent research also suggests that loss experiences may be a risk factor in depression, and that the depressive individual may lack the ability to channel aggressions effectively. (2) *Personality theory* focuses on specific personality characteristics, such as excessive emotional dependency, low self-esteem, and fear of competition, which appear to be common among depression-prone individuals. (3) *Behavioral theories* conceive of depression as a response to a change in social reinforcement. One behavioral model, learned helplessness, postulates that past traumatic experiences over which he had no control "taught" the depressed person that he is incapable of coping with problem situations. (4) *Cognitive theories* suggest that a negative cognitive set (or pessimistic attitude about self and others) can become distorted and lead to depression during times of stress. Three types of cognitive distortion may occur: overgeneralization; selective abstraction; and inexact labeling.

11. Neurochemical theories of depression suggest that abnormal levels of certain neurotransmitter substances in the brain are a major factor in depression. Schildkraut theorized that depression is associated with insufficient activity of one or more of the neurotransmitter substances, whereas mania involves an excess of activity. Two related neurochemical theories are: the permissive theory, which attributes depression to abnormal activity involving both norepinephrine and serotonin; and the two-disease theory, which suggests two types of depressive illness, one caused by a functional deficit of serotonin and the other by a functional deficit of norepinephrine.

12. Based on research with monkeys, one promising new theory suggests that neurochemical, psychosocial, and developmental factors together determine an individual's vulnerability to depression. Biorhythms have also been implicated in mood disorders.

[Handwritten marginal notes:]

GOODWIN + GROFF) no improvement after +ve changes
LEWINSOHN - neurochemy - social difficulties
COYNE, HAMMEN, PETERS - contageous"
HAMMEN, PETERS - +ve impact
MANHEIMER + DALY - -ve impact
WEISSMAN + KLEIRMAN - 15% (18-75)

CAUSES - PSYCO

① more women than men universally
② 2:1
③ " " seek treatment
④ men more alcohol use + abuse

PSYCHOANALYTIC - no consistent relationship with hormone level
PERSONALITY - (separation hypothesis) emotional dependency
BEHAVIORAL - SKINNER - loss of +ve reinforcement
LEWINSOHN - -ve reinforcement
SKINL - state dependent phenomena
SELIGMAN - LEARNED HELPLESSNESS

COGNITIVE - DEPRESSION
① OVERGENERALIZATION
② SELECTIVE ABSTRACTION
③ INEXACT LABELING
cognitive distortions

BECK - -ve cognitive set thinking = mood

WEISSMAN + PAYKEL - more stressful life events
KRAMER + MCKINNEY - 3rd alternative - interactive

FREUD'S 1st THEORY

Chapter 9 | Manic-Depressive Illness

Clinical Description

Diagnosis

The Manic-Depressive Experience

Genetic Theories of Manic-Depressive Illness

Summary

There is a particular kind of pain, elation, loneliness, and terror involved in this kind of madness. When you're high it's tremendous. The ideas and feelings are fast and frequent like shooting stars and you follow them until you find better and brighter ones. Shyness goes, the right words and gestures are suddenly there, the power to seduce and captivate others a felt certainty. There are interests found in uninteresting people. Sensuality is pervasive and the desire to seduce, be seduced irresistible. Feelings of ease, intensity, power, well-being, financial omnipotence, and euphoria now pervade one's marrow. But, somewhere, this changes. The fast ideas are far too fast and there are far too many; overwhelming confusion replaces clarity. Memory goes. Humor and absorption on friends' faces are replaced by fear and concern. Everything previously moving with the grain is now against — you are irritable, angry, frightened, uncontrollable, and enmeshed totally in the blackest caves of the mind. You never knew those caves were there. It will never end. Madness carves its own reality. It goes on and on and finally there are only others' recollections of your behavior — your bizarre, frenetic, aimless behaviors — for mania has at least some grace in partially obliterating memories. What then, after the medications, psychiatrist, despair, depression, and overdose? All those incredible feelings to sort through. Who is being too polite to say what? Who knows what? What *did* I do? Why? And most hauntingly, when will it happen again? Then, too, are the annoyances — medicine to take, resent, forget, take, resent, and forget, but always to take. Credit cards revoked, bounced checks to cover, explanations due at work, apologies to make, intermittent memories of vague men (what *did* I do?), friendships gone or drained, a ruined marriage. And always, when will it happen again? Which of my feelings are real? Which of the me's is me? The wild, impulsive, chaotic, energetic, and crazy one? Or the shy, withdrawn, desperate, suicidal, doomed, and tired one? Probably a bit of both, hopefully much that is neither. Virginia Woolf, in her dives and climbs, said it all: ''how far do our feelings take their color from the dive underground? I mean, what is the reality of any feeling?''

The young woman who wrote those words has the most severe kind of mood disorder: manic-depressive illness. Her moods swing unpredictably and inexplicably from extreme elation to devastating depression and back again. Although most of us have experienced moments, days, or even weeks of great happiness or deep despair, it is difficult to imagine the greatly exaggerated emotions and the debilitation of prolonged manic-depressive moods. We might become ecstatic over a new love affair or acceptance into college or graduate school, but we soon return to our normal state of mind. Our happiness is most likely to be clearly related to one event or a series of events, and our behavior is not likely to be inappropriate for the circumstances or to interfere with our continuing activities. For someone with manic-depressive illness, however, ecstatic feelings may begin normally enough, but often not in response to any identifiable event. The feeling of well-being may then develop into the kind of chaotic, frightening, and psychotic experience described at the beginning of this chapter. Feelings that were once within the normal range may suddenly fly out of control. In manic-de-

pressive, or *bipolar,* illness the degree, the duration, and the type of depression also appear to be very different from the normal experience, as you saw in Chapter 8.

Why do proportionately few people have such widely disparate and extreme moods? How is it that most of these individuals seem to function normally most of the time (in fact, many are highly productive members of society), but sometimes become psychotic and disorganized, lose their ability to make rational decisions, and engage in bizarre behaviors? These questions have intrigued people throughout history, but we have begun to understand them only in recent times. Just as we owe much of our knowledge of schizophrenia to Kraepelin, so we are indebted to him for his description of manic-depressive illness. His systematic studies of psychotic patients in the 1890s laid the foundation for modern research efforts. He observed large numbers of patients over long periods (often years), noticing changes in behavior and mood, patterns of the disorders in the families of his patients, duration of individual episodes of mania and depression, relationship of life events to the episodes, and many other aspects of the disorder (see Figure 9.1). Kraepelin's clinical descriptions of manic-depressive illness are still among the best we have (Kraepelin, in Wolpert 1977):

Patient during depressed stage of manic-depressive illness:

She spoke and ate but little, stared into space, and hardly slept at all. She also took a knife to bed with her at night, and expressed ideas of suicide. . . . For the past three months, she said, she had no rest, and had been absent-minded and forgetful. The patient spoke little of her own accord, and generally lay still in bed with a downcast expression. She was obliged to think for a disproportionately long time over the answers to simple questions and was not clear about the chronological order of her experience (p. 22).

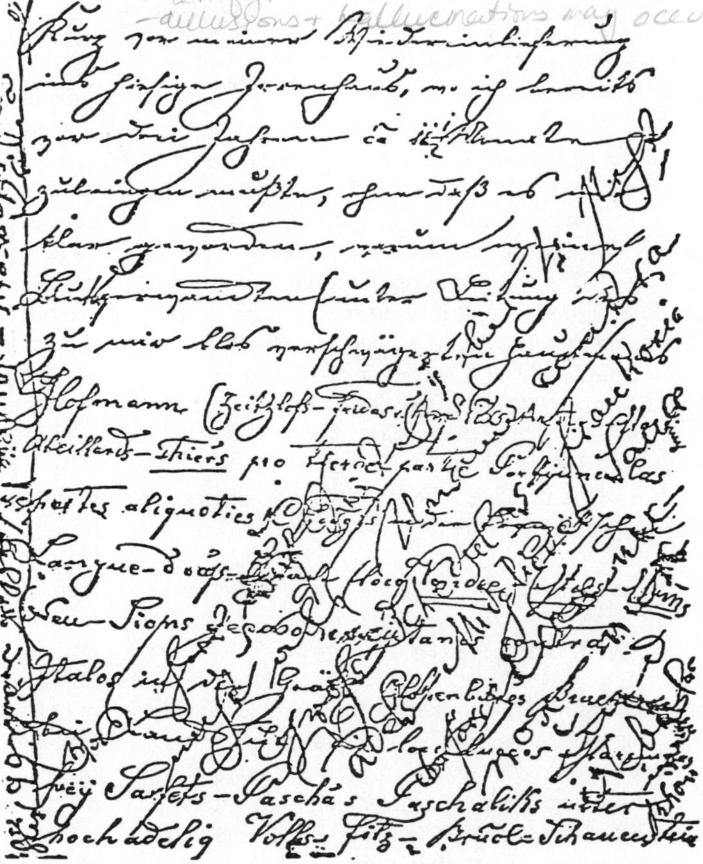

CLINICAL DISCRIPTION

- Depressive side - of unipolar + Bipolar (CH8)
- MANIC + HYPOMANIC Phase

NIC may begin suddenly, rapidly escalate
and vary in length from a few days
to a few months
- predominant mood is either
elevated, expansive or
irritable + is associated
with the other symptoms
of the manic syndrome.

- think, talk, move more rapidly
- thinking more disorganized + behavior is bizarre + psychotic
- terrifying or erotic
- delusions + hallucinations may occur

Hypomania: signs + symptoms of
manic disorder that do not
appear to be psychotic
- fewer symptoms
- better able to function
socially + proffessionally
- contradictory:
happy - irritable etc.

(Manic-depressives) some
only experience hypomania

MANIA

CARLSON + GOODWIN
3 basic stages during
acceleration course of mania
- changes in mood, cognition, + behavior
- accelerated from mild hypomanic phase
to a clearly disorganized + psychotic stage
+ finally returning to normal behavior
- lasting about 3 weeks to
— Stage 3 similar to
paranoid scizo

Fig. 9.1. Specimen of patient's writing during mania, obtained by nineteenth-century psychiatrist Kraepelin. It illustrates the frenetic writing so characteristic of the manic state.

Patient during manic stage of manic-depressive illness:

She does not sit down, but walks about quickly, examines briefly what she sees, interferes unceremoniously with the students, and tries to be familiar with them. No sooner is she induced to sit down than she quickly springs up again, flings away her shoes, unties her apron, and begins to sing and dance. The next minute she stops, claps her hands, goes to the blackboard, seizes the chalk, and begins to write her name. . . . During the whole time the patient chatters almost incessantly, though the purport of her rapid headlong talk is scarcely intelligible, and quite disconnected. Still, one can sometimes follow up her erratic thoughts. Her mood is extremely merry, she laughs and titters continuously between her talk, but easily becomes angry on slight provocation, and then breaks into a torrent of the nastiest abuse, only to be tranquil a minute after with a happy laugh (p. 27).

Most studies indicate that the rate of manic-depressive illness is approximately the same as that of schizophrenia, or about one in a hundred individuals (Klerman 1978; Weissman and Myers 1978). Unlike schizophrenia, however, bipolar illness appears to be much more common among the upper social classes (Noreik and Odegaard 1966; Petterson 1977; Weissman and Myers 1978), perhaps reflecting a higher degree of social and economic achievement as possible beneficial consequences of the illness. A few of the positive aspects of the disorder are discussed later in the chapter.

Clinical Description

In Chapter 8 we looked at the basic features of unipolar depression and the depressive side of bipolar disorder. We shall now focus on the clinical description of *hypomania* and *mania*. Essentially, a *manic* episode is "a distinct period when the predominant mood is either elevated, expansive, or irritable and is associated with other symptoms of the manic syndrome" (*DSM*-III). Among the other symptoms are hyperactivity, inflated self-esteem, decreased need for sleep, flight of ideas and racing thoughts, rapid and occasionally unintelligible speech, poor judgment, difficulty in concentrating on one thing at a time, shopping sprees, impulsiveness, social intrusiveness, and hypersexuality. Manic episodes may begin suddenly, rapidly escalate, and vary in length from days to a few months. *Hypomanic* individuals manifest many of the signs and symptoms of the manic disorder but do not appear to be psy-

chotic. Fewer symptoms are required to diagnose hypomania, and hypomanics are better able to function socially and professionally than individuals who are manic.

During a hypomanic phase, an individual's behavior is often uninhibited, gregarious, occasionally charming, energetic, aggressive, self-confident, "high," euphoric, and flippant, and he is interested in a wide range of subjects. An infectiously humorous manner, however, frequently has a more irritable, argumentative, and demanding side. Thus, family members, friends, and clinicians alike will describe hypomanic individuals in strongly contradictory language: seductive but irritating; intense but distractible; witty but often hostile. Hypomanic individuals themselves report feeling exceptionally good, having very rapid thoughts and a great deal of energy, and needing much less sleep than usual. They are generally more active, spend more money, and talk more quickly than usual, and are quite grandiose in their thinking. Many people diagnosed as manic-depressives experience only hypomania, and although it may create some chaos in their personal lives and occasionally in their work, they are often highly productive people.

Truly manic people think, move, and talk even more rapidly than hypomanics, their thinking is more disorganized, and their behavior is often bizarre and psychotic. A manic episode is generally a terrifying, occasionally ecstatic, experience. Delusions are not uncommon, and hallucinations may occur. Professional golfer Bert Yancey's description of a manic episode illustrates the grandiosity of thinking, the euphoria, and the highly personal and psychotic meaning that ordinary events acquire:

I was a Messiah. I was going to the Orient to bring an end to the evil of Communism and bring the religions of the Orient into line with Christianity. I was saying, "All right, all the whites over here, all the blacks over there, we're going to have us a Chinese fire drill," or something like that.

Which meant a great deal to me at the time. And people were laughing, right? That's high, right? Literally and figuratively. That's a natural high. That's manic-depressive illness. You're uninhibited. You do things that have a great deal of meaning to you, but they don't have any meaning to other people. They don't understand your meaning.

So in comes the Security and takes me into the quiet room. And down there I was spitting on a light bulb, thinking if I watched the saliva burn, the different colors and shapes, I could find the key to the cure for cancer (*Los Angeles Times,* April 6, 1978, Section IV).

According to Carlson and Goodwin (1973), three basic stages can be seen during the accelerating course of mania. Table 9.1 summarizes the mood and cognitive and behavioral features of these stages. For their study, Carlson and Goodwin studied twenty patients during acute, untreated manic episodes. All twenty patients progressed through stages 1 and 2. Seventy percent also went through stage 3. Figure 9.2 shows the course of a manic episode for one patient who experienced all three stages.

The acceleration period, starting with a mild hypomanic phase, progressing through a clearly disorganized and psychotic stage, and finally returning to normal behavior, lasted about three weeks. During their investigation, Carlson and Goodwin also found that the behavior of patients in stage 3 mania was frequently indistinguishable from that of paranoid schizophrenic patients, although a positive personal or family history of mood disorder, good premorbid functioning, and a good response to lithium therapy (see Chapter 11) did

Table 9.1. Stages of mania

	Stage 1	Stage 2	Stage 3
Mood	Lability (instability, or rapid fluctuation) of affect. Euphoria predominates. Irritability if demands not satisfied.	Increased dysphoria (mental discomfort) and depression, open hostility and anger.	Clearly dysphoric. Panic-stricken. Hopeless.
Cognition	Expansivity, grandiosity, overconfidence. Thoughts coherent but occasionally tangential. Sexual and religious preoccupation. Racing thoughts.	Flight of ideas. Disorganization of cognitive state. Delusions.	Incoherent, definite loosening of thought associations. Bizarre and idiosyncratic delusions. Hallucinations in one-third of patients. Disorientation to time and place, occasional ideas of reference.
Behavior	Increased psychomotor activity. Increased initiation and rate of speech. Increased spending, smoking, telephoning.	Continued increases in psychomotor acceleration. Increasingly pressured speech. Occasionally assaultive behavior.	Frenzied and frequently bizarre psychomotor activity.

Source: Adapted from G. A. Carlson and F. K. Goodwin, "The Stages of Mania: A Longitudinal Analysis of the Manic Episode," *Archives of General Psychiatry,* 1973, 28, pp. 221–228.

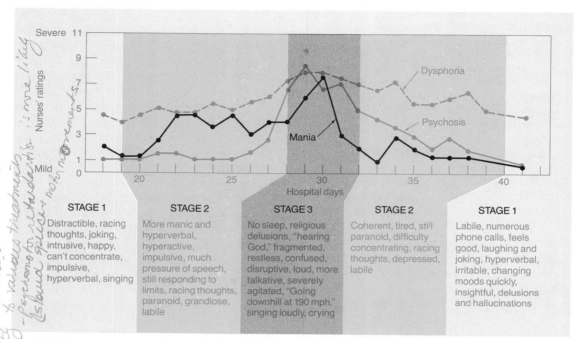

Fig. 9.2. Relationship between stages of a manic episode and daily behavior ratings. Nurses on the hospital ward rated the patient's behavior twice a day on a global measure of mania. They also wrote down general observations of the patient's behavior during the day. (After Carlson and Goodwin 1973.)

distinguish the manic individuals. Interestingly, there was no apparent relationship between the level of psychotic disorganization during the acute manic episode and the level of functioning during a follow-up study.

Diagnosis

In the remainder of this chapter we shall focus on bipolar illness, but before going on, we reemphasize the bipolar-unipolar distinction. Bipolar patients are those who have a history of depression *and* mania or hypomania, whereas unipolar patients have a history of depression only. All contemporary approaches to diagnosis differentiate these two patterns by their markedly different natural histories, genetic and biological features, and responses to treatment. Thus, people with bipolar illness tend to have their first breakdown at an earlier age; their families are much more likely to include individuals with a history of mania or hypomania; and they have many more episodes than people with unipolar depression. People with manic-depressive illness also have higher suicide and divorce rates, and respond very differently to various treatments.

The *DSM*-III criteria for major depressive

disorders in Chapter 8 are the ones used to diagnose the depressive phase of bipolar manic-depressive illness (see Table 8.1). The only significant difference, clinically speaking, is that unipolar patients are much more likely to show *psychomotor agitation* (pacing, handwringing, inability to sit still), and bipolar patients are more likely to exhibit *psychomotor retardation* (slowed speech and slowed body movements). Table 9.2 lists *DSM*-III diagnostic criteria for mania.

Patient evaluation on these diagnostic criteria occurs during a structured clinical interview, which usually inquires also into: family history for evidence of mood disorders, suicide, psychiatric hospitalization, and alcoholism (which Winokur [1978] has shown to occur more frequently in families of manic-depressive patients); current and past medical problems that might account for the patient's symptoms;

drug use; suicide attempts by the patient; and so on. At some time following the assessment interview, behavioral observations and ratings by professional personnel monitor changes in patients' behavior. The Manic-State Rating Scale (Beigel et al. 1971), for example, enables nurses to rate hospitalized patients every eight hours (on two five-point rating scales, one measuring frequency, the other intensity) on the indices shown in Table 9.3. Depressive thoughts and feelings can exist simultaneously with mania, and items 1 and 14 inquire into this possibility. The high reliability and validity of this scale make it particularly useful in clinical research.

Table 9.2. *DSM*-III criteria for mania

A. *Mood:* Euphoria or irritability (may alternate with depressive mood)
B. *Behavioral changes* (at least three of these):
  (1) hyperactivity
  (2) push of speech, increased talking
  (3) flight of ideas
  (4) inflated self-esteem, grandiosity
  (5) decreased need for sleep
  (6) distractibility
  (7) marked increased activities (e.g., hypersexuality, buying sprees, reckless driving)
C. *Severity of disturbance:* At least one of the following:
  (1) meaningful conversation impossible
  (2) serious impairment socially (family, work, home)
  (3) in absence of (1) or (2), hospitalization
D. *Duration:* At least 1 week (or any duration if hospitalized)
E. *Exclusionary:* Presence of other preexisting psychiatric illness (pp. E10–E12)

Source: Diagnostic and Statistics Manual, III, 1978.

Table 9.3. Manic-state rating scale items

1. Looks depressed
2. Is talking
3. Moves from one place to another
4. Makes threats
5. Has poor judgment
6. Dresses inappropriately
7. Looks happy and cheerful
8. Seeks out others
9. Is distractible
10. Has grandiose ideas
11. Is irritable
12. Is combative or destructive
13. Is delusional
14. Verbalizes depressive feelings
15. Is active
16. Is argumentative
17. Talks about sex
18. Is angry
19. Is careless about dress and grooming
20. Has diminished impulse control
21. Verbalizes feelings of well-being
22. Is suspicious
23. Makes unrealistic plans
24. Demands contact with others
25. Is sexually preoccupied
26. Jumps from one subject to another

Source: A. Beigel, D. L. Murphy, and W. E. Bunney, "The manic-state rating scale: Scale construction, reliability, and validity," *Archives of General Psychiatry,* 1971, 25, pp. 256–262.

Another way of assessing the extent of hypomania or elation of mood is to ask the patient to fill out a self-rating scale. One such form, the M-D Scale, appears as Table 9.4. Although most patients who are actually manic would be unable or unwilling to fill out the questionnaire, the scale can help in assessing the presence or absence of hypomania. Most normal people will agree with many of these items, but hypomanic individuals will generally answer "yes" to most.

Instruments like those in Table 9.3 and 9.4 permit initial measurement of a person's behavior, comparisons of severity among a number of patients, examination of changes in mood and behavior over time, correlation of self-reports with observers' ratings, correlation of physiological variables with subjective mood state, and so on. Thus, we can study the natural course of the illness and the effects of medications and other treatment programs.

Table 9.4. M-D scale

Here are a number of statements describing how people sometimes feel. For each statement please indicate whether or not it applies to you. Simply circle YES if it applies to you, or NO if it does not apply to you. Please judge the statements on the basis of your feelings now.

Yes No 1. I can't sit still.
Yes No 2. Lately I have been working much faster than usual.
Yes No 3. I feel angry.
Yes No 4. I have boundless energy.
Yes No 5. I feel as though I can work 20 hours a day.
Yes No 6. I feel like going on a spending spree.
Yes No 7. I am constantly on the go.
Yes No 8. People annoy me now more than before.
Yes No 9. I move faster now than before.
Yes No 10. Lately I feel like breaking things.
Yes No 11. I've been telephoning a lot of friends recently.
Yes No 12. I don't need as much sleep as other people.
Yes No 13. I have been making new plans for travel.
Yes No 14. I am continuously involved in activities.
Yes No 15. I feel like being with people.
Yes No 16. I make up my mind quickly.

Source: R. Plutchik, S. R. Platman, R. Tilles, and R. R. Fieve, "Construction and Evaluation of a Test for Measuring Mania and Depression," *Journal of Clinical Psychology,* 1970, 26, pp. 499–503.

The Manic-Depressive Experience

The range of behaviors that characterize manic-depressive illness is almost incredible: from hopelessness, despair, lethargy, and other physiological changes such as sleep and appetite disturbances in the depressed phase, to euphoria, grandiosity, irritability, hyperactivity, dysphoria (mental discomfort) in the manic phase. What is it like to experience such variable, intense, and contradictory moods? How does a manic-depressive person feel after an episode of mania or depression? What effects does this illness have on the person's relationships with other people, on work, and on self-image? In answering these questions we will present some first-hand descriptions of manic-depressive illness written by people who either have it or have been strongly affected by it.

The quotation that opens this chapter was written by a young woman who experienced many hypomanic, two major manic, and several severe depressive episodes before age thirty. In describing her illness she alludes to many of the same fears and worries that haunt most patients with manic-depressive illness: the tumultous, chaotic aspect of the episodes themselves and their powerful effects on subsequent functioning; the unpredictability of onset and duration of

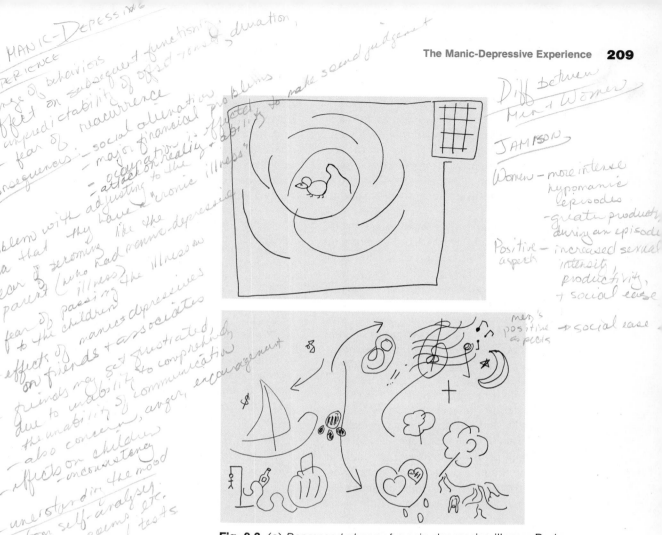

Fig. 9.3. (a) *Depressed phase* of manic-depressive illness: During this phase, and in discussing this illustration, the patient described feeling like a ''trapped, confused'' rat in a maze, unable to escape, cut off from life and others, without light, in a prison of fear, confusion, and isolation. The grilled window in the upper right-hand corner represented unobtainable light and freedom. (b) *Hypomanic phase* (just prior to escalation into full-blown mania): The same patient described her free-ranging thoughts and illustrated the flight of ideas and punning so characteristic of this stage of the illness. For example, in Area 1 of the drawing the patient described her thoughts as: ''I always get manic in October, that reminds me of pumpkins (A) on the vine (B), wine (C), winos, Gallo wine, gallows (D), gallows humor, left hanging (E).'' In Area 2: ''Hearts (A), hearts are dripping, harts running through the woods (B); blood reminds me of vampires, there are his fangs (C), teeth and dentists, roots (D) and root canals; Venice, Merchant of Venice, roots go back to the trees (B) where the harts are running.''

Handwritten margin notes:

THE MANIC-DEPRESSIVE EXPERIENCE

- range of behaviors
- effect on subsequent functioning
  - unpredictability of offset, onset, duration,
  - fear of recurrence
- Consequences - social alienation
  - major financial problems
  - occupational problems
  - alteration in reality + ability to make sound judgement
- problem with adjusting to the idea that they have a chronic illness
- fear of becoming like the parent (who had manic-depressive illness)
- fear of passing the illness on to the children
- effects of manic-depressives on friends + associates
  - friends may get frustrated, due to inability to comprehend the inability of communication
  - also concern, anger, encouragement
- effects on children
  - inconsistency
- understanding the mood
  - from self-analysis
  - poems etc.
  - psychological tests
  - TAT

Positive side
a substantial majority of bipolar patients said they had short + long term positive effects, regardless of the disabling and dysphoria they also experienced.
unipolar - overall lasting increase in sensitivity to their illness.

Diff between Men + Women
JAMISON
Women - more intense hypomanic episodes
- greater productivity during an episode
Positive aspect - increased sexual intensity, productivity, + social ease
men's positive aspects → social ease

an episode; and the ongoing fear of recurrence. The practical consequences of depression and mania may include alienation of friends, lovers, and spouses; effects of poor judgment, irrational behavior, or inability to move forward in a career; and major financial problems from overspending, overinvestment, and substantial medical expenses.

Also, manic-depressives often have problems in adjusting to the idea of having a "chronic illness." Manic-depressive illness is unquestionably a serious disorder. It is potentially life-threatening because the risk of suicide is very high; in fact, the incidence of suicide among manic-depressives is the highest of any psychiatric illness or of any other group of people (see Chapter 10). Also, it is a problem that almost always requires lifelong maintenance medication for its management. Perhaps the most subtle but pervasive feature of this illness is its fundamental (however transitory) attack on both reality and the ability to make sound judgments. This effect, in turn, usually leaves a profound mark on the person and particularly on his self-confidence once the acute episode has passed. For some time following a manic or depressive episode, many patients continue to question their judgment, their ability to assess situations, and their ability to understand reactions to and relationships with other people. And because hypomania is generally perceived as a highly intoxicating, powerful, productive, and desirable state, it is often difficult for patients to consider it a sickness or part of the same illness as depression and mania. Consequently, they may have obvious problems in attitudes toward the illness, themselves, and the treatment program.

Finally, a typical concern derives from the heritable component in the illness. Many patients, having grown up in an environment of extreme mood swings, express much fear that they will end up like the affected parent, partic-ularly when that parent has been severely disabled, hospitalized many times, is an alcoholic, or has committed suicide. The daughter of a manic-depressive woman described her fear of inheriting the illness and her difficulty in establishing her separation from her mother (Anthony 1975):

Ever since I was small, I have been told that I was just like my mother. I was named after her, and very soon I took to thinking that I was going to be committed when I was 21, like she was. I was sure that they were going to come and haul me away. I felt that the only way I could separate my thoughts and feelings from her would be for her to die, and I often hated her and wished for her death, especially when she was manic (p. 292).

Often, too, patients — and their spouses — agonize over the possibility of passing on the illness to children. Josh Logan, director-producer of *South Pacific, Mister Roberts,* and many other plays and a manic-depressive, wrote about this fear in his autobiography, where he reports this conversation with his first wife:

I asked her if she wanted to have children with me. She said "no."
I asked why, but she refused to answer. . . . She answered . . . she would never have children by me, and I should know why. I looked at her blankly, and she added, "I have no desire to bring insane children into this world" (Logan 1976, p. 153).

In this excerpt, Logan points to another problem — the effect of manic-depressive illness on friends and associates:

How can I go back to the theatre after all I've put my friends through, after all the galloping whispers and all the people who've seen me in this strange state? How will anybody, as long as I live, believe that I'm well again? What had been said about me during my absence? How much damage had the gossip done? (p. 383).

The reactions of other people to manic-depressive illness are important and they vary a great deal, of course, from person to person and also according to the severity, duration, and type of mood disturbance itself. Frequently people who are close to manic-depressives express frustration at being unable to communicate with or change the mood of the affected person (particularly when depressed). Additional reactions include concern, anger, withdrawal, encouragement and enjoyment of the hypomanic state, fear, and perhaps most common, simple inability to comprehend the often frightening and profound changes of personality that accompany severe disorders of mood. In the words of a man whose sister had manic-depressive illness:

My reaction is . . . fear, worry, compassion, respect. In my case the fear and worry were mostly at something of a distance; I live in another city and only occasionally have been present during these periods of depression, and never during mania. Yet, the fear is very real — fear for her life itself; fear for the possibility of her incapacitation; fear for the effects on our mother; fear, I suppose, for the evidence of my own vulnerability. My fear is transitory, though, and seems to pass when her moods are normal. Another strand of my reaction is compassion for the intensity of her suffering. Her periods of depression are painfully difficult to understand, and painful, to the extent I can understand, for me to share. Finally, there is an element of deep respect for her having carried through and successfully borne so much. The worst seems over, and, in retrospect, it seems incredible that she could have carried on through it all and emerged still strong.

Manic-depressive illness has a tremendous effect on a patient's children, as well. One individual recalls the experience of living in an ever-changing and unpredictable emotional environment (Anthony 1975):

We kids never knew what to believe. Mother was so completely different when she was well. She listened, she was kind, she was generous, she was fun to be with, and she was always at home. . . . We seemed to have two sets of everything: two sets of feelings and two sets of thoughts that did not really fit what was actually happening. Life was like a big pretense. We gradually got to recognize the signs that meant she was going to have another attack: she would start cleaning the home and never finish the job, buying things that were just junk and never needed, talking about relatives in the wildest sorts of ways, and chatting constantly about nothing. We gradually began to learn to live in our own worlds. Both I and my sister were always looking around for homes outside our own to "adopt" us, and we tried to spend as much time as possible with these families. This helped a great deal, but it also made us realize how differently normal families lived. There was no inconsistency. You could get up in the morning and almost know inside you what was going to happen for the rest of the day. We never knew how any day was going to turn out (p. 291).

Yet another way of understanding the experience of manic-depressive illness is to look at the writing or self-analyses done by persons in different mood states. The following poem was written by a woman with bipolar illness. She wrote it while she was hypomanic, in a few minutes and without pause. Notice the infectious cadence of the poem; the tangential and occasionally loose language; the punning; the fast, flowing rhythm; and the recurrent sexual references. All these qualities are highly characteristic of the hypomanic state.

GOD IS A HERBIVORE

Thyme passes, mixed with long grasses of herbs
    in the field.
Rosemary weeps into meadow sweeps
While curry is favored by the sun in its heaven.
The glinting scythe cuts the mustard twice

And the sage is ignored on its rock near the
   shore.
Hash is itself — high by being.
The law says shallots shall not — so they shan't.
   But . . .
The coriander meanders, the cumin seeds come
While a saffron canary eats juniper berry
Ignoring the open sesame seeds on the ground.

Consider also the responses to the *blank
card* from the Thematic Apperception Test
(TAT), a projective test requiring the patient to
tell a story about what he "sees" happening on
the card (see Chapter 3). The answers are those
of a twenty-five-year-old college-educated male
who is probably a "third-generation" manic-
depressive. He has been hospitalized many
times for both manic and depressive episodes.
The first TAT protocol he did during one of his
manic phases, the second during a depressive
episode. Notice the totally free and loose associations in the manic response, the paranoid
overtones, overt thought disorder, and dysphoria. In the depressed response, notice the
relative brevity, the self-doubt, the well-formed
and quite original story, the lack of thought disorder, and the morbid ending.

Manic phase:

   It's really clear, except for some spots. There
are lots of germs, that's why I'm not holding it
close to my face. It would look better with some
color. . . . There is an absence of all color except
there are bits of color. . . . I identified with the
hero, afraid of germs. Color of lithium. Shapes of
butterflies. Lots of symmetry, counterparts.
Candy-colored bullshit. I feel like I'm being held
involuntarily in a fog, don't see much blue. Don't
see any flowers. A guy sees a bunch of black guys
and weirdies, he follows the man and they find a
civilization, walking like robots until they find it.
They escape, find a lot of secrets about the trap.
They have a run-in with the police, find a guy who
looks like God who is arrested for having sex with
his wife, who should have been having a test-tube

baby. There is a lot of electrocardiac shock in the
fog, a lot of homosexuals and green and gray
people who travelled through fog into an insane
asylum. They emerged out into the world and
found the sun for the first time in a hundred years.

Depressed phase:

   "The Fog." I don't get it. Anything. This is the
view to a flier pilot in World War I as he's been
assigned to go over Heidelburg, Germany, and
shot from his plane. He's in the middle of a cloud
seeing nothing but whiteness and fear. Fears he
won't be successful and in fact he wasn't successful. He was shot down a little less than one
hour after he began his mission. End of story.

Although manic-depressive illness can be
frightening and disruptive both for patients and
for the people close to them, the patients themselves often feel that it has a positive side, too
(Jamison et al. 1980). In a study to determine
perceived short- and long-term positive effects
of having manic-depressive illness, thirty-five
bipolar and twenty-six unipolar patients answered questions about overall lasting effects
of having a mood disorder on personality, social
interactions, and productivity. Bipolar patients
also gave their impressions of specific behavioral and perceptual changes that they experienced during hypomanic or manic episodes. A
substantial majority of the bipolar patients perceived pronounced short- and long-term *positive* effects from their illness, regardless of the
disabling and dysphoric symptoms they also
experienced. Among the positive effects cited
were increased productivity, sociability, sexuality, and creativity. The comparison group, patients with unipolar mood disorder, attributed
only an overall, lasting increase in sensitivity to
their illness. Because the study primarily covered changes typical of hypomanic and manic
episodes, the response of the unipolar patients
is no surprise. Nonetheless, it is interesting that
most patients would say that manic-depressive

Fig. 9.4. Several scientists are interested in the relationship between creativity and manic-depressive illness and have noted the high rate of the disorder in the creative fields. Poets Robert Lowell (top left) and Anne Sexton (top right), novelist Honoré de Balzac (lower left), and composer Robert Schumann (lower right) all had manic-depression.

illness, which ostensibly carries more negative social, financial, and interpersonal consequences and involves more frequent episodes of dysfunction and mood swings than unipolar illness, makes positive contributions to their lives in one or more important ways.

Is there also a difference in the way men and women experience manic-depression? Jamison and her coworkers (1980) found that there was, and according to the results of their study, the difference is significant. The changes reported by women who had hypomanic episodes were generally perceived as more intense than those men experienced. In particular, the women perceived significantly greater productivity during an episode. The really striking differences, though, appeared between changes the male and female patients felt were the most enjoyable and important brought about by hypomania. Men judged increased social ease to be the primary positive attribute, but women rated increased sexual intensity, productivity, and social ease equally important. These differences may, in part, be a baseline effect. In other words, a powerful "novelty" or "change" factor may be operating and so women, for whom sociability may be an integral part of ordinary life, do not find the increased gregariousness and social ease either as noticeable or pleasurable as the men do. Likewise, men may not find increased sexuality and productivity as novel or reinforcing as the women do.

Genetic Theories of Manic-Depressive Illness

In Chapter 8 we examined several of the psychological theories that offer explanations for causes and maintenance of unipolar depressive illness. Psychoanalysts have developed interesting theories of manic-depressive illness, but biological formulations have all but superseded them. Also in Chapter 8 we discussed some of the neurochemical hypotheses of mood disorders, bipolar as well as unipolar. Here, then, we shall look at the second major type of biological explanation for mood disorders — the genetic approach.

The tendency for depression and mania to affect many more members of some families than of others is an inescapable fact. Kraepelin, using the limited scientific techniques available to a nineteenth-century psychiatrist, was the first to approach mood disorders systematically from a genetic perspective. He found an affective "taint" in the parents, grandparents, or siblings of one-third of his mood-disordered patients. When he examined the family histories of only those patients who had *repeated* episodes of mania or depression or both, he discovered that almost half of his patients had a significant family history of affective disorder. Since then, biologists and psychiatrists have continued to investigate how genetics affect the development of depression and manic-depressive illness, and they have found strong evidence that mood disorders have a genetic component.

The basic assumptions and strategies underlying a genetic model of the mood disorders are the same as those applied in schizophrenia research (see Chapter 6). In *family studies,* researchers look for patterns in occurrence of mood disorders, suicide, and alcoholism in the first-degree relatives of individuals diagnosed as having a mood disorder. Family histories obtained from patients suspected by specialists of having a mood disorder are a vital and continuous source of data for genetic research (see Figure 9.5). Occasionally, and more reliably, the patient's relatives are asked to complete a psychiatric examination and give a history. *High-risk studies* are longitudinal studies of children of patients with mood disorders, designed to determine the incidence of depression and

[Handwritten marginal notes, top left:] genetic marker — known that it's genetic + it's location has been demonstrated on the chromosome. ④ Twin Studies & ADOPTIONS — concordance rates (15-25) FRATERNAL — identical (70-100% concordance) — the genetic transmission mode not known — age of onset not known (childhood to old age)

[Handwritten marginal notes, top right:] Evidence for Genetic Theory of bipolar illness ① — incidence of mood disorders in first-degree relatives is much higher among bipolar than unipolar (1190) (.3-.45) — Winokur — ".. nearly all genetic studies indicate that bipolar illness has a very high genetic component, + unipolar illness a much smaller one."

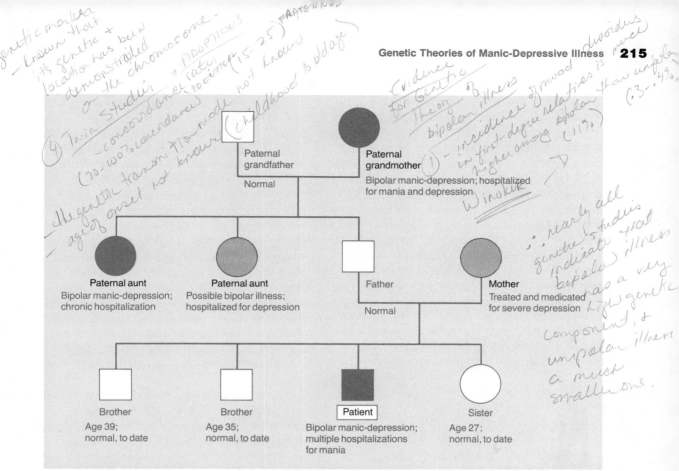

Fig. 9.5. Family history of affective disorder in a patient with bipolar manic-depressive illness. The siblings of the patient are normal to date, but still within the risk period.

mania in these offspring. There have also been efforts to find a *genetic marker,* a trait that we know is genetic and whose location on a chromosome has been demonstrated (such as color blindness) for these disorders. And, finally, *twin studies* involving identical and fraternal twins suggest the probability of one twin developing a mood disorder if the other twin already has manifested it, helping to separate environmental and genetic factors that might cause the mood disorders. To make sure that it is not environment alone that determines *concordance rates* for twin pairs, it is most desirable to study twins who were raised apart as well as those raised in the same household but apart from their biological parents.

The exact mode of genetic transmission in affective disorders is unknown but presumably is very complex. The variety that is apparent in clinical expressions of mood disorder indicates a confusing biological heterogeneity. Too, the range in age at onset of depression and mania stretches from childhood to old age, so that it is difficult to rule out the possibility that a "normal" family member actually has a mood disorder but has not yet experienced any of the clinical symptoms. These limitations aside, support is compelling for the genetic theory of bipolar illness. One of the most convincing findings is that the incidence of mood disorders in first-degree relatives of bipolar patients is consistently higher than in relatives of unipolar, depressed patients. Winokur (1978) reported a 4 to 11 percent incidence of mania among first-degree relatives of manic-depressive patients, in contrast to 0.3 to 0.4 percent among first-degree relatives of unipolar, depressed individuals. Estimates of concordance for bipolar illness range from 70 to 100 percent for identical twins compared to 15 to 25 percent for fraternal twins (Klerman 1978). These data represent a very small sample of the evidence favoring a genetic explanation. Nearly all the genetic studies indicate that bipolar illness has a very large genetic component, and unipolar illness a much smaller one.

Summary

1. Bipolar manic-depressive illness is a mood disorder that affects about one of every hundred people, approximately as many men as women, and more from the upper social classes.

2. The essential feature of a manic episode is a sustained elevated or expansive mood or predominant irritability. An episode may begin suddenly and varies in length from days to a few months. Hypomania is a milder, nonpsychotic form of mania. Hypomanic individuals can be extremely productive, although they may experience some disruption in social and job situations.

3. Carlson and Goodwin identified three basic stages in a manic episode. The stages progress in severity from mild hypomania in stage 1 to clearly psychotic symptoms, such as delusions, hallucinations, disorientation, panic-stricken mood, and frenzied activity, in stage 3.

4. The *DSM*-III criteria for the depressive phase of manic-depressive illness are the same as for unipolar depression, with the exception that bipolar depressives are more apt to exhibit psychomotor retardation than agitation.

5. The *DSM*-III criteria for mania include: (1) euphoric or irritable mood; (2) at least three behavior changes, including hyperactivity, push of speech or increased talking, flight of ideas, inflated self-esteem or grandiosity, decreased need for sleep, distractibility, or markedly increased activity; (3) evidence of severe disturbance in the form of meaningless conversation, serious social impairment, or hospitalization; (4) duration of at least one week; and (5) exclusion of preexisting psychiatric illness. Depressive thoughts and feelings can coexist with mania.

6. Manic-depressive illness may have these consequences for the victim: alienation of friends and family; problems arising from poor judgment, irrational behavior, and inability to move forward in a career; and financial problems due to spending sprees and medical expenses.

7. Other problems that may stem from the chronic nature of manic-depressive illness are: high suicide risk, lifelong need for maintenance medication, decreased self-confidence, and fear of genetic transmission of the illness to offspring.

8. Many patients consider hypomania and mania to have several positive aspects, including increased productivity, sociability, sexuality, and creativity. Women usually value increases in sexual intensity, productivity, and social ease that their illness can generate. Men appreciate the increased social ease it may bring.

9. There is compelling evidence to support neurochemical theories of the cause of bipolar illness, and it seems likely that the tendency to develop the disorder has a genetic basis. The genetic model of manic-depressive illness is based on the observation that the illness affects more members of some families than others. Data-gathering procedures include: family studies, high-risk studies, and twin studies. The way the genes transmit the illness is presumed to be quite complex because of the age range during which onset can occur (childhood through old age) and the variety of behaviors and severity of disorder that the affected individuals manifest.

10. These findings support the genetic theory of manic-depressive illness: the high incidence of mood disorders in first-degree relatives of bipolar patients; and 70 to 100 percent concordance for bipolar illness in identical twins versus 15 to 25 percent concordance for fraternal twins.

extreme euphoria, or irritability and paranoia
extreme psychomotor retardation or agitation

KRAEPLIN

CARLSON + GOODWIN — 3 stages

BIPOLAR   VS   UNIPOLAR
— Psychomotor retardation
— long term effects (.3-.4%)
— family

FEARS
— adjusting to "cronic illness"
— becoming like parents
— passing illness to children
— effect on friends
— effects on children

1/ — Psychomotor retardation
agitation
2/ — breakdown at an earlier age
3/ — more likely family history
4/ — more episodes + divorce rate
5/ — higher suicide + diff to treatment
6/ — respond diff to treatment
7/ — short + long term
8/ positive effects

JAMISON
MEN VS WOMEN
— social ease

— more intense hypomanic episodes
— greater productivity during an episode
— sexual intensity
— social ease

GENETIC (barning — 11%)
Kraeplin — 50% family history
Twin studies — 70-100% concordance

Chapter 10 (22) | Suicide

Handwritten margin notes:

Types of Suicidal Behavior

- 3 categories
① Completed suicide: circumstances of death that lead to the conclusion of suicide.
② Suicide attempt: intent or appearance of intent to jeopardize life by life-threatening behaviors.
③ Suicidal ideas: behavior which is a threat to life.
④ Victim-precipitated homicide — indicates a possible self-induced
⑤ Subintentional death

partial or unconscious role in risk to increase chances of premature death. e.g. alcoholism

more sophisticated & painless the method, the greater the chance of failure — natural reaction to an unnatural condition.

Types of Suicidal Behavior

Historical and Cultural Perspectives

Statistics on Suicide

Phenomenological Perspectives

Theories of Suicide
Psychological Theories
Biological Theories
Sociological Theory

Psychiatric Illness and Suicide

Suicide and College Students

Summary

After all this, I have to admit that I am a failed suicide. It is a dismal confession to make, since nothing, really, would seem to be easier than to take your own life. But in the event, this isn't so. No one is promiscuous in his way of dying. A man who has decided to hang himself will never jump in front of a train. And the more sophisticated and painless the method, the greater the chance of failure. I can vouch, at least, for that. I built up to the act carefully and for a long time, with a kind of blank pertinacity. It was the one constant focus of my life, making everything else irrelevant, a diversion. Each sporadic burst of work, each minor success and disappointment, each moment of calm and relaxation, seemed merely a temporary halt on my steady descent through layer after layer of depression, like an elevator stopping for a moment on the way down to the basement. . . . A suicidal depression is a kind of spiritual winter, frozen, sterile, unmoving. The richer, softer, and more delectable nature becomes, the deeper that internal winter seems, and the wider and more intolerable the abyss which separates the inner world from the outer. Thus, suicide becomes a natural reaction to an unnatural condition. Perhaps this is why, for the depressed, Christmas is so hard to bear. In theory, it is an oasis of warmth and light in an unforgiving season, like a lighted window in a storm. For those who have to stay outside, it accentuates, like spring, the disjunction between public warmth and festivity, and cold, private despair (Alvarez 1973, p. 257).

Although death will come to all of us, very few people actively seek it out. We may think of death, fear it, even briefly consider it preferable to our temporary unhappiness, ill health, or disappointment. But we seldom consider death the *most* viable alternative to our pain. Accordingly, few of us ever arrange to kill ourselves and subsequently act on those arrangements. Why, then, does anyone actually commit suicide or seriously attempt it? Is the act of suicide a completely individualistic matter, the result of a unique history and a unique pain, or are there some common patterns in suicide behavior? What does it feel like to want to kill yourself? What are some of the thoughts, perceptions, misperceptions, and experiences that lead to a suicide attempt? How pervasive is this problem of self-destruction, and are some groups of people at high risk, people who are more likely than the rest of us to actually end their own lives? Are psychiatric illness and suicide related? What theories have been postulated to explain this phenomenon, suicide?

Types of Suicidal Behavior

Most of us think of suicide as a final action, but it is, in fact, a complicated concept that includes thoughts about suicide and attempts to end one's life, as well as completed suicide. The National Institute of Mental Health (NIMH) recognizes three major categories of suicidal behaviors (Resnick and Hathorne 1973):

I. *Completed Suicide:* This category includes deaths in which the circumstances surrounding the death lead to the conclusion that the individual took a positive action with the primary purpose of ending his life.

II. *Suicide Attempts:* This category refers to life-threatening behaviors in which the intent is to jeopardize life or to give the appearance of such an intent.

III. *Suicide Ideas:* The Suicide Ideas category includes behaviors which can be directly seen, or inferred, and which indicate a possible self-induced threat to the individual's life. Taking barbiturates out of a bottle and then returning them all to the bottle would be classified as Suicide Ideas. However, swallowing several pills with the intent of committing suicide would be classified as a Suicide Attempt (p. 8).

Two other, less definitive categories are *victim-precipitated homicides* (Wolfgang 1959) and *subintentional death* (Shneidman 1974). They include instances in which individuals

Fig. 10.1. Many historians contend that Alexander Hamilton, in his duel with Aaron Burr, deliberately fired into the air—an example of "subintentional death." Interestingly, his son also died in a duel by refusing to draw; his daughter was insane virtually all of her adult life.

take a partial or unconscious role in their own demise by periodically or persistently taking risks that increase the probability of premature death. Frequently cited examples are patients who do not comply with therapeutic medical regimes (for example, cardiac patients or diabetics), people who provoke extreme anger in others, persons deeply enmeshed in a drug subculture, chronic alcoholics, and people in highly dangerous professions or avocations (Schuyler 1974). Attributing suicidal motives to these cases needs more interpretation or subjective evaluation than deaths that conform to the more rigorous NIMH criteria, but it does give us a fuller understanding of suicidal behaviors.

Historical and Cultural Perspectives

Attitudes toward suicide have varied throughout history and from culture to culture. The Old Testament of the Bible records only five instances of suicide; the New Testament, just one (Rosen 1975). Most of these self-deaths were battle-related or tied to religious convic-

tion. The consensus of Biblical scholars is that the overall moral posture of the Old and New Testaments toward suicide is neutral. Although suicidal ideation and profound despair are common subjects in the Bible, suicide is neither lauded nor deplored.

Greeks and Romans had a similarly nonjudgmental attitude toward suicide, although they frequently gave overt approval to suicide for the sake of honor and to prevent capture by a military enemy. It appears that early Christian scholars were mainly responsible for denouncing suicide as a "mortal sin." By the seventh century A.D., people who attempted suicide were subject to excommunication by the Church, and if they survived, were in danger of imprisonment, torture, and loss of property. Oddly enough, although the Church persecuted any who attempted or committed suicide (the English drove stakes through the hearts of those who had committed suicide and the French dragged their corpses through the streets before hanging them on the gallows), it excepted people it regarded as insane.

Gradually, as the psychological components of suicide came to be recognized, it acquired a romantic connotation. Hume, Voltaire, and

Subintentional Death: A Playwright's Interpretation

From the moment he [Thomas Becket] became Archbishop, he completely reversed his policy; he showed himself to be utterly indifferent to the fate of the country, to be, in fact, a monster of egotism. This egotism grew upon him, until it became at last an undoubted mania. I have unimpeachable evidence to the effect that before he left France, he clearly prophesied, in the presence of numerous witnesses, that he had not long to live, and that he would be killed in England. He used every means of provocation; from his conduct, step by step, there can be no inference except that he had determined upon a death by martyrdom. Even at the last, he could have given us

reason: you have seen how he evaded our questions. And when he had deliberately exasperated us beyond human endurance, he could still have easily escaped; he could have kept himself from us long enough to allow our righteous anger to cool. That was just what he did not wish to happen; he insisted, while we were still inflamed with wrath, that the doors should be opened. Need I say more? I think, with these facts before you, you will unhesitatingly render a verdict of Suicide while of Unsound Mind. It is the only charitable verdict you can give, upon one who was, after all, a great man (Eliot, *Murder in the Cathedral* 1963, pp. 83–84).

[Handwritten margin notes: Men 3x complete suicides as women — gun ? hanging + carbon monoxide poisoning / Women attempted 3 suicides for every man — method overdose of drugs]

other eighteenth-century philosophers advocated abolishing criminal sanctions against suicide, and physicians and priests increasingly
dealt with suicide as a medical and psychological problem, not a moral one. The stigma is still
attached to suicidal behaviors in Western civilization (some countries have laws discriminating
against immigration for relatives of persons who
committed suicide), but recriminations are
fewer and less extreme than they were in medieval times. In fact, sometimes suicide is socially
approved. Tredgold and Wolff (1975) list "personal honour (Japanese hara-kiri, or until recently, a Royal Navy captain going down with
his ship); to save relations the trouble of long
nursing; to avoid torture and betrayal of com-
rades; to curtail prolonged illness; to bear witness to one's faith; to save someone else's life."

Religious and cultural variables still influence the incidence and manifestation of suicidal behaviors. Among the Hutterites and Mus-
lims, suicide is one of the most serious sins and
is extremely rare (Costello 1970). Very little in
the American experience, however, indicates
that our predominantly Judeo-Christian heritage is an effective deterrent to suicide.

[Handwritten: due to ① stigma ② coroners ambiguity of cause of death / statistics show only a portion of suicides]

Statistics on Suicide

The official statistics for the United States
indicate that approximately 25,000 Americans,
or twelve to thirteen of every 100,000, kill themselves each year (Schuyler 1974). Most experts
agree, however, that this figure is much too low.

[Handwritten: Risk of attempted suicide is highest in (24-44 age range) / " of complete " " " 55-64 " "]

Fig. 10.2. Suicide rates in five countries: Hungary, Sweden, Japan,
the United States, and Italy.

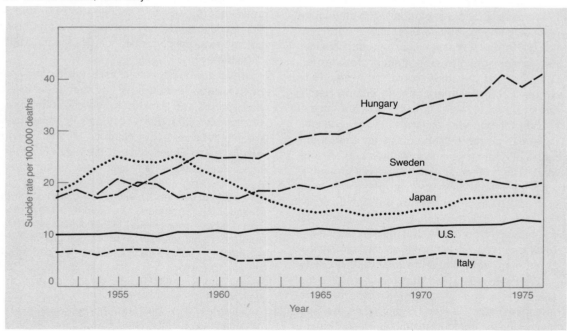

Suicide — shut-off world — every detail fits supports his decision — feelings of isolation, self-duplication + distorted self-perception; extreme feeling of inadequacy + isolation; feelings of hopelessness; desire to die → severely constricted thinking

motives → auto-biographies → histories → biographies suicidal note / not generalizable + do not readily answer why?

Estimates of completed suicides range between 50,000 and 75,000 a year (Schuyler 1974) and 100,000 (Kline 1974). Furthermore, it seems likely that at least five million Americans have made suicide attempts of varying severity at one time or another.

The risk of attempted suicide is highest between ages 24 and 44, but people between ages 55 and 64 are most likely to complete suicide. About three times more men than women actually kill themselves. In fact, suicide is now among the top five causes of death for Caucasian males aged 10 to 55 years. And yet the ratio of suicide *attempts* is three women for every man. Just as the rate of suicide differs for men and women, the methods do too: men are most likely to kill themselves first by gun, second by hanging, and third by carbon monoxide poisoning; women, on the other hand, most often choose an overdose of drugs (usually barbiturates). There are many explanations for sex-based differences in suicide rate. For one thing, women are more likely than men to seek professional help for psychological problems (quite possibly because of different cultural norms for the two sexes). Women may use suicidal behavior more often to call attention to interpersonal conflict; in other words, as a means of expression rather than of finality (World Health Organization 1974). Of course, *reported* rates of suicide for the two sexes may differ, and officials may be more likely to call an ambiguous cause of death a suicide in women and an accident in men. Also, one-car accidents and lethal auto accidents involving alcohol are more common in men than women, but suicide statistics may or may not reflect this fact. Whether sex-related differences will persist as sexual roles change and methods of assessment become more sophisticated remains to be seen.

We have mentioned that many experts feel suicide is a considerably underreported phenomenon. Why? Several hypotheses are suggested for the inaccurate suicide rates. Shneid-man (1973) estimates that 10 to 15 percent of coroner-certified deaths have ambiguous causes. Conceivably the training that coroners receive does not equip them to recognize the signs of suicide, and they mislabel a fair number as accidents. Another hypothesis is that generally people avoid "stigmatizing" suicide victims and their families with the label "suicide."

Phenomenological Perspectives

Statistics are useful in that they help to identify high-risk groups and so aid efforts at prevention. But the numbers tell psychologists little about what motivates people to take their own lives. It is impossible to issue blanket generalizations about suicide and suicide intent, but one way to try to understand suicidal ideation and behavior is to read case histories and autobiographical or biographical accounts written by people who have struggled intensely for some time with the idea of self-destruction. In these records we can discover how profound is the despair as well as how varied are the internal and external circumstances that lead to suicidal behavior.

In the passage that follows, English critic and poet Alvarez reveals how one man's distorted perceptions and thinking reinforced a decision on suicide. Changes like those he describes frequently accompany suicidal thinking and planning. His accounting of the bleak isolation in suicidal despair is, likewise, not uncommon.

Once a man decides to take his own life he enters a shut-off, impregnable but wholly convincing world where every detail fits and each incident reinforces his decision. An argument with a stranger in a bar, an expected letter which doesn't arrive, the wrong voice on the telephone, the wrong knock at the door, even a change in the weather — all seem charged with special meaning; they all contribute. The world of the suicide is superstitious, full of omens. Freud saw suicide as

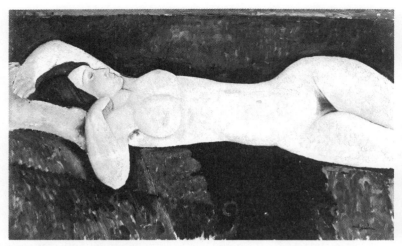 

Fig. 10.3. Amedeo Modigliani, the talented Italian painter, was 35 when he died of medical problems and heavy alcohol and other drug use. The self-destructive pattern of his life, which fits that of subintentional death described by Shneidman and others, did not keep him from producing art such as that shown here (*Reclining Nude,* c. 1919, oil on canvas, 28½ x 45⅞"; collection, The Museum of Modern Art, New York, Mrs. Simon Guggenheim Fund).

a great passion, like being in love: "In the two opposed situations of being most intensely in love and of suicide, the ego is overwhelmed by the object, though in totally different ways." As in love, things which seem trivial to the outsider, tiresome or amusing, assume enormous importance to those in the grip of the monster, while the sanest arguments against it seem to them simply absurd.

Similar feelings of isolation, self-deprecia-tion, and distorted self-perceptions fill an excerpt from the hospital records of John, a twenty-three-year-old patient with manic-depressive illness. At the time of these comments, he was under observation around the clock (suicide observation), because the hospital staff worried for his life.

I have prayed to God to kill me — Oh, isn't there some pill they can give me to take my life? I put my neck across the back of a chair and tried to put weight on it but I chickened out. I'm a failure. I'm not as intelligent as the group of males here now. I can't hold a conversation with any of them. I've lived my whole life and accomplished nothing, I just want to die. . . . I feel apathy, isolated, empty. . . . I dread to wake up in the morning and face another day of emptiness. . . . I'm tired of feeling as though I'm standing in the foyer of mankind and can't go in.

In John's case, extreme feelings of hope-lessness, inadequacy, and isolation — and high suicidality — appear to be secondary to a pri-mary disorder of mood. People who are severely depressed *and* have a primary disorder in thinking — for example, schizophrenics — sometimes consider suicide to be an alternative to some worse fate. The case of twenty-four-year-old Margaret, a paranoid schizophrenic, illustrates how a delusional system can evoke strong suicidal feelings. Just prior to making the remarks quoted below, the patient (who intermittently believes that she is possessed by the devil, is herself God, and is possessed by her dead father's soul) reported having a strong desire to either kill herself or "go totally insane." She also stated that were she to be taken off suicide observation she would slash her wrists or bang her head against the wall until she died. She expressed the desire to pierce her eardrums and eyes so that she would not have to hear or see what goes on in the world. She

felt that she was going "in and out of hell" and there was no alternative but suicide, which she felt would release her to go to heaven.

I want to kill myself. I'm going crazy, I'm feeling hopeless, I'm never going to get better. I saw a rainbow last night and it was there to give me a message. It was telling me to kill myself so I could die and go to heaven and be with my father. I don't feel like I have any control over myself. I wish I could go through the window or break some glass and kill myself.

Although different psychiatric illnesses led to both John's and Margaret's suicidal thinking and to multiple suicide attempts, both patients manifested the same feelings of hopelessness, desire to die, and severely constricted thinking.

Suicide Notes: Illuminating or Disappointing?

Shneidman has studied philosophical, psychological, and literary aspects of suicidal behavior for many years. Here are excerpts from his work on suicide notes (Shneidman 1973).

Without a doubt, suicide notes are valuable and fascinating documents. They furnish extremely important data for the study of suicide. But they are not the royal road to an easy understanding of suicidal phenomena. The perusal of a suicide note is usually a disappointing process. . . . One study . . . compared materials "before suicide" and materials "at the time of suicide." The former were Thematic Apperception Test protocols of persons who subsequently committed suicide; the latter were genuine suicide notes, albeit not of the same persons. The most important finding of this study is that the styles of reasoning and the patterns of logic are different at the time of suicide . . . a person is more constricted, irrelevant, scattered, and disorganized in his logical style. He simply is not at his cerebral best at the moment of truth (pp. 380–82). . . . About one-third of those who commit suicide write suicide notes.

What are the psychological differences between those who do write suicide notes and those who do not? Sex, age, marital status, and socioeconomic statistics of the two groups have been found to be essentially the same (as have mental condition, history of mental illness, medical care and supervision, place of suicide, and history of previous attempts or threats).

In comparison with simulated suicide notes written as people imagined they would write them if they were planning to commit suicide, Shneidman says:

Genuine suicide notes are generally characterized by dichotomous logic, a greater amount of hostility and self-blame, more use of very specific names and instructions to the survivors, less evidence of thinking about how one is thinking, and more use of the various meanings of the word "love" (p. 382).

It is hypothesized that suicide notes cannot be the insightful documents which suicidologists would hope that they would be, mainly because they are written during a special psychological state, a state of focused purpose and narrowed perception and psychodynamic

Of course, suicidal inclinations are not the lone preserve of psychotic disorders. Loss or grief or any severe life stress can plunge people into suicidal despondency. Many well-known and successful persons have suffered from "black despair." Abraham Lincoln and Winston Churchill both are "diagnosed" as having mood disorders (Fieve 1975; Kline 1974). Whether or not the diagnosis is valid — and it is a controversial issue — perhaps it is more important that the two men experienced periods of deep depression and yet functioned well under tremendous pressure. Fieve's description of Lincoln points out the profound and suicidal grief that occasionally accompanies the loss of a significant person:

Lincoln, at the age of twenty-nine, following the death of his first love, Ann Rutledge, plunged into a profound depression. He was seen wandering up and down the river through the woods, distracted and filled with indescribable grief. Fearing that he might commit suicide, his friends deprived him of knives and razors (Fieve 1975, pp. 94–95).

Winston Churchill had a multigenerational history of severe depression, and in addition to having depressive episodes himself, exhibited at least some signs of hypomania. His physician, Lord Moran, quoted Churchill as follows:

When I was young, for two or three years, the light faded out, I did my work barely, sat in the House of Commons, but black depression settled on me. . . . I don't like standing near the edge of a platform when an express train is passing through. I like it wider between me and the train. I don't like to stand on the side of a ship and look into the water. I don't want to go out in the world, even so still my wife, which makes you entitled to the things which belong to me, and I want you to have them. . . . I am listing some of the things, they are: A Blue Davenport and chair, a Magic Chef Stove, a large mattress [etc.] . . . Your husband, William H. Smith (p. 266).

Notes with some psychological descriptiveness: This note was written by a thirty-year-old psychiatrist who committed suicide with sleeping pills.

I'm sorry, but somewhere I lost the road, and in my struggle to find it again, I just got further and further away.

There should be little sadness, and no searching for who is at fault; for the act and the result are not sad, and no one is at fault.

My only sorrow is for my parents who will not easily be able to accept that this is so much better for me. Please folks, it's all right, really it is. . . .

I wanted to be too many things, and greatness besides — it was a hopeless task. I never managed to learn to really love another person — only to make the sounds of it . . . (p. 379).

denial. . . . diminish[ing] the possibility of his sharing with others (in a suicide note) what is truly going on in his mind (p. 385).

Three distinct types of suicide notes, according to Shneidman, are: declarative or testimonial; instructional and devoid of emotion; and psychologically descriptive. He gives these examples:

Notes that are declarative or testimonial: Percy W. Bridgman, Nobel laureate in physics and well-known American philosopher, shot himself at the age of eighty. Bridgman had been in great pain from terminal cancer and had asked doctors to give him something with which he could kill himself. They refused, and his suicide note gave testament to their refusal:

"It isn't decent for Society to make a man do this thing himself. Probably this is the last day I will be able to do it myself. p.w.b. (p. 386).

Notes that lack a point of view and simply contain instructions or directions:

Dear Mary. I am writeing you, as our Divorce is not final, and will not be until next month, so the way things stand now you are

at all, at such moments. . . . I have no desire to quit this world but thoughts, desperate thoughts, come into my head (Fieve 1975, p. 114).

Suicide notes are another source of phenomenological information about suicidal feelings, thinking, and behavior, although they do not always provide satisfactory answers to the question, "Why?" Nor do they enable psychologists to generalize across people and situations. We are ultimately left with a collection of theories that we cannot validate.

Theories of Suicide

We will discuss briefly three major theoretical positions on suicide: (1) psychological, (2) biological, and (3) sociological. These groups of theories clearly overlap in many important ways, but neither alone nor in combination do they completely explain why some people commit suicide and others do not. Surprisingly, although the psychological literature on the subject is vast, we find remarkably few integrated or comprehensive theories of suicide and suicide behavior.

Psychological Theories

As they have in so many areas of psychopathology, Freud (1917) and subsequent psychoanalytic writers (Menninger 1938; Binswanger 1958; Litman 1967) have shaped thinking about suicide. The prevalent view among psychoanalysts is that suicide is a uniquely intrapsychic event (rather than a reflection of more general, sociological factors), and that it generally is an act of self-aggression, the result of a great deal of hostility directed inward. Furthermore, they postulate that the suicidal person's hostility is a product of frustration and ambivalence toward a significant individual in his life. This is an oversimplification, for most psychoanalysts also stress the feelings of helplessness and hope-

lessness, dependency conflicts, and overwhelming anxiety and guilt.

Some behaviorists believe that suicidal behavior occasionally is a maladaptive way of handling interpersonal relationships; in behavioral language, it is a maladaptive response to highly problematic situations. From the point of view of the individual, suicidal behaviors may be attempts to cope with some personal problem. For some people, suicide seems to be a *solution* to an overpowering dilemma (Funabiki 1977).

Biological Theories

Just as most of the psychological theories of suicide are, in some ways, more accurately theories of depression, so too are the biological theories of suicide. Thus, the biological models we discussed in Chapters 8 and 9 can be, and often are, implicated in suicide. Although these physiological correlates are both interesting and of increasing importance as the neurochemistry is slowly worked out, they are still speculative, tentative, and correlative. Nevertheless, we have reason to hope that methods of treating depression that have evolved from these research hypotheses will eventually reduce the suicide rate (see Chapter 11).

Sociological Theory

Suicide, as we have seen, is an immoral act in some religious and cultural traditions. And despite the higher risk of suicide among the mentally ill, it is also a choice that a distressing number of apparently normal people make each year. Therefore, it should come as no surprise that suicide has long had a place in sociology textbooks and that the overlap of psychology and sociology is more pronounced in this area of abnormal behavior than where effects are more clearly personal, intrapsychic, or biological, such as schizophrenia and manic-depressive illness. Sociologists consider suicide to be the result of problems in an individual's relationship with society. Emile Durkheim

(1951), a French sociologist who did much of the original sociological research on suicide in the late 1800s, saw suicide as mainly a product of social disorganization, and concluded that the stronger an individual's ties to others in society, the smaller the risk of suicide. He divided suicide into three basic types: egoistic, altruistic, and anomic.

EGOISTIC SUICIDES

Egoistic suicide, Durkheim believed, stems from the lack of meaningful social interactions and close relationships with the community. A frequently quoted finding by Durkheim's proponents is that Protestants have a considerably higher suicide rate than Catholics. In addition to the Catholic church's stronger moral constraints against suicide, a greater belief in free will among Protestants and the relatively weaker social bond between them and their churches is the explanation sociologists generally give for this difference.

ALTRUISTIC SUICIDES

Altruistic suicide involves individuals whose ties to society are so strong as to be, paradoxically, potentially life-threatening. These are people who will take their own lives if the society deems it the only honorable thing to do. The self-death or hara-kiri of a Japanese officer after a military defeat is an altruistic suicide. French playwright Albert Camus succinctly characterized this no-win situation: "What is called a good reason for living is also an excellent reason for dying" (Alvarez 1973, p. 88).

The third type, *anomic suicide,* Durkheim attributed to a sudden marked change in the victim's position and relationship with society that necessitates rearranging events, values, and interpersonal relationships. Perhaps the most common life changes that can lead to this type of suicide involve loss of job, spouse, friends, or money, although sudden acquisition of wealth or power can sometimes have the same effect.

Plausible as Durkheim's assessment may be, it is, after all, still a theory. The obvious limitations of researching suicide behavior (the impossibility of interviewing victims and of conducting experimental research), in turn, reduce the likelihood that anyone will ever be able to prove or disprove either Durkheim's nineteenth-century hypothesis or the more modern psychological theories. On the other hand, if researchers can demonstrate that depression involves biological change and if there is a link between depression and suicide, one day we might indirectly be able to explain some suicide motivation. In the meantime, psychologists and sociologists alike must be satisfied with primarily inferential evidence.

Fig. 10.4. The behavior of Japanese kamikaze pilots during World War II illustrates the concept of altruistic suicide.

Suicide Intent and Motivational Influences

Suicide often seems to the outsider a supremely motiveless perversity, performed, as Montesquieu complained, "most unaccountably . . . in the very bosom of happiness," and for reasons which seem trivial or even imperceptible. . . . In other words, a suicide's excuses are mostly casual. At best they assuage the guilt of the survivors, soothe the tidy-minded and encourage the sociologists in their endless search for convincing categories and theories. They are like a trivial border incident which triggers off a major war. The real motives which impel a man to take his own life are elsewhere; they belong to the internal world, devious, contradictory, labyrinthine, and mostly out of sight (Alvarez 1973, p. 97).

Suicide and suicidal behaviors are almost always the culmination of many highly complicated and related motivational patterns, external circumstances, and internal mental states. Although it is difficult to quantify this relationship and to suggest a precise combination of factors that disposes an individual to commit suicide, available data enable us to identify with some confidence characteristics of high-risk individuals. We can also predict which type of person is likely to complete the act and which will probably go no further than to attempt suicide.

Shneidman (1976) has suggested three psychological phenomena that cause a person to be acutely suicidal: an increase in self-hatred, exacerbation of psychological imbalance, and constriction of thinking (that is, tunneling or narrowing of the mind's content). Coupled with the conscious thought of one's own ability to stop the pain (cessation), these elements increase the probability of suicide dramatically.

Assessing the *intent* and *seriousness* of an individual's suicidal behavior is one of the major complexities in the study of suicide. Stengel (1964) addresses this and related issues:

The conventional notion of a genuine suicidal act is something like this: "A person, having decided to end his life, or acting on a sudden impulse to do so, kills himself, having chosen the most effective method available and having made sure that nobody interferes. When he is dead he is said to have succeeded and the act is often called a successful suicide attempt. If he survives he is said to have failed and the act is called an unsuccessful suicidal attempt. Death is the only purpose of this act and therefore the only criterion of success. Failure may be due to any of the following causes: the sense of purpose may not have been strong enough; or the act may have been undertaken half-heartedly because it was not quite genuine; the subject was ignorant of the limitations of the method; or he was lacking in judgment and determination through mental illness." Judging by those standards only a minority of fatal and very few nonfatal suicidal acts would pass muster as both serious and genuine. The rest have to be dismissed as poor efforts some of which succeeded by chance rather than design. Obviously, this approach cannot do justice to a very common and varied behaviour pattern. . . .

Any act of self-damage inflicted deliberately which looks like a suicidal attempt ought to be regarded and treated as such. Only if there is evidence that the person took no risk subjectively should the act be regarded as falling outside the categories of suicidal acts . . . . *Most people who commit suicidal acts do not either want to die or to live; they want to do both at the same time, usually the one more, or much more, than the other.* It is quite unpsychological to expect people in states of stress, and especially vulnerable and emotionally unstable individuals who form the large majority of those prone to acts of self-damage, to know exactly what they want and to live up to St. James' exhortation: "Let your yea be yea and your nay, nay" (pp. 77, 87).

Studies indicate that the incidence of completed suicides among people who attempt to kill themselves is 10 to 20 percent, and that between 20 and 65 percent of those who eventually commit suicide have a prior history of at least one attempt (Dorpat and Ripley 1967; Wilkins 1967). Psychologists use several techniques to assess the seriousness of suicide intent. Weisman and Worden (1972) devised a *risk-rescue rating scale* that measures variables involved in suicide rescue and in the actual degree of risk inherent in the suicide method (see Table 10.1). A more subjectively oriented assessment of suicide attempts emphasizes data obtained by examining the individual's preconceptions about suicide methods and his inner mental state, as well as the circumstances surrounding the attempted or completed suicide (Schuyler 1974). Table 10.2 outlines the *suicide intent factors.* Still another source of data on suicidal behavior and intent is the *psychological autopsy,* a case history compiled after the fact. Table 10.3 lists several items of information that a psychological autopsy generally includes.

What reasons do people give for *wanting* to kill themselves? Shneidman (1971) surveyed 30,000 readers of *Psychology Today* magazine — an admittedly highly self-selected group of readers and respondents — and found that 540 of this group had made serious suicide attempts. The two motives most frequently cited for the attempts were loneliness and illness or physical pain. In another study, men who had attempted suicide gave as the main reasons ill health, marital difficulties, and psychological depression. Women respondents attributed

Table 10.1. Risk-rescue rating scale

Rescue factors
1. Location
2. Person initiating rescue
3. Probability of discovery by any rescuer
4. Accessibility to rescue
5. Delay until discovery

Risk factors
1. Agent used
2. Degree of impaired consciousness
3. Brain lesions, toxicity
4. Reversibility
5. Treatment required

Source: A. D. Weisman and J. W. Worden, "Risk-rescue Rating in Suicide Assessment," *Archives of General Psychiatry,* 1972, 26, pp. 553–560.

Table 10.2. Suicide intent factors

Introspective data
1. Concept of the method's lethality
2. Degree of premeditation
3. Self-report of intent
4. Concept of reversibility of behavior

Circumstantial data
1. Degree of isolation
2. Timing
3. Precautions vs. intervention
4. Action to gain help
5. Final acts on anticipation of death
6. Degree of planning
7. Suicide note
8. Communication of intent before act

Source: D. Schuyler, *The Depressive Spectrum* (New York: Jason Aronson, 1974), p. 93.

their suicide attempts to poor physical health, poor mental health, and psychological depression (Farberow and Shneidman 1965).

A Viennese study of 1040 attempted suicides reported by the World Health Organization (1974) divided 385 men and 655 women into two groups depending on whether they categorized their motivation as "unhappiness" (depression, loneliness, or loss of a close friend or relative) or "conflict" involving other persons. Conflict motives were more prevalent among the women (70 percent) than among the men (56 percent) and, conversely, unhappiness motives were more prevalent among men (44 percent) than among the women (30 percent). As Figure 10.5 shows, conflict motives were more common, generally speaking, in the younger age ranges, but in every age range, women mentioned conflict motives more frequently than the men did. Perhaps these data reflect genuinely different motivational and psychological functioning in men and women, more awareness and willingness to talk about interpersonal conflict on the part of women, or differences in cultural expectations of acceptable social behavior for men and women.

[Handwritten annotations in top margin: "Social variables that may correlate with suicidal behavior includes ① loss of job ② living alone ③ socioeconomic status"; "Peaking in May, low in December; Monday for age groups 40-64"]

Table 10.3. Outline for psychological autopsy

1. Identifying information for victim (name, age, address, marital status, religious practices, occupation, and other details)
2. Details of the death (including the cause or method and other pertinent details)
3. Brief outline of victim's history (siblings, marriage, medical illnesses, medical treatment, psychotherapy, previous suicide attempts)
4. "Death history" of victim's family (suicides, cancer, other fatal illnesses, ages at death, and other details)
5. Description of the personality and life style of the victim
6. Victim's typical patterns of reaction to stress, emotional upsets, and periods of disequilibrium
7. Any recent — from last few days to last 12 months — upsets, pressures, tensions, or anticipations of trouble

8. Role of alcohol and drugs in (a) overall life style of victim and (b) in his death
9. Nature of victim's interpersonal relationships (including physicians)
10. Fantasies, dreams, thoughts, premonitions, or fears of victim relating to death, accident, or suicide
11. Changes in the victim before death (of habits, hobbies, eating, sexual patterns, and other life routines)
12. Information relating to the "life side" of victim (upswings, successes, plans)
13. Assessment of intention (role of the victim in his own demise)
14. Rating of lethality
15. Reactions of informants to victim's death
16. Comments, special features, etc.

Source: Adapted from E. S. Shneidman, "Suicide Among the Gifted," in E. S. Shneidman, ed., *Suicidology: Contemporary Developments* (New York: Grune & Stratton, 1976), p. 353.

Fig. 10.5. Percentage of subjects with "conflict motives" and "unhappiness motives" by age group (n = 1040 attempted suicides). (After Brooke 1974.)

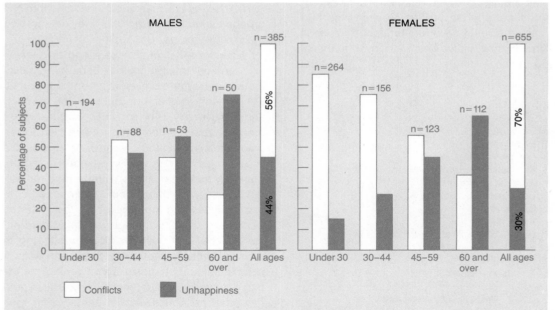

Sociological variables that may correlate with suicidal behavior include loss of job (Kline 1974), living alone (NIMH 1974), and socioeconomic status, although there is conflict on whether those in higher income brackets have a higher or lower suicide rate (Shneidman and Farberow 1957; Hamermesh and Soss 1974; Stengel 1964). Other facts that have been thought by some to be connected to suicide are summarized in Table 10.4 (Lester and Lester 1971). Overall factors that seem to differentiate those at high risk from those at low risk, based on one major study (Farberow and Shneidman 1965), appear in Table 10.5.

Table 10.4. Time, season, weather, and suicide rate

Variable	Relationship to suicide rate
Seasonal rhythms	Unclear; peak in May, low in December
Holidays	No apparent relationship
Day of week	Monday for age group 40–64; otherwise unclear
Weather	Unclear
Phases of moon, sunspot activity	No apparent relationship

Table 10.5. Characteristics of committed and attempted suicides, Los Angeles County (1957)

Characteristic	Committed suicide (540 males; 228 females)	Attempted suicide (828 males; 1824 females)
Sex	More males	More females
Race	For both sexes, almost entirely Caucasian	For both sexes, predominantly Caucasian
Age	For both sexes, greatest number in forties; for males, continues proportionately high in sixties and over	For both sexes, greatest number in twenties and thirties
Marital status	For both sexes, large percentage married (though low proportionately), more divorced, separated, and widowed; for females, high proportion of widowed	For both sexes, large percentage married (though low proportionately), high proportion single
Occupation	For females, high proportion of housewives; for males, high proportion skilled and unskilled	For females, high proportion of housewives; for males, high proportion skilled, semiskilled, and unskilled
Nativity	For both sexes, predominantly native-born	For both sexes, predominantly native-born
Method of suicide	For males, mostly gunshot wounds, hanging, carbon monoxide; for females, mostly barbiturates and gunshot wounds	For both sexes, mostly barbiturates, some wrist cutting
"Reason" for suicide	For both sexes, ill health, depression; for males, marital difficulties	For both sexes, marital difficulties, depression; for males, financial and employment difficulties
Socioeconomic areas	For both sexes, highest in apartment areas of all types (most, moderately, and least advantaged)	For both sexes, highest in apartment areas, particularly least and moderately advantaged

Source: N. L. Farberow and E. S. Shneidman, *The Cry for Help* (New York: McGraw-Hill, 1965).

Psychiatric Illness and Suicide

Is the suicide rate higher among people who have a major psychiatric problem than for the rest of the population (possibly excepting the aged and the terminally ill)? Many methodological problems are involved in researching this question. First, the absence of a clear dividing line between normal behavior and deviant behavior (see Chapter 1) makes it impossible to say conclusively that a suicide victim was or was not clinically disturbed at the time of death. Second, as Kramer and colleagues (1972) point

The Psychological Autopsy

In 1957, Los Angeles County Coroner Theodore J. Curphey invited members of the Los Angeles Suicide Prevention Center to assist him in settling equivocal cases of possible suicide. Focusing primarily on the *personality* elements associated with suicide, such as suicide intention, subtle communications about that intent, presence of clinical depression, and schizophrenia, this so-called suicide team performed psychological "autopsies" on suspected suicide victims. Their approach was to reconstruct the life styles and personalities of the deceased mainly by interviewing their spouses, grown children, parents, physicians, and others who knew them well. From these psychological data, and other physical evidence of suicide, accident, homicide, or natural death, the suicide team attempted to describe the last days of a victim's life. They reported their conclusions and recommendations to the coroner for final integration with the findings of the coroner's staff. They recommended that the coroner certify this case a suicide (Farberow and Shneidman 1965):

A 33-year-old male of German descent, working as a butler for a well-to-do investment broker, was found dead in his bathtub with his head under water. The bathtub was filled to the brim. The police report stated that he had been in ill health for the preceding two months and that the day prior to his death he had told the cook where he worked that he did not feel well. A glass containing a yellow crystalline substance was found on top of the water closet next to the bathtub. Autopsy revealed a large quantity of water in his stomach and proximal small bowel, associated with marked pulmonary edema. The heart and aorta were essentially normal. Toxicological examination showed the absence of alcohol and the presence of 1.4 mg per 100 cc barbiturates in the blood. The residue in the glass was found to be pentobarbital.

With these facts, the preponderant opinion was that this was a suicide, but in light of the realistic possibility that this could have been an accident, it was felt that an investigation by the Suicide Team was indicated. Their study revealed many interesting facts. It was ascertained that the victim had been depressed for some time previous and had made a serious suicide attempt just two months before in the home of a nurse, where he had been staying. As a result of that attempt, he had been taken to a local hospital, where he had been comatose over 24 hours and where he had then spent 8 days. On recovery he told his nurse friend that he had taken 24 Nembutal tablets.

His life history, as reconstructed from the informants, was most interesting. At the age of 15 he had entered a military academy in Germany; Hitler was then in power. He was trained as a fighter pilot and engaged in heavy fighting. While he was on a mission, his best friend had been killed. Upon his return, he requested his superior officer to send him again so that he could either avenge or join his friend. Upon denial, he threatened suicide and actually attempted it by shooting himself through the left chest. He survived this attempt and was hospitalized. Later, he was taken prisoner by the British and sent to Egypt in 1945. In 1946, he returned to Germany and fell in love with an airline stewardess, who was later killed in an airline crash. He then left Germany and went to Argentina, where he flew for Peron until the dictator was ousted. From there he went to Brazil and later to Venezuela, where he worked

out, classification of mental disorders varies not only in time but also from place to place (we saw in Chapter 5 that manic-depressive illness was found to be diagnosed much more commonly in the United Kingdom than in the United States and, conversely, schizophrenia was more often the diagnosis in America than in Britain). Third,

we have no adequate way of assessing the *total* number of persons in a community who may be mentally ill, making it difficult to judge what proportion of suicides involves individuals who have exhibited symptoms of behavior disorders (Kramer et al. 1972). Also, major inadequacies flaw sampling procedures, disagreements

until the revolution occurred and he lost everything he had. He finally made his way to the United States in 1956, and came to Los Angeles, where he worked until the time of his death.

In the course of gathering the foregoing information, members of the Suicide Team investigated the actual scene some days after his death. Because of the feelings of his employer, the victim's quarters had been left undisturbed during this time. The investigators, on checking the bathtub, found a wad of cloth stuffed in the safety, or overflow, drain, thus allowing the tub to be filled to the very top. Mindful of the victim's prior experience with barbiturates, we reconstructed that he had taken this precaution to make certain of his death by drowning, if the barbiturates failed to kill him (p. 120).

The following case initially appeared suicidal but was recommended for certification as an *accident.*

In practically any coroner's office, a death that results from playing Russian roulette would automatically be certified as suicide. Indeed, there is now legal precedent for such certifications. Because of a special interest on the part of the Suicide Team in this type of death, this case was turned over to them by the coroner for investigation, with, as it turned out, extremely surprising results. On the basis of interviews it was ascertained that the victim, a 28-year-old male, was an Army veteran who had a collection of revolvers, which he kept in perfect operating condition. It was determined from his best friend that the victim's favorite activity at parties was to play Russian roulette (following the usual rules of the game by having one chamber of the cylinder loaded) and that he had done this literally dozens of times

in the preceding few years. At this point, the Suicide Team wondered about the psychology of a man who would behave in such a fashion: was he psychotic or was he intent on killing himself? Interviews with the widow clarified the situation: the victim had told her that there was no possibility of his hurting himself, as he always glanced at the gun to ascertain that the bullet was in a nonlethal position before he pulled the trigger. If the bullet was one notch to the left of the barrel, he would spin the cylinder again. There had been no suicidal ideation and no evidence of depression, psychosis, or morbid content of thought. What had happened? The Suicide Team knew that the death had occurred in someone else's home. Interviews developed the information that he shot himself with a revolver that was not his own but belonged to his host of the evening. What seemed most important was the fact that, whereas his collection consisted entirely of Smith & Wesson revolvers, he had killed himself with a Colt revolver. The actions of the two guns are different; i.e., the cylinder of the Smith and Wesson revolves clockwise. It was believed that the victim, checking and seeing the bullet one space to the right of the barrel, thought that he could not possibly kill himself, whereas in reality pulling the trigger put the bullet in the lethal position and he died immediately.

In the absence of any indication of suicidal affect or any indications of suicidal ideation, and with the additional information about the two types of revolvers, the Suicide Team recommended that this death be considered as accidental. One member of the Suicide Team labeled this case as one of Soviet Roulette, that is, Russian roulette wherein one cheats (p. 121).

about defining suicide, and retrospective speculation. A general problem is that studies performed after the suicidal act rely mostly on inference, not direct observation. With these limitations in mind, we will examine the evidence for relationships between mental illness and suicide.

Pokorny (1964) found the suicide rates (per 100,000 per year) for different psychiatric diagnostic categories shown in Figure 10.6. Another study (Levy and Southcombe 1953) indicated that 50 percent of patients in one mental hospital who committed suicide were diagnosed as schizophrenics and 10 percent as manic-depressives. More recent data (Kramer et al.

1972) suggest that the incidence of suicide is highest among patients diagnosed as having primary mood disorders and "psycho-neuroses," and that the rates for schizophrenic patients and victims of organic brain syndromes are also disproportionately high. Robins et al. (1959) found that the most frequent psychiatric diagnoses in persons who committed suicide were manic-depressive illness and alcoholism. In the follow-up study of patients with manic-depressive illness, this group reported suicide to be the cause of death in 15 percent of the sample, and this finding was consistent across groups, regardless of size, length of follow-up, or country of origin. The lifetime risk of suicide

Fig. 10.6. Psychiatric diagnosis and suicide rate. Notice the strikingly high rate for affective disorders. (After Pokorny 1964.)

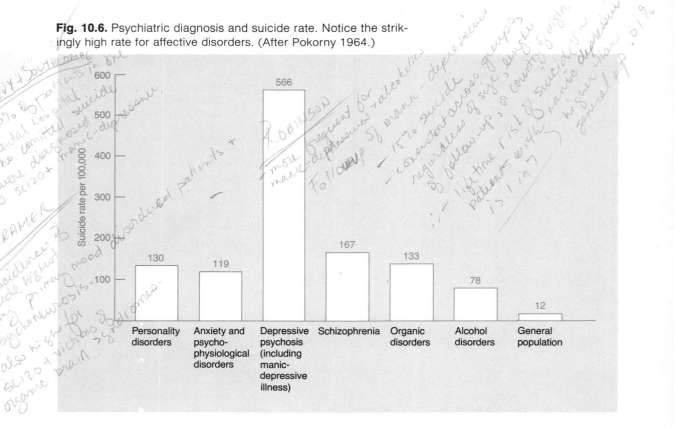

in patients with manic-depressive illness was 1 in 7, much higher than for any other group. Although the figures vary, the results of these and similar studies (Robins 1959; Guze and Robins 1970; Pederson et al. 1972) suggest that the suicide rate for persons having a primary mood disorder is much greater than the overall rate of 0.01 percent for the general population.

What makes a severely depressed person a very high risk for suicide? Among the high-risk characteristics of this group, Sainsbury (1955) lists: endogenous depression (see Chapter 8); age greater than forty; history of parental death in childhood; history of suicide threat or attempt; brief duration of depressive illness or recent discharge from hospital; living alone; emphasis placed by patient on a feeling of hopelessness, worthlessness, or lack of energy rather than adverse circumstances; heavy alcohol intake. Another study, made in the emer-

Psychosis and Suicide: Death of Virginia Woolf

These excerpts from Quentin Bell's 1972 biography of Virginia Woolf illustrate the complexities, poignancies and despairs that often are handmaidens to suicide. The noted English author and intellectual suffered from recurrent psychotic episodes of manic-depression. She feared recurrences of her illness, and her fears had devastating effects on her relationships.

Miss Bowden describes Virginia kneeling on the floor — they were mending a torn curtain — "and she sat back on her heels and put her head back in a patch of sun, early spring sun, and laughed in this consuming, choking, delightful, hooting way . . . and it has remained with me. So that I get a curious shock when I see people regarding her entirely as a martyred, or a definitely tragic sort of person claimed by the darkness."

When did the laughter end and the darkness begin? It is hard to say. It was a symptom of Virginia's madness that she could not admit that she was mentally ill; to force this knowledge upon her was, in itself, dangerous. . . . In the end she did confess some part of her fears, fears that the past would come back, that she would be unable to write again.

On the morning of Friday 28 March, a bright, clear, cold day, Virginia went as usual to her studio room in the garden. . . . Then she went back into the house and wrote again to [her husband] Leonard:

Dearest,
  I feel certain I am going mad again. I feel we can't go through another of those terrible times. And I shan't recover this time. I begin to hear voices, and I can't concentrate. So I am doing what seems the best thing to do. You have given me the greatest possible happiness. You have been in every way all that anyone could be. I don't think two people could have been happier till this terrible disease came. I can't fight any longer. I know that I am spoiling your life, that without me you could work. And you will I know. You see I can't even write this properly. I can't read. What I want to say is I owe all the happiness of my life to you. You have been entirely patient with me and incredibly good. I want to say that — everybody knows it. If anybody could have saved me it would have been you. Everything has gone from me but the certainty of your goodness. I can't go on spoiling your life any longer.
  I don't think two people could have been happier than we have been.

V.

She put this on the sitting-room mantelpiece and, at about 11:30, slipped out, taking her walking-stick with her and making her way across the water-meadows to the river. Leonard believed that she might already have made one attempt to drown herself; if so she had learnt by her failure and was determined to make sure of it now. Leaving her stick on the bank she forced a large stone into the pocket of her coat. Then she went to her death, "the one experience," as she had said . . . , "I shall never describe" (pp. 224–226).

SAINSBURY
High-Risk Categories
- endogenous depression
- age 7 40
- history of parental death in childhood
- history of suicide threat or attempt
- brief duration of depressive illness or recent discharge from hospital
- living alone,
- heavy alcohol intake
- feelings of hopelessness, worthlessness + lack of energy

Other studies
- psychotics
- hopelessness

[Handwritten top margin: person suffering from a primary mood disorder, as well as schizo appear to be much more vulnerable to suicidal thoughts + behaviors than the general popln.]

[Handwritten: + relationship between depression and suicide tends to be the strongest + most consistent correlate in almost every study of self-destructive behavior]

gency room of a general hospital (Rubenstein et al. 1958), reported that the suicide attempts of psychotics were more life-threatening than those of the general suicidal population who made their way into the same hospital emergency room.

An important correlation also seems to connect hopelessness and the seriousness of suicidal intent. Beck (1967a) maintains: "In our studies we found that suicidal wishes had a higher correlation with hopelessness than with any other symptom of depression."

Still, most depressed persons do not commit suicide. Theoretical and practical interest in finding some way to distinguish the potential suicide from the nonsuicide among depressed patients has been extensive. Researchers at the Suicide Prevention Center in Los Angeles have suggested one clue (Wold and Tabachnik 1974) that is consistent with the statistical data accumulated for mood-disordered patients. For their study, they compared a sample of patients who came to the center in a suicidal crisis and who subsequently did kill themselves, with a similar sample who did not commit suicide. They classified the patients in each group according to the type of suicidal crisis they were experiencing at the time of the initial contact at the center, and also rated them on four different components of depression from information in their case files. The results indicate that although the type of suicidal crisis did not predict suicide rate, one type of depressive cluster, *somatic depression* (similar to the major depressive disorders discussed in Chapter 8), was more common in completed suicides. The symptoms shown by the somatic depressives included severe sleep disturbances, early morning awakening, major acute fluctuations in weight or appetite, and a variety of vague somatic complaints, often seemingly hypochondriacal.

The relationship between depression, in particular, and psychiatric illness in general, has significant implications for treatment of high-risk patients and prevention of suicide, as we will see in Chapter 11. Persons suffering from a primary mood disorder, as well as schizophrenics, appear to be much more vulnerable to suicidal thoughts and behaviors than the rest of the population. The relationship between depression and suicide appears to be the strongest and most consistent correlate in almost every study of self-destructive behavior.

Suicide and College Students

[Handwritten right margin: women 3x more likely to attempt + men more likely to complete — high risk too — 2x as many as noncollege commit suicide]

Yet another group of individuals known to be at high risk for suicide is made up of college students. Statistics indicate that more than 1000 kill themselves each year, and 10,000 attempt suicide. Twice as many college students kill themselves as do noncollege students in the same age range. Women students are three times as likely as men to attempt suicide, but men are much more likely to actually complete suicide. Why? Consider how two well-known personalities, economist-philosopher John Stuart Mill and poet Sylvia Plath (who eventually did kill herself), felt about their days as college students and their suicidal thoughts during that time:

Neither selfish nor unselfish pleasures were pleasures to me. . . . These were the thoughts which mingled with the dry heavy dejection of the melancholy winter of 1826–1827. During this time I was not incapable of my usual occupations. I went on with them mechanically, by the mere force of habit. . . . Of four years' continual speaking at that [debating] society, this is the only year of which I remember next to nothing. Two lines of Coleridge, in whom alone of all writers I have found a true description of what I felt, were often in my thoughts:

Work without hope draws nectar in a sieve, and hope without an object cannot live . . .

[Handwritten left margin: most depressed people don't commit suicide / clue to predicting suicide / somatic depression (similar to major depression) most common / consistent with statistics on mood disorder]

SHNEIDMAN
College students
-53% seriously contemplated suicide
-11% attempted it
-33%-sure they would never commit suicide

reason 1) loneliness or abandonment 2) illness or physical pain 3) to get even with or hurt someone else

SEIDEN
Factors: worry about academic work + physical health, + difficulties with relationships

I frequently asked myself, if I could, or if I was bound to go on living, when life must be passed in this manner. I generally answered to myself that I did not think I could possibly bear it beyond a year.

— John Stuart Mill, age 21
(from his *Autobiography,* p. 111)

Sylvia Plath, an enormously successful poet and student during her undergraduate years at Smith College, describes a period of exuberance just prior to an episode of severe depression and a serious suicide attempt:

All in all, I felt upborne on a wave of creative, social and financial success — The six month crash, however, was to come. . . . A time of darkness, despair, disillusion — so black only as the inferno of the human mind can be — symbolic death, and numb shock — then the painful agony of slow rebirth and psychic regeneration (Plath, *The Bell Jar,* p. 208).

Both Mill and Plath speak of being caught up in perhaps too much success and thought and excitement too soon, without time to assimilate either their talents or successes into their self-concepts or life styles.

Many people regard college students as an endowed or privileged group. Why is there so much despair in so capable a group? Shneidman (1967), in one survey of ninety college students, described their experiences and attitudes toward suicide. Among them, 53 percent said they had seriously contemplated suicide and 11 percent had attempted it. Only 33 percent were sure they never would actually commit suicide. Forty-three percent doubted that it was very likely, but 2 percent expressed worry that they might kill themselves some day. When asked what they thought would make them actually commit suicide, they gave these answers: loneliness or abandonment (36 percent); illness or physical pain (18 percent); and to get even with or hurt someone else (4 percent).

Seiden (1966) studied the lives and academic records of twenty-three University of California (Berkeley) students who had committed suicide in a nine-year period and found that they had been moodier, had driven themselves harder, and had been depressed more frequently than other students, and they had given recurrent warnings of their suicidal intent to others. The major precipitating events appeared to have been worry about academic work and physical health, and difficulties in relationships. It is difficult to ascertain, of course, whether these factors indeed caused the suicides or whether academic difficulties and interpersonal problems were secondary to a severe depression or other major emotional problem. Worry about physical health is frequently a symptom of depression. Suicidal students often have higher records of academic achievement than their nonsuicidal fellow students, so that we can rule out academic failure as a significant cause of suicide among students. The ever-present problems of adolescence — separation from home, issues of identity, independence-dependency conflicts, sexual turmoil — are, of course, highly important in the sphere of college students' problems. These problems, however, confront most adolescents and young adults, both students and nonstudents, and cannot account for the substantially higher suicide rate among students.

The complex interweavings of sociological and psychological factors in all suicidal behavior are revealed by suicide studies undertaken at British universities. Stengel (1964) and Lester and Lester (1971) found a large number of symptoms common among those who had committed suicide:

loss of appetite
psychophysiological complaints
insomnia
withdrawn behavior
neglect of academic work
communication problems

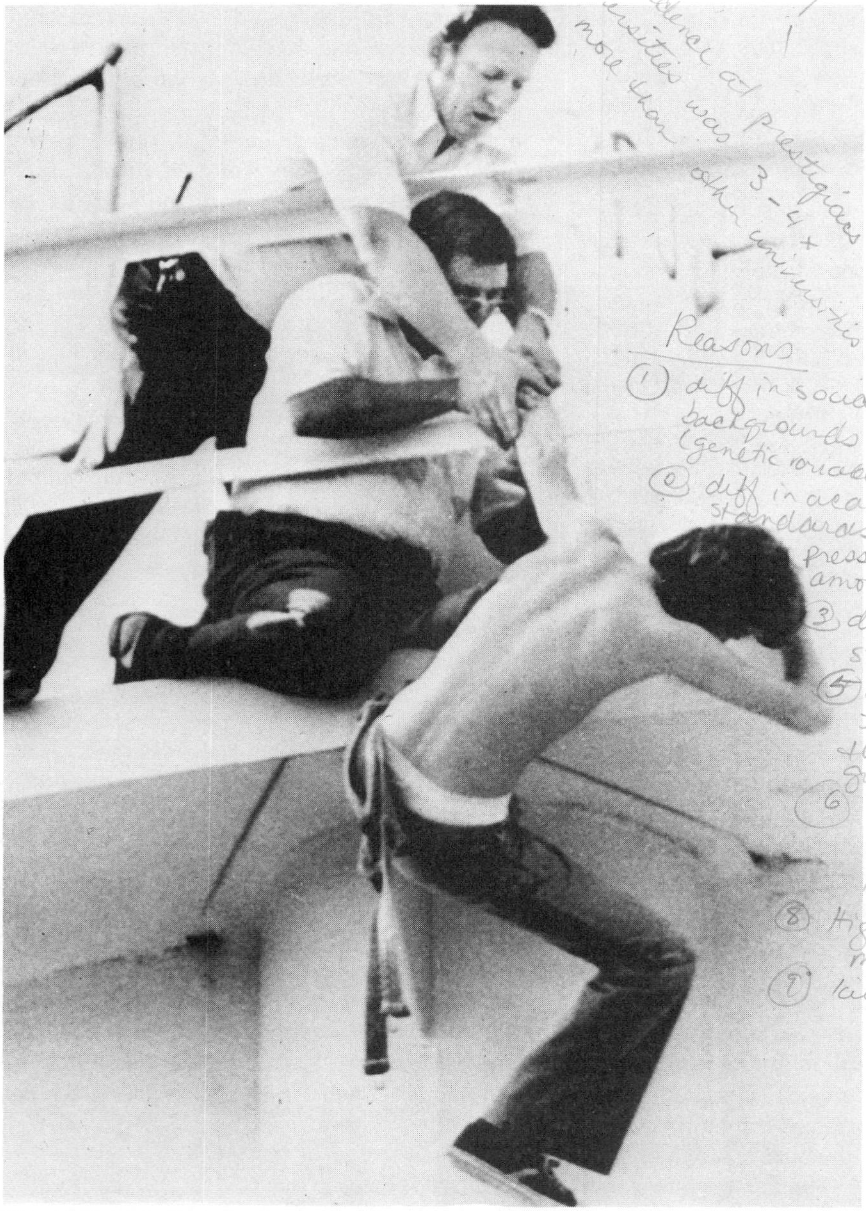

Fig. 10.7. In Georgia, police get a double-handed grip on a young would-be suicide as he dangles off a walkway around a water tower. The police answered a call when the youth was reported yelling obscenities at people. He asked the police to get his parents so they could watch him die.

Stengel + Lester

incidence at prestigious universities was 3-4 + more than other universities

Commonalities who among those committed suicide

1 - loss of appetite
2 - sleeplessness (insomnia)
3 - withdrawn behavior
4 - neglect of academic work
5 - communication problems
6 - loss of weight
7 - promiscuity - increased use of drugs
8 - increased use of alcohol
9 - poor class attendance
10 - neglect of personal hygiene

Reasons

1 diff in social backgrounds (genetic oriented)
2 diff in academic standards + pressures among the U.
3 diff #'s of students
5 diff in social structures in the U. that might produce greater alienation
6 syndrome of the little frog in the big pond — competition
8 higher proportion of male
9 lack of family contact

loss of weight
promiscuity
increased alcohol use
increased use of other drugs
poor class attendance
neglect of personal hygiene
decreased concentration

That these symptom patterns overlap with those that characterize the mood disorders is readily apparent.

When the same researchers compared suicide rates at British universities and the overall rate for persons of the same age group in England and Wales, they found that the incidence at prestigious universities like Oxford and Cambridge was between three and four times what it was at other universities, where the rate was more nearly equal to the nationwide rate for people of college age.

In attempting to explain this difference, Stengel (1964) covered the sociological and psychological gamut. He cited: (1) differences in social background of the students, presumably including some genetic variables that might result in differential distribution of students with mood disorders, schizophrenia, and so on; (2) differences in academic standards and pressures among the universities; (3) different numbers of students; (4) a hypothesized "greater pull for eccentrics" by Cambridge and Oxford; (5) differences in social structure within universities that might produce greater alienation and isolation, as in the college systems of Oxford and Cambridge; (6) the greater stress generated by the less-structured academic procedures of the "old" universities; (7) the syndrome of the "little frog in the big pond," which makes it difficult for students who excelled in less competitive environments to adjust to academic environments that are exceedingly competitive and set superior standards; (8) the higher proportion of males at the prestigious universities, which increases social problems among a group already at higher statistical risk for suicide; and (9) more contact with family members for students at the "new" universities, who are more likely to live at or near home and thus have readier access to potential support systems.

This panoply of explanations for differences in suicidal behavior, added to the more general psychological, sociological, and biological correlates and explanations for a phenomenon that affects persons whose personalities, constitutions, and circumstances are widely diverse, confirms what Alvarez has said of suicide: "The processes which lead a man to take his own life are at least as complex and difficult as those by which he continues to live" (p. 115).

Summary

1. Three major categories of suicidal behavior recognized by the National Institute of Mental Health are: (1) completed suicide, (2) suicide attempts, and (3) suicide ideas.

2. Attitudes toward suicide have varied throughout history and from culture to culture. In contemporary Western culture, a stigma is still attached to suicidal behavior.

3. The official statistics on suicide for the United States are: (1) 12 or 13 people out of every 100,000 commit suicide each year; (2) the risk of attempted suicide is highest for people between ages 24 and 44, but the age of highest risk for completed suicide is 55 to 64; (3) for every woman who actually kills herself, three men commit suicide, but the ratio for suicide attempts is the reverse — three women for each man. It is generally felt that women are more likely to use attempted suicide as a call for attention and are more likely to seek professional help with their problems than men are.

4. The official number of suicides is believed to be less than the actual number committed because: coroners may mislabel suicides as "accidents"; and there is a tendency to avoid "stigmatizing" the victims and their families by writing "suicide" on death certificates.

5. These changes in perception and thinking often occur in the individual considering suicide: (1) feelings of isolation, (2) self-depreciation, (3) distorted self-perceptions, and (4) hopelessness. Manic-depressives, schizophrenics, and others with major psychiatric disorders often feel suicide is an alternative to some worse fate. Loss, grief, or severe life stress may also bring on suicidal despair.

6. The major suicide theory categories are: psychological, biological, and sociological.

7. The two major psychological theories of suicide are: *Psychoanalytic* (Freudian) *theory,* which views suicide as an act of self-aggression in which hostility and ambivalence toward a significant individual are directed inward. Feelings of hopelessness, helplessness, dependency conflicts, and overwhelming anxiety and guilt also play a part; and *Behavioral theory,* which suggests that suicidal behavior is an attempt to cope with personal problems that the individual considers overpowering.

8. *Biological theories* are still speculative and deal more with depression than specifically with suicide.

9. *Sociologists* look at suicide as reflecting the individual's relationship with society. Durkheim believed he could recognize three types of suicide: (1) egoistic suicides, which stem from lack of meaningful social interaction and close relationships with the community; (2) altruistic suicide, among individuals whose ties to society are so strong that they will take their own lives if society considers it the only honorable thing to do; and (3) anomic suicide, prompted by sudden or marked change in the victim's position and relationship with society.

10. Although it is difficult to determine exactly what combination of factors will cause an individual to commit suicide, psychologists can identify characteristics of high-risk individuals and predict the type of person most likely to complete the suicide act by applying these techniques: (1) risk-rescue rating scales; (2) examination of the individual's preconceptions about suicide methods, inner mental state, and the circumstances surrounding the suicide or suicide attempt; and (3) the psychological autopsy.

11. People give these reasons for wanting to kill themselves: loneliness, illness or physical pain, marital difficulties, psychological depression, and poor mental health. Conflict motives are more prevalent among women, whereas men are more often motivated by unhappiness. Loss of job, living alone, and socioeconomic status also have been correlated with suicidal behavior.

12. Research suggests that the suicide rate is much higher than average among patients diagnosed as having primary mood disorders. An important correlation connects feelings of hopelessness in severely depressed individuals and seriousness of suicidal intent, and there is evidence that depressed individuals displaying somatic symptoms, such as severe sleep disturbances, are at high risk for completed suicide.

13. College students are also a high-risk group. Several characteristics of suicidal students are: moodiness, tendency to drive themselves hard, frequent depression, and recurrent warnings of intent. Worry about academic performance, physical health, and difficulty in relationships seems to precipitate the event, although these may have been only symptoms of more fundamental problems such as severe depression.

Chapter 11

Treatment of Mood Disorders

handwritten annotations:

TYPES
1) Completed – circumstances
2) ATTEMPT – content of appearance
3) IDEAS – intent or appearance
4) VICTIM-PRECIPITATED HOMICIDES – behavior
5) SUBINTENTIONAL DEATH) PARTIAL OR UNCONSCIOUS

SCHNEIDMAN – 1) stigma
2) coroners ambiguity
Suicide Notes – Declarative + TESTIMONIAL
– Instructional
– Psychological

DURKHEIM: SOCIAL DISORGANISATION
1) EGOISTIC
2) ALTRUISTIC
3) ANOMIC – sudden change

SHNEIDMAN (REASONS)

High Risk – Mood Disorder
– High Stress

Men
– 3x complete
– sun, hanging, carbon monoxide poisoning

Women
– 3x ATTEMPT
– overdose
illness
– illness, marital problems, depression

Biological Approaches
Drugs I: Lithium
Drugs II: Antidepressants
Electroconvulsive Therapy (ECT)
Sleep Deprivation

Psychological Approaches
Cognitive Therapy
Behavior Therapy

Multimodal Interventions
Combined Treatment with Drugs and Psychotherapy
Mood Disorders Clinics

Suicide Prevention

Summary

handwritten annotations:

HIGH RISK
SCHNEIDMAN: 1) self-hatred
2) psychological imbalance
3) constriction of thinking
4) ability to stop the pain

WEISMAN
WORDEN
INTENT – RISK – RESCUE SCALE
– PERCEPTION OF SUICIDE
– METHODS
– MENTAL STATE
– Psychological Autop's (case history)

LEVY + SOUTHCOMB
KRAMER
ROBINSON
) higher among primary mood disorders

At this point in my life, I cannot imagine leading a normal life without both taking lithium and being in psychotherapy. It is more than clear to me from my startings and stoppings of lithium that it is an essential part of maintaining my sanity and avoiding a totally tumultuous existence. Lithium prevents my seductive but disastrous highs, diminishes my depressions, clears out the wool and webbing from my disordered thinking, slows me down, gentles me out, keeps me from ruining my career and relationships, keeps me out of a hospital, alive, and makes psychotherapy possible. But, ineffably, psychotherapy *heals.* It makes some sense of the confusion, reins in the terrifying thoughts and feelings, returns some control and hope and possibility of learning from it all. Pills cannot, do not, *ease* one back into reality; they only bring one back headlong, careening, and faster than can be endured at times. Psychotherapy is a sanctuary, it is a battleground, it is a place I have been psychotic, neurotic, elated, confused and despairing beyond belief. But, always, it is where I have believed — or have learned to believe — that I might someday be able to contend with all of this.

No pill can help me deal with the problem of not wanting to take pills; likewise, no amount of analysis alone can prevent my manias and depres-

handwritten annotations at bottom:

HIGH RISK
1 – age > 40
2 – lives alone
3 – heavy alcohol use & lonely
4 – history of suicide attempt
5 – history of potential death in childhood
7 / depression – primary mood disorder
8 / 2x college students
9 / Prestigious U. 3–4x
SHNEIDMAN

[Handwritten margin note: Treatment — decrease both duration + severity of the situation, minimize risk of suicide and severe social impairment + greatly lessen the probability of recurrence. (multimodal treatment is most effective)]

sions. I need both. It is an odd thing owing life to green pills, one's own quirks and tenacities, and this unique, strange and ultimately profound relationship called psychotherapy.

— Patient with manic-depressive illness

Mood disorders are so varied and disturbances range so widely in severity that many methods of treatment have evolved. Because the more serious disorders appear to be at least partially neurochemical, this chapter necessarily has a somewhat more medical quality than others in the book. Psychotherapy, however, is a valuable and widely used mode of treatment, and we will discuss some of its applications as well.

At one time, treatment of the extreme mood disorders was limited to hospitalization, mechanical restraint (see Figure 11.1) and electroshock therapy. More sophisticated chemical treatments have replaced many of these older techniques. For less severe cases of depression there are recent additions to the psychological treatments — including cognitive and behavior therapy — offering effective alternatives to traditional psychoanalysis, which has not proved as effective or practical as others, though it is still widely used (Beck 1967b; Lewinsohn 1974; Klerman 1978). Philosophical and educational differences among therapists, as well as changing diagnostic criteria, have provoked basic disagreements about the type of intervention most appropriate for the mood disorders. Further problems arise from the course of the disorders. Most manic and depressive episodes will resolve spontaneously, without any treatment whatsoever (mania generally lasts from one to three months, depression from three to nine), leading many therapists to assume that their treatment, not time alone, is responsible for any improvement in a patient's condition. But treatment can decrease both duration and severity of the episode, minimize risk of suicide and severe social impairment, and greatly lessen the probability of recurrence. Recent evidence (Klerman 1978; Klerman et al.

Fig. 11.1. "The Crib," a nineteenth-century method of control for mania and other psychoses.

1974) suggests, in fact, that a multimodal treatment approach (such as psychotherapy plus drug therapy) is often more effective than a single treatment modality alone; we will discuss the evidence and its implications later.

Altogether, we shall look at several types of treatments that therapists administer to people who have mood disorders. The biological approaches, which we will consider first, include drug therapy, electroshock therapy, and sleep deprivation. In a section on psychotherapy, we will focus on cognitive and behavioral approaches. We will also discuss multimodal treatment programs, and introduce techniques for preventing suicides.

Biological Approaches

Unipolar and bipolar mood disorders do not respond equally to the same methods of treatment, as you saw in Chapters 8 and 9, where we distinguished between depression and manic-depression and their probable causes. Actually, much of the evidence that underlies the neurochemical explanations of the severe forms of these disorders stems from research on the effects of drugs on depressive and manic patients. Uniformly different drug responses indicate that different mechanisms are responsible for the different patterns of symptoms. Research with one drug in particular — lithium — has helped confirm that the unipolar-bipolar distinction is valid.

Drugs I: Lithium

Lithium, an alkaline metal in mineral rocks and salt water, was used as a mineral water cure for mental problems at least as early as the second century A.D. In the fifth century the physician Aurelianus used alkaline spring water, which contains high concentrations of lithium,

to treat both mania and depression (Fieve 1977). It was not until 1949, however, that the antimanic effects of lithium came to be scientifically described and appreciated. Since then, its effectiveness in treating acute mania, combined with its potential for preventing recurring episodes in both phases of manic-depressive illness, has led many scientists to call lithium the "insulin of psychiatry." It might be overstating the case to call lithium a wonder drug, but evidence is convincing that it is effective in treating acute manic episodes (often together with temporary use of phenothiazines, such as Chlorpromazine, and hospitalization), and especially in preventing recurrent manic and depressive episodes in bipolar manic-depressive illness.

Individuals who are put on lithium generally take it orally one or more times a day for an indefinite period. The level of lithium in their blood requires careful monitoring to insure that the dosage they are receiving is high enough to be effective but not so high that there is a risk of lithium poisoning. Severely toxic reactions such as convulsions, coma, and death are rare, but lithium can cause unpleasant side effects. These reactions range from hand tremor, diarrhea, vomiting, thirst, and anorexia, which are usually transient and frequently disappear without a reduction in dosage, to twitching, drowsiness, confusion, and dysphoria at highly toxic levels. In addition, test results suggest that lithium produces some of the psychotic symptoms characteristic of schizophrenia, and there is some evidence of long-term effects from continued lithium ingestion (Shader 1975).

Lithium does not immediately affect a patient's behavior; usually it takes five to ten days to build up a therapeutic level in the body. It generally has no significant effect on a normal person's mood. How lithium works is still not clear, but the possibility is strong that it inhibits release of norepinephrine and dopamine and markedly influences the chemical balance across membranes, including neurons (Baldessarini 1978); see Figure 8.7.

More than sixty studies in the scientific literature report successful use of lithium in treating manic episodes. The estimated success rate is an impressive 70 to 80 percent. In acute mania and hypomania, marked clinical improvement follows within three to fourteen days. In contrast, the phenothiazines that are beneficial in treating schizophrenia (see Chapter 7), are

Fieve on Lithium and Manic-Depressive Illness

Ronald Fieve is an internationally known expert on manic-depressive illness. He has written more than a hundred scientific articles and several books on mood disorders, conducted the first clinical study of lithium in America, and established the first lithium clinic in the United States. Although he received his professional training in psychoanalysis, his practice now has a pharmacological orientation. He has treated thousands of patients with severe mood disorders. A professor of clinical psychiatry at Columbia University and medical director of the Manic Depression Foundation of New York City, Fieve is noted in his field for his emphasis on the positive as well as negative aspects of manic-depression. These excerpts are from his book *Moodswing: The Third Revolution in Psychiatry* (1975):

I have emphasized that manic depression is a spectacular disease because of its bizarre, excruciating, and at times beneficial and even ecstatic symptoms. It is spectacular because people who suffer from the illness in its milder forms of moodswing tend to be magnificent performers, magnetic personalities, and true achievers. . . . Manics have not only fabulous energy when they're not too manic, but a qualitatively different, quicker, more perceptive grasp of others and their surroundings. They are manipulators par excellence, and they are also the people who get things done. Without them society would be much impoverished. . . . But the depressions that sometimes grow shattering enough to take the terrible toll of suicide are the other side of moodswing.

The optimistic news, however, is that manic depression, this spectacular disease, now has an equally spectacular cure. Lithium is the first drug in the history of psychiatry to so radically and specifically control a major mind disorder. In general medicine, miracle drugs are commonplace. Penicillin and antibiotics have spoiled us. But in psychiatry, in which disorders generally mean years lost, lives wasted in emotional agony, untold damage to self, friends, family, and finances, it is truly spectacular to watch this simple, naturally occurring salt, lithium carbonate, return a person in one to three weeks from terrible throes of moodswing to normalcy. . . .

My first research trials of this drug on hyperactive and elated manics resulted in a dramatic calming of their symptoms. Furthermore, with the correct dosage of lithium, there seemed to be no side effects, unlike the chemical straitjacketing of the patient which often resulted from use of the major tranquilizers. I had seen this latter effect in acutely agitated patients for whom massive doses of tranquilizers were required, to slow them down and induce sleep. In the process, side effects — retarded body movement, a mask-like face with little expression, a zombie-like appearance — were usually evident. Manic patients calmed on lithium, in contrast, were perfectly normal. Their overactivity, talkativeness, seductiveness, playful tie pulling, and high energy levels were quickly dampened, and they were ready for discharge in a few weeks. Previously, these same patients had received months and years of electroshock therapy, multiple drugs, psychotherapy, and psychoanalysis. During the three years I spent in psychiatric training, the additional five years of formal psychoanalytic training, and the years I have spent in psychiatric research, I have not found another treatment in psychiatry that works so quickly, so specifically, and so permanently as lithium for recurrent manic and depressive mood states (pp. 222–223).

[handwritten margin notes: i-thium - prophylactic agent (substance + technique used both in actually preventing + early treatment of a disorder!)]

sometimes useful in the temporary management of mania but have no overall effect on the course of bipolar illness (that is, they cannot *prevent* future episodes of mania or hypomania), as lithium does.

As a *prophylactic agent,* that is, a substance or technique used both in actually *preventing* and *early treatment* of a disorder, lithium has demonstrated value. A great deal of documentation shows that early treatment with lithium

[handwritten margin notes: FIEVE study - effective - lithium very effective for manic-depressives - and also for unipolar depression]

Box 11.1. Dr. Ronald Fieve is a psychiatrist who has studied manic-depressive illness for many years.

decreases the duration and intensity of manic and depressive symptoms and continuing it helps control the disorder. Nevertheless, preventive research has its limitations, because of its substantial methodological problems. The word "prevention" has no universally acceptable definition, so that it is difficult to design a study easily comparable to others. A second problem is deciding what length of time is sufficient to substantiate the treatment's effectiveness in preventing episodes that are highly variable in onset and duration. Still another very important consideration is the ethical one we have mentioned: withholding from a control group of patients at high risk for suicide a medication that is known to be effective.

The most comprehensive study of lithium's preventive effects was sponsored by the National Institute of Mental Health and the Veterans Administration hospitals. More than 200 bipolar patients participated. Upon discharge from a hospital, they were placed either on lithium or on a placebo drug. Over the two years following their release, 80 percent of the placebo patients suffered recurrence of manic-depressive symptoms, whereas only 41 percent of the lithium-treated patients experienced further episodes. For the latter group, new episodes were frequently less severe than for the placebo group. Although many of the patients who had manic or depressive episodes probably did not take their medication regularly (problems with drug compliance will be discussed a bit later), you can see that lithium made a large difference in the outcome (Prien et al. 1973a). A review of six well-controlled clinical studies of lithium prophylaxis showed that the overall rates of relapse in bipolar patients for manic or depressive episodes was 85 percent among 175 patients given a placebo, but only 30 percent among 174 patients maintained on lithium (Johnson 1975).

In the second part of the NIMH investigation of lithium (Prien et al. 1973b), researchers randomly assigned 44 bipolar and 78 unipolar acutely depressed patients to lithium, antidepressant drugs (see following section), or placebo. Only 28 percent of the bipolar patients who took lithium had affective episodes, compared to 77 percent of those taking the antidepressant or placebo. The unipolar patients had a generally higher rate of recurring depressive episodes; 92 percent of the patients on placebo experienced recurrent depression, and 48 percent of those on lithium or antidepressants experienced subsequent breakdowns. Thus, as Fieve (1977) and many other investigators have concluded, lithium unquestionably is highly effective in preventing recurrent mania or hypomania, quite effective — although less demonstrably so — in preventing and treating severe depressions in bipolar patients, and possibly effective in preventing and treating depressive episodes in some unipolar patients (particularly those who have no personal history of mania or hypomania but who do have a family history of bipolar illness).

The fact that lithium is currently the treatment of choice for bipolar patients and for some types of unipolar disorders reflects evidence of its effectiveness. Marketing firms and pharmaceutical companies estimate that between 50,000 and 120,000 Americans currently take lithium. Yet, despite the drug's well-established usefulness in treatment and prophylaxis of mood disorders, an estimated 35 to 50 percent of the patients on lithium maintenance stop taking the drug — against medical advice — at one time or another (Polatin and Fieve 1971; Van Putten 1975; Goodwin 1977; Jamison, Gerner and Goodwin 1979). Why? Generally, four interacting sets of variables probably account for failure to take lithium regularly: (1) factors unique to the *illness* (the type of mood disorder, its natural history and phasing, intensity and consistency of positive and negative experiences); (2) the *patient's characteristics* (metabolic functioning, interpersonal capacities and support systems, personality structure, self-image, attitudes towards medication, perceived cause of the disorder, socioeconomic status, cognitive abilities, age, and gender); (3) nature of the *drug* (degree and type of side effects, efficacy, immediacy of effect, dosage schedule, and form of preparation — controlled or immediate release, pill or capsule); and (4) *characteristics of the physician* (attitudes toward and experience with the disorder, the drug, and psychotherapy; beliefs about the etiology of the disorder; amount of clinical experience; and attitudes toward the patient).

The first reported instance of lithium noncompliance involved the first manic-depressive patient treated with it. After recounting the dramatic initial success of lithium in the patient, Cade (1949) described the subsequent course:

It was with a sense of the most abject disappointment that I readmitted him to the hospital six months later as manic as ever, but took some consolation from his brother, who informed me that Bill had become overconfident about having been well for so many months, had become lackadaisical about taking his medication, and finally ceased taking it about six weeks before (p. 13).

To determine reasons for lithium noncompliance, Jamison, Gerner, and Goodwin (1979) studied forty-seven patients who were currently receiving lithium and fifty clinicians who were experienced in using it. All answered questions about the importance of social, medical, and intrapsychic factors in noncompliance. About half of the patients had stopped lithium against medical advice at least once. Their main reasons were: (1) they were bothered by the idea that their moods were controlled by a medication; (2) they disliked the idea of having a chronic illness, which lithium symbolized; and (3) it had side effects (particularly, lethargy and decreased coordination). The patients who

stopped lithium were significantly more likely also to report "missing highs." For the clinicians, the most important reasons for noncompliance were that the patients: (1) felt well and saw no need to continue taking medication; (2) missed the "highs" of hypomania; and (3) were bothered by the idea of having a chronic illness.

Fig. 11.2. This drug company advertisement for lithium raises these questions: What are the effects of lithium on creativity? If Handel had been on lithium and thus less hypomanic or manic, would the *Messiah* have been written? What trade-off is there between control of personal turmoil and anguish and creativity or productivity? It is a complex and unresolved issue.

George Frederick Handel (1685-1759), known for his swings from depression to mania, composed his majestic *Messiah* oratorio in only six weeks. If he were living today, lithium would probably control his symptoms.

[handwritten margin notes, top:] ANTIDEPRESSANTS — 2 types: MAO inhibitors / tricyclic antidepressants — more commonly used — used for symptoms that are typical for depression / the two groups work by diff mechanisms + on diff kinds of depression. — have genetic components / increase neurotransmitter activity in the brain

[handwritten margin notes, left side:] work for atypical depression / significantly more effective than placebo

Interestingly, twice as many patients felt that psychotherapy was useful to them in staying on lithium as did the clinicians (most of whom were also practicing psychotherapists).

Drugs II: Antidepressants

Currently, two types of antidepressant medications are prescribed for individuals suffering from unipolar and bipolar depressive disorders: the *monoamine oxidase (MAO) inhibitors* (such as Nardil and Parnate) and the *tricyclic antidepressants* (such as Tofranil, Elavil, and Sinequan). Clinical research studies indicate that the two groups of drugs work by different mechanisms and on different kinds of depression. The patients who respond to MAO inhibitors are generally unlikely to respond to tricyclic antidepressants and vice versa. Drug response also has genetic components. "Tricyclic responders," for example, tend to run in families. Whether or not a patient is likely to benefit from antidepressant drug therapy depends on the factors outlined in Table 11.1.

Tricyclic antidepressants are by far the most commonly prescribed medication for depression in the United States. They are most appropriate for persons having a major unipolar or bipolar depressive disorder. In general, the more closely a person fits the description of the depressive syndrome (see Chapter 8), the more likely it is that these drugs will improve his condition (Goodwin 1977). It usually takes two or three weeks from the time medication begins for clinically significant improvement in the depression to become apparent. The exact action of the tricyclics is unknown, but they almost certainly increase neurotransmitter activity in the brain (Baldessarini 1978); see Figure 8.7.

Although tricyclics are generally more effective than other drugs against moderately severe and severe depressive disorders, some "atypical depressions" respond more quickly and thoroughly to MAO inhibitors. These depressions are often characterized by increased anxiety, somatic or hypochondriacal concerns, obsessive-compulsive features (all discussed at length in Chapter 13), and increases rather than decreases in sleep and eating. As we saw in Chapter 8, the MAO inhibitors prevent neurotransmitters from being metabolized following transmission of a nerve impulse (Baldessarini 1978).

The usefulness of tricyclic antidepressants is well established in the scientific literature (Baldessarini 1978). Morris and Beck (1974) reviewed 146 drug studies (each a well-controlled, random-assignment, double-blind de-

Table 11.1. General indications for drug therapy

Clinical features likely to be associated with good drug response

Presence of clear endogenous symptoms
Pervasiveness of the depressive syndrome
Clear onset of the depressive syndrome
Decrease in functional capacity
Prior history of drug response
Family history of affective illness
Family history of drug response

Clinical features likely to be associated with poor drug response

Depressive symptoms integral to another psychiatric diagnosis
Depressive symptoms of long duration (chronic)
Prominent features of hysteria, complaining, blaming others
History of multiple previous drug failures
History of exaggerated sensitivity to drug side effects
Multiple somatic symptoms with history of somatic preoccupation
Presence of schizoaffective features[a]

Source: F. K. Goodwin, "Diagnosis of Affective Disorders: General Principles," in M. E. Jarvik, ed., *Psychopharmacology in the Practice of Medicine* (New York: Appleton-Century-Crofts, 1977), p. 244.
[a] Schizoaffective disorders include symptoms of schizophrenia as well as strong symptoms of mood disorder (see Chapter 5).

sign) and found that tricyclics were significantly more effective than placebos in 60 percent of the studies. Klein and Davis (1969) reported too that 70 percent of 734 patients improved when treated with the tricyclic antidepressant imipramine, in contrast to only 40 percent of 606 patients who received placebos.

Electroconvulsive Therapy (ECT)

Perhaps the most controversial method of intervention with depression or mania is electroshock or electroconvulsive therapy (ECT), in which an electrical current applied to the patient's head induces an epilepsy-like seizure. Widespread public apprehension about this treatment is relatively recent, yet artificial generation of seizures as a way of treating mental disorders has a long history. In fact, electrical discharge from torpedo fish was used to cure medical ailments by ancient healers as long ago as 46 A.D. (Salzman 1978). Physicians used camphor to cause convulsions as early as 1764, and primitive methods of electroshock therapy were used in both the eighteenth and nineteenth centuries (Fink 1978).

Modern procedures and safeguards make ECT a painless, relatively safe, straightforward, and highly effective treatment for severe depressive disorders (see Figure 11.3). Electrodes placed on one or both sides of the patient's head induce a seizure by passing a *modified* electrical current through the brain. Patients undergoing ECT receive a short-acting anesthetic, which renders them unconscious for the procedure. A muscle-relaxing agent, succinylcholine, prevents bone fractures that convulsions might otherwise cause.

The average number of treatments given for an episode of severe depression is five to seven, but occasionally ten to twelve are necessary (Kiloh 1977). Patients with bipolar or unipolar depression usually require two to four seizures at 48 hour intervals to experience elevation in

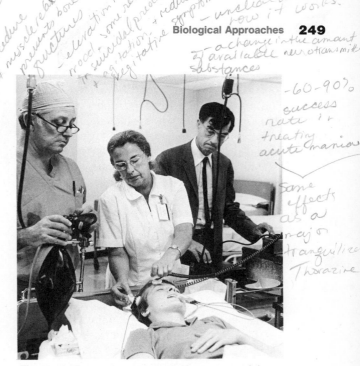

Fig. 11.3. Patient undergoing electroconvulsive therapy. Note that a psychiatrist, a nurse, and an anesthesiologist are in attendance.

mood, some relief in suicidal preoccupation and agitation, and reduced vegetative (sleeping, eating, and psychomotor abnormalities) symptoms (Fink 1978). As with so many empirically based interventions, it is unclear how ECT works. A change in the amount and availability of neurotransmitter substances (see Chapter 8) is currently the most widely accepted explanation (Fink 1978; Kiloh 1977).

How well does ECT work? General estimates of the success rate in treating acute mania range from 60 to 90 percent (Fink 1978). McCabe (1976) compared manic patients treated with ECT and a major tranquilizer (Thorazine) and found no significant difference in length of hospitalization or condition at discharge; both treatments were much more ef-

ECT effectiveness = tricyclic antidepressant effectiveness
often more effective
- much more effective than psychotherapy, placebo, or simulated ECT
- medical complication from ECT are now rare

risk of possible memory loss, patients generally have no memory around the procedure itself + sometimes amnesia / usually does not persist

fective than hospitalization alone. The most common use of ECT today, however, is in treating severe and unremitting depression rather than mania. Although legal statutes limit application of ECT in most states, many psychiatrists and clinical scientists regard it as the preferred means of intervention with some types of depressions, particularly psychotic ones, which may involve paranoid and somatic delusions and in which the degree of suicidality or vegetative symptoms or both can be life-threatening.

No data comparing the effectiveness of ECT and lithium are available, but ECT is at least as effective in treating severe depressive disorders as the tricyclic antidepressants such as imipramine, and often it is more effective (Cole and Davis 1967). Almost all investigators have found ECT much more effective than psychotherapy, placebo, or simulated ECT, in which the patient undergoes all aspects of the ECT procedure except that no electrical current is passed through the brain, so that no seizure is induced. This "sham ECT" is done to rule out the "suggestion" effects of undergoing this major procedure.

Although several significant potential sources of risk threaten the patient undergoing ECT (the direct effect of the seizure itself, side effects from the anesthesia, effects of shock and fear, and social stigma from having to have it), medical complications from ECT are now exceedingly rare. One reason for the increased safety stems from the use of succinylcholine as a muscle relaxant. Before this drug was introduced, the only effective way to induce relaxation was to administer curare, a potent, paralyzing drug that can cause cardiac complications and death. Fractured bones were once common, too, but muscle relaxants generally prevent this hazard as well. Informed understanding of the procedure, sedation prior to it, and general anesthesia allay much of the anxiety that people usually have about receiving ECT.

A risk that is much more real is possible loss of memory from ECT. Patients generally have no memory of events around the procedure itself, and occasionally memory loss, or *amnesia,* extends to all events during the illness. It is often difficult to judge, however, how much is lost because of the ECT series and how much is attributable to the illness; the cognitive changes associated with mania and depression, including impaired memory, are well established (see Chapters 8 and 9). Two weeks after their last ECT treatment, most patients perform memory tests as well as or better than before ECT. Within a few months they are able to recall events as well as they could before treatment began. Some mental complications or memory deficits persist in one out of 200 patients (Fink 1978). These risks, though, almost always are outweighed by the chance of suicide and other physical, social, and psychological problems that can come from *not* treating a person who is severely depressed or manic.

Quite apart from the risks of the procedure, concern on the part of many mental health professionals, the media, and the general public about the use of ECT seems to stem from a lack of familiarity with modern methods and equipment. At one time, patients were often fully awake during the treatment. And severe complications and death once were a real risk with ECT. Perhaps the most legitimate apprehension arises from indiscriminate application and overuse of ECT. (In fact, at one time, it was occasionally used as punishment.) Serious memory impairment can follow a large number of treatments for an episode of depression or mania, but as diagnosis has grown more precise over the years and as alternative treatments have been developed for other psychiatric disorders (such as schizophrenia), ECT has been applied as a more specific treatment, and clinicians now use it much more judiciously. And all but a few states now require the patient's informed consent before ECT is given.

need for the patient's informed consent

Public concern due to lack of knowledge

① the dramatic + frightening aspects of ECT watching

Sleep Deprivation — staying awake for 24 hours

7½ of depressed patients respond well
- severely depressed more likely to benefit
- therapeutic effect last 1-7 days

Biological Approaches **251**

Another possible explanation for public concern about ECT lies in the procedure itself — it is dramatic and can be frightening to observe and to undergo. In our society many people rely on pills to treat their problems. Antidepressant medications, therefore, are much less disturbing and fit better into the social system. Electroconvulsive therapy clearly is a major medical procedure and may arouse proportionately more fear and distrust than pills.

may be due to biological rhythms or neurotransmitter changes

ECT Consent Form

Before a patient can receive electroconvulsive therapy in the state of California, he must sign the document that follows, indicating that he has been informed of its treatment potential, alternative interventions that are available, possible side effects or complications from ECT, and that he is aware he can refuse the treatment at any time. Many other criteria must also be met before a physician can administer ECT.

INFORMED CONSENT FOR
ELECTROCONVULSIVE TREATMENT
DO NOT SIGN THIS FORM UNTIL YOU HAVE READ IT THOROUGHLY, YOUR PHYSICIAN HAS ADEQUATELY EXPLAINED TO YOU THE MATTERS MENTIONED BELOW, AND YOU HAVE ALL THE INFORMATION THAT YOU DESIRE CONCERNING ELECTROCONVULSIVE TREATMENT.

The nature of electroconvulsive therapy has been fully explained to me by Doctor _____ and I am satisfied with that explanation. I understand all of the following:

1. The nature and seriousness of my mental condition.
2. The reason for using this treatment, which involves passing a controlled electrical current through my brain.
3. The frequency (probably _____ times per week for _____ weeks, but not to exceed _____ treatments and not to exceed 30 days from the first treatment).
4. There exists a division of opinion as to the efficacy of this treatment, but it is known to induce a brief episode of unconsciousness and a form of convulsion which, since the 1930's, has been known to result in a change in brain functioning, which may end or reduce depression, excitement or agitation, and disturbing thought.
5. The improvement associated with this treatment has sometimes been permanent and has sometimes lasted for only a few months. However, without such treatment my present condition might improve or might continue with little or no change for many weeks or months, thereby endangering my health and even my life.
6. Alternatives to this treatment are no treatment, psychotherapy, and medication, individually or in various combinations. These alternatives are not preferable to the proposed electroconvulsive therapy because _____

_____

7. This treatment may have the following side effects and risks:
   a. Headache, nausea, and sore muscles lasting from an hour or so to several weeks after a treatment.
   b. Confusion lasting from an hour or so after each treatment to several weeks after a series of treatments.
   c. Memory loss lasting from an hour or so after each treatment to spotty losses lasting for several months or years after a series of treatments.
8. There may be serious complications of heart, lung, or brain functioning as a result of the treatments or of procedures used with the treatment.
9. I have the right to accept or refuse this treatment and the right to revoke my consent for any reason at any time prior to or between treatments.
10. The special circumstances that apply to my case are: (indicate "none" if there are no special circumstances.) _____

_____

_____

_____

I have carefully read and understand the foregoing. I hereby consent to the performance of electroconvulsive therapy. I understand that the required 24 hours have elapsed between my signature and the time the above information was provided to me.

[Handwritten annotations at top: "Beck (Cognitive Therapy): Treatment — set goals / Identify Automatic Thoughts (or cognitions) (that cause depression) find cognitions / (2) Distancing: training patient to recognize how his cognitions + observations distort reality. / (3) Neutralization: learning to recite reasons that cognitions are invalid: reduce frequency + intensity of distorted cognitions"]

[Left margin handwritten: "Problems in studies — no distinction between type of depression — often depression was not the primary symptom / Still primary treatment in depression"]

Sleep Deprivation

Sleep deprivation has been used as a treatment for depression in England, Germany, France, Scandinavia, and, more recently, the United States. The treatment itself is quite simple. The patient, who is under observation, stays awake from breakfast on the first day until 10 P.M. on the second day. According to initial studies, about half of the depressed patients respond well to the treatment, and severely depressed patients are more likely to benefit from deprivation of sleep than those less depressed. Mood elevation does not take place in normal individuals who undergo this procedure. Generally, the therapeutic effect, which starts around noon of the second day, lasts one to seven days. How sleep deprivation works in depression is unclear, but alterations in the physiological rhythms of the body and changes in neurotransmitter substances may be important factors in its success (Gerner et al. 1978; Post et al. 1976).

Psychological Approaches

[Handwritten: "Cognitive / Behavioral"]

Despite the important advances in treatment of depression by drugs, a National Institute of Mental Health special report on depression (1973) indicates that psychotherapy is still the primary treatment for this disorder. Almost every type of psychological therapy has been used to treat depression. In fact, it has been estimated that psychologists, psychiatrists, and other mental health professionals together offer more than 130 psychological approaches to treatment (Weissman 1978).

It is difficult to judge how effective psychological intervention is with depression, from evidence uncovered by research, at any rate. One review of more than 200 articles on the psychotherapy of depression (Lieberman 1975) turned up only a few adequately controlled studies. A major problem with these studies is that they make no distinction among types of depressed patients. Seldom were bipolar patients differentiated from unipolar ones, and rarely were rigorous diagnostic criteria applied. In fact, depression was not the primary diagnosis in many cases, but was just one of many symptoms that patients reported experiencing. Because we cannot describe all the 130 or more approaches in this one chapter, we will focus on two of the newer ones — cognitive and behavioral. Psychoanalysis and other traditional therapies that emphasize insight into the past (see Chapter 2) are also commonly used in treating affective disorders, particularly combined with other forms of therapy.

Cognitive Therapy

[Handwritten: "depression is caused by negative cognition supported by −ve assumptions + attitudes"]

You will recall that in Chapter 8 we discussed cognitive sets and their role in depression. Beck (1967, 1970) has developed a treatment approach for depression based on cognitions and on the assumptions and attitudes behind the negative cognitions that maintain a depressive episode. The first step is to identify the patient's major problems. Then therapist and patient together set therapeutic goals and come up with a strategy for achieving them. The three stages in cognitive therapy are: (1) identifying *automatic thoughts,* or cognitions that cause feelings of depression; (2) *distancing,* or training the patient to recognize how his own cognitions and observations distort reality; and (3) *neutralization,* or learning to recite reasons that cognitions are invalid, so as to reduce the frequency and intensity of distorted cognitions.

This case history illustrates how cognitive therapy works.

Case History: Cognitive Therapy

Pat, a thirty-two-year-old woman, came to the outpatient psychiatric clinic complaining of depressive symptoms, including insomnia, fatigue, poor concentration, feelings of hopelessness, pessimism about the future, and suicidal ideation. After a thorough diagnostic evaluation, the staff concluded that Pat was suffering from a moderately serious unipolar depression. She was placed on antidepressant medication and referred for individual psychotherapy. After discussing the advantages and limitations of cognitive therapy, Pat and her therapist agreed to begin that form of treatment.

Because cognitive therapy is a short-term method of treatment (usually fifteen to eighteen sessions), the therapist and Pat worked quickly to specify these clear-cut treatment goals: (1) to engage Pat collaboratively in the therapy (in order for her to both learn the skills to "be her own therapist" and to raise her depressive, low self-esteem by minimizing her dependence on the therapist); (2) to help Pat feel at least somewhat better each session, including the first, so that she would experience the therapy positively and be motivated to do the learning and work demanded; (3) to teach her important features of the cognitive theory of depression and also train her to take a more problem-solving approach to her depression rather than maintaining a hopeless, pessimistic attitude; and (4) to design homework assignments (people generally learn best by *doing*) that would help Pat learn about her depression, practice the cognitive therapy skills, and learn to cope better with her current and future depressions. Pat's general goals for the therapy were to become less depressed and to learn to manage her irritability and anger toward other people.

Because Pat's goals were to decrease depression and anger, the therapy sessions concentrated on dealing with these emotions. The first task of the cognitive therapist was to teach Pat the relationships between feelings, thinking, and her behavior. During the first session Pat made an observation that many depressed patients express: "I don't think at all," she said. "I just get depressed. Once I'm depressed, it doesn't matter what I think." To convince her that she *does* think at such times, the therapist asked Pat to tell her about her last experience of depressed feelings.

Pat: Last night I was at a dinner party. Someone did something rude and I got angry. Then a few minutes later I got depressed. I don't know why.

Therapist: Try to imagine yourself in that situation now.

P: Okay.

T: After you get mad, what do you say to yourself?

P: I think, "I get angry a lot."

T: And then what?

P: It's not smart. If you're calm, you have a better approach.

T: And then?

P: I always react this way to irritation. It bothers me that most of my behavior is repeated. There will be no change in the future. I'm never able to learn or grow. I don't think I have what it takes to do anything that would make me feel gratified.

T: Now, what do you think made you depressed? The situation, getting angry, or your thoughts about getting angry?

P: I never realized that I had any thoughts about getting angry. But I guess they made me depressed even though the situation didn't call for it.

At the end of this session, the therapist told Pat to keep records to learn more about the links between her behavior, feelings, thoughts, and the events that occurred in her life. Each day, she listed her activities and rated her mood during each activity (on a ten-point scale from very depressed to very happy) and any thoughts she had that were relevant to either the activities or her mood.

During a phone conversation between sessions, Pat reported discouragement that this homework assignment was "too hard" and "took too much time," and that her moods were difficult to rate on the scale ("I'm either depressed or I'm not"). The therapist reminded Pat that attempting the homework was all that was required to succeed with the assignment and that she could learn a lot from her difficulties. In the next session, the therapist pointed out that she had learned that she experienced depression as an "all-or-none" state and that this kind of thinking might make it difficult

to test of validity of cognition;
I gather more info.
2/ validity of both?
3/ generating alternatives
nondepressant cognitions.

for her to notice small signs of improvement. She then received a slightly different homework assignment. Instead of rating her mood, activity level, interaction with other people, and anger or amiability for each new activity, she should do it twice a day. She should also record any depressing thoughts or events. Pat agreed that this new type of record-keeping would be easier for her to complete and she did so for two months. By helping Pat to handle a therapy "roadblock," the therapist demonstrated the important idea that, rather than interpreting experiences as failure, the patient could learn from them in order to plan future change.

The therapist eventually graphed the data recorded by Pat on her daily record and used them to help her understand some of the correlates of her depressed mood state (see Figure 11.4). In accordance with some theories of depression, the graph showed that Pat tended to be less depressed during times of greater activity (or more active when less depressed). With this information Pat and her therapist were able to design homework assignments that would make her more active. Pat chose activity goals of exercise and reorganizing her house, which had become quite messy, she said, because she lacked motivation to keep it tidy when she was depressed. As Pat

Fig. 11.4. One patient's self-ratings of mood, activity level, interactions with people, and anger. This graph was used to help the patient understand some of the correlates of her moods with her life events, and as a rationale in designing cognitive therapy homework assignments.

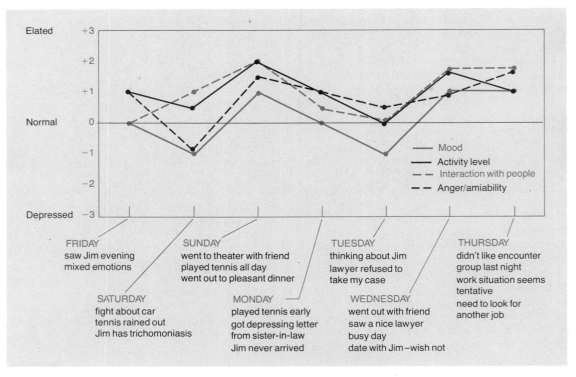

worked toward these goals, she could track the improvement in her mood and thus gain a sense of control over her depression. She also learned that her moods were not "all or none," and this knowledge added to her optimism that she could improve.

As the therapy proceeded, Pat learned to better evaluate her cognitions. She learned that one cognitive symptom of depression is that people "assume the worst." Thereafter, when she became depressed, she would first try to identify her thinking patterns and then examine their validity. For example, each of the cognitions that Pat expressed in the dialogue presented earlier could have been explored using one of three techniques: (1) *gathering more information* ("I get angry a lot" suggests a homework assignment in which Pat would chart the frequency and type of situations in which she became angry); (2) *reality-testing* ("I'm never able to learn and grow" could be evaluated by Pat's recalling times and situations in which she had learned and grown); or (3) *generating alternative, nondepressing cognitions* ("There will be no change in the future" is no more valid a conclusion than "My behavior has been repeated until now because I've never carefully examined it. If I study my patterns, I may be able to find a way to change").

Once Pat understood these techniques and after some practice in the therapy session, she was able to employ the techniques on her own. She learned to deal with anger in a similar fashion. First, she and her therapist described the problem and charted it to learn as much as possible about anger situations, variations in her angry feelings, and the cognitions involved. Through homework assignments she was able to modify her reactions to situations and her cognitions. Also, role-plays (in which the therapist played the part of another person in Pat's life, and Pat practiced expressing her thoughts and emotions) in the therapy sessions allowed Pat to monitor her cognitions and feelings step by step and to practice and evaluate alternate responses to provoking situations.

After several months, Pat was able spontaneously to notice the relationship between her moods and her behavior. Although the antidepressant medication was significant in reducing her more severe depressive symptoms, the cognitive therapy allowed her to examine the way she handled her moods and how she interacted with other people. It also gave her, as she stated, "a greater sense of control over things" and an opportunity to deal more effectively with strong feelings, such as anger and hopelessness.

Behavior Therapy

The major goal of the behavioral treatment of depression is to restore an adequate level of positive experiences (or reinforcement) by changing the type and variety of the patient's daily activities and interactions with other people (Lewinsohn 1975). As in many psychological therapies, the first stage of treatment consists of a thorough diagnostic evaluation. During this phase, the therapist assesses the degree of depression, including suicidality, and gathers data with personality tests, home observations, mood ratings, activity monitoring, interest patterns, and so on. Generally, the therapist and patient agree on a time limit for changing the patient's behavior, say three months. Then, with the patient's participation, the therapist designs a tentative treatment plan, which may employ one or more of these behavioral strategies (Lewinsohn 1975):

1. *To increase the patient's activity level* — For nondepressed, active behaviors the patient earns rewards such as social reinforcements, therapy time, and general "tokens," which he can exchange for other kinds of positive reinforcement. An underlying assumption is that there is a strong relationship between engaging in pleasant activities and mood.

2. *To reduce behavioral excesses* (morbid ruminative thinking, self-depreciatory thoughts or statements, preoccupation with physical symptoms, and statements or thoughts of guilt) — Treatments include: *nonreinforcement* by therapist and family members, friends, and staff (when the patient says "Things are hopeless and I am never going to get better," the therapist might look away or not say anything at all, rather than "rein-

forcing'' the behavior by engaging in a verbal exchange); and *self-control* methods that help the patient learn to break into his own thinking patterns and stop them in midsentence or midthought.

3. *To produce feelings that are incompatible with depression* — Many behavior therapists give their depressed patients training in relaxation (see Chapter 15), in part because some anxiety often accompanies depression and can itself become a depressing symptom. It is assumed also that relaxation is incompatible with depression and thus can partially substitute for it. Increasing the patient's activity level is also intended to create feelings incompatible with a depressed mood.

4. *To enhance the patient's interpersonal skills* — Learning several interactional skills increases the likelihood of getting sufficient positive reinforcement. *Assertion training* systematically teaches the patient to express his feelings and expectations of people in a firm and direct manner. *Marital therapy* in the form of psychotherapy or counseling focuses on problems between partners that may contribute to or aggravate a patient's depression. *Desensitization* involves systematic and gradual exposure to an anxiety-provoking object or situation in order to neutralize the patient's emotional response to it. *Social skill learning* helps the patient acquire highly specific ways of interacting with other people (how to meet them, talk to them, and express feelings in an appropriate manner).

Although these behavioral interventions have proved effective for many individual patients, as with most other depression psychotherapies, the outcome research is based on small samples of patients. Few studies have been designed to compare the results of drug therapy with the outcome of behavioral therapy. In one recent study, Rush et al. (1977) found that cognitive therapy was more effective in treating chronic and recurrent depression than a tricyclic antidepressant (imipramine). The validity of those results has come under attack (Becker and Schuckit 1978) because the re-

searchers did not vary the medication type, dosage level, and duration of treatment in order to determine whether the experimental drug treatment was the most effective combination available. In addition, critics have questioned whether the rating scale (the Beck Depression Inventory) used by Rush et al. is the most appropriate instrument to measure change in depression. Clearly, then, additional research is necessary to confirm or refute the conclusions of the Rush study, but it does establish the possibility that cognitive therapy is as effective or more effective than drug therapy in certain types of depression and that in itself is exciting.

Multimodal Interventions

Many patients with mood disorders receive several kinds of treatment at the same time. Probably the one most widely used for depression combines medication and psychotherapy (Klerman 1978). Bipolar patients, too, are likely to take drugs to control their manic and depressive symptoms and to receive some form of psychological therapy to combat their depressed moods. We shall examine this combined use of drugs and psychotherapy and then look at a recent innovation in diagnosing and treating mood disorders (often a combination of treatments) — the specialty clinic.

Combined Treatment with Drugs and Psychotherapy

A large number of unipolar and bipolar patients benefit from multimodal treatment programs combining drug therapy and some form of individual or group psychotherapy. The rationale for combined treatment ranges from well-reasoned scientific arguments to less rigorous, less rational pragmatic reasons.

To better appreciate the lack of consistent

[handwritten marginalia, top left] OVERSIDE 1 focus on symptoms + drug the patterns side effects not the behavior patterns 2 Therapist can control patient 3 Therapy counteract

[handwritten marginalia, top center] Study antidepressants that are more effective than placebo drugs + psychotherapy in preventing a depressive relapse & return to depression. But not focus in the social + help in the social area of problems of living

[handwritten marginalia, top right] Psychotherapy had no significant effect on symptoms but helped in the social aspect

outcome criteria for multimodal intervention, we must look at the advantages and disadvantages of combined treatment (Klerman 1975; Weissman 1978). On the positive side, drugs can facilitate concentration, consequently increasing the effects of psychotherapy, by reducing the patient's anxiety, improving memory, and restoring normal sleep patterns. Drugs can also increase a depressed person's energy, increasing receptivity to social interaction and leaving him more fully able to participate in the psychotherapeutic process. Finally, psychotherapy may augment the patient's compliance with the drug regime.

Among the disadvantages, a combined treatment program may lead to a focus during psychotherapy on symptoms and drug side effects, not the patient's behavior patterns. Or if the physician prescribing drugs takes the "easy way out" and becomes more of an authority figure, he can undermine the patient's motivation for active participation in the treatment program. Also, psychotherapy may backfire and increase rather than decrease anxiety and depression, counteracting the beneficial reduction of symptoms resulting from medication.

A lot of clinicians encourage psychotherapy for many of their patients on lithium (Benson 1974; Goodwin 1977) to help them comply with the drug regime; a few do not (Fieve 1975). No controlled studies have been done on lithium compliance in the context of psychotherapy. Benson (1974), however, has reported some evidence that lithium and psychotherapy produce better results than lithium alone. Regular monitoring of lithium and of tricyclic antidepressant levels is indispensable in both encouraging therapeutic compliance and in making sure that the patient is getting a safe and an effective dosage.

For depressed patients, a good relationship with a psychotherapist can significantly affect drug compliance and success of treatment. Trying to delineate the relationship between psychotherapy and drug therapy in depression, the National Institute of Mental Health sponsored three studies comparing the two types of treatment and different combinations of them. Almost all the 455 subjects displayed symptoms of medium severity on the depressive spectrum. All took treatment as outpatients. Clinical ratings, self-reports of mood and activities, and measures of social functioning for patients in all three studies indicated that maintenance antidepressants were more useful than placebo drugs or psychotherapy in preventing a depressive relapse and return of depressive symptoms. But, although some social performance was recovered as the symptoms were reduced, the medications themselves had limited influence on problems in living. The strongest effects of psychotherapy, compared to drugs alone and infrequent therapeutic contact (which had little effect), were in problems in living and interpersonal relationships. Psychotherapy alone had no significant effect on the symptoms of depression. Weissman (1978) concluded that these studies argue for the usefulness of combined drug treatment and psychotherapy because the effects of the individual modalities appear to be mostly independent of one another but highly complement each other when combined. Although the studies did not examine the full range of the depressive spectrum and dealt with maintenance rather than acute treatment, they provide insight into the effects of different kinds of treatment.

Mood Disorders Clinics

[handwritten marginalia] define a combination of treatments

Advances in diagnosing recurrent mood disorders, coupled with the highly effective treatments available to people having such disorders, have made it possible to treat unipolar and bipolar disorders in outpatient clinics (Fieve 1975; Daly 1978). In the past several years, clinics specializing in the treatment of mood disorders have appeared all over the world, particularly in Western Europe, Great

Britain, and the United States. Known variously as "mood disorders clinics," "affective disorders clinics," and "lithium clinics," they provide diagnostic and treatment services. Many are also research and teaching facilities. In general, mood disorders clinics provide a wide range of treatments, including medication; individual and group psychotherapy; patient

education about the disorder, prognosis, and medication; crisis intervention; family therapy; and hospital referral for patients who need closer supervision than an outpatient setting can provide. This case history illustrates how one such clinic, the University of California at Los Angeles Affective Disorders Clinic, operates (see Figure 11.5).

Fig. 11.5. Procedure for treatment and evaluation at the UCLA Affective Disorders Clinic.

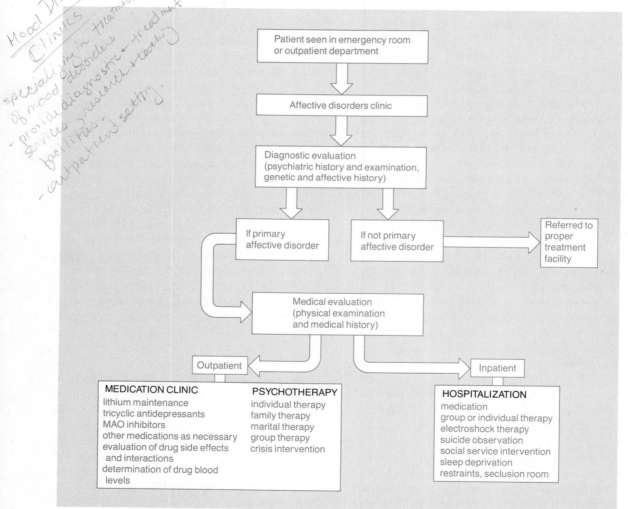

[handwritten margin notes: Suicidal Preventions ~ danger of suicide, particularly during the depressive phase of a unipolar or bipolar disorder. Goal is to the reduce the incidences of suicide. counteract the desire to commit suicide, the first suicidal attempt + the repetition + the fatal outcome of suicidal acts. specialize in emergency treatment]

When John Clark, a twenty-one-year-old university student, was first brought to the UCLA Outpatient Psychiatric Clinic by his parents, he was withdrawn, anxious, and very depressed. He talked about killing himself because he "couldn't stand it any longer." His grades had slipped markedly during the past term. He was having difficulty concentrating, sleeping, and he had lost fifteen pounds. His friends and family had expressed concern to him about his health and well-being. In the outpatient clinic, John first saw a psychiatric nurse, who after talking with him decided that he might have a mood disorder, and referred him to the Affective Disorders Clinic for further evaluation. At the clinic he spoke with a psychologist who asked him about his current functioning, sleep patterns, social life, the nature and extent of his suicidal thinking, past history of mood disorders, past treatment, and his family history of alcohol abuse, mood disorders, and other psychological problems. The interview disclosed no family history of affective disorder, and further discussion with John's parents supported this impression. Likewise, there was no indication that John had ever experienced hypomanic or manic episodes. The Research Diagnostic Criteria (see Chapter 8) confirmed a diagnosis of a major depressive (unipolar) disorder, and although John was clearly quite depressed, he had sufficient psychological support from family members and friends to persuade the clinic staff to design an outpatient treatment program instead of hospitalizing him.

A psychiatrist did a medication evaluation and ordered routine medical tests to rule out possible physical causes (for example, thyroid problems) for John's depression. Then John began taking tricyclic antidepressants, joined a therapy group made up of other persons his age who also had problems with moods, arranged to undergo extensive psychological and research testing, and started seeing a psychotherapist on a short-term, individual basis to ensure coordinated treatment and additional therapeutic support until the drugs and group therapy took effect.

John improved gradually and appeared at the clinic less frequently over the months that he was in treatment. Because he was young and this was his first episode of affective illness, he was slowly withdrawn from his antidepressant medication. He remained in group therapy for approximately one year. At follow-up, he was doing well and had not experienced any symptoms of depression. Clinic personnel told him he could contact the clinic at any time for further information or help if he needed it.

Suicide Prevention

We have discussed the danger of suicide for people who are severely depressed, particularly during the depressive phase of a unipolar or bipolar disorder. Although many factors can enter into someone's decision to commit suicide — interpersonal, situational, physiological, and internal — we will be focusing here on programs to help people who have expressed or acted on a desire to die and those who are at high risk for becoming suicidal in the future.

The goal of suicide prevention is to reduce the incidence of suicide. To succeed then, suicide prevention agencies must counteract the *desire to commit suicide,* the *first suicide attempt,* the *repetition of suicidal acts,* and the *fatal outcome of suicidal acts* (World Health Organization 1968).

Programs designed to prevent fatal outcomes of necessity specialize in emergency treatment. Therefore, many suicide prevention facilities are part of a general or psychiatric hospital. Because people find so many ways of committing suicide, prevention requires a multitude of skills other than professional training in psychology. Preventive measures include specialized education in lifesaving techniques such as resuscitation and treatment of drug overdoses for paramedics, police, and fire officials, and the establishment of poison control centers, which act as central sources of information about antidotes and lethal dosages of different drugs.

Special treatment centers for suicide attempters are not uncommon in Western Europe and are becoming more numerous in the United States. The Regional Poisoning Treatment Centre in Edinburgh admits people who have poisoned or otherwise harmed themselves, presumably deliberately, whatever the intended consequences. The center itself is a 20–25 bed ward in a general hospital. Toxicologists and psychiatrists provide primary care. Toxicologists treat the medical complications and psychiatrists evaluate the patients when they are able to discuss their problems. The average stay at the center is four or five days. Depending on patients' continued risk of suicide, they may enter a psychiatric hospital (approximately 33 percent) or receive outpatient care (67 percent). Community resources and short-term treatment facilities are the prevalent approaches to suicide management in some countries (Ireland and Norway), but Great Britain, Austria, and the United States have traditionally relied on more conservative measures, such as hospitalization.

In the hospital, an individual who has attempted suicide or who is believed for other reasons to be highly suicidal, receives comprehensive precautionary treatment from the medical and nursing staff. Particularly worrisome patients are placed on *suicide observation* (S.O.), which means that members of the ward staff watch them continually. This excerpt from a nursing-care manual illustrates both the seriousness with which hospital personnel regard severe suicide risk and some of the practical means for dealing with high-risk patients.

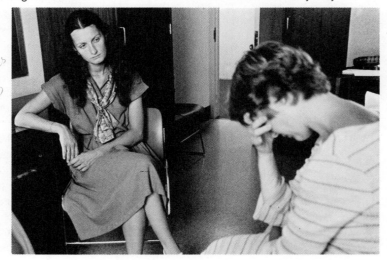

Fig. 11.6. Suicide observation is used in psychiatric hospitals when a patient is a particularly high risk for committing suicide. During suicide observation the patient is watched continuously by the nursing staff to ensure that she does not harm herself in any way.

Maintaining the Patient in a Safe Environment

The suicidal patient will be placed in a room which will allow greatest environmental safety and maximum visibility. This room is to be stripped of all potentially dangerous objects prior to being used, i.e., cosmetics in glass containers (this includes compacts with mirrors, toiletries, etc.)

Any patient not on S.O., who, because of necessity, must sleep in the S.O. room, is also required to be searched for sharp and potentially dangerous objects.

Any belongings taken into the S.O. room must be searched. This is to prevent inadvertent contamination of the room. If this is not done, the room is to be considered lethal and must be completely stripped and searched to be rendered safe.

Such sharp and potentially dangerous objects are to be removed and locked in the sharps closet.

The S.O. room is to be locked at all times when the patients are not in it, to prevent others from entering. All packages brought in by visitors must be inspected by the staff.

The following precautions are to be followed with each S.O. patient:

They are to use only the electric razor.

They are to take showers. No baths are allowed.

They are to use only the public bathroom. They are not to use the bathroom off the dayroom as it locks from the inside.

S.O. patients may have matches, but not lighter fluid.

Temperatures are not to be taken on S.O. patients for the first 48 hours. If a temperature must be taken during this time, it is to be ordered by a physician indicating the route to be used.

Keep the suicidal patient within visual observation of the assigned staff member:

This means the staff member must be clearly able to see the patient's whole body.

The staff member is to place himself between the S.O. patient and the nearest exit.

The staff member must remain sufficiently close to the patient to intervene in the event of impulsive behavior.

No physical barrier should be between the patient and staff member, e.g., on the other side of a glass door.

Remain accountable for a suicidal patient until this responsibility has been delegated to another staff member.

This delegation implies written and verbal communication about pertinent behavior (UCLA Neuropsychiatric Institute, *Adult Psychiatric Service Manual,* July 1978).

Once the patient is evaluated and felt to be no longer acutely suicidal, he is gradually given more independence until he is finally able to be released into the community and treated as an outpatient.

In discussing treatment of acutely suicidal patients in a hospital, we have not taken account of those who are not necessarily suicidal at the moment but are likely to become suicidal. People who *are at high risk for suicide* include those who have a unipolar or bipolar mood disorder, as well as the elderly, alcoholics, some types of epileptics, and schizophrenics. Severe mood disorders are known to carry a high risk of suicide. The incidence of suicide is particularly high among manic-depressives, 15 percent of whom eventually kill themselves (Guze and Robins 1970). Barraclough (1972) has estimated that up to 20 percent of suicides could be prevented by putting persons with a history strongly suggestive of bipolar illness on a long-term lithium treatment program. In a retrospective study of 100 suicides, he found that 21 of the victims had histories of recurrent affective illness of "sufficient frequency and severity to have qualified them hypothetically for lithium therapy." Tentative but interesting support for Barraclough's hypothesis comes from a double-blind controlled lithium study conducted by Pokorny and Prien (1974): the suicides that occurred during their investigation involved patients on placebo rather than lithium. It is too early to assess the long-term effects of lithium treatment on suicide and suicidal behaviors, but in a few years we may be able to attribute part of an overall decline in suicide rate to its use.

An entirely different kind of effort to prevent suicide involves educating and training the general public, medical and mental health personnel, social workers, clergy, teachers, and paraprofessionals to recognize potential suicide victims. These programs acquaint people with early warning signs of high suicide risk, available resources, methods of treatment available, diagnostic criteria, and the significance of symptoms, warnings, and threats.

Suicide Prevention

After an introduction by Dr. Edwin Shneidman, who at the time was chief of the National Institute of Mental Health Center for Studies of Suicide Prevention, we reproduce a telephone conversation between a suicide prevention worker and a caller.

Dr. Shneidman: A suicide prevention worker needs to assess the lethality of each call in order to know how quickly and deeply he has to move. The worker attempts to . . . evaluate the lethality of the call and, simultaneously, to influence — specifically to reduce — that lethality.

Briefly, overall lethality is rated according to the caller's suicidal plan; the resources felt by the caller to be available to him; the kind of crisis experienced by the caller; his recent medical, psychological, and suicidal history; and the stability of his character and personality in general.

Comment: Call No. 5 is from a man in his thirties, weeping in the anguish of his loneliness. Notice especially how the worker quickly and effectively gives the caller permission to talk and to cry, and then helps him in his own way to tell his story and to unburden himself of his feelings.

This call also contains that special and sometimes terrifying situation faced sooner or later by every suicide prevention worker — the problem of a suicidal person with a gun.

Caller: (Garbled) . . .
Worker-1: All right. You've got the right place. And the right person.
C-1: I feel so horrible . . . everything. I just don't know what to do any more.
W-2: Can you tell me a little bit about yourself? How old you are?
C-2: I'm 30.
W-3: Are you married, single, or . . . ?
C-3: I was married. I have two children. I am divorced now . . . living by myself. . . . So lonely, I can't stand it.

W-4: You're feeling upset or you are feeling very low, depressed, perhaps?
C-4: I just haven't, I haven't cried for so long, I can't remember and all of a sudden I can't stop, I just. . . . I just want to get out of it all. I just don't know what to do, you know. I feel like what the hell's the use. I mean I can sit here and cry all day or. . . . And for a simple, simple little thing, it is a simple little thing in a person's life to be rejected and be alone, I guess, but I just can't seem to cope with it any more. I've been alone too long now. I don't have any purpose any more. I guess I've had it.
W-5: You say you are thinking of getting out. By that you mean what? Do you have some ideas about suicide?
C-5: If I didn't, I would not now have called you.
W-6: Yeah, I know.
C-6: I don't like that. . . . I don't like that idea. I don't like it at all, but I just don't care.
W-7: What sort of thoughts do you have about suicide?
C-7: I just want to put a bullet in my head and forget about it, you know.
W-8: Do you have a gun?
C-8: Yes, I do.
W-9: You do? Have you ever tried anything in the past? Have you ever made any suicide attempts in the past?
C-9: I beat my head against the wall a few times. Played a little Russian roulette, I guess. I won. Unfortunately.
W-10: Uhha. Well, that's a terribly serious game.

Comment: Later in this interview, the caller was persuaded to come in person to the suicide prevention center and to bring his gun, unloaded, with him. The appropriate role of the suicide prevention worker is to contribute his skills, compassions, and energies on the side of life.

Yet another kind of large-scale attempt to prevent suicide is the *suicide prevention center,* which utilizes a crisis and community model of mental health. Suicide prevention centers typically rely on volunteers who are supervised and trained by professional mental health workers or by other volunteers. These paraprofessionals answer telephone inquiries, assess the intent and severity of the caller's suicidal feelings, make recommendations for treatment and referrals for psychotherapy, and actively intervene to prevent suicide when possible.

There is some debate about whether suicide prevention centers are primarily useful for suicide prevention or for general crisis intervention. Several researchers believe that people at highest risk for *completed suicide* (those with severe depressive disorders) are less likely to contact prevention centers than are those who *attempt suicide* (Holding 1974; Whitlock 1977). The risk of completed suicide, however, is much greater for some of the people who attempt suicide than it is for the general population (see Chapter 10), and suicide prevention centers certainly help some of them.

Summary

1. The main goals and desired effects of any type of treatment for mood disorders are: (1) to decrease both duration and severity of an episode, (2) to minimize risk of suicide and severe social impairment, and (3) to lessen the probability of recurrence.

2. One of the most effective biological methods for treating bipolar mood disorders is *lithium,* which not only relieves the symptoms of an acute manic episode, but also acts as a prophylactic agent against recurrent manic and depressive episodes in bipolar illness. It is most effective in treating bipolar patients, but does have some effect on some types of unipolar depression. Between 35 and 50 percent of patients on lithium maintenance stop taking the drug against medical advice. In giving reasons for interrupting medication, patients say: (1) they were bothered by the idea their moods were controlled by medication; (2) they disliked the idea of having a chronic illness, which lithium symbolized; and (3) side effects.

3. Other biological modes of treatment include: two types of drugs — monoamine oxidase (MAO) inhibitors and, more commonly, tricyclic antidepressants; electroconvulsive therapy (ECT); and sleep deprivation.

4. There are several major psychological approaches for treating depression. The two we have emphasized are cognitive and behavioral. *Cognitive therapy* attempts to help patients to understand and overcome negative cognitions that maintain a depressive episode by: (1) identifying automatic thoughts that cause feelings of depression, (2) distancing or training patients to recognize how their own cognitions and observations distort reality, and (3) neutralizing negative cognitions to reduce frequency and intensity of distorted cognitions. *Behavior therapy* is meant to restore adequate positive experiences by changing the type and variety of a patient's activities and interaction. A behavioral treatment plan might involve one or more of these strategies: (1) increase the patient's activity level, (2) reduce behavioral excesses, (3) produce feelings incompatible with depression, and (4) enhance the patient's interpersonal skills.

5. One multimodal approach to intervention with mood disorders combines drug treatment and psychotherapy — drugs to alleviate the symptoms and psychotherapy to deal with the problems of daily living and social interaction. A good relationship between patient and therapist seems to significantly affect drug compliance and treatment. Mood disorders clinics offer a wide range of single and multimodal methods, including: medication, individual and group psychotherapy, patient education, crisis intervention, family therapy, and hospital referral when necessary.

6. The goal of suicide prevention is to reduce the incidence of suicide by counteracting (1) the desire to commit suicide, (2) the first suicide attempt, (3) repetition of suicidal acts, and (4) the fatal outcome of suicidal acts.

7. Suicide prevention programs include: specialized education in lifesaving techniques for paramedics, police, and fire officials; establishment of poison control centers; suicide observation of acutely suicidal individuals in hospitals; educating and training the public to recognize potential suicide victims; and suicide prevention centers staffed by trained volunteers who answer telephone inquiries, assess the caller's intent and the severity of risk, make treatment recommendations and referrals, and intervene whenever possible to prevent suicide.

[Handwritten annotations:]

Fieve - LITHIUM MORE EFFECTIVE FOR M-D

Phenothiazines vs.
- temporary symptom relief of
- recurrence of episodes

- Psychological approach

Noncompliance (35-50%)
(1) illness / chronic illness
(2) patient's characteristics mixed signs
(3) drug / side effects
(4) physician's characteristics

Cognitive Therapy:
primary in treating depression (or cognitions)
(1) Identify Automatic Thoughts
(2) Distancing (distortion in reality)
(3) Neutralization - learning to recite reason

Behavior Therapy:
(1) Increase activity level
(2) decrease behavioral excess
(3) Produce feelings incompatible with depression
(4) Enhance interpersonal skills

Drugs + Psychotherapy
(1) facilitate concentration
(2) increase energy; motivation
(3) psychotherapy helps with compliance to drugs

Beck

Multimodal Intervention:
(1) re focus on symptoms + drug side effects not overall behavior pattern
(2) Therapist's control
(3) Therapy can counteract drug benefit

Baraclough - 2-10% prevention (history of bipolar illness)

Tokorny v Prien - b. LITHIUM

Suicide

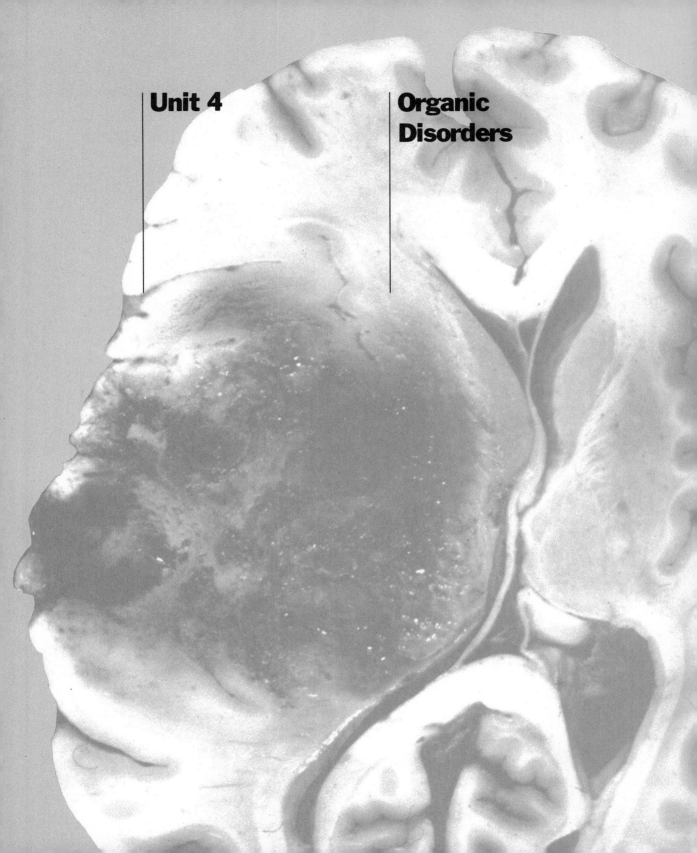

Unit 4 | **Organic Disorders**

Chapter 12

Organic Brain Syndromes

Clinical Features

Injuries to the Brain
Types of Trauma
Posttraumatic Complications

Brain Tumors

Brain Infections

Endocrine Disorders
Thyroid Disorders
Adrenal Disorders

Syndromes Associated with Aging
Presenile Degenerative Disorders
Senile Dementia
Pseudodementia
Circulatory Disturbances
Problems in Treating the Elderly

Epilepsy
Grand Mal
Petit Mal
Psychomotor Epilepsy
Treatment of Epilepsy

Summary

Gramp and Dan were on the back porch having coffee after dinner when Gramp said, ''Got three rabbits around here. Guess what color they are?''

''Brown, probably,'' replied Dan.

''Nope, they're red. Red as red can be,'' said Gramp.

In addition to the red rabbits, over the next few months we were introduced to a variety of creatures that inhabited Gramp's private world. They had delightful names — chillysmiths, Michigans, rupes, bugeyes, and the ever-present whatcha-calls. ''Hey, come here,'' Gramp would say as he peered out the picture window, ''look at this. I don't know what the name of it is, but it has a pretty good length and head of a tiger.''

Gramp's dressing habits also became more and more creative. He'd show up wearing two pairs of pants (one inside out) over two pairs of boxer shorts. Or sporting a woman's stocking as a scarf with a beach towel as a head covering. Coming from school, Nink saw him in one of his ''outfits'' and laughed. ''You look like one of those drawings that's captioned, 'See how many things you can find wrong in this picture,' '' . . .

Gramp's bizarre dressing habits, coupled with his erratic behavior, meant the end of friendships that had remained intact for decades. Most people who had known Frank Tugend as a respected, proper pillar of the community just couldn't take being around him as he shuffled about in his wife's red velvet housecoat or blew his nose loudly on a pair of Nink's underpants that he'd found and decided to use as a handkerchief.

Nan [Gramp's wife] was deeply affected by the ostracism. "People just don't want anything to do with us because of Gramp," she said bitterly on Christmas day, when none of the usual holiday visitors showed up. "We're just crossed off the list" (Jury and Jury, *Gramp* 1976, pp. 44, 59).

With advancing age, everyone will experience some impairment of mental and physical functioning. For most of the elderly, normal deterioration takes its toll by reducing the ability to remember recent events and retain new information and by gradually diminishing the ability to get around easily and to perform skills that require manual dexterity. Severe mental deterioration of the kind Gramp's case illustrates falls in the category of the organic brain syndromes, chemical and anatomical disorders that have a degenerative effect not only on memory and motor coordination but also on judgment, perception, and responsiveness and often on emotions, motivation, and social behavior. They are the result of specific dysfunctions within the brain.

The normal brain governs a seemingly ungovernable number and variety of human behaviors. This orchestrator of moods, movements, thinking, and expression is necessarily a highly complicated and finely tuned organ. It is also vulnerable to disease, time, and injury, all of which can cause people to behave abnormally. In this chapter we shall examine the *organic brain syndromes,* a group of brain disorders that have a particularly pronounced effect on behavior.

The essential feature of an organic brain syndrome is a temporary or permanent brain dysfunction that has a *known* organic cause

Fig. 12.1. Gramp is confronted by his grandson Richard, whom he has not seen for a number of months. "Richard? You're a Richard?" Gramp says, peering out from under the ear flap of a cap he keeps over his face. "What's a Richard?"

(*DSM*-III). All behavior, normal or not, requires direction and participation by the brain. Brain dysfunction can particularly reduce an individual's cognitive abilities — including judgment, perception, and responsiveness — consequently, it directly affects our behavior.

An indirect effect of organic brain disorders is that victims undergo changes in emotion, motivation, and behavior because they know they have suffered a loss of cognitive abilities. Sometimes these changes are profound and may aggravate any cognitive disability caused by the organic factor. Often it is impossible to distinguish symptoms directly related to brain pathology from secondary, or *reactive,* symptoms, but these features must be assessed in individuals who have suffered relatively mild cognitive decrements or abnormalities in order to design the best medical and psychological programs of treatment for them. People's reactions to awareness of their disability differ and, regardless of its severity, reflect their personality, educational background, and premorbid social adjustment. If the patient or a family member views a cognitive disability as a serious threat or loss or both, a severe emotional disturbance may develop. An untreated emotional problem can prolong an illness.

The organic factor underlying organic brain syndrome may be any of these (*DSM*-III):

1. Infection within the brain itself or disease that attacks another part of the body first and only secondarily affects brain function
2. Head injury
3. Degenerative disorder associated with aging
4. Drug use or toxic condition
5. Withdrawal from drug or other substance dependency

Drug effects and withdrawal syndromes are classified as organic brain syndromes because the organic agents are known. Because drug use and dependency are usually reactions to social or psychological pressures, however, we will consider them in Unit 5, where we will discuss social deviations (see Chapter 16).

In general, onset of an organic brain syndrome may be sudden (as in head trauma) or insidious (degenerative brain diseases). Diagnosis of an organic problem requires one of these: medical laboratory evidence (x-ray or brain scan, for example), physical examination, or a history in which the organic causal factor appears. Prognosis depends primarily on the cause of the dysfunction. A condition may be "steadily or irregularly progressive, remittent, static, or rapidly or gradually resolving" (*DSM*-III). Except in a progressive disorder, the prognosis also depends, in part, on the patient's reactive behavior. The greater a patient's desire or determination to recover, the better the chance for improvement.

Of the few organic brain syndromes that we can examine here, some illustrate particular aspects of the brain-behavior relationship (effect of an epileptic seizure on perception, cognition, psychomotor control, and other types of behavior). Others illustrate sophisticated medical and scientific procedures that help diagnose brain disorders (studies of cerebral blood flow and computerized tomography, or EMI scans), or raise theoretical or ethical issues (genetic counseling in Huntington's chorea). Some highlight premorbid psychological functioning in determining how well brain-damaged patients such as stroke victims adapt to their disability. And some of these disorders (head injury and syndromes associated with aging) are fairly common.

Clinical Features

Many of the changes in emotion, motivation, behavior, and cognition that characterize organic brain syndrome are profound. Specific symptoms are:

1. *Impaired orientation.* A person may have so much difficulty with memory, perception, and attention that he cannot recognize his relationship to time, space, or situation. When asked where or who he is he may give a totally fantastic or confused answer.
2. *Impaired memory.* Many brain-damaged patients have difficulty remembering recent events and occasionally cannot recall events in the distant past. Asked to remember an address or an object, a brain-damaged individual will often be unable to remember the correct response five minutes or an hour after receiving the information.
3. *Impaired intellectual function.* In addition to having difficulty with memory and orientation, people who have suffered brain damage often have problems in cognition that impair ability to understand the written or spoken language, to do arithmetic calculations, to reason, or to learn new tasks.
4. *Impaired judgment.* Brain damage can cause pronounced changes in a person's ability to assess outcomes of situations or consequences of his behavior. Some people also lose their ability to behave appropriately in social situations.
5. *Lability and shallowness of affect.* Organic brain syndromes can change temperament, so that formerly stable, even-tempered people may become extremely moody, or *labile.* They may cry suddenly with no apparent cause and then, just as precipitously, laugh or giggle inappropriately. Increases in irritability and hostility are not uncommon, and occasionally feeling may become blunted and shallow.

   Other changes in personality can be caused by brain dysfunction. Some people become more anxious, others grow obsessive and rigid, and still others become paranoid or lose impulse control.
6. *Delirium.* Essentially, delirium is a disorder of attention, but disturbances in perception, memory, and orientation complete the clinical picture. It develops rapidly and is associated with a variety of medical disorders, including alcoholism and drug abuse, high fever, infections, injuries to the brain, and even extreme exhaustion and dehydration ("desert mirages"). During a twenty-four-hour period, the delirious patient may sometimes seem lucid and attentive. This fluctuation in symptoms is significant because it distinguishes delirium from psychotic behavior. Generally the symptoms disappear without leaving the patient permanently damaged. The diagnostic criteria for delirium appear in Table 12.1.
7. *Dementia.* The *DSM*-III describes dementia as *fundamentally a disorder of intellectual functioning,* with impaired ability to think abstractly, changes in personality, and de-

Table 12.1. *DSM*-III diagnostic criteria for delirium

A. Disturbance of attention, as manifested by:
   (1) Impairment in ability to sustain attention to environmental stimuli.
   (2) Impairment in ability to sustain goal-directed thinking, e.g., being unable to finish a calculation.
   (3) Impairment in ability to sustain goal-directed behavior, e.g., starting to walk across the room, stopping, and going back to where one started.
B. Disordered memory and orientation (if testing not interfered with by attention disturbance).
C. At least two of the following:
   (1) Reduced wakefulness or insomnia.
   (2) Perceptual disturbance: simple misinterpretations, illusions, or hallucinations.
   (3) Increased or decreased psychomotor activity.
D. Clinical features develop over a short period of time and fluctuate rapidly.
E. There is evidence from physical examination, medical laboratory tests, or history, of a specific organic factor that is judged to be of importance in the origins of the delirium.

Table 12.2. *DSM*-III diagnostic criteria for dementia

A. A deterioration of previously acquired intellectual abilities of sufficient severity to interfere with social or occupational functioning.
B. Memory impairment.
C. At least one of the following:
   (1) Impairment of abstract thinking as manifested by reduced capacity for generalizing, synthesizing, differentiating, logical reasoning, and concept formation. [Such impairment often can be demonstrated by testing a person with a standardized intelligence test such as the WAIS, discussed in Chapter 3.]
   (2) Impairment in judgment or impulse control.
   (3) Personality change (as discussed in earlier sections).
D. Does not meet the criteria for Intoxication (alcohol or other drugs) or Delirium, although these may be superimposed.
E. There is evidence from physical examination, medical laboratory tests, or history, of a specific organic factor that is judged to be of importance in the origins of the dementia.

creases in judgment and impulse control (see Table 12.2). The onset is generally gradual and the course usually irreversible. Although dementia can occur in childhood (in fact, childhood schizophrenia was originally called "dementia praecox" because of the deterioration in cognitive functioning during its clinical course), it is most common in the elderly. Dementia may accompany the group of degenerative diseases known as *presenile dementias,* or it may be the primary disorder, *senile dementia.*

Injuries to the Brain

The symptoms of organic brain syndromes that we have just described can be caused by a blow to the head or by a jarring motion. Brain injury, or trauma, frequently is caused by auto-

mobile or other accidents, boxing and other athletic events, violent physical assaults to the skull, or injuries to the head sustained during birth. Head injuries are by no means uncommon: the National Center for Health Statistics estimated that in 1971, eight million Americans sustained head injuries. Two-thirds of the people injured in automobile accidents experienced some form of head trauma. Peterson (1975) has estimated that one person in 200 requires medical care for head injury each year, and that approximately 1 percent of the work force is disabled by such injuries each day.

Types of Trauma

The two varieties of brain trauma are: *closed head injuries,* in which the skull is not opened by the trauma, and *open head injuries,* with an

Fig. 12.2. Contusions, or bruises, in the frontal and temporal areas of the brain.

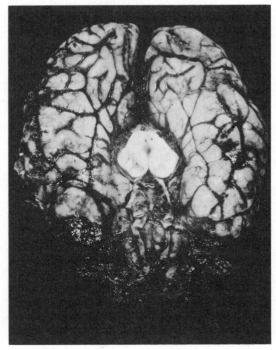

Fig. 1. The normal human brain seen from the left. At the front of the brain (far left) is the frontal lobe; at bottom, the temporal lobe; and at the top, the parietal lobe. At the back (far right) the occipital lobes of both hemispheres can be seen. The cerebellum is visible below the occipital lobes.

Fig. 2. Close-up of the brain surface. The photo shows veins and arteries on the surface of the cortex. Some vessels appear to end abruptly in rounded structures. These are the points where arteries enter the cortex or veins make their exit.

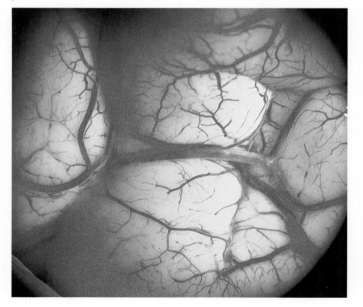

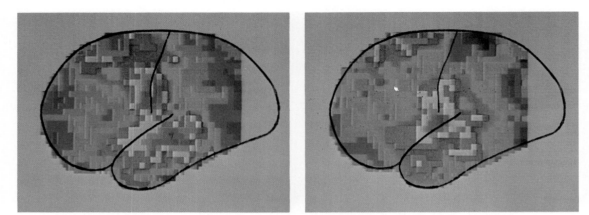

Fig. 3. Variations in the rate of blood flow in specific areas of the brain can provide clues to functional activity in these tissues. Following injection of a radioactive liquid in a major brain artery, sensors record emitted radiation, which is translated into colors on a video screen. Average blood flow is represented as green, rates of 20 percent below average are shades of blue, and rates of 20 percent above average are shades of yellow and red. These averaged images from nine different subjects show differences in activity between the two hemispheres of the brain during speaking. Three centers are activated in each hemisphere: the mouth-tongue-larynx area of the somatosensory and motor cortex, the supplementary motor area, and the auditory cortex. In the right hemisphere (right), the mouth-tongue-larynx area is less distinct and coalesces with the auditory cortex.

Fig. 4. Blocking of a cerebral artery caused the damage shown in these sections of the brain, taken through the left cerebral hemisphere.

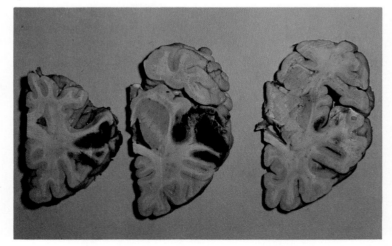

open wound. Closed head injuries include concussions and contusions. Open wounds, or *lacerations,* are far more serious, and many laceration victims do not survive.

CONCUSSION

A concussion causes temporary loss of consciousness that usually lasts less than five minutes; it typically results from disruption in blood flow or other brain function caused by a mild injury to the head, of the kind that can easily occur in athletics and children's play. Recovery from concussions usually is both spontaneous and complete, without lasting effect on the brain. In a severe concussion, the patient may be delirious, agitated, restless, confused, and unable to remember experiences around the time of the injury. In this description by Gene Tunney, you can pick out all these symptoms:

One day while boxing with a sparring partner, Frank Muskie, we bumped heads. The part of my skull which is the thinnest, near the temple, struck the toughest part of his, the top. I was terribly dazed. As I straightened up, a long hard swing landed on my jaw. Without going down or staggering, I lost all consciousness of what I was doing and instinctively proceeded to knock Muskie out. Another sparring partner, Eddie Eagan, entered the ring; we boxed three rounds. I have no recollection of this nor have I any recollection of anything that occurred until next morning when I was awakened in my little cabin by the water's edge, wondering who I was and what I was doing there.

As I lay in this awful state of returning consciousness, I became greatly frightened. Gradually my name came to me. That I was a pugilist soon followed, then the thought of being a champion — impossible, unbelievable. I must have had a long dream. Gradually, the realization came that I had not been dreaming. I rose and asked guarded questions. I wanted to know all about the events of the day before. For three days, I could not remember the names of my most intimate acquaintances. I had to stop training. I did not leave

my cabin except to eat or take a short walk. On three occasions all seemed queer. I was unable to orientate myself. The sensation I had was as though hot water had been poured through a hole in my skull and flowed slowly over my brain to my eyes, leaving a hot film.

After returning to normal I decided that any sport in which such accidents could occur was dangerous. I realized I had a concussion. The first seed of retirement was sown then. The possibility of becoming a punch-drunk haunted me for weeks (Gene Tunney, professional boxer).

Occasionally, a posttraumatic or *postconcussion syndrome* takes the form of persistent headaches and anxiety, irritability, insomnia, and minor cognitive impairments. Whether this syndrome is primarily psychological or organic is unclear. Treatment generally consists of increasing physical exercise and encouraging the patient to resume normal functioning gradually.

CONTUSION

More serious than a concussion, a *contusion,* or brain bruise, can result from a jarring movement of the brain that forces it against the bone of the skull and bruises the tissue. The primary apparent symptom is coma, or loss of consciousness lasting hours or days. Some may have convulsions, or delirium with severe disorientation. Bleeding frequently occurs, and surgical intervention is often necessary to repair damage and to stop hemorrhaging. Repeated boxing injuries to the brain, which result in concussions or contusions, can cause *traumatic encephalopathy,* the "punch-drunk syndrome," to which former boxer Gene Tunney referred. It is marked by slurred speech, unsteady gait, and occasionally impaired intellectual functioning or outright psychosis.

LACERATION

When an object pierces the skull and tears brain tissue, the injury is a *laceration.* Degree and reversibility of damage depends on the size of the area injured and its location in the brain. Many patients do not survive such trauma to the brain. Those who do often follow a pattern of recovery similar to that in contusions: coma, delirium, confusion, and gradual return to more normal consciousness. Many survivors sustain permanent damage to the brain and never regain a normal level of intellectual or emotional function.

One very well known example of profound emotional change brought about by a serious head injury is Phineas P. Gage, a twenty-five-year-old foreman injured midway through the nineteenth century by an iron rod. His physician describes the injury and the subsequent change in Gage's personality:

The missile entered by its pointed end, the left side of the face, immediately anterior to the angle of the lower jaw, and passing obliquely upwards, and obliquely backwards, emerged in the median line, at the back part of the frontal bone, near the coronal suture. . . . The iron which thus transversed the head, is round and rendered comparatively smooth by use, and is three feet seven inches in length, one and one fourth inches in its largest diameter, and weighs thirteen and one fourth pounds. . . .

His contractors, who regarded him as the most efficient and capable foreman in their employ previous to his injury considered the change to his mind so marked that they could not give him his place again. The equilibrium or balance, so to speak, between his intellectual faculties and animal propensities, seems to have been destroyed. He is fitful, irreverent, indulging at times in the grossest profanity (which was not previously his custom), manifesting but little deference for his fellows, impatient of restraint or advice when it conflicts with his desires, at times pertinaciously obstinate, yet capricious and vacillating, devising many plans of future operations, which are no sooner arranged than they are abandoned in turn for others. . . . His mind is radically changed (Harlow 1868, pp. 330–32, 339–40).

Posttraumatic Complications

People who experience trauma to the brain can have many problems, both from the injury itself and in ability to cope with the injury. Physical complications include impairment in intellect, speech, and movement, as well as posttraumatic epilepsy (onset of seizures one month or more after injury). Among the psychological consequences are transient or permanent overreactions to stress, pervasive anxiety, changes in personality, increased mood lability, and tendency to exaggerate the significance of physical symptoms. Many patients, along with medical treatment for the acute phase of their injury, now also receive individual or group psychotherapy to help them adjust to the physical and psychological effects of brain injury.

Brain Tumors

Abnormal tissue growths, or tumors, within the brain can produce widely varied physical and psychological symptoms. Frequently, the first sign of a tumor may be a change in personality or psychotic symptoms, such as hallucinations and other sensory disturbances. It is often difficult to distinguish between behavioral symptoms of the psychotic and other functional disorders and changes caused by brain tumors, as these examples illustrate (Geschwind 1975):

An atomic physicist on a mission abroad began to develop paranoid ideas about the stealing of atomic secrets. He was returned home, diagnosed as schizophrenic and hospitalized. After several months he suffered a grand mal seizure. He was seen again in consultation by an expert psychiatrist who felt that the clinical picture was so characteristically schizophrenic that organic causes could be dismissed as the cause of the psychosis. Within a short time, however, when severe headaches developed, the patient was referred for study and a temporal lobe . . . [tumor] was found (p. 7).

A hard-driving and very successful businessman in his thirties stopped sleeping with his wife shortly after his promotion to vice-president of his company. At his wife's insistence, he went into psychotherapy. It was only several months later that his work performance began to decline, followed by a deterioration in personal cleanliness. These were interpreted as signs of depression, for which the patient was eventually hospitalized. Although he then developed incontinence, the possibility of organic disorder was still not considered until he became stuporous. He was found to have a large subfrontal tumor (p. 7).

A previously highly successful young officer in the diplomatic corps was returned home because of a loss of interest in his work and a decline in his performance. Despite psychiatric help, he became increasingly apathetic about his work and he was dismissed. He took a series of successively less attractive jobs and was finally employed keeping pigs. He was repeatedly diagnosed as a character disorder. He eventually developed severe headaches and was found to have a large . . . [tumor] that had compressed the under surface of his frontal lobe (p. 7).

Malignant growths destroy brain tissue, whereas *benign* ones usually exert their influence by size and increased pressure on the brain. Vomiting, headaches, and changes in vision are among the more common physical symptoms; lability of mood, changes in cognition (particularly memory function) and depression are frequent psychological manifestations of abnormal growths in the brain. Impairment of motor functions, problems with coordination, and hallucinations are possible.

Diagnosing tumors requires medical and neuropsychological procedures (neurological examination, psychological examination and brain scan) to rule out a purely behavioral disorder. Surgery is usually necessary to restore normal functioning or to save a patient's life,

although functional loss from tissue damage may be permanent. Sometimes location of the tumor or the spreading and damage caused by it make an operation medically inadvisable. Many malignant tumors are ultimately fatal, and benign ones can be if they are not removed. Clearly, the symptoms that appear with brain tumors, the degree of damage sustained, and the ability of medical and surgical procedures to give significant aid in the treatment depend on the original site and type of the tumor and how early in its development an accurate diagnosis is made.

Fig. 12.3. Large astrocytoma, a tumor which grows very rapidly within the brain and produces many mental symptoms. Often the tumor grows so rapidly that the patient cannot adapt to his or her constricted mental functioning and may respond catastrophically.

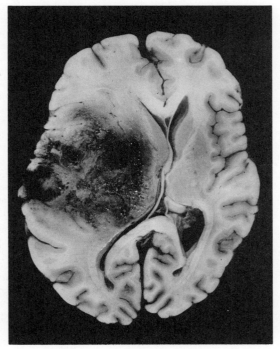

Brain Infections

Viral or bacterial infections can profoundly affect the brain's functioning. One type of brain infection is *encephalitis,* a general name for an inflammation of the brain most frequently caused by a virus; sometimes it is bacterial or chemical in origin. One common form of encephalitis is "sleeping sickness," or endemic encephalitis, bringing on extreme lethargy and excessive sleeping, often followed by a period of hyperactivity and hyperirritability. Delirium and convulsions can occur; changes in behavior are particularly pronounced in children.

It has been estimated that a third to a half of patients who survive endemic encephalitis will continue to have psychological symptoms (such as restlessness, impulsivity, and in-

Neuropsychological Testing

Information on the presence or absence of brain damage and its type and extent is gathered in many ways. Some are medical: physical examination, laboratory studies of blood and urine, specialized examinations by neurologists, brain x-rays, brain scans or computerized axial tomography, studies of brain waves by electroencephalograms (EEG), and lumbar punctures ("spinal taps") that obtain cerebrospinal fluid to check for possible brain infections, hemorrhaging, and so on, and many other medical diagnostic procedures. Many useful psychological tests can give additional types of information for diagnostic decisions about brain damage. Psychologists disagree about precisely which group or battery of neuropsychological tests to use in assessing patients with brain damage. We will discuss a few of the difficulties in testing these patients and describe several of the tests.

Benton (1975) describes factors in the psychological assessment of patients with possible brain damage that make it difficult to diagnose these patients accurately everytime: (1) lack of cooperation and effort by apathetic, hostile, asocial, or paranoid patients; (2) lack of mental energy in patients who are depressed or badly depleted by illness; (3) inattention and difficulty in concentration associated with preoccupation or intense anxiety; (4) simulated or exaggerated mental incompetence, particularly when the question of a pension or compensation for injuries comes up; (5) poor understanding and task adjustment by culturally handicapped patients.

Several general types of neuropsychological tests have evolved to measure organicity. General tests of *intelligence* (such as the Wechsler Adult Intelligence Scale described in Chapter 3) are used to assess possible decline in overall functioning. If a patient does much more poorly on a test like the WAIS than expected from prior performance of educational and cultural background, some sort of cerebral damage may be suspected.

Tests of *reasoning and problem solving* that show change in the person's ability to make abstract interpretations are similar. Often the first and most obvious changes in brain disease and aging are *memory* deficits, which can be tested by asking patients to recall information presented to them (digits or words). Asking the patient to recall such information within five seconds of presentation examines *immediate memory;* within minutes or hours but after ten seconds, is *recent memory;* examining recollection of events in the distant past taps *remote memory.* Interestingly, remote memory is often relatively more intact in patients with significant dementia than in immediate or recent memory. Tests of *orientation* (What is today's date? What time is it now? Who are you? Where are you?) frequently indicate impairment in recent memory, as well as confusional states.

Still other neuropsychological tests assess changes or deficits in *language* ability, generally suggestive of damage in the cerebral hemisphere dominant for language. Often aphasia can be detected with these tests. Tests of *spatial orientation, visual memory* for design, and ability to *perceive*

creased aggressiveness) following the *acute phase* of the illness. Older victims may develop Parkinson's disease, an organic brain syndrome that we will consider later in this chapter. In general, the earlier the onset the more severe the psychological and cognitive impairment; children under five are particularly vulnerable, and mental retardation is not uncommon in those affected within this age group. Antibiotics are generally very effective in treating this form of encephalitis and preventing extensive, permanent brain damage.

A second type of brain infection, *neurosyphilis,* is the advanced stage of syphilis, a venereal disease caused by the bacterium *Treponema pallidum* (for a discussion of the discovery of this organism see Chapter 1). It is almost always transmitted during sexual inter-

and *construct designs* in three dimensions are also important indicators of brain disease. For example, the accompanying figures show how patients with diseases of the nondominant, nonlanguage hemisphere incorrectly reproduce standardized shapes.

If the patient who drew them was right-handed and therefore dominant in the left hemisphere, where the language function is concentrated, the types of errors in the drawings would lead a psychologist to conclude that the patient had right-hemisphere disease.

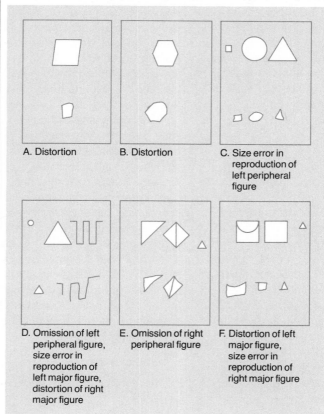

A. Distortion

B. Distortion

C. Size error in reproduction of left peripheral figure

D. Omission of left peripheral figure, size error in reproduction of left major figure, distortion of right major figure

E. Omission of right peripheral figure

F. Distortion of left major figure, size error in reproduction of right major figure

course, although occasionally a pregnant woman will transmit it to her unborn child. At one time syphilis resulted in 10 to 30 percent of admissions to psychiatric hospitals. Today, however, with early diagnosis syphilis can be effectively treated with penicillin or other antibiotics.

Initial symptoms of syphilis include small sores on the lips or in the genital area and occasionally a rash; often these symptoms are so mild that the victim may not even notice them. No further associated symptoms may show up for fifteen to twenty years, the so-called latent period. During this time the bacteria may invade any tissue or organ system in the body. When they invade and destroy tissue of the central nervous system the resulting condition is known as *general paresis;* between 2 and 5 percent of those infected with syphilis initially will develop paresis. Mental symptoms can include lethargy, depression, poor emotional control, intellectual deterioration, irritability, and occasional delusions of grandeur. Victims also become progressively paralyzed.

Endocrine Disorders

The endocrine glands secrete hormones that, when released into the bloodstream, regulate many of the body's functions, including its energy supply and availability, sexual functions, and physical growth. For the most part, the endocrine system is under the control of the central nervous system, so that disorders in endocrine functioning can cause significant changes in personality, memory, and mental functions, as well as medical and neurological problems. Endocrine disorders can lead to psychopathological states as well as result from them; the degree and manifestation of such disorders often depends on an individual's personality and cognitive functioning prior to illness. Although many types of illnesses involve the endocrine system, we shall focus on the most psychopathologically important endocrine glands — the thyroid and adrenal — and diseases that are common to them.

Thyroid Disorders

Significant changes in mood, behavior, and cognition can result from overproduction of the hormone *thyroxin,* a condition known as *Grave's disease,* or, more commonly, *hyperthyroidism,* and from underproduction of thyroxin, a disorder called *myxedema,* or *hypothyroidism.* Hypothyroidism can also be caused by insufficient intake of iodine; adding iodine to table salt has all but eliminated this type of the once common disorder. Hyperthyroidism causes marked weight loss, tremors, excessive anxiety and apprehension, increased sweating, and psychomotor agitation. Occasionally, psychotic symptoms such as visual and auditory hallucinations also occur. It is not unusual for hyperthyroid patients to be seen first by psychiatrists or psychologists because of the anxious, agitated condition they present; such patients are sometimes misdiagnosed as manics or agitated depressives.

Hypothyroidism, on the other hand, brings increased weight, sluggishness, difficulties with concentration and memory, lethargy, and depression. A patient suffering from hypothyroidism can be indistinguishable in symptoms and appearance from one with a major depressive disorder. For this reason, good clinical practice requires that patients displaying marked depressive symptomology be routinely screened for thyroid problems. Treatment for thyroid dysfunctions, generally medical or surgical, is relatively straightforward.

Adrenal Disorders

The adrenal glands are above the kidneys and consist of an outer layer, or *cortex,* and an inner core, the *medulla.* The cortex secretes hormones that control stress reactions and secondary sexual characteristics; secretions from the medulla mediate strong emotions. *Addison's disease* results from insufficient production of hormones by the adrenal cortex. Common symptoms of this disorder include depression, anxiety, irritability, lack of motivation, fatigue, and decreased sociability. When the adrenal cortex is too active, *Cushing's syndrome* can result; common symptoms include obesity, atrophied muscles, lability of mood, and fatigue. As with thyroid dysfunctions, medical and surgical intervention are the most usual methods of treatment.

Syndromes Associated with Aging

The thought of growing old evokes strong fear and anxiety in most of us. Although many older people approach their sixties and seventies with expectation and an active mind, many dread the possibility of failing physical health, financial difficulties, and isolation. Their fears are not without foundation. Psychological and social losses at this time are often profound. Financial stresses from retirement and fixed income are well documented. Isolation is increasing in modern society, particularly for the elderly. Changes in role are substantial and often demoralizing. Health concerns and changes in health are both real and often extensive. Death of friends and relatives is also a source of loss and reminder of our own mortality. Certainly, however, capacity to cope with the normal facets of growing old depends on our premorbid personality and current resources. An organic brain syndrome in this stage of life only compounds difficulties in adjustment.

Several degenerative disorders of the central nervous system strike primarily in middle age

and the declining years. They are classified as presenile dementias and senile dementias, according to the age group they usually affect. After briefly examining the presenile (that is, appearing before age sixty-five) dementias, we shall examine the major degenerative syndromes associated with aging.

Presenile Degenerative Disorders

The presenile dementias are a group of degenerative central nervous system diseases with intellectual deterioration and relatively early onset. The etiologies of these disorders are unclear.

ALZHEIMER'S DISEASE

Early in this century, Alzheimer described a syndrome involving severe dementia, occurring in people in their forties, fifties, and early sixties. Although the disorder is mostly indistinguishable from senile dementia, the patients tend to be younger and the course of the illness is much more rapid, with exceedingly evident deterioration in intellectual functioning; personality structure usually remains relatively intact. Death generally occurs within five years of onset of the symptoms. There is no specific treatment for Alzheimer's disease; patients are almost always confined to institutions because it is incapacitating.

PARKINSON'S DISEASE

Parkinson's disease is a relatively common disorder; at least 500,000 people in the United States suffer from it at any time (Mulder 1975). It is a progressive disorder most commonly caused by some type of brain fever, or encephalitis. Millions of cases were left by the major influenza epidemic during World War I. In many people the effects of this virus-induced encephalitis did not show up for years (occasionally twenty to twenty-five); the mechanism for the delay is still not fully understood. Parkinsonism causes tremor, impairment of fine movements,

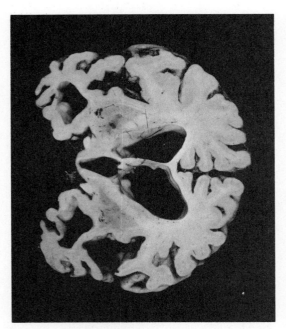

Fig. 12.4. Diffuse and widespread atrophy of brain tissue which hallmarks senile dementia.

and rigidity of the face and other parts of the body. Both dementia and depression can be present in advanced Parkinsonism, although symptoms vary greatly. Treatment often consists of encouraging as much activity as possible; speech therapy can be useful in helping overcome the impairments that frequently occur. In the past decade, drug therapy with L-Dopa has proved highly effective in controlling Parkinsonian symptoms for most patients; occasionally surgery can have beneficial effects.

HUNTINGTON'S CHOREA

This is a rare (4 to 7 per 100,000 persons in the United States population) hereditary disorder that generally first appears between ages thirty and fifty. The hallmark of the disease is severe and progressive cognitive deterioration. McHugh and Folstein (1975) describe three distinctive features of the dementia syndrome in Huntington's chorea: (1) slow progressive deterioration of all cognitive powers, (2) pronounced apathy and inertia, and (3) absence of aphasia or amnesia. They also found in many of their patients an affective disorder that was often indistinguishable from manic-depressive illness (and, in fact, the suicide rate in Huntington's chorea is very high); occasionally, patients also experienced delusions and hallucinations, leading to a misdiagnosis of schizophrenia. Patients usually live about fifteen years after the illness appears, although many have lived much longer. Almost invariably the treatment is long-term hospitalization. No cure is known, although partial or transient improvement has been achieved recently with several experimental drugs that alter central neurotransmitter substances.

That Huntington's chorea is hereditary, of course, worries and adds stress to the life of families having a stricken member. If one parent carries the gene, each offspring has a 50 percent chance of developing Huntington's chorea during his adult years. This recorded conversation between a neurosurgeon, I. S. Cooper (1976), one of his patients, and her husband illustrates a few feelings about the genetic aspect of the disorder, as well as the fears in having such a disabling disorder:

Mrs. K: The last two weeks have really been rough on me. I think I've finally made up my mind and accepted the realization that I do have Huntington's. This hope has been in the back of my mind, praying that I was misdiagnosed — you know, all the fantasies. (Mrs. K's mother, grandmother, two aunts, and an uncle all had Huntington's chorea.)
Doctor: What gave you the realization?
Mrs. K: Well, I noticed that I wasn't walking as

Fig. 12.5. Woody Guthrie (left), famous American folksinger and songwriter, suffered from Huntington's chorea, a progressively debilitating form of presenile dementia. His son, Arlo Guthrie (right), also a folksinger, has a 50 percent chance of being stricken with the same disease.

straight as I had been. I couldn't keep my balance — you know, when anyone pushed me I fell over. And also some of the drawings I did in my last tests were so shaky . . .

Doctor: You have two children. Did you have children before you knew what Huntington's chorea was?

Mrs. K: There was no feeling about this hereditary thing, or how bad it was, anything like that.

Doctor: Were you just not informed, or were you just pushing it to the back of your mind?

Mr. K: A combination of both, I think.

Doctor: Do you think some doctor should have come to you and said, ''This is a hereditary disease''?

Mr. K: I think the answer is no. I don't think anyone should have done that.

Doctor: I'm asking this question because one of the biggest and most important issues facing us at the moment is the question of genetic counseling. We doctors have to learn from you. If you had known would you have had children? It is difficult, perhaps an unfair question, since you have two children whom you love, and . . .

Mr. K: If we knew then what we know now . . .

Mrs. K: It is a profound question. I don't know. How can I answer that now?

Mr. K: If we knew then what we know now, the answer is no, as far as I'm concerned.

Mrs. K: We also have a son who is twenty-one. He says he's got to marry someone who loves him enough to understand that he is going to adopt children. But our daughter says she will not. She's the opposite. She wants her own.

Mr. K: I tell you, if I could just see these genes die everywhere! (Cooper 1976, pp. 177, 178, 179).

Senile Dementia

Mental deterioration in old age is often associated with cerebral degeneration and atrophy. The average person whose dementia is sufficiently severe to warrant hospitalization is in his mid-seventies at the time of admission. Onset of dementia is almost always gradual, and its manifestation is influenced by predementia personality and abilities, the support systems available, the degree of organic impairment, and continuing stresses. The characteristics of dementia (cognitive deterioration, impaired judgment and impulse control, and changes in personality) become increasingly noticeable. Patients may be any or all of these: disoriented, agitated, paranoid, severely depressed, delusional, delirious, or hallucinatory.

Although no specific cure is known for senile dementia, many things can be done to increase the likelihood of at least some ameliorating symptoms. A correct diagnosis is exceedingly important to rule out the possibility that the patient may have a treatable depression, metabolic or nutritional disturbance, or situational reaction. Older people with dementia usually are hospitalized or put in a nursing home when they are unable to care for themselves. Medications are occasionally useful in managing the secondary behavioral and mood disorders (including tranquilizers, antipsychotics, and antidepressants), as are structured environments with supportive individual or group psychotherapy. Many hospitals and nursing homes have clearly time-cued environments so that older patients, who may have difficulty knowing what time of day it is, have many large clocks that are easy to see. For more sense of security, lights often are kept on at night and changes in the physical layout are kept to a minimum so as not to distress the occasionally anxious and somewhat obsessive older patient.

Pseudodementia

Many symptoms of depression and dementia overlap. Like severely depressed individuals, the senile may suffer failures in memory and cognition, apathy, delusions, agitation, and insomnia. An older person who is depressed but also manifests symptoms of dementia is said to have *pseudodementia.* Because depression is a disorder amenable to treatment, we must be aware of the similarities between the illnesses. The rates of significant depressive symptoms in the geriatric population are estimated at 30 to 65 percent (Gerner 1979). Manic behavior in the elderly, like depressive behavior, can also have distinctive features that may appear to mimic dementia or other organic brain syndromes. Manic confusion can resemble delirium; paranoid features are often more pronounced in older manic patients; increased lability of affect and circumstantiality (thinking or conversation with unnecessary elaboration of trivial details) in both dementia and mania can also make correct diagnosis more difficult.

Circulatory Disturbances

Cerebral arteriosclerosis can result in senile plaques in thin formations accumulating inside the arteries, eventually impeding circulation. The vessels can be blocked by such deposits, or a blood clot can form and block the vessel. Occasionally a piece of the hardened deposit will travel to a narrower place in the vessel, again causing blood stoppage. Sometimes one of these processes causes a blood vessel to rupture. Blocking or rupturing of the vessels that cause only slight and generally transient effects is known as a *small stroke.* When a large vessel is affected, a *major stroke,* or *cerebrovascular accident,* occurs. Patients suffering from a major stroke often are disoriented, extremely confused, incoherent, and emotionally labile. They may have transient or permanent paralysis, disorders in speech and expression, mood problems, and cognitive impairment. Speech and recreational therapy, as well as physical

Aphasia: One Woman's Account

One common result of a cerebrovascular accident, or stroke, is impaired comprehension of spoken and written language and production of speech. This language disorder, caused by damage to the brain, is *aphasia,* halting, *nonfluent speech, difficulty in finding words, problems in comprehension,* and *abnormalities in grammatical structure.* Inability to express thoughts and feelings, though occasionally reversible with time and intensive speech therapy, is extremely frustrating for the person who has suffered a stroke. A few aspects of the aphasic's world are described by Helen Wulf in her account of her stroke.

The experience

Aphasia is a weird disorder made more so, regrettably, because there are those who equate speaking with intelligence. It's sad, maddening, funny, how unaware and unperceptive people can be. ''Oh, so she has aphasia. What in the world is that? . . . You mean she can't talk? . . . Just how badly is her mind affected? . . .''

My speaking sounds inebriated. I slump and slosh and mush through too many words. Do you have any idea what it feels like to realize you have been bereft of the ability to communicate as you have always done? Where do I find the right words? No clinical, objective, dissective dissertation will do. Aphasia can be a devastating trauma striking with unwarranted violence at an essence of the humanness of man: his self-esteem.

Aphasia, in one sense, could be called a disorder of exaggeration: too much of anything comes too soon. Too many people, too much noise, too many distractions, too much to see. Things that normally impinge on our visual and auditory senses can bring total fatigue quickly. . . . Prior to the stroke, difficulty in driving was never thought of consciously. Now it nags so much that driving may mean setting a goal of one block at a time until reaching the destination. Driving demands being constantly alert every old which way and able to zip an instruction through a brain that is set on slow motion. But aphasia demands doing one thing at a time.

Reactions of others

Reactions of people to me since I stumbled and fell into a stroke trap have been almost as varied as all of ourselves put together.

There are those wonderful ones who always accept me the way I am; use their eyes and ears and heads to determine how things are, what can be done and what cannot; play their part accordingly and then reassess the situation when they see me next time.

There are those to whom the word *stroke* seems to be so shocking that I, the victim, feel I am polluting the entire atmosphere. There are those who cannot bring themselves to use the word, though one is not sure whether by ignoring the subject of a stroke its effect will go away, or whether the person thinks the subject is too painful for me to discuss. So I use the word, at least stumble through it for it is a hard word for me to pronounce, and the listener seems to cringe.

Treatment

Probably no two victims suffer identical damage. Therefore, those working with aphasics cannot pick out a pattern, a textbook pattern as it were, and hope to jam the patient into it despite any resistance on the part of the aphasic. For this very reason, in my considered judgment, aphasia appalls many professionals, a feeling easily conveyed to the patient.

There is an old jingly rhyme telling that little girls are made of sugar and spice and everything nice, while little boys arrive replete with rats and snails and puppy dog tails. This is no

therapy, are common adjuncts to medical treatment regimes.

Problems in Treating the Elderly

Gerner (1978) outlines several levels of resistance encountered in treating the elderly: *patient's resistance:* many older persons still view hospitals and institutions as "snake pits," although a few patients no doubt enjoy the secondary gains from attention they may receive as a result of illness and dependency; others have obsessive worries about sameness and not

---

sillier than for an aphasic's caretaker to decide how he should behave and be nonplussed when he does not.

I am not typical and neither is anyone else. Let us assume, for the sake of argument, that a stroke caused identical damage in ten cases. These ten people would be so different in abilities, talents, age, responsibilities, reactions, family make-up, qualities innumerable that the impact of a stroke could not possibly be the same for any of them (Helen Wulf 1973, p. 31).

A page from the aphasia victim's workbook.

> With which form of word might you have difficulty:
>
> rain   rainy   raining
>
> part   party   parting
>
> test   testy   testing
>
> At this point it seems to me I either don't get the word I want or it comes to me whole. In conversations I do plenty of substituting not all of it accurate. For 3 days I've been hunting the word Capillary. No part of it came to me, instead of suddenly the whole word. What I used in a sort of odd way was pheriphery.
>
> I'll watch you + see if that continues to happen or if I get part of the word.

wishing to change environments; *physician's resistance:* physicians seem to avoid evaluating and treating older patients; one study revealed that fewer than 2 percent of psychiatric patients are over 65 (Feigenbaum 1974); *family resistance* to treatment is often strong, for either fi-nancial or psychological reasons (ambivalence about the patient, or a tendency to see senility and unhappiness as "just part of being old"); and, a *general societal resistance* opposes treating the elderly. Ageism, or discriminatory attitudes and practices against older people, is

UCLA Clinic Treats the Elderly

The Psychosocial Clinic for People over 65 of UCLA was specifically designed to spur interest in evaluating and treating a pre-viously neglected but quickly growing part of our population. Because the problems of the elderly are often complex and multifaceted — their losses are physical, mental, social, and financial — the clinic uses an interdisciplin-ary model of evaluation and treatment plan-ning, which Dr. Kay Rowland, clinical psychologist and director of the clinic, dis-cusses:

Q. Dr. Rowland, could you tell us about the pa-tients seen in the clinic?
A. Since our beginning two years ago, approxi-mately 250 older people (and often their families) have been seen for evaluation and treatment or both. Their complaints have been representative of the well-documented problems of aging: increased physical ill-ness, impaired cognitive functioning, finan-cial strains, children leaving home and having less involvement with them, death of friends and spouses, moving from familiar houses to smaller apartments or perhaps to institutions, sexual decline, decreased sen-sory acuity, and unwanted inactivity after retirement. We can view old age as a seg-ment of the life cycle in which a person is faced with life events that bombard his feel-ings of well-being and mastery. The major-ity of our patients are female; many are widowed, living alone in apartments into which they have recently been forced to move. They complain of depression, loneli-ness, and difficulty coping with the limita-tions and pain of their increasing physical diseases. Some recognize and are frus-trated by beginning signs of mental impair-ment, such as memory loss and slowed, fuzzy thinking.
Q. How are the patients evaluated?
A. We have found it important to get input from many disciplines in evaluating elderly pa-tients, because their problems are often in-terrelated.

The complaints of depression and hope-lessness of one sixty-five-year-old man had been triggered by the onset of congestive heart failure a year before. Because of his ill health, he had been forced to retire and found himself spending long idle hours at home with his wife, with whom he had little in common. His physical activities were se-verely restricted. To make matters worse, his income since retirement had been drastically reduced, and he and his wife were no longer able to afford the increasing property taxes on their house.

In another case, a daughter brought her mother in for evaluation after noticing that she was becoming increasingly withdrawn and uninterested in social activities, and was instead devoting hours of her daily activity to "keeping the family books." The mother, a retired accountant, at one time had kept the finances in order with ease. Her psychologi-cal testing revealed early signs of organic impairment, and indeed, when the family was encouraged to check the mother's book-keeping, they found notices of bills months behind in payment. This woman expressed little awareness of her impairment and, in-stead of reacting emotionally, had immersed herself in long hours of unproductive shuf-fling of papers.

The point about evaluating an older per-son is that each discipline views problems from a different vantage point. Assessing a

deep-seated in our current culture and can result in societal resistance to treatment.

Fortunately, many of the biases against older people appear to be abating somewhat, partly because of increased public awareness of the problems of the elderly. Many hospitals now have specialty clinics in their departments of medicine or psychiatry, specializing in the psychosocial treatment of the elderly, providing coordinated help with medical problems, psychosocial difficulties, or family and financial worries.

patient's medical status and drug intake is extremely important. Psychiatric nurses in the clinic occasionally make home visits, to view a patient "on home territory." The patient's living situation, nutritional status, and obvious hazards around the house can be noticed and later attended to. Psychologists are invaluable in assessing a patient's cognitive functioning and style of personality. In addition, the structure of a patient's family and support system must be understood, in both determining his problems and planning his treatment.

Q. What kinds of treatment does the clinic offer?

A. Psychotherapy is offered for individuals, couples, and in groups. Along with it, psychotropic medications are given when necessary. Also, we try to inform the older person and his family of community services that may be available to help them cope with their problems. Senior citizen centers, visiting nurses, meals on wheels programs, dial-a-ride services, job placement services, day care centers, or retirement planning programs may offer needed support. In cases of chronic organic brain syndrome, for which there is no medical treatment, we often work with the families to help them understand the strange process their spouse or parent is going through. The patient's disturbed behaviors (poor personal hygiene, repetitive questioning, carelessness with household appliances, irresponsible handling of money, getting lost, unpredictable emotional outbursts) are disturbing to the family. Their reactions may involve anger (believing that the patient is purposefully behaving in such a manner), or guilt ("if I had been a better child/spouse, this wouldn't have happened"), or denial ("he's always been forgetful"), or overreaction, assuming that if a patient needs care in one area, he will need to be supervised in all activities.

Q. What kinds of feelings are engendered by working with elderly patients?

A. One of the predominant societal attitudes about helping the elderly is that it isn't worthwhile to help them at all. This has often been the attitude of our colleagues, our patients, and their families, and it sometimes permeates our work as well so that we vacillate between an excited, enthusiastic view of the opportunities of working in a new, burgeoning area to despair on days when nothing seems to go well. Listening to the experiences of an older person is sometimes heartbreaking, as you feel with them the discouragement of facing insurmountable problems. One seventy-six-year-old retired psychologist, who is currently undergoing progressive deterioration of her cognitive abilities, has profoundly affected all our staff. She used to be held in high esteem for her work with brain-damaged children, and has described for us her heroic, though usually futile, attempts to correct her own impairments by applying the methods she had once used in her profession. Her despair that she is alone in a world where no one is interested in her brilliant, eventful past and her rambling, sometimes halting speech (as she tries to find the right word) in expressing herself has aroused in us intense feelings, including fierce pride and admiration and overwhelming sadness and dread.

Epilepsy

There is a phrase of a dream in *Autobiography* which describes the preliminary warning of an approaching epileptic attack although it was written merely of a nightmare: "the heart stood to meet its enemy." After this desperate stand comes a fluttering tremulousness of body and mind. The intensity varies, but it is physically like a breeze or a gale entering one and agitating all one's being. The old idea of demoniac possession, I am sure, arose not from the onlookers of sufferers in fits but from the sufferers themselves. Because in the violent attacks one feels as though the body has been entered by a terrific alien power; and that that power is trying, after entrance, to push its way

out again. It is not unlike labour, but not so intelligent. If the consciousness is prolonged until the fall, as mine has often been, the flesh with its limbs and its orderly muscles seems actually to be entangled — the body is on the point of being blown aside as if it were what mystics have called it, a curtain; or as Blake said, a shady grove.

One hears people ask, "What is the matter?" One cannot answer, although one seems to know. One's eyes are nailed on an object or a face. This rigid attitude in which one seems to be listening to a call important beyond all human matters — there is of course no voice, but such is the effect, as if the last trump had blown — dissolves into a kind of hideous hovering. One turns round or away from helpers, if they are present; if not, from the pres-

Fig. 12.6. Electroencephalographic (EEG) recordings of the electrical potentials of the brain, obtained by placing scalp electrodes over various sites on the scalp. Records are shown for a normal person and for individuals with different types of epilepsy.

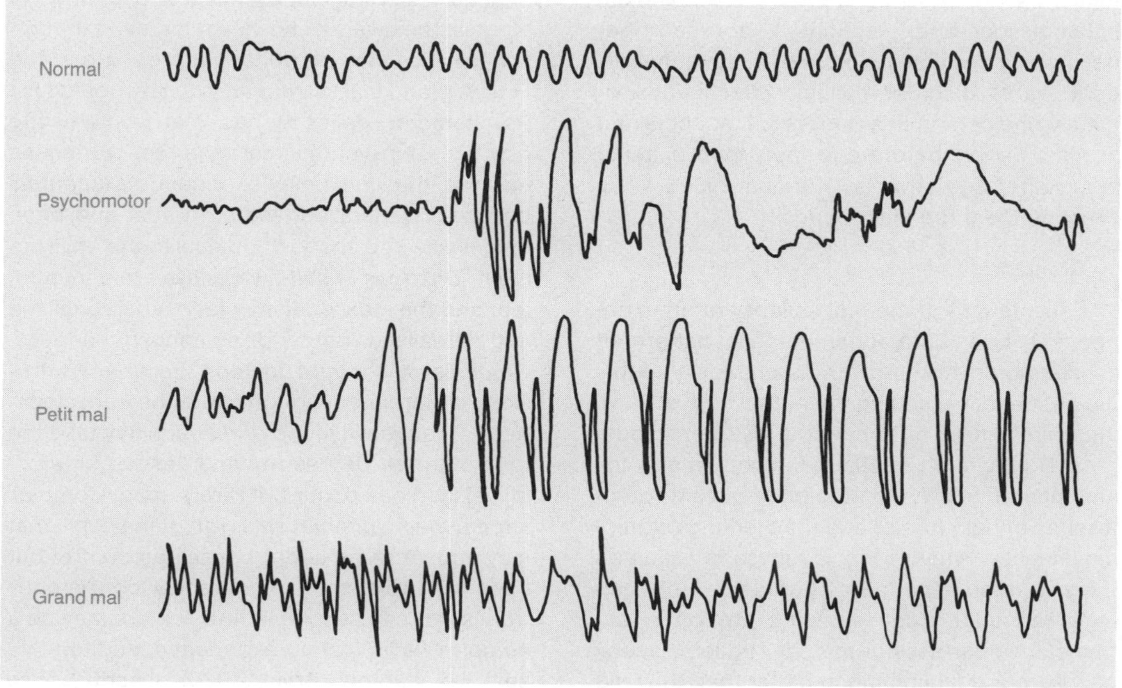

ence of the appalling calamity in the room which is the body. The utmost source of terror to me was never the summons but this awful and yet *silly* moment, when the being tries to laugh it off, to leave it behind, to walk irresponsibly away. That ghastly moment is *funny* whether one can believe it or not. But have not many people written of the giggling silly horror of pure terror? Whether or not my last sensation, and the one I most dread, the one which has most nearly touched me with true neurosis, the one I cannot forget, is that laughter, that shrugging it off. The next instant I fall into nothing.

— Margiad Evans,
A Ray of Darkness

Epilepsy is a brain disorder with abnormal rhythms in the electrical discharge of brain cells. Its causes are many, some known and some unknown; among those known to be potential causes are trauma, high fever, anoxia, inflammations and infections, tumors, and genetic predisposition. An incurable, but generally controllable, disorder, epilepsy affects approximately one person in a hundred, first occurring in most people before age four, then peaking again after age seventy (Kurland 1959). We'll examine the three major types.

Grand Mal

Patients with grand mal epilepsy often experience a brief aura (characteristic pattern of sensorimotor events, such as change in lighting or sound, preceding the actual convulsion), then may emit a brief cry and lose consciousness. During such a seizure the patient may fall and injure himself; next the body goes through a series of rigid (tonic) and then jerking (clonic) movements. When consciousness is regained there is often a period of confusion. Interestingly, although such seizures are often extremely embarrassing for the patient, many people report feeling much better than they did before the convulsion. In fact, occasionally pa-

tients will deliberately induce seizures by not taking their anticonvulsant medications.

Petit Mal

This type of epilepsy is most common in childhood and is a brief (10 to 30 second) attack that can be unnoticed by both the epileptic and by observers. Total unconsciousness actually occurs, but so briefly that it is sometimes not subjectively experienced; however, many people report confusion and short episodes of amnesia. The more frequently episodes occur, of course, the more profound the consequences. One woman reportedly had 300 petit mal seizures in a day (Ervin 1975).

Psychomotor Epilepsy

During psychomotor seizures a patient may experience lapses in consciousness and may engage in stereotypical behaviors, appearing to others to be aware of his behavior, even though his activities may be quite inappropriate at the time. A grand mal seizure may or may not follow. Psychomotor epilepsy has many interesting psychic, or psychological features. During an episode, the victim may experience *perceptual changes.* Generally these are visual and often distort size and shape of objects in the environment. *Changes in self-awareness* are common, too, and the individual may feel depersonalized and derealized (unreal or somehow changed). *Changes in thought* include dominant intrusions of unrelated thoughts into the consciousness. *Changes in mood and affect* may take the form of terror, depression and despair, or anxiety; elation can occur but rarely does. *Complex stereotyped automatisms,* or behaviors that may appear to be under conscious control but often are irrelevant, may reappear consistently from seizure to seizure. A final feature may be a *complex hallucinatory experience,* auditory, visual, or olfactory. Ervin (1975) describes one such phenomenon:

Fig. 12.7. How it feels to have an epileptic seizure. This drawing was made by a victim of grand mal. Many epileptics have visual premonitions of an oncoming seizure, called *auras*. These experiences resemble dreams, although the individual is still fully conscious. Terrifying as it often is, an aura can help steel an epileptic for the ordeal of a seizure.

One patient always heard a poker game in the next room, with the shuffling of cards, the unmistakable click of stacked poker chips, and a mumble of voices. The patient usually has a clear insight into the hallucinatory nature of the phenomenon and feels it alien to himself but, unless he is unusually sophisticated, he may be quite anxious as to its reflection on his sanity (p. 1148).

Psychological and behavioral difficulties are particularly associated with disorders of the temporal lobe psychomotor seizure, including behavioral problems, lability of mood, hallucinatory experiences, and occasional problems with impulse control and violence.

Ervin also points out that although attitudes toward those with epilepsy are obviously much less superstitious and persecutory than they were in the Middle Ages (in Scotland, men with epilepsy were castrated, and women with epilepsy were burned alive with their children), eleven states still have sterilization laws applying to persons with epilepsy. Some school systems refuse to admit epileptic children to normal classrooms, and they are discriminated against in employment, even though the disorder can be mostly controlled with medication. In many states it is difficult for an epileptic to get a driver's license. Prominent among the problems, of course, is the social embarrassment that accompanies the disorder, leading to difficulties in self-esteem and normal adjustment.

Treatment of Epilepsy

Most types of epilepsy can be very effectively controlled by a variety of anticonvulsant medications. Because the disorder is chronic, patients usually are actively involved in education and treatment. Biofeedback techniques have been useful in treating some patients with seizure disorders (Shapiro 1976; Sterman 1977), and supportive psychotherapy is frequently a useful adjunct to the medical treatment program. Rarely, in some patients with severe seizures that do not respond to any other kind of treatment, psychosurgery is done, with varying effectiveness.

Summary

1. An organic brain syndrome is a temporary or permanent brain dysfunction with a known organic cause. Brain dysfunction affects behavior both directly — often through reduced cognitive abilities — and indirectly — through awareness of the cognitive loss. Onset may be sudden or insidious. The prognosis depends on the cause of the dysfunction, the patient's determination to recover, and the patient's premorbid level of functioning.

2. Symptoms of an organic brain syndrome are: (1) impaired orientation, memory, intellectual function, and judgment; (2) lability and shallowness of affect; (3) delirium; and (4) dementia.

3. Head injuries, either open or closed, are one cause of organic brain syndrome. Closed head injuries can result in: (1) concussion, characterized by temporary loss of consciousness and spontaneous and complete recovery; or (2) contusion, characterized by coma or loss of consciousness lasting hours or days. Repeated injuries of this type may result in "punch drunk syndrome." An open head injury, or laceration, occurs when an object pierces the skull and tears brain tissue. Many people do not survive brain lacerations.

4. After recovering from brain trauma, people sometimes experience residual physical and psychological effects, including: (1) impairment of intellect, speech, and movement; (2) epilepsy; (3) transient or permanent overreactions to stress; (4) pervasive anxiety; (5) personality changes; (6) increased mood lability; and (7) a tendency to exaggerate the significance of physical symptoms.

5. Brain tumors are abnormal tissue growths that may produce: personality change, psychotic symptoms, vomiting, headaches, vision changes, mood lability, cognitive changes, and depression.

6. A malignant tumor destroys brain tissue, whereas a benign tumor affects brain function through its growth and increasing pressure on the brain. Generally, surgery is necessary to restore normal functioning or to save the life of a brain tumor patient, although not all tumors are operable.

7. Brain infections can have a damaging effect upon the brain. Examples are: encephalitis, an inflammation of the brain that may result in mental retardation in young children or Parkinson's disease in older adults; and neurosyphilis, the advanced stage of the venereal disease syphilis that is marked by lethargy, intellectual deterioration, delusions of grandeur, and progressive paralysis.

8. Disorders of the thyroid gland include: Grave's disease (hyperthyroidism), in which overproduction of the hormone thyroxin results in marked weight loss, tremors, excessive anxiety and apprehension, increased sweating, and psychomotor agitation; and myxedema (hypothyroidism), in which underproduction of thyroxin results in increased weight, sluggishness, difficulties in concentration and memory, lethargy, and depression.

9. Two disorders of the adrenal glands are: Addison's disease, which is caused by insufficient hormone production and results in depression, anxiety, irritability, lack of motivation, fatigue, and decreased sociability; and Cushing's syndrome, in which excessive hormone production results in obesity, muscle atrophy, lability of mood, and fatigue. Both thyroid and adrenal disorders are treated through medical or surgical methods.

10. Degenerative organic brain syndromes associated with aging are divided into presenile (before age 65) and senile (after age 65) dementias. Presenile dementias are characterized by intellectual deterioration and relatively early onset. They include: Alzheimer's disease, Parkinson's disease, and Huntington's chorea.

11. Symptoms of senile dementia are cognitive deterioration, impaired judgment and impulse control, and personality changes. Although senility is incurable, secondary behavioral and mood disorders associated with it can be controlled by medication and structured environments with supportive psychotherapy.

12. Pseudodementia is a depressive disorder in which symptoms of dementia are also present.

13. Circulatory disturbances that impede the normal flow of blood through the brain can produce the symptoms of organic brain syndrome. A major stroke, for example, may cause permanent or transient paralysis and impair speech, mood, and cognitive function. Physical, recreational, and speech therapies are often combined with medical treatment in order to help stroke victims regain more normal functioning.

14. There is resistance at many levels to treating the elderly: (1) patient resistance, (2) physician resistance, (3) family resistance, and (4) general societal resistance. Many hospitals now have specialty clinics which are helping the elderly to deal with the problems of aging.

15. Epilepsy is a brain disorder characterized by abnormalities in the rhythm of electrical discharge in the brain. Causes include: (1) trauma, (2) high fever, (3) anoxia, (4) inflammations and infections, (5) tumors, and (6) genetic predisposition. Temporary loss of consciousness is characteristic of epileptic seizures. The three types of epilepsy are grand mal, petit mal, and psychomotor epilepsy.

16. Epileptics may suffer from low self-esteem and social adjustment problems, and they experience frequent discrimination.

17. Drugs generally control epilepsy, but biofeedback and, in extreme cases, psychosurgery are also used.

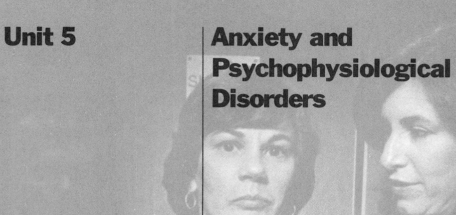

Unit 5

Anxiety and Psychophysiological Disorders

In previous sections we have dealt with patterns of behavior that are dramatic and contrast sharply with our notions of normal behavior. In this unit we shall examine the anxiety disorders — a relatively new name for the traditional "neuroses" — which describe behaviors much closer to our own experience. We all know fear, both the fear of specific real danger and that vague, diffuse sensation of fear, anxiety, which we experience when we cannot identify a clear and present danger. The poet W. H. Auden called ours "The Age of Anxiety," because he believed that the threats of modern life — industrialization, anonymity of urban life, crowds, economic uncertainty, and the overhanging threat of nuclear war — demand constant vigilance and tension. And yet, despite these ever-present threats, or, as they are sometimes called, stresses of life, most people continue to work, love, and play. We shall consider the individuals who cannot manage these normative stresses.

In Chapter 13 we focus upon individuals who manifest failure to cope by one or all of these: excessive chronic fear, crippling psychological symptoms, or rigid and self-defeating personality patterns. In Chapter 14 we examine the somatic consequences of failure to master the stress of life. Here we will concentrate on psychophysiological disorders, some major alteration in physiological function or structure caused by chronic anxiety. The separation between psychological and physiological consequences of excess anxiety is admittedly artificial, because many individuals manifest both types of symptoms. Research literature on each of these has followed different directions, and we have chosen to treat psychological and physiological reactions separately.

In Chapter 15 we survey interventions currently available to assist individuals with anxiety disorders. Most of the therapies described also have applications to other patterns of abnormal behavior, but they were originally devised to provide relief from anxiety disorders, and, as research indicates, this is the purpose for which they are most effective. For this reason we

chose to concentrate extensive discussion of the major approaches to psychological treatment in this section of the book.

In all other sections we have provided statistics on the incidence of each pattern of abnormal behavior, a task that is much more difficult for the anxiety disorders. Many clients are treated by private physicians and psychologists who keep no precise statistics. Physical ailments of a psychophysiological type are not always recognized as such. One recent report from the National Institute of Mental Health concludes: "Sound figures for the incidence of neurosis are nearly impossible to obtain since the definition and classification of these disorders vary from one investigational framework to the next and the crucial terms are usually not defined at all" (1975). We will use *DSM*-III criteria, where relevant, in the hope that these more carefully specified criteria will assist us in developing accurate figures on the incidence of anxiety-related disorders in our society and, thereby, in quantifying our personal impression that psychological and physiological symptoms of excessive anxiety substantially impair many people around us.

Chapter 13

Anxiety Disorders and the Borderline Syndrome

handwritten margin notes: normal appropriate reaction to genuine danger / fear — emotional response that alerts the body to take appropriate action to reduce the threat by/running away · 2/DSegengrity 226

handwritten margin notes (right): symptoms of anxiety = fear the diff lies in the validity · Anxiety — expression of fear disproportionate to external danger — subjective state of apprehension or tension accompanied by physiological arousal + often by escape or avoidance behavior.

Measures of Anxiety
Self-report of Anxiety
Biological Measures of Anxiety
Behavioral Signs of Anxiety
Relationship Among Indices of Anxiety

Anxiety Disorders: Patterns of Expression
Symptomatic Disorders
Personality Disorders
Onset and Course of Anxiety Disorders

Theories on Development of Anxiety Disorders
Psychoanalytic Model
Behavioral Model

Summary

handwritten: flight or fight response — physiological changes accompany these

handwritten notes (lower left): Freud anxiety: 3 forms: 1/ neurotic anxiety in observation 2/ expectant dread free floating anxiety · according to the DSM II anxiety disorders which overlap behavior: 1/ anxiety prominent symptom 2/ anxiety is believed to underlie symptoms 3/ patterns of disorder to ward off anxiety · 1/ phobias: exaggerated danger + other severe neurosis — no justification of external change · 2/ hysteria + other severe neurosis · borderline 3/ phobias developed disabling symptoms developed — anxiety disorder victims still remain in contact with reality · borderline lies between the boundary of anxiety disorders + Psychosis

At the moment, as you probably noticed, I'm going through a spell of being depressed. I really couldn't tell you why it is, but I believe it's just because I'm a coward. . . .

This evening, while Elli was still here, there was a long, loud, penetrating ring at the door. I turned white at once, got a tummyache and heart palpitations. . . .

These subjective, physiological reactions seem to reflect an exaggerated state of apprehension suggesting abnormality. But, in fact, those words are from *The Diary of Anne Frank* (1952), written during World War II while the author and her family were in hiding to avoid deportation by German troops to a concentration camp. The vigilance and hypersensitivity to danger that Frank reported were highly adaptive when survival required making no noticeable sound or movement (unfortunately, they were inadequate, for she ultimately perished in a concentration camp).

Appropriate reactions to a genuine danger, such as Anne Frank described, we call *fear*. Fear is an emotional response that alerts the body to take appropriate action to reduce the threat, either by running away from it or by

[handwritten margin note: measurement of anxiety 1) self-reports 2) biological measurements of physiological response 3) direct observation of behavior.]

fighting it off. Physiological changes (increased heartbeat, rapid breathing, sweaty palms, and so on) generally occur in preparation for the so-called flight-or-fight response to imminent danger.

The symptoms of anxiety are much the same as those of fear; the difference lies in their validity. *Anxiety* is an expression of fear disproportionate to the external danger. Psychoanalyst Karen Horney observed that an anxious person's distress is not a systematic response to objective stimuli: "His anxiety concerns not the situation as it stands in reality, but the situation as it appears to him" (1937, p. 44). Anxiety, then, is a *subjective* state of apprehension or tension accompanied by physiological arousal and often by escape or avoidance behavior (Spielberger 1966).

Anxiety is expressed as abnormal behavior in several forms. Freud was first to delineate the psychological basis of this group of disorders, traditionally called *neuroses.* Our current conceptualization of anxiety owes much to his observations, and is still worth reading:

We then turned our attention to neurotic anxiety, and pointed out that it could be observed in three forms. First, we have free floating, general apprehensiveness, ready to attach itself for the time being to any new possibility that may arise in the form of what we call expectant dread, as happens in the typical anxiety neurosis. Secondly, we find it firmly attached to certain ideas, in what are known as *phobias,* in which we can still recognize a connection with external danger, but cannot help regarding the anxiety felt towards it as enormously exaggerated. Thirdly, and finally, we have anxiety as it occurs in hysteria and in other severe neuroses; this anxiety either accompanies symptoms or manifests itself independently whether as an attack or as a condition which persists for some time, but always without any visible justification in an external danger. (Freud 1933, p. 115)

The *DSM*-III eliminates the neurosis classification as excessively vague and applies *anxiety*

disorders to the group of distinct abnormal behavior patterns once known collectively as neuroses. According to *DSM*-III, three observable patterns of behavior characterize anxiety disorders: (1) patterns in which anxiety is the prominent symptom; (2) patterns in which anxiety is believed to underlie discrete disabling symptoms, such as phobias (irrational fears of specific objects or situations); and (3) patterns of behavior developed to ward off anxiety.

Anxiety disorders are less disorganizing than the psychotic disorders we discussed in previous chapters. Despite intense fears, self-doubts, and crippling symptoms, anxiety-disordered individuals remain in contact with reality. Anxiety disorders are moderately severe disturbances of behavior in which an individual recognizes that his discomfort arises from within and does not grossly distort reality to explain it. He may feel slighted by others, powerless, timid, or chronically apprehensive, but he neither believes that others are plotting against him or grossly distorts sensory experiences to justify these feelings.

Nevertheless, some patterns of behavior seem to perch on the ambiguous boundary between anxiety disorders and psychosis. Anxiety reactions appear to form a continuum ranging from patterns in which contact with reality is stable and constant to others that feature transitory psychotic symptoms. Individuals who show a tendency to drift over the line are classified as *borderline.* Although we will focus our attention primarily on the more moderate disorders, we will also look at the borderline syndrome and contrast it with the typical anxiety disorder.

[handwritten note: sometimes hard to tell if within normal range or not]

Measures of Anxiety

Anxiety is a subjective and often normal experience (how many of us have *not* had the experience of studying hard for an exam and walking into the room, palms sweating, heart pounding, "knowing" we would fail?), but it is sometimes difficult to tell whether a person's anxiety is within normal range or an extreme deviation. Consequently, clinicians have had to devise ways of measuring anxiety. Three approaches to anxiety measurement are current: self-reports, biological measurement of physiological response, and direct observation of behavior.

Self-report of Anxiety

We are all experts on what we feel. In fact, no one can share our inner states without some verbal communication. Some particularly articulate individuals describe anxiety with great vividness. Kierkegaard (1844) summed up its effect with remarkable keenness before Freud was even born. "Anxiety," he wrote, "is an alien power which lays hold of an individual, and yet one cannot tear oneself away, nor has the will to do so."

Informative as such self-reports are, they lack systemization. Mental health professionals rely on standardized self-report tests on which respondents indicate how closely a statement applies to them. Table 13.1 shows some items from one of these inventories. By comparing the responses of one individual with the average score of a sizable and diverse test population, test administrators can better judge whether self-reported anxiety is below average, average, or excessive.

Statistical analyses of one test, the Taylor Scale of Manifest Anxiety (Taylor 1953), by Fenz and Epstein (1965), indicate that people distinguish among three classes of events when reporting on their own anxiety: (1) awareness of physiological sensations that are basically reflex actions controlled by the autonomic nervous system — rapid heart rate, sweating, churning stomach, and so on; (2) awareness of physiological sensations primarily mediated by the central nervous system — muscle tension

Table 13.1. Sample items from an anxiety self-test

Agree	Disagree

1. I work under a great deal of tension.
2. I am troubled by discomfort in the pit of my stomach every few days or oftener.
3. I am certainly lacking in self-confidence.
4. Often I feel as if there were a tight band about my head.
5. Sometimes, when embarrassed, I break out in a sweat, which annoys me greatly.
6. I feel anxiety about something or someone almost all the time.
7. I have several times given up doing a thing because I thought too little of my ability.
8. I worry quite a bit over possible misfortunes.
9. I have had periods in which I lost sleep over worry.
10. It makes me nervous to have to wait.

Source: S. R. Hathaway and J. C. McKinley, *Booklet for the Minnesota Multiphasic Personality Inventory* (New York: The Psychological Corporation, 1951).

noticeable as low backache or headache; and (3) feelings of inadequacy or inferiority. Highly anxious people report less confidence, assertiveness, and acceptance by others. As we will see in Chapter 15, this distinction has proved very valuable in formulating behaviorally oriented treatment programs, for it allows therapists to treat each class of anxiety problems separately.

Subjective reports of anxiety cannot be fully relied on because the person taking the test may believe it is demeaning to admit to being fearful, even if his inner turmoil is overwhelming. For this individual, making such an acknowledgment on a test that a stranger will evaluate may have negative consequences. Until quite recently, it was believed unmanly to admit to fear, perhaps explaining why males have scored consistently lower on anxiety self-tests than females.

Biological Measures of Anxiety

As we mentioned in Chapter 3, we have a number of indices measuring the physiological changes triggered by the autonomic nervous system during an emotionally aroused state (see Figure 13.1). These responses include increased heart rate and blood flow, sweating palms, decreased stomach motility, and numerous complex biochemical changes forming the flight-or-fight response to an external threat. Two of the most heavily studied indices of anxiety are palmar sweating and changes in heart rate. Clinicians measure palmar sweating with skin resistance tests like the one described in Chapter 3. Unfortunately, the intense, highly regular changes in psychophysiology recorded during states of anxiety produce a response that does not differ uniquely from patterns registered when the subject is angry or otherwise emotionally aroused.

Behavioral Signs of Anxiety

Anxiety shows in our behavior. You may notice that one of your friends has the shakes, is unusually jumpy, sleeps poorly — or not at all — and has sweaty palms. Deciding that she must be anxious about something, you may ask her what's wrong. If she denies that anything is bothering her, must you assume that your perceptions are inaccurate? Table 13.2 shows a systematic scale developed for observers to record anxiety. Used in a study in which college students who were fearful of speaking in public participated in one of three treatment programs (Paul, 1966), this scale helped evaluate how effective each therapy was. Notice that observers

Fig. 13.1. A schematic of the autonomic nervous system, showing the sympathetic and parasympathetic divisions and the organs they control.

are asked to observe signs of anxiety in motor behavior, posture, facial expression, and physiological symptoms (sweating, blushing, twitching, perspiration).

Another behavioral index of anxiety is *avoidance behavior,* an observable consequence of anxiety. By remarking how frequently a person avoids specific people, situations, or things, we can infer how much anxiety these stimulus

Table 13.2. Timed behavioral checklist for performance anxiety

Behavior observed	Time period
1. Paces	
2. Sways	
3. Shuffles	
4. Knees tremble	
5. Extraneous arm and hand movement (swings, scratches, toys, etc.)	
6. Arms rigid	
7. Hands restrained (in pockets, behind back, clasped)	
8. Hand tremors	
9. No eye contact	
10. Face muscles tense (drawn, tic, grimaces)	
11. Face "deadpan"	
12. Face pale	
13. Face flushed (blushes)	
14. Moistens lips	
15. Swallows	
16. Clears throat	
17. Breathes heavily	
18. Perspires (face, hands, armpits)	
19. Voice quivers	
20. Speech blocks or stammers	

Source: G. L. Paul, *Insight vs. desensitization in psychotherapy* (Stanford, Calif.: Stanford University Press, 1966).

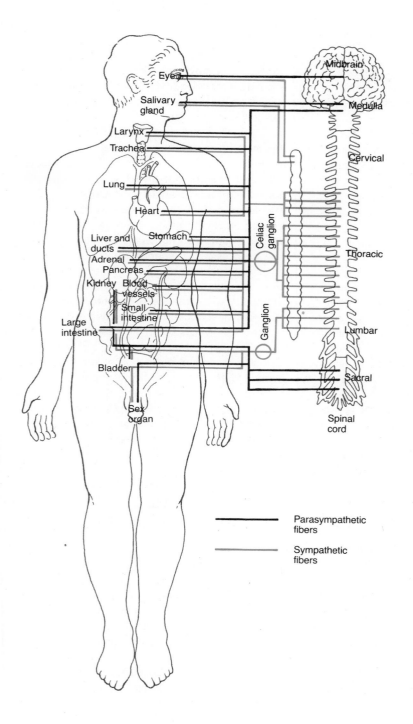

Eye

Salivary
gland

Larynx

Trachea

Lung

Heart

Liver and
ducts

Adrenal

Pancreas

Kidney Blood
vessels

Small
intestine

Large
intestine

Bladder

Sex
organ

Stomach

Celiac
ganglion

Ganglion

Midbrain

Medulla

Cervical

Thoracic

Lumbar

Sacral

Spinal
cord

Parasympathetic
fibers

Sympathetic
fibers

conditions evoke. Many behavioral studies expose patients to stimuli that they claim cause them to become anxious. Their tendency to withdraw or avoid contact when exposed to the feared object suggests how much anxiety it arouses.

Of course, psychologists see avoidance behavior in many forms, although less systematically. Noticing that someone conspicuously avoids members of the opposite sex, any type of demand for achievement, heights, or dogs is an important clue to the amount of anxiety they stimulate in that individual.

Relationship Among Indices of Anxiety

Interestingly, the three indices of anxiety just described do not always correlate. Our twitching friend may deny feeling distressed. And individuals who contend that specific objects or situations make them anxious may not manifest the expected fear behavior when we observe them with the stimulus in question. In one series of studies (Lang 1968), participants in an experimental therapy program all professed intense fear of snakes. When they were subsequently observed in the presence of an actual snake, though, their avoidance behavior varied widely. Some refused to enter a room containing a live snake in a cage. Others who expressed equal anxiety about snakes during their interviews could place themselves next to the caged animals after a single request by the experimenter.

Researchers have reported similar discrepancies between self-reports of anxiety and psychophysiological reactions to threat stimuli. Some people show concordance between these two response systems and others do not.

Initially, the lack of correspondence between indices of anxiety threw clinicians and researchers into despair. The value of the anxiety construct itself was in doubt. If the different indices agree so poorly, the tool is too vague to be useful. More recent research demonstrates,

however, that each index conveys important information about a person and that the *pattern* appearing in subjective reports and biological and behavioral manifestations of anxiety counts more than the information conveyed by any one measure. Some evidence comes from a study by Lang, Melamed, and Hart (1974), in which they wanted to determine how effective a procedure for reducing anxiety would be. Subjects imagined scenes that they had previously reported as arousing anxiety. (In Chapter 15 we will describe this therapeutic approach, systematic desensitization, in greater detail.) The scenes began with minimally arousing images and progressed to scenes rated very high in anxiety. Researchers recorded heart rate and subjective accounts of anxiety. When maximally frightening scenes were suggested, some subjects who described themselves as too fearful to continue showed a sharp increase in heart rate as well. Others who reported the same degree of distress showed no measurable increase in heart rate. Retesting the two groups after treatment, the researchers found that only those whose subjective report of anxiety was accompanied by increased heart rate during imagery showed noticeably reduced anxiety.

Anxiety Disorders: Patterns of Expression

Thinking back over what we've said about anxiety, you might reason that it need not impair an individual's ability to live normally and function in a socially acceptable way. Perhaps on the surface it doesn't. Some people focus their anxiety on specific objects or events, and unless we are present in an anxiety-producing situation, we may not be aware that they have a problem. Someone you know fairly well may suddenly turn pale and faint dead away, for no apparent reason, while you are talking about your recent appendectomy. Later you learn from a mutual friend that she faints even at the thought of blood. *Hemophobia,* an irrational fear of blood, is one of a group of phobic disorders, all interfering with social and vocational functioning.

Phobias are among the anxiety disturbances known as *symptomatic disorders,* in which overwhelming feelings of anxiety become focused in one or more discrete, disabling symptoms (such as hemophobia). For some people, however, the disturbances are more diffuse and more apparent in everyday social interaction: distrust of people, quick temper, and nervous mannerisms. Unable to cope with mild distress of *any* kind, such individuals may find social interaction difficult and may make it unpleasant for others to be around them. These people work hard at avoiding stimuli that might produce anxiety and so develop maladaptive patterns of behavior that prevent them from having a normal life. The so-called *personality disorders* from which they suffer may be more common than symptomatic disorders, but as we will see, they are also more difficult to classify. Table 13.3 summarizes the major symptomatic disorders as well as general characteristics of personality disorders. We'll look at each type in some detail.

Symptomatic Disorders

GENERALIZED ANXIETY DISORDERS

The dominant characteristic of this disorder is *free-floating generalized anxiety.* The inner experience is that the threat, or subject of the fear, is omnipresent, hovering about unattached to anything specific, and the disordered individual spends most of the time in a state of extreme tension. It is like being a soldier about to go into batttle, psychologically and physiologically mobilized for the danger that is not always clearly identifiable. As might be expected in this state of hyperarousal, people complain of difficulty sitting still, concentrating,

Table 13.3. Anxiety disorders

Symptomatic disorders: Behavior patterns in which anxiety is the dominant symptom or in which anxiety is believed to underlie disabling symptoms.

— *Generalized anxiety disorder:* Pervasive anxiety, tension, and apprehension.
— *Panic disorder:* Periodic "attacks of anxiety."
— *Phobic disorders:* Irrational fears of objects, persons, or places.
— *Obsessive-compulsive disorder:* Repetitive, intrusive, and disturbing thoughts often coupled with ritualistic acts.
— *Conversion disorder:* Impairment of bodily functioning without known organic cause.
— *Dissociative disorders:* A splitting-off or dissociation of parts of the personality from each other.

Personality disorders: Maladaptive, recurrent patterns of behavior which an individual develops to prevent anxiety and which impair personal functioning.

and falling asleep. Other common complaints are profuse sweating, blushing, dizziness, heart palpitations, and shortness of breath. The anxiety-disordered person will exhaust and amaze friends with persistent worry about future events and originality in fantasizing the hundred things that could go wrong.

PANIC DISORDER

On top of chronic tension and apprehension, some people experience *panic attacks,* a sudden overwhelming dread, or sense of imminent death accompanied by rapid heart palpitations and other disturbing physiological sensations. Often these attacks occur in a public place. The fear they engender is intense, and the victim may give in to a strong desire to run. This autobiographical moment captures the experience vividly:

I remember walking up the street, the moon was shining and suddenly everything around me

Fig. 13.2 Like a soldier about to enter battle, the anxiety-disordered person is constantly mobilized for danger.

seemed unfamiliar, as it would be in a dream. I felt panic rising inside me, but managed to push it away and carry on. I walked a quarter of a mile or so, with the panic getting worse every minute. . . . By now, I was sweating, yet trembling; my heart was pounding and my legs felt like jelly (Melville 1977, p. 1).

Panic disorders can be stable and enduring, or they may represent a preliminary stage in development of another form of symptomatic disorder.

PHOBIC DISORDERS

Hemophobia is just one of many phobic disorders, which are properly defined as the persistent and recurring fear of a specific object, activity, or situation that is avoided at all costs. A phobic person will often recognize that the fear is unreasonable but feel helpless to control the feeling or the subsequent avoidance behavior. We all have some sort of phobia — height or animals or social situations — but only when it drastically interferes with everyday life do people seek professional assistance. In fact, many research studies on phobias have used phobic people who have responded to newspaper ads for volunteers for an experimental treatment program. Most of the volunteers had never sought treatment for their phobias, but the prospect of a new (and often free) treatment is enticing.

The *DSM*-III delineates three classes of phobias: agoraphobia, social phobia, and simple phobia.

AGORAPHOBIA. In Greek, *agora* is an assembly or marketplace. Agoraphobia is a fear of going into stores or crowds, and of traveling alone in cars, trains, or buses. To avoid fear-producing environments, agoraphobiacs often seclude themselves and progressively become prisoners of their homes. The fear shifts from public places to terror at the prospect of leaving the house or leaving unaccompanied. In many ways, the agoraphobiac resembles the school-phobic child (see Chapter 21), who clings to parent and home and refuses to go to school.

As you might expect, the agoraphobic's life is severely restricted by his fear of leaving the house, and the fear frequently restricts the lives of parents, spouses, and children. Family members often must accompany agoraphobiacs everywhere and understandably come to resent the limitations this disorder places on their own activities. Freud felt that the control the agoraphobiac gains over others with his symptoms represents a *secondary gain* of the disorder, an advantage that limits the phobic person's desire to change the behavior pattern (Jones 1955). And yet these people are not insensitive to the pain they bring their loved ones. One phobic mother admitted, "I mind very much putting the burden of shopping on my young daughter; the loneliness, the torment that goes on inside. You can't imagine what it's like."

Agoraphobias begin, as many phobic reac-

tions do, with one or a series of panic attacks. The situation in which these occur is vivid and frightening. To avoid reexperiencing it, the individual comes to shun the situation in which the panic attack occurred. The avoidance pattern then seems to spread from one situation to many others and progressively limits the phobic's range of movement. The person whose account of a panic attack we quoted (pages 301–302) explained what it is like to experience this progression:

Terrified, I stood not knowing what to do. The only bit of sanity left in me told me to get home. Somehow this I did very slowly, holding onto the fence in the road. I cannot remember the actual journey back, until I was going into the house, then I broke down and cried helplessly. . . . I did not go out again for a few days. When I did it was with my mother and baby to my grandmother's a few miles away. I felt panicky there and couldn't cope with the baby. My cousin suggested we go to my Aunt's house, but I had another attack there. I was sure I was going to die. Following this, I was totally unable to go out alone and even with someone else I had great difficulty. Not only did I get the panicky-fainting spells but I lived in constant fear of getting them (Melville 1977, p. 14).

Most of the agoraphobiacs who seek treatment are female. Many males experience this type of terror, but because of their traditional workplace roles, they find ways to organize their lives around their phobia.

SOCIAL PHOBIAS. Some phobias focus on specific social situations. A social phobic, as likely to be male as female, is intensely afraid of performing some behavior in the presence of other people. One who fears that his hands will tremble holding a fork, glass, or cup may avoid eating and drinking with other people. He may refuse invitations to dinner and adopt a reclusive life style for fear of looking ridiculous. Some social phobics, on the other hand, restrict their activities minimally, as by avoiding a specific restaurant.

Many social phobics fear interactions with authority figures (bosses, teachers) and refuse to appear in front of an audience. Extreme self-consciousness may cause them to avoid wearing swimsuits in front of others. Some social phobics are excessively preoccupied with some aspect of their appearance, and many of these end up as applicants for plastic surgery.

SIMPLE PHOBIA. The source of irrational fear in cases of simple phobia is a specific object or situation. Even if an element of danger is justifiably feared in these situations or objects, the anxiety response and avoidance behavior is disproportionate to the danger. Although the person recognizes the irrationality of his specific fear, he feels powerless to do anything about it. Common sources of simple phobias are animals (dogs, cats, or snakes primarily), transportation (flying, trains, cars), closed spaces, and height. A babysitter known to one of the authors had a severe simple phobia of cats. She would work only in houses in which no cats were present. One family believed themselves amateur psychologists, and thought they could help her conquer this phobia. They obtained a kitten and kept it hidden until she arrived for the evening. When one of the children came in holding it, the babysitter panicked and ran from the house so fast that she fell on the steps and broke her ankle. It is possible to treat simple phobias by exposing the phobic to the fear-producing object or situation, but this type of behavioral therapy involves gradual physical exposure or psychological techniques under the control of a qualified therapist (see Chapter 15).

Pure phobias are relatively rare. Most phobic patients present a mixture. The distinction between a simple focused phobia and a mixed pattern evidently is very important for treatment because they respond differently to different types of intervention, as we will discover in Chapter 15.

OBSESSIVE-COMPULSIVE DISORDER

We all have moments of indecision, when alternating and contradictory thoughts flood our consciousness. These short-lived experiences are muted versions of the obsessive-compulsive's inner state, tormented by an obsessive thought or idea that persists though unwanted. The thought may be offensive because it represents a blatant sexual or aggressive idea, or it may be neutral. No matter what, it is continuously intrusive. In a sense, obsessions are more than just thoughts; they are impulses to perform some disturbing deed. Obsessive-compulsives seldom act out their hostile or sexual fantasies, but they live in dread that they will.

Compulsive actions are another facet of this syndrome. They are repetitive acts one feels compelled to perform without understanding why. If you have ever locked your door and gone back to check because the thought occurred that it might not be locked, then you have some insight into the relationship between an obsessive thought and a compulsive action. If compulsives do not perform the actions demanded of themselves, they experience extreme anxiety. Perhaps the most famous sufferer of compulsive ritual was Lady Macbeth, washing her hands over and over after she and her husband had murdered the King of Scotland.

Doctor: What is it she does now? Look how she rubs her hands.

Gentlewoman: It is an accustomed action with her, to seem thus washing her hands. I have known her to continue in this a quarter of an hour.

Lady Macbeth: Yet here's a spot.
Out damned spot! Out, I say! . . . Yet, who would have thought the old man to have had so much blood in him? (*Macbeth,* Act V, Scene 1)

In fact, the hand-washing compulsion is one of the most common in clinics even today.

This case vividly conveys the obsessive symptoms and their intimate connection to compulsive acts:

Shirley K., a twenty-three-year-old housewife, came to the clinic with a complaint of frequent attacks of headaches and dizziness. During the preceding three months she had been disturbed by recurring thoughts that she might harm her two-year-old son, Saul, either by stabbing or choking him [the obsessive thought]. She constantly had to go into his room, touch the baby and feel him breathe in order to reassure herself that Saul was still alive [the compulsive act]; otherwise she became unbearably anxious. If she read a report in the daily paper of the murder of a child, she would become agitated, since this reinforced her fear that she too might act on her impulse. Shirley turned to the interviewer and asked, with desper-

ation, whether this meant that she was "going crazy" (Goldstein and Palmer 1975, p. 155).

Notice that by acting on her compulsion to make sure her son was still alive, Shirley was able to relieve her anxiety, if only temporarily.

In obsessive-compulsive individuals, the focal symptoms of obsessive thoughts and compulsive rituals are part of a personality pattern that includes extreme indecisiveness and dread of situations that demand decisions. Each time the person makes up her mind, the opposite alternative intrudes into awareness. Obsessives are masters at avoiding decisions and often evoke consternation in friends or relatives who accompany them to restaurants or try to get them to decide which film to see or when and where to go on vacation. The indecisiveness in trivial decisions grows dramatic for significant issues such as whether to marry this

Fig. 13.3. The concern of the obsessive patient for order, neatness, and control is reflected in this drawing by a depressed obsessive patient. Note the repetition of detail, neatness of outlines, and coverage of the total pictorial surface.

person, take that new job, or make any life-changing decision.

Obsessives also appear to be very rigid, most comfortable with sameness and order and resisting change and spontaneity. A great deal of effort goes into controlling emotions by intellectual means. Although obsessives appear to worship reason and thought and ruminate endlessly over trivial matters, they cannot use their reason effectively to come to conclusions or decisions. Clinicians have remarked that obsessives seem to use thought and reason to avoid experiencing spontaneous feelings or emotions, which frighten them, and so they frequently appear to be cold, overcontrolled, and unfeeling.

But no matter how elaborate the complex of obsessive thoughts and compulsive ritual, it does not successfully reduce anxiety. Most obsessives report constant tension and dissatisfaction with their personal lives. And it is not unusual for this dissatisfaction to blend imperceptibly into feelings of depression.

CONVERSION AND DISSOCIATIVE DISORDERS AND MULTIPLE PERSONALITY

These abnormal behavior patterns are variants of a diagnostic class known originally as "hysteria." In Chapter 2 we said that early notions about hysteria were very significant in forming psychological models of abnormal development. This was true despite the fact that the term referred to the ancient view that hysteria was due to a "wandering uterus."

The link between disorders formerly classified under hysteria is that all involve major alterations in states of awareness. This may be expressed as some alteration in bodily functioning, as in *conversion disorders,* with physical symptoms that cannot be explained by a known organic cause, or they may involve altered awareness at a cognitive level, as in *dissociative* and *fugue* disorders, in which individ-

uals cannot remember their own identity or previous behavior. The most extreme of these altered states is the *multiple personality,* in which different personalities alternately dominate awareness and behavior. Because these diverse disorders share this altered awareness we shall discuss them together.

CONVERSION DISORDERS. Disturbances in sensory systems or in functioning of skeletal musculature that have no known organic cause are the primary types of conversion disorders, though any bodily system can be the target. Conversion disorders are sometimes distinguishable from genuine organic disorders because the pattern of symptoms does not make anatomical sense. The clearest example is *glove anesthesia,* in which sensation is lost from the hand to the elbow, resembling the shape of an old-fashioned glove; it does not coincide with the known nerve tracks of arm and hand. The many conversion reactions are summarized in Table 13.4.

Table 13.4. Varieties of conversion disorders

1. **Sensory symptoms**
   (a) *Anesthesia:* loss of sensitivity, as in blindness or deafness.
   (b) *Hypesthesia:* partial loss of sensitivity, as in blurring or intermittent loss of vision or hearing.
   (c) *Hyperesthesia:* excessive sensitivity, with lowered threshold for sound, light, or smell.
   (d) *Analgesia:* loss of sensitivity to pain.
   (e) *Paresthesia:* exceptional sensations such as tingling.
2. **Motor symptoms**
   (a) *Paralysis:* complete or partial loss of activity in some part of the body, usually a limb.
   (b) *Tremors:* muscular shaking or trembling.
   (c) *Tics:* unconscious, localized muscular twitches.
3. **Visceral symptoms:** headaches, constant "lump in the throat," choking sensations, coughing spells, vomiting, etc.

Conversion Disorders
1/ Sensory
  1/ Anesthesia: loss of sensitivity
  2/ Hypoesthesia: partial " "
  3/ Hyperesthesia: excessive sensitivity
  4/ Analgesia: loss of sensitivity to pain
  5/ Paresthesia: exceptional sensations
2/ Motor
  a/ Paralysis:
  b/ Tremors:
  c/ Tics:
3/ Visceral
  - headaches - etc.

- lack of worry about symptoms
  (anxiety)

To prescribe proper treatment, a
conversion reaction must be distinguished
from similar problems that have a
true anatomical sense.
Mistakes have been made.

SLATER + GLITHERO
  60% diagnosed wrong

- if not under conscious control,
  can show true function.
- NOT MANY conversion reactions
  found today due to wide
  knowledge of this disorder

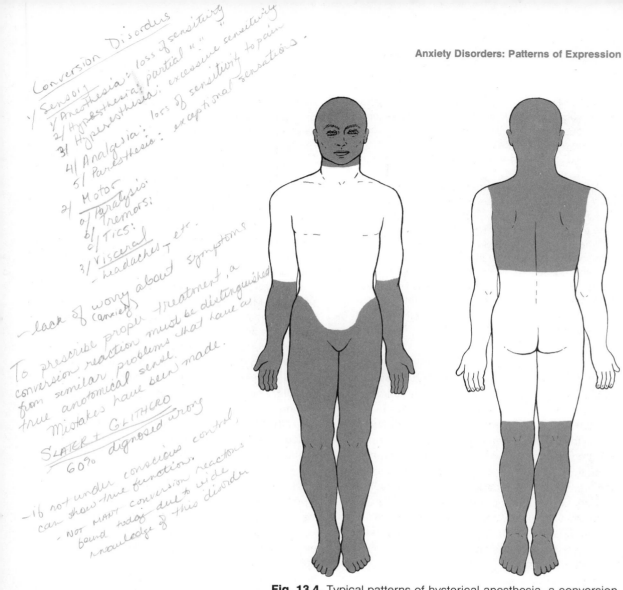

Fig. 13.4. Typical patterns of hysterical anesthesia, a conversion disorder. The areas of anesthesia do not correspond to known neural patterns in the body.

Generally, conversion reactions appear suddenly and under intense personal stress that the patient perceives to be inescapable. This case of hysterical blindness illustrates these conditions and the acute onset.

Phil, forty years of age, had a history of marginal work adjustment since his discharge from the Army at age twenty-five. In the fifteen years since discharge, he had depended on public assistance and financial aid from relatives to get by. He painted a very dismal picture of his married life, as one of almost constant harassment from his wife and mother-in-law. He had a history of minor illnesses involving his eyes, none of which had grossly affected his visual acuity.

During the Christmas season his wife and

mother-in-law were being more demanding than usual, requiring him to work nights and weekends at various chores under their foremanship. Three days before Christmas, while shopping with his wife and mother-in-law, Phil suddenly became blind in both eyes.

Neurological and ophthalmological exams were essentially negative in accounting for his blindness, and a diagnosis of conversion disorder was made. At this time, Phil did not seem greatly alarmed by his loss of sight, but instead had an attitude of patient forbearance. Observers in the hospital noticed that Phil could get about in the ward better than expected for a totally blind man. He was not concerned with this, but felt hurt and unjustly accused when other patients pointed out the discrepancy to him. (Adapted from J. P. Brady and D. L. Lind 1961)

Phil's lack of worry about his blindness is not unusual in conversion reaction. Observations of this phenomenon date back to Freud and French psychiatrist Pierre Janet (1929), who wrote that patients who manifested this disorder seemed strangely unconcerned about it. Janet used the phrase *la belle indifférence* to describe this feature of conversion reaction. The lack of anxiety about the apparently serious illness, coupled with the escape from a stressful life situation, suggest that frequently conversion disorders are extreme attempts to reduce overwhelming anxiety.

To prescribe proper treatment, a conversion reaction must be distinguished from similar problems that have a true anatomical cause. When the disorder does not follow anatomy, diagnosis is not so difficult. But sometimes it can be applied too casually, and an underlying organic disorder can be missed. Slater and Glithero (1965) examined records of individuals who nine years before had been diagnosed as conversion-disordered. Unexpectedly, 60 percent had either died in the meantime or developed symptoms of physical disease! Generally,

the diseases were of central nervous system origin. Earlier careful diagnosis might have saved lives and suffering.

Sometimes psychological techniques can be helpful in isolating true cases of conversion reaction. Sensory tests employing response indicators that are not under conscious control can reveal whether or not a sensory deficit has an organic cause. If an apparently deaf patient shows accelerated heart rate at each sound stimulus, it is very unlikely that a true organic deafness is present.

Conversion reactions are very rare in clinical practice. Most cases occur in remote rural areas (Proctor 1958), where knowledge of psychology is limited, or in special circumstances where somatic symptoms may provide the only escape from danger, as in response to wartime stress. Conversion symptoms occur more often in military hospitals than elsewhere. Mucha and Reinhardt (1970) found that in one year doctors saw fifty-six student naval aviators who manifested conversion symptoms in the form of visual problems and paralysis or paresthesia.

DISSOCIATIVE DISORDER. The most common type of dissociative disorder, *amnesia,* involves loss of memory. Typically, during amnesia episodes, individuals cannot remember their names or addresses or anything about their circumstances. The amnesic period may last an hour or two, or it may last years. When amnesiacs "return" to their normal state of consciousness, they remember little, if anything, about the amnesia episodes.

A *fugue* reaction is similar to amnesia except that it takes the form of a more definite "flight" from an unbearable situation. People simply disappear to some other part of the country. Some start new lives — get a job, marry, and have children — and completely forget former jobs and families. The case of Barbara Y. illustrates a mild fugue state.

One day Barbara disappeared from her home without leaving a trace; two weeks later, disheveled and dirty, she was picked up by the police in a nearby city and brought to a hospital. Wearing a ponytail, bobby-sox, and low-heeled shoes, she looked more like a high school girl than a woman of thirty-one. At first she did not recognize her husband, did not know her own name, and could not remember anything about the past two weeks or her previous life. During the psychotherapy, she gradually regained her memory of the two-week period as well as her past life. She had apparently left home with only enough money to buy a bus ticket to the city where she had lived as a child. She spent much of one day walking the streets where she had grown up and standing in front of the building where her father's office had been.

Later she had gone to a motel with a man and according to the motel owner had "entertained" several men over a three-day period (Goldstein and Palmer 1975, pp. 188–189).

In Chapter 15 we will come back to Barbara's case and look at the therapy she underwent.

MULTIPLE PERSONALITY. Symptoms of multiple personality are extremely rare. This syndrome is an extension of the amnesic or fugue reaction that results in separate and different personalities coming out in the same person. Two or more personalities may coexist with varying awareness of each other. In a sense, we are all multiple personalities — one person at work,

[handwritten margin notes: rare — an extension of amnesia or fugue that results in separate and diff personalities. } with varying awareness of each other. to give each side of themselves an outlet, cannot vent personalities & keep them to themselves']

Fig. 13.5. Drawings by William Milligan, 23, an accused rapist suffering from multiple personality. According to psychiatrists, Milligan has displayed ten different personalities. The drawing at left was done by the Christene personality, a vulnerable three-year-old girl; that at right is by Billy, the core personality.

another at a party or sporting event. Part of us is conforming and good, but we all have a non-comforming, rebellious, acting-out side. Somehow, most of us are able to give vent to each part of our personalities in appropriate circumstances and keep some parts "to ourselves." Most of the people who manifest multiple personalities cannot achieve this synthesis and seem to assume different personalities to give each side of themselves an outlet.

Personality Disorders

Most of those in treatment for anxiety disorders, as we said earlier, do not manifest clearly defined symptoms. They are more likely to complain of unsatisfactory personal relation-ships than of inability to behave rationally in a specific situation, although some also exhibit characteristics of one or more of the symptomatic disorders. These troubled persons come to depend too heavily on others, lack the ability to relate to authority figures, and display excessive suspiciousness or inability to get close to another person. Their behavior trends to be repetitive, rigid, and generally self-defeating. Ultimately, despair envelops not only them but the people around them as well. Although most of these people complain of anxiety (and for some it is the only complaint), the persistence of their self-destructive behavior appears to be nourished by deep-seated and often unacknowledged anxieties, which must be recognized

The Many Faces of Eve

Perhaps the best known and most studied case of multiple personality in recent times is the subject of the fascinating book *The Three Faces of Eve* (Thigpen and Cleckley 1954) and the film of the same title. The first two of many separate personalities, Eve White and Eve Black, appeared in early adulthood following a long history of maladjustment. From earliest childhood, this woman had great difficulty accepting responsibility for her actions, particularly the naughty actions involving her younger twin siblings and a cousin with whom she was raised. The "splitting" of the bad self from the good self was evident in Eve's reports of a type of childhood hallucination in which she saw another child her age committing bad deeds. Eve unyieldingly asserted that "the other child" was at fault, despite extreme punishment from her family for "lying." In later childhood, further signs of dissociation of self took the form of blackouts with amnesia as well as numerous episodes of hysterical blindness. In fact, in high school she was known as the "blind poet."

Despite her maladjusted behavior and a propensity to undergo altered states of awareness, Eve did not see a mental health professional until adulthood. When she began seeing a psychiatrist, her marriage was in disarray and she was behaving erratically. She suffered from frequent amnesia, loss of bladder control, and rapid mood swings. At first, because of real marital difficulties, the psychiatrist felt he was dealing with a conventional case of emotional breakdown arising from intense marital conflict. Interestingly, evidence of multiple personalities appeared only after some months of psychiatric interviews. Recently "Eve" revealed her true identity in an autobiography (Sizemore and Pittillo 1977), in which she describes the session when her doctor met her second personality:

After several months of irregular visits to the doctor, the discovery was made. As she sat in the chair, drooped, head bent, eyes downcast, answering his questions in a barely audible voice, her head began to ache . . . slowly, the head raised, straight and proud; the sparkling eyes gazed back at him sardonically.

"Hello Doc," she chirped, changing the

and extinguished before maladaptive behaviors can be changed.

Because this type of generalized disorder seems to reside in the whole personality and not in some isolated symptom, the abnormal behavior patterns that result are called *personality disorders.* The more formal language of *DSM*-III describes these as "deeply ingrained, inflexible maladaptive patterns of behavior of sufficient severity to cause either significant impairment in adaptive functioning or subjective distress."

Table 13.5 lists the kinds of behavior patterns that *DSM*-III classifies as personality disorders. If you read through the table, it may strike you that the group of personality disorders encompasses a rather gray area of abnormal psychol-

ogy. Certainly these patterns of behavior are complex. But some seem to involve important cultural values. Is it truly bad to be dependent? Is someone who has no friends actually abnormal? Manipulating others as political leaders often do is sometimes considered a sign of personality disorder. Is this a psychiatric diagnosis or a value judgment, pure and simple? These are difficult questions. Furthermore, this part of *DSM*-III has not been extensively field tested, so that we don't know yet whether these categories are diagnostically reliable. Only the personality disorders that overlap symptomatic anxiety disorders seem free of value judgments. We will discuss two of them, the compulsive and histrionic disorders.

---

tired droop of her body to a sensuous slouch with one almost imperceptible wiggle.

"H-Hello," the doctor answered, treading on unsure ground. . . . "Who are *you?*" "I'm me," she flipped. "And what is your name?" he pursued. "I'm Chris Costner." "Why are you using that name instead of Chris White [her married name]?" She straightened her skirt, hitching it higher up her leg, and tossing her head, "Because Chris White is her," she stated pointing off vaguely, "not me."

After another psychiatrist was summoned, the interview continued with Dr. Cleckley and Dr. Thigpen.

"How are you, Mrs. White?" Dr. Cleckley asked.

"I ain't Miz White, I'm Miss Costner," she responded. . . . "Why are you using that name?" "Cause I ain't married to that jerk; *she* is. I'm a maiden lady. I ain't never been married and I ain't gonna be!" "What about the child?" asked Thigpen. "She ain't my child. It's her child not mine." "Your body had her," he reminded. "It might have, but I wasn't in it when it did," she firmly countered. . . . "Can we talk with Mrs. White now?" asked Thigpen. "She just has a headache, but I can do it most

any ole time." . . . "Mrs. White, can I speak to you?" asked the doctor. And there she was. Startled, sad, and unaware of what had happened. She looked at them as if waiting for the blow to fall (Sizemore and Pittillo 1977, pp. 255–256).

After an extended period of therapy, a third personality, Jane, appeared to be a synthesis of the opposites represented by Eve White and Eve Black. At this time, she appeared cured and ready to embark upon a new marriage and return to relative normality. Her autobiography reveals, however, that this synthesis was illusory and that she suffered intensely from the continuous emergence of new personalities for the next twenty years. Often suicidal and dysfunctional, she continued to strive for some reintegration of her disparate personalities, hoping for some relief from her continuous anxiety and hopelessness. At times she was so disabled that her daughter became her guardian, a job that she dispatched with remarkable skill and sensitivity, considering that by the time her mother wrote the book she had manifested fifteen personalities.

Table 13.5. Personality disorders described in *DSM*-III

1. *Paranoid Personality Disorder:* Pervasive and unwarranted suspiciousness and mistrust of others.
2. *Introverted Personality Disorder:* Inability and lack of desire to form social relationships.
3. *Schizotypal Personality Disorder:* Tendency toward schizophrenic-type language, thought, and misperceptions without any sign of psychotic break with reality.
4. *Histrionic Personality Disorder* (Hysterical Personality): Excitability, self-dramatization, attention-seeking, shallow, and lacking in genuineness, and frequently manipulative of others by suicidal threats, gestures, or attempts.
5. *Narcissistic Personality Disorder:* Self-centered and with a grandiose sense of self-importance. Exhibitionistic, requiring constant attention and admiration. Lack of empathy for others and a tendency to exploit others for personal gain. Mood vacillates between over-idealization of self and extreme self-devaluation.
6. *Antisocial Personality Disorder*:* History of tantrums and chronic antisocial behavior (lying, thefts, vandalism, aggressive behavior, etc.), in which the rights of others are violated.
7. *Borderline Personality Disorder:* Stormy personality who drifts into psychotic states under stress.
8. *Avoidant Personality:* Low self-esteem, hypersensitivity to rejection, social withdrawal, and unwillingness to enter into relationships unless given strong guarantees of uncritical acceptance.
9. *Dependent Personality Disorder:* Low self-confidence, fearful of self-reliance, relies on others to assume responsibility for major areas of one's life. Feels intense discomfort when alone.
10. *Compulsive Personality Disorder:* Shows many signs of obsessive-compulsive neurotic actions (indecisiveness, preoccupation, etc.).

* See Chapter 17.

COMPULSIVE PERSONALITY DISORDER

Excessive control over emotions and insistence on conformity and adherence to internal standards pervade the life style of the compulsive personality. These traits show up as an obvious desire to keep everything in order and to be efficient. Compulsive personalities are extremely stiff in interpersonal relationships and have difficulty relaxing informally. Many are perfectionistic, rigid, and overly preoccupied with details, and are upset by attempts to change their routines. They place a premium on work and productivity, to the exclusion of pleasure and close relationships. As you might expect, they can be quite successful as students, although at great personal cost. When these individuals do seek help for themselves, generally they complain, "I can't seem to *feel anything* or get close to other people" or "There's no joy or spontaneity in my life."

HISTRIONIC (HYSTERICAL) PERSONALITY

At one time, mental health professionals believed that people who developed conversion hysteria commonly were emotionally intense, craving constant attention. Research has not supported the view that conversion hysteria patients all have the same type of personality (Chodoff 1974), but the symptoms once attributed to these people do seem to form a distinct pattern of personality organization, which, for historical reasons, we label *hysterical* or *histrionic personality disorder.*

Typically, histrionic personalities are attention-seekers who make extraordinary demands on the people in their lives. Their emotional responses to most situations are very intense, yet other people may perceive them as individuals playing a role. A histrionic woman is often openly seductive, but tends to lack genuine sexual responsiveness. She might put on a provocative dress and cruise singles bars and disco clubs aggressively picking up men. At the end of the evening, however, she would insist on going home alone or, if she went with one of her conquests, would refuse sex and further personal contact.

BORDERLINE SYNDROME

In recent years, mental health workers have seen a sharp decline in the symptomatic disorders and a progressive increase in personality disorders. Within this category are repeated

Anxiety Disorders for Which People Typically Seek Help

It is very difficult to describe all the varied anxiety problems with which people struggle daily. Only when they reach the edge of despair do we fully see their most distressing symptoms and interpersonal difficulties. In one study (Sloane et al. 1975), 94 clients sought help from an outpatient clinic and subsequently participated in a research study contrasting two approaches to therapy (the results are discussed in Chapter 15). Intake interviewers felt that these people were very typical of anxiety-disordered clients who came to the clinic for help.

These clients were carefully assessed in two ways — by means of a classical psychiatric diagnostic system (*DSM*-II) and by analyzing their life problems. The table shows how clients were distributed by diagnostic group.

Sixty-four of 94 applicants for help were classified as symptomatic and 25 as personality disorders. Of the 64 symptomatic cases, most by far were so classified because of pervasive, overwhelming anxiety without any other specific symptom.

Diagnostic categories give us a sense of how varied the difficulties reported were, but more revealing are some of the life problems with which anxiety-disordered patients have trouble coping. In the 94 patient sample, clients were asked to target the most disturbing aspects of their life from which they wanted relief. They were, in descending frequency of mention:

1. Generalized anxiety
2. Interpersonal difficulties with everyone
3. Low self-esteem
4. Interpersonal difficulties particularly with opposite-sex peers
5. Depression and sadness
6. Somatic complaints
7. Difficulty with parental family
8. Poor school or work performance
9. Anxiety about nonsocial situations (subways, etc.)
10. Difficulties with spouse and children

Notice that here, too, anxiety is the most common complaint, followed by interpersonal problems of one sort or another.

Diagnostic categories[a]	Number of patients	Diagnostic categories[a]	Number of patients
Symptomatic disorders		*Personality disorders*	
Generalized anxiety and panic disorder or both	57	Histrionic personality	8
Minor depressive disorder	4	Adjustment reaction	2
Phobic disorder	2	Marital maladjustment	1
Dissociative disorder	1	Special symptoms (obesity, impotence)	2
	64	Other personality disorders (dependent, avoidant, paranoid, etc.)	12
			25

[a]The diagnostic groups have been translated into their *DSM*-III equivalents. Five cases received miscellaneous unspecified diagnoses.

Gunderson & Singer
functional difficulties in 5 areas
1/ interpersonal relationships ←
2/ impulse control
3/ work
4/ affect   5/ perception
∴ fit well in social groups
∴ the close relationships are self-humiliating
prone to depression + anger
periodic auditory + visual hallucinations
∴ not continuous like psychotics
they also have paranoid tendencies
they also do destructive acts. acting out — suicide etc.
with this scheme, Gunderson was able to separate the borderline group from schizo, + depressive groups

references (Hartocollis 1977) to a pattern named *borderline,* which implies that some of these individuals are more disturbed than most patients who have anxiety disorders but are not overtly psychotic. Nevertheless, the so-called borderline patients suffer disturbances in thinking and interpersonal problems similar to those seen in psychotics. Under extreme stress, such individuals will manifest total disintegration of a psychotic type, although compared to an actual psychotic breakdown, this condition is short-lived. The borderline cases are chaotic and stormy, and they show considerable evidence of a desire for self-destruction in choice of partners and the types of relationships, in use of drugs and alcohol, and in more subtle behaviors. One writer observes that if the hysteric was the typical patient of Freud's time, the borderline is the problem of our own (Knight 1953), and many other clinicians agree (Green 1977).

Although "borderline syndrome" appears to have a meaning intuitively recognizable by clinicians, it is difficult to define precisely. Gunderson and Singer (1975) reported that most clinical descriptions of borderline patients mention functional difficulties in five areas: (1) interpersonal relationships, (2) impulse control, (3) work, (4) affect, and (5) perception. Specifically, they wrote that borderline patients have active social lives outside their homes and are confident that they fit well in social groups. But although they have a large circle of friends and acquaintances and often fear being alone, they cannot accept nurturance from others. On the other hand, they do tend to take care of friends. They establish sexual relationships very rapidly, but breakups are frequent. Their relationships with partners are often infantile and masochistic (self-humiliating), and they continuously accept devaluing treatment. Nevertheless, borderline persons are often seen as manipulative partners who use threats of self-destruction to control intimates. They also do much *acting out* (destructive acts against oneself or others, anti-

social behavior, or substance abuse) and often overdose, threaten suicide, and mutilate themselves (slashing, head banging, burning).

Gunderson and Singer found also that borderline patients are prone to *depression* caused by chronic feelings of loneliness or emptiness and *anger,* which they express as extreme irritability, impatience, and demandingness. A significant number report that their impatience and demandingness create severe personal and occupational difficulties for them. Reports of their work performance indicate that their functioning is well below capacity.

Borderline syndromes do not feature continuous or severe psychotic reactions, but according to Gunderson and Singer (1975), borderline patients report periodic auditory and visual hallucinations not related to drug usage. They also report having ideas of reference, which cause them to become unduly suspicious of others and to believe people are plotting against them. These psychotic experiences are very disturbing to them. This case illustrates many facets of a borderline disorder:

Doug was an attractive, twenty-one-year-old college student who appeared on the surface to have an active social life. He had many acquaintances but could not keep them long because he was excessively demanding. Doug made friends very rapidly; within an hour you were his best friend and he shared very intimate confidences. It was similar with women. He formed attachments very rapidly and could meet a girl at a party, decide he was in love, and propose marriage — all in a few hours. Also, he would be crushed if his proposal was not accepted.

Doug was not easy to get along with. He gave a great deal but demanded much in return. He had a dreadful fear of being alone and would call friends at any hour of the day or night and insist that they come over and stay with him. When he was alone, he experienced terror that he had ceased to exist. During one period, when he was alone and could not find any friends, the terror escalated to panic and he developed paranoid ideas of reference: all his friends had deliberately plotted to leave him alone to punish him. This realization led him to misinterpret all kinds of little events on the street — expressions on people's faces, the weather, etc. — as all having special meaning to him alone. These ideas of reference were deeply frightening, and in a panic he requested admission to a psychiatric hospital. He was admitted and stayed six days, during which

time his psychotic-like symptoms disappeared completely and his panic subsided.

Although these acute symptoms receded rapidly, his chaotic interpersonal relationships continued unabated.

A more recent study by Gunderson (1977) supports the borderline concept. Using the five difficulties we have discussed, he compared a

Anorexia Nervosa: A Type of Adolescent Borderline Syndrome

We opened Chapter 1 with a description of Nancy, a teenager who was evidently starving herself to death. Nancy's self-starvation was part of the behavior pattern *anorexia nervosa,* in which the self-denial of food becomes an obsession and internal sensations of hunger seem to disappear. Anorexia is most common among females and occurs most often between late childhood and early adolescence, although there is also a notable incidence in late adolescence, around the time that individuals leave home for work or college (Bruch 1973).

Anorexia nervosa often begins innocuously as an attempt to improve one's body image by dieting. As the individual keeps losing weight, though, it appears that she is no longer in control of the dieting, and denial of food and loss of weight continue.

The basic symptom of anorexia nervosa is loss of bodily weight (20 to 25 percent of original body weight is a common criterion) for which no organic cause can be found. Other signs are adamant refusal to eat (alternating with overeating episodes), excessive physical activity (jogging and bicycle riding are current favorites of modern anorectics), and intense fear of obesity. Cessation of menstruation, if it has begun, or delay of its onset during the anorectic period is also typical. The quality that suggests a borderline state is the abnormal body image, which seems more distorted among anorectics than in other anxiety disorders. Despite continued loss of weight and signs of extraordinary thinness — many anorectics resemble pictures of World War II concentration-camp victims — fatness is a constant complaint. Grasping any piece of loose flesh on upper

arm, thigh, or buttocks, the anorectic will exhibit it to others as evidence of her grotesque "fatness." It is this distorted perception that is almost psychotic, for it is a major distortion of reality.[1]

Evidently many more people are anorectic than come to the attention of mental health professionals, as the authors frequently find when they discuss this topic in class. A substantial number of students, usually female, report that they went through such a period during their teenage years, but it just seemed to pass. We have no reliable statistics on the extent of this problem in the general population, but many clinicians (Bruch 1973) believe that, in our appearance and diet-conscious society, such problems are on the upswing.

Before special treatment facilities and methods were developed for dealing with this disorder, fatal self-starvation was common (Halmi et al. 1973). But recent reports of special units set up to assist anorectic patients (Cantwell et al. 1977) indicate that the risk of death can be greatly reduced.

[1] A common question is whether anorectics misperceive only their own body images or whether they have a distorted view of others' bodies as well. One of the authors' students once asked whether anorectics recognize the excessive thinness of other anorectic patients. A former anorectic in the class submitted this written response to the question: "While hospitalized, I recognized and was horrified by the body weight (or lack of it) in other people on the anorectic regime, while not understanding how I could be treated as one of them." Evidently, it is possible for the anorectic to misperceive her own body weight, while recognizing the excessive thinness of others.

sample of schizophrenic, depressive, and borderline patients. With that scheme alone, he was able to separate the borderline group from the other two.

Onset and Course of Anxiety Disorders

We have been considering anxiety disorders as if they exist frozen in time. We described patterns of symptoms or personality as clinicians observe them, without referring to their development or future course. Like most psychological disorders, some anxiety disorders seem to appear insidiously, and it is hard to delineate the exact moment of their onset. Others, as in panic attacks, show acute onset. They begin suddenly and without prior history. As it sometimes happens with schizophrenia and depression, acute onset of anxiety disorders frequently occurs after a distinguishable series of adverse life changes.

In one study that included anxiety-disordered patients, Cooper and Sylph (1973) investigated the incidence of notable life changes prior to the onset of the disorder. They defined the severity of a change as the seriousness of threat or adverse implications an event would hold for a person one week after its occurrence. Serious events included failure to realize important personal goals, unexpected crises, changes in status of health, and so on. In a sample of anxiety-disordered patients with acute onset, 18 percent had experienced at least one negative life change of marked severity, and 47 percent had experienced at least one major life event of marked or moderate severity in the three weeks prior to onset of their anxiety disorder. The percentages in a normal control sample were 0 and 6 percent, respectively. Unfortunately, no evidence shows that knowing whether the onset was insidious or acute has any prognostic value for anxiety disorders, as it has for schizophrenia and depression.

Once an anxiety disorder has appeared, what are the prospects for recovery? Research has shown (Lambert 1976; Malan et al. 1968) that in 40 to 50 percent of adult cases, overt symptoms substantially decrease in intensity without intervention. The other 50 percent experience a chronic disability that does not fade. Even the individuals who experience marked reduction in symptoms exhibit significant residual difficulties in interpersonal relations, however.

In one very thorough longitudinal study, Malan et al. (1968) monitored for six to seven years a sample of forty-five anxiety-disordered patients who had sought help at the beginning of that period but had not received it. In symptoms alone, 49 percent of the sample showed a reduction in intensity. Of the improved patients, however, less than half could be said to be *totally* recovered from disabling symptoms.

Malan's group also evaluated these individuals from the point of view of "dynamic improvement," or positive changes in life adjustment believed to have resulted from resolution of underlying problems. Only 24 percent of the group met criteria for improvement in this area, despite the larger number whose *symptoms* had faded. Included in the study is the case of Mrs. R., illustrating that spontaneous abatement of symptoms and "dynamic improvement" do not necessarily occur together.

Mrs. K. R. sought psychotherapeutic assistance for acute attacks of anxiety and depression during her pregnancy. In this, the eighth month of her pregnancy, the patient suddenly had an attack of severe anxiety and depression soon after giving up work. She feared that something terrible would happen to her which would leave her children unprovided for. She regretted having children and thought that it would be better to kill herself and her children, as the world was such a dreadful place. Her marriage was very unsatisfactory and both partners had sexual difficulty. She rarely, if ever, had orgasm, and although she and her husband were sexually active before marriage, he lost interest afterward. Mrs. R. complained that her hus-

[Handwritten margin notes at top of page:]

Phobic Reactions - highly resistant - symptoms over time with no treatment

Psychoanalysis - indirect relationship between early life experiences & subsequent development so that an unresolved conflict from childhood may lead to adjustment problems in adulthood.

Behaviorism - direct relationship between prior learning + development of symptoms.

band kept her short of money, which is why she continued to work until the last minute in all her pregnancies. At the time of this crisis, the patient was admitted to a maternity hospital for a few days but received no subsequent psychiatric treatment.

Follow-up information: [After three years and eight months], Mrs. R.'s symptoms subsided soon after her admission to the hospital and have not recurred. There have been no further pregnancies. Her marriage is still reported as highly unsatisfactory as she and her husband have settled down to a state of mutual tolerance, but have minimal physical or psychological contact with one another. Mrs. R. reported that they only stayed together because of the children. She has now started a course of training in order to have something to fall back on when her children grow up.

Conclusion: Although the acute anxiety disorder subsided dramatically, her relationship difficulties remain the same, though reduced in intensity by mutual disengagement. Would you say that Mrs. R. has improved, worsened, or remained the same with the passage of time? (Malan et al. 1968, p. 539)

It appears that persistent anxiety-linked difficulties in living are less likely to disappear in time than are the more noticeable symptoms of an anxiety disorder. Also, close to half of the people who have symptomatic anxiety disorders experience no spontaneous reduction of disabling symptoms and appear to be chronically disturbed by them. With treatment, as we will see in Chapter 15, the prognosis improves considerably.

We do not know, in general, whether the incidence of spontaneous improvement varies with the type of anxiety disorder. The one exception is the phobic reaction, which seems highly persistent. The evidence underlying this conclusion comes from two studies of untreated phobic cases identified in community surveys. One study by Agras et al. (1972) found that only one of sixteen phobics (6 percent) were symptom-free five years after initial detec-

tion, and more than a third (37 percent) were worse. In the second study (Beiser 1976), only 25 percent of the people judged to have phobic symptoms showed some recovery without treatment after five years.

Theories on Development of Anxiety Disorders

Freud pioneered the study and treatment of anxiety disorders (see Chapter 2), and as we might expect, one of the two major schools of contemporary thought about the origin and treatment of these disorders — the psychoanalytic — incorporates many Freudian ideas. Fundamentally, it postulates an *indirect relationship* between early life experience and subsequent development, so that an unresolved conflict from childhod may lead to adjustment problems in adulthood. The second school, based on behavioral theory, suggests a *direct relationship* between prior learning and development of symptoms.

These two theoretical approaches to the development of anxiety disorders will be presented in a highly general and schematic way in this chapter. Their implications will become clearer when we discuss different approaches to intervention with anxiety disorders in Chapter 15, for the differences in intervention strategies highlight the differences of opinion about the origins and modification of anxiety and related disorders.

Psychoanalytic Model

[Handwritten margin note:] anxiety disorder - internal conflict a person carries from childhood to adulthood — failed to develop normally due to a childhood experience

Freud firmly believed that anxiety disorders stem from internal conflicts an individual carries through childhood into adulthood. From extensive case studies and psychotherapy efforts with anxiety-disordered individuals, he hypothesized that these people failed to develop normally because of some childhood experience.

He delineated a *developmental theory* according to which children pass through critical stages of psychological adjustment in which they experience specific developmental conflicts (see Table 13.6). A *conflict* arises when an individual experiences incompatible basic needs, and in order to meet one need must act in a way that thwarts fulfillment of another. During each developmental period the child must resolve new conflicts relating to dependency, aggression, and sexuality in order to mature into a well-adjusted, well-integrated adult. A child who encounters one or more significant obstacles (a parent dies or deserts the family before the child has resolved an oedipal conflict, or the child is prevented by an overprotective parent from achieving some independence) may become *fixated,* or stuck, at that stage. As an adult, the fixated person will be vulnerable to normative life crises. Thus, an individual who carries forward conflicting desires or emotions about being taken care of by others will show difficulties in balancing dependency on and independence from other people in later life. Similarly, a person who becomes overly attached to a parent of opposite sex as a child may have difficulties in developing satisfactory heterosexual interests as an adult. The latter problem was evidently a major factor in the fugue episode of Barbara Y., whose symptoms we described on page 309.

During her psychotherapy, Barbara attributed much of her problem to the fact that she was "Daddy's little girl" and that she had never grown up. She made many slips of speech and frequently referred to her father as her husband or vice versa. Her history confirmed an overattachment to father during her formative years. While she was growing up, her father was overprotective of her and insisted on driving her to and from dates, a rule that quickly drove potential boyfriends away. After her mother died (when Barbara was 17), Barbara assumed a wifely role toward her father

for a number of years. She took over the housekeeping duties at home "because father would have been lost without me." She also became her father's administrative assistant in his real estate business. During this period she had few dates, but the absence of male companionship with someone other than her father did not bother her (adapted from Goldstein and Palmer 1975, p. 194).

A second part of the psychoanalytic theory of anxiety, the so-called *structural model,* elaborates on the role of *conflict* in adjustment problems. Barbara's overattachment to her father conflicted with her desire for a normal heterosexual relationship with an appropriate male. To protect oneself against consciously recognizing an unresolved conflict and avoid the anxiety that this awareness would produce, an individual will develop *defense mechanisms.* Barbara had deceived herself into believing that her attachment to father had no relationship to her sexual fantasies. This defense mechanism enabled her to avoid recognizing that her father was the object of her erotic desires and to suppress her need for normal heterosexual relationships.

Anxiety and anxiety-linked symptoms appear, according to the psychoanalytic model, when defense mechanisms fail, and forbidden desires or feelings start breaking into consciousness. The conditions surrounding the emergence of Barbara's symptoms represent the kind of clinical data used to support this part of the psychoanalytic model.

Two years before her fugue episode, Barbara's father died. "I almost had a breakdown then." After a brief period of sexual promiscuity, which ended in depression, Barbara sought employment in a real estate firm owned by her father's former partner. Soon afterward, she accepted an offer of marriage from this man, who was seventeen years her senior. She had always admired this man and had been secretly in love with him when she was a little girl. As the wedding date approached, she

[Handwritten margin notes, top: "is not fixated to vulnerable to life crisis" — "symptoms gains — act as primary gain — substituting for inoperative defense mechanisms + acting out as a further barrier between awareness and conflict." — "Psychoanalytic theory — if underlying conflict must be dealt with so symptoms don't keep reappearing"]

[Handwritten margin notes, left side: "must resolve conflicts relating to dependency aggression + sexuality"]

Table 13.6. Five stages of psychosexual development according to Freudian theory

Stage and age	Form of gratification	Possible conflicts from overgratification or excessive deprivation
Oral Year 1	The infant obtains gratification by stimulation of the mouth — by sucking and feeding.	Adult may be overly acquisitive, always attempting to take things in (as seen in drug addiction, excessive eating, smoking), or overly dependent on others.
Anal Year 2	The child obtains gratification by controlling elimination and retention of feces.	Adult may be preoccupied with cleanliness, orderliness, and possession of goods. Obsessive and compulsive traits may pervade the individual's personality. Overcautiousness, stinginess, and introversion may result. The adult may suppress emotions excessively.
Phallic Years 3–6	Gratification by self-manipulation of the genitalia.	For adult males: may be inordinately tied to mother; male homosexuality may result. For females: may lead to inadequate superego development; female homosexuality may result.
Latency Years 6–12	Sexuality believed dormant.	Adult may be withdrawn, overly individualistic, or deviant.
Genital Years of adolescence and adulthood	Gratification in the genital area through heterosexual activities.	

Souce: Adapted from Howard Gardner, *Developmental Psychology* (Boston: Little, Brown, 1978), p. 199.

became more and more anxious and postponed the ceremony with a flimsy excuse. Finally, after a long-delayed wedding, she had great difficulty performing and enjoying sexual relations with her new husband. After one painful incident when her husband plied her with liquor to reduce her apprehension and ended up criticizing and berating her, she fled and began her fugue episode (adapted from Goldstein and Palmer 1975, p. 194).

According to the structural model of psychoanalysis, Barbara's symptoms appeared when her conflict between father attachment and her sexual desires were about to be brought into full awareness by the pressures from her "father figure" of a husband. From this perspective, symptoms serve an important function known as *primary gain* by substituting for inoperative defense mechanisms and acting as a further barrier between awareness and conflict. As we indicated in talking about phobia, symptoms may also bring the anxious person secondary gains in the form of control over others. The psychoanalytic notions of primary and secondary gain are the source of a major difference between the psychoanalytic and behavioral theories of anxiety disorders, for psychoanalytic adherents insist that the behavioral

[Handwritten margin note, right: "agoraphobia"]

practice of treating symptoms directly, not uncovering the underlying conflict, carries the risk that new symptoms will appear later.

Behavioral Model

There is no one behavioral theory of anxiety disorders. Of the several models, varying in complexity, the simplest is the *classical conditioning model* (see Chapter 2), which explains anxiety symptoms as an extreme example of conditioned emotional reactions to external stimuli. This model has been applied especially to phobic behavior, which could be the result of a traumatic conditioning experience involving a specific stimulus.

In the classic experiment of this conditioning model, Watson and Rayner (1920) conditioned "little Albert" to fear a white rat (discussed in Chapter 2). This model is plausible, but is weakened because no one has successfully reproduced the results (English 1929; Bregman [see Thorndike 1935]). Also, intensive interviews with simple phobic patients, who best seem to fit the conditioning model, indicate that they rarely had the type of traumatic experiences that a conditioning model demands (Marks 1977).

Classical conditioning does, however, have a part in the development of anxiety disorders. In our account of phobic development, the panic attack on the road was an important conditioning stimulus for the subsequent fear of leaving the house. The classical conditioning model does not, though, explain why the anxiety was stimulated on the road just at that time.

The limitations of a simple classical conditioning model have led theorists to more complex models combining classical and operant conditioning (the acts learned are instrumental in achieving rewards or avoiding punishment). A two-factor theory developed by Mowrer (1947) holds that anxiety-disordered behavior develops from two related learning experiences: by classical conditioning, a person learns to fear a neutral stimulus and then learns to avoid the fear arousal in the future by escaping from or avoiding the conditioned stimulus. Avoidance behavior can be actual motor behavior (running away from or not approaching a fearful stimulus), or verbal-symbolic (not thinking about fearful stimuli). Symptoms of anxiety appear when avoidance behavior stops being effective.

Mowrer's theory is somewhat similar to psychoanalytic theory in requiring some initial fearful experience (the classical conditioning), followed by defensive behavior (patterns of avoidance), which is reinforced because it reduces anxiety.

Although behavioral theorists can explain how fears and avoidance patterns can be learned, until recently they have assumed that the learned reactions grow out of direct experience with fearful objects. A modification of this position has come from Bandura (1969) and other *social learning* theorists, who emphasize that learning occurs by observing significant people in a person's life, who are called *models*. From a social learning point of view, excessive fears or avoidance patterns may be the result of imitating — sometimes consciously and sometimes unconsciously — behavior patterns manifested by parents or other significant authority figures. Thus, the fearful adult is modeling apprehensions and anxieties that she observed in her parents or others during her formative years; or the conversion hysteric develops a style of coping observed in a family unit in which illness was a common way of dealing with tensions in relationships. In their study of conversion hysteria in student aviators, Mucha and Reinhardt (1970) found that 70 percent of their parents had had an illness involving the same organ system. Modeling a parental behavior obviously was significant in the choice of symptom.

Fig. 13.6. Exaggerated fears can be learned by imitating the behavior of significant others.

Behavioral Model

CLASSICAL CONDITIONING MODEL
- conditioned emotional reactions to external stimuli
  - especially for phobies
- but, phobics don't seem to have had a traumatic experience
- but, has a part in the development of anxiety disorders
- limitation of C.C. has formed combination of C.C + O.C
- The acts learned are instrumental in achieving rewards or avoiding punishment

Mowrer : 2-factor theory
anxiety disorders develop from 2 related learning experiences:
C.C: learning to fear a neutral stimuli + to avoid the fear arousal by conditioned stimuli
avoidance (running away or not approaching) or verbal-symbolic (not thinking about it)
- Symptoms arise when avoidance behavior becomes ineffective.
∴ initial fearful experience (C.C.) + defensive behavior (avoidance) which is reinforced due to reduction of anxiety.

the psychoanalytic theory)
- learned reactions grow out of direct experience w/ fearful objects but, recently BANDURA + other social learning theorists say that learning occurs by observing significant others - models conscious or unconscious extreme fears.

Social Learning Theories advance our behaviorism because: " recognize the family system as an important source of conflicts + overt behavior patterns " describe specific developmental processes that contribute to the formation of anxiety disorders.

Social learning theories of anxiety disorders are a major advance over earlier behavioral theories for two reasons. First, they recognize the family system as an important source of conflicts and overt behavior patterns. Second, they provide an enriched vocabulary for describing specific developmental processes that contribute to the formation of anxiety disorders, a vocabulary that simpler behavioral formulations do not offer.

Summary

1. Anxiety is an exaggerated feeling of fear aroused by the way an individual perceives a situation. Freud identified three forms of "neurotic anxiety": free-floating anxiety, or general apprehensiveness; anxiety that focuses on objects or situations to which real danger may be attached; and unjustifiable anxiety, which may accompany other symptoms or may itself be the primary symptom of severe neurosis.

2. Anxiety disorders are moderately severe behavior disturbances. They are less disorganizing than psychotic disorders because the individual remains in contact with reality and recognizes that the discomfort arises from within. The continuum of anxiety reactions ranges from patterns in which there is no break with reality to others with transitory psychotic symptoms. Individuals who exhibit a tendency toward transitory psychosis are classified as "borderline."

3. The three approaches to measurement of anxiety are: self-reports, biological measures, and behavioral signs of anxiety. Although these indices do not always correlate, the pattern that the three together generate is more significant than the information each measure alone provides.

4. Anxiety disorders can be divided into two general categories: symptomatic disorders, in which anxiety is focused in one or more discrete, disabling symptoms; and personality disorders, in which an individual avoids anxiety-producing stimuli by developing maladaptive behavior patterns, which, in turn, prevent him from having a normal life style.

5. The group of symptomatic disorders includes: (1) generalized anxiety, characterized by an inner feeling that threat is omnipresent; (2) panic disorder, characterized by sudden attacks of feelings of overwhelming dread or imminent death; (3) phobic disorders, with irrational fear of one or more specific objects or situations; (4) obsessive-compulsive disorder, in which the individual is obsessed with an impulse to perform some disturbing deed and feels compelled to perform some repetitive action to lessen the anxiety connected with that impulse; (5) conversion and dissociative disorders and multiple personality, all of which involve major alterations in one's state of awareness.

6. Among the many types of personality disorders two are common patterns: the compulsive personality disorder, in which excessive emotional control, insistence on conformity, and adherence to internalized standards are characteristic; and the histrionic (hysterical) personality disorder, with attention-seeking behavior and extraordinary demands on others.

7. Borderline syndromes are more severe than most anxiety disorders. Borderline patients tend to experience functional difficulties in: (1) interpersonal relationships, (2) impulse control, (3) work, (4) affect, and (5) perception.

8. The onset of anxiety disorders can be either insidious or acute. In one study, a major life event of marked or moderate severity had occurred in the three weeks prior to onset in half of the cases examined.

9. Without treatment, 40 to 50 percent of adult cases of anxiety disorders show substantial reduction of symptoms, but even for many of these people, underlying difficulties in interpersonal relationships persist.

10. Two distinct perspectives on the origin and treatment of anxiety disorders come from psychoanalytic theory and behavioral theory. Psychoanalytic theory suggests an indirect relationship between unresolved childhood conflicts and adjustment problems in adulthood.

Anxiety and anxiety-linked symptoms appear when a person's defense mechanisms fail to suppress conflict. Behavioral theory suggests two models: the conditioning model, in which anxiety and avoidance behavior are conditioned responses to external stimuli; and the social learning model, in which anxiety is learned from significant people in an individual's life.

[Handwritten annotations throughout the page:]

Malan — did study again 49% — reduction in intensity, only 24% the changes — anxiety-linked difficulties are less likely to disappear or time than are the noticeable symptoms or more noticeable of an anxiety disorder

Mowrer 2-factor theory

direct relationship between prior learning + development of symptoms

BANDURA — observation of significant others — conscious or unconscious

Secondary gain — an advantage that limits the persons desire to get better
① physical symptom — no organic cause
disorders { Sensory, Motor, Visceral
② flight
③ outlet of each side of the personality

— addiction of Narcissistic + Masochistic

study by this criteria they could separate borderlines from schizos + depressives
— fit well in social groups
— relationships are self-humiliating
— depression anger
— periodic hallucinations
— paranoid tendencies

— acute onset 47% had major life changes 3 months before

must resolve conflicts in each stage relating to dependency + aggression + sexuality
frustrated vulnerable to life crisis
primary gain — symptoms
substitution for inoperative defense m. + act conflict out as further barrier between awareness + conflict

ANXIETY DISORDERS [DSM III]
✓ anxiety the prominent symptom
2) anxiety underlies one discrete disabling symptoms
3) patterns of behavior were adopted to ward off anxiety.

distinguishing between 3 classes ① ANS ② II ② CNS of events self reports

Frenz Ebstein
Borderline Syndrome — Gunderson + Singer 49%
scale.
Malan.
Cooper + Sylph Mowrer BANDURA significant others
life changes 45
Slater + Glithero — 60% of conversions developed symptoms or died 9 years after being diagnosed.

Agras — Sy cures later amount of phobics — no treatment free 69% — symptom free 37 — worse

26

Chapter 14

Psychophysiological Dysfunction

Stress and Coping
Nonspecific Stress Theories
Specific Theories of Life Stress

Biological Predisposition to Psychophysiological Disorders

Understanding Psychophysiological Disorders by Treating Them

Sexual Dysfunction
Preparatory Phase
Coital Culmination
Origins of Sexual Dysfunction
Effect of Sexual Dysfunction on Relationships

Summary

Throughout this book, we have talked about disturbed psychological functioning. Although psychological symptoms are often accompanied by physical signs of disturbance in psychotic and many anxiety-disordered individuals, physical symptoms are not the significant components of abnormal behavior patterns. But sometimes, when the multiple chains of biochemical and physiological change that anxiety produces are long sustained, severe alterations in physical functioning can occur. We will now examine how psychological factors influence the development of biological malfunction.

Three types of ailments are linked to the emotions. First, *short-term physiological changes* interfere with physiological states that are necessary for some desired behaviors. The physiological responses to fear stimuli are incompatible with those necessary for penile erection in the male. When a frightened male attempts sexual intercourse, sex dysfunction can arise from this incompatibility of biological states. Second, relatively *long-term changes in physiological functioning* can follow sustained exposure to life stress, as in high blood pressure. Third, the biological changes can ultimately produce *actual damage to specific organs* of the body, as in the stomach, where lesions, or ulcers, in the stomach wall develop, apparently in response to prolonged exposure to stress.

At one time, the term *psychosomatic* was applied to a specific set of physical, or somatic, disorders believed to arise from unresolved and sustained psychological conflict. Unlike hysterical conversion disorder, in which organs are intact but nonfunctional, psychosomatic disorders mean actual diseases involving damage to tissue (as in ulcers), or disordered physiological dysfunction (as in essential hypertension, the medical term for a type of high blood pressure) that were believed to result from chronic physiological arousal correlated with persistent conflict.

Recently, the concept of psychophysiological disorder has been broadened considerably with the recognition that emotions and life stress help increase vulnerability to *all* physical disease and not to a limited group of so-called psychosomatic disorders. Thus, a *psychophysiological disorder* is *any* physical illness that is attributable, at least in part, to sustained stress. Reflecting this change, *DSM*-III does not recognize a discrete class of psychophysiological disorders, and leaves it to the attending physician to determine how deeply stress is involved in a patient's illness. Table 14.1 lists some disorders in which stress has been implicated.

Recognizing that illness is caused by multiple factors, including not only the virulence of the agent (say, a bacterium) but also the person's vulnerability, is a major breakthrough. Vulnerability to disease can be affected by multiple physiological factors, such as inherited predisposition or temporarily lowered resistance, and multiple psychological and social factors, such as psychological stress, faulty coping, social isolation or alienation, or combinations of these. The primary goal of research today is to understand life stress and how much

Table 14.1. Some physical disorders in which stress factors have been particularly implicated

Bronchial asthma — A chronic disorder characterized by shortness of breath, wheezing, a suffocating feeling, and labored coughing to remove mucus from the air passages.

Colitis — Inflammation of the mucous membrane of the colon which can result in lesions or ulcers (ulcerative colitis). Symptoms include lower abdominal pain, diarrhea, constipation, anemia, and sometimes fever.

Eczema — A skin disease characterized by inflammation, redness, itching and the formation of visciles which exude a watery substance that evaporates and leaves the skin covered with crusts.

Essential hypertension — Elevated blood pressure either constantly (stabile) or episodically (labile) of no known organic cause.

Gastritis — Inflammation of the stomach. Symptoms include gastric discomfort, nausea, loss of appetite, belching and distention of the stomach with gas.

Heart attack (myocardial infarction) — A sudden instance of heart failure usually caused by a blood clot in a vessel supplying the heart leading to inadequate blood supply and death of heart tissue. Symptoms often include pain or tightness in center of chest which may radiate to arms, throat or jaw.

Migraine headache — A particularly intense headache which returns periodically. It is usually confined to one side of the head and accompanied by nausea, vomiting and sensory disturbances.

Peptic or duodenal ulcer — An open sore on the wall of the esophagus, stomach or duodenum caused in part by excessive production of pepsin and hydrochloric acid. Symptoms include nausea, discomfort or sharp pain an hour or two after eating, and in severe cases, bleeding which may be noted in vomit or the passing of tarry-black stools.

Raynaud's disease — Spasmodic obstruction of peripheral arteries. Fingers (sometimes toes) become white or lead-blue, cold, and numb, and sometimes ache. Later blood flow is excessive; fingers become blotchy, turn red, and throb or tingle. In severe cases, gangrene may result.

Sexual dysfunction — Incapacity to perform the sexual act or to achieve sexual satisfaction through orgasm.

it contributes to vulnerability to all types of physical disorders, from traditional "psychosomatic" disorders such as ulcers to disorders not previously put in this category, such as cancer and heart disease.

Stress and Coping

The term *stress* describes noxious life events that demand both physiological and psychological adaptation by an organism. Sustained stress subjects mind and body to a continued, unrelenting demand and produces lasting physiological and psychological changes that ultimately result in physical changes so severe that they are classified as diseases. What are these stressful life events and how do they interfere with bodily functioning? One of the two

types of answers to this question treats stress as a *nonspecific* set of events that produce a broad range of physical dysfunctions, and the other links specific stressors or personality types with specific disease outcomes. Let's look separately at each kind of explanation.

Nonspecific Stress Theories

These theories owe a great deal to physiologist Hans Selye (1976), who observed that a highly regular pattern of bodily changes follows exposure to a great variety of noxious agents, including fear, food deprivation, oxygen deprivation, and pain. Selye's research with rats led him to conclude that all stressors activate a *general adaptation syndrome,* a three-stage physiological reaction showing alarm, resistance, and exhaustion (see Figure 14.1). The body's immediate reaction to stress is to mobilize for defense by stepping up production and

Fig. 14.1. General adaptation syndrome. Under prolonged stress, initial shock and countershock reactions may be followed by a stage of resistance and then a stage of exhaustion that culminates in death. Adding a new stress to the original stress will accelerate the process. (From Selye 1950.)

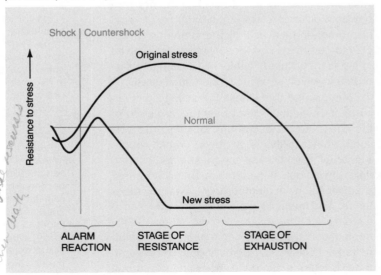

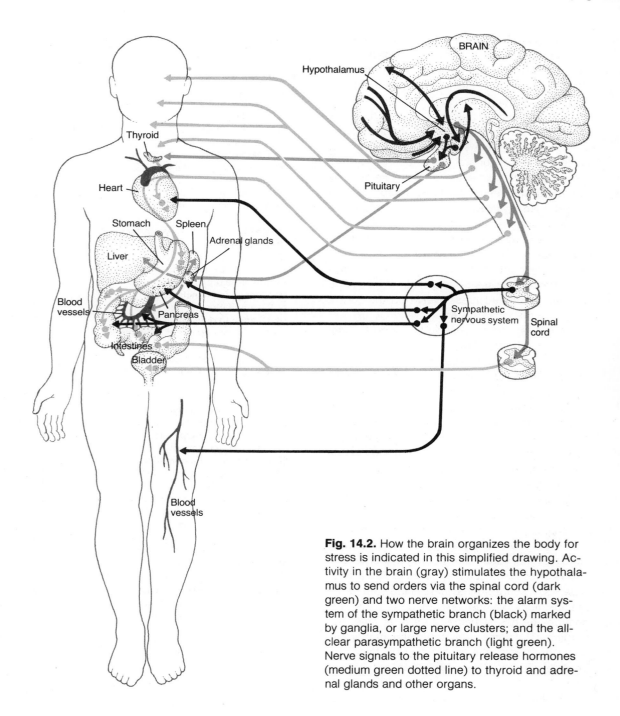

Fig. 14.2. How the brain organizes the body for stress is indicated in this simplified drawing. Activity in the brain (gray) stimulates the hypothalamus to send orders via the spinal cord (dark green) and two nerve networks: the alarm system of the sympathetic branch (black) marked by ganglia, or large nerve clusters; and the all-clear parasympathetic branch (light green). Nerve signals to the pituitary release hormones (medium green dotted line) to thyroid and adrenal glands and other organs.

secretion of hormones under the direction of the autonomic nervous system. Now the organism is in the shock phase of the alarm reaction. Continued stress induces a countershock response, activating local defenses in systems throughout the body that will take over the work begun by the autonomic and endocrine systems if stressful conditions persist. In resistance, stage two of the general adaptation syndrome, the takeover is complete, and physiologically the organism seems to have adapted to a stressful life style. But prolonged exposure to stress or introduction of new stressors overtakes the body's defensive resources and the third stage — exhaustion, or even death — may occur. Psychophysiological symptoms — Selye calls them "diseases of adaptation" — develop because continued stress overworks the body's defensive response system.

Selye's position received support from Holmes and Rahe (1967), who studied the relationship between physical illness and varying degrees of *life change,* a key stress, they say. Life changes include any alteration in the external environment that requires personal readjustment. Holmes and Rahe considered positive changes, such as graduation and marriage, and negative changes, such as death of a loved one and loss of employment, to be stressful events. Assigning quantitative weights to a number of important life changes according to the difficulty in readjustment they felt was inherent in the change, the researchers developed a scale that would allow them to measure the amount of stress an individual has recently experienced. The Holmes-Rahe scale appears in Table 14.2. A person's score on the scale is the sum of the readjustment values assigned to the life changes he has sustained in a brief time. According to Holmes and Rahe, the higher the total, the greater the likelihood of subsequent physical illness. The score does not predict which form the illness might take, but how likely some type of breakdown in physiological or

Table 14.2. Social readjustment rating scale

Rank	Life event	Readjustment value
1	Death of spouse	100
2	Divorce	73
3	Marital separation	65
4	Jail term	63
5	Death of close family member	63
6	Personal injury or illness	53
7	Marriage	50
8	Fired at work	47
9	Marital reconciliation	45
10	Retirement	45
11	Change in health of family member	44
12	Pregnancy	40
13	Sex difficulties	39
14	Gain of new family member	39
15	Business readjustment	39
16	Change in financial state	38
17	Death of close friend	37
18	Change to different line of work	36
19	Change in number of arguments with spouse	35
20	Mortgage over $10,000	31
21	Foreclosure of mortgage or loan	30
22	Change in responsibilities at work	29
23	Son or daughter leaving home	29
24	Trouble with in-laws	29
25	Outstanding personal achievement	28
26	Wife begin or stop work	26
27	Begin or end school	26
28	Change in living conditions	25
29	Revision of personal habits	24
30	Trouble with boss	23
31	Change in work hours or conditions	20
32	Change in residence	20
33	Change in schools	20
34	Change in recreation	19
35	Change in church activities	19
36	Change in social activities	18
37	Mortgage or loan less than $10,000	17
38	Change in sleeping habits	16
39	Change in number of family get-togethers	15
40	Change in eating habits	15
41	Vacation	13
42	Christmas	12
43	Minor violation of the law	11

Source: T. H. Holmes and R. H. Rahe, "The social adjustment rating scale," *Journal of Psychosomatic Research,* 1967, 11:216, Table 3.

psychological functioning may be (see Figure 14.3).

This letter has evidence that supports the conclusions Holmes and Rahe reached. The readjustment value of each life change appears in parentheses next to the event. Notice that the first signs of illness appeared only after 285 life-change units had accumulated.

Dear Jane:

You never will believe what has happened this past year. Don was transferred to Southern California (25) because they closed the branch in our area. He got a promotion, which was nice, but we sure hated to move after 25 years in the San Francisco area. We sold our home (20) and we cried when we left it. Shelly, our 20-year-old daughter, moved with us (39). She was planning to get married later that same summer and would be living down south anyway, so she changed colleges to go to the one her husband was attending down here, and that worked out very well. We decided not to buy a house again but rent an apartment (25) because we didn't think we would stay very long in Southern California. Don was planning to retire early, but as you know, inflation changed those plans. Anyway, the day we moved into our apartment we got a call that my brother-in-law passed away (63) and so we had to go back home for the funeral. It was so sad and I felt a little guilty that we had to move at such a time; I knew my sister would have loved to have us near her at that sad point in her life. Shelly decided to be married (29) where the family was, up north, so we

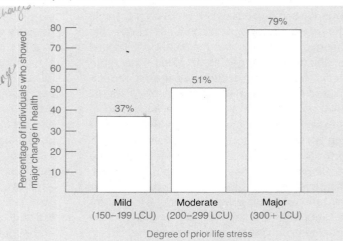

Fig. 14.3. This graph illustrates the results of a study by Holmes and Rahe in which changes in health status were closely related to the degree of recent life stress. Life stress was measured using the Social Readjustment Rating Scale (Table 14.2). The sum of Life Changes (*LCU*s) are grouped into three categories: mild, moderate, and major. Note the progressive increase in illness rates following these different levels of life change. Compute the score for yourself for the past six months. Do the results correspond to your recent health history? (After Holmes and Masuda 1974.)

made many trips back and forth planning the wedding. It was a beautiful wedding!

I hated to leave my job (20) and postponed quitting for about a month. That meant Don was commuting weekends and it really wasn't too good for either of us. I did get a new and different type of job (36) down here at the university. I'm enjoying it and I have a very understanding boss. I feel this job has helped my mental attitude immensely.

We took a trip to Hawaii (13) after the wedding to try to relax and pull ourselves together after such a hectic year. It was wonderful but when we got home I developed colitis, which lasted for about 10 months. I felt just miserable physically and mentally. Anyway that finally passed and now I have been told that I have high blood pressure. It was labile up north, but now I have to be on medication I guess for the rest of my life. I look at it like taking vitamin pills and that helps. We also had Christmas down here this year which meant having the family with us for a few days. It was strenuous but fun as we don't see the family much any more (15). In spite of the confusion we all survived the holidays.

Let me know how life is with you. Write soon.

Jeri

One drawback of studies like the Holmes-Rahe project is that most of the corroborating evidence comes from sick or recovered patients who have answered questions about life changes that occurred in the past. Longitudinal studies of life changes as they occur have not yielded such strong evidence as the retrospective studies. These studies (Rahe 1974; Theorell 1974) indicate that although the incidence of illnesses in groups of people studied for some time are higher among individuals who undergo more life changes, many individuals experience significant changes without subsequent illness. Therefore, it is not clear that life changes — or any other stress, for that matter — are the important factor. Perhaps it is the way each individual interprets them that is critical.

One series of studies indicates that the sub-jective *appraisal* of a stressful event determines the intensity of physiological response to it. Appraisal is the interpretation of an event as threatening and the degree of threat perceived. Using disturbing films as stressor stimuli, Lazarus (1964) was able to show that when a sound track accompanying the film played down the pain of the events portrayed, viewers responded with considerably less intensity physiologically than those who saw the same film with a sound track enhancing the stress in the events.

The way each of us appraises life events can become part of the way we cope with problems and determine how much stress (both psychological and physiological) we experience. De-Long (cited in Goldstein 1973) classified a study sample by their responses to an incomplete-sentence test into three coping-style groups: *copers* were very alert to stressful stimuli; *avoiders* minimized or denied the presence of threat; and *nonspecific defenders* (NSD), a middle group, shifted flexibly between the other two styles, depending upon the situation. Representatives of each group were studied on the day they had to face a stressful life event: awareness that they had to have major surgery. After being informed by their physicians that surgery was necessary, patients filled out a measure of momentary anxiety to be compared to a previously obtained measure of their general level of anxiety. Looking at Figure 14.4, you can see that the groups varied markedly in their appraisal of the stressfulness of the event. The avoiders claimed that at that moment they were less anxious than usual, whereas the NSD and copers indicated that this was indeed a stressful event for them. Interestingly, their reactions to the stressful news predicted not only the amount of anxiety they experienced before surgery but also their postoperative response to the stress of surgery itself. Individuals who acknowledged momentary anxiety when informed of surgery then engaged in coping behaviors

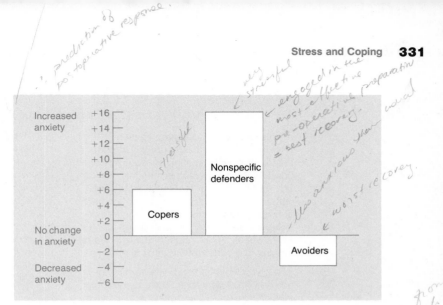

Fig. 14.4. Characteristic style of coping with stress predicted the degree of subjective anxiety aroused by the stressful news that major surgery was needed. (From Goldstein 1973.)

that left them better prepared than the others to endure the stress of surgery (reading about their surgery, talking with doctors and nurses about what to expect, seeking support from relatives and friends, etc.). The least rigidly defended group, the *NSD*s, showed the most subjective anxiety initially but also engaged subsequently in the most effective pre-operative preparation with the result that they had the shortest and easiest post-operative recovery. This type of momentary anxiety differs from the chronic and high levels of apprehension that afflict anxiety-disordered individuals and frequently interferes with effective preparatory action. Consequently, before linking life stress to disease we must consider the possible effects of appraisal and coping style in such a relationship.

Specific Theories of Life Stress

Without ruling out the idea that life stress generally increases an individual's vulnerability to illness, we must give some thought to the possibility that specific psychological pro-

cesses predispose us to specific diseases. Theories of specificity fall into three classes, according to their emphasis on: (1) situational specificity, (2) attitudinal specificity, or (3) personality specificity.

SITUATIONAL SPECIFICITY
Some stressful situations permit flight, but from others there is no escape. You can drop out of a class that you are failing, but you cannot walk out of the room when the boss is chewing you out. In some situations, you can do something to reduce your anxiety about a stressful event (read up on your illness to get ready for surgery, for example), but for others preparation is difficult, if not impossible. Some theorists have suggested that the stress we experience under different conditions arouses different physiological systems, and that sustained arousal of a system will predispose us to some form of illness in that system.

Evidence linking specific kinds of stress situations is not overwhelming, but some interesting lines of research have been followed. In

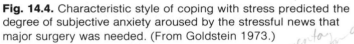

[handwritten margin notes: Cousins / Selye's Stress of Life / — replacing anxiety with the emotion / — laughter / — recovered. / ✓✓ / Holistic medicine / — sickness + health / involve the whole person / not just part of the body]

Can a Systematic Program of Stress Reduction Facilitate Recovery from a Disabling Physical Illness? A Personal Account

If life stress is a contributing element in physiological breakdown, does it stand to reason that by eliminating as much stress as possible once a disease is manifest, we can alter our chance for recovery? Editor and writer Norman Cousins (1976) wrote a fascinating account of his heroic struggle to recover from a severely disabling and painful joint disease by doing just that. From the beginning, the odds were against him.

In August of 1964, I flew home from a trip abroad with a slight fever. The malaise, which took the form of a general feeling of achiness, rapidly deepened. Within a week, it became difficult to move my neck, arms, hands, fingers and legs. . . . I had considerable difficulty in moving my limbs and even turning over in bed. Nodules appeared on my body, gravel-like substances under the skin, indicating the systemic nature of the illness. . . .

I asked Dr. Hitzig about my chances for full recovery. He leveled with me, admitting one of the specialists had told him I had 1 chance in 500. The specialist had also stated that he had not personally witnessed a recovery from this comprehensive condition.

Faced with this grim news, Cousins organized a two-pronged program of recovery. First, he determined from a review of the medical literature that increased intake of ascorbic acid (Vitamin C) could assist in regenerating connective tissue, and so began a program of massive intake of this substance. Second, he decided that his disorder was stress-related, that stress had lowered his resistance to a toxic substance to which he had been exposed overseas. He reasoned that because life stress had lowered his resistance he might be able to achieve some recovery by reversing the process.

I remembered having read, 10 years earlier, Hans Selye's classic book *The Stress of Life.* With great clarity, Selye showed that adrenal exhaustion could be caused by emotional tension such as frustration or suppressed rage. . . . How was I to get my adrenal glands — my endocrine glands — working again — both physically and emotionally?

The inevitable question came to my mind: What about the positive emotions? If the negative emotions produce negative changes in the body, would't the positive emotions produce positive chemical changes? Is it possible that love, hope, faith, laughter, confidence and the will to live have therapeutic value? Do chemical changes occur only on the downside?

Obviously, putting the positive emotions to work is nothing . . . simple. . . . But even a reasonable degree of control over any emotions might have a salutory physiological effect. Just replacing anxiety with a fair degree of confidence would be helpful (pp. 1458–1463).

Cousins embarked on a program to stimulate positive emotions, particularly laughter, by systematic and regular exposure to humorous materials. With assistance from producer Allen Funt, Cousins obtained videotapes of Funt's television program, Candid Camera, and watched them often. He also read anthologies of humorous writing.

He must have done something right, for Cousins is one of the few to recover from the disorder. Although recovery was slow and arduous and took more than seven years, he regained reasonably normal functioning and freedom from pain.

It is difficult to determine from a single case whether any of Cousins's therapeutic methods really helped to effect his remarkable recovery, or whether he was the one in five hundred who would have recovered anyway. Nevertheless, his systematic application of current knowledge about relationships among stress, body chemistry, and disease to reverse the negative effects of stress was a highly creative way of carrying this view to a logical, if extreme, conclusion.

Much of the medicine now called "holistic" follows a similar view, that sickness and health involve the whole person, not just parts of the body. Thus, the holistic approach takes as much interest in people's emotional lives and modes of coping with stress as in physiological well-being. Although this movement is very appealing, systematically collected evidence that they improve health status is not yet available.

particular, substantial evidence links essential hypertension (a form of high blood pressure of unknown organic cause) to potentially harmful environmental contexts in which (1) outcome is uncertain, (2) fight or flight is inappropriate, and (3) a person must maintain constant vigilance (Syme 1977). This pattern shows up clearly among one group, the air traffic controllers, whose job it is to prevent aircraft collisions during takeoff and landing. Theirs is a very de-

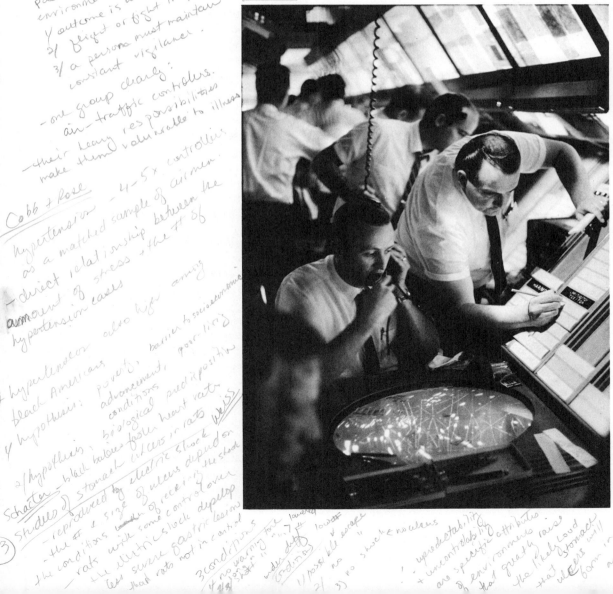

Fig. 14.5. In the stress-charged atmosphere of an air traffic control center, two men study a radar screen as they track a plane through congested skies. Their heavy responsibilities may make them vulnerable to illness.

(1) Evidence
— linking hypertension to potentially harmful environmental context in which
1/ outcome is uncertain
2/ flight or fight inappropriate
3/ a persons must maintain constant vigilance.
— one group clearly:
  air-traffic controllers.
— their heavy responsibilities make them vulnerable to illness

Cobb + Rose
hypertension — 4-5× controllers as a matched sample of airmen.
— direct relationship between the amount of stress + the # of hypertension cases

(2) hypertension also high among black Americans
1/ hypothesis: poverty, barrier to socioeconomic advancement, poor living conditions
2/ hypothesis: biological predisposition
Schachter — black babies faster heart rate

(3) Studies of stomach ulcers in rats (Weiss)
— reproduced by electric shock
— the # + size of ulcers depend on the conditions under which objects receive the shock
— rats with some control over the electric shock develop less severe gastric lesions that rats not in control

3 conditions:
1/ no warning tone lowered
2/ warning tone lowered
3/ no shock/no ulcers
1/ possible to escape
2/ ...
3/ no shock/no ulcers
— unpredictability + uncontrollability are specific attributes of environments that greatly raise the likelihood that stomach ulcers will form in animals

manding job, and the consequences when these airport personnel relax their vigilance because they have worked too many hours, are not feeling well, or any other reason can be tragic. In one study, Cobb and Rose (1973) found clinical levels of essential hypertension in four or five times as many controllers as in a matched sample of airmen. Using statistics on density of traffic as an indirect measure of job stress, they discovered a direct relationship between the amount of stress and the number of hypertension cases. And youth gave no apparent protection against hypertension. Other psychophysiological illnesses did show up in the sample (peptic ulcers, in particular), but the incidence of other disorders was substantially below that of hypertension.

Other supportive evidence for situational specificity comes from the disproportionately high rate among black Americans of essential hypertension. In a recent large-scale survey of young adults aged 15 to 29, 19 percent of white males and 12.7 percent of white females had hypertension; among blacks, however, the rates were 34 percent and 31.6 percent for men and women, respectively. Many other studies have confirmed this difference. One hypothesis about the high rate among black Americans is that this group suffers from excessive stress caused by poverty, poor living conditions, and barriers to socioeconomic advancement, resulting in chronic anger and frustration that cannot be expressed in constructive ways (Myers 1975). This model makes some sense, but evidence of differences in cardiovascular functioning between black and white babies suggests that blacks may have a biological predisposition to stress reactions. In studies by Schacter and colleagues (1974), black infants showed significantly faster heart rates for some time after birth. Thus the potential for cardiovascular dysfunction among blacks may be greater.

We have more definitive evidence that specific stressor conditions are responsible for specific disorders, from a very different source — studies of stomach ulcers in rats. Stomach ulcers are chronic, or long-lasting, lesions in the wall of the stomach and upper part of the small intestine (duodenum), or both. They can be produced readily in rats by exposing the animals to recurrent electric shock. Research demonstrates, however, that the number and size of ulcers depends on the conditions under which the rats receive the shocks. In a series of elegant studies, Weiss (1977) has shown that rats with some control over the electric shock develop less severe gastric lesions than rats not in control. In one study, shock was administered under three conditions. One group of animals received no warning signal before shock; another received an extended warning signal that shock was coming; and a third received a short warning signal, a simple tone. Furthermore, three separate groups of test rats had different degrees of control over the test conditions. One group was able to avoid or escape shock by pressing a lever (avoidance escape), and another group received the same shock but could not escape it in any way (yoked). A third group received no shock at all. Figure 14.6 presents the results of the experiment. Animals that received no shocks did not develop ulcers. Animals that could control shock by making an avoidance response developed a low number of ulcers. The largest amount of ulcer formation occurred in the group that had to experience the shocks but could do nothing about them. The data also suggest that a warning of imminent danger limited the number of ulcers formed, even among animals that could not escape the shock. Thus, unpredictability and uncontrollability are specific attributes of environments that greatly raise the likelihood that stomach ulcers will form in lower animals.

Although a case has been made for the hy-

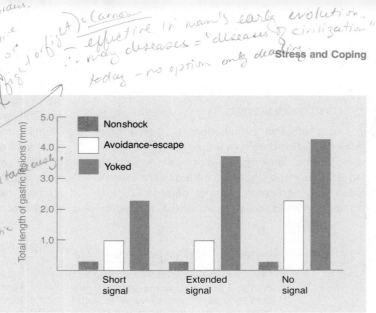

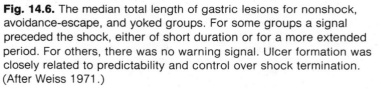

Fig. 14.6. The median total length of gastric lesions for nonshock, avoidance-escape, and yoked groups. For some groups a signal preceded the shock, either of short duration or for a more extended period. For others, there was no warning signal. Ulcer formation was closely related to predictability and control over shock termination. (After Weiss 1971.)

pothesis that specific environmental attributes heighten the likelihood of developing hypertension or ulcers, we do not know whether specific environmental conditions are unique to each of the psychophysiological disorders. If we examine the attributes listed earlier for a hypertension-prone environment, they seem little different from those isolated by Weiss in his experimental studies of ulcerating rats. One common factor in both is inhibition of the primitive response modes of fleeing the situation or aggressing against the source of the stress, the so-called *flight or fight reactions* first described by physiologist Walter Cannon (1939). Cannon theorized that early in man's evolution many of the body's physiological reactions to threat were effective preparations for either fleeing danger or subduing an aggressor. In fact, Cannon argued that many psychophysiological diseases are "diseases of civilization," because modern human beings do not generally have

the option of fleeing or attacking when we feel threatened. Instead, we must deal with social forces beyond our control and modulate our emotional reactions to frustration, not express them.

Interestingly, Weiss (1977) confirmed this position to a degree by a study in which two rats received shocks simultaneously. The rats reacted to this stress by fighting and wounding each other. Helpless to control the shock but able to "fight," these animals did not develop gastric ulcers, even when a plastic shield kept them from actually biting or clawing each other. The act of aggression was effective even when it could not be completed.

Evidence indicates that specific attributes of stressful situations increase or decrease the likelihood of subsequent disease. It is not clear that specific types of situational stress are uniquely tied to particular diseases, but it is a viable hypothesis nonetheless.

ATTITUDINAL SPECIFICITY

An alternative explanation for psychophysiological disorders is that they result from specific ways of thinking about oneself. According to Graham (1972), specific attitudes are associated with particular patterns of physiological change; should the attitude persist, a psychophysiological disorder will develop in the physiological system correlated with that attitude. *Attitude,* as Graham defined it, is twofold and includes how we perceive our own position in a situation (what we feel is happening to us) and what actions, if any, we wish to take. All having a specific psychological disease are hypothesized to have the same attitude (see Table 14.3).

Situational Stress in Family Life

Psychophysiological disorders occur in children and teenagers as well as adults. According to psychiatrist Salvador Minuchin (1978), who has studied families with offspring having different psychophysiological disorders, the young people who suffer psychophysiological breakdowns may be victims of distorted family relationships. Minuchin subscribes to the so-called *family systems theory* of abnormal behavior. You may remember that in Chapter 6 we introduced the concept of the schizogenic family, which attributes development of schizophrenia to growing up in a disturbed family environment. This idea derives from family systems theory, which holds that a family unit reacts to external and internal forces by altering the structure to maintain the unit's stability. These changes affect styles of communication, assignment of roles, modes of dealing with conflict, and the delicate balance between caring for others and preserving a sense of personal identity. If stresses within the family are great, major alterations in the balance of forces are required to sustain family cohesion. At times the distortions in modes of relating are so great that either psychological or physiological symptoms appear in one or more family members. From the family systems viewpoint, symptoms tell us less about the individual who manifests them than about the dysfunctional family system. The symptomatic member is the "bearer" or "carrier" of the family psychopathology who, for some reason, is the fulcrum of stressful relationships within the family.

Minuchin's research likewise indicates that four characteristics common to families in which a child develops psychophysiological symptoms may contribute to the illness. Furthermore, these habits differentiate such families from normal ones and from those having other types of emotionally disturbed offspring. They are: (1) *enmeshment,* the involvement of all family members in the private and public activities of every other family member with poor boundary definition; (2) *overprotectiveness,* the tendency of family members to do too much for offspring and therefore to inhibit development of autonomy; (3) *rigidity,* a commitment to maintaining the status quo even when change and growth of offspring require new rules and ways of relating to each other; and (4) *lack of conflict resolution,* a tendency to avoid overtly acknowledging conflicts or attempts to resolve them.

Rigidity, overprotectiveness, and enmeshment combine to lower greatly these families' threshold for conflict, and, Minuchin believes, all four must be present to produce psychophysiological symptoms: "No one of these characteristics . . . seemed sufficient to spark and reinforce psychosomatic symptoms. But the cluster of transactional patterns was felt to be characteristic of a family process that encourages somatization."

From this point of view, enmeshment in one another's lives and thoughts, coupled with overprotectiveness, severely limits development of autonomy and self-confidence. The rigidity with which they are practiced in turn creates frustration, anger, and anxiety in offspring. These emotions cannot be defused because of the family's inability to acknowledge conflict or resolve differences. Consequently, the child resorts to somatic rather than psychological channels of expression.

Table 14.3. Psychophysiological disturbances and attitudes expressed by patients manifesting them

1. *Urticaria* (hives). Patients have image of themselves as mistreated and are preoccupied with what is happening to them, not with retaliation.
2. *Eczema*. Individuals feel that they are the object of outside interference or are somehow being prevented from doing something and cannot overcome the resulting frustration. They care more about the interference or the obstacle than about remedying the situation.
3. *Raynaud's disease* (cold hands). The individual wants to undertake hostile physical action but may not have any idea what the action should be.
4. *Asthma*. Patients are facing a situation that they would rather avoid or escape. The most important part of their attitude is their desire to have nothing to do with the situation at all and to deal with it by simply ignoring it.
5. *Hypertension*. Individuals feel that they must be constantly on guard and prepared to ward off the ever-present threat of danger.
6. *Duodenal ulcer*. Individuals are seeking revenge and wish to injure the person or thing that has injured them.

Source: W. J. Grace and D. T. Graham, "Relationship of specific attitudes and emotions to certain bodily diseases," *Psychosomatic Medicine,* 1952, 14, pp. 243–251; and D. T. Graham, J. D. Kabler, and F. K. Graham, "Physiological response to the suggestion of attitudes specific for hives and hypertension," *Psychosomatic Medicine,* 1962, 24, pp. 159–169.

Because attitudes and symptoms are correlated, it is difficult to know what comes first. Therefore, Graham and his colleagues undertook studies in which they experimentally induced discrete attitudes in normal subjects who were in a receptive state after hypnotic induction. In one study (Graham et al. 1966), they suggested two attitudes on different days, one of which was hypothesized to lead to urticaria (hives), the second to hypertension.

Hives suggestion: "You feel mistreated, unfairly treated, wrongly treated. There is nothing you can do about it, nothing you even want to do about it. You are only thinking of what happened to you. You just have to take it. You are the helpless, innocent victim of unfair, unjust treatment. Nobody should do a thing like that to you. That is the way you're feeling; that feeling gets stronger and stronger."

Hypertension suggestion: "We're going to do something to you; you have to be on your guard, prepared for whatever it is. It might be a burn, an electric shock, a needle stick. It's going to come; you just have to sit there and wait and try to be ready for whatever it is. You feel that you may be attacked and hurt at any instant; it may be painful, it may be dangerous. You feel that you are in danger. You're threatened every instant, you have to watch out."

The former attitude was expected to produce marked changes in skin temperature but not blood pressure; the hypertension suggestion was expected to have the opposite effect. Figure 14.7 shows the results of the two sessions. The hives suggestion effected a change in skin temperature (possibly a precursor of a skin rash), but the hypertension suggestion did not. And, as predicted, blood pressure was higher in response to the suggested hypertension attitude.

The attitudes suggested by Graham, in fact, may contribute to the development of disease states, but we must also consider the possibility that the situational variables outlined in the previous section contribute to a predisposing attitude. An air traffic controller in a situation that demands continuous vigilance, and in which mistakes can result in great criticism and harm, may develop an attitude very similar to the one Graham found in hypertensive patients. Possibly individuals living or working in situations that elevate blood pressure who develop hypertensive attitudes are particularly vulnerable to the development of essential hypertension; others in the same situation who develop other attitudes may be less so.

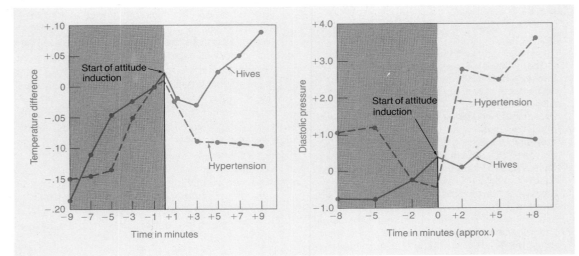

Fig. 14.7. Changes in skin temperature (left) and blood pressure (right) following the hypnotic induction of either the hives or the hypertension attitudes. (After Graham et al. 1962.)

PERSONALITY SPECIFICITY

The idea that some personality types are predisposed to different psychophysiological disorders is not new. Dunbar (1934, 1943) suggested a relationship between achievement-oriented perfectionism and the tendency toward migraine headaches. And psychoanalytic proponent Franz Alexander (1934) argued that a specific unresolved conflict is associated with each psychophysiological disorder. He suggested that ulcer patients suffer from unresolved dependency problems, which they cover over with a pattern of denial in which hyperindependence and autonomy are prominent. They expressed their denied dependency longings physiologically as a chronic "hunger," and literally secreted an excess of hydrochloric acid in the stomach, which ultimately ate away the stomach lining, giving them ulcers.

Although these theories are attractive and intuitively compelling, attempts to validate them empirically have not been fruitful nor have they supported the theory. Some current work, however, does find a relationship between a specific personality type and coronary heart disease. Using a basic dichotomy of the human personality, Freidman and Rosenman (1975) have shown that coronary heart disease is much more likely to occur in *type A personalities* than in *type B personalities* (see Table 14.4). Type A personalities are distinguished by excessive competitive drive, aggressiveness, impatience, and a worried sense of being under constant pressure of time. Notable free-floating hostility is ready to be triggered by any event perceived as irritating, such as waiting in line. The type A personality is defined as much by the way they look and behave in an interview as by what they say.

Type B personalities are more relaxed and do not show the pressured type A quality of life. They relax easily, play for fun, not to display superiority, are not hostile, and are more inter-

Table 14.4. Characteristic behaviors of Type A personality [handwritten: coronary heart disease more likely]

1. Speaks explosively, hurriedly, uses limited vocabulary. Impatient with discursive or slow speech in others.	7. Does not notice interesting or lovely things in the environment (would not stop to look at a beautiful scene).
2. Walks, eats, moves rapidly.	8. Is preoccupied with getting things (having) rather than becoming something worth *being*.
3. Gets impatient with the rate at which events occur, such as movement of traffic. Sets unnecessary deadlines.	9. Attempts to schedule more and more activities in less and less time.
4. Strives to do two or more things at once (such as drinking coffee while dictating letters).	10. Challenges other Type A persons aggressively.
5. Always strives to bring conversations around to preferred topics; often only pretends to listen to others.	11. Has nervous gestures such as fist-clenching, table-banging, or facial tics.
6. Feels guilty for relaxing. Very competitive in sports.	12. Attributes success to speed.
	13. Evaluates people by numbers, such as amount of sales, number of publications, or appendectomies performed.

Source: M. Friedman and R. H. Rosenman. *Type A behavior and your heart* (Greenwich, Conn.: Fawcett, 1975), pp. 100–102.

Stress in the Control Tower

The degree of stress under which air traffic controllers operate can be appreciated only during and after an air disaster like the one over San Diego on September 25, 1978. These excerpts from a newspaper account of the accident and a controller's reaction to it vividly convey the immediate stress and the more lasting effect.

Air traffic controllers high atop Lindbergh tower watched helplessly Sept. 25 as a Pacific Southwest Airlines jetliner nosedived to the earth killing 144 persons, documents released by the government showed Friday.

"What happened to PSA?" traffic tower coordinator Stephen Majoros asked fellow air traffic controller Alan Saville moments after the midair collision. Then the PSA pilot calmly said, "We're going down."

The six Federal Aviation Administration employees on duty that day looked out the tinted tower window when radio transmission indicated the commercial jet was in trouble.

None of them, according to statements filed with the FAA, could see the actual collision between a small Cessna 172 and the large jetliner.

But they intently watched the wounded jetliner roll to the right and dive into a densely populated neighborhood.

In an interview with The Times, Saville, 31,

the controller directing the ill-fated PSA at the time of the collision, said he had a feeling of helplessness as he watched the airliner fall to the ground.

There was nothing we could do," he said. "My heart was beating very fast. I couldn't sit still. My insides felt like they wouldn't slow down. I had great anxiety."

The crash occurred approximately three miles northeast of the airport, and the airliner struck the ground at 310 mph. The 135 persons on the jetliner were killed, plus a pilot and his student in the Cessna and seven persons on the ground.

At the time of the crash, air traffic controllers at Lindbergh were talking to the PSA. Controllers at San Diego Approach Control were in radio communication with the Cessna. . . .

"I have to live with the fact that I was the last person talking to this aircraft," he [Saville] said. "I don't know what that means. When all the facts are known and it's put into a report, I'm going to be in it. Where I'm going to be in it I don't know.

"In some way, shape or form, I was involved in the accident, and no matter what happens I will be involved in the accident."

Source: The Los Angeles Times, October 21, 1978.

[handwritten marginal notes, left side:] Some personality types are predisposed to certain psychophysiological disorders. Friedman + Rosenman — taxonomy of human personality. more likely in Type A than B. 8½ yrs after classification × heart attacks + fatal attacks recurrent + fatal attacks more common to A. not a direct relationship because they also found that type A also had high level of cholesterol + smoked more. may be a link w/ personality types + stressful situations. eg. Type A seeks out more stressful situations ∴ more attacks ∴ heart attacks

Fig. 14.8. Type A personalities are infuriated by waiting.

ested in enjoying life than proving their worth.

In a major longitudinal study, Friedman and Rosenman (1975) classified 3254 healthy males aged 39 to 59 in four categories: definite type A; type A tendencies; definite type B; and type B tendencies. Eight and a half years after classification, twice as many heart attacks had struck type A personalities as the type B group, and recurrent and fatal attacks were more common among type A's. From these results alone, however, we cannot assume that a direct relationship connects personality and coronary heart disease, because Friedman and Rosenman also found that the type A personalities had higher levels of serum cholesterol in the blood (despite similar diets) and smoke more cigarettes than type B personalities. Both of these factors greatly increase the risk for heart disease. Thus it may be that a relationship binds personality type and diet, drug use, and exercise patterns, all of which independently affect the health of the cardiovascular system. If so, the association between personality type and heart attack is indirect.

If personality type predisposes people to life habits that weaken the cardiovascular system, might it also relate to the way we respond to situational stress? In other words, might our reaction to stress be determined by personality type rather than the situation? Obviously, there is interplay between our psychological makeup and a stressful situation, just as there is a link between situational factors and attitudes. It is possible that type A individuals, who have strong ambition and competitiveness, seek out stressful environments. The stress in these environments could increase the likelihood of dietary, drug, and recreational patterns that weaken the cardiovascular system.

Biological Predisposition to Psychophysiological Disorders

Despite evidence that specific stressful environments, attitudes, or personalities help cause psychophysiological disorders, it appears that they are not sufficient to explain why a particular disorder strikes a specific person. There is strong evidence that we all are biologically programmed to react to stress in specific organ systems. It is as if we all have a weakest link that would break if we were exposed to sufficient stress.

That each of us has an individual pattern of physiological response for stress became clear from studies by Lacey (1967). Comparing individual patterns of response in different stressful situations, Lacey found that some individuals reacted repeatedly with cardiovascular changes and others exhibited prominent changes in skin resistance and minimal cardiovascular reactivity. No long-term studies have been done to find a relationship between a person's tendency to experience stress most acutely in a specific biological system and subsequent formation of illness. Nevertheless, it is an attractive hypothesis.

Studies of specific disorders do support the notion of a biological predisposition. A large factor in formation of peptic ulcers is excessive secretion and concentration of hydrochloric acid and pepsin in the lower part of stomach and duodenum.

Although we cannot directly measure amounts of these digestive juices, we can measure a derivative substance, serum pepsinogen, in the bloodstream. Peptic ulcer patients have high levels of it, and the evidence is strong that the concentration is genetically determined (Weiner et al. 1957) and that it varies widely among newborn babies. In a classic study, Weiner et al. (1957) predicted that the level of serum pepsinogen in healthy subjects would determine who would develop peptic ulcers when exposed to life stress. Thus, their model required both a specific biological predisposition *and* life stress for a psychophysiological disorder to develop. They measured serum pepsinogen levels in 2073 draftees at the time of induction into the armed services, on the hypothesis that basic training is a strong life stress for all men, but only those with high serum pepsinogen levels will subsequently develop peptic ulcers. They were right: *all* subjects who subsequently developed ulcers came from the high pepsinogen group.

Further support for the genetic theory of biological predisposition appears in the experimental breeding of "ulcerogenic" rats (Sines 1959; 1963). Sines was able to selectively breed a strain of rats that responded with stomach lesions 100 percent of the time to the stress of restricted movement. Similar studies suggest that serum pepsinogen level is a marker for ulcers in rats (Ader et al. 1960) just as it may be in human beings.

These studies and others also indicate a higher rate of cardiovascular disease (including both heart attack and hypertension), migraine headache, and ulcers among those who have a family history of these disorders. This predisposition strongly supports the stress-diathesis model we have described in Chapter 6. The model would describe psychophysiological disorders as a response to life stress, the incidence and form of which depend critically upon inborn biological dispositions (the diathesis).

Understanding Psychophysiological Disorders by Treating Them

As we have seen, research on efficacy of treatment can provide clues to the origins of a disorder as well as improved methods of intervention. In psychophysiological disorders, if we can reduce chronically high blood pressure, for instance, we will see more deeply what sustains the disorder. Holistic medicine, which has been gaining popularity in the prevention and treatment of disease, has given us some treatment techniques that promise better knowledge of how stress works in physical disorders.

Advocates of holistic medicine argue that it is as important to encourage emotional well-being as it is to treat physical symptoms of disease. They also support a preventive approach, training people to deal with inevitable life stress without becoming ill. Following the dictum that "it's mostly what you do hour by hour, day by day that determines how healthy you are, when you get sick, what you get sick with, and perhaps when you die," health workers have invented many techniques to help us alter our life styles.

Many total-health tenets are little more than clichés: "you should take life easier," "you should find a hobby to take your mind off your work," and so on. Some scientific efforts have been made, however, to translate this view into real programs. On the hypothesis that a state of relaxation is incompatible with the physiological hyperarousal believed to underlie psychophysiological disorders, Benson (1975) developed a systematic program for teaching people to relax. Strongly influenced by Eastern philosophies, which emphasize meditation, Benson incorporated their essence in a daily exercise routine designed to produce the *relaxation response*. His current method includes these steps:

1. Sit quietly in a comfortable position.
2. Close your eyes.
3. Deeply relax all your muscles, beginning at your feet and progressing to your face — keep them relaxed.
4. Breathe through your nose. Become aware of your breathing. As you breathe out, say the word "one" silently to yourself. For example, breathe In . . . Out, "one"; In . . . Out, "one"; etc. Breathe easily and naturally.
5. Continue for ten to twenty minutes. You may

open your eyes to check the time, but do not use an alarm. When you finish, sit quietly for several minutes, at first with your eyes closed and later with your eyes opened. Do not stand up for a few minutes.
6. Do not worry about whether you are successful in achieving a deep level of relaxation. Maintain a passive attitude and permit relaxation to occur at its own pace. When distracting thoughts occur, try to ignore them by not dwelling upon them, and return to repeating "one." With practice, the response should come with little effort. Practice the technique once or twice daily, but not within two hours after any meal, since the digestive processes seem to interfere with the elicitation of the Relaxation Response (Benson 1975, pp. 114–115).

Research (Benson et al. 1974) shows that twenty weeks of practice with this technique reduced blood pressure in fourteen hypertensive patients who were also on drug therapy and in twenty-two borderline cases of hypertension not receiving drugs. Apparently, meditation reduces blood pressure by inducing a general state of relaxation and reduced tension.

Biofeedback is another technique that has been used to control specific physiological systems. The principle is that many physiological dysfunctions are not readily perceived by higher mental centers (Schwartz 1977). The goal is to teach us awareness of our physiological states in order to control some of them.

One series of biofeedback studies (Shapiro et al. 1977) designed to train subjects to reduce their own blood pressure did so to reduce the risk of subsequent cardiac failure. During the training, borderline and essential hypertensive subjects wore a blood pressure cuff that constantly registered readings on a display screen. They were instructed to attempt to lower the readings. Researchers rewarded subjects when they succeeded in bringing down their own blood pressure. Of 7 patients who had essential

2) Biofeedback
- used to control specific physiological symptoms.
- the principle is that many physiological disfunctions are not readily perceived by the higher mental centres. to teach us awareness of our physiological states in order to control some of them.
- reward for lowering reading scale

5/7 = tie

∴ short term control over systolic press.
∴ less control over diastolic press.

Fig. 14.9. In one type of biofeedback program, patients with chronic headaches are taught to monitor blood flow in the periphery and in the head. By increasing peripheral blood flow and decreasing central blood flow, the pain of a vascular headache (such as migraine) can be reduced.

hypertension, 5 responded positively to the biofeedback treatment showing decreases in systolic blood pressure of 34, 29, 16, 16, and 17 mmHg with 33, 22, 34, 31, and 12 sessions of training. The training enabled both borderline and hypertensive individuals to achieve short-term control over systolic pressure (the force exerted on blood vessels in the contracted state) and less control over diastolic pressure (the force exerted on blood vessels in the expanded state). The long-term effects of this training are not yet well documented.

It is clear that biofeedback can be beneficial, but not whether it is more effective than training in general relaxation (Blanchard and Young 1974). Furthermore, it seems that biofeedback training may be futile unless it is part of a larger attempt to alter life style and methods of coping with stress. Witness this interesting case:

One of our hypertension patients . . . during the feedback sessions, was successful in lowering his pressure. Over the five daily sessions of a typical week, he might lower his pressure by 20 mmHg [millimeters of mercury, the standard measure of blood pressure], and thus earn a total of $35 [patients received monetary reward for successful performances]. However, we consistently noted that after the weekend he would enter the laboratory on Monday with elevated pressure again. In interviews, the problem became clear. After earning a sizable amount of money, the patient would go to the racetrack on the weekend, gamble, and invariably lose. The likelihood of teaching this patient to ''relax'' while at the racetrack through simple laboratory blood pressure feedback would seem slim, indicating there is a need to work on other aspects of the patient's behavior and personality which are related to high pressure (Schwartz 1973, p. 671).

Sexual Dysfunction

We have described different models for understanding the relationship between stress and psychophysiological disorders. Most of these disorders are diseases in the traditional sense because they involve severe distortions of normal physiological functioning or actual damage to tissue. Here we will consider problems in sexual functioning, in which psychophysiological dysfunction is obvious but which are not traditionally thought of as physical disorders or diseases. Stress and tension are, after all, important components of sexual dysfunction.

Most cases of sexual dysfunction show no sign that anything is organically wrong. The physiological apparatus is intact and capable of adequate sexual response. In the overwhelming majority of cases, psychological factors exert an inhibitory action over what is essentially series of reflexive acts (Kaplan 1974). Sexual dysfunction very often leads to other psychological problems that can totally disrupt a couple's relationship.

> Mr. C sought help for sexual impotence, which began five years ago on his wedding night. He had become sexually aroused in lovemaking with his bride but had been unable to maintain an erection and thus could not have intercourse. The condition persisted for the next three months, at which time his wife left him because of her sexual frustration (adapted from Goldstein and Palmer 1963, p. 95).

To complete heterosexual intercourse, two types of physiological changes are necessary. The normally flaccid penis of the male must achieve minimal erection and the female vagina must lubricate and expand enough to receive the erect penis. Physiologically, the erection response requires activation of the parasympathetic division of the autonomic nervous system (see Fig. 14.2). The parasympathetic nervous system regulates the normal activities of the body during states of relaxation. Conversely, activation of the sympathetic counterpart of the autonomic nervous system is a response to perceived threat or danger, and inhibits readiness for sexual intercourse.

Preparatory Phase

Activation of the parasympathetic nervous system produces sexual receptivity in male and females in a similar fashion by increasing the flow and concentration of blood in the sexual organs by *vasodilation.* Increased blood volume extends and firms the penis and is a precondition for expansion of the vagina and secretion of lubricating fluids necessary for intercourse. Ordinarily, vasodilation is a reflexive response to sexual stimulation. But when the sympathetic nervous system is aroused, this normal response cannot readily occur.

According to many writers (Kaplan 1974; Masters and Johnson 1970), it is valuable to separate disorders of this preparatory phase from difficulties in achieving orgasm. These are disorders of preparation:

1. *Primary impotence.* The male has *never* been able to maintain an erection sufficient to accomplish the act of intercourse.

2. *Secondary impotence.* The man currently cannot achieve or maintain an erection but previously has succeeded at sexual intercourse at least once. Usually he has a number of successful entries before the impotence occurs. Sometimes it occurs only with specific partners (such as his wife).

3. *Inhibited sexual excitement.* Kaplan finds a parallel for preparatory sexual dysfunction in the female, although the consequences are less drastic. The *DSM*-III describes this pattern as partial or complete failure to obtain or maintain the lubrication and swelling of the vaginal cavity until the sexual act is completed.

[handwritten marginalia at top: "— the ejaculator reflex is governed by the sympathetic system."]

4. *Vaginismus*. An involuntary tightening or spasm that occurs in the outer third of the vagina, vaginismus can be so painful as to preclude intercourse. The muscle groups contract spastically rather than rhythmically as in orgasm. The tightening is a completely involuntary reflex stimulated by imagined, anticipated, or real attempts at vaginal penetration. Vaginismus has numerous parallels in failure of erection in the male.

[handwritten in margin: phase 11]

Coital Culmination
[handwritten: preparatory capable but no orgasm]

Some individuals are capable of the necessary preparatory responses for sexual intercourse, but are unable to achieve sexual satisfaction through orgasm. From the careful physiological research of Masters and Johnson (1970), we now know that the physiological response of orgasm involves similar mechanisms in males and females. Rhythmic contractions recur every .8 second in the muscles surrounding penis or vagina. In males, this rhythmic vibration is accompanied by ejaculation of seminal fluid. A noticeable refractory period follows male orgasm, during which no other ejaculations are possible. Females, however, are capable of multiple orgasms and experience little or no refractory period.

In contrast to erection, the ejaculatory reflex is governed by the sympathetic division of the autonomic nervous system. The same is believed true for female orgasm, although the evidence is not yet conclusive. Problems associated with successful orgasm are:

1. *Premature ejaculation*. The male ejaculates either before penetrating the vagina or soon after. Reasonable control of ejaculation and orgasm during sexual activity is persistently absent. It is a problem more often defined by the females (who fail to achieve orgasm because the act is so brief) than by the males, and, possibly for this reason, Masters and Johnson describe this dysfunctional pattern as "inability to delay ejaculation long enough for the woman to have orgasm 50 percent of the time."

2. *Ejaculatory incompetence*. The male can achieve erection and engage in intercourse but cannot achieve orgasm while inside the female.

3. *Primary orgasmic dysfunction*. The woman has never had an orgasm by any method.

4. *Situational orgasmic dysfunction*. The woman is able to have orgasm only under specific conditions and at specific times. She may be able to masturbate to orgasm but may not be able to achieve it in intercourse; or she may be able to have orgasm only on special occasions (vacations or special settings), or with special partners (as with sadistic males).

[handwritten: Freud — unconsciously perceived as dangerous]

Origins of Sexual Dysfunction

Numerous hypotheses on the causes of sexual dysfunction have come from the psychoanalytic treatment of dysfunctional individuals. Freud (1938) hypothesized that inhibitions to sexual activity arise because it is unconsciously perceived as dangerous. Thus, he believed that inhibition of sexual activity is a defense against engaging in the feared activity. Because he believed that the oedipal conflict is the origin of all anxiety and personality disorders, he felt that all sex dysfunction derives from failure to resolve it. Impotent males find it safer to avoid intercourse with females who may symbolically represent their mother, and nonorgasmic females, fearing erotic attachment to father, permit intercourse but resolve their conflict by denying themselves the pleasure of orgasm. Essentially, then, the Freudian theory of sexual dysfunction is similar to psychoanalytic theories on the origin of disorders in which psychological symptoms of anxiety are prominent (see Chapter 13). A limitation of the Freudian view is that it does not explain why one individual experiences anxiety without sexual dysfunction and another has no general anxiety symptoms but a highly specific anxiety response to sexual arousal.

In a remarkable fifteen-year program of research on many sexually dysfunctional individuals, Masters and Johnson (1970) compiled evidence suggesting that the Freudian view may be accurate for some individuals, but that the routes to disorders of sexual life are diverse. They suggest that sexual dysfunction has two components: an immediate attitude that interferes with sexual activity, and a developmental history inimical to healthy and positive attitudes toward one's own body, sex in general, and the opposite sex. A vital part of their theory is *performance anxiety,* a preoccupation with performing adequately as a sex partner, which arouses the sympathetic nervous system, inhibiting the body's normal reflexive responses to sexual stimulation.

Performance anxiety begets more performance anxiety, as fears of not performing lead to sexual failure, which, in turn, increases the level of performance anxiety. As a result of this anxiety, the man or woman cannot behave naturally during sexual contact but instead adopts a *spectator attitude,* critically observing performance rather than participating in the lovemaking act without self-consciousness.

The second tenet of Masters and Johnson's theory is that developmental experiences lay the groundwork for performance anxiety in adulthood. In their research, Masters and Johnson found some histories of traumatic fear conditioning in which the first adolescent experience with sex had devastating consequences. "One single thirty-one-year-old male had been surprised by police in a local 'lover's lane' while being manipulated to ejaculation by a young woman. The girl's terror and his overwhelming fear of embarrassment and public exposure left an indelible residual. . . . Since he

was on the verge of ejaculating when surprised, he thereafter was frozen by fear of observation when a similar level of excitation developed" (Masters and Johnson 1970, p. 124).

Many cases reported by Masters and Johnson reveal that the people who had traumatic experiences had been predisposed to negative sexual attitudes because of inadequate or erroneous sexual education or counseling, negative attitudes toward sexuality based upon orthodox religious beliefs, or problems with gender identity involving conscious or unconscious desires for sexual relations with same-sex partners.

How diverse are the development factors that might contribute to sexual dysfunction? Three out of thirty-two men whom Masters and Johnson treated for primary impotence disclosed in their interviews that they had seductive mothers. Each would have fit the Freudian notion of unresolved oedipal conflict, for the boy slept in his mother's bedroom at least through puberty, and although he and his mother had no intercourse, their relationship involved strong erotic features. The father in these families was absent or ineffective. Six of the same group of men came from families with the strong religious belief that sex is sinful. Curiously, these men had married women with similar backgrounds, five of whom had vaginismus. Four other men had humiliating experiences with prostitutes. No two of the remaining nineteen impotent men reported similar histories in beliefs, family background, or trauma. All shared a sense of threat associated with heterosexual activity.

Effect of Sexual Dysfunction on Relationships

Difficulties in the preparatory and orgasmic phase of sexual relationships profoundly affect the self-concept of the dysfunctional individual. Humiliated and hounded by a sense of inade-

Fig. 14.10. Difficulties in sexual performance can have a destructive effect upon a couple's interpersonal relationship as well.

quacy, individuals with sexual dysfunction often experience declining self-esteem.

Each night I would lie in bed and wonder if my wife expected me to make love to her. I would think — "Can I do it?" Thoughts of other nights when I lost my erection before entering her recurred and how frustrated she was bothered the hell out of me. And then it happened, my erection started to go down and I thought, "I can't do it! I'm going to fail her again." The next morning neither of us would talk about what happened but I felt rather inadequate and I knew she was disappointed and frustrated.

The consequences of sexual dysfunction are disturbing not only to dysfunctional individuals but also to their partners, and the results are not simply physiological. Witness the comments of the spouse of the man quoted above:

I lie in bed and wonder if he's ever going to approach me. Maybe he wants me to start things going — but maybe that'll frighten him and cause him to lose his erection. I wonder — don't I turn him on — is that it and he can't tell me outright? Or is there something wrong with my technique — maybe there's something he'd like me to do and can't ask. I'm not much of a sex partner, I guess.

Continued sexual failures cause a relationship to deteriorate. Each partner blames the other, and mutual devaluation and emotional withdrawal soon follow. For this reason most programs of therapy for sexual dysfunction involve couples whenever possible. Establishing sexual trust and gratification requires participation by both partners who have shared the pain of prior failures, as we will see again in Chapter 15.

Summary

1. The three types of emotion-linked physical ailments are: short-term physiological changes, long-term changes in physiological functioning, and actual damage to organs of the body.

2. Psychophysiological disorders are defined as physical illness that is attributable, at least in part, to sustained stress.

3. The two types of stress theory are the nonspecific and the specific. Hans Selye's research on nonspecific stress theories suggests that, following exposure to different stressors, a three-stage physiological reaction, the general adaptation syndrome, occurs. It consists of: (1) alarm, in which the autonomic nervous system mobilizes the body for defense; (2) resistance, in which the local defense mechanisms have completely taken over and the organism has adapted physiologically to a stressful life style; and (3) exhaustion, resulting from prolonged exposure to stress or introduction of new stressors. At this stage, psychophysiological disorders may develop because continued stress has overworked the body's defensive response systems. Positive and negative life changes, such as marriage or the death of a loved one, are considered stressful events that may bring on illness in some individuals.

4. DeLong classified styles of coping with stress into three groups: (1) copers, who were alert to stressful stimuli; (2) avoiders, who denied or minimized the threat; and (3) nonspecific defenders, who shifted between the other two styles depending on the situation. Coping style predicted immediate and long-term response to a realistic life stress of surgery.

5. Specific theories of life stress can be divided into three categories: (1) situational specificity, suggesting that such diseases as hypertension and ulcers may be linked to stressful situations in which outcome is uncertain, fight or flight is inappropriate, and vigilance must be constant; (2) attitudinal specificity, suggesting that psychophysiological disorders may result from the way a person perceives his own position in a situation and what action, if any, he decides to take; and (3) personality specificity, proposing that some personality types are predisposed to different psychophysiological disorders. Type A personalities, who are highly competitive and ambitious, are at greater risk for heart attack than type B personalities, who are more easygoing.

6. There is strong evidence that individuals are biologically programmed to react to stress in specific organ systems.

7. Advocates of holistic medicine believe it is important to encourage the emotional well-being of the patient as well as to treat the physical symptoms of disease. Two programs designed to help individuals deal with stress teach: the relaxation response, a daily exercise routine intended to promote relaxation and reduce tension; and biofeedback, a technique for increasing awareness of physiological states and learning to control some of them.

8. Stress and tension are vital components of sexual dysfunction because the physiological reactions to threat inhibit sexual response.

9. Hypotheses about the causes of sexual dysfunction include: (1) Freud's theory that sexual dysfunction derives from the individual's failure to resolve the oedipal conflict; and (2) Masters and Johnson's conclusion that sexual dysfunction has two components — an immediate attitude that interferes with sexual activity, performance anxiety, and a developmental history that instills negative and unhealthy attitudes about one's body, sex in general, and the opposite sex.

10. Sexual dysfunction in the preparatory or orgasmic phase of intercourse has deleterious effects on both the afflicted individual and his relationship with his partner. Therefore, therapy programs involve both partners whenever possible.

[Handwritten annotations:]

sympathetic → threat
- ejaculation
parasympathetic - erection
- relaxation
1) Preparatory Phase
2) Coital Culmination

Black:
Weiss
ulcers - unpredictability
+ uncontrollability
specific attributes of ulcers
∴ situations may increase or decrease the likelihood of a certain disease
- may not be the unique cause

→ induced attitudes through hypnosis
that produced symptoms correlated to the attitudes
∴ attitudes come first

∴ may contribute to development of disease but have to consider situational too

Minuchin → linked to disorders
- family systems theory
1/ enmeshment
2/ overprotectiveness
3/ rigidity
4/ lack of conflict resolution

1) comparing individual patterns of physiological response to different stressful sit.
2) ulcers
ulcer patients have high levels of serum pepsinogen in bloodstream - evidence genetic
Weiner - predicted the formation of ulcers in warriors
3) breeding of "ulcerogenic" rats (hereditary evidence)
4) inborn biological dispositions

Selye
Holmes + Rahe
LAZARUS
DELONG
WEISS
GRAHAM
Minuchin
FRIEDMAN + ROSENMAN
reaction to specific stress in specific organ LACEY
WEINER
relaxation BENSON

Chapter 15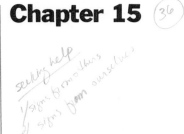

Intervention in Anxiety and Psychophysiological Disorders

Nonspecific Features of Psychological Therapies

Psychoanalytic Approach
Client-Therapist Relationship
The Psychoanalytic Therapist
Transference
Dream Interpretation
Extensions of the Psychoanalytic Model — Groups and
    Families

Existential-Humanistic Approaches
The Inner Experience
Client's Responsibility for Change
The Humanistic-Existential Therapist
Client-Centered Therapy
Gestalt Therapy

Behavior Therapy
Behavioral Assessment of Anxiety Disorders
Anxiety Reduction Techniques

Effectiveness of Psychological Therapies
Effects of Different Therapies
Specific Therapies for Specific Problems

Preventing Anxiety Disorders

Summary

We all have remarkable ability to tolerate pain and discomfort. But ultimately, the suffering that an anxiety disorder may burden us with is too much to bear. The crippling symptoms; painful feelings of dependence or inferiority; inability to work effectively; overwhelming sense of futility, guilt, or inadequacy; or fear of death from progressive tissue damage in psychophysiological disorders may motivate people to seek relief from mental health professionals. Most often, the decision to seek help is driven by many things, including advice from friends and loved ones and, frequently, by self-observations that our own behavior or emotions are inappropriate to our situation. "I know I shouldn't feel or act this way, but I just can't help it," has been expressed by almost every person seeking professional assistance. This is the paradox that so disturbs us. Part of us, the thinking part, recognizes the inappropriate feelings or actions, but recognition is not enough to change our behavior.

Two general classes of intervention are now available to deal with anxiety: psychological and pharmacological. With psychological approaches we attempt to assist the anxiety-ridden to modify their behavior by creating optimal conditions for change in behavior in a client-professional relationship. This modification requires us to rely upon words, symbols, and actions as the media for clarifying problems and organizing programs for coping with them. Pharmacological therapies apply some active chemical substance to relieve a primary symptom in a behavior pattern such as anxiety or depression. In our nation of pill-takers, tranquilizers are one of the drugs most prescribed (Kornetsky 1976). We have no firm figures on

preferred treatments, but it is very likely that more people seek help for anxiety from chemical than from psychological agents. Many who go for help to general physicians or internists for excessive anxiety will receive a prescription for one of the compounds in the group *benzodiazepines,* which include *Valium* and *Librium.*

Controlled studies indicate that these drugs are effective in reducing anxiety (Kornetsky 1976). In fact, they are so widely used that Valium is the most prescribed medication in the United States. However effective these drugs

Fig. 15.1.

Drawing by H. Martin; © 1975 The New Yorker Magazine, Inc.

may be, they are a major hazard in the form of dependence on drugs. Not only can we become physiologically dependent on them, but they trigger characteristic withdrawal symptoms when we stop using them.

Although these drugs are effective in short-run reduction of anxiety, they do not appear to be a viable, lasting way of reducing anxiety symptoms and altering life styles. The question is, can these antianxiety agents supplement psychological therapy? Few controlled studies have been done on this issue. Antianxiety agents such as Valium and Librium are rarely used regularly; instead they are used during periods of crisis and not between stressful periods. The few studies in which effects of regular use in psychotherapy have been examined (Hollon and Beck 1978) indicate that such drugs did not contribute substantially to the psychotherapeutic program. Therefore, we will concentrate on psychological therapies.

Nonspecific Features of Psychological Therapies

Most theories about how anxiety and psychophysiological disorders develop (see Chapter 13) emphasize faulty learning. Similarly, all psychological approaches to modifying anxiety-linked behavior operate on the premise that with the proper conditions, relearning can take place and will reduce the likelihood of future breakdowns. To assist in the relearning, all psychological therapists follow certain guidelines.

1. The therapy relationship is an emotionally charged, professional one. It involves an expert offering a service to someone who needs it, and receiving a salary or fee.

2. The client, seeking the help of an expert in the ways in which human problems arise, has great faith and trust in the therapist.

3. The therapist continuously provides support, encouragement, and hope for a better life.

4. The therapist models patterns of behavior that can facilitate personal growth. These may be personal integrity, refusal to be panicked by the client's symptoms, trust of others, knowledge of techniques for managing anxiety, and the like, which help the client try out new patterns of behavior.

5. The client's needs take precedence over those of the therapist. Thus, therapists do not use the relationship to exploit clients or meet their own needs for adulation, affection, power, or sexuality.

6. All therapies are attempts to reduce excessive anxiety by encouraging the client to confront fears and self-doubts (adapted from Frank 1974; Korchin 1976, and Marmor 1962).

These core elements are sometimes called *nonspecific features* of psychological therapies. A continuing debate questions whether it is these nonspecific aspects of the therapeutic relationship which primarily account for the changes observed, or the specific techniques therapists believe themselves to be using. Many ingenious research studies have been designed (see Chapter 4 for general design issues, and Gottman and Markman 1978) to separate the specific and nonspecific effects of an intervention program for anxiety disorders, and we will examine some of the results later on.

Despite these common features, the literature on treatment reveals an incredible number of "therapies" for anxiety disorders. It seems we have as many schools of therapy as therapists. The different approaches to treatment reflect theoretical disagreement over the ways in which these disorders develop. They differ in emphasizing *what* is learned and the *degree* to which the learning involves overt or covert behaviors, such as wishes, fantasies, and defense mechanisms. Consequently, they disagree on

Alexander
- corrective emotional experience
- past anxieties can be confronted
+ strong blocked emotions will be reexperienced before meaningful relearning is possible

- all psychoanalytic therapies rely on conflict-defense model of anxiety disorders + structural & developmental components

what is to be relearned and how relearning occurs and can be facilitated. To minimize confusion, we will discuss the three major therapeutic schools and their subgroups: (1) psychoanalytic, (2) humanistic-existential, and (3) behavioral (Korchin 1976).

Although we recognize three distinct schools, two are more closely related (psychoanalytic and existential) than both are to the third, because they emphasize *insight* as a *necessary* condition for relief of symptoms and change in behavior. Insight is newly achieved awareness of previously unacknowledged, repetitive patterns of behavior and the links to past experience, particularly with significant family members. Behavioral therapies, as we shall see, deny that insight is a significant goal in therapeutic intervention. Although psychoanalytic and existential therapies put more weight on insight, they differ, as we shall see, in (1) the types of insight considered critical, (2) techniques for stimulating insight, and (3) the type of therapist-client relationship appropriate to this goal.

attempt to weaken defensive operations so that the patient will be more aware of conflicting feelings + examine the dangers of the past illumined by current reality

Psychoanalytic Approach

Treatments of anxiety disorders by psychoanalysis grow out of the clinical investigations Sigmund Freud (1912) began late in the nineteenth century (see Chapter 2). The model of psychoanalytic therapy began in relatively simple form with anxiety-laden thoughts and feelings derived from early childhood conflicts translated from an unconscious to a conscious state of awareness. As Freud and his followers treated more patients, they saw clearly that this type of cognitive insight into the links between warded-off past and current neurotic anxieties was not sufficient to produce meaningful change in feelings and behavior. Consequently

therapists sought a new goal: producing a condition that psychoanalyst Franz Alexander (1946) named *corrective emotional experience*, in which past anxieties can be confronted and strong, blocked emotions will be reexperienced before meaningful relearning is possible. Psychoanalysis originally was a highly specialized form of treatment in which clients were seen frequently (four or five times a week), and which followed the basic rule of free association. While lying on a couch, the patient was to say every thought that came to mind, no matter how embarrassing or disturbing the thought. Because traditional psychoanalysis is enormously expensive, and evidence is lacking that this form is more effective than intensive application of psychoanalytic principles, few patients today receive this traditional form of therapy. Most psychoanalytic therapists today apply techniques of intervention derived from Freudian theory but much modified by four decades of experience.

Today no one pattern of psychoanalytic therapy is standard for anxiety and psychophysiological disorders. All psychoanalytic therapists, however, appear to rely on the *conflict-defense model* of anxiety disorders (see Chapter 13 for a description). This model has structural and developmental components. All modern psychoanalytic therapies rely upon the structural model, in one form or another. Their supporters assume that intense, often unrecognized inner conflicts produce anxiety. Defense mechanisms and patterns of personality partially reduce this anxiety. Symptoms appear when these defenses no longer prevent forbidden thoughts or desires from reaching awareness.

The psychoanalytic therapist attempts to weaken the defensive operations so that the patient will be more aware of conflicting feelings and examine the dangers of the past illumined by current reality. Relief from symptoms or rigid personality disorders will occur when the patient no longer needs to ward off significant parts of the self and to fear inner desires. This goal, described by Freud as "Where id was, Ego shall be," replaces primitive, taboo desires (the Id in Freudian theory) with the more mature and integrated self (the Ego).

All psychoanalytic therapists recognize the etiological or causative effect of early experiences — particularly within the family — in anxiety, but some differ about the need to link awareness of current conflict to specific roots in childhood. They differ in how they apply the developmental component of psychoanalytic theory. Freud and his followers believed that relief from current difficulties can occur only after we have recovered memories of early childhood that explain the origins of our exaggerated fears. We can then appreciate how inappropriate these childish fears are to our adult status. This freedom from the past will make way for new, more mature behavior. A number of writers, however (Horney 1965; Perls 1970), have questioned the value of exploring and extracting childhood memories to produce therapeutic change. Awareness of crippling defense mechanisms and conflicts is a sufficient condition, they argue, for modifying ultimate behavior patterns. Psychoanalytic therapists still disagree strongly and no well-done research has helped resolve the issue.

Client-Therapist Relationship

Psychoanalytic therapy requires self-exploration, which is often painful. The client must examine old ways and habits that are known and reasonably secure, in order to reach uncharted ground. Therefore, the psychoanalytic model is designed to form a *working alliance* between therapist and client. They need to develop mutual trust and the client must be willing to confront forbidding parts of the self. Powerful resistances always keep the alliance rather tenuous. On the one hand, the anxiety-disordered person is compulsively driven by conflicting forces (unacknowledged needs, distrust of

help, hopelessness, and self-defeat) and frequently cannot see himself or his problems with detachment. Yet, on the other hand, in more rational moments, he has hope, however vague, for a better life and greater personal creativity. Throughout psychoanalytic therapy, holding onto "sameness" and wanting change battle incessantly.

The Psychoanalytic Therapist

Psychoanalytic therapists facilitate self-exploration (1) by encouraging patients to examine their experience and (2) by recognizing, integrating, and clarifying the patient's feelings and remarks. If you were the client, what would be expected of you in a therapy session? You would describe when you feel happy, when you feel distressed, and in which circumstances you experience problems or relief. You might talk about your family, friends, work, hobby, or recreational interests. The therapist will make occasional comments or ask questions designed to get you to take a closer look at your own assumptions about events and your emotional reactions to them. The therapist's comments are designed to break up narrow and overly rigid ways of construing disturbing life events, as in these examples:

Client: Every time I begin a course of study, I'm really turned on and excited, but about halfway through, I just lose interest and stop working. I can't understand what happens to my enthusiasm.

Therapist: Is it always like that, or was there some time when you could finish a course?

Client: Well, yes, there was one year when I finished every course and could stay interested right through to the end. That was three years ago.

Therapist: Tell me about that year, how things were different and how you felt then.

Client: I don't know what it is, but I'm always very nervous around my professors. But, particularly around Prof. Smith. I know my stuff, but when he asks me any question, I stammer and stutter and make a damn fool of myself. I feel so stupid and incompetent.

Therapist: Tell me about Prof. Smith, what's he like and what might he do that makes you feel so uncomfortable?

Client: Well, whenever he asks a question, he looks me straight in the eye and keeps staring at me until I answer.

Therapist: And how does that make you feel?

Notice that the therapist's questions encourage both of these clients to probe deeper into themselves. The therapist tried to help the first patient avoid a tendency toward overgeneralizing about events in order to search out critical differences between times when the student could and could not function. The second client was led to describe a particularly threatening authority figure in detail to evoke the specific feelings he aroused.

Psychoanalytic therapists sometimes direct patients to address topics that they appear to consistently avoid. In psychoanalytic therapy with Shirley K., who was overwhelmed with obsessive thoughts that she would harm her infant son (see Chapter 13), the therapist noticed that Shirley talked about her son to the exclusion of all other relationships. He commented, "You talk a great deal about your son Saul, but you've never talked about your husband or how your marriage is going." This observation started an intense outpouring of feelings of frustration and resentment about her marriage that immediately furthered Shirley's self-exploration.

Clients must be brought to understand that current problems are not new but have a consistent history. They are helped to explore links between present and past difficulties: "Was it always this way?" "Can you remember a time when you felt or behaved differently?" "You've mentioned that Prof. Smith is a very intimidating figure; can you search for anyone else in your earlier life who made you feel the same way?" Each probe is designed to stimulate a broader

Fig. 15.2.

"I hereby dub thee, officially and forevermore, grown up."

Drawing by W. Miller; © 1978 The New Yorker Magazine, Inc.

attitude toward current problems and a sense of connection with the past. Because so many anxious people feel their behavior is irrational (they often call it ''crazy''), this sense of connection is effective in reducing anxiety. It makes the irrational more comprehensible and reasonable.

As psychoanalytic therapy proceeds, themes begin to recur in the client's reports and complaints. The therapist generally listens, but may attempt to accelerate self-discovery by offering interpretive comments to nudge the client into recognizing some important feeling or meaning that lies close to awareness. Sometimes the therapist's statements are merely reflective.

Client: I couldn't get anything accomplished this weekend just thinking and worrying about all the things that could go wrong next year.
Therapist: It sounds like your anxiety about the future makes it hard for you to live in the present.

The therapist will also try to help the client see disordered life style patterns that she herself has described but has not summarized: ''It seems that whenever you get close to a man whom you like . . . as soon as he shows that he cares for you as well, you no longer want him anymore.'' Or the therapist interprets a discrepancy between verbal and nonverbal expressions of feelings: ''You say you like Jim, but every time you talk of him you get a tense look on your face and start moving about uncomfortably in your chair''; ''You tell me how much you love your wife, but all you talk about are her faults.''

The most inferential style of interpretation typically is used only in the later stages of therapy, after the client has greater self-awareness and has explored problems more deeply. These interpretations, many of them derived from Freudian theory, are aimed at clarifying the relationship between past and present events.

These are samples of this ''deeper'' interpretation: ''Possibly, your inability to have sexual feelings toward your wife relates to the fact that she resembles your mother in so many ways?'' ''It sounds as if your tendency to snatch defeat from the jaws of victory has something to do with your feelings about your brother, who always did better than you in everything and left you feeling that you could never beat him in anything. You're still involved in that competition now and in making sure that you lose.''

Naturally, these deeper interpretations about early relationships are more likely to be used by psychoanalytic therapists who feel it is vital to connect current life problems with their specific developmental roots.

Transference

A vital element in psychoanalytic therapy of anxiety disorders is the focus upon the relationship between therapist and client. Freud noticed early in his exploratory work that patients attributed qualities to him, both positive and negative, which were both exaggerated and apparently unrelated to his behavior. He called these attributions *transference,* because he believed that these attitudes and feelings were in fact derived from feelings about significant figures in childhood and only transferred or projected onto him. Psychoanalytic therapists invited transference because they minimized self-disclosure, providing a ''blank screen'' upon which clients could project their feelings and attitudes. If the client could become aware, within the therapeutic relationship, that she often transferred irrational feelings, attitudes, and expectations, she could then see how similar projections probably disrupted current relationships outside of therapy. The therapeutic relationship was now used as a *microcosm* or miniature version of the client's interpersonal attitudes and behaviors.

Psychoanalytic treatment of Barbara Y's

the therapeutic goal in transactional analysis is to recognize the unconscious games so that we will be able to see that our fate is under our own control more than we realize

a naturalistic studies support the value of encouraging & interpretive transference relationships: outcome in both better when therapist + patient were able to use transference data to link unresolved conflicts with parental figures

Kernberg found resolution of transference was critical for successful therapy with borderline syndrome patients.

(they are more dependent on past projections than current reality)

Psychoanalytic Approach 357

fugue reaction (described in Chapter 13) illustrates how transference is manifested in the therapeutic relationship.

During the ensuing two and a half years, Barbara was seen in outpatient psychotherapy interviews three times weekly. At first, she was quite loquacious, reciting much of her history. She attributed much of her problem to the fact that she was "Daddy's little girl," who had never grown up. During therapy, she began to dress in a more adult fashion, using more cosmetics and wearing revealing blouses that emphasized her shapely figure. Her walk and mannerisms became very seductive. She made many slips of speech, particularly referring to her husband as her father and vice versa. Once she slipped and said "daddy" instead of "doctor" when addressing the therapist. When these slips were called to her attention and it was suggested that she confused her husband, father, and therapist, she would smile sweetly, remain silent, or attempt to make a joke of it. Several months later, after repeated interpretations of this sort, she reported that sexual relations with her husband had improved markedly (Goldstein and Palmer 1975, p. 194).

Most psychoanalytic therapists today rely heavily on client-therapist behavior as a clue to the significant but unrecognized attitudes and feelings that people carry about. Traditional psychoanalytic therapists do interpret transference as one part of therapy, but recent offshoots of the psychoanalytic movement rely on it almost entirely. In transactional analysis (Berne 1964; Harris 1967), these neurotic attitudes and feelings are called "games," in that people project unacknowledged expectations on others and then relate to them following these expectations. Interpersonal relationships are not based on actual transactions with others but are pre-scripted "games" set up by the conflicted person with inevitable outcomes unaffected by others' attempts to modify the script. The therapeutic goal in transactional

analysis is to recognize these unconscious games so that we will be able to see that our fate is under our own control more than we realized: if we are chronically rejected, we recognize that we set ourselves up for rejection; supposedly weak, we recognize that we powerfully control others.

Although no one has systematically studied how effective the different components of psychoanalytic therapy are, two naturalistic studies (see Chapter 4) support the positive value of encouraging and interpreting transference relationships (Kernberg et al. 1972; Malan 1976 a, b). In both studies, outcomes were better when therapist and patient were able to use transference data to link unresolved conflicts with parental figures. Interestingly, Kernberg found that resolution of transference feelings was particularly critical for successful therapy with borderline-syndrome patients. This is not surprising when you recall that descriptions of the interpersonal behavior of such patients (see Chapter 13) suggest it is frequently based more on past projections than current reality.

Dream Interpretation

In his earliest investigations, Freud observed that clients who could not verbalize inner conflicts clearly were able to express them in condensed form in dreams (Freud 1953). If the therapist could find the key to the symbolic language of a client's dreams, client and therapist could learn a great deal about current anxieties and their childhood antecedents.

How does the therapist break the dream code? Freud relied on *free association,* asking the client to mention whatever came to mind, when he thought about each part of the dream. Often the client saw no relationship between his associations and the dream itself, but Freud found that even thoughts that seemed most remote clarified elements of the dream (see Chapter 2 for Freud's own description). Dreams

(margin notes: condensed form of inner conflicts — symbolic language. to break the dream code, Freud relied on free association. today, still used in psychotherapy, but few consider them central to the problem.)

Psychoanalytic dream interpretation depends on the search for meanings, alternative to those implied by the dream's obvious structure.

are still used in psychoanalytic therapy, although few consider them as central to the process of self-discovery as they once were. Dreams that are particularly upsetting, dramatic, or meaningful to the client are, however, used to accelerate insight. Notice in this case how the therapist encourages the patient to associate to his own dream and uses his associations as well to formulate a hypothesis about the client's core conflict and its roots in childhood emotions and perceptions of his parents. Notice, too, that the therapist uses interpretation to suggest the underlying conflict; we can see that the patient resists this interpretation and also his subsequent behavior.

Mr. N. reports a fragment of a dream. All he can remember is that he is waiting for a red traffic light to change when he feels that someone has bumped into him from behind. He rushes out in fury and finds out, with relief, it was only a boy on a bicycle. There was no damage to his car. The associations led to Mr. N.'s love of cars, especially sports cars. He loved the sensation, in particular, of whizzing by those fat old expensive cars. The expensive cars seem so sturdy, but they fall apart in a few years. The little sports car of his can outrun, outclimb, outlast the Cadillacs, the Lincolns, and the Rolls Royces. He knows this is an exaggeration, but he likes to think so. It tickles him. This must be a carry-over from his athletic days when he loved to be the underdog who defeated the favorite. His father was a sports fan who always belittled my patient's achievements. His father always hinted that he had been a great athlete, but he never substantiated it. He was an exhibitionist, but Mr. N. doubted whether his father really could perform. His father would flirt with a waitress in a café or make sexual remarks about women passing by, but he seemed to be showing off. If he were really sexual, he wouldn't resort to that.

It is clear that the patient's material concerns comparing himself with his father in terms of sexual ability. It also deals with people who pretend to be what they are not. The strongest affect in his

associations was the moment when he said he was "tickled" by the fantasy of beating out the big cars. He knew this was a distortion, but he liked imagining it. In the dream his fury changes to relief when he discovers he has been bumped by "only a boy on a bicycle." It seemed to me that these two affect-laden elements must contain the key to the meaning of the dream and the analytic hour.

I interpreted to *myself* that the boy on the bicycle means a boy masturbating. The red light probably refers to prostitution since "red-light district" is a common term for those areas where prostitutes congregate. I knew my patient claimed to love his wife but preferred sex with prostitutes. Up until this point in the analysis the patient had no memories concerning the sexual life of his parents. However, he often mentioned his father's flirtations with waitresses, which I took to be screen memories. I therefore felt that I would point my interpretation in the direction of his adult attitude of superiority versus his childhood concern with the sexual life of his father. (I deliberately neglected, for the time being, all the references to bumping, behind, anger, etc.)

I said to Mr. N. toward the end of the hour that I felt he was struggling with his feelings about his father's sexual life. He seemed to be saying his father was sexually not a very potent man, but I wondered if he had always thought so. The patient responded rather quickly, in fact, a bit too quickly. In essence he was in haste to agree that his father always seemed to him to be arrogant, boastful, and pretentious. He didn't know what his sex life was like with his mother, but he is quite sure it couldn't have been very satisfactory. His mother was sickly and unhappy. She spent most of her life complaining to him about his father. Mr. N. was quite sure his mother disliked sex, although he couldn't prove it.

I intervened at this point and said that I supposed the idea that his mother rejected sex with his father tickled him. The patient said that it didn't tickle him, but he had to admit it gave him a sense of satisfaction, a sense of triumph over the "old boy." In fact, he now recalls finding some "girlie magazines" (magazines with photos of nude women) hidden in his father's bedroom. He also recalls that he once found a packet of condoms under his father's pillow when he was an adolescent and he thought, "My father must be going to prostitutes."

I then intervened and pointed out that the condoms under the father's pillow seemed to indicate more obviously that his father used the condoms with his mother, who slept in the same bed. However, Mr. N. *wanted* to believe his wish-fulfilling fantasy: mother doesn't want sex with father and father is not very potent. The patient was silent and the hour ended.

The next day he began by telling me that he was furious with me as he left my office. As he drove away he drove wildly, trying to pass all the cars on the freeway, especially the expensive ones. Then he got the sudden impulse to race against a Rolls Royce if he could only find one. A fleeting thought crossed his mind. On the front of the Rolls Royce are the initials R. R. Those are Dr. Greenson's initials, he suddenly realized. With that he began to laugh, all by himself in the car. "The old boy is probably right," he thought, "it does tickle me to imagine that my mother preferred me and I could beat out my father. Later I wondered whether this had something to do with my own screwed-up sex life with my wife" (Greenson 1967, pp. 40–41).

Psychoanalytic dream interpretation depends on the search for meanings alternative to those implied by the dream's obvious structure. The word "tickle" is ambiguous and has a special meaning in the dream, and we can see the boy on the bicycle as a symbol for a very different act, masturbation.

Extensions of the Psychoanalytic Model — Groups and Families

Originally designed as a treatment for a therapist and a client, psychoanalytic therapy has been extended to involve groups of clients. In group therapy, one or two therapists meet with six to ten clients and attempt to resolve emotional problems by analyzing intergroup relationships. Distorted ways of perceiving and re-

lating become explicit in the group, and the therapist can rely on group members to observe one another's defenses (Yalom 1975).

Perhaps the most interesting elaboration of psychoanalytic principles is *family therapy,* in which whole family units are the object of intervention. Family systems theory goes beyond the psychoanalytic model of individual psychopathology; distorted patterns of relationships between family members are hypothesized to be the source of symptoms in one family member, the *identified* patient. Family therapy is meant to resolve conflicts and defenses, not in individuals but between members of the family system.

In Chapter 14 we presented Minuchin's theory of disturbances in the family system that produce psychophysiological disorders in some family member, usually an offspring. Minuchin went beyond this theory to develop a program of family therapy designed to alter the pathological system of relationship in such families. He applied the therapy program to fifty families with anorectic daughters. He used no control group, but the 86 percent recovery rate was significantly higher than any previously reported for individual psychoanalytic therapy with anorectics.

It is hard to convey the quality of this family therapy for anorexia. It challenges the rigidity, over-protectiveness, enmeshment, and conflict-avoidance of the whole family system. The therapy traditionally begins with a luncheon session assembling the therapist and all relevant family members. The parents are instructed to try to get the child to eat.

In a report of the initial session with the Kaplan family, Minuchin describes how he uses this luncheon session to try to break up the enmeshment of the family members with one another. First, both parents are encouraged to get their daughter, Deborah, to eat. They meet initial resistance and frustration. Then Minuchin takes the father out of the room and asks Mrs.

Kaplan to try alone. Mrs. Kaplan tries many techniques to get Deborah to eat, to no avail. At this point, Minuchin asks the father to try while the mother is absent. He also tries, but reacts to Deborah's defiance and becomes far more aggressive than the mother. Witness the following interchange:

Deborah *(referring to father's demand that she eat the hot dog):* I don't want it! Look at it. It's ugly!
Father: Eat that hot dog! I'm not leaving this place, I swear to God, until you eat it. Eat it. . . . God damn you! You son of a bitch! You eat the goddamn hot dog! I told you to eat it! (Minuchin, 1978, pp. 175–76)

The tension and frustration mount unbearably. At this point, Minuchin enters the process and relieves the tension.

Father: I'm sorry. *(He sits down, visibly exhausted.)*
Minuchin: I think that you have done your best. . . .

He then tries to get the family to look at the problem in a different way so they can begin a process of family self-examination. The parents state that they have failed, but Minuchin counters that they haven't. It is Deborah who has defeated them because she is stronger than both of them — a new way of looking at the problem.

Such a dramatic session is only a mechanism for initiating family therapy in a rigid, highly enmeshed, and conflict avoidant family system. Subsequent sessions involve a close analysis of behavior patterns within families like the Kaplans in order to change perceptions of relationships and encourage a sense of personal autonomy and modes of dealing with conflict. Most cases in Minuchin's study had at least nine months of family therapy before real progress could be seen, and in a number of instances progress took even longer.

Existential-Humanistic Approaches

Most existential therapists would agree with Rollo May (1961) that *existential therapy* "is not a system of therapy but an attitude toward therapy, not a new set of techniques but a concern with the understanding of the structure of the human being and his experience that must underlie all techniques" (pp. 18–19). *Humanistic* means a viewpoint, more philosophical than scientific, about the nature of man. The humanistic view is a reaction against Freudian psychology with its emphasis on unconscious forces and their influence on man as their passive victim. The humanistic therapist prefers to emphasize man's sense of purpose, values, options, and the right to and capacity for self-determination. It is from these uniquely human capacities that humanistic psychology derives. The emphasis on inner experience, or phenomenology, and self-determination is the cornerstone of the existential-humanistic psychotherapies. It reflects a somewhat different opinion on the origins of anxiety disorders; different, that is, from the Freudian view. According to the existential-humanistic approaches, anxiety disorders follow the individual's refusal to accept responsibility for her own behavior and its consequences for others. A major consequence of this failure is that significant parts of the self are cut off from each other and from awareness. Despite differences in philosophy and emphasis, these therapists often use the psychoanalytic theory with different names. Insight is critical for change and emphasizing the splitting off part of the self strongly resembles the psychoanalytic notion of conflict-defense. The most significant difference lies in emphasizing the client's responsibility and therapeutic behaviors and techniques that follow this belief.

No coherent system of therapy fits the title existential-humanistic. Instead, a number of individuals have offered theories of psychotherapy for anxiety disorders that follow a common orientation. At the heart of these theories are: (1) exploring the inner experience in the "here and now"; (2) emphasizing personal responsibility for change; and (3) active participation by the therapist in the intervention.

The Inner Experience

A major aspect of this therapy is encouraging personal exploration of feelings, assumptions, and values about the self and significant others at the moment. As in Freudian psychotherapy, the therapist encourages the client to examine his experience honestly and in detail. The client must learn the difference between his genuine feelings and the false emotions with which he deceives himself. He must also learn to be an "authentic" or "genuine" person who experiences close harmony between feelings and overt behavior.

The therapist's role in these proceedings is clear and reveals the emphasis on phenomenology. The therapist tries as much as possible to get "inside the skin" of the client, to experience as much of the client's feelings as humanly possible, and to communicate this understanding to the client.

You may wonder how this technique differs from the psychoanalytic therapist's encouragement of examining experience. In some ways it is very similar, but in one crucial respect it is not. In the existential-humanistic therapies, the client is the expert on his own inner experience, and the therapist's job is merely to assist in the journey. The therapist does interpret what may be going on, but reports his understanding of what the client is experiencing. The therapist offers no hypotheses on inner conflict because he does not presume to know more about the client than the client knows about himself.

Client's Responsibility for Change

One way of interpreting the Freudian approach is that it encourages the client to think of herself as helpless to effect change until unconscious conflicts are resolved. Existential therapies take a different tack and emphasize that the client is in charge of herself and can make effective choices. The existential therapist avoids the psychoanalytic notion that only the therapist's efforts and expertise will help the patient to change. Treating the client as expert places responsibility for behavior squarely on the client.

In an interview with a volunteer client, therapist Carl Rogers (1965) explores her anxiety that she has not been honest with her nine-year-old daughter, Pammy, about her sexual relationships with men since her divorce. Gloria has always been honest with her children and is feeling great conflict over lying to Pammy. She wants to know whether or not telling Pammy the truth about her sexual relationships will affect her daughter adversely. Gloria wonders if Pammy could accept her "devilish" or "shady" side, referring to her sexual needs. She presses Rogers for an answer:

Gloria: I want you very much to give me a direct answer.

Rogers: I guess, I am sure this will sound evasive to you, but it seems to me that perhaps the person you are not being honest with is *you* — because I was very much struck by the fact that you were saying "If I feel all right about what I have done, whether it's going to bed with a man or what, if *I* really feel all right about it, then I do not have any concern about what I would tell Pammy or my relationship with her."

The Humanistic-Existential Therapist

The humanistic therapist does not serve as a blank screen for a client, as the psychoanalyst does, providing minimal clues about their own reactions and judgments. Humanistic therapists believe that technique sets up a nongenuine relationship and that the therapist's self-disclosure is a valuable model of honesty for the client. Witness a later exchange between Gloria and her therapist, after exploring her distance from her own father:

Gloria: You know what I was just thinking? I . . . a dumb thing . . . that all of a sudden while I was talking to you, I thought, "Gee, how nice, I can talk to you and I want you to approve of me and I respect you, but I miss that my father couldn't talk to me like you are." I mean, I'd like to say, "Gee, I'd like you for my father." I don't even know why that came to me.

Rogers: You look like a pretty nice daughter. But you really do miss the fact that you couldn't be open with your own Dad.

Later in that same interview follows another disclosure by the therapist:

Gloria: Well, see, I sort of feel that's pretending too, because, I can't expect you to feel very close to me. You don't know me that well.

Rogers: All I can know is what I am feeling and that is I feel close to you at this moment.

Client-Centered Therapy

Rogers is a distinguished clinical psychologist whose optimistic view of the human capacity for achieving well-being led him to design an alternative to psychoanalytic theory in the late 1930s. His system, *client-centered therapy,* emphasizes that it is the client and not the therapist who sets the pace and decides the issues and goals of therapy. Rogers's belief is: "Contrary to those therapists who see depravity at man's

Fig. 15.3. Carl Rogers, the originator of client-centered therapy and a leader in the existentialist-humanistic movement.

core, who see man's deepest instincts as destructive, I have found that when man is truly free to become what he most deeply is, free to actualize his nature as an organism capable of awareness, then he clearly appears to move towards wholeness and integration" (Rogers 1966, p. 193). Client-centered therapy is intended to create conditions that unleash this inherent striving for growth in each client.

Rogers contends, and extensive research by his group (Parloff, Waskow, and Wolfe 1978) provides some support, that conditions occur when the therapist projects these attitudes and values in the therapeutic relationship: (1) *congruence,* (2) *unconditional positive regard,* and (3) *accurate empathetic understanding.* In other words, the therapist should be honest, open to exploring his own inner experience, free of facade and self-deceit (congruence). He should know himself and be willing and able to share personal experience when necessary. The therapist should communicate deep and genuine caring for the client as a human being, with faith in his potential. He must create an accepting environment in which it is safe to express all feelings and attitudes. The therapist sets no conditions on acceptance. "It is an unpossessive caring for the client as a separate person, which allows the client freely to have his own feelings and his own experiencing" (Rogers 1966, p. 186). The therapist should perceive those feelings and experiences sensitively and accurately and understand their meaning. With accurate empathetic understanding, the therapist can sense the client's inner world as if it were his own, and reflect it:

Client: If I am going to be a member of the group, I must contribute. I don't know what, but if you're going to be a part of it, you've got to contribute to the well-being of the group.
Therapist: If you knew what it was [that is expected], you would do it.
Client: Well, I really do think that you like me now. I told you that, you know, that you weren't reaching me. I don't remember how far back it was, now, but that I wasn't digging you or reading you. You weren't . . . but I think you do really like me now. I feel this. So I feel we have made . . . at least you and I have made contact.
Therapist: You can really believe the guy inside.

An important component of Rogers's therapy is stimulating exploration of inner states of feeling, as in this exchange:

Client: There are times when I'm afraid, and you said yesterday, "Why don't you just tell everybody what you think and let it go." There are times I don't seem to be able to do that. There are other times when I can. I don't, to my

knowledge, turn these on and off as a mechanism or anything like that. It happens.
Therapist: Can you get any closer at all to what it's like when you are afraid? If that clicks, I wonder if you could just let us sink in and let us know more of what it seems like inside when you feel that way? (Meador and Rogers 1973, pp. 149–151).

Gestalt Therapy

Another variation of the humanistic-existential approach, Gestalt therapy, is a form of intervention developed by psychiatrist Fritz Perls (1970). Perls was originally trained as a psychoanalyst, and in his Gestalt therapy we can see many aspects of psychoanalytic theory. Why, then, is Gestalt therapy considered an existential approach? It relies on the immediate "here and now," and rejects traditional psychoanalytic concentration on understanding past events:

In my lectures on Gestalt Therapy, I have one aim only: to impart a fraction of the meaning of the word, *now*. To me, nothing exists except the now. Now = experience = awareness = reality. The past is no more and the future not yet. Only the now exists (Perls 1970, p. 4).

Gestalt therapy has little theoretical superstructure: its major tenet is that anxiety and personality disorders occur when individuals dissociate from awareness parts of themselves, most particularly their needs for personal gratification. They don't experience themselves as "whole" but as fragmented, exerting great energy to separate parts of self from each other. This view is not very different from the psychoanalytic notion that fearful impulses are blocked from awareness by defense mechanisms. The client has to experience the warded-off part of self within the therapeutic interaction. Numerous techniques have been invented to enhance awareness. Nonverbal expressions of emotion and attitude are used extensively to point out discrepancies between words and body language:

> A woman in therapy is going over, in a very complaining voice, some examples of how she was recently mistreated by her mother-in-law. I am impressed in her account by her lack of awareness of how much she invited this and how she misperceives her capacity to interrupt this behavior, but said nothing. My attention is caught by a rapid repetitive movement of her hand against her other arm, although I can't make the movement out.
>
> Therapist: What are you doing with your hand?
> Client: *(Slightly startled)* Uh, making a cross.
> Therapist: What might you do with a cross?
> Client: Well. I certainly hung myself on one this weekend, didn't I?
>
> She returns to her account but with more awareness of her martyr attitude and its contribution to events (Enright 1970, pp. 364–365).

To enhance awareness, therapists conduct games or exercises, usually in group sessions, having the patient enact different roles or parts of the self. Gestalt therapists emphasize that such action heightens awareness of parts that are "split off." In one game called "I take responsibility," the client comments on facets of her behavior and must add the phrase "and I take responsibility for it" after each behavior ("I am a fearful person, and I take responsibility for it"; "I do not do as well in school as I could, and I take responsibility for it"). In another game, "I have a secret," each member of the group thinks of a personal secret and then tries to imagine how others would react to knowing it. Still without revealing it, members are then asked to boast about how terrible their secrets are. The intent is to encourage them to explore feelings of shame and guilt.

During role-playing exercises, the three rules are: (1) *The principle of Now,* which requires communicating in the present tense, avoiding future or past tense; (2) *I and thou,* maintaining a flow of communication between equals; that is, talking *to* rather than at someone; and (3) *Using "I"* language, not "it" language to see oneself as responsible for acts, not a passive recipient of experience:

> Therapist: What do you hear in your voice?
> Client: My voice sounds like it is crying.
> Therapist: Can you take responsibility for that by saying, "I am crying"? (Levitsky and Perls 1970, p. 365).

Dreams are used in Gestalt therapy, but not as in psychoanalytic therapy. Perls assumes that each element in the dream, nonhuman as well as human, represents some part, often a split-off part, of the personality. In the therapy session, the client has to tell the dream repeatedly and from the vantage point of each image. We are asked to imagine ourselves as the dog or tree in the dream, for example. By enacting and becoming the dream element, presumably we will understand and reclaim that fragment of the self. Look at how dream therapy works in Jean's dream, in which she and her mother are going into a tunnel on a sheet of cardboard. With Jean in front, they slide down a chute into the depths of the earth, only to find it a sunlit, gladelike place.

> Fritz: So, let's switch back to Jean. Jean, would you talk again, tell again the dream, live it through as if this was your existence, as if you live it now, see if you can understand more about your life. . . .
> Jean: I don't — it doesn't really seem clear until I find myself — the place has become kind of a top of the chute. I don't remember whether at first I was afraid or not, possibly — oh, I should say this is now?
> F: You are now on the chute. Are you afraid to go down?

J: (*Laughs*) I guess I am a little afraid to go down. But then it seems like. . .

F: So the existential message is, "You've got to go down."

J: I guess I'm afraid to find out what's there.

F: This points to false ambitions, that you're too high up.

J: That's true.

F: So the existential message says, "Go down." Again our mentality says, "High up is better than down." You must always be somewhere higher.

J: Anyway, I seem a little afraid to go down.

F: Talk to the chute.

J: Why are you muddy? You're slippery and slidy and I might fall on you and slip.

F: Now play the chute. "I'm slippery and. . ."

J: I'm slippery and muddy, the better to slide and faster to get down on. (*Laughs*)

F: Ahah, well, what's the joke?

J: (*Continues laughing*) I'm just laughing.

F: Can you accept yourself as slippery?

J: Hm. I guess so. Yes. I can never seem to. . . . Yeah, you know, always just when I think I'm about to, you know, say, "Aha! I've caught you now!" it slips away — you know, rationalization. I'm slippery and slidy. Hm. Anyway, I'm going because it looks like it would be fun, and I want to find out where this goes and what's going to be at the end of it. And it seems, perhaps only now, I'm turning around and looking to see what I could use to kind of protect my clothes (*laughs*) or maybe make a better slide. I discover the cardboard. . . .

F: Can you play this cardboard? If you were this cardboard . . . what's your function?

J: I'm just — to make things easier. I'm just kind of lying around and left-over, and aha, I have a use for it.

F: Oh — you can be useful.

J: I can be useful. I'm not just left-over and lying around, and we can make it easier to get down.

F: Is it important for you to be useful?

J: (*Quietly*) Yes. I want to be an advantage to somebody. . . . Is that enough for being the cardboard? . . . Maybe I also want to be sat upon. (*Laughter*) [F: Oh!] What is the part in the book about who wants to kick who? I want to be pitied, I want to be scrunched down. [F: Say this again.] (*Laughing*) I want to be sat upon and scrunched down.

F: Say this to the group.

J: Well, that's hard to do. (*Loudly*) I want to be sat upon and scrunched down. . . . Hm. (*Loudly*) I want to be <u>sat upon</u> and <u>scrunched down</u>. (*Pounds her thigh with fist.*)

F: Who are you hitting? [J: Me.] Besides you?

J: I think my mother, who's turning, who's behind me and I look around and see her.

F: Good. Now hit her.

J: (*Loudly*) Mother, I'm scrunching down upon — (*hits thigh*) ouch! — you (*laughs*) and I am going to take <u>you</u> for a ride (*laughter*) instead of you telling me to go, and taking <u>me</u> whenever <u>you</u> want to. I'm taking <u>you</u> along for a ride with me.

F: Did you notice anything in your behavior with your mother?

J: Just now? (*Laughs*)

F: I had the impression it was too <u>much</u> to be convincing. . . . It was spoken with anger, not with firmness.

J: Mmm. I think I'm still a little afraid of her.

F: That's it. You tell her that (Perls 1969, pp. 148–150).

Behavior Therapy

Since the 1950s, behavior therapy has grown from a small school rebelling against the psychoanalytic model of treatment to become a major influence in the literature on psychological intervention in anxiety disorders. In his early writings, British psychologist and pioneer in behavior therapy Hans Eysenck (1959) broke sharply with the psychoanalytic emphasis on conflict resolution, unconscious motivation, and insight. Eysenck rejected the idea that unless a client resolves underlying conflicts, reducing neurotic symptoms will result in new symptoms. The behavioral position was that the maladaptive behavior itself is the neurosis — that it represents no deeper conflict. The past is important only insofar as it can elucidate present behavior, and insight is unnecessary therapeutically. Treatment should focus on unlearning maladaptive behaviors.

These clear distinctions from other schools of psychotherapy have become muddled over the years, as behavior therapists have paid more attention to the individual's thoughts and feelings. Behavior therapy is perhaps best distinguished by a general orientation to clinical practice, aligned philosophically with an experimental approach to the study of human behavior (Goldfried and Davison 1976). Treatments for clinical problems are derived from psychological principles and the therapeutic process is held up to experimental scrutiny.

Actually, much the behavior therapist believes and does is not too different from the psychotherapeutic approaches we have considered. The therapist-patient relationship, though not primary, is very important, especially so that the client will share the therapist's perspective on the problem and will be motivated to carry out all that treatment demands. In behavior therapy, the client usually is asked to *do* specific tasks (practice relaxation at home, refrain from a compulsive ritual), and acceptance and trust are critical if the client is to make this effort. Also, reflection and clarification of feelings and experience are important in understanding the client's problems, in providing reassurance, and in creating the trustful atmosphere crucial to all therapeutic work.

Since there has been much emphasis on a scientific approach to behavior change, sometimes detractors have portrayed behavior therapists as cold and impersonal. In fact, the major study comparing behavior therapy and psychotherapy (Sloane et al. 1975), which we will describe later, revealed that clients found behavior therapists as warm and accepting as their psychoanalytic colleagues and indeed that they demonstrated more of the accurate empathy, interpersonal contact, and self-disclosure advocated by Rogerian psychotherapists. Tape recordings of the therapy sessions, however, revealed clear differences in what the therapists did. Behavior therapists gave more explicit advice and talked during the therapy sessions an average of twice as much as the more traditional psychotherapists. Guidance and active involvement by the therapist are characteristic of behavior therapy.

The behavior therapist's goals are usually expressed as observable change in behavior. From a detailed behavioral assessment, therapist and client set specific goals for treatment, which they accept as successful only when the patient's behavior conforms to the goals. Additionally, behavior therapists are now paying more attention to teaching patients coping skills they can use in future stressful situations.

Behavioral Assessment of Anxiety Disorders

The first step in a program of behavior therapy is a thorough behavioral assessment. In a lengthy interview, the therapist seeks to understand the nature and dimensions of the problem, relevant historical events, current situational determinants, consequences of the problem in the client's life, the client's behavioral assets and deficits, and his motivation for and expectations of treatment. The aim is to develop, with the client, specific objectives for the therapy program. The therapy is not guided by a particular theoretical notion of how the client should change ("self-actualization" or "personal growth"). Consider the following brief excerpt from an initial interview, along with the therapist's thoughts about what he is doing.

Client: I just feel nervous a lot of the time.
Therapist: What is the feeling like?

Client: I don't know. It's hard to describe . . . I just feel nervous.

Therapist: [*I think I'm going to have some difficulty in getting her to elaborate on her problems. Maybe I'll hold off on trying to push for specifics for a little bit, and instead try to get her to feel more comfortable about describing and elaborating on her feelings, and just talking in general.*] So you know what the feeling is like, but it's kind of difficult to describe it in words.

Client: Yet, it is. You know, it's just a feeling of uneasiness and apprehension. Like when you know something bad may happen, or at least you're afraid that it might.

Therapist: So emotionally, and perhaps physically, there's a fear that something might happen, although you may not be certain exactly what.

Client: Yes.

Therapist: When you're feeling that way, what do you experience physically?

Client: Well, my heart starts pounding and I feel myself tense up all over. It's not always that bad; sometimes it's only mild.

Therapist: [*I can make a smooth transition at this point and try to find out the situations in which the intensity of her anxiety varies. Whether or not I'll ever use this information for hierarchy construction remains to be seen.*] In other words, depending upon the circumstances, you may feel more or less anxious.

Client: Yes.

Therapist: Tell me something about the situations that make you *most* anxious.

Client: Well, it's usually when I deal with other people.

Therapist: I would find it particularly helpful to hear about some typical situations that may upset you.

Client: It's hard to come up with something specific.

Therapist: [*I'm having doubts as to how hard to press her for details. If she has too much difficulty in coming up with specifics, the whole process of questioning might just make our relationship too aversive. Perhaps I can give her a homework assignment to self-observe during*

the course of the week. Let me try to get one or two examples, perhaps confining them to the past week, suggesting certain kinds of situations to her. I can then use this as a lead to question the extent to which the situations were typical of a broader class of events. I sense by the expression on her face that she may be somewhat uneasy about her inability to give me the information I want. I should probably attend to that before moving on.*] I can understand how it may be hard to come up with specific examples right on the spot. That's not at all uncommon. Let me see if I can help to make it a little easier for you. Let's take the past week or so. Think of what went on either at work, at home, or when you were out socially that might have upset you.

Client: O.K. Something just occurred to me. We went out to a party last weekend, and as we were driving to the place where the party was being held, I felt myself starting to panic.

Therapist: Can you tell me more about that situation?

Client: Well, the party was at my husband's boss' house, and I always feel uncomfortable about events like that.

Therapist: In what way?

Client: Well, I find it difficult for me to be natural in that kind of situation.

Therapist: [*In my personal and clinical experience, there are a number of components that might be relevant in creating anxiety. There is the obligatory nature of the occasion, the perceived evaluations in such situations, to say nothing of the broader class of social interactions to which she may be responding with apprehension. Let's see if I can find out from her what this situation was a sample of.*] Do you typically become nervous when you go to social gatherings?

Client: Well, a lot depends on the situation.

Therapist: In what way?

Client: It depends on how comfortable I feel with the people.

Therapist: [*We seem to have come full circle. I think I have to be less open-ended in my line of questioning.*] O.K., so there are certain situations and certain types of people that make you feel more comfortable, and others that make you more apprehensive.

Client: Yes.

Therapist: I think it would be helpful if we focused a little more on the kinds of people and the kinds of situations which upset you to varying degrees.

Client: A lot has to do with how loud or how aggressive the people are. I think I get very intimidated when people seem so self-confident.

Therapist: [*Among the possibilities that I should check out a little later in the session is whether or not a social deficit may be operating here, as well as any associated problems in general unassertiveness. For now, though, I should stick with getting general classes of situations that upset her.*] What other kinds of individuals do you find you react negatively to? (Goldfried and Davison 1976, pp. 40–42).

This initial interview is similar to other psychotherapeutic interviews. Behavioral assessment, though, may also involve completing self-report inventories, measuring physiological response to anxiety-evoking stimuli, role-playing of critical situations in the therapist's office, and directly observing the client's behaviors in the natural environment. The treatment program grows out of the behavioral assessment.

In Chapter 13 we discussed Mowrer's (1947) two-factor theory of anxiety learning, which involves both classical conditioning (learning to respond with anxiety to specific situations) and operant conditioning (learning to reduce anxiety by specific escape or avoidance behaviors). The behavior-therapy treatments we will consider here deal mostly with the first factor — weakening the anxiety response itself in distressing situations. The operant components of treatment include reinforcement by the therapist and significant others; all therapies give such reinforcement, however, so that although behavior therapy more purposefully includes it, we will not dwell on the techniques. As you read about behavioral methods, keep in mind that

therapists often combine them in clinical practice. The therapist in the initial interview quoted above might have employed relaxation and systematic desensitization to reduce the client's anxiety as well as training in interpersonal communication skills.[1]

Anxiety Reduction Techniques

In treating anxiety disorders, the behavior therapist utilizes techniques directly aimed at reducing anxiety. The two most frequently used are training in relaxation, for general anxiety level, and systematic desensitization, for anxiety in specific situations.

TRAINING IN RELAXATION

"Try to relax" seems obvious advice when we are experiencing anxiety or its somatic consequences, such as headaches or insomnia. Knowledge about the beneficial effects of training people directly to achieve muscle and mental relaxation antedates modern behavior therapy, but the relaxation response has received renewed interest as part of systematic desensitization (see below) and as a treatment in its own right. A great many techniques are used to induce relaxation, including hypnosis, yoga, transcendental meditation, and biofeedback. We have considered the latter two in Chapter 14, as employed with essential hypertension. We will say more about training in relaxation

---

[1] Techniques in behavior therapy for other disorders will be discussed in the appropriate chapters on intervention. Modeling and counterconditioning techniques for anxiety are considered further under intervention for childhood behavior disorders. Reinforcement methods and the token economy, which modify the living or school environment to teach adaptive behaviors, are highlighted under intervention for schizophrenia, delinquency, childhood behavior disorders and mental retardation. Aversive procedures employing punishment to reduce undesirable behaviors are considered under intervention with social deviance (alcohol, drugs, sexual deviance). Cognitive strategies that alter the patient's self-defeating thoughts are dealt with further under intervention with depressive disorders.

learning to identify tension in the muscle groups by · *relaxing one group of muscle at a time* · *then combination* · *deep breathing* · *home exercises to deal with everyday situations* · *inhibits arousal of S.N.S.* · *can produce clinically significant results with 1) insomnia 2) tension headaches 3) asthma 4) essential hypertension*

here, however, because it is basic in many behavior therapy methods.

Methods for training the relaxation response all involve focusing of attention and reducing muscular tension. Most methods of relaxation in clinical practice are brief derivatives of the progressive-relaxation approach introduced by Edmund Jacobson in 1938. The client usually receives four to eight hours of training with a therapist, although it may be automated with tape-recorded instructions. Although training varies in the particulars, generally the client sits or reclines comfortably, eyes closed, learning to identify tension in the muscle groups (such as hands and arms, face, neck, back, stomach, lower extremities) by tension-release exercises. A typical instruction begins:

"Now that you are comfortable, close your eyes and keep them closed for the remainder of the procedure. I am going to teach you to relax very deeply. To do this, I will ask you to concentrate on, and relax, one group of muscles at a time. We will start with your hands. Begin by making a tight fist. Pay attention to how these muscles feel when they are tense — study the tension in these

Fig. 15.4. Behavior therapist Arnold Lazarus conducts a group relaxation-training session.

muscles.'' After some 10 or 15 seconds, the instructor continues: ''Now relax. Release all tension in these muscles. Let all the tension go. Keep on letting go until the muscles seem completely relaxed. Even now, when these muscles seem completely relaxed, see if you can relax them more; let those muscles relax completely.''

Using the same basic instructions, other muscle groups are relaxed systematically, usually beginning with the forearms (Agras 1978, p. 136).

After tension-release exercises are applied to muscle groups separately, several are combined, accompanied by a deep breath, slowly released as the client relaxes. Clients often report a tremendous feeling of relaxation, even after one or two sessions.

Training sessions are augmented by home practice. The client progressively learns to identify even minor tension and, ultimately, to reduce it at will. This method becomes an active coping device for everyday situations. Clients are taught to scan their muscles during possibly stressful activities (driving in heavy traffic, taking exams) and to relax those which need not be tense to perform the activity.

Although the effects and mechanisms of training in relaxation are not fully understood, we assume that it inhibits arousal of the sympathetic nervous system, decreasing the subjective experience of anxiety.

Relaxation methods are often applied by the behavior therapist directly to clinical problems thought to relate to anxiety, such as the psychophysiological disorders discussed in Chapter 14. We now have reason to believe that relaxation can produce clinically significant results with problems such as insomnia (Kahn, Baker, and Weiss 1968; Borkovec and Fowles 1973), tension headaches (Sargent, Walters, and Green 1973), asthma (Alexander, Miklich, and Hershkoff 1972), and essential hypertension.

SYSTEMATIC DESENSITIZATION

The behavior-therapy approach to anxiety disorders most often used and studied is systematic desensitization, introduced in 1958 by Joseph Wolpe, who went beyond general relaxation to reducing or *counterconditioning* anxiety in specific stress-arousing situations. Systematic desensitization has been employed especially for phobias. Treatment involves gradually exposing the relaxed patient, either in imagined scenes or in real life, to situations progressively arousing more anxiety until each situation has lost its threat. The approach traditionally has three parts: (1) teaching a response that is antagonistic to anxiety, usually relaxation; (2) constructing a graded list of anxiety-evoking situations, known as a *hierarchy;* and (3) the actual desensitization process, in which the patient progressively imagines hierarchy items, while relaxed, gradually trying to extinguish anxiety to the situations in the hierarchy.

We have discussed relaxation training. Constructing a hierarchy of anxiety is difficult and sometimes tedious, for the therapist and the patient must list anxiety-arousing situations, beginning with one arousing only a tinge of anxiety and progressing by just-noticeable differences to those producing overwhelming anxiety. A relatively specific phobia illustrates the hierarchy. Jamie experienced acrophobia (fear of high places) severe enough to restrict her daily activities. She put together the list of eighteen anxiety-eliciting situations in Table 15.1. The first item (''You're walking over a sidewalk grating'') was mildly anxiety-arousing. The last item (''You are standing at the edge of the roof on a twenty-story building'') elicited intense anxiety. The items between these two represented scenes varying in height and physical stability, the two dimensions identified as crucial for Jamie. Some social anxieties require

[handwritten margin notes: "if anxiety is produced during any sit, the patient signals by raising a finger + therapist shifts to a diff mode of thought • an assumption is that the imagined scene has many properties of the real life situation but necessary to also practice in real life"]

Table 15.1. Sample anxiety hierarchy for acrophobia

1. Walking over a sidewalk grating.
2. Sitting in a third-floor office, near the window (not a floor-to-ceiling window).
3. Walking up a steep incline while hiking in the country.
4. Sitting in a tenth-floor office near the window (not a floor-to-ceiling window).
5. Riding an elevator to the forty-fifth floor.
6. Seeing window washers ten stories up on a scaffold.
7. Standing on a chair to change a lightbulb.
8. Sitting in a third-floor office near a floor-to-ceiling window, looking down.
9. Sitting on the balcony of a fifth-floor apartment (with railing).
10. Sitting in a tenth-floor office near a floor-to-ceiling window, looking down.
11. Sitting at the front of the second balcony in a theater.
12. Standing on the third step of a ladder to trim bushes.
13. Standing at the edge of the roof of a three-story building (no railing).
14. Taking flight in a large airliner (especially takeoffs and landings).
15. Driving down steep hills.
16. Driving around curves on a mountain road.
17. Riding as a passenger around curves on a mountain road.
18. Standing at the edge of the roof of a twenty-story building.

much longer and much more complex hierarchies.

Desensitization starts with having the patient relax and imagine the first item in the hierarchy. The therapist vividly describes the scene: "You're walking along Main Street. It's crowded and you can't easily avoid walking over the sidewalk grating ahead. Imagine walking over the grating and looking down. Hear the traffic, feel the closeness of other people, see the empty space below. You are comfortable and walk on. You feel very relaxed and peaceful." If

the patient experiences any anxiety, she signals by raising a finger, and the therapist may then terminate the image and shift to something pleasant ("It's a clear blue sky day, and you're soaking up the sun on the beach"). The therapist repeats each scene until it consistently elicits no anxiety and then introduces the next item. An assumption in this approach is that a well-imagined scene has many properties of the real-life situation. The parallel has its limits, and

Fig. 15.5. This elevator-phobic woman is confronting the feared situation with her therapist as part of a systematic desensitization program.

it is necessary to practice next in real life, always using situations already mastered in the clinic and utilizing the now well-learned relaxation response to counter anxiety.

EFFECTIVENESS OF DESENSITIZATION. Much evidence shows that systematic desensitization is effective with problems of many types in which anxiety is fundamental (Marks 1975). A classic outcome study was conducted by Gordon Paul (1966, 1967), who selected ninety-six college students suffering from performance anxiety "in nearly every social, interpersonal, or evaluative situation . . . [and most severely] in a public speaking situation" (Paul 1969, p. 112). As a preassessment, Paul had each person give a short, impromptu speech to an unfamiliar audience. Cognitive aspects of anxiety were assessed with a questionnaire, and physiological measures (pulse rate and palmar sweat) were

Sexual Arousal in Counterconditioning Anxiety

In one case study of a claustrophobic patient the therapist varied systematic desensitization to meet the client's capacity. He substituted sexual arousal for relaxation, and essentially dispensed with the graded hierarchy of anxiety. Even though behavior therapists employ specific techniques, in clinical practice they are tailored to the client.

Ms. C., age twenty-one, had experienced her first panic reaction two years earlier upon seeing an autopsy in a special high school science class. She recalled vividly her feelings: nausea, blurring of vision, dizziness, sweating, and an intense desire to escape. During the first two years of college she felt mild anxiety on entering classrooms and in time began to have attacks on subways and while riding in a car. She undertook six months of intermittent counseling, gradually increased the dosage of the tranquilizer Valium to 40 mg a day, and on two occasions following severe anxiety reactions spent weeks on the psychiatric ward of a major New York hospital. She described her life as a "shambles" — formerly an excellent student, she had a C average, dropped out of school, and was unable to travel anywhere. Although behavioral assessment indicated standard systematic desensitization as appropriate, repeated attempts at relaxation training methods failed. Searching for an alternative response that would be antagonistic to anxiety, the therapist explored pleasurable responses. The most pleasant appeared to be "making love with her boyfriend," and she further mentioned that she used fantasies of sex with her boyfriend while masturbating. Sexual arousal, then, was employed instead of relaxation to countercondition her phobic anxiety.

Ms. C. was instructed that at the point of orgasmic inevitability in masturbation and while making love to her boyfriend she was to fantasize herself in one of the feared situations (subway, car, classroom). After two weeks she reported she was successfully carrying out the program and feeling more confident in her ability to confront the phobic stimuli. She said, "subways and cars and classes are beginning to take on a new meaning, one that I'm beginning to enjoy."

In the following three weeks she was directed to confront the real phobic situations, while maintaining sexual arousal. For example, she and her boyfriend were to take a bus to the other end of town and an express subway back; upon returning she was to initiate intimate contact as soon as possible. Several weeks later she was able to drive with a girl friend from New York to Boston, reporting that when she felt anxious she would close her eyes and fantasize making love in the back of the car. This would both arouse and amuse her, dissipating the anxiety. Her comment was "I never thought I'd be able to do this. I really feel confident now; I don't seem to be so worried over when I'll become anxious; in fact it all seems so unreal now." Treatment was terminated one year later. Ms. C. was again a successful student, had no major setbacks, and rarely used medication.

taken just before the speech. During the speech, trained observers scored visible signs of anxiety on the observational checklist described in Chapter 13 (p. 298). Then subjects were randomly assigned to four groups, which received (1) no treatment, (2) systematic desensitization, (3) brief insight-oriented psychotherapy, and (4) an attention-placebo control. We have mentioned the nonspecific factors in all therapies, such as the therapist's encouragement and the patient's expectation of success. Paul included a form of pseudotherapy (performing a stressful task while supposedly under the influence of a tranquilizer) as an attention-placebo control (see Chapter 4).

The treatments were carried out by five experienced therapists, all of neo-Freudian or Rogerian persuasion, whom Paul had hired and trained to perform desensitization. These therapists felt that five sessions of insight therapy would be enough to eliminate anxiety in speech-making situations, so that all treatments were conducted for five sessions. When the same measures were readministered after treatment, the results were quite surprising. As Figure 15.6 shows, only the desensitization group differed from no-treatment controls on the psychophysiological measures, and it was superior to the other treatment groups on the cognitive and observational measures. In fol-

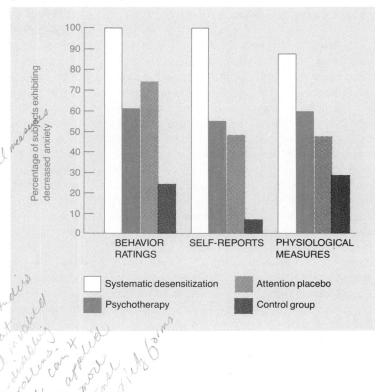

Fig. 15.6. Percentage of subjects in each of four conditions who exhibited decreases in anxiety as measured by behavior ratings, self-reports of anxiety, and measures of physiological arousal. (After Bandura 1969.)

low-up after two years, the final proportion of subjects showing significant improvement over pretreatment levels was: desensitization, 85 percent; insight-oriented psychotherapy, 50 percent; attention-placebo pseudotherapy, 50 percent; and untreated controls, 22 percent.

A limitation in many studies of desensitization is that they have involved nondisabling problems, such as fear of snakes, anxiety over examinations, or the performance anxiety we saw in Paul's study. How effective is this approach with the more severe and complex anxiety problems seen in clinical settings? We will discuss several large comparative studies later, but reports from many clinic clients by Wolpe (1958), Lazarus (1961), and others leave little doubt that desensitization is effective. One advantage to studies with nonclinical populations, however, is that they can study components of treatment without depriving of treatment persons with disabling anxiety. Many such studies have been conducted to determine why desensitization works when it does.

THERAPEUTIC COMPONENTS OF DESENSITIZATION. The model of desensitization we have seen spells out standard procedures. These include having the therapist teach the incompatible response of relaxation, develop a personalized anxiety hierarchy, and progress gradually up the hierarchy. Yet, as subsequent research has sought to tease out the critical techniques in desensitization therapy, "each and every one of the components of systematic desensitization have been shown to be neither necessary nor sufficient — like the Cheshire cat left with only its smile, systematic desensitization seems to work, but there seem to be no component parts that cannot be removed . . ." (Yates 1975, p. 162). Relaxation was thought crucial for counterconditioning, but a number of studies have found equal success whether relaxation training is part of the program or not (sum-

marized in Yates 1975). The personal hierarchy was also considered crucial, and yet some studies have employed uniform hierarchies for a whole group having the same phobia with undiminished effectiveness (Ihli and Garlington 1969). Nor do other procedural violations seem to make much difference; Krapfl and Nawas (1970) presented items from the hierarchy in descending and random order, with no loss in effectiveness. Marks (1975, 1978) has reviewed all behavioral procedures successfully used to treat anxiety and concludes that the common element is *exposure*. Each of these procedures in some way gets the individual to confront what he fears.

Flooding: The behavioral technique *flooding* follows a procedure that directly contradicts principles of systematic desensitization. The therapist presents to the patient only the top items in the hierarchy, repeating and embellishing them, sometimes with terrifying realism, until they lose their anxiety-evoking properties. Flooding has been used successfully for obsessive compulsive behavior, making the client tolerate anxiety-eliciting stimuli and refrain from the compulsive response, such as hand washing (Rainey 1972). Although flooding is not as clearly successful as desensitization (Redd et al. 1979), the reports of successful cases further question the principles of desensitization.

Self-directed desensitization: Although the therapist's part in desensitization has been considered very important, many have demonstrated that automated desensitization can be successful (Melamed and Lang 1967; Nawas, Fishman, and Pucel 1970). Baker, Cohen, and Sanders (1973), treating acrophobics, found that a self-directed procedure utilizing a tape recorder was just as effective as therapist-directed desensitization, both being superior to an untreated control group. More important, at an eight-month follow-up, although the therapist-directed subjects reported slightly more fear than at post-testing, the self-directed subjects showed further improvement. The strength of such self-directed approaches may be that they give clients an active way to cope in new stressful situations.

IMPROVING COMMUNICATION SKILLS

As we saw in Chapter 13, many anxious individuals do not experience clear symptoms but exhibit anxiety-provoking and self-defeating patterns of interpersonal behavior. A common core problem is poor communication to others of one's feelings and wishes.

Some people are generally shy and nonassertive, and passively accept many situations that inwardly cause great turmoil. They eat the cold steak rather than send it back, watch silently while others cut into line in front of them, or greatly appreciate what a friend has done for them but say nothing. Negative and positive feelings alike are denied expression, and sometimes pent-up anxieties erupt in an angry outburst. Many other people are not so generally unassertive but do communicate poorly in specific intimate relationships — with parents or spouse, for example. We have seen that existential approaches to therapy are concentrated on getting people better "in touch" with their feelings, because satisfying relationships seem to bring more open communication and self-disclosure (Levinger and Snoek 1972). Behavior therapists have come to share this view, but they take it a step further by directly teaching better communication and problem solving to people whose anxiety is, in part, a result of deficient social skills.

ASSERTION TRAINING. The assumption in assertion training is that unassertive individuals might experience better relationships and be less anxious in social situations if communication were more open and straightforward, if they were better able to refuse unreasonable requests and stand up for their rights. People do not usually come to behavior therapists asking for training in assertion, but if the therapist believes that the anxiety is partly a reaction to a lack of skill in communication, he might raise this as a possible approach. It is important at first to clarify with the client the distinction between assertion and aggressiveness, and similarly between nonassertion and politeness, and to discuss the client's beliefs about the meaning and consequences of being more assertive. The emphasis is on *socially realistic assertion,* not aggression for its own sake.

The main tactic in assertion training is *behavioral rehearsal;* the therapist discusses and models appropriate (and inappropriate) assertive behavior and then role-plays typical situations with the client, at first providing coaching in possible responses. As the client is better able to make assertive responses in the therapist's office, she is given graded "homework" tasks, with progressively more difficult assertion (first returning an unwanted article to a store . . . and later telling father you resent his constant criticisms).

Variations of assertion training have been applied to problems as varied as increasing skills in heterosexual dating (Curran 1977) to teaching a homosexual, who wants to make his sexual preference known, how to deal with his detractors and minimize anxiety (Duehn and Mayadas 1976). Assertion training seems particularly effective in groups (Lazarus 1971), because group members can provide more varied models and opportunities for practice than the therapist alone. Assertion-training groups and even manuals on how to be more assertive (among them Smith 1975) have become quite popular in recent years. The women's liberation movement has led many women to desire to enhance their social assertiveness, and training groups have sprung up in response.

[handwritten margin notes:]
Jacobson Study on happy + unhappy couples.
unhappy — fewer rewarding ones + more punishing ones — control by aversive means — feelings are rarely expressed straight forwardly. — tone of communication in engaged couples.

Markham
greater satisfaction — predicted future relationship. (+ve) neutral -ve distress in marriage.
2 yrs later

Behavioral Marriage counselling — to increase the rewarding interaction + decreasing punishing ones.
counseling program. — negotiation of behavior — exchange agreements — when the consequences are spelled out + contingency contacts
2/training in communication skills and effective problem solving. — in behavioral language — no blame etc

approach to — training couples in assertion techniques — to involve others — behavioral communication etc — and others for enhancing communication for beyond individual needs i.e. treat individual couples together.

difficulty in maintaining open communication + sustaining pleasure in an intimate relationship.

evidence of effectiveness is accumulating

Fig. 15.7. In assertion training groups, participants often learn about appropriate and inappropriate assertiveness through role playing.

BEHAVIORAL MARRIAGE COUNSELING. For many people it is especially difficult to maintain open communication and sustain pleasure in an intimate relationship. In the past, problems in marriage might have led one or both partners into individual psychotherapy, but therapists of all persuasions are increasingly seeing such difficulties as problems in relationship that go beyond individual neuroses, and are treating couples together. Behavioral marriage counseling is one approach to treating couples; it incorporates training in assertion and other behavioral techniques for enhancing communication and problem solving. Many recent studies have sought behaviors which characterize happy and distressed couples (Jacobson 1979). Observational and self-assessment measures reveal that distressed couples display fewer rewarding behaviors with each other and, especially, that they display more punishing ones (Gottman et al. 1976). In distressed relationships, control is apt to be exerted by aversive means, such as nagging, pouting, complaining, and sometimes physical abuse (see Chapter 17). In these, feelings are rarely expressed straightforwardly (Eisler and Hersen 1973). A remarkable study by Markman (1978) examined the tone of communication in engaged couples. Each partner rated the other's communication as positive, neutral, or negative, and the ratings predicted later relationship distress in marriage. Engaged couples who rated their experience of each other's statements as more positive reported greater satisfaction in their relationships two and a half years later.

Behavioral marriage counseling generally aims to increase the rewarding interactions between partners and to decrease the punishing

Eysenck's
- focus on observable behaviors
- but BT has changed this view ... more cognitive ... minimizing diff w/ psychotherapeutic
go into more cognitive levels ... diff w/ approaches

ones. A counseling program has two main segments. The first is to help each partner pinpoint specific changes that he or she would like to see in the relationship and to negotiate *behavior-exchange agreements,* wherein each partner agrees to change specific behaviors. When the consequences are spelled out, these are called *contingency contracts.* The second part is training in *communication skills and effective problem solving.* Training may be given in expression of feelings, assertiveness, and expressing support and understanding. Couples are taught to express their desires and dissatisfactions in specifically behavioral language. Rather than make vague general statements such as, "You never care about what I say," which fix blame, invite counter-blame, and do not point the way to a resolution, a husband might be helped to specify, "When I come home at night, I'd like it if you asked me about my day at work." This more specific statement more easily points to constructive change. It may become part of a contingency contract:

Wife agrees:	Husband agrees:
to ask three days this week about how Jerry's day went.	to help Betty with the dishes at least four nights this week.

A more elaborate contract would include several behaviors for each to increase and decrease, as well as penalties for noncompliance, and perhaps additional rewards that each would choose. Although such contracts may seem contrived and an artificial way for two people to relate, they do seem effective in a therapy program when the couple genuinely desire to improve their relationship.

Because much stress in marital relationships comes about in dealing with specific conflicts, counseling also facilitates problem-solving skills. Teaching communication and problem solving utilizes behavioral rehearsal methods, with therapist modeling and coaching, role-play sessions in the office, continuing feedback, and homework assignments. Many specific techniques have been devised in recent years to facilitate the technique, and evidence of their effectiveness is beginning to accumulate (Jacobson 1979).

An illustrative couple from Jacobson's (1977) behavioral marriage counseling recorded daily frequencies at home of the behaviors they disliked in the other partner. Marlene complained that Leon spent little time talking with her and that when he did talk he made many demanding statements. Figure 15.8 is Marlene's record of these behaviors. At point A a contract was negotiated in which Leon agreed to talk more with Marlene, who would reward this action by taking interest in his activities. Notice the marked rise in Leon's talking. Demanding statements did not decrease, though, until Leon agreed to change them in another contract at Point B. Similarly, Leon pinpointed behaviors for Marlene to change, and these too were recorded and included in agreements.

COGNITIVE STRATEGIES *anxiety, etc. are a response to external events; less than a reaction to the way in which we perceive + interpret these events.*

Introducing behavior therapy, we mentioned Eysenck's (1959) insistence that treatment focus on observable behaviors. In recent years, however, behavior therapists have deemed it important to also modify cognitions — what people believe and say to themselves. As with interpersonal communication earlier, the new cognitive emphasis has blurred some distinctions between behavior therapy and the psychotherapeutic approaches.

catastrophizing
Ellis

Cognitive therapists argue that our anxiety is less a response to external events than a reaction to the way in which we perceive and interpret these events. A college student may panic during exams with thoughts such as: "I'm getting confused and am going to go blank," and

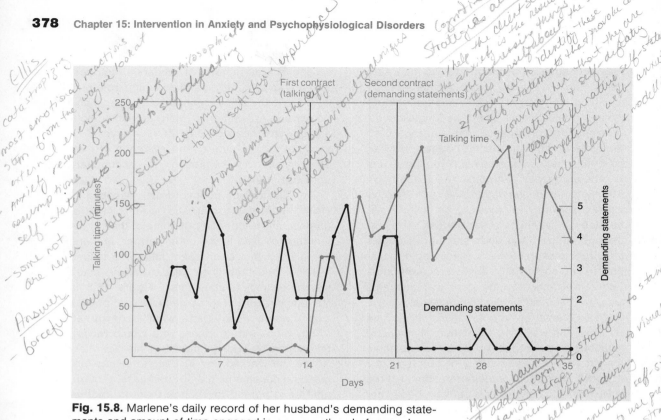

Fig. 15.8. Marlene's daily record of her husband's demanding statements and amount of time engaged in conversation, before and after agreeing to contracts developed during behavioral marriage counseling. (After Jacobson 1977.)

"This can make or break my future." This type of thinking is called *catastrophizing* by Albert Ellis (1962), whose rational-emotive therapy was predecessor of current cognitive therapies (Mahoney 1974; Meichenbaum 1977).

Ellis's premise is that most emotional reactions stem from the way we look at external events. Anxiety results from faulty philosophical assumptions that lead to self-defeating self-statements. These are among the faulty assumptions Ellis (1962) describes:

The idea that it is a dire necessity for an adult human being to be loved or approved by virtually every significant other person in his community (p. 61).

The idea that one should be thoroughly competent, adequate, and achieving in all possible respects, if one is to consider oneself worthwhile (p. 63).

The idea that one should be dependent on others and needs someone stronger than oneself on whom to rely (p. 80).

Ellis says many anxious persons, not even aware that they hold some such belief, cannot ever appraise their experiences as totally satisfying. His approach is to offer forceful counterarguments against the faulty beliefs and the resulting self-statements, as in this excerpt from a therapy session with a woman whose love affair had ended against her wishes:

"But you don't seem to understand," Myra wailed. "He has left me. I not only loved him, but had my whole future planned in and around him. Nothing has meaning any more. Everything I try to do, everywhere I go, everything I even try to think about is just plain empty without him." And she dived, for the twelfth time that session, for her wad of Kleenex tissues.

"Yes, I don't seem to understand. But I do understand; and it is you, in all probability, who don't."

Treating Sexual Dysfunction

Successful ways of treating sexual dysfunctions have been found only in the last decade, due in large part to the pioneering work of Wolpe (1958) and Masters and Johnson (1966, 1970). Although many persons are now doing research and clinical work in sexual dysfunction and therapy (see, for example, Barbach 1974; Kaplan 1974; Lobitz and LoPiccolo 1972; Zeiss et al. 1978), Masters and Johnson have provided the model for current approaches.

They believe that sex dysfunctions result from faulty learning about sexuality and persist because of fear of failure, anxiety about performance (see Chapter 14), worry about pleasing one's partner, fear of rejection, and inability to express to one's partner one's sexual likes and dislikes. A premise in their approach to sex therapy is that "there is no such thing as an uninvolved partner in any marriage in which there is some form of sexual inadequacy" (Masters and Johnson 1970, p. 2). Treatment of sexual dysfunction therefore generally employs a conjoint approach, both members of the marital unit working together to improve their sexual relationship. Masters and Johnson also recommend a male-female cotherapy team to facilitate the therapeutic process by assuring each member of the couple that his or her views will be empathetically understood. Also, the cotherapy team can model the frank and open questioning and sharing of information that many couples with a sexual problem find difficult.

All approaches to sex therapy include at least three components: (1) an in-depth psychosexual history of each partner, (2) instruction in the facts about male and female sexuality and responsiveness, and (3) homework assignments.

Consider the case of Mike and Judith, a couple in their early twenties who came for therapy before they had been married a year. Although they had slept together occasionally prior to marriage, they had refrained from premarital intercourse and limited their sexual relationship to kissing, caressing, and manually stimulating each other's nude body. Both partners were dissatisfied with their sexual relationship. Mike complained that he ejaculated too quickly, sometimes after only one or two thrusts, and Judith was displeased with her inability to achieve orgasm with her husband. Although they were clearly frustrated by their sexual relationship, both partners professed their emotional commitment to each other and willingness to comply with the demands of sex therapy.

The psychosexual history

Before treatment begins, the therapists obtain from each partner a complete picture of historical and present influences, beliefs, and activities that might be related to the present complaint. Mike and Judith revealed that both had come from religious homes where sex was rarely discussed. Neither had received any formal sex education. Although both were able to masturbate to orgasm, they rarely did so because it made them feel guilty. Mike had intercourse once before marriage and recalled the experience with more anxiety than pleasure. Judith was a virgin when she married, but eagerly anticipated broadening her sexual experience with her husband.

Sex education

When the specific sexual dysfunction is clear, therapy begins. The plan for treatment focuses on providing the partners with infor-

You don't — or, rather, I should really say you won't understand that it is over, and there's not a damned thing you can do about it right now to start it up again. And what you especially don't or won't understand is that the only sane thing to do, at the moment, is to start thinking about what else and who else can be interesting and enjoyable to you. No use repeating over and over that 'life is empty without Robert' — thereby making it as empty as you're saying it is.

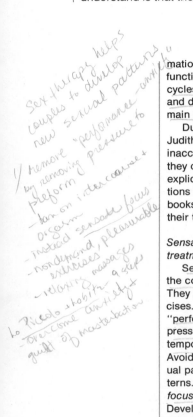

mation and skills to improve their sexual functioning. Accurate information on the cycles of male and female sexual response and debunking of myths about sex are a main part of treatment.

During their first sessions, Mike and Judith became aware of their incomplete and inaccurate sexual knowledge. After a while, they overcame embarrassment when talking explicitly about sex and began to ask questions freely. They even picked up paperback books on male and female sexuality that their therapist recommended.

Sensate focus and specific strategies for treatment

Sex therapy is meant ultimately to help the couple develop new sexual patterns. They receive a range of homework exercises. The first step is to erase the partners' "performance anxieties" by removing the pressure to perform; the therapist imposes a temporary ban on intercourse and orgasm. Avoiding established, anxiety-producing sexual patterns makes it easier to learn new patterns. Instead the couple learns *sensate focus,* or nondemand, pleasuring, exercises. Developed by Masters and Johnson (1970), these exercises are relaxing massages that partners take turns giving and receiving. They neither demand nor expect that either partner will become aroused. Anxiety caused by sexual failure abates so that new, pleasurable responses can be reinforced and new sexual intimacy can be established.

Other home exercises work on specific sexual dysfunctions. Treatment of orgasmic dysfunction provides the woman with permission and procedures for reaching orgasm by encouraging self-stimulation. In a highly effective nine-step masturbation program developed by LoPiccolo and Lobitz (1972), women learn to explore their own bodies vi-

sually and tactually, ultimately focusing on pleasure-producing sensations in the clitoral area. Obviously, therapists must be extremely sensitive in helping *both* partners overcome guilt and anxiety about masturbation and erotic fantasy during masturbation. When the woman can achieve orgasm by self-stimulation, she learns to teach her partner to stimulate her successfully by giving him verbal directions and physically guiding his hand. Once this step has been accomplished, the woman should be able to achieve pleasurable stimulation by coitus.

The *stop-start technique* (Semans 1956) and a variation, the *squeeze technique* (Masters and Johnson 1970), are homework used in treating premature ejaculation. Both are designed to help the male achieve voluntary control over the ejaculatory reflex by becoming more aware of sensations in his penis that precede orgasm. While his partner masturbates him, he is instructed to focus on these sensations. As excitement mounts and he approaches orgasm, he is instructed to tell his partner, who will then either stop stimulation or firmly squeeze the erect penis just below the glans with her thumb and forefinger. The ejaculatory urge abates and the erection subsides. Moments later, the couple repeats this process. After four repetitions, the man is permitted to ejaculate. The man becomes increasingly aware of the sensations that signal orgasm and is able to exercise voluntary control over the ejaculatory reflex. Masters and Johnson (1970) reported using these techniques successfully with 182 of 186 men who had complained of premature ejaculation.

Inasmuch as Mike and Judith's attempts at intercourse had been so unsatisfactory, both were delighted with the bans the therapist imposed. Although neither found the early sensate focus exercises particularly

''Why, just the other day I had a fifty-four-year-old man in here who literally began to cry when he talked about his mother. Know how long his dear old mother had been dead? Twenty-five years. Only yesterday to him. Genuine emotion? Deep love for dear old mother? Absolutely. But the poor guy had kept it alive for twenty-five years by regularly saying to himself: 'Mother is dead. How awful, how dreadful. What a fine, wonderful, self-sacrificing woman she was! And now she's dead —

arousing, both reported that the procedure was unhurried, relaxing, and comfortable. Also, these sessions were a chance to reexplore each other's body and discuss response to tactile stimulation. In small steps, treatment progressed through the stages described above. By the end of therapy, Mike was able to delay his orgasm for up to four minutes. Although Judith continued to have difficulty reaching orgasm during coitus, she had learned to give herself an orgasm and had taught her husband how to give her an orgasm as well. Perhaps as important, the couple reported being especially pleased with the new intimacy that accompanied their recently acquired sexual awareness.

Outcome of sex therapy

Masters and Johnson reported an extremely high rate of success with their therapy program and found after a five-year follow-up period that their success was sustained. Recent reviews of many studies using variations of their techniques with a much broader range of clients have been less favorable, however (Wright et al. 1977). Helen Kaplan (1974, 1975), a major figure in this field, argues that sex therapy would be more effective if it included both insight and behavioral techniques for dealing with the conflicts aroused by various homework exercises.

the masters + Johnsons techniques have proved to be effective even after a 5 yr follow up — but variations have not been so successful

Kaplan :- suggested the inclusion of both insight + behavioral techniques for dealing with the conflicts.

gone forever. Poor mother! And poor motherless me! How awful!' ''

''Well, you'll have to admit,'' and Myra smiled a little through her tears, ''that I'm not quite as bad as that yet.''

''No, not yet. But you probably will be if you keep feeding yourself this hogwash about how indispensable Robert was to your life and how you can't go on without him. If you want to follow the noble example of my fifty-four-year-old patient and his dear departed mother. . . . I am sure, in fact I have every confidence, that you can go on telling yourself for the next twenty-five years or so what a stinking, horrible, catastrophic shame it is that Robert has left you and rendered your poor, poor life infinitely barren. You can do it, all right, if you just keep telling yourself such nonsense. On the other hand, if you decide that instead of sitting around in feebleminded grief you'd like to develop an interesting and enjoyable life — this you can do by saying different kinds of sentences to yourself and learning to believe and act on them.''

''You are certainly a hard-boiled and hard-hearted person. You make fun of my genuine bereavement by comparing it with a sick old man's sentiment for his mother.''

''Yes, I make fun because I have found from long experience in helping people that they find it exceedingly difficult to leave my office and start catastrophizing with the same consistency and intensity if I have ridiculed their prolonged disturbance. For you to feel badly for a little while about Robert's desertion may make some sense. And it especially makes sense if you want to examine as critically and objectively as possible — with my help — what are some of the things you did or didn't do to contribute to Robert's leaving you. But for you to sit around and tell yourself how hornswoggled bad it is, how devastatingly catastrophic that you no longer have your dear Robert — that makes no more sense than my two examples. So Robert deserted you. The problem is: What can you do to enjoy your life without him? Stop crying over how unfair reality is to you. It is as it is. Let's see what you can do to make it better.''

As I proceeded to hammer away at Myra Benson's irrational preoccupation with her loss, she began to substitute other self-verbalizations for the ones with which she had been making, and keeping, herself depressed. She soon began to develop new interests, activities, associations. Life ceased to be empty. Not that it had intrinsically changed; but she began to interpret it differently. And that made all the difference in the world (Ellis and Harper 1961, pp. 116-117).

Subsequent cognitive therapists have used rational-emotive therapy as a starting point and added other behavioral techniques, such as shaping and behavioral rehearsal. Cognitive strategies generally aim to: (1) help the client see that anxieties are the result of the distressing things she tells herself about the situation, not of the situation itself; (2) train her to identify the self-statements she makes in these anxiety-provoking situations; (3) convince her of how these are irrational and self-defeating, and (4) teach alternative self-statements (''self-talk'') that are incompatible with anxiety. When the client has generally accepted the inappropriateness of the self-defeating thoughts, she is exposed to anxiety-evoking situations (in a desensitization-like hierarchy) and trained by role-playing and modeling to reformulate anxiety-producing self-statements (Goldfried, Decentecer, and Weinberg 1974). Meichenbaum (1977) has studied adding cognitive strategies to standard techniques of behavior therapy. In one study he found that test-anxious college students showed greater improvement in an analogue test situation, on self-report measures, and on gradepoint averages when they were asked to visualize coping as well as mastery behaviors during desensitization (Meichenbaum 1972). They were to imagine themselves coping with anxiety as it arose and to use personally generated self-statements to facilitate staying with the task and inhibiting anxiety. For them anxiety was a signal to employ previously learned coping strategies, such as relaxation and alternative self-talk. We have evidence that such modification of cognitive behavior is especially helpful with clients whose anxiety is "free-floating" (Meichenbaum et al. 1971).

Effectiveness of Psychological Therapies

We have talked at length about the various ways that therapists attempt to create conditions that will alleviate anxiety disorders. But how effective are these procedures, and does evidence show that any therapeutic school has a genuine advantage over the others? In a series of classic papers, Eysenck (1952; 1965) concluded that psychotherapy has not proven effective. Reviewing a number of studies on therapy, he reported that about two-thirds of the clients were seen as improved. The improvement rate cited for untreated clients, based upon two papers, was also about two-thirds. Eysenck's conclusion that psychotherapy has no effect got a lively controversy started. One point hotly contested (Bergin and Lambert 1978) was the high rate of improvement without therapy, called *spontaneous recovery*. Many of these individuals had experience with doctors and mental hospitals, and besides, the criteria for improvement were questionable.

Malan (1973), in particular, distinguished between relieving symptoms and relieving underlying problems (see Chapter 13). Studying applicants for help with anxiety or personality disorders who went untreated, he found that 48 percent did show reduction of symptoms; however, only 22 percent could be said to have resolved underlying problems. Obviously the rate of spontaneous recovery relates to one's criteria for success.

Since Eysenck did his original analysis, numerous controlled studies have compared groups who received a known psychological treatment with some control conditions. The control is most often a definite waiting period after a person is accepted for treatment. Smith and Glass (1977) carefully combined the results of more than 375 studies on this subject into one global analysis and concluded, in marked contrast to Eysenck, that the average client treated by a psychological therapy was better off than 83 percent of untreated clients, by criteria of alleviation of anxiety and improvement in self-esteem.

Effects of Different Therapies

Smith and Glass also attempted to determine if this large series of studies gave one therapeutic approach an advantage over another. They found no great difference. Determining the relative effectiveness of different therapies requires controlled trials more narrowly specifying the client population. In one outstanding study, Sloane and colleagues (1975) contrasted behavioral and psychoanalytic therapeutic techniques with a waiting-list control for a four-month course of treatment. The psychoanalytic therapy followed the model described in this chapter, and the behavior therapy was multimodal, involving counterconditioning and procedures such as assertiveness training. All therapists were highly experienced. Independent analyses of tape recordings revealed that these were distinctive therapeutic approaches, and that their implementation was true to their model. The waiting-list control group was handled with considerable therapeutic skill, with all clients extensively interviewed about their problems, definitely promised treatment, and called regularly for support and encouragement. This attention probably reduced differences between therapy and control groups.

The patients in the study were very typical of those with anxiety or personality disorders who apply for psychotherapeutic help (Table 13.3). The participants were troubled mainly by crippling anxiety and disturbed interpersonal relationships.

Outcomes of treatment were evaluated by

independent assessors, blind as to which treatment each patient received. Although an overall subjective assessment favored behavior therapy, the external observers' more specific rating of change in target problems found 80 percent of the patients in each active therapy group either improved or recovered. No difference appeared in rates of effectiveness for the two treatments. In the waiting-list control, 48 percent were judged improved or recovered, very close to Malan's finding. Furthermore, the gains at four months in improved clients were still apparent twelve months later, with no significant difference between the treatment approaches.

Specific Therapies for Specific Problems

Although these two forms of therapy are similarly effective for many kinds of anxiety problems, one *may* be more effective than another for a specific type of problem. Research on subclinical forms of psychopathology, in which clients respond to ads for free therapy for such problems as classical phobias (heights, small animals), social anxieties, or insomnia consistently show that behavior therapy is superior to other forms of intervention (Paul 1966). For clinical patients who seek help for the crippling effects of severe phobias, the difference is not so clear. Zitrin, Klein, and Woerner (1978) treated three types of phobic clients: (1) agoraphobics, who experience panic attacks when they leave the house and anticipatory anxiety the rest of the time; (2) simple phobics, who manifest fear of closed spaces, heights, animals, and specific social situations; and (3) mixed phobics, who have characteristics of both simple phobias and agoraphobia. They are, for the most part, clients with circumscribed phobias who have spontaneous attacks of panic but no restrictions on travel.

All clients were assigned to one of three group-treatment conditions for a six-month

course. Two groups received Imipramine, an antidepressant drug that inhibits panic attacks, and either behavioral or insight therapy. The third group had only behavior therapy. Unfortunately, no group had insight therapy alone. The insight therapy was either psychoanalytic or client-centered. The behavior-therapy clients were directed to confront phobic situations; the insight-therapy clients never were. The behavior therapy was multimodal, with homework assignments.

The results of the study are quite complex. For agoraphobias and mixed phobics, both therapies accompanied by Imipramine were equally effective and more effective than behavior therapy alone. The panic-suppressing benefit of the drug apparently was important in cases of severe phobia. The data for simple phobics was very consistent with the earlier studies on volunteer populations. The group with behavior therapy alone (no drug) had the highest rate of moderate to marked improvement and also the lowest rate of clients dropping out of the study. When dropouts are considered as failures, the success rate is: behavior therapy alone, 80 percent; behavior therapy and drug, 48 percent; insight therapy and drug, 29 percent. It is not clear why the drug inhibited progress with behavior therapy for simple phobics. Data of this sort indicate that although differences between therapeutic approaches are not obvious in studies of a heterogenous sample of anxiety and personality disorders, advantages and additional questions may appear in studies of carefully defined groups.

Preventing Anxiety Disorders

Throughout this chapter we have considered methods of help for people who already have anxiety or psychophysiological disorders. An obvious question, though, is what we can do to

[handwritten margin annotations at top:] Meichenbaum / Stress-inoculation training — 3 steps / 1) educational phase — learns about emotions + stress reactions / 2) rehearsal phase — direct action (relaxation) and cognitive coping, models 4 stages in dealing with stress / 1) preparing for stressor / 2) confronting a stressor + handling a stressor / 3) coping with the feeling of being overwhelmed / 4) reinforcing self statements / 3) Application phase — practice dealing with stressful conditions in the therapist's office

prevent these in the first place. In Chapter 22 we shall consider programs with children that may, we hope, reduce likelihood of later problems in adulthood. To consider possibilities of prevention more fully, however, we would need to think of reducing many sources of stress in the environment, such as poverty, crowding, noise pollution, unemployment, competition for jobs, and discrimination. As long as these continue, we will live in an anxiety-producing climate. A consideration of these possibilities, however important, is beyond the scope of this book.

Psychological efforts at preventing anxiety have focused primarily on individuals, and usually are aimed at early intervention for anxiety or preventing further anxiety in the future. Self-help books suggest how to cope with problems not yet so disabling as to bring people to a clinic, such as fears, sexual anxieties and dysfunctions, or problems in parenting, marital communication, and assertiveness. Some therapies strengthen the client's resistance to future anxieties. One is Meichenbaum's (1977) extension of the self-instruction techniques we have discussed.

To provide the client with a more fully effective coping strategy against future anxiety in varied situations, Meichenbaum developed a three-phase method of *stress-inoculation training.* In the *educational phase,* the client learns about emotion and stress reactions. In the *rehearsal phase,* the client rehearses coping skills such as direct actions (relaxation) and cognitive coping modes. He receives positive coping statements for each of four stages in dealing with stress, and learns to use his maladaptive behaviors, thoughts, and feelings as cues to employ these statements. These are examples of coping self-statements taught to clients:

1. *Preparing for a stressor*
   What is it you have to do?
   You can develop a plan to deal with it.
   Maybe what you think is anxiety is eagerness to confront the stressor.

2. *Confronting and handling a stressor*
   One step at a time: you can handle the situation.
   This anxiety is what the doctor said you would feel. It's a reminder to use your coping exercises.
   Relax; you're in control. Take a slow deep breath.

3. *Coping with the feeling of being overwhelmed*
   When fear comes, just pause.
   Keep the focus on the present; what is it you have to do?
   Don't try to eliminate fear totally; just keep it manageable.

4. *Reinforcing self-statements*
   It worked; you did it.
   Wait until you tell your therapist (or group) about this.
   It's getting better each time you use the procedures (Meichenbaum 1977, p. 155).

In the *application phase* the client has a chance to practice dealing with stressful conditions in the therapist's office. He may receive unpredictable electric shocks, see a stressful film, or experience failure or embarrassment; in each stressful situation he is coached to employ the previously learned coping skills. Meichenbaum and Cameron (1972) report one study of multiphobic clients in which training in stress inoculation brought more general success than systematic desensitization. The clients had learned some general coping skills that they could apply as the skills were needed in new situations. *[handwritten: Meichenbaum & Cameron study — better than desensitization]*

Summary

1. Psychological and pharmacological intervention are used to treat anxiety disorders.

2. The drugs taken by anxiety-disordered patients effectively reduce anxiety for a short time but have no evident lasting benefits.

3. The three major psychological schools of

[handwritten margin: therapeutic guidelines]

treatment for anxiety disorders are: psychoanalytic, humanistic-existential, and behavioral.

4. Both psychoanalytic therapy and humanistic-existential therapy emphasize the need for insight, or awareness of underlying, conflicting feelings, as a precondition for relief of symptoms and change in behavior.

5. In all psychological therapies the client-therapist relationship must include mutual trust and a client willing to confront the hidden parts of the self. The role of the psychoanalyst is primarily nondirective, providing a blank screen onto which the client can transfer his feelings and attitudes about those significant in his life. Insight into the past is seen as essential for change.

6. The trend in psychoanalytic therapy is to extend intervention techniques to groups and particularly to families.

7. Existential-humanistic approaches to treatment of anxiety disorders differ from psychoanalytic therapy in emphasizing that both client and therapist should be more active in the therapeutic work. The varied existential-humanistic approaches have these in common: (1) insight into current feelings, assumptions, and values about the self and significant others; (2) emphasis on the client's responsibility to change; and (3) active participation by the therapist in the intervention.

8. The diverse existential-humanistic approaches include: client-centered therapy, in which the therapist shares his own perceptions and experiences with the client to create a supportive environment for self-exploration; and Gestalt therapy, which uses games, awareness of body language, and dream reenactment to help the client discover parts of himself that he has refused to acknowledge.

9. Behavior therapy is far more directive than the psychoanalytic and existential-humanistic approaches. Also, behavior therapists measure success in treatment by observable change in behavior, not by assessing how thoroughly a client understands how his problem developed or why it persists. The behavior therapist's major techniques in treating anxiety include: relaxation training, in which the individual learns how to identify minor tension and reduce it; and systematic desensitization, in which a patient is gradually exposed to situations that progressively arouse more anxiety until each has lost its threat.

10. Behavioral techniques for alleviating anxiety that derives from inability to communicate effectively include: assertion training, and behavioral marriage counseling.

11. Cognitive variations of behavior therapy are an attempt to modify what people believe and say about themselves, on the theory that it is our perceptions of reality, not reality itself, which determine our response to our environment.

12. Controlled studies indicate that anxiety-disordered patients fare better with therapy than without, and psychoanalytic and behavioral therapies seem to be equally effective, except in treating simple phobic patients, who respond better to behavioral techniques.

13. One attempt to prevent anxiety disorders teaches coping skills that can be employed in future stressful situations.

Unit 6

Social Deviance

In our country almost everyone reveres individual liberty. It is a priceless ethic, backed by a constitutional guarantee. Complete freedom, though, is never feasible. People organized into communities must submit to major compromises for harmony to prevail. Freud recognized this compromise in his structural view of the mind. He saw a continuous war among id (constantly pressing for relief from tension); ego (evaluating the risks and benefits in immediate or delayed expression of impulses); and superego (internalizing major rules and sanctions). To live together, we must delay some impulses, inhibit others, and find socially acceptable outlets for the rest.

All societies have criteria for acceptably expressing impulses as well as sanctions for transgressing the bounds. The criteria differ remarkably from culture to culture; use of some drugs is abuse in our society, but a positive act, a religious rite, in another. Anthropologists tell us that even though specific cultural norms differ so, all cultures attempt to regulate three broad classes of impulse expression: sexual behavior, aggressive behavior (against property or person), and ingestion of mind-altering chemicals. Of course, it is not always easy to separate these behavioral systems. Is rape a pattern of sexual behavior or an aggressive act? As we will see, it may be both.

In these chapters we will examine patterns of behavior that are considered deviant in contemporary society. We are in a period of great change in the social criteria that define deviance. Our values on acceptable sexual patterns are changing, as are our attitudes toward psychoactive chemicals. Perhaps nowhere else in this book do we need to keep such an open mind about standards of deviance and criteria for social intervention.

In Chapter 16 we will discuss individuals who recurrently use psychoactive chemicals. Individual liberty and social control collide more violently here than on any other issue. Do you have the right to ingest some chemicals for recreation, so long as it does not bring you in conflict with others or with basic rules of social living? Some will resoundingly answer yes; others will be equally vociferous in the negative. Society has a right, they will argue, to control any use of chemicals deemed excessive, to protect people from harming themselves.

In fact, it is not so simple to separate effects on the individual from effects on others. Alcoholics disrupt not themselves alone, but their families. Heroin addicts frequently resort to criminal acts against others for cash to buy illegal drugs. We have chosen to emphasize the most serious patterns of substance abuse.

In Chapter 17 we focus on patterns of sexual behavior that cause difficulties for the individual or for those around him. Mostly, but not exclusively, the sexual behavior is male, and the victim, if any, is usually a female. To learn about sexual deviance we must know both past and current cultural attitudes on male-female roles and relationships.

In Chapter 18 we present patterns of social deviance that involve aggression. Here we range from the traditional criminal, both adult and juvenile, to the sociopath who seems remarkably insensitive to normal rewards and punishments, to a subject newly opened up: family violence, in which members aggress against spouse or child.

In Chapter 19, we survey different classes of interventions used with socially deviant individuals. Interventions originally devised for the anxiety disorders have not worked well with socially deviant individuals. Rehabilitation techniques, applying peer group pressure and multimodal treatment combining pharmacology and psychology, appear to be more effective.

Discussing intervention for social deviance is difficult because the sexual deviant, the substance abuser, and the criminal may be handled by more than one system of intervention. Very often they come in contact with the legal system, which dispenses punishments such as imprisonment for criminal activity, and a mental health system that tries to offer rehabilitation. Social values have vacillated markedly in the last thirty-five years on how to construe and handle social deviants. Are they "sick" people best considered less than fully responsible for their actions and so eligible for helpful treatment outside the criminal justice system? Or are they "bad" people who must be punished in the criminal justice system to prevent recurrences and to act as a deterrent to others? No doubt you feel strongly about this issue yourself and sense conflict between these alternatives. Be assured that your conflict mirrors the ambivalence in our society and in these chapters.

Chapter 16

Substance Abuse

Criteria for Abuse
Psychological Dependence
Negative Social Effects
DSM-III Criteria

Causes of Abuse

Opiate Addiction
Theories of Addiction
Factors Leading to Opiate Addiction
Continuing Use of Narcotics

Central Nervous System Depressants: Alcohol
Alcohol
Theories of Alcoholism
Factors Leading to Alcoholism

Stimulants of the Central Nervous System
Amphetamines
Cocaine
Caffeine

Hallucinogens

Marijuana
Patterns of Use
Therapeutic Uses
Social Policy

Summary

Poppies, wild mushrooms, hemp (cannabis), tobacco, cocoa, fermented grains and fruits — these chemical agents have provided people with the means of celebration, escape, pleasure, and relaxation throughout history. In recent years the pharmaceutical industry has added more powerful and sophisticated substances to this formidable supply of mind-altering substances. These substances can produce desirable altered states of consciousness, but why should we be concerned with them in abnormal psychology? Some drugs, including alcohol and marijuana, are used by so many that it is the nonuser who can feel abnormal; Figure 16.1 gives some idea of how many youths use mind-altering chemicals. And yet their power to provide pleasure, increase fantasy, and permit escape from life's daily irritations can make problems for all of us. Some people cannot regulate their use of one or more and become their slaves. And some drugs, such as heroin and morphine, produce major changes in our bodies that make it difficult for even the most stable of us to stop using them. This loss of control turns substance abuse into a problem,

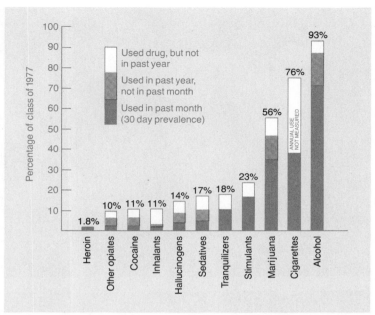

Fig. 16.1. Percentage of the United States high school class of 1977 using different types of drugs. These data were collected in a nationwide study of high school students, focusing on a pivotal point in their life, their final year in high school. (After "Marijuana and Health" 1977.)

and the changes in behavior that invariably accompany excessive use of drugs make it appropriate for psychologists to study.

Ordinarily, when we think of drug abuse, we think of heroin, cocaine, amphetamines, glue-sniffing, and perhaps LSD, PCP, and marijuana. Usually we don't connect the word "abuse" with alcohol and tobacco, and certainly not with coffee. Attitudes toward use and abuse of drugs, like the definition of abnormal behavior, are determined by social mores and values and vary from time to time and from place to place. In France, a meal without wine can be unthinkable, but in Moslem countries drinking alcohol violates religious law, if not civil law. Attitudes toward drugs also differ in subcultures within the United States. Society as a whole sanctions

consumption of alcohol, tobacco, coffee, and tea, but looks on users of peyote, or mescaline, as deviant. Yet members of the Mormon Church are forbidden to use alcohol, tobacco, or caffeine, and in some Indian nations of the Southwest, peyote is permanently part of religious ceremonies.

Criteria for Abuse

Despite wide differences in cultural attitudes, agreement seems general about behaviors of and consequences for the substance abuser. They are: (1) *psychological dependence,* and (2) *negative social effects.*

Fig. 16.2. The cultural acceptability of a drug often determines the environment and pattern of its use. Alcohol is a widely accepted drug in our society. Although marijuana is becoming increasingly accepted, its use is more often limited to more casual, ''nonestablishment'' social situations.

Psychological Dependence

A person who has a compelling *desire* (not necessarily a physical need) to use a chemical substance and cannot stop using it or cut down frequency or dosage is said to have a psychological dependence. *Psychological dependence,* as the term implies, is the belief that the substance is necessary for continued functioning.

Many of those who are psychologically dependent on some drugs develop physiological *tolerance* for a drug they use regularly. In other words, they come to require more and more of the substance to achieve the effect they want. This condition is important not only in drug abuse but in medical treatment of infection and disease, for the patient's drug or dosage must be changed as tolerance develops. Consequently most new drugs are tested on labora-

Fig. 16.3. This woman shows some of the painful and terrifying feelings that people can experience when withdrawing from drugs.

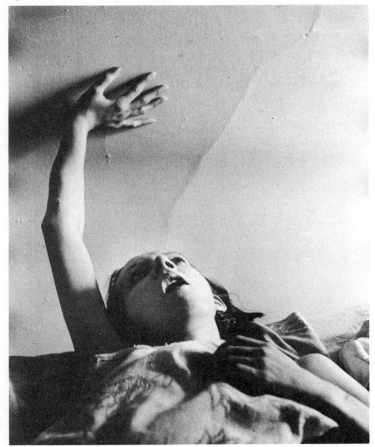

tory animals to determine the likelihood of tolerance.

Some *addictive drugs* can create not only tolerance but also physiological dependence. If the individual fails to consume more of the drug before his body has completely metabolized the previous dose, he will suffer a generally painful physical reaction, the *withdrawal syndrome.* The symptoms of withdrawal differ with each class of substance, but generally the reaction is quite uncomfortable. The pain frequently motivates the user to go back on the drug, despite a desire to give it up and resume a normal life.

Negative Social Effects

Using a drug repeatedly with noticeable signs of psychological dependence frequently affects social, educational, and occupational effectiveness. Social relations may be disturbed by failure to meet obligations to friends, family, employers, or teachers. The person may manifest erratic, impulsive, or inappropriate aggressive behavior deviating significantly from past patterns. Intoxication or criminal behavior motivated by the need to buy drugs brings many drug abusers into the criminal justice system.

If we accept this highly negative picture of drug abuse, we can eliminate coffee, tea, cocoa, and tobacco from the list of dangerously abused drugs. The person who needs his daily twelve cups of coffee to feel alert and avoid headaches can be said to depend on caffeine, but his dependence is not likely to have negative social or legal implications. Excluding tobacco from the list of drugs that have harmful effects on nonusers might be questioned by an increasingly vocal group who would outlaw smoking in public places, but this viewpoint does not yet predominate.

DSM-III Criteria

In the current revision of *DSM*-III two general patterns of drug misuse are recognized: *sub-stance abuse* and *substance dependence.* Substance abuse has a minimal duration of one month of drug use and includes marked psychological dependence as well as evidence of social complications. Though dependence may not be noticeable, a "pathological pattern of use" may reveal abuse. The symptoms are excessive use (using the substance every day or remaining intoxicated all day) and episodes of drug complications, such as alcoholic blackout or opiate overdose. *Substance dependence* shows the same symptoms as substance abuse but includes evidence of tolerance and withdrawal.

Causes of Abuse

The pathway from drug use to abuse or dependence is very complex, but there seem to be three sets of important factors: (1) the properties of the drug, (2) attributes of the drug user, and (3) the social environment. A drug's properties include biochemical action, positive and negative effects, route of administration, potential for tolerance and physical dependence, cost, access, and reinforcement schedules. Table 16.1 displays the major abused drugs and their relevant properties. The user's attributes consist of personality structure, psychopathology, financial resources, and biological predisposition. Many of these are similar to those implicated in psychophysiological disorders (see Chapter 14). Finally, drug abuse rarely occurs in a vacuum. It involves peers, it usually happens in specific social settings, and frequently it fosters association with subcultural groups and values that support continued abuse. Some factors lead to abuse and others maintain it. Availability of the drug, peer influence, and personality variables are thought to be important in the initial stages of substance abuse, whereas pharmacological properties of the drug, conditioning by experience with the drug, lack of life options, and involvement in a drug subculture are believed to be important in continued abuse.

Nowhere is this complexity of interactions more apparent than in the use and abuse of opiate drugs. That is why we have chosen to highlight *opiate addiction*. The costs are enormous, both to addicts and to society (in crime, treatment, and enforcement). It is a singularly important and interesting form of deviant behavior. Likewise, theories about the causes of opiate addiction are particularly variable, intermeshing, and numerous; they range from social and psychological explanations, on the one hand, to biological theories, on the other.

We shall also look at *central nervous system depressants* (alcohol, barbiturates, and sedative-hypnotic drugs), *psychomotor stimulants* (cocaine, amphetamines, and caffeine), and the *hallucinogens* and related drugs (LSD and marijuana). Each drug and its abuse need sep-arate treatment, but *polydrug abuse* (Gran et al. 1978), in which several drugs are used sequentially or concurrently, probably is the most common problem today.

Opiate Addiction

Opium, a substance that comes from the juice of poppy capsules, has a long history of use and abuse. Back in 4000 B.C., the Sumerians called the poppy a "joy plant," well aware of opium's euphoric effects. Arabian physicians used it to control dysentery, and Galen, a second-century physician, regarded it as a cure for almost every known physical and mental ailment, from insect bites to melancholy. By the sixteenth century, opium was common in Europe, and by the eighteenth century, smoking it was popular in the Orient. Morphine, a derivative, was discovered in 1803, and by the end of the nineteenth century, its use was

Patterns of Drug Abuse in the United States

Abuse of alcohol continues as the largest drug problem in this country. Adolescent problem drinking and alcoholism have spread significantly.

In spite of controls recently placed on amphetamines, the drugs are still readily available on the street and are widely abused.

Methaqualone (Quaaludes) continues in wide use, and in most localities it is second only to marijuana (excluding alcohol). Its abuse is greater than that of cocaine.

Phencyclidine (PCP or "angel dust") abuse is still widespread among adolescents.

Some over-the-counter psychoactive drugs are widely abused; normally these are sold for their tranquilizing or sedating effects.

Most hospital emergency room admis-sions for drug overdose involve substances available legally by prescription or over the counter without prescription.

Patterns of female drug use, at least as they compare to male patterns, are set quite early in life. During adolescence, females probably use twice as many prescription psychoactive drugs as males do.

Although females are more likely to be consumers of prescription drugs, males are more likely to use them for nonmedical or euphoric effects.

Much has been said on excessive use of psychoactive drugs by women who do not work outside the home, but the data suggest that current use of these drugs is strikingly similar, even for adult females who are primarily a part of the labor force (adapted from Chambers and Hunt 1977).

Table 16.1. Commonly abused substances; their uses and effects

Drugs	Common brand names	Medical uses	Dependence potential	
			Physical	Psychological
Opiates				
Opium	Dover's Powder, Paregoric	Analgesic, antidiarrheal	High	High
Morphine	Morphine	Analgesic	High	High
Codeine	Codeine	Analgesic, antitussive	Moderate	Moderate
Heroin	None	None	High	High
Meperidine (Pethidine)	Demerol, Pethadol	Analgesic	High	High
Methadone	Dolophine, Methadone, Methadose	Analgesic, heroin substitute	High	High
Other opiates	Dilaudid, Leritine, Numorphan, Percodan	Analgesic, antidiarrheal, antitussive	High	High
Depressants				
Chloral Hydrate	Noctec, Somnos	Hypnotic	Moderate	Moderate
Barbiturates	Amytal, Butisol, Nembutal, Phenobarbital, Seconal, Tuinal	Anesthetic, anticonvulsant, sedation, sleep	High	High
Glutethimide	Doriden	Sedation, sleep	High	High
Methaqualone	Optimil, Parest, Quaalude, Somnafac, Sopor	Sedation, sleep	High	High
Tranquilizers	Equanil, Librium, Miltown, Serax, Tranxene, Valium	Antianxiety, muscle relaxant, sedation	Moderate	Moderate
Other depressants	Clonopin, Dalmane, Dormate, Noludar, Placydil, Valmid	Antianxiety, sedation, sleep	Possible	Possible

Tolerance	Duration of effects (in hours)	Usual methods of administration	Possible effects	Effects of overdose	Withdrawal syndrome
Yes	3 to 6	Oral, smoked	Euphoria, drowsiness, respiratory depression, constricted pupils, nausea	Slow and shallow breathing, clammy skin, convulsions, coma, possible death	Watery eyes, runny nose, yawning, loss of appetite, irritability, tremors, panic, chills and sweating, cramps, nausea
Yes	3 to 6	Injected, smoked			
Yes	3 to 6	Oral, injected			
Yes	3 to 6	Injected, sniffed			
Yes	3 to 6	Oral, injected			
Yes	12 to 24	Oral, injected			
Yes	3 to 6	Oral, injected			
Probable	5 to 8	Oral	Slurred speech, disorientation, drunken behavior without odor of alcohol	Shallow respiration, cold and clammy skin, dilated pupils, weak and rapid pulse, coma, possible death	Anxiety, insomnia, tremors, delirium, convulsions, possible death
Yes	1 to 16	Oral, injected			
Yes	4 to 8	Oral			
Yes	4 to 8	Oral			
Yes	4 to 8	Oral			
Yes	4 to 8	Oral			

Table 16.1. *(continued)*

Drugs	Common brand names	Medical uses	Dependence potential	
			Physical	Psychological
Stimulants				
Cocaine	Cocaine	Local anesthetic	Possible	High
Amphetamines	Benzedrine, Biphetamine, Desoxyn, Dexedrine	Hyperkinesis, narcolepsy, weight control	Possible	High
Phenmetrazine	Preludin	Weight control	Possible	High
Methylphenidate	Ritalin	Hyperkinesis	Possible	Possible
Caffeine (coffee, tea, cola drinks, aspirin, over-the-counter antifatigue preparations)	No-Doz, Tirend	Headache	None	Moderate
Nicotine (cigarettes, cigars, snuff, smoking tobacco)		None	Possible	High
Other stimulants	Bacarate, Cylert, Didrex, Ionamin, Pondimin, Pre-Sate, Sanorex, Voranil	Weight control	Possible	Degree unknown
Hallucinogens				
Lysergic acid diethylamide (LSD)	None	None	None	Degree unknown
Mescaline	None	None	None	Degree unknown
Psilocybin	None	None	None	Degree unknown
MDA	None	None	None	Degree unknown
Phencyclidine (PCP)	Sernylan	Veterinary anesthetic	None	Degree unknown
Other hallucinogens	None	None	None	Degree unknown
Cannabis				
Marijuana	None	None	Degree unknown	Moderate
Hashish	None	None	Degree unknown	Moderate

Tolerance	Duration of effects (in hours)	Usual methods of administration	Possible effects	Effects of overdose	Withdrawal syndrome
Yes	2	Injected, sniffed	Increased alertness, excitation, euphoria, dilated pupils, increased pulse rate and blood pressure, insomnia, loss of appetite	Agitation, increase in body temperature, hallucinations, convulsions, possible death	Apathy, long periods of sleep, irritability, depression, disorientation
Yes	2 to 4	Oral			
Yes	2 to 4	Oral			
Yes	2 to 4	Oral			
Yes	2 to 4	Oral			
Yes	1 to 2	Oral, sniffed, smoked			
Yes	Variable	Oral			
Yes	Variable	Oral	Illusions and hallucinations (except MDA); poor perception of time and distance	Longer, more intense "trip" episodes, psychosis, possible death	Not reported
Yes	Variable	Oral, injected			
Yes	Variable	Oral			
Yes	Variable	Oral, injected, sniffed			
Yes	Variable	Oral, injected, smoked			
Yes	Variable	Oral, injected, sniffed			
Yes	2 to 4	Oral, smoked	Euphoria, relaxed inhibitions, increased appetite, disoriented behavior	Fatigue, paranoia, possible psychosis	Insomnia, hyperactivity, and decreased appetite reported in a limited number of individuals
Yes	2 to 4	Oral, smoked			

widespread. The hypodermic needle, invented in 1856, revolutionized drug therapy, and morphine during the Civil War was much applied as pain killer and treatment for dysentery. Many soldiers become addicted to morphine.

Attempts to eliminate morphine addiction opened up manufacture of another opium derivative: heroin. The new drug was even more addictive than its precursors. The problem was growing so rapidly that the government began an intensive campaign to limit the production and distribution of opiates in the United States. Legal restrictions greatly reduced their availability, but failed to suppress addiction completely because a steady black-market supply appeared for any who could pay the high asking price. Currently the United States has about 500,000 to 1 million addicts (Chambers and Hunt 1977).

Heroin is, of course, an illegal drug almost always requiring the addict to have to steal $300 to $400 worth of goods a day in order to support a habit costing $100 a day; he must steal that much more because the person who resells the stolen property will give him much less than its true value.

Opiates, or narcotics, as they are commonly known (although not all narcotics are derived from opium), are powerful *analgesics,* or pain relievers, as well as strong sedatives. Although morphine mainly affects the central nervous system as a depressant, it can also act as a stimulant, depending on the amount given, the way it is administered, and the user's experience. Heroin, the most abused opiate, can be lethal, and is the major cause of death from drug overdose. It can be smoked, eaten, inhaled ("snorted"), injected under the skin ("skin popping"), or injected intravenously ("mainlining"). A usual, immediate effect of mainlining heroin is intense euphoria, followed by prolonged but milder euphoria, lethargy, and relaxation. Within four to six hours, an addict begins to desire more heroin; signs of with-

drawal can begin within eight hours of the injection. Severity of the withdrawal depends on how strong the addict's habit is and on his health. The symptoms are tearing eyes, perspiration, increased respiration, chills, vomiting, sweating, and diarrhea. After three to five days, nearly all these withdrawal symptoms will have left.

Theories of Addiction

Is the addict or potential addict different from the rest of us in basic personality structure? Why and how is heroin first used? What options are open to an addict, and how do they, or the lack of them, affect the likelihood of becoming addicted? Why does an addict remain an addict?

Characteristics of addicts change over time. Early in this century most addicts were white adults, including a large number of women (Terry and Pellens 1928). In the 1930s the typical addict was an indigent white Southerner who did not participate in any subculture of antisocial activities (Winick 1964). In 1969, Einstein reported that most addicts were adolescents and young adults, and that addiction was more common among whites than nonwhites. He also found six to seven times as many male as female addicts, and more addiction among Christians than non-Christians. Addicts were less likely to have stable marriages, if they married at all, and intact families were relatively few. They were most likely to be members of the lower socioeconomic classes, and their IQs were likely to be within the average range, particularly when schooling was considered. We should not, however, assume that the use of opiates is peculiar to any homogeneous group in the United States. Rather, there are several general groups of users: (1) street addicts, (2) medical and paramedical addicts, (3) military personnel, particularly those who served in Southeast Asia, and (4) middle-class white youths.

Factors Leading to Opiate Addiction

AVAILABILITY OF THE DRUG

For addiction to occur, opiates must be available. Abundant evidence suggests that addiction rates are highest where availability is greatest, as in large metropolitan slums and among health-related professionals. It is also apparent that demand increases availability, which further complicates the search for causes.

According to Maddux (1965), 1.5 percent of those admitted to federal hospitals for treatment for addiction were physicians, or ten times the proportion of medical doctors in the United States. Modler and Montes (1964) estimated that about 15 percent of known addicts in the United States and Western Europe were physicians, and another 15 percent were in paramedical professions. In Viet Nam, the high incidence of addiction and the easily accessible, relatively pure heroin at low cost further supports the connection between availability and rate of addiction. Other variables, such as combat strain, boredom, and loneliness may be important as well. Availability of drugs is a necessary but not sufficient condition for addiction. Only a small percentage of doctors and nurses exposed to opiates and opportunities for abuse become addicted. Most slum dwellers who have access to opiates do not choose to use them. And most soldiers in Viet Nam did not use and become addicted to heroin. We have no evidence that widespread "pushing" of heroin goes on in all these places — that the high incidence is caused by high-pressure or "insidious" peddling. We must look for other reasons why people take up heroin.

ATTRIBUTES OF THE PERSON

Of the millions exposed to heroin, only a small percentage use it. Therefore researchers have searched for personality attributes that separate the opiate abuser from his non-abusing peers. But imperfections in design weaken many of the studies. First and largest of the problems in clinical assessments of opiate abusers, or any other group of abusers, is the "chicken or egg" quandary. Most clinical evaluations of addicts are done after the habit has been set for some time. Without thorough preaddiction histories it is virtually impossible to determine whether the difficulties in personality and social adjustment are caused by the heroin habit and its life style or if the difficulties were there prior to addiction and, in fact, caused it. How do hospitalization or imprisonment affect a person and the probability that the responses will reveal a homogeneity caused solely by these and not by any preexisting personality disorder? Although it is not only plausible but very tempting to assume that there is such a thing as an "addictive personality," we cannot reasonably suggest it from after-the-fact data alone.

Explanations for opiate addiction have stressed escape — either from the realities of the environment (poverty, lack of opportunity, or stressful situations in general) or from the responsibilities of adulthood (sexual role expectations, gainful employment). Theorists explain that heroin makes an addict less responsive to situational conflicts and stress. If he has psychological conflicts that he can't settle, narcotics may provide an attractive escape (Ausubel 1958; Maurer and Vogel 1967). Variations have depended on which group of addicts they studied. All emphasize that the potential addict cannot face the pressures of adulthood, and escapes into heroin.

Inability to fulfill the expected sex role is suggested by several investigators as a reason why adolescent boys turn to heroin (Chein 1965; Isbell 1965; Rado 1933). Chein found that a high percentage of the adolescent addicts he studied in New York were "pretty boys" who had difficulty assuming the normal masculine role.

Because opiates depress pain, sexual desire, and anger, some writers (Isbell 1965; Ausubel 1958; Wilner and Kassebaum 1965) suggest that individuals who fear these impulses will find specific relief in heroin. Similarly, people with low tolerance for frustration may turn to it for relief (Maurer and Vogel 1967).

Another question often comes up: Is opiate abuse a form of self-medication (tranquilization) for people with preexisting psychiatric disorders? Two studies eighteen years apart yielded similar results, indicating that generally it does not (Gerard and Kornetsky 1955; Ling et al. 1973). Both groups used rigorous criteria to define opiate addiction; they discovered that no one diagnosis characterized all or even a majority of addicts. They diagnosed approximately 30 to 40 percent of the addicts in their studies as having antisocial personality disorders, but about 50 percent did not fit any other psychiatric group. Interestingly, the first study found that 20 percent of the sample manifested signs and symptoms of schizophrenia before they started using drugs. Other psychological tests generally confirm no pattern of psychiatric symptoms that precedes heroin abuse, although psychological profiles suggest that quite a few have antisocial personality disorders (Austin et al. 1977). For these individuals, heroin is a means of rebelling against society and authority figures (Hill et al. 1962).

THE SOCIAL ENVIRONMENT

Another large influence in addiction is associating with those who are already addicted. Evidence that the first use of heroin generally occurs in a peer-group situation is overwhelming. Chambers (1971) found that 90 percent of their subjects first experimented with opiates while in the company of a peer who was already using opiates; 40 percent of the addicts began in a group. Chein and Rosenfeld (1957) concluded that the first use of heroin came through

some adult in only 10 percent of the cases. Nearly all were introduced to the drug in the company of a boy their own age or in a group of boys, and the heroin was free to 90 percent . . . they were not tricked into addiction by drug peddlers. In one study of Puerto Rican addicts, more than 80 percent of the boys reported that they were initiated by friends who were addicts (Ball and Chambers 1970).

Continuing Use of Narcotics

ATTRIBUTES OF THE DRUG

The abuser is ensnared into continued dependence on heroin by three offshoots of the opiate's biological effects:

PHYSIOLOGICAL DEPENDENCE. It may take more or less heroin and the time may be short or long, but it is usually predictable that a user will develop a physiological dependence on the drug — the body needs it.

AVOIDANCE OF WITHDRAWAL SYMPTOMS. Many investigators report that addicts continue taking heroin because they must avoid the withdrawal symptoms that accompany stopping. Although the evidence is strong that this may be an important variable in addiction, some argue that withdrawal is not the primary reason for continuing on the drug. Wikler (in Wilner 1965) discusses continuing theories of addiction and says: "There is no reason why experienced addicts can't withdraw themselves in a relatively painless manner by gradual reduction or use of methadone [a synthetic narcotic often used to assist addicts in painless withdrawal]." Khazan and colleagues (1967), evaluating animal experimentation, conclude: "The experimental data do not support the conception that animals self-administer opioids simply to avoid or escape from the aversive properties of the withdrawal syndrome."

EUPHORIC REACTIONS. Clinicians and addicts alike have emphasized that euphoria, the "high" or "rush" that follows injection, encourages continuing use of heroin (Isbell 1965), though other investigators dispute the idea. Wikler (1965) argues that tolerance to the euphoric effect develops quickly. A study of patients (Dole and Nyswander 1967) in a methadone maintenance program (see Chapter 19) concluded it was difficult to understand that the quest for euphoria was important because the patients consistently accepted a program using

The Case of One Schizophrenic Heroin Addict

Ed, a 31-year-old white male heroin addict, first came to the Clinic in December 1969. Profoundly depressed and physically unkempt, he was unable to look directly at his interviewer. He mumbled that he wanted to be hospitalized for the rest of his life because, he said, "I quit." Prior to coming to the Clinic, Ed used not only heroin but barbiturates, alcohol, and occasionally psychedelics.

Ed was diagnosed as a schizophrenic with the feeling of utter worthlessness common in the psychotic addict and one of the first hurdles to be overcome in therapy. He agreed to try therapy at the Clinic and was quite faithful to his schedule of five thirty-minute sessions a week. His treatment consisted of active, psychodynamically oriented therapy.

Ed discussed his feeling that people wanted to attack him in buses and in stores. He had difficulty remembering what had been said in previous sessions, had no memory of a marriage which lasted from the time he was 16 until he was 25, and had only sketchy memories of several hospitalizations during the previous five years.

A point of crisis occurred during the sixth month of therapy when the sexual advances of a woman caused such a panic that Ed overdosed on heroin in an attempt to quell his anxiety. In therapy he was beginning to become aware of his extreme dependency on heroin to manage such situational fear. Subsequently, it was decided to start Ed on chlorpromazine (Thorazine) as a specific antipsychotic medication. Ed then decreased his heroin habit to about one fix every seven to ten days.

At the end of six months, Ed began to have homosexual fantasies concerning the psychologist. During the seventh month, he began to explore his more painful life fears. He recalled his first association with heroin, which occurred at the age of fourteen when he witnessed his elder brother shoot and kill his mother in her bed while Ed was hiding under it. After leaving the house, the brother went to his own home where he killed his wife and then himself. A week later his father attempted to kill one of his sisters. The father was subsequently hospitalized and Ed was left, alone with a younger brother, in the care of an older sister who allowed the boys to run free, often unfed and uncared for.

The memory of this family tragedy reduced Ed to such a depressed state that he was barely able to climb the Clinic stairs for his daily therapy sessions and was unable to hustle for heroin. As his depression began to improve, Ed went back to hustling heroin and stopped therapy. The next contact with him occurred when he was brought back to the Clinic in a rigid, catatonic state and was hospitalized for ten days.

After further therapy, Ed saw his psychotic breakdown and hospitalization as the culmination of many life pressures. The first and major pressure was the burden of reactivated memories of his family. Another major fear was the necessity for employment and time-structuring, particularly the associations with strangers which looking for a job involved, and his fear of potential rejection. Ed later became a successful patient on the city's methadone maintenance program and, in addition to methadone, received 400 mg of Thorazine daily.

Source: Adapted from G. R. Gay, D. K. Wellisch, D. R. Wesson, and D. E. Smith. *The Psychotic Junkie* (New York: Insight Publishing Co., 1972).

a drug that blocked the euphoric action of heroin. Euphoria may still be a variable in continuing use of opiates, because addicts in the methadone program might merely have found that the disadvantages of heroin outweighed the advantages. Nor have all addicts been willing to participate in such programs, almost certainly because, in part, they would miss the euphoria that methadone cannot give.

This euphoria itself may be somewhat learnable by classical conditioning (see Chapter 2). In double-blind studies of the opiates' subjective effects (Lasagna 1955; Von Felsinger 1955), very few of the normal subjects reported feeling euphoria after opiates were administered — though it is possible that these were the few most physiologically disposed to becoming addicted. The authors of these studies found a surprising absence of marked euphoria after the drug was given (a complication was that it was not administered intravenously), and suggested:

An important factor that may overlap many responses is the long-term conditioning that usually begins before the first experience with narcotics; i.e., the almost universal anticipation by addicts (based on conversation with, or observations of, other addicts) that opiates will produce a pleasant state of some sort. How to dissect out this factor of suggestion from subsequent drug reactions poses a problem almost impossible of solution.

We cannot expect to understand other animals' motivational systems, but work with monkeys (Schuster 1975) indicates that they will voluntarily become addicted and will push a lever controlling injection of heroin into their bodies, preferring the drug to food or female monkeys. An interesting aside (Goldstein 1974) is that "these were normal animals who had never experienced hunger, loss of parents, or intense frustration or depression."

GENETIC PREDISPOSITION

Few have studied the genetic aspects of opiate addiction, yet it has been suggested in the literature that some people may be more biologically predisposed to opiate abuse than others. This research shows promise. Nichols (1965) found that the liability to morphine addiction can be bred into rats, demonstrating that, in some animals at least, genetics affects dependence on opiates. Some combination of genetic predisposition and biological properties of opiates may help explain addiction. Claghorn (1965), in research on rhesus monkeys, found individual differences in the tendency to self-administer morphine, and other authors suggest that some addicts' reaction to the drug was abnormal, even on first exposure (Dole and Nyswander 1967).

Dole and Nyswander (1967) built biological susceptibility into their metabolic model of drug addiction and contrasted it with standard psychological theories. The Dole-Nyswander theory, which assumes a preexisting biological disposition that produces an altered response to opiates, differentiates the potential addict from his peers. Dole and Nyswander also argue that because of this biological predisposition, opiate abusers can never live a drug-free existence, requiring continuous maintenance on an opiate substitute such as methadone. Treatment programs using methadone (see Chapter 19) are full of controversy about whether opiate abusers should accept lifelong maintenance or should ultimately be "weaned" to a drug-free life.

THE SOCIAL SITUATION

CONDITIONING AND THE DRUG EXPERIENCE. Experimental psychology has contributed useful theories explaining both why an addict continues to take heroin and why, once free of heroin, he relapses to the former habit. The theories say that an individual, for whatever reason, begins taking heroin, develops physical dependence on the drug and acquires a *drive-need state* that must be satisfied by taking heroin. The drug then becomes a reinforcer. If withdrawal symptoms begin, in time the close association between relief and use of a narcotic is firmly established. As Kolb (1939) wrote: "By thus building up a strong association between pleasure and pain and the taking of a narcotic, the addict becomes conditioned to taking one in response to most any situation that may arise."

Research (Schuster and Villarreal 1967) indicates that both the opiate and the life style associated with use of opiates can act as reinforcers in at least three ways. First, work on animals shows that morphine can act as a reinforcer even without physical dependence (although its effect is greatly enhanced if the animal is suffering withdrawal symptoms). Second, Wikler's *hustling theory* suggests (1961) that all the activities and rituals associated with taking opiates (stealing to obtain the money, mixing the heroin, making a tourniquet, injecting the drug, involvement in the drug subculture, using the argot, and so on), and particularly the activities closely related in time to the injection and subsequent physiological reactions, may strengthen conditioning reinforcement. Third, Wikler postulates that environmental stimuli associated with the withdrawal syndrome may come to symbolize the withdrawal experience. When an addict or former addict finds himself in circumstances similar to those in which he had suffered withdrawal distress, he may feel or relive some of these symptoms and turn to heroin for relief.

Nichols (1956, 1965) has studied how important conditioning can be in opiate addiction, using operant conditioning (see Chapter 2). Rats were given morphine long enough to become physiologically addicted. If the animals then were given a choice between water and a morphine solution, even if they were undergoing withdrawal, they would not drink morphine. Two experimental conditions were set up. One group of rats was given training trials and forced to drink a morphine solution (no water was available). After training, the animals continued drinking morphine although tap water was available. The other group of rats was given similar dosages of morphine that the experimenter injected. These rats refused to drink the morphine solution when water was available. The rats in the first group had received morphine only because they made the operant response of drinking, whereas the second group received the drug passively, not contingent upon any operant behavior, and failed to show any subsequent preference for the drug.

Nichols conjectures that this difference might explain why so few patients who passively receive opioids during medical treatment show drug-seeking behavior when drug administration is terminated. But physicians and other medical personnel, in a unique position to self-administer drugs, show a higher incidence of drug dependence than people in other professions. Availability, self-selection, and knowledge undoubtedly affect the balance as well.

These studies and experiments do not explain why addicts first use heroin, yet they are useful because now we can identify some of the factors in continuing an opiate habit.

LACK OF OPTIONS AND INVOLVEMENT IN DRUG SUBCULTURE. Several investigators suggest that people continue to use opiates because they find here an alternative style of life, having had no other viable options. Cloward and Ohlin (1970) suggested that heroin addicts are retreatists, *double failures* who cannot qualify for either legitimate or illegitimate careers and in frustration turn to opiates to escape reality. This theory, however, does not account for addicts in the health professions and others who are holding down responsible jobs though addicted. Another compelling argument against the double-failures notion is that, if an addict is to survive and maintain his habit, he *cannot* be a complete failure in the criminal world — he must steal and hustle and, as Preble and Casey (1969) point out, "be alert, flexible, and resourceful."

Hustling for heroin is a full-time occupation and gives the addict something to do with his day. Preble and Casey (1969) maintain that, far from being an escape route, addiction requires that addicts be "actively engaged in meaningful activities and relationships seven days a week." Stealing and fencing stolen property, prostitution, buying and selling drugs, and so on, afford the addict a job, something to look forward to, a challenge, and a way of life. For those who grow up in poverty in the ghettos of our large cities, activities like these may seem the only meaningful ones available.

Several researchers have discussed how involvement in the drug subculture maintains addiction. Rubington (1967) outlined four aspects of the drug subculture:

1. Ideology. Addict language is considered to be the "symbolic form in which the ideology casts its contents." A compilation of opiate addicts' language gathered more than 500 words.
2. Self-image. "The subculture defines the symbolic meaning and behavior which attend the definition, 'junkie.' Not only does it make plain what it means to be hooked, but it makes clear how people who meet this criterion go about coping with a dilemma which it defines as drug-induced."
3. Skills. The addict culture reinforces skills for obtaining the heroin, shooting it, and not getting caught.
4. Norms. Informal rules outlining the procedure for interactions with other addicts and non-addicts. (p. 16)

Clinard (1968) identified these components of the addict subculture: an elaborate distribution system (illegal importation, peddlers,

pushers); an ideology justifying drug use; a "reproductive system" (addicts must constantly recruit new members to support their habits); a "defensive communication system" with its own language, which "must be learned by initiates"; a "neighborhood warning system" with which addicts protect themselves and others; and a complicated information system "whereby the addict learns to secure the illegal drugs."

These theories of opiate abuse are complicated, overlapping, difficult to verify, and sometimes contradictory; however, they have broadened knowledge, not only about addiction to narcotics but about abuse of many other types of drugs as well.

Central Nervous System Depressants: Alcohol

Because they sedate and induce sleep, depressants, which work on the central nervous system (CNS), have been applied to ease the human condition for thousands of years. In the nineteenth century, *bromides* were widely used for sedation, but in this century much more sophisticated antianxiety and sedative drugs have been invented. We will concentrate on abuse of alcohol, but *barbiturates* and *sedative-hypnotics* have similar effects. A recent study indicated that more than one American in seven, aged eighteen to seventy-four, used an antianxiety or sedative drug; 40 percent of these used such a drug daily for a month or more (Sutherland 1977). For many years, Valium has been prescribed more than any other drug. Massive amounts of anti-anxiety drugs are taken daily, and yet no one has answered the pragmatic and ethical questions about whether such drugs are abused and overprescribed and, if they were not taken, whether physical disease secondary to stress and unnecessary suffering from anxiety or insomnia would increase. Chronic use of these drugs can, we know, cause social, psychological, and medical problems. Tolerance to them builds rapidly, as does dependence. Symptoms of withdrawal range from mild restlessness to violent anger, psychosis, convulsions, and occasionally death. Anyone being withdrawn from a strong CNS depressant, particularly one of the barbiturates, must be given decreasing doses of the drug to prevent acute withdrawal. Chronic use of sedative-hypnotics can deteriorate psychomotor function, alter and disturb sleep patterns, and cause significant physical problems by leaving the body deficient in vitamins. Grant and colleagues (1978) compared polydrug-abuse patients with nonpatients, using a large battery of neuropsychological tests sensitive to behavioral changes associated with damage to the central nervous system (Reitan 1966). Extensive polydrug users with definite history of barbiturate abuse made up the highest percentage of individuals with impaired performance suggesting brain dysfunction.

Alcohol

Dylan [Thomas] was now having blackouts at frequent intervals. On more than one occasion he had been warned by his doctor that he must go on a regime of complete abstinence from alcohol if he was to survive. There was to be no escape from his illness. . . . "I have seen the gates of Hell tonight," he said. "I've come to the melancholy conclusion that my health is totally gone. I can't drink at all . . . now most of the time I can't even swallow beer without being sick. I tell myself that if I'd only lay off whiskey and stick to beer I'd be all right . . . but I never do." Dylan seemed exhausted, self-preoccupied, and morbidly depressed. He went out alone, and an hour and a half later returned to announce, "I've had eighteen straight whiskies. I think that's the record." On November 9 he died.

— W. Read, *The Days of Dylan Thomas*

Far and away the most commonly used and abused CNS depressant is alcohol. It has been friend and enemy to humanity since the discovery that fermented berries and grains could profoundly alter our moods, thinking, and behavior. The countless social contexts for drinking vary from formal sherry-to-brandy dinners with several intervening table wines to football games, bars, and solitary drinking. One of us may drink to combat shyness, another to ward off depression, and yet another just because everyone else is drinking. Try not to drink at a social gathering and you may be made to feel ill at ease or out of place, especially if the occasion calls for more than one or two cocktails.

Most of the 68 percent of Americans who consume alcohol do it in moderation. They drink primarily because they like the effects one or two drinks produce. A CNS depressant, alcohol reduces tension and lowers inhibitions. A few drinks will make most of us more sociable, explaining the unflagging popularity of alcoholic beverages at parties and of the infamous "three-martini" business lunches.

If we drink beyond one or two in a brief time, a pleasant high can turn into acute drunkenness, or *intoxication.* How much alcohol we can tolerate without becoming drunk in a specific time depends on our size and our normal drinking habits. The acute stages of alcohol intoxication have been described (only half-jokingly) as "jocose, lachrymose, bellicose, and comatose" because of the behavioral symptoms. After a few drinks, we may be noticeably less inhibited, more jovial or more depressed, argumentative, and occasionally combative. Other alcohol-induced changes include impaired motor coordination, slurred speech, impaired memory, and ultimately, loss of consciousness. For many revelers the aftereffects of an intoxicated night are the headache, dizziness, nausea, and vomiting that betray a *hangover.*

Anyone who gets drunk now and then at a party but normally drinks in moderation is not an alcoholic. Alcoholics, like opiate addicts, have no control over their drinking. One does not become an alcoholic overnight, and although it is not always easy to pinpoint when a problem drinker becomes an alcoholic, common patterns of behavior seem to characterize three stages of alcoholism (Moore 1977). As Table 16.2 shows, by the *early stage* alcohol has begun to interfere with normal social and occupational functioning.

After extended steady drinking, tolerance often sets in, and the effects of alcohol on behavior become less and less pronounced. During this time *blackouts* can and frequently do occur. Quite common in the histories of alcoholics, but otherwise rare, blackouts have been called the "hallmark of alcoholism." They appear as temporary amnesia in a heavy drinker who generally appears both functional and sober. Seixas (1977) cites a surgeon who discovered he had performed a tracheotomy during a blackout; he did not recall having done it.

As we drink more over a long period — usually within five years after beginning to drink regularly — we can become physiologically dependent on it. Now a sudden drop in the blood alcohol level if drinking is decreased or stopped will bring on the withdrawal syndrome. At its mildest, alcohol withdrawal is manifested by anxiety, insomnia, anorexia, and tremor; not uncommonly the drinker appears hyperalert, irritable, and tremulous. These symptoms, which appear within a few hours of the last alcohol intake, are most pronounced twenty-four to thirty-six hours later and then disappear relatively soon. *Delirium tremens,* more commonly known as "the DTs," is a more severe form of withdrawal, causing paranoia, disorientation, extreme agitation, or hallucinations, in addition to the symptoms described above. The delirious state may continue two or three days, and often stops abruptly (Butz 1977). Grand mal seizures can also follow withdrawal of alcohol. In many cases, fear of withdrawal and DTs seems to motivate alcoholics to continue drinking.

Chronic intake of alcohol can cause other major problems, including malnutrition (from inadequate intake of food), potentially lethal liver damage (cirrhosis), inflammation of the pancreas, and brain damage. Changes in the brain caused by excessive alcohol intake can

Table 16.2. Three stages of alcoholism

Early stage	Middle stage	Late stage
Gulping drinks	Repeated attempts at abstinence	Blatant, indiscriminate use of alcohol
Surreptitious drinking	Loss of job	Chooses employment that facilitates drinking
Medical excuses from work	Drinking to relieve anger, insomnia, fatigue, depression, social discomfort	Frequent automobile accidents
Preference for bars, drinking companions		Outbursts of rage and suicidal gestures when drinking
Loss of interest in activities not directly associated with drinking		Slippage in socioeconomic status

Source: Adapted from Moore, R. "Dependence on alcohol," in S. Pradhen & S. Dutta (eds.) *Drug Abuse: Clinical and Basic Aspects* (St. Louis, Mo.: C. V. Mosby & Co., 1977).

be either acute or chronic. Acute alcohol brain syndromes are reversible, develop rapidly, and may be manifested by intoxication, delirium tremens, or other signs of cognitive and perceptual impairment. Chronic brain damage caused by abuse of alcohol, on the other hand, generally sets in more insidiously and is relatively irreversible. Autopsies performed on alcoholics with secondary brain damage often show pronounced cortical atrophy and other major changes in brain structure (Smith 1977). A chronic brain syndrome, *dementia* (see Chapter 12), is associated with a diffuse loss of functioning brain tissue; it is still not clear exactly how alcohol damages the brain, but we assume it is by direct damage to brain cells as well as to heart and liver, organs that significantly affect functioning of the brain. Chronic alcohol dependence also increases the risk or seriousness of heart disease, pneumonia, tuberculosis, neurological disorders, and mental retardation.

Depressive symptoms are a frequent complication (although also a cause) of alcohol dependence and, in part, account for the high rate of suicide among the alcohol-dependent. Suicide associated with dependence can occur in both intoxicated and sober states.

Theories of Alcoholism

Theories explaining causes and continuance of alcoholism, like those for opiate abuse, are complicated and often confusing. Many of the research problems we have encountered throughout the book, especially in opiate addiction, also plague us here. Clinical researchers define alcoholism in many ways and study groups of alcoholics who differ drastically. And most research has been focused ex-

Self-Report Measures of Alcoholism

Short Michigan Alcoholism Screening Test	Alcoholic responses	
	Yes	No
1. Do you feel you are a normal drinker? (By normal we mean you drink *less than* or *as much* as most other people?)		1
2. Does your wife, husband, a parent, or other near relative ever worry or complain about your drinking?	1	
3. Do you ever feel guilty about your drinking?	1	
4. Do friends or relatives think you are a normal drinker?		1
5. Are you able to stop drinking when you want to?		1
6. Have you ever attended a meeting of Alcoholics Anonymous?	1	
7. Has drinking ever created problems between you and your wife, husband, or other near relative?	1	
8. Have you ever gotten into trouble at work because of drinking?	1	
9. Have you ever neglected your obligations, your family, or your work for two or more days in a row because you were drinking?	1	
10. Have you ever gone to anyone for help about your drinking?	1	
11. Have you ever been in a hospital because of drinking?	1	
12. Have you ever been arrested for drunk driving, driving while intoxicated, or driving under the influence of alcoholic beverages?	1	
13. Have you ever been arrested, even for a few hours, because of other drunk behavior?	1	

Scoring: 0–1 points = nonalcoholic; 2 points = possibly alcoholic; 3–13 points = alcoholic.

clusively on alcoholics who have been drinking for several years. With all this variety it is hard to determine whether differences in personality between alcoholics and nonalcoholics cause alcoholism or are effects of excessive drinking. All the variables count, and are so difficult to control in research that we must cautiously interpret data from them.

Factors Leading to Alcoholism

AVAILABILITY OF THE DRUG

Alcohol can be found almost anywhere, a freedom that seems to contribute to its potential for abuse, especially in adolescents and children. In most states you can purchase wine and beer in the same store where you buy your groceries. Other states and counties regulate distribution far more closely, but these controls, like Prohibition (which outlawed the sale and manufacture of alcoholic beverages in the United States between 1920 and 1933), seem barely to touch the rate of consumption (Vaillant 1978). In fact, it was during Prohibition that the cocktail party replaced the tea party as the preferred social gathering.

ATTRIBUTES OF THE PERSON

With the so-called Jellinek formula, which correlates liver cirrhosis and mortality with alcoholism, the number of problem drinkers in the United States is approximately 9 million. Of these, 5 million are believed to be alcoholics (Enterline and Capt 1959; Keller and Efron 1955; Haglund and Schuckit 1977). What generalizations can we possibly make about so many people and their drinking behavior? Table 16.3 gives some interesting statistics about the part of the adult population who drink and who the heavy drinkers are, but the figures are little help in explaining heavy drinking. Why is the ratio of heavy male drinkers to heavy female drinkers 4.2 to 1 when the overall ratio of male to female drinkers is 1.3 to 1? And why is the highest rate of heavy drinking found among blacks and people forty to fifty-nine years old? To answer these questions, we must look for differences in background and style of life.

Increased urbanization, higher education, and higher income are correlated with increased alcohol use, but do not appear to be significantly or consistently related to heavy or problematic drinking (Haglund and Schuckit 1977). The values acquired from ethnic and religious influences, however, do seem to make a difference in the amount of both moderate drinking and heavy drinking. Table 16.4 summarizes Irish, Italian and Jewish drinking practices. Notice that although the percentage of drinkers is slightly higher for Jews than for the others, the percentage of heavy drinkers is lowest among people with Jewish backgrounds. One logical explanation is that wine drinking is part of many Jewish rituals, and children exposed to such moderate drinking are more likely to acquire moderate drinking habits than are those who do not regularly see moderate drinking in an acceptable social context. Many other sociocultural factors are thought to encourage alcoholism, such as cross-cultural differences in attitudes, expectations, and child-rearing practices, and sex-role conflicts, but many of the data either have not been explained or are open to many interpretations.

Just as it has been suggested that people can learn good drinking habits, reinforcement theories have stressed learning in the development and maintenance of alcoholism. In this view, alcohol, by removing discomfort, increasing social facility, and loosening inhibitions, creates a reinforcement system strong enough to turn some people into alcoholics (Bandura 1969; Mello and Mendelson 1971; Nathan et al. 1970; Roebuck and Kessler 1972). Other psychological theories cite the importance in alcoholism of personality types (Lawlis and Rubin 1971; Williams, McCourt, and Schneider 1971); psychodynamic factors, interpersonal conflicts,

Table 16.3. Characteristics of American adults, by drinking group (percentages)

		Drinkers			
	Abstainers	Total	Infrequent	Light and moderate combined	Heavy[a]
Total	32	68	15	41 (28 light, 13 moderate)	12 (18)
Sex					
Men	23	77	10	46	21 (28)
Women	40	60	18	37	5 (8)
Age					
21–29	24	76	15	47	14 (18)
30–39	22	78	17	46	15 (19)
40–49	29	71	12	44	15 (21)
50–59	40	60	14	36	10 (25)
60 +	47	53	15	32	6 (11)
Socioeconomic status					
High		70			
Middle		66			
Low		62			
Education					
High school or more		70			
Did not complete high school		62			
Population					
Greater than 100,000		77			
Less than 2500		46			
Race					
White	31	69	15	42	12 (17)
Black	38	62	12	36	14 (23)

Source: Based on data from D. Cahalan and I. H. Cisin, "American Drinking Practices: Summary of Findings from a National Probability Sample. I. Extent of Drinking by Population Subgroup," *Q. J. Stud. Alcohol,* 29, 1968, pp. 130–152; and V. Efron, M. Keller, and C. Gurioli, *Statistics on Consumption of Alcohol and on Alcoholism* (New Brunswick, N. J.: Rutgers Center for Alcohol Studies, 1974).
[a] Percentage of heavy drinkers among all drinkers is given in parentheses.

How Big a Problem is Alcoholism?

An estimated 10 million Americans are problem drinkers or alcoholics.

Alcohol is not a significant problem for the 80 percent of the drinking population who have fewer than two drinks a day.

The risk of death from disease, accident, or violence is two to six times greater for the problem drinker than for the population at large.

Drinking problems cost society about $43 billion in 1975 in lost production, medical bills, accidents, and other expenses.

Alcohol may be involved in up to a third of the suicides, half of the murders, and half of the traffic deaths.

Alcohol is the third leading cause of birth defects, including mental retardation.

The number of programs treating problem drinkers and alcoholics increased from 500 in 1973 to nearly 2400 in 1977. Most are in the private sector, for businesses have realized they can save money by helping drinkers overcome their problems.

Source: Adapted from Special Report of the National Institute on Alcohol Abuse and Alcoholism (1978)

Table 16.4. Drinking practices of ethnic groups in the United States

Ethnic group	Drinkers (percentage)	Percentage of heavy drinkers among all drinkers
Irish Catholic	83	23
Irish conservative Protestant	52	13
Italian Catholic	83	23
Jewish (East European)	92	11

Source: R. M. J. Haglund and M. A. Schuckit. "The Epidemiology of Alcoholism," in Estes and Heineman, 1977.

and disordered levels of communication (Gorad, McCourt, and Cobb 1971; Steiner 1971); and a history of antisocial behavior (Schuckit et al. 1969; Schuckit and Haglund 1977); but it is difficult to validate these hypotheses without identifying and studying high-risk individuals before they become alcoholics. Some researchers (Vaillant 1978) feel that personality factors, childhood environment, and specific relief of symptoms (reduction of tension) are more influential in opiate addiction than in alcoholism.

Individual differences in biological predisposition and genetic factors also have been implicated as possible causes of alcoholism. Davis and Walsch (1970) suggest that in the brains of certain individuals alcohol may produce a morphine-like substance that can lead to alcohol addiction. Others suggest that differences in susceptibility to alcoholism might be caused by abnormalities in metabolizing sugar (Lundquist 1971), food allergies, endocrine abnormalities (Noble 1973), or differential responsiveness of the brain to alcohol (Kuehnle, Anderson, and Chandler 1974). As in the psychological theories, it is difficult to establish whether the physiological differences caused or were produced by chronic drinking.

Genetic studies in other species and in

humans have yielded interesting data on drinking behavior. Different strains of mice and rats will seek out and drink different amounts of alcohol; likewise, if a mouse from a heavy-drinking strain is mated with one from a nondrinking strain, their offspring will be intermediate in intake of alcohol (Schuckit and Haglund 1977). These findings may prove to be related less to alcohol intake than to separate variables, such as metabolic or sensory (taste and smell) differences between strains of rodents, but it is a fascinating line of research.

Genetic studies of human alcoholism have followed genetic research on manic-depression and schizophrenia (see Chapters 6 and 9), concentrating on family histories and twin studies. Histories of hospitalized male alcoholics reveal that about half of their first-degree male relatives (fathers, brothers, sons) are alcoholics (Amark 1951; Winokur et al. 1970). Twin studies give us even more information about heredity in alcoholism. Kaij (1960) studied 174 male twin pairs of which one was an established alcoholic; he found a 54 percent concordance rate for identical twins and 24 percent for fraternal twins, and that the more severe the alcoholism, the greater the concordance.

Using a slightly different approach, Partanen, Bruun, and Markkanen (1966) interviewed 133 identical and 471 fraternal pairs of nonalcoholic twins about their general drinking patterns. They found concordance for the amount of alcohol consumed and frequency of drinking, but not for social consequences of drinking behavior.

The most compelling genetic data come from studies of twins raised apart from one another so that influences from environment and learning can be ruled out as a major cause of any concordance. Goodwin et al. (1973, 1974) compared fifty-five men whose biological parents were alcoholics with fifty-five controls who had also been adopted before the age of

six weeks. The two samples were matched in socioeconomic status and age, they had been placed by the same adoption agency, and they had been raised in similar homes. None of the children knew anything about their biological parents. The children whose biological parents were alcoholics were four times more likely to become alcoholics than were the controls (20 percent and 5 percent). Things in the adopted children's upbringing that might have been thought to predict alcoholism did not, such as being raised by an alcoholic or suffering a broken home following death of or separation from an adoptive parent.

Women and Alcohol

More than a million women alcoholics live in the United States, perhaps 20 to 25 percent of the total. Many of them suffer social, medical, family, and economic consequences different from those besetting alcoholic men. Although (proportionately) about as many women as men are admitted to mental hospitals for alcoholism, women are *much more* likely to die from cirrhosis of the liver and much less likely to get in trouble with the law because of their alcoholism (Edwards et al. 1972). Women of all races, ages, and socioeconomic backgrounds become alcoholics, although the social consequences may vary depending on a woman's background or living situation. Fort and Porterfield (1961) found that upper-class women were more protected against public disgrace but more punished *within* the family system than women with lower-class backgrounds.

Many of the general etiological assumptions about alcoholism hold true for women in particular. Hormonal and metabolic factors specific to women have also been implicated, however. Some researchers have found that the blood alcohol level (from drinking the same amount of alcohol) varies at different times in the menstrual cycle (Jones 1975; Jones and Jones 1976). Difficulties that go with being a woman have also been thought to cause alcoholism. Among

these are trouble in accepting a traditional female role; frustrations with marriage and children; difficulties in adjusting to changing societal expectations of women; loneliness; and the "empty-nest" syndrome that sets in as children grow up, leave home, and become less dependent on their parents (Wilsnack 1975).

Two groups of researchers (Rimmer et al. 1971; Horn and Wanberg 1973) looked further into differences between men and women alcoholics and concluded:

1. Women began to drink and experience first intoxication later in life.
2. Women more often drink at home, alone or with spouse.
3. Women have shorter drinking bouts.
4. Women more often use alcohol to improve job performance.
5. Men lose jobs more frequently because of drinking.
6. Men are more often gregarious drinkers and women solitary drinkers.
7. Women more often perceive their alcoholism as becoming worse.
8. Men experience more blackouts and more episodes of delirium tremens.
9. Men have more histories of school problems and "reckless youth."
10. Women are more likely to attempt suicide.

Stimulants of the
Central Nervous System

Amphetamines

Amphetamines, first of the major drug stimulants (Benzedrine, Dexedrine, and Methedrine are among them), though rigidly controlled by the federal government, are significantly abused in our society. They have been much used in biochemical research on schizophrenia (see Chapter 6) because of their effect on the dopaminergic tracts in the brain. Initially developed for their ability to counteract fatigue and heighten wakefulness, they were soon found to suppress appetite (temporarily) and came into widespread use as aids in dieting. In human beings, the acute effects of amphetamines, like those of cocaine, another stimulant, are a general sense of well-being and self-confidence, euphoria, and alertness. A person who stops taking stimulants after prolonged use experiences a *stimulant withdrawal* syndrome, with jitteriness, depression, lassitude, lethargy, hunger, and interpersonal withdrawal (Ellinwood and Petrie 1977).

Several patterns of use appear in the scientific literature: (1) *occasional users* (such as students and truckdrivers) who take stimulants intermittently and seldom develop an abuse problem; (2) *habitual users* such as people who take amphetamines orally and either have a physician's prescription (dieters) or obtain them from illicit sources; (3) *intravenous users of stimulants* such as "speed freaks," who repeatedly take large doses of amphetamines intravenously; and (4) *combined drug users;* who simultaneously use barbiturates to counteract the stimulant effects of the "uppers." Despite the many dangerous complications of stimulant abuse, a study of polydrug abusers (Grant et al. 1978) failed to find neuropsychological test signs of notable brain dysfunction in chronic users of amphetamine. According to their re-

port: "We interpret our data and previous reports to suggest that heavy, persistent amphetamine use is not related to neuropsychological impairment in most youthful users, although a few persons might indeed be at risk for idiosyncratic reasons (e.g., pre-existing hypertension)" (Grant et al. 1978, p. 1071).

Cocaine

Some of the images I tried to describe in the first part of my delirium were full of poetry. I sneered at the poor mortals condemned to live in this valley of tears while I, carried on the winds of two leaves of coca, went flying through the spaces of 77,438 worlds, each more splendid than the one before.

An hour later I was sufficiently calm to write these words in a steady hand: "God is unjust because he made man incapable of *sustaining the effect* of coca all life long. I would rather have a life span of ten years with coca than one of 10000 . . . (and here I had inserted a line of zeros) centuries without coca. [Dr. Paola Mantegazzo (in Segal 1977, p. 123)]

But to one who abuses cocaine for his pleasure, nature soon speaks, and is not heard. The nerves weary of the constant stimulation; they need rest and food. There is a point at which the jaded horse no longer answers whip and spur. He stumbles, falls into a quivering heap, gasps out his life. . . . So perishes the slave of cocaine. With every nerve clamoring, all he can do is renew the lash of the poison. The pharmaceutical effect is over; the toxic effect accumulates. The nerves become insane. [A. Crowley 1917 (in Segal 1977, p. 122)]

Cocaine, like so many drugs that powerfully influence mood, thinking, and behavior, is heir to a long, emotional, and contradictory mythology of ecstasies and terrors. Its storied effectiveness as a stimulant aroused great interest in it as an antifatigue medication, as well as an antidepressant. Freud, like others, initially praised the euphoric effects, but when the less desirable side-effects became apparent (including secondary depression) medical application as an antidepressant was virtually abandoned. Cocaine is still used by physicians as a local anesthetic however. Because it constricts the blood vessels, it is particularly good at limiting bleeding in the nose and throat and other areas richly supplied with blood.

Illicit cocaine is sold as a white translucent powder, frequently "cut" or diluted with other amphetamine-like substances. It is extremely expensive, selling in 1979 for $110–125 per gram; it is known as the "rich man's drug." Like other stimulants, cocaine produces an intense feeling of self-confidence, power, energy, and euphoria (see Table 16.5). Other acute effects are increased gregariousness, hypervigilance, and increased psychomotor activity. Prolonged heavy use often leads to severe psychomotor agitation, "crash depression," paranoia, and a visual hallucinatory phenomenon that causes one to see snakes or insects creeping over or digging inside one's skin ("Magnan's sign," or "cocaine bugs"). The symptom pattern of chronic cocaine intoxication can be indistinguishable from the symptoms of paranoid schizophrenia.

The kinds of people who take cocaine, their reasons, and the amounts they use differ as much as users of most other drugs. These case histories illustrate two individuals' reactions to cocaine and why they used it. Both were interviewed by psychologists as part of an in-depth study of cocaine use patterns conducted by the National Institute on Drug Abuse (Spotts and Shontz 1976).

Bill F.: A Casual but Regular User

Bill is a twenty-three-year old, white musician who is a guitarist with an excellent midwestern rock band. He first tried cocaine when he was seventeen years old. He is an intermittent (two to three times weekly), low-dosage, intranasal cocaine user; he also uses moderate amounts of al-

Table 16.5. Reported effects of cocaine in 85 male users[a]

	Percentage
Intoxication effects	
Euphoria	100
Stimulation	82
Reduced fatigue	70
Diminished appetite	67
Garrulousness	59
Sexual stimulation	13
Untoward effects	
Restlessness	70
Anxiety	34
Hyperexcitability	28
Irritability	16
Paranoia	5
Perceptual changes	
Increased sensitivity to light	44
Hallucinatory experiences	18

Source: Adapted from R. K. Siegel, "Cocaine: Recreational Use and Intoxication," in R. C. Petersen and R. C. Stillman, eds., *Cocaine: 1977* (Rockville, Md: National Institute on Drug Abuse, Monograph No. 13).
[a] All subjects were social and recreational cocaine users, and all "snorted" the drug. Each subject met the initial requirement of having used a minimum of 1 gram of cocaine per month for twelve months. All were male and 21 to 38 years old.

cohol and marijuana on a regular basis. Bill states that he uses cocaine because: (1) it increases his self-confidence and assurance in his interactions with other musicians; (2) it enhances his performance and the aesthetic experience of sexual relationships with women; and (3) it "perks" him up and helps him play well as a musician when he is tired and exhausted. In addition to the reasons Bill gave, the psychologist who interviewed him speculated that cocaine helped Bill eradicate feelings of anger so that he does not jeopardize his relationships with people he cares about or needs, and it helped a "stimulus-hungry" man tolerate unavoidably dull, routine, or boring life situations. Bill summarized his feelings about cocaine by saying: "I like the feeling. It makes me feel more self-confident. It sometimes makes me feel like I am floating. I am all pepped up, relaxed. If

I am depressed or down, it gets me into a better mood and peps me up. Records sound better. You are able to pick out nuances in a record that you might not otherwise notice. The music is richer, fuller. It enhances all your feelings when you are doing sex. You can go on a long time and not get tired. You last longer and the orgasm is better for both of you. I can also handle a crowd better when I am doing coke."

George B.: An Intravenous and Daily User

George is a twenty-eight-year old, white, highly successful salesman. He began snorting cocaine when he was twenty-three and started intravenous use three years later. He is an intravenous, daily, high-dosage pharmaceutical cocaine user who also regularly uses heroin and other narcotics. George states that he uses cocaine because: (1) it makes him feel self-confident, strong, and potent; (2) it gives him exceptional energy, drive, and stamina for his work as a salesman; and (3) it enables him to maintain a high performance level for long gruelling hours without respite. The psychologist who interviewed George hypothesized that cocaine served as a prop for a lonely existence so that George could be independent, autonomous, and self-sufficient, and not have to lean on or be dependent upon any other human being. George summarized his feelings: "It made me feel powerful, strong, creative. You feel no pain at all. Your body functions like a beautiful machine. I felt like I was on top of the world and could do anything. But after shooting two grams of coke, I would start getting paranoid. I was afraid something was going to happen. You feel like someone is reading your thoughts; that people are out to get you; that the police are going to break the door down any minute." The withdrawal reaction was difficult for George because of the amount of cocaine he used: "You can't relax. If you lay down, you're wide awake. You're depressed and anxious as hell that you have run out of coke. You're physically tired and worn out, but you're still hyper. It was all crazy as hell. I got into coke so I could keep my drive to sell. I got into heroin to get off the cocaine. Now, I'm taking methadone to handle the heroin habit. It's all crazy."

Caffeine

The often elaborate and highly ritualistic social customs around tea and coffee drinking express caffeine's complete incorporation and acceptance in our society. The drug tea has been consumed for thousands of years and gives many cultures a late-afternoon focus for social activity. Siegel (1973, 1977) writes that many psychoactive plant substances — such as caffeine and hallucinogens — were discovered when someone observed changes in the behavior of animals after they had ingested plants. Coffee, thought to have been discovered around A.D. 900, was recognized by an Abyssinian tending his herd of goats. His animals became abnormally active after eating the bright red fruit of a tree that was later isolated and identified as coffee (Siegel 1977).

Levenson and Bick (1977) report that the United States annually imports approximately three billion pounds of green coffee to satisfy a per capita consumption of 136 pounds. Two-thirds of the caffeine imports that are not in the form of coffee are used in cola beverages; the remaining one-third goes into headache compounds, cold remedies, and nonprescription stimulants.

Levenson and Bick (1977) summarize caffeine's status as a psychoactive drug:

Caffein, as a constituent of the social beverages and as an ingredient in popular cola soft drinks and countless nonprescription pharmaceutical combinations, is the most widely used stimulant in the world. Caffein, nicotine, and ethanol [alcoholic beverages] are the only naturally occurring psychoactive substances accepted by our culture for recreational use. Each of these three nonmedical, mind-affecting drugs has had a great influence on human civilization, undoubtedly greater than that of all other psychopharmacologic agents combined. This is true by any measure chosen: The number of people using them regularly, number of hours spent "under the influence," the quantities of each produced and consumed, as well as the amount of money spent to obtain them (p. 451).

Caffeine stimulates the central nervous system; it can elevate mood and increase energy and wakefulness. Subjective effects depend on the personality, metabolism, and expectations of the one taking it. In too large an amount (varying from person to person, or in the same person from time to time, depending on the amount of coffee or tea one is used to drinking) caffeine can give "coffee nerves": irritability, headache, and anxiety. Effects of regular caffeine intake are as yet unclear. Both caffeine and amphetamines stimulate the CNS, and yet they seem to affect some kinds of behavior differently. Comparing the effects of caffeine and amphetamines on performance, Weiss and Laties (1962) found: (1) caffeine has little or no effect on reaction time, whereas amphetamines seem to lower it, especially in fatigued subjects; (2) both caffeine and amphetamines can somewhat counteract the decrement of motor performance produced by alcohol; and (3) both caffeine and amphetamine counteract fatigue from exhausting physical activity.

Dependence on caffeine is primarily psychological, but both for its stimulation and its social qualities, people who regularly take in quantities of it unquestionably become physiologically dependent. Mild withdrawal symptoms have been clearly demonstrated: irritability, anxiety, headache, fatigue, and decreased ability to concentrate. Goldstein and Kaiser (1969) gave heavy users who abstained from morning coffee decaffeinated coffee in a blind experiment. They were able to relieve the subsequent withdrawal headaches by taking 150 milligrams of caffeine. But if you give light coffee drinkers or nondrinkers caffeine, they get stomach upsets and jitteriness and no sense of increased alertness or well-being. Habitual coffee drinkers, on the other hand, reported jitteriness when de-prived of caffeine; when given it they reported feeling more alert, awake, and generally better (Goldstein, Kaiser, and Whitby 1969).

Alertness and overall well-being are also the reasons most commonly given by coffee drinkers for their morning "pick-me-ups"; most people drink less coffee at night because it can keep them awake. Others appear able to drink all through the day and evening without insomnia. Perhaps the development of tolerance or an intrinsic low sensitivity to all stimulants causes some people both to need more and to be able to drink more coffee than others (Goldstein, Warren, and Kaiser 1965; Levenson and Bick 1977).

Hallucinogens

An examination of hallucinations requires some definite frame of reference through which to view the phenomenon. This frame of reference is not yet firmly established. In past centuries hallucinations were thought to be real visitations from the spirit world. Depending on the interpretation of the community, their celestial or satanic origin was determined. The French loyalists believed that Joan of Arc's visions were from God; the English judged them to be inspired by the devil. Today certain subcultures still give credence to the spiritual nature of visionary phenomena. Often the hallucinator gains considerable status within his group. The Eskimos elect as their religious leader the person fortunate enough to hallucinate. Ruth Benedict describes the extent to which the Plains Indians went to procure an hallucination: "On the western plains men sought these visions with hideous tortures. They cut strips from the skin of their arms, they struck off fingers, they swung themselves from tall poles by straps inserted under the muscles of their shoulders. They went without food or water for extreme periods. They sought in every way to achieve an order of experiences set apart from daily living" (Sidney Cohen, 1965, p. 69).

Many altered states of awareness that people used to crave were associated with religious ceremonies. More recently, the changes have been actively sought for the experience alone. Some people have tried to induce altered states of consciousness without drugs by means of yoga; sleep deprivation; combinations of heat, thirst, and social isolation; and sensory deprivation. But a great many have turned to drugs such as mescaline, LSD, psilocybin, and phencyclidine ("angel dust" or PCP). These drugs strongly affect perception and may also profoundly change mood and behavior. Such drugs are often called *psychotomimetic,* or mimicking of psychosis, and *hallucinogenic,* or causing hallucinations. Both terms have limited meaning. The drugs do not truly mimic schizophrenia or any other major psychotic disorder, and the vast majority of people taking them do not become psychotic. The word "hallucinogen" overemphasizes perceptual changes, whereas changes in mood and thinking are often at least as profound. Also, hallucinogens create perceptions less than they distort them. "Hallucinogen," though, is the most common descriptor for this class of drugs (which also includes mescaline and peyote).

Lysergic acid diethylamide (LSD) well illustrates hallucinogenic drugs because much research has been done on it and because, despite differences in potency and chemical structure, these drugs share very clear subjective effects. LSD was first synthesized in 1938; in 1943, Hofmann, a Swiss chemist, accidentally ingested a small amount of the drug and reported its remarkable effects. His observations remain useful because he was not affected by experimenter's or participant's bias that later influenced the reported subjective effects of LSD:

Last Friday, April 16, 1943, I was forced to stop my work in the laboratory in the middle of the afternoon and to go home, as I was seized by a peculiar restlessness associated with a sensation of mild dizziness. On arriving home, I lay down and sank into a kind of drunkenness which was not unpleasant and which was characterized by extreme activity of imagination. As I lay in a dazed condition with my eyes closed (I experienced daylight as disagreeably bright) there surged upon me an uninterrupted stream of fantastic images of extraordinary plasticity and vividness and accompanied by an intense, kaleidoscopelike play of colours. This condition gradually passed off after about two hours (Hofmann 1959, p. 240).

The hallucinogenic experience, perhaps more than other experience, is influenced by the mind set of the person giving the drug, the personality and attitudes of the person taking the drug, and the setting in which the drug is given. In fact, Jones (1977) suggests that LSD is unique in that sociocultural factors significantly determine the drug's psychological effects. Several researchers have found characteristics that set apart those who are strongly attracted to hallucinogen use (McGlothlin and Arnold 1971):

Persons who are attracted to hallucinogen use tend to prefer a casual, uncertain world as opposed to systematic, orderly, and structured life. They like an intuitive style rather than a conventional and factual approach. They score high on risk-taking and sensation-seeking measures, believe in paranormal phenomena, are susceptible to naturally occurring altered states of consciousness and seek to encourage them through both drug and non-drug methods. In short, persons who welcome the structure-loosening qualities of the hallucinogens also demonstrate this preference in other aspects of their lives. Those who have no taste for this type of experience place more emphasis on structure and control — both internal and external (McGlothlin and Arnold 1971).

Many species of animals become tamer on LSD, which often lowers their sensory thresh-

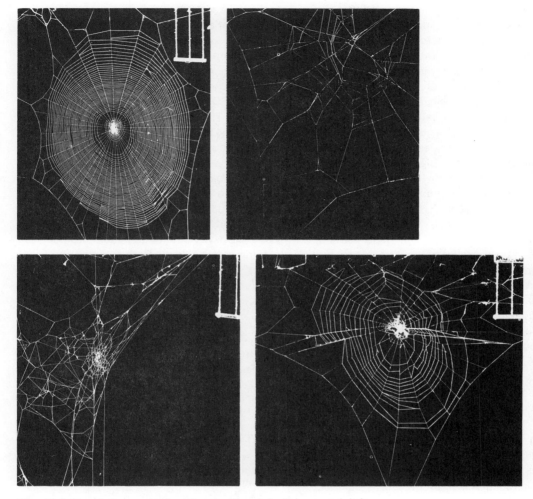

Fig. 16.4. Top, left: a normal or ''control'' web built by an adult female cross-spider once every 24 hours in the laboratory. The scale in the upper right corner indicates the direction of gravity and the 2 x 20 mm. original distance. Top, right: a web built by a spider after a high dose of caffeine, which disturbed the animal severely. Only remnants of the original center, radii, and frame are recognizable. The spider recovered completely 48 hours later. Bottom, left: a web built 6 hours after a relatively high dose of d-amphetamine (Dexedrine). The web was so severely distorted that measuring became impossible. Bottom, right: this web was built 24 hours after the one in the last photo by the same spider. It shows partial recovery. A fully ''normal'' web was built a day later.

olds. Spiders build better webs with LSD and worse ones with mescaline (a hallucinogen derived from peyote cactus). The effects on people are noticeable about one hour after ingestion, peak at two to three hours, and gradually disappear in six to ten hours. The human brain is exquisitely sensitive to LSD. The drug concentrates in the midbrain, which modulates emotional responses, regulates physiological functioning, and oversees awareness. The major site of drug accumulation is also close to the dopaminergic tracts, which filter, compare, and match sensory information (Cohen 1970).

Somatic changes include increased blood pressure and heart rate, dizziness, nausea, tremors, and weakness. The most striking changes, however, alter perception, mood, and behavior; these have been well demonstrated in both research and natural settings (Cohen 1970; Jones 1977; Pradhan and Hollister 1977). (We will illustrate all psychological and behavioral effects of LSD mentioned here with first-hand accounts [Cohen 1970].) Perceptual changes include intensification of color, blurring and changing of shapes, increased attention to detail, hallucinations and pseudo-hallucinations; enhanced auditory and tactile senses; distortions of time; and synesthesia, or merging of one sensory modality with another ("hearing colors" or "seeing sounds"). Changes in mood include occasional anxiety and panic reactions; euphoria; lability of mood; inappropriate affect; and occasional, profound depression, which can bring both suicidal ideation and behavior. Cognitive changes can take the form of increased fantasy; loosening of associations; decreased performance on tests involving attention, concentration, and motivation; and a loss of control over thoughts. Some behavioral changes are increased passivity, social withdrawal, and increased reaction time. Less common are increases in talkativeness, aggression, paranoid behavior, and frenetic psychomotor behavior. Other general psycho-

logical changes can include depersonalization and loss of ego boundaries, fears of self-disintegration, feelings of "oneness with the universe," and subjectively experienced expansion of the mind's horizons.

No deaths have been ascribed to drug toxicity with LSD, but accidents and suicides have occurred. The three major types of adverse effects are: (1) acute panic reactions, (2) spontaneous recurrences of drug-induced mental phenomena while not taking LSD (flashbacks), and (3) prolonged psychotic reactions. All appear to be relatively uncommon. Cohen and Ditman (1963) found that psychotic reactions lasting more than 48 hours occurred in only 1.8 per 1000 psychiatric patients and 0.8 per 1000 experimental subjects. Both suicides and flashbacks were rare. "Bad trips" can occur, though, and they can be terrifying. Cohen (1970) presents the reactions of one woman while on LSD:

As the guilt piled up, I felt that I killed my father, turned my mother towards insanity and made my brother neurotic and latently homosexual. And it was too much. I went off into a tangential world and knew that I was insane. I could feel the enclosedness of it, the separateness, and worst of all — the symbolization. I saw giant mosquitoes which drilled into my skull and sucked out the brains. They were not alive but were mechanical — huge, impersonal, glittering insects with the flecks of brilliant colour that were the sign of my analytic tendencies as decorations on their transparent, beautiful but completely unalive wings. And they swarmed around in complete silence. I told the therapists they would have to pull me through — or I didn't know what would happen.

These excerpts from three LSD experiences were obtained in another experiment conducted by Dr. Cohen (1965). You can see normal defense mechanisms breaking down, the intensified visual and other sensory perceptions, the elation and despair, the ecstasy, near-death, and terror. Dr. Cohen's remarks precede the experiential reports of the three subjects.

The highlights of a psychologist's story illustrate a point. Her day was a varied one emotionally, ranging from depression to mystical feelings of unity. A knock on the door could change her mood markedly. Under LSD a person is vulnerable to such relatively minor incidents. Even minimal variation in attitude of those with whom one is in contact may be sensed and may cause an intense response.

This subject reported:

I could feel my tongue getting thick, and I couldn't answer questions quite properly. I felt as though the messages were all coming into the switchboard, and messages were going out all right, but that the switchboard was all jammed up and the two weren't coordinating. As though the operator had something else on her mind, or too much to do, and was just letting things get all jammed up. . . .

Then I suddenly saw the colour of the wall waxing and waning — ebbing and flowing. The extraordinary character of light and colour is unbelievable. There was a third dimensionality to colour — and a constant change. And there would be a symphony of variations on what ordinarily is a plain brown wall. Or the flat yellow paint above it would suddenly light up the room and vary from pale translucent yellow to daffodil bright. The color would ebb from left to right, and then it would move from the floor up to the ceiling and back — and always I was aware of the objects and the room, and although the things moved towards and away from me as though on waves, still they were actually fixed and I knew they were real. This was interesting — how dimension and colour and other things all were mixed up in that they were all part of the whole pulsating ebb and flow, and it took enormous effort to try and separate things out sufficiently to describe what was happening accurately.

About another subject, Dr. Cohen states: "A sensitive, introspective hospital physiotherapist appeared relaxed and happy, undisturbed by the loss of his usual controls and defenses and the appearance of repressed material. The remark that there was something of death in the experience has been repeated many times." Parts of this subject's report follow:

I said this started this morning at 8:00, but, of course it didn't. It started some place in the distant past, millions of years ago, before we measured time on watches. It started someplace before there was language to juggle and make games with. It started before we learned to thrust and parry with words. It started when the early man could only express himself in the inarticulate, guttural "ghoss" and "ghas" of an infant — when his fellow man could only understand by understanding. Back there someplace, this started, this hard core of a desire to be — became. Call it by any name. I tried earlier today to describe it. I can't now, but I can try. Your faces and bodies were changing forms but this did not seem too strange to me. Your face colours changed, but that was not disturbing. I was at different times suspicious of you both, and I will never again belittle a patient's anxieties. . . .

Now, I felt this fine little hair. I could measure it. I could describe the colours of this delicate tube. I could let it float between my fingers and it became a ballet dancer or a Chinese horse — not as realities, but with all the grace and form. I was, at the time, an instrument that could measure the diameter of the hair, I could weigh it — and these were realities. And so we approach the next thing that I do not understand yet. Perhaps when fear goes I will do better. Some place in this there was an element of death. About as close as I ever have been or will be, I suppose, without actual death.

In contrast, Dr. Cohen states: "The extreme range of LSD effects ought to be brought out by extracting from the narration of another psychologist whose response was neither pleasant nor enlightening." This subject stated:

Over my right shoulder I could vaguely see what looked like a winged animal. It reminded me of a pterodactyl and it frightened me considerably. I was quite scared of it. We went on with the test though I still felt somewhat terrified of this thing. It seemed that instead of being in the room, it shifted outside as if I was too scared to have it inside with me and I put it outside. I felt often that it was beating its wings out there trying to get in. I could see through the window the flickering shadow of it. And once or twice I heard its wings. I was so terrified by this thing that I just couldn't move. Another peculiar reaction was that every time I heard this thing, the tester would turn a pale green colour and his face would assume the consistency of cream cheese with his eyebrows and hair being very finely etched against his pale face. It was the most frightening experience I've ever had (pp. 140–141; pp. 118–120).

Marijuana

In China it was called "the Liberator of Sin." An American described it as "the Lullaby of Hell." The Hindus gave it many names — usually more sympathetic, such as "the Heavenly guide, the Poor Man's Heaven, the Soother of grief." One Indian described its use as "so grand a result, so tiny a sin." There are hundreds of descriptions of cannabis. Max Glatt, a British representative at the World Health Organization, says that more has been written about cannabis than is known about it. In fact cannabis is a weed, a commercial product, until recently a medicine, and now a recreational drug.

— M. Schofield, *The Strange Case of Pot* (1971, p. 15)

Marijuana (a preparation of the hemp, or *Cannabis Sativa,* plant), like so many other drugs, has a long history. A Chinese compendium of medicines from 2737 B.C. mentions *Cannabis* (Taylor 1949). Even in ancient times controversy and social disapproval accompanied its use. Some cultures believed that hemp lined the road to Hades (Grinspoon 1975). The colonial settlers in seventeenth-century Jamestown, Virginia, grew hemp as a source of fiber, and in the nineteenth century marijuana was prescribed for many ailments throughout the Western world; in fact, marijuana was listed in the U.S. Pharmacopoeia as recently as 1941.

How strange — I remember thinking — it is exactly as people tell you it will be, and yet until it has happened to you, you cannot have the faintest idea what they mean. Just as in making love or giving birth for the first time, you enter a new world of experience which, no matter how many times you may have heard it described, still comes as a revelation to you personally.

I felt utterly relaxed — rather sleepy in fact — and serene and composed. I could feel the texture and weight of the settee with startling clarity; could measure the precise curve of the cushion under my elbows, and the exact depth to which they sank into it. The radiator behind and to one side of me felt hotter to my left shoulder than to my right: a measurable difference in temperature, though I had never noticed it before. The texture of corduroy was microscopically detailed, each ridge of the material distinct and separate.

Time crawled. The music went on and on. I tried to smoke an ordinary cigarette but it tasted dry and boring and I soon stubbed it out. The cat jumped onto my lap and I stroked her, enjoying the sleek, glossy softness of her fur and the subtle curves and hollows of her body. Obviously I was stroking beautifully, for she purred like mad.

The room was full of delicate vibrations of light, which shimmered through the air. My mind too seemed twanging with these vibrations, and my skin. They were palpable, rhythmic waves. . . . I had taken my shoes off by now and the dense, opulent pile of the carpet felt even better to the soles of my feet than had the corduroy of the settee to my elbows — though still not as luxuriant as the cat. My senses were alight with more complexity and beauty of feeling than I had ever assimilated before. It was totally new and unimaginable. No words could have prepared me to expect this.

After a couple of hours (or so my watch recorded: it felt infinitely more) I went to bed and slept deeply and refreshingly, without dreaming.

Next morning I woke with ease, earlier than usual, but full of energy and very clear-headed.

Anonymous marijuana smoker, *The Manchester Guardian* (December 3, 1969)

The effects of marijuana, like those of the hallucinogens, are particularly related to a user's personality, to the setting, dosage, and expectations. The psychological effects at different levels of intoxication are shown in Table 16.6. Potentially dangerous effects usually occur only at very high levels of intoxication — and rarely then. The reported relationship between repeated use of hallucinogens and marijuana and subtle changes in the ability to engage in abstract thinking, changes in personality, and the *amotivational syndrome,* with decreased energy and interest in pursuing goal-directed behavior, remains controversial (McGlothlin and West 1968; McGlothlin and Arnold 1971; Jones 1977). The evidence is clear for impaired reaction time, motor coordination, and visual perception, which makes driving, flying, and operating machinery potentially dangerous under marijuana intoxication (Marijuana and Health 1977).

Similarly, the long-term physical effects of prolonged marijuana use are unknown, although several dangers to health are being questioned (Marijuana and Health 1977): pulmonary effects (chronic administration has been shown to impair function of the lungs in otherwise healthy subjects); changes in the immune response system, which defends the body against disease; changes in endocrine functioning (some evidence — as yet quite tentative — hints that using marijuana can decrease testosterone [male hormone] levels and sperm counts); and possible genetic hazards.

Patterns of Use

The Marijuana and Health Report of 1977 drew several conclusions about marijuana use:

1. About 43 million Americans had tried marijuana. Approximately 16 million of them were currently using the drug (had used in the month prior to the survey).
2. The number of younger users (ages twelve to seventeen) had jumped 25 percent since 1976.
3. Three out of five in the eighteen to twenty-five age group (peak users of marijuana) had

Table 16.6. Subjective effects of marijuana

Low levels of intoxication	Moderate to high intoxication	Very high intoxication
Mild euphoria	Intensification of the effects experienced at lower levels	Changes in body image
Heightening of sensory awareness and sensory appreciation	Impaired functioning of short-term memory	Depersonalization
Alterations in perception of time	Lapses of attention	Marked sensory disturbance
Relaxed passivity	Disturbed thought patterns	Rarely: Panic reactions, paranoid thoughts, delusions, severe depressive reactions, hallucinations, and disorientation
	Feelings of unfamiliarity	
	Visual illusions	

Source: Adapted from R. T. Jones, "The Hallucinogens," in M. E. Jarvik, ed., *Psychopharmacology in the Practice of Medicine* (New York: Appleton-Century-Crofts, 1977); and J. R. Tinklenberg, "Abuse of Marijuana," in S. Pradhan and S. Dutta, eds., *Drug Abuse: Clinical and Basic Aspects* (St. Louis, Mo.: C. V. Mosby, 1977).

used marijuana; more than one in four used it currently.
4. Use continued to be strongly age-related; only 7 percent of those over thirty-five had ever tried marijuana.
5. Among high school seniors nationwide, one in eleven reported using it daily, up from one in twelve in 1976 and one in seventeen in 1975.

Therapeutic Uses

For centuries marijuana has been thought to have healing powers. Systematic studies on its medicinal properties, however, are recent; the most promising therapeutic potential appears to be its use as an antiemetic (decreasing or eliminating nausea and vomiting) in patients undergoing chemotherapy for cancer. Many have been made exceedingly ill by the treatments: they often lose weight, are very uncomfortable, and sometimes refuse to continue prescribed treatment. Standard antiemetic drugs have not been particularly successful in controlling their nausea and vomiting. In one preliminary double-blind study tetrahydrocannibinol (the active agent in marijuana) was found effective in nearly all the patients who received it (Sallan, Zinberg, and Frei 1975). Its use as a therapeutic agent is also being investigated in glaucoma, asthma, multiple sclerosis, anorexia nervosa, and epilepsy.

Social Policy

Controversy still exists about federal and state control of marijuana. For many years it was regarded as a "killer weed," the first step down the road to certain heroin addiction. As times changed and more and more people experimented, many of these extreme views moderated. In fact, several states have decriminalized marijuana; that is, taken away criminal penalties for personal use. McGlothlin (1968) discusses many of the complexities in making social policy on drugs, particularly marijuana:

Fig. 16.5. The illegal sale of a drug has many social and legal implications for its user. It also greatly affects society in general, through increased law enforcement costs and the criminal activity necessary to support drug purchases.

Murphy [1963] raises the question of why cannabis is so regularly banned in countries where alcohol is permitted. He feels that one of the reasons is the positive value placed on action, and the hostility toward passivity:

In Anglo-Saxon cultures inaction is looked down on and often feared, whereas overactivity, aided by alcohol or independent of alcohol, is considerably tolerated despite the social disturbance produced. It may be that we can ban cannabis simply because the people who use it, or would do so, carry little weight in social matters and are relatively easy to control; whereas the alcohol user often carries plenty of weight in social matters and is difficult to control, as the United States prohibition era showed. It has yet to be shown, however, that the one is more socially or personally disruptive than the other (p. 19).

Summary

1. Substance abuse has two behavioral characteristics: (1) psychological dependence, defined as the belief that the substance is necessary for continued functioning, with or without physiological dependence; and (2) negative social impact in the form of criminal behavior or failure to meet social or job responsibilities.

2. *DSM*-III differentiates two general patterns of drug misuse: (1) substance abuse, which includes psychological dependence, evidence of social complications, and duration of at least one month of drug use; and (2) substance dependence, which includes the same symptoms as abuse plus evidence of physical tolerance and/or withdrawal.

3. A combination of factors seems to affect the likelihood that a particular drug user will abuse or become dependent on drugs: the availability of the drug; personal attributes, such as an inability to handle pressure; and a social environment in which there is peer group pressure to use the drug.

4. Opium and its derivatives, morphine and heroin, are powerful analgesics and strong sedatives. Intravenous injection of heroin causes feelings of intense euphoria, followed by milder euphoria, lethargy, and relaxation. Symptoms of withdrawal — chills, vomiting, sweating, diarrhea — occur within eight hours of the last injection and last from three to five days.

5. Factors involved in continued use of opiates are: (1) the specific attributes of the drug, such as physiological dependence, avoidance of withdrawal symptoms, and the euphoric reaction following injection; (2) genetic predisposition to opiate addiction; (3) the conditioning aspects of the drug experience, including its rituals; and (4) the alternative lifestyle that the drug subculture offers.

6. Central nervous system (CNS) depressants, which include barbiturates and sedative hypnotics, are sedative and anti-anxiety drugs whose use can result in drug tolerance and withdrawal symptoms. Alcohol is the most commonly used and abused CNS depressant. The early stage of alcohol addiction is marked by interference in normal social and occupational functioning caused by the use of the drug. Continued and increased drinking may lead to physiological dependence. Withdrawal may result in delirium tremens (DTs), characterized by paranoia, disorientation, extreme agitation, and/or hallucinations. Chronic alcohol intake has been linked to the following major health problems: malnutrition, brain and liver damage, and inflammation of the pancreas. Factors leading to alcoholism include its widespread availability, cultural acceptance of its use, and a possible biological predisposition.

7. CNS stimulants include amphetamines, cocaine, and caffeine. Both amphetamines and cocaine promote a generalized sense of well-being and self-confidence, euphoria, and alertness. Chronic cocaine intoxication can produce symptoms of paranoid schizophrenia. Caffeine is the most widely used stimulant in the world. It is consumed in tea, coffee, and colas. Caffeine produces elevated mood, increased energy, and wakefulness, but in large amounts can cause irritability, headache, and anxiety.

8. Hallucinogens are drugs that profoundly

affect perception, mood, and behavior. The hallucinogen LSD affects the mid-brain, which controls emotion, physiological functioning, and levels of awareness. Three possible adverse effects of LSD are: acute panic reactions, flashbacks, and prolonged psychotic reactions.

9. Marijuana, or cannabis, is a widely used drug that produces mild euphoria, heightened sensory awareness, alterations in time perception, and relaxed passivity. High levels of intoxication can cause depersonalization and marked sensory disturbance. Marijuana seems to have therapeutic value as an antiemetic in cancer chemotherapy patients, and it is being studied as a treatment for glaucoma, asthma, multiple sclerosis, anorexia, and epilepsy.

Chapter 17

Sociopathy, Delinquency, and Family Violence

Crime in America
Crime Rates
Increases in Crime Rates
Types of Criminals
Causes of Criminal Behavior

Sociopathy
Clinical Characteristics
Causes of Sociopathy

Juvenile Delinquency
Types of Delinquents
Causes of Delinquency

Family Violence
Child Abuse
Spouse Abuse
Murder
Legal Status and Powerlessness
Causes of Family Violence

Summary

Crime is familiar to all of us; we read and hear about it daily, undoubtedly have been victimized by it, and possibly have perpetrated it. Much criminal activity does not strictly fall in the domain of abnormal psychology because it represents an intentional choice of occupation that causes little subjective distress, does not involve extreme or bizarre social behavior and, strictly speaking, does not impair the individual's ability to function. Three types of antisocial behavior of psychological interest, however, are sociopathy, juvenile delinquency and violence in the family.

Sociopathy is a personality disorder that is often associated with criminality. It has inspired much study of the individual's biological uniqueness and characteristics of his learning. *Juvenile delinquency* has been seen primarily as resulting from family and environmental influences. And *violence in the family* can be understood better by considering cultural values and practices. Actually, individual, environmental and cultural factors probably contribute some to each of these three problems. We begin with a brief survey of what is known about crime in America, and then concentrate on sociopathy, delinquency and family violence.

Crime in America

Crime Rates

The "crime index," compiled annually by the Federal Bureau of Investigation and published as part of the Uniform Crime Reports, summarizes rates of violent crimes (murder, forcible rape, robbery, and aggravated assault) and property crimes (burglary, larceny-theft, and motor vehicle theft). More than 11 million crime index offenses were reported in America in 1977. Violent crimes, which raise the greatest public concern, accounted for 9 percent of these; the average likelihood of our being the victim of a reported violent crime during that year was one in 220. With this possibility of personal attack hanging over them, many people report they are afraid to walk in their neighborhoods at night, even fearful in their own homes. Actually, although we usually fear the unex-

Fig. 17.1. Seven major types of crime in the United States are tallied and published each year by the FBI as the Crime Index. Twenty of these serious crimes occurred every minute throughout 1977.

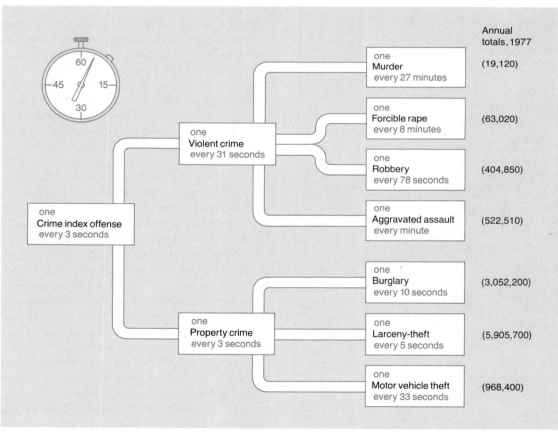

pected assault by a stranger, we are almost twice as likely to be attacked by our spouses, members of our family, friends, or acquaintances as by strangers.

Crimes against property, involving various kinds of theft, are much more frequent. Each year the average likelihood of our being a victim of a reported property crime is about one in twenty. Disturbing as these statistics are, the crime index is only a partial picture. It includes just seven major crimes; the Uniform Crime Reports include twenty-one others, such as fraud, arson, forgery, vandalism, and sex offenses, but these do not show up in the crime index. Also, a survey by the National Opinion Research Center of the University of Chicago found that much crime goes unreported, never making the official indices. When members of 10,000 households were asked about their experience as victims of crime in the previous year, they reported rates several times as high as the official statistics. Actual forcible rapes were more than 3.5 times the reported rate, burglaries three times, and aggravated assaults and larcenies of $50 and over more than double (President's Commission on Law Enforcement 1968). In short, criminal activity, assessed by official reports and from our daily experiences, is extensive.

Increases in Crime Rates

We often read or hear that crime in America is getting worse, and the statistics in Uniform Crime Reports agree. To allow for the increase that we would expect as the population grows, the statistic to compare is the crime rate. From 1967 to 1976, the rate of violent crimes grew by 82 percent and the rate of property crimes by 79 percent.

To understand what increased crime rates mean, we must consider a number of factors related to reports of crime and crime itself. First, some of the rise may not reflect more actual

crime, but more and better reporting of crime. Minorities, getting somewhat better representation in city governments and on police forces, may be more apt to report crimes and to be taken seriously. Also, with broader insurance coverage, thefts are more likely to be reported. Furthermore, police in many departments are using more sophisticated systems to report crime.

Second, even though the statistics also reflect a rise in actual crime, we must consider this in light of national trends in age and urbanization. Rates of crime are highest among the young; 74 percent of those arrested for crime index offenses are under twenty-five. Also, crimes proliferate in large cities; the rate of offenses in metropolitan areas is almost three times as high as in rural ones. In recent decades the proportion of youths in the population has grown and still more people have moved into the cities, both contributing to greater crime. It seems that the average person has not become more criminal, but that America in the late 1970s has more of the conditions associated with crime.

One notable exception is the increased chance that a woman will be arrested for a crime. Men still are five times as likely to be arrested as women, but arrests of females for index offenses have increased by 2.5 times in a decade. As women have achieved greater equality and have moved into most roles that used to be all-male, crime has been no exception. Then too, agencies of law enforcement may now give less favored status to women.

Types of Criminals

We will concentrate on individuals whose antisocial behavior has particularly interested psychologists. A common thread to follow in understanding sociopathy, delinquency, and family violence is that these are related to biological or psychological disturbances. For perspective, however, we cannot forget that most crime is committed by individuals who knowingly and intentionally set out to break the law, for individual gain. Sociologists classify them as career criminals, organized criminals, and white collar criminals. For some people, crime is a full-time occupation, supplying most of their income and involving attendant expenses, such as doing time in prison. The career criminal is most likely to commit property offenses for income, avoiding physical violence if possible. At the top of this professional ladder is the high-status criminal — the safecracker, jewel thief, art forger, confidence person or counterfeiter, as well as the career shoplifter or pickpocket. Of particular interest are the areas of organized and white collar crime, for they demonstrate how society's tolerance of, or even need for, some criminal activities can lead to selectivity in who is arrested and incarcerated for breaking the law.

ORGANIZED CRIME

Organized crime in America thrives by supplying illegal goods and services that millions of people want, operating in areas of morality where public opinion is divided and organized opposition is weak, mainly gambling, narcotics, and loan sharking (Haskell and Yablonsky 1974).

Many of us will bet a few dollars on Sunday's football game with hardly a thought about the broader consequences. Yet it is estimated that profits just from organized criminal betting operations may run as high as six to seven billion dollars a year. The President's Commission on Law Enforcement and Administration of Justice reported: "It is organized crime's accumulation of money, not the individual transactions by which the money is accumulated, that has a great and threatening impact on America," for "organized crime exists by virtue of the power it purchases with its money" (President's Commission on Law Enforcement

1968, p. 187). Organized crime flourishes only where it has corrupted local public officials; one of the organization's primary purposes is to secure and maintain immunity to interference by law enforcement agents, with regular payments to police, judges, and politicans, contributions to election campaigns, and purchase of votes.

The enormous profits of organized crime, as well as strong-arm tactics, buy ever-expanding control of legitimate businesses. These provide a veneer of respectability for the racket executive in the community and the appearance of a legal income. An interesting question is how such leaders can strongly uphold many social and community values, be accepted as good and charitable citizens, maintain self respect — and yet be thoroughly unscrupulous and outright criminal in everyday practices. Some of their illegal business dealings utilize strong-arm tactics and illegal practices, such as extortion, terrorism, fraud, bribery and arson, perhaps to secure a monopoly or milk a company's assets.

No one can certainly say how much organized crime affects life in America, but the economic cost is very high. We pay hidden costs, too, for the robbery, burglary, and larceny committed to secure money that maintains costly narcotics habits and covers gambling debts. The moral costs to the nation of corrupt officials, weakened public trust in government, and known criminal leaders living in high style seemingly untouchable by the law are profound.

WHITE COLLAR CRIME

Sociologist Edwin Sutherland termed the crimes committed by persons of respectability and high social status in their occupations "white collar" crimes (Sutherland 1949). This criminal is the businessman who engages in price fixing, the public assessor who exchanges a low tax valuation for a bribe, the builder who deliberately uses defective materials, the doctor who gives false testimony in an accident case, or the landlord who contracts to have a building torched for insurance.

The economic drain on society of white collar crime is estimated to be far greater than that of traditional crimes, yet, paradoxically, public response is much milder. No one's personal safety is immediately threatened and, amid the complexities of business, this invisible crime

Working for La Cosa Nostra

For thirty years Joseph Valachi was a member of the Vito Genovese family, one of New York City's racketeer groups in La Cosa Nostra (more familiarly, the Mafia). In 1963, while in prison for narcotics violations and murder, he testified extensively before a Senate investigating committee — an exceedingly rare and dangerous act because total secrecy is the first rule of the organization's strong code of ethics. These excerpts vividly portray the initiation and obligations of a Cosa Nostra "soldier." The oath Valachi mentions promises loyalty and secrecy.

Question: In other words, when you took that oath, you expected someday to die either by the gun or by the knife.

Valachi: That is right. . . .

Question: . . . What kind of ceremony did you go through in taking that oath?

Valachi: Well, then he gave me a piece of paper, and I was to burn it. . . . That is the way I burn if I expose this organization. . . . Then he pricks your finger, the Godfather . . . with a needle, and he makes a little blood come out, and in other words, that is the expression, the blood relationship. It is supposed to be like brothers. . . . Then they all shake hands, everybody gets up and shakes hands, and say a few more words together, which I can't recall. . . .

Question: . . . You became there a soldier or a button man. I see. Were any of the rules explained to you there, or were they explained to you later? . . .

Valachi: . . . For instance, you can't hit another member with your fist. That is a serious charge, not that you die for it, but you have a chance for a trial, which I was involved in one of those. . . . Well, the defense was that we had a business together and he was stealing.

Question: He was stealing?

Valachi: He was stealing most of the profit.

Question: Was that against your code, to steal from each other?

Valachi: Well, yes; against my code it was. . . .

Question: What was your first contact . . . after you became a member of Cosa Nostra?

Valachi: Joe Baker.

Question: You had a contract to kill Joe Baker?

Valachi: That is right. . . .

Question: You referred to these contracts. Did you get paid for performing these chores?

Valachi: No.

Question: This was part of your obligation as a member of the organization?

Valachi: Yes.

Question: This was part of the oath you described earlier this afternoon?

Valachi: Right. If this organization finds out that any member gets paid for any killing, he is in trouble. I must tell you that. . . .

Question: Let me ask you this. When you were chosen for this job, did you have any choice? Is this something you had to do when you were asked to do it? . . . Were you obeying orders as a soldier?

Valachi: Yes; we were working as a team, just like any army would, you know.

Question: This is something you wanted to do, but if you didn't want to do it could they have forced you to do it?

Valachi: A thought like that never even entered our mind as to whether you wanted to do it or not. You are there for that purpose, Senator.

Despite Valachi's violent career, he had previously been loyal to the organization. He simply "did what had to be done." Valachi's behavior, although certainly undesirable, would not be considered psychologically abnormal by most mental health professionals. What do you think? (President's Commission on Law Enforcement 1968, p. 207).

Fig. 17.2. White-collar crimes often violate public trust and cause people to be more skeptical of business, professional, and political practices. In 1974, several French wine merchants were convicted of doctoring and mislabeling wine. Among them were cousins Lionel and Ivan Cruse, shown here at a tasting table in a Bordeaux winery. The Cruses, officers in the 155-year-old firm of Cruse et Fils Frères, drew fines and suspended sentences.

often seems far removed from and incomprehensible to the average citizen. People who engage in such practices usually do not see themselves as criminals or even as morally wrong, justifying their behavior under the capitalistic system as only doing what must be done to survive in business. This conception of self as a law-abiding citizen and astute businessman is perhaps the main distinction from other criminals, though it is similar to the attitude of executives in organized crime. Generally the offender does not lose status among business associates, and the courts have been notoriously lenient with white collar criminals.

Causes of Criminal Behavior

Illegal behaviors vary so greatly that we must search for diverse explanations. To create some

semblance of organization, we will consider causes in categories of constitutional predisposition, family and immediate environment, and the broader culture. None of these elements adequately explains all antisocial behavior or, in truth, the actions of even one deviant person. Nonetheless, each level of analysis has some merit.

GENETIC-BIOLOGICAL FACTORS

Antisocial behavior "runs in families," leading to continuing controversy about inherited versus learned criminal tendencies. Recent research seems to uphold biological predisposition in some criminals, though it does not rule out environmental influence. In Denmark, where extensive social records are kept, Hutchings and Mednick (1974) studied criminal behavior of adoptees, to determine the relative influence of their biological and adopted parents. They reasoned that if criminal tendences are inherited, rates of crime should be higher for adoptees with biological fathers who were known criminals. Conversely, if the home environment has more influence, rates should be higher for those adopted by criminal fathers (for a similar analysis of schizophrenia, see Chapter 6). Table 17.1 shows that having a biological father who was a criminal increased crime rates, but being adopted by a criminal father did not. When both the genetic and environmental factors were present, however, the rate was highest. The authors warn that these results may in some way be unique to adoptees. Also, in Denmark, a fairly homogeneous society, genetic factors may be more likely to emerge than in the United States, with its more diverse cultural influences.

Other investigators have sought correlations with crime in faulty chromosomes, brain damage, abnormal brain waves, and abnormal activity of the autonomic nervous system. Much of this research was focused on the personality disorder sociopathy, which we will consider in detail.

FAMILY AND ENVIRONMENT

Other researchers have studied correlates of crime in social classes, neighborhoods, and the family. An early study by Shaw and McKay (1942) found a similar pattern in twenty-two cities in which crime rates were highest in the impoverished center of the city and diminished progressively out toward more affluent areas. The inner city also has the highest incidence of other social problems, such as mental illness, retardation, truancy, infant mortality, poor housing, and unemployment. From other studies of early family influences on personality development, particularly broken homes, marital discord, disciplinary practices, and the outright neglect and rejection of children, it is apparent that none of these neighborhood or family stresses is particularly healthy for the growing child. However, it is quite difficult to determine how much any one of them contributes to crime. Juvenile delinquency has been most often studied from the perspective of the family and the environment, so that we will consider it at length as an example of this level of explanation.

CULTURAL VALUES

The extent of antisocial behavior and the forms it takes must also be understood from the perspective of the values and practices of a given culture, for these exert a pervasive influence. Understanding antisocial behavior in the United States means considering American culture. A thorough analysis of white collar crime would require considering the competitive pressures of capitalism, and an analysis of property crimes would mean looking at the influence of materialism. As an example, we have chosen to examine how the problem of violence in the family relates to American cultural attitudes toward aggression.

Table 17.1. Percentage of adoptees with criminal records, as a function of biological and adoptive fathers' criminality

Fathers' criminality	Criminal rates among adoptees (Percent)
Neither biological nor adoptive father criminal	10.4
Adoptive father criminal, biological not a known criminal	11.2
Biological father criminal, adoptive not a known criminal	21.0
Both biological and adoptive fathers criminal	36.2

Sociopathy

For the 10 percent or so of adult offenders classified as sociopaths, the obvious purpose and payoff that spur ordinary criminal activities are absent. We see in their antisocial behavior a repetitive pattern of impulsive and often purposeless and self-defeating acts, committed with little planning or regard for the consequences. The sociopath is outside the community of professional criminals, for his behavior lacks the loyalty, cooperation, and planning they value. The terms *psychopath* and *sociopath* are interchangeable, but we will use sociopath for consistency. The *DSM*-III has more broadly defined the antisocial personality, no

XYY Chromosomes and Violence

The idea that crime might have a genetic cause was rekindled in the 1960s by discovery of a specific aberration in the chromosome patterns of several men who were mentally retarded, very tall, and violent (Jacobs et al. 1965). Instead of the one X and one Y sex chromosome that normal males have, these criminals had one X and two Y chromosomes. The rare XYY genotype is found in only one to three men in 1000, but is legally and ethically significant. If this chromosomal aberration predisposes a man toward violence, then perhaps he should not be held responsible for his actions:

In April, 1969, six-foot, eight-inch, 240 pound John Farley, nicknamed "Jolly Green Giant" because he was usually good-natured and "Big Bad John" because he was subject to fits of violent temper, confessed to having beaten, strangled, raped, and mutilated a Queens, New York, woman. He was defended on the grounds that due to the presence in his cells of an extra Y chromosome, he had no control over his actions or his judgment, and should therefore be found not guilty by reason of insanity resulting from a chromosome imbalance (Jarvik et al. 1973, p. 675).

A number of researchers sought to determine more conclusively how common the XYY genotype is and the behavioral characteristics associated with it. Yet methodological shortcomings have made conclusions uncertain. Most samples have been drawn from prison or hospital populations, obviously increasing the likelihood of associated violence. Researchers have not often included normal XY men for comparison, and those who did include such controls were generally aware of the participants' genotypes when they began their studies.

The most sophisticated and thorough study of the XYY genotype, by Witkin and eleven coauthors (1976), took advantage of the superior Danish system for keeping records. Chromosomes were analyzed for more than 4000 men over six feet tall who were born between 1944 and 1947. Twelve XYY men were in this sample, five of whom (41.7 percent) had been convicted of one or more criminal offenses. This number was significantly higher than the 9.3 percent rate for the XY controls, supporting the hypothesis that XYY men are more likely to show criminal behavior. The XYY men also had lower performance on army intelligence tests and lower educational attainment, variables that relate to the crime rate. Hence part of the excessive crime rate for these men may reflect greater likelihood that less intelligent men will commit crimes, or it may indicate that they are more likely to be apprehended. Most of the offenses were mild, however, with no more violence than evidenced in the control sample. The excessive violent behavior described in previous selected case studies was not found in this well-controlled study.

The twelve XYY men are still being studied for psychological, somatic, and developmental characteristics that may further explain the higher rate of crime among men of this genotype. In any case, the rare XYY chromosome would account for only a tiny proportion of crime.

longer delineating the sociopath as a separate entity. However, although the diagnostic distinction may not always be clear, the research literature on the sociopath is copious.

Clinical Characteristics

The best clinical description of the sociopath was presented by Cleckley in 1941, and elaborated in revisions of *The Mask of Sanity.** We will draw from his description in summarizing major characteristics:

1. *Ability to make a good impression.* The sociopath is apt to be alert, friendly, witty, intelligent, and easy to talk with. You can see nothing odd about him (or her); he is poised and in control, almost immune to normal anxiety and worry. Cleckley, after a lifetime of experience with sociopaths, writes that it is difficult not to be taken in by their charm and sincerity. He confesses to still being conned sometimes by their professed good intentions to reform, and has loaned them money. ("No such loan has ever been repaid and . . . all such checks have bounced" p. 342.) It is easy for judges, probation officers, therapists, and others to momentarily forget the incredibly antisocial behavior of this affable, convincing fellow. Writing of the exploits of Tom, a young sociopath, Cleckley says: "In view of his youth and the wonderful impression he made, he was put on probation. Soon afterward he took another automobile . . ." (p. 67).

2. *Impulsivity and disregard for conventions.* The sociopath has a remarkably chronic history of impulsive antisocial actions —criminal, unethical, or just annoying. There are alcoholic binges, repeated drug trips, outlandish pranks (urinating from the public library on passersby). There is thrill seeking, fighting,

* Cleckley, Hervey. *The Mask of Sanity,* 5th ed. St. Louis: The C. V. Mosby Co., 1976.

passing bad checks, car theft, and other impulsive acts (getting married to the prostitute he has just met). There is nonchalant acting out against those who have befriended him, such as stealing from the clergyman who has helped him, or seducing his best friend's wife. These behaviors often leave him open to high risk of being caught, with little potential gain. He will "lie about any matter, under any circumstances, and often for no good reason" (Cleckley, p. 341) in a thoroughly straightforward and convincing way. His life has an erratic quality; he will seize the gratification of the moment, sometimes with an aggressive outburst if frustrated.

3. *Lack of capacity to love.* Egocentric to an extreme, the sociopath is a loner, without real emotional ties. He can pretend to love, can mimic insight about how others feel, but in fact no real emotion seems to lie behind it. He brings no end of suffering, humiliation, physical hurt, and economic deprivation to those he professes to love — parents, spouse, or children. People are there to be manipulated for his own pleasure or gain. He may easily display outward social graces in trivial situations — volunteering to drive the old lady across the street to the market — while repeatedly abusing his family in every way possible.

4. *Lack of remorse or shame.* Most of us would feel rather bad about behaving in this way. Perhaps most striking is the sociopath's "guiltlessness," his denial of responsibility or, if trapped, acceptance of it without apparent regret. Many have inferred that the sociopath does not experience anxiety and guilt, the "pangs of conscience" most people experience.

5. *Failure to learn from experience.* Finally, though the sociopath can verbally give good explanations of how he or others should behave, his own actions are repeatedly self-defeating. Punishment is meaningless, for the sociopath neither learns to restrain criminal activity nor to become more accomplished at it so as to avoid being caught again. After brief periods of "reform," he is again acting out. About Tom, Cleckley writes further:

> Reliable information indicates that he has been arrested and imprisoned approximately fifty or sixty times. It is estimated that he would have been put in jails or police barracks for short or long periods of detention on approximately 150 other occasions if his family had not made good his small thefts and damages and paid fines for him (pp. 67–68).

Cleckley notes that the sociopath is unreliable, on many occasions showing no responsibility whatsoever, "no matter how binding the obligation, how urgent the circumstances, or how important the matter" (p. 340). Cleckley sees considerable psychological disturbance hidden by the sociopath's "mask of sanity." In time the impression that emerges of a life full of "gratuitous folly and nonsensical activity" (p. 364) leads inescapably to the conclusion that the individual is truly pathological. It is, in fact, the pattern of behavior over time that best illustrates the peculiarity of the sociopath.

Cleckley's description (below) of Roberta captures the characteristic features of the sociopath. In the psychiatric examination she appeared personable and quite verbal, though somewhat childlike. At the age of twenty she already had a lengthy history of impulsive antisocial and self-defeating actions, lack of consideration for others and chronic lying. She showed little guilt about her behavior; the consequences seemed to have had no effect and her self-awareness was limited. Her parents, who seemed firm and yet quite fair, were constantly bewildered by Roberta's behavior:

"I can't understand the girl, no matter how hard I try," said the father, shaking his head in genuine perplexity. "It's not that she seems bad or exactly that she means to do wrong. She can lie with the straightest face, and after she's found in the most outlandish lies she still seems perfectly easy in her own mind."

He . . . related . . . how Roberta at 10 years of age stole her aunt's silver hairbrush, how she repeatedly made off with small articles from the dime store, the drug store, and from her own home.

"At first it seemed just the mischievous doings of a little girl," he said, "a sort of play — and her not realizing about its being serious. You know how children sometimes tell a lot of fanciful stories without thinking of it as lying." . . .

As she grew into her teens, this girl began to buy dresses, cosmetics, candy, perfume, and other articles, charging them to her father. He had no warning that these bills would come. Roberta acted without saying a word to him, and, no matter what he said or did, she went on in the same way. For many of these things she had little or no use; some of them she distributed among her acquaintances. In serious conferences it was explained to the girl that the family budget had been badly unbalanced by these bills. As a matter of fact, the father, previously in comfortable circumstances, had at one time been forced to the verge of bankruptcy.

In school Roberta's work was mediocre. She studied little and her truancy was spectacular and persistent. No one regarded her as dull and she seemed to learn easily when she made any effort at all. (Her I.Q. was found to be 135.) She often expressed ambitions, and talked of plans for the future. . . . For short periods she sometimes applied herself and made excellent grades, but she would inevitably return to truancy, spending the school hours in cheap movie houses, in the drug store, or wandering through shops, stealing a few things for which she seemed to have neither need or specific desire. . . .

One of this girl's most appealing qualities is, perhaps, her friendly impulse to help others. . . . She often went to sit with an ill neighbor, watched the baby of her mother's friend, and rather patiently helped her younger sister with her studies. In none of these things was she consistent. She often promised her services and, with no explanation, failed to appear. . . .

"She has such sweet feelings," Roberta's mother said, "but they don't amount to much. She's not hard or heartless, but she's all on the surface. I really believe she means to stop doing all those terrible things, but she doesn't mean it enough to matter." . . .

"I wouldn't exactly say she's like a hypocrite," the father added. "When she's caught and confronted with her lies and other misbehavior, she doesn't seem to appreciate the inconsistency of her position. Her conscience seems still untouched. Even when she says how badly she's acted and promises to do better, her feelings just must not be what you take them for." . . .

Roberta was sent to . . . boarding schools from which she had to be expelled. She entered a hospital for training to be a registered nurse but did not last a month. Employed in her father's business as a bookkeeper, she used her skill at figures and a good deal of ingenuity to make off with considerable sums. . . .

With no explanation to her parents she suddenly disappeared. To me she explained that she had left with the intention of visiting a boyfriend stationed at a camp in another state. She admitted that she had in mind the possibility of marrying this man but that no definite decision had been made by her, much less by him. She had, it seems, given the matter little serious thought, and from her attitude one would judge she was moved by little more than what might make a person stroll off into the yard to see if the magnolia tree had bloomed. She left with a little over $4.00 in her purse. . . .

In a strange town and unable to locate her soldier friend, Roberta visited the family of an acquaintance and fabricated a story about visiting a sick aunt and missing the bus. They invited her to stay the night.

. . . While alone she attempted to place another long-distance call to the soldier. She still had in mind ideas about marrying him but had come no closer to a decision. The call not being completed, she began to fear the operator might ring back. She also was not quite sure her hostess had not overheard her at the telephone. After thinking of this and realizing that her family might trace her in such a nearby place, she slipped off after pretending to go to bed early, leaving no message for these people who had taken her in.

Catching a bus bound in another direction, she rode for a few hours and got off at a strange town where she knew no one. Not having concluded plans for her next step, she sat for a while in a hotel lobby. Soon she was approached by a middle-aged man. He was far from prepossessing, smelt of cheap liquor, and his manners were distinctly distasteful. He soon offered to pay for her overnight accommodations at the hotel. She realized that he meant to share the bed with her but made no objection. As well as one can tell by discussing this experience with Roberta, she was neither excited, frightened, repulsed, nor attracted by a prospect that most carefully brought-up virgins would certainly have regarded with anything but indifference.

The man, during their several hours together, handled her in a rough, peremptory fashion, took no trouble to conceal his contempt for her and her role, and made no pretense of friendliness, much less of affection. She experienced moderate pain but no sexual response under his ministrations. After giving her $5.00 with unnecessarily contemptuous accentuations of its significance, he left her in the room about midnight.

When she finally did reach her boyfriend, he strongly encouraged her to return home. Instead, and for no apparent reason, she drifted to another city and supported herself through rather aimless prostitution. After three weeks, her frantic parents located her. She entered a hospital for psychiatric treatment, which she later claimed had given her "a new outlook and a new life." Nevertheless, following her release from the hospital, she immediately resumed her former patterns of behavior (Cleckley 1976, pp. 46–55).

Causes of Sociopathy

Much experimental research has been done on aberrant physiology and learning deficits, guided by clinical observations of deficiencies in feelings and the apparent inability of sociopaths to learn from experience. We will focus on these, although some of the family influences that we will consider when we discuss juvenile delinquency apply here as well. Many sociopaths were raised in families broken by desertion or divorce or marked by inconsistent, sometimes brutal punishment, and these no doubt interact with any biological predisposition to produce the behavior we have described.

Some noteworthy problems complicate research on sociopaths. First, there is no generally accepted definition of sociopathy or standard system for classifying someone as a sociopath, so that different studies apply different criteria, although many researchers have attempted to follow those Cleckley suggested (Ziskind 1978). Also, most of the data were compiled on sociopaths who have been arrested and incarcerated, so that experience with the criminal justice system may have contributed to some of the abnormalities. Widom (1978) has a strategy for recruiting sociopathic subjects from the general community; she runs this classified advertisement in a Boston "counterculture" newspaper:

> Wanted: charming, aggressive, carefree people who are impulsively irresponsible but are good at handling people and looking after number one. Send name, address, phone and short biography proving how interesting you are. . . . (Widom 1978, p. 72).

People who have responded to this ad have resembled sociopaths on a number of measures, and further studies using this method could in-vestigate the generality of the findings we will consider.

FAILURE TO LEARN TO AVOID PUNISHMENT

Clinical descriptions of the sociopath report impulsive acting out and apparent inability to learn how to avoid future punishment. To understand these characteristics better, researchers have studied the sociopath's response to laboratory tasks involving punishment. Lykken (1957), in a brilliant study, compared sociopathic prison inmates, nonsociopathic inmates, and college students in learning to avoid shock in a maze task. The "maze" was a row of four levers, two lights, and a visible error counter. For each choice one lever would be correct, lighting the green light and advancing to the next choice. The task was to determine for each choice which of the four levers was correct and to learn a sequence of twenty correct lever presses. For a wrong choice, each of the three incorrect levers would light the red light and one of these levers would also trigger a shock. The purpose was to find if subjects would learn to minimize the punishment by incidentally learning the sequence of shocked alternatives and avoiding them. No explicit instructions for avoiding the shock, or even that it was possible, were given the subjects.

On the measure of learning the maze, the number of errors made before mastering the sequence, all three groups performed equally well. In learning to avoid punishment, however, the number of errors that produced shock, the college students eventually learned to decrease their shock errors, but the sociopaths showed almost no such learning. The nonsociopathic prisoners fell between those two groups.

It has been reasoned that sociopaths learn to avoid shock less effectively in Lykken's task because this type of punishment may have no meaning for them. The sociopath displays a "you can't hurt me" attitude, seeming to have less anxiety, or even less perception of pain itself.

LACK OF EMOTIONAL RESPONSE

Some investigators have attended particularly to the sociopath's atypical emotions, especially the apparent lack of anxiety. They have used physiological indices of activity in the sympathetic nervous system, such as heart rate and skin resistance, to measure the sociopath's emotional responsibility. When threatened with pain, as in Lykken's maze, sociopaths display less than the normal increase in palmar sweat-gland activity (Hare 1965). In one study, subjects were told they would receive a painful shock after ten minutes. While they watched a clock in anticipation, the sociopaths showed a relatively smaller increase in palmar sweating (Lippert and Senter 1966).

The lower degree of anticipatory anxiety could imply that sociopaths do not experience pain as intensely as nonsociopaths, leading researchers to study response to noxious stimulation. When people are presented with a noxious stimulus, most show a momentary decrease in skin resistance (see Chapter 3). The sociopath, though, shows *more* skin resistance in response to stimuli such as a loud noise or shock than do nonsociopaths (Borkovec 1970; Hare and Craigen 1974). The sociopath, then, shows less response than others to anticipated shock or to shock itself.

Schachter and Latané (1964) figured that if sociopaths were not learning to avoid punishment because of low anticipatory anxiety, then increasing their arousal by injecting adrenalin should improve their learning. Under the guise of studying effects of hormones, half the subjects were injected with adrenalin and half with a placebo drug on the first day of learning Lykken's maze. The injections were reversed on the second day. As in Lykken's study, sociopaths

learned the maze as well as contrast groups, but were markedly inferior in learning to avoid the shocks under placebo. With increased arousal under adrenalin, however, sociopaths showed dramatic improvement (see Figure 17.3), supporting the hypothesis that sociopaths do not learn to inhibit behavior normally because they experience less anxiety.

We still do not know, though, whether the sociopath's "emotional indifference" in these shock situations reflects an inborn deficit or is the result of his experiences in social learning. Many sociopaths experienced considerable physical punishment as children and may have learned to tune it out.

Fig. 17.3. Avoidance of shock in the Lykken maze under placebo and adrenalin. The increased performance of sociopaths when they received the arousing drug adrenalin supported the hypothesis that they do not learn to inhibit behavior normally because they experience less anxiety. (After Schachter and Latané 1964.)

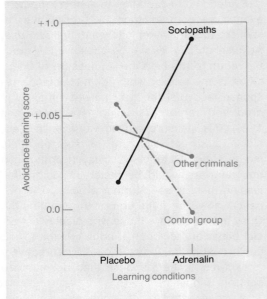

UNDERAROUSAL AND STIMULUS-SEEKING

One theory about inborn deficits is Quay's (1965): The sociopath is generally under-aroused and his behavior is an extreme of stimulation seeking. Quay particularly sought to explain the sociopath's impulsive acting out. The sociopath, either because his threshold of arousal is generally lower or he adapts faster to sensory inputs, frequently finds himself suffering stimulus deprivation. His need to create excitement and adventure, his thrill-seeking behavior, and his inability to tolerate routine and boredom may manifest his need to increase or change patterns of stimulation. But the evidence for this theory is not strong. During periods of minimal stimulation ("resting levels"), some investigators have found higher skin resistance (a sign of lower arousal) in sociopaths than in controls (Hare 1978), but a review of the literature does not reveal consistent evidence that sociopaths are underaroused (Siddle 1977).

Evidence on adaptation to sensory inputs is even more contradictory. Skin-resistance responses to stimulation follow a definite course. An initial drop in resistance is followed by gradual return to the baseline. A measure of adaptation is the rate at which skin-resistance response recovers, the time between maximum drop and return to resting level (Venables 1974); this measure proved valuable in Mednick's study of offspring of schizophrenic mothers (see Chapter 6). Quay hypothesized that recovery would be faster in sociopaths, leading them to seek further arousal. The evidence, however, quite consistently refutes the Quay hypothesis, for those who display antisocial behavior (sociopaths, adult criminals, and adolescent delinquents) show *slower* recovery of skin-resistance response than do matched controls (Siddle 1977).

All these studies of emotional discharge have been conducted with prison populations. Consequently, inhibited emotionality may be an adaptation to punitive prison life and not a pre-conditioned attribute. Therefore, in a recently published study, Loeb and Mednick (1976) tested a sample of adolescents five to ten years before they committed any known delinquent acts. Those who subsequently had at least two court convictions displayed significantly *slower* skin-resistance recovery than matched nondelinquents. Slow recovery cannot then be explained by conviction and imprisonment. Notice that this pattern is opposite that of adolescents who subsequently develop schizophrenia. Among this group, the rate of recovery turned out to be *faster* than normal (see Chapter 6).

Mednick (1974) has used these findings to support an alternative theory of sociopathic behavior, focusing on the sociopath's failure to learn to inhibit previously punished behavior. Mednick argues that a person contemplating an antisocial act experiences anticipatory fear, and that inhibiting the antisocial act dissipates fear. Reduction of fear reinforces inhibition of response. Accordingly, relatively rapid dissipation of fear (fast recovery) should better reinforce inhibition of response, and the person should learn to avoid punishment more effectively. Sociopaths, we have seen, have less anticipatory response and slower dissipation, which would be consistent with poorer learning to avoid acts that will be punished. This position is attractive, but a great deal of further investigation is needed to confirm psychophysiological findings and to evaluate alternative hypotheses.

LEARNING TO AVOID PUNISHMENT
(REVISITED)

We have seen that the sociopath's poor learning to avoid punishment in the Lykken task might be explained by his experiencing less arousal to noxious stimulation or to anticipation of it. Perhaps the punishment was not meaningful. We remember that another clinically recorded characteristic is the sociopath's tendency to exploit people or situations for his own gain, to "get something" from them. Schmauk (1970), exploring alternative consequences for errors, had subjects learn three maze sequences and used three kinds of punishment for errors: physical (shock), monetary (losing one quarter from an initial pile of forty), and social (experimenter saying, "wrong"). When the punishments for errors were physical or social, the sociopaths learned to avoid these much less well than a normal control group did. When errors meant losing money, though, the sociopath's avoidance learning was superior (see Figure 17.4). It appears that sociopaths can indeed learn to inhibit punished behavior as well as normals "if the punishment is appro-

priate to their value system; that is, if the punishment is genuinely experienced as noxious or distressing" (p. 334). More recently Widom (1976) found also that sociopaths' performance was comparable to that of nonsociopaths on an interpersonal task requiring cooperation, for which monetary incentives were offered.

Under the right circumstances, sociopaths can be cooperative and can learn from experience. But we still understand poorly why physical punishment is not one of those "right" circumstances.

BRAIN-WAVE ABERRATIONS

Some investigators have attributed the sociopath's impulsivity and inability to learn to inhibit punished behaviors to abnormalities in the brain. Reviewers conclude that 50 to 60 percent of sociopaths showed abnormalities in brain waves (Ellingson 1954; Syndulko 1978), compared with 10 to 15 percent in normal controls (Hare 1970). The most common abnormality is widespread, excessively slow brain-wave activity (5 to 8 cycles per second). This pattern resembles that generally found in children, leading some to suggest that the sociopath's higher brain centers mature slowly. Slow brain-wave activity may also be associated with boredom and drowsiness, leading Syndulko (1978) to caution investigators about the need to control for the general alertness of their subjects.

There is also evidence that the sociopath's brain is apt to show bursts of greater activity in the temporal area. The incidence of this phenomenon is very low in the general population (1 to 2 percent), but among highly impulsive and aggressive sociopaths in one study it was 48 percent (Kurland et al. 1963). Hare (1970) believes these abnormalities may reflect a malfunction in the limbic system of the midbrain, which is important in regulating fear-motivated behavior, including learning to inhibit a response in order to avoid punishment.

Fig. 17.4. Avoidance of different punishments in the Lykken maze. The increase in performance by sociopaths when punishment is loss of money indicates that they can perform as well as normal controls if the punishment is personally meaningful to them. (After Schmauk 1970.)

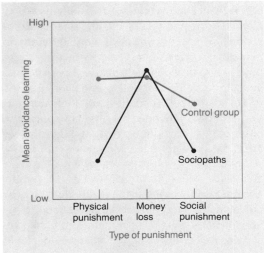

The results of brain-wave studies are interesting, but explanations of how they relate to the sociopath's behavior are still mostly speculation. We must bear in mind that 15 percent of the population show slow brain-wave activity without sociopathic behavior, and that about half the sociopaths fail to show abnormal activity in the higher brain centers. Future research might more profitably examine how the sociopaths who do show brain-wave abnormality differ in background, behavior, psychophysiology, and prognosis (Syndulko 1978).

Juvenile Delinquency

Seeking precursors for adult criminality, many have studied antisocial behavior of adolescents. "Juvenile delinquency" is the legal name for offenders younger than the statutory age limit, which varies from sixteen to twenty in different states. An adolescent officially becomes a delinquent only when he or she is arrested and appears before appropriate jurisdictional bodies. Juvenile offenses range from the infrequent crimes of murder, rape, or robbery, to "status offenses" — acts that would not be illegal for an adult, such as truancy, running away from home, or violating liquor laws. Most states are eliminating status offenses, so that the activities which lead to being classified as a delinquent more closely parallel those which classify an adult as a criminal. The rate of serious juvenile offenses has risen sharply in recent decades, though, as with adult crime, the arrest statistics still greatly underestimate the problem (Uniform Crime Reports 1977). Indeed, self-report surveys of youth in this country reveal that 90 percent have committed acts for which they could have been brought to juvenile court (President's Commission on Law Enforcement 1968).

The literature on delinquency describes mainly boys, because they commit many more offenses and more serious ones than girls do. Boys are arrested more often for aggressive offenses, such as breaking and entering, theft, or robbery, and girls are arrested most for nonaggressive behaviors like shoplifting or sexual promiscuity. In fact, boys have not been judged delinquent for the same types of sexual behavior that has marked girls as delinquent. In recent years, however, female delinquency has increased greatly, including aggressive crimes. Research will be needed to reexamine the typologies and causes that we now know primarily from studies of male delinquents.

Types of Delinquents

Many observers have noticed different types of delinquent youths, and some have attempted to classify these in order to better understand causes. One classification scheme, with three main "patterns of personality organization," was proposed by Hewitt and Jenkins (1947) after studying three hundred boys at the New York State Training School, and this general division, with varying labels, is supported by subsequent studies (Quay 1972; Jenkins 1973). Most delinquents would qualify as *socialized-subcultural delinquent.* Not very different in personality from the nondelinquent, these boys — and probably girls also — have adopted subcultural values accepting behaviors that the rest of society considers deviant. Their activities are strongly influenced by the environmental press of family, neighborhood, and peers. They are likely to be gang members.

For *disturbed-neurotic delinquents,* the characteristics are different. They tend to rebel against family, seeking their attention or even punishment, according to some observers, for unconscious guilt. They come from middle-class as well as lower-class families, and usually have a history of neurotic symptoms, such as chronic depression or diffuse anxiety (Kessler

Hidden Delinquency

Delinquent conduct is far more widespread than official records indicate (Akers 1964; Empey and Erickson 1966; Gold 1966; Belson 1969). In fact, most adolescents admit to at least some acts for which they could have appeared before a court. Although many of these crimes are minor, a substantial number of people who are not officially delinquent admit to relatively serious offenses when surveyed by researchers. Those who are officially delinquents, however, admit to a greater number of different offenses and a higher frequency, so that their being arrested in part reflects the extent of their delinquency. Also, though, many of the middle-class youths who commit delinquent acts are dealt with not by arrest but by other means, such as counseling by clergy or psychologists, and never appear officially on police records.

This is a list of delinquent acts administered to a random sample of midwestern high school students. Take the inventory yourself, but don't feel too uncomfortable about your own delinquency — nearly every student surveyed admitted to at least one offense!

This survey was done more than twenty years ago; which offenses do you think would be committed more frequently today?

Delinquent offenses admitted by high school students

Type of offense	Percentage admitting offense	
	Boys	Girls
Driven a car without a driver's license or permit	81	60
Skipped school	54	40
Had fist fight with one person	87	33
"Run away" from home	13	10
School probation or expulsion	15	3
Defied parents' authority	22	33
Driven too fast or recklessly	50	21
Taken little things (worth less than $2) that did not belong to you	63	36
Taken things of medium value ($2–$50)	17	3
Taken things of large value ($50+)	4	2
Used force (strong-arm methods) to get money from another person	6	1
Taken part in "gang fights"	24	10
Taken a car for a ride without the owner's knowledge	11	5
Bought or drank beer, wine or liquor (include drinking at home)	68	63
Bought or drank beer, wine or liquor (outside your home)	43	29
Deliberate property damage	61	22
Used or sold narcotic drugs	1	1
Had sex relations with another person of the same sex (not masturbation)	12	5
Had sex relations with a person of the opposite sex	39	12
Gone hunting or fishing without a license (or violated other game laws)	74	21
Beat up on kids who hadn't done anything to you	16	6
Hurt someone to see them squirm	23	10

Source: Adapted from Short and Nye 1958.

Fig. 17.5. Delinquency in girls typically has been nonviolent, as in this teenager's shoplifting. In recent years, however, there has been an increase in female delinquency, including violent crimes.

1966). Their illegal actions often are compulsive — repeatedly stealing cars, shoplifting, setting fires, or acting out sexually. They also frequently ensure that they will be caught, as if punishment were their intent.

Unsocialized-aggressive delinquents resemble adult sociopaths. They are impulsive, defiant, and cruel, lack family ties, and feel little guilt. They are usually loners who have difficulty with peers as well as others. Robins (1978) studied the child precursors of adult sociopathy and reported that every one began antisocial behavior before age eighteen, and many of these probably were "unsocialized-aggressive delinquents."

Causes of Delinquency

The search for causes of juvenile delinquency has been long and exhaustive. Most research though has been correlational (see Chapter 4), so although we know that low social class, broken homes, and poor school performance, for example, are associated with delin-

quency, we are less certain about causal relationships. A number of sociological theories attribute delinquency primarily to certain features of the social structure, such as social disorganization or unavailability of opportunities to satisfy needs (Cohen 1955; Cloward and Ohlin 1960). It is difficult to dispute the influence of these variables, but it is also difficult to demonstrate their importance experimentally. Nevertheless they do point to conditions in which delinquency may thrive, given the existence of other influences.

Psychologists, on the other hand, have focused chiefly on individual personality problems and characteristics of the delinquent's family life as causes of delinquent behavior. An interactive perspective, in which both social and psychological factors are seen to contribute to delinquency, is likely to prove the most reasonable, but because the interplay of adolescent and environmental pressures is unquestionably important, we will highlight some of them here.

ENVIRONMENTAL INFLUENCES: LIVING CONDITIONS

The conditions of poverty may not cause delinquency, but they do provide fertile soil in which it can thrive. Dirty and deteriorating buildings, overcrowded living, excessive noise, littered streets, insufficient space for recreation and inadequate schools provide a backdrop of stress and grim despair to which the child does not fail to respond. Many adult models in this environment provide daily examples of violence, drunkenness, drug addiction, and prostitution. One fourteen-year-old boy described his neighborhood:

When I first started living around here it was really bad, but I have gotten used to it now. Been here two years. People getting shot and stuff. Lots of people getting hurt. People getting beat up. . . . Gee, there's a lot of violence around here. You see it all the time (*Challenge of Crime in a Free Society* 1967, p. 62).

AFFLUENCE, ALIENATION, AND SELF-ESTEEM

One argument is that people steal not because they are starving but because they are envious (Toby 1967). The all-too conspicuous affluence of the middle class naturally breeds frustration and alienation among youths growing up in poverty. Some criminologists believe that this contrast is one cause of aggressiveness and adoption of antisocial (or anti-middle-class) values. Certainly children who are aware of their poverty in an affluent world may have low self-esteem. One sociological perspective on delinquency is Merton's (1957) *theory of anomie,* proposing that delinquency is a response to unavailability of conventional or socially approved routes to success.

A study of male youths living in a high-delinquency Chicago area found that delinquents had little optimism about their chances for achievement in conventional society (Institute for Social Research 1974). They were pessimistic about their chances of finishing high school and expected to hold adult jobs of low status. Even at ages ten to thirteen, more delinquent boys said they had little chance of graduating, though their academic standing was as good as that of nondelinquents. They expected to fail. Without anything positive to look forward to, a youth may feel he has nothing to lose by engaging in antisocial acts, which either gain him what he cannot get by legitimate means or deny altogether the desirability of middle-class goals. Once he has been labeled "delinquent," his chances for success and his expectancies diminish further.

Kaplan (1975) theorizes that youths adopt deviant *reference groups* to enhance self-esteem. A number of researchers have found a relationship between delinquency and low self-esteem, but there is controversy about which comes first. Rosenberg and Rosenberg (1978) recently analyzed longitudinal data and found support for Kaplan's position that low self-esteem precedes delinquent behavior.

PEER PRESSURE AND THE GANG

The peer group is vital to all adolescents, and most delinquent acts are committed in a group. As we'd expect, many more delinquents than nondelinquents have had previous habitual association with other delinquents (Glueck and Glueck 1950). For many youths this association is formalized in the gang (Cartwright et al. 1975). Status and companionship can be found in gang membership, and these, not criminal activity, seem to be the main reason for joining a gang. Gangs stake out their turf and adopt names, dress, hair styles, and language that signal their group membership and "toughness." The gang is something to do, some place to be — it is excitement, prestige, power, and protection. It sets up models of delinquent behavior as well as reinforcement for that behavior. Most gangs are not highly organized and

Fig. 17.6. The Katos Wunchcus in New York City bill themselves as more of a recreation club than a gang. This does not mean that they do not protect themselves and each other. Here, one of the members displays a chuka stick, made from two iron pipes and a chain, in the Katos Wunchcus clubhouse.

rarely are they primarily criminal. Their varied activities include fighting, gambling, sports, social activities, drugs and alcohol, sex, auto theft, and petty larceny. A few core members are decidedly delinquent, but the majority are peripheral members with relatively weak commitment to the subculture (Hood and Sparks 1970).

FAMILY RELATIONSHIPS

The family, as the primary socializing agent, is critical in determining which youths in a community will be delinquent. Because almost half of adolescent delinquents have engaged in delinquent acts before they are eight years old, an examination of early family influences seems critical.

PARENTAL ANTISOCIAL MODELS. Many delinquent children have parents who model antiso-

cial behavior and accept or even reinforce it in their children. Glueck and Glueck (1950), for example, reported that 84 percent of delinquents in Massachusetts reformatories came from homes in which there were criminals. A boy's relationship with his father is most predictive of later delinquency, and many delinquents have fathers who display alcoholism, absences, brutality, or dishonesty. Aggression, in particular, is modeled and reinforced as a response to stress.

My father don't get smart with me no more. He used to whup me, throw me downstairs, until I got big enough to beat him. The last time he touch me, he was coming downstairs talking some noise about something. I don't know what. He had a drink, and he always make something up when he start drinking. He was trying to get smart with me, so he swung at me and missed. I just got tired of it. I snatched him and threw him up against the wall, and then we started fighting. My sister grabbed him around the neck and started choking him. So I started hitting him in the nose and everything, and around the mouth. Then he pushed my mother and I hit him again. Then he quit, and I carried him back upstairs. Next morning he jump up saying, "What happened last night? My leg hurts." He made like he don't know what had happened. And ever since then, you know, he don't say nothing to me (Werthman 1967, p. 161).

BROKEN HOMES AND MARITAL DISCORD. Many studies record the greater likelihood that delinquents will have homes broken by separated or divorced parents (Rodman and Grams 1967). With no male figure at home the boy is more apt to find role models among older peers or adults in the community, and for inner-city youths these are likely to be criminal. Some children raised in poverty by a single parent must fend for themselves at an early age and deny their dependency. This "premature autonomy" inspires resentment of others who seek to exert control, such as teachers or police.

In intact families, the degree of marital disharmony has been shown to relate to delinquency; the child may find himself neglected or overtly rejected, and may lose respect for his parents. Johnson and Lobitz (1974) systematically observed children's behavior at home and found more behavior problems in homes with marital maladjustment. Indeed, some authorities now feel that a child in a harmonious broken home is less likely to become delinquent than another in an intact family with much parental discord (Rutter 1971).

PARENTAL AFFECTION, REJECTION, AND DISCIPLINE. Daily interaction between child and parents is vital to a child's behavior. Homes of delinquent children are often neglectful and chaotic, with no clear routine and poorly managed behavior. Constructive behaviors may be ignored, not encouraged, and punishments

may be meted out severely or inconsistently, as this adolescent boy describes:

Well, like last week, you know. Last Saturday I came home about 4 A.M. and they got kind of excited. And they didn't say nothing that night. But the next morning they kept talking "where you been" and all this. And I told them where I had been and they said okay. They told me to stay in this weekend but they didn't say nothing about it this weekend so I went out last night and tonight. (When she tells you not to do something, do you go along with her or what?) Like you mean stay or something? Oh, if she say stay in, I talk to her about it for an hour or two and then she get mad and say, "Oh, get out of the house. Leave." That's what I been waiting for (Werthman 1967, p. 161).

Much evidence shows that harsh and inconsistent punishment relates to delinquency. The Cambridge-Somerville youth study, begun in the 1930s to investigate causes and prevention of juvenile delinquency, gathered extensive family data on 500 high-risk boys. Years later, after it was known which boys had become delinquent, the family backgrounds were compared. The delinquents were much more likely to have families described as quarrelsome, neglectful, and lax in discipline, with punitive but erratic discipline being most detrimental (McCord, McCord, and Zala 1959). One result of harsh and unfair punishment is hostility and overt aggression in the child (Bandura and Walters 1959).

Family discipline cannot be separated from the social conditions in which the family lives, however. Discipline is more difficult in poverty. A half-century ago Shaw wrote:

The continuous movement of the older residents out of the area and the influx of newer groups, the confusion of many divergent cultural standards, the economic insecurity of the families, all combine to render difficult the development of a stable and efficient neighborhood organization for the education and control of the child and the suppression of lawlessness (National Commission on Law Observance and Enforcement 1931).

Today, the inner-city parent still lacks the support in child rearing taken for granted in the suburbs, such as neighbors who know the child well, help to supervise play, and report difficulties they notice to the parents.

Parents who reject and neglect their children, however, can be found in all social classes (Bratter 1973). The Cambridge-Somerville study found, in fact, that consistency of affection is even more important than consistency of discipline. A number of researchers have mentioned the father's special role:

The fathers of aggressive boys were typically hostile to, and rejecting of, their sons, expressed little warmth for them, and had spent little time in affectionate interaction with them during the boys' childhood (Bandura and Walters 1959, p. 354).

In these homes, loving and supportive mothers can be a counterforce against delinquency (McCord, McCord, and Zala 1959).

Delinquency in subgroups whose overall rates of antisocial behavior are low (as among girls and middle-class youths) may be directly linked to family influences. One study of thirty delinquent girls uncovered all the family factors we have mentioned (Scharfman and Clark 1967). Nineteen girls came from broken homes and twenty-two had at least one parent with severe psychopathology. Many had early sexual experience, modeled and encouraged by parents, as well as unpredictable, irrational, and violent punishment. The authors conclude: "Any form of consistent discipline or rational setting of limits was unknown to the girls in their homes. Rather, there was an almost regular pattern of indifference to the activities or whereabouts of these girls" (p. 443).

Delinquency seems not to have one main cause, just as there is no one type of delinquent.

Probably some have an inherited tendency toward antisocial behavior, consistent with evidence we have discussed (see pages 432–33). For most youths, though, impoverished living conditions, sense of alienation and low self-esteem, peer pressures, discord and antisocial models in the family, and a lack of love and caring are among the causes. For any delinquent youth, one or several of these may be present, and as we will see in Chapter 19, rehabilitation programs must address as many of these problems as possible.

In examining family correlates of delinquency we have often mentioned violence, either modeled by parents or inflicted on children as severe and arbitrary punishment. We will consider further the general problem of violence in the family.

Family Violence

Not long ago, violence in the family was a hidden crime, avoided by law enforcement, psychiatry, and just about everyone else. The so-called battered child syndrome was first described in a medical journal in 1962 (Kempe et al. 1962), and wife — or spouse — beating only came to public awareness in the 1970s. Yet family violence is emerging as an enormous social problem with millions of victims each year. Family disturbances are the most frequent source of police calls and account for one of every five police deaths in the line of duty (Uniform Crime Reports 1977).

The physical injuries from violence among family members are exceeded only by the emotional ones. The family has been called the cradle of violence (Steinmetz and Strauss 1975), graphically demonstrating for the growing child how stress is to be coped with and problems are to be solved. Examining how and why loved ones hurt each other may help us further understand crime and delinquency.

Child Abuse

I have given suck, and know
How tender 'tis to love the babe that milks me:
I would, while it was smiling in my face,
Have pluck'd my nipple from his boneless gums,
And dash'd the brains out.
— Shakespeare, *Macbeth*
Act I, Scene 7

Each day thousands of children are abused or neglected by their parents. Child abuse in its narrow sense means nonaccidental physical injury inflicted on a child by his parents. Abused children are beaten, kicked, burned, strangled, suffocated, sexually molested, thrown against walls and radiators. They suffer fractures, lacerations, contusions, permanent brain damage, and sometimes death. Neglected children left for days in dirty cribs without food or water suffer hunger, dehydration, festering sores, rashes, and sometimes death.

In Los Angeles County 48,000 cases were referred to the Division of Public Social Services in one year, and these were only reported cases (*Los Angeles Times,* September 3, 1978). It is estimated that in America each year 2.5 million children are physically abused or neglected (Papalia and Olds 1975). If the definition of child abuse included verbal abuse and emotional neglect, the incidence would be several times higher.

A Brooklyn man, 6 feet 5 inches tall, and a woman he was living with were charged yesterday in Criminal Court with homicide in the beating death of the woman's 5-year-old daughter. The body of the child, Maria Chevonna, was found covered with cuts, welts, and burns, in a square-foot hole of the couple's ground-floor apartment in a four-story tenement in the Brownsville section of Brooklyn.

The police answering a disturbance call on Tulsa's fashionable east side found a 20-year-old man who had been confined to a water heater closet without a bath, haircut, or change of clothing for three years. . . . Deputy Warren said that the youth . . . had been forced to sleep standing up for almost three years. He said the youth was apparently retarded. . . . It all started three years ago, when he was trying to use the bathroom and missed the stool, and his father got onto him about it. He was simply overpowered emotionally.

An army staff sergeant at Fort Hamilton, Brooklyn, and his wife were arrested Tuesday on charges that they had beaten their adopted 18-month-old son into insensibility. . . . The child had undergone brain surgery . . . and is comatose.
— from *The New York Times* 1973

Reports of child abuse are most frequent in poorer families (Gil 1970), but it occurs in families of all social classes, races, religions, and schooling. Middle-class families, using private physicians, are less apt to be suspected of abuse or reported to social service agencies.

Spouse Abuse

Physical violence between marital partners or men and women living together is so pervasive and ingrained in American life that usually people don't think of reporting it (Langley and Levy 1977). In a study of randomly selected families in New Castle County, Delaware, 60 percent reported that husband and wife engaged in some physical violence and 10 percent reported regularly inflicting extreme abuse (Steinmetz and Straus 1975). In New Hampshire, Gelles (1974) chose forty neighbors of violent families as a nonviolent control group, only to find that 37 percent of these had experienced at least one incident of violence; for 12 percent it was a regular occurrence. Also in New Hampshire, when state university students were questioned about violence in their homes, 16 percent reported witnessing physical violence between their mother and father during the previous year (Straus 1974). It is interesting to note that the Uniform Crime Report statistics

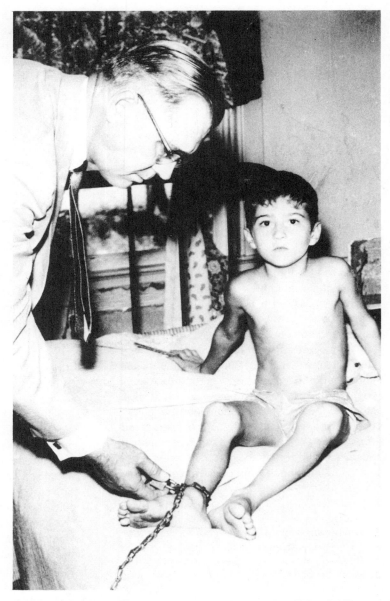

Fig. 17.7. Family violence takes many bizarre forms. This sheriff removes a 20-foot chain and lock from the foot of six-year-old John Henry Clay Perry, Jr. The boy was found at home, where his parents had kept him chained for over two months ''to teach him a lesson.''

on rates of violent crime indicate that New Hampshire is the second safest state in the nation, so it seems likely marital violence must be at least this high elsewhere. Reviewing seven studies (with admittedly small samples), Langley and Levy (1977) concluded that "between 55 and 65 percent of the married population engages in spouse abuse" (p. 28).

Evidence tells us that women are about as apt to strike out physically as men, and the homicide rate is equivalent for husbands and wives. The man is usually stronger, though, and the woman most often suffers the serious injuries in extreme abuse.

Predictably, child and spouse abuse are often found in the same family. Gayford (1975), studying 100 abused women, found that 54 percent of their mates also abused the child, and that 37 percent of the women themselves beat their children.

Fig. 17.8. Spouse abuse is a recent psychological concern but an age-old reality. This 1887 woodcut depicts wife-beating in a "proper" family.

Murder

Violent death is forever a threat in the abusive family. Each year about 25 percent of murders occur in the family, and in half of these spouse kills spouse. In 90 percent of these homicides the police had previous disturbance calls but had done nothing in most of them beyond preventing immediate physical injury (Wolfgang 1978). Family homicides depend as much on the relationship between perpetrator and victim as on the murderer's psychopathology and are often the result of the killer's inability to escape from an unbearable relationship (Duncan and Duncan 1978). Killing may be an intentional act or "accidental" consequence of hitting too hard or too often.

Legal Status and Powerlessness

After the pain itself, the victim of family violence feels most acutely the powerlessness to do anything about it. When one parent abuses a child, usually the other passively goes along, leaving the child no place to turn. To keep the child from talking about violent incidents to anyone outside the family, the parents threaten further hurt or desertion. Many a beaten wife who turns to friends, clergy, or medical professionals after keeping previous incidents to herself finds, to her shock, that they are unwilling to

A Letter from a Battered Wife

I am in my thirties and so is my husband. I have a high school diploma and am presently attending a local college, trying to obtain the additional education I need. My husband is a college graduate and a professional in his field. We are both attractive and, for the most part, respected and well-liked. We have four children and live in a middle-class home with all the comforts we could possibly want.

I have everything, except life without fear.

For most of my married life I have been periodically beaten by my husband. What do I mean by "beaten"? I mean that parts of my body have been hit violently and repeatedly, and that painful bruises, swelling, bleeding wounds, unconsciousness, and combinations of these things have resulted.

Beating should be distinguished from all other kinds of physical abuse — including being hit and shoved around. When I say my husband threatens me with abuse I do not mean he warns me that he may lose control. I mean that he shakes a fist against my face or nose, makes punching-bag jabs at my shoulder, or makes similar gestures which may quickly turn into a full-fledged beating.

I have had glasses thrown at me. I have been kicked in the abdomen when I was visibly pregnant. I have been kicked off the bed and hit while lying on the floor — again, while I was pregnant. I have been whipped, kicked and thrown, picked up again and thrown down again. I have been punched and kicked in the head, chest, face, and abdomen more times than I can count.

I have been slapped for saying something about politics, for having a different view about religion, for swearing, for crying, for wanting to have intercourse.

I have been threatened when I wouldn't do something he told me to do. I have been threatened when he's had a bad day and when he's had a good day.

I have been threatened, slapped, and beaten after stating bitterly that I didn't like what he was doing with another woman.

After each beating my husband has left the house and remained away for days.

Few people have ever seen my black and blue face or swollen lips because I have always stayed indoors afterwards, feeling ashamed. I was never able to drive following one of these beatings, so I could not get myself to a hospital for care. I could never have left my young children alone, even if I could have driven a car.

Hysteria inevitably sets in after a beating.

get involved and ready to blame her for the problem.

The police and courts are apt to be no better. Every state has laws to handle reports of child abuse, and many abused children will receive good attention from social services, but judges and agencies are reluctant to place the child outside the family. Do you leave the child with a parent who may inflict further harm, or do you remove her from parents she nonetheless loves and depends on and place her in the uncertain land of foster care? Abused wives face even greater official reluctance to take any action. Police give their calls or complaints low priority.

On September 4, 1972, Ruth Bunnell telephoned the police to report that her estranged husband had called her, saying that he was coming to her residence to kill her. She requested immediate police aid, and was refused; she was told to call the department again when Bunnell actually arrived. Approximately forty-five minutes later, Bunnell entered the woman's home and stabbed her. When police finally did arrive, in response to a neighbor's call, Ruth Bunnell was dead.

During the year prior to her death, this woman had called the police at least twenty times to complain that her ex-husband was committing violent acts against her and her two daughters (Martin 1977, p. 100).

This hysteria — the shaking and crying and mumbling — is not accepted by anyone, so there has never been anyone to call.

My husband on a few occasions did phone a day or so later so we could agree on the excuse I would use for returning to work, the grocery store, the dentist appointment, and so on. I used the excuse — a car accident, oral surgery, things like that.

Now, the first response to this story, which I myself think of, will be "Why didn't you seek help?"

I did. Early in our marriage I went to a clergyman who, after a few visits, told me that my husband meant no real harm, that he was just confused and felt insecure. I was encouraged to be more tolerant and understanding. Most important, I was told to forgive him the beatings just as Christ had forgiven me from the cross. I did that, too.

Things continued. Next time I turned to a doctor. I was given little pills to relax me and told to take things a little easier. I was just too nervous.

I turned to a friend, and when her husband found out, he accused me of either making things up or exaggerating the situation. She was told to stay away from me. She didn't, but

she could no longer really help me. Just by believing me she was made to feel disloyal.

I turned to a professional family guidance agency. I was told there that my husband needed help and that I should find a way to control the incidents. I couldn't control the beatings — that was the whole point of my seeking help. At the agency I found I had to defend myself against the suspicion that I wanted to be hit, that I invited the beatings. Good God! Did the Jews invite themselves to be slaughtered in Germany?

I did go to two more doctors. One asked me what I had done to provoke my husband. The other asked if we had made up yet.

I called the police one time. They not only did not respond to the call, they called several hours later to ask if things had "settled down." I could have been dead by then!

I have nowhere to go if it happens again. No one wants to take in a woman with four children. Even if there were someone kind enough to care, no one wants to become involved in what is commonly referred to as a "domestic situation" (Martin 1977, pp. 1–3).

Police, reluctant to make arrests, are even trained in some departments in ways of convincing a wife that she should not file a complaint. They say that many women will not follow through with a formal complaint, choosing instead to give him "another chance." Hence police are reluctant to spend time and risk personal injury to no end. Yet when victims do press charges, the judge is likely to give the abuser no more than a warning to refrain or, if the wife has left him, to stay away, even when he has ignored previous warnings and kept on abusing her. The woman, especially if she has children, feels utterly powerless — she can turn to no one, and any attempt only results in more abuse. Even divorce may not end the torment; women report continued harassment, threats, beatings, and officials turning down pleas for help. One woman, divorced for three years, wrote to a woman's group for help:

Tragedy in the Home

Parent-killing by a child is rare but a dramatic end of violence in a family. Most of these homicides resolve events that blew up in the previous three days or so (Tanay 1969), and the killing involves a gun. A study of boys who killed their fathers (Corder et al. 1976) demonstrated that they were different from other adolescent murderers. They had fewer social outlets, more modeling of overt hostility at home, an alcoholic father who was abusive to the boy and his mother, and a mother who quietly endured.

At 7:44 p.m. on March 12, William Hubert Mathers, 42, father of six, was shot once through the head as he sat in his living room watching TV.

Four and a half hours later, his youngest son, Michael, 14, was arrested and booked on suspicion of murder.

On the surface, the Mathers seemed a normal blue-collar family in the middle-class city of Pleasant Hill, a community of 30,000 that looks much like its name and is about 25 miles from San Francisco.

Bill Mathers seemed to acquaintances a talkative, outgoing, even jovial plumber-contractor, slightly forgetful and a procrastinator, perhaps, but a pleasant man.

He was a man dreaming of making big money as he tried to keep up with his bills, people said, raising his kids, four boys, two girls, the best he knew how. A normal man.

Normal except that five years before his murder, his wife Pat had tried to kill him, too, wounding him twice and telling authorities she and the children had been beaten too often and she couldn't take it any more.

Normal, except that over the next five years, there were constant arguments and discord; the Pleasant Hill police built up a 2-inch-thick file from calls to the unkempt white ranch house on Hoover Ave.

One time Bill called his eldest son, Billy, now 19 and away at college, incorrigible and wanted him booked at Juvenile Hall. Another time there was a fight over which channel should be tuned on the television set.

Another time, he choked Sue, now 17, dragged her into his bedroom, pushed her into the closet and took out his guns. He said he was going to shoot her boyfriend.

Five days before the murder, the police came again, called by a neighbor. This time, Michael had been beaten with a belt for taking a pellet gun outside.

Michael told the officers he was all right, and they left.

But sometime during the next five days, Billy Mathers' .357 magnum revolver disappeared out of the gunbox in his bedroom. Although Bill was prone to hear noises at night, get up, take out one of his three guns and search the house for prowlers he never found, he apparently did not notice his most powerful weapon was missing.

After the murder, and after the police talked

In every place where I have lived, my house has been watched so closely by my ex-husband that I have been virtually a prisoner. I have been endlessly followed and relentlessly pursued. My life has been threatened many times, and I have occasionally been severely beaten. My friends and all those who have ever exhibited sympathy or who have attempted to aid me have likewise been harassed and threatened. This had the effect of driving away what little support I had, leaving me more susceptible than ever to my ex-husband's bullying, intimidation and reign of domestic terror. Two weeks ago he cornered me in the drugstore. He repeatedly and very forcefully threatened my life in front of a dozen witnesses. When I finally escaped his grasp, I ran home. I called the police, but they didn't come. I am afraid to leave the house. I have been unable to go to work; I can't send my children to school. I am running out of food, and my landlord has asked me to move. Yesterday my husband parked his car in front of my home for six hours. I don't know what to do. My

to Michael, the gun was found in the Contra Costa Canal, not far from the house.

Roy Mathers, Bill's younger brother, . . . was angry. It seemed to him Michael was being made a "hero" for killing Roy's brother, whose name and reputation were being dragged through the mud. . . .

"If he was the monster everyone's attempting to depict him as," Roy said later, "all these things, why didn't social services, or the police, why wasn't something done before it culminated in his death?"

It was a good question.

Pleasant Hill police said intervention would be an invasion of privacy. They, the courts and local social service agencies had no jurisdiction. In the years since Pat's shooting of Bill, for which she served 30 days in jail, no one pressed abuse charges. When the police came, the kids said they were OK.

Bill's mother, Ruby, 64, said she lived in the house two years, returned and left again just before the murder. She witnessed beatings, she added, but said she left because "I'm tired of kids." . . .

Roy said he and Bill had been raised in a "harsh household. My father was very stern; we used to get a lot of whippings. . . . I talked to my brother about being overly stern. He told me, 'I can't do anything with them. I tell them something, Pat tells them something different.' "

Pat, Bill's wife for 20 years, said she didn't leave because "I really felt there was no place to go. Bill always told me if I ever left, he'd kill me, the kids and then himself. I was afraid to take the bluff." . . .

Michael, the smallest of the four boys, was variously described by family and neighbors as "sweet," "a nice kid." He did not seem to be an angry child, jealous or aggressive.

He was only a C student at Pleasant Hill High School, where he was a freshman, and interested in mechanical things. He liked bicycles, enjoyed taking them apart, putting them back together. He worked a paper route and had saved enough to buy a small motorcycle.

His sister Sue, 17, said, "He seemed to be the person who'd come out of here the best because he knew what he wanted. As soon as he was old enough, he said he would go in the Navy."

"He's a good little kid," his grandmother Ruby said. "He's the only one that had any gumption." . . .

At one point, Pat tried to explain why, when the police came, they all "played down how hard we were hit. There were never any broken bones. Okay, so the police might have taken Bill away, God knows what it would have been like when he came back."

Her son Scott, 16, was there then, and said softly, "That's not why I didn't tell."

"Why didn't you?" Pat asked.

"He was my father," the boy replied.

—Los Angeles Times
April 22, 1979, p. 3

life is in jeopardy; my resources are nearly depleted. And my husband is circling my house like a buzzard (Martin 1977, p. 78).

The women's movement has become an important force for victims. Community homes giving battered wives temporary haven have opened in some cities, along with special nurseries and homes for abused children; however, there are far too few-to begin to meet the need (see Chapter 19). Wife beating is more openly talked about, some women speak up publicly for their rights, and women's groups monitor law enforcement and social service practices. These developments are a growing source of comfort and courage to abused wives.

Causes of Family Violence

Perpetrators of family violence are, most of them, neither psychotic nor sociopathic, but people who function adequately in most other spheres. As a group, however, they are especially likely to have suffered abuse or neglect in childhood. Brandt Steel, a psychiatrist who has worked extensively with abusive parents, comments on the emotional consequences:

People who were neglected or abused as children have a fairly characteristic set of memories and feelings about their childhood. They recall that their own desires, needs, and emotions were never really considered; that they were never listened to or considered valuable and important in their own right. On the contrary, they had to be acutely aware of parental expectations and strive to meet them; at the same time, they felt that their parents were never really pleased by anything they did. Consequently, they felt ineffectual and often worthless; they never had much sense of joy or pleasure in life or any reliable expectation that people would be good to them. They thought of success only in terms of avoidance of punishment, criticism, and ridicule. The effects of this kind of experience can be seen in later years in the form of low self-esteem; chronic, low-grade depres-

sion; a sense of hopelessness; and a lack of basic trust, with corresponding disbelief in the availability of help from other adults and a conviction that one should try to solve problems alone rather than share them with others (Steele 1978, pp. 293–294).

A consequence many clinicians observe is that the child or spouse is there for one's own gratification, to compensate for previous lack of love. In child abuse, there is an odd role-reversal, the parent seeking to have her needs met by the child, making unrealistic demands, and feeling rejected by the child who does not meet them (Kempe and Helfer 1972). Similar dynamics, often exacerbated by alcohol, are evident in instances of spouse abuse. Another consequence, naturally, is that early in life physical aggression is learned as a way of coping with stress. A five-year-old boy, asked why he had choked and shaken his "disobedient" baby sister, answered quite simply, "Mommy, that is what you used to do to me" (Steele 1978).

PSYCHOSOCIAL FACTORS

Sociologists emphasize immediate stressors in the family and surroundings, including the relationship of abuse to the chronic stress of poverty, early marriage, unwanted pregnancies, many children born close together, and the like (Gil 1970). Reducing poverty and all that goes with it might decrease family violence by lessening sources of stress. However, each day brings new stresses, even for those with financial security, and all abusers seem to respond to stress in a similar manner.

When faced by great loneliness or a crisis such as financial trouble due to job lows, they are hampered or even totally blocked in trying to solve the problem through useful assertive action in the real world. Instead, they respond by feeling uncared for, misunderstood, put down, and fearful — in a repetition of the nightmare of their early years (Steele, p. 298).

Fig. 17.9. This mock aggression in children's play is an eerie reminder of television models and a reflection of our cultural attitudes toward violence.

To fully understand why so many people abuse so many others, we must go beyond individual psychopathology or even environmental stress and examine more general cultural influences. It may be that the cycle of abuse in families will be broken only with an overall reduction of violence in the American culture.

CULTURAL ACCEPTANCE OF VIOLENCE

Diverse statistics support the contention that in American society violence is widely practiced and accepted as a response to stress. From 1968 to 1973, 100,200 persons were killed in the United States, more than twice the number of Americans killed in the Viet Nam War. Indeed the rate of gun homicide is thirty-five times higher in the United States than in England, Germany, and Denmark (Johnson 1972). Fur-

thermore, nearly half of all American households have at least one gun (Gallup 1975).

We accept violence as a way to handle problems. Children are exposed to it every day: on their Saturday-morning television programs, surveys record an aggressive act every 3½ minutes. In a representative sample of American men in 1969, nearly half felt that shooting was a good way to handle campus disturbances "almost always" or "sometimes," although most campus disturbances were nonviolent expressions of protest or dissent. Our culture also strongly values protection of private property and the male's prerogative to exert his individuality. The two combine in family violence. A man's wife and children have historically been his property. Subjugating wife and children by any force necessary has long been considered the father's right, even his responsibility. Women, and especially children, had none or very limited rights. A law still on the books in Pennsylvania decrees that no husband shall beat his wife after 10 o'clock at night or on Sundays. Even today outsiders tread lightly when called upon to intervene in a man's "castle." An experiment in social psychology staged fights on the sidewalk to study reactions of passersby. Men, they found, rushed to aid other men being assaulted by men or women and also women being hit by another woman. But not one male bystander interfered when a man was hitting a woman (Pogrebin 1974, p. 55). In the notorious Kitty Genovese murder in New York, where thirty-eight watchers remained uninvolved while she was beaten and stabbed to death, many said afterward they didn't help her because they thought her assailant was her husband.

Most family violence is accepted as a routine part of the culture, questioned only when it becomes extreme. Surveys show that 84 to 97 percent of American families use physical punishment at some time in child rearing, and a Harris survey revealed that 25 percent of college-educated adults approved of a husband's slapping his wife "on appropriate occasions" (Stark and McEvoy 1970). In cultures that have strong taboos against striking children, such as the American Indians, child abuse is extremely rare (Gil 1970). It appears that very abusive parents or mates are just carrying socially approved practices too far. The pathology is in the extent of their violence.

Two recent reports in the news give us food for thought. (1) The U.S. Supreme Court sanctioned state laws which permit corporal punishment in the schools; and (2) Sweden, which long ago forbade corporal punishment in schools, passed a law forbidding it in the home as well. From what you know of learning by modeling, in which place would you predict that a child will grow up more violence-prone?

Summary

1. Sociopathy, delinquency, and family violence are forms of social deviance of particular relevance to abnormal psychology. Unlike most criminals who knowingly and intentionally break the law for personal gain, actions of individuals exhibiting these behaviors are seen as resulting from biological, psychological, and social disturbances.

2. Possible causes of antisocial behavior are divided into categories: (1) genetic-biological factors, including faulty chromosomes, brain damage, and abnormal brain waves; (2) family and environmental factors, including poverty, marital discord, parental neglect and rejection; and (3) cultural values, including materialism, violence, and racism.

3. The sociopath's major characteristics are: ability to make a good impression, impulsivity and disregard of convention, lack of capacity to love, lack of remorse or shame for behavior that would make most people feel anxious or guilty, and failure to learn from experience.

4. Studying sociopathic prison inmates, Lykken found that sociopaths did not learn to avoid electric shock. Further studies based on his work suggested several hypotheses about sociopaths: (1) they learn less effectively to avoid shock because this type of punishment has no meaning for them; (2) they do not learn to inhibit behavior in normal ways because they experience less anxiety; and (3) they are generally underaroused and their behavior is an extreme form of stimulation-seeking.

5. Sociopaths can learn to avoid punishment and cooperate with others when punishment or reward is tailored to their value system (as with money).

6. Two types of brain-wave abnormalities have been found in some sociopaths: slow brain-wave activity and bursts of great activity in the temporal area of the brain. Further research is necessary to relate these brain-wave patterns to specific behaviors.

7. Several types of delinquent youths are: (1) socialized-subcultural delinquents, who adopt subcultural values that the broader culture considers deviant and who are highly influenced by their environment; (2) disturbed-neurotic delinquents, who rebel against family and usually have a history of neurotic symptoms; and (3) unsocialized-aggressive delinquents, who are similar to adult sociopaths and lack ties with either their peers or their families.

8. Some environmental pressures that contribute to delinquency are: poor living conditions; unavailability of conventional or socially approved routes to success, which engenders low self-esteem; peer pressure; and family problems, which may include antisocial parents, marital discord, lack of parental affection, and harsh or inconsistent discipline.

9. Family violence — which includes child abuse, child neglect, and spouse abuse — is the most frequent source of police calls. Often abuse of both child and spouse occurs in the same family.

10. Two factors that figure in family violence are: (1) childhood experiences of neglect or abuse, which suggest that the adult may set up unrealistic expectations for spouse or child to compensate for a previous lack of love or may have learned early that physical aggression was the way to cope with stress; and (2) societal acceptance of violence in America as a response to problems.

Chapter 18   Sexual Deviance

Social Mores and Laws

Actual Sexual Practices

Psychological Abnormality

Gender Identity Disorders
Transvestism
Transsexualism
Causes of Gender Identity Disorders

Alternative Sexual Activities: I
Fetishism
Voyeurism
Exhibitionism
Causes of Alternative Activities

Alternative Sexual Activities: II
Pedophilia
Incest
Rape

Summary

Kevin, aged twenty, was beginning to recognize how serious his problem was. This latest arrest and the likelihood of prison had shaken him. But as he talked he still couldn't grasp why he did it again and again. His marriage of two years was marked by infrequent intercourse, sexual naiveté, and general social ineptness. "About six months ago Ruth started waitressing evenings, and I'd be sitting around at home alone, studying. Every night this girl in the next building would get undressed in front of her window, and I'd watch her." Kevin began to fantasize about this scene while masturbating and gradually altered the fantasy so that he was undressing for her. When we talked with him he had been arrested three times for exhibiting himself in his apartment window to passing college girls.

Sexual deviance may be the most difficult subject in abnormal psychology to clearly delineate. Whether a behavior is considered simply a sexual variation or an instance of deviance depends greatly on who does it, who labels it, and what criteria are applied in the evaluation. Is it acceptable to society according to social mores and laws? How common is it? Does it fit the definition of psychological abnormality?

Social Mores and Laws

The sexual practices that society considers deviant differ across cultures, over time, and even within a culture. A classic analysis of sexual practices in 190 societies throughout the world by Ford and Beach (1951) found clear diversity. In contrast to Western mores, most non-Western societies permitted multiple mates, some encouraged homosexual relations between men and boys, and some revered as a powerful shaman the man who dresses as a woman:

Among the Siberian Chukchee such an individual puts on women's clothing, assumes feminine mannerisms and may become the "wife" of another man. . . . A number of Lango men dress as women, simulate menstruation, and become one of the wives of other males (Ford and Beach 1951, pp. 130–131).

Also, some practices once considered definitely abnormal in Western culture are accepted and sometimes even encouraged today. Masturbation was formerly condemned and considered a certain cause of blindness, insanity, intellectual deterioration, and all manner of social ills (Hare 1962). Now masturbation is generally considered harmless and, in fact, is encouraged as an integral component of some new sex therapies (see Chapters 14 and 15).

In our own culture today, whether some behaviors are considered deviant varies according to sex, social class, circumstance, and the like. If Kevin had been a woman undressing where passersby could see, the likelihood of arrest would have been nil. In fact, had the viewers been male and had they lingered a bit too long, they might have been reported for voyeurism. Alternatively, had Kevin chosen to "streak" across the campus, some people would have seen his nudity as a harmless, humorous act.

Actual Sexual Practices

The definition of sexual deviance is further complicated by the discrepancy between expressed standards and actual practices. Even when society condemned masturbation, Alfred Kinsey and his coworkers (1948, 1953), in the most thorough study of American sexual practices ever undertaken, found some history of masturbation reported by the majority of women and practically all men.

American social mores and even laws conflict dramatically with other current practices too. In 1948, Kinsey reported that more than 90 percent of white males had, by age eighteen, committed at least one sexual act for which they could be imprisoned, under state law. Today intercourse outside marriage is still prohibited in many states, by laws against "fornication, cohabitation and adultery," which are almost universally ignored. Indeed, premarital intercourse and living together outside of marriage are now common. A recent survey of married persons aged twenty-five and younger indicated that 95 percent of men and 81 percent of women had engaged in intercourse before marriage (Hunt 1974). Extramarital sexual activity is still considered undesirable by most people, but it too is very common. Kinsey's data (1948, 1953) suggested that 50 percent of married men and 26 percent of married women had engaged in extramarital intercourse by age forty, and the percentages are higher today, especially for women. In some marriages, nonexclusive sex relations are mutually acceptable, and alternative sexual patterns have evolved (Cole and Spaniard 1974).

Furthermore, consider sexual activities other than intercourse, called euphemistically "crimes against nature" in legal writings. These, too, are now commonplace and sometimes encouraged by marriage manuals and sex therapists. Yet, most states have laws against many types of physical practices including oral-genital contact, even between husband and wife. Some state penal codes call for prison terms as long as twenty years. Because such laws infringe on the privacy of consenting adults, are contrary to common practice, and are basically unenforceable, some critics have called them anachronisms that weaken respect for the law. Others argue that these laws are an important symbolic expression of the community's moral values (MacNamara and Sagarin 1977).

Psychological Abnormality

In Chapter 1 we discussed several criteria for labeling actions as psychologically abnormal. In sexual deviance, the behaviors that concern mental health professionals are, for the most part, the same ones that matter to society and law enforcement agencies, and are not common practices. The behaviors we have mentioned that society frowns on and perhaps are even illegal but commonly practiced, such as intercourse outside of marriage, may certainly have concomitant psychological problems, but they are not considered psychological disorders. However, some behaviors, such as fetishism, are not technically violations of the law or much trouble to society, but psychologists consider them abnormal. We will generally limit this chapter to sexual activities that *markedly* violate our social mores and practices and cause personal suffering or cause others to suffer.

In *DSM*-III the American Psychiatric Association defines three main psychosexual disorders. One category is the *sexual dysfunctions,* which we discussed together with psychophysiological disorders in Chapter 14. A second, *gender identity disorders,* mainly in-

cludes transsexualism, though we will consider transvestism here as well. A third category, *paraphilias,* is a catchall for deviant activities such as voyeurism, fetishism, and child molesting. In this chapter we will cover disorders of gender identity and the alternative sexual activities *DSM*-III calls paraphilias, with an extended discussion of forcible rape.

Gender Identity Disorders

The most common and controversial variation of gender identity is homosexuality, sexual activity with a member of the same sex. It was common and accepted in ancient Greece and Rome, yet has been taboo in the Judaeo-Christian tradition — proscribed in the Bible, forbidden by law, and classified by psychiatry as sexual deviance. Kinsey and his colleagues surprised many in 1948, when they reported that 37 percent of 5300 American males they interviewed had at least one homosexual experience to orgasm after adolescence began. Although most of these men were exclusively heterosexual adults, the commonness of early homosexual experiences helped begin a reexamination of the "problem."

In subsequent years England and a number of states in America repealed antihomosexual legislation, and some cities have passed bills protecting homosexuals from discrimination in housing and employment. After much deliberation and disagreement, the American Psychiatric Association in 1973 removed homosexuality from the list of sexual disorders. Individuals who explicitly complain that their sustained pattern of homosexual arousal is unwanted and distresses them are now labeled *ego-dystonic homosexuals* (*DSM*-III). Those content with their homosexual choice are no longer classified psychiatrically.

Being Gay in a Straight World

Despite some gains toward acceptance that homosexuals have made in recent years, daily life in heterosexual society still causes much stress. Maybe being gay means some stress is inevitable, but this is certainly not a proven fact. Some writers suggest that without the close system of support that the nuclear family gives, the gay person is cursed with loneliness in old age. In our society, though, children often supply little support to their aging parents. Furthermore, the greater likelihood of the homosexual's aging without a partner to live with may reflect the social discrimination that makes maintaining such relationships so difficult. The problems caused by social attitudes and practices are much clearer.

A major choice confronts the homosexual man or woman alike: just how far to "come out" — to publicly identify oneself as gay, risking desertion by friends, eviction from housing, harassment by police, and the inevitable stares and whispers. Two reactions that especially trouble the gay person are those of employers and family. In lengthy interviews with gay men, Alan Ebert captured some of these concerns:

Bob Lawson, opera singer:

They still don't know of my homosexuality and I wish they did. But I know my mother. If I told her, she would lay such a guilt trip on herself . . . a real "Where-did-I-go-wrong" kind of thing. Too bad.

I really don't want any more secrets in my life. I am only sorry that I must still hide professionally but . . . I have heard my employer pontificate on the subject of "queers." Unfortunately, I need my job or I'd tell him to shove it (Ebert 1976, p. 124).

Erik Edwards came out inadvertently at age eighteen:

I was keeping pretty late hours. My parents were on my back a lot, which is what caused me late one night to say to Joe on the telephone, "I think I'll have to tell my parents that I'm gay." At that very moment my father had picked up the phone to make a call. He heard my words and flipped out. He was screaming as he came for me and continued to scream as he dragged me into their bedroom. My mother was also screaming.

Were you frightened by their reaction?

Do you know I was more angry than I was scared. My mother kept saying, "We'll get you the best psychiatrist money can buy," and I kept saying, "But I'm happy. I don't want one." . . . It got worse. I eventually went to a shrink, not for me, but to acclimate them to my being gay. . . . My father was saying things like "If the word homosexual is used I'll throw up." My mother was mouthing, "Some parents have polio or palsy to contend with in their child. We have this." It was horrible. . . . [Later] My father . . . turned to me and said: "I wish you were dead and so does your mother" (Ebert 1976, pp. 127–128).

Despite this initial reaction, Erik gradually gained acceptance and support from his family.

Dr. Gabriel Anthony, resident in surgery:

On his profession: I have recently discovered it is difficult being a homosexual in any profession. I always had an inkling that being a homosexual was not among the Top Ten choices in life, but it is only since I came out three years ago that I have realized how deep the hatred toward homosexuals is in the hearts and minds of society. . . . The medical profession is among the most biased, bigoted and prejudiced. You would think that in a so-called "helping profession," there would be some understanding, but no. They think of homosexuality as an illness — worse, as plague! (Ebert 1976, pp. 2–3, 14).

Nevertheless, a homosexual is likely to continue to experience great stress about his or her choice, mostly because of continuing social discrimination. Many homosexuals have "come out of the closet" to fight for "gay rights" in organizations and by demonstrations on college campuses and in large cities. At the same time, an antihomosexual movement has succeeded in the late 1970s in repealing antidiscrimination bills in some cities. How far society will go toward truly accepting this minority group probably will be contested for some time; meanwhile homosexuals will experience the many problems of being gay in a straight world.

Despite the controversy, homosexual activity in private between consenting adults is now considered neither a psychiatric disorder nor (in most states) a criminal offense, and we will not consider it further.

Transvestism

The *transvestite* is sexually stimulated by wearing clothing considered appropriate for the opposite sex. Unlike the fetishist, who feels masculine but is aroused by a single feminine item, the transvestite has some variation in gender identity and needs an outlet for a "feminine side." Cross-dressing is almost exclusively reported in men, yet women in our society can and increasingly do dress in masculine clothing and engage in what have traditionally been considered "masculine" activities without appearing particularly deviant.

Most transvestites limit their cross-dressing to the home. Often transvestite behavior consists of masturbating or engaging in intercourse while wearing a nightgown, lingerie, or a complete feminine wardrobe. Perhaps a third of

Fig. 18.1. This male transvestite, transformed by feminine clothing, wig, and makeup, easily "passes" as a woman in public.

transvestites more thoroughly impersonate a woman (with wig and makeup as well as full feminine costume) and successfully "pass" in public places — riding subways, eating in restaurants, and the like — without the deception being detected.

We have numerous case reports of transvestites who have sought therapy, but Prince and Bentler (1972) published the first large study of nonpatient male transvestites, a survey of 504 subscribers to a magazine for cross-dressers called *Transvestia*. Their findings were surprising. Although some homosexuals cross-dress, it appears that transvestites are not usually homosexual. Fully 78 percent were married or had been; 86 percent reported average or above-average interest in women; and 89 percent identified themselves as heterosexual. They cross-dress not to appeal to men but for the stimulation and the outlet the act itself gives them. These men did not seem markedly disturbed. They represented a wide range of education, occupation, economic status, and religion, and seemed to be functioning "normally" except for their cross-dressing. An earlier study did indicate that transvestites differed from controls on some personality scales. The transvestites exerted greater control over their impulses, were more withdrawn from social involvement, and were less concerned about what other people thought of them (Bentler and Prince 1969).

Cross-dressing does have obvious negative social consequences. More than half the wives either completely accept the behavior or at least are somewhat permissive, but others do not. Cross-dressing puts a strain on many marriages and is frequently cited as the reason for divorce. It is also generally illegal to appear in public impersonating the opposite sex, although no evidence relates cross-dressing to any more serious criminal activity (MacNamara and Sagarin 1977).

Transsexualism

A more extreme problem with gender identity is transsexuality. Transsexuals may cross-dress, but their reasons are different. The transsexual is not aroused by masquerading as a member of the opposite sex but, instead, desperately wants to completely become a member of the opposite sex. The transsexual man believes that in all respects, save some anatomical details, he is actually a woman. He reports that he has felt since childhood like a "woman trapped in a man's body." Likewise, an anatomical female may have truly regarded herself as a man and rejected her feminine characteristics as foreign throughout her life. The depth of this feeling of being the opposite sex is certainly difficult for nontranssexual readers to comprehend. One female transsexual wrote in desperation: "It seems to me that I have spent almost twenty-six years of hell trying to be the girl everyone thought me to be" (Pauly 1969). She reported growing up isolated, unable to accept the female role, and in constant turmoil with her family. Despite her efforts, she could never feel aroused with a man. Posing as a man, she would become involved in quasi-platonic relationships with women that would end when they discovered she was (anatomically) a woman.

Transsexuals feel incomplete, neither male nor female. Depression, suicidal ideas, and suicide attempts are common (Walinder 1967). Striving for completeness leads many transsexuals to undergo lengthy, costly, and physically and emotionally painful transformation. Surgical procedures for sex reassignment first received public attention in 1952 when George became Christine Jorgensen. In the mid-1960s, sex-reassignment surgery became available in the United States, and today at least twenty American medical centers perform the procedure (Slavitz 1976). More than 10,000 transsex-

A Transsexual's Texas Homecoming: Classmates Confront a Buddy's Sex Change

For an instant — one blinding instant of utter panic — she wanted to run. She trembled and her throat tightened with fear. Canary Conn had traveled a long road of ridicule and rejection. She had crossed the unfathomable world between masculine and feminine. Tonight, in the middle of South Texas hill and prairie country, she was to U-turn abruptly into her past. . . .

The inescapable fact of her life was that she had been born man and become woman. She entered the Jersey Lilly Room of the Pearl Brewery, head held high. Inside, by the light of gas lamps glowing on red-papered walls, 285 of her former classmates from Robert E. Lee High School were celebrating the 10th anniversary of their graduation.

Most had not seen her since her sex-change operation nine years ago. They remembered her as Danny O'Connor, sometime football player and all-round cusser, brawler and beer-drinker. A gen-u-ine Texas heartthrob who wooed the girls with guitar and song. Returning from Los Angeles last weekend, she was a lithe woman of 28 with flowing blonde hair and gentle manners. Who could predict her reception? . . . .

Betty Ward Ramsey was the first to greet Canary Conn: "Well, hi!" "You've changed," Miss Conn shrieked.

"You have too," Mrs. Ramsey said. They both giggled.

Around the room the faces of old classmates reflected a mixture of amusement, bewilderment and outright anger. One man asked Miss Conn for an autograph. Another, one Danny had scrimmaged with on the football field, began an evening-long exercise of dodging her whenever she looked his way.

Tim and Linda Fadeley of Grand Prairie leaned against the bar, engaged in marital debate as they watched it all. . . . "I'm shocked, but she's turned out a beautiful woman," Mrs. Fadeley said.

Her husband shook his head. "I guess I might have a prejudged opinion. I think they ought to have places for people like that. Rub-

ber rooms. Anybody like that's got a problem."

"No," Mrs. Fadeley said. "It takes guts to show up here."

Ricki Swenson Burton, a bookkeeper, gave Miss Conn the most enthusiastic welcome. "I think it's terrific you came," she boomed. "A lot of people are saying, 'Wow, is she for real?' But just because you're a woman doesn't mean you aren't the same. I'm glad you're here."

Mrs. Burton, like most of the women, easily adjusted to Miss Conn's transformation. They embraced and laughed together. The men were less comfortable with her, often avoiding contact and resorting to barnyardisms to express their outrage at her transsexuality.

As the evening wore on and the beer flowed, however, Miss Conn earned grudging acceptance for sheer persistence. She cornered classmates and asked them about themselves. She answered their questions about herself.

Why the operation? It was more than a feeling of a woman being trapped in a man's body, Miss Conn said. "It was something that went deeply and intensely inside me, that was hurting me."

Nikki O'Connor watched the local television reports of her daughter's reunion with trepidation — especially when one announcer said Canary Conn's return had created a stir. "It turned out he only meant excitement," Mrs. O'Connor said the next day. "I was so relieved I cried". . . . Miss Conn savored the adoration of loving parents. She and her father had been estranged for years after her surgery. When he learned he no longer had a son, O'Connor broke out in hives the size of silver dollars, he said. "Oh, my God, it was hard to accept. Danny was the little guy I used to take fishing."

"But I was confident," Mrs. O'Connor said. "You couldn't reject somebody you love. She's our child."

"It was not as frightening as I thought," Miss Conn said. "Generally there was positive response, but there were some people who didn't like me. I heard one guy say, 'That person is sick.' "

She bit her lower lip. ''I can't help but feel pain from that. I'm still in touch with my humanity. Even though there's a sensational aspect (to transsexualism) I'm living my life with dignity. As long as you're a moral person and don't hurt anyone, you don't have to be ashamed'' (B. Liddick, *Los Angeles Times,* July 2, 1978).

Danny O'Connor and Canary Conn.

uals may live in the United States, with (preoperative) males outnumbering females by four to one. Of these, approximately 2500 have undergone sex-reassignment surgery (Gagnon 1977).

Usually the transsexual who wants surgery is advised initially to undergo one or two years of hormonal treatment to increase opposite-sex characteristics and to assume the chosen gender role in everyday life. If adjustment is successful, surgery may be undertaken. For the male the operation involves removing penis, testes, and scrotum, using the tissue to construct an artificial vaginalike aperture, and hormone treatment to encourage growth and development of breasts and other womanly characteristics. Successful surgery makes it possible for the male-to-female transsexual to have intercourse and even to experience orgasm, but it has not been possible to create a penis capable of erection.

Overall, postoperative studies of transsexuals indicate that their adjustment is improved. One survey of forty-two male-to-female transsexuals found that although many reported physical problems after the operation and felt they needed more postoperative counseling, most reported that life as a woman equalled or surpassed their expectations, and all but one said, in retrospect, they would do it again (Bentler 1976). These people encounter a great many legal and social problems, but they are able to confront them with greater self-confidence.

Causes of Gender Identity Disorders

All but a few adult transsexuals trace their cross-gender identity to childhood (Prince and Bentler 1972; Green 1974). One retrospective study of biological males found that before puberty most played exclusively with girls (63 percent), were embarrassed to undress in front of boys (60 percent), and felt they belonged to the female sex (90 percent). "These boys preferred to play with dolls, to sew and embroider, and to help their mothers with the housework as much as possible" (Walinder 1967). Green describes a number of cases who experienced cross-gender identification in the preschool years. One boy insisted he was a girl at age twenty-two months. His mother reported:

He's said that he'd like to be a girl. . . . He is very taken with ballet . . . he wants to always dress as the girl. . . . It's always the female part. . . . [He dresses up] as often as you let him. . . . He even tucks animals up underneath his outfit, you know, expecting a baby and then has the baby. . . . He's always playing with girl dolls (Green 1969, p. 28).

After puberty, *all* these boys became increasingly disgusted with their developing male anatomy and wanted to be accepted by society as females.

Why is early cross-gender identification so strong for some individuals? One possible influence on behavioral masculinity and femininity is sex hormones. Female rhesus monkeys exposed *in utero* to male hormones (androgens) behaved in a more "masculine," rough-and-tumble, and aggressive way than untreated females (Young et al. 1964). Following up this observation, Yalom and colleagues (1973) studied six-year-old and sixteen-year-old boys whose diabetic mothers had received the female hormones estrogen and progesterone during pregnancy to prevent complications. Teachers' blind ratings of the six-year-olds revealed that they were less assertive and less athletically able than matched controls. The sixteen-year-olds differed in several measures from matched controls who had untreated diabetic mothers. They were less aggressive, less assertive, and had less athletic skill and grace. The authors noted some problems with keeping the interviewers totally blind as to which groups the sixteen-year-olds were in, but the behavioral measure of athletic ability was completely unbiased. If hormones have any influence, and this experiment would have to be replicated to validate such a conclusion, they seem to result in less aggressiveness, not specifically feminine traits.

Another obvious influence on the child is early social learning experience. The clinical literature has many reports of mothers dressing their boy children as girls and promoting feminine behavior. Stoller summarizes his examination of nine families of male transsexuals:

> These factors are: excessive, blissful physical and emotional closeness between mother and infant, extended for years and uninterrupted by other siblings; strong transsexual tendencies in the mothers throughout their own mid-childhood, such as dressing in boys' clothes and keen competition as an equal in sports and/or intellectual matters with boys (behavior which goes underground in adolescence); passive and/or effeminate fathers who are scarcely at home, day or night, during the transsexuals' first years; and an empty, angry marriage between mother and father, without moves toward separation or divorce (Stoller in Green 1969, p. 169).

Much additional systematic research is needed. Prince and Bentler's (1972) large and more representative sample of transvestites did show that cross-dressing begins early (for 54 percent before age ten), but also found that the subjects' recollections of their childhood were quite average. For transsexuals, however, the cross-gender identification is more extreme, and early parental influence seems more likely.

One project studying childhood disturbances produced an effective, though controversial, treatment program (Rekers 1977; Rekers, Bentler, Rosen and Lovaas 1977). A series of studies defined gender behavior disturbances in extremely feminine boys, aged three to eight. Play behavior, vocal inflections, speech content and behavioral mannerisms

Fig. 18.2. Danny O'Connor cross-dressing at the age of seven. Canary Conn writes, ''Even then I knew something was wrong inside. This photo depicts the inner torment of a child searching for identity . . . for what then seemed a futile dream. Dressing was a way of life from first memory; introspection and guilt would continue for many years. 'I am bad,' I would say to myself over and over. Just two years later, I would secretly make the first serious attempt on my own life.''

were found to have feminine qualities resembling behaviors of normal girls (Rekers et al. 1977b). The intervention aimed to teach these children to be more "masculine." This was criticized by homosexuals and some others, but the researchers defended the program on grounds that it could possibly reduce the likelihood of gender identity disturbances in adulthood as well as unhappiness in childhood, given that these children inevitably experience rejection from peers, isolation and low self-esteem. The complex program taught the child's parents to contingently use social reinforcement to encourage more masculine behaviors and to discourage feminine ones, first under supervision in the clinic and later at home. Initial follow-ups of a year or two indicated lasting effects (Rekers et al. 1974), and these researchers are presently conducting a long-term follow-up through adolescence.

Alternative Sexual Activities: I

We will next consider the milder of the *DSM-III* paraphilias: fetishism, voyeurism, and exhibitionism. In all three, sexual gratification is attained without contact between the individual and a partner. Though all are apt to involve a person with the law, they are not usually considered serious crimes but psychological problems requiring therapeutic intervention.

Fetishism

Fetishism is sexual fascination with a part of the human body (e.g., breasts, feet) or, more commonly, an object (e.g., underwear, stockings), overriding interest in normal sexual activity with another person. Fetishism itself is not illegal, but the compulsion to get the arousing object may lead to illegal acts such as breaking and entering. Many of us are aroused by some attribute of a lover. Some men are particularly

aroused by full breasts or long hair, and some women by firm buttocks. An article of clothing may enhance sexual pleasure. Normally, however, these are not the sole source of sexual gratification.

The fetishist seems more psychologically aberrant. Sexologist von Krafft-Ebing (1965) reported in 1886 a man who could become aroused to intercourse only when his wife put on a wig with long tresses. Five years later, they still had an active sex life and had accumulated seventy-two wigs! Helped by the wigs, they enjoyed a relatively conventional sex life; this fetish was not so extreme as a man's seeking out women's stockings, shoes, gloves, or panties in order to achieve sexual gratification by touching, smelling, or kissing the fetish, perhaps masturbating at the same time. As with most sexual deviance, fetishism seems to occur almost exclusively in men.

Voyeurism

The voyeur derives sexual gratification by surreptitiously watching another person undressing, nude, or engaging in sexual activity. There is something of the voyeur in all of us. Some of the pleasure in courtship rituals and lovemaking is in looking. The construction worker who whistles at a passing woman and the beachgoer ogling bikini-clad bathers may be displaying poor manners but they are hardly voyeurs. Nor are the millions of men and women who, as sexual explicitness spreads even further in the media, view erotic pictures or X-rated movies. Nor, really, are those who engage in group sexual activities. All these are channels for meeting voyeuristic (and exhibitionistic) needs, but the true or "offensive" voyeur or peeper (almost always a man) has a compulsive need to obtain arousal by taking risks to spy upon an *unknowing* victim. One voyeur describes it:

Looking at a nude girlfriend wouldn't be as exciting as seeing her the sneaky way. It's not just the

Pornography and Sexual Deviance

Viewing pornography is one common voyeuristic-like activity. Does using pornography lead to antisocial activity? With confusion in our courts about defining and penalizing pornography, the question seems significant.

The Commission on Obscenity and Pornography (1970), having reviewed empirical studies and commissioned others, concluded that research offers no evidence that exposure to sexually explicit materials plays a significant role in crime, deviance, delinquency, or severe emotional disturbance. Although many politicians and theologians were less than pleased, the findings agreed with most psychiatric and social science opinions.

In one commission-sponsored study, Goldstein and coworkers (Goldstein and Kant 1973) interviewed sixty newly incarcerated rapists and pedophiles about their experiences with pornography and compared their comments to those of control samples of homosexuals, male pornography users, and heterosexual males. Surprisingly, the sex offenders reported *less* exposure to erotica during adolescence than the controls. Their experience reflected "either an active avoidance of heterosexual stimuli or limitation to an environment where such materials were unavailable" (p. 70). The authors concluded that exposure to erotic material did not precipitate sexual crimes. Their evidence suggested that sex offenders actually used such materials less than others.

Another commission-sponsored study (Kutchinsky 1973) examined the results of a naturally occurring "social experiment." Since 1965, visual pornography has been widely available in Denmark. As the accompanying graph shows, the increase in sex offenses that some might have predicted never appeared, and a rather striking decrease began about 1965. The number of violations dropped from about 85 per 100,000 to fewer than 50 per 100,000. Further study suggested that the lower incidence of reported exhibitionism and minor physical indecency toward adult women was mostly because of greater tolerance for these minor crimes and, hence, less reporting. Public and police attitudes, however, were still quite negative toward voyeurism and molesting of young girls, so that the sharp decrease in these crimes did not seem attributable to less tendency to report and may well have resulted from increased availability of pornographic substitutes. The only sex offense that did not decrease was forcible rape, which has been infrequent in Denmark anyway and could not be reduced by much.

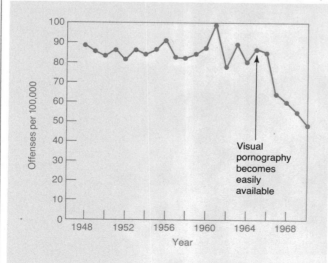

Fig. 18.3. Although the woman in the top photo enjoys exposing her body and the men enjoy looking at her, she is not an exhibitionist nor they voyeurs as we have defined the terms. The activities of these people are not surreptitious, with an unwilling victim, and not, presumably, their primary source of sexual gratification. The voyeur in the bottom photo obtains sexual gratification from surreptitiously watching a woman undressing.

nude body but the sneaking out and seeing what you're not supposed to see. The risk of getting caught makes it exciting. I don't want to get caught, but every time I go out I'm putting myself on the line (Yalom 1960, p. 316).

Most writers have deemed voyeurism a relatively harmless activity, engaged in by men who have strong sex drives but are passive and inept in relationships with women. Yet MacNamara and Sagarin (1977) argue that voyeurism should be taken more seriously because: (1) by definition, it is an invasion of one's privacy, and (2) it is often the precursor to other crimes, such as rape, assault, or burglary.

Exhibitionism

Exhibitionism is displaying one's genitals to an unwilling viewer for sexual gratification. Almost all exhibitionists are men, and the victims are often young girls. The exhibitionist usually has a compulsion to act and a consistent mode of operation — sitting in his car by a school or waiting in the park — and derives gratification from the act itself and from the shocked flight response of his victim.

Unlike the voyeur, the exhibitionist must be noticed to experience gratification and therefore is more likely to come in contact with police. The most frequently reported sexual offense, exhibitionism accounts for 25 to 35 percent of the total (Hughes 1977), but the majority of such incidents still go unreported.

Again, we must remember that our society has more or less acceptable channels for fulfilling exhibitionistic tendencies, especially for women. The woman who wears revealing clothes, the photographer's model, even the stripper and the topless waitress are not considered exhibitionists in the sense we use here. Even those who go to nude beaches and nudist camps do not fit our definition, for though they take pleasure in exposing their bodies (and, in-

cidentally, looking at others), the intent is not exclusively sexual; their sexual gratification is not primarily from exhibiting, and the viewers are not an unwilling audience.

Like the voyeur, the man who exhibits is generally a passive, socially inadequate person who is afraid that a conventional sexual approach will bring rejection. It is speculated that he seeks to verify his masculinity by exhibiting. The exhibitionist may claim that he was seeking intercourse, but, in fact, he arranges matters to preclude it and usually flees if his bluff is called (Sadoff 1976).

Causes of Alternative Activities

Why do men choose fetishism, voyeurism, and exhibitionism as sexual outlets? Psychological explanations have mainly drawn on psychoanalytic models, which posit an inner conflict dating back to early childhood and symbolically expressed in the deviant symptom (Kolb 1973; Fenichel 1934). More recent causal theories derive from a behavioral conditioning model. Rachman (1966; Rachman and Hodgson 1968) demonstrated experimentally how a mild "fetish" can be acquired. In a Pavlovian conditioning procedure, adult males were shown slides of women's boots together with slides of attractive nude women. After repeated pairings, the women's boots came to elicit sexual arousal (measured by change in penile volume); this conditioned arousal was even generalized somewhat to objects similar to boots.

Similarly McGuire, Carlisle, and Young (1965) theorized that sexual deviations are learned gradually *after* an initial seduction or arousing experience which supplies a fantasy for later masturbation. They noticed that their sexually deviant patients commonly (1) remembered experiencing their first real sexual arousal in a deviant situation, (2) reported using that memory and embellishing it in subsequent masturbation fantasies, and (3) reported believing even before the sex deviation that a normal sex life was not possible for them, because of "early aversive heterosexual experiences or feelings of physical or social inadequacy." This is among the cases they cite:

A seventeen-year-old male had, three years earlier, seen through a window a girl dressed only in her underwear. He was sexually stimulated by the sight and later took to masturbating to the memory. However, with the passage of time his memory of the actual girl became vague whereas advertisements and shop window displays continually reminded him of details of underwear to use in his fantasy, so that the latter became the stronger cue. His interests thereupon changed gradually but consistently, so that when seen three years later he no longer had the slightest interest in girls but was sexually stimulated by female underwear which he bought or stole (McGuire, Carlisle, and Young 1965, p. 189).

This conditioning model has led to the design of *counterconditioning* therapies, which we will discuss in Chapter 19. Altogether, though, evidence for any theory about causes of fetishism, voyeurism, and exhibitionism is still scanty.

A noteworthy fact about voyeuristic and exhibitionistic behaviors is that they involve an element of power or control over an unwilling female victim. They permit the male aggressor to exert his "masculinity," though in a manner unacceptable even to him. This factor is also present in many cases of child molesting and is primary in incidents of forcible rape.

Alternative Sexual Activities: II

The major sexual offenses we will now consider — pedophilia, incest, and rape — involve force or underaged victims and carry severe criminal penalties.

Pedophilia

Pedophilia literally means "love of children," but it describes an erotic sexual desire for prepubertal children. Reports to police of child molesting almost always mention men. Society is much more tolerant of such encounters between an older female and a young male; if any criminal charges result, they are in the less serious category of "contributing to the delinquency of a minor."

For male pedophiles, heterosexual encounters are more common than homosexual ones and usually involve girls six to twelve years of age. Homosexual encounters involve somewhat older boys (twelve to fourteen or so). Parents seeking to make their children aware of the danger of child molesters repeatedly warn them never to take rides with strangers. Some pedophiles do abduct, molest, and even violently assault children whom they do not know. Yet most pedophilic acts are committed by relatives, neighbors, or friends of the family; one survey found that only 19 percent of reported molesters were strangers (Mohr et al. 1964).

Child molesting may begin with a child's innocent kiss or a hug for a favorite uncle and lead — by plan or circumstance — to the adult's holding the child on his lap, fondling the hair, stroking the genitals, or engaging in mouth-genital contact. Attempts at intercourse are rare. In fact, usually no force is applied; the child is either willing (sometimes inviting) or unknowing and neutral. Such incidents may continue for a long time, usually until the child tells his or her parents. The effects of such sexual experience on the child depend on many factors. Although few facts are available, agreement does seem general that the child is more apt to suffer lasting effects if the parents or other adults react strongly, say, with fear, anger, or disgust, to the discovery (Gagnon 1977).

In our attempt to understand child molesting, we should be mindful of a study by Mohr, Turner and Jerry (1964), in which they concluded that the act may have different causes, in this case depending upon the age of the offender. The fifty-five pedophiles, at the Forensic Clinic of the Toronto Psychiatric Hospital, were in three age groups: late adolescence, mid-to-late thirties, and late fifties to early sixties. Heterosexual incidents among the first group were said to represent "an arrested development in which the offender has never grown psychosexually beyond the immature prepubertal stage." These boys were sexually and socially immature and showed evidence of impaired interpersonal relationships and judgment.

The other two groups did not necessarily prefer children for sexual arousal but found them acceptable when other outlets were unavailable. Most of the middle-aged pedophiles were married and had children of their own but suffered from severe social and marital maladjustment. Often unemployed and heavy users of alcohol, they turned to children following stressful events at home. The older offenders were socially sounder, but they were lonely, sexually isolated and fearful of impotence. Many had no history of child molesting and for many the act was a one-time occurrence.

For most of these individuals, pedophilic acts are incidental occurrences, but a small number of offenders are chronic. Recidivism rates indicate that homosexual pedophiles are more chronic. Philip had a twenty-five-year history of molesting boys. He discussed his exclusively pedophilic interest:

I'm not attracted to just any boy; he has to be small and good looking, usually between twelve and sixteen years old. At times I've tried to break this, to become a true homosexual, with adults, but I didn't know how to approach adult homosexuals and I often felt rejected by them. . . . I've never had any desire to harm a boy. I mean, I don't force myself — I try to see if he's interested. It's really important that he is interested in me, that I don't get rejected.

Treatment results for pedophiles are discouragingly poor; prison is a frightening place, as child molesters are held in contempt by other inmates and often sexually assaulted in retribution for their own actions.

Incest

The prohibition against sexual activity between close family members is the most universal and strongest taboo in human societies (Ford and Beach 1951). But despite this "incest taboo," sexual relations between brother and sister or, less commonly, between father and daughter do occur. Kinsey et al. (1948) found that 0.5 percent of males interviewed reported some such activity. Brother-sister intercourse is usually seen as adolescent experimentation, and usually stops when one of them finds an extrafamilial partner. Too, there are frequent reports of fathers becoming involved sexually with stepdaughters, and although these relationships do not exactly violate the incest taboo, they are nonetheless illegal and are often labeled under statutory rape or child abuse.

In father-daughter incest, the victim is usually the oldest daughter, although the father may then become involved with one or more of her sisters in turn. Incest may last for years, but it usually ceases when overtly exposed. At this time, the family may break up. The psychological effects on the "victim" are not clear. Many younger children show little guilt until parents and authorities censure them for their participation. Adolescents are more apt to react by running away, behaving promiscuously with other men, avoiding all social contacts with men, withdrawing into a state of depression or attempting suicide, but no clear pattern of reaction has appeared.

A number of factors contribute to incest, but very little systematic research has been done, partly because reported cases are rare. We do know that reports of incest are more common in poor, isolated families living in cramped quarters with limited outside contact. It may be, however, that these criminal cases overrepresent the lower classes and that father-daughter incest in middle-class families is handled in other ways (Henderson 1976).

Some of the fathers clearly show mental deficiency or psychosis, but most are not markedly disturbed. Gebhard (1965) reported that these men are likely to be highly moralistic and devoutly committed to fundamentalist religious doctrines. They usually confine their extramarital activity to their daughters and do not engage in other criminal activity.

These families are marked by shifted roles. Many mothers put household responsibilities onto the daughter and avoid sexual intimacy with the father. The beginning of the father-daughter relationship seems to meet mutual attention needs, and some authors hypothesize that mothers acquiesce to maintain family stability (Lustig et al. 1966).

Jack is a forty-five-year-old, separated black male with three children. When his oldest daughter was about nine, his wife attended church meetings on a regular nightly basis. She refused her daughter's request to leave the house and Jack had to stay with the children. During his wife's religious preoccupation, Jack was denied sexual relations, and he began to suspect that his wife was seeing another man. He drank beer when his wife was away and began to observe his daughter maturing. His daughter became rebellious against the mother and lay in her bed in seductive positions while her father waited for his wife to come home. On several occasions, she would approach him, kiss him good night, and then go to her room. Later, the contact between father and daughter

began to increase and expand to lap-sitting and mouth-kissing, which became deeper and longer. Jack knew he was becoming increasingly involved with his daughter and, after several experiences at penovaginal relations with her, he attempted to stop the relationship. He was unable to stop, however, because his daughter became more seductive and encouraged continuation with the threat that she would tell her mother if he stopped (Sadoff, in Sadock 1976, p. 434).

Incest clearly points to disturbance in the family system that, as this example shows, cannot be attributed solely to the father's behavior. Perhaps a fuller understanding of this problem will come from therapeutic intervention with entire families.

Rape

Rape is the fastest-growing violent crime in America, but the rate of arrest and conviction for rape is lower than for any other. Except for incest, no sexual activity is more universally condemned. Yet many a woman reporting rape is treated with callousness, disbelief, and even hostility. Though rape is considered a sexual offense, dominance, power, and control over a woman may be the real motives. It is sexual, violent, personal, political, and above all, fraught with contradictions that say a great deal about American culture.

Forcible rape is usually defined as sexual intercourse (with even the slightest penetration of the female genitalia by the penis) committed without consent. *Attempted rape* is an effort to commit forcible rape in which the male does not, for whatever reason, effect penetration. *Statutory rape* usually means nonviolent voluntary sexual intercourse between an adult male and a female who is under the age of ''consent'' (in most states, age eighteen), and who, therefore, is unable legally speaking to consent to the act. We will concentrate on forcible rape.

The number of reported rapes and serious attempted rapes more than tripled from 1960 to 1975. According to the Uniform Crime Reports compiled by the FBI, 56,090 cases were reported in 1975. It is well known, however, that rape is the most *underreported* of serious crimes. In 1967, the President's Commission on Law Enforcement and the Administration of Justice conducted a nationwide random survey of 10,000 households, inquiring about experience as victims of crime. Forcible rape for the preceding year, as reported to the researchers, was more than 3.5 times the figure listed in the Uniform Crime Reports, and undoubtedly some rape victims did not reveal their experiences even to these interviewers. (Police investiga-

Sadism and Masochism

The name "sadism" is taken from the activities of the Marquis de Sade (1740–1814), who obtained sexual gratification by inflicting pain on his partners. Masochism, too, owes its name to a writer, Count Leopold von Sacher-Masoch (1836–1895), who sought out women to inflict pain upon him. In voluntary sexual liaisons, sadistic and masochistic persons seek each other and even advertise for partners in underground newspapers. Sadomasochism is present in both homosexual and heterosexual relationships with one person submitting to the abuse of the other. The abuse may be only verbal (teasing, threatening, denigrating), or it may be physical, ranging from tying, slapping, kicking, and biting to extremes of whipping, burning, and the like. Some sadists inflict pain as a precursor to intercourse, and others are aroused to orgasm by inflicting pain. Although many "normal" relationships include some mild pain (scratching, biting) during intercourse, sadism and masochism become pathological as they grow extreme and necessary for arousal. Adult stores in most major cities cater to an "SM" trade by selling articles for bondage and inflicting pain. Most sadists can fulfill these tendencies with fantasy materials or in a sadomasochistic relationship, but a few act out in the extremes of mutilation and lustful murder.

Sadomasochistic themes increasingly have appeared in popular advertising, such as advertisements for women's fashions and this record album cover.

tions do encounter false reports, but fewer than some would have us believe.) It appears that not even 25 percent of rapes are reported, for many reasons, including shame, a desire to conceal the event from family, anticipated trouble with police and courts and attendant publicity, the feeling of some that the event is not terribly important, fear of retaliation from the rapist, and unwillingness to accuse a friend or relative. The women's movement has encouraged reporting, and changes in treatment of rape victims by hospitals and police (see Chapter 19) have made this procedure somewhat less onerous. Therefore official statistics are higher partly because of increased reporting.

The legal system and the social sciences have not always taken rape seriously. The legal penalties have been very severe (some states allow the death penalty), but the rates of conviction have been very low. (The striking exception is the discriminatory treatment of black men accused of raping white women.) The rape victim's credibility is questioned more than that of any other victim of crime, to the extent that the woman herself often seems to be on trial, if the case even gets that far.

Among social scientists, Freud and his disciples, who had something to say about almost every other aspect of sexuality, have been silent on rape. In 1965, during a major study of rape in Philadelphia, Amir was unable to find one book dealing exclusively with rape (Amir 1971). Since then it has had more attention, mostly because of the women's movement and its emphasis on rape both as personal assault and as symbol of violence and sexism in American culture.

Susan Brownmiller, in her popular book *Against Our Will* (1975), describes acceptance of rape through the ages and asserts: "Rape is to women as lynching was to blacks: the ultimate physical threat by which all men keep all women in a state of psychological intimidation." Rape is of particular interest to us in studying abnormal psychology because attempting to

understand the act takes us on a journey from the psychology of the individual rapist, through aspects of his immediate environment, to deep societal values and practices. Is the rapist disturbed, compelled by a sexual impulse? Does he need treatment? Is he basically antisocial, conditioned by his surroundings to adopt violence as a way of life? Does he need punishment? Or is he just acting out, in an extreme way, attitudes about male-female relations that most of us unconsciously share?

THE EXPERIENCE OF RAPE

That rape is both sexual and aggressive cannot be illustrated better than by statements from rapists themselves and their victims. One analysis of rapists' motives distinguishes four types (Cohen et al. 1969): displaced aggression, compensation, sex-aggression defusion, and impulse. In the *displaced-aggression type,* the intent of the act is primarily aggressive. "The acts are experienced by the offender as the result of an 'uncontrollable impulse' and almost always follow some precipitating, disagreeable event" (Cohen et al. 1969, p. 250) involving a wife, girl friend or mother, or some other interpersonal stress. Sexual excitement is minimal or absent, because sexual behavior is used·to harm or degrade to satisfy an aggressive urge.

He started pushing me back to the bedroom. All the time I kept talking but I can't remember what I said. We got back to the bedroom and he said to take off my clothes. I said no. He said if I didn't take them off he would. Right then I screamed as loud as I could and he grabbed me by my throat and started choking me. He picked me up and threw me on the bed, still choking me with one hand so I couldn't even breathe. The other hand was pointing the gun in my stomach.

I finally got his hand off my throat and he said, "Just answer me one question, are you going to take your clothes off or am I?" And I said, "Just answer me one question, Why?" At this point he got up off the bed and stood up, still pointing the gun at me. So I got up, still trying to talk to him and not trying to make him mad. I started moving around the bedroom picking up things, telling him that I had a date real soon and had to get ready. . . . He then started talking about himself and his family. He said he had just had a big fight with one of his brothers and got in his car and just started driving and ended up at my apartment. I asked him why he picked my apartment. He said he just picked one (MacDonald 1971, p. 16).

In *compensatory rape* the intent is primarily sexual, and the rapist uses force only as needed to accomplish his sexual aims. These men have a high state of sexual excitement but pervasive feelings of sexual inadequacy. "The recurrent fantasy . . . is that he will be especially virile and so pleasing to the victim that she will become enamored with him and invite him to repeat the sexual acts" (Cohen et al. 1969, p. 250).

I'd find a woman and observe her till I felt I saw a pattern and an opportunity to be able to rape her successfully. . . . I'd want her in bed and asleep. I'd try to wake her with caution, want to control her to keep her from becoming too scared. I thought she would submit, even hoped she'd want me, love me, give herself willingly. I had a fantasy women secretly like to be kissed on their vagina. I thought this would please them. I was actually desperately wanting to please the woman, win her over. I'd concentrate on this. I would tell her to respond, to let go and to have a climax with me (MacDonald 1971, pp. 141–143).

In *sex-aggression defusion rape,* sexual fantasy and experience are always coupled with aggressive thoughts and feelings. They become intertwined, and the rapist may see a woman's struggles as seductive: "Women like to get roughed up; they enjoy a good fight" (Cohen et al. 1969, p. 70). Often this type of rape includes primitive, brutal assault, and sometimes even murder. Notice the sadism in this account by an abducted couple of a group rape:

John: There was a lot of talk going on between them as to what they were going to do with us. They started the car and started driving around. They started raping Anne, taking turns and asking her if she liked it and told her to answer yes. Also while the rape was taking place one of the men in the front would hit me every so often and say he wanted to kill us both. Then the man holding my head would argue with him and say we hadn't done anything to hurt them. I think during this time the man in front pulled a gun and said he wanted to kill us.

Anne: I was raped in the back seat by the two back there and then they stopped the car and changed drivers so he could rape me. I brushed up against John and could see blood on his shirt. I knew then that he had been cut or stabbed. I did not try to resist in any way because I was afraid they might hurt John and I was hoping we could get out of this alive. They argued among themselves several times trying to persuade one of them not to kill John. . . . I was raped again. I don't know who or how many times. I was repeatedly told to keep my eyes closed and my head down and slapped and hit with fists on my face. They finally stopped the car and pushed me out (MacDonald, pp. 20–21).

Finally, in cases of *impulsive rape,* neither sexual nor aggressive features are prominent, the act being primarily opportunistic. Frequently it occurs during some other crime, such as robbery. The impulsive rapist fits the profile of the sociopath presented in Chapter 17 — that is, one who takes advantage of the situation in an impulsive, guiltless way.

One night he entered a home with the intention of burglarizing the house, entered one of the bedrooms, and found the daughter of the owner sleeping. When she awoke, he covered her mouth to keep her quiet, found her attractive, and decided to rape her. Her screams brought the owner, who held him at gunpoint until the police arrived. He was charged with attempted rape and his only comment was that he had been dumb in not checking out the rest of the house to see if anyone else was present. He apparently felt no guilt about the attempted rape (Rada 1978, p. 131).

Sexual and aggressive motives in rape are even more clearly illustrated in wartime, which heightens sexual deprivation and aggressive feelings, loosens social sanctions against deviance, and glorifies *machismo* (extreme feelings of masculinity). It is a high-risk time for rape. Violating the enemy's women has been an integral part of the war ethic from early civilizations to the present. The most recent American experience of this sort involved atrocities in Viet Nam (Brownmiller 1975). This account is psychologically compelling just because it was not an isolated act by a severely disturbed person:

"Me and one of the buck sergeants and two other guys took these four chicks in the elephant grass," a Vietnam deserter who uses the name "Jerry Samuels" told writer Roger Williams in Toronto. "We balled these chicks. They were forcibly willing — they'd rather do that than get shot. Then one of the girls yelled some derogatory thing at the guy who'd balled her. . . . He just reached down for his weapon and blew her away. Well, right away the three other guys, including myself, picked up our weapons and blew away the other three chicks. Just like that. . . . Me and this other guy, we got high together in the bunker a lot, and we talked a lot about why we did it. The thing we couldn't understand was that when this other guy shot the first chick, we picked up our weapons without giving it a second thought and fired up the rest" (Brownmiller 1975, p. 111).

Fig. 18.4. Rape is, above all, an act of violence.

WHO COMMITS RAPE?

Rape is often an aggressive act that allows the rapist to feel powerful by humiliating a woman. What type of man is so driven? News accounts of sadistic cruelty accompanying rape call undue attention to the rare rapist who is severely disturbed, even psychotic. But the typical rapist does not manifest any typical pattern of psychopathological symptoms, although he is likely to have a history of previous crimes against persons (Henn et al. 1976). Three large studies in major cities (Amir 1971; MacDonald 1971; Rada 1978) characterize the rapist: he is young — the median age of arrested rapists is about twenty-four — and the age with the highest incidence is fifteen to nineteen; he is poor — most are unemployed or unskilled; and very often he is black — the rate of reported rapes involving black men is more than ten times that for whites. Because a higher propor-

Common Myths About Rape

Women are raped by strange men in dark alleys.

Actually, about half the rapists are known to their victims, as casual acquaintances, neighbors, family friends, relatives, or boy friends. Rapes in public are most apt to be reported. Nonetheless, more than half those reported take place in either the victim's or the rapist's home.

Rapists are impulsive and motivated by uncontrollable sexual desires.

Amir (1971) reports that more than 70 percent of rapes in his Philadelphia research were planned (more often the place was chosen, not the person), not perpetrated on impulse. Amir found 43 percent of rapes had more than one assailant, and these incidents were more likely to be planned. In fact, about 40 percent of rapists are married and therefore should already have some sexual outlet.

Only women with bad reputations are raped.

A major study of rape victims in Boston (Burgess and Holmstrom 1974) disclosed that all women are in danger of rape. The age range was seventeen to seventy-three; the work status included career women, housewives, college students, and women on welfare; and physical attractiveness ranged from very plain to very pretty. Although women with a reputation for promiscuity may be especially likely targets, nevertheless they account for a small percentage of forcible rapes.

Women invite rape by their behavior.

Reports of rape certainly include some instances in which the woman has been less than cautious, as in hitchhiking or leaving a bar with a new acquaintance. Yet to equate a woman's freedom to move about and make decisions with an implicit invitation to be raped reflects a view of male superiority in male-female relationships that the women's movement has challenged. Imagine cross-examining a robbery victim in the same way that rape victims are questioned:

In other words, Mr. Smith, you were walking around the streets late at night in a suit that practically advertised the fact that you might be a good target for some easy money, isn't that so? I mean, if we didn't know better, Mr. Smith, we might even think that you were *asking* for this to happen, mightn't we? (Borkenhagen 1975).

Rape is sexually motivated.

Most rapes involve physical force, from roughness to extreme beatings and, in rare cases, murder. The purpose is usually to humiliate and debase the victim, and the sex act itself is secondary (Hilberman 1976).

Source: Based mainly on large-scale studies of rapists by Amir (1971), MacDonald (1971), Burgess and Holmstrom (1974), and Rada (1978).

tion of blacks in America are living in poverty, this racial difference is partly an artifact; if economic status were equalized in examining rape and race, the black-white difference would be reduced.

Sociologists Wolfgang and Ferracuti (1967) have suggested that rape is partly a consequence of a subculture of violence, lower-class values that support and encourage the expression of violence. Lower-class males, especially youths, are expected to resort quickly to physical combat to prove their courage and defend their status. This subcultural norm means that physical assault and violence are a way of life, especially in black ghettos, where channels of recognition and achievement usual elsewhere are unavailable.

Most men convicted of rape committed the act in a pair or group. These statistics may be a bit unrepresentative because the lone rapist is less likely to be caught, but they certainly support the idea that rape is an act of machismo, committed to earn identity and status in the subculture. Force and beatings should be less necessary in multiple-offender rapes, but in reality they are then used more often, supporting the view that violence itself is a primary aim of rape. Rada (1978) reports one group of males who began raping in late adolescence and continued weekly rape episodes for fourteen years! Many dropped out of the group for a time, to serve in the military among other things, and then rejoined. They married, had children, and held steady jobs, but they continued this activity. Rada suggests they did so because of a strong covert homosexual bond, which they denied by expressing the group's machismo in rape.

Only a small proportion of lower-class young men commit rape, though, and we must look closer at the individual rapist. Examining family histories of rapists to try to explain their propensity for sexual violence reveals unusually high rates of parental rejection, domination, cruelty, and sexual seduction or overstimulation. One study found that 92 percent of varied sex offenders had been beaten frequently and severely as children (Hartogs 1951). One rapist recalled the lessons of violence his father taught him when he was four or five years old:

He'd lecture me, "What the hell's the matter with you? I don't treat you like a son, I treat you like a brother, I treat you like a man." He'd tell me when he was a kid he could whip anyone in the neighborhood. He'd drive around, find two or three kids, then he'd say you go whip them and whip them good. I'd try to squirm out of it. He'd double his fist up and hit me in the ear or in the ribs and knock the air out of me. "Go out and whip them kids, if you don't, I'll beat the shit out of you. You're no pansy, do I have to be ashamed of you?" I'd go, crying, pick a fight, I was scared stiff and I didn't want to fight.

I'd fight in sheer desperation. When I got back to the car, he'd pat me on the back and hug me and make me feel good. I'd feel relieved (MacDonald 1971, pp. 146–147).

Parents may unwittingly sanction sexual and aggressive acting out by their own promiscuity and violent behavior and by warnings and accusations to the child that in fact reflect their own sexual inclinations. MacDonald (1971) writes about an aggressive thirteen-year-old whose behavior included sexual acting out:

All his life [his mother] had controlled his bowels with laxatives and she still bathed him. From the time of starting in school, [he] had become increasingly aggressive and demanding. His father would beat him brutally, at times until he bled, because of his use of swear words with a sexual connotation (MacDonald 1971, p. 137).

Abel and his coworkers (1975, in press) conducted laboratory experiments on the conditions that sexually arouse the rapist. They compared the responses of incarcerated rapists and men jailed for sex offenses other than rape (such as child molesting) to vivid audiotaped descriptions. To obtain an objective measure of arousal, they used a penile strain gauge. As shown in Figure 18.5 the nonrapists became aroused by scenes of mutually enjoyable intercourse but not by rape scenes, whereas the rapists showed arousal by both. This measure, the authors suggest, could be used to assess the rapist's progress in treatment; the therapist would hope to see progressive decline in the rapist's arousal to rape cues but continued arousal to mutually enjoyable intercourse. Rada

(1978), with a self-report inventory, found that brutally violent rapists scored higher on expressed hostility than nonviolent rapists, and both groups scored higher than "normals."

Abel and colleagues (1975) found a strong correlation between arousal to scenes of rape and to scenes of nonsexual aggression toward women. Their data support the hypothesis that aggression and rape are connected. Two of the rapists in their study had a history of extreme force and brutality and were aroused only by a scene depicting intercourse when aggression or force was added.

Fig. 18.5. Sexual arousal of rapists and nonrapists to alternating audio descriptions of mutually enjoyable intercourse and rape. Nonrapists showed arousal to descriptions of mutually enjoyable intercourse but not to those of rape, while rapists showed arousal to both types of description. (After Abel et al. 1975.)

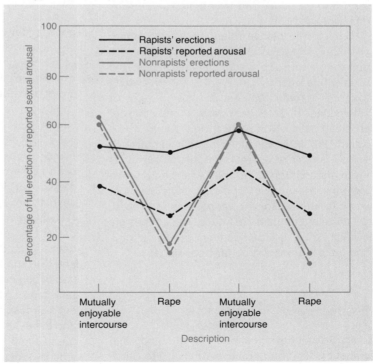

RAPE AND AMERICAN SOCIETY

It is not an aberration, a deviation from the norms of sexual and social behavior in this country. Rape is simply at the end of the continuum of male-aggressive, female-passive patterns, and an arbitrary line has been drawn to mark it off from the rest of such relationships (Medea and Thompson, 1974).

As we saw in Chapter 17, violence is an everyday affair in the American home, and is an heirloom for the next generation. Subjugation of women also has been normative in American society. Rada (1978, p. 71) writes: "To the extent that women are thus depersonalized, the threshold for the use of force to obtain sexual entry is lowered." Is rape more likely in America than elsewhere? The annual incidence of reported rape in the United States of at least 30 in 100,000 compares with 12 in Japan, 7 in Poland, 3 in England, and less than 1 in Norway (MacDonald 1971).

Coercion in sexual relations is much more common. In two studies of college women a quarter-century ago, about 30 percent reported at least one offensive incident in the preceding year of "forceful attempt at intercourse" or "menacing threats or coercive infliction of physical pain" (Kirkpatrick and Kanin 1957; Kanin 1957). Periodically the public is outraged at news stories of violent rapes, especially those involving children, but rape in fact may be an extreme reflection of society's attitudes. Violence in interpersonal relationships is likely to get more attention in the future. The causes are neither exclusively personal nor purely cultural, and the solutions will be far from simple.

Summary

1. Sexual deviance is one of the most difficult subjects in abnormal psychology to delineate because: (1) notions of which behavior is sexually deviant vary across cultures, over time, and within a culture; and (2) often there is a discrepancy between expressed social standards and actual practices.

2. The *DSM*-III identifies these main categories of psychosexual disorders: sexual dysfunctions, disorders of gender identity, and paraphilias.

3. The three types of gender identity disorders are: (1) homosexuality, a psychiatric classification only for individuals who wish to change their homosexual behavior; (2) transvestism, in which individuals, usually heterosexuals, derive sexual stimulation from wearing clothing considered appropriate for the opposite sex; and (3) transsexualism, in which individuals identify so completely with the opposite sex that many undergo hormone therapy and a costly and painful operation that transforms them anatomically into the desired sex.

4. Most transsexuals trace their cross-gender identification to childhood. Two influences thought to produce it are: (1) imbalance of sex hormones, and (2) early social learning experiences in the family, such as cross-dressing of child by mother.

5. The milder paraphilias involve deriving sexual gratification in activities that do not involve contact with a partner. Although not usually considered serious crimes, they are seen as psychological problems. Three examples are: (1) fetishism, in which the individual is sexually aroused solely by a body part or object; (2) voyeurism, in which sexual gratification is derived by spying on an unknowing person undressing, nude, or engaging in sexual activity; and (3) exhibitionism, in which sexual gratification is derived from both displaying one's genitals to an unwilling viewer and seeing the victim's shocked flight response. Both the voyeur and the exhibitionist are generally thought to be passive and socially inadequate, fearing the rejection that a conventional sexual approach might bring.

6. Theories on the causes of the milder paraphilias are of two types: the psychoanalytic theory suggests that the deviant symptom symbolically expresses an unresolved childhood conflict, and the behavioral conditioning theory proposes that memories from an early deviant sexual experience provide content for fantasy during masturbation. This strengthens aberrant desires, which are eventually acted upon.

7. The serious paraphilias — pedophilia, incest, and rape — are punishable offenses involving force or underaged victims. Pedophilia is an erotic desire for prepubertal children. In most cases, the pedophile is acquainted with the child and does not use force; he usually is both socially and sexually maladjusted.

8. Incest is sexual activity between close family members and is a universal taboo. Several factors are seen in father-daughter incest: (1) crowded living conditions and isolation from outside contacts; (2) a father who is highly moralistic and devoutly committed to fundamentalist doctrines; and (3) a shift in role of household responsibilities from mother to daughter and avoidance of marital relations by the mother.

9. Rape is the fastest growing and least prosecuted violent crime in America. The three categories are: forcible rape, attempted rape, and statutory rape.

10. Four types of motives for rape have been identified: (1) displaced aggression, in which the intent of the act is to harm or degrade the victim; (2) compensatory rape, in which the intent is primarily sexual and force is used only to accomplish sexual aims; (3) sex-aggression defusion, in which sexual fantasy and experience are intertwined with aggressive thoughts and feelings so that the rapist sees the woman's struggles as seductive; and (4) impulsive rape, in which the rapist takes advantage of a situation in an impulsive, guiltless way.

11. The typical rapist has this profile: (1) he does not manifest any specific pattern of psychopathological symptoms, although likely to have a history of crimes against persons; (2) he is young, and poor; (3) he has an unfortunate family history of parental rejection, domination, cruelty, and sexual seduction or overstimulation.

12. Rape is thought to reflect both the violence in American society and the traditional subjugation of women.

Chapter 19

Intervention with Social Deviance

Criminal Justice System

Mental Health and Criminal Justice

Rehabilitation Programs
Psychotherapy
Behavior Therapy
Family Therapy
Residential Programs
Community-Based Programs

Help for Victims
Support and Counseling
Protection from Further Harm

Prevention

Summary

Most people who manifest socially deviant behavior do not voluntarily seek psychological assistance to change their ways. The alcoholic and heroin addict may be so caught up in the cycle of their addiction that they lack insight into their dependency or strength to deal with it. The sexual offender often takes pleasure in deviant behavior and does not recognize or value the possibility that normal modes of sexual expression are feasible for him. The delinquent youth may derive much gratification from acceptance by peers. Because they find the deviant pattern somewhat accepted and gratifying, such persons are most likely to come into contact with mental health professionals following some contact with the criminal justice system. The mental health system's goal of rehabilitation and the criminal justice system's primary goal, control, are not always in sympathy, either in philosophy or in practice. A recurring issue in public policy is which set of goals and practices should prevail in dealing with a type of social deviance.

Criminal Justice System

Society needs a way to control unacceptable behavior, and the criminal justice system has evolved to fill that need. Its main mechanism is punishment, usually in the form of incarceration. Removal from society and restraint of freedom is rationalized as deterring future episodes of social deviance. This method of deterrence, it is assumed, operates in two ways. First, in a general way, the very existence of prisons is seen as a deterrent to the law-abiding citizen who might otherwise be tempted to engage in socially deviant behavior. Second, removing a convicted offender from society is believed to eliminate the possibility of criminal behavior during the sentence, providing a punishment likely to deter future deviant behavior, and providing an opportunity for rehabilitation to improve the likelihood of successful adaptation after release (Zimring and Hawkins 1973).

About the general value of prisons as a deterrent for law-abiding citizens, we must confess ignorance. How many of us decide against robbing a store, using heroin, or committing rape because of the possibility we will have to pay with a prison term? We would like to believe that our socialization and our values, not fear of arrest and punishment, prevent these behaviors, but it is very difficult to design an experiment or find social statistics to answer this question.

As for the deterrent value of incarceration for actual offenders, the results are reasonably clear and quite disappointing. Our prisons and juvenile training schools have received severe criticism for perpetuating the very problems they are supposed to deter (Menninger 1968; Wooden 1976). Emphasis on custody and punishment has often created facilities with poor physical conditions, crowding, coercion, and a paucity of therapeutic and educational pro-

Fig. 19.1. The prison's emphasis on control and punishment often clashes with mental health's emphasis on rehabilitation.

grams; conditions such as these combined with the criminal role models plentiful in a prison have not boded well for eventual rehabilitation. One study of nearly 7000 offenders who had been in prison rehabilitation programs showed that 48 percent were arrested for new offenses within two years of release (President's Commission on Law Enforcement 1967). These results are very typical of a large number of studies; Glaser (1964) estimated that with or without rehabilitation programs, 40 to 67 percent of adults who are imprisoned eventually are arrested for another crime, usually of the same type.

Mental Health and Criminal Justice

In part because the results of imprisonment are so discouraging, repeated attempts have been made to find alternatives. Actually, the attempt to separate individuals who need mental health care from those appropriate for the criminal justice system has a long history. The criminal justice system is based on a notion of personal responsibility for one's actions; individuals known in the legal system as *insane* are not considered responsible for their socially deviant acts. The "defense by reason of insanity" was clearly delineated in 1843 in the trial of a Scotsman, Daniel M'Naughten, who today would probably be diagnosed as a paranoid schizophrenic (Goldstein 1967). M'Naughten had a delusional belief that the Conservative Party was persecuting him and thereupon decided to kill the British prime minister. He mistakenly shot someone else, but was acquitted by reason of insanity and then confined to an insane asylum for the rest of his life. The major rule, derived from M'Naughten's acquittal, was that "to establish a defense on the grounds of

insanity, it must be clearly proven that at the time of committing the act, the party accused was laboring under such a defect of reason from disease of the mind, as not to know the nature and quality of the act he was doing or if he did know it, that he did not know what he was doing was wrong" (Goldstein 1967, p. 45). For many years, this "right-wrong" distinction was the basis for the insanity defense in England and the United States. An additional criterion often used was "irresistible impulse," signifying a mentally ill person's inability to control his behavior. In newer guidelines issued by the American Law Institute (ALI) these criteria are combined: "A person is not responsible for criminal conduct if at the time of such conduct, as a result of mental disease or defect, he lacks substantial capacity either to appreciate the criminality (wrongfulness) of his conduct or to conform his conduct to the requirements of the law" (Model Penal Code 1962, p. 66).

The ALI guidelines also specify that mental disease or defect "do not include an abnormality manifested only by repeated criminal or otherwise antisocial conduct" (p. 66). This definition eliminates the insanity defense for sociopathic individuals, who might otherwise seem to qualify by their incapacity to recognize consequences. Although the insanity defense provides one mechanism for providing mental health care rather than incarceration for socially deviant behavior, it is rarely applied, especially to the behavior patterns discussed in this section.

Other attempts have been made more recently to distinguish patterns of social deviance that are more appropriately the province, at least initially, of the mental health system:

1. *Redefining crimes as psychological problems.* Public drunkenness, drug addiction, and resulting antisocial behavior have, until recently, been considered the domain of the

criminal justice system. Currently it is recognized that many criminal behaviors of substance-abusing persons derive from their inability to free themselves of dependence or addiction. Programs designed to relieve or control substance abuse, wholly or partly independent of the criminal justice system, are now seen as more effective than punishing the individual for abuse or its secondary criminal consequences. Moreover, for some social deviants who require incarceration (sex offenders, serious drug abusers), special inpatient facilities combine custody with active efforts at rehabilitation.

2. *Intervening early, to prevent further criminal acts.* Many communities have developed diversion programs, assigning first offenders to community-based rehabilitation programs rather than to jail. These programs can involve such diverse acts as petty theft by juveniles and family violence.

We will focus on these rehabilitation and early intervention efforts.

Rehabilitation Programs

Most rehabilitation programs for socially deviant persons involve some control. In cases of more extreme deviance, rehabilitation programs are apt to be undertaken in correctional settings; most reports of treatment for violent sex offenders deal with incarcerated persons. In other cases, rehabilitation programs seem more successful when civil control is added, as we shall see with heroin-abuse programs. Many other programs rely on control by court-mandated treatment or peer pressure, as we shall see in programs for alcoholics and delinquents. A constant need in rehabilitation programs, though, is suppression of antisocial behaviors while seeking to establish alternatives. Hence, civil liberties are a continuing issue. How far can society go in forcing an individual to participate in rehabilitation programs? Intervention programs for social deviance must continually balance the individual's rights with social pressures toward conformity.

Psychotherapy

The socially deviant person generally has not been a very promising client for insight-oriented psychotherapies, such as those we discussed in Chapter 15 for anxiety disorders. Traditional psychotherapy has several limitations with this population. First, as we have seen, deviant individuals are apt to be much less distressed about their behavior than are other people. The substance, sexual, or social abuses in which they engage often are not only a source of gratification but also an integral part of their self-concept.

The second limitation is that treatment is often involuntary and the desire for change minimal. Treatment is frequently sought, or mandated, after difficulties, usually involving the law. An individual may be unhappy about ill consequences of his behavior, but this feeling is as likely to be expressed in resentment against his controllers as in desire to change himself. The person in prison might go through the motions of psychotherapy to gain favor with the parole board. Even volunteer clients with strong desire to change derive it not only from personal suffering but also from pressures applied by others. The wife or child abuser "voluntarily" entering therapy still does so under real or implied sanctions imposed by family or court.

Third, deviant individuals often do not have enough of the requisite therapeutic process skills. Even individuals who do desire to change may lack the verbal and cognitive skills required for traditional psychotherapy. For many individuals with a history of acting out, problems have been met impulsively by action, not by reflection and planning. The psychotherapeutic process of talking through situations is apt to be experienced as quite alien and endured only if required.

A fourth prerequisite for successful psychotherapy is a repertoire of adaptive alternative behaviors. Many socially deviant persons have multiple problems and are ill-equipped to cope with them. Their lives and problems do not divide up as neatly as in our chapters. The delinquent who is addicted to heroin and commits rape is quite likely, as well, to be poor, to have limited education, to be without an occupational specialty, and to lack meaningful family or heterosexual relationships. Therapy may not have a lot to build upon, and even the most successful therapeutic intervention for, say, heroin addiction would ultimately have little value if it did not aim as well at better adaptation in a variety of areas.

For these and other reasons, attempts by mental health professionals to intervene with socially deviant individuals have not been spectacularly successful, a fact well known by professionals and deviant individuals alike. Many psychotherapists will not even attempt treatment with a sex offender, sociopath, alcoholic, or drug addict, and the institutional programs that deal with these individuals attract few mental health personnel. Likewise, offenders are reluctant to enter professional treatment.

At one walk-in psychiatric clinic, fifty-eight heroin addicts who requested help were offered outpatient methadone detoxification; none returned to the clinic after the initial visit. Of twenty-two who were offered psychotherapy, three returned. These rates contrast vividly with a return rate of 97 percent for a control group drawn from all diagnostic categories in this same setting (O'Malley, Anderson, and Lazare 1972). They caution us in looking at the results

reported on any treatment to realize that the clients who enter and complete the program are highly selected. There are, to be sure, some reports of successful psychological counseling with socially deviant persons, although these efforts seem most successful when counseling is based on present concerns and actions (Glasser 1965) and when the client presents few of the limitations listed above.

Behavior Therapy

A promising and relatively recent approach to rehabilitating social deviants involves individual or institutional behavior therapy. Behavior therapies for social deviance do not rely on insight but attempt to recreate the deviant situations and behaviors and help the individual to learn more adaptive behaviors.

The literature on behavior therapy contains a number of reports of successful treatment of alcoholism (Sobell and Sobell 1973, 1976) and sexual deviations including exhibitionism, fetishism, voyeurism, transvestism, pedophilia, and sadism (Marks and Gelder 1967; Barlow 1974; Hallam and Rachman 1976). Also, although we have not discussed homosexuality as a sexual deviation, a major focus of behavioral therapy has been treatment of homosexuals who want to change their sexual preference (Feldman and MacCulloch 1965, 1971). The main aim of behavioral treatment for these problems is to decrease the deviant behavior; an important secondary aim is to increase incompatible positive behaviors and relevant coping skills.

AVERSION THERAPY

The primary approach to decreasing deviant responses has been *aversion therapy*, reducing enjoyment of inappropriate sexual arousal or drinking by pairing the stimuli for these behaviors with some unpleasant event. The client is exposed to the situations by means of slides,

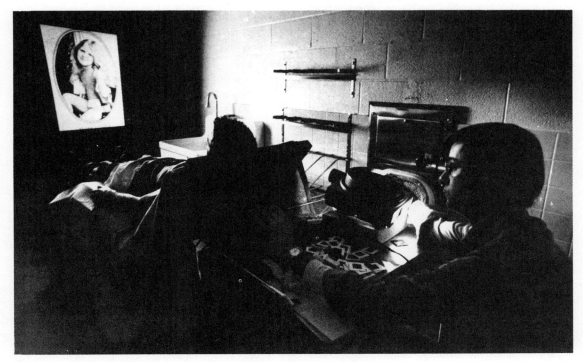

Fig. 19.2. A man convicted of molesting children undergoes voluntary treatment in a Connecticut state prison. When the prisoner is shown a picture of a young girl, a psychologist triggers a mild but unpleasant electric shock in an attempt to destroy the connection in the convict's mind between children and sexual pleasure.

verbal descriptions, imagined scenes, or real-life activities. These stimuli are paired with a noxious event, such as electric shock or chemicals that induce nausea and vomiting. Theoretically, the deviant stimuli come to elicit anxiety, by classical conditioning, or the deviant responses are punished by instrumental conditioning; the learning mechanism actually operating in successful treatment is unclear, as we shall discuss later.

In aversion therapy to decrease sexual arousal to inappropriate stimuli the items themselves might be used, or they might be presented symbolically (pictures of boots for a fetish). An illustrative case treated by Marks and Gelder (1967) is a twenty-one-year-old unmarried male college student who had been cross-dressing since age thirteen. He masturbated while dressed in women's clothing, especially panties, pajamas, a skirt and blouse, or a slip. He had never experienced intercourse and did not have a girl friend. The authors first assessed his erectile response by means of a penile plethysmograph (see Chapter 3) to these articles of clothing and to a photograph of a nude woman. He showed maximal erection to all these stimuli before treatment. Treatment followed a multiple-baseline design, first concentrating on eliminating arousal to panties, then pajamas, then skirt and blouse, and finally slip. While the patient looked at or touched the garment, he would receive an electric shock (arm or leg). Results of treatment were quite specific: when the erectile response to panties was eliminated, it was still strong to the other stimuli. After the erectile response to all women's clothing was eliminated, it was still strong to the nude photo. Marks and Gelder reported concomitant increased heterosexual functioning, but did not direct treatment specifically toward this goal.

With alcoholism, the purpose of aversion therapy is to decrease the drinking by making it a noxious or at least neutral experience. Although electric-shock punishment is sometimes used, the most effective aversion therapy with alcoholics seems to involve chemicals, to produce nausea and vomiting when the client sips alcohol. The largest clinical trial, in which close to 5000 alcoholics participated, took place at the Shadel Sanatorium in Seattle, Washington (Lemere and Voegtlin 1950; Voegtlin, Lemere, Broz, and O'Halleren 1941). Treatment consisted of four to six sessions over a two-week period, with six- and twelve-month booster sessions. The patient was administered the drug emetine, and then given alcohol to drink. The combined effect was prolonged vomiting, for up to 45 minutes. Over a long follow-up period Lemere and Voegtlin (1950) reported the exceptionally high total abstinence rate of 51 percent, combining data of original treatment successes and successful retreatment of initial relapses. With these results it is interesting that this form of treatment is little used today, probably because it is aversive to therapist as well as patient. A related treatment employs the drug *Antabuse,* a pill that produces nausea and vomiting only if the client ingests any alcohol. Although Antabuse is quite effec-

tive in suppressing drinking, its main limitation is that 99 percent of clients refuse to continue taking the pill when they are no longer under supervision (Lubetkin, Rivers, and Rosenberg 1971). It could be an effective treatment, but has had limited value in practice.

A variation of aversion therapy is *covert sensitization,* wherein both the deviant approach behavior and a noxious event are imagined. During treatment the therapist will teach the client to relax and then describe a scene in vivid and elaborate detail. These are excerpts from a typical narrative for an alcoholic:

> You are walking into a bar. You decide to have a glass of beer. You are now walking toward the bar. . . . You have a funny feeling in the pit of your stomach. Your stomach feels all queasy and nauseous. Some liquid comes up your throat and it is very sour. . . . As the bartender is pouring the beer, puke comes up into your mouth. . . . You reach for the glass of beer to wash it down. As soon as your hand touches the glass, you can't hold it down any longer. You have to open your mouth and you puke. It goes all over your hand, all over the glass and the beer. . . . Your shirt and pants are full of vomit. . . . You notice people looking at you. . . . You turn away from the beer and immediately start to feel better and better . . . (Cautela 1967, pp. 461–462).

Covert sensitization has several advantages. It dispenses with the apparatus needed for electric shock or chemical aversion, tailors the image directly to the client's own situation, and, perhaps most important, gives the client a technique to employ outside the therapy session.

UNRESOLVED QUESTIONS ABOUT AVERSION TECHNIQUES

Although aversive therapies seem to have promising effects, some clinical, theoretical, and ethical questions are unresolved. The main clinical limitation of these methods is a lack of generalization from the therapist's office to the real-life situation. Alcoholics can discriminate quite well between drinking in a bar and in a hospital; the attempts of cognitive strategies such as covert sensitization to bridge this gap are not yet thoroughly evaluated. A further clinical limitation to programs designed only to reduce deviant responses is that they are incomplete, an issue that we shall consider shortly.

The main theoretical dilemma is that we still do not understand the learning mechanisms in successful treatment. For many cases, there is both classical conditioning (the noxious event is paired with the arousing stimulus) and instrumental conditioning or punishment (the noxious event follows a deviant response, and it can sometimes be avoided or terminated depending upon the patient's response). It is difficult, if not impossible, to separate these processes. The classical conditioning paradigm would predict, however, that the client will eventually feel anxious in the presence of the deviant stimulus, but there is no consistent evidence that the stimulus elicits anything but a neutral response.

The ethical issues of aversive conditioning are many. For some people it brings up the images of control popularized in Anthony Burgess's novel, *A Clockwork Orange,* in which a severely antisocial youth was "deconditioned" to undergo an instant and total personality change. Although in reality clients are neither forced into aversion therapy nor changed so dramatically, these techniques raise the question of whether the society has the right to compel deviant individuals to submit to aversive therapy in order to control their aberrant behavior. Because aversive techniques are not pleasant to administer or to receive, therapists have been reluctant to employ them even where they might be the best treatment, and a great many clients refuse them. In considering whether the gains are worth the discomfort, we must understand more fully the long-term benefits, and the literature is still quite deficient here. If aversion therapy *is* being considered, good clinical practice advises that nonaversive methods be tried first, that patients be fully informed of the procedures and be as free as possible of pressures to consent, and that treatment be administered by a therapist with the training and experience to administer it safely and judiciously (Bellak and Hersen 1977). A positive trend is the search by investigators for less noxious stimuli that may be as effective as electric shock and emetics, as in covert sensitization.

INCREASING COPING BEHAVIORS

We have seen that a major limitation of exclusively using aversion therapy to reduce deviant responses is that the person might still lack adaptive responses necessary for effective functioning. Barlow (1974) argued that in treating sexual deviations four components function independently: gender role behavior, heterosocial skills, deviant arousal patterns, and heterosexual arousal patterns. Patients often need treatment programs designed to increase adaptive behavior as well as to eliminate deviant practices. The treated pedophile may no longer be aroused by children, but if he never acquired appropriate social and sexual skills with adult women, he would be left in an uncomfortable state of limbo, prone to revert to former deviant behavior. His treatment should include instruction in heterosexual or communication skills by methods such as those described in Chapter 15. When heterosexual arousal is deficient, for example, it might be increased by techniques used to treat sexual dysfunction, such as orgasmic conditioning, in which masturbation fantasy gradually changes into appropriate heterosexual stimuli.

With alcoholics, Gottman and Markman (1978) have noticed that relapses often follow

Covert Sensitization for Exhibitionism and Sadism

A clinical case reported by Hayes, Brownell, and Barlow (1978) demonstrates successful use of covert sensitization to reduce exhibitionistic and sadistic arousal in a man with a long history of deviant sexual behavior and antisocial acts. As the authors describe him:

The client was a 25-year-old white married male, referred to an acute psychiatric inpatient facility because of multiple sexual deviations. He had run away from home at an early age and had gone to a large metropolitan area where he had made his living through homosexual prostitution. His history also included polydrug abuse and addiction, theft, and other illegal acts. The client was highly heterosocially skilled and had frequent and successful heterosexual intercourse before marriage (p. 285).

At age twenty-two he was sent to prison for armed robbery, and he blamed his incarceration on his wife.

[He] began to have fantasies about torturing her. These became increasingly sexual in nature . . . [and soon he] was having strong sadistic sexual fantasies, involving only imaginary women and occupying between four and six hours of each waking day. . . . In short, the client's sexual fantasies involved sadistic rape in which the degradation of the female was paramount. The client masturbated to the sadistic fantasies almost exclusively while serving his 2.5 year sentence and reported that they became increasingly intense and involving. Within two weeks after his release from prison he was arrested for attempted rape. Subsequently he reported that the sadistic rape fantasies continued, but he did not act on them (p. 285).

The authors go on to describe the client's exhibitionistic fantasies and behavior, which culminated in his arrest for publicly masturbating. A week later, he sought treatment.

Physiological measures of sexual arousal were obtained by a penile strain gauge, which measured his erections while viewing slides he had selected as arousing:

Exhibitionistic slides depicted fully clothed women looking through a car window with shocked looks on their faces. Sadistic slides showed nude females tied or chained down in a number of provocative positions. Heterosexual slides displayed pictures of nude females.

The client's self-report of arousal to written descriptions of exhibitionistic, sadistic, and appropriate heterosexual scenes was also assessed.

Treatment sessions employed self-administered covert sensitization, in which the description of an arousing scene was followed by a description of a realistic aversive scene that had been generated by the client. It was felt that aversive scenes would be most effective if they related meaningfully to the deviant arousal being treated. The client's aversive scenes followed the theme of getting caught by the police or his family and friends, losing his home and job, and going to jail.

During the first six days he received treatment for exhibitionistic arousal. The first scene was presented by the therapist, and subsequent scenes were described aloud by the client. In addition to two or three repetitions in the therapy session, the client would practice on his own at least twice a day. Here is a typical scene:

I call her over to the car. She doesn't see what I am doing. I say, "Can you help with this?" She looks down and sees my dick. It's hard and she's really shocked. Her face looks all kind of distorted. I quick drive away. As I drive away I see her look back, I think "Oh, shit, she's seen my license plate!" I begin to worry that she might call the police. . . I get home and I'm still worried. My wife keeps saying "What's wrong?" . . . As we all sit down to dinner I hear a knock on the door. I go open it and there are four pigs. They come charging in and throw me up against the wall and say "You're under arrest for indecent exposure!" My wife starts to cry and says "This is it! This is the last straw!" (p. 286).

The second six days of inpatient treatment focused on sadistic scenes. The results of this multiple-baseline design are depicted in the accompanying figure. Both erection and self-report measures showed dramatic change that was specific to the treatment administered. During the exhibitionism sessions, arousal to exhibitionistic scenes declined but remained strong to sadistic and heterosexual ones. During the sadism sessions, arousal to sadistic scenes decreased, but the patient continued to be strongly responsive to heterosexual scenes. After these twelve days the client was discharged from the hospital. He reported, following treatment, that he was able to easily control his now very infrequent deviant fantasies and impulses by using aversive scenes. Unfortunately no long-term results of the client's sexual and other behavior were included in the report.

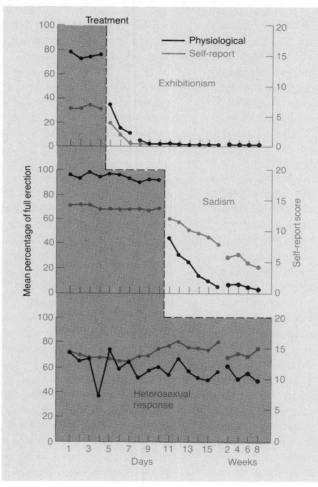

two types of critical events: (1) social pressures to drink where the person does not know a graceful way of refusing, and (2) situations in which he could not obtain his rights and could not be appropriately assertive (one man went on a binge when his ex-wife denied him visiting rights with the children one weekend). Furthermore, many alcoholics have the cognitive set that one drink means failure, following disease models of alcoholism (represented especially by Alcoholics Anonymous), which hold that even one drink will inevitably cause a relapse. In fact, a number of studies have shown that total abstinence need not necessarily be a goal. At least some alcoholics can become social (moderate) drinkers (Davies 1962; Sobell, Sobell, and Christelman 1972).

Many programs are now aimed at controlled social drinking and include training in restraint and assertiveness. Sobell and Sobell (1973, 1976) reported on one successful combined program. For realism, in-hospital treatment sessions were administered in a simulated bar and simulated home environment. Along with aversion therapy (electric shock) for drinking behaviors, clients were taught to identify the situations that normally led to heavy drinking and to think of other ways of coping with those situations and the long-term consequences of these behaviors.

An even more comprehensive program, described by Hunt and Azrin (1973), was superior to a hospital-based detoxification and didactic program for the small sample studied. The "community reinforcement program" included not only an in-hospital educational program about alcoholism, but also vocational, marriage, family, and social counseling, regular follow-up, and contacts in the community. Marriage and family counseling consisted of information about important matters, such as money management, sexual adjustment, and social activities, as well as reciprocal reinforce-

ment agreements (see Chapter 15). The social-counseling program even renovated a former tavern into an alcohol-free social club, to provide varied activities for patients and their wives (such as picnics, games, and movies).

It appears that problems such as alcoholism relate to so many aspects of an individual's life that the likelihood of success is enhanced by a program aimed at both decreasing problem drinking and increasing other coping skills.

Family Therapy

The same type of behavioral objective, increasing adaptive coping skills, has been applied to work with families. The main application of family therapy to social deviance has been with families that have delinquent youths. Because the family system perspective sees the deviant behavior of one member as reflecting problems in the family as a whole, intervention programs having this orientation require members to change their behavior toward one another. Although a number of clinical approaches to family therapy are used (see Chapters 7, 15, and 22), we will focus on behavioral programs because they have been most thoroughly evaluated.

One useful approach with families is to develop a contract between parent and child that spells out their mutual responsibilities, privileges each will receive for meeting them, and sanctions for failure (Tharp and Wetzel 1969). The conflict between parents and a delinquent child usually is extreme, and the contracting helps to focus energy on solving problems and to define what each wants of the other. Stuart (1971) reports behavioral contracting with Candy, a sixteen-year-old referred by the juvenile court following alleged promiscuity, exhibitionism, drug abuse, home truancy, and chronically antagonistic exchanges at home. Candy's parents, in their sixties and physically ill, wanted her placed out of the home, and would consider keeping her at home only if they could exercise very rigid control. Contracting sessions were designed to help Candy and her parents give in somewhat and to work out a specific and mutually acceptable contract (see Table 19.1). Negotiating and renegotiating such a contract takes extensive arbitration by the therapist.

A more elaborate approach to family therapy is Alexander and Parsons's (1973) short-term behavioral family intervention. Family interaction studies have shown that deviant families are more silent than normal families, share talking time less equally, have fewer positive interruptions, and in general are less active (Mischler and Waxler 1968; Winter and Ferreira 1969). Therapy aimed at altering this lack of reciprocity in family interaction seems to decrease disruptive behaviors in the target child (Patterson and Reid 1970). Therefore, Alexander and Parsons designed a short-term behavioral program for family intervention with inputs that:

(a) assess the family behaviors that maintain delinquent behavior; (b) modify the family communication patterns in the direction of greater clarity and precision, increased reciprocity, and presentation of alternative solutions; (c) all in order to institute a pattern of contingency contracting in the family designed to modify the maladaptive patterns and institute more adaptive behaviors p. 219).

Twenty families in this treatment program were compared on three family interaction measures with ten families in client-centered family group therapy (focusing on attitudes and feelings about family relationships and adolescent problems) and ten untreated controls. After treatment, families in the behavioral treatment program demonstrated more equality in interaction, gauged by the amount of time each member talked, with more interruptions and less silence, which are characteristics of non-problem families. For a larger sample, the behavioral treatment also reduced recidivism at follow-up to 26 percent, compared with about 50 percent for families in client-centered treatment or various no-treatment control conditions. The Alexander and Parsons study is unique because it looked not only at outcome for the delinquent youth but also at interaction patterns in the family that might facilitate more adaptive behavior.

Table 19.1. Excerpts from behavioral contract

Privileges	Responsibilities
In exchange for the privilege of going out at 7 P.M. on one weekend evening without having to account for her whereabouts . . .	Candy must maintain a weekly average of B in the academic ratings of all her classes and return home by 11:30 P.M.
In exchange for the privilege of going out a second weekend night . . .	Candy must tell her parents by 6 P.M. of her destination and her companion, and must return home by 11:30 P.M.
In exchange for the privilege of having Candy complete household chores and maintain her curfew . . .	Mr. and Mrs. B agree to pay Candy $1.50 on the morning following days on which the money is earned.

Source: R. Stuart, "Behavioral Contracting with the Families of Delinquents," *Journal of Behavior Therapy and Experimental Psychiatry*, 1971, 2, p. 9.

Residential Programs

The rate of failure from our fixed institutions for young and old offenders has remained more constant through the years than any other index upon which we rely — cost of living, Dow Jones, or the annual precipitation of rain. An average of the recidivism rates reported by the most reliable researchers runs consistently in a range from one-half to two-thirds. No other facility created by our society for dealing with any other area of social pathology which showed such a consistently high rate of failure could so long endure (Keller and Alper 1970, p. xi).

Many attempts have been made at rehabilitation programming in adult and juvenile correctional facilities, involving job training, education, and therapy. We have mentioned that some promise seems to lie in more recent programs for juveniles, especially those providing alternatives to prison or massive changes in the prison environment.

One approach is to provide relatively small, community-based halfway houses as alternatives to incarceration in large correctional facilities (Keller and Alper 1970). As part of their rehabilitation, residents participate in the daily life of the larger community, going to jobs or school and taking their recreation away from the house (Dean and Reppucci 1974). There is some evidence of success with this approach.

Another approach is to redesign the correctional facility itself to better blend the goals of custody and rehabilitation. A number of attempts have been made to introduce behavior-modification programs, such as the token economy described in Chapter 7, into prisons. Often, however, these have been criticized because they are total programs and deprive prisoners of their right to refuse participation. Generally, behavior modification approaches have been accepted more often in juvenile correc-

tions, where the state assumes greater prerogative to require participation in programs.

A thoughtfully planned and highly effective behavioral program for juveniles was developed by Reppucci and his colleagues at the Connecticut School for Boys (Dean and Reppucci 1974; Reppucci and Saunders 1974). Located in a small industrial city in central Connecticut, CSB was the only training school in the state in 1970. It had a full-time staff of about 200 and about 180 delinquent boys. Reppucci's team was called in after a rash of runaways and brutality; state police were on duty and a staff "goon squad" patrolled the grounds to protect employees (Dean and Reppucci 1974).

Working closely with the superintendent and CSB staff, and utilizing group-dynamic approaches as well as behavior modification, the consultants converted the cottages, one at a time, to a positively oriented token economy, with the boys and staff determining points earned and reinforcers given. The program was increasingly individualized as the boys progressed through it.

Over several years, the program was successful by a variety of indices: (1) incidents of brutality were reduced almost to zero; (2) the maximum-security cottage was closed; (3) staff goon squads and state police were eliminated; (4) cottage-based school programs were developed; (5) runaways were markedly reduced; (6) staff sick days were cut drastically; and (7) a number of positive changes were made in the social climate, as assessed by residents and staff. Perhaps the most dramatic measure of success was that in the mid-1970s the entire institution was closed, with the remaining residents transferred to Connecticut's residential school for girls. It appears that comprehensive rehabilitation programs, which attend to preparing the person to live in the community and pave the way for this to happen, are a promising alternative to custodial institutions.

Community-Based Programs

We shall consider a variety of rehabilitation programs at the community level. We have seen that some improvement can be gained with social deviance when professionals administer individual treatment in a clinic or hospital. Such programs are inherently limited, however, primarily for two reasons. First, it is often necessary to alter the individual's social environment to change socially deviant behavior. Many of the problems we have described originate in

Achievement Place

A noteworthy experiment in community-based rehabilitation of delinquent youths is Achievement Place, a home-style setting operated according to behavior-modification principles. Established by Montrose Wolf and Ellery Phillips, psychologists at the Universtiy of Kansas, the original program in Lawrence, Kansas is a temporary home for nine or so boys adjudicated delinquent, of junior high school age and three or four years behind in school. The boys live for about nine to twelve months with a professional adult couple, called "teaching parents." This highly successful program is unique for several reasons. It has described its approach in detail, it has been extensively evaluated, and, most strikingly, the original program now has been replicated in more than eighty group homes for boys and girls in twelve states and in Canada.

The premise of Achievement Place is that delinquent behavior is the product of inadequate social learning experiences, and that antisocial behaviors result from such factors as inadequate education, poor adult models of prosocial behavior, and a delinquent peer group. Traditional correctional institutions entrench antisocial behavior, because peer pressure there encourages socially undesirable behavior, such as aggressive talk and defiance of rules. Achievement Place, by contrast, seeks to systematically reinforce socially acceptable behavior while teaching social skills (such as promptness), academic skills (how to study), self-care skills (personal hygiene), and home maintenance and prevocational skills. Residents attend regular schools, bringing daily report cards back to

Achievement Place. Within the home, the residents share household chores. Each evening they meet with the teaching parents for a group discussion of issues related to living in the house. The sessions are meant to teach problem-solving skills. A highly structured token economy is administered in a warm, empathetic family-like setting.

In the token economy, rules and consequences are clear; the youths can earn or lose points for specific behaviors, such as good grooming and reading books and newspapers, on the plus side, or arguing and failing grades, on the minus side. These points then can be exchanged for privileges, such as snacks, an allowance, use of a bicycle, or permission to go downtown. Initially, points are exchanged several times a day; as the youth becomes accustomed to the system, he is shifted to a daily exchange and then, with progress, to a weekly exchange. After four consecutive weeks of improvement on the weekly exchange system, he moves to the merit system, in which all privileges are free, and desirable behaviors are reinforced with praise and approval, rather than points. His behavior is still carefully monitored, and after four successful weeks on the merit system he advances to the homeward-bound system, spending progressively more time in his family's home each week. Now the program staff also consult with the family as a whole. The entire system is conducted giving the youth a voice in its operation, and no doubt its success is attributable in large part to its supportive, nonpunitive atmosphere.

This fictionalized account illustrates a boy's first meal at Achievement Place:

and are maintained by adverse family, peer-group, or neighborhood settings. Very often, gains made in inpatient hospital treatment programs do not carry over into the outside world. Tharp and Wetzel wrote: "A persistent theme in any account of mental health work is the failure of treatment techniques in the face of an adverse environment" (1969, p. 7). Treatment in "real-life" settings can reduce this effect by helping to alter behavior patterns while exposing the client to the stresses and stimuli of everyday life. Some such programs, as we have

I finished off the sandwich and chips in a hurry and got up. The wife was still eating, but she looked up at me, everybody else did too, like I did some terrible thing.

"Would you please carry your dishes to the sink, Paul?"

Man, oh man, oh man, I felt like telling her, I ain't no damn waitress, lady, but I kept quiet. I looked at the warden, and he nodded his head, meaning I had to do what she said.

"But that's woman's work," I said louder than I planned. My voice sounded weird to me, cause I'd hardly said nothing out loud since I left the courthouse. All the guys looked around at each other, rolling their eyes and grinning, and I thought, these sons of bitches, ain't nobody going to laugh at me, you'll see.

"We all do things here you'll probably call 'women's work,' " the warden said. "Elaine couldn't possibly do everything for all of us, and there's no reason why she should. We want you to learn how to do things for yourself while you're here. Now please carry your dishes to the sink."

He said that all pretty nice, not grouchy or like he lost his temper. I took the damn dishes over to the sink, since I didn't figure that he'd let me out of there until I did.

"Good Paul, that's fine, thank you, give yourself 500 points."

This guy was like a broken record. But I wrote down 500 points for "carrying dishes to sink," and the warden put a big "L" by it, but he erased the "S" and "M" and said it was for

seen, are intended to teach more successful ways of coping with the environment, and others to change family interactions. Many of the successful community-based programs act to create a new support group for nondeviant behavior (Alcoholics Anonymous) or establish an alternative total community (Synanon).

The second disadvantage of treating social deviance with traditional methods is that many mental health professionals have a social and intellectual background that makes it difficult for them to relate to persons labeled socially

---

maintenance or something. The guys were being quiet, watching again (Allen et al., in press).

The results of this program are certainly encouraging. One outcome study compared recidivism rates for sixteen boys whom the court had committed to Achievement Place, fifteen boys sent to a state institution, and thirteen boys placed on probation. Two years after their release, only 19 percent of the youths from Achievement Place have reappeared in the juvenile justice system, in contrast to 53 percent of those who had spent time in the state institution, and 54 percent of those on probation. These samples are quite small, and the youths were not assigned at random, so that the results cannot be considered conclusive. Nevertheless, the Achievement Place record seems to promise a viable alternative to more costly and less effective institutions.

Sources: From Phillips 1968; Phillips, Phillips, Fixsen, and Wolf 1971; Eitzen 1975; Wolf, Phillips, Fixsen, Braukmann, Kirigin, Willnes, and Schumaker 1976; and Fixsen, Phillips, Phillips, and Wolf 1976.

Behaviors and the number of points earned or lost

Behaviors that earned points	Points
1. Watching news on TV or reading the newspaper	300 per day
2. Cleaning and maintaining neatness in one's room	500 per day
3. Keeping one's person neat and clean	500 per day
4. Reading books	5 to 10 per page
5. Aiding houseparents in various household tasks	20 to 1000 per task
6. Doing dishes	500 to 1000 per meal
7. Being well dressed for an evening meal	100 to 500 per meal
8. Performing homework	500 per day
9. Obtaining desirable grades on school report cards	500 to 1000 per grade
10. Turning out lights when not in use	25 per light

Behaviors that lost points	Points
1. Failing grades on the report card	500 to 1000 per grade
2. Speaking aggressively	20 to 50 per response
3. Forgetting to wash hands before meals	100 to 300 per meal
4. Arguing	300 per response
5. Disobeying	100 to 1000 per response
6. Being late	10 per minute
7. Displaying poor manners	50 to 100 per response
8. Engaging in poor posture	50 to 100 per response
9. Using poor grammar	20 to 50 per response
10. Stealing, lying, or cheating	10,000 per response

Source: E. L. Phillips, "Achievement Place: Token Reinforcement Procedures in a Home-Style Rehabilitation Setting for 'Pre-Delinquent' Boys," *Journal of Applied Behavior Analysis,* 1, 1968, Table 1, p. 214.

deviant. The trend in the mental health care system of employing nonprofessionals or paraprofessionals is especially meaningful here. Although part of the rationale for sharing the therapeutic task has been a manpower shortage, many troubled individuals would indeed rather relate to someone with a similar background. This knowledge is often applied by hiring persons who have had and have overcome the problem for which they will be treating others. A program will utilize ex-alcoholics to counsel alcoholics, another ex-addicts to rehabilitate addicts, and a third ex-convicts to work with juvenile delinquents. Some of these programs were begun in collaboration with mental health agencies; others had entirely separate beginnings. Notice as we describe these community-based programs that all exert control over the individual's deviant behavior while pursuing rehabilitation goals. For them to succeed, however, control must be in the hands of people the clients view as peers.

SELF-HELP GROUPS

Closed membership groups, or societies, have been part of the United States since its beginnings and are strongly protected by the First Amendment to the Constitution. Yet in the twentieth century we have seen a singular addition to the panoply of political, religious, and social organizations — the self-help groups. These generally gather individuals who, for one reason or another, have been stigmatized and placed outside the mainstream of society (for compulsive gambling, alcoholism, mental illness, or other aberrations). Such groups almost always have voluntary membership policies, although new members are referred to a few by the courts and social service agencies. Unlike other groups that may actually stigmatize the person who joins (the Ku Klux Klan or the American Communist Party), self-help groups attempt to decrease the stigma of their mem-

bers in one of two ways: (1) by helping them conform to the norms of the dominant society; or (2) by trying to change the norms to accept the members' behavior (Sagarin 1969).To meet these aims, most self-help groups guarantee anonymity for their members (Alcoholics Anonymous, Gamblers Anonymous, Narcotics Anonymous), but also, when they gain visibility, often use their collective power to reduce social disapproval. The groups whose priority is adapting members to society often take the view that deviant persons are worthwhile but their deviance (alcohol, drugs) is immoral. Many function as religious or quasi-religious organizations, strictly emphasizing nondeviance from the group norms; in fact, the more socially deviant the group membership is, the greater the tendency for rigid adherence to nondeviance. The sharing of experiences in formats resembling group therapy is the way many of these groups organize themselves.

The very emphasis on anonymity that helps self-help groups recruit socially deviant people makes it very difficult to do systematic research on their therapeutic effects. Many such groups in fact resent outside evaluation and scrutiny, making unbiased and thorough studies even more unlikely. In a general evaluation, however, many self-help groups seem to have been remarkably successful in accomplishing both goals: helping individual members gain control over deviant behavior and decreasing the social stigma of such deviancy.

Alcoholics Anonymous (AA) was the first and is still the largest and most successful self-help group of its kind (Robinson 1979). The prototype for many problem-oriented programs, it attempts to help those who are the largest socially deviant group in society. For these reasons we shall concentrate on this self-help group. Many other groups, however, have been founded on similar principles for others who are socially deviant or different, including Gamblers Anonymous, Parents Anonymous (for child abusers), Ex-Mental Patients Anonymous, Neurotics Anonymous, Schizophrenics Anonymous, Synanon (for drug abusers), Self-Development Group (for ex-convicts) and TOPS (Take Off Pounds Sensibly).

Alcoholics Anonymous is the most widely known treatment for alcoholism. Founded and run by alcoholics themselves, it now has approximately 30,000 groups with more than one million members in the United States and more than seventy other countries (Leach 1973). Fully one-third of the members are women, and although its membership is largely middle- to upper-middle class, all social classes and most occupations are represented.

Alcoholics Anonymous began in the 1930s with two alcoholics who believed that (1) alcoholism is a disease, (2) once an alcoholic, always an alcoholic, and (3) abstinence requires help from others. The helping involves public self-examination, acknowledging defects of character, and restitution for harm done. In addition, the group has a strong religious orientation which is reflected in the "Twelve Suggested Steps of Alcoholics Anonymous" (see Table 19.2).

The only requirement for membership in AA is a desire to stop drinking. Members are available to one another around the clock for support and counseling. During meetings, generally at least once a week, members discuss their drinking problem and the difficulties alcoholism has created in their lives. This is a typical recitation:

Larry was a thin man, rather muscular, and had a wistful, almost smiling expression when he appeared before the group. Then his face became somber as he began:

My name is Larry and I am an alcoholic. I have been an alcoholic for as long as I can remember. I guess I took my first drink when I was twelve, when I was playing with some older

Table 19.2. Twelve suggested steps of Alcoholics Anonymous

1. We admitted we were powerless over alcohol — that our lives had become unmanageable.
2. Came to believe that a power greater than ourselves could restore us to sanity.
3. Made a decision to turn our will and our lives over to the care of God *as we understood Him.*
4. Made a searching and fearless moral inventory of ourselves.
5. Admitted to God, to ourselves, and to another human being the exact nature of our wrongs.
6. Were entirely ready to have God remove all these defects of character.
7. Humbly asked Him to remove our shortcomings.
8. Made a list of all persons we had harmed, and became willing to make amends to them all.
9. Made direct amends to such people wherever possible, except when to do so would injure them or others.
10. Continued to take personal inventory and, when we were wrong, promptly admitted it.
11. Sought through prayer and meditation to improve our conscious contact with God *as we understand Him,* praying only for knowledge of His will for us and the power to carry that out.
12. Having had a spiritual awakening as the result of these steps, we tried to carry this message to alcoholics and to practice these principles in all our affairs.

Source: Alcoholics Anonymous, © 1955, 1976 by Alcoholics Anonymous World Services, Inc.

kids and they had some wine. I thought I'd be a wise guy, a big shot, and show them that I could drink too. So I started then, and it seems like I didn't stop for twenty years.

I graduated from wine to whiskey, and when I was in high school and didn't have the money for a bottle, I stole it from my mother. After I'd been drinking, I had to come sneaking into my own house so my mother wouldn't see me and smell my breath.

When I was seventeen I got my driver's license, and a month later I had my first smashup. My girl friend was in the car with me,

Fig. 19.3. Alcoholics, all Navy personnel, meet in an Alcoholics Anonymous session at the Navy's Alcohol Rehabilitation Center in Virginia. Coffee is an important crutch in the treatment program; some men drink up to twenty cups a day.

and before we left the party where we'd spent the evening, she said, Larry, you're stinking and I'm going to drive. I told her I was okay, and besides she didn't even have a license and no girl was going to drive me around. A half-hour later I had that car halfway up a tree — but, thank God, nobody was hurt. We climbed out of the car and she said, Larry, listen, say I was driving. Well, she took the rap for driving without a license, and when I called her the next day she wouldn't talk to me. But that was only the first time — and it wasn't the last — that a girl covered up for me because I couldn't hold my liquor.

So Larry went on, five minutes, ten, fifteen. He was expelled from college and lost one job after another because of the bottle; his first marriage ended in divorce, and he has never seen the child born afterward. By thirty his life was a shambles. He was ready to try anything: doctors, hospitals, psychiatrists, clergymen — anything if only he could control his drinking. He often thought of suicide as the only way out.

Then, one day, the girl he wanted to marry told him about Alcoholics Anonymous:

> So I figured they were a bunch of nuts. How were they going to help me if doctors couldn't? But she begged me to go. She said that if I'd give this a try and it worked, we could get married. So I figured I had nothing to lose.
>
> The first thing I learned in AA was that I was an alcoholic, and that an alcoholic can't control his liquor. He has to give it up. That was four years ago, and from the day I entered this room my life has changed completely. I've been able to hold down a job, and I don't have to worry that if I call in sick everyone will know that it's a hangover. I have a family, I have a car, and I'm on the way to having my health back. I owe all of this to AA, and to this room, and to the people I've met here, and to the support they gave me (Sagarin 1969, pp. 41–42).

Group meetings of AA may be closed (for alcoholics only) or open to the public, friends, and family members. These comments were made by the child of an alcoholic after attending one such public meeting:

The first time I went to an Alcoholics Anonymous meeting with my father, I was appalled. People were getting up and describing their experiences as alcoholics in an embarrassingly direct, and demeaningly confessional, sort of way. I really didn't want to hear all about those awful things that had happened to them and to their families because of their alcoholism. Most of all, I didn't want to think of my father — my gentle, brilliant, soft-spoken father — as one of *those* people. But I knew he was, and I knew that for years, off and on, he drank so heavily he really hadn't been what I had thought him to be at all. I could see the support he got from the others there, as well as the sense of camaraderie that existed within the membership. The fact was he hadn't had a drink for years. And, if the dogma was not of one's choosing and the intolerance for other types of treatments not to one's liking, still — he had not been drinking. I might prefer my religion in church and my personal problems kept personal, but — still and all — my father has not been drinking.

To help families cope with the problems of living with an alcoholic, there are separate AA-affiliated support groups: Al-Anon counsels spouses and other family members, and Ala-Teen counsels the teenage children of alcoholics. Alcoholics Anonymous apparently derives its success from acceptance of the belief that only an alcoholic can help and understand another alcoholic; the continuous support, hope, and help provided by peers; exposure to successfully abstinent alcoholics; substitution of other AA members for former drinking companions; and increased self-esteem from helping other people in like circumstances (Vaillant 1978). Critics of AA say, however, that because of its self-examination and religious quality only

a limited subgroup of alcoholics will be attracted to — or able to tolerate — the approach. It is further argued that AA's insistence on total abstinence and its opposition to adjunct treatments such as tranquilizers, Antabuse, and psychotherapy have jeopardized the complete rehabilitation of many of its members and discouraged others from joining. It is important to know just how successful AA is in accomplishing its aims.

Assessing AA's success, however, poses many problems. First, the membership's anonymity limits accessibility for research, and because it is a volunteer program traditional comparisons between treatment and nontreatment are unfeasible. Second, the membership is self-selecting, which means that applying generalizations about its outcomes to other alcoholic groups who may have different characteristics will be somewhat invalid. Third, the data on outcome we do have are based on self-reporting, with its shortcomings. Hence we do not have evidence showing how a randomly selected group of alcoholics would fare if assigned to AA.

Despite these difficulties, the data available from AA members suggest that AA is a very worthwhile program. In 1968 a survey was made of 11,355 who attend AA meetings in the United States and Canada, representing 4.4 percent of the AA population in North America. It revealed that 41 percent of respondents reported they had not had a drink since their first attendance at AA. Many others had maintained unbroken sobriety after an initial period marred by relapses; for an additional 23 percent this abstinence had come within a year or less after their first meeting, for 18.5 percent, within two to five years, and for the remainder it took more than five years of involvement with AA before they finally stopped drinking (Leach 1973). Harris (1976) reports that of AA members abstinent for a year, 35 percent will maintain unbroken sobriety; for those abstinent one to five years, the figure rises to 79 percent, and for those with more than five years of abstinence, to 91 percent. There is a clear need for evaluative research comparing AA with other programs, examining effects other than strict abstinence, and determining who is likely to do best in a program like AA.

THERAPEUTIC COMMUNITIES

The therapeutic community extends the self-help group philosophy into a total, residential program. Although therapeutic communities (also called halfway houses) have been set up for ex-convicts and delinquent youths with many of the characteristics we will describe below (Goldenberg 1971), we will focus on the primary population the communities serve, drug addicts. At any time, approximately 2 percent of the addict population resides in therapeutic communities (McGlothlin et al. 1972). The first such program was Synanon, founded in California in 1958; other well-known programs include Odyssey House, Phoenix House, and Daytop Village. Like AA, these therapeutic communities require of those applying for admission evidence of strong motivation to change, and almost all applications are voluntary.

Treatment goals vary. Synanon assumes that addicts need to stay indefinitely in its highly structured community, and it has grown financially successful, employing members in related business ventures. Odyssey House, on the other hand, actively works at returning recovered residents to society after prolonged residence.

Therapeutic communities impose heavy demands on their residents. Drugs, naturally, are prohibited. Most facilities maintain an exceedingly structured social system and require that addicts avoid contact with former friends, associates, and family members, at least for the first several months of residence. Most programs

have a hierarchic structure, assigning the most menial and demeaning work to newcomers; after demonstrating individual responsibility they can assume jobs of higher status.

A basic practice in therapeutic communities is using former addicts as staff:

Here is another significant thing in terms of an institution, and in terms of understanding the Synanon thing: About this time . . . about three or four weeks after my arrival, I began to notice that the place was full of me. I saw a million manifestations of me — in everyone. The Contract that had been set up all my life, the "we-they" — my father and me, my psychiatrist and me, the warden and me — you know, this contract was smashed by Synanon. I became aware that the place was run by a hundred mes — different aspects of me. Different aspects of me were all there. So when I hated somebody's behavior, I hated me; when I approved of somebody's behavior, I approved of me. (Yablonsky 1967, p. 281).

In some communities it is assumed that only addicts can help other addicts; in others directors feel that although addict staff members are essential, professionals must also be available to maintain objectivity and to treat underlying psychopathology when necessary. Programs such as Odyssey House, which emphasize returning addicts to "straight" society, are more apt to have professionals for vocational counseling, educational programming, and psychological evaluation and treatment. Educational counseling is focused on finding the best way of using skills the addict has acquired on the street in legitimate employment (Platt and Labate 1976).

An integral part of all therapeutic communities is group therapy sessions, although their formats and frequency vary. At Synanon, the "games" or group sessions take place at least three times a week with about ten members in a group. Generally the atmosphere of the residence is supportive, but the meetings are extremely provocative and confrontive, often openly hostile. Synanon acts on the belief that only by being direct, often brutally honest, and even contemptuous, can the addict's defenses be broken down sufficiently to allow maturing to take place. Addicts are held in disdain and contempt, as in this reaction by Synanon's founder to an addict who asked to be readmitted (quoted in Sagarin 1969): Dederich took one look at him and said, "What is it? Oh, put it on a couch. There's a bare possibility that there may be something human inside all this garbage."

Daytop Village employs varied therapeutic modalities, including variations on the group approach. *Encounter groups* meet three times a week for two hours, are led by a facilitator, and give the resident a chance to express feelings toward other residents. *Probes* are longer sessions (twelve to eighteen hours) during which residents tackle more emotional issues (such as homosexual panic from living too close to many other males and required abstinence from heterosexual intercourse). *Cop-outs* are group meetings that involve the entire living group in solving problems.

The therapeutic community approach certainly has its limitations. The modality appeals to relatively few addicts, and the drop-out rate is high. The drop-out rate is appreciable in all drug treatment modalities; however, clients do tend to drop out sooner after admission in the therapeutic community. In a study of Synanon it was found that more than half (54 percent) of

Fig. 19.4. An encounter group meeting at Daytop Village, a therapeutic community for narcotic addicts.

residents left prematurely, and a study of Phoenix House in New York found that of 2110 admissions, only 79 (3.7 percent) completed the program (Legislative Commission on Expenditure Review: Narcotic Drug Control, 1971). However, substantial benefits and changes occur even with those who leave the communities without completing the program. The addicts who are attracted to and stay in the program tend to be predominantly young, single, middle-class males, reflecting their greater representation within therapeutic community populations.

A recently completed nationwide study assessing effectiveness of drug programs included more than 1400 addicts (Simpson, Savage, and Sells 1978). Drug use was recorded three years after the addict had entered: (1) a therapeutic community; (2) a methadone maintenance program; or (3) intake examination only, no program. The addicts' preprogram social deviance (drugs, crime, nonproductivity) was also recorded, so that each program's effects could be examined separately for low, medium, and high preprogram deviance. In each condition, the greater the original deviance the more likely the addict was to be using drugs after three years. Therapeutic communities and methadone maintenance were about equally effective, but both were superior to having no program at all, especially for addicts who had been heavy users. Like most research evaluating programs, however, this study did not randomly assign addicts to treatment conditions, so that we must regard the results cautiously.

METHADONE MAINTENANCE

Therapeutic communities have a good record for the few addicts who stay in them, but they are not a viable rehabilitation program for most addicts. In an alternative approach, it is assumed that opiate addicts cannot remain off drugs after a withdrawal period and that other medications can be used to avert the desirable consequences of heroin addiction. On heroin, the addict requires a number of injections each day and goes through cycles of euphoria and social withdrawal that prevent normal work and social functioning. Maintenance on the drug *methadone* is currently used to block the effects of heroin while satisfying the craving for an opiate.

Methadone is a synthetic narcotic that is also addictive. Unlike the natural opiate heroin, however, it can be administered orally, is more lasting, does not cloud consciousness, and can partially block the "rush" if the addict takes heroin. Early work by Dole and Nyswander (1965) in New York City revealed that methadone maintenance reduced incarcerations by 98 percent and criminal activities by 94 percent for one group of heroin addicts. Because they no longer had to purchase expensive drugs on the street, much of their secondary crime undertaken to obtain the needed money disappeared. Also freed of this pressure and the stupefying effects of heroin, these patients showed renewed interest in life and after years of unproductivity suddenly began to hold jobs and go to school.

The incredible success of the Dole-Nyswander program led to establishment of methadone maintenance clinics all over the United States. As with so many social programs, the later results have not approached the early ones. Keeping addicts in these programs proved difficult. Though figures vary widely, however, a minimum of 48 percent of addicts do remain in these programs for at least one year, and in a number of programs as many as 70 percent stay in.

Because methadone maintenance substitutes one form of drug dependence for another, the early programs were opened only to long-term addicts who had failed in other rehabilitation programs. As heroin addiction increased among teenagers and young adults of our cities during the 1960s, programs were opened to younger and younger addicts whose educational success or work experience was limited. Reducing juvenile crime and effecting social rehabilitation have proved more difficult because these youths lacked skills. It is now recognized that methadone programs must be tied closely to job training, educational programs, and other supportive services to deal with the deficits that preceded addiction (Bourne 1975). Williams and Johnston (1972) identified seven factors associated with successfully remaining in a methadone program:

1. Age — older patients stay longer in treatment.
2. Addiction history — the longer a patient has been addicted, the longer he stays in treatment.
3. Age at which heroin use started — patients who began heroin use at a later age stay longer in treatment.
4. Previous treatment — the more treatment attempts a patient has made, the better are his results in the present sequence.
5. Criminal history — the higher the percentage of time spent in jail during addiction, the better are treatment results.
6. Pattern of drug use — the less involvement with drugs other than opiates, the better the treatment results.
7. Marital status — married patients, especially those with dependent children, stay longer in treatment (p. 441).

Several unfortunate consequences of using methadone as a treatment for heroin addiction have appeared since its initial clinical trials (Platt and Labate 1976): diversion of methadone to the black market; inadvertent creation of methadone addiction in some adolescent drug abusers; an increasing number of deaths from overdoses of methadone; and many methadone addicts who have never been in a meth-

adone program. One social and philosophical objection arises from the minority community. Senay (1972) points out that many people living in the ghettos and barrios regard methadone as "white, establishment medicine" designed to provide a new form of social control over minority groups and relieving society of responsibility for addressing the real problems of poverty. They feel methadone is a palliative at best and oppression at worst. Another criticism of methadone maintenance is that occasionally addicts serving time in jail are required to accept it as a condition for parole; critics argue that this is, in effect, coercive and that social control is taking precedence over civil liberties. Some individuals both in and out of the mental health professions raise yet another important question about values. They feel that replacing heroin addiction with methadone addiction is no more than an illusion, that it remains a treatment of symptoms, not underlying problems.

Recent efforts have concentrated on discovering biological agents that produce similar results but are not themselves addictive. Research has been done on compounds known as narcotic "antagonists" such as cyclazocine and naltrexone. These drugs block the euphoric and physiological effects of opiates, are not themselves addicting, and have no potential for abuse and no black-market value. If a person who has gone through withdrawal from heroin (or methadone) takes a narcotic antagonist, he will be protected against readdiction. Even if he again uses heroin, he will experience no euphoria and develop no opiate dependence. Clinical trials have not been encouraging, though (Resnick, Washton, and Schuyten-Resnick 1979), because the dropout rate of patients from these programs is extremely high, particularly during the latter stages of withdrawal from heroin (detoxification phase). Those who stayed in the program did remain drug-free. Recent research revealing that the brain manufactures morphine-like substances, called endorphins, which suppress pain naturally, has opened a whole new direction for studying the biochemistry of drug dependence. This new research may turn up better ways of keeping drug-dependent people off drugs.

Although biological blocking agents are useful, both methadone maintenance and narcotic antagonist trials are most helpful if accompanied by psychological treatment. "Narcotic antagonists change neither the intrapsychic, environmental or lifestyle problems of which opiate use is symptomatic. Unless these problems are ameliorated, the individual will be predisposed to terminate treatment and become readdicted. . . . The medication, in itself, is not the whole treatment" (Resnick et al. 1979).

Help for Victims

It would have been easier if there had been someone to tell me what was going on and to prepare me for the things that happened after — with my family, my friends, the police, the courts. Someone to help sort it out, to say: "You're not the only one." I felt so terribly alone. . . . More than anything else, I just needed to understand what was happening (Sister of a murder victim — Bard and Sangrey 1979, p. xi).

There are many more victims than criminals. Indeed, the likelihood of any one of us becoming a victim of crime this year is better than one in twenty. Thus far we, like the helping professions, have concentrated on ways to help socially deviant individuals. Attention by society to the victims of social deviance is relatively recent and still quite limited. As of October, 1977, only twenty states had some kind of victim compensation law[1] to help victims of crimes and, in some places, survivors meet medical expenses, living expenses if earnings are lost because of injury, or burial costs. Some provide funds for vocational rehabilitation or psycho-

logical counseling, if the victim can show financial need (Bard and Sangrey 1979).

Unfortunately, obtaining these and other benefits to which one is entitled (such as Workman's Compensation) can mean an exceedingly difficult struggle with the bureaucracy at a time when the victim is most debilitated. In part the poor treatment of victims by service-agency personnel may reflect a deeply rooted sociocultural tendency to blame victims of crime for their misfortune. These remarks by the close friend of a woman who had been raped illustrate how we stigmatize victims:

I remember feeling badly for a long time that I would look at her and I would think, you know, that's the woman I know who was raped . . . and I was really feeling bad about this preying on my mind and I couldn't, you know, forget it. I felt it was a real injustice to her that she had to carry this burden. . . . There is still that certain aura of being, ah, I think of it as tarnished. You're not quite whole and pure anymore and people remember that. And it's so unjust. . . . But I found those feelings in myself (Bard and Sangrey 1979, p. 77).

The victim herself may feel embarrassed, shameful, and guilty, sensing that she is in some way a failure and should have been able to prevent the incident.

Support and Counseling

Most victims of crime do not need professional counseling but could benefit greatly from another person's support, from a good listener who will let the victim regain some sense of autonomy and control by expressing herself. Someone supportive who is not judgmental, argumentative, or questioning can make a great deal of difference in the victim's recovery.

In severe trauma, short-term crisis counsel-

[1] Alaska, California, Delaware, Florida, Hawaii, Illinois, Kentucky, Maryland, Massachusetts, Michigan, Minnesota, New Jersey, New York, North Dakota, Ohio, Pennsylvania, Tennessee, Virginia, Washington, and Wisconsin.

ing may also be helpful. Burgess and Holmstrom (1974) established a crisis-counseling program for rape trauma victims at Boston City Hospital, to help women through the two phases of reaction they identified. The acute phase, immediately after the rape, is characterized by a great deal of disorganization in the woman's lifestyle, with insecurity, fears, and loneliness, and heightened accessibility to other's influence in making decisions. After several weeks, the long-term reorganization phase is under way, with many psychological

Fig. 19.5. A page from a public awareness pamphlet, "What Every Woman Should Know About Rape," distributed by the University of California Police Department.

Your
IMMEDIATE
CONCERNS
will probably be

--EMOTIONAL

You will have to cope with **STRONG NEGATIVE FEELINGS** --realize that they're _normal_ reactions to being raped.

AT FIRST--
- CONFUSION
  (about what happened, what to do)
- SHAME
  (feeling abused, degraded)
- FEAR
  (of further violence from the rapist)

THEN--
- ANGER
  (at world in general)
- HELPLESSNESS
  ("my life's out of control")
- GUILT
  ("was it my fault?")
- DIRTINESS
  (feeling damaged)

- WORTHLESSNESS
  (loss of self-respect)
- ISOLATION
  (feeling "different")
- DISTRUST
  (of everyone)
- FEAR
  (of another rape)

TALKING TO A CLOSE FRIEND
should, in time, help you overcome these feelings.
BUT--
IF TROUBLE PERSISTS IN...
-- expressing affection
-- relating sexually
-- relating to your family, etc.

GET HELP!
Your hospital or Rape Crisis Center can refer you to a counselor or a discussion group.

DON'T HIDE.. the fact that you've been raped. Close friends and relatives whom you can trust to support you should be first to know.

problems, depending upon her prior personality, the characteristics of the rape itself, and the amount of support she receives. Many hospitals and police departments are becoming sophisticated, learning not only how to effectively examine for medical and legal evidence but also how to treat the victim with compassion and follow their examinations with supportive counseling.

Protection from Further Harm

For some victims of violent crime, the most immediate need is protection from further harm. Especially in family violence, the beaten wife or abused child is very likely to be harmed again if she remains in the home. Protective children's services intervene to place abused children in foster care until the home is deemed safe to return to. Courts often mandate professional help for abusive parents, though traditional individual and group counseling have not been very successful with families that often have multiple problems and are resistant.

A nationwide movement to establish shelters for battered wives is being fueled by women's rights organizations and is receiving belated support from some church and social-service agencies (Davidson 1978). In Chapter 17 we described the helpless feelings of most battered wives and their inability to escape or to get support and protection from social agencies. A shelter typically is a home staffed by nonprofessionals providing temporary sanctuary for a few women and sometimes their young children. Terry Davidson (1978), a journalist and formerly abused child herself, has written of this movement, listing more than fifty shelters in the United States. Their purposes are reflected in names such as *Women's Advocates House* (the pioneer shelter, in St. Paul, Minnesota) and *Women's Resource and Survival Center* (the first federally funded relief and emergency assistance center, in Keyport, N.J.). Variations have been tried. *Women's Survival Space* in Brooklyn has a capacity of thirty-six in a converted hospital, *Rosie's* in Boston is more typi-

Fig. 19.6. Marilyn and her daughter are tearful as they recount the abuse that brought them to this family shelter; the owner attempts to cheer up the girl.

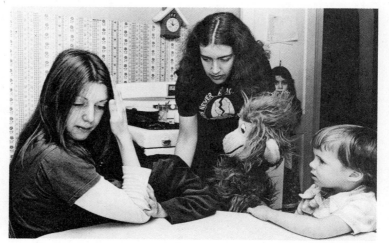

When Professional Counseling is Needed

The decision to see a professional counselor is a very personal one, and it can be made only by the person who needs the help. Loved ones who insist that a reluctant victim seek professional help do both the counselor and the victim a disservice. Victims have a right to resist such intrusion, and pressure will often simply harden their resistance. Sometimes a friend or family member feels deeply troubled by the victim's behavior. When this happens, the loved one may benefit from counseling; he or she should probably seek a professional for help in sorting the feelings out.

Francine Jacobson has lived in San Francisco for more than fifty years. She married, raised a family, and still keeps house in the same little apartment. Her husband Sam owns the drugstore across the street. Four years ago Sam was robbed and pistol-whipped in his store. His wife came to the living-room window and saw the ambulance and the police cars. She ran across the street just as they were putting Sam into the ambulance.

The doctor put twenty-three stitches in Sam's head and kept him in the hospital for a week. One of his eyes had been injured and they wanted to be sure his sight was intact. He recovered from his physical injuries, spent another week at home, and then had the stitches out and went back to work. Francine seemed to be all right. She visited him every day in the hospital and took care of him while he convalesced at home.

But when Sam came home for dinner after his first day back at work, he noticed that his wife was acting strangely. She didn't eat very much, and she seemed very sad and uncommunicative. He tried to talk to her, but she just brushed him off. As the days went on, she seemed to get worse. She was sleepless and irritable most of the time. By the third week, Sam was really concerned. The changes in his wife were more than he could understand or deal with.

Finally one day a doctor friend called the store to order a prescription, and Sam talked with him about Francine. The doctor recognized the symptoms of depression and when Sam told him about the crime, he explained that Francine was probably suffering from a delayed reaction that surfaced when Sam went back to work. So long as Sam was in the hospital or at home, she knew he was safe, but when he went back to the store he was in danger again. This time he might be killed, leaving her alone. The depth of her depression indicated to the doctor that she would benefit from professional counseling. He suggested that Sam go to see Dr. Connors, a woman psychologist whom he recommended, about the best way to approach Francine. He offered to call Dr. Connors and tell her that Sam would be getting in touch with her.

The next day Sam made an appointment, and two days later he went in to talk with the counselor. She agreed with her colleague that Francine needed help, but she said that the idea would have to be presented to her with care. Dr. Connors also asked Sam how *he* was feeling, and he was able to admit that he hadn't been doing so well either. He was really worried about his wife, but he also felt angry because he had to deal with her problems while he was still struggling with his fear of strange customers and other residual reactions from the crime.

Dr. Connors suggested that both Sam and his wife could benefit from counseling. She advised him to go home and tell his wife that he had decided to work with a psychologist because he had unresolved feelings about the assault. She also recommended that he tell his wife that the psychologist thought Francine might want to come to the counseling sessions.

The fact that Sam was able to acknowledge his own problems made it easier for Francine to admit to hers when he talked with her about his visit to Dr. Connors. They went together to the next session, and they both began to talk about the feelings that had been bottled up. Francine's depression eased, and her husband became less angry and also less fearful. The support of their doctor friend who made the referral and the tact with which Dr. Connors was able to include Francine in the counseling process were both crucial in the final resolution of this couple's crisis (Bard and Sangrey 1979, pp. 145–147).

cal with ten beds, and the *York Street Center* in Denver is not a building but a service that arranges crisis housing in volunteer homes for up to two weeks. Although the main aim is protection, some facilities such as the *Salvation Army Emergency Lodge* in Chicago offer counseling, advocacy, and even child services.

These facilities are not without problems, among them continuing financial insecurity, constant danger from retaliatory husbands, stresses caused by many people living in close quarters, and the women's ambivalence about what to do next. Davidson (1978) spent a week in a shelter for abused women and reflects on the difficult role of a staff person in such a setting:

> I was very eager to meet the women who ran the house. Although they had no training as social workers, psychologists, or counselors, they had to perform the functions of all these professionals. They had to know all possible resources for local aid: legal problems of separation and divorce, the ins and outs of applying for welfare, job-training programs, back-to-school programs, self-defense and spiritual help. Each had to be a veritable encyclopedia of ways a battered woman might better her life. These women had an unquenchable belief in nondirectiveness: their mission was to help the woman decide what she wanted to do with her life. They would help her gain control of her life. They would support, assist and champion her freely made choices. They would not interfere with her decisions or impose their own values on her (p. 158).

Prevention

In considering prevention of social deviance we will simply raise some illustrative directions, for thorough consideration of this topic would open a Pandora's box. If you look again at our chapters on crime, substance abuse, and sex-ual deviance, you will quickly see a multitude of potential causes and therefore of potential areas for prevention.

The *criminal justice system* itself offers some strategies for prevention, such as diversion, decriminalization, deterrence, or expanded duties for law enforcement officers. Diversion programs for juvenile first offenders assigning them to counseling rather than the criminal justice system certainly prevent the ill effects of being labeled delinquent and may reduce the likelihood of future delinquency. Decriminalization of victimless crimes, such as alcoholism and prostitution, is often urged as a way of freeing police to deal with more serious crime. As a deterrent to these serious crimes, many argue for stronger criminal penalties and more police on the streets. Also, to prevent further instances of family violence, and to reduce injury to police officers, some cities have experimented with training select police in counseling techniques so as to better handle the frequent family disturbance calls (Bard 1970).

The *mental health and educational systems* have stressed public education as a deterrent. Courses in sex education and drug education have proliferated in elementary and high schools, and courses on child development and better parenting are spreading in high schools and community agencies. The drug-education programs are meant to alert children to the dangers of drugs through films, readings, discussions, and sometimes talks by ex-addicts about their experience. Such programs must be carefully conducted, however, because some people fear they may backfire and glamorize the drug experience. The necessary evaluations of these public education programs as a deterrent have not been done.

One unique attempt at preventive education for delinquents is the prison-exposure program, run by convicts. The Academy Award-winning documentary *Scared Straight* graphically depicts one such program at Rahway State Prison in New Jersey. A group of violent offenders, most of them sentenced for life, meet in a locked prison room with seventeen delinquent youths, all with multiple-arrest records. The four-hour confrontation includes a hard-hitting lecture about prison life, emphasizing sex and violence in prison. The aim, quite openly, is to scare the youths into going straight. Despite their initial nonchalance, sixteen of the youths were arrest-free six months after their day in prison. There is some question, however, if initial gains are lasting; a closer study of such programs is certainly needed.

Ultimately, the *larger society* must address the conditions that breed social deviance if any great change is to occur. Many efforts to improve the quality of life, especially in poverty-ridden areas, will simultaneously be designed to reduce social deviance. Also, as we have seen, cultural attitudes toward relationships between the sexes and toward violence contribute in ways that are not directly measurable but are nonetheless significant. Among the possible preventions at this level are tightening gun control or reducing aggressive models on television. We can readily see, though, that a discussion of prevention soon takes us far beyond our scope in this book.

Summary

1. Socially deviant people usually come in contact with the criminal justice system before meeting mental health professionals. A fundamental issue in social deviance is which goal should take priority: the mental health system's goal of rehabilitation or the criminal justice system's goal of controlling deviant behavior.

2. The criminal justice system is meant to prevent and control deviant behavior in two ways: (1) by its existence, prison deters most citizens from breaking the law; and (2) by removing the convicted offender from society it tries to eliminate the possibility of deviant behavior during the period of sentence, to deter future deviant behavior, and to provide an opportunity for rehabilitation. Unfortunately, incarceration has proved ineffective both in deterring deviance and in rehabilitating the deviant.

3. Attempts to isolate those who might benefit from psychological intervention have resulted in redefinition of some acts as psychological problems and early intervention to prevent further deviant activity.

4. Intervention methods for socially deviant individuals include psychotherapy and behavior therapy. Psychotherapy is generally unsuccessful with social deviance because: (1) these people are less distressed about their behavior than others are; (2) therapy is usually involuntary; (3) the talking-through is alien to their experience; and (4) they lack alternative, adaptive behaviors. Aversion therapy, a form of behavior therapy, has been successful in decreasing deviant responses by pairing stimuli for deviant behaviors with an unpleasant event, such as electric shock or nausea. A variation is covert sensitization, in which the therapist presents noxious mental images to create aversion. Although aversion therapies may decrease deviant responses to stimuli, they do not provide adaptive behaviors for effective functioning.

5. Techniques for teaching socially deviant individuals adaptive skills include: (1) training in restraint and assertiveness; (2) vocational, marriage, and social counseling; and (3) family therapy.

6. Two alternatives to the traditional correctional system are: (1) small, community-based halfway houses, and (2) using behavior modification in prisons.

7. Community rehabilitation programs include: self-help groups, such as Alcoholics Anonymous, based on the sharing of common experiences and peer support for change; and therapeutic communities, such as Synanon, where former offenders help voluntary residents acquire the adaptive skills they need for acceptable social functioning.

8. Methadone maintenance substitutes the synthetic opiate methadone for heroin. This drug allows an individual to function without the stupefying effects of heroin and without needing to commit crimes to support the habit. Methadone alone, however, does not deal with the problems that led to addiction.

9. Some states have programs for helping the victims of social deviance. They include: (1) compensation of victims by financial aid; (2) support and counseling by hospitals and police departments; and (3) protection, in the form of foster care for abused or neglected children and shelters for battered wives.

10. Preventing social deviance requires: (1) changes in the criminal justice system to counsel juveniles after the first offense instead of labeling them delinquent and to decriminalize victimless crimes, provide stronger criminal penalties, and educate police in counseling for family disturbances; (2) better public education programs about substance abuse, delinquency, parenting, and child development; and (3) efforts in society to improve the quality of life and alter cultural attitudes toward violence.

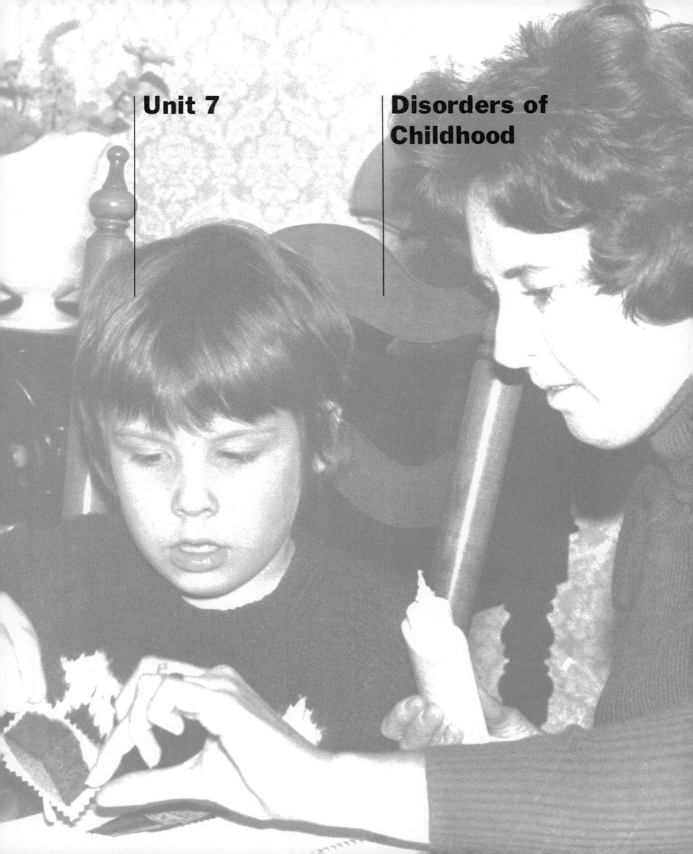

Unit 7

Disorders of Childhood

In this unit we will examine psychological problems of childhood. These have received less attention by mental health professionals than adult psychopathology, and most abnormal psychology texts provide little coverage of childhood disorders. Today, however, many professionals are urging a vast increase in mental health research and intervention efforts with children. Childhood problems are often precursors of adult ones, and therefore early attention to them can be preventive. Moreover, advocates for child rights and child welfare remind us that children deserve psychological help as much as adults do. In 1970 the Joint Commission on Mental Health in Children issued this challenge to American society:

This nation, richest of all world powers, has no unified national commitment to its children and youth. The claim that we are a child-centered society, that we look to our young as tomorrow's leaders, is a myth. Our words are made meaningless by our actions — by our lack of national, community, and personal investment in maintaining the healthy development of our young, by our tendency to rely on the proliferation of simple, one-factor, short-term, and inexpensive remedies and services. As a tragic consequence, we have in our midst millions of ill-fed, ill-housed, ill-educated, and discontented youngsters and almost 10,000,000 under age 25 who are in need of help from mental health workers (pp. 1–2).

Chapter 20 focuses on mental retardation. Most of the preschool children whom mental health professionals see are referred because of delays in development, and many children continue to lag behind their peers during the school years. The consequences of this problem for the child and the family are enormous. In this chapter we will explore the many causes of retarded functioning, from genes and the early physical environment to influences within the family and subculture. We will also consider our society's current efforts to reduce the problem and to live with it.

In Chapter 21 we will examine other childhood behavior disorders. Although most of the disorders discussed in this book show up in children as well as adults, some problems are unique to the developmental years. Developmental disorders include: bedwetting; childhood fears, such as school phobia; the conduct and learning problems of "hyperactivity"; and the severely disabling and extraordinary problem of infantile autism. We will see that theories about the origins of these problems are highly controversial and that not enough is known about their life course.

In Chapter 22 we will survey interventions for childhood psychological problems. In addition to discussing the traditional approach of play therapy, we will look at newer family and behavior therapies. One trend is toward involving persons in the child's natural environment, such as parents and teachers, in the treatment program. Another, more controversial trend is toward early intervention. It seems wise to seek early signs of disturbance in children and begin remedial programs as soon as possible, but in truth, some problems diminish as the child matures so that early treatment may not be worth risking the negative consequences of giving the child a mental health label. Further research is necessary to establish the likelihood of changes in child behavior disorders with and without intervention.

Chapter 20

Mental Retardation

History

Diagnosis and Classification
IQ as a Measure of Retardation
Adaptive Behavior
Classification

Experience of the Family

Causes of Retardation
Genetic Causes
Physical and Environmental Causes
Psychosocial Causes

Characteristics of Retarded Persons
Learning
Personality and Interpersonal Experiences

Growing Up
Education
Social Acceptance
Adulthood

Summary

A summer day at a camp for retarded children:

"Hey, Debbie, will you help watch the little kids while I wash them up for lunch?"

"Yeah, yeah. I'll blow bubbles with Keith. He likes that."

Deb's torn blue sneakers carry her in a flash from "that damn classroom" across the camp to Keith's bunkhouse. She likes to help — especially to care for the little kids. Her helping is a surprising legacy from a home life that has given little else positive to model.

As Debbie engages Keith in blowing bubbles, she seems to momentarily put aside the rough-talking, hard-edged style she has learned so well. Growing up in rural poverty, with eight people living in several rooms and a hard-drinking and abusive father: all have instilled in her a wariness and explosiveness.

Deb's glad to be out of the classroom. "I ain't goin' tomorrow. You'll see. Just try to make me." Although her reading is now at mid-first grade level, it is always a struggle. Deb's intellectual deficiencies, her limited constructive learning at home, and her aggressive, defiant speech and behavior have not been helped by a poor rural school system. This pretty nine-year-old has been quickly ushered in and out of several schools until the alternatives have been exhausted.

Keith watches Deb's bubble blowing in silence.

Almost five, he has no speech, seems to understand very little, cannot begin to dress himself, and has just learned to eat with a spoon. It's certainly to Debbie's credit that Keith will sit and look at the bubbles, a brief interlude in his usual frantic running in seemingly aimless patterns or crying uncontrollably for no apparent reason. Keith's teachers find it very difficult to hold his attention. They are trying to teach him to respond to very simple instructions, such as "look at me" and "come sit down."

Keith's mom is trying to carry out the teachers' suggestions at home, despite her profound sadness. She has many questions about her little boy's development. The doctors say it's brain damage, but the causes are unknown. No one seems too sure what Keith will be able to learn.

Debbie and Keith are mentally retarded. Yet they are very different children. Debbie's limitations are really noticeable only in a classroom, but Keith's more severe disabilities are evident in all areas of functioning. For both of them, however, "growing up" will be a special challenge. Our complex world was not built with them in mind. They bring to it more limited resources than their nondisabled peers, and they are likely to receive from it misunderstanding and mistreatment. To understand the problems facing Debbie and Keith, we must come to understand the major social problem of mental retardation from all sides — biological and psychosocial causes to philosophical and political contexts.

History

It has been said that social services reflect not so much the knowledge of the times as their spirit (Raush and Raush 1968). Care and education for retarded persons is a recent phenomenon. In ancient Greece and Rome those who were handicapped or deformed were objects of scorn and persecution. Although Christianity brought some pity for retarded individuals, superstition lingered for centuries. Both Luther and Calvin denounced retarded persons as "filled with Satan" (Rosen et al. 1976). In modern times those who are retarded have been looked on as irreversibly sick, as subhuman organisms who lack many of the needs, aspirations, and sensitivities of other human beings, or as menaces to society (Wolfensberger 1969).

Each view has led to a different type of societal response. Retarded children allegedly were killed in pre-Christian times, were enlisted as fools and jesters in medieval times, and later were suffered to wander unmolested but uncared for. Early in the nineteenth century, Jean Itard's attempts to teach a severely retarded child (the wild boy of Aveyron) captured the imagination of a small group of humanitarians. During a period of optimism midway through the nineteenth century, pioneers like Edouard Seguin and Samuel Gridley Howe believed that with care and education retarded persons could show dramatic improvement. The "state schools" that followed, however, did not fulfill the promise, and by the turn of the twentieth century, arguments for eliminating retardation by prohibiting retarded people to marry, by sterilization, by segregation in isolated institutions, and by restricted immigration (Sarason and Doris 1969) had gained momentum. Although this so-called *eugenics movement* fizzled by the 1930s, Adolf Hitler advanced the same "survival of the fittest" rationale in 1933 to justify Nazi extermination of 100,000 "incurables and mental defectives" in Germany.

In the past twenty years interest has awakened and consideration has grown for retarded persons as developing individuals who have a right to society's acceptance and support. These changes in the United States followed minorities' rights movements and were spurred by President John Kennedy's personal commitment, by legislative advances, and by an enormous increase in federal funding. The 1960s saw an emphasis on services: institutional reform, community-based living alternatives, expanded special education, and early intervention (one example: Head Start). Biomedical advances in early screening and prevention are especially noteworthy. With the 1970s came greater emphasis on legal and ethical matters, as legislatures and courts began delineating the basic rights of retarded citizens.

Diagnosis and Classification

The incidence of mental retardation in the United States is estimated at about 3 percent; 6.5 million persons will have been classified as retarded at some time in their lives. A child who at some point will be diagnosed as retarded is born every three minutes.

But it is not so easy to know precisely how large the problem is, and efforts to find out are hampered, as we will see, by a number of factors. Definitions have differed so over the years and in various localities that no full census has been attempted. Children like Keith, severely delayed in all areas, would be considered retarded by any definition. Yet whether children like Debbie are labeled "retarded" depends on the criteria employed.

The most recent definition advanced by the American Association on Mental Deficiency (AAMD) states:

Mental retardation refers to significantly subaverage general intellectual functioning existing concurrently with deficits in adaptive behavior, and manifested during the developmental period (Grossman 1973, p. 5).

This definition has three main components.

"Significantly subaverage general intellectual functioning" statistically includes persons whose scores on intelligence tests are in approximately the lowest 3 percent. "Deficits in adaptive behavior" means that a low IQ score alone is not sufficient to label a child mentally retarded. The child must also show deficits in adaptation to the environment. Finally, the "developmental period" includes the first eighteen years, excluding retarded functioning that appears as an adjunct to other problems in adulthood.

For children like Keith, whose impairment is organic, retardation is diagnosable at birth or during the preschool years, from indicators of a specific syndrome known to be associated with retardation (such as Down's syndrome) or from markedly delayed development in all spheres, or both of these. Such children are perhaps 15 to 25 percent of the diagnosed retarded children. The majority of children diagnosed as retarded are, like Debbie, not likely to come to professional attention until they enter school. These children are less noticeably retarded and do not have obvious brain damage; their retardation combines inherited intellectual capacity and early experiences.

For less retarded children, diagnostic criteria are particularly important. The past tendency to base a diagnosis almost exclusively on IQ test performance has diminished in recent years, and the current AAMD definition responds somewhat to the prevailing disenchantment with IQ tests by focusing jointly on intellectual functioning and adaptive behavior in assessing retardation. Let's consider each of these criteria.

IQ as a Measure of Retardation

Over the years little agreement has been achieved on a definition of intelligence. We can find many ways in which a child may be said to be acting intelligently. He might learn rapidly, or demonstrate much knowledge that he has acquired, or cope well with new situations. A number of "intelligence" tests have been devised to assess one or several of these. The IQ tests most widely used are the Stanford-Binet and the Wechsler Scales, which are described in Chapter 3. They are scored so that the average child will have an IQ of 100. The distribution of intelligence test scores is shown in Figure 20.1. Despite the widespread use of IQ tests, they have been greatly criticized. Some objections pertain to the tests themselves and others to the ways in which they are used.

A major criticism of IQ tests is that their content is least appropriate for the children most affected by them. They have not been well standardized on children with IQs of less than 70. Also, as most tests were developed, the items chosen were mostly related to the experience of white, middle-class, Western populations. On the average, nonwhite children score a few points lower on IQ tests than their white peers, although the two distributions overlap greatly. Because a higher proportion of nonwhite children are classified as mentally retarded by these tests, there has been much controversy about whether such differences are attributable to genetic differences or to environmental ones (Jensen 1969; Bloom 1964). Clearly, however, until completely culture-free tests are developed and until nonwhite and white children have the same developmental opportunities, the test scores remain open to contradictory interpretations.

Furthermore, IQ scores vary with many characteristics of the child and the testing situation. Children with behavior disorders and children with an impairment in vision, hearing, motor coordination, or speech are already at a disadvantage and may well appear less intellectually capable on standardized tests than they actually are. Also, a child may be uncom-

fortable in the testing situation, distrustful of the examiner, preoccupied with something else, or trying to appear "bright" or "dull." Braginsky and Braginsky (1971) conducted a study of "impression management" among institutionalized, retarded adolescents. Children who were told that high scorers would enter a new *un*desirable program scored lower on retesting. Conversely, those who were told that low scorers would enter the program scored higher on retesting. Within limits, these children adapted their test-taking behavior to manage a "brighter" or "duller" impression, depending upon what they thought would pay off for them. The possible influences on test scores are endless. The thoughtful examiner must be careful to select a test that will be least affected by other handicaps the child might have, try to put the child at ease, and consider the characteristics of the individual child and situational factors in interpreting results of the test.

Some critics argue too that IQ scores have limited predictive power. For school-age children and adults, test-retest reliability is reasonably good (see Chapter 3). Unless there are marked changes in life circumstances or testing conditions, an IQ score at one testing pretty well predicts the score at another testing, although ten- or fifteen-point changes in scores during the school years are frequent (Honzik et al. 1948). In preschool years, and especially in infancy, low scores have some predictive value, but normal and high scores do not predict scores at later ages (Bayley 1949). Although preschool assessment and an early start in special programming might help a child whose development is delayed, labeling a child "retarded" too quickly is certainly a hazard.

Finally, IQ scores are primarily good predictors only of school performance. The first practical IQ test was devised in 1905, when Alfred Binet was commissioned to develop a measure that would predict which Paris schoolchildren

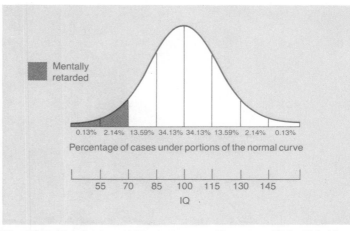

Fig. 20.1. Distribution of IQ test scores. The mean IQ is 100. IQ scores below 70 are one typical criterion for diagnosing retardation.

would fail in the regular curriculum, so that they could be placed in special schools. Subsequent tests have followed this lead, and IQ scores have come to predict rather well a child's performance in school. On the other hand, these tests are not especially good predictors of nonschool functioning, especially for children with test scores at a mildly retarded level or higher.

An IQ test, then, can be helpful in diagnosing problems in cognitive functioning, provided that the examiner is aware of the limitations in the construction, administration, and predictive powers of the test. For a child to be classified as retarded, however, she must also have deficits in adaptive functioning.

Adaptive Behavior

Ultimately more important than intellectual functioning alone is how an individual copes with life tasks. Adaptive behavior has been defined as an individual's independent functioning, or ability to accomplish activities typically expected for his age by the general community;

personal responsibility, that is, doing what he is capable of doing; and social responsibility, that is, accepting the obligations of community membership (Nihira et al. 1969). Adaptive behavior and IQ are related at the low ends of the scales, as in Kevin's case, but relate less strongly in the higher ranges where Debbie is.

Adaptive behavior is assessed in varied categories, according to age. The AAMD definition suggests assessing deficits in adaptive behavior in these stages:

During infancy and early childhood in:
1. Sensory-motor skills development
2. Communication skills (including speech and language)
3. Self-help skills
4. Socialization (development of ability to interact with others)
During childhood and early adolescence in:
5. Application of basic academic skills in daily life activities
6. Application of appropriate reasoning and judgment in mastery of the environment

Fig. 20.2. Adaptive behaviors are sometimes more important than intellectual level. These mildly retarded adolescents will enjoy back-packing in the mountains without mishap to the extent that they have and use adaptive skills. They need to apply what they learned in a school setting to nonschool activities (e.g., cooking), use appropriate reasoning and good judgment in mastering their new environment (e.g., pacing their hiking, choosing a campsite), and work together cooperatively (e.g., gathering firewood, breaking camp).

7. Social skills (participation in group activities and interpersonal relationships)
During late adolescence and adult life in:
8. Vocational and social responsibilities and performances (Grossman 1973, p. 12).

Adaptive behavior also varies with environmental demands. Diagnosed retardation is higher in urban areas and in industrialized countries. In the greater complexity of city life a child who cannot tell time, read signs, or understand bus routes is likely to stand out as dif-ferent; the same child in a less demanding environment might not seem to have such deficient adaptive behavior.

A number of scales have been developed to assess adaptive behavior, including the Vineland Scale of Social Maturity (Doll 1964) and the AAMD Adaptive Behavior Scales (Nihira et al. 1969). Although research has been increasing on these and other scales to measure adaptive behavior, they are still not as widely accepted for use in the classification of individuals as IQ tests are.

Classification

We have seen that children diagnosed as retarded are very diverse. The general label may qualify a child for services, but to decide which services best meet the child's need, we must be able to subclassify retardation. The system most used by educators has three levels that describe presumed learning capacity. The AAMD system has four categories, assigned by degree of retardation. Based primarily on IQ scores, these systems are similar, and both give some attention to adaptive behavior as well. Indeed, deficits in adaptive behavior often lead to IQ testing in the first place. The AAMD classification system and its educational-system equivalents (in parentheses) are:

1. Mild retardation (educable retarded), with IQ scores about 55 to 69.
2. Moderate retardation (trainable retarded), with IQ scores about 40 to 54.
3. Severe retardation (trainable or profoundly retarded), with IQ scores about 25 to 39.
4. Profound retardation (profoundly retarded), with IQ scores below 25 (Grossman 1973, p. 18).

In practice, cutoff points vary depending upon the classification system, the IQ test used, the policies in each school district, and other information about a child. The education categories actually refer as much to the special school programs in which children are placed as to the children themselves. Each program has its own goals, skills to be taught, and methods of teaching.

MILD RETARDATION

From 75 to 85 percent of retarded children are classified as mildly retarded. Many are placed in special classes for educable children, which teach academic skills, such as reading and arithmetic, toward mastery as far as sixth grade level. As adults, they are likely to lead fairly independent lives, often working at an unskilled or semiskilled job. Debbie tests at about IQ 65, and would be classified as mildly retarded and placed in an educable class. Mildly retarded children, however, are increasingly being "mainstreamed," placed for part of their school day in a regular classroom rather than having an entirely separate education.

MODERATE RETARDATION

From 10 to 20 percent of retarded children are classified as moderately retarded. Most are placed in special classes for trainable children, which teach basic skills necessary for some future independence in the community. The curriculum concentrates on information about the environment, basic sight vocabulary, self-help and housekeeping skills, language development, applied skills such as telling time or counting money, and community mobility. As adults, they are likely to require some continuing guidance and financial support, but can live in the community and work in sheltered workshops.

SEVERE AND PROFOUND RETARDATION

Fewer than 5 percent of retarded children are classified as severely or profoundly retarded. Until recently, most of them were considered untrainable, and many were confined in custodial institutions where little effort was made to teach them. With recent behavior modification methods (see Chapter 22) and with education mandated for all children, more and more attempts are being made to teach these children basic skills in trainable-level classrooms or in special developmental centers. Keith would probably be in the profoundly retarded classification.

This whole process of classification is not without critics (Mercer 1973). As we saw in Chapter 1, a classification is apt to become a label that has social implications beyond its original intent. The concern over labeling the mentally retarded relates mostly to mildly retarded children, whose limitations are often not readily apparent in non-academic situations. That "six-hour retarded child" is a mildly retarded child who functions quite adequately except when facing the special demands of the school day. The concern is that the label "retarded" sets expectancies for these children and their peers that will further impede their performance. Actually we have conflicting evidence about the effects of labeling; it seems that nonretarded children are more apt to gauge their acceptance by a retarded child's behavior and placement in class than by the label itself (Gottlieb 1975). Nonetheless, it is good to remember that classification systems are justifiable only as they help us better understand causes or provide services, and that the misuse or overuse of labels is potentially harmful.

Experience of the Family

The retarded child is born into a family, so that others are inescapably affected by retardation. Much has been written about the experiences of a retarded child's parents and siblings. Despite limited empirical study, we know that such effects vary widely, as families do. Some variables are readily quantified. The impact on the family seems harsher when the child is more retarded, the family's socioeconomic status is *higher,* and the community's services are less adequate. But effects also seem to relate to the more elusive characteristics of individual parents and of their marriage, such as stability, values, and capacity to adapt. The literature is admittedly one-sided, because it primarily reports families' reactions to moderate to profound retardation. Here the disability becomes apparent in early childhood, sometimes at birth, and even in the best of situations the effects are considerable.

A number of authors have tried to delineate the "stages" parents of retarded children go through, but these are not entirely satisfying in that many of the reactions are not really stages entered and left but moods and mind sets that linger. Nevertheless, they do identify common reactions to the discovery that one's child is mentally retarded. We will discuss six so-called stages: shock and confusion, disbelief, guilt, blame, the search for diagnosis, and later reactions.

The initial reaction, quite often, is shock and a feeling of confusion and loss. Years of hopes and dreams seem suddenly shattered:

> When next I awoke after seeing Karen for the second time, my mother and doctor were hovering over me. I saw the doctor's haggard face and my mother's red-rimmed eyes, and I knew that the nightmare I had been having was real (Brown 1976, p. 27).

Many parents go though a period of disbelief and nonacceptance that the child might be retarded. Wolfensberger (1967) has argued that for a while this attitude might well be adaptive because of the limited resources available for the young, retarded child; perhaps time spent learning to accept the child before accepting the disability is healthy in building an enduring relationship with her:

> As the years have gone by I have gradually come to realize that in those days I was incapable of admitting to myself that I was really the mother of a handicapped child. While her teachers and therapists struggled to develop her limited capabilities, I saw her moving along the road to normalcy. Somehow, someday, my dream daughter would emerge. The knowledge that I was now and forever parent to this imperfect child was too defeating for me to accept (Brown 1976, p. 85).

The most often noted parental reaction is guilt, both about having brought this child into the world and about the daily feelings of rejection that are so inevitable. Solnit and Stark (1961) recorded two extreme reactions that may be defenses against feelings of guilt. In one, guilt leads to constant and exclusive dedication to the child's welfare. In the other, parents feel intolerant of the defect and an almost irresistible impulse to deny their relationship to the child. Many parents may have some of both reactions, for as Schild (1964) points out, ambivalence is frequent. At one time natural instincts to love and care for the child are primary, and at another time the frustrations and disappointments surface. These thoughts of Helene Brown are probably more forthright than unique:

> When she was home I sometimes thought: Why doesn't she drown in the bathtub? It would be easy for her to slip. Why doesn't that happen? Or I would be sitting in the kitchen and hear her in her bath, making a noise that sounded like an emergency. I would keep right on with what I was doing, not going to her, thinking: "I'll go in later and find that she's drowned."
>
> At that moment Karen would appear, drying herself and laughing and I would be overcome with horror and guilt at my thoughts. How could I feel that way, loving her as much as anyone could love another human being? (Brown 1976, p. 154).

As parents come to feel guilt and to recognize that something is wrong with the child, they begin to search for causes, for places to fix the blame. A retarded child forces parents to reexamine their lives. Indeed, ruminations about "the possible cause" leave no family stone unturned. Perhaps the cause is punishment for some action, bad genes, an accidental bump on the head, too much dieting, or even ill thoughts:

> To add to our guilt, there is also the fact that we did not want Noah. The pregnancy came less than a year after Karl's birth. We would have had an abortion except we were broke. . . . So perhaps Noah sensed chemically in the womb that he wasn't welcome (Greenfeld 1973, p. 28).

Many families shop around for a specific diagnosis or a dissenting opinion. Even when parents have reached some acceptance of the problem and have reoriented to search for services, the question "why" lingers:

> The fate of Noah hangs over us like a joke whose grim punchline one vaguely remembers having heard before. But even as we know Noah's retarded, we still can't believe that there is no hope, so we look for little outs, random possibilities that might upset the diagnostic applecart (Greenfeld 1973, p. 63).

Olshansky (1962) has written of the "chronic sorrow" of parents of retarded children, a phrase that seems overly dramatic. It is true that, unlike other losses and disappointments, the loss of the hoped-for healthy child is constantly raised, when others in the family and neighborhood begin kindergarten, go out on their first date, or buy clothes for college. Many families, though, quite successfully come to accept their retarded children as they are and seek constructive services. When that search uncovers poor services or mistaken advice, as it often does, parents may naturally experience frustration, anger, and despair. Professionals who have focused on treating parents for their sorrow rather than giving useful advice and services have contributed further to the problem.

Constructs such as shock, disappointment, guilt, and sorrow, although they are commonly used to describe the parents' experience, are difficult to measure and study. Interview and survey studies aimed at delineating behavioral indices of distress have consistently uncovered the frequent disagreements between husband

and wife over child rearing; severely restricted social life; disrupted short- and long-range family plans; disproportionate amounts of time devoted to the retarded child to the exclusion of other family members; and excessive financial burdens (Jacobs 1969; Schild 1971). A study comparing families with both retarded and normal children to a matched group of families with only normal children showed that the "special" families read stories to and discussed problems with their normal children and visited friends and neighbors less often than the "normal" families (McAllister, Butler, and Lei 1973).

The preceding discussion of a retarded child's influence on the family is a one-sided, generally negative view. For many families, the joys of raising a child are more than enough to balance the sorrows of the handicap. Grossman (1972), for instance, has found that some brothers and sisters of retarded children grow up to be more patient and more accepting of others. Therefore we must keep the negative effects, however real, in perspective.

Causes of Retardation

Often it is not possible to pinpoint the cause of a child's retardation, and even more often retardation is due to a combination of causes. We will, however, distinguish among groups of determinants labeled genetic, physical-environmental, and psychosocial (Robinson and Robinson 1976). More than a hundred genetic and physical-environmental causes of mental retardation are known; they pertain mainly to children classified as moderately to profoundly retarded. Specific organic causes of mild retardation are found more rarely. For these children we must look elsewhere, to the psychosocial environment, and we must anticipate finding general indicators, not specific causes.

Genetic Causes

It is possible for a child to become retarded for many reasons at any time from conception on. In some genetic disorders the retardation was ordained from the moment of conception. Down's syndrome is an example, and we will discuss it in detail. In other cases, genetic factors cause retardation only as the child begins to metabolize a substance from the environment. For example, infants with the "inborn error of metabolism" known as phenylketonuria (PKU) will be affected by toxic metabolic by-products only after they have begun to ingest foods. We have chosen to focus on these two genetic disorders because they have been the subject of much productive research, which has led to methods of prevention.

DOWN'S SYNDROME

Down's syndrome occurs in one in 700 live births and is the most common organic disorder among persons in residential facilities for the retarded (at least 10 percent, according to Benda 1969). In 1866, British physician Langdon Down classified this syndrome, and because of the peculiarly slanted eyes characteristic of children born with this disorder, he named it "Mongolism," an attempt (now discredited) to equate disorders with racial characteristics. In Down's syndrome there is a general developmental arrest, with many distinctive physical symptoms and moderate to severe intellectual retardation. Although over the years many causes were hypothesized — syphilis, tuberculosis, psychic shock, even alcoholism — new techniques for chromosomal analysis developed in 1956 rapidly led to the discovery that it is the result of a genetic imbalance (Lejeune et al. 1959).

Although Down's syndrome is a genetic disorder, it is rarely an inherited one. Ninety-five percent of cases result from faulty distribution

Camp Freedom

In recent years community-based programs have sought to demonstrate viable alternatives to institutional care for troubled children. One such program was Camp Freedom (1969–77), a seven-week summer residential program which combined many intervention approaches we have described (Baker 1973; Brightman 1972). The fifty retarded and autistic campers each year presented such serious skill deficiencies or behavior problems, or both, interfering with learning that they were failing in special schools and, in many cases, had been excluded from school altogether.

The interdisciplinary staff included professionals in behavior therapy and undergraduates, specially trained for their counselor role. From a complete behavioral assessment for each child, four to six target areas were selected and individual skill training and behavior management goals were derived. The camp activity schedule was then developed to best meet each child's learning needs. Pictured here is teaching to increase self-help skills (eating), reading readiness (eye-hand coordination in crafts), leisure-time skills (fishing), social skills (cooperation in gardening), and applied academic skills (time telling). The more than forty teaching areas also included activities such as reading, speech and language, total communication, work skills, music and dancing, swimming, backpacking, and individual counseling.

Campers' motivation for activities was enhanced by a variety of rewards for learning, including a complex token economy, with the delivery of tokens (or points for advanced campers) as well as the schedule and nature of back-up reinforcers geared to individual capacity. Each child's parents and teacher attended training to promote generalization of gains from the special camp setting back to the child's home and school.

of chromosomes when the egg or sperm is formed. Normal human cells contain forty-six chromosomes, which carry the genetic codes that program an individual's physical appearance, intellectual capacity, blood type, and so on. A person with Down's syndrome has forty-seven chromosomes because, for some yet unknown reason, either the egg or the sperm cell fails to divide into equal complements of twenty-three chromosomes prior to fertilization. Consequently, the fertilized zygote that holds the developing infant's genetic characteristics has an extra chromosome. Also for unknown reasons, the likelihood that a child will have Down's syndrome rises sharply as the mother ages (see Figure 20.3). About half the children with Down's syndrome are born to mothers aged thirty-five and older; because in recent years women are completing their childbearing earlier, the incidence of Down's syndrome has begun to decline (Penrose 1967).

INTELLECTUAL AND PERSONALITY CHARAC-TERISTICS. In fact, people with Down's syndrome vary in functioning from the severely retarded child, unable to walk without assistance, to the occasional mildly retarded child, capable of regular elementary school work. No relationship seems to connect the type or number of physical abnormalities and the level of intelligence (Domino and Newman 1965).

Today, most children with Down's syndrome live at home and function in the range of moderate retardation. There are early intervention programs to stimulate development in Down's syndrome infants (Hayden and Haring 1976). The school-aged child is likely to be placed in a trainable special education class, with emphasis on learning functional self-care, information, and community awareness skills. Compared with others who have the same tested IQ, children with Down's syndrome are particularly poor in conceptual and abstract processes. As

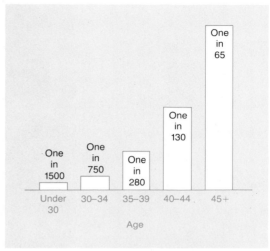

Fig. 20.3. The likelihood of giving birth to a Down's syndrome child increases with maternal age. (After Smith and Wilson 1973.)

Robinson and Robinson (1976) suggest, however, at this level of functioning concrete learning and practical everyday skills are perhaps most important, so that many persons with Down's syndrome adapt rather well. For the adult with Down's syndrome, a sheltered workshop and supervised living in a community residence are likely.

Studies of the personality characteristics of Down's syndrome children show that they generally seem happier, more friendly and affectionate, and more easily managed than similarly retarded children (Belmont 1971). Two characteristics notable in many are a tendency to mimic others and unusual stubbornness, an inability to adapt quickly to new demands or situations.

PRENATAL DETECTION. Prenatal detection of Down's syndrome and a number of other congenital disorders can now be done by *amniocentesis*. In the fourth month of pregnancy a

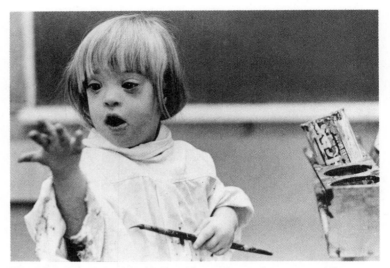

Fig. 20.4. This little girl with Down's syndrome has some of the characteristic physical features. Her almond-shaped eyes slant upwards, her nose is small with a low bridge, her hands are small and rather square, and her hair is sparse and straight. Physical abnormalities associated with Down's syndrome become more obvious with age; this child's stature will be short and stocky, her walk broad-based, and her muscle tone poor.

sample of amniotic fluid surrounding the fetus can be extracted and tested for the chromosome aberration. If the test indicates Down's syndrome, the parents can decide to terminate the pregnancy. Amniocentesis is an expensive procedure, and although risks to mother and fetus appear to be slight, these need further study. At present the procedure usually is limited to cases in which the mother is over thirty-five, a parent is a known carrier for a rare, hereditable type of Down's syndrome (translocation), or the couple has already had a Down's syndrome child, which increases the risk slightly over that of the general population.

PHENYLKETONURIA

Phenylketonuria, or PKU, is the most common inborn error of metabolism leading to

mental retardation. It occurs about once in 10,000 live births. The condition is particularly interesting because study for nearly a half a century has led to relatively good understanding of it, to methods of early screening, and to a dietary treatment that can prevent retardation.

Fölling first described PKU in 1934 after parents had called to his attention a peculiar odor in the urine of their two retarded children. Testing revealed an excess of phenylpyruvic acid in the urine, and later research (Jervis 1939, 1947) revealed that these children lacked an enzyme necessary to oxidize phenylalanine, an amino acid in protein foods. The resulting formation of excessive phenylpyruvic acid and other abnormal metabolites, in turn, usually damages the nervous system.

PKU is transmitted genetically as a recessive

trait. Current estimates are that as many as one in fifty persons carry the gene (Rosenthal 1970). If two carriers produce a child, there is a 25 percent chance that the child will have PKU. A carrier does not manifest any of the intellectual or behavioral signs of the disorder, but will show reduced capacity to metabolize phenylalanine in a tolerance test; hence, carriers can be identified.

CHARACTERISTICS. Affected children will almost certainly be quite retarded. Very few test at IQs of more than 50 (Knox 1972), a third cannot walk or control excretion, and two thirds cannot talk. These children are apt to be blond and blue-eyed, with fair skin (because phenylalanine is not oxidized to tyrosine, a substance that is important for pigmentation). The infant with PKU is likely to have symptoms of irritability, eczema, seizures, urine odor, and failure to develop mentally. As the child grows older, these symptoms continue and are usually accompa-

nied by hyperactivity, with a stiff gait and short, jerky steps. He or she may exhibit unpredictable, erratic behavior, such as excessive rocking, arm waving, finger mannerisms, and overall aimless and unresponsive behavior. These children have often been misdiagnosed as autistic (Koch et. al. 1971), raising the question of how many other so-called autistic children may be suffering from undiscovered or undiagnosed organic defects. Children who are nonverbal and very retarded have a limited behavioral repertoire, so that expressions in observable behavior overlap for different disorders. As a result, accurate diagnosis is often quite difficult. Fortunately, early diagnosis of PKU can be made biochemically.

SCREENING AND DIET. The possibility of preventing retardation by early diagnosis and treatment has sparked intense interest and much study. Serum phenylalanine levels in the PKU infant are likely to be abnormally high as

Excerpts from Paul Scott's Diary

An exceptional example of developmental capability in Down's syndrome is Paul Scott, whose innate abilities were developed by broad travel and educational experiences provided by his wealthy and dedicated father and several companions and teachers. Excerpt's from Paul's diary, kept for most of his life (Seagoe 1964), reveal a capacity for communication, albeit in simple words and structure, as well as dramatic effect and humor.

Age 15. I fed lumps of sugar to my donkey. I went on a new trail. My donkey refused to go down the stone steps. I walked down and my Dad led him. My Dad had a switch to switch the poor little donkey. The donkey ate the switch (p. 44).

Age 20. I went over the new road. Pop went to see tires and got stuck on the sand. Senor Pop stayed with the Chevy and Senor Paul went to the fishing boat. I went on it and I

found fishermen senors in boots, coat and hat and Senor Paul led the senors to the Chevy and push and push and push and push and out comes the Chevy (p. 95).

Despite Paul Scott's good ability to communicate, his writing is primarily descriptive. Notice the lack of reflection about events in this entry, written just days after Pearl Harbor:

Age 25. We were invited to a friend's apartment for dinner: had tongue: first time I ever tasted it: then we heard the air raid signal: all lights were put out: We stood on the porch and watched Los Angeles, California, grow blacker and blacker: finally there was complete darkness: This is my first experience in a blackout: I lay down on the davenport for a little snooze with Chip close to me: After it was over our friend took us home (p. 150).

early as two days after birth, when the infant has begun to drink milk. A simple urine test with ferric chloride detects high phenylalanine levels, and more sensitive blood tests (Guthrie test) have refined the screening. If an infant's sibling is a known PKU victim or the parents are known carriers, the infant can be monitored carefully from birth for signs of the disease. As the testing methods were perfected during the 1970s, most states began to mandate screening for all newborns.

Once PKU is diagnosed, the child is put on a special diet with only about 15 percent of the phenylalanine in a normal infant's diet. The biochemical abnormalities of PKU are soon reversed: eczema clears up, pigmentation increases, seizures lessen, and motor skills increase (Robinson and Robinson 1976).

Studies of the low-phenylalanine diet indicate that normal or nearly normal intellectual development will occur if the diet is begun early in infancy and properly maintained, until at least age six. The later the diet is begun, the greater the retardation; beginning the diet after age four or five does not appear to improve intellectual functioning at all (Berry et al. 1967).

Other research on dietary control indicates, as would be expected, that retardation is less in children who adhere reasonably well to the diet so that serum phenylalanine stays low. Counseling with parents and children who have poor dietary control is indicated, and most PKU treatment teams have psychologists and social workers to assess child behavior and counsel families (Fox and Rosen 1977). A hope for the future is to develop a replacement for the missing liver enzyme so that the special diet will not be necessary.

Physical and Environmental Causes

The developing fetus also can be affected by influences in the *physical environment,* such as maternal malnutrition, drugs ingested during pregnancy, maternal antibody response to the fetus, radiation, trauma, or infections in the mother.

The birth itself is also accompanied by possible hazards, including prematurity, anoxia (oxygen deprivation), and direct injury to the head and brain. As the infant develops, still other potential hazards arise, including infections such as meningitis and encephalitis, malnutrition, poisoning, or anoxia from near drowning or head injury.

Again, rather than attempt to survey the multitude of physical and environmental factors implicated in retardation, we will concentrate on several illustrative examples, chosen in part because they may suggest precautions to readers who may become parents.

CONGENITAL RUBELLA SYNDROME

Mothers have always feared that diseases they contract during pregnancy will adversely affect the developing fetus. Several chronic infections, such as syphilis and cytomegalovirus, do result in developmental disabilities. Studies of acute infections have thus far failed to show lasting ill effects, however, with one clear exception: rubella (German measles). For many years deafness, cataracts, and congenital heart disease were believed to be the primary characteristics of the congenital rubella syndrome, but one study of 243 children born to mothers who had contracted rubella found many other physical defects (Chess et al. 1971). Also, 37 percent of their sample at age 2.5 to 4 were mentally retarded, and of these, more than half were severely or profoundly retarded. The exact effect on the fetus of this otherwise mild virus is unknown, but it apparently causes cell death or changes the rate of cell growth, and perhaps also interferes with the blood supply to developing fetal tissues. The defects a child is likely to have depend on the time of fetal development when infection occurs. The frequency of obvious congenital anomalies (such as deafness, cataracts, and heart disease) and the likelihood of mental retardation are 50 percent if infection occurs in the first month of pregnancy, and progressively less in months two and three (Sever and White 1968). This is especially unfortunate because in the first month or so women often do not realize they are pregnant. Some evidence also warns that children born of mothers who contract rubella in the second trimester (months four, five, and six) are likely to evidence more subtle developmental problems, such as a decrease in auditory sensitivity, or some motor or mental impairment not apparent at birth (Hardy, McCracken, Gilkeson, and Sever 1969).

In 1964 the United States experienced a rubella epidemic and a conservatively estimated 30,000 children with rubella-associated birth defects. Two years after the shock of the 1964 epidemic, rubella became a nationwide reportable disease, whereby doctors must report new cases to the appropriate government agency. Rubella virus vaccines were licensed in mid-1969, and by early 1974 more than 50 million doses of vaccine had been distributed. Widespread vaccination of schoolchildren of both sexes is now generally accepted. No further rubella epidemics have erupted since 1964, and since the vaccine became available, congenital rubella has markedly decreased in newborns. The vaccination program appears to be accomplishing its purpose.

NUTRITION AND DRUGS

Development of the fetus is greatly influenced by what the mother ingests. In many parts of the world, starvation is an obvious cause of retarded development or death of the fetus. Even when caloric intake is adequate, though, poor choice of diet can have serious consequences. Maternal nutritional deficiencies during pregnancy have been found to re-

late to prematurity and retarded development (Birch and Gussow 1970). An often-cited study by Knobloch and Pasamanick (1958) examined the birthdates of 5000 persons admitted to an institution for the retarded and found significantly more to be born during the winter months, January, February, and March. These researchers hypothesized that deficient diets during summer hot spells, when mothers were not hungry, interfered with fetal development in the first trimester and produced lasting damage. A further analysis showed the percentage of winter-born retarded children to be especially high following extremely hot summers.

Retardation also traces to poor nutrition in the child. Brain growth is most rapid during the last three months of pregnancy and the first year of life, and malnutrition during this period seems related to intellectual retardation. Data are contradictory as to how well a malnourished child can catch up in intelligence if shifted to a more adequate diet. Some children, of course, suffer from malnutrition not so much because of poverty and inadequate choice of diet but because of maternal neglect. The child found in a crib, left unfed for days, is an all-too-common experience of children's hospitals.

In addition, many chemical substances are known to cause, or are suspected of causing, birth defects. Continuing research on the specific effects on the unborn fetus of diet and drugs probably will further confirm a fact that we take for granted — a woman of childbearing age cannot be too careful about what she ingests.

POISONING AND HEAD INJURY

The developing child can suffer brain injury from many causes, such as malnutrition, illnesses accompanied by high fever, some poisons, and head injury. One insidious cause of retardation, especially in inner-city areas, is lead poisoning. Lead at high levels can cause retardation as well as lethargy, seizures, and attention deficits (see also Chapter 21). Children not only inhale airborne lead from automobile exhausts but also may eat chips of lead-based paint. Lead-based paint is now prohibited in homes, yet it is still found in many older buildings. Screenings in American cities have found toxic levels of lead in the bloodstreams of more than ten percent of the children (Chow and Earl 1970). Prevention is aimed at decreasing lead pollution, primarily by requiring that lead-free gasoline be used in automobiles. Intervention involves screening and treating affected children with a chemical that reduces the blood's lead content.

The two most common causes of severe head injury in children, it is sad to say, are automobile accidents and child abuse (Robinson and Robinson 1976).

Psychosocial Causes

Most retarded children are only mildly retarded and have no obvious organic impairment. For these children, retardation is the combined result of limited intellectual capacity that they have inherited and psychosocial influences as they grow up. Retardation caused by psychosocial disadvantage is also referred to as *cultural-familial retardation*. This diagnosis is applied if: (1) the child shows retarded intellectual and adaptive behavior; (2) there is no clear evidence of cerebral pathology; and (3) evidence of retarded intellectual functioning appears in the immediate family.

A further indicator is that the family usually is living in poverty (Grossman 1973). It is estimated that at least 75 percent of retarded children are growing up in poverty, and these children are typically those labeled with cultural-familial retardation. The President's Committee on Mental Retardation (1968) said that a child living in a low-income rural or urban family is fifteen times more likely to be diagnosed as re-

tarded than is a child from a higher-income family. Children growing up in poverty are more likely to manifest early developmental lag, and their families have fewer resources than middle-class families to help them overcome it. Of infants scoring in the lowest 25 percent on a developmental test at eight months of age, those from lower-class families were seven times more likely than those from higher-class families to score below IQ 80 at age four (Willerman, Broman, and Fiedler 1970). For older children from families with income of less than $3000, the illiteracy rate is three times the national average (Vogt 1973).

You will recall from our discussion of IQ test practices that some children are misclassified as retarded by overreliance on an IQ score that does not accurately reflect their capacity. Most children classified as cultural-familial retarded, however, do legitimately function at a retarded level, and many probably have limited genetic endowment. But how closely the distribution of measured intelligence represents a similar distribution of inherited capacity or is the result of children's psychosocial experience is controversial. Although each extreme in the nature-nurture controversy has its proponents, there seems to be little doubt that growing up in poverty has detrimental effects, especially for the genetically less endowed child (Hurley 1969). We will not dwell on the nature-nurture argument, but will concentrate on disadvantageous aspects of poverty, because ultimately these are the variables over which social planners can exert some influence. Overcoming poverty should be the first priority in the drive to reduce retardation.

In contrast to retardation of organic origin, retardation attributed to psychological factors is difficult to trace to one or more specific causes. Sometimes, to be sure, the psychosocial disadvantage is so extreme that it creates a specifiable physical-environmental cause like

Fig. 20.5. Children growing up in poverty run a higher risk of retardation than those in more affluent homes. Known contributing influences include inadequate nutrition and medical care, and limitations in cognitive and language stimulation. However, since the majority of poor children are not retarded, an intriguing focus of further study might be those children who "beat the odds."

the ones we have discussed (lead poisoning, extreme abuse, or neglect). Usually no specific agent can be delineated, however. Poverty is multidimensional.

The culturally disadvantaged or culturally different child may be born to a mother who lacked prenatal diet and medical care. The home atmosphere may be noisy and crowded. Early home life with parents wrapped up in the immediate problems of daily living may provide little verbal stimulation, limited reinforcement for problem-solving, and low expectation of cognitive achievement. Later, the child may enter a substandard, segregated school and may subsequently acquire the label "retarded." Studies show correlations among these factors, countless other components of poverty, and the label "retarded," but drawing conclusions about the specific contribution of any one is next to impossible. Any one of these disadvantages taken in the extreme (severe malnutrition) can cause severe damage. Usually, however, many of these conditions are present to some degree, and undoubtedly the interaction among them ultimately retards a child's functioning.

DEFICIENCIES IN HEALTH CARE

It is well established that prematurity, postnatal mortality, and other complications in early life are much higher in poor families. A high proportion of pregnancies are "at risk" for subsequent developmental disabilities because of timing, health care, or nutrition.

In poverty-level families fewer pregnancies are intentionally planned than in middle-class families. MacMillan (1977) summarizes the evidence on timing of pregnancies in lower-class women.

Pregnancies at early ages, teen-age deliveries, pregnancies at close intervals, a great number of pregnancies and pregnancies that occur late in the childbearing years are related to prematurity, high infant mortality, low birth weight, prolonged labor, toxemia, anemia, malformations, and mental retardation (MacMillan 1977, p. 85).

Inadequate health care is also related to birth complications and mental retardation, and it is much more likely to be seen in lower-class families. In 1968, 45 percent of women in public hospitals had no prenatal care (President's Committee on Mental Retardation 1969). A study of poor children enrolled in Head Start programs (North 1967) revealed grossly deficient health care. Among children studied in more than 2000 communities, 14 percent had not been born in a hospital, 35 percent had not

been seen by a doctor for two years, 50 percent had not been immunized for diphtheria, polio, and smallpox; 75 percent had never seen a dentist, and 88 percent had not received measles vaccine. The expansion of government efforts in recent years to provide medical services for the poor has begun to show results, but health care is still far from adequate. As we have seen, malnutrition in the mother or the child is further detrimental to healthy development.

DEFICIENCIES IN COGNITIVE STIMULATION

The child classified as cultural-familial retarded usually has one or both parents who would also test retarded. Heber, Dever, and Conry (1968) found that 62 percent of mothers with IQs below 70 had husbands whose IQs were also below 70. Although these mating patterns have obvious genetic consequences, the effects are environmental as well. In the home the child probably will be exposed to less intellectually and socially capable role models and undoubtedly will suffer some disadvantage in cognitive stimulation.

One condition considered crucial is verbal stimulation. A child's early language score is the best predictor of her later IQ (Schaefer 1970). Because of the pressing problems of daily life, lower-class parents, on the average, have less time than middle-class parents to talk with their children, to challenge them to reason and solve problems, or to engage in cognitive, school-like games with them. Passive and conforming behavior is likely to be valued. Many families cannot afford play materials such as toys, books, and paints, and the television set often becomes the child's intellectual parent (Frost and Hawkes 1966).

Studies of the language environment in poor homes suggest differences from middle-class homes. Jensen (1968) observed that in lower-class homes the infant's vocalizations are less likely to be rewarded or shaped to closer approximations of adult speech. Hess and Shipman (1965) studied the mother-child interaction between lower- and middle-class black mothers and their four-year-old children. In teaching the children how to solve a problem, middle-class mothers talked more, gave more verbal explanation, used more complex syntax, and praised success more often. Lower-class mothers were less likely to give specific instructions, made more nonverbal intrusions, and were more critical of errors. Also, Jensen (1968) reports that in some way the spoken language in some lower-class homes is less like written language than middle-class speech is. It does not transfer as well to reading and formal writing.

Several highly successful programs have been aimed at preventing cultural-familial retardation in high-risk children by beginning to provide experiences shortly after birth to counteract the adverse factors we have previously described. We will consider these enrichment programs in Chapter 22; their success suggests that much cultural-familial retardation may be preventable.

Characteristics of Retarded Persons

It is not only presumptuous but misleading for us to try to convey the charcteristics and experience of retardation. For the most part, the abilities, attitudes, anxieties, and aspirations of retarded people are not very different from those of anyone else, and the differences we can highlight as special characteristics are only a matter of degree. Moreover, people called retarded are a diverse group. The majority can tell us about themselves, often with great clarity and feeling, and their experiences and views vary extensively. For the minority whose only language is their behavior, the expressions also bespeak diversity. We will not, then, pretend to convey *the* experience of retardation, but simply highlight some of the themes and characteristics relatively common in the experience of mildly retarded persons.

Learning

By definition, the retarded person is an inefficient learner, and his learning has been the subject of much research. Two main theoretical positions have been advanced to explain learning inefficiencies. The *difference model* assumes that some cognitive defect makes the retarded person qualitatively different from people with a higher IQ. Studies have investigated deficits in processes such as incidental learning (Denny 1964), short-term memory (Ellis 1970), attention (Zeaman and House 1963), and rehearsal strategies (see Gardner 1978 for review). A number of studies have found performance by retarded persons poorer than that of younger normal persons of the same mental age, which seems to support the difference notion.

The *developmental model* starts with the argument that the retarded person learns much like the nonretarded person, except that she learns slower and ultimately reaches a lower ceiling of performance (Zigler 1969). Considering primarily people who are mildly retarded, the developmental theorist attributes the finding that they perform cognitive tasks less well than normal persons of the same mental age to factors in the retarded person's history of social learning that cause a motivational difference in approaching new tasks.

Consider the experience of failure. The joy of succeeding that motivates many children is pretty much a stranger to the retarded child. Repeated experiences of failure during the developmental years affect a retarded person's motivation and problem-solving strategy. She has a generalized expectancy of failure, and the

Fig. 20.6. Retarded children often feel anxious and frustrated in a problem-solving situation.

problem-solving strategy she develops is one of failure avoidance (Cromwell 1963). The retarded child often enters a situation that requires performance looking for ways to avoid failure, rather than ways to succeed. Strategies vary. One child tries to avoid the situation altogether; another remains passively resigned; and still another constructs unrealistic excuses. Also, retarded children may not be as motivated by success on a task as normal children are and may settle for limited achievement and a low rate of reinforcement because they expect to fail anyway. Osler (reported by MacMillan 1974) studied retarded children's reduced aspirations, giving them a simple two-choice discrimination problem and a candy reward for each

correct choice. After more than 150 trials, the children still had not learned the task, settling instead for the 50 percent (random) payoff. Yet when she told the children they would have to give back a piece of candy for each incorrect response, they learned in two or three more trials! An expectancy of failure and reduced aspirations had led these children to appear more ''retarded'' than in fact they were.

In teaching retarded individuals we must be aware of the possible cognitive difficulties that difference theorists propose and also of the attributes from social learning history that developmental theorists mention. Behavior-modification methods (discussed in Chapter 22) have been particularly effective with retarded persons because they are directly aimed at structuring tasks for success and at motivational factors.

Personality and Interpersonal Experiences

Contrary to some popular notions, retarded persons seem no more likely than others to manifest severe personality disorganization, such as psychosis or criminality. Yet they have some personality characteristics that relate to coping with one's own limitations and the reactions of other people.

ANXIETY AND FRUSTRATION

To have limited intellectual abilities in an increasingly technological world certainly means to be often anxious, confused, and frustrated, to struggle to do or to understand what others handle with seeming ease. Sarason et al. (1960), in an extensive study of elementary schoolchildren, found that all indices of anxiety were higher in those who scored lower on group intelligence and achievement tests. American novelist John Steinbeck captured this anxiety and frustration in his characterization of Lennie, a giant of a man and an able worker, but struggling constantly to sort things out:

Lennie looked timidly over to him. "George?"

"Yeah, what ya want?"

"Where we goin', George?"

The little man jerked down the brim of his hat and scowled over at Lennie. "So you forgot that already, did you? I gotta tell you again, do I? Jesus Christ, you're a crazy bastard!"

"I forgot," Lennie said softly. "I tried not to forget. Honest to God I did, George."

"O.K. — O.K. I'll tell ya again, I ain't got nothing to do. Might jus' as well spen' all my time tellin' you things and then you forget 'em, and I tell you again."

"Tried and tried," said Lennie, "but it didn't do no good" (Steinbeck 1937, p. 4).

ROUTINE AND RULES

To feel anxiety in confronting situations is natural, because the retarded person must cope with very real difficulties in understanding and communicating. Robinson and Robinson (1976) help us to empathize a bit with this position by reminding us how difficult it can be to live in another country and not speak the native language. During a year in Paris, they report, their communications were necessarily more concrete, they watched carefully for cues from others about what to say, they began to avoid potential experiences of failure such as talking on the telephone, and they became more dependent on their family. These are phenomena one sees exaggerated in retarded individuals, though their trouble often is caused as much by difficulty in conceptualizing as in communicating.

Many retarded persons become quite reliant on routine, because familiar activities and surroundings minimize the need to cope with new problems. Behavior is guided by absolute rules, and some see it as overly conforming. Although a retarded person's observations are often quite acute, they are primarily concrete and descriptive. Difficulties especially arise in coping

with more abstract problems. Consider the gaps in logic of this institutionalized retarded woman's planning:

Q. Say that you were walking out of the hospital today — today was the last day in the hospital, and you were leaving this afternoon, what would be the first thing that you would do?

A. I'll get a house first. I'd have to see about a house first . . .

Q. How do you do that?

A. Well — you'd see "For Sale" and you'd ask how much it is — and pay for it, and if the furniture is OK, you just clean the house up, and you dust a little bit (de laCruz and LaVeck 1974, pp. 224–225).

Of course this woman's simplistic solution is also the result of the limited opportunity to learn in her institutional life, so she has become doubly handicapped.

DEPENDENCE ON OTHERS

It is perhaps to be expected that those who experience difficulties in coping with the world and with the reactions of people in that world learn to distrust their own judgment and to become especially attuned to others for cues on how to behave. Zigler (1966) called this strategy *outer-directedness* and has shown that retarded children, more than their nonretarded peers, depend on external guides to action. That is why retarded individuals often seem quite suggestible. This characteristic, useful in coping with certain life tasks, is counterproductive in some situations requiring performance; on standardized tests the child who is preoccupied with the adult tester may get a spuriously low score.

LOW SELF-ESTEEM

Those with mild retardation are not only aware of their limitations, but often painfully aware of other persons' reactions to them. They have heard all the words — retard, mental, dummy — and have felt the hurt. They have necessarily incorporated some of these views of others into their own self-image, as we all do. Anger, despair, and low self-esteem often follow, though these reactions are less frequently expressed, partly because retarded persons often live in settings where the expression of such feelings is discouraged. At a nationwide conference in England, mentally handicapped persons came together to discuss their experiences and hopes for change (Our Life Conference 1972). One delegate reflected on the well-intentioned efforts of others, which he reported sometimes cause pain that cannot be acknowledged:

You have to say "never mind," when you feel like going mad, when you're seething with rage inside.

Others cling to the present routine partly because of their anxiety about people's reactions:

If I'd go in a factory, they'd all pick on me, so I wouldn't be very happy in a factory. I'm happy now where I am, so I'm going to stick. I've got nothing to grumble at.

Having lived with the label "retarded" and especially having lived segregated, their expressions of low self-esteem, futility, and resignation are not surprising.

Growing Up

Special decisions and difficulties of all kinds confront any disabled person and his family from childhood through the adult years. In this chapter we discuss only the developmental disability of retardation, but other developmental disabilities such as blindness, deafness, and physical handicaps raise similar issues. We have considered some of the psychological and learning characteristics of the retarded person. Other issues are sociolegal, involving interchange with other people and society's institutions, as well as ensuring basic human rights. Many legal rights of disabled people are still being defined in legislatures, in courts, and in practice (Friedman 1976); they really afford disabled people only the same rights as everyone else, but since society's thinking as well as its institutions must be adapted somewhat, the evolution of rights for this "last minority" is slow.

Education

For the parent of the *non*disabled child, free public education has long been a right. For the parent of the disabled child, however, securing appropriate school placement is a constant struggle. A prevailing attitude has been that exclusion from public schools is warranted for children who are different and that any educational placement is a tenuous privilege subject to termination at the whim of a school district or even a teacher. It has not been atypical for retarded children to have very sporadic schooling. Furthermore, placement in a school has been no guarantee that the child would be taught well, because in the past "special education" frequently implied neither special nor education (see Chapter 22). Talk with the parent of any disabled child and you will almost certainly hear a litany of struggles with the system for appropriate services. Their common needs have led parents to form advocacy organizations, such as the National Association for Retarded Citizens, which have been a strong force for better educational services.

The movement toward equity crystallized with passage by Congress in 1975 of Public Law 94–142, the Education for All Handicapped Children Act. This far-reaching legislation, which took effect in the fall of 1977, provides federal funds to states to defray the cost of providing an education for every child. Among its provisions are assessing children by nondiscriminatory tests, annually developing an individualized educational plan, involving parents in development of such a plan, and placing the child in the least restrictive setting possible. The philosophy behind this last, very important provision is *mainstreaming* — providing placements for disabled children as close as possible to those for nondisabled children.

In practice, a continuum of placements is considered, from a totally separate residential school to fully integrated placement in a regular public school classroom. Most moderately and severely retarded children, like Kevin, whom we described earlier, need a great deal of specialized help. The most mainstreamed alternative for them might still involve a separate special education class, but preferably one in a regular public school, with some opportunities during the day for the children to mix with the nondisabled children (at recess, perhaps in some gym classes, and the like). Many mildly retarded children, like Debbie, could spend some time in a regular classroom and several hours a day in a "resource room" where special instruction is available. The extent of separate education is determined so as to best fit the needs of each child. Although this and similar legislation holds considerable promise for parents of retarded children, it seems that advocacy and persistent involvement with the educational system will continue to be necessary.

Social Acceptance

Laws can mandate integrated education, but they cannot guarantee social acceptance of the retarded child by nondisabled peers. A prominent reality throughout the life of every retarded or disabled person is subtle and sometimes not-so-subtle rejection. Mildly retarded individuals are accepted by the public more than those who have greater impairment (Gottlieb 1975).

But abundant evidence documents that even mildly retarded children are devalued by nonretarded age-mates (Cook and Wollersheim 1976; Goodman, Gottlieb, and Harrison 1972). After interviewing fifty children of late elementary school age about their understanding of retardation, Brightman (1977) concluded that most: (1) based their perceptions of individuals labeled retarded on a single referent (either a relative or someone in the neighborhood, not always a peer); (2) saw retarded children not as multifaceted individuals, but as unidimensional persons best characterized by single, typically unfavorable words, such as "helpless," "funny," "sad," or "stupid"; (3) perceived no variability among retarded children: "all of them — the retarded — are alike"; and (4) saw retardation as a generic term for the entire range of disabilities —"they walk funny, talk strange, or don't hear any good" (p. 61).

Because of these preconceptions, it is not likely that integration alone will generate more favorable, or factual, impressions. Indeed, evidence is plentiful that social contact by itself may not only fail to promote prosocial attitudes but also may reinforce previously acquired negative stereotypes. Gottlieb, Cohen, and Goldstein (1974) found that typical children in two elementary schools in which retarded children were either partially integrated or in a special class rated "mentally retarded children" significantly more negatively on a semantic differential rating scale than did children attending a school that did not accommodate retarded children. Similarly, a sociometric investigation by Gottlieb and Budoff (1973) revealed not only that typical children accept retarded children less frequently and reject them more frequently than they do their nonretarded age-mates, but also that they are more rejecting of partially integrated retarded children than they are of children who spend their day in a special classroom.

Some educators have attempted to promote typical children's acceptance of disabled agemates with classroom-simulation activities and informative curricula to acquaint them with the special and not-so-special needs of labeled children (Bookbinder 1977). Cohen (1977) has collected pilot data on just such a curriculum, entitled *Accepting Individual Differences,* a series of booklets and activities covering many handicapping conditions. After viewing a videotape of a disabled child, a classroom of second grade children who had participated in the AID curriculum were able to characterize the child in a multidimensional manner, commenting not only on the disability but on other facets of personality and behavior as well. The comments of a matched classroom of control children, though, showed they could not see beyond the disability.

An exciting and potentially more cost-effective approach to preparing typical children for mainstreaming is with television or film. Disabled people have rarely been seen in the mass media, except as occasional figures of evil, as superheroes, or as victims (Blatt 1977). Recently a number of children's television shows have included retarded children in selected segments ("Sesame Street," "Zoom"). A more concentrated effort to present disabled children to young viewers has been made in the award-winning series "Feeling Free," developed by Alan Brightman and his associates at the Cambridge, Massachusetts Workshop of Children's Awareness (Brightman 1977). The series is a spontaneous, nonscripted introduction to Laurie, Hollis, Ginny, John, and Gordon, articulate and engaging children who are disabled. Minidocumentaries delve into the experiences, special interests, and insights of each of these children and some others, and informal rap sessions show the children answering questions from each other and from friends ("Is it that you can't read or you don't want to?"

"What's the hardest thing about being deaf?" "What kinds of things do you do after school?"). One consistent theme of the series is that disabilities are not to be hushed up and hidden away, but seen, asked about, and then looked beyond.

Adulthood

The retarded adult in our society faces the same problems in life as any of us, although often theirs are more extreme. We will consider three of these.

VOCATION

Most retarded adults work, either in competitive jobs or under some supervision in sheltered workshops. In 1970, 2.6 million retarded adults with IQs between 40 and 69 were living outside of institutions in the United States; of these, 59 percent held competitive jobs (Conley 1973). Typical jobs are in many unskilled and semiskilled vocations, such as clerical work, domestic service, factory work, farming, food services, gardening, maintenance, and the like (President's Committee on Mental Retardation 1969). The employability of a retarded individual depends on abilities and emotional stability, but it also strongly relates to social attitudes and needs prevailing in the labor force. Manpower demands in World War II meant jobs for many formerly unemployed retarded people, most of whom performed quite well (Cobb 1972).

Although retarded people have always been laid off first in a tight job market, with increased social acceptance people have also become aware that many retarded workers have excellent attendance and performance records and are valuable employees to retain. During the 1960s the Civil Service Commission began to encourage hiring of retarded people, and an evaluation of mildly retarded workers found that after ninety days on the job, 73 percent had adjusted satisfactorily or very well (Oswald 1968).

Some mildly retarded persons and many moderately and severely retarded persons work in sheltered workshops; most of the vocational training programs available to retarded adults in the United States are provided by these facilities, which are intended to both employ and train, mainly in subcontract work with industry. Contracts involve jobs such as light assembly and packaging. Retarded workers' pay is prorated by comparing their output with that of nonretarded workers; the average retarded worker earned about $1000 for the year 1975, in 30 hours of work per week (Seltzer and Seltzer 1978). Sheltered workshops have been criticized as inadequate training, however, because they rely heavily on assembly-line jobs, ostensibly paralleling private industry, where industrial occupations have in fact been declining. On the other hand, service occupations are becoming more plentiful, and sheltered workshops have generally not kept pace (Power and Marinelli 1974). An alternative type of work placement is the work crew, organizing groups of five to ten retarded adults under supervision to do work projects such as cleaning, maintenance, or agriculture (Seltzer and Seltzer 1978).

MARRIAGE

Little has been written about the retarded person as a sexual being, a topic fraught with anxiety for parents, who earnestly inquire about sex education for their adolescent retarded child, and for society in general, as reflected in our history and laws. MacMillan (1977) reports that in 1971 twenty-one states had laws providing for compulsory sterilization of the mentally retarded, forty-one states prohibited marriage for retarded persons. These laws are rarely enforced today, but they stand as a reminder and an insult to the dignity of all retarded persons. Although most moderately retarded individ-

uals could not fulfill the demands of a lasting heterosexual relationship, many do have sexual feelings, and a program of sex education is important for them. Many mildly retarded individuals, however, do marry and live reasonably fulfilled lives, especially when they have extended family to rely on.

RESIDENCE*

The following exchange took place between an interviewer and Frank, resident of a halfway house.

Interviewer: What are the things you do really well?

Frank: Making salads, cooking, working; I'm a good friend.

Interviewer: What are the things you're not so good at?

Frank: I screw things up once in a while — it's in my mind. I don't know how to take a vacation. They'll have to teach me.

Interviewer: Do you think it's a good thing to have more houses like this one?

Frank: A lot of kids from the school want to move out here and make it by themselves. They're bored at school. Most of the bright ones are gone — they're going to close down that place. . . .

Interviewer: You called the people at school "kids"; are they children or adults?

Frank: While they're at the school they're kids; you're an adult only when you get out here.

When a retarded person no longer lives with parents and cannot yet live on his or her own, social agencies typically intervene to provide some other place to live. During the past century the dominant mode of service to retarded people has been nonservice — either leaving parents to cope unaided or encouraging them

* This section is adapted from Baker, Seltzer, and Seltzer 1977.

Two Mentally Retarded Adults Talk About Their Life Together

"We worked in the same workshop — at the Jewish Vocational Service. . . . In a way I guess that's how we met. . . . Our parents were quite shocked [when we got engaged]. . . . We said that we wanted to get married, that we wanted each other and we loved each other very much, and that we don't want to split, you know?

"I went to a lot of schools. . . . I stayed back quite a lot of times. . . . I couldn't keep up with the kids. See, that's my problem, I couldn't keep up. They put me in a special class when I was twelve. . . . I went to high school, and I was in a special class. . . . I graduated when I was twenty. . . . They had to push me, I had a very hard time. . . . They used to call me a nok-nok, and they used to call me a retard, and all kinds of names. . . . A nok-nok is somebody that's supposed to be up here. And I'm not up there, I'm not crazy. . . . Well, I was told that anybody that says that to somebody else has something wrong with *them*."

"I worked in a nursing home. I had two different jobs and I got laid off from both of them. I found out that I can't work. I found out that I can't cope with pressure, and I can't understand the different things that they ask me to do. . . . I get all nerved up. . . . It's in my head. I can't grasp. There's just some things that I can't do. Going out on a job, working for someone — it's not easy. I have too many ups and downs. They call it a . . . minimal neurology, something, some big word, and it means that I have too many ups and downs. I want to find out what's making me click, what's causing all this — just to see why I can't work.

"The only thing that worries me is about children — about having children. . . . We want to have two kids, a boy and a girl . . . and a dog and a cat. . . . I want my child to be able to do things, to be able to think on her or his own, and be with other people — and just to have a good life, that's all.

"Everybody's happy [for us]. And they wish us the luck all the time. . . . When you're living with a person, . . . sometimes you have to realize . . . that you're not alone, I'm with him! . . . and it's nice. As long as we love each other that's all that matters."

Source: MacMillan, *Mental Retardation in School and Society* (Boston: Little, Brown, 1977), pp. 320–321.

to segregate their retarded offspring in institutions "for their own good" and for the good of a frightened and suspicious community. A comfortably accepted myth was that the big "state school" in the country was really just that, a school that was somehow "best" for those attending. Only recently have graphic descriptions of total institutions and their deleterious effect on human life been forced into public consciousness (Goffman 1961; Blatt and Kaplan 1966; Blatt 1970; Rivera 1972). This description by Wendy Kimball of her visit to one institution is typical:

As the door locked behind me, I stepped into a room of bare cots, naked bodies and unintelligible voices. Some of the bodies strolled about or danced, waving their hands, grunting, shouting; others sat on the floor with folded legs, staring silently and emptily. There were eighteen men, aged fifteen to thirty; some had bodies of old men and others those of children. They had slept without pajamas and they had not yet been dressed,

Fig. 20.7. Gloria, a retarded adult, writes of her concern about her future.

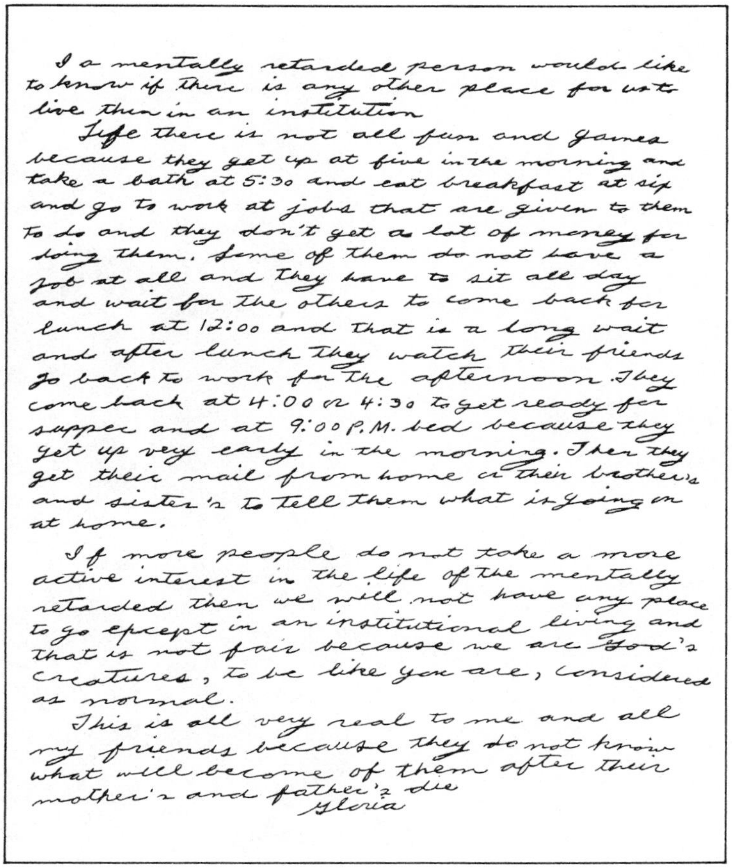

I a mentally retarded person would like to know if there is any other place for us to live then in an institution

Life there is not all fun and games because they get up at five in the morning and take a bath at 5:30 and eat breakfast at six and go to work at jobs that are given to them to do and they don't get a lot of money for doing them. Some of them do not have a job at all and they have to sit all day and wait for the others to come back for lunch at 12:00 and that is a long wait and after lunch they watch their friends go back to work for the afternoon. They come back at 4:00 or 4:30 to get ready for supper and at 9:00 P.M. bed because they get up very early in the morning. Then they get their mail from home or their brother's and sister's to tell them what is going on at home.

If more people do not take a more active interest in the life of the mentally retarded then we will not have any place to go except in an institutional living and that is not fair because we are God's creatures, to be like you are, considered as normal.

This is all very real to me and all my friends because they do not know what will become of them after their mother's and father's die

Gloria

but they milled about as though they had been milling for decades in that room with its flimsy cots and puddles of urine (Kimball 1972).

In 1969, more than 200,000 people, nearly half of them children, lived in over 150 institutions for the mentally retarded in the United States, and tens of thousands more lived in private facilities and institutions for the mentally ill (Butterfield 1969).

In the late 1960s, however, a new movement became evident, to decrease the census of institutions and establish community-based residential alternatives. This movement found some direction from halfway houses for the mentally ill, but it gained much impetus from two sources: the Scandinavian countries' revolution in providing services and increased legal advocacy for civil rights in the United States. During

Fig. 20.8. In a small group home, these retarded women find opportunities for friendship, skill development, and greater involvement in the community.

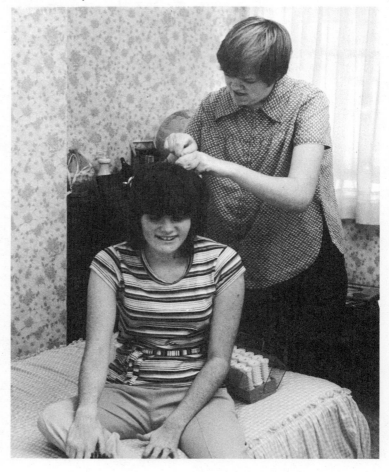

the 1960s Denmark and Sweden reevaluated their residential models and began to place settings near population centers to provide their programs with a full complement of backup services. Older institutions were remodeled, regional centers were built, and small community-based hostels were established. Numerous influential planners in the United States visited Scandinavia and returned with generally glowing reports of tasteful community dwellings that were airy and rich in color, accommodating diverse programs in a system that treated these services as rights, not privileges. They returned embracing the philosophy of *normalization* as well. First proposed by Nirje, the normalization principle means "making available to the mentally retarded patterns and conditions of everyday life which are as close as possible to norms and patterns of the mainstream of society" (1969, p. 181). This philosophy was embraced in court decisions in the United States, which responded to class-action suits on behalf of institutionalized retarded people. Many decisions held that every mentally retarded person has a right to treatment in the least restrictive alternative, and these led toward providing community-based alternatives to total institutions.

In recent years a remarkable array of community residences have been opened to meet various needs of retarded persons (Baker, Seltzer, and Seltzer 1977; O'Connor 1976). The most prevalent are the traditional foster care and the newer small-group home. The latter usually gathers six to ten retarded adults in a large house in the community supervised by several house managers, often a married couple. Small-group homes vary widely in the autonomy and responsibilities for daily living they afford their residents, but they certainly are a more "normalized" living arrangement than the large institution. Other community models include workshop dormitories, where retarded adults live for a year or two and get vocational training, and semi-independent apartments,

where three or four retarded adults share an apartment, with a part-time counselor available for several hours a day (perhaps to help with preparing dinner). In some areas, more comprehensive systems have evolved, providing a variety of such services, so that a person can move to more or less independence as his or her needs dictate. The notable success of these facilities in helping retarded adults who need supervision to live within the community is encouraging indeed, and we may hope that it points the way to elimination forever of institutional warehouses.

Summary

1. Mental retardation, as defined by the American Association on Mental Deficiency (AAMD), has these components: (1) significantly subaverage general intellectual functioning; (2) deficits in adaptive behavior; and (3) manifestation during the developmental years (birth to eighteen years).

2. As a way of measuring the intelligence of retarded individuals, IQ tests have been criticized for many reasons, including poor standardization of items for children with IQs lower than 70. IQ scores are still widely used, however.

3. Adaptive behavior, which is more important than intellectual ability in day-to-day functioning, is the ability to accomplish activities typically mastered at a specific age level, combined with personal and social responsibility. The AAMD suggests assessing a variety of adaptive behaviors at different stages: (1) in infancy and early childhood — sensory-motor skills, communication and self-help skills, and socialization; (2) in childhood and early adolescence — applying basic academic skills to daily life, mastery of the environment by appropriate reasoning and judgment, and social skills; (3) in late adolescence and adult life — vocational and social responsibilities and performances. Adaptive behavior varies with environmental demands — diagnosed retardation is higher in urban areas where more sophisticated skills are needed.

4. The AAMD describes four categories of retardation. (1) Mild retardation (educable retarded), with IQ scores of about 55 to 69, includes 75 to 85 percent of retarded children. These children can learn academic skills through sixth grade level, and as adults they can hold jobs and lead fairly independent lives. (2) Moderate retardation (trainable retarded), with IQ scores of about 40 to 54, includes 10 to 20 percent of retarded children. Moderately retarded children are taught practical skills needed to function with some independence in the community. (3) Severe retardation (trainable or profoundly retarded), with IQ scores of about 25 to 39, and (4) profound retardation (profoundly retarded), with IQ scores below 25, include fewer than 5 percent of retarded children. Only recently have serious attempts been made to teach these children basic skills.

5. The parents of retarded children typically pass through several stages of reaction on discovering their child's retardation: shock and confusion, disbelief, guilt, blame, and search for a different diagnosis.

6. The causes of mental retardation can be divided into three categories: genetic, physical-environmental, and psychosocial. Retardation due to genetic causes includes: Down's syndrome, a chromosomal disorder that results in moderate retardation along with specific behavioral and physical characteristics; and phenylketonuria (PKU), in which an inability to oxidize the amino acid phenylalanine leads to nervous system damage and retardation. The recent development of a test for PKU allows early detection and early treatment with a special diet to prevent retardation.

7. Physical factors in the environment that cause retardation include: (1) maternal disease during pregnancy, especially rubella; (2) poor maternal nutrition during pregnancy and poor infant nutrition during the first year of life; (3) maternal drug use; (4) childhood illness accompanied by high fever; (5) poisoning, especially from accidental ingestion of lead; and (5) head injuries.

8. Cultural-familial, or psychosocial retardation is diagnosed when there is no clear evidence of cerebral pathology and when both the child and another family member show signs of retarded intellectual functioning. This type of retardation is caused by the interaction of factors associated with growing up in poverty, such as poor diet and health care, lack of verbal stimulation, and limited reinforcement for solving problems.

9. Two models offer explanations for the inefficient learning of retarded children: the difference model assumes that a particular cognitive defect makes the retarded person qualitatively different; and the developmental model suggests that the retarded person learns in the same way as nonretarded individuals but learns more slowly and has a lower ceiling on performance.

10. Repeated failure during the developmental years causes many retarded children to use a problem-solving strategy designed to avoid failure.

11. Personality characteristics that retarded persons develop to cope with their own limitations and the reactions of others are: anxiety and frustration, reliance on routine and rules, dependence on others for behavioral cues, and low self-esteem.

12. Providing retarded citizens their basic human rights requires: (1) public education that not only meets the child's special needs but also fosters interaction with nonretarded peers; (2) social acceptance of retarded people; (3) job opportunities; (4) sex education; and (5) normalized living environments in the community.

Chapter 21

Childhood Behavior Disorders

Experiencing Childhood Behavior Disorders

Diagnostic Issues
Eye of the Beholder
Variability in Children's Behavior

Classification of Childhood Behavior Disorders

Developmental Disorders: Enuresis
Adjustment of Enuretics
Treatment
Adjustment Following Conditioning Treatment
Life Course

Anxiety Disorders
Developmental Trends
School Phobia

Hyperactivity
Incidence
Description
Etiology
Life Course

Childhood Psychoses
A Description of Infantile Autism
Etiology of Autism
Life Course of Autism

Summary

We entered Mrs. C's classroom to consult about a child referred for "hyperactivity." "Where's Jimmy?" we asked, looking at the rows of children, and Mrs. C. answered, "Up there," nodding toward the ceiling. Sure enough, clinging to a pipe about 12 feet high was a small boy, waving to his classmates with a let-me-entertain-you smile. Later systematic observations showed Jimmy to be doing something other than the assigned task for more than 85 percent of the school day. When he was not out of his seat disrupting the class, he was fidgeting, talking to his neighbors, drawing on his desk, blurting out incorrect answers, and laughing loudly. Jimmy's school progress during first grade had been nil.

Jimmy's mom was drinking heavily and in and out of the home. Jimmy's absent dad had been replaced by a long series of men with little more time for Jimmy than the obligatory pat on the head. At home, Jimmy's antics did not seem strikingly atypical, and, indeed, his acting out seemed to escalate under the demands of first grade. To Jimmy school brought impossible tasks, and to Mrs. C. Jimmy brought trouble.

Age six certainly seems young to give Jimmy a psychiatric label and begin treatment, maybe with drugs. Perhaps intervention should wait a while. Yet the literature reports that many similar children

[handwritten margin notes: no fewer than 10%... (even more) have disorders — children w/ more serious behavior... greater frequency among boys than girls. Behavior Disorder — sets child apart — acceptance determined by reaction of adults + living with problem + ensuing isolation + the knowledge that he is helpless to do something about it. effects on family are agonizing which in turn may trouble the child... a circle with no escape]

slip progressively further behind in school and eventually into early adolescent delinquency. Perhaps for Jimmy intervention should have begun years ago.

Childhood is never without its struggles and distress, and most children will at one time or another be afraid, disobey, or in some other way trouble their parents. However, millions of children have behavior disorders so severe and lasting that professional help is advisable. Estimates of their magnitude vary according to the criteria, but no fewer than 10 percent of children (and probably far more) will have serious behavior disorders. For reasons not well understood, almost all childhood behavior disorders occur with greater frequency in boys than in girls. Some children, like Jimmy, have difficulty meeting demands of growing up such as those encountered in school. Countless other children live with more circumscribed but still distressing problems, such as a disrupting fear of school or chronic bedwetting. And a few children, who are autistic, show extremely disordered behavior in almost every area of functioning.

Experiencing Childhood Behavior Disorders

A behavior disorder sets a child apart — this kid is different. For the school-age child, being "like the other kids" is the safest path to acceptance. Even small differences invite magnification and, under the scrutiny and naive cruelty of peers, lead to feelings of being unaccepted, of being alone. These are the years, especially, when all children try to discover themselves — they are very perceptive about the world around them, quick to notice differences and to question. Children's acceptance of their own differences and those of others is, of course, very much determined by

the reactions of adults. Children look to parents and teachers for answers to their questions: why does Janet cry all the time and what's wrong with Tommy's eye and why doesn't that new kid talk? And they look to the same people for acceptance of their own differences:

Q. What would you like most?
A. [6 years, 11 months] Anything at all? Like are you maybe going to *do* what I say? Well, I'll tell you. First, I would like it a lot if Mrs. Miller [teacher] would just once in a while, even once in the whole of second grade, say, "Here's a boy who's really moving up fast" to me like she did to Stu and Jackie. . . . And I also would like to do some things good like Elliot [older brother] does right from the start. Elliot hit a baseball right off, and he just catches good, and my dad says, "That boy is a natural," and I would like it if I was natural at something (Ross and Ross 1976, p. 166).

The child with a behavior disorder must live not only with his problem and the ensuing isolation, but also with the terrible knowledge that he is helpless to do something about it. Again, during the years when most children are setting out to master their world, some realize that they cannot even control their own fears, fantasies, or tears. Writer George Orwell remembers his own childhood experiences as a bedwetter:

Soon after I arrived at Crossgates . . . I began wetting my bed. In those days . . . it was looked on as a disgusting crime which the child committed on purpose and for which the proper cure was a beating. For my part I did not need to be told it was a crime. Night after night I prayed, with a fervor never previously attained in my prayers, "Please God, do not let me wet my bed!" but it made remarkably little difference. Some nights the thing happened, others not. There was no volition about it, no consciousness. You did not properly speaking *do* the deed: you merely woke up in the morning and found that the sheets were wringing wet.

Fig. 21.1. The child with a behavior disorder often feels different, left out.

And after a beating:

I was crying . . . partly because of a deeper grief which is peculiar to childhood and not easy to convey: a sense of desolate loneliness and helplessness, of being locked up not only in a hostile world but in a world of good and evil where the rules were such that it was actually not possible for me to keep them (Orwell 1945, p. 250, 253).

The effects of childhood behavior disorders on the family are also agonizing. Parents are driven to worry about causes, seek to place blame, search out services, suffer embarrassment in front of relatives and neighbors, pity the child's pain, and search out more services. Quite naturally, the parents often disagree about what to do, a controversy heightened by emotions about the problem itself. Below, the parent of a severely disturbed child reflects on his feelings:

All day yesterday there were tears beneath my eyes, waiting to stream through the facade of workaday reality. On the train into the city I wanted to cry. But of course I couldn't. And I didn't know what good crying would do. Finally everything surfaced when I got home. Foumi and I got into a senseless argument as to whether hereditary factors were the cause of Noah's possible — indeed very likely — retardation or autism (Greenfeld 1973, pp. 59–60).

Inevitably, the family's reactions trouble the child, a vicious circle from which there seems to be no escape. A hyperactive child, not yet seven years old, captures for us the feelings we have described of differentness and helplessness, as well as awareness of the effects on his parents, in his response to the question, "What would you like most?"

Well, can this be anything I'd like? OK here goes. I am very tired of everything always being wrong and having to go for tests and my mom and dad look awful worried and soon I might have to go to another school. And what I would like a lot would be if I could just sit still and be the way the other kids are and not have all these things happen. And most of all I wish I did not break that mirror at Teddy Work's birthday party (Ross and Ross 1976, p. 166).

The sensitivity and tolerance of the parents are, in fact, often vital to a child's being classified as having a behavior disorder in the first place. The diagnosis of childhood behavior disorders in many ways depends on how "significant" persons experience the child.

Diagnostic Issues

Clinicians and researchers working with childhood behavior disorders are plagued by many of the same difficulties in definition found with adult disorders, but two are especially significant: (1) subjective viewpoint of significant adults in the child's life, and (2) variability of childhood behavior.

Eye of the Beholder

Children are rarely self-referred; they are labeled a problem at an adult's initiative. If a child's behavior is severely disordered, he probably will have come to the attention of some agency. With less disordered behavior, however, a major determinant of whether he will be referred to an agency is the tolerance his teachers, and especially his parents, show for his behavior. Large surveys of children never brought to clinics reveal many kinds of behavior disorders (Ross 1974); these parents, though, were not concerned enough to seek help. Hence researchers who study diagnosed children find that their clinic sample might reflect uniqueness in the parents' tolerance as much as in the child's behavior.

Variability in Children's Behavior

Furthermore, the child's behavior shows situational variability, so that parents and teachers may be experiencing a somewhat different child. We saw that Jimmy's hyperactive and attention-seeking behavior in school was less evident at home. The clinician getting conflicting reports from teachers and parents, then, must determine if the reason is different tolerances or a real situational difference in behavior. In Jimmy's case it was probably a bit of both.

Also, as children mature, their behavior patterns change rapidly. Today's problems may be different or even gone tomorrow, and very little is known about the rate or nature of these changes. A frequent question with problems of children is whether to intervene now or wait for the child to perhaps "grow out of it." Therefore, knowing that the child's behavior varies with age and situation is important for the clinician deciding whether to diagnose a problem and when, or where, to intervene. And this variability is especially troublesome to the researcher trying to interpret surveys of childhood problems.

Classification of Childhood Behavior Disorders

Several standard systems of classification are applied to childhood behavior disorders. The *DSM*-III says that any appropriate diagnosis for adults can be used in diagnosing a child and also lists forty-three disorders "usually arising in childhood or adolescence" (see Table 21.1). An even more detailed system, proposed by the Group for the Advancement of Psychiatry (GAP 1966), is noteworthy for having a "healthy response" category, which reminds the diagnostician that some childhood problems are natural at certain stages of development (such as puberty) or life events (death of a parent). One drawback of both complex systems is that neither has a consistent scheme of classification; sometimes they classify by the presence or severity of symptoms, sometimes by the age appropriateness of behavior, and sometimes by the (assumed) etiology of the difficulty. And although a primary reason for diagnosis is to guide treatment, correspondence between the diagnostic label and the treatment a child receives has not been good.

A different approach to the problem of classification has been to describe empirical clusters of behavioral symptoms that children manifest. Using checklists of symptoms drawn from clinic records, mentioned by parents or teachers, or seen in clinic visits, investigators have statistically searched for these clusters. Interestingly, although studies have used different sampling methods, two rather similar dimensions have emerged (Peterson 1961; Patterson 1964; Achenbach and Edelbrock 1978):

1. acting out or conduct behaviors that distress those in the child's world (such as aggression, hyperactivity)
2. internal or personality problems that distress the child (such as fears).

One limitation of such studies is that the dimensions can reflect only the behaviors that were surveyed. They usually exclude children of

Table 21.1. Disorders usually arising in childhood or adolescence, from *DSM*-III (general categories)

Mental retardation
Pervasive developmental disorders (e.g., infantile autism)
Attention deficit disorders (e.g., with hyperactivity)
Specific developmental disorders (e.g., enuresis)
Stereotyped movement disorders (e.g., motor tic)
Speech disorders not otherwise classified (e.g., stuttering)
Eating disorders (e.g., pica)
Anxiety disorders (cf., phobias)
Conduct disorders
Disorders characteristic of late adolescence (e.g., identity disorder)
Other disorders of childhood or adolescence (e.g., academic underachievement disorder)

limited intelligence or those with childhood psychosis, and therefore do not include a dimension representing these behavioral deficits.

The areas that we will consider in this chapter do not correspond exactly to any one classification scheme, although our discussion is consistent with most of them. We will consider specific developmental symptom disorders, fears and withdrawn behaviors, hyperactivity, and childhood psychoses, generally in order of increasing severity in effects on the child and family.

Developmental Disorders: Enuresis

A great many children at some time worry their parents about their "progress" in development. The child who is very late in reaching most developmental milestones (walking, speaking, becoming toilet trained) may be labeled developmentally delayed or mentally retarded (see Chapter 20). More commonly, though, a child will be slow or will demonstrate some behavioral deviance in only one of these. Child-guidance clinics see many preschool and early school-age children whose parents worry about eating, sleeping, elimination, or speech problems (eating nonfood substances such as plaster; sleepwalking; having "night terrors"; delayed speech; stuttering; and bedwetting). Table 21.2 summarizes these major developmental disorders, which we will illustrate by a more detailed discussion of "nocturnal enuresis" or bedwetting. Like many of the other developmental disorders, enuresis is mildly disabling but has damaging consequences for the child's peer relationships and self-esteem.

Behaviors often come to be seen as developmental disorders when they continue past a specific age or reach a certain intensity. The

[handwritten marginalia: Nocturnal ENURESIS — bedwetting at least once a month beyond age 3 or 4. — more apt to occur in boys (75%) — family usually has a history of bedwetting. primary enuresis: bedwetting since birth; secondary ": following a stressful event. medical — 5-10%. psychological / psychoanalytic — symptom of emotional disturbance. behavioral — faulty learning. However (1) a substitute for gratification of repressed genital sexuality (2) a direct manifestation of anxieties + fears (3) disguised aggress toward parents. parent substitute... therapy must treat... underlying disturbance]

Table 21.2. Developmental disorders

Eating disorders

Refusal to eat	Dawdling over food, fussy and variable appetite, holding unchewed food in mouth. More seriously, vomiting almost at will, and losing weight (see anorexia nervosa in Chapter 13).
Obesity	Eating to 25% + overweight for age, sex, and height, resulting often in peer-group animosity and lowered self-esteem.
Pica	Craving for and purposely eating "inedible" substances (dirt, clay, plaster) beyond age one. Particular danger of lead poisoning from eating chips of paint. Beyond age six pica is rare and a sign of serious disturbance.

Elimination disorders

Encopresis	Involuntary persistent soiling alternating with periods of prolonged retention of feces, in child beyond age two or three. Prevalence of about 1.5% beyond age seven.

Sleep disorders

Nightmares	Repeated "bad dreams," usually causing the child to awaken fully, recall the dream content, and experience a brief period of wakeful anxiety.
Night terror	A panic-arousing bad dream, from which the child cannot be fully awakened, is confused and agitated, and cannot be calmed by parents. May last up to 20 minutes, with the child then returning to peaceful sleep and having no memory of the episode.
Somnambulism	Sleepwalking, with slow and deliberate movement. The child's eyes are usually open but gait is unsteady. The child does not awaken, is unresponsive to stimulation, and has no memory of the event. There is potential for harm, because the child may walk outside, etc. Prevalence about 6% of children.

Speech disorders

Delay	Prolonged delay in speaking — no words to communicate wants by age two — or very slow development of ability to produce some sounds well. May relate to a variety of problems, such as hearing loss, mental retardation, or emotional disturbance.
Stuttering	Interruption of flow of speech by blocks, repeated words or syllables, and prolonged sounds. Onset usually between ages two and five, in 5 to 10% of children.

Habit disorders

Tics	Periodic involuntary muscle twitches or spasms (eye-blink, head twist, grimace). Prevalence about 12% between ages six and twelve.
Nailbiting Thumbsucking Nosepicking	Motor habits that seem to reduce tension or boredom.

[handwritten marginalia left column: Developmental Disorders — 1) Obesity + low self-esteem — eating to 25% + overweight. 2) Pica — craving for + purposely eating inedible things. 3) Nightmares — bad dream, brief period of anxiety. 4) Thumbsucking. 5) Stutter — interruption, reating + prolonged sounds.]

criteria are not usually firm. Generally, however, nocturnal enuresis means bedwetting at least once a month beyond age three or four. The prevalence by age six is about 15 percent of children, but by age twelve it has dropped to 2 or 3 percent; for some, bedwetting persists into adulthood. Enuresis is more apt to occur in boys (75 percent), and the family often has a history of bedwetting (Rutter et al. 1973). Most enuretic children have been wetting since birth (primary enuresis: 75 percent), though some have been dry for a time and then resumed wetting following a stressful event such as illness, birth of a sibling, or separation from a parent (secondary enuresis: 25 percent).

In 5 to 10 percent of the cases, enuresis does have a medical basis. The two main views of etiology for the other cases are the psychoanalytic view, that enuresis is a symptom of emotional disturbance, and the behavioral view, seeking an explanation in faulty learning.

Mowrer (1950) summarized the psychoanalytic explanation as follows: (1) a substitute form of gratification of repressed genital sexuality; (2) a direct manifestation of deep-seated anxieties and fears; and (3) disguised aggression toward parents or parent substitutes. All these views share the belief that a deeper problem is reflected in the bedwetting, and therefore therapy must treat the underlying disturbance. Behavior therapists believe that most often enuresis is an isolated habit deficiency. It represents the child's failure to learn sufficiently well to inhibit relaxation of the sphincter muscle that controls urination (Lovibond 1964; Yates 1970).

These very different views raise several questions on which their predictions would differ. Are enuretic children more maladjusted than nonenuretics? Can enuresis be eliminated without treating an underlying disturbance? Does the child suffer any adverse effects from such a direct approach to treatment?

Adjustment of Enuretics

Other behavioral symptoms and emotional immaturity have been found in enuretic children (Kanner 1948; Biering and Jespersen 1959). But the enuretic children in those studies were all clinic patients, an unrepresentative sample of a group that indeed might be more generally disturbed. Several controlled comparisons of enuretic schoolchildren with randomly selected nonenuretic classmates have found no differences on child or teacher measures of behavioral disturbance (Tapia, Jekel, and Domke 1960; Baker 1969).

Emotional problems that lead to enuresis seem to have been considerably overstated, and its emotional consequences too often ignored. Bedwetting results, for most children, in some feelings of guilt, embarrassment, anxiety about physical health, low self-esteem, and the like. These feelings are not well assessed by available measures, although Compton (1968) did find that enuretic children scored significantly lower than a control group on a scale measuring self-concept. Also, every enuretic child meets with some parental displeasure. Indeed, problems of elimination are second only to crying among the reasons given by child-abusing parents for their aggression toward their children (Helfer and Kempe 1970).

Treatment

Although we consider treatment of childhood disorders in Chapter 22, treatments for enuresis relate directly to our discussion of etiology here. A direct conditioning approach derived from the behavioral theory was first described by Mowrer and Mowrer in 1938. A pad on the child's bed detects the first drops of urine, activates a bell, and awakens the child, whose parents then help him shut off the bell and go to the bathroom. Although the exact learning mechanism has been debated, it probably is "avoidance conditioning," in which the child eventually learns to inhibit urination to avoid the aversiveness of waking to the bell. The psychoanalytic view stresses the need for psychotherapy to address underlying causes and is quite critical of conditioning. Sperling (1965) summarizes: "The removal of the symptom of enuresis, without providing other outlets for the child, leads to a replacement by other symptoms ... usually of a characterological nature, manifesting themselves in behavior disorders more harmful to the child than enuresis."

The evidence, however, is quite clear. No well-controlled study has demonstrated success of psychotherapy with enuresis. On the other hand, Lovibond (1964) reviewed thirteen published studies of the bell and pad method and found that 87 percent of treated children became dry, taking on the average several weeks. The relapse rate may be as high as 40 percent, though most of these respond well to renewed treatment.

Adjustment Following Conditioning Treatment

As to the contention that a child will develop other symptoms if an underlying cause is not discovered and treated, Baker (1969) studied adjustment following successful conditioning treatment. Parents of cured enuretics, rating behavior problems and personality attributes, saw improvement following treatment. Children were happier, less anxious, and more grown-up. They assumed responsibility and ventured into new activities. Because parents' measures are open to bias, however, assessments were obtained also from the enuretic children, from their teachers, and from randomly selected same-sex classmates. The school measurement was presented as a study in creativity — none of the teachers or children associated this school study with the enuresis treatment program. Also, the examiner was blind as to which children were enuretic. Consistent with parent reports (and contrary to the symptom-substitution hypothesis), cured enuretics did not show a decline in adjustment on any measures, which included pre- and post-treatment and three-month follow-up teacher rating scales, child self-report measures, and children's drawings. Two clinical psychologists who blindly scored the drawings found a significant shift toward greater adjustment in the drawings of enuretic children after successful treatment and at follow-up. No such change was found for controls (see Figure 21.2).

Life Course

Without treatment, all but about 2 percent of enuretics will have ceased bedwetting by age fourteen, though some continue into adulthood (Werry 1979a). We do not yet know how to predict which of the childhood enuretics will remit spontaneously and which will not. Treatment of the enuretic child beyond age six is recommended, because it is simple to administer and can shorten the years of wetting and consequent difficulties. This pattern is similar for most other developmental symptom disorders of childhood, among them encopresis (elimination disorder), tics, sleep disorders, and stuttering; all decrease as the child matures. Without treatment, 80 percent of stutterers have normal speech by their late teens (Sheehan and Martyn 1966). One exception is childhood obesity, which is strongly predictive of obesity in later life and is particularly resistant to current methods of treatment.

Anxiety Disorders

Some children are extremely anxious and withdrawn. They might be described by those around them as fearful, tense, timid, seclusive, sad, hypersensitive, and lacking in self-confidence, but generally they are less likely to be noticed at all than the aggressive, acting out child. It appears that most of the anxiety disorders we described in Chapter 13 happen among children as well, though some, like obsessive-compulsive and hysterical disorders, are rare (Knopf 1979).

Childhood depression has only recently been acknowledged as a real phenomenon (Schueterbrandt and Raskin 1977). We simply do not expect children to be depressed, and because they are less able to describe their feelings, depressive reactions often go unnoticed. Raskin (1977) suggests that those children at high risk for depression are those who have recently experienced death of a parent, meet constant failure at school, are physically abused, experience lengthy hospitalization, or have recently witnessed dissolution of their

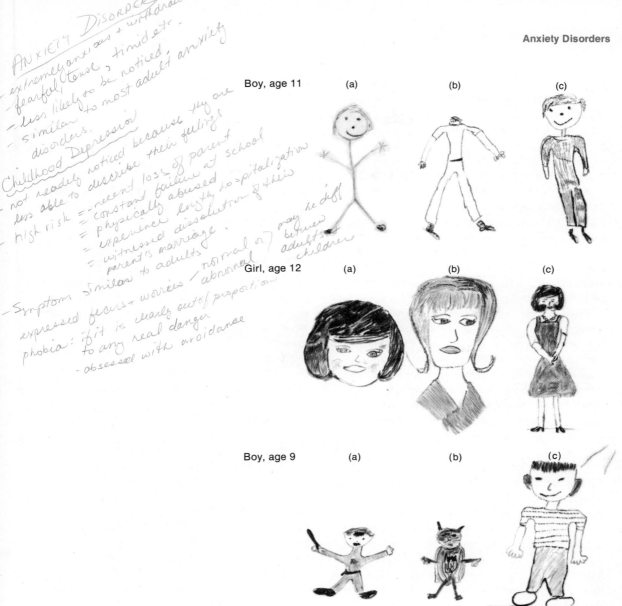

ANXIETY DISORDERS
- extremely anxious + withdrawn
- fearful, tense, timid etc.
- less likely to be noticed.
- similar to most adult anxiety disorders.

Childhood Depression
- not readily noticed because shy are less able to describe their feelings
- high risk = - recent loss of parent
 = constant failure at school
 = physically abused
 = experience lengthy hospitalization
 = witnessed dissolution of their parent's marriage

- Symptoms similar to adults

expressed fears + worries - normal or may be diff between adults + children

phobia: if it is clearly out of proportion to any real danger
- obsessed with avoidance

abnormal

Boy, age 11   (a)   (b)   (c)

Girl, age 12   (a)   (b)   (c)

Boy, age 9   (a)   (b)   (c)

Fig. 21.2. Psychologists sometimes use young children's drawings to assess their emotional adjustment. These series of drawings were done by three enuretic children in the Baker (1969) study. Three times they were asked to draw pictures of themselves: (a) before beginning behavior therapy for their bedwetting, (b) toward the end of treatment, and (c) three months after treatment had ended. In all three cases treatment was completely successful. What changes do you note in the drawings they did after becoming dry?

parents' marriage. Depressive symptoms in children may be masked by apathy, social withdrawal, somatic complaints (headaches or abdominal pain), or even aggressive acting out in older children (Knopf 1979). Little has been written on childhood depression, and conceptualizations seem to parallel those for adult depression, so that we refer you to Chapters 8 to 11 for symptoms, causes, and treatment. One unique diagnostic problem, however, is ascertaining whether expressed fears and worries reflect an abnormal mood state or are transient developmental phenomena in essentially normal children, which leads us to consider childhood fears.

Fears are an inescapable companion to the growing child, as she becomes more aware of her outer and inner worlds and the potential dangers that reside there. A fear is called a *phobia* if it is clearly out of proportion to any real danger. The phobic child will be obsessed with avoiding the dreaded object or situation. Diagnosing a phobia in an adult is not difficult (see Chapter 13). In children, though, fearful behavior is a good example of our earlier point that the diagnostician must understand what is abnormal for the child's age. Consider the common childhood fear of animals. To a three-year-old a large dog may seem, and in fact may be, dangerous; the child's crying and wanting to be picked up as the dog approaches are understandable. Yet when a nine-year-old shows extreme panic, painstakingly arranges his day to avoid dogs, and — always alert for dogs — fills his fantasies with the imagined danger, he is said to have a phobia. Such a phobia is illustrated in this excerpt from a short story relating Peter's bedtime on the night after his new foster parents had decided to get him "what every son should have" — a dog.

He lay stiffly in the darkness. He did not dare to close his eyes. He watched the shadows warily, fearfully, trying to make out the crouched figure of a dog. He lay still, so it would not see him. He pressed his hands against his throat, to protect it from the tearing fangs. He waited. The shadows drew together, came closer. There was a scraping across the floor. He could not breathe. There was a roaring in his ears. A cold breath brushed his cheek. His stomach tightened. He clutched the sheets, and drew himself up. The dog shadows were all around him. All around him. . . . Peter screamed (Reilley 1972).

Developmental Trends

The objects of fear change as children mature. Jersild and his coworkers in the 1930s extensively studied these fears, using reports by parents and children and the child's behavior in potentially fearful experimental situations. For one study, parents kept records of fears that they observed in their preschool children's daily lives. Observations between birth and age six are shown in Figure 21.3.

The infant fears immediate, tangible objects or situations, such as noise and strange objects or persons. Jersild writes: "As he grows older, the range of his fears grows wider. As he acquires the ability to dwell upon his past and to anticipate his future, many fears will pertain to distant dangers, forebodings of what the future may bring and apprehension concerning his own impulses and what he has done or might do" (1968, p. 328). Fears of imaginary creatures, the dark, and being left alone increase. Holmes (1935) found that, consistent with developmental changes, the more intelligent, developmentally advanced child may have fears that other children do not show until they are older.

Bauer studied fear more recently through the elementary school years. He told each of fifty-four children: "All of us are afraid of something, but we are afraid of some things more than others. What are you afraid of most? Draw a

[Handwritten margin notes:]

BAUER
- by grade 6, there was abandonment of imaginary fears and a turn to more realistic ones.
- may be influenced by age + sex-role expectations

- the passing fears of childhood can be transformed into phobias (same as adults phobias)

Behaviorist: anxiety is learned through conditioning + modeling (2 step process)

phobic avoidance behaviors are learned due to reduction in anxiety

Psychodynamic: predictable conflicts and impulses of growing up (unconsciously) are repressed + the anxiety is transferred to an external object that bears some symbolic relationship to the conflict.

Phobia eg. School Phobia

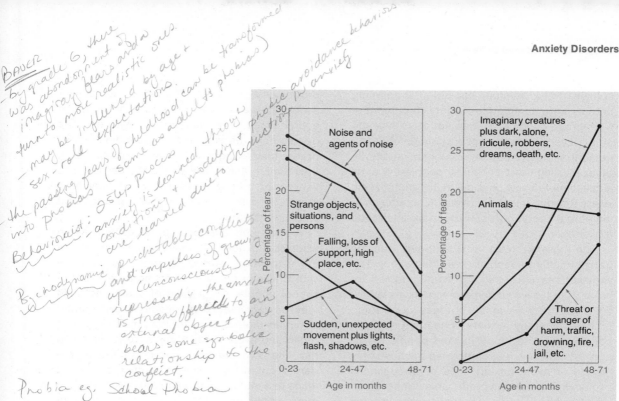

Fig. 21.3. The relative frequency of preschool children's fears of various situations. (After Jersild and Holmes 1935.)

picture and tell me about it." Coding the interviews and drawings according to Jersild's categories, Bauer found the developmental trends shown in Table 21.3. By sixth grade, children had abandoned the more imaginary fears of monsters, ghosts, and animals but had become apprehensive about more realistic sources of physical danger not well understood by the younger child.

As Bauer reports, these results may be influenced by age and by sex-role expectations. Older children may less readily admit to "sillier" fears, and boys may feel some pressure to deny fears — especially "imaginary" ones. In re-

Table 21.3. Occurrence of types of fear in elementary school children

Grade	Bodily injury and physical danger	Monsters and ghosts	Animals
Kindergarten (4–6 years)	11%	74%	47%
Second (6–8 years)	53	53	40
Sixth (10–12 years)	55	5	10

Source: Adapted from D.H. Bauer, "An Exploratory Study of Developmental Changes in Children's Fears," *Journal of Child Psychology and Psychiatry*, 1976, 17(1).

sponse to a related question, frightening dreams were admitted to by only 10 percent of sixth grade boys but 70 percent of sixth grade girls. Nevertheless the general trends of development seem consistent with observations by other investigators. For many people the early adolescent fears of physical injury and psychic stress (making mistakes, failing in school, making others angry) persist throughout adulthood (Miller et al. 1972).

The passing fears of childhood can be transformed into phobias (see Chapter 13). The explanations advanced for adult phobias involve essentially the same mechanisms as for children. The behaviorists propose a two-stage process whereby anxiety is learned through conditioning and modeling and phobic avoidance behaviors are strengthened because they reduce or avoid anxiety. The psychodynamic explanation is that the predictable conflicts and impulses of growing up (castration fears or guilt over aggressive thoughts toward parents), which the child cannot deal with consciously, are repressed, and the anxiety is transferred to an external object that bears some symbolic relationship to the conflict. To illustrate the complexity of understanding a phobia, we will examine a prevalent and very disabling childhood phobia — attending school.

School Phobia

The school-phobic child dreads leaving home to go to school. She may awaken in the morning with somatic complaints, a headache, drowsiness, or nausea. If forced to get ready for school anyway, she is likely to express vague apprehensions of impending disaster. The parents are thrown into a quandary — they probe, they "diagnose," they make light of it, they confer, and finally they force her to go to school, or they give in. The child may miss months or even years of school, causing great strain in the family.

A school phobia does not necessarily begin when school does — it may occur during any of the elementary grades. A recent experience with illness or death is a common precursor of school phobia. At the time of onset, the child may be legitimately or imaginatively worried about his mother's health, the possibility of her death and even his own, because he is losing her. The psychoanalytic view is that the dependent relationship between mother and child leads to a mutual *separation anxiety*. The problem is not so much facing events at school but separating from home. The child senses that his mother wishes him to remain at home, and this is congruent with his own needs (cf. Eisenberg 1958). This anxiety about separation is repressed and then is transferred onto school. Here is one of Eisenberg's many graphic clinical observations of mother "holding onto" the child:

One father reported during the course of treatment that on the day his son had agreed to begin his return to school, his mother wondered aloud whether it might not be wiser to wait a day since it

Children's Fears

According to one source, these are the ten most prominently reported fears of children aged nine to twelve:
Being hit by a car or truck
Failing a test
Getting poor grades
Bombing attacks — being invaded
Not being able to breathe

Being sent to the principal
Fire — getting burned
Death or dead people
Having my parents argue
Germs or getting a serious illness

Source: Adapted from Scherer and Nakamura 1968, pp. 177–178.

[handwritten margin notes, top:] SOCIAL LEARNING THEORISTS - real fear of school. - imagined dangers there - + imagined or real - school avoidance behavior is further reinforced by parents! causes: ① traumatic experiences at school ② separation anxiety ③ combination eg - academic failure - bullying - rejection ① consumption from home reinforcement for ① avoidance of fear ② attention gain Treatment → early return to school KENNEDY → 3 day program

[handwritten margin notes, right:] Type I child - lower grades - first episode - communicate / parents + willing in therapy

Type 2 - upper grade - several episodes - parents noncommunicative / unwilling in therapy

Type I - reminder on sunday - somatic complaints are ignored & Monday progress complimented

was raining and he might catch cold. When the youngster insisted he should keep to his agreement, the mother suggested she consult his father. Called at his office, the father responded with an exasperated "of course he should go!" Whereupon, the mother turned to the patient and stated, "your father thinks it's raining too hard" (Eisenberg 1958, p. 714).

Some mothers do seem anxious about their child's leaving, but this explanation for school phobia is partial at best, because similar dynamics are found with mothers of children having different behavior disorders or none at all. Social learning theorists hold that the child actually does fear school, because of imagined or real dangers there, and that the school-avoidance behavior is further reinforced, often unwittingly, by parents. It is likely that in some cases school phobia stems from traumatic experiences at school, in other cases from extreme separation anxiety at home, and in most from a combination of these.

Many school-phobic children express fear of academic failure, even though they are generally bright and doing well. Hersov (1960a,b) compared school achievement in fifty truant, fifty phobic, and fifty control children, and found that only four of the phobic children had "a poor standard of school work," compared with thirty-one of the truants and eighteen of the control children. For many children other aspects of school come to cause discomfort — for example, abuse by a bully, rejection by a peer group, teasing by a teacher, or embarrassment at having to undress in gym. Whatever the source, the child is now anxious about returning to school.

The parent who reacts to a child's periodic reluctance to attend school by showing concern and who quickly permits staying at home may, however, be encouraging future incidents. Furthermore, the child who does remain home "gains" twice: (1) avoiding the fear-arousing conditions of school, and (2) getting the special

attention and privileges of a "sick" child. The irony is that after a few days of missed school there is more cause for anxiety, because the child has now fallen behind. Indeed, theorists with different views on how school phobia begins seem to agree that the first objective of treatment should be early return to school.

Kennedy (1965) developed a three-day program for rapid return to school. He distinguished between two types of school-phobic children. *Type I children* are in the lower grades and are experiencing their first episode. The onset is sudden, usually on Monday, following an illness that kept them home the previous Thursday or Friday. The child expresses worry about death and mother's health. Parents of the Type I child communicate well with each other, are well adjusted, and cooperate in treatment.

Type II children, on the other hand, are in the upper grades, have had several episodes of school phobia, and the onset is gradual. The child has not been ill, nor is mother's health an issue. But the parents evince behavior disorders themselves, do not communicate well with each other, and are very difficult to work with in the child's treatment.

Kennedy's program of treatment is reserved for Type I children because Type II children and their families generally require long-term treatment. Essential to his program is forcing the child to return to school on Monday morning, after refraining from weekend discussion of the problem, except a Sunday evening reminder that "tomorrow you go back to school." Somatic complaints are ignored, and the child's Monday progress is complimented no matter how resistant she was. The therapist meets with the parents and sometimes with the child to stress the advantages to both of carrying through on the procedure. "Wednesday," Kennedy claims, "should be virtually symptom free" (p. 288). Kennedy reports complete success with rapid treatment of fifty Type I children.

Normal Childhood Fears

These drawings and stories, by two children aged 6 and two aged 10, illustrate developmental trends in children's fears. The six-year-old fears animals and imaginary creatures, and turns to parents for protection.* The ten-year-old also fears for personal safety, but the worries he expresses seem as much curiosity about a world he is trying to master as actual fear. He can rely on his own resourcefulness to cope with the dangers.

Story (boy, age six)

Once there was a boy Jimmie who was real afraid of everything. Every time he'd go to sleep he'd have nightmares. There was a monster that had long claws and chased him all around the place. Jimmie ran around the house and the monster got tired and ran away. Jimmie was shaky and hollered out so loud he woke his Mother up. His Mother thought some-

* The story could be interpreted symbolically as well, expressing the anxiety about Oedipal feelings or masturbation common at age six. The image of the threatening monster merges with that of Dad, "gun" ready, who finds Jimmy in bed, exposed!

one was in the house and woke up the Daddy and the Daddy got his gun and only saw that Jimmie was sleeping but his covers were off his bed.

Story (boy, age ten): In the Woods

One day I was walking in the woods by myself. I unpacked my things and ate my dinner and then it was time to go to sleep. Next morning I woke up and then I went hunting to find my breakfast before I knew it a giant bird was attacking me I didn't know what to do so I started to run. The bird still was after me I started to run faster and faster unil finally I reached a dead end. so I tried to slip away but I was trapped so I picked up a rock and threw it at a bird but it missed him. Now I remembered the bird whistle I got in camp so I blew it and the bird flew away and now it was night time the wolves were howing and I got a little scard because I wouldn't know what would happen next. The next night the wolf attacked and I was fighting it and I stabbd it with a knife and he was dead and that was the end of my campout.

Source: From Lystad 1974.

Drawing (girl, age six): Spider

Drawing (boy, age ten): My First Time Out

[handwritten margin notes at top:] unstructured play situations. "problem seems to be, not so much greater activity but the inability to regulate activity according to expectations in situations requiring inhibition or control. —inability to channel his activity & focus attention in a goal directed manner "; quality of the activity that differs from a highly active child*

Hyperactivity

The mother of a severely retarded six-year-old recently confided in us, with a tremor in her voice: "His teacher says he also might be *hyperactive!*" It was sadly humorous to find the realities of severe retardation momentarily pale before that dreaded new label. "Hyperactivity" has become childhood mental health's most common and probably most controversial diagnosis (Ross and Ross 1976). Some argue for a *hyperactive child syndrome,* implying a cluster of related characteristics (hyperactivity, distractibility, impulsivity, and excitability) with a common cause (Wender 1971). Conversely, others insist that there have always been children who misbehave and have trouble coping with the demands of school and that to call them "hyperactive" does nothing but promote the inaccurate view that there is a unitary problem and it is located within the child. Poor parenting and even poorer school environments are overlooked in the rush to medicate the child (Conrad 1975).

Wherever the truth lies, several hundred thousand American schoolchildren are being maintained on psychostimulant drugs, and many teachers, physicians, and drug companies advocate extending the practice. The clinical and social implications compel us to take a closer look at hyperactivity. Who is the "hyperactive child"? Why does he behave as he does? What justifies drug treatment?

Incidence

Hyperactivity is the presenting problem in as many as 40 percent of referrals to child guidance clinics (Safer 1971). Furthermore, mass screening of elementary school children has been suggested in order to detect the problem and begin drug treatment early (Wender 1971). This possibility is especially troublesome if we consider the high rate at which teachers perceive the clinical signs. When Werry and Quay had teachers complete checklists of behavior problems, they described 50 percent of boys as restless, 48 percent as distractible, and 30 percent as hyperactive (1971). The actual incidence of hyperactivity, according to clinicians, is lower, but it is still about 5 to 6 percent; for boys the diagnosis is applied up to nine times more often than for girls (Miller et al. 1973). We have seen that whether a child receives any label has much to do with the ability of those around him (parents and teachers) to tolerate his behavior, and clinicians may tolerate disruptive behavior better than teachers. Nonetheless, the child's disruptiveness is likely to be more evident in school.

Description

The classification hyperactive, or hyperkinetic, has been applied to a wide range of problem behaviors. The *DSM*-III lists short attention span and distractibility as essential features and has recommended replacing it with a new category: *attentional deficit disorder.*

Teachers report that the hyperactive child cannot sit still through a lesson, that he daydreams, fidgets, and talks a great deal. He is also impulsive, perhaps blurting out tactless remarks, charging into traffic, or giving the first answer that comes to mind. Parents complain of poor response to discipline and problems with peers. He is often aggressive and impatient, unable to keep his hands to himself, to wait his turn, or to follow rules, as these quotations illustrate:

A ten-year-old hyperactive boy talks about his behavior:

> I was trying to run in the water, swimming pretty fast, bumping into the girls, my sisters, and diving in, and diving in and bouncing in and diving in and turn around and spring off your feet like a bowling pin in the water.

[handwritten margin notes: ETIOLOGY (causes) — behavioral symptoms of hyperactivity match those with minimal brain damage (not good evidence) — genetic factors — history of hyperactivity is common in families. — support from twin & adoption studies]

And an eleven-year-old boy sums up his behavior in school:

Child: Running out of the room, kicking people, beating people up, cussing them out, things like that.
Interviewer: How come?
C.: *(laughs)* I don't know. I just wanna. I just feel like it.
I.: What *does* that feel like?
C.: Like, I don't know what it feels like, really.
I.: Think about it for a minute.
C.: I can't. Let's see, how it feels. It feels just like you can't hold it in. It has to come out (Whalen and Henker, in press, pp. 38–39).

Many observers have described an erratic quality in the hyperactive child's performance; he gets some test items correct and misses similar ones in no predictable pattern, or he has overall "good days" and "bad days," which particularly irritates parents and teachers (Douglas 1974). Often these same children are quite excitable; they react to high activity around them or to minor frustrations by bubbling over with excitement or throwing temper tantrums and crying.

Where among all these behaviors is hyperactivity itself? Parents report that these children are always on the go; they quickly wear out shoes, clothing, and the family. Even in infancy these children display irregular eating and sleeping habits (Stewart et al. 1966). Systematic studies of activity level in unstructured play situations, though, have failed to show more general activity in the so-called hyperactive child than in normal children (Douglas et al. 1969). One well-designed study by Schleifer and coworkers (1975) compared three- and four-year-olds diagnosed as hyperactive with matched control children. The fifty-four children were divided into groups of six children each (three hyperactive, three control), and each group participated in nine weekly two-

hour nursery school sessions. To avoid bias, the teachers and observers were not told the children's status or the purpose of the study. Systematic observations revealed no differences in play activity between the hyperactive and control children. In fact, two psychologists observing the nursery groups could not even identify the hyperactive children any better than predicted by chance.

In structured learning, however, the child displays distractibility and short attention span, and these result in greater activity. In a structured play period during which children were to sit, Schleifer found that the hyperactive children were more often out of their seats and were more aggressive than the control children. The problem, then, seems to be not so much greater overall activity as inability to regulate activity according to expectations in situations requiring inhibition or control. A number of laboratory studies have suggested that the problem may be attention: selecting what to attend to and sustaining attention (Sroufe 1975). It is the *quality* of the hyperactive child's activity that differentiates him from the normal, highly active child. The latter has the ability to channel his activity and focus his attention in a goal-directed manner, at least some of the time (Campbell 1976).

Etiology

Why do children behave in these ways? One difficulty in understanding etiology is the remarkably wide array of problem behaviors drawn under the umbrella of "hyperactivity." Current thinking is that in fact we are considering a heterogeneous group of children with different etiologies. In different cases the observed behaviors may be caused by brain damage, genetic factors, hazards in the physical or educational environment, or practices of child rearing.

One term often used synonymously with

HASTING + BARKLEY
- psycho physiological arousal
- hyperactive children seem to have a defect in arousability being unable to respond optimally to stimulation.
  ∴ motor activity may be an attempt to increase sensory inputs.

SOME EVIDENCE FOR
- not conclusive
- environmental toxins
- LEAD poisoning
- food additives
  ∴ evidence for family disturbances and techniques used to manage the child's behavior can cause it or help it.

LIFE COURSE
- hyperactive children do not differ from peers on ... intelligence + academic achievements in early grades but the results decrease with age
- defects inattention + cognitive function increase, gross motor activity decrease gross, motoric but persistent academic failure + continued impairment in concentration and attention.

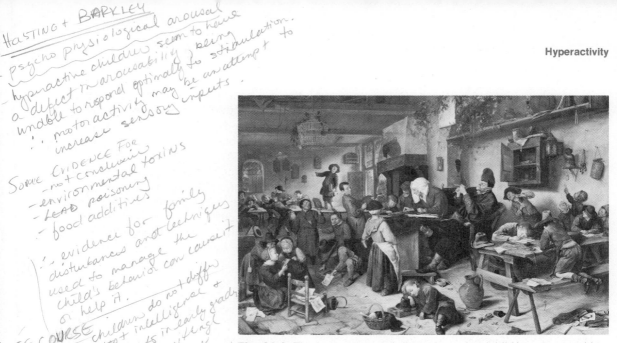

Fig. 21.4. The inattentive and disruptive schoolchildren portrayed in this 17th century Dutch painting might be diagnosed "hyperactive" today. Have we discovered a previously unrecognized syndrome or merely coined a new label for age-old behavior? (Jan Steen: "A School for Boys and Girls.")

hyperactivity is *minimal brain damage,* because some children with known brain damage have the behavioral symptoms we have described. It is illogical, however, to assume brain damage from these behaviors, without other independent evidence. Stewart and Olds (1973) estimate that 10 percent of histories might suggest brain damage, but there is little evidence supporting it as a major etiological factor.

Genetic evidence that implicates transmission in the family is accumulating, however. A history of hyperactivity is common in the families of hyperactive children (Morrison and Stewart 1971; Safer 1973). Attempts to distinguish genetic from learning influences have employed the twin study and adoption study methods used in schizophrenia research (see Chapter 6). They show no heightened incidence of hyperactivity in the *non*biological relatives of adopted hyperactive children (Morrison and Stewart 1973) and a higher concordance rate for monozygotic twins than for dyzygotic twins (Cantwell 1975). These results support a genetic theory of hyperactivity. As with adult psychotic disorders, some biochemical investigators have begun to look for clues in neurotransmitter substances like serotonin, dopamine, and norepinephrine (Brase and Loh 1975; Greenberg and Coleman 1976), but it is still too early to know whether further research will substantiate the positive findings.

Other researchers have measured psychophysiological arousal, using indices like those applied to sociopathy. Hastings and Barkley (1978), reviewing these numerous and often conflicting studies, conclude that, as a group, hyperactive children appear to have a defect in arousability, being unable to respond optimally to stimulation. Their motor activity, then, may be an attempt to increase sensory inputs. These findings are consistent with the *DSM*-III reclassification of hyperactivity as a deficit in attention (not a motor disorder).

Other possible causes for hyperactivity have been suggested. Some evidence shows that environmental toxins may account for hyperactive behavior in some children. Lead poisoning, a common hazard from automobile exhaust and peeling paint in urban areas, has been found to be associated with hyperactivity (Baloh et al. 1975), and Feingold (1975) has received much publicity for his still unproven claim that food additives can produce hyperactivity in genetically predisposed children. Finally, evidence is ample that, in general, family disturbances and, in particular, the techniques used by parents and teachers to manage their child's behavior can markedly increase the rate of behaviors in the hyperactive child syndrome. As we will see in Chapter 22, these environmental causes are cited by behavior therapists who seek to decrease the child's problem behavior by altering the ways in which his parents and teachers respond to him.

Life Course

Although long-term data on the adjustment of hyperactive children are still limited, the prognosis is not as favorable as once believed. Hyperactive children do not differ from peers on tests of intelligence and academic achievement in early grades, but a downward spiral appears as the child gets older. His defects in attention and cognitive functioning are increasingly detrimental (Douglas 1972) and interact with his sense of failure and lack of motivation (Ross and Ross 1976). Studies following the hyperactive child into adolescence find a decrease in gross motor activity but persistent academic failure and continued impairment in attention and concentration (Kinsbourne and Caplan 1979). Hyperactive children who show aggressive tendencies in childhood are likely to display antisocial behavior as adolescents. One study has even found that many former hyperactive children judged to be making a favorable later adjustment nonetheless were lonely and unpopular (Minde et al. 1971). It is likely that much of the hyperactive child's continuing difficulty grows from inevitable negative reactions to his behavior by family, teachers, and peers and the frustration, isolation, and low self-esteem he then suffers. In Chapter 22 we will consider attempts at intervention to interrupt this cycle.

Childhood Psychoses

Until now we have considered rather typical childhood problems, such as fears, enuresis, and hyperactivity, which become clinical matters only if they are exaggerated in degree or persistence. The behavior of the psychotic child, however, is qualitatively quite different and markedly atypical. Current estimates are that fewer than one in 1000 children have behavior sufficiently disordered to be diagnosed psychotic, and boys outnumber girls three or four to one. There appear to be two major types of childhood psychosis, *infantile autism* and *childhood schizophrenia*. The diagnostic criteria for these disorders have varied, and the diagnoses have often been used interchangeably in clinical practice and research. The most useful distinction seems to be developmental, infantile autism indicating early-onset psychosis (zero to two and a half years) and childhood schizophrenia indicating late-onset psychosis (five to twelve years) (Kolvin 1971). The former is a reasonably distinct syndrome, first described by Leo Kanner (1943, 1944) as mainly identifiable by "(a) an inability from the beginning of life to relate themselves to people and situations in the ordinary way, and (b) an anxiously obsessive desire for the preservation of sameness." Because of autism's early onset

[handwritten margin notes: schizo — disordered behavior appears after a period of normal development + clinically seems like adult schizo. — delusions, hallucinations, thought disorder — same etiology as adult schizo (CH 5, 6). AUTISM — apparent in the 1st or 2nd year of life, physically attractive & may have extraordinary skills — discontinuities in normal sequence of development with spurts & lags, with severe mental retardation]

and severity, children like Peter in our example (see box) have aroused interest and study far out of proportion to their "incidence."

In childhood schizophrenia, though, the disordered behavior appears after a period of normal development and clinically seems very much like adult schizophrenia. Diagnostic criteria include delusions, hallucinations, and thought disorder. Childhood schizophrenia has received much less attention from researchers than autism; many believe it probably has the same etiology as schizophrenia in later life (Werry 1979b). Because we have discussed schizophrenia at length in Chapters 5 and 6, we will now focus on the unique syndrome of infantile autism.

A Description of Infantile Autism

In the office, he wandered aimlessly about for a few moments, then sat down, uttering unintelligible sounds, and abruptly lay down, smiling. Questions and requests, if reacted to at all, were repeated in echolalia fashion. Objects absorbed him, and he showed good attention in handling them. He seemed to regard people as unwelcome intruders. When a hand was held out before him so that he could not possibly ignore it, he played with it as if it were a detached object. He promptly noticed the wooden form boards and worked at them spontaneously, interestedly and skillfully (Kanner 1971, p. 123).

Autism is usually apparent in the first or second year of life. These children usually are physically attractive and may have extraordinary skills, such as memory for musical pieces or ability to do complex perceptual-motor tasks (puzzles). Yet they show discontinuities in the normal sequence of development, with spurts and lags. A child might sit up unaided early but not stand for many months, or say a few words only to lose them later. Their mental functioning is usually retarded, often severely so. The *DSM*-III lists these diagnostic criteria for infantile autism:

Reflections of a Mother on Her Autistic Child

More troubling was the fact that Peter didn't look at us, or smile, and wouldn't play the games that seemed as much a part of babyhood as diapers. While he didn't cry, he rarely laughed, and when he did, it was at things that didn't seem funny to us. He didn't cuddle, but sat upright in my lap, even when I rocked him. But children differ and we were content to let Peter be himself. We thought it hilarious when my brother, visiting us when Peter was eight months old, observed that "that kid has no social instincts, whatsoever."

It was Kitty, a personality kid, born two years later, whose responsiveness emphasized the degree of Peter's difference. When I went into her room for the late feeding, her little head bobbed up and she greeted me with a smile that reached from her head to her toes. And the realization of that difference chilled me more than the wintry bedroom.

Peter's babbling had not turned into speech by the time he was three. His play was solitary and repetitious. He tore paper into long thin strips, bushelbaskets of it every day. He spun the lids from my canning jars and became upset if we tried to divert him. Only rarely could I catch his eye, and then saw his focus change from me to the reflection in my glasses. It was like trying to pick up mercury with chopsticks.

His adventures into our suburban neighbourhood had been unhappy. He had disregarded the universal rule that sand is to be kept in sand-boxes, and the children themselves had punished him. He walked around a sad and solitary figure, always carrying a toy aeroplane, a toy he never played with. At that time, I had not heard the word that was to dominate our lives, to hover over every conversation, to sit through every meal beside us. That word was autism.

Source: Eberhardy 1967, p. 258.

Fig. 21.5. Autistic children often give the impression of being "in a world of their own." These children seem unaware of each other. They are preoccupied and absorbed in sensations of light and touch.

1. Onset usually prior to 30 months but up to 42 months.
2. Lack of responsiveness to other human beings ("autism").
3. Self-isolation.
4. Gross deficits in language development.
5. If speech is present, peculiar speech patterns.
6. Peculiar interest or attachments to animals or inanimate objects.

[Handwritten marginal notes:]

DSM III
Autism
① Onset usually prior to 30 months but up to 42
② Lack of responsiveness to other human beings (autism)
③ Self isolation
④ Gross deficits in language development
⑤ Of speech is present, peculiar speech patterns
⑥ Peculiar interest and attachment to animals or inanimate objects.

KENNER — Related Behaviors of AUTISM
① Disturbances in Relating
— aloofness + self-absorption
— aversion to being held + avoid eye contact
— as they grow; disengage from people
— prefer to be alone; display preoccupation with inanimate objects
— disturbance of interpersonal relating may be due to avoidance of eye contact.
Hypothesis: autistic child is in a high state of physiological + behavioral arousal + because another person's eyes convey most information are the most arousing / gaze aversion functions to lower arousal

② INSISTANCE ON PRESERVING SAMENESS
— slight changes may produce outbursts
— have surprisingly good memory for selected NOT DSM III perceptions

③ DISTURBANCES IN SPEECH (LANGUAGE)
— little effort to communicate
½ — remain mute (or say one or two phrases)
½ — echolalic - directly (or saying) repeating head words
— many acquire small words or phrases but rarely use them for communication

④ DISTURBANCES IN MOTILITY
— bizarre gestures + odd patterns of mobility
— immobility, body rocking, whirling, swaying, head rolling
— use objects (plates, sticks) for bizarre, rhythmically manipulate

⑤ DISTURBANCES IN PERCEPTION
— disturbed auditory response to preferences
— prefer: touch, smell, taste over hearing + vision
— sensory input is improperly modulated
— overreaction to some stimuli and disregard of others

For a clearer sense of this unique disorder, we will describe in detail these and related behaviors.

DISTURBANCES IN RELATING

Kanner emphasized the aloofness, the self-absorption of autistic children. Among autistic infants the social smile and anticipatory response to being picked up are delayed or absent; they show aversion to being held and avoid eye contact. As they grow they seem disengaged from people; they generally prefer to be alone and display preoccupation with inanimate objects. Kaufman, in a personal account of his autistic son, gives us a glimpse of how disconcerting this seeming indifference can be:

His eyes did not seem to absorb my image, but merely reflected it back to me. Again I asked him, but it was like asking the wind. And each time I looked at my son I found myself turning inward. Searching within myself for the answer. . . . The pushing-away of people and the silent aloneness. When Raun turned to you, he turned through you as if you were transparent (Kaufman 1976, p. 11).

The autistic child's avoidance of eye contact with people seems to some researchers the source of disturbed interpersonal relationships. In a laboratory documentation of this gaze avoidance, autistic and nonautistic children, all inpatients, were given ten minutes to explore an otherwise empty room containing five drawings of faces mounted on stands. As Figure 21.6

Fig. 21.6. The proportions of time spent by autistic and nonautistic children attending to each of five model faces and to the environmental fixtures in an experimental room. Autistic children spent much less time looking at faces and more time absorbed in environmental fixtures, consistent with the "gaze avoidance" described clinically. (After Hutt and Ounsted 1966.)

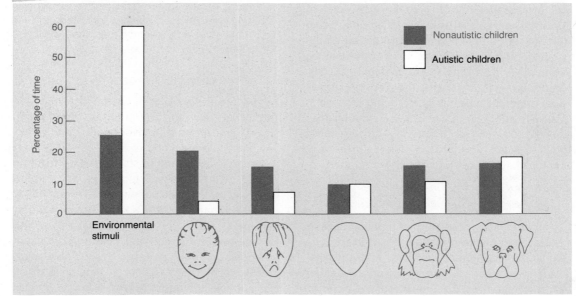

[handwritten margin notes: ETIOLOGY OF AUTISM; Psychological — concentrate on child's early family relationships — disturbed feelings, primary relationship problems; KANNER; parents 3rd and professional, cold; Bettelheim, early parental maladaptation leads to autism]

shows, the nonautistic children showed about equal interest in all the faces, except the blank one. The autistic children looked least at the happy face, somewhat more at the animal faces, but by far the most at environmental stimuli such as light switches and faucets (Hutt and Ounsted 1966). The investigators hypothesized that the autistic child is in a high state of physiological and behavioral arousal and that because another person's eyes convey most information — are the most arousing — gaze aversion functions to lower arousal. Whether or not this explanation proves correct, avoidance of gaze is a distinct and disconcerting sign of autism.

INSISTENCE ON PRESERVING SAMENESS

The other key sign originally noticed by Kanner but absent from the *DSM*-III criteria is the child's anxious ordering of materials to maintain sameness in his world. In some autistic children, even slight changes may provoke an outburst. Creak (1952) described a child who loved chocolate but would eat it only if it were cut into squares; round chocolate was rejected. Teddy, a six-year-old, cried violently while being readied for bed the first night at summer camp. Wondering if he really was so upset at leaving his home and parents, the counselor finally figured out that Teddy wanted to wear his underwear under his pajamas. Upon being dressed in his accustomed way, Teddy immediately quieted down. This insistence on sameness does indicate that autistic children have surprisingly good memory for selected perceptions.

DISTURBANCES IN SPEECH AND LANGUAGE

Another sign of disturbed relationships is that autistic children make little effort to communicate, in words or gestures. About half remain mute or say only one or two phrases at key times in their lives. The speech of the other 50

percent is usually *echolalic* — directly repeating words they have heard. They speak in a high-pitched, parrotlike monotone. In time, many of these children acquire single words and phrases, but they use speech rarely for communication. Even those few who do develop truly communicative speech lack spontaneity and originality.

DISTURBANCES IN MOTILITY

Bizarre gestures and odd patterns of motility are particularly striking. Often the autistic child plays with his fingers in front of his eyes, or flaps his hands or arms excitedly. He might walk on his toes and make staccato lunging and darting movements and sudden stops. Brief periods of immobility mix with whirling, body rocking, swaying, or head rolling. An object such as a plate or stick might be rhythmically manipulated for a long time:

Slowly, with a masterful hand, he places the edge of the plate to the floor, sets his body in a comfortable and balanced position and snaps his wrist with great expertise. The plate begins to spin with dazzling perfection. It revolves on itself as if set into motion by some exacting machine. And it was (Kaufman 1976, p. 1).

DISTURBANCES IN PERCEPTION

Many autistic children have a distorted hierarchy of receptor preferences; they prefer touch, smell, and taste over hearing and vision. A child exploring a new room is likely to get very close to fixtures, and to smell, touch, or put his mouth on them. Sensory input, too, is improperly modulated, the child sometimes overreacting to stimuli (agitation at barking dogs, vacuum cleaners) and sometimes disregarding stimuli altogether (apparently not hearing commands or looking through people). This variable sensitivity to stimuli may explain why the child strives to maintain sameness in his world.

[handwritten marginalia: Behaviorists - function of the interaction mother-child interaction. FERSTER - parents may fail to reinforce prosocial behavior with adequate attention + therefore, teach the child bizarre patterns of responding. But - many rejecting parents raise children who are not autistic / parents of autistic children have other normal children / autism occurs very early in life]

Etiology of Autism

No convincing evidence yet explains why some children behave in such strange ways. The many explanations can be roughly categorized as psychological and biological.

PSYCHOLOGICAL EXPLANATIONS

Some psychological theories concentrate on the child's early experiences in learning, particularly his interactions with his parents, and see autism as a relationship disorder in which disturbed feelings and relationships are the primary problem. Kanner (1943) wrote that parents of autistic children were intelligent, usually professionals, and characteristically obsessive, detached, and cold. A later paper (Eisenberg and Kanner 1956) coined the expression "emotional refrigeration" for the child's supposed early experience. The major proponent of the idea that early parental rejection leads to autistic withdrawal is psychoanalyst Bruno Bettelheim (1967). He writes, the "parents' wish that the child did not exist" results in rejection during critical periods of development in the first year of life. The child finds that his own efforts have no influence and begins to withdraw from the world. The child's aloofness, preservation of sameness, and mutism are a means of coping. Behavioral theorists also explain childhood psychosis as a function of mother-child interaction. Ferster (1961) hypothesized that parents of autistic children may "fail" to reinforce prosocial behavior with adequate attention and therefore teach the child bizarre patterns of responding.

In a study of parental characteristics, Eisenberg and Kanner (1956) compared parents of fifty autistic children referred to their clinic with parents of fifty clinic-referred nonautistic children. They reported the former to be considerably higher in educational attainment and professional status, but their findings are potentially biased. Kanner was nationally known as the authority on autism, and well-educated professionals would be more likely to have heard of him; they also had the means to bring their autistic children to his Baltimore clinic. Later con-

Speech Irregularities in Autism

Affirmation by repetition. The child does not answer "yes"; he expresses agreement by repeating the question. "Do you want a cookie?" means "Yes, I want a cookie."

Pronominal reversal. "You" is used for "I," as in the first example. A child who wants to go outside might say, "You go out?"

Extreme literalness. The child insists on the literal meaning of words. Rimland (1964) reports that one boy got upset because his father spoke of hanging a picture *on* the wall rather than *near* the wall.

Metaphorical usage. The child may use a specific phrase he has heard to indicate a more general concept. One child used the sentence "Don't throw the dog off the balcony" to indicate "No." His mother had long before used this sentence to dissuade him from dropping a toy dog from a railroad station balcony.

Part-whole confusion. The child refers to one component of a larger whole. One boy used the expression "Do you want some catsup, honey?" to ask for dinner; his favorite food was meat seasoned with catsup (Rimland 1964).

Delayed echolalia. The child will repeat a sentence or phrase heard some time before, usually out of context and for no recognizable purpose. Some of the examples above are echolalic, but the purpose is clearer. Much delayed echolalia is from television commercials — one little girl constantly mumbled "no more tangles" from a shampoo ad.

LIFE COURSE OF AUTISM
- partial abatement of some symptoms at age 5 or 6
- bizarre mannerisms diminished + they develop some communication with others
- the long term prognosis is quite bleak
- the clearest diagnostic sign was useful speech by age 5
EISENBERG

trolled studies are equivocal; some found that parents of autistic children had higher educational, occupational, and intellectual levels, and others failed to find differences. Studies of parents' emotional characteristics and child rearing, though, have not supported Bettelheim's assertions (Ornitz 1973).

Psychological causation is further weakened by several facts. Many very rejecting parents raise children who do not show the signs of autism, and parents of autistic children raise other perfectly normal children. And, as we have discussed previously, autism is evidenced very early in life.

BIOLOGICAL EXPLANATIONS

Biological theorists see autism as a cognitive disorder. They believe that the preservation of sameness and disturbances in language and perception are primary and that they result from an organic deficit.

We have no conclusive evidence that complications from pregnancy and birth or specific neurological impairments are more numerous among autistic children. The evidence for genetic factors is equivocal. Psychosis in parents of autistic children is about as frequent as in the general population, although the rate of autism

BIOLOGICAL EXPLANATIONS
- cognitive disorder
- preservation of sameness and disturbances in language and perception are primary and that they result from an organic deficit
- No evidence for complications at birth
- genetic factors equivocal
- as general population except for twins, > 100% concordance
Rimland - brain damage - reticular formation
Lovaas - wires up a person - deficit in selectivity in stimulus
- oversensitive to sth would be more likely the stress-diathesis formulation

A Mother's View of Psychogenic Theories

The literature on child psychology is replete with psychogenic theorizing about autism, in effect blaming parents for the child's disturbance. This view, though becoming outdated in the literature, still pervades psychiatric practice, despite little empirical support and the considerable destructive effect it has on parents. We do not know for certain if parents of autistic children are "different," and even if they are, it might well be because they live with a very atypical child. Even if parents are in some way contributing to their child's disorder, little purpose is served by professionals who have an accusatory attitude. We started this section describing an autistic boy, Peter. His mother, stung by an article presenting Bettelheim's idea, tells her own story:

I told my psychiatric social worker about Peter but her questions were directed to me.

How did I get along with my parents, siblings, the people at work? As well as most people, I thought.

Had I wanted the baby? Yes, I had gone through sterility studies to get pregnant.

Why had I wanted a baby? Why? I had

never reasoned it out. They are a part of life, just like food, sunshine, friends and marriage.

How did I get along with my husband? Very well. She snapped to attention. "Why?" she asked, "Are you afraid to quarrel with him?" Well — we were both in our thirties. We had no serious problems and could laugh at our small differences. Years of separation by the war had made us treasure the ordinary joys of life:

I asked the psychiatric social worker for suggestions, but she had none to offer. What I did was not so important as how I felt about it. What could I read that would help me understand Peter? She could suggest no reading nor would she advise it. . . .

My questions as to the cause of Peter's trouble, she evaded — an eloquent answer, indeed!

I alternated between being overwhelmed with guilt, and feeling resentful at being treated like a child who couldn't face an unpleasant truth. If I could have felt that it was true, that we had been cold and dominating, or cold and indifferent parents, I think I could have faced that fact. At least I would have had something concrete to work with. Anything would have been better than that nameless, formless faceless fear (Eberhardy 1967, pp. 259–260).

in the siblings of autistic children is 2 percent, much higher than the expected rate of less than 0.1 percent. Stronger evidence comes from studies of twins. Rimland (1964) reported 100 percent concordance for autism in eleven sets of monozygotic twins. Of course evidence for a genetic influence doesn't indicate the resulting biological malfunction, and a number of theories have been advanced. Rimland (1964) suggests damage to part of the brain stem, the recticular formation, which "wakes up" a person. He believes that the primary defect is the child's inability to sustain attention to relevant stimuli and to relate new stimuli to remembered experience. The child, then, cannot derive meaning from his experiences, and his insistence on sameness is an attempt to minimize new, incomprehensible stimuli. Currently no direct evidence supports Rimland's intriguing theory. Lovaas, focusing on the disturbance in perception, has proposed a deficit in stimulus selectivity. In a laboratory study (Lovaas et al. 1971), autistic, retarded, and normal children were reinforced for responding to a complex stimulus involving the simultaneous presentation of auditory, visual, and tactile cues. After the discrimination was learned, the cues were presented separately. Autistic children responded primarily to one stimulus component, retarded children to two, and normal children to all three. Although no modality was preferred by the autistic children, apparently they had overselectively attended to only one modality while learning the task. Because much learning involves a complex stimulus, this selective attention may be important in understanding why autistic children fail to learn.

These and other theories are suggestive, but for now the cause of childhood psychosis is still a question. It seems likely that a stress-diathesis formulation such as the one advanced for schizophrenia (Chapter 6) will ultimately be the most plausible. The autistic child quite likely enters the world biologically different in some way, but the consequences probably vary with the way the child's environment, especially his mother, responds to that difference. Lovaas is studying the effects of very early psychological intervention with autistic children, and we will describe this program in Chapter 22.

Life Course of Autism

Some autistic children do show partial abatement of symptoms around age five or six; their bizarre mannerisms diminish, and they develop some communication with others. The long-term prognosis for the autistic child is generally quite bleak, however. Eisenberg (1956) followed up sixty-three autistic children from an average of age six to age fifteen. By mid-adolescence, only three were making "good" adjustment, fourteen were classified "fair" and forty-six had made "poor" progress. A common outcome has been institutionalization and final diagnosis in adulthood as mentally retarded or schizophrenic. With adequate training most of these individuals could live in community-based residential settings like the ones described in Chapter 20. The clearest prognostic sign Eisenberg found was useful speech by age five. Of thirty-two speaking children, sixteen (50 percent) were making fair or good social adjustment, but of thirty-one nonspeaking children, only one (3 percent) met even the criterion for fair adjustment. Rutter and Lockyer (1967; Rutter et al. 1967) found that some nonspeaking autistic children with higher intelligence later developed speech, and concluded that the relationship between linguistic achievement and intelligence needs to be further studied, because IQ may be more relevant than language as a predictor of long-term prognosis.

The few autistic children who make good adjustment as adolescents or adults continue to be somewhat "odd." Their thinking tends to be concrete, and they display a matter-of-fact, tactless manner. Both characteristics indicate little ability to empathize with the feelings of others. Eisenberg related one autistic adolescent's speech at a junior college football rally. The boy gave the logical (and correct) argument that the team would lose and was bewildered by the boos of his classmates!

Summary

1. Children with behavior disorders must endure: (1) isolation from their peers; (2) helplessness at being unable to control their behavior; and (3) the family turmoil that their behavior causes.

2. Two significant problems in defining these disorders are: the subjective viewpoint of significant adults in the child's life; and the natural variability of childhood behavior depending on situation and age.

3. There are different approaches to classifying childhood behavior disorders: (1) the DSM-III uses appropriate adult diagnoses as well as child categories; (2) the Group for the Advancement of Psychiatry's (GAP) more detailed system lists a "healthy-response" category for problems that are normal for a stage of development or life event; and (3) a statistical approach describes empirical clusters of behavioral symptoms derived from information supplied by clinics, parents, and teachers. The latter approach often produces two categories — acting out or conduct behaviors that are distressing to others, and internal or personality problems that are distressing to the child.

4. Developmental disorders are behaviors that continue past a specific age or magnitude or both. Enuresis (bedwetting) is an example of this type of disorder.

5. Psychoanalytic theorists see enuresis as a symptom of emotional disturbance, and behaviorists treat it as the result of faulty learning. Enuretic children have a lower self-concept than their peers, and most face parental displeasure because of their bedwetting. A conditioning treatment has proved most effective in stopping enuresis and improving adjustment. Without treatment, 98 percent of enuretics cease bedwetting by age fourteen. This pattern is typical of developmental disorders.

6. Anxiety disorders in children include: (1) depression, which may appear as apathy, social withdrawal, acting out, or somatic complaints; and (2) phobias, which are distinct from the normal childhood fears that abate in the course of development. School phobia, a prevalent and disabling childhood phobia, may be caused by mutual separation anxiety between mother and child, fear of imagined or real dangers at school, or both.

7. Hyperactivity occurs in about 5 to 6 percent of children. The label is applied much more frequently to boys than girls. Its essential features, according to DSM-III, are a short attention span and distractibility. Hyperactive children are impulsive, aggressive, excitable, and unable to channel their activity and focus their attention to achieve a goal. Possible causes of hyperactivity are: brain damage, genetic factors, and environment. Studies have found that although hyperactive children do not differ from peers on tests of intelligence in the lower grades, as they grow older they fall further and further behind. The resulting sense of failure and frustration often leads to antisocial behavior in adolescence.

8. The two major childhood psychoses are: infantile autism (onset between birth and 2.5 years); and childhood schizophrenia (onset between ages five and twelve). Schizophrenia appears after a period of normal development and is characterized by delusions, hallucinations, and thought disorder.

9. These behaviors are characteristic of autism: (1) disturbances in relating, such as avoidance of eye contact and aversion to being held; (2) insistence on preserving sameness; (3) disturbances in speech and language, such as echolalia or muteness; (4) disturbances in motility, such as hand flapping, whirling, body rocking, or rhythmical manipulation of objects; and (5) disturbances in perception, such as using touch, smell, or taste rather than hearing and sight to explore objects.

10. The cause of autism is unknown, but theories include: (1) psychological explanations, suggesting that early parental rejection leads to autistic withdrawal; (2) biological explanations, based on genetic abnormality; and (3) a stress-diathesis formulation, suggesting a combination of biological difference and parental response to that difference.

11. Autistic children show partial abatement of symptoms at age five or six, but in general the prognosis is positive only for children who develop useful speech by age five.

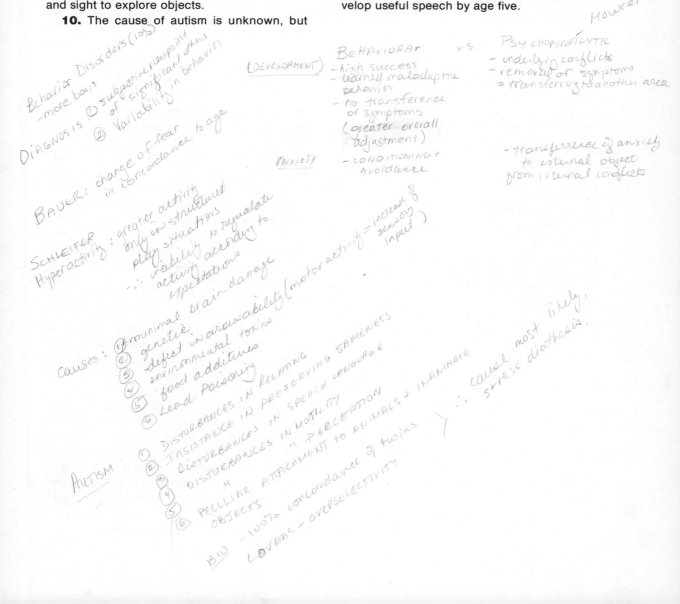

Chapter 22

When? / Where? / how? / Psychoanalytic — focus on the child himself? / helps him to express work through his problems in words + often in play. / family treatment / Behavioral — focus on behavior.

Psychotherapy
Psychoanalytic Play Therapy
Nondirective Play Therapy
Outcome of Child Psychotherapy
Family Therapy

Behavior Therapies
Anxiety Reduction
Behavior Management
Skill Training

Drug Therapy

Early Intervention and Prevention
Moderate to Severe Retardation
Mild or Borderline Retardation
Behavior Disorders

Summary

Intervention with Children

In the 1960s, government and the mental health professions alike decried the lack of a unified national commitment to improve mental health of children and youth. Writers of one government report sadly noted that almost 10 million young persons need some form of help from mental health workers (Joint Commission on Mental Health of Children 1970). But, as Smith and Hobbs (1966) pointed out in an often-quoted paper on the mental health needs of children, most services and facilities have emphasized treatment for adults. In the ensuing years child services have grown noticeably, and much experimenting has been done with new models for service. Nevertheless, millions of children still grow up in conditions of poverty, racism, and abuse. Contemplating this, you might wonder how so many children do, in fact, make an adequate adjustment.

There can be little doubt that to truly influence psychological problems of children would mean very broad social changes: alleviating poverty, eliminating racial discrimination, upgrading the educational system, legislating increased rights for children, and planning families to reduce unwanted births. These are just a few. We must leave to other authors consideration of the social change needed to approach an environment conducive to positive mental health, and focus here on those who already need specialized intervention, the retarded and behavior-disordered children whose problems we described in Chapters 20 and 21.

Intervention with children confronts us with several critical questions. The first is: when is it time to intervene? Obviously, early intervention is desirable, because it may reduce suffering and prevent children's problems from growing more serious. Yet the benefits of therapy must always be weighed against the unwelcome social stigma of labels like "retarded" and "disturbed." We want to be reasonably sure that mild developmental delay or fearfulness is not simply part of normal growing up. Also, children usually are not self-referred; adults usher them into treatment. The child himself may be quite unmotivated to enter therapy and, whenever possible, should have some say in the decision about treatment.

The second important question is: where to intervene? Traditionally, the troubled child could get therapy and even education only by removal to a special place. For many retarded, psychotic, and delinquent children, that place has been a private or state-operated residential institution, which all too often became a permanent home. Less severely disordered children found help in a therapist's office or a playroom at the child-guidance clinic. Now treatment is more often available in the natural settings that affect the child's behavior most directly, the home and the school. A separate setting, such as a residential school or therapeutic summer camp, these days is more likely to be short-lived and designed to reintegrate the child into more natural settings.

A third, more complex question is: how should we intervene? Until recently, children's mental health services in the United States have been dominated by a psychoanalytic orientation and individual treatment. Intervention has been focused on the child himself, on helping him to express and work through his problems in words and often in play. An increased emphasis on services to children has necessitated new approaches to intervention.

The newer behavioral therapies have shifted the focus from feelings to behavior and, like drug therapies, have sought more rapid change in behavior. Also, therapists of various persuasions now include the child's family in treatment. And the expansion in clientele and settings for treatment has naturally enlisted new providers of service, including teachers,

Fig. 22.1. Training parents as therapists for their own children is a recent development in child intervention. This mother has learned to make home a better learning environment for her autistic son.

parents, and volunteers and paraprofessionals trained especially for specific service roles.

Psychotherapy

Verbal forms of psychotherapy (Chapter 15) are frequently employed with older children who have the cognitive ability. With preadolescents, however, psychotherapy usually utilizes the child's play. Children naturally use play to express anxieties and conflicts, to reflect on experiences, and to experiment with new ways of coping. The therapist uses play to establish a relationship and facilitate the child's expression of feelings. Although play therapy has been tried with all types of disordered childhood behavior, it is most applicable to the anxious and withdrawn child.

Play therapy takes place in a specially designed playroom. Materials are chosen to expedite creative play and expression of feelings:

dolls and dollhouse, paints, sandbox, toy soldiers, baby bottle, punching doll, and the like. Only broad limits are set, usually on length of session, aggression against the therapist, and destruction of expensive toys. The therapist tries to create an atmosphere in which the child is responsible for choosing her activities and feels free to express herself. Some therapists include other activities designed for self-expression, such as art, music, dance, or dramatic role playing. The two main approaches are psychoanalytic play therapy and nondirective play therapy.

Psychoanalytic Play Therapy

Psychoanalytic treatment of children was pioneered by Melanie Klein (1932, 1955) and Anna Freud (1946), for whom play rather than free association was the natural means for tapping the child's unconscious processes and basic conflicts. With play the child acts out intrapsychic conflicts, while the therapist helps identify and talk about what he is doing and

Fig. 22.2. Play therapy.

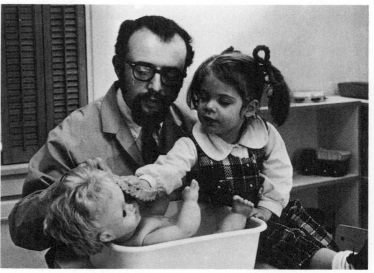

[handwritten margin notes at top: "giving interpretations + gaining insight", "Problem", "Presupposed a capacity for understanding that the child may not have"]

feeling. Gradually the therapist offers more interpretations, to increase the child's conscious awareness of unconscious anxieties and conflicts.

Klein, who introduces interpretations early in therapy, explains how the therapist delves into the symbolic meaning of play with dolls:

If I gathered from the play that the three people remaining in the room are father, mother, and the patient, I would interpret that at times he wanted his younger brother out of the way, wishing to remain alone with his parents and to be an only child as he had been before the birth of his brother. This might lead to his putting another of

Play Therapy: Linda

Linda, age four, was described by her nursery teacher and school psychologist as "seriously maladjusted." She was rarely with other children and usually sat alone, staring at the toys and sometimes reaching out anxiously to handle them. At times she attacked her classmates and interfered with their play, or approached adults, whining. Linda's mother described her behavior at home as obstinate, willful, and destructive. It appeared that Linda's parents were not too happy with each other or with Linda; life at home was filled with bitter quarrels, threats to Linda for "bad" behavior, and a pervasive pessimism that Linda would never meet their expectations.

Play therapy was an opportunity for Linda to express and explore her hostile feelings toward people. Her mother brought her to eight consecutive one-hour sessions. Through the first two sessions in the playroom, Linda was silent, tense, and suspicious. Then, when she began to talk and play with the toys, came an outpouring of anger, at first toward the therapist and later toward her parents. Linda's therapist was nondirective; she accepted the child's feelings nonjudgmentally, in an atmosphere nonetheless made safe by limits.

This excerpt from Linda's sixth play session is typical:

Linda: I'll stomp you with this.
Therapist: You really want to stomp the water on me, but I cannot let you do that.
L: Why?
T: You just may not do that here.
L: (Laughs loudly) Then I'll stomp in it, and I

don't care if I get all wet. Hey! My sock is wet. I'm gonna throw some more water on the floor. (Takes pail into bathroom and enters with it filled with water.) I'm gonna spill it all over.
T: There, it splattered all over.
L: (Laughs) Let 'er splatter all over. Lock the door. Lock it for me.
T: You want the door to be locked, hm?
L: Yes, you do it for me. No one can get in here. I'll splash them if they try.
T: You want us to be here alone.
L: (Steps round in puddles of water. Then goes to dollhouse.) I'm gonna move the house. I'm gonna put it right in the water.
T: Right in the middle of the water, hm?
L: Yes. I'm gonna put it in the water. And if somebody comes up this chimney, they'll put the stove on real quick, and they'll go right in it.
T: Right into the fire and get all burned (Moustakas 1973, p. 70).

By session 8, Linda had moments of appropriate and constructive play; however, her mother then began to bring her irregularly, and therapy was never adequately completed. Nonetheless, after several sessions, Linda's teacher and mother were describing her as less frightened and more sociable. Linda had begun to participate in class activities; for the first time in two years of nursery school she told a story to the children. She was more decisive and freer in her play and had made two friends. Her teacher reported that "the most outstanding difference seemed to be that Linda was expressing her feelings clearly."

[handwritten margin notes: Nondirective PT — therapist should provide conditions under which clients can solve their own problems. Axline (Rogers). — content of activity not important — play activity not important — no interpretations or attempt to influence child — nondirective orientation of therapist — therapist stressed that the establishment of a trusting permissive relationship — post treatment — for adolescents remembering memories of personal discovery — the value of sharing a relationship]

the toy people out of the supposed room — a figure standing for his father — which would lead me to interpret that there are times when he feels his father to be in the way and wants his mother all to himself. I might also have grounds to interpret that in this situation the analyst represented his mother whom he wished to devote herself exclusively to him. At any point in this sequence, even perhaps quite early, we might observe on the child's face that telling look so convincing to the psychoanalyst, which shows clearly that the child has understood something about himself, and that he feels this insight to be helpful and valuable (Klein 1955 in Schaefer, pp. 132–133).

Psychoanalytic play therapy concentrates on giving interpretations and achieving insight. One criticism of this approach is that it presupposes a capacity for understanding that the young child simply may not have.

Nondirective Play Therapy

An alternative approach to play therapy was derived by Virginia Axline (1950, 1969) from Rogers' client-centered therapy for adults and its idea that the therapist should provide conditions under which clients can solve their own problems (see Chapter 15). The nondirective play therapist does not regard the content of the play activity as especially important and does not offer interpretations or attempt in other ways to influence the child.

Therapists with a nondirective orientation primarily stress establishing a trusting and permissive relationship and see the therapeutic value in the child's experience of himself in that relationship. Axline regards play therapy "as a play experience that is therapeutic because it provides a secure relationship between the child and the adult so that the child has the freedom and room to state himself in his own terms exactly as he is at that moment, in his own way and in his own time" (Axline 1950, p. 531).

The simple act of "playing" can be a struggle for the child unaccustomed to assuming responsibility for his own actions. Axline captures the experience of such a child in therapy. We can see how respecting the child's ability to solve his own problems without stepping in to help is difficult for the therapist as well:

Then there was John, seven years old, not knowing how to handle his freedom. He stood just inside the playroom door and mumbled nervously, "What'll I do? What'll I do?" He was told that in here this hour he could do what *he* wanted to do with the toys and materials — that he could play or not play, whichever way he felt. But John was not able to make a choice and he repeated in a louder voice, "What'll I do?" Then he yelled at the therapist angrily, "Why don't you tell me what to do? Why do you let me just *stand* here? You tell me *what to do*!"

"So you want me to tell you what to do! Well in here, John, it's up to *you* to decide what you want to do."

John screamed at the therapist. "But I'm *telling you to tell* me what to do!"

"Yes," said the therapist. "You want me to tell you what to do and I am telling you to decide whether you want to stand there or do something else."

John's face grew red with anger. "I don't want to just stand here," he cried. "And I don't want to do something else. I want *you to tell me* [sobs] what — I *should* — do — "

"There isn't anything that you *should* do in here, John. That's why I don't tell you what to do. Because it doesn't make any difference what you *do* just so it's what you want to do."

John's voice dropped to a whisper and he said, "I'm afraid."

"Are you afraid, John?" the therapist said gently.

"Yes," John whispered. He came closer to the therapist and took her hand. "*Mommy* always tells me what to do," he said.

"I see, John, Mommy tells you what to do and when someone else tells *you* to make up your own mind, then it scares you?"

"Yes," John said. There was a long silence. Finally John said, "Would it be all right if I played with that little red car?"

[handwritten margin notes: Outcome of Child Psychotherapy — Levitt = Improvement of treated children (73%) = Improvement of untreated children (72%). Love, KASWAN, Bugenthal — children whose parents had treatment showed higher improvement than those who had treatment themselves]

"Yes, if you want to," the therapist replied. John edged over to the little car and began to play with it.

Five months and twenty-one contacts later John spontaneously referred to this first contact.

"Do you remember that scared silly little kid who was afraid of letting himself do what he really wanted to do?" he said to the therapist. "I can hardly remember that *baby.* 'Tell me what to do,' " he mimicked. "Scared as a rabbit then, that was me. But not any more. 'Cause now I know what I can do — what I want to do — what I will do" (Axline 1950, pp. 521–522).

Interviews with adolescents looking back on the experience of play therapy revealed that the therapy was remembered well. The details were not as salient as memories reflecting personal discovery and the value of a sharing relationship. Sam, age fifteen, had been seen in therapy when he was twelve. At that time he was described as failing in school, sleeping or eating most of the time, having no friends, and very unhappy.

Talking and whittling a piece of wood — that's all I remember doing. Telling you about stories I had read, shows I had seen, what I had eaten, how I liked eating and sleeping and being by myself. Telling you that and all the time thinking something else. That here I was preferring to keep awake and talk to you — to talk about anything at all just to be able to come there and talk to you — and saying something else to myself all the time. Saying to myself that I didn't really like the way I was living away off in a corner of the world by myself — burying myself in a book — or in a movie — or dreaming — or sleeping. What did I do it for then? I asked myself. This time I spent talking to you was the most wonderful important experience I ever had. Why did it seem like that to me? I asked myself. Certainly the things I told you weren't important or wonderful. It was a kind of mechanical talk that I didn't even listen to myself. The important thing was that I was *talking* to someone. I was *doing it.* And I got up early in the morning to keep that appointment. I spent two hours on the train

coming and two hours going — five hours all together of real hard effort in all kinds of weather and I never missed once. Why did I? Because I wanted to get away from that dead-alone person I was and I wanted to be a together-person in a real people's world (Axline 1950, pp. 526–527).

Outcome of Child Psychotherapy

John laughed at that "scared silly little kid" he used to be, and Sam remembered therapy as a unique context for change. Are they specially chosen examples of success? Would they have improved just as readily without therapy? To find out, Levitt (1957, 1963) reviewed fifty-two evaluative studies: "The inescapable conclusion is that available evaluation studies do not furnish a reasonable basis for the hypothesis that psychotherapy facilitates recovery from emotional illness in children" (1963, p. 49). Levitt reported that 73 percent of children who had received treatment showed some improvement, but two studies of untreated children uncovered an almost identical improvement rate of approximately 72 percent.

We should be somewhat skeptical of both figures. Rates of improvement following therapy are often based on subjective judgments by therapists or parents — those who want to see positive change. Too, the measures of improvement are often vague because they involve judgments about changes in constructs (ego integration, self-reliance, dependency) that have no clear behavioral referents. Even if the measures were more objective we would have some difficulty interpreting outcome of therapy, because rarely are proper control groups used to see if children improve more as a result of the therapy than they would from increased attention from adults or other children's activities (such as dancing lessons).

Because untreated control groups are almost never part of research design in this area, we also know little about the *spontaneous improvement* of children who receive no intervention at all. The high rate cited by Levitt suffers from the same vagueness and subjectivity as improvement rates in therapy. You will remember from Chapter 21 that some disorders, such as childhood autism, rarely show substantial recovery, and others, such as hyperactivity, show changes in symptoms as the child grows older. The striking need is to gather better information about the natural course of the childhood behavior disorders so that we can better evaluate effects of therapy.

Some of these shortcomings in research on outcomes of therapy reflect the real difficulties of research in clinical service settings. Among these are ethical constraints on assigning troubled children to waiting list control groups in order to measure spontaneous improvement. Difficulties are also inherent in the theoretical orientation of the psychotherapies. They focus on inner conflicts and feelings; therefore, procedures and outcomes are not usually defined in readily observable forms. In a careful study, Love, Kaswan, and Bugenthal (1972) sought to overcome some of these methodological problems. They evaluated schoolchildren referred for chronic social and emotional difficulties on several measures, including the more objective index of changes in school grades. They were assigned randomly to a mean of twelve psychoanalytically oriented therapy sessions or to one of two types of parent counseling that did not involve any contact with the child. Changes in school grades in the year following intervention were not dramatic, but children whose parents received counseling showed improvement, and children who received therapy themselves did progressively worse. In fact, only three of thirty-three children in therapy attained at least a half-point gain in their average, and two of these were treatment dropouts!

A recent review of studies with assessment both at close of treatment and at a later follow-up is more encouraging (Wright et al. 1976). From the close to the follow-up, gains in out-come status generally were found, especially when treatment had continued for thirty or more sessions. The authors suggest that reconstruction of personality during therapy may pave the way for later development of behavioral adaptation, and that assessment should wait until therapy has had time to take effect. It may be, then, that child psychotherapy does not give clear short-term benefits but that it has a prophylactic effect that eventually shows up.

Finally, we should assess therapy in relation to its own goals. Most play therapists see the primary aim of treatment as increased awareness and expression of feelings. Yet measures of outcome usually concentrate on other areas, such as personality attributes, expression of symptoms, performance in school, and the like. It may well be that play therapy *is* effective, even in the short run, in producing some kinds of changes (such as increasing communication of feelings), but is relatively ineffective in producing others (reducing defiant behavior at home). Nonetheless, research reports of limited effectiveness and practitioners' own sense that individual psychotherapy with children is too narrow to be truly effective have led to an interest in treating the whole family.

Family Therapy

A relatively new approach to treating children with behavior disorders, family therapy has achieved widespread acceptance in a short time. Family therapists adhere to the systems view, which, as we have discussed elsewhere (see Chapters 6 and 14), defines the family as a mutually interdependent set of relationships striving toward internal balance. A healthy family system achieves balance by maintaining a definite but permeable barrier between the generations, so that parents and offspring all have unique roles, but relationships have some openness.

In a pathological family system, generational

FAMILY THERAPY
- family is a mutually interdependent set of relationships striving toward internal balance by maintaining internal balance

HEALTHY → definite but permeable barrier between the generations so the parents + offspring all have unique roles, have openess

→ TREATMENT APPROACHES
MINUCHIN → structural family systems
- symptoms of patient a result of the distortion in the system; design therapy to realign the system in a healthier way.

FT - dealing with family as a unit ∴ child's problems are not of great interest ∴ may reside in importance.

PATHOLOGICAL generational barriers are faulty or lacking
- subsystems in form of alliances in opposition
- : symptoms of distorted relationships
TREATMENT - reorganization of family system to achieve a more harmonious balance of forces.

Fig. 22.3. In a family therapy session all family members are present and have an opportunity to express their concerns.

barriers are faulty or lacking, and the child may assume the parental role by default or design. Rigid family subsystems emerge in the form of alliances (father and daughter vs. mother) that are often oppositional. According to this family systems model, emotional disorders in children are symptoms of distorted relationships in the family unit and can be relieved by reorganizing the family system to achieve a more harmonious balance of forces.

One major approach to reorganizing distorted family systems is the structural family therapy of Salvatore Minuchin (1974). In Chapter 14 we described Minuchin's view of the way in which distorted family relationships can produce psychophysiological problems, but the model is equally applicable to many behavior disturbances in offspring. According to Minuchin, a structural diagram of a healthy family would look like Figure 22.4A. The lines in this diagram indicate the clear generational roles within the family, but the lines are broken to suggest permeable boundaries. Each person

within the family has a unique role, but no one is shut off from anyone else by a rigid barrier. A structural diagram of one type of disturbed family system might look like Figure 22.4B. This family has a clear alliance between the mother and the two children, one of whom is the identified patient (IP). The continuous lines indicate a rigid boundary excluding father from emotional contact with the rest of the family system. Structural family therapists believe the symptoms of the identified patient to be a result of this distortion in the system and design therapy to realign the system in a healthier way.

It is helpful to see this model applied to a real case, described by Minuchin:

A child comes to therapy with a dog phobia that is so severe he is almost confined to the house. The therapist's diagnosis is that the symptom is supported by an implicit unresolved conflict between the spouses, manifested in an affiliation between mother and son that excludes father. His strategy is to increase the affiliation between the father and son before tackling the spouse subsystem prob-

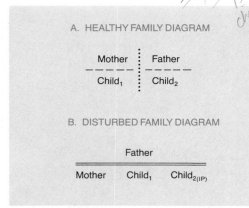

A. HEALTHY FAMILY DIAGRAM

Mother : Father
– – – – – : – – – – –
Child₁ : Child₂

B. DISTURBED FAMILY DIAGRAM

Father
Mother   Child₁   Child₂(IP)

Fig. 22.4. Structural diagrams depicting a healthy family and one type of disturbed family.

lems. Therefore, he encourages the father, who is a mailman "and therefore an expert in dealing with dogs" to teach his son to deal with strange dogs. The child, who is adopted, in turn adopts a dog, and the father and son join in transactions around the dog. This activity strengthens their relationship and promotes a separation between mother and son. As the symptom disappears, the therapist praises both parents for their successful handling of the child. He then moves to work with husband-wife conflicts (Minuchin 1974, p. 153).

Family therapy would go on to encourage family members meeting as a unit to explore their relationships with one another, to attempt to strengthen the parental coalition, and to deal with the resentments that underlie the rigid alliances. Family members would be encouraged to try new ways of behaving with one another in order to experience gratifications that they had believed impossible. Interestingly, most family therapists do not focus on the problems that brought the offspring to the clinic, because they believe that approach contrary to attempts to raise the family's consciousness about its own properties as a system. Frequently the troubled child does not receive therapy outside the fam-

ily context. Offspring problems tend to recede in importance as the family gropes with the problems in its relationship (Ackerman, 1970).

The family systems approach is very popular today in treatment of childhood emotional problems. Despite many clinical reports of successful outcome, though, the few well-controlled comparisons of outcome are equivocal on whether family therapy is superior to no treatment (Wells and Dezen 1978). There is a clear need for better research on family therapy outcome.

Behavior Therapies

Unlike psychotherapies, which aim to resolve unconscious conflicts implied by the child's actions, behavior therapies define the problem in terms of specific, observable behaviors, which they aim to change. Within the several major behavior therapy approaches are unlimited procedural variations. This diversity does not reflect theoretical differences, like those between psychoanalytic and nondirective play therapies, but is an attempt to tailor interventions to individual problems. A behavior-therapy program begins with thorough assessment of the child's problem behavior and then develops an intervention uniquely for that child. Generally, for an anxious child the behavior therapist seeks to neutralize the child's response to phobic situations, using techniques for reducing anxiety based mainly on the classical conditioning model and similar to the techniques described in Chapter 15. With a hyperactive child the therapist focuses on changing the way the child interacts with his environment and helps teacher or parents to use techniques derived from operant conditioning (see Chapters 7 and 19). With an autistic or retarded child, the therapist devises an educational program to overcome specific deficiencies in skills.

Hyperactive
- changing the way
the child interacts
with his environment +
helps significant others to
use techniques from
operant conditioning.

Autistic or Retarded:
- educational
program to overcome
specific deficiencies
in skills

- Behavior Therapy occurs where child's problems occur more naturally school, home

Behavior Therapy: Ann

Ann, age four, had begun to worry her pre-school teachers by her isolation from the other children. Though she was bright and approached adults freely and frequently, she had little involvement with her peers and their play. She complained at length of minor or invisible bumps and cuts, retreated frequently to a make-believe bed to "sleep" for several minutes, or simply stood and watched the others, picking her lip and pulling a strand of hair.

Ann's teachers decided to focus on one aspect of her behavior, isolation from peers. They observed Ann when she was with peers, with adults, and by herself and concluded that she had adequate social-play skills, but just was not using them. Much of Ann's behavior seemed to serve the purpose of getting their attention. They realized that they would have to change their own behavior toward Ann and decided they would no longer pay attention to her isolate behavior and would only talk briefly when she approached them. They would give maximum attention when Ann played with another child.

They trained two observers to code Ann's interaction with peers. Prior to the behavior-therapy program, Ann interacted with children about 10 percent of the time (see graph). When the teachers reinforced inter-action with other children, the rate immediately rose to 60 percent and stayed there. To demonstrate that Ann's behavior had changed because of the reinforcement contingencies, her teachers instituted a reversal on days 12 to 16 (see Chapter 4). They ignored her play with children and paid attention once again to solitary pursuits and to her approaches to adults. Immediately Ann became an isolate once again. On Day 17, the program was reinstituted. When Ann was spending more time playing with children, the teachers gradually withdrew their special attention so that eventually Ann was receiving the same amount of adult attention as her classmates. At several later observations, Ann was continuing to interact more with her classmates. The success of Ann's behavior-therapy program was determined by observing changes in a specific behavior.

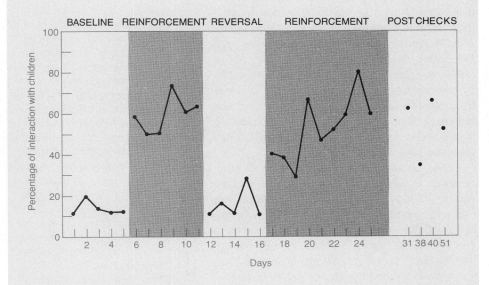

(After Allen et al. 1964.)

Behavior therapy often takes place where the problem occurs naturally, especially school and home. Many therapists enlist teachers or parents to implement the therapy program throughout the child's day. Behavioral procedures typically are more explicit than psychotherapeutic ones, and the outcome is usually assessed by an objective measure of changed behavior.

Anxiety Reduction

Behavior therapy with an anxious child concentrates first, as psychotherapy does, on changing the way the child feels. Therapy, however, focuses on the phobic situation. The primary techniques for reducing anxiety are systematic desensitization, modeling, and reinforcement for approaching the feared situation.

SYSTEMATIC DESENSITIZATION

In Chapter 15 we described systematic desensitization, which exposes the individual to the feared situation, in real life or in imagination, while minimizing anxiety, usually by relaxation. It is often difficult to teach relaxation to children, so that therapists have sought to evoke other responses incompatible with anxiety. In a pioneering experiment, Mary Cover Jones (1924) reduced a young child's fear of rabbits by moving the rabbit progressively closer while the child was eating. The pleasure of eating was antagonistic to anxiety, and gradual exposure to the anxiety-arousing stimulus progressively weakened the rabbit-anxiety bond.

Other incompatible responses are evoked in *emotive imagery* (Lazarus and Abramovitz 1962), an ingenious approach in which the therapist describes a series of events involving the child's favorite hero or alter ego "to arouse feelings of self-assertion, pride, affection, mirth and similar anxiety-inhibiting responses" (p. 111). While the child imagines these, he is also gradually asked to imagine the situations he fears. The procedure is illustrated in this report:

Stanley M., aged fourteen, suffered from an intense fear of dogs, of two and a half to three years' duration. He would take two buses on a roundabout route to school rather than risk exposure to dogs on a direct 300 yard walk. He was a rather dull (IQ 93), sluggish person, very large for his age, trying to be cooperative, but sadly unresponsive — especially to attempts at training in relaxation. In his desire to please, he would state that he had been perfectly relaxed even though he had betrayed himself by his intense fidgetiness. Training in relaxation was eventually abandoned, and an attempt was made to establish the nature of his aspirations and goals. By dint of much questioning and after following many false trails because of his inarticulateness, a topic was eventually tracked down that was absorbing enough to form the subject of his fantasies, namely racing motor-cars. He had a burning ambition to own a certain Alfa Romeo sports car and race it at the Indianapolis "500" event. Emotive imagery was induced as follows: "Close your eyes. I want you to imagine, clearly and vividly, that your wish has come true. The Alfa Romeo is now in your possession. It is your car. It is standing in the street outside your block. You are looking at it now. Notice the beautiful sleek lines. You decide to go for a drive with some friends of yours. You sit down at the wheel, and you feel a thrill of pride as you realize that you own this magnificent machine. You start up and listen to the wonderful roar of the exhaust. You let the clutch in and the car streaks off. . . . You are out in a clear open road now; the car is performing like a pedigree; the speedometer is climbing into the nineties; you have a wonderful feeling of being in perfect control; you look at the trees whizzing by and you see a little dog standing next to one of them — if you feel any anxiety, just raise your finger. Etc., etc." An item fairly high up on the hierarchy: "You stop at a cafe in a little town and dozens of people crowd around to look enviously at this magnificent car and its lucky owner; you swell with pride, and at this moment a larger boxer comes up and sniffs at your heels — if you feel any anxiety, etc., etc."

After three sessions using this method he reported a marked improvement in his reaction to dogs. He was given a few field assignments during the next two sessions, after which therapy was terminated. Twelve months later, reports both from the patient and his relatives indicated that there was no longer any trace of his former phobia (Lazarus and Abramovitz 1962, p. 192).

The authors report that seven of nine children treated with emotive imagery recovered in an average of only 3.3 sessions. Four of these children had shown no gains from previous therapy, suggesting that changes were not attributable only to the therapist's attention. Surprisingly, though, this clinical report of emotive imagery has not been followed by controlled studies.

MODELING

Children can also be made less fearful by observing someone else coping successfully with the troubling situation. In one experimental study of modeling, preschool children who were afraid of dogs spent eight brief sessions watching a four-year-old model perform progressively

more fearful interactions with a dog. Following intervention, these children approached test dogs more often than before. They also approached them more often than control groups of fearful children who had the same exposure to the dog without the model or had no exposure at all (Bandura, Grusec, and Menlove 1967). Seeing another child perform fearlessly seems to have beneficial effects, if there are no untoward consequences and especially if the model is reinforced for his actions.

REINFORCEMENT

Even after anxiety has been reduced, however, a child may resist approaching the phobic situation. Often the child actually gains something by being phobic. The child who is afraid of the dark is apt to receive much attention from parents and may even be permitted to stay up late watching television or playing with siblings. In such cases, the behavior-therapy program will also seek to eliminate reinforcement for

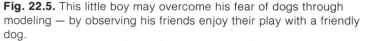

Fig. 22.5. This little boy may overcome his fear of dogs through modeling — by observing his friends enjoy their play with a friendly dog.

[handwritten margin note: Psychotherapies + fixed problem + change child's personality + Physiology]

phobic avoidance behavior, while having the parents reinforce the child for attempts at non-phobic behavior by attention and praise.

COMBINED APPROACHES

In clinical practice, therapists often combine several behavioral methods. An interesting illustration is the approach Lazarus and his colleagues (1965) employed with Paul, a nine-year-old with a long history of school phobic episodes. Paul had begun the fourth grade and then refused to attend for three weeks prior to beginning therapy. His school phobia seemed to be motivated by intense fear of school but was also maintained by reinforcers at home, primarily attention from parents and siblings. We will present only excerpts from the eighteen-step program, but you will see components of the methods we have just described: systematic desensitization (gradual exposure and emotive imagery), modeling, and reinforcement only for desired behavior.

1. On Sunday Paul walked to his school and back home, with the therapist.
2. On the next two mornings Paul walked to the schoolyard with the therapist. Paul's anxiety was reduced by encouragement and emotive imagery (pleasant images of Disneyland and Christmas).
3. On the next day Paul sat in the empty classroom after school and acted out aspects of the school routine with the therapist.
4. On the next three mornings Paul and the therapist entered the classroom with other children, and then left after the opening exercises. . . .
10. At 1:45 P.M. the therapist left, with the promise that if Paul stayed until the end of school they would play guitar together that evening.
11. Paul's mother was instructed not to allow him into the house during school hours, and the teacher was asked to provide special jobs to make school more attractive.

The earlier stages of therapy were aimed at reducing Paul's anxiety about school; during the later stages, when Paul was less anxious, the therapist concentrated on reducing avoidance of school. Normal school attendance was soon attained, and a ten-month follow-up found that his attendance had been maintained.

Behavior Management

The child who is aggressive, impulsive, disobedient, disruptive, or whose behavior in other ways disturbs those around him is a likely candidate for a *behavior-management program,* which is a systematic application of reinforcement and possibly punishment to reduce the undesirable behavior and encourage more acceptable behaviors. Psychotherapies and drug therapies locate such problems in the child and are focused on changing his personality or physiology. Behavior therapists, though they recognize that some children are more prone than others to display behavior problems, view the problem as a skill deficiency in the child and employ cognitive strategies for teaching the child to regulate his own behavior better. Moreover, behavior therapists believe that the child's environment often encourages and maintains deviant behavior, so they focus more broadly on changing the patterns of reinforcement in relevant settings. We described home behavior-management programs for conduct disorders in Chapter 19; here we will consider classroom behavior management and cognitive training.

CLASSROOM BEHAVIOR MANAGEMENT

Behavior therapists conduct programs for teachers in the general principles of classroom management, with the aim of making the entire classroom a better environment for learning. More often, though, they consult on managing the behavior of one particularly troublesome child. The object of these management programs is twofold: (1) to rearrange the antecedents of problem behavior so that the child is more likely to perform well (e.g., by developing an easier, more structured reading program), and (2) to rearrange consequences so that the child loses reinforcement or receives punishment for disruptive behaviors and receives special reinforcement for on-task behavior (as by paying attention to the child only when he is seated and working).

Often the teacher's attention is the most important reinforcer for the child; by systematically ignoring off-task behavior and giving approval for on-task behavior, teachers can sometimes improve the child's functioning. A more elaborate intervention is a *token reinforcement program,* or token economy, in which on-task behaviors will earn a child tokens (or points on a card, etc.), which he can exchange periodically for "backup" reinforcers,

Fig. 22.6. Token economies have special stores. For this retarded child, exchanging tokens earned in school for a desired toy provides an opportunity to practice counting skills.

such as prizes and special activities. Problem behaviors may result in loss of points earned with on-task behaviors. In Chapter 7 we discussed token economy programs in mental hospital wards. Many variations of token reinforcement programs in the classrooms have proved effective with retarded children (Birnbrauer et al. 1965), with special classes made up of children labeled emotionally disturbed or schizophrenic (O'Leary and Becker 1967; Kaufman and O'Leary 1972), and with underachieving or disruptive children in normal classes (O'Leary and O'Leary 1977).

Later in this chapter we will discuss drug treatment for hyperactive children. There is evidence, however, that hyperactive children can be withdrawn from medication with no loss in on-task behavior and greater academic gains, provided the teacher has instituted a proper behavioral management program. Ayllon et al. (1975), for example, experimented with a token reinforcement program for hyperactive children that reinforced academic performance rather than nondisruptive behavior. They found that the rate of correct answers in math and reading averaged 12 percent while the children were on medication, but increased to 85 percent when medication was discontinued and a reinforcement program was established for correct academic performance.

One of the children in the reinforcement program was eight-year-old Crystal, who had been on the drug Ritalin for three years before this intervention. While Crystal was on medication, observers recorded very low hyperactivity, but her academic performance was zero. When she stopped receiving medication (day 7), her disruptive behavior in math class increased dramatically. On day 8, a reinforcement program was introduced in which each correct answer earned one check on an index card. The checks could be exchanged for items priced from one to seventy-five checks, including

candy, school supplies, free time, lunch in the teachers' room, and picnic in the park. Crystal's disruptive behavior in math class dropped, and the percentage of her correct math answers immediately increased. To assess whether Crystal's behavior changes were linked to the reinforcement program, the researchers employed a multiple-baseline design. In reading class, Crystal's high disruptive and low academic behavior continued until day 10, when therapists extended the reinforcement program to reading class. In general, this study indicates that some hyperactive children can maintain low rates of disruptive behavior and increased academic performance without medication.

COGNITIVE TRAINING

Despite their effectiveness, token reinforcement programs can be time-consuming and complex for teachers or parents to manage. Consequently, they sometimes abandon token programs after several weeks, despite positive results. If the child's behavior changed in response to the token reinforcement system, the problem behavior may quickly reappear if the system is withdrawn. It has seemed desirable to some behavioral psychologists, then, to also explore ways to make changes more *internal* — in fact, to teach the child better ways of approaching classroom tasks. This cognitive training is quite consistent with the view of hyperactivity as an attention-deficit disorder (see Chapter 21).

One very interesting example is Meichenbaum and Goodman's (1971) work on impulsive behavior in hyperactive children. The authors sought to increase the child's self-control by a cognitive-training procedure. The child learned, by doing a series of repeated tasks, to "size up" the demands of a task, to cognitively rehearse options, and then to guide his own performance by "self-talk." First the teacher would perform a task such as copying line pat-

Behavior Therapy: Two Teachers' Views

Although published accounts of behavior modification in the classroom are very precise in describing behaviors, careful in measurement, and often complicated in intervention design, this second grade teacher's account is closer to our experience in the typical classroom situation. Following a short in-service training course in behavior modification this teacher could roughly carry through a program and was enthusiastic about it, although she was unclear in her specification of behaviors to be changed and continued to speak of attitudes in a way that would make most behaviorists cringe:

Teacher: Yes, Nancy was a problem. She had difficulty in getting along with her peers. And she was not liked by anyone in the class. And she was also stealing.

Interviewer: What did you do?

Teacher: I started a reward-type program, where if she could get through one day there was a small reward for her at the end of that day. If she could get through five consecutive school days there would be, like a super-big reward for her at the end of the week.

Interviewer: What would be a small reward for her?

Teacher: Oh, a pencil, a small pad of note paper.

Interviewer: And what would be a big reward?

Teacher: Oh, a very nice felt-tip marking pen.

Interviewer: Did it work?

Teacher: Yes, it has worked. In fact, it worked immediately. This is why I was so surprised. In the beginning I thought: "Okay, I've been doing this already — this is the kind of psychology I'm sure I've used before because rewards, you use kind of instinctively in teaching." But I did learn a great deal because this worked . . . you know, she was such a problem all year and we just began this the end of February and it just worked from the very first day.

Interviewer: Was your behavior changed very much as a teacher?

Teacher: I wouldn't say it's changed very much. I'd say my attitude changed at that point, and it was a bad point in the year . . . it was February and I was getting a little bit discouraged, especially with Nancy. I'd reached the point where I almost disliked her — I really did. I didn't like her — it's an awful thing to say but I didn't care for her. Now I really don't feel that way about her. And that changed my attitude about the entire group.

Interviewer: When your attitude changed did you notice that you were doing different things?

Teacher: No. I think it was my attitude that was important here, because when my attitude changed about Nancy I think the attitude of the class changed too. They weren't so quick to jump on her. . . .

Interviewer: Did they behave differently toward her?

Teacher: Yes. They did. Children started playing with her at recess time, and started sharing games with her and this was unheard of before. They wouldn't even come near her.

Not all teachers enthusiastically carry through a token reinforcement program, though, as this teacher's remarks illustrate:

I continued it for about a month . . . I continued it, and then they lost interest in the stickers and stars and toys and trucks so I found there wasn't anything I could interest them with . . . M&Ms, candy bars, whatever. Partially it was my fault because I tend to — you know, things like that don't turn me on so I'd downgrade it to them which I know I shouldn't have done and that's probably why they got turned off. To me it was silly, pop an M&M in his mouth and he'll quote Shakespeare. The whole thing turned me off, I didn't really enjoy it.

terns, talking aloud while the child observed. Next the child would do the same task while the teacher instructed him aloud. Then the child would perform the task twice, talking aloud to himself and then whispering to himself. Finally, the child would complete the task with covert self-talk (no lip movements). With the help of graded practice the child learned to analyze a problem and to self-direct his action. Here is an example of the teacher's talk, which the child would then model:

Okay, what is it I have to do? You want me to copy the picture with the different lines. I have to go slow and be careful. Okay, draw the line down, down, good; then to the right, that's it; now down some more and to the left. Good, I'm doing fine so far. Remember, go slow . . . (Meichenbaum and Goodman 1971, p. 117).

After only four half-hour training sessions, impulsive children randomly selected to participate had demonstrated enhanced performance on a number of psychometric measures, compared with groups of impulsive children who had simply received a comparable amount of attention from the teacher or no intervention at all. Although we have some evidence that cognitive behavior-modification procedures can result in generalization to the natural environment of the classroom (Bornstein and Quevillon 1976), this question requires further study.

Skill Training

The overriding need of children who are retarded or autistic is to learn adaptive behaviors that they have failed to acquire in the ways customary for other children. Psychologists working with these developmentally disabled children have cooperated increasingly with specialists in education and rehabilitation to develop effective skill-teaching programs. They carefully analyze the task (breaking down skills into finely graded steps) and apply progressive

teaching as well as reinforcement to motivate children whose learning histories have been characterized by frustration and failure. These programs concentrate on self-help skills (dressing, eating, toilet habits); home-care skills (cooking, basic repairs); cognitive skills (color discrimination); community mobility (riding a bus); information skills (telling time, reading signs); vocational skills (light assembly); and communication skills. The visible gains in skill from this type of educational therapy have been most heartening. Even severely retarded persons have learned such complex tasks as assembling bicycle brakes (Gold 1975).

LANGUAGE TRAINING

Behavioral skill training is well-illustrated with development of language in autistic children. The long-term prognosis for these severely disabled children has been poor (see Chapter 21) and is not improved by traditional play therapies (Brown 1960; Rutter 1966). The prognosis is especially poor for children still lacking language by age five. Therefore, as researchers turned to more specific interventions, language development had primary importance.

Ivar Lovaas and his coworkers at the University of California, Los Angeles, developed a graded language-development program that is modified to fit the child's entering skills. First they seek to teach the child a number of verbal responses and then how to use them appropriately and spontaneously. The initial steps with a mute child include:

1. Rewarding every vocalization.
2. Rewarding vocalizations within a specified time (five seconds) after the therapist makes a sound.
3. Rewarding only those sounds emitted during the time interval which are similar to the therapist's sound.

SKILL TRAINING
(autistic or retarded)
- to learn adaptive behaviors
- break down a task with reinforcements to motivate the child
skill concentration
- self help skills
- home-care "
- cognitive "
- community mobility "
- information skill "
- vocational "
- communication "

LANGUAGE TRAINING - Sign language
- start at early age

Social Skill T.
- behavior management, so they could manage the group
behaviors of rejecting teachers & peers
Parent T - in consultation with therapist or < manuals
use on nonprofessional trained by therapist who in turn train parents.

Fig. 22.7. Laurie, a severely retarded child without speech, is learning to sign and say her name as part of a total communication program.

4. Introducing new sounds interspersed with those already learned, and rewarding imitation (Lovaas et al. 1966).

For echolalic children, who parrot what they hear, the language program aims to make speech more meaningful and functional. Lovaas et al. (1973) found that children in their program progressively increased appropriate speech when an adult initiated conversation; after the child had acquired and practiced more appropriate speech, spontaneous speech (without adult initiation) began to increase as well.

Behavioral language-development programs, despite some success, have not been effective with all autistic children, require enor-

mous investments of time, and have not usually produced definite reduction in the child's generally disordered behavior. Two recent directions show promise. One incorporates sign language, adapted from language used by deaf persons, into the early stages of training, to give the child initial means of communication. The child learns to make basic signs (such as toilet, help, yes, no, want, eat) as well as to say the words in a total communication program. Another is the recent focus by Lovaas and his coworkers on much younger children (thirty months of age and younger). For each child, six to eight undergraduates are trained to reduce interfering stereotyped behaviors and to increase language and social skills. Working in shifts, these therapists spend from four to six

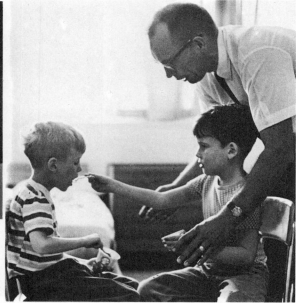

Fig. 22.8. Stages in the language program for autistic children developed by psychologist Ivar Lovaas. The child above is being taught to make a speech sound. The children at right are being taught to communicate with one another — in this case, to ask for what they want.

hours each day in the child's home. After six months or so of treatment, the child is placed in a preschool with nonhandicapped peers, and the therapist staff consult with the teacher; home therapy continues. The ultimate criteria for success are stringent and include successful completion of the first grade, normal play, and absence of self-stimulating behaviors. Initial data, as yet unpublished, indicate that 50 to 60 percent of children in the program meet these criteria and an additional 30 percent achieve significant improvement. These results are certainly very hopeful, but a great deal more research is required.

SOCIAL SKILLS TRAINING

An intriguing application of behavioral techniques is training in social skills. Graubard and his associates (1977) devised a program to counteract the hostility and other nonaccepting attitudes that public school teachers and nonhandicapped peers sometimes display toward students with special needs. They taught principles of behavior management to handicapped children, so that they could then modify the behaviors of rejecting teachers and peers! The special education children were helped to specify and record teacher and peer behaviors that were particularly troublesome (scolding by teachers or name calling by peers) and were taught how to extinguish these by ignoring and how to prompt and reinforce more accepting behaviors. The positive results suggest that by utilizing reinforcement principles, "socially deviant groups can readily change the behavior of those groups who generally exercise the most control over them" (Graubard et al. 1977, p. 249).

PARENT TRAINING

Many behavioral programs, especially those involving training in skills for retarded or autistic children, are carried out at home by the child's parents, in consultation with professionals.

Some skills, such as dressing and toilet habits, are most appropriately taught at home, and others are certainly learned more rapidly when the home and school work together. Although some parent-training programs simply supervise their teaching of one skill, others teach parents behavioral principles and various teaching methods, so that they can develop, execute, and evaluate teaching programs by themselves (Baker 1976).

In a typical program, the therapist meets with one or both parents and child to assess which skills to teach, to instruct the parent(s) in behavioral principles, to demonstrate methods of teaching, and to supervise the parent's teaching, sometimes using aids to observation such as one-way mirrors or videotapes. This type of

program may involve weekly meetings over many months.

Because individual training can be very time-consuming, three alternatives have recently been attempted to make it more cost-effective by reducing the time a professional must spend with each family. In the first, non-professionals under professional supervision have proved to be very effective in training parents (Schortinghuis and Frohman 1974). Second, parents can be trained in groups. The gains in parent-teaching ability and children's skills seem to be comparable whether parents are trained individually or in groups of five to ten families (Salzinger et al. 1970; Baker, Brightman, and Clark 1978). Third, behavioral teaching strategies can be presented to parents in

Getting Tito to Talk

Tito, at admission, was a . . . five-year-old boy who evidenced an extremely short attention span. Eye contact was absent. He had many compulsive rituals. For example, he would spend considerable time arranging objects in a straight line and would become very upset if the arrangement was disturbed. He "refused" to let his parents read the Sunday paper by becoming very upset when they removed the string that tied it in a bundle. He was untestable on intelligence tests. . . . He was echolalic, but occasionally would use speech for communication. Tito's understanding of speech, however, was minimal. He resisted any involvement with people, and was unresponsive to displays of affection. He was extremely negative and clever at getting himself out of situations he did not like, often responding to the most elementary demands (*e.g.,* "sit in the chair") with extreme tantrums.

Tito was treated as an outpatient. He was seen for three sessions per week for 1 year. We served primarily as consultants to his mother, who was very conscientious and warm. His treatment program included two main objectives. First, we tried to teach him to deal with frustrating situations more maturely

rather than engaging in tantrums. This was an extremely demanding job, and he received many spankings. Secondly, he was taught those basic skills upon which he could build more complex behaviors, particularly in language. Included in this category were pronoun usage, preposition usage, number concepts, relational concepts such as big and little, and social greetings. He was taught to comment upon his environment. He was also taught to draw, and to play more appropriately.

At discharge, Tito was observant and alert, but still appeared definitely educationally handicapped. He had made some progress in most areas, but his biggest gains were in language. His speech was quite spontaneous, and he could comment correctly on most social interactions. He obtained an IQ of 47 on the Stanford Binet. . . . He now attends a school for retarded children three hours per day. His mother reports that he has continued to show improvement in most areas. He remains emotionally aloof with strangers, but is close to his mother. His future is uncertain. He may escape institutionalization if his progress continues.

Source: Lovaas et al. 1973, pp. 157–158.

written manuals, reducing the time trainers must spend in instruction. One study found that parents accomplished as much self-help teaching when they were trained by manuals alone as when they participated in group meetings and even consultation at home with professionals (Baker and Heifetz 1976). One trend clearly in the future of intervention with childhood behavior disorders is to involve parents more heavily in therapeutic programs.

Drug Therapy

Discussing drug treatment for children, we will emphasize stimulant drugs because other types have been studied infrequently and unsystematically, and they seem to have little demonstrated benefit. The major tranquilizers, now so important in treating adults (see Chapters 7 and 11), appear to have limited usefulness and involve considerable risks for children. They not only impair cognitive functioning and learning, but may produce severe physical side effects (Campbell and Small 1978). A recent review of minor tranquilizers (such as Librium and Valium) concluded: "There is no absolute documentation of benefit for the use of sedatives and minor tranquilizers in children" (Patterson and Pruitt 1977, p. 176). As for antidepressants, we have few properly controlled studies demonstrating effectiveness with children.

Central nervous system stimulants were first prescribed for children with behavior problems in the 1930s (Bradley 1937), but not until the 1960s did they become the preferred treatment for hyperactive children. With popularity came controversy. Many found the picture of steadily increased drugging of schoolchildren onerous, especially because so little is known about long-term effects. Although recent research has

shown that drugs have some beneficial short-term effects on impulsiveness and attention span, it is true that some children are unnecessarily taking drugs, that dosages are often too high, and that monitoring is inadequate (Sroufe 1975).

The most widely used stimulant drugs are methylphenidate (Ritalin) and dextroamphetamine (Dexedrine). Paradoxically, these stimulants calm hyperactive children, apparently helping them to focus their attention. Typically, children begin to take stimulant medication between ages seven and nine and terminate treatment before puberty. The response is judged "positive" for 65 to 75 percent of school-age children, but in 5 to 10 percent the drug exacerbates the symptoms. The critical change is not an actual decrease in activity, but an increase in directed or controlled motor activity (Millichap and Boldrey 1967). Rating scales consistently show greater improvement with these drugs than with a placebo in classroom behavior, group participation, and behavior toward authority (Conners et al. 1967). Indeed, some parents, such as this mother of a five-year-old boy, report immediate and dramatic effects:

When my son received his first half-tablet, the first thing he did was to get a rather complex jigsaw puzzle out of his toy closet. It was a puzzle that he had never been able to complete and that had particularly frustrated him. It had always angered him that his sister could do it without much difficulty. He worked at it for a whole hour, methodically fitting each piece or discarding it without evidence of temper or frustration. . . . The change was extremely noticeable. It surprised me because never before had he been able to devote more than ten minutes to one activity (Ross and Ross 1976, pp. 107–108).

Despite double-blind designs, many studies of stimulant drugs have been questioned for their methodology; for example, the physical side effects of the drugs make it possible for raters to distinguish children on drugs from children on placebo. Now investigators have conducted more and better-controlled laboratory studies and have found that children on psychostimulants show less task-irrelevant activity and better performance on psychological tasks such as response latency and simple discriminations. An excellent review of this literature summarized the effects of drugs as follows:

> In general, the types of tasks yielding positive results are repetitious, mechanical, and/or of long duration, and seem to require concentration, care, and sustained performance. . . . To date there is no compelling evidence that stimulant drugs have beneficial effects on problem solving, reasoning, nonrote learning, or actual school achievement (Sroufe 1975, p. 358).

Stimulant drugs sometimes have negative effects. The most common short-term side effects are loss of appetite and sleeplessness. Long-term effects seem generally benign, but we are still not certain. Safer and his colleagues (1972) have found suppression of both growth and weight gain in children while on psychostimulants, but there is a rebound during drug-free periods (summer vacations).

The most important lasting effect, however, may be that the child and those around him know he is on medication. First, he is apt to look different. One frequent effect is a sunken-cheeked, sallow look with dark shadows under the eyes; one six-year-old boy, commenting on this "look," said:

> I would like not to take those pills. I do not think those pills are good. Ladies say to my mom, "Why is he so *pale?* Doesn't he get enough sleep?" and my mom hates that and she says, "He's on medication," and they all look like I'm a new animal in the zoo and then real quick they start talking about some other things but they all keep looking at me in a real funny way and I don't feel good when they do (Ross and Ross 1976, p. 110).

Also, the child feels different. Embarrassment at being singled out by peers is pointed out in an eight-year-old boy's answer to the question, "What would you like most?"

> Just one thing. I would like to only take these medications at home where no other kids know. I am calling them medications because ever since last year when we all had to write poems about real-life things I hate the word Pill. Last year my teacher was always saying, "Did you take your pill, Davie?" and pretty soon the other kids started saying it and then that dumb Susan Neilson wrote her poem on me and this is the poem. I heard it a million times already:
>
> > David Hill
> > Did you take the pill
> > That makes you work
> > And keeps you still?
> > Take your pill, Hill.
>
> And in baseball when I swing out and I almost always do the other kids all yelled it. Sometimes I wish I could go to another school and start over (Ross and Ross 1976, p. 102).

A further concern is that the child on drugs will come to attribute all his successes to the drug and his failures to lapses in taking the drug. The child, then, comes to feel that his actions are out of his control, that he is not responsible for them. Clearly such attitudes could have lasting detrimental effects.

> I: So, sometimes you can really tell that you need it?
> C: (Eleven-year-old boy) Yeah. (Pause) Sometimes I get mad at my dog and if I start getting mad at my dog, my mother will say, "Go take your pill." I'll say, "Ah — O.K.," and I'll go downstairs and take it and then I come back upstairs and start saying I'm sorry to my dog (Whalen and Henker, in press, p. 33).

Finally, when a child takes medication and his academic deficiencies still do not improve (which is most common), he may feel even less self-esteem, even more of a failure.

When they are effective, then, psychostimulant drugs seem to increase the child's ability to sustain and focus attention on a task. There is no good evidence that they reverse the trend toward academic failure or antisocial behavior as the child approaches adolescence. Perhaps if these drugs were accompanied by a systematically planned educational program, the child's increased control over attention could be utilized in teaching problem-solving strategies and ultimately in realizing academic gains. Yet administering drugs with little or no attention to the educational environment is still the rule, so that even if the child is more ready to learn, his school is not necessarily readier to teach him.

Comparative studies of drug treatment and behavior therapy are under way. The data generally suggest that drugs are as effective in managing behavior as behavior-therapy methods. But knowing that behavior therapy is superior in improving academic performance (Wolraich et al. 1978; Ayllon et al. 1975) and that medication has various side effects, many authorities argue that drugs should be the treatment of last resort (Lahey et al. 1979).

Early Intervention and Prevention

We have considered therapeutic intervention with children whose problem behaviors have attracted attention. Yet, there are frequent calls for expanding services to the very young, especially those at high risk for subsequent retardation or behavior disorders. Despite the inherent logic of the idea, practitioners are caught up in trying to service the problems that already exist, funds come more easily for remedial service,

and the task of proving that a prevention program has been successful is enormous; therefore, efforts at prevention and early intervention are rare. Nonetheless, a core of programs are aimed at prevention or early intervention and should provide models for more efforts in the future.

Moderate to Severe Retardation

An encouraging study in England suggests that the incidence of moderate to severe retardation decreased by about a third (Tizard 1964) between the 1920s and the 1960s. This reduction probably is due to ordinary social and health advances, such as immunization techniques, better prenatal and natal care, and the earlier age at which mothers complete their families (Clarke 1977). In Chapter 20 we considered some recent biomedical developments that will further decrease the incidence of severe mental retardation. They include amniocentesis for mothers at risk and subsequent termination of pregnancies in which the fetus is known to be damaged, rubella vaccine, and the special diet for children with the metabolic disorder phenylketonuria. Attempts to eradicate lead poisoning by legislation regulating lead-based paints and by screening high-risk children have been somewhat less successful. All these efforts involve public education and, very often, counseling for parents.

Over the past decade the number of infant and preschool programs of early intervention with organically impaired children has increased. The Bureau of Education for the Handicapped has sponsored more than 200 "First Chance" programs to educate handicapped preschoolers, to develop curriculum materials, and to train other professionals. These programs usually include professionals in several disciplines (psychology, education, speech and hearing, physical therapy) as well as parents. One promising example is the Model

[handwritten margin notes: day care facilities; MILWAUKEE PROJECT; to mothers & children; "low mother" education; IQ; low & disadvant; IQ 80; child high risk; education too]

Preschool Center for Handicapped Children at the University of Washington, which serves parents of Downs syndrome infants. Weekly clinic visits may begin when a child is five weeks old. Mother and child do exercises to stimulate early motor and cognitive development. The therapists emphasize visual and sound stimulation. Encouraging preliminary evidence shows that Downs syndrome children who continue in this program achieve close to age norms on a developmental scale (Hayden and Haring 1977).

Mild or Borderline Retardation

Because mild retardation is not usually detected until the school years, programs for prevention or early intervention must seek children who are at risk. Because of the strong relationship between poverty and retardation, these efforts have focused on the poor child. Prevention has meant changing the child's early experiences by altering the home environment, by providing a day care substitute, or both. The largest classroom program, Head Start, began in 1965 as part of the "war on poverty" declared by President Lyndon B. Johnson. Overall evaluations in early elementary school were not encouraging (Westinghouse Learning Corporation 1969) and suggested that results would be better with a more structured curriculum begun earlier in the child's life and continued longer in combination with parent training.

Several prevention programs are more intensive than Head Start and begin earlier in the child's life. The Carolina Abecedarian Project, for instance, provides nutritional and medical help to families, although it concentrates educational efforts in the classroom. It provides an intensive day care experience beginning as early as six weeks of age for high-risk children. This program seems to prevent the developmental lag usually noticed in high-risk infants as

Fig. 22.9. This curious child's mother is participating in an early intervention program to learn ways to stimulate cognitive development.

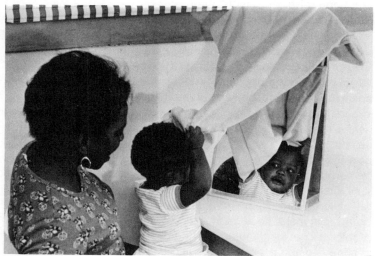

young as twelve to eighteen months, especially in language (Ramey and Campbell 1977).

The most thorough effort at early intervention is the Milwaukee Project, a six-year program of vocational and social education for mothers and education for their high-risk children (Heber and Garber 1975; Garber and Heber 1977). Studies by these researchers had shown that children of mothers with IQ below 80 decline markedly in IQ from infancy on, in contrast to children of mothers from the same sociocultural background with higher IQ. Therefore, for the Milwaukee Project, they selected forty high-risk infants, three to six months old, applying dual criteria for poverty-level homes in the inner city and mothers whose IQs were below 75. Twenty of the infants were assigned at random to the experimental condition. By ages fourteen to eighteen months, these children showed greater language development than the twenty control children, and differences increased as time passed. Increased mother-child interaction in families in the experimental condition resulted from the child's "prodding and shaping of the mother's verbal responses." The results of repeated IQ testing are impressive. Although the controls performed in the borderline retarded range, the experimental children were consistently above average (Figure 22.10). Indeed, by age eight, a third of the controls had IQs below 75, which is often considered justification for placement in special classes for the mentally retarded. No experimental child scored this low. Future research can build on these very impressive results to determine which aspects of this extensive and expensive program are most necessary and which families are most likely to benefit. One interesting sidelight is that the experimental children, now more confident and verbal than their peers, have been seen as behavior problems by their public school teachers. Teachers' emphasis on classroom control has

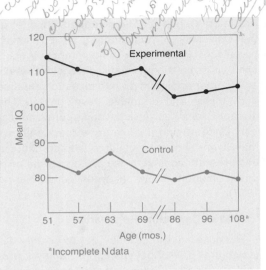

Fig. 22.10. In the Milwaukee Project, children who were high risk for retardation participated in a special experimental program during their preschool years. Subsequent IQ testing revealed a marked advantage over a nonparticipating control group. (After Garber and Heber 1977.)

received much criticism for its destructive influence on children (Kozol 1967; Holt 1964). Thus, changes in these important children's settings seem to be vital for effective early intervention.

Behavior Disorders

A host of community activities involving children or their families in some way contribute an ounce of prevention or early intervention for behavior disorders. They range from alternative parenting (big brothers and sisters, foster grandparents) and books about crises (divorce, surgery) to youth groups (scouting, camping) and even zoos! Yet the truly basic prevention is to ensure that the child's primary environments (home, school) will be encouraging and support growth. We have mentioned specific mental health efforts involving families. Also, more general education programs are designed to promote effective parenting (Gordon 1970). Considering behavioral techniques in the classroom, we have seen the teacher's potential for intervening early with behavior disorders. For its critical influence in socialization, the school deserves further attention.

Mental health professionals have more often become involved in schools primarily as consultants for teachers who work with identified problem children. Some efforts, however, have been directed toward identifying childhood problems early, in the first grade or before, and developing remedial efforts before the problems become debilitating. Cowen and his coworkers (1966, 1975) developed a system to screen first graders for early signs of emotional disturbance and put a "red tag" on their files. Following up red-tag children, they found a high incidence of emotional and educational problems (Cowen et al. 1973). An early intervention effort to prevent these later problems was devised, including social work with mothers, consultation with teachers, parent-teacher discussion groups, and volunteer aids in the school. Although the children in the school where this program was tested showed better adjustment and achievement than those in a control school, the red-tag children still lagged behind, and the results of the test are equivocal. Even successful early screening and intervention programs would have to balance their benefits against the possible ill effects of labeling children, however. Knowing the power of expectancy, some critics abhor the thought of five-year-olds carrying a red-tag label into the classroom with them.

Belief is spreading among professionals that meaningful child intervention should begin early and must involve the child's social settings. This belief clashes, however, with the fiscal conservatism of recent times; prevention programs, which do not attack the most visible problems with demonstrable payoffs, do not compete well for funding. The danger is that efforts at mental health programming will generally continue to follow the strategy many consider short-sighted: intervening only when grave problems are already apparent.

Summary

1. Important questions to consider in treating children are: when to intervene; where to intervene; and how to intervene.

2. Types of psychotherapy used with children include: (1) verbal forms, employed primarily with older children who have the necessary cognitive abilities; and (2) play therapy, used with preadolescents.

3. Two approaches to play therapy are the psychoanalytic and the nondirective. Psychoanalytic play therapy uses play to help the child act out intrapsychic conflicts. The therapist talks to the child about what he is doing and feeling and then helps the child interpret the underlying meaning. Nondirective play therapy is a derivative of client-centered therapy. The play activity itself is not as important as a trusting and permissive relationship between child and therapist so that children can assume responsibility for their own actions.

4. Family therapy treats emotional disorders in children as symptoms of distortion in the family unit. Relieving the child's symptoms requires understanding and realigning relationships within the family system.

5. Several behavioral techniques have been used in treating children. Behavior therapies for reducing anxiety include systematic desensitization, modeling, reinforcement, and a combination of these approaches.

6. Behavior therapies for managing disruptive behavior are: (1) behavior management in the classroom, arranging the classroom to ensure the child's success and punishing or not reinforcing disruptive behavior; and (2) cognitive training, in which the child learns to control his behavior by analyzing a situation or task and talking himself through it, aloud at first, then mentally.

7. Behavioral techniques with retarded or autistic children concentrate on skill training. Language training helps children learn to make verbal responses and to use them appropriately and spontaneously. Training in social skills can help handicapped children learn principles of behavior management to modify rejecting behaviors of teachers and peers. Parents are taught behavioral techniques for use at home, to teach one specific skill or a variety of skills.

8. Central nervous system stimulants, primarily the drugs Ritalin and Dexedrine, are used to control hyperactivity in children. These drugs do not actually decrease activity, but help the hyperactive child focus his activity with more direction or control. The negative effects of these drugs are: loss of appetite and sleeplessness; awareness of being different from one's peers; the possibility that the child will feel his actions are caused by the drug and not under his control; and the increasing loss of self-es-

teem and feeling of failure if the medication does not help the child's academic deficiencies.

9. Methods of preventing moderate to severe retardation in children have included: (1) amniocentesis for mothers at risk and subsequent termination of pregnancies that show abnormalities; (2) rubella vaccine; (3) special diet for children with phenylketonuria; and (4) attempts to eradicate lead poisoning. Early intervention with these children generally has both mother and child participate in exercises to stimulate the child's motor and cognitive development.

10. Prevention of mild or borderline retardation focuses on changing the child's early experiences by altering the home environment, providing a day care substitute, or both. One early effort at intervention, the Milwaukee Project, was a six-year education program for poverty-level inner-city mothers with IQs below 75 and their high-risk children.

11. Prevention of behavior disorders has focused on early identification of high-risk schoolchildren. Program results are equivocal, and there is some danger in early labeling of children.

Unit 8

Mental Health Law and Clients' Rights

Chapter 23 | Mental Health Law and Clients' Rights

Access to Mental Health Services
Paradoxes

Rights of Mental Patients
Donaldson v. *O'Connor*
Civil Commitment and Right to Liberty
Rights in Institutions
Right to Refuse Treatment

Acceptance in the Community

Summary

Throughout this book we have presented current theories and findings about experiences, origins, and interventions relating to patterns of abnormal behavior. During the last quarter-century in particular, federal funding for mental health research has increased substantially, and many of the projects completed during this period have greatly affected our conceptions of abnormal behavior and mental health practices. Most of these new developments have arisen within the "mental health community," which consists of researchers and practitioners in psychology, medicine, social work, nursing, and allied fields. Activities outside this "community" also have greatly influenced mental health care. Especially interesting is the evolving mental health law, clarifying rights of persons in the care of the mental health system. This movement promises to be much more visible in years to come.

Questions about mental health practices and demands that the client's rights be safeguarded have come from several sources. Certainly, the citizen's interest in and awareness of theory and practice in abnormal psychology is greater today than in the past. Millions of people have taken courses in abnormal psychology and are familiar with the vocabulary and concepts. Similarly, the news and entertainment media have stimulated sympathetic recognition for the needs of troubled children and adults. The mental health establishment is no longer a private fraternity with a special language to use in recommending treatment that uninformed laymen do not understand well enough to question. The consumer movement is causing many citizens to ask hard, penetrating questions about the whys and wherefores of current practice. They want to know more about costs and benefits and, most significantly, about the risks or hazards of different interventions.

The consumer movement has enjoyed support from the legal system, which has steadily extended the "rights" that were recently guaranteed blacks and women to handicapped and psychiatrically disabled persons. The practice known as civil commitment has deprived psychiatric patients of basic civil rights in much the same way that laws and social custom once forced women and ethnic minorities to accept second-class citizenship, and lately this and ensuing institutional practices have come under attack in courtrooms all over the country.

The consumer movement and several landmark legal decisions have already changed the field of abnormal psychology significantly, especially in (1) access to mental health care, (2) the rights of mental patients, and (3) social acceptance of people who are "different." These issues also illustrate some fascinating paradoxes. Victories won by social pressure, legislation, or court decisions, although laudable for their general advance toward more humane care for patients, have produced some less than desirable side effects. In these sections we will discuss these changes in mental health law and clients' rights as well as some of the paradoxes they entail.

Access to Mental Health Services

One major consequence of the 1960s civil rights movement was a new awareness of America's cultural and racial diversity. Americans had lived with the myth that the population was white and, if not of Anglo-Saxon heritage, was at least well on the way to assimilating that heritage. We recognized ethnic and racial minorities, but our image of America the "melting pot" caused mental health professionals to assume that models of etiology and intervention constructed mainly from experience with whites were applicable to other groups.

The movements of the 1960s challenged this assumption. Furthermore, projections of changes in population within our society make it clear that, in proportion to whites, minority groups — blacks and Hispanic Americans, in particular — are growing rapidly. In many states with large urban areas, ethnic minorities now outnumber the previous white majority. These population dynamics promise an even more diverse ethnic and racial mix in the immediate future. The age distribution of our society is changing as well. Declining birth rates, coupled with the baby boom following World War II, will produce a population in the latter part of this century whose average age will be much greater. By the year 2020, as many as one in five Americans will be over sixty-five.

All these changes will demand of the mental health system new models for delivering services. Different ethnic, age, and religious groups are likely to demand etiological models and intervention systems that are sensitive to their unique problems. One task panel of the President's Commission on Mental Health (1978) felt that the time had already arrived:

Because of the pluralistic nature of the American society and cultural order, social problems and social deviances, when applied to mental health issues, must be approached from a cultural relativity frame of reference (p. 828).

Established by President Carter in 1977 to evaluate the status and future needs of mental health care in the United States, the commission took this position very seriously. It set up task forces to evaluate mental health needs of many groups. Their variety was incredible, as this list of titles shows: Asian-Pacific Americans, Black Americans, Americans of Euro-ethnic origin, Hispanic Americans, American Indians and Alaska Nations, Physically Handicapped Americans, Women, the Elderly, Rural Dwellers, Migrant Farmworkers, and Viet Nam Era Veterans.

Although the task force reported unique problems in each group, several issues echoed through the studies on ethnic and racial minority groups:

1. Ethnic minority and poverty status are common correlates, and as we have seen, poverty seems to be a contributing factor in some behavior disorders. Attempts to improve the mental health status of various groups, therefore, must address the larger issues of providing jobs and housing, improving educational opportunities, and upgrading economic status.
2. Etiological models must show sensitivity to the unique cultural heritage and values of each group. For example, professionals must modify diagnostic criteria to take account of behavior patterns characteristic of an ethnic group and also recognize cultural, neighborhood, and family values that help to understand the stresses of life within the subculture.
3. Our mental health delivery systems need to adapt to specific needs of subcultural groups. Therefore, we must locate mental health facilities within the communities that need them to facilitate access, increase the number of mental health professionals from subcultural groups, and develop models of intervention for specific groups.

Paradoxes

These broad recommendations are a positive and valuable step toward improving access to mental health care and, consequently, demand implementation. But like the changes instigated by social and legal pressures, changes in the delivery system of mental health care that have a cultural basis pose a potentially serious dilemma: How do we acknowledge cultural, ethnic, and religious differences without discriminating against one group or another? For example, consider the assertion that ethnically oriented etiological models are essential to account for the development of abnormal behavior. Adapting general models to specific cultural factors seems necessary, but a paradox underlies the more radical assumption that there is a black psychology, which is different from a Hispanic psychology, which, in turn, is different from Asian-American and Caucasian-American psychologies, and so on. This view denies that a basic science of human behavior, normal and abnormal, is feasible, because we are all more different than alike. Denying the commonality of all our needs, fears, hopes, and aspirations could encourage the notion that intergroup differences are so great that intergroup relationships and harmony are not possible.

Now consider the notion that members of ethnic minority groups can get better treatment from members of their own group than from anyone else. Unquestionably, Spanish-speaking mental health professionals are in the best position to appreciate the cultural background of Spanish-speaking patients. And no doubt mental health professionals who are black have special insight into the stresses of racial discrimination. But carrying this idea to the extreme position that *only* members of a minority group can serve members of that group is hazardous, because it could lead many talented mental health professionals who are not members of a minority group to cease making their services available to minority patients. In the report by the task force on Americans of Euro-ethnic origin, this danger was recognized:

The use of bilingual mental health workers has provided a "Catch 22" situation which needs to be corrected. For example, an Italian-American bilingual mental health worker is often automatically given to all Italian clients. The other workers therefore discharge their responsibility by referring all Italian-American clients to one worker. This may result in isolation of the worker as well as inadequate service to the client. Either bilingual staff has to be greatly increased or structures devised that more effectively reach the ethnic communities (Task Panel Reports Submitted to the President's Commission on Mental Health 1978, p. 886).

Rights of Mental Patients

We have been considering people's rights of access to appropriate psychological help, primarily in community-based agencies. Now we will consider the rights of people who are forced into the role of patients.

Imagine how frightened, confused, powerless, and angry you would feel if you were suddenly taken from your home and locked in a mental institution. This procedure raises a host of complex legal and ethical questions: Under what conditions can a person be committed involuntarily? What procedural safeguards prevent someone from being unjustifiably confined to an institution? What rights do institutionalized persons have? Do they have the right to receive treatment and to choose that treatment? The rights of individuals during involuntary commitment to a mental hospital and for the time they remain in an institution are currently being redefined, primarily in the nation's courts. The case of Kenneth Donaldson illustrates why changes are necessary.

Donaldson v. O'Connor

The most influential case on the rights of liberty and treatment has been *Donaldson* v. *O'Connor.* In January 1957, Kenneth Donaldson, aged forty-nine, was committed to a Florida state mental hospital on the petition of his father, who believed his son to be delusional. After a brief hearing before a county judge, Donaldson was committed on grounds that he was mentally ill and dangerous; he was diagnosed "paranoid schizophrenic." The judge told Donaldson that he was being sent to the hospital for a few weeks of care and treatment. In fact, he was not released until July 1971, after he had initiated a legal suit against Dr. O'Connor, the hospital superintendent, and Dr. Germanis, a hospital psychiatrist. Donaldson contended that he was neither mentally ill nor dangerous and that during more than fourteen years of hospitalization he had received little or no psychiatric care or treatment. He claimed a constitutional right to be released.

Court testimony revealed that Donaldson, a Christian Scientist, had refused medication and electroconvulsive therapy (see Chapter 11) and had been offered no other psychiatric treatment. Indeed, he was usually confined in a locked ward. His requests for occupational therapy met with refusal and he received only about fourteen minutes a year of the psychiatrists' time. Arguments by Dr. O'Connor and Dr. Germanis that Donaldson had received "milieu therapy" were discounted by the courts, after Donaldson described his living conditions:

Q: Approximately how many beds were there in the rooms where you slept?
A: Some sixty beds.

Q: How close together were they?

A: Some of the beds were touching, the sides were touching, and others there was room enough to put a straight chair if we had a chair.

Q: Did you have chairs in the dormitory areas?

A: There wasn't a chair in the room I was in.

Q: All right, was there an outside exercise yard for your department?

A: Yes, there was a space outside the building, a good-sized space enclosed with a cyclone fence topped with barbwire.

Q: Did you go out to that exercise yard?

A: I went out from time to time when the other patients were out.

Q: Was there ever a period of time when you did not go out to the exercise yard?

A: Yes, there was one period in particular when nobody went out for two years. . . .

Q: Was there a place on the ward you had access to for keeping personal possessions?

A: No, not at that time.

Q: What did you do with your personal possessions?

A: I kept mine in a cedar box under the mattress of my bed.

Q: Was there a place in the wards where you could get some privacy?

A: No, not any time in all the years I was locked up.

Q: Were you able to get a good night's sleep?

A: No.

Q: Why not?

A: On all of the wards there was the same mixture of patients. There were some patients who had fits during the night. There were some patients who would torment other patients, screaming and hollering, and the fear, always the fear you have in your mind, I suppose, when you go to sleep that maybe somebody will jump on you during the night. They never did, but you think about those things. It was a lunatic asylum.

Further testimony revealed that Donaldson had not been dangerous to himself or others. Yet the psychiatrists felt that he could not function well outside the hospital, and they repeatedly blocked attempts by a college friend and a halfway house to secure Donaldson's release to their custody.

The court decided that whether or not Donaldson had been or currently was mentally ill, he should not have been detained in the hospital without treatment. The court awarded Donaldson $28,500 in compensatory damages and $10,000 in punitive damages. This judgment was sustained on appeal and the case made its way to the United States Supreme Court, which upheld the decision in June 1975.[1]

This case is especially influential because the highest court in the land reviewed it and upheld Donaldson's right to have been treated or released. The Supreme Court ruled:

A finding of "mental illness" alone cannot justify a State's locking a person up against his will and keeping him indefinitely in simply custodial confinement. . . . In short, a State cannot constitutionally confine without more [than custodial care] a nondangerous individual who is capable of surviving safely in freedom by himself or with the help of willing and responsible family members or friends (O'Connor v. Donaldson 1975).

The Supreme Court did not actually specify the conditions under which an individual can be committed, nor did it specifically rule that all committed patients have a right to treatment. The substance and spirit of its ruling, however, are still having a major influence as courts continue to address these questions.

Civil Commitment and Right to Liberty

In a free society the right to liberty is precious. The Fourteenth Amendment to the Constitution reads: "No state shall . . . deprive any

---

[1] Donaldson later settled out of court for the sum of $20,000 from the estate of Dr. O'Connor, who had died during the legal proceedings, and from Dr. Germanis. The defendants made no admission of guilt.

person of life, liberty, or property, without due process of law; nor deny to any person within its jurisdiction the equal protection of the laws." Yet every state has standards and procedures for committing persons against their will to institutions for the mentally ill or retarded, and until recent years a majority of patients in these facilities were there involuntarily. Now many states are revising their mental health codes. Traditional standards for civil commitment were that a person must be mentally ill and (1) dangerous to others, (2) dangerous to himself, (3) gravely disabled, or (4) in need of treatment.

These criteria, especially regarding mental illness and need for treatment, are broad and vague. Therefore the police or a person's family often could have someone committed simply by obtaining a "certificate of mental illness" signed by one or two physicians. Perhaps he would appear before a special commission or a judge, where brief psychiatric testimony to the effect that he was mentally ill and needed treatment would affirm the need for hospitalization for an indefinite period. Such hearings often lasted only a few minutes, but the commitments often lasted a lifetime.

PARENS PATRIAE

Recent challenges to civil commitment standards have questioned whether the power of the state to police society (to protect persons from others) extends to civil law, and especially whether the doctrine of parens patriae (to protect persons from themselves) is adequate legal basis for commitment. The doctrine of parens patriae (literally, father of the country) originated in England, during the middle ages. At that time, it allowed the king to assume control over the property of nobility who were "idiots or lunatics." Although the doctrine's original intent was to protect the king's property, it was transformed over the centuries to justify the state's protecting people from their own actions. The

state exercises parens patriae when it requires cigarette companies to label their products with the warning that smoking is hazardous to your health or forces removal of dangerous drugs from the market. Under this rationale the state can act in what it takes to be the best interest of a person who is incapacitated, often without the procedural rights that the individual would have in a criminal trial.

The doctrine of parens patriae for civil commitment has been widely criticized because it unduly restricts personal liberty. Vague criteria such as "mental illness and need for treatment" can be easily abused, and with conditions as they are in our institutions, hospitalization frequently has not been in the person's best interest. Furthermore, some critics argue that mental patients have been singled out for more state regulation than that exercised over others: "We allow people to drink, smoke, squander their money, work when they are physically ill, and fly balloons across the Atlantic without interference. Why should people who are called mentally disordered forfeit similar personal autonomy when their behaviors are often less harmful than the 'strange' behaviors of 'normal' people?" (Ennis and Emery 1978, p. 40).

The courts have heard many challenges recently to civil commitment besides the Donaldson case, although it is the most notable. As states revise their mental health codes, new procedures and standards give clear evidence of a trend toward guaranteeing constitutional rights in commitment. Typical procedural guarantees include the right to a judicial hearing before or soon after hospitalization, to legal representation, to prior written notification about the details of the hearing, and to attendance at the hearing without having been drugged beforehand. The specifics of these and other rights are quite complex legally, but overall the trend is to grant the same rights a person would have if charged with a crime.

DANGEROUSNESS

Following the spirit of the Supreme Court's decision in the Donaldson case, mental illness and need for treatment are no longer sufficient grounds for civil commitment. Proof must also be shown of physical danger to self or others, "based upon evidence of overt acts, threats or attempts of a dangerous nature in the recent past" (Ennis and Emery 1978, p. 57). Furthermore, if a person is committed as dangerous,

periodic reviews must be arranged to determine if at some time he is no longer dangerous and is eligible for release.

Underlying the dangerousness criterion is the assumption that future behavior is predictable. But the laws do not give satisfactory answers to many questions about dangerousness. How imminent must the danger be? How serious? How probable? Furthermore, who is capable of accurately assessing dangerousness? Contrary to past belief, the evidence simply

Dilemma — What to Do with a "2,000-Year-Old" Man

During three days of testimony, the jurors had heard that behind those soft brown eyes and that endearing smile, Jose Rivera was a potentially dangerous man:

He had a mental capacity of a 3- or 4-year-old and in the past had rammed a toothbrush down his own throat and jammed a pencil through his ear. During his current stay at Atascadero State Mental Hospital, he had engaged in yelling, shouting, biting and kicking, and he had to be kept in both arm and leg restraints at all times.

As diagnosed by the hospital, he was suffering from "schizophrenia, chronic disassociative type." He heard voices that commanded him to do things, and he had hallucinations.

His medical records showed that Jose, 24, had been in and out of mental hospitals 25 times in the last eight years.

Jose (not his real name) took the stand and told the court that he was 2,000 years old and a professional tennis player, jockey, carpenter and several other professions. He said that he had lived several lifetimes. He remembered under questioning that about 1,000 years ago he was "captured by a boatload of aliens."

At issue before the jury in Department 95 of the Los Angeles County Superior Court was not whether Jose was mentally ill. Both sides readily conceded that he was.

The issue was whether he was so sick that he had to be institutionalized. Was society's interest in protecting itself sufficient to deprive him of his liberty? Was he what the law considers "gravely disabled" — unable to provide for his own personal needs of food, clothing and shelter?

The jury was given its instructions and dispatched to a back room to deliberate.

People usually find themselves in Department 95 when they are picked up by a policeman, brought in by relatives or turned in by friends for violent, bizarre or self-destructive behavior.

Sometimes it is a crisis that lasts only a few days — grief at the death of a mate or a marital breakup. Other times it is a manifestation of deeper problems. Between 7,000 and 10,000 cases a year are handled in the two small courtrooms at 1150 San Fernando Road.

Under state law, a person can be kept in a mental hospital against his will only for 72 hours. After that, if doctors believe more treatment is needed, the hospital recommends to the court that the patient be held. If the patient objects, he may file for a hearing in which the court decides whether he should remain in the hospital. If he requests it, the patient receives a jury trial. The proceedings are held in Department 95.

Monday through Thursday every week, buses arrive at about 9 a.m. from the various mental hospitals — Metropolitan State, Camarillo State, Atascadero State, County-USC Medical Center, UCLA Neuropsychiatric Institute and David Brotman Memorial Hospital. The number of people varies each day from as few as 10 to as many as 50.

The patients — who are taking various types of medication and exhibiting various levels of

does not support the contention that mental health professionals can make accurate predictions (Shah 1977; Kress 1979). Very few mentally disordered persons are actually dangerous; the probability that a disordered individual will commit a dangerous act is low. But the tendency is to overpredict low probability events. Consequently, for each hospitalized person who is thereby prevented from committing suicide or assault, many others would not have proved dangerous if left at liberty.

The same dilemma arises in noninstitutional psychiatric practice. One long-recognized right of clients in therapy has been privileged communication. Traditionally a client could expect that what she told her doctor or lawyer or psychologist would be held in confidence, although the codes of professional practice in these disciplines have always allowed for exceptions. Yet in a California case (*Tarasoff* v. *Regents of University of California,* 1976) the court ruled that a therapist who believes the

psychotic behavior — are deposited in the lobby of the building, where they are watched by hospital technicians. They pace the halls and lobby for eight hours.

Some laugh loudly, cry hysterically or scream incoherently. Many just stare into space.

They are suffering from everything from PCP (angel dust) psychosis to depressions caused by marital problems and financial stress. But most are suffering from some type of schizophrenia.

The role of the court is to ensure that the rights of the patient are protected.

"If a person comes in here and says he wants a jury trial and in the next sentence says he is taking off for Uranus and will be back in time for the trial, he will get that trial and all his rights will be protected," said David A. Ziskrout, a commissioner who acts as a judge in Department 95.

"It's a waste of time, but we do it."

One day recently a man in leg and arm restraints paced in his imposed measured little steps and challenged anyone who came by to conversation.

A woman who had been on her way into a courtroom was cornered by him. Growing increasingly agitated, he expounded his theories on language and God's communication with earth.

In a corner, a short, olive-skinned man with his legs also in restraints sat shouting in what officials said they thought was Greek.

Neither the hospital nor his public defender

attorney had been able to break through his torrent of words, not even enough to get his name or where he came from. So he was labeled John Doe 218. And though his words made no sense, the tone in which he said them was hostile, loud and threatening.

On the other side of the lobby, a young man in leg and arm restraints pleaded with his mother to ask the judge to release him from the hospital.

"Please let me come home," he said, banging his already restrained fists against the wall, "I promise I won't do it no more. I'm not a dope fiend."

In another corner, a young woman sat sobbing and talking to no one in particular. She had already had her court appearance and the judge had decided against her.

"I can't go back to that place," she said between sobs, "I'll die if I go back to that place. You hear me judge?" she said aiming her threat at the open courtroom door. "I'll kill myself if I go back there. I'll kill myself."

Inside the courtroom a soft-spoken young man sat on the witness stand explaining his suicide attempt.

Yes, he said, he had taken 10 of his Dalmane sleeping capsules and gone to bed leaving a suicide note: "I love you all. Please remember me."

His wife was threatening to leave him. He had so many bills he could not afford his psychotherapy sessions. He had just bought his wife a new car and she had totaled it.

But things had improved since he was

client to be dangerous has the obligation to inform a third party who is endangered by the client. In the words of the court, "the protective privilege ends where the public peril begins." Again, owing to the problem of false predictions, psychotherapists are apt to violate the confidence of a patient unnecessarily to avoid the risk of a damage suit (Stone 1978).

In addition, because our society generally considers preventive detention an improper exercise of police power, some critics charge that the dangerousness criterion for commitment,

like parens patriae, discriminates against the mentally ill. Some others are much more likely than mentally ill persons to commit a violent crime, but no court would agree to their confinement merely because they *might be* dangerous.

PARADOXES

Alan Stone (1978) writes that, read broadly, "all of the legal developments in civil commitment suggest both a distrust of psychiatry and a growing repudiation of the traditional legal

taken to the hospital. His wife decided to stay; his father, for whom he worked, promised to raise his salary.

"My whole outlook on life is different. Everything has changed. . . . It was a simple family feud," he said.

His writ was granted and he went home.

But many of the problems that surface in the courtroom are not as understandable.

Next on the stand was a man in his 30s who had come from Eugene, Ore. to visit his parents. After a few days, his parents had called the police. They said he was carrying weapons and acting irrationally.

According to the hospital psychiatrist who testified in the case, the man was suffering from a delusion that he was the new Messiah and he was sent to earth to stop "crimes of violence and nuclear fission."

When the man took the stand in his own defense, he said that things had changed for him, too. If allowed to return to Oregon, he would "go fishing, read books and write articles." As for being the Messiah, he said, "I no longer have that delusion. In the history of the world no one has ever believed in a Messiah."

The judge denied his writ and sent him back to the hospital.

Another man in his 20s talked about the UFOs that had landed in his backyard. A beautiful young woman talked about her telepathic conversations with the Pope.

Then came the young man in restraints who had been pleading with his mother in the lobby.

His mother, an attractive woman in her 40s,

told the judge that she did not want to be conservator for her son anymore because of the long trips to Camarillo, the days spent in court and the fact that her boss was no longer understanding about her absences.

"I remember how I used to love you," her son said. "Couldn't nobody love you the way I did, and now all that love has turned to hate. He couldn't ever love you the way I did," he continued, gesturing to his stepfather, who was sitting silently next to his wife.

"He'll go off and find himself another woman," the son went on, "and I would've still been there. But now that's all turned to hate.

"Won't you give me just one more chance? Let me come home. I won't do it no more. . . . I won't touch PCP. . . . I don't want to see that hospital again. . . . I'm too bright to be in the hospital.

"I love you, Carrie Mae, even if you do want to send me back," he said crying.

The court ruled that he be kept in the hospital.

At issue in the courtrooms is not whether the patient thinks he's Napoleon (having delusions is not a crime) or has a past history of a certain kind of behavior.

"The core of the problem is not mental disorder," said Alan Simon, head deputy public defender in Department 95. "A person can be psychotic and not be detained.

"The key is behavior. Is he a danger to self, to others or gravely disabled?"

Because of the emphasis on behavior at the time of the hearing or trial, many patients are

doctrine of *parens patriae.*" The result has been a marked decrease in involuntary commitments, a trend that is certain to continue. Nevertheless, many psychotic individuals who remain in the community because they are not classified as dangerous cause severe stress for their families and others. There is certainly not unanimous agreement that this trend has been as humane as legal advocates imply.

Another paradox of more stringent commitment procedures is that mental health professionals must spend more time attending court hearings and preparing evidence, leaving them with less time available to render treatment. And regrettably, as their responsibilities change to include legal maneuvering and personal liability, as in the Donaldson case, fewer skilled psychologists and psychiatrists are likely to take positions in already understaffed institutions for the mentally ill or the retarded. Although the changes in civil commitment procedures represent a beginning of enlightenment, we run the risk of an attendant loss in the quality of services.

released only to return the next day, week or month.

Some public defender lawyers who represent the patients tend to feel that it is better to have people coming back over and over again to mental hospitals than to have them incarcerated needlessly.

"Some people don't like the revolving-door approach, but at the same time these people are entitled to be free as long as they can be," Richard Brodkin, a deputy public defender in Department 95 for the last four years, said.

But some public defenders say they win more cases than they should.

"We win a lot of cases because the other side isn't doing what they should do," Simon said. "The system should work better."

In defense of the prosecution, David Guthman, head deputy district attorney in Department 95 said that many patients get out of the hospital because of the limitations of the law itself.

"It's a very good law if you recognize its limitations," Guthman said. "It's totally useless if you are looking at long-term treatment but very, very good for short-term crisis intervention."

Several hours passed in the courthouse lobby while Jose Rivera paced up and down waiting for the jury's verdict.

When they returned to the courtroom, they announced that Jose was not gravely disabled and he was to go free.

The court was dismissed and the leg restraints were removed from his legs. Suddenly, he was no longer dangerous.

He stood in the doorway of the lobby smiling under his sky-blue golfer's hat while his attorney tried to call Jose's sister to tell her Jose would be coming home on a public bus.

Unable to reach her, he gave Jose car fare home.

The attorney was torn by the decision. He would have preferred to lose the case. Off the record, he conceded that he was frightened of Jose. All during the trial, he said, he had been fearful that one day as they consulted across the defense table one of Jose's voices would order that he be punched in the mouth.

For the next few days, the attorney called Jose's house to find out how he was.

Jose did not make it home the first night. He stayed with a friend, his sister said. The second day he was home and things were fine.

The lawyer called a few more days and Jose was still all right. But the lawyer couldn't help thinking of him as a time bomb. So did the members of the jury who had set him free.

A week after the trial, a woman who was in the jury that freed Jose said, "We really didn't want to do it, but the county counsel never made a case that he was gravely disabled."

As for Jose's lawyer, it was one of those cases he had to look at philosophically. It came with the job.

"Nothing says I have to root for them," the lawyer said. "I just have to work as hard as I can for them."

Source: Celeste Durant, "Dilemma — What to Do with a '2,000-Year-Old' Man," *Los Angeles Times,* 15 July 1979, p. 1.

Rights in Institutions

RIGHT TO TREATMENT

Foremost among rights claimed for persons in institutions for the mentally ill or retarded is the right to treatment or rehabilitation. The Constitution does not explicitly grant a "right to treatment," but the courts have interpreted several provisions of the Constitution in a way that guarantees this right. According to court interpretations of the due process clause of the Constitution, the state owes an individual treatment in exchange for taking away the right to liberty. Other courts have cited the Constitution's protection against "cruel and unusual punishment" in rejecting custodial care, on the basis that it harms patients. Although *Donaldson* provided only that the state cannot confine a nondangerous person without treatment, subsequent decisions have extended this judgment to all committed patients and, in some cases, to those who voluntarily commit themselves.

The first important case in which civil commitment without treatment or rehabilitation was judged unconstitutional was *Wyatt* v. *Stickney* (1971). This suit has had far-reaching significance because it was filed as a class action, on behalf of all patients in three Alabama hospitals for the mentally ill and retarded. The defendant, Dr. Stickney, was the new Alabama Commissioner of Mental Health at the time the suit was filed. He was a willing adversary, for he, too, was eager to modernize the state's archaic mental health system (Prigmore and Davis 1973). United States District Judge Frank Johnson, remarking that Alabama ranked fiftieth among the states in daily per patient expenditures, concluded that "programs of treatment failed to conform to any minimums established for providing treatment for the mentally ill." He judged Alabama's mental health hospitals to be deficient in three main areas: they failed to provide a humane psychological and physical environ-

ment, sufficient qualified staff to provide adequate treatment, and individualized treatment plans. Other shortcomings were nontherapeutic, uncompensated work assignments; lack of privacy; and overcrowding. At the state school for the retarded, conditions were worse. The court commented: "The result of almost fifty years of legislative neglect has been catastrophic; atrocities occur daily. . . . The gravity and immediacy of the situation cannot be overemphasized. At stake is the very preservation of human life and dignity."

The court ruled in favor of Ricky Wyatt, the plaintiff named in the case, and asserted that involuntarily confined patients have a constitutional right to treatment: "To deprive any citizen of his or her liberty upon the altruistic theory that the confinement is for humane and therapeutic reasons and then fail to provide adequate treatment violates the very fundamentals of due process" (325 F. Supp. 781). Furthermore, Judge Johnson issued a series of court orders spelling out minimum standards of care for Alabama's institutions. These wide-ranging standards embrace a number of patients' rights, such as privacy, rehabilitation, adequate medical care, visitors, and recreation. A milestone in the battle for patients' rights, the Alabama standards not only affirm the right to treatment but also proclaim the court's duty to protect that right by intervening in the system dispensing mental health care, to the extent of defining minimal conditions of adequate treatment. And the effects of this victory have spread beyond Alabama's borders to many other states, where the case has sparked similar class-action suits. In general, compliance has been slower and less complete than the court intended, but these rulings are making a noticeable difference in institutional facilities and practices.

LEAST RESTRICTIVE ALTERNATIVE

The right to treatment in the *least restrictive alternative* warrants special mention as we consider decisions on commitment and treatment. The principle that in curtailing individual freedom the government should choose the least restrictive alternative has been applied in three mental health areas. First, civil commitment is deemed appropriate only when less restrictive alternatives are not available. Second, courts have held that the same doctrine applies to choice of treatment within an institution (*Covington* v. *Harris*, 1969). Finally, some courts have recently mandated the development of community-based alternatives, such as halfway houses and community residences, on the grounds that they are less restrictive than large institutions.

PARADOXES

With right-to-treatment rulings the courts have tried to eliminate years of neglect and abuse. But although upgrading institutions, reducing the number of residents, and creating community-based alternatives are certainly praiseworthy developments, not all the consequences of the court effort are for the best. One paradox has been that because institutions must either provide treatment or release a patient, institutions that are unable or unwilling to meet court guidelines for treatment may simply discharge patients to fend for themselves in the community.

Another paradox relates to psychological intervention. The token economy, as we have seen, is an effective approach to rehabilitation for severely disordered or retarded persons (Chapters 7 and 22), and for these populations only a few items are effective reinforcers. Yet nearly all the items and activities that therapists have used as contingent reinforcers in token economy programs (such as food, clothes, off-unit passes, and room furnishings) are now prescribed rights.

Whether or not other reinforcers (such as a "fancy meal" instead of a plain one) will motivate severely disturbed individuals equally well remains to be seen. There are provisions for waiving some of these rights under special circumstances. Nonetheless, institutional professionals are left with the irony that they may be held liable either way: for not providing treatment or for violating another right in providing effective treatment. These issues require considerably more attention before they can be resolved and we can only hope that able professionals and researchers do not give up in frustration along the way.

Right to Refuse Treatment

Traditionally, patients in the mental health system have had little say about what type of treatments they will receive. They have received little information about the treatment and have not felt free to refuse to submit to prescribed forms of therapy. You may have had the experience of being told by a doctor: "I'm going to give you these pills; take them three times a day." The doctor expected you to follow recommendations for medical or psychological treatment out of trust. Recent legal challenges to mental health practices have established that we all have a right to information about potential benefits and risks of any intervention, biological or psychological, and to refuse treatment if we so desire. Protecting this right is the requirement that patients give *informed consent* prior to treatment; they must acknowledge receipt of sufficient information regarding treatment benefits and risks to make such a significant decision.

We encountered the concept of informed consent in Chapter 4, in relation to research ethics, and in Chapter 11, which includes a consent form for electroconvulsive therapy that you might want to refer to again. Psychiatric patients, prisoners, minors — indeed all subjects — must be aware of the potential risks and benefits of participating in research and treatment programs and are free to refuse or withdraw at any time. Legally, informed consent entails at least three requirements. First, consent must be voluntary, without any coercion. The patient must receive specific and adequate information about the proposed treatment, including method of administration, probability of success and failure, possible risks and side effects, alternative treatments, and consequences of receiving no treatment. Finally, the patient must have the mental capacity to give consent.

Ensuring individual rights in the treatment process is certainly a positive and necessary development, not only from the legal perspective but also the therapeutic. It accords individ-

uals the respect they deserve and the opportunity to take responsibility for their own treatment and for the consequences of their actions. In turn, their investment and participation in their overall rehabilitation might increase. But the legal right to refuse treatment raises problems in clinical practice. First, which treatments require informed consent? Aversive behavior therapy, electroconvulsive therapy, and phenothiazines obviously fall into this category. But why not psychotherapy as well? Many clinicians would argue that psychotherapy is not only expensive but risky: it can increase anxiety, depression, and family conflicts and can keep a patient from receiving other treatments. Per-

Rights of Committed Patients

In the case of *Wyatt* v. *Stickney* (1971), a Federal District Court specified some of the rights of committed patients in Alabama, several of them in detail. Subsequent court actions in other states have resulted in the establishment of similar standards.

1. Right to privacy and dignity.
2. Right to the least restrictive conditions necessary to achieve the purposes of commitment.
3. Rights of visitation, telephone usage, receiving and sending sealed letters.
4. Right to be free from unnecessary or excessive medication.
5. Right to wear their own clothes and keep personal possessions.
6. Right to regular physical exercise several times a week.
7. Right not to be required to perform labor for which the hospital would otherwise have to pay an employee.
8. Right not to be subjected to experimental research without the informed consent of the patient and his guardian or next of kin.
9. Right to adequate number of qualified staff. Among the staff the court required for every 250 patients were: 1 dental hy-

gienist, 1 chaplain, 1 vocational rehabilitation counselor, 3 psychologists, 4 registered physicians, 5 social workers, 12 registered nurses, 92 aides.
10. Right to a humane psychological and physical environment within the hospital facilities. For example:
    (a) The number of patients in a bedroom shall not exceed six.
    (b) One toilet will be provided for every eight patients, one lavatory for every six patients, and one bathtub or shower for every fifteen patients. Each shower stall must be separated by curtains to ensure privacy.
    (c) At minimum, the patients will receive the daily dietary allowance as developed by the National Academy of Science.
    (d) Each patient shall have an individualized treatment plan.
11. Right, for retarded residents, to receive suitable educational services regardless of chronological age, degree of retardation, or accompanying disabilities or handicaps.
12. Right, for retarded residents, to have suitable opportunities for interaction with the opposite sex, under supervision.

haps psychotherapists soon will be obliged to obtain informed consent for every client. Some now do it routinely.

Second, how much information about their condition should patients receive? An explication of every risk and unlikely side effect may in some cases erode the patient's trust in the therapist or physician and, consequently, diminish the placebo effect (the consistent finding that a large percentage of patients respond well to the support of the doctor-patient relationship or to a pill containing no active substance at all).

Third, who should consent to treatment on behalf of the patient who is too confused or disorganized (lacks the mental capacity) to do so? The psychiatrist or psychologist? The family? A representative of the court? Traditionally, the consent of the family has been considered an adequate substitute for the patient's informed consent. But research evidence of extensive disturbance in the family relationships of psychotic patients (see, for example, Chapter 6) raises questions about the wisdom of this custom. Also, family members can be so confused and distraught when a severe psychotic episode occurs that they may not be capable of dealing with information about treatment or resisting subtle coercion to consent. Furthermore, what happens if no family member is available?

Recent recommendations for alternatives to family consent include appointing a *consent auditor,* or *patient advocate,* who would participate in the procedure of consent with and for a disabled patient. The advocate would function much like the Swedish ombudsman, who impartially reviews citizens' complaints against government agencies. It is not yet clear what background and training or authority patient advocates should have.

The following case highlights the complexity in these issues as encountered in clinical practice:

D.Y. is a 23-year-old unmarried white female who has been psychotic almost continuously since age 16. She has been hospitalized in numerous state and private hospitals with only a brief period of remission. Frequent periods of assaultiveness, pacing, confusion, auditory hallucinations, and disheveled dress have occurred. About the sixth year of her hospitalization it was noted that she began to develop periorbital mouth movements and smacking movements of the lips, generally considered early signs of tardive dyskinesia. Her medications were discontinued and her psychotic behavior became more florid. The staff was caught in a dilemma. During the period when medication was withdrawn, the patient became very psychotic and attacked a nurse on the night shift, attempting to strangle her. Only the fortunate intervention of another patient saved the nurse from death by strangulation. The decision was therefore made to reinstitute medication. Was the patient capable of participating in this decision? Was the decision made in the patient's best interests or to control her aggressive behavior? Was this done for the patient's benefit or to improve staff morale? (Klerman 1977, p. 626).

This patient was clearly too psychotic to participate in informed consent, and she had no family. Who, then, was in the best position to make some decision about treatment? The psychiatrist? A mental health advisor? You can begin to see from this case the kinds of problems that arise when patients' rights to refuse treatment conflict with those of society at large.

Acceptance in the Community

We have been considering primarily the rights of people already in the mental health system. A much larger number of people outside of mental health settings must cope with diminished status and outright discrimination in the community because of "mental illness." Some of them are attempting to live in their community in spite of their problems. Others are simply haunted by their "ex" label; their psychiatric problems are behind them, but the social consequences linger. In the past quarter-century, research interest in social attitudes toward mentally and physically disabled people has grown considerably, and yet the rights of this large minority have attracted much less attention in the legal arena. The problem of community acceptance is just one of the difficulties these people face, but it certainly will receive a lot of legal attention in the next few years. It also raises some personal questions that you might ponder now that you have some knowledge of abnormal psychology.

Let us examine Jerry's situation. Following a schizophrenic breakdown in his early twenties, he was hospitalized for three months. He then moved to a hospital-sponsored halfway house in the community, where he has lived for the past two years. Now Jerry has enough courage and competence to try to live on his own again. What is his reception likely to be? You may recall that in Chapter 1 we alluded to many of the problems that might ensue from the label "former schizophrenic." Along with negative reactions from other people, however, Jerry's special status will cause him legal problems. In many states, Jerry, as an ex-mental patient, could not legally vote, drive a motor vehicle, hold office, serve on a jury, or pursue some professions. Because the government routinely denies security clearances to ex-patients, many job opportunities would be denied him. Many employers would be reluctant to hire him if he truthfully accounted for the past two years of his life. Jerry might choose to go back to school, but he would find that many colleges and graduate schools deny admission to former patients. He might even have trouble finding housing, for many landlords will not rent to ex-patients. Finally, although no law dictates it, Jerry's former friends may keep their distance.

Ennis and Emery (1978) list three general points that underlie the developing law on the rights of former mental patients in the community. First, a history of hospitalization or treatment for mental disorder in the past cannot justify discrimination in the present. Phillips (1966) conducted a study of social attitudes based upon past experiences. Women were asked to read a case description of a normal man. One group was told that he had never sought professional help. More than 98 percent of them said they would let their daughters marry such a man, and all said they would rent him a room, work with him, have him in a club, or have him as a neighbor. A second group read this same case history but were told that the man had once been confined in a mental hospital. In striking contrast, only 17 percent of these respondents would have considered him as a son-in-law, and less than half would have rented him a room. Because his current behavior was consistently identified as normal, his history of hospitalization had to be the only basis for rejection. The developing principle that denial of rights, if at all permissible, must reflect present functioning rather than a person's history is likely to invalidate many of the statutes that now set Jerry apart.

Second, "even present mental disorder will not justify discrimination unless there is some rational connection between the disorder and denial of the job, benefit or right involved" (Ennis and Emery, p. 171). This point and the first guided the development of a federal statute (Section 504 of the Rehabilitation Act of 1973), which prohibits discrimination because of mental disorder in any program that receives federal funding. It states that a mentally or physically handicapped person cannot be denied access to a program or job solely because of his handicap if he is "otherwise qualified." A simple example is a person in a wheelchair seeking admission to your college. If he is intellectually capable of college work and meets academic standards for admission, the college cannot refuse him enrollment because his handicap, in this case, would be irrelevant. Furthermore, if the college receives federal funds, according to guidelines issued by the Department of Health, Education and Welfare, it would have to make whatever architectural and scheduling changes are necessary to give him access to the classes he wanted to attend.

In countless other complex examples it is difficult to determine whether the individual is "otherwise qualified." Imagine that Jerry continued to hear voices and talked to himself at times and that he was denied a job as a dishwasher. It could be argued that if he is a good dishwasher he should be hired — that his unusual behavior is not sufficient grounds for denying him a job that does not involve contact with the public. Jerry is "otherwise qualified." This is one area in which we can be sure that many revised guidelines and court decisions will be necessary for clarification.

Third, the doctrine of "least restrictive alternative" applies. In other words, when a state does intervene to deny a person's rights, it must restrict them in the least drastic way possible. Hence the state should identify which affairs the individual is deemed incompetent to manage and not take away his right to manage others. For example, he may not be able to handle complex financial matters, but still have the capacity to manage a simple checking account.

All these rights exist in a social context, and in part, their realization depends upon social attitudes toward people who are different. In a review of the literature on social attitudes, Rabkin (1974) wrote that in recent years an intensive campaign to educate the public has changed expressed attitudes somewhat. Clearly, however, it takes time for changes in thinking to translate into action. Nothing seems to unite a neighborhood as quickly as the hint that a group of ex-mental patients or retarded persons wants to establish a halfway house down the street. But fortunately for those people whose problems we have discussed in this book, there seems to be enough tolerance in our society already to give them a chance to live in the community, rather than segregated from it.

In this book we have shared with you some of what is known in abnormal psychology as well as how it came to be known. And we have made the subject as real as possible by sharing the words both of people who are experiencing personal difficulties and of those searching for solutions. Our main reason for undertaking this effort is a deep belief that an informed public will be a more accepting one. In the last analysis, your understanding and caring are more powerful than any intervention we could describe.

Summary

1. The consumer movement has changed abnormal psychology in these areas: access to mental health care; rights of mental patients; and social acceptance for people who are different. Paradoxically, some of these gains threaten to undermine established benefits in the same areas.

2. To provide appropriate mental health care for the diverse American population, mental health professionals must take into account the ethnic, age, or religious group to which the patient belongs, and the behavior patterns, social values, and stress inherent in belonging to that group. Coupled with this objective, however, is the danger of discriminating against different groups in efforts at prevention and treatment.

3. Mostly because of the *Donaldson* v. *O'Connor* case, many states have begun to change laws restricting the rights of the mentally ill. A direct outgrowth of this 1975 decision is that proof of dangerousness to self or to others is necessary for involuntary commitment. Consequently, a person is less likely to be committed wrongly or for an indefinite period. But this requirement could make mental health professionals more reluctant to recommend commitment for anyone and thus may increase stress in the patient's family and create problems in the community.

4. The decision granting institutionalized patients the right to treatment or release was intended to prevent further neglect and abuse, but a possible negative consequence is that hospitals might choose to release patients into the community rather than increase their own costs for treatment. Another paradox of this advance is that effective treatments like the token economy sometimes violate other recently established rights, such as the right to food, clothes, and a measure of personal freedom.

5. Mental patients have the legal right to refuse treatment and, when hazardous therapy is considered, must give informed consent to treatment. This right raises several questions in clinical practice: (1) which treatments require informed consent? (2) how much information about the treatment is the patient entitled to? and (3) who should be approached for consent to treatment if the patient is not competent to do so?

6. As the law pertaining to the rights of former mental patients and outpatients develops, it provides two guarantees: a history of hospitalization or treatment for mental disorder cannot justify discrimination in the present; and present mental disorder will not justify discrimination unless there is a rational connection between the disorder and the denial of job, benefit, or right involved. In addition, the doctrine of the least restrictive alternative allows the state to deny only the rights these individuals are deemed incompetent to manage.

Glossary

acute onset: the sudden occurrence of a psychotic disorder.

acute phase: an early stage of psychotic disorder marked by a distinct decrease in the individual's ability to adjust and function.

acute psychosis: a sudden, severe behavior disorder of relatively short duration.

acute treatment stage: the first phase of intervention, intended to reduce disorganizing psychotic symptoms and allow the patient to reestablish contact with reality.

addictive drugs: drugs that can create a physiological dependence when consumed at a rate greater than the body's ability to metabolize them.

Addison's disease: insufficient production of hormones in the adrenal cortex, causing fatigue, depression, and darkening of the skin.

adoption studies: a method of testing genetic theories of abnormal behavior by studying the offspring of abnormal parents who are being raised by relatively normal adoptive parents.

aftercare: outpatient treatment of formerly institutionalized individuals within their communities.

Alcoholics Anonymous: a self-help organization founded and run by alcoholics.

alpha rhythms: brain waves of 8–12 cycles per second; the dominant pattern in a resting but wakeful adult.

altruistic suicide: self-destruction intended to serve a social purpose or cause rather than to resolve a personal crisis.

Alzheimer's disease: a presenile dementia involving rapid intellectual deterioration, speech impairment, loss of body control, and death, usually within five years of onset.

amnesia: memory loss, total or partial, often associated with behavior disorders.

amniocentesis: analysis of a sample of fluid drawn from the sac surrounding the fetus during the fourth month of pregnancy to detect chromosome aberrations.

amphetamines (or "speed"): central nervous system stimulants (e.g., benzedrine, dexedrine, and methedrine) that produce high levels of energy and, in large doses, nervousness, sleeplessness, and delusions.

analgesics: a class of pain-relieving drugs.

analogue experiments: attempts to recreate and study, in a controlled situation, behavior that is analogous to naturally occurring psychopathology.

anal stage: the second stage in Freud's theory of psychosexual development, during which the anus is the principal erogenous zone; usually the second year of life.

anhedonia: the inability to find any pleasure in life.

anomic suicide: self-destruction resulting from an individual's inability to deal with a sudden or marked change, or both, in social position or situation.

anomie: the absence of norms believed by some sociologists to lead to deviant behavior in individuals who cannot gain access to conventional or socially approved routes to success.

anorexia nervosa: a psychosomatic disturbance in eating patterns typified by extreme dieting, hyperactivity, and distorted body image.

anoxia: oxygen deprivation; severe anoxia can cause permanent brain damage.

Antabuse: a drug that causes the ingestion of alcohol to produce nausea, vomiting, and other unpleasant effects.

anxiety: a subjective state of apprehension or tension accompanied by physiological arousal.

aphasia: partial or complete loss of the ability to use or understand language caused by brain damage.

assessment techniques: methods of observation and measurement used to profile a person's psychological and behavioral traits. Assessment supports diagnosis, intervention, and research.

automatic thoughts: thoughts that cause feelings of depression.

aversion therapy: a behavior therapy that discourages deviant behavior by affixing unpleasant associations to the stimuli of such behavior.

barbiturates: addictive central nervous system depressants.

behavioral exchange agreements: a component of behavioral marriage counseling in which partners negotiate specific, desired changes in each other's behavior.

behaviorism: school of psychology based on the study of observable behavior and the patterns of stimulus and response that govern it.

behavior modification: an intervention approach using procedures based on principles of learning to modify behavior.

benzodiazepines: widely prescribed drugs used to treat severe anxiety (e.g., Valium and Librium).

beta rhythms: brain waves of 13–25 cycles per second; the dominant pattern in an alert, awake adult.

biofeedback: a technique for graphically representing usually imperceptible physiological processes so that an individual can achieve conscious control over them.

bipolar depression: a mood disorder characterized by episodes of depression and mania.

board and care homes: residential treatment centers in which patients live in hotel-like, supervised environments.

borderline syndrome: behavior that resembles psychosis but is shorter in duration and less severe; includes functional difficulties in interpersonal re-

lationships, impulse control, task performance, expression, and perception.

brain laceration: an injury to the brain that occurs when an object pierces the skull and tears brain tissue.

Brief Psychiatric Rating Scale: an instrument used to assess a subject along sixteen dimensions (e.g., anxiety, depressive mood, somatic concern, and motor retardation).

butyrophenones: powerful, antipsychotic tranquilizers.

caffeine: a central nervous system stimulant found in coffee, tea, and cola beverages; produces elevated mood, increased energy, and wakefulness.

Casanova complex: delusion of extraordinary sexual potency and desirability.

catatonic schizophrenia: a subtype of schizophrenia, characterized by extreme withdrawal and rigid immobility, alternating in some cases with agitated excitement.

catharsis: an emotional release achieved by reexperiencing and communicating emotions associated with past trauma.

central nervous system (CNS) depressants: substances, including alcohol, which reduce agitation and induce sleep.

cerebral arteriosclerosis: abnormal thickening of the walls of the arteries in the brain; usually an old-age disorder.

cerebrovascular accident (stroke): blockage or rupture of a large blood vessel in the brain resulting in disorientation, cognitive impairment, speech disorders, and transient or permanent paralysis.

childhood schizophrenia: psychosis that appears between ages 5–12, after a period of normal development, and is characterized by delusions, hallucinations, and thought disorder.

chlorpromazine: major tranquilizer that is widely used as an antipsychotic drug.

chronic psychosis: a pattern of disturbed behavior that persists for many years.

civil commitment: legal process of hospitalizing individuals who are dangerous to themselves or others or are gravely disabled, even against their will.

classical (Pavlovian) conditioning: a basic learning process in which a previously neutral stimulus (conditioned stimulus) is paired with one that elicits a known response (unconditioned stimulus) until the neutral stimulus comes to elicit a similar response (conditioned response).

client-centered therapy: a humanistic insight therapy

developed by Carl Rogers in which the therapist seeks to understand the client's subjective experiences and to create an accepting atmosphere in which the client can actualize his or her potential.

cocaine: pain-reducing central nervous system stimulant derived from the coca plant; produces increased mental energy, euphoria, and heightened sexual desire.

cognitive-behavior theory: an approach that emphasizes the role of beliefs, thoughts, and self-statements in behavior patterns.

concordance: the degree of similarity in characteristics or diagnosis of a twin pair.

concurrent validity: a measure's relation to other, independent indices of the same phenomenon.

concussion: a brain injury that disrupts consciousness and memory, often accompanied by a brief period of amnesia and disorientation.

congenital rubella syndrome: effects on an infant of rubella (German measles) contracted by the mother during the first trimester of pregnancy; primarily includes deafness, cataracts, heart disease, retardation, or some combination of these.

conjugal delusion: the unfounded conviction that one's spouse is unfaithful.

constriction of thinking: a narrowing focus of the mind that is symptomatic of acute suicidal tendencies.

content or face validity: accuracy of a measure's representation of the variable it attempts to measure.

contusion: brain bruise caused by compression of neural tissue against the skull; results in loss of consciousness and sometimes in permanent impairment.

conversion disorders: psychological disturbances in which physical symptoms cannot be attributed to an organic cause.

correlational study: an investigation that measures the relationship between two or more variables without experimental manipulation.

covert sensitization: a form of aversion therapy that uses mental imagery to associate unpleasant sensations with the stimuli for undesirable behavior.

creative regression: deliberate re-creating of the psychotic state to facilitate reintegration of the disordered personality.

cross-sectional study: a research method using subjects of different ages to investigate developmental questions.

cultural-familial retardation: mild mental retardation of no known organic cause in an individual who has at least one similarly impaired parent or sib-

ling; cases generally appear in socioeconomically deprived environments.

Cushing's syndrome: obesity, muscle atrophy, mood disturbance, and fatigue caused by overproduction of hormones in the adrenal cortex.

defense mechanisms: in psychoanalytic theory, self-protective, usually unconscious psychological devices that block the ego's awareness of anxiety-provoking memory and instinct.

delirium: temporary impairment of perception, judgment, concentration, memory, and orientation associated with medical disorders; often accompanied by delusions and hallucinations.

delirium tremens (DTs): a severe form of alcohol withdrawal in which paranoia, disorientation, extreme agitation, hallucinations, anxiety, insomnia, anorexia, and tremors can occur.

delta rhythms: brain waves of less than four cycles per second; the dominant pattern in a sleeping adult.

delusions of persecution: unjustified belief that one is the target of potential attack or injury.

demand characteristics: in research, those aspects of the experimental situation which tend to inform the subjects of expected behavior.

dementia: progressive deterioration of ability to think abstractly, make judgments, and control impulses.

dementia praecox: an early term for schizophrenia; connotes early appearance and inevitable progress of the disease.

dependent variable: in an experiment, the behavior that is measured and is expected to change with manipulation of an independent variable.

depression: a mood disorder characterized by severe or prolonged feelings of hopelessness, despair, low self-esteem, worthlessness, guilt, withdrawal from others, and loss of sleep, appetite, and sexual desire.

descriptive study: a research method, such as a case study or survey, which describes a phenomenon as it exists or occurs in nature.

desensitization: a therapeutic process in which subjects are gradually exposed to increasingly anxiety-provoking situations, usually via the imagination, in order to neutralize their phobic emotional responses.

destructuring of perception and affect: feelings of extreme urgency and anticipation, together with the conviction that neutral events have special, personal significance; suggestive of potential psychotic breakdown.

developmental model: the theory that a mentally retarded person's learning simply proceeds more slowly, toward a lower ceiling of performance, than that of a normal person.

developmental study: research methods, such as cross-sectional, longitudinal, and retrospective studies, used to investigate changes in behavior over time.

Diagnostic and Statistical Manuals (DSMs): classification systems developed by the American Psychiatric Association that specify behavioral criteria for determining diagnosis from clinical observations; *DSM*-III is the latest edition.

difference model: the theory that a retarded person's learning difficulties result from a cognitive defect and, therefore, the learning processes themselves are qualitatively different from those of normal people.

directionality problem: a shortcoming of correlational studies in which two variables interrelate in such a way that it is not clear which is causing the other.

dissociation: separation of specific mental functions from the mainstream of consciousness or of specific behaviors from the rest of the personality.

distancing: therapeutic process in which the subject learns to recognize and control reality-distorting cognitions that cause depression.

disturbed-neurotic delinquency: an adolescent's adoption of impulsive, antisocial behavior as a means of rebelling against the family.

Down's syndrome: moderate to severe retardation caused by an extra chromosome; marked by distinct physical characteristics — most notably slanted eyes — and formerly called mongolism.

Draw a Person Test: a projective test in which the subject, who is usually a child, draws a person, then draws one of the opposite sex; results can be scored for cognitive development or for psychopathology.

dysrhythmia: irregular or chaotic brain-wave sequences.

echolalia: meaningless repetition of what is spoken by others; may be immediate or delayed; often characteristic of autistic children's speech.

ego: in psychoanalytic theory, the rational self-concept, which mediates between the instinctual demands of the id and the externally oriented pressures of the superego.

ego-dystonic homosexuality: *DSM*-III classification of sexual preference for people of the same gender that is unwanted by, and distressing to, the individual.

egoistic suicide: self-destruction stemming from the lack of close relationships and meaningful social interaction.

ejaculatory incompetence: a male's inability to achieve orgasm during penetration of the vagina.

Electra conflict: in Freud's theory of psychosexual development, the female child's conflict between desire for the father and fear of punishment by the mother.

electrocardiogram (EKG): graphic recording of subject's heart rhythms.

electroconvulsive therapy (ECT): the passing of an electric current through the brain from outside the skull to induce convulsions; sometimes used to treat severe depression.

emotional divorce: the state of a marriage in which the partners have ceased to have meaningful verbal or other interaction.

emotive imagery: a psychotherapeutic technique in which a child acquires anxiety-inhibiting responses by imagining an alter ego or favorite hero conquering his or her fears.

encephalitis: inflammation of brain tissue, usually caused by a virus carried by an insect.

endocrine glands: organs that regulate body functions, such as energy supply and availability, sexual arousal, and physical growth, by secreting hormones into the blood and lymph system.

endorphins: opiates produced in the brain that act as natural pain suppressants; may be involved in the chemistry of drug addiction.

epilepsy: a brain disorder in which abnormalities in the electrical activity of the brain produce loss of consciousness and convulsions.

erectile dysfunction: inability of a male to maintain an erection for sexual intercourse; impotence.

essential hypertension: high blood pressure that is of an emotional or psychological origin and not a secondary consequence of an identifiable physical disorder.

etiology: the assignment of a cause to or the determination of origin of a disease.

exhibitionism: display or exposure of the genitals to an unwilling and unsuspecting observer for the purpose of sexual gratification.

existential therapy: intervention that encourages exploration of the subjective experience of psychosis as a means of reintegrating the self and emphasizes the potential for self-determination.

experimental study: a research method that manipulates an independent variable and measures changes in a dependent variable according to a procedure designed to eliminate alternative explanations.

external validity: the extent to which conclusions of a research study can be generalized to other populations and settings.

family therapy: treatment of the entire family that focuses on the relationships and communication among family members, rather than on the pathology of one individual.

fear: an emotional response to an external threat; consists of subjective apprehension and physiological changes, including increased pulse and respiration, which prepare the body for a "flight or fight" response.

Fear Survey Schedule II (FSS II): descriptions of fifty-one stressful situations to which respondents relate their emotional responses.

fetishism: sexual fascination with a body part or an object so absorbing that the individual has no interest in normal sexual activity.

fixation: in psychoanalytic theory, the inability to progress normally from one stage of psychosexual development to the next due to overgratification or excessive deprivation during that stage.

"flight or fight" reaction: in response to a threat that arouses fear, the choice between fleeing the source of stress or counterattacking.

flooding: behavioral-therapy technique of repeatedly presenting strong anxiety-provoking stimuli to neutralize their effect.

free association: a technique in psychoanalytic therapy in which the client is urged to talk about whatever comes to mind without censoring or interpreting those thoughts in order to reveal repressed ideas and memories for analysis.

fugue: a dissociative reaction in which an individual alters the locale and mode of living and is amnesic for his or her previous life, yet apparently functions normally.

functional psychosis: severe disturbance of thought, emotion, and behavior without detectable brain pathology.

galvanic skin response (GSR): change in electrical conductivity of the skin caused by an increase in sweat-gland production stimulated by the sympathetic nervous system; an indication of anxiety.

gender identity disorders: psychosexual disorientation in which the individual lacks clear identification with physiological gender.

genital stage: in Freud's theory of psychosexual development, the final stage, in which heterosexual interests predominate; adulthood.

Gestalt therapy: a humanistic-existential insight therapy approach developed by Fritz Perls to reintegrate dissociated thoughts, feelings, and actions into a whole, well-functioning self; focuses on nonverbal clues to unacknowledged needs, which the therapist encourages the patient to confront.

grandiosity: delusion of exaggerated importance or power.

grand mal epilepsy: severe form of epilepsy involving periodic loss of consciousness and violent, generalized convulsions.

halfway houses: living environments in which formerly institutionalized patients prepare to readjust and reenter society.

hallucinogens: drugs that induce sensory perceptions with no external stimuli (e.g., LSD, mescaline, psilocybin, and phencyclidine); some are also called psychedelics.

Hawthorne effect: change in a subject's behavior caused by awareness of being in an experiment.

hebephrenic schizophrenia: a subtype of schizophrenia involving severe personality disintegration marked by delusions, hallucinations, incoherent speech, and absurd behavior; typically occurs in young adults.

histrionic (hysterical) personality: behavior pattern characterized by exaggeration, self-dramatization, and attention seeking.

Holmes-Rahe Scale: an instrument for assessing the stress on an individual by quantifying major life changes according to the difficulty people typically have readjusting after them.

Holtzman inkblot technique: a projective test containing two sets of forty-five inkblots; similar to the Rorschach, but featuring better-standardized administration, scoring, and interpretation.

homosexuality: sexual preference for members of one's own sex.

humanism: the philosophical view that humans have free will and both the right and capacity for self-determination based on purposes and values (in contrast to Freud's emphasis on unconscious forces).

Huntington's chorea: a rare and fatal hereditary disorder characterized by severe and progressive mental deterioration, muscular spasms, and psychotic behavior.

hustling theory: that the rituals and activities associated with the use of drugs reinforce addiction and abuse.

hyperactivity: a term applied to a cluster of childhood

behavior problems that includes short attention span, inability to channel activity, irritability, and restlessness; also called attention-deficit disorder.

hyperthyroidism: disorder caused by overproduction of the hormone thyroxin; marked by extreme weight loss, tremors, excessive anxiety, increased sweating, and psychomotor agitation.

hypomania: a mild form of mania in which an individual is still able to function socially and professionally; can be marked by slight psychomotor overactivity, pressured speech, elation, and irritability.

hypothyroidism: disorder caused by underproduction of the hormone thyroxin; marked by increase in weight, sluggishness, poor concentration and memory, and depression.

id: in psychoanalytic theory, the instinctual energy and drives that strive continually for gratification; the most primitive and inaccessible aspect of personality.

identity dissolution: the progressive confusion about who one is that occurs during a schizophrenic breakdown.

incest: sexual relations between close relatives, most often between father and daughter or brother and sister.

independent variable: in an experimental study, the variable that the researcher manipulates to produce changes in dependent variables.

infantile autism: a disorder diagnosed in infancy or early childhood and marked by withdrawal from others, distorted perception, intolerance of environmental changes, bizarre body movements, and speech peculiarities.

insidious onset: the gradual appearance of a psychotic disorder.

institutionalism: a patient's overaccommodation to the undemanding safety of the institutional environment; characterized by apathy.

interjudge reliability: substantial agreement in evaluation of a phenomenon among independent, trained observers or scorers.

internal reliability: similarity or consistency between the results of one part of a measurement or observation and those of another part or of the whole.

internal validity: the extent to which experimental results can be attributed unambiguously to manipulation of the independent variable; more generally, the extent to which the results of a study can be confidently assigned a cause.

intervention: effort to reduce abnormal behavior patterns.

introspection: a research procedure in which trained observers report their own responses to stimuli.

isolation: defense mechanism typified by the conscious denial of emotions associated with unwanted desires.

lability: instability of mood or emotion.

latency period: in Freud's theory of psychosexual development, the fourth stage, in which sexuality is dormant; preadolescence.

learned helplessness: a reaction of passively accepting a painful emotional state when one feels unable to escape from it; learned from experiences in which one's actions were ineffective in altering an unpleasant situation.

libido: instinctual drives of the id for pleasure; in a narrow sense, the drive for sexual gratification.

lobotomy: a surgical procedure in which the fibers connecting the frontal and prefrontal lobes of the brain are severed in the hope of reducing severely disturbed behavior.

longitudinal study: a research method for examining the development of the same subjects over a long period.

lysergic acid diethylamide (LSD): a synthetic hallucinogen.

magical thinking: a delusion of catatonic schizophrenics that small actions on their part will cause dramatic events.

mainstreaming: the concept of educating developmentally disabled children as much as possible in the same classrooms as nondisabled children.

Major Role Therapy (MRT): a counseling technique that focuses on assuming a productive social role and reestablishing personal relationships; used with institutionalized patients preparing to reenter the community.

mania: extreme euphoria and excessive mental and physical activity characterized by difficulty in concentration, impulsiveness, inflated self-esteem, rapid speech, and hypersexuality.

manic-depressive psychosis: severe mood disorder marked by repeated and often inexplicable shifts between extremes of euphoria and depression or prolonged periods of either one.

marijuana: drug derived from the cannabis plant that produces mild euphoria, heightened sensory awareness, altered time perception, and relaxed passivity.

medical model: a classification system for examining abnormal behavior in the same way as medicine studies physical diseases, by seeking underlying causes and resulting observable symptoms.

mental retardation: condition that becomes apparent during childhood, characterized by subnormal intelligence and deficient adaptive behavior.

methadone: synthetic, orally administered addictive drug used to treat heroin addiction; satisfies opiate craving without clouding consciousness.

Minnesota Multiphasic Personality Inventory (MMPI): a self-report inventory with questions covering a range of topics, widely used because it is an easily administered and scored diagnostic measure of disorders such as anxiety, depression, gender identity, and paranoia.

monoamine oxidase (MAO) inhibitors: antidepressant medication (e.g., Iproniazid) used to treat some types of depressive disorders.

monogenetic model: the theory that attributes the development of schizophrenia to one inherited gene.

multiaxial diagnosis: a diagnostic system for assessing behavior on several dimensions and using a complex numerical code to reach a diagnosis.

multiple-baseline design: a single-subject experiment in which the researcher measures two or more behaviors and then introduces treatment sequentially to determine if behavior changes coincide with treatment manipulations.

multiple personality: dissociative disorder involving the expression by one individual of two or more distinct personalities that have varying degrees of awareness of each other.

mystification: the systematic parental denial of a child's feelings and perceptions that causes the child to doubt his or her concept of reality and to experience fear and confusion as a result.

neurochemistry: study of the chemical composition and activity of brain and nervous system.

neurosis: nonpsychotic emotional disorder characterized by anxiety and associated avoidance and obsessive-compulsive behaviors; also called anxiety disorder.

neurotransmitters: chemical substances (e.g., dopamine and norepinephrine) that facilitate or inhibit transmission of nerve impulses between neurons; malfunction may be a factor in psychological disorders.

neutralization: therapeutic process by which subject learns to reduce the frequency and intensity of reality-distorting thoughts by reciting reasons why they are invalid.

nocturnal enuresis: bedwetting at least once a month beyond the age of three or four years.

normalization: creation of a life style for retarded people that resembles as much as possible that of the mainstream of society.

obsessive-compulsive disorder: an anxiety disorder characterized by persistent, uncontrollable thoughts or a drive to continually repeat a behavior pattern such as handwashing or checking door locks.

Oedipal conflict: in Freud's theory of psychosexual development, the male child's conflict between desire for his mother and fear of punishment by his father.

operant conditioning: basic learning process in which behaviors are repeated or reduced as a function of environmental consequences (reinforcements and punishments).

opiates: narcotics, including opium and its derivatives, morphine, codeine, and heroin; abuse can lead to addiction.

oral stage: in Freud's theory of psychosexual development, the first stage, during which the mouth is the principal erogenous zone; extends from birth into the second year.

organic brain syndrome: degenerative effects of brain pathology on a variety of functions, including memory, judgment, perception, social behavior, and motor coordination.

organic psychosis: severe mental disorder known to be caused by a physical disease or condition.

paranoid schizophrenia: a subtype of schizophrenia characterized by delusions (e.g., persecution or personal importance), hallucinations, and ideas that external events have personal significance.

paraphilias: a class of deviant sexual activities including voyeurism, fetishism, and pedophilia.

parasympathetic nervous system: the part of the nervous system that regulates basic body functions during states of relaxation; must be operating for sexual arousal to occur.

paresis: condition of the central nervous system resulting from syphilis that is characterized by lethargy, depression, intellectual deterioration, delusions, and progressive paralysis.

Parkinsonian symptoms: side effects of the phenothiazines that mimic Parkinson's disease.

Parkinson's disease: degenerative brain disease characterized by impairment of motor activity, tremors, rigidity of muscle tone, and an expressionless face.

pedophiliac: person who seeks sexual gratification by contact with prepubertal children.

performance anxiety: apprehension about sexual activity that causes the sympathetic nervous system to take over from the parasympathetic, with the result that reflexive responses necessary for sexual arousal are inhibited.

permissive theory: idea that production of abnormal amounts of two neurotransmitters, norepinephrine and serotonin, may be involved in depression.

personality disorders: well-established maladaptive behavior patterns, such as self-defeating personal habits and forms of social deviance.

petit mal epilepsy: a mild form of epilepsy involving a brief alteration in or loss of consciousness.

phallic stage: in Freud's theory of psychosexual development, the third stage, during which the genitals are the principal erogenous zone; usually the third to sixth years of life.

phenomenology: the focus on subjective experience and perception in the investigation and treatment of behavioral disorders.

phenothiazines: a class of nonaddictive antipsychotic tranquilizers.

phenylketonuria (PKU): genetic metabolic disorder that leads to central nervous system damage and mental retardation unless diet is carefully restricted in early childhood.

Phillips Scale of Premorbid Adjustment: a measure that assesses, in retrospect, the social and sexual adjustment of an individual prior to onset of psychotic symptoms.

phobic disorder: anxiety marked by persistent and recurring fear of an object, activity, or situation to the extent of avoiding it completely, often with understanding that the anxiety is unfounded.

placebo: inert substance given as a drug to patients or research subjects, who may then experience a change in condition or behavior simply as a result of their own expectations; used as a control to isolate the actual effects of experimental drugs.

play therapies: psychotherapeutic techniques that use play to establish a relationship between therapist and child and to facilitate the child's expression of conflicts and feelings.

polygenetic model: the theory that attributes the development of schizophrenia to a specific group of interacting genes.

postconcussion syndrome: persistent headaches, anxiety, insomnia, irritability, and minor cognitive impairments that typically occur after an individual has suffered a concussion.

predictive validity: the extent to which a measure successfully predicts related future behaviors.

premature ejaculation: a male's inability to delay ejaculation long enough to achieve mutually satisfying sexual relations with his partner; usually occurs either before or soon after penetration.

presenile dementia: degeneration of brain tissue accompanied by mental deterioration that occurs before age sixty-five; characterized by personality changes, cognitive difficulties, and impaired judgment and impulse control.

primary erectile dysfunction: condition of a man who has never maintained an erection sufficient to achieve sexual intercourse.

primary labeling theory: the position that the assignment of labels is a causal factor in abnormal behavior.

primary orgasmic dysfunction: condition of a female who has never achieved orgasm by any method.

prognosis: prediction of the future course and outcome of an illness or disorder.

projection: defense mechanism marked by the attribution of one's own unwanted characteristics, attitudes, and desires to others.

projective tests: assessment techniques (e.g. Rorschach inkblot test, Thematic Apperception Test) that present ambiguous stimuli designed to reveal unconscious motivations and fears.

pseudodementia: a mental and emotional disorder in older individuals; depressive disorder can produce a dementialike syndrome.

pseudo-mutual relationship: the state of a marriage in which the partners emphatically persist in a pretense of happiness and compatibility, though both are quite dissatisfied with the relationship.

psilocybin: a hallucinogen derived from a mushroom.

Psychiatric Status Schedule: a standardized interview in which the interviewer rates the subject's answers according to precoded response types.

psychoanalysis: the theoretical model and therapeutic approach developed by Sigmund Freud; uses free association, dream interpretation, and other means to uncover unconscious sources of thought, feeling, and behavior.

psychological autopsy: analysis, after the fact, of an individual's suicidal behavior and intent.

psychological dependence: the need, not physiological, for continued use of a drug.

psychological handicap: impaired ability, because of mental or emotional disturbance, to function adequately in everyday social and occupational roles.

psychomotor agitation: disordered behavior (e.g., pacing, handwringing, and squirming) likely to be exhibited by unipolar depressive patients.

psychomotor epilepsy: lapse in consciousness in which the individual, although appearing to remain conscious, is unaware of his behavior, which often has the form of some routine or repetitive act.

psychomotor retardation: disordered behavior (e.g., slowed speech and body movements) likely to be exhibited by bipolar depressive patients.

psychophysiological disorder: physical symptoms such as hives and ulcers and other disorders involving actual tissue damage that result from continual emotional activation of the autonomic nervous system.

psychosis: severe mental disorder characterized by delusions and hallucinations in which thought and emotion are so disturbed that the individual loses contact with reality.

psychotic breakdown: a radical and damaging disruption of consciousness, perception, thinking, and social behavior.

psychotomimetics: drugs that alter perception, mood, and behavior in a way that mimics psychosis.

Q-sort: a personality inventory in which the subject arranges a set of descriptive statements in piles according to how much they apply to him or her.

r: a statistical index ranging from -1.00 to $+1.00$ that expresses the relationship between two variables; the positive or negative sign indicates whether the relationship is direct or inverse, and the number indicates its strength.

radical behaviorism: a theory of development that attributes all behavior to two processes of learning: classical conditioning and operant conditioning.

random sample: a method of selecting research subjects that allows all members of the population under study an equal chance of being selected, with the expected result that the selection will be representative of the population.

rape: sexual intercourse forced on one person by another.

rational-emotive therapy: method developed by Albert Ellis for restructuring self-defeating thoughts and feelings that underlie disordered behavior.

reaction formation: a defense mechanism through which the individual escapes the anxiety that stems from undesired wishes and impulses by expressing their opposites.

reinforcers: consequences of a response that increase the likelihood that an individual will make that response in the future.

relaxation response: the goal of a system of daily exercises designed to enhance an individual's ability to relax; intended to reduce the individual's vulnerability to stress and related problems and disorders.

repression: a defense mechanism that blocks awareness of impulses and deadens the memory of painful or upsetting events.

reserpine: drug used to treat hypertension; reduces the functional availability of some neurotransmitters and can produce depression.

retrospective study: a research method of investigating subjects' development, examining their histories by means of interviews and records.

reversal design: single-subject study in which the effects of a treatment program on target behavior are demonstrated by alternately introducing and withdrawing the treatment program.

Rorschach Psychodiagnostic Inkblot Test: a projective test in which the subject interprets ten symmetrical inkblots as images and then points out which features of the blots suggested the interpretation.

schism: role distortion within families of schizophrenics resulting from pronounced antagonism between the marital partners that colors all family interactions.

schizo-affective disorders: psychotic disorders characterized by schizophrenic symptoms together with depression or elation.

schizophrenia: psychosis characterized by generalized withdrawal, apathy, thought disorder, emotional disturbance, delusions, and hallucinations.

schizophrenogenic: causing or contributing to a condition of schizophrenia.

schizotaxia: according to Meehl, a basic neurological impairment, possibly inherited, of the ability to integrate thought and emotions, which results in limited capacity to cope with life stress; characterized by thought disorder and anhedonia; predisposition to schizophrenia.

secondary erectile dysfunction: condition of a man who cannot maintain an erection sufficient to achieve sexual intercourse, although he has been able to do so at least once in the past.

secondary labeling theory: hypothesis that the assignment of labels can stigmatize an individual, thereby limiting the possibility of recovery or rehabilitation.

sedative-hypnotics: central nervous system depressants, chronic use of which can cause deterioration in psychomotor function, disturbed sleep patterns, and physiological problems from vitamin deficiency.

senile dementia: deterioration of the central nervous system in old age, which results in personality changes and impaired thinking, judgment, and impulse control.

Sentence Completion Test: a projective test in which the subject supplies words or phrases to complete sentence stems.

serotonin: a neurotransmitter that may be involved in clinical depression and mania.

serum pepsinogen: a product of the digestive process found in the bloodstream; measured in the study of peptic ulcers.

situational orgasmic dysfunction: condition of a female who can achieve orgasm only under limited conditions or at certain times.

skew: role distortion within the families of schizophrenics resulting from domination of the family system by one parent.

socialized-subcultural delinquency: adoption of subcultural values that sanction behaviors viewed as deviant by the broader culture.

sociopath: an individual who displays repetitive, impulsive, and purposeless antisocial behavior with emotional indifference and without guilt.

spectator attitude: a response to performance anxiety in which the individual apprehensively observes his or her own sexual functioning instead of participating unself-consciously in love making.

spontaneous recovery: improvement of a patient's condition with little or no therapeutic intervention.

Stanford-Binet: an intelligence test that compares a subject's performance in developmentally graded tasks to a chronological norm; primarily used with children.

statistical regression: the tendency for extreme scores to become less extreme with retesting because chance variation leads to a broader range of scores on the original test.

stress: a difficult or uncomfortable event or situation that demands an organism's response on both physiological and psychological levels.

stress-diathesis model: the hypothesis that some individuals possess high biological vulnerability, or diathesis, to schizophrenia, but that stress, coupled with the vulnerability, may be necessary to bring on schizophrenia itself.

stress-inoculation training: a three-phase therapeutic technique by which an individual learns to cope with stressors in the clinic in order to cope better in the future with anxiety-producing situations.

subintentional death: behavior of individuals who play an unconscious role in their own death by periodically or persistently taking risks that increase the probability of premature death (e.g., chronic alcoholism, neglect of prescribed medication, and performance of dangerous work).

subjective distress: experience of excessive and inhibiting fearfulness, depression, agitation, or other disturbing emotion.

substance abuse: drug abuse characterized by a minimum of one month's physiological dependence, difficulty in social functioning, with or without withdrawal symptoms.

suicide observation: precautionary, continuous observation by medical and nursing staff of patients considered severe suicide risks.

superego: in psychoanalytic theory, the part of the personality that reflects internalized moral standards learned from parents and significant others.

symbiosis: parent-child relationship typified by extreme parental interference, which prevents the child from developing a sense of autonomy.

sympathetic nervous system: the part of the nervous system that regulates vital body functions in response to emergency.

symptomatic disorders: overwhelming anxiety manifesting itself as a particular symptom or group of symptoms.

Synanon: a prominent therapeutic community in which residents, primarily drug addicts, learn by intense confrontation to take responsibility for, and change, their problem behavior.

tardive dyskinesia: apparently irreversible symptoms of brain damage that sometimes result from sustained intake of phenothiazines.

test-retest reliability: consistency of scores on the same test given to the same subject at different times.

Thematic Apperception Test (TAT): projective test in which pictures depicting ambiguous situations provide the stimuli for stories the subject makes up.

therapeutic community: an expansion of the mutual-help, group approach into a total residential program (e.g., Synanon).

third-variable problem: the difficulty in interpreting correlational studies caused by the possibility that the relationship between two variables may be attributable to a third, unmeasured variable.

thyroxin: a hormone secreted by the thyroid gland that helps to regulate the activity level of adults and the growth, development, and intelligence of infants.

token economies: behavior-therapy programs that reward institutional residents or schoolchildren for positive behavior and penalize them for anti-social behavior by giving them tokens that they can exchange for items they desire in exchange for desirable behavior and taking the tokens away in punishment for unacceptable behavior.

toxic psychosis: a severe mental disturbance induced by a poisonous substance.

tranquilizers: drugs used both to control various psychotic symptoms and to reduce anxiety and tension.

transactional analysis: an interpersonal therapy in which the major goal is to become aware of one's unconscious games and so realize an ability to control one's own fate; based on the interaction of "parent," "child," and "adult" ego states.

transactional thought disorder: a pattern of ambiguous and incomplete communication.

transference: in psychoanalytic theory, the process by which the patient attributes to the therapist qualities belonging to a significant person in his or her life, such as a parent, and responds to the therapist accordingly.

transsexualism: psychological gender orientation opposite to the individual's biological sexual identity.

transvestism: the persistent desire to dress in the clothes of the opposite sex for the purpose of sexual stimulation.

tricyclic antidepressants: drugs used to treat unipolar and bipolar depressive disorders (e.g., Tofranil, Elavil, and Sinequan); believed to alter the function of neurotransmitters at nerve synapses in the brain.

twin studies: a method of testing genetic theories of abnormal behavior by comparing the concordance rates of identical twins and fraternal twins.

two-disease theory: a neurochemical explanation of mood disorders suggesting that depressive illness is caused by functional deficits of serotonin and norepinephrine.

type A personality: excessive competitive drive, aggressiveness, impatience, and a sense of operating under constant pressure, which are characteristics of an individual at high risk for coronary disease caused by stress.

unipolar depression: a mood disorder characterized by periodic episodes of severe depression.

unsocialized-aggressive delinquency: juvenile behavior akin to that of adult sociopaths.

vaginismus: involuntary tightening and spasm in the outer third of the vagina that can be too painful to permit sexual intercourse.

vasodilation: expansion of blood vessels in the sexual organs to accommodate increased flow and concentration; a reflexive response during unhindered arousal.

Vineland Scale of Social Maturity: an assessment technique for determining a child's level of appropriate, socially adaptive behavior.

voyeurism: distinct sexual preference for surreptitiously watching others while they are in a state of partial or complete undress or while they are having sexual relations.

Wechsler Adult Intelligence Scale (WAIS): an adult intelligence test that yields separate subtest scores in individual areas, as well as overall verbal and performance scores and an intelligence quotient.

Wechsler Intelligence Scale for Children-Revised (WISC-R): an intelligence test for school-age children that yields separate subtest scores in individual areas, as well as overall verbal and performance scores and an intelligence quotient.

Wechsler Preschool-Primary Scale of Intelligence (WPPSI): an intelligence test for preschool and early primary schoolchildren that yields separate subtest scores in individual areas, as well as overall verbal and performance scores and an intelligence quotient.

word salad: incoherent language of psychotics and other disordered individuals that renders verbal communication with them impossible.

XYY: a rare chromosome anomaly in men (extra male chromosome); at one time considered the cause of a strong predisposition for violence.

References

Abel, G. G.; Barlow, D. H.; Blanchard, E. B.; and Guild, D. "The Components of Rapists' Sexual Arousal." Paper presented at the American Psychiatric Association Meeting, May, 1975, Anaheim, Calif. (In press, *Archives of General Psychiatry.*)

Abelson, H.; and Atkinson, R. B. *Public Experience with Psychoactive Substances.* Princeton, N.J.: Response Analysis Corporation, 1975.

Achenbach, T. M.; and Edelbrock, C. G. "The Classification of Child Psychopathology. A Review and Analysis of Empirical Effects," *Psychological Bulletin,* 85 (1978): 1275–301.

Ackerman, N. W., ed. *Family Therapy in Transition.* Boston: Little, Brown, 1970.

Ader, R.; Beels, C. C.; and Tatum, R. "Social Factors Affecting Emotionality and Resistance to Disease in Animals: II. Susceptibility to Gastric Ulceration as a Function of Interruptions in Social Interactions and the Time at Which They Occur," *Journal of Comparative and Physiological Psychology,* 53 (1960): 455–58.

Agras, S. *Behavior Modification: Principles and Clinical Applications.* Boston: Little, Brown, 1978.

Agras, W.; Chapin, H.; and Olivean, D. "The Natural History of Phobia: Course and Prognosis," *Archives of General Psychiatry,* 26 (1972): 315–317.

Akers, R. "Socio-Economic Status and Delinquent Behaviour: A Retest," *Journal of Research in Crime and Delinquency,* 1 (1964): 38–46.

Alexander, A. B.; Miklich, D. R.; and Hershkoff, H. "The Immediate Effects of Systematic Relaxation Training on Peak Expiratory Flow Rates in Asthmatic Children," *Psychosomatic Medicine,* 34 (1972): 388–94.

Alexander, F. "The Influence of Psychological Factors upon Gastrointestinal Disturbances: General Principles, Objectives, and Preliminary Results," *Psychoanalytic Quarterly,* 3 (1934): 501–39.

Alexander, F. "The Principle of Flexibility," in *Psychoanalytic Therapy,* ed. F. Alexander and T. M. French. New York: Ronald Press, 1946.

Alexander, J. F.; and Parsons, B. V. "Short-Term Behavioral Intervention With Delinquent Families: Impact on Family Process and Recidivism," *Journal of Abnormal Psychology,* 81(3) (1973): 219–25.

Alksne, H.; et al. "A Conceptual Model of the Life Cycle of Addiction," *International Journal of the Addictions,* 2 (1967): 221–40.

Allen, J. D.; Phillips, E. L.; Phillips, E.; Fixen, D. L.; and Wolf, M. M. *Achievement Place: A Novel.* Champaign, Ill.: Research Press, in press.

Allen, K. E.; Hart, B.; Buell, J. S.; Harris, F. R.; and Wolf, M. M. "Effects of Social Reinforcement on Isolate Behavior of a Nursery School Child," *Child Development,* 35 (1964): 511–18.

Alvarez, A. *The Savage God: A Study of Suicide.* New York: Bantam Books, 1973.

Amark, C. "A Study in Alcoholism," *Acta Psychiatrics Scandinavica* (Suppl.), 70 (1951): 1–283.

American Medical Association. *Manual on Alcoholism.* Chicago: American Medical Association, 1973.

American Psychiatric Association. *Diagnostic and*

Statistical Manual of Mental Disorders (DSM–I), 1st ed. Washington, D.C.: American Psychiatric Association, 1952.

American Psychiatric Association. *Diagnostic and Statistical Manual of Mental Disorders (DSM–II)*, 2nd ed. Washington, D.C.: American Psychiatric Association, 1968.

American Psychiatric Association. *Diagnostic and Statistical Manual of Mental Disorders (DSM–III)*, 3rd ed. Washington, D.C.: American Psychiatric Association, 1978.

American Psychiatric Association Task Force on Nomenclature and Statistics. *DSM–III: Diagnostic Criteria Draft*. New York, 1978.

American Psychological Association, ad hoc Committee on Ethical Standards in Psychological Research. *Ethical Principles in the Conduct of Research with Human Participants*. Washington, D.C.: American Psychological Association, 1973.

Amir, M. *Patterns in Forcible Rape*. Chicago: University of Chicago Press, 1971.

Anastasi, A. *Psychological Testing*, 3rd ed. New York: Macmillan, 1968.

Andrews, G.; and Solomon, D., eds. *The Coca Leaf and Cocaine Papers*. New York: Harcourt Brace Jovanovich, 1975.

Anonymous. "Death of a Mind; A Study in Disintegration," *Lancet*, 1 (1950): 1012.

Anonymous. *Manchester Guardian*, 3 December 1969.

Anthony, E. J. "A Clinical Evaluation of Children with Psychotic Parents," *American Journal of Psychiatry*, 125 (1969): 177–84.

Anthony, E. J. "The Influence of a Manic-Depressive Illness on the Developing Child," in *Depression and Human Existence*, ed. E. J. Anthony and T. Benedek. Boston: Little, Brown, 1975.

Asberg, M.; Thoren, P.; Traskman, L.; Bertilsson, L.; and Ringberger, V. "Serotonin Depression — A Biochemical Subgroup Within the Affective Disorders?" *Science*, 191 (1976): 478–80.

Austin, G. A.; Macari, M. A.; Sutker, P.; and Lettieri, D. J., eds. *Drugs and Psychopathology*. Rockville, Md.: National Institute of Drug Abuse, 1977.

Ausubel, D. P. *Drug Addiction: Physiological, Psychological, and Sociological Aspects*. New York: Random House, 1958.

Axline, V. M. "Play Therapy Experiences as Described by Child Participants," *Journal of Consulting and Clinical Psychology*, 14 (1950): 53–63.

Axline, V. M. *Play Therapy*, rev. ed. New York: Ballantine Books, 1969.

Ayllon, T.; and Azrin, N. H. "The Measurement and Reinforcement of Behavior of Psychotics," *Journal of Experimental Analysis of Behavior*, 8 (1968): 357–83.

Ayllon, T.; Layman, D.; and Kandel, H. J. "A Behavioral-Educational Alternative to Drug Control of Hyperactive Children," *Journal of Applied Behavior Analysis*, 8 (1975): 137–46.

Baker, B. L. "Symptom Treatment and Symptom Substitution in Enuresis," *Journal of Abnormal Psychology*, 74 (1969): 42–49.

Baker, B. L. "Camp Freedom: Behavior Modification for Retarded Children in a Therapeutic Camp Setting," *American Journal of Orthopsychiatry*, 74 (1973): 418–27.

Baker, B. L. "Parent Involvement in Programming for Developmentally Disabled Children," in *Communication Assessment and Intervention Strategies*, ed. L. L. Lloyd. Baltimore: University Park Press, 1976, pp. 691–733.

Baker, B. L.; Brightman, R. P.; and Clark, D. B. "Training Parents as Teachers for Their Developmentally Disabled Children." Invited Symposium. San Francisco, Calif.: Western Psychological Association Annual Meeting, 1978.

Baker, B. L.; Cohen, D. C.; and Saunders, J. T. "Self-Directed Desensitization for Acrophobia," *Behavior Research and Therapy*, 11 (1973): 79–89.

Baker, B. L.; and Heifetz, L. J. "The READ Project: Teaching Manuals for Parents of Retarded Children," in *Intervention Strategies for High Risk Infants and Young Children*, ed. T. D. Tjossem. Baltimore: University Park Press, 1976.

Baker, B. L.; Seltzer, G. B.; and Seltzer, M. M. *As Close as Possible: Community Residences for Retarded Adults*. Boston: Little, Brown, 1977.

Baldessarini, R. J. "Chemotherapy," in *The Harvard Guide to Modern Psychiatry*, ed. A. M. Nicholi. Cambridge, Mass.: Belknap Press, 1978.

Ball, J. C.; and Chambers, C. D. *The Epidemiology of Opiate Addiction in the United States*. Springfield, Mass.: Charles C Thomas, 1970.

Baloh, R.; Sturm, R.; Green, B.; and Gleser, G. "Neuropsychological Effects of Asymptomatic Increased Lead Absorption: A Controlled Study," *Archives of Neurology*, 32 (1975): 326–30.

Bandura, A. *Principles of Behavior Modification*. New York: Holt, Rinehart & Winston, 1969.

Bandura, A.; Grusec, J. E.; and Menlove, F. L. "Vicarious Extinction of Avoidance Behavior," *Journal of Personality and Social Psychology*, 5 (1967): 16–23.

Bandura, A.; and Walters, R. H. *Adolescent Aggression.* New York: Ronald Press, 1959.

Barbach, L. G. "Group Treatment of Preorgasmic Women," *Journal of Sex and Marital Therapy,* 1 (1974): 139–45.

Barber, T. X.; and Silver, M. J. "Fact, Fiction and the Experimenter Bias Effect," *Psychological Bulletin,* Monograph Supplement, 70 (1968): 1–29.

Bard, M. "Alternatives to Traditional Law Enforcement," in *Psychology and Problems of Society,* ed. F. Korten; S. W. Cook; and J. I. Lacey. Washington, D.C.: American Psychological Association, 1970, pp. 128–32.

Bard, M.; and Sangrey, D. *The Crime Victim's Book.* New York: Basic Books, 1979.

Barlow, D. H. "The Treatment of Sexual Deviation: Toward a Comprehensive Behavioral Approach," in *Innovative Treatment Methods in Psychopathology,* ed. K. S. Calhoun; H. E. Adams; and K. M. Mitchell. New York: John Wiley & Sons, 1974.

Barraclough, B. "Suicide Prevention, Recurrent Affective Disorder and Lithium," *British Journal of Psychiatry,* 121 (1972): 391–92.

Bauer, D. H. "An Exploratory Study of Developmental Changes in Children's Fears," *Journal of Child Psychology and Psychiatry,* 17(1) (1976): 69–74.

Bayley, N. "Consistency and Variability in the Growth of Intelligence From Birth to Eighteen Years," *Journal of Genetic Psychology,* 75 (1949): 165–96.

Beck, A. T. *Depression: Causes and Treatment.* Philadelphia: University of Pennsylvania Press, 1967a.

Beck, A. T. *Depression: Clinical, Experimental and Theoretical Aspects.* New York: Harper & Row, 1967b.

Beck, A. T. "Cognitive Therapy: Nature and Relation to Behavior Therapy," *Behavior Therapy,* 1 (1970): 184–200.

Beck, A. T.; War, K. H.; Mendelson, M.; Mock, J. E.; and Erbaugh, J. K. "Reliability of Psychiatric Diagnoses. II: A Study of Consistency of Clinical Judgments and Ratings." *American Journal of Psychiatry,* 119 (1962): 315–57.

Becker, J.; and Schuckit, M. A. "On the Comparative Efficacy of Cognitive Therapy and Pharmacotherapy in the Treatment of Depressions," *Cognitive Therapy and Research* (1978): 193–97.

Beigel, A.; Murphy, D. L.; and Bunney, W. E. "The Manic-State Rating Scale: Scale Construction, Reliability, and Validity," *Archives of General Psychiatry,* 25 (1971): 256–62.

Beiser, M. "Personal and Social Factors Associated With Remission of Psychiatric Symptoms," *Archives of General Psychiatry,* 33 (1976): 941–45.

Bell, J. E. *Family Group Therapy.* Public Health Monograph no. 64. Washington, D.C.: Department of Health, Education and Welfare, 1961.

Bell, Q. *Virginia Woolf: A Biography.* London: Hogarth Press, 1972.

Bellack, A. S.; and Hersen, M. *Behavior Modification: An Introductory Textbook.* New York: Oxford University Press, 1977.

Bellak, L. *The Thematic Apperception Test and the Children's Apperception Test in Clinical Use.* New York: Grune & Stratton, 1954.

Belmont, J. M. "Medical-Behavioral Research in Retardation," in *International Review of Research in Mental Retardation,* vol. 5, ed. N. R. Ellis. New York: Academic Press, 1971.

Belson, W. A. "The Extent of Stealing by London Boys and Some of Its Origins." Reprint series of the Survey Research Centre, London School of Economics, no. 39, 1969.

Benda, C. *Down's Syndrome.* New York: Grune & Stratton, 1969.

Benson, H. *The Relaxation Response.* New York: William Morrow and Co., 1975.

Benson, H.; Rosner, B. A.; Marzetta, B. R.; and Klemchuk, H. P. "Decreased Blood Pressure in Borderline Hypertensive Subjects Who Practiced Meditation." *Journal of Chronic Diseases,* 27 (1974): 163–69.

Benson, R. "The Forgotten Treatment Modality in Bipolar Illness: Psychotherapy," *Diseases of the Nervous System,* 35 (1974): 634–38.

Bentler, P. M. "A Typology of Transsexualism: Gender Identity Theory and Data," *Archives of Sexual Behavior,* 5 (1976): 567–84.

Bentler, P. M.; and Prince, C. "Personality Characteristics of Male Transvestites," *Journal of Abnormal Psychology,* 74 (1969): 140–43.

Benton, A. L. "Psychological Tests for Brain Damage," in *Comprehensive Textbook of Psychiatry II,* ed. A. M. Freedman; H. I. Kaplan; and B. J. Sadock. Baltimore: Williams & Wilkins, 1975.

Bergin, A. E.; and Lambert, M. J. "The Evaluation of Therapeutic Outcomes," in *Handbook of Psychotherapy and Behavior Change,* 2nd ed., ed. S. Garfield and A. E. Bergin. New York: John Wiley & Sons, 1978, pp. 139–90.

Berne, E. *Games People Play.* New York: Grove Press, 1964.

Berry, H. K.; Sutherland, B. S.; Umbarger, B.; and O'Grady, D. "Treatment of Phenylketonuria," *American Journal of Diseases of Children,* 113(1), 1967: 2–5.

Bettelheim, B. *The Empty Fortress.* New York: The Free Press, 1967.

Biering, A.; and Jesperson, I. "The Treatment of Enuresis Nocturna With Conditioning Devices," *Acta Paediatrics,* 48 (1959): 152–53.

Binswanger, L. "The Case of Ellen West," in *Existence,* ed. M. Rollo. New York: Simon & Schuster, 1958.

Birch, H. G.; and Gussow, J. D. *Disadvantaged Children: Health, Nutrition and School Failure.* New York: Grune & Stratton, 1970.

Birnbrauer, J. S.; Wolf, M. M.; Kidder, J. D.; and Tague, C. E. "Classroom Behavior of Retarded Pupils With Token Reinforcement," *Journal of Experimental Child Psychology,* 2 (1965): 219–35.

Blanchard, E. B.; and Young, L. D. "Clinical Applications of Biofeedback Training," *Archives of General Psychiatry,* 30 (1974): 573–89.

Blatt, B. *Exodus From Pandemonium: Human Abuse and the Reformation of Public Policy.* Boston: Allyn & Bacon, 1970.

Blatt, B.; and Kaplan, F. *Christmas in Purgatory: A Photographic Essay on Mental Retardation.* Boston: Allyn & Bacon, 1966.

Blatt, J. "Small Changes and Real Difference," in *Promise and Performance: Children with Special Needs,* ed. M. Harmonay, Cambridge, Mass.: Ballinger Publishing Co., 1977, pp. 11–22.

Bleuler, E. *Dementia Praecox or the Group of Schizophrenias.* New York: International University Press, 1950.

Bleuler, M. "A 23-Year Longitudinal Study of 208 Schizophrenics and Impressions in Regard to the Nature of Schizophrenia," in *The Transmission of Schizophrenia,* eds. D. Rosenthal and S. S. Kety. Oxford: Pergamon Press, 1968.

Block, J. *The Q-Sort Method in Personality Assessment and Psychiatric Research.* Springfield, Ill.: Charles C Thomas, 1961.

Bloom, B. S. *Stability and Change in Human Characteristics.* New York: John Wiley & Sons, 1964.

Bockoven, J. S. *Moral Treatment in American Psychiatry.* New York: Springer, 1963.

Bookbinder, S. "What Every Child Needs to Know," *Exceptional Parent,* 7(4) (1977): 31–35.

Borkenhagen, C. K. "House of Delegates Redefines Death, Urges Redefinition of Rape and Undoes the Houston Amendments," *American Bar Association Journal,* 61 (1975): 464–65.

Borkovec, T. D. "Autonomic Reactivity to Sensory Stimulation in Psychopathic, Neurotic, and Normal Juvenile Delinquents," *Journal of Consulting and Clinical Psychology,* 35 (1970): 217–22.

Borkovec, T. D.; and Fowles, D. C. "A Controlled Investigation of the Effects of Progressive and Hypnotic Relaxation on Insomnia," *Journal of Abnormal Psychology,* 82 (1973): 153–58.

Bornstein, P. H.; and Quevillon, R. P. "The Effects of a Self-Instructional Package on Overactive Preschool Boy," *Journal of Applied Behavior Analysis,* 9 (1976): 179–88.

Bothwell, S.; and Weissman, M. "Social Impairments Four Years After an Acute Depressive Episode," *American Journal of Orthopsychiatry,* 47 (1977): 231–37.

Bourne, P. G. *Methadone: Benefits and Shortcomings.* New York: Drug Abuse Council, 1975.

Bowers, M. B., Jr. "Pathogenesis of acute schizophrenic psychosis," *Archives of General Psychiatry,* 19 (1968): 348–55.

Bowers, M. B., Jr. *Retreat from Sanity.* New York: Human Science Press, 1974.

Bowers, M. B., Jr. "Clinical Components of Psychotic Disorders: Their Relationship to Treatment," *Schizophrenia Bulletin,* 3 (1977): 600–607.

Bowlby, J. *Attachment.* New York: Basic Books, 1969.

Bradley, C. "The Behavior of Children Receiving Benzedrine," *American Journal of Psychiatry,* 94 (1937): 577–85.

Brady, J. P.; and Lind, D. L. "Experimental Analysis of Hysterical Blindness," in *Case Studies in Behavior Modification,* ed. L. P. Ullmann and L. Krasner, New York: Holt, Rinehart & Winston, 1968.

Braginsky, D. D.; and Braginsky, B. M. *Hansels and Gretels: Studies of Children in Institutions.* New York: Holt, Rinehart & Winston, 1971.

Brain, W. R. *Brain's Diseases of the Nervous System,* 8th ed. Oxford: Oxford University Press, 1977.

Bramwell, J. H. *Hypnotism: Its History, Theory and Practice.* London: William Rider & Son, 1921.

Brase, D. A.; and Loh, H. H. "Possible Role of 5-Hydroxytryptamine in Minimal Brain Dysfunction," *Life Sciences,* 16 (1975): 1005–15.

Bratter, T. E. "Treating Alienated, Unmotivated Drug Abusing Adolescents," *American Journal of Psychotherapy,* 4 (1973): 585–98.

Bratter, T. E. "Reality Therapy: A Group Psychotherapeutic Approach with Adolescent Alcoholics,"

Annals of the New York Academy of Sciences, 233 (15 April 1974): 104–14.

Brightman, A. "Toward the Non-issues of Retardation," *Syracuse Law Review,* Fall 1972.

Brightman, A. J. "Behavior Modification in Organization Development: Toward the Implementation of Planned Change in Settings for Retarded Children." Unpublished doctoral dissertation, Harvard University, 1975.

Brightman, A. " 'But Their Brain Is Broken': Young Children's Conceptions of Retardation," in *Promise and Performance: Children With Special Needs,* vol. 1, ed. M. Harmonay. Cambridge, Mass.: Ballinger Publishing Co., 1977, pp. 59–64.

Brooke, E. M., ed. *Suicide and Attempted Suicide.* Geneva: World Health Organization, 1974.

Brown, G. W.; Sklair, F.; Harris, T. O.; and Birely, J. L. T. "Life Events and Psychiatric Disorders. I: Some Methodological Issues," *Psychological Medicine,* 3 (1973): 74–87.

Brown, H. *Yesterday's Child.* New York: New American Library, 1976.

Brown, J. L. "Prognosis from Symptoms of Preschool Children with Atypical Development," *American Journal of Orthopsychiatry,* 30 (1960): 382–91.

Brown, P.; and Elliott, R. "Control of Aggression in a Nursery School Class," *Journal of Experimental Child Psychology,* 2 (1965): 103–107.

Brownfield, C. A. *Isolation: Clinical and Experimental Approaches.* New York: Random House, 1965.

Brownmiller, S. *Against Our Will: Men, Women and Rape.* New York: Simon & Schuster, 1975.

Bruch, H. "Perceptual and Conceptual Disturbances in Anorexia Nervosa," *Psychosomatic Medicine,* 24 (1962): 187–94.

Bruch, H. *Eating Disorders.* New York: Basic Books, 1973.

Bunney, W. E., Jr.; Pert, A.; Rosenblatt, J.; Pert, C. B.; and Gallaper, D. "Mode of Action of Lithium: Some Biological Considerations," *Archives of General Psychiatry,* 36 (1979): 898–901.

Burgess, A. W.; and Holstrom, L. L. *Rape: Victims of Crisis.* Bowie, Md.: Robert J. Brady Co., 1974.

Butler, J. M.; and Haigh, G. V. "Changes in the Relation Between Self-Concepts and Ideal Concepts Consequent Upon Client-Centered Counseling," in *Psychotherapy and Personality Change,* ed. C. R. Rogers and R. F. Dymond. Chicago: University of Chicago, 1954.

Butterfield, E. C. "Basic Facts About Public Residential Facilities for the Mentally Retarded," in *Changing Patterns in Residential Services for the Mentally Retarded,* ed. R. B. Kugel and W. Wolfensberger. Washington, D.C.: President's Committee on Mental Retardation, 1969, pp. 15–33.

Butz, F. "Intoxication and Withdrawal," in *Alcoholism: Development, Consequences, and Interventions,* ed. N. J. Estes and M. E. Heinemann. St. Louis: C. V. Mosby, 1977.

Cade, J. F. J. "Lithium Salt in Treatment in Psychotic Excitement," *Medical Journal of Australia,* 2 (1949): 349–52.

Cahalan, D.; and Cisin, I. H. "American Drinking Practices: Summary of Findings From a National Probability Sample. I. Extent of Drinking by Population Subgroups," *Quarterly Journal of Studies on Alcohol,* 29 (1968): 130–52.

Cameron, N. "The Paranoid Pseudocommunity Revisited," *American Journal of Sociology,* 65 (1959): 52–58.

Campbell, D. T. "Reforms as Experiments," *American Psychologist,* 24 (1969): 409–29.

Campbell, D. T., and Ross, H. L. "The Connecticut Crackdown on Speeding: Time Series Data in Quasi-Experimental Analysis," *Law and Society Review,* 3(1) (1968): 33–53.

Campbell, D. T.; and Stanley, J. C. *Experimental and Quasi-Experimental Designs for Research.* Chicago: Rand McNally and Co., 1966.

Campbell, M.; and Small, A. M. "Chemotherapy," in *Handbook of Treatment of Mental Disorders in Childhood and Adolescence,* ed. A. O. Ross and J. Egan. Englewood Cliffs, N.J.: Prentice-Hall, 1978.

Campbell, S. B. "Hyperactivity: Course and Treatment," in *Child Personality and Psychopathology: Current Topics,* vol. 3, ed. A. Davis. New York: John Wiley & Sons, 1976.

Cannon, W. B. *The Wisdom of the Body.* New York: W. W. Norton, 1939.

Cantwell, D. *The Hyperactive Child — Diagnosis, Management, Current Research.* New York: Spectrum Publications, 1975.

Cantwell, D.; Sturzenberger, S.; Burroughs, J.; Salkin, B.; and Green, J. "Anorexia Nervosa: An Affective Disorder?" *Archives of General Psychiatry,* 34 (1977): 1087–93.

Carlson, G. A., and Goodwin, F. K. "The Stages of Mania," *Archives of General Psychiatry,* 28 (1973): 221–28.

Carlson, N. R. *Physiology of Behavior.* Boston: Allyn & Bacon, 1977.

Cartwright, D. S.; Tomson, B.; and Schwarts, H. *Gang Delinquency.* Monterey, Calif.: Brooks/Cole, 1975.

Castenada, C. *The Teachings of Don Juan.* Berkeley: University of California Press, 1968.

Cautela, J. R. "Covert Sensitization," *Psychological Reports,* 20 (1967): 459–68.

Chambers, C. "An Assessment of Drug Use in the General Population: Drug Use in New York State." Narcotics Addiction Control Commission, Special Report no. 1, 1971.

Chein, I. "The Use of Narcotics as a Personal and Social Problem," in *Narcotics,* ed. D. Wilner and G. Kassebaum. New York: McGraw-Hill, 1965.

Chein, I., et al. *The Road to H.* New York: Basic Books, 1964.

Chein, I., and Rosenfeld, E. "Juvenile Narcotics Use," *Law and Contemporary Problems,* 22 (1957): 52–69.

Chess, S.; Korn, S. J.; and Fernandez, P. B. *Psychiatric Disorders of Children With Congenital Rubella.* New York: Brunner/Mazel, 1971.

Chodoff, P. "The Depressive Personality: A Critical Review," in *The Psychology of Depression: Contemporary Theory and Research,* ed. R. J. Friedman and M. M. Katz. New York: John Wiley & Sons, 1974, pp. 55–70.

Chodoff, P.; and Lyons, H. "Hysteria, the Hysterical Personality and 'Hysterical' Conversion," *American Journal of Psychiatry,* 114 (1958): 734–40.

Chow, T.; and Earl, J. L. "Lead Aerosols in the Atmosphere: Increasing Concentration," *Science,* 169 (1970): 577.

Claghorn, J. L., et al. "Spontaneous Opiate Addiction in Rhesus Monkeys," *Science,* 149 (1965): 440.

Clark, R. E. "The Relationship of Schizophrenia to Occupational Income and Occupational Prestige," *American Sociological Review,* 13 (1948): 325–30.

Clarke, A. D. B. "From Research to Practice," in *Research to Practice in Mental Retardation,* vol. I, ed. P. Mittler. Baltimore: University Park Press, 1977, pp. A7–A19.

Clausen, J. A. "Social and Psychological Factors in Narcotics Addiction," *Law and Contemporary Problems,* 22 (1957): 38–39.

Clayton, P. J.; Desmarais, L.; and Winokur, G. "A Study of Normal Bereavement," *American Journal of Psychiatry,* 125 (1968): 168.

Cleckley, H. *The Mask of Sanity,* 5th ed. St. Louis, Missouri: Mosby, 1976.

Clements, F. E. "Primitive Concepts of Disease," *University of California Publications in American Archeology and Ethnology,* 32 (1932): 185–252.

Clinard, M. B. *Sociology of Deviant Behavior.* New York: Holt, Rinehart & Winston, 1968.

Cloward, R. A.; and Ohlin, L. E. *Delinquency and Opportunity, a Theory of Delinquent Gangs.* Glencoe, Ill.: The Free Press, 1960.

Cobb, H. V. *The Forecast of Fulfillment: A Review of Research on Predictive Assessment of the Adult Retarded for Social and Vocational Adjustment.* New York: Teachers College Press, 1972.

Cobb, S., and Rose, R. M. "Hypertension, Peptic Ulcer, and Diabetes in Air Traffic Controllers," *Journal of American Medical Association,* 224 (1973): 489–91.

Cohen, A. K. *Delinquent Boys, the Culture of the Gang.* Glencoe, Ill.: The Free Press, 1955.

Cohen, M.; Seghorn, T.; and Calmas, W. "Sociometric Study of the Sex Offender," *Journal of Abnormal Psychology,* 74 (1969): 249–55.

Cohen, S. *Drugs of Hallucination.* London: Secker and Warburg, 1965.

Cohen, S. *Drugs of Hallucination.* St. Albans, England: Paladin, 1970.

Cohen, S. "Fostering Positive Attitudes Toward the Handicapped: A New Curriculum," *Children Today,* 6 (1977): 7–12.

Cohen, S.; and Ditman, K. S. "Prolonged Adverse Reactions to Lysergic Acid Diethylamide," *Archives of General Psychiatry,* 8 (1963): 475.

Cole, C. L., and Spaniard, G. B. "Comarital Mate-Sharing and Family Stability," *Journal of Sex Research,* 10 (1974): 21–31.

Cole, J. O., and Davis, J. "Antidepressant Drugs," in *Comprehensive Textbook of Psychiatry,* ed. A. M. Freedman and H. Kaplan. Baltimore: Williams & Wilkins, 1967.

Committee on Nomenclature and Statistics of the American Psychiatric Association. *Diagnostic and Statistical Manual.* Washington, D.C.: American Psychiatric Association, 1977.

Compton, R. D. "Changes in Enuretics Accompanying Treatment by the Conditioned Response Technique," *Dissertation Abstracts,* 28(7–A) (1968): 2549.

Conley, R. W. *The Economics of Mental Retardation.* Baltimore: Johns Hopkins University Press, 1973.

Connelly, T. L. *The Marble Man: Robert E. Lee and His Image in American Society.* New York: Knopf, 1977.

Conners, C. K.; Eisenberg, L.; and Barcai, A. "Effect of Dextroamphetamine in Children," *Archives of General Psychiatry,* 17 (1967): 478–85.

Conrad, P. "The Discovery of Hyperkinesis: Notes on the Medicalization of Deviant Behavior," *Social Problems,* 23 (1975); 12–21.

Cook, J., and Wollersheim, J. "The Effect of Labeling of Special Education Students on the Perceptions of Contact Versus Noncontact Normal Peers," *Journal of Special Education,* 10 (1976): 187–98.

Cooper, B., and Sylph, J. "Life Events and the Onset of Neurotic Illness: An Investigation in General Practice," *Psychological Medicine,* 3 (1973): 421–35.

Cooper, I. S. *Living with Chronic Neurologic Disease: A Handbook for Patient and Family.* New York: W. W. Norton, 1976.

Corder, B. F.; Ball, B. C.; Halzip, T. H.; Rollins, R.; and Beaumont, R. "Adolescent Parricide: A Comparison With Other Adolescent Murder," *American Journal of Psychiatry,* 133 (1976): 957–61.

Corsini, R., ed. *Current Psychotherapies.* Itasca, Ill.: F. E. Peacock Publishers, 1973.

Costello, C. G. *Symptoms of Psychopathology.* New York: John Wiley & Sons, 1970.

Cousins, N. "Anatomy of an Illness (as Perceived by the Patient)," *New England Journal of Medicine,* 295 (1976): 1458–63.

Covington v. Harris, 419 F. 2d 617 (D.C. Cir. 1969).

Cowen, E. L.; Izzo, L. D.; Miles, H.; Telschow, E. F.; Trost, M. A.; and Zax, M. "A Preventive Mental Health Program in the School Setting: Description and Evaluation," *Journal of Psychiatry,* 56 (1963): 307–56.

Cowen, E. L.; Pederson, A.; Babigian, H.; Izzo, L. D.; and Trost, M. A. "A Long-Term Follow-Up of Early Detected Vulnerable Children," *Journal of Consulting and Clinical Psychology,* 41 (1973): 438–46.

Cowen, E. L.; Trost, M. A.; Lorion, R. P.; Dorr, D.; Izzo, L. D.; and Isaacson, R. V. *New Ways in School Mental Health: Early Detection and Prevention of School Maladaption.* New York: Human Sciences Press, 1975.

Cowen, E. L.; Zax, M.; Izzo, L. D.; and Trost, M. A. "Prevention of Emotional Disorders in a School Setting: A Further Investigation," *Journal of Consulting Psychology,* 30 (1966): 381–87.

Coyne, J. C. "Toward an Interactional Description of Depression," *Psychiatry,* 39 (1976): 28–40.

Creak, M. "Discussion: Psychoses in Childhood," *Social Medicine,* 45 (1952): 797–800.

Crime in the United States: Uniform Crime Reports. Washington, D.C.: Government Printing Office, 1977.

Cromwell, R. L. "A Social Learning Approach to Mental Retardation," in *Handbook of Mental Deficiency,* ed. N. R. Ellis. New York: McGraw-Hill, 1963, pp. 41–91.

Crowley, A. *Cocaine.* San Francisco: Level Press, 1973.

Curran, J. P. "Skill Training as an Approach to the Treatment of Heterosexual-Social Anxiety," *Psychological Bulletin,* 84 (1977): 140–57.

Curry, S. H. "Chlorpromazine: Concentrations in Plasma Excretion in Urine and Duration of Effect," *Proceedings Research in Social Medicine,* 64 (1971): 285–89.

Custace, J. "The Universe of Bliss and the Universe of Horror: A Description of a Manic-Depressive Psychosis," reprinted from *Wisdom, Madness, and Folly,* ed. J. Custace. New York: Farrar, Straus & Cudahy, 1952.

Dai, B. *Opium Addiction in Chicago.* Shanghai: Commercial Press, 1937.

Dale, V. P.; and Nyswander, M. "A Medical Treatment for Diacetylmorphine (Heroin) Addiction — A Clinical Test With Methadone Hydrochloride," *Journal of the American Medical Association,* 198 (1965): 646–50.

Daly, R. M. "Lithium-Responsive Affective Disorders: Model Comprehensive Plan for Treatment," *New York State Journal of Medicine* (March 1978): 594–601.

Davidson, T. *Conjugal Crime: Understanding and Changing the Wifebeating Pattern.* New York: Hawthorn Books, 1978.

Davies, D. L. "Normal Drinking in Recovered Alcohol Addicts," *Quarterly Journal of Studies on Alcohol,* 23 (1962): 94–104.

Davis, J. M. "Central Biogenic Amines and Theories of Depression and Mania," in *Phenomenology and Treatment of Depression,* ed. W. F. Fann; I. Karacan; A. D. Pokorny; and R. L. Williams. New York: Spectrum Publications, 1977.

Davis, J. M. "Dopamine Theory of Schizophrenia: A Two-Factor Theory," in *The Nature of Schizophrenia: New Approaches to Research and Treatment,* ed. L. C. Wynne; R. L. Cromwell; and S. Matthysse, New York: John Wiley and Sons, 1978.

Davis, V. E.; and Walsch, M. J. "Alcohol, Amines, and Alkaloids: A Possible Biochemical Basis for Alcohol Addiction," *Science,* 167 (1970): 1005–07.

Dean, C. W.; and Reppucci, N. D. "Juvenile Correctional Institutions," in *Handbook of Criminology,* ed. D. Glaser. New York: Rand McNally, 1974.

De la Cruz, F. F.; and LaVeck, G. D. *Human Sexuality and the Mentally Retarded.* Baltimore: Penguin Books, 1974.

deLint, J.; and Schmidt, W. "The Epidemiology of Alcoholism," in *Biological Basis of Alcoholism,* ed. Y. Israel. New York: John Wiley & Sons, 1971.

Denny, M. R. "Research in Learning and Performance," in *Mental Retardation: A Review of Research,* ed. H. A. Stevens and R. Heber. Chicago: University of Chicago Press, 1964.

Deutsch, A. *The Mentally Ill in America,* 2nd ed. New York: Columbia University Press, 1965.

Dohrenwend, B. P.; and Dohrenwend, B. S., eds. *Stressful Life Events: Their Nature and Effects.* New York: John Wiley & Sons, 1974.

Dole, V. P.; and Nyswander, M. E. "Heroin Addiction — A Metabolic Disease," *Archives of Internal Medicine,* 120 (1965): 19–24.

Doll, E. A. *Vineland Scale of Social Maturity.* Minneapolis: American Guidance Service, 1964.

Domino, G.; and Newman, D. "Relationship of Physical Stigmata to Intellectual Subnormality in Mongoloids," *American Journal of Mental Deficiency,* 69 (1965): 541–47.

Donaldson v. O'Connor, 493 F. 2nd 507 (the Cir. 1975), Vacated, 422 U.S. 563 (1975).

Dorpat, T. L.; and Ripley, H. S. "The Relationship Between Attempted Suicide and Committed Suicide," *Comprehensive Psychiatry,* 8 (1967): 74.

Douglas, V. I. "Stop, Look, and Listen: The Problem of Sustained Attention and Impulse Control in Hyperactive and Normal Children," *Canadian Journal of Behavioral Science,* 4 (1972): 259–82.

Douglas, V. I. "Sustained Attention and Impulse Control: Implications for the Handicapped Child," in *Psychology and the Handicapped Child,* ed. J. A. Swets and L. L. Elliott. Washington, D.C.: U.S. Department of Health, Education, and Welfare, DHEW Publication no. (OE) 73–05000, 1974.

Douglas, V. I.; Weiss, G.; and Minde, K. "Learning Disabilities in Hyperactive Children and the Effect of Methylphenidate," *Canadian Psychology,* 10 (1969): 201.

Duehn, W. D.; and Mayadas, N. S. "The Use of Stimulus/Modeling Videotapes in Assertive Training For Homosexuals," *Journal of Homosexuality,* 1 (1976): 373–81.

Dunbar, F. *Emotions and Bodily Changes: A Survey of Literature on Psychosomatic Interrelationships.* New York: Columbia University Press, 1935.

Dunbar, F. *Psychosomatic Diagnosis.* New York: Hoeber-Harper, 1943.

Duncan, J. W.; and Duncan, G. H. "Murder in the Family," in *Violence: Perspectives on Murder and Aggression,* ed. I. L. Kutash; S. B. Kutash; L. B. Schlesinger; et al. San Francisco: Jossey-Bass Publishers, 1978, pp. 171–86.

Dunham, H. W. *Community and Schizophrenia: An Epidemiological Analysis.* Detroit: Wayne State University Press, 1965.

Durant, Celeste. "Dilemma — What to Do with a '2,000-Year-Old' Man," *Los Angeles Times,* 15 July 1979, p. 1.

Durkeim, E. *Suicide.* Glencoe, Ill.: The Free Press, 1951.

Eaton, J. W.; and Weil, R. J. *Culture and Mental Disorders.* Glencoe, Ill.: The Free Press, 1955.

Eberhardy, F. "The View From 'The Couch,' " *Journal of Child Psychology and Psychiatry,* 8 (1967): 257–63.

Ebert, A. *The Homosexuals.* New York: Macmillan Publishing Co., 1976.

Edgerton, R. B. *The Cloak of Competence: Stigma in the Lives of the Mentally Retarded.* Berkeley: University of California Press, 1967.

Edwards, G., et al. "Alcoholics Known or Unknown to Agencies: Epidemiological Studies in a London Suburb," *British Journal of Psychiatry,* 123 (1972): 169–83.

Efron, V.; Keller, M.; and Gurioli, C. *Statistics on Consumption of Alcohol and on Alcoholism.* New Brunswick, N.J.: Rutgers Center for Alcohol Studies, 1974.

Einstein, S. "The Addiction Dilemma," *International Journal of the Addictions,* 4 (1969): 25–44.

Eisenberg, L. "The Autistic Child in Adolescence," *American Journal of Psychiatry,* 112 (1956): 607–12.

Eisenberg, L. "School Phobia: A Study in the Communication of Anxiety," *American Journal of Psychiatry,* 114 (1958): 712–18.

Eisenberg, L.; and Kanner, L. "Early Infantile Autism," *American Journal of Orthopsychiatry,* 26 (1956): 556–66.

Eisler, R. M.; and Hersen, M. "Behavioral Techniques in Family-Oriented Crisis Intervention," *Archives of General Psychiatry,* 28 (1973): 111–16.

Eisner, V. *The Delinquency Label: The Epidemiology of Juvenile Delinquency.* New York: Random House, 1969.

Eitzen, D. S. "The Effects of Behavior Modification on the Attitudes of Delinquents," *Behavior Research and Therapy,* 13 (1975): 295–99.

Ellingson, R. J. "The Incidence of EEG Abnormality Among Patients With Mental Disorders of Apparently Non-Organic Origin: A Critical Review," *American Journal of Psychiatry,* 111 (1954): 263–75.

Ellinwood, E. H.; and Petrie, W. M. "Dependence on Amphetamine, Cocaine, and Other Stimulants," in *Drug Abuse: Clinical and Basic Aspects,* ed. S. N. Pradham and S. N. Dutta. St. Louis: C. V. Mosby, 1977.

Eliot, T. S. *Murder in the Cathedral.* New York: Harcourt, Brace and World, 1963.

Ellis, A. *Reason and Emotion in Psychotherapy.* Secaucus, N.J.: Lyle Stuart, 1962.

Ellis, A.; and Harper, R. A. *A Guide to Rational Living.* North Hollywood, Calif.: Wilshire Book Co., 1961.

Ellis, N. R. "Memory Processes in Retardates and Normals," in *International Review of Research in Retardation,* vol. 4, ed. N. R. Ellis. New York: Academic Press, 1970, pp. 1–32.

Ellison, G. D. "Animal Models of Psychopathology: Studies in Naturalistic Colony Environments," in *Psychopathology in Animals: Research and Clinical Applications,* ed. J. D. Keehn. New York: Academic Press, in press.

Elmer, E. *Children in Jeopardy: A Study of Abused Minors and Their Families.* Pittsburgh: University of Pittsburgh Press, 1967.

Empey, L. T.; and Erickson, M. L. "Hidden Delinquency and Social Status," *Social Forces,* 44 (1966): 546–54.

English, H. B. "Three Cases of the 'Conditioned' Fear Response," *Journal of Abnormal and Social Psychology,* 34 (1929): 221–25.

Ennis, B. J.; and Emery, R. D. *The Rights of Mental Patients.* New York: Avon Books, 1978.

Enright, J. B. "An Introduction to Gestalt Techniques," in *Gestalt Therapy Now,* ed. J. Fagan and I. L. Sheperd. Palo Alto: Science and Behavior Books, 1970.

Enterline, P. E.; and Capt, K. G. "A Validation of Information Provided by Household Respondents in Health Surveys," *American Journal of Public Health,* 49 (1959): 205–12.

Erlenmeyer-Kimling, L.; and Cornblatt, B. "Attentional Measures in a Study of Children at High Risk for Schizophrenia," in *The Nature of Schizophrenia,* ed. L. Wynne. New York: John Wiley & Sons, 1978, pp. 359–65.

Ervin, F. R. "Organic Brain Syndromes Associated With Epilepsy," in *Comprehensive Textbook of Psychiatry — II,* ed. A. M. Freedman; H. I. Kaplan; and B. J. Sadock. Baltimore: Williams & Wilkins, 1975.

Estes, N. J.; and Heinemann, M. E. *Alcoholism: Development, Consequences, and Interventions.* St. Louis: C. V. Mosby, 1977.

Evans, M. *A Ray of Darkness.* London: Arthur Barker, Ltd., 1952.

Eysenck, H. J. "The Effects of Psychotherapy: An Evaluation," *Journal of Consulting Psychology,* 16 (1952): 319–24.

Eysenck, H. J. "Learning Theory and Behavior Therapy," *Journal of Mental Science,* 105 (1959): 61–75.

Eysenck, H. J. "The Effects of Psychotherapy," *International Journal of Psychiatry,* 1 (1965): 99–142.

Eysenck, H. J. *The Measurement of Intelligence.* Baltimore: Williams & Wilkins, 1973.

Faegerman, P. M. *Psychogenic Psychoses.* London: Butterworth & Co., 1963.

Fairweather, G. E.; Sanders, D. H.; Cressler, D. L.; and Maynard, H. *Community Life for the Mentally Ill.* Chicago: Aldine Publishing Co., 1969.

Farber, B. *Mental Retardation: Its Social Context and Social Consequences.* Boston: Houghton Mifflin, 1968.

Farberow, N. L.; and Shneidman, E. S. *The Cry for Help.* New York: McGraw-Hill, 1965.

Faris, R. E. L.; and Dunham, H. W. *Mental Disorders in Urban Areas: An Ecological Study of Schizophrenia and Other Psychoses.* Chicago: University of Chicago Press, 1939.

Feigenbaum, E. M. "Geriatric Psychopathology: Internal or External?" *Journal of American Geriatric Sociology,* 22 (1974): 49–55.

Feingold, B. *Why Your Child is Hyperactive.* New York: Random House, 1975.

Feldman, M. P.; and Macculloch, M. J. "The Application of Anticipatory Avoidance Learning to the Treatment of Homosexuality," *Behaviour Research and Therapy,* 2 (1965): 165–83.

Feldman, M. P.; and Macculloch, M. J. *Homosexual Behaviour: Therapy and Assessment.* Oxford: Pergamon Press, 1971.

Felix, R. H. "An Appraisal of the Personality Types of the Addict," *American Journal of Psychiatry,* 100 (1944): 462.

Fenichel, O. *Outline of Clinical Psychoanàlysis.* London: Routledge, 1934.

Fenichel, O. *The Psychoanalytic Theory of Neurosis.* New York: W. W. Norton, 1950.

Fenz, W. D.; and Epstein, S. "Manifest Anxiety: Unifactorial or Multifactorial Composition?" *Perceptual and Motor Skills,* 20 (1965): 773–80.

Ferster, C. "Positive Reinforcement and Behavioral Deficits of Autistic Children," *Child Development,* 32 (1961): 437–56.

Ferster, C. B. "Animal Behavior and Mental Illness," *Psychological Records,* 16 (1966): 345–46.

Fieve, R. R. *Moodswing: The Third Revolution in Psychiatry.* New York: William Morrow and Company, 1975.

Fieve, R. R. "Lithium: An Overview," *Handbook of Studies in Depression,* ed. G. D. Burrows. Amsterdam: Excerpta Medica, 1977.

Fink, M. "Efficacy and Safety of Induced Seizures (EST) in Man," *Comprehensive Psychiatry,* 19 (1978); 1–18.

Fixsen, D. L.; and Phillips, E. L.; Phillips, E. A.; and Wolf, M. M. "The Teaching-Family Model of Group Home Treatment," in *Behavior Modification: Principles, Issues and Applications,* ed. W. E. Craighead, A. E. Kazdin, and M. J. Mahoney. Boston: Houghton Mifflin, 1976.

Fölling, A. "Über Ausscheidung von Phenylbrenztraubensäure in den Harn als Stoffweckselanomalie in Verbindung mit Imbezillität," *Atschrift fur physiolische Chemistrie,* 227 (1934): 169–76.

Ford, C. S.; and Beach, F. A. *Patterns of Sexual Behavior.* New York: Harper & Row, 1951.

Fort, J. P. "Heroin Addiction Among Young Men," *Psychiatry,* 17 (1954): 25.

Fort, T.; and Porterfield, A. L. "Some Backgrounds and Types of Alcoholism Among Women," *Journal of Health and Human Behavior,* 2 (1961): 283.

Foucalt, M. *Madness and Civilization: A History of Insanity in the Age of Reason.* New York: Random House, 1965.

Fowler, R. D., Jr. "The Current Status of Computer Interpretation of Psychological Tests," *American Journal of Psychiatry,* 125 (1969): 21–27.

Fox, R. A.; and Rosen, D. L. "A Parent-Administered Token Program for Dietary Regulation of Phenylketonuria," *Journal of Behavior Therapy and Experimental Psychiatry,* 8 (1977): 441–43.

Frank, J. D. *Persuasion and Healing.* Baltimore: Johns Hopkins University Press, 1961.

Frank, J. "Therapeutic Components of Psychotherapy. A 24-Year Progress Report of Research," *Journal of Nervous and Mental Disease,* 159 (1974): 325–42.

Freedman, A. M.; Kaplan, H. I.; and Sadock, B. J. *Comprehensive Textbook of Psychiatry — II.* Baltimore: Williams & Wilkins, 1975.

Freedman, B.; and Chapman, L. J. "Early Subjective Experience in Schizophrenic Episodes," *Journal of Abnormal Psychology,* 82 (1973): 46–54.

Freud, A. *The Psychoanalytic Treatment of Children: Lectures and Essays.* London: Imago, 1946.

Freud, S. *The Interpretation of Dreams,* standard ed., vols. 4 and 5. London: Hogarth Press, 1953 (original 1900).

Freud, S. *The Dynamics of Transference,* standard ed., vol. 12. London: Hogarth Press, 1955 (original 1912).

Freud, S. "Mourning and Melancholia," in *Collected Papers,* vol. 4. London: Hogarth Press, 1917.

Freud, S. *New Introductory Lectures on Psychoanalysis.* New York: W. W. Norton, 1933.

Freud, S. "Three Contributions to the Theory of Sex, 1905," in *The Basic Writings of Sigmund Freud,* ed. A. A. Brill. New York: Modern Library, 1938.

Freud, S. *The Psychoanalytical Treatment of Children: Lectures and Essays.* London: Imago, 1946.

Freud, S. "Mourning and Melancholia," in *Standard Edition of the Complete Psychological Works of Sigmund Freud.* London: Hogarth Press, 1953.

Freud, S.; and Breuer, J. *Studies on Hysteria.* New York: Avon Books, 1966.

Friedman, M.; and Rosenman, R. H. *Type A Behavior and Your Heart.* Greenwich, Connecticut: Fawcett, 1975.

Friedman, P. R. *The Rights of Mentally Retarded Persons: An ACLU Handbook.* New York: Avon Books, 1976.

Fromm-Reichman, F. *Principles of Intensive Psychotherapy.* Chicago: University of Chicago Press, 1950.

Frost, J.; and Hawkes, G. *The Disadvantaged Child: Issues and Innovations.* Boston: Houghton Mifflin, 1966.

Funabiki, D. "The Behavioral Assessment of Coping Among College Students in Problematic Situations," *Dissertation Abstracts International,* 34 (1977): 3607B.

Gagnon, J. H. *Human Sexualities.* Chicago: Scott, Foresman, 1977.

Gallup, G. "Guns Found in 44% of Homes," *San Francisco Chronicle,* 7 July 1975.

Garber, H.; and Heber, F. R. "The Milwaukee Project: Indications of the Effectiveness of Early Intervention in Preventing Mental Retardation," in *Research to Practice in Mental Retardation,* vol. I, ed. P. Mittler. Baltimore: University Park Press, 1977, pp. 119–27.

Gardner, Howard. *Developmental Psychology.* Boston: Little, Brown, 1978.

Gardner, W. I. "Research in Learning and Performance Characteristics of the Mentally Retarded," in *Retardation: Issues, Assessment and Intervention,* ed. J. T. Neisworth and R. M. Smith. New York: McGraw-Hill, 1978, pp. 205–39.

Garfield, S. L.; and Bergin, A. E. *Handbook of Psychotherapy and Behavior Change: An Empirical Analysis,* 2nd ed. New York: John Wiley & Sons, 1978.

Garmezy, N. "DSM III: Never Mind the Psychologists; Is It Good for the Children?" *The Clinical Psychologist,* 31 (Spring/Summer 1978a): 1–6.

Garmezy, N. "Current Status of a Sample of Other High-Risk Research Programs," in *The Nature of Schizophrenia: New Approaches to Research and Treatment,* ed. L. C. Wynne; R. L. Cromwell; and S. Matthysse. New York: John Wiley & Sons, 1978b, pp. 473–483.

Garmezy, N.; and Streitman, S. "Children at Risk: The Search for the Antecedents of Schizophrenia. Part I. Conceptual Models and Research Methods," *Schizophrenia Bulletin,* 8 (1974): 14–90.

Gay, G. R.; Wellisch, D. K.; Wesson, D. R.; and Smith, D. E. *The Psychotic Junkie.* New York: Insight Publishing Co., 1972.

Gayford, J. J. "Wife Battering: A Preliminary Survey on 100 Cases," *British Medical Journal,* 25 January 1975, pp. 194–97.

Gebhard, P. H.; Gagnon, J. H.; Pomeroy, W. B.; and Christenson, C. V. *Sex Offenders.* New York: Harper & Row, 1965.

Geer, J. H. "The Development of a Scale to Measure Fear," *Behaviour Research and Therapy,* 3 (1965): 45–53.

Gelles, R. J. *The Violent Home: A Study of Physical Aggression Between Husbands and Wives.* Beverly Hills: Sage Publications, 1974.

Gerard, D. L.; and Kornetsky, C. "Adolescent Opiate Addiction: A Study of Control and Addict Subjects," *Psychiatric Quarterly,* 29 (1955): 457–86.

Gerard, D. I.; and Siegel, J. "The Family Background of Schizophrenia," *Psychiatric Quarterly,* 24 (1950): 47–73.

Gerbie, A. B. "Amniocentesis for Prenatal Detection of Genetic Defects," *American Journal of Obstetrics and Gynecology,* 127(2) (1977): 158–61.

Gergen, K. J. "The Codification of Research Ethics: View of a Doubting Thomas," *American Psychologist,* 28 (1973): 907–12.

Gerner, R. H. "Depression in the Elderly," in *Psychopathology in the Aging,* ed. O. Kaplan. New York: Academic Press, 1979.

Gerner, R. H.; Post, R. M.; Goodwin, F. K.; and Bunney, W. E. "A Comparison of Biological Correlates and Antidepressant Effects of Sleep Deprivation in Patients and Normals," *Journal of Psychiatric Research,* 1978.

Geschwind, N. "Borderland of Neurology and Psychiatry," in *Psychiatric Aspects of Neurological Disease,* ed. D. F. Benson and D. Blumer. New York: Grune & Stratton, 1975.

Gil, D. *Violence Against Children.* Cambridge: Harvard University Press, 1970.

Gilluly, R. H. "A New Look at the Meaning of Reality," *Science News,* 99 (1971): 335–37.

Glaser, D. *The Effectiveness of Prison and Parole System.* Indianapolis, Indiana: Bobbs-Merrill, 1964.

Glasser, W. *Reality Therapy: A New Approach to Psychiatry.* New York: Harper & Row, 1965.

Glassman, A. H.; Shostak, M.; and Kantor, S. J. "Plasma Levels of Imipramine and Clinical Outcome," *Psychopharmacological Bulletin,* 14 (1975): 27–28.

Glidewell, J.; and Swallow, C. *The Prevalence of Maladjustment in Elementary Schools.* Chicago: University of Chicago Press, 1969.

Glowinski, J.; and Axelrod, J. "Inhibition of Uptake of Tritiated Noradenaline in the Intact Rat Brain by Imipramine and Related Compounds," *Nature,* 204 (1964): 1318–19.

Glueck, S.; and Glueck, E. T. *Unraveling Juvenile Delinquency.* New York: Commonwealth Fund, 1950.

Goffman, E. *Asylums: Essays on the Social Situation of Mental Patients and Other Inmates.* New York: Doubleday and Co., 1961.

Golann, S. E.; and Eisdorfer, C. "Mental Health and the Community. The Development of Issues," in *Handbook of Community Mental Health,* ed. S. E. Golann and C. Eisdorfer. New York: Appleton-Century-Crofts, 1972.

Gold, M. "Undetected Delinquent Behaviour," *Journal of Research in Crime and Delinquency,* 3 (1966): 27–46.

Gold, M. W. "Vocational Training," in *Mental Retardation and Developmental Disabilities: An Annual Review,* vol. 7, ed. J. Worties. New York: Brunner/Mazel, 1975.

Goldberg, S. R.; and Schuster, C. R. *Journal of the Experimental Analysis of Behavior,* 10 (1967): 235.

Goldenberg, I. I. *Build Me a Mountain: Youth, Poverty and the Creation of a New Setting.* Cambridge, Mass.: MIT Press, 1971.

Goldfried, M.; and Davison, G. *Clinical Behavior Therapy.* New York: Holt, Rinehart & Winston, 1976.

Goldfried, M. R.; Decenteceo, E. T.; and Weinberg, L. "Systematic Rational Restructuring as a Self-Control Technique," *Behavior Therapy,* 5 (1974): 247–54.

Goldstein, A. *The Insanity Defense.* New Haven: Yale University Press, 1967.

Goldstein, A. "Interactions of Narcotic Antagonists with Receptor Sites," in *Narcotic Antagonists,* ed. M. C. Braude; L. S. Harris; E. L. May; J. P. Smith; and J. E. Villareal. New York: Raven Press, 1974.

Goldstein, A.; and Kaiser, S. "Psychotropic Effects of Caffein in Man," *Clinical Pharmacology Therapy,* 10 (1969): 477–87.

Goldstein, A.; Kaiser, S.; and Whitby, O. "Psychotropic Effects of Caffeine in Men: Part IV: Quantitative and Qualitative Differences Associated with Habituation to Caffeine," *Clinical Pharmacology Therapy,* 10 (1969): 489–97.

Goldstein, A.; Warren, R.; and Kaiser, S. "Psychotropic Effects of Caffeine in Men: Part I: Individual Differences in Sensitivity to Caffeine-Induced Wakefulness," *Journal of Pharmacology and Experimental Therapeutics,* 49 (1965): 156–59.

Goldstein, M. J. "Premorbid Adjustment, Paranoid Status and Pattern of Response to Phenothiazines in Schizophrenia," *Schizophrenia Bulletin,* 3 (1971): 24–37.

Goldstein, M. J. "Individual Differences in Response to Stress," *American Journal of Community Psychology,* 1 (1973): 113–37.

Goldstein, M. J.; and Kant, H. S. *Pornography and Sexual Deviance.* Berkeley: University of California Press, 1973.

Goldstein, M. J.; and Palmer, J. O. *The Experience of Anxiety: A Casebook.* New York: Oxford University Press, 1963.

Goldstein, M. J.; and Palmer, J. O. *The Experience of Anxiety: A Casebook,* 2nd ed. New York: Oxford University Press, 1975.

Goldstein, M. J.; Rodnick, E. H.; Evans, J. R.; May, P. R. A.; and Steinberg, M. "Drug and Family Therapy in the Aftercare Treatment of Acute Schizophrenia," *Archives of General Psychiatry,* 35 (1978): 1169–77.

Goldstein, M. J.; Rodnick, E. H.; Jones, J. E.; McPherson, S. R.; and West, K. L. "Familial Precursors of Schizophrenia Spectrum Disorders," in *The Nature of Schizophrenia: New Approaches to Research and Treatment,* ed. L. C. Wynne; R. L. Cromwell; and S. Matthysse. New York: John Wiley & Sons, 1978, pp. 487–98.

Gomberg, E. S. "Women with Alcohol Problems," in *Alcoholism: Development, Consequences, and Interventions,* ed. N. J. Estes and M. E. Heinemann. St. Louis: C. V. Mosby, 1977.

Goodman, H.; Gottlieb, J.; and Harrison, R. "Social Acceptance of EMRs Integrated into a Nongraded Elementary School," *American Journal of Mental Deficiency,* 76 (1972): 412–17.

Goodwin, D. W.; and Guze, S. B. "Heredity and Alcoholism," in *Biology of Alcoholism,* vol. 3, *Clinical Pathology,* ed. B. Kissin and H. Begleiter. New York: Plenum Press, 1974.

Goodwin, D. W.; et al. "Alcohol Problems in Adoptees Raised Apart from Alcoholic Biological Parents," *Archives of General Psychiatry,* 28 (1973): 238–43.

Goodwin, D. W.; et al. "Drinking Problems in Adopted and Nonadopted Sons of Alcoholics," *Archives of General Psychiatry,* 31 (1974): 164–69.

Goodwin, F. K. "Diagnosis of Affective Disorders," in *Psychopharmacology in the Practice of Medicine,* ed. M. E. Jarvik. New York: Appleton-Century-Crofts, 1977, pp. 219–28.

Goodwin, F. K.; Cowdry, R. W.; and Webster, M. H. "Predictors of Drug Response in the Affective Disorders: Toward an Integrated Approach," in *Psychopharmacology: A Generation of Progress,* eds. M. A. Lipton; A. Dimascio; and K. F. Killam. New York: Raven Press, 1978.

Gorad, S. L.; McCourt, W. F.; and Cobb, J. C. "A Communication Approach to Alcoholism," *Quarterly Journal of Studies on Alcohol,* 32 (1971): 651–68.

Gordon, T. *Parent Effectiveness Training.* New York: Wyden Press, 1970.

Gottesman, I. I.; and Shields, J. "A Critical Review of Recent Adoption, Twin, and Family Studies of Schizophrenia: Behavioral Genetics Perspectives," *Schizophrenia Bulletin,* 2 (1976): 360–98.

Gottlieb, J. "Public, Peer and Professional Attitudes Toward Mentally Retarded Persons," in *The Mentally Retarded and Society: A Social Science Perspective,* ed. M. J. Begab and S. A. Richardson. Baltimore: University Park Press, 1975.

Gottlieb, J.; and Budoff, M. "Social Acceptability of Retarded Children in Nongraded Schools Differing in Architecture," *American Journal of Mental Deficiency,* 78 (1973): 15–19.

Gottlieb, J.; Cohen, L.; and Goldstein, L. "Social Contact and Personal Adjustment as Variables Relating to Attitudes toward EMR Children," *Training School Bulletin,* 71 (1974): 9–16.

Gottman, J.; and Markman, H. J. "Experimental Designs in Psychotherapy Research," in *Handbook of Psychotherapy and Behavior Change: An Empirical Analysis,* 2nd ed., ed. S. L. Garfield and A. E. Bergin. New York: John Wiley & Sons, 1978.

Gottman, J.; Notarius, C.; Markman, H.; Bank, S.; Yoppi, B.; and Rubin, M. E. "Behavior Exchange Theory and Marital Decision Making," *Journal of Personality and Social Psychology,* 34 (1976): 14–23.

Government Operations Committee, Senate. "Organized Crime and Illicit Traffic in Narcotics," hearings before the Permanent Subcommittee on Investigations, 88th Congress, 1st and 2nd sessions, 1963 and 1964. Washington, D.C.: Superintendent of Documents, U.S. Government Printing Office.

Grace, W. J.; and Graham, D. T. "Relationship of Specific Attitudes and Emotions to Certain Bodily Diseases," *Psychosomatic Medicine,* 14 (1952): 243–51.

Graham, D. T. "Psychosomatic Medicine," in *Handbook of Psychophysiology,* ed. N. S. Greenfield and R. A. Sternbach. New York: Holt, Rinehart & Winston, 1972.

Graham, D. T.; Kabler, J. D.; and Graham, F. K. "Physiological Response to the Suggestion of Attitudes Specific for Hives and Hypertension," *Psychosomatic Medicine,* 24 (1962): 159–69.

Gram, L. F.; Reisby, N.; and Ibsen, I. "Plasma Levels and Antidepressive Effect of Imipramine," *Clinical Psychopharmacology Therapy,* 19 (1976): 318–24.

Grant, I.; Adams, K. M.; Carlin, A. S.; Rennick, P. M.; Judd, L. L.; and Schoof, K. "The Collaborative Neuropsychological Study of Poly-Drug Abusers," *Archives of General Psychiatry,* 35 (1978): 1063–74.

Graubard, P. S.; Rosenberg, H.; and Miller, M. B. "Student Applications of Behavior Modification to Teachers and Environments or Ecological Approaches to Social Deviancy," in *Classroom Management: The Successful Use of Behavior Modification,* 2nd ed., ed. K. D. O'Leary and S. G. O'Leary. New York: Pergamon Press, 1977, pp. 235–49.

Green, A. "The Borderline Concept," in *Borderline Personality Disorders: The Concept, the Syndrome, the Patient,* ed. P. Hartocollis. New York: International Universities Press, 1977, pp. 15–44.

Green, H. *I Never Promised You a Rose Garden.* New York: Signet, 1964, pp. 47–48; 185–186.

Green, R. "Childhood Cross-Gender Identification," in *Transsexualism and Sex Reassignment,* ed. R. Green and J. Money. Baltimore: Johns Hopkins University Press, 1969, pp. 23–35.

Green, R. *Sexual Identity Conflict in Children and Adults.* New York: Basic Books, 1974.

Greenberg, A.; and Coleman, M. "Depressed 5-Hydroxyindole Levels Associated with Hyperactive and Aggressive Behavior," *Archives of General Psychiatry,* 33 (1976): 331–36.

Greenberg, J. *I Never Promised You a Rose Garden.* New York: Holt, Rinehart & Winston, 1964.

Greenfeld, J. *A Child Called Noah.* New York: Warner Books, 1973.

Greenson, R. R. *The Technique and Practice of Psychoanalysis,* vol. 1. New York: International Universities Press, 1967.

Gregg, N. M. "Congenital Cataract Following German Measles in the Mother," *Transactions of the Ophthalmological Society of Australia,* 3 (1941): 35.

Grinker, R. R., Sr.; and Holzman, P. S. "Schizophrenic Pathology in Young Adults: A Clinical Study," *Archives of General Psychiatry,* 28 (1973): 168–75.

Grinspoon, L. "Drug Dependence: Non-narcotic Agents," in *Comprehensive Textbook of Psychiatry,* ed. A. M. Freedman; H. I. Kaplan; and B. J. Sadock. Baltimore: Williams & Wilkins, 1975.

Grof, P.; Angst, J.; and Haines, T. "The Clinical Course of Depression: Practical Issues," in *Classification and Prediction of Outcome in Depression,* ed. J. Angst. New York: F. K. Schattauer Verlag, 1973.

Grossman, F. K. *Brothers and Sisters of Retarded Children.* Syracuse, New York: Syracuse University Press, 1972.

Grossman, H. J., ed. *Manual on Terminology and Classification in Mental Retardation.* Washington, D.C.: American Association of Mental Deficiency, 1973.

Group for the Advancement of Psychiatry. "Psychopathological Disorders in Childhood: Theoretical

Considerations and a Proposed Classification," GAP Report No. 62, 1966.

Gunderson, J. G. "Characteristics of Borderlines," in *Borderline Personality Disorders: The Concept, the Syndrome, the Patient,* ed. P. Hartocollis. New York: International Universities Press, 1977, pp. 173–92.

Gunderson, J. G.; Autry III, J. H.; and Mosher, L. R. "Special Report: Schizophrenia," *Schizophrenia Bulletin,* 9 (1974): 16–54.

Gunderson, J.; and Mosher, L. *Psychotherapy of Schizophrenia.* New York: Aronson, 1975.

Gunderson, J. G.; and Singer, M. T. "Defining Borderline Patients: An Overview," *American Journal of Psychiatry,* 132 (1975): 1–10.

Gurland, B. J.; Fleiss, J. L., Cooper, J. E.; Kendell, R. E.; and Simon, R. "Cross-National Study of Diagnosis of the Mental Disorders: Some Comparisons of Diagnostic Criteria from the First Investigation," *American Journal of Psychiatry,* 125 (1969): 1–11.

Guttman, H. A. "A Contradiction for Family Therapy: The Prepsychotic or Postpsychotic Young Adult and His Parents," *Archives of General Psychiatry,* 29 (1973): 352–55.

Guze, S. B.; and Robins, E. "Suicide and Primary Affective Disorders," *British Journal of Psychiatry,* 117 (1970): 437.

Haggard, E. A.; Brekstad, A.; and Skard, A. G. "On the Reliability of an Anamnestic Interview," *Journal of Abnormal and Social Psychology,* 61 (1960): 311–18.

Haglund, R. M. J.; and Schuckit, M. A. "The Epidemiology of Alcoholism," in *Alcoholism: Development, Consequences, and Interventions,* ed. N. J. Estes and M. E. Heinemann. St. Louis: C. V. Mosby, 1977.

Hall, R. V.; Lund, D.; and Jackson, D. "Effects of Teacher Attention on Study Behavior," *Journal of Applied Behavior Analysis,* 1 (1968): 1–12.

Hallam, R. S.; and Rachman, S. "Current Status of Aversion Therapy," in *Progress in Behavior Modification,* vol. 2, ed. M. Hersen; R. M. Eisler; and P. M. Miller. New York: Academic Press, 1976.

Halmi, K. A.; Brodland, G.; and Loney, J. "Prognosis in anorexia nervosa," *Annals of Internal Medicine,* 78 (1973): 907–909.

Hamilton, M. A. "A Rating Scale for Depression," *Journal of Neurology, Neurosurgery, and Psychiatry,* 23 (1960): 56–62.

Hammen, C.; and Peters, S. "Differential Responses to Male and Female Depressive Reactions," *Journal of Consulting and Clinical Psychology,* 45 (1977): 994–1001.

Hammen, C.; and Peters, S. "Interpersonal Consequences of Depression: Responses to Men and Women Enacting a Depressed Role," *Journal of Abnormal Psychology,* 87 (1978): 322–32.

Hammermesh, D. S.; and Soss, N. M. "An Economic Theory of Suicide," *Journal of Political Economy,* 82 (1974): 83–98.

Hardy, J. B.; McCracken, G. H., Jr.; Gilkeson, M. R.; and Sever, J. L. "Adverse Fetal Outcome Following Maternal Rubella After the First Trimester of Pregnancy," *Journal of the American Medical Association,* 207 (1969): 2414–20.

Hare, E. D.; and Craigen, D. "Psychopathy and Physiological Activity in a Mixed-Motive Game Situation," *Psychophysiology,* 11 (1974): 197–206.

Hare, E. H. "Masturbatory Insanity: The History of an Idea," *Journal of Mental Science,* 108 (1962): 1–25.

Hare, R. D. "Temporal Gradient of Fear Arousal in Psychopaths," *Journal of Abnormal Psychology,* 70 (1965): 442–45.

Hare, R. D. *Psychopathy: Theory and Research.* New York: John Wiley & Sons, 1970.

Hare, R. D. "Electrodermal and Cardiovascular Correlates of Psychopathy," in *Psychopathic Behaviour: Approaches to Research,* ed. R. D. Hare and D. Schalling. New York: John Wiley & Sons, 1978, pp. 103–43.

Harlow, H.; and Harlow, M. K. "Effects of Various Mother-Infant Relationships on Rhesus Monkey Behaviors," in *Determinants of Infant Behavior,* vol. 4, ed. B. M. Foss. New York: Barnes & Noble, 1969.

Harlow, J. M. "Recovery from the Passage of an Iron Bar through the Head," Publications of the Massachusetts Medical Society, 1868.

Harris, J. G. "An Abbreviated Form of the Phillips Rating Scale of Premorbid Adjustment in Schizophrenia," *Journal of Abnormal Psychology,* 84 (1975): 129–37.

Harris, T. *I'm O.K., You're O.K.: A Practical Guide to Transactional Analysis.* New York: Harper & Row, 1967.

Hartocollis, P. "Affects in Borderline Disorders," in *Borderline Personality Disorders: The Concept, the Syndrome, the Patient,* ed. P. Hartocollis. New York: International Universities Press, 1977, pp. 495–507.

Hartogs, R. "Discipline in the Early Life of Sex-Delinquents and Sex-Criminals," *Nervous Child,* 9 (1951): 167–73.

Haskell, M. R.; and Yablonsky, L. *Criminology: Crime and Criminality.* Chicago: Rand McNally College Publishing Co., 1974.

Hastings, J.; and Barkley, R. "A Review of Psychophysiological Research with Hyperkinetic Children," *Journal of Abnormal Child Psychology,* 6 (1978): 413–47.

Hathaway, S. R.; and McKinley, J. C. *Minnesota Multiphasic Personality Inventory: Manual.* New York: Psychological Corporation, 1951.

Hathaway, S. R.; and Meehl, P. E. *An Atlas for the Clinical Use of the MMPI.* Minneapolis: University of Minnesota Press, 1951.

Haughton, E.; and Ayllon, T. "Production and Elimination of Symptomatic Behavior," in *Case Studies in Behavior Modification,* ed. L. P. Ullmann and L. Krasner. New York: Holt, Rinehart & Winston, 1965, pp. 94–98.

Hayden, A. H.; and Haring, N. G. "Early Intervention for High Risk Infants and Young Children: Programs for Down's Syndrome Children at the University of Washington," in *Intervention Strategies for High Risk Infants and Young Children,* ed. T. D. Tjossem. Baltimore: University Park Press, 1976.

Hayden, A. H.; and Haring, N. G. "The Acceleration and Maintenance of Developmental Gains in Down's Syndrome School-Age Children," in *Research to Practice in Mental Retardation,* vol. 1., ed. P. Mittler. Baltimore: University Park Press, 1977, pp. 129–41.

Hayes, S. C.; Brownell, K. D.; and Barlow, D. H. "The Use of Self-Administered Covert Sensitization in the Treatment of Exhibitionism and Sadism," *Behavior Therapy,* 9 (1978): 283–89.

Heber, R. F.; Dever, R. B.; and Conry, J. "The Influence of Environmental and Genetic Variables on Intellectual Development," in *Behavior Research in Mental Retardation,* ed. H. H. Prehm, L. A. Hamerlynch; and J. E. Crossen. Eugene: University of Oregon Press, 1968, pp. 1–23.

Heber, R.; and Garber, H. "The Milwaukee Project: A Study of the Use of Family Intervention to Prevent Cultural-Familial Mental Retardation," in *Exceptional Infant, vol. 3: Assessment and Intervention.* New York: Brunner/Mazel, 1975.

Heinicke, C. M. "Parental Deprivation in Early Childhood: A Predisposition to Later Depression?" in *Separation and Depression: Clinical Research Aspects,* ed. E. C. Senay and J. P. Scott. Washington, D.C.: American Association for the Advancement of Science, 1973.

Helfer, R. E.; and Kempe, C. H., eds. *Helping the Battered Child and His Family.* Philadelphia: J. B. Lippincott Co., 1970.

Henderson, D. J. "Incest," in *The Sexual Experience,* ed. B. J. Sadock; H. I. Kaplan; and A. M. Freedman. Baltimore: Williams & Wilkins, 1976.

Henn, F. A.; Herjanic, M.; and Vanderpearl, R. H. "Forensic Psychiatry: Profiles of Two Types of Sex Offenders," *American Journal of Psychiatry,* 133(6) (1976): 694–96.

Hersov, L. A. "Persistent Non-Attendance at School," *Journal of Child Psychology and Psychiatry,* 1 (1960): 130–137.

Hersov, L. A. "Refusal to Go to School," *Journal of Child Psychology and Psychiatry,* 1 (1960): 137–46.

Hess, R. D.; and Shipman, V. C. "Early Experience and the Socialization of Cognitive Modes in Children," *Child Development,* 36 (1965): 869–86.

Hewitt, L. E.; and Jenkins, R. L. *Fundamental Patterns of Maladjustment: The Dynamics of their Origin.* Springfield: State of Illinois, 1947.

"High Court Upholds Donaldson: Harmless Mentally Ill Cannot be Confined Without Treatment," *Civil Liberties,* 308 (September 1975): 1–7.

Hilberman, E. *The Rape Victim: A Project of the Committee on Women of the American Psychiatric Association.* Washington: American Psychiatric Association, 1976.

Hilgard, E. R. "Hypnosis and Experimental Psychodynamics," in *Lectures on Experimental Psychiatry,* ed. H. Brosen. Pittsburgh: University of Pittsburgh Press, 1961.

Hill, H. E., et al. "Personality Characteristics of Narcotic Addicts as Indicated by the MMPI," *Journal of General Psychology,* 62 (1960): 127.

Hill, H. E., et al. "An MMPI Factor Analytic Study of Alcoholics, Narcotic Addicts and Criminals," *Quarterly Journal of Studies on Alcohol,* 23 (1962): 411.

Hoffer, A.; Osmond, H.; Callbeck, M. J.; and Kahan, I. "Treatment of Schizophrenia with Nicotinic Acid and Nicotinamide," *Journal of Clinical and Experimental Psychopathology,* 18(2) (1957): 131–58.

Hofmann, A. "Psychotomimetic Drugs: Chemical and Pharmacological Aspects," *Acta Physiologica et Pharmacologica Neerlandica,* 8 (1959): 240.

Hogarty, G. E.; and Goldberg, S. L. "Collaborative

Study Group: Drug and Sociotherapy in the Aftercare of Schizophrenia Patients: One Year Relapse Rates," *Archives of General Psychiatry,* 28 (1973): 54–64.

Hogarty, G. E.; Goldberg, S. C.; and Schooler, N. R. "Drug and Socio-Therapy in the Aftercare of Schizophrenic Patients. III. Adjustment of Nonrelapsed Patients," *Archives of General Psychiatry,* 31 (1974): 609–18.

Hogarty, G. E.; Goldberg, S. C.; Schooler, N. R.; and Ulrich, R. F. "Drug and Socio-Therapy in the Aftercare of Schizophrenic Patients. II. Two Year Relapse Rates," *Archives of General Psychiatry,* 31 (1974): 603–608.

Holding, T. A. *British Journal of Psychiatry,* 124 (1974): 470.

Hollingshead, A. B.; and Redlich, F. C. *Social Class and Mental Illness: A Community Study.* New York: John Wiley & Sons, 1958.

Hollon, S. D.; and Beck, A. T. "Psychotherapy and Drug Therapy: Comparisons and Combinations," in *Handbook of Psychotherapy and Behavior Change: An Empirical Analysis,* 2nd ed., ed. S. L. Garfield and A. E. Bergin. New York: John Wiley & Sons, 1978, pp. 437–90.

Holmes, F. B. "An Experimental Study of the Fears of Young Children," in *Children's Fears,* Child Development Monograph no. 20, eds. A. T. Jersild and F. B. Holmes. New York: Teachers College, Columbia University, 1935.

Holmes, T. H.; and Masuda, M. "Life Change and Illness Susceptibility," in *Stressful Life Events: Their Nature and Effects,* ed. B. S. Dohrenwend and B. P. Dohrenwend. New York: John Wiley & Sons, 1974, pp. 45–72.

Holmes, T. H.; and Rahe, R. H. "The Social Adjustment Rating Scale," *Journal of Psychosomatic Research,* 11 (1967): 213–18.

Holt, J. *How Children Fail.* New York: Dell Publishing Co., 1964.

Holtzman, W. H. *Inkblot Perception and Personality: Holtzman Inkblot Technique.* Austin: University of Texas Press, 1961.

Holzman, P. S.; Proctor, L. R.; Levy, D. L.; Yasillo, N. J.; Meltzer, H. Y.; and Hurt, S. W. "Eye-Tracking Dysfunctions in Schizophrenic Patients and Their Relatives," *Archives of General Psychiatry,* 31 (1974): 143–51.

Honzik, M. P.; Macfarlane, J. W.; and Allen, L. "The Stability of Mental Test Performance Between Two and Eighteen Years," *Journal of Experimental Education,* 17 (1948): 309–14.

Hood, R.; and Sparks, R. *Key Issues in Criminology.* New York: McGraw-Hill Book Co., World University Library, 1970.

Horn, J. L., and Wanberg, K. W. "Females are Different: On the Diagnosis of Alcoholism in Women." Proceedings of the First Annual Alcoholism Conference of the National Institute on Alcohol Abuse and Alcoholism." Washington, D.C.: Department of Health, Education, and Welfare Publication no. NIH 74-675, 1973.

Horney, K. *The Neurotic Personality of Our Time.* New York: W. W. Norton, 1937.

Horney, K. *Collected Works.* New York: W. W. Norton, 1965.

Hudgens, R. W.; Robins, E.; and Delong, W. B. "The Reporting of Recent Stress in the Lives of Psychiatric Patients," *British Journal of Psychiatry,* 117 (1970): 635–43.

Hughes, R. C. "Covert Sensitization Treatment of Exhibitionism," *Journal of Behavior Therapy and Experimental Psychiatry,* 8 (1977): 177–79.

Hunt, G. M.; and Azrin, N. H. "A Community Reinforcement Approach to Alcoholism," *Behavior Research and Therapy,* 11 (1973): 91–104.

Hunt, M. *Sexual Behavior in the 1970s.* New York: Playboy Press, 1974.

Hurley, R. *Poverty and Mental Retardation: A Causal Relationship.* New York: Vintage Books, 1969.

Hutchings, B.; and Mednick, S. A. "Registered Criminality in the Adoptive Biological Parents of Registered Male Adoptees," in *Genetics, Environment, and Psychopathology,* ed. S. A. Mednick; F. Schusinger; J. Higgins; and B. Bell. New York: Elsevier, 1974, pp. 215–27.

Hutt, C.; and Ounsted, C. "The Biological Significance of Gaze Aversion with Particular Reference to the Syndrome of Infantile Autism," *Behavioral Science,* 11 (1966): 346–56.

Ihli, K. L.; and Garlington, W. K. "A Comparison of Group vs. Individual Desensitization of Test Anxiety," *Behavior Research and Therapy,* 7 (1969): 207–209.

Institute for Social Research. Newsletter (Winter). Ann Arbor: University of Michigan, 1974.

Isbell, H. "Perspectives in Research on Opiate Addiction," in *Narcotics,* ed. D. M. Wilner and G. G. Kassebaum. New York: McGraw-Hill, 1965.

Isbell, H.; and Chrusciel, T. L. "Dependence Liability of 'Non-Narcotic' Drugs," *WHO Bulletin* 43 (1970).

Jackson, D. D. "A Critique of the Literature on the Genetics of Schizophrenia," in *The Etiology of*

Schizophrenia, ed. D. D. Jackson. New York: Basic Books, 1960, pp. 37–87.

Jacobowitz, D. M. "Monoaminergic Pathways in the Central Nervous System," in *Psychopharmacology: A Generation of Progress,* ed. M. A. Lipton; A. DiMascio; and K. F. Killam. New York: Raven Press, 1978.

Jacobs, J. *The Search for Help: A Study of the Retarded Child in the Community.* New York: Brunner/Mazel, 1969.

Jacobs, P. A.; Brunton, M.; Melville, M. M.; Brittain, R. P.; and McClemont, W. F. "Aggressive Behavior, Mental Subnormality, and the XYY Male," *Nature,* 208 (1965): 1351–52.

Jacobson, E. *Progressive Relaxation.* Chicago: University of Chicago Press, 1938.

Jacobson, N. S. "Behavioral Treatments for Marital Discord: A Critical Appraisal," in *Progress in Behavior Modification,* ed. M. Hersen; R. M. Eisler; and P. M. Miller. New York: Academic Press, 1979.

Jacobson, N. S. "Problem Solving and Contingency Contracting in the Treatment of Marital Discord," *Journal of Consulting and Clinical Psychology,* 45 (1977): 92–100.

Jamison, K. R. "Manic-Depressive Illness in the Elderly," in *Psychopathology in the Aging,* ed. O. Kaplan. New York: Academic Press, 1979.

Jamison, K. R.; Gerner, R. H.; and Goodwin, F. K. "Patient and Physician Attitude Toward Lithium: Relationship to Compliance," *Archives of General Psychiatry,* 36 (1979): 866–69.

Jamison, K. R.; Gerner, R. H.; Hammen, C.; and Padesky, C. "Clouds and Silver Linings: Positive Experiences Associated with the Primary Affective Disorders," *American Journal of Psychiatry,* 1980.

Jamison, K. R.; Hammen, C.; Gong-Guy, E.; Padesky, C.; and Gerner, R. H. "Self-Perceptions of Inter-personal Functioning in Unipolar and Bipolar Men and Women," submitted for publication, 1979.

Janet, P. *The Major Symptoms of Hysteria,* 2nd ed. New York: Macmillan Publishing Co., 1929.

Jarvik, L. F.; Klodin, V.; and Matsuyama, S. S. "Human Aggression and the Extra Y Chromosome: Fact or Fiction," *American Psychologist,* 28 (1973): 674–76.

Jarvik, M. E. *Psychopharmacology in the Practice of Medicine.* New York: Appleton-Century-Crofts, 1977.

Jenkins, R. L. *Behavior Disorders of Childhood and Adolescence.* Springfield, Ill.: E. P. Dutton, 1968.

Jensen, A. R. "Social Class, Race, and Genetics: Implications for Education," *American Educational Research Journal,* 5 (1968): 1–412.

Jensen, A. R. "How Much Can We Boost IQ and Scholastic Achievement?" *Harvard Educational Review,* 39 (1969): 1.

Jersild, A. T. *Child Psychology,* 6th ed. Englewood Cliffs, N.J.: Prentice-Hall, 1968.

Jersild, A. T.; and Holmes, F. B. *Children's Fears.* New York: Bureau of Publications, Teachers College. Columbia University, 1935.

Jervis, G. A. "The Genetics of Phenylpyruvic Oligophrenia," *Journal of Mental Science,* 85 (1939): 719.

Jervis, G. A. "Studies of Phenylpyruvic Oligophrenia: The Position of the Metabolic Error," *Journal of Biological Chemistry,* 169 (1947): 651.

Johnson, F. N., ed. *Lithium Research and Therapy.* New York: Academic Press, 1975.

Johnson, R. N. *Aggression in Man and Animals.* Philadelphia: W. B. Saunders Co., 1972.

Johnson, S. M.; and Lobitz, G. K. "The Personal and Marital Adjustment of Parents as Related to Observed Child Deviance and Parenting Behaviors," *Journal of Abnormal Child Psychiatry,* 2 (1974): 192–207.

Joint Commission on Mental Illness and Health. *Action for Mental Health.* New York: Basic Books, 1961.

Joint Commission on Mental Health of Children. *Crisis in Child Mental Health: Challenge for the 1970s.* New York: Harper & Row, 1970.

Jones, B. M. "Alcohol and Women: Intoxication Levels and Memory Impairment as Related to the Menstrual Cycle," *Alcohol Technical Reports,* 4 (1975): 1.

Jones, B. M., and Jones, M. K. "Male and Female Intoxication Levels for Three Alcohol Doses or Do Women Really Get Higher Than Men?" *Alcohol Technical Reports,* 5 (1976): 11.

Jones, E. *The Life and Work of Sigmund Freud.* New York: Basic Books, 1955.

Jones, K. L.; Smith, D. W.; Ulleland, C. N.; and Streissguth, A. P. "Pattern of Malformation in Offspring of Chronic Alcoholic Mothers," *Lancet,* 1 (1973): 1267–71.

Jones, M. *The Therapeutic Community.* New York: Basic Books, 1953.

Jones. M. C. "A Laboratory Study of Fear: The Case of Peter," *Pedagogical Seminars,* 31 (1924): 308–15.

Jones, R. T. "The Hallucinogens," in *Psychopharmacology in the Practice of Medicine,* ed. M. Jarvik, New York: Appleton-Century-Crofts, 1977.

"The 'Junkie Monkey' Experiments," *San Francisco Chronicle,* 14 August 1971.

Kaelbling, R.; and Volpe, P. A. "II. Constancy of Psychiatric Diagnoses in Readmissions," *Comprehensive Psychiatry,* 4 (1963): 29–39.

Kahn, M.; Baker, B. L.; and Weiss, J. "The Treatment of Insomnia by Relaxation Training," *Journal of Abnormal Psychology,* 73(6) (1968): 556–58.

Kaij, L. *Alcoholism in Twins.* Stockholm: Almqvist & Wiksell, 1960.

Kanin, E. J. "Male Aggression in Dating-Courtship Relations," *American Journal of Sociology,* 63 (1957): 197–204.

Kanner, L. "Autistic Disturbances of Affective Content," *Nervous Child,* 2 (1943): 217–40.

Kanner, L. "Early Infantile Autism," *Journal of Pediatrics,* 25 (1944): 211–17.

Kanner, L. *Child Psychiatry.* London: Blackwell, 1948.

Kanner, L. "Follow-Up Study of Eleven Autistic Children Originally Reported in 1943," *Journal of Autism and Childhood Schizophrenia,* 1 (1971): 119–45.

Kaplan, H. B. *Self-Attitudes and Deviant Behavior.* Pacific Palisades, Calif.: Goodyear Publishing, 1975.

Kaplan, H. S. *The New Sex Therapy: Active Treatment of Sexual Dysfunctions.* New York: Brunner/Mazel, 1974.

Kaplan, H. S. *The Illustrated Manual of Sex Therapy.* New York: Quadrangle/The New York Times Book Company, 1975.

Karlsson, J. L. "Genealogic Studies of Schizophrenia," in *The Transmission of Schizophrenia,* ed. D. Rosenthal and S. S. Kety. New York: Pergamon Press, 1968, pp. 85–94.

Katz, M. M.; and Hirschfeld, R. A. "Phenomenology and Classification of Depression," in *Psychopharmacology: A Generation of Progress,* ed. M. A. Lipton; A. DiMascio; and K. F. Killam. New York: Raven Press, 1978.

Kaufman, B. N. *Son Rise.* New York: Harper & Row, 1976.

Kaufman, C.; and Rosenblum, L. A. "The Reactions to Separation in Infant Monkeys: Anaclitic Depression and Conservation-Withdrawal," *Psychosomatic Medicine,* 29(6) (1967): 648–75.

Kaufman, I. C. "Mother-Infant Separation in Monkeys: An Experimental Model," in *Separation and Depression: Clinical and Research Aspects,* ed. J. P. Scott and E. Senay. Washington: American Association for the Advancement of Science, 1973.

Kaufman, K. F.; and O'Leary, K. D. "Reward, Cost, and Self-Evaluation Procedures for Disruptive Adolescents in a Psychiatric Hospital School," *Journal of Applied Behavior Analysis,* 5 (1972): 293–309.

Kazdin, A. E.; and Bootzin, R. R. "The Token Economy: An Evaluation Review," *Journal of Applied Behavioral Analysis,* 5 (1972): 343–72.

Kazdin, A. E.; and Wilcoxon, L. A. "Systematic Desensitization and Non-specific Treatment Effects: A Methodological Evaluation," *Psychological Bulletin,* 83 (1976): 729–58.

Kellam, S. G.; and Schiff, S. K. "Adaptation and Mental Illness in the First-Grade Classrooms of an Urban Community," *Psychiatric Research Reports,* 21 (1967): 79–91.

Keller, M.; and Efron, V. "The Prevalence of Alcoholism," *Quarterly Journal of Studies of Alcohol,* 16 (1955): 619–43.

Keller, O.; and Alper, B. *Halfway Houses: Community-Centered Correction and Treatment.* Lexington, Mass.: D. C. Heath, 1970.

Kelman, H. C. "The Rights of the Subject in Social Research: An Analysis in Terms of Relative Power and Legitimacy," *American Psychologist,* 27 (1972): 989–1016.

Kempe, C. H., et al. "The Battered Child Syndrome," *Journal of the American Medical Association,* 181 (1962): 12–24.

Kempe, C. H.; and Helfer, R. E., eds. *Helping the Battered Child and His Family.* Philadelphia: J. B. Lippincott, 1972.

Kennedy, W. A. "School Phobia: Rapid Treatment of Fifty Cases," *Journal of Abnormal Psychology,* 70 (1965): 285–89.

Kernberg, O. F.; Burstein, E. D.; Coyne, L.; Applebaum, A.; Horowitz, L.; and Voth, H. "Psychotherapy and Psychoanalysis: Final Report of the Menninger Foundation's Psychotherapy Research Project," *Bulletin of the Menninger Clinic,* 36 (1972): 1–276.

Kessler, J. W. *Psychopathology of Childhood.* Englewood Cliffs, N.J.: Prentice-Hall, 1966.

Kety, S. S. "Biochemical Theories of Schizophrenia. A Two-Part Critical Review of Current Theories and of the Evidence Used to Support Them," *Science,* 129 (1959): 1528–32, 1590–96.

Kety, S. S. "Commentary," *Journal of Nervous and Mental Disorders,* 153 (1971): 323.

Kety, S. S.; Rosenthal, D.; Wender, P. H.; and Schulsinger, F. "The Types and Prevalence of Mental Illness in the Biological and Adoptive Families of Adopted Schizophrenics," in *The Transmission of Schizophrenia,* ed. D. Rosenthal and S. S. Kety. New York: Pergamon Press, 1968, pp. 345–62.

Kety, S. S.; Rosenthal, D.; Wender, P. H.; and Schulsinger, F. "Studies Based on a Total Sample of Adopted Individuals and Their Relatives: Why They Were Necessary, What They Demonstrated and Failed to Demonstrate," *Schizophrenia Bulletin,* 2 (1976): 413–28.

Kety, S. S.; Rosenthal, D.; Wender, P. H.; Schulsinger, F.; and Jacobsen, B. "Mental Illness in the Biological and Adoptive Families of Adopted Individuals Who Have Become Schizophrenic: A Preliminary Report Based Upon Psychiatric Interviews," in *Genetic Research in Psychiatry,* ed. R. Fieve; D. Rosenthal; and H. Brill. Baltimore: The Johns Hopkins University Press, 1975, pp. 147–65.

Khazan, N., et al. "Electroencephalographic Electromyographic, and Behavioral Correlates during a Cycle of Self-maintained Morphine Addiction in the Rat," *Journal of Pharmacological Experiments in Therapy,* 155 (March 1967): 521–31.

Kierkegaard, S. A. *The Concept of Dread,* 2nd ed. Princeton: Princeton University Press, 1957.

Kiloh, L. G. "The Use of Electroconvulsive Treatment in Depressive Illness," in *Handbook of Studies on Depression,* ed. G. D. Burrows. Amsterdam: Excerpta Medica, 1977.

Kimball, W. "Human Warehouses: An Inside Look at the Fernald School for the Retarded," *Boston After Dark,* May 1972.

Kinsbourne, M.; and Caplan, P. J. *Children's Learning and Attention Problems.* Boston: Little, Brown, 1979.

Kinsey, A. C.; Pomeroy, W. B.; and Martin, C. E. *Sexual Behavior in the Human Male.* Philadelphia: W. B. Saunders, 1948.

Kinsey, A. C.; Pomeroy, W. B.; Martin, C. E; and Gebhard, H. *Sexual Behavior in the Human Female.* Philadelphia: W. B. Saunders, 1953.

Kirkpatrick, C.; and Kanin, E. "Male Sex Aggression on a University Campus," *American Sociology Review,* 22 (1957): 52–58.

Klaber, M. M. *Retardates in Residence: A Study of Institutions.* West Hartford, Conn.: University of Hartford, 1970.

Klein, D. F.; and Davis, J. M. *Diagnosis and Drug Treatment of Psychiatric Disorders: Review of Mood-Stabilizing Drug Literature. Baltimore: Williams & Wilkins, 1969.*

Klein, M. *The Psychoanalysis of Children.* London: Hogarth Press, 1932.

Klein, M. "The Psychoanalytic Play Technique," *American Journal of Orthopsychiatry,* 25 (1955): 223–37.

Klerman, G. L. "Clinical Research in Depression," *Archives of General Psychiatry,* 24 (1971): 305.

Klerman, G. L. "Combining Drugs and Psychotherapy in the Treatment of Depression," in *Drugs in Combination With Other Therapies,* ed. M. Greenblatt. New York: Grune & Stratton, 1975, pp. 67–81.

Klerman, G. L. "Better But Not Well: Social and Ethical Issues in the Deinstitutionalization of the Mentally Ill," *Schizophrenia Bulletin,* 3 (1977): 617–31.

Klerman, G. L. "Long-Term Treatment of Affective Disorders," in *Psychopharmacology: A Generation of Progress,* ed. M. A. Lipton; A. DiMascio; and K. F. Killam. New York: Raven Press, 1978, pp. 1303–12.

Klerman, G. L.; DiMascio, A.; Weissman, M. M.; Prusoff, B.; and Paykel. E. S. "Treatment of Depression by Drugs and Psychotherapy," *American Journal of Psychiatry,* 131 (1974): 186–91.

Kline, N. S. "Clinical Experience with Iproniazid (Marsilid)," *Journal of Clinical Experimental Psychopathology,* Suppl. 1. 19(2) 1962.

Kline, N. S. *From Sad to Glad.* New York: Ballantine Books, 1974.

Knight, R. "Borderline States," *Bulletin Menninger Clinic,* 17 (1953): 1–12.

Knobloch, H.; and Pasamanick, B. "Seasonal Variations in the Births of the Mentally Deficient," *American Journal of Public Health,* 48 (1958): 1201–1208.

Knopf, I. J. *Childhood Psychopathology: A Developmental Approach,* Englewood Cliffs, N.J.: Prentice-Hall, 1979.

Knox, W. E. "Phenylketonuria," in *The Metabolic Basis of Inherited Disease,* ed. J. B. Stanbury; J. B. Wyngaarden; and D. S. Frederickson. New York: McGraw-Hill, 1972.

Koch, R.; and Dobson, J. C. *The Mentally Retarded Child and His Family.* New York: Brunner/Mazel, 1971.

Kohen, W.; and Paul, G. L. "Current Trends and Recommended Changes in Extended-Care Placement of Mental Patients: The Illinois System as a

Case in Point," *Schizophrenia Bulletin,* 2 (1976): 575–93.

Kohn, M. L. "A Social Class and Schizophrenia: A Critical Review and a Reformulation," *Schizophrenia Bulletin,* 7 (1973): 60–79.

Kolb, L. *Drug Addiction in Its Relation to Crime.* New York: National Committee for Mental Hygiene, Reprint no. 204, 1925.

Kolb, L. "Types and Characteristics of Drug Addicts," *Mental Hygiene,* 9 (1925): 300.

Kolb, L. "Drug Addiction as a Public Health Problem," *Scientific Monthly,* 48 (1939): 391.

Kolb, L.; and Ossenfort, W. F. "The Treatment of Drug Addicts at the Lexington Hospital," *Southern Medical Journal,* 31 (1938): 914.

Kolb, L. C. *Modern Clinical Psychiatry.* Philadelphia: W. B. Saunders, 1973.

Kolvin, I. "Psychoses in Childhood — A Comparative Study," in *Infantile Autism: Concepts, Characteristics and Treatment,* ed. M. Rutter. Edinburgh: Churchill Livingstone, 1971.

Korchin, S. J. *Modern Clinical Psychology: Principles of Intervention in the Clinic and Community.* New York: Basic Books, 1976.

Kornetsky, C. *Pharmacology: Drugs Affecting Behavior.* New York: John Wiley & Sons, 1976.

Kozol, J. *Death at an Early Age.* Boston: Houghton Mifflin, 1967.

Kraemer, G. W.; and McKinney, W. T. "Interactions of Pharmacological Agents Which Alter Biogenic Amine Metabolism and Depression," *Journal of Affective Disorders,* 1 (1979): 33–54.

Kraepelin, E. *Clinical Psychiatry.* New York: Macmillan, 1907.

Kraepelin, E. *Manic-Depressive Insanity and Paranoia.* London: Churchill Livingstone, 1921.

Kramer, M. "Cross-National Study of Diagnosis of the Mental Disorders: Origin of the Problem," *American Journal of Psychiatry,* 125 (1969): 1–11.

Kramer, M.; Pollack, E. S.; Redick, R. W.; and Locke, B. Z. *Mental Disorders/Suicide.* Cambridge, Mass.: Harvard University Press, 1972.

Krapfl, J. E.; and Nawas, M. M. "Differential Ordering of Stimulus Presentation in Systematic Desensitization," *Journal of Abnormal Psychology,* 75 (1970): 333–37.

Kress, F. "Evaluations of Dangerousness," *Schizophrenia Bulletin,* 5 (1979): 211–17.

Kuehnle, J. C.; Anderson, W. H.; and Chandler, E. "First Drinking Experience in Addictive and Non-addictive Drinkers," *Archives of General Psychiatry,* 31 (1974): 521–23.

Kurland, H. D.; Yeager, G. T.; and Arthur, R. J. "Psychophysiological Aspects of Severe Behavior Disorders," *Archives of General Psychiatry,* 8 (1963): 599–604.

Kurland, L. T. "The Incidence and Prevalence of Convulsive Disorders in a Small Community," *Epilepsia,* 1 (1959): 143.

Kutchinsky, B. "The Effect of Easy Availability of Pornography on the Incidence of Sex Crimes: The Danish Experience," *Journal of Social Issues,* 29(3) (1973): 163–81.

Lacey, J. I. "Somatic Response Patterning and Stress: Some Revisions of Activation Theory in Psychological Stress," in *Psychological Stress,* ed. M. H. Appley and R. Trumbul. New York: Appleton-Century-Crofts, 1967, pp. 14–37.

Lahey, B. B.; Hobbs, S. A.; Kupfer, D. L.; and Delamater, A. "Current Perspectives on Hyperactivity and Learning Disabilities," in *Behavior Therapy with Hyperactive and Learning Disabled Children,* ed. B. B. Lahey. New York: Oxford, 1979, pp. 3–18.

Laing, R. D. "Is Schizophrenia a Disease?" *International Journal of Social Psychiatry,* 10 (1964): 184–93.

Laing, R. D. "Mystification, Confusion and Conflict," in *Intensive Family Therapy,* ed. I. Boszormenyi-Nagy and J. L. Framo. New York: Harper & Row, 1965, pp. 343–363.

Laing, R. D. *The Politics of Experience.* New York: Ballantine Books, 1967.

Laing, R. D.; and Esterson, A. *Sanity, Madness, and the Family.* Middlesex, England: Penguin Books, 1970.

Lambert, M. "Spontaneous Remission in Adult Neurotic Disorders: A Revision and Summary," *Psychological Bulletin,* 83 (1976): 107–17.

Lang, P. J. "Fear Reduction and Fear Behavior: Problems in Treating a Construct," in *Research in Psychotherapy,* vol. III, ed. J. M. Shlien. Washington, D.C.: American Psychological Association, 1968, pp. 90–103.

Lang, P. J.; Melamed, B. G.; and Hart, J. H. "Automating the Desensitization Procedure: A Psychophysiological Analysis of Fear Modification," in *Experimental Approaches to Psychopathology.* ed. M. J. Kietzman. New York: Academic Press, 1974.

Langer, E. "Human Experimentation: New York Verdict Affirms Patient's Rights," *Science,* 151 (1966): 663–66.

Langley, R.; and Levy, R. C. *Wife Beating: The Silent Crisis.* New York: Pocket Books, 1977.

Langner, T. S.; and Michael, S. T. *Life Stress and Mental Health: The Midtown Manhattan Study.* New York: The Free Press, 1963.

Lasagna, L., et al. "Drug-Induced Changes in Man: I. Observations on Healthy Subjects, Chronically Ill Patients and 'Post-Addicts,'" *Journal of the American Medical Association,* 157 (1955): 1006.

Lassen, N. A.; Ingvar, D. H.; and Skinhoj, E. "Brain Function and Blood Flow," *Scientific American,* (October 1978), pp. 62–71.

Lawlis, G. F.; and Rubin, S. E. "16-PF Study of Personality Patterns in Alcoholics," *Quarterly Journal of the Study of Alcohol,* 32 (1971): 318–27.

Lazarus, A. A. "Group Therapy of Phobic Disorders by Systematic Desensitization," *Journal of Abnormal and Social Psychology,* 63 (1961): 504–10.

Lazarus, A. A. *Behavior Therapy and Beyond,* New York: McGraw-Hill, 1971.

Lazarus, A. A.; and Abramovitz, A. "The Use of 'Emotive Imagery' in the Treatment of Children's Phobias," *Journal of Mental Science,* 108 (1962): 191–95.

Lazarus, R. S.; and Alfert, E. "The Short-Circuiting of Threat," *Journal of Abnormal and Social Psychology,* 69 (1964): 195–205.

Lazarus, A. A.; Davison, G. C.; and Polefka, D. A. "Classical and Operant Factors in the Treatment of School Phobia," *Journal of Abnormal Psychology,* 70 (1965): 225–29.

Leach, B. "Does Alcoholics Anonymous Really Work?" in *Alcoholism: Progress in Research and Treatment,* ed. P. G. Bourne and R. Fox. New York: Academic Press, 1973.

Leff, J. "Schizophrenia and Sensitivity to the Family Environment," *Schizophrenia Bulletin,* 2(4) (1976): 566–74.

Legislative Commission on Expenditure Review, Narcotic Drug Control in New York State, Program Audit Highlights. Albany, New York, 1971.

Lehmann, H. E. "Strategies in Clinical Psychopharmacology," in *Psychopharmacology: A Generation of Progress,* ed. M. A. Lipton; A. DiMascio; and K. F. Killam. New York: Raven Press, 1978, pp. 13–24.

Lejeune, J.; Gautier, M.; and Turpin, R. "Le Mongolisme. Premier Example d'Aberration Autosomique Humaine," *Année Genetique,* 1 (1959): 41.

Lemere, F.; and Voegtlin, W. "An Evaluation of the Aversion Treatment of Alcoholism," *Quarterly Journal of Studies on Alcohol,* 11 (1950): 199–204.

Lester, G.; and Lester, D. *Suicide: The Gamble With Death.* Englewood Cliffs, N.J.: Prentice-Hall, 1971.

Levenson, H. S.; and Bick, E. C. "Psychopharmacology of Caffeine," in *Psychopharmacology in the Practice of Medicine,* ed. M. Jarvik. New York: Appleton-Century-Crofts, 1977.

Levi, L. D.; Fales, C. H.; Stein, M.; and Sharp, V. H. "Separation and Attempted Suicide," *Archives of General Psychiatry,* 15 (1966): 158–64.

Levinger, G.; and Snoek, J. D. *Attraction in Relationship: A New Look at Interpersonal Attraction.* Morristown, N.J.: General Learning Press, 1972.

Levitsky, A.; and Perls, F. S. "The Rules and Games of Gestalt Therapy," in *Gestalt Therapy Now,* ed. J. Fagan and I. L. Sheperd. Palo Alto; Science and Behavior Books, 1970.

Levitt, E. "Results of Psychotherapy With Children: An Evaluation," *Journal of Consulting Psychology,* 21 (1957): 189–96.

Levitt, E. "Psychotherapy With Children: A Further Review," *Behavior, Research, and Therapy,* 1 (1963): 45–51.

Levy, S.; and Southcombe, R. H. "Suicide in a State Hospital for the Mentally Ill," *Journal of Nervous and Mental Disease,* 117 (1953): 504–514.

Lewinsohn, P. M. "A Behavioral Approach to Depression," in *The Psychology of Depression: Contemporary Theory and Research,* ed. R. J. Friedman and M. M. Katz. New York: Halsted Press, 1974.

Lewinsohn, P. M. "The Behavioral Study and Treatment of Depression," in *Progress in Behavior Modification,* ed. M. Hersen; R. M. Eisler; and P. M. Miller. New York: Academic Press, 1975.

Lewinsohn, P. M.; and Shaffer, M. "Use of Home Observations as an Integral Part of the Treatment of Depression: Preliminary Report and Case Studies," *Journal of Consulting and Clinical Psychology,* 37 (1971): 88.

Liberman, R. P. "Behavior Therapy for Schizophrenia," in *Treatment of Schizophrenia,* ed. L. J. West and D. E. Flinn. New York: Grune & Stratton, 1976, pp. 175–206.

Liddell, H. S. "Conditioned Reflex Method and Experimental Neurosis," in *Personality and the Behavioral Disorders,* ed. J. McV. Hunt. New York: Ronald Press, 1944.

Liddick, B. "A Transsexual's Texas Homecoming: Classmates Confront a Buddy's Sex Change," *Los Angeles Times,* 2 July 1978.

Lidz, T.; Cornelison, A.; Fleck, S.; and Terry, D. "The Intrafamilial Environment of Schizophrenic Patients: II. Marital Schism and Marital Skew," *American Journal of Psychiatry,* 114 (1957): 241–48.

Lidz, T.; Fleck, S.; Alanen, Y. O.; and Cornelison, A. "Schizophrenic Patients and Their Siblings," *Psychiatry,* 26 (1963): 1–18.

Lieberman, M. "Survey and Evaluation of the Literature on Verbal Psychotherapy of Depressive Disorders." Report prepared for the Clinical Research Branch, National Institute of Mental Health, 1975.

Lindesmith, A. R. *Opiate Addiction.* Bloomington, Ind.: Principia Press, 1947.

Lindesmith, A. R., *The Addict and the Law.* Bloomington: Indiana University Press, 1965.

Ling, W.; Holmes, E. D.; Post, G. R.; and Litaker, M. B. "A Systematic Psychiatric Study of the Heroin Addicts," *Proceedings of the Fifth National Conference on Methadone Treatment,* vol. 1. New York: The National Association for the Prevention of Addiction to Narcotics (NAPAN), March 1973, pp. 429–32.

Lippert, W. W.; and Senter, R. J. "Electrodermal Responses in the Sociopath," *Psychonomic Science,* 4 (1966): 25–26.

Litman, R. E. "Sigmund Freud on Suicide," in *Essays in Self-Destruction,* ed. E. S. Shneidman. New York: Science House, 1967.

Lobitz, W. C.; and LoPiccolo, J. "New Methods in the Behavioral Treatment of Sexual Dysfunction," *Journal of Behavior Therapy and Experimental Psychiatry,* 3 (1972): 265–71.

Loeb, J.; and Mednick, S. A. "Asocial Behavior and Electrodermal Response Patterns," in *Crime, Society and Biology — A New Look,* ed. K. O. Christiansen and S. A. Mednick. New York: Gardner Press, 1976.

Logan, J. *Josh, My Up and Down, In and Out Life.* New York: Delacorte Press, 1976.

LoPiccolo, J.; and Lobitz, W. C. "The Role of Masturbation in the Treatment of Orgasmic Dysfunction," *Archives of Sexual Behavior,* 2 (1972): 163–71.

Los Angeles Times, "5.6% of Returning GI's Used Drugs — Pentagon," *Los Angeles Times,* 22 August 1971.

Los Angeles Times, "Interview with Bert Yancey," *Los Angeles Times,* 6 April 1978.

Lovaas, O. I. *The Autistic Child: Language Development Through Behavior Modification.* New York: Irvington Publication, 1977.

Lovaas, O. I.; Berberich, J. P.; Perloff, B. F.; and Schaeffer, B. "Acquisition of Imitative Speech in Schizophrenic Children," *Science,* 151 (1966): 705–707.

Lovaas, O. I.; Freitag, G.; Nelson, K.; and Whalen, C. "The Establishment of Complex Behavior in Schizophrenic Children," *Behavior, Research and Therapy,* 5 (1967): 171–81.

Lovaas, O. I.; Koegel, R.; Simmons, J.; and Long, J. "Some Generalization and Follow-Up Measures on Autistic Children in Behavior Therapy," *Journal of Applied Behavior Analysis,* 6 (1973): 131–66.

Lovaas, O. I.; Schreibman, L.; Koegel, R.; and Rehm, R. "Selective Responding by Autistic Children to Multiple Sensory Input," *Journal of Abnormal Psychology,* 77 (1971): 211–22.

Love, L.; Kaswan, J.; and Bugenthal, D. "Differential Effectiveness of Three Clinical Interventions for Different Socioeconomic Groupings," *Journal of Consulting and Clinical Psychology,* 39 (1972): 347–60.

Lovibond, S. H. *Conditioning and Enuresis.* Oxford: Pergamon Press, 1964.

Lubetkin, B. S.; Rivers, P. C.; and Rosenberg, C. M. "Difficulties of Disulfiram Therapy With Alcoholics," *Quarterly Journal of Studies on Alcohol,* 32 (1971): 168–71.

Lundquist, F. "Influence of Ethanol on Carbohydrate Metabolism," *Quarterly Journal of Studies on Alcohol,* 32 (1971): 1–12.

Lustig, N.; Dresser, J. W.; Spellman, S. W.; and Murray, T. B. "Incest: A Family Group Survival Pattern," *Archives of General Psychiatry,* 14 (1966): 31.

Lykken, D. T. "A Study of Anxiety in the Sociopathic Personality," *Journal of Abnormal and Social Psychology,* 55 (1957): 6–10.

Lystad, M. "A Child's World: As Seen in His Stories and Drawings," Washington, D.C.: Department of Health, Education, and Welfare, Pub. no. (ADM) 74–118, 1974.

Maas, J. W. "Clinical Implications of Pharmacological Differences Among Antidepressants," in *Psychopharmacology: A Generation of Progress,* ed. M. A. Lipton; A. DiMascio; and K. F. Killam. New York: Raven Press, 1978, pp. 955–60.

McAllister, R. J.; Butler, E. W.; and Tzuen-Jan Lei. "Patterns of Social Interaction Among Families of

Behaviorally Retarded Children," *Journal of Marriage and Family,* 35(1) 1973.

McCabe, M. S. "ECT in the Treatment of Mania: A Controlled Study," *American Journal of Psychiatry,* 133 (1976): 688–91.

McClelland, D. C. *The Achieving Society.* New York: The Free Press, 1961.

McClelland, D. C.; Davis, W. N.; Kalin, R.; and Wanner, E. *The Drinking Man.* New York: The Free Press, 1972.

McCord, W.; McCord, J.; and Zala, I. K. *Origins of Crime.* New York: Columbia University Press, 1959.

MacDonald, J. *Rape Offenders and Their Victims.* Springfield, Ill.: Charles C Thomas, 1971.

McGhie, A.; and Chapman, J. S. "Disorders of Attention and Perception in Early Schizophrenia," *British Journal of Medical Psychology,* 34 (1961): 103–16.

McGlothlin, W. H. "Cannabis: A Reference," in *The Marijuana Papers,* ed. D. Solomon. New York: Signet Books, 1968.

McGlothlin, W. H. "Chemical Comforts of Man: The Future," *The Journal of Social Issues,* vol. 27, 1971.

McGlothlin, W. H.; and Arnold, D. O. "LSD Revisited: A Ten Year Follow-Up of Medical LSD Use," *Archives of General Psychiatry,* 24 (1971): 35.

McGlothlin, W. H.; Jamison, K.; and Rosenblatt, S. "Marijuana and the Use of Other Drugs," *Nature,* 228 (1970): 1227–28.

McGlothlin, W. H.; Tabbush, V.; Chambers, C.; and Jamison, K. "Alternative Approaches to Opiate Addiction Control: Costs, Benefits and Potential," United States Department of Justice Report, SCID-TR-7, 1972.

McGlothlin, W. H.; and West, L. J. "The Marijuana Problem: An Overview," *American Journal of Psychiatry,* 125 (1968): 126.

McGuire, R. J.; Carlisle, J. M.; and Young, B. G. "Sexual Deviation as Conditioned Behaviour: A Hypothesis," *Behavior Research and Therapy,* 2 (1965): 185–90.

Machover, K. *Personality Projection in the Drawing of the Human Figure.* Springfield, Ill.: Charles C Thomas, 1949.

McHugh, P. R.; and Folstein, M. F. "Psychiatric Syndromes of Huntington's Chorea: A Clinical and Phenomenological Study," in *Psychiatric Aspects of Neurological Disease,* ed. D. F. Benson and D. Blumer. New York: Grune & Stratton, 1975.

McKinney, W. T.; Suomi, S. J.; and Harlow, H. F. "Depression in Primates," *American Journal of Psychiatry,* 127 (1971): 49–56.

MacMillan, D. L. "The Problem of Motivation in the Education of the Mentally Retarded," in *Special Education in Transition,* ed. R. L. Jones and D. L. MacMillan. Boston: Allyn & Bacon, 1974.

MacMillan, D. L. *Mental Retardation in School and Society.* Boston: Little, Brown, 1977.

MacNamara, D. E. J.; and Sagarin, E. *Sex, Crime, and the Law.* New York: The Free Press, 1977.

Madakacherry, P. "Reduced Wetting, Isolate Play and Thumbsucking by a Preschool Child," unpublished manuscript, Temple University, 1974.

Maddux, J. F. "Hospital Management of the Narcotic Addict," in *Narcotics,* ed. D. M. Wilner and G. G. Kassebaum. New York: McGraw-Hill, 1965.

Mahoney, M. J. *Cognition and Behavior Modification.* Cambridge, Mass.: Ballinger Publishing Co., 1974.

Malan, D. H. "The Outcome Problem In Psychotherapy Research: A Historical Review," *Archives of General Psychiatry,* 29 (1973): 719–29.

Malan, D. H. *The Frontier of Brief Psychotherapy.* New York: Plenum Press, 1976a.

Malan, D. H. *Toward a Validation of Dynamic Psychotherapy: A Replication.* New York: Plenum Press, 1976b.

Malan, D. H.; Bacal, H. A.; Heath, E. S.; and Balfour, F. H. G. "A Study of Psychodynamic Changes in Untreated Neurotic Patients," *The British Journal of Psychiatry,* 114 (1968): 525–51.

"Marijuana and Health: Seventh Annual Report to the U.S. Congress," from the Secretary of Health, Education, and Welfare. Washington, D.C.: 1977.

Markman, H. J. "A Longitudinal Study of Premarital Couples: A Social Exchange Perspective." Paper presented at the Annual Meeting of the American Psychological Association, Toronto, September 1978.

Marks, I. "Phobias and Obsessions: Clinical Phenomena in Search of Laboratory Models," in *Psychopathology: Experimental Models,* ed. J. D. Maser and M. E. P. Seligman. San Francisco: W. H. Freeman and Co., 1977, pp. 174–213.

Marks, I. M. "Behavioural Treatments of Phobic and Obsessive-Compulsive Disorders: A Critical Appraisal," in *Progress in Behavior Modification,* vol. 2, ed. M. Hersen, R. M. Eisler and P. M. Miller. New York: Academic Press, 1975.

Marks, I. M. "Exposure Treatments: Conceptual Issues," in *Behavior Modification: Principles and*

Clinical Applications, 2nd ed., ed. W. S. Agras. Boston: Little, Brown, 1978.

Marks, I. M.; and Gelder, M. G. "Transvestism and Fetishism: Clinical and Psychological Changes During Faradic Aversion," *British Journal of Psychiatry,* 113 (1967): 711–29.

Marmor, J. "Psychoanalytic Therapy as an Educational Process: Common Denominators in the Therapeutic Approaches of Different Psychoanalytic 'Schools,' " in *Science and Psychoanalyses,* vol. 5, ed. J. H. Masserman. New York: Grune & Stratton, 1962.

Marmor, J. "New Directions in Psychoanalytic Theory and Therapy," in *Modern Psychoanalysis,* ed. J. Marmor. New York: Basic Books, 1968, pp. 1–15.

Martin, D. *Battered Wives.* New York: Pocket Books, 1977.

Masserman, J. H. *Principles of Dynamic Psychiatry.* Philadelphia: W. B. Saunders Co., 1961.

Massie, H. N.; and Beels, C. C. "The Outcome and Family Treatment of Schizophrenia," *Schizophrenia Bulletin* (Fall 1972): 24–36.

Masters, W. H.; and Johnson, V. E. *Human Sexual Response.* Boston: Little, Brown, 1966.

Masters, W. H.; and Johnson, V. E. *Human Sexual Inadequacy.* Boston: Little, Brown, 1970.

Maurer, D. W.; and Vogel, V. H. *Narcotics and Narcotic Addiction.* Springfield, Ill.: Charles C Thomas, 1967.

May, P. R. A. *Treatment of Schizophrenia.* New York: Science House, 1968.

May, R. "The Emergence of Existential Psychology," in *Existential Psychology,* ed. R. May. New York: Random House, 1961.

Mayer-Gross, W.; Slater, E.; and Roth, M. *Clinical Psychiatry,* 3rd ed. Baltimore: Williams & Wilkins, 1969.

Meador, B. D.; and Rogers, C. R. "Client-Centered Therapy," in *Current Psychotherapies,* ed. R. Corsini. Itasca, Ill.: F. E. Peacock Publishers, 1973.

Medea, A.; and Thompson, K. *Against Rape.* New York: Farrar, Straus & Giroux, 1974.

Mednick, S. A. "Electrodermal Recovery and Psychopathology," in *Genetics, Environment and Psychopathology,* ed. S. A. Mednick; F. Schulsinger; J. Higgins; and B. Bell. Oxford: North-Holland, 1974.

Mednick, S. A.; and McNeil, T. F. "Current Methodology in Research on Etiology of Schizophrenia: Serious Difficulties Which Suggest the Use of the High-Risk-Group Method," *Psychological Bulletin,* 70 (1968): 681–93.

Mednick, S. A.; and Schulsinger, F. "Some Premorbid Characteristics Related to Breakdown in Children With Schizophrenic Mothers," in *The Transmission of Schizophrenia,* ed. D. Rosenthal and S. S. Kety. Oxford: Pergamon Press, 1973, pp. 267–91.

Mednick, S. A.; Schulsinger, F.; and Venables, P. "Risk Research and Primary Prevention of Mental Illness," *International Journal of Mental Health,* in press.

Mednick, S. A.; Schulsinger, F.; and Venables, P. "The Mauritious Project," in *An Empirical Basis for Primary Prevention: Prospective Longitudinal Research in Europe,* ed. S. A. Mednick and A. E. Baert. New York: Oxford University Press, in press.

Meehl, P. E. "Schizotaxia, Schizotypy, Schizophrenia," *American Psychologist,* 17 (1962): 827–38.

Meehl, P. E. *Manual for Use with Checklist of Schizotypy Signs.* Minneapolis: University of Minnesota Medical School, 1964.

Meichenbaum, D. H. "Cognitive Modification of Test Anxious College Students," *Journal of Consulting and Clinical Psychology,* 39 (1972): 370–80.

Meichenbaum, D. H. *Cognitive-Behavior Modification: An Integrative Approach.* New York: Plenum Press, 1977.

Meichenbaum, D. H.; and Cameron, R. "Stress Inoculation: A Skills Training Approach to Anxiety Management." Unpublished manuscript, University of Waterloo, 1972.

Meichenbaum, D. H.; Gilmore, J. B.; and Fedoravicius, A. "Group Insight Versus Group Desensitization in Treating Speech Anxiety," *Journal of Consulting and Clinical Psychology,* 36 (1971): 410–21.

Meichenbaum, D. H.; and Goodman, J. "Training Impulsive Children to Talk to Themselves: A Means of Developing Self-Control," *Journal of Abnormal Psychology,* 77 (1971): 115–26.

Melamed, B.; and Lang, P. J. "Study of the Automated Desensitization of Fear." Paper read at the Meeting of the Midwestern Psychological Association, 1967, Chicago.

Mello, N. K.; and Mendelson, J. H. "A Quantitative Analysis of Drinking Patterns in Alcoholics," *Archives of General Psychiatry,* 25 (1971): 527–39.

Melville, J. *Phobias and Obsessions.* New York: Coward, McCann & Geoghegan, Inc., 1977.

Mendels, J.; Stern, S.; and Frazer, A. "Biochemistry of Depression," *Diseases of the Nervous System,* 37 (1976): 3–9.

Menninger, K. *The Crime of Punishment.* New York: Viking Press, 1968.

Menninger, K. A. *Man Against Himself.* New York: Harcourt, Brace, 1938.

Mercer, J. R. *Labeling the Mentally Retarded.* Berkeley: University of California Press, 1973.

Merton, R. K. *Social Theory and Social Structure.* New York: The Free Press, 1957.

Messinger, E.; and Zitrin, A. "A Statistical Study of Criminal Drug Addicts, Psychosis, Psychoneurosis, Mental Deficiency, and Personality Types," *Crime and Delinquency,* 11 (1965): 283–92.

Mikkelsen, M.; and Stene, J. "Genetic Counseling in Down's Syndrome," *Human Heredity,* 20 (1970): 457–64.

Milkovich, L.; and van den Berg, B. J. "Effects of Prenatal Meprobomate and Chlordiaziposide Hydrochloride on Human Embryonic and Fetal Development," *New England Journal of Medicine,* 291 (1974): 1268–71.

Mill, John Stuart. *Autobiography.* New York: Signet, 1964.

Miller, L. C.; Barrett, C. L.; Hampe, E.; and Noble, H. "Factor Structure of Childhood Fears," *Journal of Consulting and Clinical Psychology,* 39(2) (1972): 264–68.

Miller, R. G.; Palkes, H. S.; and Stewart, M. A. "Hyperactive Children in Suburban Elementary Schools," *Child Psychiatry and Human Development,* 4 (1973): 121–27.

Millichap, J. G.; and Boldrey, E. E. "Studies in Hyperkinetic Behavior. II. Laboratory and Clinical Evaluations of Drug Treatments," *Neurology,* 17 (1967): 467–72.

Minde, K.; Lewin, D.; Weiss, G.; Lairgueur, H.; Douglas, V.; and Sykes, R. "The Hyperactive Child in Elementary School: A Five-Year Controlled Follow-Up," *Exceptional Children,* 38 (1971): 215–21.

Minuchin, S. *Families and Family Therapy.* Cambridge, Mass.: Harvard University Press, 1974.

Minuchin, S.; Rosman, B. L.; and Baker, L. *Psychosomatic Families: Anorexia Nervosa in Context.* Cambridge, Mass.: Harvard University Press, 1978.

Mischel, W. *Personality and Assessment.* New York: John Wiley & Sons, 1968.

Mischler, E.; and Waxler, N. *Interaction in Families.* New York: John Wiley & Sons, 1968.

Mitford, J. *Kind and Unusual Punishment: The Prison Business.* New York: Random House, 1974.

Model Penal Code: Proposed Official Draft. Philadelphia, Penn.: American Law Institute, 1962.

Modler, H. C.; and Montes, A. "Narcotics Addiction in Physicians," *American Journal of Psychiatry,* 121 (1964): 358–65.

Mohr, J. W.; Turner, R. E.; and Jerry, M. B. *Pedophilia and Exhibitionism.* Toronto: University of Toronto Press, 1964.

Moore, K. E.; and Kelly, P. H. "Biochemical Pharmacology of Mesolimbic and Mesocortical Dopaminergic Neurons," in *Psychopharmacology: A Generation of Progress,* ed. M. A. Lipton; A. DiMascio; and K. F. Killam. New York: Raven Press, 1978.

Moore, R. "Dependence on Alcohol," in *Drug Abuse: Clinical and Basic Aspects,* ed. S. N. Pradham and S. N. Dutta. St. Louis: C. V. Mosby, 1977.

Moos, R. *Evaluating Treatment Environments: A Social Ecological Approach.* New York: John Wiley & Sons, 1974.

Moos, R. *Evaluating Correctional and Community Settings.* New York: John Wiley & Sons, 1975.

Moos, R. *The Human Context: Environmental Determinants of Behavior.* New York: John Wiley & Sons, 1976.

Morgan, C. D.; and Murray, H. A. "A Method for Investigating Fantasies: The Thematic Apperception Test," *Archives of Neurology and Psychiatry,* 34 (1935): 289–306.

Morris, J. B.; and Beck, A. T. "The Efficacy of Antidepressant Drugs," *Archives of General Psychiatry,* 36 (1974): 667–74.

Morrison, J. R.; and Stewart, M. A. "A Family Study of the Hyperactive Child Syndrome," *Biological Psychiatry,* 3 (1971): 189–95.

Morrison, J. R.; and Stewart, M. A. "Evidence for Polygenetic Inheritance in the Hyperactive Child Syndrome," *American Journal of Psychiatry,* 130(7) (1973): 791–92.

Mosher, L. R. "Psychiatric Heretics and the Extra Medical Treatment," in *Strategic Intervention in Schizophrenia: Current Developments in Treatment,* ed. R. Cancro; N. Fox; and L. Shapiro. New York: Behavioral Publications, 1974, pp. 279–302.

Moustakas, C. *Children in Play Therapy.* New York: Jason Aronson, Inc., 1973.

Mowrer, O. H. *Learning Theory and Personality Dynamics.* New York: Ronald Press, 1950.

Mowrer, O. H. "On the Dual Nature of Learning — A Reinterpretation of 'Conditioning' and 'Problem-Solving,'" *Harvard Educational Review,* 17 (1947): 102–48.

Mowrer, O. H.; and Mowrer, W. M. "Enuresis: A Method for Its Study and Treatment," *American Journal of Orthopsychiatry,* 8 (1938): 436–59.

Mucha, T. F.; and Reinhardt, R. F. "Conversion Reactions in Student Aviators," *American Journal of Psychiatry,* 127 (1970): 493–97.

Mulder, D. W. "Organic Brain Syndromes Associated With Diseases of Unknown Cause," in *Comprehensive Textbook of Psychiatry — II,* ed. A. M. Freedman; H. I. Kaplan; and B. J. Sadock. Baltimore: Williams & Wilkins, 1975.

Murphy, D. L.; Shilling, D. J.; and Murray, R. M. "Psychoactive Drug Responder Subgroups: Possible Contributions to Psychiatric Classification," in *Psychopharmacology: A Generation of Progress,* ed. M. A. Lipton; A. DiMascio; and K. F. Killam. New York: Raven Press, 1978, pp. 807–20.

Murphy, H. B. M. "The Cannabis Habit: A Review of Recent Psychiatric Literature," *Bulletin on Narcotics,* 15 (1963): 15–23.

Murphy, J. M. "Psychiatric Labeling in Cross-Cultural Perspective," *Science,* 191 (1976): 1019–28.

Myers, H. F. "Holistic Definition and Measurement of States of Nonhealth, in African Philosophy: Assumptions and Paradigms for Research on Black Persons." A compilation of papers from the First Annual J. Alfred Cannon Research Series Conference, April 28–29, 1975, Culver City, Calif.

Nameche, G. F.; Waring, M.; and Ricks, D. F. "Early Indicators of Outcome in Schizophrenia," *Journal of Nervous and Mental Disease,* 139 (1964): 232–40.

Nathan, P. E., et al. "Behavioral Analysis of Chronic Alcoholism," *Archives of General Psychiatry,* 22 (1970): 419–30.

National Center for Health Statistics. Series 11, No. 37, Washington, D.C., 1970.

National Commission on Law Observance and Enforcement. *Report on the Causes of Crime,* vol. 2, no. 13. Washington, D.C.: U.S. Government Printing Office, 1931.

National Institute of Mental Health. *Patient Care Episodes in Psychiatric Services,* 1971. Washington, D.C.: Department of Health, Education and Welfare Publication no. HSM 74–655, Statistical Note no. 92, 1973.

National Institute of Mental Health. *Living Alone.* Washington, D.C., 1974.

National Institute of Mental Health. *Research in the Service of Mental Health.* Washington, D.C., 1975.

Nawas, M. M.; Fishman, S. T.; and Pucel, J. C. "A Standardized Desensitization Program Applicable to Group and Individual Treatments," *Behavior Research and Therapy,* 8 (1970): 49–56.

Neale, J. M.; and Liebert, R. M. *Science and Behavior: An Introduction to Methods and Research.* Englewood Cliffs, N.J.: 1973.

Nicholi, A. M., ed. *The Harvard Guide to Modern Psychiatry.* Cambridge, Mass.: Belknap Press, 1978.

Nichols, J. R. "How Opiates Change Behavior," *Scientific American,* 212 (1965): 80.

Nichols, J. R., et al. "Drug Addiction I. Addiction by Escape Training," *Journal of the American Pharmaceutical Association,* XLV (1956): 778–91.

Nihira, K.; Foster, R.; Sheelhaas, M.; and Leland, H. *AAMD Adaptive Behavior Scale.* Washington, D.C.: American Association on Mental Deficiency, 1969.

Nilsson, L. *Behold Man: A Photographic Journey of Discovery Inside the Body.* Boston: Little, Brown, 1973.

Nirje, B. "The Normalization Principle and Its Human Management Implications," in *Changing Patterns in Residential Services for the Mentally Retarded,* ed. R. B. Kugel and W. Wolfensberger. Washington, D.C.: President's Committee on Mental Retardation, 1969.

Noble, E. P. "Alcohol and Adrenocortical Functioning of Animals and Man," in *Alcoholism: Progress in Research and Treatment,* ed. P. G. Bourne and R. Fox. New York: Academic Press, 1973.

Nomenclature and Statistics Task Force: American Psychiatric Association. *Diagnostic and Statistical Manual.* Washington, D.C.: American Psychiatric Association, 1977.

Noreik, K.; and Odegaard, O. "Psychoses in Norwegians: A Background of Higher Education," *British Journal of Psychiatry,* 112 (1966): 43–55.

Norris, J. L. "Alcoholics Anonymous and Other Self-Help Groups," in *Alcoholism: Interdisciplinary Approaches to an Enduring Problem,* ed. R. E. Tarter and A. A. Sugerman. Reading, Mass.: Addison-Wesley, 1976.

North, A. F., Jr. "Project Head Start and the Pediatrician," *Clinical Pediatrics,* 6 (1967): 191–94.

Noyes, A. P.; and Kolb, L. C. *Modern Clinical Psychiatry.* Philadelphia: W. B. Saunders, 1963.

O'Connor, G. *Home is a Good Place: A National Perspective on Community Residential Facilities for Developmentally Disabled Persons.* Washington, D.C.: American Association on Mental Deficiency, Monograph no. 2, 1976.

O'Connor v. Donaldson, 95 S. Ct. 2486 (1975).

O'Donnell, J. A. "Narcotic Addicts in Kentucky," Public Health Service Publication no. 1881, 1969.

O'Donnell, J. A.; and Ball, J. C., eds. *Narcotic Addiction.* New York: Harper & Row, 1966.

Office of Economic Opportunity. "Uniform Evaluation of Programs to Combat Narcotic Addiction, Final Report and Exhibit A — Data Collection Forms," Baltimore, Md.: Friends of Psychiatric Research, Inc., 1970.

Oldendorf, W. H. "The Quest for an Image of Brain," *Neurology,* 28 (1978): 517–33.

O'Leary, K. D.; and Becker, W. C. "Behavior Modification of an Adjustment Class," *Exceptional Children,* 33 (1967): 637–42.

O'Leary, K. D.; and Borkovec, T. D. "Conceptual, Methodological, and Ethical Problems of Placebo Groups in Psychotherapy Research," *American Psychologist,* 33(9) (1978): 821–30.

O'Leary, K. D.; and O'Leary, S. *Classroom Management,* 2nd ed. New York: Pergamon Press, 1977.

Olshansky, S. "Chronic Sorrow: A Response to Having a Mentally Defective Child," *Social Casework,* 43 (1962): 191–94.

Olson, L. "Post-Mortem Fluorescence Histo-Chemistry of Monoaminergic Neuron Systems in the Human Brain: A New Approach in the Search for a Neuropathology of Schizophrenia," *Journal of Psychiatric Research,* 11 (1974): 199–204.

O'Malley, J. E.; Anderson, W. H.; and Lazare, A. "Failure of Outpatient Treatment of Drug Abuse: I. Heroin," *American Journal of Psychiatry,* 128 (1972): 865–72.

Orne, M. T. "On the Social Psychology of the Psychological Experiment: With Particular Reference to Demand Characteristics and Their Implications," *American Psychologist,* 17 (1962): 776–83.

Orne, M. T.; and Scheibe, K. E. "The Contribution of Nondeprivation Factors in the Production of Sensory Deprivation Effects: The Psychology of the 'Panic Button,'" *Journal of Abnormal and Social Psychology,* 68 (1964): 3–12.

Ornitz, E. M. "Childhood Autism: A Review of the Clinical and Experimental Literature," *California Medicine,* 118 (1973): 21–47.

Orwell, G. *Such, Such Were the Joys.* New York: Harcourt Brace Jovanovich, 1945.

Osmond, H.; and Smythies, J. "Schizophrenia: A New Approach," *The Journal of Mental Science,* 98 (1953): 309–15.

Oswald, H. W. *A National Follow-Up Study of Mental Retardates Employed by the Federal Government.* Washington, D.C.: Department of Vocational Rehabilitation, 1968.

Overall, J. E.; and Gorham, D. R. "The Brief Psychiatric Rating Scale," *Psychological Reports,* 10 (1962): 799.

Papalia, D. E.; and Olds, S. W. *A Child's World: Infancy Through Adolescence.* New York: McGraw-Hill, 1975.

Parloff, M.; Waskow, I. E.; and Wolfe, B. E. "Research on the Therapist Variables in Relation to Process and Outcome," in *Handbook of Psychotherapy and Behavior Change,* 2nd ed. S. L. Garfield and A. Bergin. New York: John Wiley & Sons, 1978.

Partanen, J.; Bruun, K.; and Markkanen, T. *Inheritance of Drinking Behavior.* New Brunswick, N.J.: Rutgers Center for Alcohol Studies, 1966.

Pascal, G. R.; and Suttell, B. J. *The Bender-Gestalt Test.* New York: Grune & Stratton, 1951.

Patel, C. H. "Yoga and Biofeedback in the Management of Hypertension," *Lancet,* ii (1973): 1053.

Patel, C. H. "Twelve Month Follow Up of Yoga and Biofeedback in the Management of Hypertension," *Lancet,* i (1975): 62.

Patel, C. H.; and North, W. R. "Randomized Controlled Trial of Yoga and Biofeedback in Management of Hypertension," *Lancet,* i (1975): 62.

Patterson, G. R. "An Empirical Approach to the Classification of Disturbed Children," *Journal of Clinical Psychology,* 20 (1964): 326–37.

Patterson, G. R.; and Reid, J. B. "Reciprocity and Coercion: Two Facets of Social Systems," in *Behavior Modification in Clinical Psychology,* ed. C. Neuringer and J. Michael. New York: Appleton-Century-Crofts, 1970.

Patterson, J. H.; and Pruitt, A. W. "Treatment of Mild Symptomatic Anxiety States," in *Psychopharmacology in Childhood and Adolescence,* ed. J. M. Weiner. New York: Basic Books, 1977, pp. 169–78.

Paul, G. L. *Insight Vs. Desensitization in Psychotherapy.* Stanford: Stanford University Press, 1966.

Paul, G. L. "Insight Versus Desensitization in Psychotherapy Two Years After Termination," *Journal of Consulting Psychology,* 31 (1967): 333–48.

Pauly, I. B. "Adult Manifestations of Male Transsexualism," in *Transsexualism and Sex Reassignment,* ed. R. Green and J. Money. Baltimore: Johns Hopkins University Press, 1969, pp. 37–87.

Pavlov, I. P. *Conditioned Reflexes,* translation by G. V. Anrep. London: Oxford University Press, 1927.

Paykel, E.; and Weissman, M. "Social Adjustment and Depression: A Longitudinal Study," *Archives of General Psychiatry,* 28 (1973): 659–63.

Pederson, A. M.; Barry, D. J.; and Babigian, H. M. "Epidemiological Considerations of Psychotic Depression," *Archives of General Psychiatry, 27* (1972): 193.

Penrose, L. S. "The Effects of Change in Maternal Age Distribution Upon the Incidence of Mongolism," *Journal of Mental Deficiency Research,* 11(2) (1967): 54–57.

Perls, F. S. *Gestalt Therapy Verbatim.* Lafayette, Calif.: Real People Press, 1969.

Perls, F. S. "Four Lectures," in *Gestalt Therapy Now,* ed. J. Fagan and I. L. Sheperd. Palo Alto: Science and Behavior Books, 1970.

Pescor, M. J. *A Statistical Analysis of the Clinical Records of Hospitalized Drug Addicts.* Washington, D.C.: U.S. Government Printing Office, Public Health Reports, Supplement no. 143, 1943.

Petersen, R. C.; and Stillman, R. C., eds. *Cocaine: 1977.* Rockville, Md.: National Institute of Drug Abuse Research Monograph no. 13, 1977.

Peterson, D. R. "Behavior Problems of Middle Childhood," *Journal of Consulting Psychology,* 25 (1961): 205–209.

Peterson, G. C. "Organic Brain Syndromes Associated with Brain Trauma," in *Comprehensive Textbook of Psychiatry — II,* ed. A. M. Freedman; H. I. Kaplan; and B. J. Sadock. Baltimore: Williams & Wilkins, 1975.

Petterson, U. "Manic-Depressive Illness: A Clinical, Social and Genetic Study," *Acta Psychiatrica Scandinavica,* 269 (1977).

Pfungst, O. *Clever Hans (the Horse of Mr. Van Osten): A Contribution to Experimental, Animal and Human Psychology,* translated by C. L. Rahn. New York: Holt, Rinehart & Winston, 1911 (republished 1965).

Phillips, D. L. "Public Identification and Acceptance of the Mentally Ill," *American Journal of Public Health,* 56 (1966): 755–63.

Phillips, E. L. "Achievement Place: Token Reinforcement Procedures in a Home Style Rehabilitation Setting for Predelinquent Boys," *Journal of Applied Behavior Analysis,* 1 (1968): 213–23.

Phillips, E. L.; Phillips, E. A.; Fixsen, D. L.; and Wolf, M. M. "Achievement Place: Modification of the Behaviors of Pre-Delinquent Boys Within a Token Economy," *Journal of Applied Behavior Analysis,* 4 (1971): 45–59.

Phillips, L. "Case History Data and Prognosis in Schizophrenia," *Journal of Nervous and Mental Disease,* 117 (1953): 515–25.

Pinel, P. *A Treatise on Insanity, 1801,* translated by D. D. Davis. New York: Hafner, 1962.

Plaut, T. F. A. *Alcohol Problems: A Report to the Nation by the Cooperative Commission on the Study of Alcoholism.* New York: Oxford University Press, 1967.

Plath, S. *The Bell Jar.* New York: Harper & Row, 1971.

Platt, J. J.; and Labate, C. *Heroin Addiction.* New York: John Wiley & Sons, 1976.

Plutchik, R.; Platman, S. R.; Tilles, R.; and Fieve, R. R. "Construction and Evaluation of a Test for Measuring Mania and Depression," *Journal of Clinical Psychology,* 26 (1970): 499–503.

Pogrebin, Letty Cottin. "Do Women Make Men Violent?" *Ms.,* November 1974, p. 55.

Polatin, P.; and Fieve, R. R. "Patient Rejection of Lithium Carbonate Prophylaxis," *Journal of the American Medical Association,* 218 (1971): 864–66.

Pollack, D. "Alcohol, Coping, and Avoidance," *Journal of Abnormal Psychology,* 71 (1966): 418.

Pollin, W.; Allen, M. G.; Hoffer, A.; Stabenau, J. R.; and Hrubec, Z. "Psychopathology in 15,909 Pairs of Veteran Twins," *American Journal of Psychiatry* 126 (1969): 597–609.

Pokorny, A. D. "Suicide Rates in Various Psychiatric Disorders," *Journal of Nervous and Mental Disease,* 139 (1964): 499–506.

Pokorny, A. D.; and Prien, R. F. "Lithium in Treatment and Prevention of Affective Disorder: A VA-NIMH Collaborative Study," *Diseases of the Nervous System,* 35 (1974): 327–33.

Post, E. *Etiquette: The Blue Book of Social Usage.* New York: Funk & Wagnalls, 1940.

Post, R. M.; Kotin, J.; and Goodwin, F. K. "Effects of Sleep Deprivation on Mood and Central Amine Metabolism in Depressed Patients," *Archives of General Psychiatry,* 33 (1976): 627–32.

Power, P. W.; and Marinelli, R. P. "Normalization: The Sheltered Workshop: A Review and Proposals for Change," *Rehabilitation Literature,* 35 (1974): 66.

Pradhan, S.; and Dutta, S. *Drug Abuse: Clinical and Basic Aspects.* St. Louis: C. V. Mosby, 1977.

Pradhan, S.; and Hollister, L. "Abuse of LSD and Other Hallucinogenic Drugs," in *Drug Abuse: Clinical and Basic Aspects,* ed. S. Pradhan and S. Dutta. St. Louis: C. V. Mosby, 1977.

Prange, A. J.; Wilson, I. C.; and Knox, A. "Enhancement of Imipramine by Thyroid Stimulating Hormone: Clinical and Theoretical Implications,"

American Journal of Psychiatry, 127 (1970): 191–99.

Preble, E.; and Casey, J. J. "Taking Care of Business — The Heroin User's Life on the Street," *International Journal of the Addictions,* 4 (1969): 1–24.

President's Commission on Law Enforcement and Administration of Justice. *The Challenge of Crime in a Free Society.* Washington, D.C.: U.S. Government Printing Office, 1967.

President's Commission on Law Enforcement and Administration of Justice. *Task Force Report: Narcotics and Drug Abuse.* Washington, D.C.: U.S. Government Printing Office, 1967.

President's Commission on Law Enforcement and Administration of Justice. *The Challenge of Crime in a Free Society.* New York: E. P. Dutton, 1968.

President's Commission on Mental Health. *Task Panel Reports. Vol. III, Appendix.* Washington, D.C.: U.S. Government Printing Office, 1978.

President's Committee on Mental Retardation. *The Edge of Change — A Report to the President on MR Programs, Trends, and Innovations, with Recommendations of Residential Care, Manpower and Deprivations.* Washington, D.C.: U.S. Government Printing Office, 1968.

President's Committee on Mental Retardation. *These, Too, Must Be Equal.* Washington, D.C.: U.S. Government Printing Office, 1969.

President's Panel on Mental Retardation. *Report to the President: A Proposed Program for National Action to Combat Mental Retardation.* Washington, D.C.: U.S. Government Printing Office, 1962.

Preuss, K. *Life Time: A New Image of Aging.* Santa Cruz: Unity Press, 1978.

Prien, R. F.; Caffey, E. M., Jr.; and Klett, C. J. "Prophylactic Efficacy of Lithium Carbonate in Manic-Depressive Illness," *Archives of General Psychiatry,* 28 (1973a): 337–41.

Prien, R. F.; Klett, C. J.; and Caffey, E. M., Jr. "Lithium Carbonate and Imipramine in Prevention of Affective Episodes," *Archives of General Psychiatry,* 29 (1973b): 420–25.

Prigmore, C. S.; and Davis, P. R. "Wyatt v. Stickney: Rights of the Committed," *Social Work* (July 1973): 10–18.

Prince, V.; and Bentler, P. M. "Survey of 504 Cases of Transvestism," *Psychological Reports,* 31 (1972): 903–17.

Proctor, J. T. "Hysteria in Childhood," *American Journal of Orthopsychiatry,* 28 (1958): 394–406.

Provisional Patient Movement and Administrative Data, State and County Mental Hospital Inpatient Services, July 1, 1973–June 30, 1974. Washington, D.C.: U.S. Government Printing Office, DHEW Publication no. 75–518, Statistical Note no. 114, 1975.

Prange, A. J. "Pharmacotherapy of Depression," in *The Nature and Treatment of Depression,* ed. F. F. Flach and S. C. Draghi. New York: John Wiley & Sons, 1975.

Quay, H. C. "Psychopathic Personality as Pathological Stimulus Seeking," *American Journal of Psychiatry,* 122 (1965): 180–83.

Quay, H. C. "Patterns of Aggression, Withdrawal and Immaturity," in *Psychopathological Disorders of Childhood,* ed. H. C. Quay and J. S. Werry. New York: John Wiley & Sons, 1972.

Rabkin, J. "Public Attitudes Toward Mental Illness: A Review of the Literature," *Schizophrenia Bulletin,* 10 (1974): 9–33.

Rachman, S. "Sexual Fetishism: An Experimental Analogue," *Psychological Record,* 16 (1967): 293–96.

Rachman, S.; and Hodgson, S. "Experimentally-Induced 'Sexual Fetishism': Replication and Development," *Psychological Record,* 18 (1968): 25–27.

Rada, R. T. *Clinical Aspects of the Rapist.* New York: Grune & Stratton, 1978.

Rado, S. "The Psychoanalysis of Pharmacothymia (Drug Addiction)," *Psychoanalytic Quarterly,* 2 (1933): 1.

Rahe, R. H. "The Pathway Between Subjects' Recent Life Changes and Their Near Future Illness Reports: Representative Results and Methodological Issues," in *Stressful Life Events: Their Nature and Effects,* ed. B. S. Dohrenwend and B. P. Dohrenwend. New York: John Wiley & Sons, 1974, pp. 73–86.

Rainey, C. A. "An Obsessive Compulsive Neurosis Treated by Flooding in Vivo," *Journal of Behavior Therapy and Experimental Psychiatry,* 3 (1972): 117–21.

Ramey, C. T.; and Campbell, F. A. "Prevention of Developmental Retardation in High Risk Children," in *Research to Practice in Mental Retardation,* vol. I, ed. P. Mittler. Baltimore: University Park Press, 1977, pp. 157–64.

Raskin, A. "Depression in Children: Fact or Fallacy?" in *Depression in Childhood: Diagnosis, Treatment, and Conceptual Models,* ed. J. G. Schueterbrandt and A. Raskin. New York: Raven Press, 1977, pp. 141–46.

Rasor, R. W. "Narcotics Addiction as a Health Problem," *Police,* IX (1965).

Raush, H.; and Raush, C. *Halfway House Movement: A Search for Sanity.* New York: Appleton-Century-Crofts, 1968.

Raymond, M. J. "Case of Fetishism Treated by Aversion Therapy," *British Medical Journal,* 2 (1956): 854–56.

Read, W. *The Days of Dylan Thomas.* New York: McGraw-Hill, 1964.

Redd, W. H.; Porterfield, A. L.; and Anderson, B. L. *Behavior Modification: Behavioral Approaches to Human Problems.* New York: Random House, 1979.

Redlinger, L. J. "Dealing in Dope: Market Mechanisms and Distribution Patterns of Illicit Narcotics," Doctoral Thesis, Northwestern University, 1969.

Reich, R. "Care of the Chronically Mentally-Ill. A National Disgrace," *American Journal of Psychiatry,* 130 (1973): 911–12.

Reilley, C. "The Dog," in *Child Development Through Literature,* ed. E. D. Landau; S. L. Epstein; and A. P. Stone. Englewood Cliffs, N.J.: Prentice-Hall, 1972.

Reitan, R. M. "A Research Program on the Psychological Effects of Brain Lesions in Human Beings," in *International Review of Research in Mental Retardation,* ed. N. R. Ellis. New York: Academic Press, 1966.

Rekers, G. A. "Assessment and Treatment of Childhood Gender Problems," in *Advances in Clinical Child Psychology,* vol. 1, ed. B. B. Lahey and A. E. Kazdin. New York: Plenum Press, 1977, pp. 268–306.

Rekers, G. A.; Bentler, P. M.; Rosen, A. C.; and Lovaas, O. I. "Child Gender Disturbances: A Clinical Rationale for Intervention," *Psychotherapy: Theory, Research and Practice,* 14 (1977): 1–8.

Rekers, G. A.; Lovaas, O. I.; and Low, B. P. "The Behavioral Treatment of a 'Transsexual' Preadolescent Boy," *Journal of Abnormal Child Psychology,* 2 (1974): 99–116.

Rekers, G. A.; Willis, T. J.; Yates, C. E.; Rosen, A. C.; and Low, B. P. "Assessment of Childhood Gender Behavior Change," *Journal of Child Psychology and Psychiatry,* 18 (1977): 53–65.

Reppucci, N. D.; and Saunders, J. T. "The Social Psychology of Behavior Modification: Problems of Implementation in Natural Settings," *American Psychologist,* 29 (1974): 649–60.

Research Center for Human Relations. *Family Background as an Etiologic Factor in Personality Predisposition to Heroin Addiction.* New York: New York University, 1956.

Research Center for Human Relations. *Heroin Use and Street Gangs.* New York: New York University, 1956.

Resnick, H. L. P.; and Hathorne, B. C. *Suicide Prevention in the Seventies.* Washington, D.C.: NIMH Center for Studies of Suicide Prevention, 1973.

Resnick, J. H.; and Schwartz, T. "Ethical Standards as an Independent Variable in Psychological Research," *American Psychologist,* 28 (1973): 134–39.

Resnick, R. B.; Washton, A. M.; and Schuyten-Resnick, E. "Treatment of Opoid Dependence with Narcotic Antagonists: A Review and Commentary," in *Handbook on Drug Abuse,* ed. R. L. Dupout; A. Goldstein; and J. O'Donnell. Washington, D.C.: National Institute of Drug Abuse, 1979.

Rimland, B. *Infantile Autism.* New York: Appleton-Century-Crofts, 1964.

Rimmer, J.; Pitts, F. N., Jr.; Reich, T.; and Winokur, G. "Alcoholism. II. Sex, Socioeconomic Status, and Race in Two Hospitalized Samples," *Quarterly Journal Studies of Alcohol,* 32 (1971): 942.

Rivera, G. *Willowbrook: A Report on How It Is and Why It Doesn't Have to Be That Way.* New York: Random House, 1972.

Robbins, R. H. *The Encyclopedia of Witchcraft and Demonology.* New York: Crown Publishers, 1959.

Robins, E.; Murphy, G. E.; Wilkinson, R. H.; Gassner, S.; and Kayes, J. "Some Clinical Considerations in the Prevention of Suicide Based on a Study of 134 Successful Suicides," *American Journal of Public Health,* 49 (1959): 888–99.

Robins, L. N. "Aetiological Implications in Studies of Childhood Histories Relating to Antisocial Personality," in *Psychopathic Behaviour: Approaches to Research,* ed. R. D. Hare and D. Schalling. New York: John Wiley & Sons, 1978, pp. 255–71.

Robinson, D. *Talking Out of Alcoholism.* Baltimore, Md.: University Park Press, 1979.

Robinson, H. B.; and Robinson, N. M. "Mental Retardation," in *Carmichael's Manual of Child Psychology,* 3rd ed., ed. P. H. Mussen. New York: John Wiley & Sons, 1970.

Robinson, H. B.; and Robinson, N. M. *The Mentally Retarded Child,* 2nd ed. New York: McGraw-Hill, 1976.

Rodman, H.; and Grams, P. "Juvenile Delinquency

and the Family: A Review and Discussion," in *President's Commission on Law Enforcement and Administration of Justice, Task Force Report: Juvenile Delinquency and Youth Crime.* Washington, D.C.: U.S. Government Printing Office, 1967.

Roebuck, J. B.; and Kessler, R. G. *The Etiology of Alcoholism: Constitutional, Psychological, and Sociological Approaches.* Springfield, Ill.: Charles C Thomas, 1972.

Roethlisberger, F. J.; and Dickson, W. J. *Management and the Worker.* Cambridge, Mass.: Harvard University Press, 1939.

Rogers, C. *Three Approaches to Psychotherapy. No. 1.* Orange, Calif.: Psychological Films, 1965.

Rogers, C. R. "Client-Centered Therapy," in *American Handbook of Psychiatry,* vol. 3., ed. S. Arieti. New York: Basic Books, 1966.

Rogler, L. H.; and Hollingshead, A. B. *Trapped: Families and Schizophrenia.* New York: John Wiley & Sons, 1965.

Rorschach, H. *Psychodiagnostics: A Diagnostic Test Based on Perception.* New York: Grune & Stratton, 1942.

Rosen, A. "Differentiation of Diagnostic Groups by Individual MMPI Scales," *Journal of Consulting Psychology,* 22 (1958): 453–57.

Rosen, G. "History in the Study of Suicide," in *A Handbook for the Study of Suicide,* ed. S. Perlin. New York: Oxford University Press, 1975, pp. 3–29.

Rosen, J. *Direct Analysis: Selected Papers.* New York: Grune & Stratton, 1953.

Rosen, M.; Clark, G.; and Kizitz, M.S., eds. *The History of Mental Retardation: Collected Papers.* Baltimore: University Park Press, 1976.

Rosenberg, F. R.; and Rosenberg, M. "Self Esteem and Delinquency," *Journal of Youth and Adolescence,* 7 (1978): 279–91.

Rosenhan, D. L. "On Being Sane in Insane Places," *Science,* 179 (1973): 250–58.

Rosenthal, D. *Genetic Theory and Abnormal Behavior.* New York: McGraw-Hill, 1970.

Rosenthal, R. *Experimental Effects in Behavioral Research.* New York: Appleton-Century-Crofts, 1966.

Rosenthal, R.; and Jacobson, L. *Pygmalion in the Classroom: Teacher Expectation and Pupils' Intellectual Development.* New York: Holt, Rinehart & Winston, 1968.

Ross, A. O. *Psychological Disorders of Children.* New York: McGraw-Hill, 1974.

Ross, D. M.; and Ross, S. A. *Hyperactivity: Research,*

Theory, and Action. New York: Wiley-Interscience, 1976.

Rotter, J. B.; and Rafferty, J. E. *Manual for the Rotter Incomplete Sentences Blank, College Form.* New York: The Psychological Corporation, 1950.

Rubenstein, R.; Moses, R.; and Lidz, T. "On Attempted Suicide," *Archives of Neurological Psychiatry,* 70 (1958): 103–12.

Rubington, E. "Drug Addiction as a Deviant Career," *International Journal of the Addictions,* 2 (1967): 3–20.

Rubington, E. "Two Types of Drug Use," *International Journal of the Addictions,* 3 (1968): 301–18.

Rush, A.; Beck, A.; Kovacs, M.; and Hollon, S. "Comparative Efficacy of Cognitive Therapy and Pharmacotherapy in the Treatment of Depressed Outpatients," *Cognitive Therapy and Research,* 1 (1977): 17–37.

Rush, B. *Medical Inquiries and Observations Upon the Diseases of the Mind.* Philadelphia: Kimber and Richardson, 1812.

Rutter, M. "Prognosis: Psychotic Children in Adolescence and Early Adult Life," in *Early Childhood Autism: Clinical, Educational and Social Aspects,* ed. J. K. Wing. London: Pergamon Press, 1966.

Rutter, M. "Parent-Child Separation: Psychological Effects on the Children," *Journal of Child Psychology and Psychiatry,* 12 (1971): 233–56.

Rutter, M.; and Lockyer, L. "A Five to Fifteen Year Follow-Up of Infantile Psychosis. I. Description of Sample," *British Journal of Psychiatry,* 113 (1967): 1169–82.

Rutter, M.; Greenfeld, D.; and Lockyer, L. "A Five to Fifteen Year Follow-Up of Infantile Psychosis. II. Social Behavioural Outcome," *British Journal of Psychiatry,* 113 (1967): 1183–99.

Rutter, M.; Yule, W.; and Graham, P. "Enuresis and Behavioural Deviance: Some Epidemiological Considerations," in *Bladder Control in Enuresis,* ed. I. Kalvin; R. MacKeith; and S. Meadow. London: William Heinemann, 1973.

Sadoff, R. L. "Other Sexual Deviations," in *The Sexual Experience,* ed. B. J. Sadock; H. I. Kaplan; and A. M. Freedman. Baltimore: Williams & Wilkins, 1976.

Safer, D. J. "Drugs for Problem School Children," *Journal of School Health,* 41 (1971): 491–95.

Safer, D. J. "A Familial Factor in Minimal Brain Dysfunction," *Behavior Genetics,* 3 (1973): 175–86.

Safer, D.; Allen, R.; and Barr, E. "Depression of Growth in Hyperactive Children on Stimulant

Drugs," *New England Journal of Medicine,* 287 (1972): 217–20.

Sagarin, E. *Odd Man In.* Chicago: Quadrangle Books, 1969.

Sainsbury, P. *Suicide in London.* London: Chapman & Hall, 1955.

Sallan, S. E.; Zinberg, N. E.; and Frei, D. "Antiemetic Effect of Delta-9-Tetrahydrocannabinol in Patients Receiving Cancer Chemotherapy," *New England Journal of Medicine,* 293(16) (1975): 795–97.

Salzinger, K.; Feldman, R. S.; and Portnoy, S. "Training Parents of Brain-Injured Children in the Use of Operant Conditioning Procedures," *Behavior Therapy,* 1 (1970): 4–32.

Salzman, C. "Electroconvulsive Therapy," in *The Harvard Guide to Modern Psychiatry,* ed. A. M. Nicholi. Cambridge, Mass.: Belknap Press, 1978.

Sandifer, M. J., Jr.; Pettus, C.; and Quade, D. "A Study of Psychiatric Diagnosis," *Journal of Nervous and Mental Disease,* 139 (1964): 350–56.

Sarason, S. B.; Davidson, K. S.; Lighthall, F. F.; Waite, P. R.; and Ruebush, B. K. *Anxiety in Elementary School Children: A Report of Research.* New York: John Wiley & Sons, 1960.

Sarason, S. B.; and Doris, J. *Psychological Problems in Mental Deficiency.* New York: Harper, 1969.

Sargent, J. D.; Walters, E. D.; and Green, E. E. "Psychosomatic Self-Regulation of Migraine Headaches," *Seminars in Psychiatry,* 5(4) (1973): 415–28.

Sartorius, N.; Jablensky, A.; and Shapiro, R. "Cross-Cultural Differences in the Short-Term Prognosis of Schizophrenic Psychoses," *Schizophrenia Bulletin,* 4 (1978): 102–13.

Sartorius, N.; Shapiro, R.; and Jablensky, A. "The International Pilot Study of Schizophrenia," *Schizophrenia Bulletin,* 11 (1974): 21–34.

Schachter, J.; Kerr, J. L.; Winberly, F. C.; and Lachin, J. M. "Heart Rate Levels of Black and White Newborns," *Psychosomatic Medicine,* 36(6) (1974): 513–24.

Schachter, S.; and Latané, B. "Crime, Cognition, and the Autonomic Nervous System," in *Nebraska Symposium on Motivation,* vol. 12, ed. D. Levine. Lincoln: University of Nebraska Press, 1964, pp. 221–73.

Schaefer, E. S. "Need for Early and Continuing Education," in *Education of the Infant and Young Child,* ed. V. H. Denenberg. New York: Academic Press, 1970.

Scharfman, M.; and Clark, R. W. "Delinquent Adoles-

cent Girls: Residential Treatment in a Municipal Hospital Setting," *Archives of General Psychiatry,* 17(4) (1967): 441–47.

Scheff, T. J. "Schizophrenia as Ideology," *Schizophrenia Bulletin,* 1 (1970): 15–20.

Scher, J. "Patterns and Profiles of Addiction and Drug Abuse," *International Journal of the Addictions,* 2 (1967): 171–90.

Scherer, M. W.; and Nakamura, C. Y. "A Fear Survey Schedule for Children (FSS–FC): A Factor Analytic Comparison With Manifest Anxiety (CMAS)," *Behavior, Research, and Therapy,* 6 (1968): 173–82.

Schied, S. "Counseling With Parents of Retarded Children Living at Home," *Social Work,* 9 (1964): 86.

Schild, S. "The Family of the Retarded Child," in *The Mentally Retarded Child and His Family,* ed. R. Koch and J. Dobson. New York: Brunner/Mazel, 1971.

Schildkraut, J. J. "The Catecholamine Hypothesis of Affective Disorders: A Review of Supporting Evidence," *American Journal of Psychiatry,* 122 (1965): 509–22.

Schleifer, M.; Weiss, G.; Cohen, N.; Elman, M.; Cuejic, H.; and Kruger, E. "Hyperactivity in Preschoolers and the Effect of Methylphenidate," *American Journal of Orthopsychiatry,* 45 (1975): 38–50.

Schmale, A. H. "Giving Up as a Final Common Pathway to Changes in Health," *Advances in Psychosomatic Medicine,* 8 (1973): 20–40.

Schmauk, F. J. "Punishment, Arousal and Avoidance Learning in Sociopaths," *Journal of Abnormal Psychology,* 76 (1970): 325–35.

Schmidt, H. O.; and Fonda, C. P. "The Reliability of Psychiatric Diagnosis," *Journal of Abnormal and Social Psychology,* 52 (1956): 262–67.

Schneider, K. *Clinical Psychopathology,* translated by M. W. Hamilton. New York: Grune & Stratton, 1959.

Schneidman, B.; and McGuire, L. "Group Therapy for Nonorgasmic Women: Two Age Levels," *Archives of Sexual Behavior,* 5(3) (1976): 239–47.

Schofield, M. *The Strange Case of Pot.* Middlesex: Penguin Books, 1971.

Schortinghuis, H.; and Frohman, A. "A Comparison of Professional and Paraprofessional Success With Preschool Children," *Journal of Learning Disabilities,* 7 (1974): 245–47.

Schuckit, M. A. "Alcoholism and Sociopathy-Diagnostic Confusion," *Quarterly Journal of Studies on Alcohol,* 34 (1973): 157–64.

Schuckit, M. A., et al. "Alcoholism: Two Types of Alcoholism in Women," *Archives of General Psychiatry,* 20 (1969): 301–306.

Schuckit, M. A.; and Feighner, J. "Safety of High-Dose Tricyclic Antidepressant Therapy," *American Journal of Psychiatry,* 128 (1972): 1456–59.

Schuckit, M. A.; and Haglund, R. M. J. "An Overview of the Etiological Theories on Alcoholism," in *Alcoholism: Development, Consequences, and Interventions,* ed. N. J. Estes and M. E. Heinemann. St. Louis: C. V. Mosby, 1977.

Schueterbrandt, J. G.; and Raskin, A. *Depression in Childhood: Diagnosis, Treatment, and Conceptual Models.* New York: Raven Press, 1977.

Schulsinger, H. "A 10-Year Follow-Up of Children of Schizophrenic Mothers: Clinical Assessment," *Acta Psychologica et Neurologica Scandinavica,* 53 (1976): 371–86.

Schur, E. M. *Narcotic Addiction in Britain and America.* Bloomington: Indiana University Press, 1962.

Schuster, C. R. "Drugs as Reinforcers in Monkey and Man," *Pharmacology Review,* 27 (1975): 511.

Schuster, C. R.; and Villarreal, J. E., "The Experimental Analysis of Opioid Dependence," Proceedings of the Sixth Annual Meeting of the American College of Neuropsychopharmacology, San Juan, Puerto Rico, 1967. Washington, D.C.: U.S. Government Printing Office, Public Health Service Publication no. 1836, 1968.

Schuyler, D. *The Depressive Spectrum.* New York: Jason Aronson, 1974.

Schwartz, G. E. "Biofeedback as Therapy: Some Theoretical and Practical Issues," *American Psychologist,* 29 (1973): 666–73.

Schwartz, G. E. "Psychosomatic Disorders and Biofeedback: A Psychobiological Model of Disregulation," in *Psychopathology: Experimental Models,* ed. J. D. Maser and M. E. P. Seligman. San Francisco: W. H. Freeman, 1977, pp. 270–307.

Scott, R. *The Making of Blind Men.* New York: The Russell Sage Foundation, 1969.

Seagoe, M. *Yesterday Was Tuesday, All Day and All Night.* Boston: Little, Brown, 1964.

Seagraves, R. T.; and Smith, R. C. "Concurrent Psychotherapy and Behavior Therapy," *Archives of General Psychiatry,* 33 (1976): 756–63.

Seiden, R. H. "Campus Tragedy: A Study of Student Suicide," *Journal of Abnormal Psychology,* 71 (1966): 388–99.

Seixas, F. A. "The Course of Alcoholism," in *Alcoholism: Development, Consequences, and Interventions,* ed. N. J. Estes and M. E. Heinemann. St. Louis: C. V. Mosby, 1977.

Seligman, M. E. P. "Depression and Learned Helplessness," in *The Psychology of Depression: Contemporary Theory and Research,* ed. R. J. Friedman and M. M. Katz. New York: John Wiley & Sons, 1974 pp. 83–113.

Seltzer, M. M.; and Seltzer, G. *Context for Competence: A Study of Retarded Adults Living and Working in the Community.* Cambridge, Mass.: Educational Projects, 1978.

Selye, H. *The Physiology and Pathology of Exposure to Stress.* Montreal: Acta, 1950.

Selye, H. *The Stress of Life,* rev. ed. New York: McGraw-Hill, 1976.

Selye, H. *Stress Without Distress.* Philadelphia: J. B. Lippincott Co., 1974.

Semans, J. H. "Premature Ejaculation: A New Approach," *Southern Medical Journal,* 49 (1956): 353–57.

Senay, E. C.; and Renault, P. F. "Treatment Methods for Heroin Addicts: A Review," in *It's So Good, Don't Even Try It Once,* ed. D. E. Smith and G. R. Gay. Englewood Cliffs, N.J.: Prentice-Hall, 1972.

Sever, J.; and White, L. R. "Intrauterine Viral Infections," *Annual Review of Medicine,* 19 (1968): 471.

Shader, R. I., ed. *Manual of Psychiatric Therapeutics.* Boston: Little, Brown, 1975.

Shah, S. A. "Dangerousness: Some Definitional, Conceptual, and Public Policy Issues," in *Perspectives in Law and Psychology: The Criminal Justice System,* ed. B. D. Sales. New York: Plenum Press, 1977, pp. 91–119.

Shapiro, D.; Mainardi, J. A.; and Surwit, R. S. "Biofeedback and Self-Regulation in Essential Hypertension," in *Biofeedback: Theory and Research,* ed. G. E. Schwartz and J. Beatty. New York: Academic Press, 1977, pp. 313–47.

Shapiro, D.; and Surwit, R. S. "Learned Control of Physiological Function and Diseases," in *Handbook of Behavior Modification and Behavior Therapy,* ed. H. Leitenberg. Englewood Cliffs, N.J.: Prentice-Hall, 1976.

Shaw, C. R.; and McKay, H. *Juvenile Delinquency and Urban Areas.* Chicago: University of Chicago Press, 1942.

Sheehan, J. G.; and Martyn, M. M. "Spontaneous Recovery from Stuttering," *Journal of Speech and Hearing Research,* 9 (1966): 121–35.

Shepherd, J. *The Adams Chronicles: Four Generations of Greatness.* Boston: Little, Brown, 1975.

Shneidman, E. S. "Sleep and Self-Destruction," in *Essays in Self-Destruction.* New York: Science House, 1967.

Shneidman, E. S. "You and Death," *Psychology Today,* June (1971): 43–45, 74–80.

Shneidman, E. S. "Suicide Notes Reconsidered," *Psychiatry,* 36 (1973): 379–94.

Shneidman, E. S. *Deaths of Man.* Baltimore: Penguin Books, 1974.

Shneidman, E. S. "Suicide Among the Gifted," in *Suicidology: Contemporary Development?* ed E. S. Shneidman. New York: Grune & Stratton, 1976, p. 353.

Shneidman, E. S.; and Farberow, N. L., eds. *Clues to Suicide.* New York: McGraw-Hill, 1957.

Short, J. F.; and Nye, F. I. "Extent of Unrecorded Delinquency, Tentative Conclusions," *Journal of Criminal Law, Criminology and Police Science,* 49 (1958): 296–302.

Shulman, H. M. *Juvenile Delinquency in American Society.* New York: Harper & Row, 1961.

Siddle, D. A. T. "Electrodermal Activity and Psychopathy," in *Biosocial Bases of Criminal Behavior,* ed. S. Mednick and K. O. Christiansen. New York: Gardner Press, 1977, pp. 199–211.

Sidman, M. *Tactics of Scientific Research.* New York: Basic Books, 1960.

Siegel, M. "Unresolved Issues in the First Five Years of the Rubella Immunization Program," *American Journal of Obstetrics and Gynecology,* 124(4) (1976): 327–32.

Siegel, R. K. "An Ethological Search for Self-Administration of Hallucinogens," *International Journal of the Addictions,* 8 (1973): 373–93.

Siegel, R. K. "Cocaine: Recreational Use and Intoxication," in *Cocaine: 1977,* ed. R. C. Peterson and R. C. Stillman. Rockville, Md.: National Institute of Drug Abuse Research Monograph no. 13, 1977.

Siegler, M.; and Osmond, H. "Models of Drug Addiction," *International Journal of the Addictions,* 3 (1968): 3–24.

Simpson, D. D.; Savage, L. J.; and Sells, S. B. *Data Book on Drug Treatment Outcomes.* Fort Worth: Institute of Behavioral Research, Texas Christian University, 1978.

Sines, J. O. "Selective Breeding for Development of Stomach Lesions Following Stress in the Rat," *Journal of Comparative and Physiological Psychology,* 52 (1959): 615–17.

Sines, J. O. "Physiological and Behavioral Characteristics of Rats Selectively Bred for Susceptibility to Stomach Lesion Development," *Journal of Neuropsychiatry,* 4 (1963): 396–98.

Singer, M.; and Newitt, J. *Policy Concerning Drug Abuse in New York State. Volume 1: The Basic Study.* Croton-on-Hudson, New York: Hudson Institute, 1970.

Singer, M. T.; and Wynne, L. C. "Thought Disorder and Family Relations of Schizophrenics: III. Methodology Using Projective Techniques," *Archives of General Psychiatry,* 12 (1965): 187.

Sintchak, G. H.; and Geer, J. H. "A Vaginal Plethysmograph System," *Psychophysiology,* 12 (1975): 113–15.

Sizemore, C. C.; and Pittillo, E. S. *I'm Eve.* New York: Doubleday and Co., 1977.

Skeels, H. M.; and Dye, H. B. "A Study of the Effects of Differential Stimulation on Mentally Retarded Children," *Proceedings and Addresses of the American Association on Mental Deficiency,* 44 (1939): 114–36.

Skinner, B. F. *Science and Human Behavior.* New York: Macmillan, 1953.

Slater, E.; and Glithero, E. "A Follow-Up of Patients Diagnosed as Suffering from Hysteria," *Journal of Psychosomatic Research,* 9 (1965): 9–13.

Slavitz, H. "Transsexualism: A Radical Crisis in Gender Identity," in *Sexuality Today and Tomorrow: Contemporary Issues in Human Sexuality,* ed. S. Gordon and R. W. Libby. North Scituate, Mass.: Duxbury Press, 1976, pp. 249–60.

Sloane, R. B.; Staples, F. R.; Cristol, A. H.; Yorkston, N. J.; and Whipple, K. *Psychotherapy versus Behavior Therapy.* Cambridge, Mass.: Harvard University Press, 1975.

Smith, D. W.; and Wilson, A. A. *The Child with Down's Syndrome (Mongolism).* Philadelphia: Saunders, 1973.

Smith, J. W. "Neurological Disorders in Alcoholism," in *Alcoholism: Development, Consequences, and Interventions,* ed. N. J. Estes and M. E. Heinemann. St. Louis: C. V. Mosby, 1977.

Smith, M. B.; and Hobbs, N. "The Community and the Community Mental Health Center," *American Psychologist,* 15 (1966): 113–18.

Smith, M. J. *When I Say No I Feel Guilty.* New York: Dial Press, 1975.

Smith, M. L.; and Glass, G. V. "Meta-Analysis of Psychotherapy Outcome Studies," *American Psychologist,* 32 (1977): 752–60.

Snyder, S. H. *Madness and the Brain*. New York: McGraw-Hill, 1974.

Sobell, L. C.; Sobell, M. B.; and Christelman, W. C. "The Myth of 'One Drink,' " *Behavior Research and Therapy*, 10 (1972): 119–23.

Sobell, M. B.; and Sobell, L. C. "Individualized Behavior Therapy for Alcoholics," *Behavior Therapy*, 4 (1973): 49–72.

Sobell, M. B.; and Sobell, L. C. "Second-Year Treatment Outcome of Alcoholics Treated With Individualized Behavior Therapy: Results," *Behavior Research and Therapy*, 14 (1976): 195–215.

Solnit, A. J.; and Stark, M. H. *Mourning and the Birth of a Defective Child*. New Haven: Yale University School of Medicine, Department of Pediatrics and Child Study Center, 1961.

Sperling, M. "Dynamic Considerations and Treatment of Enuresis," *Journal of the American Academy of Child Psychiatry*, 4 (1965): 19–31.

Spielberger, C. D. "Theory and Research in Anxiety," in *Anxiety and Behavior*, ed. C. D. Spielberger. New York: Academic Press, 1966, pp. 361–98.

Spitz, R. A. *The First Year of Life*. New York: International Universities Press, 1965.

Spitzer, R. L.; and Endicott, J. "Diagno: A Computer Program for Psychiatric Diagnosis Utilizing the Differential Diagnostic Procedure," *Archives of General Psychiatry*, 18 (1968): 746–56.

Spitzer, R. L.; Endicott, J.; and Cohen, G. *The Psychiatric Status Schedule. Technique for Evaluating Social and Role Functioning and Mental Status*. New York: New York State Psychiatric Institute and Biomedics Research, 1967.

Spitzer, R. L.; Endicott, J.; and Robins, E. *Research Diagnostic Criteria RDC for a Selected Group of Functional Disorders*, 2nd ed., New York: Biometric Research, New York State Psychiatric Institute, 1975.

Spitzer, R. L.; Sheehy, M.; and Endicott, J. "DSM-III: Guiding Principles," in *Psychiatric Diagnosis*, ed. V. M. Rakoff; H. C. Stancer; and H. B. Kedward. New York: Brunner/Mazel, 1977, pp. 1–24.

Spotts, J. V.; and Shontz, F. C. *The Life Styles of Nine American Cocaine Users*. Washington, D.C.: U.S. Department HEW–NIDA Research Issues 16, DHEW Publication no. 76–392, 1976.

Srole, L.; Langner, T. S.; Michael, S. T.; Opler, M. K.; and Rennie, T. A. C. *Mental Health in the Metropolis: The Midtown Manhattan Study*. New York: McGraw-Hill, 1962.

Sroufe, L. A. "Drug Treatment of Children With Behavior Problems," in *Review of Child Development Research*, vol. 4, ed. F. D. Horowitz. Chicago: University of Chicago Press, 1975, pp. 347–406.

Stark, R.; and McEvoy, J. "III. Middle-Class Violence," *Psychology Today*, November 1970, pp. 30–31.

Steele, B. F. "The Child Abuser," in *Violence: Perspectives on Murder and Aggression*, ed. I. L. Kutash; S. B. Kutash; L. B. Schlesinger, et al. San Francisco: Jossey-Bass Publishers, 1978, pp. 285–300.

Stein, L.; and Wise, C. "Possible Etiology of Schizophrenia: Progressive Damage to the Noradrenergic Reward System by 6-Hydroxy Dopamine," *Science*, 171 (1971): 1032–36.

Steinbeck, J. *Of Mice and Men*. New York: The Viking Press, 1937.

Steiner, C. *Games Alcoholics Play*. New York: Grower Press, 1971.

Steinmetz, S. K. "Fifty-seven Families: Assertive, Aggressive, and Abusive Interaction." Unpublished manuscript, University of Delaware, n.d.

Stengel, E. *Suicide and Attempted Suicide*. Middlesex, England: Penguin Books, Ltd., 1964.

Stephens, J. H.; and Kamp, M. "On Some Aspects of Hysteria: A Clinical Study," *Journal of Nervous and Mental Disease*, 134 (1962): 305–15.

Sterman, M. B. "Neurophysiological and Clinical Studies of Sensorimotor EEG Biofeedback Training: Some Effects on Epilepsy," in *Seminars in Psychiatry*, ed. L. Birk. New York: Grune & Stratton, 1973.

Sterman, M. B. "Effects of Sensory Motor EEG Feedback Training on Sleep and Clinical Manifestations of Epilepsy," in *Biofeedback and Behavior*, ed. J. Beatty and H. Legewie. New York: Plenum Press, 1977.

Stewart, M. A.; and Olds, S. W. *Raising a Hyperactive Child*. New York: Harper & Row, 1973.

Stewart, M. A.; Pitts, F. N.; Craig, A. G.; and Dieruf, W. "The Hyperactive Child Syndrome," *American Journal of Orthopsychiatry*, 36 (1966): 861–67.

Stoller, R. J. "Parental Influences in Male Transsexualism," in *Transsexualism and Sex Reassignment*, ed. R. Green and J. Money. Baltimore: The Johns Hopkins University Press, 1969, pp. 153–69.

Stone, A. A. "Psychiatry and the Law," in *The Harvard Guide to Modern Psychiatry*," ed. A. M. Nicholi, Jr. Cambridge, Mass.: Harvard University Press, 1978, pp. 651–64.

Straus, M. A. "Levelling, Civility and Violence in the Family," *Journal of Marriage and the Family,* 36(1) (1974): 13–29.

Strauss, J. S.; and Gift, T. E. "Choosing an Approach for Diagnosing Schizophrenia," *Archives of General Psychiatry,* 34 (1977): 1248–53.

Stuart, R. "Behavioral Contracting with the Families of Delinquents," *Journal of Behavior Therapy and Experimental Psychiatry,* 2 (1971): 1–11.

Summers, M. "Malleus Maleficarum," translation. London: Puskin Press, 1951.

Sutherland, E. H. *White Collar Crime.* New York: The Dryden Press, 1949.

Sutherland, E. W. "Dependence on Barbiturates and Other CNS Depressants," *Drug Abuse: Clinical and Basic Aspects,* ed. S. N. Pradhan and S. N. Dutta. St. Louis: C. V. Mosby, 1977.

Syme, S. L. "Psychosocial Determinants of Hypertension." Paper presented at Hahnemann College's Fifth International Symposium on Hypertension, 9–12 January 1977, San Juan, Puerto Rico.

Syndulko, K. "Electrocortical Investigations of Sociopathy," in *Psychopathic Behavior: Approaches to Research,* ed. R. D. Hare and D. Schalling. Chichester, England: John Wiley & Sons, 1978, pp. 145–56.

Szasz, T. S. *The Myth of Mental Illness: Foundations of a Theory of Personal Conduct.* New York: Harper & Hoeber, 1961.

Tamayo, M. B.; and Feldman, D. J. "Incidence of Alcoholism in Hospital Patients," *Social Work,* 20(2) (1975): 89–91.

Tanay, E. "Psychiatric Study of Homicide," *American Journal of Psychiatry,* 125 (1969): 1252–58.

Tapia, F.; Jekel, J.; and Domke, H. R. "Enuresis: An Emotional Symptom?" *Journal of Nervous and Mental Disease,* 130 (1960): 61–66.

Tarasoff v. Regents of the University of California, 551 P. 2d 334, 131 Cal. Rptr. 14 (1976).

Task Force on Nomenclature and Statistics of the American Psychiatric Association. *DSM–III Diagnostic Criteria.* Washington, D.C.: American Psychiatric Association, 1978.

Task Force on Nomenclature and Statistics of the American Psychiatric Association. *Diagnostic and Statistical Manual of Mental Disorders,* 3rd ed., in press.

Taube, C. A. "Readmissions to Inpatient Services of State and County Mental Hospitals 1972," *Statistical Note 110.* Rockville, Md.: National Institute of Mental Health, November 1974.

Taylor, C. B.; Nelson, E.; Farquhar, J.; and Agras, W. S. "The Effects of Relaxation on High Blood Pressure," *Archives of General Psychiatry,* in press.

Taylor, J. A. "A Personality Scale of Manifest Anxiety," *Journal of Abnormal and Social Psychology,* 48 (1953): 285–90.

Taylor, N. *Flight From Reality.* New York: Duell, Sloan and Pearce, 1949.

Terry, C. E.; and Pellens, M. *The Opium Problem.* New York: Bureau of Social Hygiene, 1928.

Tharp, R. G.; and Wetzel, R. J. *Behavior Modification in the Natural Environment.* New York: Academic Press, 1969.

Theorell, T. "Life Events Before and After the Onset of a Premature Myocardial Infarction," in *Stressful Life Events: Their Nature and Effects,* ed. B. S. Dohrenwend and B. P. Dohrenwend. New York: John Wiley & Sons, 1974, pp. 101–18.

Thigpen, C. H.; and Cleckley, H. M. *The Three Faces of Eve.* Kingsport, Tennessee: Kingsport Press, 1954.

Third Special Report on the National Institute on Alcohol Abuse and Alcoholism. "U.S. Estimates 10 Million Are Problem Drinkers," *Los Angeles Times,* 18 October 1978.

Thompson, T.; and Schuster, C. *Behavioral Pharmacology.* New York: Prentice-Hall, 1968.

Thornburg, J. E.; and Moore, K. E. "Pharmacologically Induced Modifications of Behavioral and Neurochemical Development," in *Perinatal Pharmacology and Therapeutics,* ed. B. L. Mirkin. New York: Academic Press, 1976.

Thorndike, E. L. *Animal Intelligence.* New York: Macmillan, 1911.

Thorndike, E. L. *The Psychology of Wants, Interests and Attitudes.* New York: Appleton Century, 1935.

Thudichum, J. W. L. *A Treatise on the Chemical Constitution of the Brain.* London: Balliere, Tindall & Cox, 1884.

Tinklenberg, J. R. "Abuse of Marijuana," in *Drug Abuse: Clinical and Basic Aspects,* ed. S. N. Pradhan and S. N. Dutta. St. Louis: C. V. Mosby, 1977.

Tizard, J. *Community Services for the Mentally Handicapped.* London: Oxford University Press, 1964.

Tredgold, R. F.; and Wolff, H. H. *U.C.H. Handbook of Psychiatry,* 2nd ed. London: Gerald Duckworth & Co., 1975.

Toby, J. "Affluence and Adolescent Crime," in *President's Commission on Law Enforcement and Ad-*

ministration of Justice, Task Force Report: Juvenile Delinquency and Youth Crime. Washington, D.C.: U.S. Government Printing Office, 1967.

Tucker, G.; Harrow, M.; Detre, T.; and Hoffman, B. "Perceptual Experiences in Schizophrenic and Non-schizophrenic Patients," Archives of General Psychiatry, 20 (1969): 159–66.

Tuckman, J.; and Youngman, W. F. "Suicide Risk Among Persons Attempting Suicide," Public Health Report, 78 (July 1963): 585–87.

Turner, R. J.; and Wagenfeld, M. O. "Occupational Mobility and Schizophrenia: An Assessment of the Social Causation and Social Selection Hypotheses," American Sociological Review, 32 (1967): 104–13.

Uniform Crime Reports. Washington, D.C.: Federal Bureau of Investigation, 1977.

University of California Police Department. "What Every Woman Should Know About Rape," Los Angeles: UCLA, 1977.

U.S. Commission Report on Obscenity and Pornography. Washington, D.C.: U.S. Government Printing Office, 1970.

U.S. Journal. "Top 26 Abused Drugs," April 1978.

United States Bureau of Narcotics and Dangerous Drugs. Washington, D.C.: Unpublished data for years ending December 31, 1968, and 1969.

Vaillant, G. E. "The Prediction of Recovery in Schizophrenia," Journal of Nervous and Mental Disease, 135 (1962): 534–43.

Vaillant, G. E. "Alcoholism and Drug Dependence," in The Harvard Guide to Modern Psychiatry, ed. A. M. Nicholi. Cambridge, Mass.: Belknap Press, 1978.

Valavka, J.; Mednick, S. A.; Sergeant, J.; and Rasmussen, L. "EEGs of XYY and XXY Men Found in a Large Birth Cohort," British Journal of Psychiatry, 130 (1977): 43–47.

Vanauken, S. A Severe Mercy. San Francisco: Harper & Row, 1977.

Van Putten, T. "Why Do Patients With Manic-Depressive Illness Stop Their Lithium?" Comprehensive Psychiatry, 16 (1975): 179–82.

Van Putten, T.; Crumpton, E.; and Yale, C. "Drug Refusal in Schizophrenia and the Wish to Be Crazy," Archives of General Psychiatry, 33 (1976): 1443–46.

Van Putten, T.; and May, P. R. A. "Subjective Response as a Predictor of Outcome in Pharmacotherapy," Archives of General Psychiatry, 35 (1978): 477–80.

Vaughn, C. E.; and Leff, J. P. "The Measurement of Expressed Emotion in the Families of Psychiatric Patients," British Journal of Psychiatry, 15 (1976a): 157–65.

Vaughn, C. E.; and Leff, J. P. "The Influence of Family and Social Factors on the Course of Psychiatric Illness," British Journal of Psychiatry, 129 (1976b): 125–37.,

Venables, P. H. "The Recovery Limb of the Skin Conductance Response in 'High Risk' Research," in Genetics, Environment and Psychopathology, ed. S. A. Mednick; F. Schulsinger; J. Higgins; and B. Bell. Oxford: North-Holland, 1974.

Voegtlin, W. L.; Lemere, F.; Broz, W. W.; and O'Halleren, P. "Conditioned Reflex Therapy of Chronic Alcoholism," Quarterly Journal of Studies on Alcohol, 2 (1941): 505–11.

Vogt, D. K. Literacy Among Youths 12–17 Years. Washington, D.C.: U.S. Government Printing Office, Department of Health, Education, and Welfare Publication no. (HRA) 74–1613, 1973.

Volgyesi, F. A. " 'School for Patients' Hypnosis-Therapy and Psychoprophylaxis," British Journal of Medical Hypnotism, 5 (1954): 8–17.

Von Felsinger, J. M., et al. "Drug Induced Changes in Man: 2. Personality and Reactions to Drugs," Journal of the American Medical Association, 157 (1955): 1113.

von Krafft-Ebing, R. Psychopathia Sexualis, translated by F. S. Klaf. New York: Bell, 1965. Original 1886.

Vonnegut, M. The Eden Express. New York: Bantam Books, 1976.

Wachtel, P. Psychoanalysis and Behavior Therapy: Toward an Integration. New York: Basic Books, 1977.

Waddington, M. M. Atlas of Cerebral Angiography with Anatomic Correlation. Boston: Little, Brown, 1974.

Walinder, J. Transsexualism: A Study of Forty-Three Cases. Goteberg: Scandinavian University Books, 1967.

Walsh, B. M.; and Walsh, D. "Validity of Indices of Alcoholism. A Comment from Irish Experience," British Journal of Preventive Social Medicine, 27 (1973): 18–26.

Walsh, D. "Alcoholism in Dublin," Journal of the Irish Medical Association, 61(371) (1968): 153–56.

Watson, J. B. Psychology From the Standpoint of a Behaviorist. Philadelphia: Lippincott, 1919.

Watson, J. B.; and Rayner, R. "Conditioned Emotional Reactions," Journal of Experimental Psychology, 3 (1920): 1–14.

Watt, N. F. "Childhood and Adolescent Routes to Schizophrenia," in *Life History Research in Psychopathology,* vol. 3, ed. D. F. Ricks; A. Thomas; and M. Roff. Minneapolis: University of Minnesota Press, 1974.

Weakland, J. "The Double Bind Hypothesis of Schizophrenia and Three Part Interaction," in *The Etiology of Schizophrenia,* ed. D. D. Jackson. New York: Basic Books, 1960.

Webb, E. J.; Campbell, D. T.; Schwartz, R. D.; and Sechrest, L. *Unobtrusive Measures: Nonreactive Research in the Social Sciences.* Chicago: Rand McNally, 1966.

Wechsler, D. *The Measurement and Appraisal of Adult Intelligence,* 4th ed. Baltimore: Williams & Wilkins, 1958.

Wehr, T. A.; and Goodwin, F. K. "Biological Rhythms and Affective Illness," *Weekly Psychiatry Update Series,* 2 (1978): 2–7.

Weinberg, M.; and Williams, C. J. *Male Homosexuals: Their Problems and Adaptations in Three Societies.* New York: Oxford University Press, 1974.

Weiner, H.; Thaler, M.; Reiser, M. F.; and Mirsky, I. A. "Etiology of Duodenal Ulcer I. Relation of Specific Psychological Characteristics to Rate of Gastric Secretion (Serum Pepsinogen)," *Psychosomatic Medicine,* 19 (1957): 1–10.

Weiner, I. B., ed. *Principles of Psychotherapy.* New York: John Wiley & Sons, 1975.

Weisman, A. D.; and Worden, J. W. "Risk-Rescue Rating in Suicide Assessment," *Archives of General Psychiatry,* 26 (1972): 553–60.

Weiss, B.; and Laties, V. G. "Enhancement of Human Performance by Caffein and the Amphetamines," *Pharmacology Review,* 14 (1962): 1–36.

Weiss, J. M. "Effects of Coping Behavior in Different Warning-Signal Conditions on Stress Pathology in Rats," in *Journal of Comparative and Physiological Psychology,* 77 (1971): 1–13.

Weiss, J. M. "Psychosomatic Disorders: Psychological and Behavioral Influences on Gastrointestinal Lesions in Animal Models," in *Psychopathology: Experimental Models,* ed. J. D. Maser and M. E. P. Seligman. San Francisco: W. H. Freeman & Co., 1977, pp. 232–69.

Weissman, M. M. "Psychotherapy and Its Relevance to the Pharmacotherapy of Affective Disorders: From Ideology to Evidence," in *Psychopharmacology: A Generation of Progress,* ed. M. A. Lipton; A. DiMascio; and K. F. Killam. New York: Raven Press, 1978.

Weissman, M. M.; and Klerman, G. L. "Sex Differences and the Epidemiology of Depression," *Archives of General Psychiatry,* 34 (1977): 98–111.

Weissman, M. M.; and Myers, J. K. "Affective Disorders in a U.S. Urban Community," *Archives of General Psychiatry,* 35 (1978): 1304–11.

Weissman, M. M.; and Paykel, E. S. *The Depressed Woman.* Chicago: The University of Chicago Press, 1974.

Wells, R. A.; and Dezen, A. E. "The Results of Family Therapy Revisited: The Nonbehavioral Methods," *Family Process,* 17 (1978): 251–74.

Wender, P. H. *Minimal Brain Dysfunction in Children.* New York: Wiley-Interscience, 1971.

Werry, J. S. "The Childhood Psychoses," in *Psychopathological Disorders of Childhood,* 2nd ed., ed. H. C. Quay and J. S. Werry. New York: John Wiley & Sons, 1979a, pp. 43–89.

Werry, J. S. "Psychosomatic Disorders, Psychogenic Symptoms, and Hospitalization," in *Psychopathological Disorders of Childhood,* 2nd ed., ed. H. C. Quay and J. S. Werry. New York: John Wiley & Sons, 1979b, pp. 134–84.

Werry, J. S.; and Quay, H. C. "The Prevalence of Behavior Symptoms in Younger Elementary School Children," *American Journal of Orthopsychiatry,* 41 (1971): 136–43.

Werthman, C. "The Function of Social Definitions in the Development of Delinquent Careers," in *President's Commission on Law Enforcement and Administration of Justice, Task Force Report: Juvenile Delinquency and Youth Crime.* Washington, D.C.: U.S. Government Printing Office, 1967.

Westinghouse Learning Corporation/Ohio University. *The Impact of Head Start: An Evaluation of the Effects of Head Start on Children's Cognitive and Affective Development,* vols. I and II. Springfield, Va.: U.S. Department of Commerce (no. PD 184329), 1969.

Weyer, J. *De Praestigiis Daemonum.* Reprinted by Bibliothèque Diabolique, 1885. Original 1579.

Whalen, C. K.; and Henker, B. *The Social Ecology of Psychostimulant Treatment: A Model for Conceptual and Empirical Analysis.* Los Angeles: University of California at Los Angeles, in press.

White House Conference on Narcotic and Drug Abuse. Washington, D.C.: U.S. Government Printing Office, 1963.

Whitlock, F. A. "Depression and Suicide," in *Handbook of Studies on Depression,* ed. G. D. Burrows. Amsterdam: Excerpta Medica, 1977.

WHO Expert Committee on Drug Dependence. Sixteenth Report, WHO Technical Report Series No. 407. Geneva, 1969.

Widom, C. S. "Interpersonal Conflict and Cooperation in Psychopaths," *Journal of Abnormal Psychology,* 85 (1976): 330–34.

Widom, C. S. "A Methodology for Studying Non-Institutionalized Psychopaths," in *Psychopathic Behaviour: Approaches to Research,* ed. R. D. Hare and D. Schalling. New York: John Wiley & Sons, 1978, pp. 71–84.

Wikler, A. *Opiates and Opiate Antagonists: A Review of Their Mechanisms of Action in Relation to Clinical Problems.* Washington, D.C.: U.S. Government Printing Office, Public Health Monograph no. 52, PHS Publication No. 589, 1958.

Wikler, A. "On the Nature of Addiction and Habituation," *British Journal of Addictions,* 57 (1961): 73.

Wikler, A. "Conditioning Factors in Opiate Addiction and Relapse," in *Narcotics,* ed. D. M. Wilner and G. G. Kassebaum. New York: McGraw-Hill, 1965.

Wikler, A.; and Rasor, R. W. "Psychiatric Aspects of Drug Addiction," *American Journal of Medicine,* 14 (1953): 566.

Wilkins, J. "Suicidal Behavior," *American Sociological Review,* 32 (1967): 286–98.

Willerman, L.; Broman, S. H.; and Fiedler, M. "Infant Development, Preschool IQ and Social Class," *Child Development,* 41 (1970): 69–77.

Williams, A. F.; McCourt, W. F.; and Schneider, L. "Personality Self-Descriptions of Alcoholics and Heavy Drinkers," *Quarterly Journal on the Study of Alcohol,* 32 (1971): 310–17.

Williams, H. R.; and Johnston, W. E. "Factors Related to Treatment Retention in a Methadone Maintenance Program," *Proceedings of the Fourth National Conference on Methadone Treatment.* New York: National Association for the Prevention of Drug Addiction, 1972, pp. 439–42.

Wilner, D. M.; and Kassebaum, G. G. *Narcotics.* New York: McGraw-Hill, 1965.

Wilsnack, S. C. "The Drinking Woman: Alcohol and Sex Roles." Presented at the Second Annual Interim House Conference on Women and Alcohol, 30 October 1975, Philadelphia, Penn.

Winick, C. "The Life Cycle of the Narcotic Addict and of Addiction," *U.N. Bulletin on Naroctics,* 16(1) (1964): 1–12.

Wing, J. K. "Five-Year Outcome in Early Schizophrenia," *Proceedings of the Royal Society of Medicine,* 59 (1966): 17–23.

Winokur, G. "Mania, Depression: Family Studies, Genetics, and Relation to Treatment," in *Psychopharmacology: A Generation of Progress,* ed. M. Lipton; A. DiMascio; and K. Killiam. New York: Raven Press, 1978.

Winokur, G., et al. "Alcoholism. III. Diagnosis and Familial Psychiatric Illness in 259 Alcoholic Probands," *Archives of General Psychiatry,* 23 (1970): 104–11.

Winter, W. D.; and Ferreira, A. J. "Talking Time as an Index of Intrafamilial Similarity in Normal and Abnormal Families," *Journal of Abnormal Psychology,* 74 (1969): 574–75.

Witkin, H. A.; Mednick, S. A.; Schulsinger, F.; Bakkestrom, E.; Christiansen, K. O.; Goodenough, D. R.; Hirschhorn, K.; Lundsteen, C.; Owen, D. R.; Philip, J.; Rubin, D. B.; and Stocking, M. "XYY and XXY Men: Criminality and Aggression," *Science,* 193 (1976): 547–55.

Wold, C. I.; and Tabachnik, N. "Depression as an Indicator of Lethality in Suicidal Patients," in *The Psychology of Depression: Contemporary Theory and Research,* ed. R. J. Friedman and M. M. Katz. Washington, D.C.: V. H. Winston, 1974.

Wolf, M. M.; Phillips, E. L.; Fixsen, D. L.; Braukmann, C. J.; Kirigin, K. A.; Willner, A. G.; and Schumaker, J. "Achievement Place: The Teaching-Family Model," *Child Care Quarterly,* 5 (1976): 92–103.

Wolfensberger, W. "Counseling the Parents of the Retarded," in *Mental Retardation: Appraisal, Education and Rehabilitation,* ed. A. A. Baumeister. Chicago: Aldine Publishing Co., 1967.

Wolfensberger, W. "The Origin and Nature of Our Institutional Models," in *Changing Patterns in Residential Services for the Mentally Retarded,* ed. R. B. Kugel and W. Wolfensberger. Washington, D.C.: President's Committee on Mental Retardation, 1969, pp. 59–171.

Wolfgang, M. "Violence in the Family," in *Violence: Perspectives on Murder and Aggression,* ed. I. L. Kutash; S. B. Kutash; L. B. Schlesinger, et al. San Francisco: Jossey-Bass, 1978, pp. 238–53.

Wolfgang, M. E. "Suicide by Means of Victim-Precipitated Homicide," *Journal of Clinical and Experimental Psychopathology and Quarterly Review of Psychiatry and Neurology,* 20 (1959): 335–49.

Wolfgang, M. E.; and Ferracuti, F. *The Subculture of Violence: Towards an Integrated Theory in Criminology.* New York: Barnes & Noble, 1967.

Wolpe, J. *Psychotherapy by Reciprocal Inhibition.* Stanford: Stanford University Press, 1958.

Wolpert, E. A., ed. *Manic-Depressive Illness: History of a Syndrome.* New York: International Universities Press, Inc., 1977.

Wolraich, M.; Drummond, T.; Salomon, M. K.; O'Brien, M. L.; and Sivage, C. "Effects of Methylphenidate Alone and in Combination With Behavior Modification Procedures in the Behavior and Academic Performance of Hyperactive Children," *Journal of Abnormal Child Psychology,* 6 (1978): 149–61.

Wooden, K. *Weeping in the Playtime of Others: America's Incarcerated Children.* New York: McGraw-Hill, 1976.

Woods, J. H.; and Schuster, C. R. Reported to the Committee on Problems of Drug Dependence. Washington, D.C.: National Research Council–National Academy of Sciences, 1967.

Wright, D. J.; Moelis, I.; and Pollack, L. J. "The Outcome of Individual Child Psychotherapy: Increments at Follow-Up," *Journal of Child Psychology and Psychiatry and Allied Disciplines,* 17 (1976): 275–85.

Wright, J.; Perreault, R.; and Mathieu, M. "The Treatment of Sexual Dysfunction," *Archives of General Psychiatry,* 34 (1977): 881–90.

Wulf, H. H. *Aphasia, My World Alone.* Detroit: Wayne State University Press, 1973.

Wyatt, R. J.; Schwartz, M. A.; Erdelyi, E.; and Barchas, J. D. "Dopamine B-hydroxylase Activity in Brains of Chronic Schizophrenia Patients," *Science,* 187 (1975): 368–69.

Wyatt, R. J.; Termini, B. A.; and Davis, J. "Biochemical and Sleep Studies of Schizophrenia: A Review of the Literature: 1960–1970," *Schizophrenia Bulletin,* 4th experimental issue (1971): 45–66.

Wyatt v. Stickney, 325 F. Supp. 781 (M.D. Ala. 1971), enforced 344 F. Supp. 373 and 344 F. Supp. 387 (M.D. Ala. 1972), *Aff'd sub nom.* Wyatt v. Aderholt 503 F. 2nd 1305 (5th Cir. 1974).

Wynne, L. C.; and Singer, M. T. "Thought Disorder and Family Relations of Schizophrenics. I. A Research Study," *Archives of General Psychiatry,* 9 (1963a): 191–98.

Wynne, L. C.; and Singer, M. T. "Thought Disorder and Family Relations of Schizophrenics. II. A Classification of Forms of Thinking," *Archives of General Psychiatry,* 9 (1963b): 199–206.

Yablonsky, L. *The Tunnel Back: Synanon.* Baltimore: Penguin Books, 1967.

Yalom, I. D. "Aggression and Forbiddenness in Voyeurism," *Archives of General Psychiatry,* 3 (1960): 305.

Yalom, I. D. *The Theory and Practice of Group Psychotherapy,* 2nd ed. New York: Basic Books, 1975.

Yalom, I. E.; Green, R.; and Fish, N. "Prenatal Exposure to Female Hormones," *Archives of General Psychiatry,* 28 (1973): 554–60.

Yanagita, T., et al. Reported to the Committee on Drug Addiction and Narcotics, Washington, D.C.: National Research Council–National Academy of Sciences, 1965.

Yates, A. J. *Behavior Therapy.* New York: John Wiley & Sons, 1970.

Yates, A. J. *Theory and Practice in Behavior Therapy.* New York: John Wiley & Sons, 1975.

Young, L. D.; Suomi, S. S.; Harlow, H. F.; and McKinney, W. T. "Early Stress and Later Response to Separation in Rhesus Monkeys," *American Journal of Psychiatry,* 130 (1973): 400–405.

Young, W. C.; Goy, R. W.; and Phoenix, C. H. "Hormones and Sexual Behavior," *Science,* 143 (1964): 212–18.

Youngren, M.; and Lewinsohn, P. "The Functional Relationship Between Depression and Problematic Interpersonal Behavior." Manuscript under review, 1978.

Zeaman, D.; and House, B. J. "The Role of Attention in Retardate Discrimination Learning," in *Handbook of Mental Deficiency,* ed. N. R. Ellis. New York: McGraw-Hill, 1963, pp. 159–223.

Zeiss, R. A.; Christensen, A.; and Levine, A. G. "Treatment for Premature Ejaculation Through Male-Only Groups," *Journal of Sex and Marital Therapy,* 4 (1978): 139–43.

Zigler, E. "Developmental Versus Difference Theories of Mental Retardation and the Problem of Motivation," *American Journal of Mental Deficiency,* 73 (1969): 536–56.

Zigler, E. "Research on Personality Structure in the Retardate," in *International Review of Research in Mental Retardation,* vol. 1, ed. N. R. Ellis. New York: Academic Press, 1966, pp. 77–108.

Zilboorg, G.; and Henry, G. W. *A History of Medical Psychology.* New York: W. W. Norton & Co., 1941.

Zimring, F. E.; and Hawkins, G. J. *Deterrence: The Legal Threat in Crime Control.* Chicago: University of Chicago Press, 1973.

Ziskind, E. "The Diagnosis of Sociopathy," in *Psychopathic Behaviour: Approaches to Research,* ed. R. D. Hare and D. Schalling. New York: John Wiley & Sons, 1978, pp. 47–54.

Zitrin, C. M.; Klein, D. F.; and Woerner, M. G. "Behavior Therapy, Supportive Psychotherapy, Impramine, and Phobias," *Archives of General Psychiatry,* 35 (1978): 307–16.

Zubin, J. "But Is It Good for Science?" *The Clinical Psychologist,* 31 (1977–1978): 1–7.

Zubin, J.; Eron, L. D.; and Schumer, F. *An Experimental Approach to Projective Techniques.* New York: John Wiley & Sons, 1965.

Zubin, J.; and Spring, B. J. "Vulnerability — A New View of Schizophrenia," *Journal of Abnormal Psychology,* 86 (1977): 103–26.

Zung, W. K. "A Self-Rating Depression Scale," *Archives of General Psychiatry,* 124 (1965): 40–48.

Acknowledgments

(continued from page iv)

Excerpt, page 121: From E. J. Anthony, "A clinical evaluation of children with psychotic parents," *American Journal of Psychiatry,* vol. 125 (1969), pp. 177–184. Copyright 1969, the American Psychiatric Association.
CHAPTER 6. *Fig. 6.4:* From W. Mayer-Gros, E. Slater, and M. Roth, *Clinical Psychiatry,* Third Edition (London: Baillière Tindall, 1969). Reprinted by permission. *Table 6.1:* Adapted by permission of I. I. Gottesman. *Figure, page 131 (left):* From J. T. Benitez, "Eye Tracking and Optokinetic Tests: Diagnostic Significance in Peripheral and Central Vestibular Disorders," *Laryngoscope* 80 (1970), pp. 834–848. Reprinted by permission of The Laryngoscope Company. *Figure, page 131 (right):* From P. S. Holzman et al., "Eye-tracking Dysfunctions in Schizophrenic Patients and Their Relatives," *Archives of General Psychiatry* 31 (1974), pp. 143–151. Copyright 1974, American Medical Association. Reprinted by permission. *Figure, page 134:* From J. Zubin and B. Spring, "Vulnerability—A New View of Schizophrenia," *Journal of Abnormal Psychology,* vol. 86, no. 2 (1977), pp. 103–126. Copyright 1977 by the American Psychological Association. Reprinted by permission. *Fig. 6.5:* Adapted from S. Mednick and F. Schulsinger, "Some Premorbid Characteristics Related to Breakdown in Children with Schizophrenic Mothers," in D. Rosenthal and S. S. Kety, eds., *Transmission of Schizophrenia* (Oxford: Pergamon Press Ltd., 1968), pp. 267–291. Reprinted with permission. *Table 6.3:* Copyright © 1978 by John Wiley & Sons, Inc. Reprinted by permission of John Wiley & Sons, Inc.
CHAPTER 7. *Excerpts, pages 149, 157–158:* From Hannah Green (Joanne Greenberg), *I Never Promised You a Rose Garden.* Copyright © 1964 by Hannah Green. Reprinted by permission of Holt, Rinehart and Winston, Publishers. *Fig. 7.2:* From P. R. A. May, *Treatment of Schizophrenia* (New York: Jason Aronson, Inc., 1968). Reprinted by permission. *Fig. 7.3:* From C. E. Vaughn and J. P. Leff, *British Journal of Psychiatry,* vol. 129 (1976), pp. 125–137. Adapted by permission. *Excerpt, page 154:* From *The Eden Express* by Mark Vonnegut. © 1975 by Praeger Publishers, Inc. Reprinted by permission of Holt, Rinehart and Winston. *Excerpt, pages 156–157:* From B. D. Meador and Carl R. Rogers, "Client Centered Therapy" in R. Corsini, ed., *Current Psychotherapies,* Second Edition. Copyright © 1979 by F. E. Peacock, Inc. Reprinted by permission. *Table 7.1:* Reprinted by permission. *Excerpt, pages 160–161:* From L. R. Mosher, "Psychiatric Heretics and the Extra Medical Treatment" in Robert Cancro, M.D., *Schizophrenia: Current Developments in Treatment.* Copyright © 1974 by Behavioral Publications. Reprinted by permission of Human Sciences Press, 72 Fifth Avenue, New York, N.Y. 10011. *Table 7.2:* © 1976 by Grune & Stratton, Inc. Reprinted by permission. *Excerpt, page 165:* From D. D. Jackson, "A critique of the literature on the genetics of schizophrenia" in D. D. Jackson, ed., *The Etiology of Schizophrenia,* © 1960 by Basic Books, Inc., Publishers, New York. Reprinted by permission. *Fig. 7.5:* Alfred Eisenstadt, © Time-Life.
UNIT 3 opening photo: Martin Dain, Magnum.
CHAPTER 8. *Excerpt, page 174:* From Sylvia Plath, *The Bell Jar* (hardcover ed.). Copyright © 1971 by Harper & Row, Publishers, Inc. Reprinted by permission of Harper & Row, Publishers, Inc., and Faber and Faber Limited. *Fig. 8.1:* Martin Dain, Magnum. *Excerpt, page 178:* A selection

from *Wisdom, Madness and Folly* by John Custance. Copyright 1952 by John Custance. Reprinted by permission of Farrar, Straus and Giroux, Inc. *Fig. 8.2:* Courtesy of Dr. Dean T. Jamison, The World Bank, Washington, D.C. *Fig. 8.3:* From Frederick K. Goodwin, "The Diagnosis of Affective Disorders" in M. E. Jarvik, ed., *Psychopharmacology in the Practice of Medicine,* p. 222. Copyright © 1977 by Appleton-Century-Crofts, A Publishing Division of Prentice-Hall, Inc. Reprinted by permission of Appleton-Century-Crofts. *Excerpt, page 180, and Table 8.1:* From a draft version of *Diagnostic and Statistical Manual of Mental Disorders,* Third Edition, by permission of the American Psychiatric Association. The material appears in its final form in *Diagnostic and Statistical Manual of Mental Disorders,* Third Edition (Washington, D.C.: American Psychiatric Association, 1980). *Table 8.2:* From Aaron T. Beck, M.D., *Beck Depression Inventory.* Copyright © 1978 by Aaron T. Beck, M.D. Reprinted by permission. *Fig. 8.4:* Courtesy of Geigy Pharmaceuticals. *Excerpt, page 187:* From M. M. Weisman and G. L. Klerman, "Sex Differences and the Epidemiology of Depression," *Archives of General Psychiatry* 34 (1977), pp. 98–111. Copyright 1977, American Medical Association. Reprinted by permission. *Photo, page 193:* Harry F. Harlow, University of Wisconsin Primate Laboratory. *Table 8.3:* Copyright 1977, Spectrum Publications, Inc. Reprinted by permission. *Table 8.4:* Copyright 1977, Spectrum Publications, Inc. Reprinted by permission.
CHAPTER 9. *Fig. 9.1 and excerpt, pages 202–204:* From Emil Kraeplin in E. A. Wolpert, ed., *Manic-Depressive Illness.* Copyright 1977, by International Universities Press, Inc. Reprinted by permission of International Universities Press, Inc. *Table 9.1:* Copyright 1973, American Medical Association. Adapted by permission. *Fig. 9.2:* From G. A. Carlson and F. K. Goodwin, "The Stages of Mania: A Longitudinal Analysis of the Manic Episode," *Archives of General Psychiatry* 28 (1973), pp. 221–228. Copyright 1973, American Medical Association. Reprinted by permission. *Table 9.2:* From a draft version of *Diagnostic and Statistical Manual of Mental Disorders,* Third Edition, by permission of the American Psychiatric Association. The material appears in its final form in *Diagnostic and Statistical Manual of Mental Disorders,* Third Edition (Washington, D.C.: American Psychiatric Association, 1980). *Table 9.3:* Copyright 1971, American Medical Association. Reprinted by permission. *Table 9.4:* Reprinted by permission. *Fig. 9.3:* Drawing done by patient in the UCLA Affective Disorders Clinic. *Fig. 9.4 (top left):* The Bettmann Archive. *Fig. 9.4 (top right):* Ted Polumbaum. *Fig. 9.4 (bottom left and right):* The Bettmann Archive. *Excerpts, pages 210 and 211:* From E. J. Anthony, "The influence of a manic-depressive illness on the developing child," in E. J. Anthony and J. Benedek, eds., *Depression and Human Existence.* Copyright © 1975 by Little, Brown and Company (Inc.). Reprinted by permission.
CHAPTER 10. *Fig. 10.1:* Brown Brothers. *Excerpt, page 220:* From T. S. Eliot, *Murder in the Cathedral,* pp. 83–84. Copyright 1935 by Harcourt, Brace and Company, Inc. Reprinted by permission of Harcourt Brace Jovanovich, Inc., and Faber and Faber Ltd. *Fig. 10.3:* Museum of Modern Art. *Excerpt, pages 224–225:* From E. S. Shneidman, "Suicide Notes Reconsidered," *Psychiatry,* vol. 36 (1973), pp. 379–394. Reprinted by permission of the American Psychiatric Association. *Excerpt, pages 225–226:* From Ronald R. Fieve, M.D., *Moodswing: The Third Revolution in Psychiatry.* Copyright © 1975 by Ronald R. Fieve. By permission of William Morrow & Company. *Fig. 10.4:* United States Naval In-

stitute. *Excerpt, page 228:* From E. Stengel, *Suicide and Attempted Suicide.* Copyright © 1964, 1969 by Erwin Stengel. Reprinted by permission of Penguin Books Ltd. *Table 10.1:* Copyright 1972, American Medical Association. Reprinted by permission. *Table 10.2:* Reprinted by permission. *Table 10.3:* © 1976 by Grune & Stratton, Inc. Reprinted by permission. *Fig. 10.5:* From E. M. Brooke, *Suicide and Attempted Suicide,* Public Health Paper No. 58 (1974), p. 96. Reprinted by permission of the World Health Organization. *Table 10.5:* Copyright © 1961 by McGraw-Hill, Inc. Reprinted by permission of McGraw-Hill Book Company. *Excerpt, pages 232–233:* From N. L. Farberow and E. S. Shneidman, *A Cry For Help.* Copyright © 1961 by McGraw-Hill, Inc. Reprinted by permission of McGraw-Hill Book Company. *Excerpt, page 235:* From Quentin Bell, *Virginia Woolf: A Biography.* Copyright © 1972 by Quentin Bell. Reprinted by permission of Harcourt Brace Jovanovich, Inc., and The Hogarth Press Ltd. *Excerpt, page 237:* From Sylvia Plath, *The Bell Jar* (hardcover ed.). Copyright © 1971 by Harper & Row, Publishers, Inc. Reprinted by permission of Harper & Row, Publishers, Inc., and Faber and Faber Limited. *Fig. 10.7:* UPI.

CHAPTER 11. *Fig. 11.1:* The Bettmann Archive. *Excerpt, page 244:* From Ronald R. Fieve, M.D., *Moodswing: The Third Revolution in Psychiatry.* Copyright © 1975 by Ronald R. Fieve. By permission of William Morrow & Company. *Photo, page 245:* Courtesy of Dr. Ronald Fieve. *Fig. 11.2:* Dome Division, Miles Laboratory. *Table 11.1:* Copyright © 1977 by Appleton-Century-Crofts, A Publishing Division of Prentice-Hall, Inc. Reprinted by permission of Appleton-Century-Crofts. *Fig. 11.3:* Judith Sedwick. *Figure, page 251:* ECT Consent Form. Reprinted by permission of the Department of Mental Health of the State of California. *Excerpt, pages 255–256:* From P. M. Lewinsohn, "The behavioral study and treatment of depression" in M. Hersen, R. M. Eisler, and P. M. Miller, eds., *Progress in Behavior Modification.* © Academic Press, Inc., 1975. Reprinted by permission. *Fig. 11.6:* Lucy Cobbs, Courtesy of Beth Israel Hospital. *Excerpt, page 261:* From UCLA Neuropsychiatric Institute, *Adult Psychiatry Service Manual,* July 1978. Reprinted by permission.

UNIT 4 opening photo: Courtesy of Dr. Thomas J. Reagan, Hampton Roads Neurological Center, Inc. CHAPTER 12. *Excerpt, pages 266–267:* From Mark and Dan Jury, *Gramp* (New York: Penguin Books, 1976). Copyright © 1975, 1976 by Mark and Daniel Jury. Reprinted by permission. *Fig. 12.1:* © Mark Jury Productions. *Tables 12.1 and 12.2:* From a draft version of *Diagnostic and Statistical Manual of Mental Disorders,* Third Edition, by permission of the American Psychiatric Association. The material appears in its final form in *Diagnostic and Statistical Manual of Mental Disorders,* Third Edition (Washington, D.C.: American Psychiatric Association, 1980). *Fig. 12.2:* Courtesy of Dr. Thomas J. Reagan, Hampton Roads Neurological Center, Inc. *Excerpt, page 273:* From Friedrich Unterharnscheidt, "Boxing: Historical and Medical Aspects," *Texas Reports on Biology and Medicine,* vol. 28, no. 4, Winter 1970, pp. 421–495. Reprinted by permission. *Excerpt, pages 274–275:* From N. Geschwind, "Borderland of neurology and psychiatry," in D. F. Benson and D. Blumer, eds., *Psychiatric Aspects of Neurological Disease.* © 1975 by Grune & Stratton, Inc. Reprinted by permission. *Fig. 12.3:* Courtesy of Dr. Thomas J. Reagan, Hampton Roads Neurological Center, Inc. *Figure, page 277:* From A. L. Benton, "The Visual Retention Text as a Constructional Praxis Task," *Confinia*

Neurologica 22 (1962), pp. 141–155. Reprinted by permission of S. Karger, Publishers. *Fig. 12.4:* Courtesy of Dr. Thomas J. Reagan, Hampton Roads Neurological Center, Inc. *Excerpt, pages 280–282:* Reprinted from *Living with Chronic Neurologic Disease, A Handbook for Patient and Family,* by I. S. Cooper, M.D., with permission of W. W. Norton & Company, Inc. Copyright © 1976 by I. S. Cooper. *Fig. 12.5 (left):* Woody Guthrie Estate. *Fig. 12.5 (right):* Sygma. *Excerpt, pages 283–284:* Reprinted from *Aphasia, My World Alone* by Helen Harlan Wulf by permission of the Wayne State University Press. Copyright © 1973 by Wayne State University Press, Detroit, Michigan 48202. *Art, page 284:* From *Aphasia, My World Alone* by Helen Harlan Wulf. Courtesy of Helen Harlan Wulf. *Fig. 12.7:* Dr. Angela Folsom. *Fig. 12.8:* Courtesy Veterans Administration Hospital.

UNIT 5 opening photo: © Budd Gray. CHAPTER 13. *Excerpt, page 296:* Material is reprinted from *New Introductory Lectures on Psychoanalysis* by Sigmund Freud, translated by James Strachey; used by permission of W. W. Norton & Company, Inc. Copyright © 1933 by Sigmund Freud. Copyright renewed 1961 by W. J. H. Sprott. Copyright © 1965, 1964 by James Strachey. *Table 13.2:* © 1966 by the Board of Trustees of the Leland Stanford Junior University. Reprinted by permission of the publishers, Stanford University Press. *Fig. 13.2:* UPI. *Excerpts, pages 304–305, 309, 318–319:* From Michael J. Goldstein and James O. Palmer, *The Experience of Anxiety: A Casebook,* Second Edition. Copyright © 1963, 1975 by Michael J. Goldstein and James O. Palmer. Reprinted by permission of Oxford University Press, Inc. *Fig. 13.3:* Dr. Cunningham Dax. *Fig. 13.5 (right and left):* © Columbus Citizen Journal. *Excerpt, pages 310–311:* From *I'm Eve* by Chris Costner and Elen Sain Pittillo. Copyright © 1977 by Chris Costner Sizemore and Elen Sain Pittillo. Reprinted by permission of Doubleday & Company, Inc. *Excerpt, pages 316–317:* From D. H. Malan, H. A. Bacal, E. S. Heath, and F. H. G. Balfour, "A study of psychodynamic changes in untreated neurotic patients," *The British Journal of Psychiatry,* vol. 144, 1968, pp. 525–551. Reprinted by permission. *Table 13.6:* Copyright © 1978 by Little, Brown and Company (Inc.). Adapted by permission.

CHAPTER 14. *Fig. 14.1:* From Hans Selye, *Stress.* Copyright 1950 by Hans Selye. Reprinted by permission. *Table 14.2:* Copyright 1967, Pergamon Press, Ltd. Reprinted with permission. *Fig. 14.3:* From B. P. Dohrenwend and B. S. Dohrenwend, eds., *Stressful Life Events: Their Nature and Effects.* Copyright © 1974 by John Wiley & Sons, Inc. Reprinted by permission of John Wiley & Sons, Inc. *Fig. 14.4:* From M. J. Goldstein, "Individual Differences in Response to Stress," *American Journal of Community Psychology* 1 (1973), pp. 113–137. Reprinted by permission of Plenum Publishing Corporation. *Excerpt, page 332:* From N. Cousins, "Anatomy of an illness (as perceived by the patient)," *New England Journal of Medicine,* vol. 295 (1976), pp. 1458–1463. Reprinted by permission of The New England Journal of Medicine. *Fig. 14.5:* Henri Cartier-Bresson, Magnum. *Fig. 14.6:* From J. M. Weiss, "Effects of Coping Behavior in Different Warning-Signal Conditions on Stress Pathology in Rats," *Journal of Comparative and Physiological Psychology,* vol. 77 (1971), pp. 1–13. Copyright 1971 by the American Psychological Association. Reprinted by permission. *Table 14.3:* Adapted by permission of Elsevier North Holland, Inc. *Fig. 14.7:* From D. T. Graham et al., "Psychological response to the suggestion of attitudes specific for hives and hypertension," *Psychosomatic Medicine,* vol. 24 (1962), pp. 159–169. Reprinted by permission of Elsevier North Holland, Inc. *Table 14.4:* Copyright © 1974 by Meyer Friedman. Adapted by permission of Alfred A. Knopf, Inc. *Excerpt, page 339:* From George Frank, "Controllers Helplessly Watched PSA Jet Fall," *Los Angeles Times* (October 21, 1978). Copyright, 1978, Los Angeles Times. Reprinted by permission. *Fig. 14.8:* © Time-Life. *Fig. 14.9:* Judith Sedwick.

CHAPTER 15. *Excerpt, page 344:* From Michael J. Goldstein and James O. Palmer, *The Experience of Anxiety: A Casebook,* Second Edition. Copyright © 1963, 1975 by Michael J. Goldstein and James O. Palmer. Reprinted by permission of Oxford University Press, Inc. *Excerpt, pages 358–359:* Reprinted from *The Technique and Practice of Psychoanalysis* by R. R. Greenson by permission of International Universities Press, Inc. Copyright 1967, by International Universities Press, Inc. *Fig. 15.3:* Courtesy Carl Rogers. *Excerpt, page 363:* From B. D. Meador and Carl R. Rogers, "Client Centered Therapy," in R. Corsini, ed., *Current Psychotherapies,* Second Edition. Copyright © 1979 by F. E. Peacock, Inc. Reprinted by permission. *Excerpt, pages 364–365:* From F. S. Perls, *Gestalt Therapy Verbatim.* Copyright © 1969 Real People Press, P.O. Box F, Moab, Utah 84532. Reprinted by permission. *Excerpt, pages 366–368:* From Marvin R. Goldfried and Gerald C. Davison, *Clinical Behavior Therapy,* pp. 40–42. Copyright © 1976 by Holt, Rinehart and Winston. Reprinted by permission of Holt, Rinehart and Winston. *Fig. 15.4:* Photo Researchers, Van Bucher. *Fig. 15.5:* © Budd Gray. *Fig. 15.6:* From *Principles of Behavior Modification* by Albert Bandura. Copyright © 1969 by Holt, Rinehart and Winston, Inc. Reprinted by permission of Holt, Rinehart and Winston. *Fig. 15.8:* From N. S. Jacobson, "Problem-solving and Contingency Contracting in the Treatment of Marital Discord," *Journal of Consulting and Clinical Psychology,* vol. 45 (1979), pp. 92–100. Copyright 1979 by the American Psychological Association. Reprinted by permission. *Excerpt, pages 379–382:* From Albert Ellis, Ph.D., *Reason and Emotion in Psychotherapy.* Copyright © 1962 by the Institute for Rational Living, Inc. Reprinted by permission of Lyle Stuart, Inc.

UNIT 6 opening photo: UPI.

CHAPTER 16. *Fig. 16.2 (top):* Elliot Erwitt, Magnum. *Fig. 16.2 (bottom):* Frank Siteman. *Fig. 16.3:* Archie Lieberman, Black Star. *Excerpt, page 403:* Adapted from G. R. Gay, D. K. Wellisch, D. R. Wesson, and D. E. Smith, "The Psychotic Junkie," *Medical Insight,* vol. 4, no. 10 (1972), pp. 17–21. Copyright 1972 by Insight Publishing Co., Inc. Adapted by permission. *Excerpts, pages 417, 420–422:* From Sidney Cohen, *The Beyond Within: The LSD Story,* Revised Edition. Copyright © 1964, 1967 by Sidney Cohen. Reprinted by permission of Atheneum Publishers, Inc. *Fig. 16.4:* Dr. Peter Witt. *Excerpt, pages 422–423:* From *The Manchester Guardian* (December 3, 1969). Reprinted by permission of the Manchester Guardian. *Fig. 16.5:* Frank Siteman.

CHAPTER 17. *Fig. 17.2:* Sygma. *Excerpt, pages 435–437:* From Hervey Cleckley, *The Mask of Sanity,* Fifth Edition (St. Louis: The C. V. Mosby Co., 1976). Reprinted by permission. *Fig. 17.3:* From S. Schachter and B. Latané, "Crime, Cognition, and the Autonomic Nervous System," in D. Levine, ed., *Nebraska Symposium on Motivation, 1964.* Copyright © 1964 by the University of Nebraska Press. Reprinted by permission. *Fig. 17.4:* From R. J. Schmauk, "Punishment, Arousal, and Avoidance Learning in Sociopaths," *Journal of Abnormal Psychology,* vol. 76, no. 3, pt. 1 (1979), p. 328. Copyright 1979 by the American Psychological Association. Reprinted by permission. *Table, page 443:* From

James F. Short, Jr. and F. Ivan Nye, "Extent of Unrecorded Juvenile Delinquency: Tentative Conclusion." Reprinted by special permission of The Journal of Criminal Law, Criminology and Police Science, copyright © 1959 by Northwestern University School of Law, vol. 49, no. 4. *Fig. 17.5:* Michael Malyszko. *Fig. 17.6:* UPI. *Fig. 17.7:* UPI. *Fig. 17.8:* The Bettmann Archive. *Excerpt, pages 452–453, 455–456:* From Del Martin, *Battered Wives.* Copyright © 1976 by Del Martin. Reprinted by permission of New Glide Publications, Inc. *Excerpt, pages 454–455:* From Penelope McMillan, "Tragic Slaying in Home: Warning Signs Were Ample," *Los Angeles Times* (April 22, 1979), p. 3. Copyright, 1979, Los Angeles Times. Reprinted by permission. *Excerpt, page 456:* From B. F. Steele, "The Child Abuser," in I. L. Kutash et al., *Violence: Perspectives on Murder and Aggression* (San Francisco: Jossey-Bass, Inc., Publishers, 1978), pp. 293–294, 298. Reprinted by permission. *Fig. 17.9:* John Garrett, Woodfin Camp & Associates.

CHAPTER 18. *Excerpt, page 463:* From Alan Ebert, *The Homosexuals.* Copyright © 1976, 1977 by Alan Ebert. Reprinted by permission of Macmillan Publishing Co., Inc. *Fig. 18.1:* Charles Gatewood, Magnum. *Excerpt, pages 466–467:* From Betty Liddick, "A Transsexual's Texas Homecoming," *Los Angeles Times* (July 2, 1978). Copyright, 1978, Los Angeles Times. Reprinted by permission. *Photos, page 467:* © Canary Conn. *Fig. 18.2:* © Canary Conn. *Figure, page 471:* From B. Kutchinsky, "The effect of easy availability of pornography on the incidence of sex crimes: the Danish experience," *Journal of Social Issues,* vol. 29, no. 3 (1973), pp. 163–181. Reprinted by permission of the Society for the Study of Social Issues. *Fig. 18.3:* Michael Malyszko. *Photo, page 477:* Ariola/Eurodisc GMBH. *Excerpt, pages 478–479, 482:* From John M. Macdonald, *Rape Offenders and Their Victims* (Springfield, Ill.: Charles C Thomas, Publisher, 1975). Courtesy of Charles C Thomas, Publisher, Springfield, Illinois. *Fig. 18.4:* Globe Photos. *Fig. 18.5:* From G. G. Abel, D. H. Barlow, E. B. Blanchard, and D. Guild, "The components of rapists' sexual arousal," *Archives of General Psychiatry* 34 (1977), pp. 895–903. Copyright 1977, American Medical Association. Reprinted by permission.

CHAPTER 19. *Fig. 19.1:* Steve Hanson, Stock, Boston. *Fig. 19.2:* Ernie Herion, New York Times News Service. *Excerpt, pages 494–495 and figure, page 495:* From S. C. Hayes, K. D. Brownell, and D. H. Barlow, "The use of self-administered covert sensitization in the treatment of exhibitionism and sadism," *Behavior Therapy* 9 (1978), pp. 283–289. Reprinted by permission of the Association for the Advancement of Behavior Therapy. *Table 19.1:* Copyright 1971, Pergamon Press, Ltd. Reprinted with permission. *Excerpt, pages 500–501:* From J. Deborah Allen with E. L. Phillips, E. A. Phillips, D. L. Fixen, and M. M. Wolf, *Achievement Place: A Novel Describing a New Approach for the Community-Based Treatment of Youths in Trouble* (Lawrence, Kansas: University of Kansas Printing Service, 1973). Reprinted by permission. *Table, page 501:* Copyright 1968 by the Society for the Experimental Analysis of Behavior, Inc. Reprinted by permission. *Excerpt, pages 503–504:* From Edward Sagarin, *Odd Man In: Societies of Deviants in America,* pp. 41–42. Copyright © 1969 by Edward Sagarin. Reprinted by permission of Times Books. *Table 19.2:* Copyright © 1939, by Alcoholics Anonymous World Services, Inc. Reprinted with permission of Alcoholics Anonymous World Services, Inc. *Fig. 19.3:* Dick Bushnell, New York Times News Service. *Fig. 19.4:* Daytop Village, Inc. *Excerpts, pages 510, 513:* From Morton Bard and Dawn Sangrey, *The*

Crime Victim's Book, © 1979 by Morton Bard and Dawn Sangrey, Basic Books, Inc., Publishers, New York. Reprinted by permission. *Fig. 19.5:* From *What Every Woman Should Know About Rape,* a Scriptographic Booklet by Channing L. Bete Co., Inc., Greenfield, Mass., © 1975. Reprinted by permission. *Fig. 19.11:* Edward Hausner, New York Times News Service.

UNIT 7 opening photo: Alan Brightman, Camp Freedom, an educational/residential program of Behavioral Education Projects, Inc., Cambridge, Mass.

CHAPTER 20. *Fig. 20.2:* Alan Brightman, Camp Freedom, an educational/residential program of Behavioral Education Projects, Inc., Cambridge, Mass. *Excerpt, pages 526–527:* From Helene Brown, *Yesterday's Child.* Copyright © 1976 by Helene Brown. Reprinted by permission of the publisher, M. Evans and Company, Inc., New York, N.Y. 10017. *Fig. 20.4:* Andy French, courtesy of National Committee, ARTS FOR THE HANDICAPPED. *Fig. 20.5:* Paul M. Schrock, Freelance Photographer's Guild. *Excerpts, pages 538 and 546:* From Donald L. MacMillan, *Mental Retardation in School and Society.* Copyright © 1977 by Little, Brown and Company (Inc.). Reprinted by permission. *Fig. 20.6:* Alan Brightman, Camp Freedom, an educational/residential program of Behavioral Education Projects, Inc., Cambridge, Mass. *Photos, page 546:* Glen Suprenard and the Southshore Rehabilitation Center. *Fig. 20.7:* Baltimore Association for Retarded Citizens. *Fig. 20.8:* Valley Village.

CHAPTER 21. *Excerpts, pages 552, 553:* From D. M. Ross and S. A. Ross, *Hyperactivity: Research, Theory, and Action.* Copyright © 1976 by John Wiley & Sons, Inc. Reprinted by permission of John Wiley & Sons, Inc. *Fig. 21.1:* Judith Sedwick. *Drawings, page 564:* From *A Child's World* by Mary Lystad, National Institute of Mental Health, DHEW. *Fig. 21.4:* National Gallery of Scotland. *Excerpts, pages 569, 574:* From F. W. Eberhardy, "The view from 'the couch,'" *Journal of Child Psychology and Psychiatry,* vol. 8 (1967), pp. 257–263. Copyright 1967, Pergamon Press, Ltd. Reprinted with permission. *Fig. 21.5:* Alan Brightman, Camp Freedom, an educational/residential program of Behavioral Education Projects, Inc., Cambridge, Mass.

CHAPTER 22. *Fig. 22.2:* Doris Pinney, courtesy of Dr. Gilbert Kliman, Center for Preventive Psychiatry. *Excerpt, pages 582–583:* From V. M. Axline, "Play therapy experiences as described by child participants," *Journal of Consulting and Clinical Psychology,* vol. 14 (1950). Copyright 1950 by the American Psychological Association. *Fig. 22.3:* Linda Ferrer Rogers, Woodfin Camp and Associates. *Excerpt, pages 588–589:* From Lazarus and Abramovitz, "The use of emotive imagery in the treatment of children's phobias," *Journal of Mental Science,* vol. 108 (1962), pp. 191–195. Reprinted by permission. *Fig. 22.5:* Judith Sedwick. *Fig. 22.6 and Fig. 22.7:* Alan Brightman, Camp Freedom, an educational/residential program of Behavioral Education Projects, Inc., Cambridge, Mass. *Fig. 22.8:* Alan Grant, Lovaas Project. *Excerpt, page 597:* From O. I. Lovaas, R. Koezel, J. Simmons, and H. Long, "Some generalizations and follow-up measures on autistic children in behavior therapy," *Journal of Applied Behavior Analysis,* vol. 6 (1973), pp. 131–166. Copyright 1973 by the Society for the Experimental Analysis of Behavior, Inc. Reprinted by permission. *Excerpts, pages 598, 599:* From D. M. Ross and S. A. Ross, *Hyperactivity: Research, Theory, and Action.* Copyright © 1976 by John Wiley & Sons, Inc. Reprinted by permission of John Wiley & Sons, Inc. *Fig. 22.9:* Courtesy of Frank Porter Graham Child Development Center.

UNIT 8 opening photo: Woodfin Camp & Associates

CHAPTER 23. *Excerpt, pages 612–615:* From Celeste Durand, "Dilemma — What to Do With a '2,000-Year-Old' Man," *Los Angeles Times* (July 15, 1979). Copyright, 1979, Los Angeles Times. Reprinted by permission.

Color Sections

CHAPTER 2. *Fig. 2:* © Lennart Nilsson, *Behold Man,* Little, Brown and Co., 1974. *Fig. 3:* © National Geographic Society, Anne Krumbhaar. *Fig. 4:* Courtesy of Larry Butcher, Ph.D., UCLA.

CHAPTER 12. Fig. 1: © Lennart Nilsson, *Behold Man,* Little, Brown and Co., 1974. *Fig. 2:* © Lennart Nilsson, *Behold Man,* Little, Brown and Co., 1974. *Fig. 3:* © Dr. Niels A. Lassen, "Brain Function and Blood Flow," *Scientific American,* October 1978. *Fig. 4:* Dr. M. Waddington, *Atlas of Cerebral Angiography with Anatomic Correlation,* Little, Brown and Co., 1974.

CHAPTER 20. All from Alan Brightman, Camp Freedom, an educational/residential program of Behavioral Education Projects, Inc., Cambridge, Mass.

Photos of Drs. Goldstein and Baker on pages viii and ix are courtesy of Sybil Zaden.

Name Index

Abel, G. G., 482–483
Abramovitz, A., 588–590
Agras, W., 317
Alexander, Franz, 338, 353
Alexander, J. F., 497
Alvarez, A., 219, 222–223, 228, 239
Amir, M., 478, 481
Anthony, E. J., 210, 211
Aurelianus, Caelius, 243
Axline, Virginia, 582–583
Ayllon, T., 592
Azrin, N. H., 496

Baker, B. L., 374–375, 545, 558
Bard, M., 513
Barkley, R., 567
Barlow, D. H., 493, 494
Barraclough, B., 261
Bauer, D. H., 561
Beach, F. A., 461
Beck, A. T., 191–194, 236, 248, 252
Bell, Quentin, 235
Benson, H., 342
Bentler, P. M., 465, 468, 469
Benton, A. L., 276
Bernheim, H., 36
Bettelheim, Bruno, 573, 574
Bick, E. C., 416–417
Binet, Alfred, 522
Bleuler, Eugen, 100–105
Bleuler, Manfred, 105–107
Bootzin, R. R., 163
Bowers, M. B., Jr., 102–103, 136
Bowlby, John, 192
Braginsky, B. M., 522
Braginsky, D. D., 522
Breuer, Josef, 36–37
Brightman, Alan, 543, 544

Brown, Helene, 527
Brownell, K. D., 494
Brownmiller, Susan, 478
Brunn, K., 412–413
Budoff, M., 543
Bugenthal, D., 584
Burgess, A. W., 511

Cade, J. F. J., 247
Cameron, R., 385
Campbell, D. T., 89
Camus, Albert, 227
Cannon, Walter B., 335
Carlisle, J. M., 473
Carlson, G. A., 205–206
Casey, J. J., 406
Castenada, Carlos, 125
Chambers, C., 402
Chapman, J. S., 104, 105
Chapman, L. J., 104
Charcot, Jean Martin, 35–37
Chein, I., 402
Churchill, Winston, 225–226
Claghorn, J. L., 404
Clark, R. E., 144
Cleckley, H., 435–438
Clinard, M. B., 406
Cloward, R. A., 405–406
Cobb, S., 334
Cohen, D. C., 374–375
Cohen, L., 543
Cohen, S., 420–422, 544
Compton, R. D., 557
Connelly, Thomas L., 186
Conry, J., 538
Cooper, B., 316
Cooper, I. S., 280–282
Cousins, Norman, 332

Cowen, E. L., 603
Coyne, J. C., 184
Creak, M., 572

Davidson, Terry, 512, 514
Davis, J. M., 248
Davis, V. E., 412
DeLong, 330
de Sade, Marquis, 477
Dever, R. B., 538
Ditman, K. S., 420
Dole, V. P., 404, 508
Donaldson, Kenneth, 609–610
Down, Langdon, 528
Dunbar, F., 338
Dunham, H. W., 144, 145
Durant, Celeste, 615
Durkheim, Emile, 226–227
Dye, H. B., 82–84, 92

Eberhardy, F., 569, 574
Ebert, Alan, 463
Eisenberg, L., 562–563, 573, 575, 576
Ellis, Albert, 378–382
Ellison, G. D., 86
Emery, R. D., 620
Empedocles, 25
Endicott, J., 118
Ennis, B. J., 620
Epstein, S., 297
Ervin, F. R., 288–289
Esdaile, 36
Evans, Margiad, 288
Eysenck, Hans J., 365–366, 377, 383

Fairweather, G. E., 168
Faris, R. E. L., 144
Fenz, W. D., 297

Ferracut, F., 482
Ferster, C., 190, 573
Fieve, Ronald R., 225, 244, 246
Fölling, A., 532
Folstein, M. F., 280
Ford, C. S., 461
Frank, Anne, 295
Freedman, B., 104
Freud, Anna, 580
Freud, Sigmund, 36–42, 48, 76, 188–189,
     222–223, 226, 296, 303, 308, 317, 345,
     353, 354, 357, 388, 414–415
Friedman, M., 338, 340

Gage, Phineas P., 274
Galen, 25–26, 395
Gayford, J. J., 451
Gebhard, P. H., 476
Gelder, M. G., 491
Gelles, R. J., 449
Gerard, D. I., 141
Gerard, D. L., 402
Gergen, K. J., 93–94
Gerner, R. H., 247, 284–285
Glaser, D., 488
Glass, G. V., 383
Glithero, E., 308
Glueck, E. T., 446
Glueck, S., 446
Goldstein, A., 417
Goldstein, L., 543
Goldstein, M. J., 168–170, 471
Goodman, J., 592, 594
Goodwin, D. W., 413
Goodwin, F. K., 205–206
Gottlieb, J., 543
Gottman, J., 493
Graham, D. T., 336–337
Grant, I., 407
Graubard, P. S., 596
Green, R., 468
Greenfeld, J., 553
Greenson, R. R., 358–359
Griesinger, Wilhelm, 26
Grossman, F. K., 528
Gunderson, J. G., 314–316

Hammen, C., 184, 186
Handel, George Frederick, 247
Hare, R. D., 441
Harlow, H., 86
Harlow, M. K., 86
Harris, J. G., 505–506
Hart, J. H., 300
Hastings, J., 567
Hayes, S. C., 494
Heber, R. F., 538
Hersov, L. A., 563
Hess, R. D., 539
Hewitt, L. E., 442
Hippocrates, 25, 31
Hitler, Adolf, 520
Hobbs, N., 578
Hofmann, A., 418
Hogarty, G. E., 168–170

Hollingshead, A. B., 56, 143, 144
Holmes, F. B., 82, 560
Holmes, T. H., 328–330
Holstrom, L. L., 511
Holzman, Phillip S., 130
Horney, Karen, 296
Hunt, G. M., 496
Hutchings, B., 432–433

Jacobson, Edmund, 369
Jacobson, L., 72
Jacobson, N. S., 376, 377
Jamison, K. R., 214, 247
Janet, Pierre, 308
Jenkins, R. L., 442
Jensen, A. R., 538–539
Jersild, A. T., 82, 560
Johnson, Frank, 616
Johnson, S. M., 447
Johnson, V. E., 344–346, 379–381
Johnston, W. E., 509
Jones, Mary Cover, 588
Jones, R. T., 418
Jorgensen, Christine, 465

Kaij, L., 412
Kaiser, S., 417
Kanner, Leo, 568–569, 571–573
Kaplan, H. B., 445
Kaplan, H. S., 344
Kaswan, J., 584
Kaufman, B. N., 571, 572
Kaufman, I. C., 192
Kazdin, A. E., 163
Kelman, H. C., 92, 93
Kennedy, W. A., 563
Kernberg, O. F., 357
Khazan, N., 402
Kierkegaard, Sören, 179, 297
Kimball, Wendy, 547–548
Kinsey, Alfred, 461, 475
Klaber, M. M., 80
Klein, D. F., 248, 384
Klein, Melanie, 580–582
Klerman, G. L., 186, 187
Knobloch, H., 535
Kohen, W., 164
Kohn, M. L., 143
Kolb, L., 405
Kolb, L. C., 110
Kornesky, C., 402
Kraepelin, Emil, 10, 76, 100, 113, 202–
     203, 214
Krafft-Ebing, R. von, 470
Kramer, Morton, 111, 232–234
Krapfl, J. E., 374

Lacey, J. I., 341
Laing, Ronald D., 117, 138, 158–159
Lang, P. J., 300
Langley, R., 451
Latané, B., 439
Laties, V. G., 417
Lazarus, A. A., 588–590
Lazarus, R. S., 330

Lee, Robert E., 186
Leff, J. P., 121
Lemere, F., 492
Lester, D., 237
Lester, G., 237
Levenson, H. S., 416–417
Levitt, E., 583, 584
Levy, R. C., 451
Lewinsohn, P., 184, 190
Lidz, T., 139, 141, 142
Liebeault, A. A., 36
Liebert, R. M., 92
Lincoln, Abraham, 186, 225
Lobitz, G. K., 447
Lobitz, W. C., 380
Loeb, J., 440
Logan, Josh, 210
LoPiccolo, J., 380
Lovaas, O. Ivar, 575, 594–597
Love, L., 584
Lovibond, S. H., 557
Lykken, D. T., 438–439

McCabe, M. S., 249–250
McClelland, David C., 61
MacDonald, J., 482
McGhie, A., 104, 105
McGlothlin, W. H., 424–425
McGuire, R. J., 473
McHugh, P. R., 280
McKay, H., 433
MacMillan, D. L., 538, 545, 546
MacNamara, D. E. J., 473
Maddux, J. F., 401
Malan, D. H., 316, 383
Markkanen, T., 412–413
Markman, H. J., 376, 493
Marks, I. M., 374, 491
Masters, W. H., 344–346, 379–381
May, P. R. A., 153, 168
May, Rollo, 360
Mednick, S. A., 81–82, 134–136, 170–
     171, 432–433, 440
Meehl, P. E., 117, 131
Meichenbaum, D. H., 382–383, 385, 592,
     594
Melamed, B. G., 300
Merton, R. K., 445
Mesmer, Friedrich Anton, 35
Mill, John Stuart, 236–237
Minuchin, Salvador, 336, 359, 585–586
Mitford, J., 92
Modler, H. C., 401
Montes, A., 401
Moos, R., 67–68
Morris, J. B., 248
Mowrer, O. H., 320, 368, 557
Mowrer, W. M., 557
Mucha, T. F., 308, 320
Murphy, Jane, 16

Nameche, G. F., 141
Nawas, M. M., 374
Neale, J. M., 92
Nichols, J. R., 404

Nirje, B., 549
Noyes, A. P., 110
Nyswander, M. E., 404, 508

Ohlin, L. E., 405–406
Olshansky, S., 527
Orne, Martin T., 75
Orwell, George, 552–553
Osler, 540

Parsons, B. V., 497
Partanen, J., 412–413
Pasamanick, B., 535
Pasteur, Louis, 12, 26
Paul, Gordon L., 164, 372
Pavlov, Ivan P., 43, 86
Paykel, E., 188–189
Perls, Fritz S., 363–365
Peters, S., 184, 186
Pfungst, O., 72
Phillips, D. L., 620
Phillips, Ellery, 500
Pinel, Philippe, 46, 48
Plath, Sylvia, 236, 237
Pokorny, A. D., 234, 261
Port, 413
Poterfield, 413
Preble, E., 406
Prien, R. F., 261
Prince, V., 465, 468, 469

Quay, H. C., 565

Rabkin, J., 621
Rachman, S., 473
Rada, R. T., 482–484
Rahe, R. H., 328–330
Raskin, A., 558
Rayner, R., 320
Redlich, F. C., 144
Reinhardt, R. F., 308, 320
Reppucci, N. D., 498
Resnick, J. H., 94
Rimland, B., 573, 575
Ring, 402
Robins, E., 234
Robins, L. N., 444
Robinson, H. B., 531, 541
Robinson, N. M., 531, 541
Rogers, Carl, 156–157, 361–363
Rogler, L. H., 56, 143
Rorschach, Hermann, 60
Rose, R. M., 334
Rosenberg, F. R., 445
Rosenberg, M., 445
Rosenfeld, E., 402
Rosenhan, D. L., 17, 19
Rosenman, R. H., 338, 340
Rosenthal, D., 133, 147
Rosenthal, Robert, 72

Ross, H. L., 89
Rowland, Kay, 285–286
Rubenstein, R., 236
Rubington, E., 406
Rush, Benjamin, 24–25
Rushing, 145
Rutter, M., 575

Sacher-Masoch, Count Leopold von, 477
Safer, D., 599
Sagarin, E., 473
Sainsbury, P., 235
Sangrey, D., 513
Sarason, S. B., 540
Saunders, J. T., 374–375
Schacter, J., 334
Schacter, S., 439
Schild, S., 527
Schildkraut, J. J., 195
Schliefer, M., 566
Schmauk, F. J., 441
Schulsinger, F., 81–82, 170–171
Schwartz, T., 94
Seiden, R. H., 237
Seixas, F. A., 408
Seligman, M. E. P., 191
Seltzer, G. B., 545
Seltzer, M. M., 545
Selye, Hans, 326, 328, 332
Senay, E. C., 509
Shaw, C. R., 433, 447–448
Shipman, V. C., 539
Shneidman, Edwin S., 222, 224–225, 228, 229, 237, 262
Sidman, M., 87
Siegal, J., 141
Siegel, R. K., 416
Singer, M. T., 137–138, 142, 146, 314
Skeels, H. M., 82–84, 92
Skinner, B. F., 43–44, 189–190
Slater, E., 308
Sloane, R. B., 366, 383
Smith, M. B., 578
Smith, M. L., 383
Sobell, L. C., 496
Sobell, M. B., 496
Solnit, A. J., 527
Southcombe, 234
Sperling, M., 557
Spitz, Renée, 192
Spitzer, R. L., 118
Spring, B. J., 134
Srole, L., 7–8, 21, 77, 144
Stanley, J. C., 89
Stark, M. H., 527
Steel, Brandt F., 456
Steinbeck, John, 540–541
Stengel, E., 228, 237, 239
Stoller, R. J., 469
Stone, Alan, 614–615
Stuart, R., 496

Sutherland, Edwin H., 430
Sylph, J., 316
Syndulko, K., 441
Szasz, Thomas S., 117

Tabachnik, N., 236
Tharp, R. G., 499
Thomas, Dylan, 407
Thudichum, J. W. L., 126
Tredgold, R. F., 221
Tuke, William, 48
Tunney, Gene, 273
Turner, R. J., 145

Valachi, Joseph, 431
Van Putten, T., 153
Vaughn, C. E., 121
Voegtlin, W., 492
Vonnegut, Mark, 106–107, 154

Wagenfeld, M. O., 145
Walsch, M. J., 412
Watson, John B., 43, 320
Watt, N. F., 81
Webb, Eugene J., 77
Weiner, H., 341
Weisman, A. D., 229
Weiss, B., 417
Weiss, J. M., 334, 335
Weissman, M. M., 186–189
Werry, J. S., 565
Wetzel, R. J., 499
Weyer, Johann, 34–35
Widom, C. S., 438, 441
Wikler, A., 402, 403, 405
Williams, H. R., 509
Wing, J. K., 108
Winokur, G., 207, 216
Witkin, H. A., 434
Woener, M. G., 384
Wold, C. I., 236
Wolf, Montrose, 500
Wolfensberger, W., 526
Wolff, H. H., 221
Wolfgang, M. E., 482
Wolpe, Joseph, 43, 45, 370, 374, 379
Woolf, Virginia, 235
Worden, J. W., 229
Wulf, Helen H., 283–284
Wyatt, Ricky, 616
Wynne, L. C., 82, 137–138, 142, 146

Yalom, I. E., 468
Yancey, Bert, 204–205
Yates, A. J., 374
Young, B. G., 473

Zigler, E., 541
Zitrin, C. M., 384
Zubin, J., 134

Subject Index

ABAB (ABA'B') design, 88
Abnormal behavior, 4–22
  characteristics of, 8–10
  classification of, 10–19
    criticism of, 15
    DSM-III system of, 12–15 (*see also*
      DSM-III diagnostic criteria)
    labeling theory, 15–19
    purposes of, 10–12
  definition of, 6–8
  disciplines involved in study and treat-
    ment of, 11
  incidence of, 7–8, 21
Accepting Individual Differences (curric-
  ulum), 544
Access to mental health services, 607–
  609
Achievement Place, 500–502
Acrophobia, desensitization therapy for,
  370–371, 374
Acting out, 314
Adaptive behavior. *See also* Coping skills
  mental retardation and, 521, 523–524
Adaptive Behavior Scales, AAMD, 524
Addison's disease, 279
Adoption studies, 32
  of alcoholism, 413
  of crime, 433
  of schizophrenia, 132–133
Adrenal disorders, 278–279
Affective disorders. *See* Mood disorders
Affluence, juvenile delinquency and, 445
Aftercare treatment of schizophrenics,
  151, 155–156, 164
Ageism, 285–286
Aggression (aggressiveness). *See also*
  Crime; Family violence
  rape and, 479, 480, 482, 483
  sex hormones and, 468–469

Aging, organic brain syndromes associated with, 279–286
Agoraphobia, 303, 384
Air traffic controllers, stress and, 339
Alabama mental health system, 616
Al-Anon, 505
Ala-Teen, 505
Alcohol abuse (alcoholism), 395, 406–
  413
  aversion therapy for, 492
  behavior therapy for, 490
  brain damage caused by, 408–409
  coping skills and, 493, 496
  counseling programs for, 496
  covert sensitization therapy for, 492
  depressive symptoms of, 409
  stages of, 408
  statistics on, 410, 411
  suicide and, 234
  theories of, 409, 412–413
  women and, 413
Alcoholics Anonymous (AA), 499, 502–
  506
Alpha rhythms, 66
Altruistic suicides, 227
Alzheimer's disease, 279
American Association of Mental Deficiency (AAMD), 521, 523, 525
American Law Institute (ALI), 488
American Psychiatric Association (APA),
  8, 462. *See also DSM*-III diagnostic
  criteria
American Psychological Association,
  ethical guidelines for research of,
  93–94
Amnesia, 308. *See also* Fugue reaction
  from electroconvulsive therapy, 250
Amniocentesis, 600
  detection of Down's syndrome by,

  531–532
Amotivational syndrome, 423
Amphetamines, 395, 398–399, 414, 417
  schizophrenia and, 126–127
Analogue experiments, 84–86. *See also*
  Animal analogue studies
Anal stage, 39, 319
Anger
  in borderline syndrome, 314
  depression and, 188, 189
  suicide and, 226
Animal analogue studies (animal
  models), 86
  of depression, 192–193
  of opiate addiction, 404, 405
Animal magnetism, 35
Anomic suicide, 227
Anomie, juvenile delinquency and, 445
Anorexia nervosa, 11–12, 315
  family therapy for, 359
Antabuse, 492
Antidepressants, 195–197, 248, 256–257
Antipsychotic drugs. *See* Butyrophe-
  nones; Phenothiazines
Antisocial models, parental, 446–447
Antisocial personality disorder, 312, 402.
  See also Sociopathy
Anxiety, 38, 294
  behavior-therapy techniques for re-
    ducing, 368–383
    assertion training, 375
    behavioral marriage counseling,
      376–377
    for children, 588–590
    cognitive strategies, 377–383
    flooding, 374
    improving communication skills,
      375–377
    systematic desensitization, 370–375,

588–590
counterconditioning, 370. *See also* Desensitization, systematic
definition of, 296
drugs for reducing, 351–352
measures of, 296–300
performance, 346
in retarded persons, 540–542
sociopaths and, 439
Anxiety disorders, 294, 296, 300–317
behavioral model of, 320–322
behavior therapy for, 365–383
assertion training, 375
behavioral assessment, 366–368
client-therapist relationship, 366
cognitive strategies, 377–383
flooding, 374
improving communication skills, 375–377
marriage counseling, 376–377
relaxation, 368–370
systematic desensitization, 370–375
in children, 558–564
behavior therapy for, 588–590
psychotherapy for, 580–586
conflict-defense model of, 353 (*see also* psychoanalytic model of below*)
effectiveness of psychological therapies for, 383–384
existential-humanistic view of, 360–361
onset and course of, 316
personality disorders, 301, 310–316
borderline syndrome, 312–316
compulsive personality disorder, 312
histrionic (hysterical) personality, 312–313
prevention of, 384
psychoanalytic model of, 317–320, 353
psychoanalytic therapy for, 353–359, 383–384
symptomatic disorders, 301–309
conversion disorders, 306–308
dissociative disorders, 306, 308–309
generalized anxiety disorders, 301
multiple personality, 306, 309–310
obsessive-compulsive disorder, 304–306
panic disorders, 301–302
phobic disorders, 302–304, 317 (*see also* Phobias)
Anxiety hierarchy, 370–371, 374
Anxiety learning, 320, 368
Aphasia, 276, 283–284
Archives, 77–78
Assertion training, 256, 375
Assessment techniques. *See also* Direct observation; Interviews; Psychological tests; Psychophysiological recording
criteria for evaluating, 54
for environments, 67–68
purposes of, 53–54

Asthma, 325, 337, 370
Attentional deficit disorder, 565. *See also* Hyperactivity
Attention-placebo condition, 75
Attitudes, psychophysiological disorders and, 336–337
Autism, infantile (autistic children), 568–576
description of, 569–572
etiology of, 573–575
life course of, 575–576
misdiagnosed as phenylketonuria, 533
skill training for, 594–598
Aversion therapy, 490–493. *See also* Covert sensitization
Avoidance behavior, 320
anxiety and, 298, 300
Avoidant personality, 312

Barbiturates, 396–397, 406
Baseline, 87
Beck Depression Inventory, 182, 183
Bedwetting, 555–558
Behavioral marriage counseling, 376–377
Behavioral rehearsal, 375, 377
Behavioral theories or models (behaviorism; reinforcement theories), 43–45
of alcoholism, 410
of anxiety disorders, 320–322
of depression, 189–191
of enuresis, 557
of suicide, 226
Behavior analogues, 84–85
Behavior-exchange agreements, 377
Behavior-management programs. *See also* Behavior therapies
for children, 590–594
Behavior therapies (behavior modification), 44, 353, 365–383
anxiety-reduction techniques in, 368–383
assertion training, 375
for children, 588–590
cognitive strategies, 377–383
flooding, 374
improving communication skills, 375–377
marriage counseling, 376–377
systematic desensitization, 370–375, 588–590
behavioral assessment as first step in, 366–368
for children, 586–598
anxiety reduction, 588–590
behavior-management program, 590–594
classroom behavior management, 590–593
cognitive training, 592, 594
language training, 594–597
modeling, 589, 590
parent training, 596–598

reinforcement, 589–590
skill training, 594–598
social skills training, 596
systematic desensitization, 588–590
token reinforcement programs, 591–593
client-therapist relationship in, 366
for depression, 255–256
effectiveness of psychoanalytic therapy compared to, 383–384
for enuresis, 557–558
family, 496–497
in juvenile corrections programs, 498
for schizophrenics, 159–164
for social deviants, 490–496
aversion therapy, 490–493
Benzodiazepines, 351–352
Berkeley Growth Study, 81
Beta rhythms, 66
Bias, experimenter, 71–72
Biofeedback techniques
for epilepsy treatment, 289
for psychophysiological disorders, 342–343
Biological predisposition (or susceptibility). *See also* Genetic predisposition
to alcoholism, 412–413
to criminal behavior, 432–433
to opiate addiction, 404
to psychophysiological disorders, 340–341
Biological theories (or models), 25–32, 48, 50. *See also* Biological predisposition; Genetic theories
of autism, 574–575
of depression, 187, 194–198
of schizophrenia. *See* Schizophrenia, biological theories of
of suicide, 226
Black Americans
essential hypertension in, 334
rape and, 481–482
Blackouts, 408
Blank card, 212
Blood pressure. *See* Hypertension
Board and care homes, 164
Borderline syndrome (borderline personality disorder), 296, 312–316
Brain. *See* Neurotransmitters; Organic brain syndrome
Brain infections, 276–278
Brain injuries, 270–274
mental retardation caused by, 535–536
Brain tumors, 274–275
Brain-wave aberrations in sociopaths, 441–442
Brief Psychiatric Rating Scale, 64
Bronchial asthma, 325, 337, 370
Butyrophenones, 152

Caffeine, 398–399, 416–417
Cambridge-Somerville study of juvenile delinquency, 447, 448

Carolina Abecedarian Project, 601–602
Casanova complex, 113
Case studies, 76
Catastrophizing, 378
Catatonic schizophrenia, 114–116
Catharsis, 36
Central nervous system (CNS)
    depressants of. See Depressants
    stimulants of, 398–399, 414–417, 598–
        600
Cerebrovascular accident (major stroke),
    283–284
Child abuse, 449, 451–453, 456, 458
Childhood disorders, 518–603. See also
    Mental retardation
    behavior disorders, 551–576
        anxiety disorders, 558–564
        classification of, 554–555
        developmental disorders, 555–556
        diagnostic issues, 554
        enuresis, 555–558
        experiencing, 552–554
        hyperactivity, 565–568
        prevention or early intervention,
            602–603
        psychoses, 568–576
    intervention with, 578–603
        behavior therapies. See Behavior
            therapies, for children
        drug therapy, 598–600
        early intervention and prevention,
            600–603
        family therapy, 584–586
        nondirective play therapy, 582–583
        outcome of psychotherapy, 583
        psychoanalytic play therapy, 580–
            582
        psychotherapy, 580–586
Child molesting, 474–475
Children. See also Juvenile delinquency
    parent-killing by, 454–455
Children's Apperception Test, 62
Chloral hydrate, 396–397
Chromosomes
    criminal behavior and, 433, 434
    Down's syndrome and, 531
Circulatory disturbances, 282–284
Classical conditioning, 43
    anxiety disorders and, 320
    aversion therapy and, 493
Classification of abnormal behavior. See
    Abnormal behavior, classification
    of
Classroom behavior management, 590–
    593
Client-centered therapy, 352–353
Clinical psychologists, 11
Cocaine, 398–399, 414–416
Codeine, 396–397
Cognitive-behavioral therapy, 46
Cognitive distortion, depression and,
    192–194
Cognitive stimulation, mental retardation
    and deficiencies in, 538–539
Cognitive theory of depression, 191–194

Cognitive therapies
    for anxiety disorders, 377–383
    for depression, 252–255
Cognitive training for hyperactive chil-
    dren, 592, 594
Colitis, 325
College students, suicide by, 236–239
Commission on Obscenity and Pornog-
    raphy, 471
Commitment to mental institutions, 151,
    610–615
    dangerousness criterion and, 612–614
    doctrine of parens patriae and, 611
Communications skills, improving, 375–
    377
Community, acceptance of former men-
    tal patients by the, 619–621
Community-based programs, 499–510
    methadone maintenance, 508–510
    self-help groups, 499–506
    therapeutic communities, 506–508
Community mental health centers, 50
Compulsive personality disorder, 312
Computer, diagnosis of schizophrenia
    by, 118–119
Concurrent validity, 54
Concussion, 273
Conditioning
    classical, 43
        anxiety disorders and, 320
        aversion therapy and, 493
    operant (instrumental), 44
        anxiety disorders and, 320
        aversion therapy and, 493
        opiate addiction and, 405
    opiate addiction and, 404–405
Conflict, anxiety disorders and, 318
Congenital rubella syndrome, 534–535
Conjugal delusion, 113
Consciousness, in Freudian theory, 37
Consent auditor, 619
Consumer movement, 607
Content validity, 54
Contingency contracts, 377
Contracts
    in behavioral family therapy, 496–497
    in behavioral marriage counseling, 377
Controlled observations, 64
Contusions, 273
Conversion disorders, 306–308
Coping skills (or strategies), 330–331,
    385. See also Adaptive behavior
    for social deviants, 493, 496
Cop-outs, 507
Coronary heart disease, personality type
    and, 338
Correlational studies, 78–82, 92
Cortical activity, 66–67
Counseling
    for alcoholics, 496
    marriage, 376–377
    for victims of crime, 510–512
Counterconditioning, 45
    of sexual deviance, 474
Covert sensitization, 492, 494–495

Creative regression, 159
Crime, 427–433. See also Family vio-
    lence
    causes of, 432–433
    help for victims of, 510–514
    prevention of, 514–515
    as psychological problem, 488–489
Crime rates, 428–429
Criminal justice system, 487–489
    prevention of crime and, 514
Criminals, types of, 429–432
Cross-dressing, 464–465
Cross-sectional studies, 82
Cultural-familial retardation, 536–539
Cultural values. See also Sociocultural
    factors
    crime and, 433
    family violence and, 457–458
    sexual practices and, 461
Cushing's syndrome, 279

Day hospitals, 164
Daytop Village, 507
Decriminalization of victimless crimes,
    514
Defense mechanisms, 38, 42, 353, 354
    anxiety defenses and, 318
Deinstitutionalization, 49–50
Delirium, organic brain syndrome and,
    269
Delirium tremens, 408
Delta rhythms, 66
Delusions in schizophrenia, 103, 111–
    113
Demand characteristics, 75–76
Dementia
    alcohol dependence and, 409
    organic brain syndrome and, 269–270
    presenile, 279–282
    senile, 282
Dementia praecox, 100. See also Schiz-
    ophrenia
Dependence on drugs
    physiological, 394, 402
    psychological, 393, 394
Dependency
    depression and, 188, 189
    ulcers and, 338
Dependent personality disorder, 312
Dependent variables, 82
De praestigiis daemonum (Weyer),
    34–35
Depressants, 396–397, 406. See also Al-
    cohol abuse
Depression, 174–198
    bipolar, 181. See also Manic-depres-
        sive illness
    in borderline syndrome, 314
    causes of, 187–198
        behavioral theories, 189–191
        biological theories, 187, 194–198
        cognitive theory, 191–194
        personality theory, 189
        psychoanalytic theories, 188–189
        psychological theories, 187–194

in children, 558, 560
clinical description and diagnosis of, 176, 178–186
  DSM-III description and diagnostic criteria, 180–182
  earlier classification schemes, 185
  endogenous/reactive distinction, 185
  interpersonal aspects, 182–184, 186
  neurotic/psychotic distinction, 185
definition, 174–175
duration of, 180
hypothyroidism and, 278
incidence of, 187
normal reactive, 176, 178
primate models of, 192–193
pseudodementia and, 282
recurrence of, 180
in schizo-affective reactions, 117
suicide and, 235–237
treatment of
  antidepressant drugs, 195–197, 248, 256–257
  behavior therapy, 255–256
  cognitive therapy, 252–255
  electroconvulsive therapy (ECT), 249–251
  lithium, 243, 246
  sleep deprivation, 252
  unipolar, 181
Descriptive studies, 76–78
Desensitization, 256
  self-directed, 374–375
  systematic, 370–375
    for children, 588–589
Destructuring of perception and affect, 102, 106
Deterrence of social deviance, 487
Developmental disorders in children, 555–556
Developmental model, of learning inefficiencies, 539–540
Developmental studies, 80–82
Developmental theory, Freudian (psychoanalytic), 39–40, 42, 318, 319
Deviant behavior. *See* Social deviance
Diagnostic and Statistical Manuals (DSMs), 12
Diary of Anne Frank, The, 295
Difference model, of learning inefficiencies, 539
Differential treatment planning, 11
Directionality problem, 80
Direct observation, 64–65, 77
Discipline, juvenile delinquency and, 447–448
Discrimination, against former mental patients, 619–621
Dissociative disorders, 306, 308–309
Donaldson v. *O'Connor,* 609–610
Dopamine, schizophrenia and, 126–127, 133
Double-blind design, 75
Down's syndrome, 528, 531–533, 601
Draw a Person Test, 62

Dream interpretation, in psychoanalytic therapy, 357–359
Dreams
  Freud on, 39–40
  in Gestalt therapy, 364–365
Drug abuse. *See* Substance abuse
Drug-education programs, 514
Drugs. *See also* Substance abuse
  hallucinogenic, 398–399, 417–422
  mental retardation caused by, 535
  psychological dependence on, 393, 394
  tolerance for, 393–394
Drug subculture, 405–406
Drug therapy, 350–352. *See also* specific drugs
  for children, 598–600
  for depression, 195–197
  for mood disorders, 243–248, 256–257
  for schizophrenia, 151–156, 158, 165, 168
DSM-III diagnostic criteria (or categories), 12–15
  for anxiety disorders, 286
  for attentional deficit disorder (hyperactivity), 565
  for childhood behavior disorders, 554–555
  for delirium, 269
  for dementia, 269–270
  for depression, 180–182
  for infantile autism, 569–570
  for manic-depressive illness, 206–207
  for organic brain syndrome, 268–270
  for psychosexual disorders, 462
  for schizophrenia, 111–113, 119
  for substance abuse and substance dependence, 394
Duodenal ulcer, 325, 334, 337
Dysrhythmia, 67

Eating disorders in children, 556
Echolalic speech of autistic children, 572, 573, 595
Ecological approach, 67
Eczema, 325, 337
Education, of retarded children, 542–544
Educational system, prevention of social deviance and, 514–515
Education for All Handicapped Children Act, 542–543
Ego, 37–38, 388
Ego-dystonic homosexuals, 462
Egoistic suicides, 227
Ejaculation, premature, 345
  treatment of, 379–381
Ejaculatory incompetence, 345
Elderly, the
  organic brain syndrome in, 279–286
  problems in treating, 284–286
Electra conflict, 40
Electrocardiogram (EKG), 66
Electroconvulsive therapy (ECT), 26
  for mood disorders, 249–251
  for schizophrenia, 151

Electroencephalograph (EEG), 66
Elimination disorders in children, 556, 558
Emotional climate, schizophrenia and distortions in, 141–142
Emotional divorce, 141–142
Emotional response, sociopath's lack of, 439
Emotive imagery, 588–589
Employment, of retarded adults, 544–545
Encephalitis, 276–277, 279
Encopresis in children, 556, 558
Encounter groups, 507
Endocrine disorders, 278–279
Endogenous depressions, 185
Enuresis, 555–558
Epidemiology of abnormal behavior, 11
Epilepsy, 287–289
Eskimos, 16, 18
Essential hypertension. *See* Hypertension
Ethical issues
  aversion therapies and, 492, 493
  in research, 92–94
Ethnic differences, in drinking habits, 410
Ethnic minorities, access to mental health services and, 607–609
Etiology, 11–12, 607, 608
Eugenics movement, 520
Euphoria
  from heroin use, 400, 403–404
  in schizo-affective reactions, 117
  in schizophrenia, 102, 106
Exhibitionism, 473, 474
  covert sensitization for, 494–495
Existential-humanistic therapies, 360–365
  client-centered therapy, 362–363
  client's responsibility for change in, 361–362
  Gestalt therapy, 363–365
  inner experience in, 361
Existential therapy, 353
  for schizophrenia, 158–159
Experimental situation, external validity of studies and, 73, 75–76
Experimental studies, 71, 82–92
  analogue experiments, 84–85
  design of, 82–84
  quasi-experimental designs, 89–90
  single-subject studies, 86–91
Experimenter bias, 71–72
External validity, of studies, 73–76
Extramarital sexual activity, 461
Eye movements, in schizophrenic patients, 130, 131

Face validity, 54
Family (family life)
  childhood behavior disorders and, 553
  criminal behavior and, 433
  incest in, 475–476
  juvenile delinquency and, 446–448
  mental retardation's effect on, 526–528

Family (Family life) — *continued*
  schizophrenia and distortions in rela-
    tionships within, 136–142
    emotional climate, 141–142
    focusing attention and communica-
      tion, distortions in, 137–138
    high-risk study, 146–147
    implications and limitations of the
      distortion model, 142
    role relationships, 138–139, 141
  schizophrenia outcome and attitudes
    of, 121–122
  situational stress in, 336
Family studies, 32
  of alcoholism, 412
  of manic-depressive illness, 214
Family systems theory, 336
Family therapy
  behavioral, 496–497
  for children, 584–586
  psychoanalytic, 359
  for schizophrenia, 163, 165, 168–169
  for social deviance, 496–497
  structural, 585–586
Family violence, 427, 441–458
  causes of, 456–458
  child abuse, 449, 451–453, 456, 458
  legal status and powerlessness of vic-
    tims, 452–456
  murders, 452, 454–455
  protection of victims from further
    harm, 512–514
  spouse abuse, 449, 451–456, 458
Fear. *See also* Anxiety
  in children, 560–562, 564
  definition of, 295–296
Fear Survey Schedule II (FSS II), 64
Fetishism, 470, 473
First Chance programs, 600–601
Fixation, 40, 318
Flight or fight reactions, 335
Food additives, hyperactivity and, 568
Free association, 357
Freudian theory. *See* Psychoanalytic
  theory
Fugue reaction, 306, 308–309
Functional psychosis, 100

Galvanic skin response (GSR or skin-
  resistance response), 66
  in schizophrenia, 170–171
  in sociopaths, 439, 440
Gangs, juvenile delinquency and, 445–
  446
Gastritis, 325
Gender identity disorders, 462–470
  causes of, 468–470
  transsexualism, 465–469
  transvestism, 464–465, 469
  treatment program for, 469–470
General adaptation syndrome, 326
Generalized anxiety disorders, 301
General paresis, 278
Genetic causes. *See also* Genetic

theories
  of autism, 574–575
  of mental retardation, 528, 531–534
Genetic counseling, schizophrenia and,
  170
Genetic markers
  for manic-depressive illness, 215
  for schizophrenia, 130
Genetic predisposition. *See also* Chromosomes
  to alcoholism, 412–413
  to hyperactivity, 567
  to opiate addiction, 404
  to psychophysiological disorders, 341
  to schizophrenia, 127–133, 147
    adoption studies, 132–133
    schizotaxia, 129, 131, 134
    social drift hypothesis, 143
    twin studies, 128–129
Genetic theories, 32. *See also* Genetic
  predisposition
  of hyperactivity, 567
  of manic-depressive illness, 214–216
Genital stage, 40, 319
Gestalt therapy, 363–365
Glove anesthesia, 35, 306
Glutethimide, 396–397
Grandiosity, 113
Grand mal, 288
Grave's disease, 278
Greece, ancient, 25
Grief reaction, normal, 176, 178
Group for the Advancement of Psychia-
  try, 554
Groups, assertion-training, 375
Group therapy, psychoanalytic, 359

Habit disorders in children, 556
Halfway houses, 150, 498. *See also*
  Therapeutic communities
Hallucinations in schizophrenia, 112, 116
Hallucinogens, 398–399, 417–422
  schizophrenia and, 125, 126
Hamilton Depression Scale, 182, 183
Hangover, 407
Hartford Retreat, 48
Hashish, 398–399
Hawthorne effect, 75
Hawthorne study, 73, 75
Headaches
  migraine, 325–338
  tension, 370
Head injury, mental retardation caused
  by, 536
Head Start program, 601
Health care, mental retardation and defi-
  ciencies in, 538
Heart attack (myocardial infarction), 325
  personality types and, 340
Hebephrenic schizophrenia, 116–117
Helplessness, depression and sense of,
  190–191
Hereditary disorders. *See also* Genetic
  causes

Huntington's chorea, 280–282
Heroin (heroin addiction), 396–397, 400.
  See also Opiates
  methadone maintenance program for,
    508–510
High-risk studies
  of manic-depressive illness, 214–215
  of schizophrenia, 134–136, 146–147
Histrionic personality disorder (hysterical
  personality), 312
Hives (urticaria), 337
Holistic medicine, 332, 341–342
Holtzman Inkblot Technique, 61
Homosexuality, 8, 462–464
  behavior therapy for, 490
Homosexual pedophiles, 474, 475
Hostility. *See also* Anger
  suicide and, 226
Humanistic therapy. *See* Existential-
  humanistic therapies
Humors, theory of, 25
Huntington's chorea, 280–282
Hustling theory, 405
Hyperactivity, 565–568
  behavioral-management program for,
    592
  cognitive training for, 592, 594
  drug therapy for, 598–600
Hypertension (essential hypertension),
  325, 333–334, 337, 370
  biofeedback techniques to reduce,
    342–343
Hyperthyroidism, 278
Hypnotism, 35–37
Hypomania, 181, 206, 208, 210, 211. *See
  also* Manic-depressive illness
  clinical description of, 204
Hypothyroidism, 278
Hysteria, 35, 306. *See also* Conversion
  disorders; Dissociative disorders;
  Fugue reaction; Multiple personality
Hysterical personality (histrionic personality disorder), 312

Id, 37–38, 388
Ideas of reference, 103, 106–107
Identity dissolution, 103
Imipramine, 195, 248, 250, 384
Impotence, 344–346
Inborn error of metabolism. *See also*
  Phenylketonuria
  schizophrenia and, 124–126
Incest, 475–476
Independent variables, 82
I Never Promised You a Rose Garden
  (Green), 157–158
Inexact labeling, depression and, 194
Infantile autism (autistic children), 568–
  572
  description of, 569–572
  etiology of, 573–575
  life course of, 575–576
  misdiagnosed as phenylketonuria, 533

skill training for, 594–598
Informed consent, 93, 617–619
  for electroconvulsive therapy (ECT), 250, 251
Inner experience in existential-humanistic therapies, 361
Insanity defense, 488
Insight, 353, 361
Insomnia, 370
Institutionalism, 49
Instrumental conditioning. See Operant conditioning
Intellectual function. See also Mental retardation
  Down's syndrome and, 531
  organic brain syndrome and, 269–270
Intelligence quotient (IQ), 58
  as retardation measure, 521–523, 525
Intelligence tests, 58, 276
Interjudge reliability, 54
Internal reliability, 54
Internal validity of studies, 71–72
Intervention, 22. See also Treatment; and under specific disorders
Interviews, 56
Intoxication, alcohol, 407
Introspection, 43
Introverted personality disorder, 312
Inventories, self-report, 52–54
Iodine, 278
Iproniazid, 195
Isolation, 38

Jobs for retarded adults, 544–545
Judgment, organic brain syndrome and, 269
Juvenile delinquency (delinquents), 427, 442–448, 499
  Achievement Place program and, 500–502
  causes of, 444–448
  hidden, 443

Kingsley Hall, 159

Labeling, depression and inexact, 194
Labeling theory, 15–19
  primary, 16
  secondary, 17–19
Lability, organic brain syndrome and, 269
Laceration, 273–274
Language ability, tests of, 276
Language-development program for autistic children, 594–596
Language environment, mental retardation and, 538–539
Latency period, 40, 319
Laws, sexual activities and, 461–462
L-Dopa, 280
Lead poisoning, 600
  hyperactivity and, 568
  mental retardation caused by, 535–536
Learned helplessness, depression and, 191

Learning, mental retardation and, 539–540
Least restrictive alternative, doctrine of, 616–617, 621
Libido, 39
Librium, 351, 352, 598
Lie-detector test, 66
Life changes, physical illness and, 328–330
Life crises
  as predictive of schizophrenia outcome, 119, 121
  schizophrenia and, 136
Life stress. See Stress
Lithium, 196, 243–247, 261
Lobotomy, 26
  for schizophrenia, 151
Longitudinal studies, 81–82
Loss experiences, depression and, 188–189, 192–193
Lysergic acid diethylamide (LSD), 418–420

Machismo, rape and, 480, 482
Mainstreaming, 543
Major Role Therapy (MRT), 168
Malleus Maleficarum (The Witches' Hammer), 33–34
Malnutrition, mental retardation caused by, 535, 538
Mania. See also Manic-depressive illness
  in bipolar depression, 181
  clinical description of, 204–206
Manic-depressive illness, 174, 189, 201–216. See also Mood disorders
  clinical description of, 204–206
  diagnosis of, 206–208
  experiences of, 208, 210–212, 214
  genetic theories of, 214–216
  Huntington's chorea and, 280
  suicide and, 233–235
  surveys of, 76
  treatment of, 243–251
    electroconvulsive therapy (ECT), 249–251
    lithium, 243–247
Manic-State Rating Scale, 207
MAO inhibitors, 195, 248
  depression and, 194, 195
Marijuana, 398–399, 422–425
Marijuana and Health Report of 1977, 423–424
Marital therapy, 256
Marriage, retarded persons and, 545
Marriage counseling, behavioral, 376–377
Masochism, 477
Masturbation, 461, 473, 474
MDA, 398–399
M-D Scale, 208
Medical model, 15
Medieval times, 33–34
Megavitamin therapy, 72
Memory, organic brain syndrome and,

269, 276
Mental health services, access to, 607–609
Mental hospitals, 46–50, 150. See also Day hospitals
  schizophrenia and, 159–160
Mental patients, rights of. See Rights of mental patients
Mental retardation, 519–549
  adaptive behavior and, 521, 523–524
  adults, 544–549
  causes of, 528–539
    genetic causes, 528, 531–534
    physical and environmental causes, 534–536
    psychosocial causes, 536–539
  characteristics of retarded persons, 539–542
  diagnosis and classification of, 521–526
  education and, 542–544
  family, effects on, 526–528
  history of, 520–521
  IQ as a measure of, 521–523, 525
  prevention or early intervention programs for, 600–602
  skill training for, 594–598
  social acceptance and, 543–544
Meperidine, 396–397
Mescaline, 126, 398–399
Methadone, 396–397, 404
Methadone maintenance, 508–510
Methaqualone, 396–397
Methylpenidate, 398–399
Midtown Manhattan Study, 7–8, 21, 77, 144
Migraine headaches, 325, 338
Milwaukee Project, 602
Minimal brain damage, 567
Minnesota Multiphasic Personality Inventory (MMPI), 62–63
Mislabeling, depression and, 194
Mixed designs, 92
Modeling, 377, 382
  anxiety disorders and, 320
  in children, 589, 590
Mongolism. See Down's syndrome
Monoamine oxidase (MAO) inhibitors, 195, 248
  depression and, 194, 195
Mood disorders, 111, 174. See also Depression; Manic-depressive illness; Suicide
  neurochemical theories of, 195–197
  suicide and, 234
  treatment of, 241–263
    antidepressants, 195–197, 248, 256–257
    behavior therapy, 255–256
    cognitive therapy, 252–255
    electroconvulsive therapy (ECT), 249, 251
    lithium, 243–247
    mood disorders clinics, 257–259

Mood disorders — *continued*
　multimodal interventions, 256–259
　psychological approaches, 252–257
　sleep deprivation, 252
　suicide prevention, 259–263
Mood disorders clinics, 257–259
Moodswing: The Third Revolution in Psychiatry (Fieve), 244
Moral treatment, 34, 48
Morphine, 395–397, 400
Multiple-baseline design, 89–91
Multiple personality, 306, 309–310
Murders in families, 452, 454–455
Myxedema, 278

Narcissistic personality disorder, 312
Narcotics. *See* Opiates
National Association for Mental Health, 19
National Mental Health Study Act (1955), 50
Naturalistic observations, 64
Neurons, 31
Neuropsychological tests, 276–277
Neuroses. *See* Anxiety disorders
Neurosyphilis, 277–278
Neurotic depression, 185
Neurotransmitters, 31, 249
　depression and, 194–197, 248
　schizophrenia and, 124, 126–127, 133
Nicotine, 398–399
Nightmares, 556
Night terror, 556
Nondirective play therapy, 582–583
Nonequivalent control group design, 89
Nonreactive measures, 77–78
Norepinephrine, 243
　depression and, 195–197
　schizophrenia and, 126
Normalization approach to mental retardation, 549
Nurses, 11
Nutrition, mental retardation caused by deficiencies in, 535, 538

Obesity in children, 556, 558
Observation, direct, 64–65, 77
Obsessive-compulsive disorder, 304–306
　flooding technique for treating, 374
Odyssey House, 506
Oedipal conflict, 40, 345
Operant conditioning (instrumental conditioning), 44
　anxiety disorders and, 320
　aversion therapy and, 493
　opiate addiction and, 405
Opiates (opiate addiction), 395–397, 400–406
　availability of, 401
　avoidance of withdrawal symptoms and, 402, 405
　continued dependence on, 402–406
　euphoric effects of, 400, 403–404
　factors leading to, 401–402

　genetic predisposition to, 404
　peer groups and, 402
　personality attributes and, 401
　physiological dependence on, 402
　social situation and, 402, 404–406
　subculture of, 405–406
　theories of, 400
Opium, 395–397
Oral stage, 39, 319
Organic brain syndrome, 266–289
　aging-associated syndromes, 279–286
　alcoholism and, 408–409
　brain infections as cause of, 276–278
　brain injuries as cause of, 270–274
　brain tumors as cause of, 274–275
　clinical features of, 268–270
　endocrine disorders as cause of, 278–279
　epilepsy, 287–289
Organic psychoses, 100
Organizational Components of Behavior Modification, 68
Organized crime, 430, 431
Orgasmic dysfunction, 345
　treatment of, 379–381
Orientation
　organic brain syndrome and, 269
　tests of, 276
Outer-directedness of retarded children, 541
Overgeneralization, depression and, 193–194

Panic disorders, 301–302
Paranoid personality disorder, 312
Paranoid schizophrenia, 113, 115–116
Paraphilias, 462. *See also* Fetishism; Pedophilia; Voyeurism
Parens patriae, doctrine of, 611
Parents. *See also* Family
　of autistic children, 573–574
　　training programs for, 596–598
　of retarded children, 526–528
　　training programs for, 596–598
Parent-training programs, 596–598
Paresis, 12, 278
Parkinsonian symptoms, 153
Parkinson's disease, 277, 279–280
Patient advocate, 619
Pedophilia, 474–475
Peer groups
　juvenile delinquency and, 445
　opiate addiction and, 402
Penile plethysmograph, 66
Peptic ulcers, 325, 334, 341
Perception
　autism and disturbances in, 572
　destructuring of affection and, in schizophrenia, 102, 106
Performance anxiety, 346
Permissive theory, 197
Personality characteristics. *See also* Personality types
　of Down's syndrome children, 531

Personality disorders, 301, 310–316
　antisocial, 312, 402 (*see also* Sociopathy)
　borderline syndrome, 312–316
　compulsive personality disorder, 312
　histrionic (hysterical) personality, 312–313
Personality tests, 58, 60–64
Personality theory of depression, 189
Personality types
　of opiate abusers, 401–402
　psychophysiological disorders and, 338–340
Pethidine, 396
Petit mal, 288
Phallic stage, 39–40, 319
Pharmacological therapy. *See* Drug therapy
Phencyclidine (PCP or angel dust), 395, 398–399
Phenmetrazine, 398–399
Phenomenology, 43, 46
Phenothiazines
　for mania, 244–245
　for schizophrenia treatment, 126–127, 150, 152–156, 169
　side effects of, 153, 154
Phenylketonuria (PKU), 532–534
Phillips Premorbid Adjustment Scale, 119, 120
Phobias (phobic disorders), 301–304, 317
　behavior therapy for, 384 (*see also* desensitization therapy for *below*)
　children, 588–590
　in children, 560
　　school phobia, 562–563
　desensitization therapy for, 370–375
　effectiveness of different therapies for, 384
Phoenix House, 507–508
Physical disorders. *See* Psychophysiological disorders
Physicians, public health, 11
Physiological dependence on drugs, 394, 402
Pica, 556
Placebo effect, 75
Play therapy
　nondirective, 582–583
　outcome of, 583–584
　psychoanalytic, 580–582
Poisoning
　hyperactivity and, 568
　mental retardation caused by, 535–536
Polydrug abuse, 395, 407
Pornography, sexual deviance and, 471
Possession, 33
Postconcussion syndrome, 273
Poverty
　juvenile delinquency and, 445, 447–448
　mental retardation and, 536, 538–539
　schizophrenia and, 143

Predictive validity, 54
Premarital sexual activity, 461
Premature ejaculation, 345
  treatment of, 379–381
Pre–post control group design, 83
Presenile dementia, 279–282
President's Commission on Mental Health, 607–609
Probability sample, 73
Probes, 507
Problem solving
  in behavioral marriage counseling, 377
  tests of, 276
Projection, 38
Projective tests, 60–62
Pseudodementia, 282
Pseudomutual relationship, 142
Psilocybin, 398–399
Psychiatric nurses, 11
Psychiatric Status Schedule, 56, 57
Psychiatrists, 11
Psychoanalysis. *See* Psychoanalytic therapy
Psychoanalytic play therapy, 580–582
Psychoanalytic theory (or model), 37–40
  of anxiety disorders, 317–320
  behaviorism and, 42–46
  of depression, 188–189
  developmental model in, 39–40, 42, 318, 319
  of enuresis, 557
  influence of, 42
  of school phobia, 562–563
  of sexual deviance, 473
  of sexual dysfunction, 345–346
  structure model in, 37–39, 318, 319, 388
  of suicide, 226
Psychoanalytic therapists, 354–356
Psychoanalytic therapy (psychoanalysis), 353–359
  client–therapist relationships in, 354
  dream interpretation in, 357–359
  effectiveness of behavior therapy compared to, 383–384
  group and family therapy, 359
  for mood disorders, 252
  transference in, 356–357
Psychological autopsy, 229, 232–233
Psychological dependence on drugs, 393, 394
Psychological handicap, 10
Psychological tests, 56–64
  intelligence tests, 58, 276
  personality tests, 58, 60–64
Psychological theories, 32–46, 50. *See also* Behavioral theories; Psychoanalytic theory
  of autism, 573
  medieval demonology, 33–34
  roots of modern, 35–36
  of suicide, 226
Psychological therapies (psychotherapies), 350–351. *See also* specific

types of therapy
  behavior therapy compared to, 366
  for children, 580–586
    family therapy, 584–586
    nondirective play therapy, 582–583
    outcome, 583
    psychoanalytic play therapy, 580–582
  for depression, 252–257
  effectiveness of, 383–384
  for enuresis, 557
  for mood disorders, 242, 252
  nonspecific features of, 352–353
  for schizophrenia, 156–165
  for socially deviant persons, 489–490
Psychologists, 11
Psychology, 11
Psychomotor epilepsy, 288–289
Psychopaths. *See* Sociopathy
Psychophysiological disorders, 324–348
  biological predisposition to, 340–341
  definition of, 325
  relaxation method for treating, 370
  sexual dysfunction, 344–348
  stress and (*see* Stress)
  treatment of, 341–343
Psychophysiological recording, 65–66
Psychoses. *See also* Manic-depressive illness; Schizophrenia
  childhood, 568–576
  functional, 100
  organic, 100
Psychosexual development, Freudian theory of, 39–40
Psychosocial Clinic for People over 65 of UCLA, 285–286
Psychosocial stress, schizophrenia and, 136–147
Psychosomatic disorders, 325. *See also* Psychophysiological disorders
Psychotherapy. *See* Psychological therapies
Psychotherapy by Reciprocal Inhibition (Wolpe), 45
Psychotic depression, 185
Psychotomimetic drugs. *See* Hallucinogens
Public health physicians, 11
"Punch-drunk syndrome," 273
Punishment, sociopathy and avoidance of, 438–441

Q-Sort, 63–64
Quasi-experimental designs, 89–90

Radical behaviorism, 43–44
Rape, 476–484
  American society and, 484
  attempted, 476
  characteristics of rapists, 481–483
  compensatory, 479
  displaced-aggression, 478–479
  experience of, 478–480

  forcible, 476
  help for victims of, 510–512
  impulse, 479–480
  myths about, 481
  reporting of, 477–478
  sex-aggression defusion, 479
  statutory, 476–477
Rational-emotive therapy, 378
Raynaud's disease, 325, 337
Reaction formation, 38
Reactive depressions, 185
Reasoning, tests of, 276
Reference groups, juvenile delinquency and, 445
Regional Poisoning Treatment Centre (Edinburgh), 260
Rehabilitation, right to, 616
Rehabilitation programs, 489–510
  behavior therapy, 490–496
    aversion therapy, 490–493
  community-based programs, 499–510
    methadone maintenance, 508–510
    self-help groups, 499–506
    therapeutic communities, 506–508
  family therapy, 496–497
  psychotherapy, 489–490
  residential programs, 498
Reinforcement, 44
  behavior-therapy program for children and, 589–590
Relaxation
  behavior-therapy methods of, 368–370
  desensitization therapy and, 370, 374
Relaxation response, 342
Reliability of assessment techniques, 54
Repression, 38
Research, 70–94
  correlational studies, 78–82, 92
  descriptive studies, 77–78
  ethical issues in, 92–94
  experimental studies (*see* Experimental studies)
  external validity and, 73–76
  internal validity of studies and, 71–72
  mixed designs, 92
Reserpine, depression and, 194
Residences for retarded adults, 545, 547–549
Retardation. *See* Mental retardation
Retrospective study, 80–81
Reversal design, 87–89
Rights of mental patients, 609–619
  acceptance in the community, 619–621
  civil commitment and, 610–15
    dangerousness criterion, 612–614
    doctrine of parens patriae, 611
  doctrine of parens patriae and, 611
  Donaldson case and, 609–610
  in institutions, 616–617
Risk-rescue rating scale, 229
Role-playing, 382
  in behavioral therapies, 375, 377, 382
Rome, ancient, 25–26

Rorschach Psychodiagnostic Inkblot Test, 60–62
Routine, retarded persons and, 541
Rubella (German measles), mental retardation and, 534–535
Rules, retarded persons and, 541

Sadism, 477
    covert sensitization for, 494–495
Sample, external validity of studies and selection of, 73, 78
Schismatic families, 139, 141
Schizo-affective disorders, 112, 117
Schizophrenia (schizophrenic psychoses), 100–171
    acute-onset, 102
    biological theories of, 124–133
        biochemical theories, 124–127
        dopamine theory, 126–127
        genetic markers, 130
        genetic predisposition, 127–133, 143
        inborn error of metabolism, 124–126
        research limitations, 125
        twin studies, 128–129
    breakdown in the filter system in, 104–105
    catatonic, 114–116
    causes of, 123–124
    childhood, 568, 569
    computer diagnoses of, 118–119
    course of development of, 105–109
    cross-cultural studies of, 109, 111
    definition of, 100–101
    developmental studies of, 81–82
    diagnostic reliability in, 108–111
    disorganization process in, 102–103
    DSM-III criteria for, 111–113, 119
    experiences reported by patients, 104–105
    first-rank symptoms of, 119
    hebephrenic, 116–117
    high-risk studies of, 134–136, 146–147
    insidious-onset, 102
    interactive models of, 133–134
    intervention in, 149–171
        aftercare, 151, 155–156, 164
        behavior therapy, 159–164
        biological treatment, 151–156
        current approach, 150–151
        drug therapy, 151–156, 158, 165, 168
        existential therapy (Laing's treatment model), 158–159
        family therapy, 163, 165, 168–169
        genetic counseling, 170
        lodge program, 168
        multimodal approaches, 165, 168–170
        preventive interventions, 170–171
        psychological approaches, 156–165, 168–170
        rehabilitation, 168
        traditionally oriented psychotherapy, 156–158
    megavitamin therapy for, 72
    opiate addiction and, 402, 403
    opposition to use of term, 117
    paranoid, 113, 115–116
    predictors of outcome of, 119–122
    primary labeling theory and, 16
    psychosocial stress and, 136–147
        high-risk studies, 146–147
        sociological status, 143, 145
        stress-diathesis model of, 133–134, 147
    suicide and, 233, 234, 236
    thought disturbance in, 100, 101, 112, 131, 137–138
Schizophrenogenic mother, 137
Schizotaxia, 129, 131, 134
Schizotypes, 131
Schizotypical personality disorder, 312
School phobia, 562–563
Schools, retarded children and, 542–544
Sedative-hypnotics, 406–407
Selective abstraction, 194
Self-esteem
    juvenile delinquency and, 445
    mental retardation and, 541–542
Self-fulfilling prophecy, 72
Self-help groups, 499–506
Self-report inventories, 62–64
Self-reports of anxiety, 297–298
Senile dementia, 282
Sensory deprivation experiments, 84–85
Sentence Completion Test, 62
Separation anxiety, 562–563
Separation experiences, depression and, 188–189, 192–193
Serotonin, depression and, 195, 197
Sex education, 379–380, 514
    for retarded individuals, 545
Sex hormones, cross-gender identification and, 468–469
Sex-reassignment surgery, 465, 468
Sex therapy, 379–381
Sexual deviance, 460–484
    actual sexual practices and, 461–462
    behavior therapy for, 490–492
    coping skills and, 493, 496
    DSM-III classification of, 462
    exhibitionism, 473, 474
        covert sensitization for, 494–495
    fetishism, 470, 473
    gender identity disorders, 462–470
    incest, 475–476
    laws and, 461–462
    pedophilia, 474–475
    pornography and, 471
    psychological abnormality and, 462
    rape (see Rape)
    sadism, 477
        covert sensitization for, 494–495
    voyeurism, 470, 471, 473, 474
Sexual dysfunction, 325, 344–348
    treatment of, 379–381
Simple phobia, 304
Single-subject studies, 86–91
Situational specificity, psychophysiological disorders and, 331, 333–336
Situation analogues, 84–85
Skewed families, 139
Skill training for retarded or autistic children, 594–598
Skin-resistance tests. See Galvanic skin response
Sleep deprivation for depression, 252
Sleep disorders in children, 556, 558
Sleepwalking, 556
Social acceptance of retarded individuals, 543–544
Social class. See also Poverty; Sociocultural factors
    schizophrenia and, 143, 145
Social climate scales, 67–68
Social deviance, 8, 10, 388–389. See also Family violence; Juvenile delinquency; Sexual deviance; Sociopathy; Substance abuse
    help for victims of, 510–514
    interventions with, 486–515
        criminal justice system, 487–489
        mental health, 488
        rehabilitation programs (see Rehabilitation programs)
    prevention of, 514–515
Social drift hypothesis, schizophrenia and, 143
Social learning theories of anxiety disorders, 320, 322
Social mores, sexual practices and, 461
Social phobias, 303–304
Social readjustment rating scale, 328
Social skill learning, 256
Social skills
    depression and lack of, 190
    training of children in, 596
Sociocultural factors. See also Cultural values; Social class
    drinking habits and, 410
    mental retardation due to, 536–539
Sociological theory of suicide, 226–227
Sociopathy, 427, 434–442, 444
    causes of, 438–442
    clinical characteristics of, 435–437
Somnambulism, 556
Soteria House, 160–161
Speech disorders in children, 556
Speech of autistic children, 572, 573, 575
Spontaneous improvement of children, 583–584
Spontaneous recovery, 383
Spouse abuse, 449, 451–456, 458
Stanford-Binet Intelligence Scale, 58, 522
State hospitals, 49–50
Stimulants, 398–399, 414–417
    for children, 598–600
Stimulus-seeking by sociopaths, 440
Stomach ulcers, 325, 335
Stress (life stress), 325–340. See also Life crises

coping with, 330–331
family violence and, 456–457
nonspecific theories of, 326–331
psychosocial stress, schizophrenia and, 136–147
specific theories of, 331–340
attitudinal specificity, 336–337
personality specificity, 338–340
situational specificity, 331, 333–336
Stress-diathesis model
of autism, 575
of schizophrenia, 133–134, 147
Stress-inoculation training, 385
Stroke, 283–284
Structuralism, 43
Structural theory, Freudian (psychoanalytic), 37–38, 318, 319, 388
Stuttering in children, 556, 558
Subculture, drug, 405–406
Subintentional death, 219–220
Subject analogues, 86
Subjective distress, 8, 10
Substance abuse (drug abuse), 390–425.
  See also specific substances
causes of, 394
criteria for, 391, 393–394
Substance dependence, 394
Suicide (suicidal behavior), 174, 218–239
altruistic, 227
anomic, 227
categories of, 219–220
college students and, 236–239
egoistic, 227
historical and cultural perspectives on, 220–221
manic-depressive illness and, 210
motives for, 228–230
phenomenological perspectives on, 222–226
psychiatric illness and, 232–233
statistics on, 221–222
theories of, 226–231
Suicide notes, 224–226
Suicide prevention, 259–263
Superego, 38, 388
Surveys, 76–78
Symptomatic disorders, 301–309
Synanon, 506–507
Syphilis, 12, 277–278
Systematic desensitization, 370–375
for children, 58, 85–90

Tardive dyskinesia, 153
Taylor Scale of Manifest Anxiety, 297
Tea, 416

Tension headaches, 370
Tension-release exercises, 369–370
Test-retest reliability, 54
Tests
neuropsychological, 276–277
psychological (see Psychological tests)
Thematic Apperception Test (TAT), 61–62
Therapeutic communities, 49, 150, 506–508
Therapy. See Drug therapy; Intervention; Psychological therapies; and specific disorders
Third-variable problem, 80
Thorazine, 154, 249
Thought disturbance in schizophrenia, 100, 101, 112, 131, 137–138
Three Faces of Eve, The (Thigpen and Cleckley), 310–311
Thyroid disorders, 278
Tics in children, 556, 558
Time-series design, 89–90
Token economies, 160–163, 500
in classroom behavior-management programs, 591–593
rights of mental patients and, 617
Tolerance for drugs, 393–394
Toxins. See Poisoning
Tranquilizers, 351–352, 396–397
for children, 598
major, 150 (see also Butyrophenones; Phenothiazines)
Transactional analysis, 357
Transactional thought disorders, schizophrenia and, 137, 146–147
Transference, 356–357
Transsexualism, 465–469
Transvestism, 464–465, 469
Traumatic encephalopathy, 273
Treatment, 22
right of persons in mental institutions to, 616–617
right to refuse, 617–619
Treatment planning, differential, 11
Tricyclic antidepressants, 195, 248
Tumors, brain, 274–275
Twin studies, 32
of alcoholism, 412–413
of autism, 575
of manic-depressive illness, 215
of schizophrenia, 128–129
Two-disease theory, 197
Type A personalities, 338–340
Type B personalities, 338–340

Ulcers, 325, 334–335, 337, 341
dependency and, 338
Unconscious, the, in Freudian theory, 37–38, 388
Urticaria (hives), 337
Utility of assessment techniques, 54

Vaginismus, 345
Validity of assessment techniques, 54
Validity of studies
external, 73–76
internal, 71–72
Valium, 351–352, 406, 598
Variables. See also Third-variable problem
dependent, 82
independent, 82
Verbal stimulation, mental retardation and deficiencies in, 538–539
Victim-precipitated homicides, 219–220
Victims of crime, help for, 510–514
Viet Nam War, 480
Vineland Scale of Social Maturity, 524
Violence. See also Crime
cultural acceptance of, 457–458
in the family (see Family violence)
Voyeurism, 470, 471, 473, 474

Wechsler Adult Intelligence Scale, 276
Wechsler Intelligence Scales, 54, 58, 522
White collar crime, 430–432
Wife beating, 449, 451–456, 458
Witches, 33–34
Withdrawal syndrome (withdrawal symptoms), 268, 394
alcoholism and, 408
caffeine, 417
depressant abuse and, 407
opiate addiction and, 402, 403, 405
stimulant, 414
Women. See also Rape
alcoholism and, 413
Women's movement, 456
Worcester State Hospital, 48
Word salad, 116
World Health Organization (WHO), 109, 170
Wyatt v. Stickney, 616, 618

XYY genotype, 434

York Retreat, 48
Yorubas, 16, 18

To the owner of this book:

All of us who worked together to produce *Abnormal Psychology* hope that you have enjoyed it as much as we did. If you did — or if you didn't — we'd like to know why, so we'll have a better idea of how to improve it in future editions.

School: _____

Instructor's Name: _____

Other required reading: _____

1. Why did you take the Abnormal Psychology course?

   _____

   _____

   _____

2. Please give us your reaction to the following elements of the text by ranking them from 1 (excellent) to 5 (poor).

	1	2	3	4	5
Overall impression					
Level of difficulty					
Explanations of terms & concepts					
Writing style/interest level					
Appearance (cover, layout, use of illustrations)					

3. Were all the chapters assigned? _____ If not, which were *not* assigned? _____

4. Which chapter did you like best? Why? _____

   _____

5. Which chapter did you like least? Why? _____

   _____

6. Please comment on the illustrations. Which kind did you find most helpful to your learning? _____

   _____

7. Do you think the instructor should continue to assign this book? Why or why not? _____

_____

_____

8. Will you keep *Abnormal Psychology?* _____

_____

9. Please add any comments or suggestions on how we might improve this book: _____

_____

_____

_____

_____

10. Optional: Your name: _____ Date: _____

Address: _____

11. May we quote you, either in promotion for this book or in future publishing ventures?

_____ Yes _____ No

- -

Please mail to:

Abnormal Psychology
College Division
Little, Brown and Company
34 Beacon Street
Boston, Massachusetts 02106

Thank You!